Definition of Absolute Value

$$|x| = \begin{cases} x \text{ when } x \geq 0 \\ -x \text{ when } x < 0 \end{cases}$$

Absolute Value Equations
- If $k \geq 0$, then $|x| = k$ is equivalent to $x = k$ or $x = -k$.
- If a and b are algebraic expressions, $|a| = |b|$ is equivalent to $a = b$ or $a = -b$.

Absolute Value Inequalities
- If $k > 0$, then $|x| < k$ is equivalent to $-k < x < k$.
- If $k > 0$, then $|x| > k$ is equivalent to $x > k$ or $x < -k$.

These two properties hold for $\leq$ and $\geq$ also.

Circles

The standard form of an equation of a circle with center (h, k) and radius r:
$$(x - h)^2 + (y - k)^2 = r^2$$

The standard form of an equation of a circle with center $(0, 0)$ and radius r:
$$x^2 + y^2 = r^2$$

Quadratic Functions
A **quadratic function** is a second-degree polynomial function in one variable of the form

$$f(x) = ax^2 + bx + c \text{ or } y = ax^2 + bx + c,$$

where a, b, and c are real numbers and $a \neq 0$.

The graph of a quadratic function of the form

$$f(x) = ax^2 + bx + c \quad (a \neq 0)$$

is a **parabola** with vertex at

$$\left(-\frac{b}{2a}, c - \frac{b^2}{4a}\right)$$

- If $a > 0$, the parabola **opens upward.**
- If $a < 0$, the parabola **opens downward.**

The standard form of an equation of a quadratic function is

$$y = f(x) = a(x - h)^2 + k \quad (a \neq 0)$$

The vertex is at (h, k).
- The parabola opens upward when $a > 0$ and downward when $a < 0$.
- The axis of symmetry of the parabola is the vertical line graph of the equation $x = h$.

Tests for Symmetry

Test for x-axis symmetry:
To test for x-axis symmetry, replace y with $-y$. If the resulting equation is equivalent to the original one, the graph is symmetric about the x-axis.

Test for y-axis symmetry:
To test for y-axis symmetry, replace x with $-x$. If the resulting equation is equivalent to the original one, the graph is symmetric about the y-axis.

Test for origin symmetry:
To test for symmetry about the origin, replace x with $-x$ and y with $-y$. If the resulting equation is equivalent to the original one, the graph is symmetric about the origin.

Graphs of Common Functions

Greatest-Integer Function

Interest Formulas

Compound interest formula:
If P dollars are deposited in an account earning interest at an annual rate r, compounded n times each year, the amount A in the account after t years is given by

$$A = P\left(1 + \frac{r}{n}\right)^{nt}.$$

Continuous compound interest formula:
If P dollars are deposited in an account earning interest at an annual rate r, compounded continuously, the amount A after t years is given by the formula

$$A = Pe^{rt}$$

Finite Mathematics and College Algebra

Contributing Authors: Pavel Sikorskii and Jennifer Powers

Stefan Waner | Steven Costenoble | R. David Gustafson
Jeff Hughes

CENGAGE
Learning·

Australia • Brazil • Japan • Korea • Mexico • Singapore • Spain • United Kingdom • United States

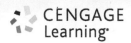

Finite Mathematics and College Algebra:
Contributing Authors: Pavel Sikorskii and
Jennifer Powers

College Algebra, 11th Edition
R. David Gustafson | Jeff Hughes
© 2013, 2010, 2007, 2004 Cengage Learning. All rights reserved.

Finite Mathematics, 6th Edition
Stefan Waner | Steven Costenoble
© 2014, 2011, 2007 Cengage Learning. All rights reserved.

Executive Editors:
 Maureen Staudt
 Michael Stranz

Senior Project Development Manager:
 Linda deStefano

Marketing Specialist:
 Courtney Sheldon

Senior Production/Manufacturing Manager:
 Donna M. Brown

Production Editorial Manager:
 Kim Frv

Sr. Rights Acquisition Account Manager:
 Todd Osborne

For product information and technology assistance, contact us at
Cengage Learning Customer & Sales Support, 1-800-354-9706

For permission to use material from this text or product,
submit all requests online at **cengage.com/permissions**
Further permissions questions can be emailed to
permissionrequest@cengage.com

This book contains select works from existing Cengage Learning resources and was produced by Cengage Learning Custom Solutions for collegiate use. As such, those adopting and/or contributing to this work are responsible for editorial content accuracy, continuity and completeness.

Compilation © 2013 Cengage Learning
ISBN-13: 978-1-305-03478-5

ISBN-10: 1-305-03478-3
Cengage Learning
5191 Natorp Boulevard
Mason, Ohio 45040
USA

Cengage Learning is a leading provider of customized learning solutions with office locations around the globe, including Singapore, the United Kingdom, Australia, Mexico, Brazil, and Japan. Locate your local office at:
international.cengage.com/region.
Cengage Learning products are represented in Canada by Nelson Education, Ltd.
For your lifelong learning solutions, visit **www.cengage.com/custom.**
Visit our corporate website at **www.cengage.com.**

Printed in the United States of America

Brief Contents

Excerpted from:
MSU MTH 110 Coursenotes
Jennifer Powers & Pavel Sikorskii

Appendix B: Transformations and Matrices
Appendix C: Sample Exams

A Review of Basic Algebra

0

CAREERS AND MATHEMATICS:

© Istockphoto.com/Lucas Rucchin

Pharmacist

Pharmacists distribute prescription drugs to individuals. They also advise patients, physicians, and other health-care workers on the selection, dosages, interactions, and side effects of medications. They also monitor patients to ensure that they are using their medications safely and effectively. Some pharmacists specialize in oncology, nuclear pharmacy, geriatric pharmacy, or psychiatric pharmacy.

Education and Mathematics Required
- Pharmacists are required to possess a Pharm.D. degree from an accredited college or school of pharmacy. This degree generally takes four years to complete. To be admitted to a Pharm.D. program, at least two years of college must be completed, which includes courses in the natural sciences, mathematics, humanities, and the social sciences. A series of examinations must also be passed to obtain a license to practice pharmacy.
- College Algebra, Trigonometry, Statistics, and Calculus I are courses required for admission to a Pharm.D. program.

How Pharmacists Use Math and Who Employs Them
- Pharmacists use math throughout their work to calculate dosages of various drugs. These dosages are based on weight and whether the medication is given in pill form, by infusion, or intravenously.
- Most pharmacists work in a community setting, such as a retail drugstore, or in a healthcare facility, such as a hospital.

Career Outlook and Salary
- Employment of pharmacists is expected to grow by 17 percent between 2008 and 2018, which is faster than the average for all occupations.
- Median annual wages of wage and salary pharmacists is approximately $106,410.

For more information see: www.bls.gov/oco

In this chapter, we review many concepts and skills learned in previous algebra courses. Be sure to master this material now, because it is the basis for the rest of this course.

0.1 Sets of Real Numbers

In this section, we will learn to

1. Identify sets of real numbers.
2. Identify properties of real numbers.
3. Graph subsets of real numbers on the number line.
4. Graph intervals on the number line.
5. Define absolute value.
6. Find distances on the number line.

5	3			7				
6			1	9	5			
	9	8					6	
8				6				3
4			8		3			1
7				2				6
	6					2	8	
			4	1	9			5
				8			7	9

SUDOKU

Sudoku, a game that involves number placement, is very popular. The objective is to fill a 9 by 9 grid so that each column, each row and each of the 3 by 3 blocks contains the numbers from 1 to 9. A partially completed Sudoku grid is shown in the margin.

To solve Sudoku puzzles, logic and the set of numbers, $\{1, 2, 3, 4, 5, 6, 7, 8, 9\}$ are used. Sets of numbers are important in mathematics, and we begin our study of algebra with this topic.

A **set** is a collection of objects, such as a set of dishes or a set of golf clubs. The set of vowels in the English language can be denoted as $\{a, e, i, o, u\}$, where the braces $\{ \}$ are read as "the set of."

If every member of one set B is also a member of another set A, we say that B is a **subset** of A. We can denote this by writing $B \subset A$, where the symbol $\subset$ is read as "is a subset of." (See Figure 0.1 below.) If set B equals set A, we can write $B \subseteq A$.

If A and B are two sets, we can form a new set consisting of all members that are in set A or set B or both. This set is called the **union** of A and B. We can denote this set by writing, $A \cup B$ where the symbol $\cup$ is read as "union." (See Figure 0.1 below.)

We can also form the set consisting of all members that are in both set A and set B. This set is called the **intersection** of A and B. We can denote this set by writing $A \cap B$, where the symbol $\cap$ is read as "intersection." (See Figure 0.1 below.)

$B \subset A$

$A \cup B$

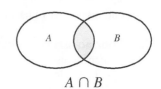
$A \cap B$

FIGURE 0-1

EXAMPLE 1   **Understanding Subsets and Finding the Union and Intersection of Two Sets**

Let $A = \{a, e, i\}$, $B = \{c, d, e\}$, and $V = \{a, e, i, o, u\}$.

a. Is $A \subset V$?   **b.** Find $A \cup B$.   **c.** Find $A \cap B$.

SOLUTION   **a.** Since each member of set A is also a member of set V, $A \subset V$.

b. The union of set A and set B contains the members of set A, set B, or both. Thus, $A \cup B = \{a, c, d, e, i\}$.

c. The intersection of set A and set B contains the members that are in both set A and set B. Thus, $A \cap B = \{e\}$.

Self Check 1   **a.** Is $B \subset V$?   **b.** Find $B \cup V$
c. Find $A \cap V$

Now Try Exercise 33.

1. Identify Sets of Real Numbers

There are several sets of numbers that we use in everyday life.

Basic Sets of Numbers

Natural numbers
The numbers that we use for counting: $\{1, 2, 3, 4, 5, 6, \dots\}$

Whole numbers
The set of natural numbers including 0: $\{0, 1, 2, 3, 4, 5, 6, \dots\}$

Integers
The set of whole numbers and their negatives:
$\{\dots, -5, -4, -3, -2, -1, 0, 1, 2, 3, 4, 5, \dots\}$

In the definitions above, each group of three dots (called an *ellipsis*) indicates that the numbers continue forever in the indicated direction.

Two important subsets of the natural numbers are the *prime* and *composite* numbers. A **prime number** is a natural number greater than 1 that is divisible only by itself and 1. A **composite number** is a natural number greater than 1 that is not prime.

- **The set of prime numbers**: $\{2, 3, 5, 7, 11, 13, 17, 19, 23, 29, 31, \dots\}$
- **The set of composite numbers**: $\{4, 6, 8, 9, 10, 12, 14, 15, 16, 18, 20, 21, \dots\}$

Two important subsets of the set of integers are the *even* and *odd integers*. The **even integers** are the integers that are exactly divisible by 2. The **odd integers** are the integers that are not exactly divisible by 2.

- **The set of even integers:** $\{\dots, -10, -8, -6, -4, -2, 0, 2, 4, 6, 8, 10, \dots\}$
- **The set of odd integers:** $\{\dots, -9, -7, -5, -3, -1, 1, 3, 5, 7, 9, \dots\}$

So far, we have listed numbers inside braces to specify sets. This method is called the **roster method**. When we give a rule to determine which numbers are in a set, we are using **set-builder notation**. To use set-builder notation to denote the set of prime numbers, we write

$$\{x \mid x \text{ is a prime number}\}$$

Read as "the set of all numbers x such that x is a prime number." Recall that when a letter stands for a number, it is called a variable.

variable such that rule that determines membership in the set

Caution

> Remember that the denominator of a fraction can **never** be 0.

The fractions of arithmetic are called *rational numbers*.

Rational Numbers

Rational numbers are fractions that have an integer numerator and a nonzero integer denominator. Using set-builder notation, the rational numbers are

$$\left\{ \frac{a}{b} \mid a \text{ is an integer and } b \text{ is a nonzero integer} \right\}$$

Rational numbers can be written as fractions or decimals. Some examples of rational numbers are

$$5 = \frac{5}{1}, \qquad \frac{3}{4} = 0.75, \qquad -\frac{1}{3} = -0.333\dots, \qquad -\frac{5}{11} = -0.454545\dots$$

The = sign indicates that two quantities are equal.

These examples suggest that the decimal forms of all rational numbers are either *terminating decimals* or *repeating decimals*.

EXAMPLE 2   **Determining whether the Decimal Form of a Fraction Terminates or Repeats**

Determine whether the decimal form of each fraction terminates or repeats:

a. $\dfrac{7}{16}$ **b.** $\dfrac{65}{99}$

SOLUTION   In each case, we perform a long division and write the quotient as a decimal.

a. To change $\frac{7}{16}$ to a decimal, we perform a long division to get $\frac{7}{16} = 0.4375$. Since 0.4375 terminates, we can write $\frac{7}{16}$ as a terminating decimal.

b. To change $\frac{65}{99}$ to a decimal, we perform a long division to get $\frac{65}{99} = 0.656565 \dots$. Since 0.656565 ... repeats, we can write $\frac{65}{99}$ as a repeating decimal.

We can write repeating decimals in compact form by using an overbar. For example, $0.656565 \dots = 0.\overline{65}$. ■

Self Check 2   Determine whether the decimal form of each fraction terminates or repeats:

a. $\dfrac{38}{99}$ **b.** $\dfrac{7}{8}$

Now Try Exercise 35.

Some numbers have decimal forms that neither terminate nor repeat. These nonterminating, nonrepeating decimals are called **irrational numbers**. Three examples of irrational numbers are

$$1.010010001000010 \dots \qquad \sqrt{2} = 1.414213562 \dots \qquad \text{and} \qquad \pi = 3.141592654 \dots$$

The union of the set of rational numbers (the terminating and repeating decimals) and the set of irrational numbers (the nonterminating, nonrepeating decimals) is the set of *real numbers* (the set of all decimals).

Real Numbers   A **real number** is any number that is rational or irrational. Using set-builder notation, the set of real numbers is

$$\{x \mid x \text{ is a rational or an irrational number}\}$$

EXAMPLE 3   **Classifying Real Numbers**

In the set $\{-3, -2, 0, \frac{1}{2}, 1, \sqrt{5}, 2, 4, 5, 6\}$, list all

a. even integers   **b.** prime numbers   **c.** rational numbers

SOLUTION   We will check to see whether each number is a member of the set of even integers, the set of prime numbers, and the set of rational numbers.

a. even integers: –2, 0, 2, 4, 6

b. prime numbers: 2, 5

c. rational numbers: –3, –2, 0, $\frac{1}{2}$, 1, 2, 4, 5, 6 ■

Self Check 3   In the set in Example 3, list all   **a.** odd integers   **b.** composite numbers
c. irrational numbers.

Now Try Exercise 43.

Figure 0-2 shows how the previous sets of numbers are related.

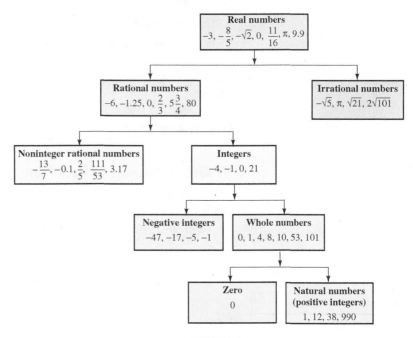

FIGURE 0-2

2. Identify Properties of Real Numbers

When we work with real numbers, we will use the following properties.

Properties of Real Numbers

If a, b, and c are real numbers,

The Commutative Properties for Addition and Multiplication

$$a + b = b + a \qquad\qquad ab = ba$$

The Associative Properties for Addition and Multiplication

$$(a + b) + c = a + (b + c) \qquad (ab)c = a(bc)$$

The Distributive Property of Multiplication over Addition or Subtraction

$$a(b + c) = ab + ac \qquad \text{or} \qquad a(b - c) = ab - ac$$

The Double Negative Rule

$$-(-a) = a$$

Caution

When the Associative Property is used, the order of the real numbers does **not** change. The real numbers that occur within the parentheses change.

The Distributive Property also applies when more than two terms are within parentheses.

EXAMPLE 4   **Identifying Properties of Real Numbers**

Determine which property of real numbers justifies each statement.

a. $(9 + 2) + 3 = 9 + (2 + 3)$ **b.** $3(x + y + 2) = 3x + 3y + 3 \cdot 2$

SOLUTION   We will compare the form of each statement to the forms listed in the properties of real numbers box.

a. This form matches the Associative Property of Addition.

b. This form matches the Distributive Property.

Self Check 4   Determine which property of real numbers justifies each statement:

a. $mn = nm$ **b.** $(xy)z = x(yz)$ **c.** $p + q = q + p$

Now Try Exercise 17.

3. Graph Subsets of Real Numbers on the Number Line

We can graph subsets of real numbers on the **number line**. The number line shown in Figure 0-3 continues forever in both directions. The **positive numbers** are represented by the points to the right of 0, and the **negative numbers** are represented by the points to the left of 0.

Comment

Zero is neither positive nor negative.

FIGURE 0-3

Figure 0-4(a) shows the graph of the natural numbers from 1 to 5. The point associated with each number is called the *graph* of the number, and the number is called the *coordinate* of its point.

Figure 0-4(b) shows the graph of the prime numbers that are less than 10.
Figure 0-4(c) shows the graph of the integers from -4 to 3.
Figure 0-4(d) shows the graph of the real numbers $-\frac{7}{3}$, $-\frac{3}{4}$, $0.\overline{3}$, and $\sqrt{2}$.

Comment

$\sqrt{2}$ can be shown as the diagonal of a square with sides of length 1.

FIGURE 0-4

The graphs in Figure 0-4 suggest that there is a **one-to-one correspondence** between the set of real numbers and the points on a number line. This means that to each real number there corresponds exactly one point on the number line, and to each point on the number line there corresponds exactly one real-number coordinate.

EXAMPLE 5   **Graphing a Set of Numbers on a Number Line**

Graph the set $\left\{-3, -\frac{4}{3}, 0, \sqrt{5}\right\}$.

SOLUTION   We will mark (plot) each number on the number line. To the nearest tenth, $\sqrt{5} = 2.2$.

Self Check 5   Graph the set $\left\{-2, \frac{3}{4}, \sqrt{3}\right\}$. (*Hint*: To the nearest tenth, $\sqrt{3} = 1.7$.)
Now Try Exercise 51.

4. Graph Intervals on the Number Line

To show that two quantities are not equal, we can use an **inequality symbol.**

Symbol	Read as	Examples		
$\neq$	"is not equal to"	$5 \neq 8$	and	$0.25 \neq \frac{1}{3}$
$<$	"is less than"	$12 < 20$	and	$0.17 < 1.1$
$>$	"is greater than"	$15 > 9$	and	$\frac{1}{2} > 0.2$
$\leq$	"is less than or equal to"	$25 \leq 25$	and	$1.7 \leq 2.3$
$\geq$	"is greater than or equal to"	$19 \geq 19$	and	$15.2 \geq 13.7$
$\approx$	"is approximately equal to"	$\sqrt{2} \approx 1.414$	and	$\sqrt{3} \approx 1.732$

It is possible to write an inequality with the inequality symbol pointing in the opposite direction. For example,

- $12 < 20$ is equivalent to $20 > 12$
- $2.3 \geq -1.7$ is equivalent to $-1.7 \leq 2.3$

In Figure 0-3, the coordinates of points get larger as we move from left to right on a number line. Thus, if a and b are the coordinates of two points, the one to the right is the greater. This suggests the following facts:

- If $a > b$, point a lies to the right of point b on a number line.
- If $a < b$, point a lies to the left of point b on a number line.

Figure 0-5(a) shows the graph of the *inequality* $x > -2$ (or $-2 < x$). This graph includes all real numbers x that are greater than -2. The parenthesis at -2 indicates that -2 is not included in the graph. Figure 0-5(b) shows the graph of $x \leq 5$ (or $5 \geq x$). The bracket at 5 indicates that 5 is included in the graph.

(a)   (b)

FIGURE 0-5

Sometimes two inequalities can be written as a single expression called a **compound inequality**. For example, the compound inequality

$$5 < x < 12$$

is a combination of the inequalities $5 < x$ and $x < 12$. It is read as "5 is less than x, and x is less than 12," and it means that x is between 5 and 12. Its graph is shown in Figure 0-6.

FIGURE 0-6

The graphs shown in Figures 0-5 and 0-6 are portions of a number line called **intervals**. The interval shown in Figure 0-7(a) is denoted by the inequality $-2 < x < 4$, or in **interval notation** as $(-2, 4)$. The parentheses indicate that the endpoints are not included. The interval shown in Figure 0-7(b) is denoted by the inequality $x > 1$, or as $(1, \infty)$ in interval notation.

(−2, 4)
$-2 < x < 4$
x is between −2 and 4.

(1, ∞)
$x > 1$
x is greater than 1.

(a)   (b)

FIGURE 0-7

Caution

> The symbol ∞ (infinity) is **not** a real number. It is used to indicate that the graph in Figure 0-7(b) extends infinitely far to the right.

A compound inequality such as $-2 < x < 4$ can be written as two separate inequalities:

$$x > -2 \qquad \text{and} \qquad x < 4$$

This expression represents the **intersection** of two intervals. In interval notation, this expression can be written as

$$(-2, \infty) \cap (-\infty, 4) \qquad \text{Read the symbol} \cap \text{as "intersection."}$$

Since the graph of $-2 < x < 4$ will include all points whose coordinates satisfy both $x > -2$ and $x < 4$ at the same time, its graph will include all points that are larger than −2 but less than 4. This is the interval $(-2, 4)$, whose graph is shown in Figure 0-7(a).

EXAMPLE 6   **Writing an Inequality in Interval Notation and Graphing the Inequality**

Write the inequality $-3 < x < 5$ in interval notation and graph it.

SOLUTION   This is the interval $(-3, 5)$. Its graph includes all real numbers between −3 and 5, as shown in Figure 0-8.

FIGURE 0-8

Self Check 6   Write the inequality $-2 < x \leq 5$ in interval notation and graph it.

Now Try Exercise 63.

If an interval extends forever in one direction, it is called an **unbounded interval**.

Unbounded Intervals

Interval	Inequality	Graph
(a, ∞)	$x > a$	
$(2, \infty)$	$x > 2$	
$[a, \infty)$	$x \geq a$	
$[2, \infty)$	$x \geq 2$	
$(-\infty, a)$	$x < a$	
$(-\infty, 2)$	$x < 2$	
$(-\infty, a]$	$x \leq a$	
$(-\infty, 2]$	$x \leq 2$	
$(-\infty, \infty)$	$-\infty < x < \infty$	

$(-3, 2)$
$-3 < x < 2$

(a)

$[-2, 3)$
$-2 \leq x < 3$

(b)

FIGURE 0-9

A bounded interval with no endpoints is called an **open interval**. Figure 0-9(a) shows the open interval between -3 and 2. A bounded interval with one endpoint is called a **half-open interval**. Figure 0-9(b) shows the half-open interval between -2 and 3, including -2.

Intervals that include two endpoints are called **closed intervals**. Figure 0-10 shows the graph of a closed interval from -2 to 4.

$[-2, 4]$
$-2 \leq x \leq 4$

FIGURE 0-10

Open Intervals, Half-Open Intervals, and Closed Intervals

Interval	Inequality	Graph
Open		
(a, b)	$a < x < b$	
$(-2, 3)$	$-2 < x < 3$	
Half-Open		
$[a, b)$	$a \leq x < b$	
$[-2, 3)$	$-2 \leq x < 3$	
Half-Open		
$(a, b]$	$a < x \leq b$	
$(-2, 3]$	$-2 < x \leq 3$	
Closed		
$[a, b]$	$a \leq x \leq b$	
$[-2, 3]$	$-2 \leq x \leq 3$	

EXAMPLE 7   **Writing an Inequality in Interval Notation and Graphing the Inequality**

Write the inequality $3 \leq x$ in interval notation and graph it.

SOLUTION   The inequality $3 \leq x$ can be written in the form $x \geq 3$. This is the interval $[3, \infty)$. Its graph includes all real numbers greater than or equal to 3, as shown in Figure 0-11.

FIGURE 0-11

Self Check 7   Write the inequality $5 > x$ in interval notation and graph it.

Now Try Exercise 65.

EXAMPLE 8   **Writing an Inequality in Interval Notation and Graphing the Inequality**

Write the inequality $5 \geq x \geq -1$ in interval notation and graph it.

SOLUTION   The inequality $5 \geq x \geq -1$ can be written in the form

$$-1 \leq x \leq 5$$

This is the interval $[-1, 5]$. Its graph includes all real numbers from -1 to 5. The graph is shown in Figure 0-12.

FIGURE 0-12

Self Check 8   Write the inequality $0 \leq x \leq 3$ in interval notation and graph it.

Now Try Exercise 69.

The expression

$$x < -2 \text{ or } x \geq 3 \qquad \text{Read as "}x\text{ is less than } -2 \text{ or } x \text{ is greater than or equal to 3."}$$

represents the *union* of two intervals. In interval notation, it is written as

$$(-\infty, -2) \cup [3, \infty) \qquad \text{Read the symbol } \cup \text{ as "union."}$$

Its graph is shown in Figure 0-13.

FIGURE 0-13

5. Define Absolute Value

The **absolute value** of a real number x (denoted as $|x|$) is the distance on a number line between 0 and the point with a coordinate of x. For example, points with coordinates of 4 and -4 both lie four units from 0, as shown in Figure 0-14. Therefore, it follows that

$$|-4| = |4| = 4$$

FIGURE 0-14

In general, for any real number x,

$$|-x| = |x|$$

We can define absolute value algebraically as follows.

Absolute Value   If x is a real number, then

$$|x| = x \qquad \text{when } x \geq 0$$

$$|x| = -x \qquad \text{when } x < 0$$

Caution

Remember that x is **not** always positive and $-x$ is **not** always negative.

This definition indicates that when x is positive or 0, then x is its own absolute value. However, when x is negative, then $-x$ (which is positive) is its absolute value. Thus, $|x|$ is always nonnegative.

$$|x| \geq 0 \qquad \text{for all real numbers } x$$

EXAMPLE 9   **Using the Definition of Absolute Value**

Write each number without using absolute value symbols:

a. $|3|$ **b.** $|-4|$ **c.** $|0|$ **d.** $-|-8|$

SOLUTION   In each case, we will use the definition of absolute value.

a. $|3| = 3$ **b.** $|-4| = 4$ **c.** $|0| = 0$ **d.** $-|-8| = -(8) = -8$

Self Check 9   Write each number without using absolute value symbols:
a. $|-10|$ **b.** $|12|$ **c.** $-|6|$

Now Try Exercise 85.

In Example 10, we must determine whether the number inside the absolute value is positive or negative.

EXAMPLE 10   **Simplifying an Expression with Absolute Value Symbols**

Write each number without using absolute value symbols:

a. $|\pi - 1|$ **b.** $|2 - \pi|$ **c.** $|2 - x|$ if $x \geq 5$

SOLUTION   **a.** Since $\pi \approx 3.1416$, $\pi - 1$ is positive, and $\pi - 1$ is its own absolute value.

$$|\pi - 1| = \pi - 1$$

b. Since $2 - \pi$ is negative, its absolute value is $-(2 - \pi)$.

$$|2 - \pi| = -(2 - \pi) = -2 - (-\pi) = -2 + \pi = \pi - 2$$

c. Since $x \geq 5$, the expression $2 - x$ is negative, and its absolute value is $-(2 - x)$.

$$|2 - x| = -(2 - x) = -2 + x = x - 2 \text{ provided } x \geq 5$$

Self Check 10   Write each number without using absolute value symbols. (*Hint*: $\sqrt{5} \approx 2.236$.)

a. $\left|2 - \sqrt{5}\right|$ **b.** $|2 - x|$ if $x \leq 1$

Now Try Exercise 89.

6. Find Distances on the Number Line

On the number line shown in Figure 0-15, the distance between the points with coordinates of 1 and 4 is $4 - 1$, or 3 units. However, if the subtraction were done in the other order, the result would be $1 - 4$, or -3 units. To guarantee that the distance between two points is always positive, we can use absolute value symbols. Thus, the distance d between two points with coordinates of 1 and 4 is

$$d = |4 - 1| = |1 - 4| = 3$$

FIGURE 0-15

In general, we have the following definition for the distance between two points on the number line.

Distance between Two Points   If a and b are the coordinates of two points on the number line, the distance between the points is given by the formula

$$d = |b - a|$$

EXAMPLE 11   **Finding the Distance between Two Points on a Number Line**

Find the distance on a number line between points with coordinates of **a.** 3 and 5   **b.** -2 and 3   **c.** -5 and -1

SOLUTION   We will use the formula for finding the distance between two points.

a. $d = |5 - 3| = |2| = 2$

b. $d = |3 - (-2)| = |3 + 2| = |5| = 5$

c. $d = |-1 - (-5)| = |-1 + 5| = |4| = 4$

Self Check 11   Find the distance on a number line between points with coordinates of **a.** 4 and 10   **b.** -2 and -7

Now Try Exercise 99.

Self Check Answers   **1. a.** no   **b.** {a, c, d, e, i, o, u}   **c.** {a, e, i}   **2. a.** repeats
b. terminates   **3. a.** $-3, 1, 5$ **b.** 4, 6   **c.** $\sqrt{5}$ **4. a.** Commutative
Property of Multiplication   **b.** Associative Property of Multiplication
c. Commutative Property of Addition   **5.**

6. $(-2, 5]$ **7.** $(-\infty, 5)$

8. $[0, 3]$ **9. a.** 10   **b.** 12   **c.** -6

10. a. $\sqrt{5} - 2$ **b.** $2 - x$ **11. a.** 6   **b.** 5

Exercises **0.1**

Getting Ready
You should be able to complete these vocabulary and concept statements before you proceed to the practice exercises.

Fill in the blanks.

1. A _____ is a collection of objects.
2. If every member of one set B is also a member of a second set A, then B is called a _____ of A.
3. If A and B are two sets, the set that contains all members that are in sets A and B or both is called the _____ of A and B.
4. If A and B are two sets, the set that contains all members that are in both sets is called the _____ of A and B.
5. A real number is any number that can be expressed as a _____ .
6. A _____ is a letter that is used to represent a number.
7. The smallest prime number is ___ .
8. All integers that are exactly divisible by 2 are called _____ integers.
9. Natural numbers greater than 1 that are not prime are called _____ numbers.
10. Fractions such as $\frac{2}{3}, \frac{8}{2}$, and $-\frac{7}{9}$ are called _____ numbers.
11. Irrational numbers are _____ that don't terminate and don't repeat.
12. The symbol _____ is read as "is less than or equal to."
13. On a number line, the _____ numbers are to the left of 0.
14. The only integer that is neither positive nor negative is ___ .
15. The Associative Property of Addition states that $(x + y) + z = $ _____ .
16. The Commutative Property of Multiplication states that $xy = $ ____ .
17. Use the Distributive Property to complete the statement: $5(m + 2) = $ _____ .
18. The statement $(m + n)p = p(m + n)$ illustrates the _____ Property of _____ .
19. The graph of an _____ is a portion of a number line.
20. The graph of an open interval has ____ endpoints.
21. The graph of a closed interval has ____ endpoints.
22. The graph of a _____ interval has one endpoint.
23. Except for 0, the absolute value of every number is

24. The _____ between two distinct points on a number line is always positive.

Let

$\mathbf{N} = $ *the set of natural numbers*
$\mathbf{W} = $ *the set of whole numbers*
$\mathbf{Z} = $ *the set of integers*
$\mathbf{Q} = $ *the set of rational numbers*
$\mathbf{R} = $ *the set of real numbers*

Determine whether each statement is true or false. Read the symbol $\subset$ as "is a subset of."

25. $\mathbf{N} \subset \mathbf{W}$
26. $\mathbf{Q} \subset \mathbf{R}$
27. $\mathbf{Q} \subset \mathbf{N}$
28. $\mathbf{Z} \subset \mathbf{Q}$
29. $\mathbf{W} \subset \mathbf{Z}$
30. $\mathbf{R} \subset \mathbf{Z}$

Practice
Let $A = \{a, b, c, d, e\}$, $B = (d, e, f, g\}$, and $C = \{a, c, e, f\}$. Find each set.

31. $A \cup B$
32. $A \cap B$
33. $A \cap C$
34. $B \cup C$

Determine whether the decimal form of each fraction terminates or repeats.

35. $\dfrac{9}{16}$
36. $\dfrac{3}{8}$
37. $\dfrac{3}{11}$
38. $\dfrac{5}{12}$

Consider the following set:
$\{-5, -4, -\frac{2}{3}, 0, 1, \sqrt{2}, 2, 2.75, 6, 7\}.$

39. Which numbers are natural numbers?
40. Which numbers are whole numbers?
41. Which numbers are integers?
42. Which numbers are rational numbers?

43. Which numbers are irrational numbers?
44. Which numbers are prime numbers?
45. Which numbers are composite numbers?
46. Which numbers are even integers?
47. Which numbers are odd integers?
48. Which numbers are negative numbers?

Graph each subset of the real numbers on a number line.

49. The natural numbers between 1 and 5

50. The composite numbers less than 10

51. The prime numbers between 10 and 20

52. The integers from –2 to 4

53. The integers between –5 and 0

54. The even integers between –9 and –1

55. The odd integers between –6 and 4

56. $-0.7, 1.75,$ and $3\frac{7}{8}$

Write each inequality in interval notation and graph the interval.

57. $x > 2$ **58.** $x < 4$

59. $0 < x < 5$ **60.** $-2 < x < 3$

61. $x > -4$ **62.** $x < 3$

63. $-2 \le x < 2$ **64.** $-4 < x \le 1$

65. $x \le 5$ **66.** $x \ge -1$

67. $-5 < x \le 0$ **68.** $-3 \le x < 4$

69. $-2 \le x \le 3$ **70.** $-4 \le x \le 4$

71. $6 \ge x \ge 2$ **72.** $3 \ge x \ge -2$

Write each pair of inequalities as the intersection of two intervals and graph the result.

73. $x > -5$ and $x < 4$

74. $x \ge -3$ and $x < 6$

75. $x \ge -8$ and $x \le -3$

76. $x > 1$ and $x \le 7$

Write each inequality as the union of two intervals and graph the result.

77. $x < -2$ or $x > 2$

78. $x \le -5$ or $x > 0$

79. $x \le -1$ or $x \ge 3$

80. $x < -3$ or $x \ge 2$

Write each expression without using absolute value symbols.

81. $|13|$ **82.** $|-17|$

83. $|0|$ **84.** $-|63|$

85. $-|-8|$ **86.** $|-25|$

87. $-|32|$ **88.** $-|-6|$

89. $|\pi - 5|$ **90.** $|8 - \pi|$

91. $|\pi - \pi|$ **92.** $|2\pi|$

93. $|x + 1|$ and $x \ge 2$ **94.** $|x + 1|$ and $x \le -2$

95. $|x - 4|$ and $x < 0$ **96.** $|x - 7|$ and $x > 10$

Find the distance between each pair of points on the number line.

97. 3 and 8   **98.** -5 and 12

99. -8 and -3 **100.** 6 and -20

Applications

101. What subset of the real numbers would you use to describe the populations of several cities?

102. What subset of the real numbers would you use to describe the subdivisions of an inch on a ruler?

103. What subset of the real numbers would you use to report temperatures in several cities?

104. What subset of the real numbers would you use to describe the financial condition of a business?

Discovery and Writing

105. Explain why $-x$ could be positive.

106. Explain why every integer is a rational number.

107. Is the statement $|ab| = |a| \cdot |b|$ always true? Explain.

108. Is the statement $\left|\dfrac{a}{b}\right| = \dfrac{|a|}{|b|}$ $(b \ne 0)$ always true?

109. Is the statement $|a + b| = |a| + |b|$ always true? Explain.

110. Under what conditions will the statement given in Exercise 109 be true?

111. Explain why it is incorrect to write $a < b > c$ if $a < b$ and $b > c$.

112. Explain why $|b - a| = |a - b|$.

0.2 Integer Exponents and Scientific Notation

In this section, we will learn to

1. Define natural-number exponents.
2. Apply the rules of exponents.
3. Apply the rules for order of operations to evaluate expressions.
4. Express numbers in scientific notation.
5. Use scientific notation to simplify computations.

bioraven/Shutterstock.com

The number of cells in the human body is approximated to be one hundred trillion or 100,000,000,000,000. One hundred trillion is $(10)(10)(10) \cdots (10)$, where ten occurs fourteen times. Fourteen factors of ten can be written as 10^{14}.

In this section, we will use integer exponents to represent repeated multiplication of numbers.

1. Define Natural-Number Exponents

When two or more quantities are multiplied together, each quantity is called a *factor* of the product. The exponential expression x^4 indicates that x is to be used as a factor four times.

$$x^4 = \overbrace{x \cdot x \cdot x \cdot x}^{4 \text{ factors of } x}$$

In general, the following is true.

Natural-Number Exponents   For any natural number n,

$$x^n = \overbrace{x \cdot x \cdot x \cdot \cdots \cdot x}^{n \text{ factors of } x}$$

In the **exponential expression** x^n, x is called the **base**, and n is called the **exponent** or the **power** to which the base is raised. The expression x^n is called a **power of x**. From the definition, we see that a natural-number exponent indicates how many times the base of an exponential expression is to be used as a factor in a product. If an exponent is 1, the 1 is usually not written:

$$x^1 = x$$

EXAMPLE 1   **Using the Definition of Natural-Number Exponents**

Write each expression without using exponents:

a. 4^2 **b.** $(-4)^2$ **c.** -5^3 **d.** $(-5)^3$ **e.** $3x^4$ **f.** $(3x)^4$

SOLUTION In each case, we apply the definition of natural-number exponents.

a. $4^2 = 4 \cdot 4 = 16$ Read 4^2 as "four squared."

b. $(-4)^2 = (-4)(-4) = 16$ Read $(-4)^2$ as "negative four squared."

c. $-5^3 = -5(5)(5) = -125$ Read -5^3 as "the negative of five cubed."

d. $(-5)^3 = (-5)(-5)(-5) = -125$ Read $(-5)^3$ as "negative five cubed."

e. $3x^4 = 3 \cdot x \cdot x \cdot x \cdot x$ Read $3x^4$ as "3 times x to the fourth power."

f. $(3x)^4 = (3x)(3x)(3x)(3x) = 81 \cdot x \cdot x \cdot x \cdot x$ Read $(3x)^4$ as "$3x$ to the fourth power." ∎

Self Check 1 Write each expression without using exponents:
a. 7^3 **b.** $(-3)^2$ **c.** $5a^3$ **d.** $(5a)^4$

Now Try Exercise 19.

Comment Note the distinction between ax^n and $(ax)^n$:

$$\underbrace{ax^n = a \cdot x \cdot x \cdot x \cdot \cdots \cdot x}_{n \text{ factors of } x} \qquad \underbrace{(ax)^n = (ax)(ax)(ax) \cdot \cdots \cdot (ax)}_{n \text{ factors of } ax}$$

Also note the distinction between $-x^n$ and $(-x)^n$:

$$\underbrace{-x^n = -(x \cdot x \cdot x \cdot \cdots \cdot x)}_{n \text{ factors of } x} \qquad \underbrace{(-x)^n = (-x)(-x)(-x) \cdot \cdots \cdot (-x)}_{n \text{ factors of } -x}$$

ACCENT ON TECHNOLOGY **Using a Calculator to Find Powers**

We can use a graphing calculator to find powers of numbers. For example, consider 2.35^3.

- Input 2.35 and press the [∧] key.
- Input 3 and press [ENTER].

Comment

To find powers on a scientific calculator use the [y^x] key.

FIGURE 0-16

We see that $2.35^3 = 12.977875$ as the figure shows above.

2. Apply the Rules of Exponents

We begin the review of the rules of exponents by considering the product $x^m x^n$. Since x^m indicates that x is to be used as a factor m times, and since x^n indicates that x is to be used as a factor n times, there are $m + n$ factors of x in the product $x^m x^n$.

$$x^m x^n = \overbrace{\underbrace{x \cdot x \cdot x \cdot \cdots \cdot x}_{m \text{ factors of } x} \cdot \underbrace{x \cdot x \cdot x \cdot \cdots \cdot x}_{n \text{ factors of } x}}^{m + n \text{ factors of } x} = x^{m+n}$$

This suggests that to multiply exponential expressions with the same base, we *keep the base and add the exponents.*

Product Rule for Exponents   If m and n are natural numbers, then

$$x^m x^n = x^{m+n}$$

Comment

The Product Rule applies to exponential expressions with the same base. A product of two powers with different bases, such as x^4y^3, cannot be simplified.

To find another property of exponents, we consider the exponential expression $(x^m)^n$. In this expression, the exponent n indicates that x^m is to be used as a factor n times. This implies that x is to be used as a factor mn times.

$$(x^m)^n = \overbrace{\underbrace{(x^m)(x^m)(x^m) \cdot \cdots \cdot (x^m)}_{n \text{ factors of } x^m}}^{mn \text{ factors of } x} = x^{mn}$$

This suggests that to raise an exponential expression to a power, we *keep the base and multiply the exponents.*

To raise a product to a power, we raise each factor to that power.

$$(xy)^n = \underbrace{(xy)(xy)(xy) \cdot \cdots \cdot (xy)}_{n \text{ factors of } xy} = \underbrace{(x \cdot x \cdot x \cdot \cdots \cdot x)}_{n \text{ factors of } x}\underbrace{(y \cdot y \cdot y \cdot \cdots \cdot y)}_{n \text{ factors of } y} = x^n y^n$$

To raise a fraction to a power, we raise both the numerator and the denominator to that power. If $y \neq 0$, then

$$\left(\frac{x}{y}\right)^n = \underbrace{\left(\frac{x}{y}\right)\left(\frac{x}{y}\right)\left(\frac{x}{y}\right) \cdot \cdots \cdot \left(\frac{x}{y}\right)}_{n \text{ factors of } \frac{x}{y}}$$

$$= \frac{\overbrace{xxx \cdot \cdots \cdot x}^{n \text{ factors of } x}}{\underbrace{yyy \cdot \cdots \cdot y}_{n \text{ factors of } y}}$$

$$= \frac{x^n}{y^n}$$

The previous three results are called the *Power Rules of Exponents.*

Power Rules of Exponents   If m and n are natural numbers, then

$$(x^m)^n = x^{mn} \qquad (xy)^n = x^n y^n \qquad \left(\frac{x}{y}\right)^n = \frac{x^n}{y^n} \qquad (y \neq 0)$$

EXAMPLE 2   **Using Exponent Rules to Simplify Expressions with Natural-Number Exponents**

Simplify: **a.** $x^5 x^7$ **b.** $x^2 y^3 x^5 y$ **c.** $(x^4)^9$ **d.** $(x^2 x^5)^3$

e. $\left(\frac{x}{y^2}\right)^5$ **f.** $\left(\frac{5x^2y}{z^3}\right)^2$

SOLUTION   In each case, we will apply the appropriate rule of exponents.

a. $x^5x^7 = x^{5+7} = x^{12}$ **b.** $x^2y^3x^5y = x^{2+5}y^{3+1} = x^7y^4$

c. $(x^4)^9 = x^{4\cdot9} = x^{36}$ **d.** $(x^2x^5)^3 = (x^7)^3 = x^{21}$

e. $\left(\dfrac{x}{y^2}\right)^5 = \dfrac{x^5}{(y^2)^5} = \dfrac{x^5}{y^{10}}$ $(y \neq 0)$

f. $\left(\dfrac{5x^2y}{z^3}\right)^2 = \dfrac{5^2(x^2)^2y^2}{(z^3)^2} = \dfrac{25x^4y^2}{z^6}$ $(z \neq 0)$

Self Check 2   Simplify:

a. $(y^3)^2$ **b.** $(a^2a^4)^3$ **c.** $(x^2)^3(x^3)^2$ **d.** $\left(\dfrac{3a^3b^2}{c^3}\right)^3$ $(c \neq 0)$

Now Try Exercise 49.

If we assume that the rules for natural-number exponents hold for exponents of 0, we can write

$$x^0x^n = x^{0+n} = x^n = 1x^n$$

Since $x^0x^n = 1x^n$, it follows that if $x \neq 0$, then $x^0 = 1$.

Zero Exponent $x^0 = 1$ $(x \neq 0)$

If we assume that the rules for natural-number exponents hold for exponents that are negative integers, we can write

$$x^{-n}x^n = x^{-n+n} = x^0 = 1 \quad (x \neq 0)$$

However, we know that

$$\dfrac{1}{x^n} \cdot x^n = 1 \quad (x \neq 0) \qquad \dfrac{1}{x^n} \cdot x^n = \dfrac{x^n}{x^n}, \text{ and any nonzero number divided by itself is 1.}$$

Since $x^{-n}x^n = \frac{1}{x^n} \cdot x^n$, it follows that $x^{-n} = \frac{1}{x^n}$ $(x \neq 0)$.

Negative Exponents   If n is an integer and $x \neq 0$, then

$$x^{-n} = \dfrac{1}{x^n} \quad \text{and} \quad \dfrac{1}{x^{-n}} = x^n$$

Because of the previous definitions, all of the rules for natural-number exponents will hold for integer exponents.

EXAMPLE 3   **Simplifying Expressions with Integer Exponents**

Simplify and write all answers without using negative exponents:

a. $(3x)^0$ **b.** $3(x^0)$ **c.** x^{-4} **d.** $\dfrac{1}{x^{-6}}$ **e.** $x^{-3}x$ **f.** $(x^{-4}x^8)^{-5}$

SOLUTION   We will use the definitions of zero exponent and negative exponents to simplify each expression.

a. $(3x)^0 = 1$ **b.** $3(x^0) = 3(1) = 3$ **c.** $x^{-4} = \dfrac{1}{x^4}$ **d.** $\dfrac{1}{x^{-6}} = x^6$

e. $x^{-3}x = x^{-3+1}$

$\qquad = x^{-2}$

$\qquad = \dfrac{1}{x^2}$

f. $(x^{-4}x^8)^{-5} = (x^4)^{-5}$

$\qquad = x^{-20}$

$\qquad = \dfrac{1}{x^{20}}$

Self Check 3 Simplify and write all answers without using negative exponents:

a. $7a^0$ **b.** $3a^{-2}$ **c.** $a^{-4}a^2$ **d.** $(a^3a^{-7})^3$

Now Try Exercise 59.

To develop the Quotient Rule for Exponents, we proceed as follows:

$$\frac{x^m}{x^n} = x^m\left(\frac{1}{x^n}\right) = x^m x^{-n} = x^{m+(-n)} = x^{m-n} \quad (x \neq 0)$$

This suggests that to divide two exponential expressions with the same nonzero base, we *keep the base and subtract the exponent in the denominator from the exponent in the numerator*.

Quotient Rule for Exponents If m and n are integers, then

$$\frac{x^m}{x^n} = x^{m-n} \quad (x \neq 0)$$

EXAMPLE 4 **Simplifying Expressions with Integer Exponents**

Simplify and write all answers without using negative exponents:

a. $\dfrac{x^8}{x^5}$ **b.** $\dfrac{x^2 x^4}{x^{-5}}$

SOLUTION We will apply the Product and Quotient Rules of Exponents.

a. $\dfrac{x^8}{x^5} = x^{8-5}$

$\qquad = x^3$

b. $\dfrac{x^2 x^4}{x^{-5}} = \dfrac{x^6}{x^{-5}}$

$\qquad = x^{6-(-5)}$

$\qquad = x^{11}$

Self Check 4 Simplify and write all answers without using negative exponents:

a. $\dfrac{x^{-6}}{x^2}$ **b.** $\dfrac{x^4 x^{-3}}{x^2}$

Now Try Exercise 69.

EXAMPLE 5 **Simplifying Expressions with Integer Exponents**

Simplify and write all answers without using negative exponents:

a. $\left(\dfrac{x^3 y^{-2}}{x^{-2}y^3}\right)^{-2}$ **b.** $\left(\dfrac{x}{y}\right)^{-n}$

SOLUTION   We will apply the appropriate rules of exponents.

a. $\left(\dfrac{x^3 y^{-2}}{x^{-2} y^3}\right)^{-2} = \left(x^{3-(-2)} y^{-2-3}\right)^{-2}$

$\qquad\qquad = \left(x^5 y^{-5}\right)^{-2}$

$\qquad\qquad = x^{-10} y^{10}$

$\qquad\qquad = \dfrac{y^{10}}{x^{10}}$

b. $\left(\dfrac{x}{y}\right)^{-n} = \dfrac{x^{-n}}{y^{-n}}$

$\qquad\quad = \dfrac{x^{-n} x^n y^n}{y^{-n} x^n y^n}$ Multiply numerator and denominator by 1 in the form $\dfrac{x^n y^n}{x^n y^n}$.

$\qquad\quad = \dfrac{x^0 y^n}{y^0 x^n}$ $x^{-n} x^n = x^0$ and $y^{-n} y^n = y^0$.

$\qquad\quad = \dfrac{y^n}{x^n}$ $x^0 = 1$ and $y^0 = 1$.

$\qquad\quad = \left(\dfrac{y}{x}\right)^n$

Self Check 5   Simplify and write all answers without using negative exponents:

a. $\left(\dfrac{x^4 y^{-3}}{x^{-3} y^2}\right)^2$ b. $\left(\dfrac{2a}{3b}\right)^{-3}$

Now Try Exercise 75.

Part b of Example 5 establishes the following rule.

A Fraction to a Negative Power   If n is a natural number, then

$$\left(\dfrac{x}{y}\right)^{-n} = \left(\dfrac{y}{x}\right)^n \qquad (x \neq 0 \quad \text{and} \quad y \neq 0)$$

3. Apply the Rules for Order of Operations to Evaluate Expressions

When several operations occur in an expression, we must perform the operations in the following order to get the correct result.

Strategy for Evaluating Expressions Using Order of Operations   If an expression does not contain grouping symbols such as parentheses or brackets, follow these steps:

1. Find the values of any exponential expressions.
2. Perform all multiplications and/or divisions, working from left to right.
3. Perform all additions and/or subtractions, working from left to right.

- If an expression contains grouping symbols such as parentheses, brackets, or braces, use the rules above to perform the calculations within each pair of grouping symbols, working from the innermost pair to the outermost pair.
- In a fraction, simplify the numerator and the denominator of the fraction separately. Then simplify the fraction, if possible.

Comment   Many students remember the Order of Operations Rule with the acronym **PEMDAS:**

- **P**arentheses
- **E**xponents
- **M**ultiplication
- **D**ivision
- **A**ddition
- **S**ubtraction

For example, to simplify $\dfrac{3[4 - (6 + 10)]}{2^2 - (6 + 7)}$, we proceed as follows:

$$\frac{3[4 - (6 + 10)]}{2^2 - (6 + 7)} = \frac{3(4 - 16)}{2^2 - (6 + 7)} \qquad \text{Simplify within the inner parentheses: } 6 + 10 = 16.$$

$$= \frac{3(-12)}{2^2 - 13} \qquad \text{Simplify within the parentheses: } 4 - 16 = -12, \text{ and } 6 + 7 = 13.$$

$$= \frac{3(-12)}{4 - 13} \qquad \text{Evaluate the power: } 2^2 = 4.$$

$$= \frac{-36}{-9} \qquad 3(-12) = -36.\; 4 - 13 = -9.$$

$$= 4$$

EXAMPLE 6   **Evaluating Algebraic Expressions**

If $x = -2$, $y = 3$, and $z = -4$, evaluate

a. $-x^2 + y^2z$ **b.** $\dfrac{2z^3 - 3y^2}{5x^2}$

SOLUTION   In each part, we will substitute the numbers for the variables, apply the rules of order of operations, and simplify.

a. $-x^2 + y^2z = -(-2)^2 + 3^2(-4)$

$$= -(4) + 9(-4) \qquad \text{Evaluate the powers.}$$

$$= -4 + (-36) \qquad \text{Do the multiplication.}$$

$$= -40 \qquad \text{Do the addition.}$$

b. $\dfrac{2z^3 - 3y^2}{5x^2} = \dfrac{2(-4)^3 - 3(3)^2}{5(-2)^2}$

$$= \frac{2(-64) - 3(9)}{5(4)} \qquad \text{Evaluate the powers.}$$

$$= \frac{-128 - 27}{20} \qquad \text{Do the multiplications.}$$

$$= \frac{-155}{20} \qquad \text{Do the subtraction.}$$

$$= -\frac{31}{4} \qquad \text{Simplify the fraction.}$$

Self Check 6   If $x = 3$ and $y = -2$, evaluate $\dfrac{2x^2 - 3y^2}{x - y}$.

Now Try Exercise 91.

4. Express Numbers in Scientific Notation

Scientists often work with numbers that are very large or very small. These numbers can be written compactly by expressing them in *scientific notation*.

Scientific Notation   A number is written in *scientific notation* when it is written in the form

$$N \times 10^n$$

where $1 \leq |N| < 10$ and n is an integer.

Light travels 29,980,000,000 centimeters per second.

To express this number in scientific notation, we must write it as the product of a number between 1 and 10 and some integer power of 10. The number 2.998 lies between 1 and 10. To get 29,980,000,000, the decimal point in 2.998 must be moved ten places to the right. This is accomplished by multiplying 2.998 by 10^{10}.

Standard notation ⟶ $29{,}980{,}000{,}000 = 2.998 \times 10^{10}$ ⟵ Scientific notation

One meter is approximately 0.0006214 mile. To express this number in scientific notation, we must write it as the product of a number between 1 and 10 and some integer power of 10. The number 6.214 lies between 1 and 10. To get 0.0006214, the decimal point in 6.214 must be moved four places to the left. This is accomplished by multiplying 6.214 by $\frac{1}{10^4}$ or by multiplying 6.214 by 10^{-4}.

Standard notation ⟶ $0.0006214 = 6214 \times 10^{-4}$ ⟵ Scientific notation

To write each of the following numbers in scientific notation, we start to the right of the first nonzero digit and count to the decimal point. The exponent gives the number of places the decimal point moves, and the sign of the exponent indicates the direction in which it moves.

a. $3\,7\,2\,0\,0\,0 = 3.72 \times 10^5$ 5 places to the right.

b. $0\,.\,0\,0\,0\,5\,3\,7 = 5.37 \times 10^{-4}$ 4 places to the left.

c. $7.36 = 7.36 \times 10^0$ No movement of the decimal point.

EXAMPLE 7   **Writing Numbers in Scientific Notation**

Write each number in scientific notation: **a.** 62,000   **b.** −0.0027

SOLUTION   **a.** We must express 62,000 as a product of a number between 1 and 10 and some integer power of 10. This is accomplished by multiplying 6.2 by 10^4.

$$62{,}000 = 6.2 \times 10^4$$

b. We must express −0.0027 as a product of a number whose absolute value is between 1 and 10 and some integer power of 10. This is accomplished by multiplying −2.7 by 10^{-3}.

$$-0.0027 = -2.7 \times 10^{-3}$$

■

Self Check 7   Write each number in scientific notation:
a. −93,000,000   **b.** 0.0000087

Now Try Exercise 103.

EXAMPLE 8   **Writing Numbers in Standard Notation**

Write each number in standard notation:

a. 7.35×10^2 **b.** 3.27×10^{-5}

SOLUTION   **a.** The factor of 10^2 indicates that 7.35 must be multiplied by 2 factors of 10. Because each multiplication by 10 moves the decimal point one place to the right, we have

$$7.35 \times 10^2 = 735$$

b. The factor of 10^{-5} indicates that 3.27 must be divided by 5 factors of 10. Because each division by 10 moves the decimal point one place to the left, we have

$$3.27 \times 10^{-5} = 0.0000327$$

Self Check 8   Write each number in standard notation: **a.** 6.3×10^3 **b.** 9.1×10^{-4}

Now Try Exercise 111.

5. Use Scientific Notation to Simplify Computations

Another advantage of scientific notation becomes evident when we multiply and divide very large and very small numbers.

EXAMPLE 9   **Using Scientific Notation to Simplify Computations**

Use scientific notation to calculate $\dfrac{(3,400,000)(0.00002)}{170,000,000}$.

SOLUTION   After changing each number to scientific notation, we can do the arithmetic on the numbers and the exponential expressions separately.

$$\frac{(3,400,000)(0.00002)}{170,000,000} = \frac{(3.4 \times 10^6)(2.0 \times 10^{-5})}{1.7 \times 10^8}$$
$$= \frac{6.8}{1.7} \times 10^{6+(-5)-8}$$
$$= 4.0 \times 10^{-7}$$
$$= 0.0000004$$

Self Check 9   Use scientific notation to simplify $\dfrac{(192,000)(0.0015)}{(0.0032)(4,500)}$.

Now Try Exercise 119.

ACCENT ON TECHNOLOGY   **Scientific Notation**

Graphing calculators will often give an answer in scientific notation. For example, consider 21^8.

FIGURE 0-17

We see in the figure that the answer given is 3.782285936E10, which means $3.782285936 \times 10^{10}$.

Comment
To calculate an expression like $\dfrac{21^8}{0.000000000061}$ on a scientific calculator, it is necessary to convert the denominator to scientific notation because the number has too many digits to fit on the screen.

- For scientific notation, we enter these numbers and press these keys: 6.1 $\boxed{\text{EXP}}$ 11 $\boxed{+/-}$.

- To evaluate the expression above, we enter these numbers and press these keys:

$$21 \boxed{y^x} 8 \boxed{=} \boxed{\div} 6.1 \boxed{\text{EXP}} 11 \boxed{+/-} \boxed{=}$$

The display will read $\boxed{6.200468748^{20}}$. In standard notation, the answer is approximately 620,046,874,800,000,000,000.

Self Check Answers
1. a. $7 \cdot 7 \cdot 7 = 343$ b. $(-3)(-3) = 9$ c. $5 \cdot a \cdot a \cdot a$
   d. $(5a)(5a)(5a)(5a) = 625 \cdot a \cdot a \cdot a \cdot a$ 2. a. y^6 b. a^{18} c. x^{12}

   d. $\dfrac{27a^9b^6}{c^9}$ 3. a. 7   b. $\dfrac{3}{a^2}$ c. $\dfrac{1}{a^2}$ d. $\dfrac{1}{a^{12}}$ 4. a. $\dfrac{1}{x^8}$ b. $\dfrac{1}{x}$

   5. a. $\dfrac{x^{14}}{y^{10}}$ b. $\dfrac{27b^3}{8a^3}$ 6. $\dfrac{6}{5}$ 7. a. -9.3×10^7 b. 8.7×10^{-6}

   8. a. 6,300   b. 0.00091   9. 20

Exercises **0.2**

Getting Ready

You should be able to complete these vocabulary and concept statements before you proceed to the practice exercises.

Fill in the blanks.

1. Each quantity in a product is called a _____ of the product.

2. A _____ number exponent tells how many times a base is used as a factor.

3. In the expression $(2x)^3$, ___ is the exponent and ____ is the base.

4. The expression x^n is called an _____ expression.

5. A number is in _____ notation when it is written in the form $N \times 10^n$, where $1 \le |N| < 10$ and n is an _____.

6. Unless _____ indicate otherwise, _____ are performed before additions.

Complete each exponent rule. Assume $x \ne 0$.

7. $x^m x^n =$ _____   8. $(x^m)^n =$ _____

9. $(xy)^n =$ _____   10. $\dfrac{x^m}{x^n} =$ _____

11. $x^0 =$ ___   12. $x^{-n} =$ _____

Practice

Write each number or expression without using exponents.

13. 13^2 14. 10^3

15. -5^2 16. $(-5)^2$

17. $4x^3$ 18. $(4x)^3$

19. $(-5x)^4$ 20. $-6x^2$

21. $-8x^4$ 22. $(-8x)^4$

Write each expression using exponents.

23. $7xxx$ 24. $-8yyyy$

25. $(-x)(-x)$ 26. $(2a)(2a)(2a)$

27. $(3t)(3t)(-3t)$ 28. $-(2b)(2b)(2b)(2b)$

29. $xxxyy$ 30. $aaabbbb$

Use a calculator to simplify each expression.

31. 2.2^3 32. 7.1^4

33. -0.5^4 34. $(-0.2)^4$

Simplify each expression. Write all answers without using negative exponents. Assume that all variables are restricted to those numbers for which the expression is defined.

35. x^2x^3 36. y^3y^4

37. $(z^2)^3$ 38. $(t^6)^7$

39. $(y^5y^2)^3$ 40. $(a^3a^6)a^4$

41. $(z^2)^3(z^4)^5$ 42. $(t^3)^4(t^5)^2$

43. $(a^2)^3(a^4)^2$ 44. $(a^2)^4(a^3)^3$

45. $(3x)^3$ 46. $(-2y)^4$

47. $(x^2y)^3$ 48. $(x^3z^4)^6$

49. $\left(\dfrac{a^2}{b}\right)^3$

50. $\left(\dfrac{x}{y^3}\right)^4$

51. $(-x)^0$

52. $4x^0$

53. $(4x)^0$

54. $-2x^0$

55. z^{-4}

56. $\dfrac{1}{t^{-2}}$

57. $y^{-2}y^{-3}$

58. $-m^{-2}m^3$

59. $(x^3x^{-4})^{-2}$

60. $(y^{-2}y^3)^{-4}$

61. $\dfrac{x^7}{x^3}$

62. $\dfrac{r^5}{r^2}$

63. $\dfrac{a^{21}}{a^{17}}$

64. $\dfrac{t^{13}}{t^4}$

65. $\dfrac{(x^2)^2}{x^2x}$

66. $\dfrac{s^9s^3}{(s^2)^2}$

67. $\left(\dfrac{m^3}{n^2}\right)^3$

68. $\left(\dfrac{t^4}{t^3}\right)^3$

69. $\dfrac{(a^3)^{-2}}{aa^2}$

70. $\dfrac{r^9r^{-3}}{(r^{-2})^3}$

71. $\left(\dfrac{a^{-3}}{b^{-1}}\right)^{-4}$

72. $\left(\dfrac{t^{-4}}{t^{-3}}\right)^{-2}$

73. $\left(\dfrac{r^4r^{-6}}{r^3r^{-3}}\right)^2$

74. $\dfrac{(x^{-3}x^2)^2}{(x^2x^{-5})^{-3}}$

75. $\left(\dfrac{x^5y^{-2}}{x^{-3}y^2}\right)^4$

76. $\left(\dfrac{x^{-7}y^5}{x^7y^{-4}}\right)^3$

77. $\left(\dfrac{5x^{-3}y^{-2}}{3x^2y^{-3}}\right)^{-2}$

78. $\left(\dfrac{3x^2y^{-5}}{2x^{-2}y^{-6}}\right)^{-3}$

79. $\left(\dfrac{3x^5y^{-3}}{6x^{-5}y^3}\right)^{-2}$

80. $\left(\dfrac{12x^{-4}y^3z^{-5}}{4x^4y^{-3}z^5}\right)^3$

81. $\dfrac{(8^{-2}z^{-3}y)^{-1}}{(5y^2z^{-2})^3(5yz^{-2})^{-1}}$

82. $\dfrac{(m^{-2}n^3p^4)^{-2}(mn^{-2}p^3)^4}{(mn^{-2}p^3)^{-4}(mn^2p)^{-1}}$

Simplify each expression.

83. $-\dfrac{5[6^2+(9-5)]}{4(2-3)^2}$

84. $\dfrac{6[3-(4-7)^2]}{-5(2-4^2)}$

Let $x = -2$, $y = 0$, and $z = 3$ and evaluate each expression.

85. x^2

86. $-x^2$

87. x^3

88. $-x^3$

89. $(-xz)^3$

90. $-xz^3$

91. $\dfrac{-(x^2z^3)}{z^2-y^2}$

92. $\dfrac{z^2(x^2-y^2)}{x^3z}$

93. $5x^2-3y^3z$

94. $3(x-z)^2+2(y-z)^3$

95. $\dfrac{-3x^{-3}z^{-2}}{6x^2z^{-3}}$

96. $\dfrac{(-5x^2z^{-3})^2}{5xz^{-2}}$

Express each number in scientific notation.

97. 372,000

98. 89,500

99. $-177,000,000$

100. $-23,470,000,000$

101. 0.007

102. 0.00052

103. -0.000000693

104. -0.000000089

105. one trillion

106. one millionth

Express each number in standard notation.

107. 9.37×10^5

108. 4.26×10^9

109. 2.21×10^{-5}

110. 2.774×10^{-2}

111. 0.00032×10^4

112. $9,300.0 \times 10^{-4}$

113. -3.2×10^{-3}

114. -7.25×10^3

Use the method of Example 9 to do each calculation. Write all answers in scientific notation.

115. $\dfrac{(65,000)(45,000)}{250,000}$

116. $\dfrac{(0.000000045)(0.00000012)}{45,000,000}$

117. $\dfrac{(0.00000035)(170,000)}{0.00000085}$

118. $\dfrac{(0.0000000144)(12,000)}{600,000}$

119. $\dfrac{(45,000,000,000)(212,000)}{0.00018}$

120. $\dfrac{(0.00000000275)(4,750)}{500,000,000,000}$

Applications

Use scientific notation to compute each answer. Write all answers in scientific notation.

121. Speed of sound The speed of sound in air is 3.31×10^4 centimeters per second. Compute the speed of sound in meters per minute.

122. Volume of a box Calculate the volume of a box that has dimensions of 6,000 by 9,700 by 4,700 millimeters.

123. Mass of a proton The mass of one proton is 0.0000000000000000000000000167248 gram. Find the mass of one billion protons.

124. Speed of light The speed of light in a vacuum is approximately 30,000,000,000 centimeters per second. Find the speed of light in miles per hour. (160,934.4 cm = 1 mile.)

125. Astronomy The distance d, in miles, of the nth planet from the sun is given by the formula

$$d = 9,275,200[3(2^{n-2}) + 4]$$

To the nearest million miles, find the distance of Earth and the distance of Mars from the sun. Give each answer in scientific notation.

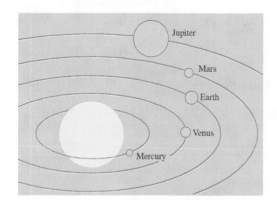

126. License Plates The number of different license plates of the form three digits followed by three letters, as in the illustration, is $10 \cdot 10 \cdot 10 \cdot 26 \cdot 26 \cdot 26$. Write this expression using exponents. Then evaluate it and express the result in scientific notation.

Discovery and Writing

127. New way to the center of the earth The spectacular "blue marble' image is the most detailed true-color image of the entire Earth to date. A new NASA-developed technique estimates Earth's center of

mass within 1 millimeter (0.04 inch) a year by using a combination of four space-based techniques.

The distance from the Earth's center to the North Pole (the **polar radius**) measures approximately 6,356.750 km, and the distance from the center to the equator (the **equatorial radius**) measures approximately 6,378.135 km. Express each distance using scientific notation.

128. Refer to Exercise 127. Given that 1 km is approximately equal to 0.62 miles, use scientific notation to express each distance in miles.

Write each expression with a single base.

129. $x^n x^2$

130. $\dfrac{x^m}{x^3}$

131. $\dfrac{x^m x^2}{x^3}$

132. $\dfrac{x^{3m+5}}{x^2}$

133. $x^{m+1} x^3$

134. $a^{n-3} a^3$

135. Explain why $-x^4$ and $(-x)^4$ represent different numbers.

136. Explain why 32×10^2 is not in scientific notation.

Review

137. Graph the interval $(-2,4)$.

138. Graph the interval $(-\infty,-3]\cup[3,\infty)$.

139. Evaluate $|\pi - 5|$.

140. Find the distance between -7 and -5 on the number line.

0.3 Rational Exponents and Radicals

In this section, we will learn to

1. Define rational exponents whose numerators are 1.
2. Define rational exponents whose numerators are not 1.
3. Define radical expressions.
4. Simplify and combine radicals.
5. Rationalize denominators and numerators.

Medionimages/Photodisc/Jupiter Images

"Dead Man's Curve" is a 1964 hit song by the rock and roll duo Jan Berry and Dean Torrence. The song details a teenage drag race that ends in an accident. Today, dead man's curve is a commonly used expression given to dangerous curves on our roads. Every curve has a "critical speed." If we exceed this speed, regardless of how skilled a driver we are, we will lose control of the vehicle.

The radical expression $3.9\sqrt{r}$ gives the critical speed in miles per hour when we travel a curved road with a radius of r feet. A knowledge of square roots and radicals is important and used in the construction of safe highways and roads. We will study the topic of radicals in this section.

1. Define Rational Exponents Whose Numerators Are 1

If we apply the rule $(x^m)^n = x^{mn}$ to $(25^{1/2})^2$, we obtain

$$(25^{1/2})^2 = 25^{(1/2)2} \qquad \text{Keep the base and multiply the exponents.}$$
$$= 25^1 \qquad \tfrac{1}{2} \cdot 2 = 1$$
$$= 25$$

Caution

In the expression $a^{1/n}$, there is **no** real-number nth root of a when n is even and $a < 0$. For example, $(-64)^{1/2}$ is **not** a real number, because the square of **no** real number is -64.

Thus, $25^{1/2}$ is a real number whose square is 25. Although both $5^2 = 25$ and $(-5)^2 = 25$, we define $25^{1/2}$ to be the positive real number whose square is 25:

$$25^{1/2} = 5 \qquad \text{Read } 25^{1/2} \text{ as "the square root of 25."}$$

In general, we have the following definition.

Rational Exponents If $a \geq 0$ and n is a natural number, then $a^{1/n}$ (read as "the nth root of a") is the nonnegative real number b such that

$$b^n = a$$

Since $b = a^{1/n}$, we have $b^n = (a^{1/n})^n = a$.

EXAMPLE 1 **Simplifying Expressions with Rational Exponents**

In each case, we will apply the definition of rational exponents.

a. $16^{1/2} = 4$ \qquad Because $4^2 = 16$. Read $16^{1/2}$ as "the square root of 16."

b. $27^{1/3} = 3$ \qquad Because $3^3 = 27$. Read $27^{1/3}$ as "the cube root of 27."

c. $\left(\dfrac{1}{81}\right)^{1/4} = \dfrac{1}{3}$ \qquad Because $\left(\dfrac{1}{3}\right)^4 = \dfrac{1}{81}$. Read $\left(\dfrac{1}{81}\right)^{1/4}$ as "the fourth root of $\dfrac{1}{81}$."

d. $-32^{1/5} = -(32^{1/5})$ Read $32^{1/5}$ as "the fifth root of 32."

$\qquad\qquad = -(2)$ Because $2^5 = 32$.

$\qquad\qquad = -2$

Self Check 1   Simplify: **a.** $100^{1/2}$ **b.** $243^{1/5}$

Now Try Exercise 15.

If n is even in the expression $a^{1/n}$ and the base contains variables, we often use absolute value symbols to guarantee that an even root is nonnegative.

$(49x^2)^{1/2} = 7|x|$ Because $(7|x|)^2 = 49x^2$. Since x could be negative, absolute value symbols are necessary to guarantee that the square root is nonnegative.

$(16x^4)^{1/4} = 2|x|$ Because $(2|x|)^4 = 16x^4$. Since x could be negative, absolute value symbols are necessary to guarantee that the fourth root is nonnegative.

$(729x^{12})^{1/6} = 3x^2$ Because $(3x^2)^6 = 729x^{12}$. Since x^2 is always nonnegative, no absolute value symbols are necessary. Read $(729x^{12})^{1/6}$ as "the sixth root of $729x^{12}$."

If n is an odd number in the expression $a^{1/n}$, the base a can be negative.

EXAMPLE 2   Simplifying Expressions with Rational Exponents

Simplify by using the definition of rational exponent.

a. $(-8)^{1/3} = -2$ Because $(-2)^3 = -8$.

b. $(-3,125)^{1/5} = -5$ Because $(-5)^5 = -3,125$.

c. $\left(-\dfrac{1}{1,000}\right)^{1/3} = -\dfrac{1}{10}$ Because $\left(-\dfrac{1}{10}\right)^3 = -\dfrac{1}{1,000}$.

Self Check 2   Simplify: **a.** $(-125)^{1/3}$ **b.** $(-100,000)^{1/5}$

Now Try Exercise 19.

Caution

If n is odd in the expression $a^{1/n}$, we **don't** need to use absolute value symbols, because odd roots can be negative.

$(-27x^3)^{1/3} = -3x$ Because $(-3x)^3 = -27x^3$.

$(-128a^7)^{1/7} = -2a$ Because $(-2a)^7 = -128a^7$.

We summarize the definitions concerning $a^{1/n}$ as follows.

Summary of Definitions of $a^{1/n}$

If n is a natural number and a is a real number in the expression $a^{1/n}$, then

If $a \geq 0$, then $a^{1/n}$ is the nonnegative real number b such that $b^n = a$.

If $a < 0$ $\begin{cases} \text{and } n \text{ is odd, then } a^{1/n} \text{ is the real number } b \text{ such that } b^n = a. \\ \text{and } n \text{ is even, then } a^{1/n} \text{ is not a real number.} \end{cases}$

The following chart also shows the possibilities that can occur when simplifying $a^{1/n}$.

	a	n	$a^{1/n}$	Examples
Strategy for Simplifying Expressions of the Form $a^{1/n}$	$a = 0$	n is a natural number.	$0^{1/n}$ is the real number 0 because $0^n = 0$.	$0^{1/2} = 0$ because $0^2 = 0$. $0^{1/5} = 0$ because $0^5 = 0$.
	$a > 0$	n is a natural number.	$a^{1/n}$ is the non-negative real number such that $(a^{1/n})^n = a$.	$16^{1/2} = 4$ because $4^2 = 16$. $27^{1/3} = 3$ because $3^3 = 27$.
	$a < 0$	n is an odd natural number.	$a^{1/n}$ is the real number such that $(a^{1/n})^n = a$.	$(-32)^{1/5} = -2$ because $(-2)^5 = -32$. $(-125)^{1/3} = -5$ because $(-5)^3 = -125$.
	$a < 0$	n is an even natural number.	$a^{1/n}$ is not a real number.	$(-9)^{1/2}$ is not a real number. $(-81)^{1/4}$ is not a real number.

2. Define Rational Exponents Whose Rational Exponents Are Not 1

The definition of $a^{1/n}$ can be extended to include rational exponents whose numerators are not 1. For example, $4^{3/2}$ can be written as either

$(4^{1/2})^3$ or $(4^3)^{1/2}$ Because of the Power Rule, $(x^m)^n = x^{mn}$.

This suggests the following rule.

Rule for Rational Exponents   If m and n are positive integers, the fraction $\frac{m}{n}$ is in lowest terms, and $a^{1/n}$ is a real number, then

$$a^{m/n} = (a^{1/n})^m = (a^m)^{1/n}$$

In the previous rule, we can view the expression $a^{m/n}$ in two ways:

1. $(a^{1/n})^m$: the mth power of the nth root of a
2. $(a^m)^{1/n}$: the nth root of the mth power of a

For example, $(-27)^{2/3}$ can be simplified in two ways:

$$(-27)^{2/3} = [(-27)^{1/3}]^2 \qquad \text{or} \qquad (-27)^{2/3} = [(-27)^2]^{1/3}$$
$$= (-3)^2 \qquad\qquad\qquad\qquad = (729)^{1/3}$$
$$= 9 \qquad\qquad\qquad\qquad\qquad = 9$$

As this example suggests, it is usually easier to take the root of the base first to avoid large numbers.

Comment   It is helpful to think of the phrase *power over root* when we see a rational exponent. The numerator of the fraction represents the *power* and the denominator represents the *root*. Begin with the *root* when simplifying to avoid large numbers.

Negative Rational Exponents   If m and n are positive integers, the fraction $\frac{m}{n}$ is in lowest terms and $a^{1/n}$ is a real number, then

$$a^{-m/n} = \frac{1}{a^{m/n}} \quad \text{and} \quad \frac{1}{a^{-m/n}} = a^{m/n} \qquad (a \neq 0)$$

EXAMPLE 3   Simplifying Expressions with Rational Exponents

We will apply the rules for rational exponents.

a. $25^{3/2} = (25^{1/2})^3$

$= 5^3$

$= 125$

b. $\left(-\dfrac{x^6}{1{,}000}\right)^{2/3} = \left[\left(-\dfrac{x^6}{1{,}000}\right)^{1/3}\right]^2$

$= \left(-\dfrac{x^2}{10}\right)^2$

$= \dfrac{x^4}{100}$

c. $32^{-2/5} = \dfrac{1}{32^{2/5}}$

$= \dfrac{1}{(32^{1/5})^2}$

$= \dfrac{1}{2^2}$

$= \dfrac{1}{4}$

d. $\dfrac{1}{81^{-3/4}} = 81^{3/4}$

$= (81^{1/4})^3$

$= 3^3$

$= 27$

Self Check 3   Simplify: **a.** $49^{3/2}$ **b.** $16^{-3/4}$ **c.** $\dfrac{1}{(27x^3)^{-2/3}}$

Now Try Exercise 43.

Because of the definition, rational exponents follow the same rules as integer exponents.

EXAMPLE 4   Using Exponent Rules to Simplify Expressions with Rational Exponents

Simplify each expression. Assume that all variables represent positive numbers, and write answers without using negative exponents.

a. $(36x)^{1/2} = 36^{1/2}x^{1/2}$

$= 6x^{1/2}$

b. $\dfrac{(a^{1/3}b^{2/3})^6}{(y^3)^2} = \dfrac{a^{6/3}b^{12/3}}{y^6}$

$= \dfrac{a^2 b^4}{y^6}$

c. $\dfrac{a^{x/2}a^{x/4}}{a^{x/6}} = a^{x/2 + x/4 - x/6}$

$= a^{6x/12 + 3x/12 - 2x/12}$

$= a^{7x/12}$

d. $\left[\dfrac{-c^{-2/5}}{c^{4/5}}\right]^{5/3} = \left(-c^{-2/5 - 4/5}\right)^{5/3}$

$= \left[(-1)\left(c^{-6/5}\right)\right]^{5/3}$

$= (-1)^{5/3}\left(c^{-6/5}\right)^{5/3}$

$= -1c^{-30/15}$

$= -c^{-2}$

$= -\dfrac{1}{c^2}$

Self Check 4   Use the directions for Example 4:

a. $\left(\dfrac{y^2}{49}\right)^{1/2}$ b. $\dfrac{b^{3/7}b^{2/7}}{b^{4/7}}$ c. $\dfrac{(9r^2s)^{1/2}}{rs^{-3/2}}$

Now Try Exercise 59.

3. Define Radical Expressions

Radical signs can also be used to express roots of numbers.

Definition of $\sqrt[n]{a}$ If n is a natural number greater than 1 and if $a^{1/n}$ is a real number, then

$$\sqrt[n]{a} = a^{1/n}$$

In the **radical expression** $\sqrt[n]{a}$, the symbol $\sqrt{}$ is the **radical sign**, a is the **radicand**, and n is the **index** (or the **order**) of the radical expression. If the order is 2, the expression is a **square root**, and we do not write the index.

$$\sqrt{a} = \sqrt[2]{a}$$

If the index of a radical is 3, we call the radical a **cube root**.

---

nth Root of a Nonnegative Number   If n is a natural number greater than 1 and $a \geq 0$, then $\sqrt[n]{a}$ is the nonnegative number whose nth power is a.

$$\left(\sqrt[n]{a}\right)^n = a$$

Caution

In the expression $\sqrt[n]{a}$, there is **no** real-number nth root of a when n is even and $a < 0$. For example, $\sqrt{-64}$ is **not** a real number, because the square of **no** real number is -64.

If 2 is substituted for n in the equation $\left(\sqrt[n]{a}\right)^n = a$, we have

$$\left(\sqrt[2]{a}\right)^2 = \left(\sqrt{a}\right)^2 = \sqrt{a}\sqrt{a} = a \text{ for } a \geq 0$$

This shows that if a number a can be factored into two equal factors, either of those factors is a square root of a. Furthermore, if a can be factored into n equal factors, any one of those factors is an nth root of a.

If n is an odd number greater than 1 in the expression $\sqrt[n]{a}$, the radicand can be negative.

EXAMPLE 5   **Finding *n*th Roots of Real Numbers**

We apply the definitions of cube root and fifth root.

a. $\sqrt[3]{-27} = -3$ — Because $(-3)^3 = -27$.

b. $\sqrt[3]{-8} = -2$ — Because $(-2)^3 = -8$.

c. $\sqrt[3]{-\dfrac{27}{1,000}} = -\dfrac{3}{10}$ — Because $\left(-\dfrac{3}{10}\right)^3 = -\dfrac{27}{1,000}$.

d. $-\sqrt[5]{-243} = -\left(\sqrt[5]{-243}\right)$
$$= -(-3)$$
$$= 3$$

Self Check 5   Find each root: **a.** $\sqrt[3]{216}$ **b.** $\sqrt[5]{-\dfrac{1}{32}}$

Now Try Exercise 69.

We summarize the definitions concerning $\sqrt[n]{a}$ as follows.

Summary of Definitions of $\sqrt[n]{a}$ If n is a natural number greater than 1 and a is a real number, then

If $a \geq 0$, then $\sqrt[n]{a}$ is the nonnegative real number such that $\left(\sqrt[n]{a}\right)^n = a$.

If $a < 0$ $\begin{cases} \text{and } n \text{ is odd, then } \sqrt[n]{a} \text{ is the real number such that } \left(\sqrt[n]{a}\right)^n = a. \\ \text{and } n \text{ is even, then } \sqrt[n]{a} \text{ is not a real number.} \end{cases}$

The following chart also shows the possibilities that can occur when simplifying $\sqrt[n]{a}$.

Strategy for Simplifying
Expressions of the Form $\sqrt[n]{a}$

a	n	$\sqrt[n]{a}$	Examples
$a = 0$	n is a natural number greater than 1.	$\sqrt[n]{0}$ is the real number 0 because $0^n = 0$.	$\sqrt[3]{0} = 0$ because $0^3 = 0$. $\sqrt[5]{0} = 0$ because $0^5 = 0$.
$a > 0$	n is a natural number greater than 1.	$\sqrt[n]{a}$ is the non-negative real number such that $\left(\sqrt[n]{a}\right)^n = a$.	$\sqrt{16} = 4$ because $4^2 = 16$. $\sqrt[3]{27} = 3$ because $3^3 = 27$.
$a < 0$	n is an odd natural number greater than 1.	$\sqrt[n]{a}$ is the real number such that $\left(\sqrt[n]{a}\right)^n = a$.	$\sqrt[5]{-32} = -2$ because $(-2)^5 = -32$. $\sqrt[3]{-125} = -5$ because $(-5)^3 = -125$.
$a < 0$	n is an even natural number.	$\sqrt[n]{a}$ is not a real number.	$\sqrt{-9}$ is not a real number. $\sqrt[4]{-81}$ is not a real number.

We have seen that if $a^{1/n}$ is real, then $a^{m/n} = (a^{1/n})^m = (a^m)^{1/n}$.
This same fact can be stated in radical notation.

$$a^{m/n} = (\sqrt[n]{a})^m = \sqrt[n]{a^m}$$

Thus, *the mth power of the nth root of a* is the same as *the nth root of the mth power of a*. For example, to find $\sqrt[3]{27^2}$, we can proceed in either of two ways:

$$\sqrt[3]{27^2} = \left(\sqrt[3]{27}\right)^2 = 3^2 = 9 \text{ or } \sqrt[3]{27^2} = \sqrt[3]{729} = 9$$

By definition, $\sqrt{a^2}$ represents a nonnegative number. If a could be negative, we must use absolute value symbols to guarantee that $\sqrt{a^2}$ will be nonnegative. Thus, if a is unrestricted,

$$\sqrt{a^2} = |a|$$

A similar argument holds when the index is any even natural number. The symbol $\sqrt[4]{a^4}$, for example, means the *positive* fourth root of a^4. Thus, if a is unrestricted,

$$\sqrt[4]{a^4} = |a|$$

EXAMPLE 6 **Simplifying Radical Expressions**

If x is unrestricted, simplify **a.** $\sqrt[6]{64x^6}$ **b.** $\sqrt[3]{x^3}$ **c.** $\sqrt{9x^8}$

SOLUTION We apply the definitions of sixth roots, cube roots, and square roots.

a. $\sqrt[6]{64x^6} = 2|x|$ Use absolute value symbols to guarantee that the result will be nonnegative.

b. $\sqrt[3]{x^3} = x$ Because the index is odd, no absolute value symbols are needed.

c. $\sqrt{9x^8} = 3x^4$ Because $3x^4$ is always nonnegative, no absolute value symbols are needed.

Self Check 6 Use the directions for Example 6:

a. $\sqrt[4]{16x^4}$ **b.** $\sqrt[3]{27y^3}$ **c.** $\sqrt[4]{x^8}$

Now Try Exercise 73.

4. Simplify and Combine Radicals

Many properties of exponents have counterparts in radical notation. For example, since $a^{1/n}b^{1/n} = (ab)^{1/n}$ and $\frac{a^{1/n}}{b^{1/n}} = \left(\frac{a}{b}\right)^{1/n}$ and $(b \neq 0)$, we have the following.

Multiplication and Division Properties of Radicals

If all expressions represent real numbers,

$$\sqrt[n]{a}\sqrt[n]{b} = \sqrt[n]{ab} \qquad \frac{\sqrt[n]{a}}{\sqrt[n]{b}} = \sqrt[n]{\frac{a}{b}} \qquad (b \neq 0)$$

In words, we say

The product of two nth roots is equal to the nth root of their product.

The quotient of two nth roots is equal to the nth root of their quotient.

Caution

These properties involve the nth root of the product of two numbers or the nth root of the quotient of two numbers. There is **no** such property for sums or differences. For example,

$$\sqrt{9 + 4} \neq \sqrt{9} + \sqrt{4}, \text{ because}$$

$$\sqrt{9 + 4} = \sqrt{13} \quad \text{but} \quad \sqrt{9} + \sqrt{4} = 3 + 2 = 5$$

and $\sqrt{13} \neq 5$. In general,

$$\sqrt{a + b} = \sqrt{a} + \sqrt{b} \quad \text{and} \quad \sqrt{a - b} = \sqrt{a} - \sqrt{b}$$

Numbers that are squares of positive integers, such as

$$1, 4, 9, 16, 25, \text{ and } 36$$

are called **perfect squares**. Expressions such as $4x^2$ and $\frac{1}{9}x^6$ are also perfect squares, because each one is the square of another expression with integer exponents and rational coefficients.

$$4x^2 = (2x)^2 \text{ and } \frac{1}{9}x^6 = \left(\frac{1}{3}x^3\right)^2$$

Numbers that are cubes of positive integers, such as

$$1, 8, 27, 64, 125, \text{ and } 216$$

are called **perfect cubes**. Expressions such as $64x^3$ and $\frac{1}{27}x^9$ are also perfect cubes, because each one is the cube of another expression with integer exponents and rational coefficients.

$$64x^3 = (4x)^3 \text{ and } \frac{1}{27}x^9 = \left(\frac{1}{3}x^3\right)^3$$

There are also perfect fourth powers, perfect fifth powers, and so on.

We can use perfect powers and the Multiplication Property of Radicals to simplify many radical expressions. For example, to simplify $\sqrt{12x^5}$, we factor $12x^5$ so that one factor is the largest perfect square that divides $12x^5$. In this case, it is $4x^4$. We then rewrite $12x^5$ as $4x^4 \cdot 3x$ and simplify.

$$\sqrt{12x^5} = \sqrt{4x^4 \cdot 3x} \qquad \text{Factor } 12x^5 \text{ as } 4x^4 \cdot 3x.$$

$$= \sqrt{4x^4}\sqrt{3x} \qquad \text{Use the Multiplication Property of Radicals: } \sqrt{ab} = \sqrt{a}\sqrt{b}.$$

$$= 2x^2\sqrt{3x} \qquad \sqrt{4x^4} = 2x^2$$

To simplify $\sqrt[3]{432x^9y}$, we find the largest perfect-cube factor of $432x^9y$ (which is $216x^9$) and proceed as follows:

$$\sqrt[3]{432x^9y} = \sqrt[3]{216x^9 \cdot 2y} \qquad \text{Factor } 432x^9y \text{ as } 216x^9 \cdot 2y.$$

$$= \sqrt[3]{216x^9}\sqrt[3]{2y} \qquad \text{Use the Multiplication Property of Radicals: } \sqrt[3]{ab} = \sqrt[3]{a}\sqrt[3]{b}.$$

$$= 6x^3\sqrt[3]{2y} \qquad \sqrt[3]{216x^9} = 6x^3$$

Radical expressions with the same index and the same radicand are called **like** or **similar radicals**. We can combine the like radicals in $3\sqrt{2} + 2\sqrt{2}$ by using the Distributive Property.

$$3\sqrt{2} + 2\sqrt{2} = (3 + 2)\sqrt{2}$$

$$= 5\sqrt{2}$$

This example suggests that to combine like radicals, we *add their numerical coefficients and keep the same radical.*

When radicals have the same index but different radicands, we can often change them to equivalent forms having the same radicand. We can then combine them. For example, to simplify $\sqrt{27} - \sqrt{12}$, we simplify both radicals and combine like radicals.

$$\sqrt{27} - \sqrt{12} = \sqrt{9 \cdot 3} - \sqrt{4 \cdot 3} \qquad \text{Factor 27 and 12.}$$
$$= \sqrt{9}\sqrt{3} - \sqrt{4}\sqrt{3} \qquad \sqrt{ab} = \sqrt{a}\sqrt{b}$$
$$= 3\sqrt{3} - 2\sqrt{3} \qquad \sqrt{9} = 3 \text{ and } \sqrt{4} = 2.$$
$$= \sqrt{3} \qquad \text{Combine like radicals.}$$

EXAMPLE 7 **Adding and Subtracting Radical Expressions**

Simplify: **a.** $\sqrt{50} + \sqrt{200}$ **b.** $3z\sqrt[5]{64z} - 2\sqrt[5]{2z^6}$

SOLUTION We will simplify each radical expression and then combine like radicals.

a. $\sqrt{50} + \sqrt{200} = \sqrt{25 \cdot 2} + \sqrt{100 \cdot 2}$
$$= \sqrt{25}\sqrt{2} + \sqrt{100}\sqrt{2}$$
$$= 5\sqrt{2} + 10\sqrt{2}$$
$$= 15\sqrt{2}$$

b. $3z\sqrt[5]{64z} - 2\sqrt[5]{2z^6} = 3z\sqrt[5]{32 \cdot 2z} - 2\sqrt[5]{z^5 \cdot 2z}$
$$= 3z\sqrt[5]{32}\sqrt[5]{2z} - 2\sqrt[5]{z^5}\sqrt[5]{2z}$$
$$= 3z(2)\sqrt[5]{2z} - 2z\sqrt[5]{2z}$$
$$= 6z\sqrt[5]{2z} - 2z\sqrt[5]{2z}$$
$$= 4z\sqrt[5]{2z}$$

Self Check 7 Simplify: **a.** $\sqrt{18} - \sqrt{8}$ **b.** $2\sqrt[3]{81a^4} + a\sqrt[3]{24a}$

Now Try Exercise 85.

5. Rationalize Denominators and Numerators

By **rationalizing the denominator**, we can write a fraction such as

$$\frac{\sqrt{5}}{\sqrt{3}}$$

as a fraction with a rational number in the denominator. All that we must do is multiply both the numerator and the denominator by $\sqrt{3}$. (Note that $\sqrt{3}\sqrt{3}$ is the rational number 3.)

$$\frac{\sqrt{5}}{\sqrt{3}} = \frac{\sqrt{5}\sqrt{3}}{\sqrt{3}\sqrt{3}} = \frac{\sqrt{15}}{3}$$

To rationalize the numerator, we multiply both the numerator and the denominator by $\sqrt{5}$. (Note that $\sqrt{5}\sqrt{5}$ is the rational number 5.)

$$\frac{\sqrt{5}}{\sqrt{3}} = \frac{\sqrt{5}\sqrt{5}}{\sqrt{3}\sqrt{5}} = \frac{5}{\sqrt{15}}$$

EXAMPLE 8   Rationalizing the Denominator of a Radical Expression

Rationalize each denominator and simplify. Assume that all variables represent positive numbers.

a. $\dfrac{1}{\sqrt{7}}$ **b.** $\sqrt[3]{\dfrac{3}{4}}$ **c.** $\sqrt{\dfrac{3}{x}}$ **d.** $\sqrt{\dfrac{3a^3}{5x^5}}$

SOLUTION   We will multiply both the numerator and the denominator by a radical that will make the denominator a rational number.

a. $\dfrac{1}{\sqrt{7}} = \dfrac{1\sqrt{7}}{\sqrt{7}\sqrt{7}}$ **b.** $\sqrt[3]{\dfrac{3}{4}} = \dfrac{\sqrt[3]{3}}{\sqrt[3]{4}}$

$= \dfrac{\sqrt{7}}{7}$ $= \dfrac{\sqrt[3]{3}\sqrt[3]{2}}{\sqrt[3]{4}\sqrt[3]{2}}$ Multiply numerator and denominator by $\sqrt[3]{2}$, because $\sqrt[3]{4}\sqrt[3]{2} = \sqrt[3]{8} = 2$.

$= \dfrac{\sqrt[3]{6}}{\sqrt[3]{8}}$

$= \dfrac{\sqrt[3]{6}}{2}$

c. $\sqrt{\dfrac{3}{x}} = \dfrac{\sqrt{3}}{\sqrt{x}}$ **d.** $\sqrt{\dfrac{3a^3}{5x^5}} = \dfrac{\sqrt{3a^3}}{\sqrt{5x^5}}$

$= \dfrac{\sqrt{3}\sqrt{x}}{\sqrt{x}\sqrt{x}}$ $= \dfrac{\sqrt{3a^3}\sqrt{5x}}{\sqrt{5x^5}\sqrt{5x}}$ Multiply numerator and denominator by $\sqrt{5x}$, because $\sqrt{5x^5}\sqrt{5x} = \sqrt{25x^6} = 5x^3$.

$= \dfrac{\sqrt{3x}}{x}$ $= \dfrac{\sqrt{15a^3x}}{\sqrt{25x^6}}$

$= \dfrac{\sqrt{a^2}\sqrt{15ax}}{5x^3}$

$= \dfrac{a\sqrt{15ax}}{5x^3}$

Self Check 8   Use the directions for Example 8:

a. $\dfrac{6}{\sqrt{6}}$ **b.** $\sqrt[3]{\dfrac{2}{5x}}$

Now Try Exercise 101.

EXAMPLE 9   Rationalizing the Numerator of a Radical Expression

Rationalize each numerator and simplify. Assume that all variables represent positive numbers: **a.** $\dfrac{\sqrt{x}}{7}$ **b.** $\dfrac{2\sqrt[3]{9x}}{3}$

SOLUTION   We will multiply both the numerator and the denominator by a radical that will make the numerator a rational number.

a. $\dfrac{\sqrt{x}}{7} = \dfrac{\sqrt{x} \cdot \sqrt{x}}{7\sqrt{x}}$ **b.** $\dfrac{2\sqrt[3]{9x}}{3} = \dfrac{2\sqrt[3]{9x} \cdot \sqrt[3]{3x^2}}{3\sqrt[3]{3x^2}}$

$\qquad\quad = \dfrac{x}{7\sqrt{x}}$ $\qquad\quad = \dfrac{2\sqrt[3]{27x^3}}{3\sqrt[3]{3x^2}}$

$\qquad\qquad\qquad\qquad\qquad\quad = \dfrac{2(3x)}{3\sqrt[3]{3x^2}}$

$\qquad\qquad\qquad\qquad\qquad\quad = \dfrac{2x}{\sqrt[3]{3x^2}}$ Divide out the 3's.

Self Check 9   Use the directions for Example 9:

a. $\dfrac{\sqrt{2x}}{5}$ **b.** $\dfrac{3\sqrt[3]{2y^2}}{6}$

Now Try Exercise 111.

After rationalizing denominators, we often can simplify an expression.

EXAMPLE 10   **Rationalizing Denominators and Simplifying**

Simplify: $\sqrt{\dfrac{1}{2}} + \sqrt{\dfrac{1}{8}}$.

SOLUTION   We will rationalize the denominators of each radical and then combine like radicals.

$$\sqrt{\dfrac{1}{2}} + \sqrt{\dfrac{1}{8}} = \dfrac{1}{\sqrt{2}} + \dfrac{1}{\sqrt{8}} \qquad \sqrt{\dfrac{1}{2}} = \dfrac{\sqrt{1}}{\sqrt{2}} = \dfrac{1}{\sqrt{2}}; \sqrt{\dfrac{1}{8}} = \dfrac{\sqrt{1}}{\sqrt{8}} = \dfrac{1}{\sqrt{8}}$$

$$= \dfrac{1\sqrt{2}}{\sqrt{2}\sqrt{2}} + \dfrac{1\sqrt{2}}{\sqrt{8}\sqrt{2}}$$

$$= \dfrac{\sqrt{2}}{2} + \dfrac{\sqrt{2}}{\sqrt{16}}$$

$$= \dfrac{\sqrt{2}}{2} + \dfrac{\sqrt{2}}{4}$$

$$= \dfrac{3\sqrt{2}}{4}$$

Self Check 10   Simplify: $\sqrt[3]{\dfrac{x}{2}} - \sqrt[3]{\dfrac{x}{16}}$.

Now Try Exercise 115.

Another property of radicals can be derived from the properties of exponents. If all of the expressions represent real numbers,

$$\sqrt[n]{\sqrt[m]{x}} = \sqrt[n]{x^{1/m}} = (x^{1/m})^{1/n} = x^{1/(mn)} = \sqrt[mn]{x}$$

$$\sqrt[m]{\sqrt[n]{x}} = \sqrt[m]{x^{1/n}} = (x^{1/n})^{1/m} = x^{1/(nm)} = \sqrt[mn]{x}$$

These results are summarized in the following *theorem* (a fact that can be proved).

Theorem   If all of the expressions involved represent real numbers, then

$$\sqrt[m]{\sqrt[n]{x}} = \sqrt[n]{\sqrt[m]{x}} = \sqrt[mn]{x}$$

We can use the previous theorem to simplify many radicals. For example,

$$\sqrt[3]{\sqrt{8}} = \sqrt{\sqrt[3]{8}} = \sqrt{2}$$

Rational exponents can be used to simplify many radical expressions, as shown in the following example.

EXAMPLE 11   **Simplifying Radicals Using the Previously Stated Theorem**

Simplify. Assume that x and y are positive numbers.

a. $\sqrt[6]{4}$ b. $\sqrt[12]{x^3}$ c. $\sqrt[9]{8y^3}$

SOLUTION   In each case, we will write the radical as an exponential expression, simplify the resulting expression, and write the final result as a radical.

a. $\sqrt[6]{4} = 4^{1/6} = (2^2)^{1/6} = 2^{2/6} = 2^{1/3} = \sqrt[3]{2}$

b. $\sqrt[12]{x^3} = x^{3/12} = x^{1/4} = \sqrt[4]{x}$

c. $\sqrt[9]{8y^3} = (2^3y^3)^{1/9} = (2y)^{3/9} = (2y)^{1/3} = \sqrt[3]{2y}$

Self Check 11   Simplify: a. $\sqrt[4]{4}$ b. $\sqrt[9]{27x^3}$

Now Try Exercise 117.

Self Check Answers   **1. a.** 10   **b.** 3   **2. a.** -5 **b.** -10 **3. a.** 343   **b.** $\dfrac{1}{8}$

c. $9x^2$ **4. a.** $\dfrac{y}{7}$ **b.** $b^{1/7}$ **c.** $3s^2$ **5. a.** 6   **b.** $-\dfrac{1}{2}$ **6. a.** $2|x|$

b. $3y$ **c.** x^2 **7. a.** $\sqrt{2}$ **b.** $8a\sqrt[3]{3a}$ **8. a.** $\sqrt{6}$ **b.** $\dfrac{\sqrt[3]{50x^2}}{5x}$

9. a. $\dfrac{2x}{5\sqrt{2x}}$ **b.** $\dfrac{y}{\sqrt[3]{4y}}$ **10.** $\dfrac{\sqrt[3]{4x}}{4}$ **11. a.** $\sqrt{2}$ **b.** $\sqrt[3]{3x}$

Exercises **0.3**

Getting Ready
You should be able to complete these vocabulary and concept statements before you proceed to the practice exercises.

Fill in the blanks.

1. If $a = 0$ and n is a natural number, then $a^{1/n} =$ _____ .

2. If $a > 0$ and n is a natural number, then $a^{1/n}$ is a _____ number.

3. If $a < 0$ and n is an even number, then $a^{1/n}$ is _____ a real number.

4. $6^{2/3}$ can be written as _____ or _____ .

5. $\sqrt[n]{a} =$ _____   6. $\sqrt{a^2} =$ _____

7. $\sqrt[n]{a}\sqrt[n]{b} =$ _____   8. $\sqrt[n]{\dfrac{a}{b}} =$ _____

9. $\sqrt{x + y}$ _____ $\sqrt{x} + \sqrt{y}$

10. $\sqrt[m]{\sqrt[n]{x}}$ or $\sqrt[n]{\sqrt[m]{x}}$ can be written as _____ .

Practice

Simplify each expression.

11. $9^{1/2}$

12. $8^{1/3}$

13. $\left(\dfrac{1}{25}\right)^{1/2}$

14. $\left(\dfrac{16}{625}\right)^{1/4}$

15. $-81^{1/4}$

16. $-\left(\dfrac{8}{27}\right)^{1/3}$

17. $(10,000)^{1/4}$

18. $1,024^{1/5}$

19. $\left(-\dfrac{27}{8}\right)^{1/3}$

20. $-64^{1/3}$

21. $(-64)^{1/2}$

22. $(-125)^{1/3}$

Simplify each expression. Use absolute value symbols when necessary.

23. $(16a^2)^{1/2}$

24. $(25a^4)^{1/2}$

25. $(16a^4)^{1/4}$

26. $(-64a^3)^{1/3}$

27. $(-32a^5)^{1/5}$

28. $(64a^6)^{1/6}$

29. $(-216b^6)^{1/3}$

30. $(256t^8)^{1/4}$

31. $\left(\dfrac{16a^4}{25b^2}\right)^{1/2}$

32. $\left(-\dfrac{a^5}{32b^{10}}\right)^{1/5}$

33. $\left(-\dfrac{1,000x^6}{27y^3}\right)^{1/3}$

34. $\left(\dfrac{49t^2}{100z^4}\right)^{1/2}$

Simplify each expression. Write all answers without using negative exponents.

35. $4^{3/2}$

36. $8^{2/3}$

37. $-16^{3/2}$

38. $(-8)^{2/3}$

39. $-1,000^{2/3}$

40. $100^{3/2}$

41. $64^{-1/2}$

42. $25^{-1/2}$

43. $64^{-3/2}$

44. $49^{-3/2}$

45. $-9^{-3/2}$

46. $(-27)^{-2/3}$

47. $\left(\dfrac{4}{9}\right)^{5/2}$

48. $\left(\dfrac{25}{81}\right)^{3/2}$

49. $\left(-\dfrac{27}{64}\right)^{-2/3}$

50. $\left(\dfrac{125}{8}\right)^{-4/3}$

Simplify each expression. Assume that all variables represent positive numbers. Write all answers without using negative exponents.

51. $(100s^4)^{1/2}$

52. $(64u^6v^3)^{1/3}$

53. $(32y^{10}z^5)^{-1/5}$

54. $(625a^4b^8)^{-1/4}$

55. $(x^{10}y^5)^{3/5}$

56. $(64a^6b^{12})^{5/6}$

57. $(r^8s^{16})^{-3/4}$

58. $(-8x^9y^{12})^{-2/3}$

59. $\left(-\dfrac{8a^6}{125b^9}\right)^{2/3}$

60. $\left(\dfrac{16x^4}{625y^8}\right)^{3/4}$

61. $\left(\dfrac{27r^6}{1,000s^{12}}\right)^{-2/3}$

62. $\left(-\dfrac{32m^{10}}{243n^{15}}\right)^{-2/5}$

63. $\dfrac{a^{2/5}a^{4/5}}{a^{1/5}}$

64. $\dfrac{x^{6/7}x^{3/7}}{x^{2/7}x^{5/7}}$

Simplify each radical expression.

65. $\sqrt{49}$

66. $\sqrt{81}$

67. $\sqrt[3]{125}$

68. $\sqrt[3]{-64}$

69. $\sqrt[3]{-125}$

70. $\sqrt[5]{-243}$

71. $\sqrt[5]{-\dfrac{32}{100,000}}$

72. $\sqrt[4]{\dfrac{256}{625}}$

Simplify each expression, using absolute value symbols when necessary. Write answers without using negative exponents.

73. $\sqrt{36x^2}$

74. $-\sqrt{25y^2}$

75. $\sqrt{9y^4}$

76. $\sqrt{a^4b^8}$

77. $\sqrt[3]{8y^3}$

78. $\sqrt[3]{-27z^9}$

79. $\sqrt[4]{\dfrac{x^4y^8}{z^{12}}}$

80. $\sqrt[5]{\dfrac{a^{10}b^5}{c^{15}}}$

Simplify each expression. Assume that all variables represent positive numbers so that no absolute value symbols are needed.

81. $\sqrt{8} - \sqrt{2}$

82. $\sqrt{75} - 2\sqrt{27}$

83. $\sqrt{200x^2} + \sqrt{98x^2}$

84. $\sqrt{128a^3} - a\sqrt{162a}$

85. $2\sqrt{48y^5} - 3y\sqrt{12y^3}$

86. $y\sqrt{112y} + 4\sqrt{175y^3}$

87. $2\sqrt[3]{81} + 3\sqrt[3]{24}$

88. $3\sqrt[4]{32} - 2\sqrt[4]{162}$

89. $\sqrt[4]{768z^5} + \sqrt[4]{48z^5}$

90. $-2\sqrt[5]{64y^2} + 3\sqrt[5]{486y^2}$

91. $\sqrt{8x^2y} - x\sqrt{2y} + \sqrt{50x^2y}$

92. $3x\sqrt{18x} + 2\sqrt{2x^3} - \sqrt{72x^3}$

93. $\sqrt[3]{16xy^4} + y\sqrt[3]{2xy} - \sqrt[3]{54xy^4}$

94. $\sqrt[4]{512x^5} - \sqrt[4]{32x^5} + \sqrt[4]{1,250x^5}$

Rationalize each denominator and simplify. Assume that all variables represent positive numbers.

95. $\dfrac{3}{\sqrt{3}}$

96. $\dfrac{6}{\sqrt{5}}$

97. $\dfrac{2}{\sqrt{x}}$

98. $\dfrac{8}{\sqrt{y}}$

99. $\dfrac{2}{\sqrt[3]{2}}$

100. $\dfrac{4d}{\sqrt[3]{9}}$

101. $\dfrac{5a}{\sqrt[3]{25a}}$

102. $\dfrac{7}{\sqrt[3]{36c}}$

103. $\dfrac{2b}{\sqrt[4]{3a^2}}$

104. $\sqrt{\dfrac{x}{2y}}$

105. $\sqrt[3]{\dfrac{2u^4}{9v}}$

106. $\sqrt[3]{-\dfrac{3s^5}{4r^2}}$

Rationalize each numerator and simplify. Assume that all variables are positive numbers.

107. $\dfrac{\sqrt{5}}{10}$

108. $\dfrac{\sqrt{y}}{3}$

109. $\dfrac{\sqrt[3]{9}}{3}$

110. $\dfrac{\sqrt[3]{16b^2}}{16}$

111. $\dfrac{\sqrt[5]{16b^3}}{64a}$

112. $\sqrt{\dfrac{3x}{57}}$

Rationalize each denominator and simplify.

113. $\sqrt{\dfrac{1}{3}} - \sqrt{\dfrac{1}{27}}$

114. $\sqrt[3]{\dfrac{1}{2}} + \sqrt[3]{\dfrac{1}{16}}$

115. $\sqrt{\dfrac{x}{8}} - \sqrt{\dfrac{x}{2}} + \sqrt{\dfrac{x}{32}}$

116. $\sqrt[3]{\dfrac{y}{4}} + \sqrt[3]{\dfrac{y}{32}} - \sqrt[3]{\dfrac{y}{500}}$

Simplify each radical expression.

117. $\sqrt[4]{9}$

118. $\sqrt[6]{27}$

119. $\sqrt[10]{16x^6}$

120. $\sqrt[6]{27x^9}$

Discovery and Writing

We often can multiply and divide radicals with different indices. For example, to multiply $\sqrt{3}$ by $\sqrt[3]{5}$, we first write each radical as a sixth root

$$\sqrt{3} = 3^{1/2} = 3^{3/6} = \sqrt[6]{3^3} = \sqrt[6]{27}$$

$$\sqrt[3]{5} = 5^{1/3} = 5^{2/6} = \sqrt[6]{5^2} = \sqrt[6]{25}$$

and then multiply the sixth roots.

$$\sqrt{3}\sqrt[3]{5} = \sqrt[6]{27}\sqrt[6]{25} = \sqrt[6]{(27)(25)} = \sqrt[6]{675}$$

Division is similar.

Use this idea to write each of the following expressions as a single radical.

121. $\sqrt{2}\sqrt[3]{2}$

122. $\sqrt{3}\sqrt[3]{5}$

123. $\dfrac{\sqrt[4]{3}}{\sqrt{2}}$

124. $\dfrac{\sqrt[3]{2}}{\sqrt{5}}$

125. For what values of x does $\sqrt[4]{x^4} = x$? Explain.

126. If all of the radicals involved represent real numbers and $y \neq 0$, explain why

$$\sqrt[n]{\dfrac{x}{y}} = \dfrac{\sqrt[n]{x}}{\sqrt[n]{y}}$$

127. If all of the radicals involved represent real numbers and there is no division by 0, explain why

$$\left(\dfrac{x}{y}\right)^{-m/n} = \sqrt[n]{\dfrac{y^m}{x^m}}$$

128. The definition of $x^{m/n}$ requires that $\sqrt[n]{x}$ be a real number. Explain why this is important. (Hint: Consider what happens when n is even, m is odd, and x is negative.)

Review

129. Write $-2 < x \leq 5$ using interval notation.

130. Write the expression $|3 - x|$ without using absolute value symbols. Assume that $x > 4$.

Evaluate each expression when $x = -2$ and $y = 3$.

131. $x^2 - y^2$

132. $\dfrac{xy + 4y}{x}$

133. Write 617,000,000 in scientific notation.

134. Write 0.00235×10^4 in standard notation.

0.4 Polynomials

In this section, we will learn to

1. Define polynomials.
2. Add and subtract polynomials.
3. Multiply polynomials.
4. Rationalize denominators.
5. Divide polynomials.

Football is one of the most popular sports in the United States. Brett Favre, one of the most talented quarterbacks ever to play the game, holds the record for the most career NFL touchdown passes, the most NFL pass completions, and the most passing yards. He led the Green Bay Packers to the Super Bowl and most recently played for the Minnesota Vikings. His nickname is Gunslinger.

An algebraic expression can be used to model the trajectory or path of a football when passed by Brett Favre. Suppose the height in feet, t seconds after the football leaves Brett's hand, is given by the algebraic expression

$$-0.1t^2 + t + 5.5$$

At a time of $t = 3$ seconds, we see that the height of the football is

$$-0.1(3)^2 + 3 + 5.5 = 7.6 \text{ ft.}$$

Algebraic expressions like $-0.1t^2 + t + 5.5$ are called **polynomials,** and we will study them in this section.

1. Define Polynomials

A **monomial** is a real number or the product of a real number and one or more variables with whole-number exponents. The number is called the **coefficient** of the variables. Some examples of monomials are

$$3x, \qquad 7ab^2, \qquad -5ab^2c^4, \qquad x^3, \qquad \text{and} \qquad -12$$

with coefficients of $3, 7, -5, 1$, and -12, respectively.

The **degree** of a monomial is the sum of the exponents of its variables. All nonzero constants (except 0) have a degree of 0.

The degree of $3x$ is 1. The degree of $7ab^2$ is 3.

The degree of $-5ab^2c^4$ is 7. The degree of x^3 is 3.

The degree of -12 is 0 (since $-12 = -12x^0$). 0 has no defined degree.

A monomial or a sum of monomials is called a **polynomial**. Each monomial in that sum is called a **term** of the polynomial. A polynomial with two terms is called a **binomial**, and a polynomial with three terms is called a **trinomial**.

Monomials	Binomials	Trinomials
$3x^2$	$2a + 3b$	$x^2 + 7x - 4$
$-25xy$	$4x^3 - 3x^2$	$4y^4 - 2y + 12$
a^2b^3c	$-2x^3 - 4y^2$	$12x^3y^2 - 8xy - 24$

The **degree of a polynomial** is the degree of the term in the polynomial with highest degree. The only polynomial with no defined degree is 0, which is called the **zero polynomial**. Here are some examples.

- $3x^2y^3 + 5xy^2 + 7$ is a trinomial of 5th degree, because its term with highest degree (the first term) is 5.
- $3ab + 5a^2b$ is a binomial of degree 3.
- $5x + 3y^2 + \sqrt[4]{3}z^4 - \sqrt{7}$ is a polynomial, because its variables have whole-number exponents. It is of degree 4.
- $-7y^{1/2} + 3y^2 + \sqrt[5]{3}z$ is not a polynomial, because one of its variables (y in the first term) does not have a whole-number exponent.

If two terms of a polynomial have the same variables with the same exponents, they are **like** or **similar** terms. To combine the like terms in the sum $3x^2y + 5x^2y$ or the difference $7xy^2 - 2xy^2$, we use the Distributive Property:

$$3x^2y + 5x^2y = (3 + 5)x^2y \qquad\qquad 7xy^2 - 2xy^2 = (7 - 2)xy^2$$
$$= 8x^2y \qquad\qquad\qquad\qquad\qquad = 5xy^2$$

This illustrates that *to combine like terms, we add (or subtract) their coefficients and keep the same variables and the same exponents.*

2. Add and Subtract Polynomials

Recall that we can use the Distributive Property to remove parentheses enclosing the terms of a polynomial. When the sign preceding the parentheses is +, we simply drop the parentheses:

$$+(a + b - c) = +1(a + b - c)$$
$$= 1a + 1b - 1c$$
$$= a + b - c$$

When the sign preceding the parentheses is $-$, we drop the parentheses and the $-$ sign and change the sign of each term within the parentheses.

$$-(a + b - c) = -1(a + b - c)$$
$$= -1a + (-1)b - (-1)c$$
$$= -a - b + c$$

We can use these facts to add and subtract polynomials. *To add (or subtract) polynomials, we remove parentheses (if necessary) and combine like terms.*

EXAMPLE 1   **Adding Polynomials**

Add: $(3x^3y + 5x^2 - 2y) + (2x^3y - 5x^2 + 3x)$.

SOLUTION   To add the polynomials, we remove parentheses and combine like terms.

$$(3x^3y + 5x^2 - 2y) + (2x^3y - 5x^2 + 3x)$$
$$= 3x^3y + 5x^2 - 2y + 2x^3y - 5x^2 + 3x$$
$$= 3x^3y + 2x^3y + 5x^2 - 5x^2 - 2y + 3x \qquad \text{Use the Commutative Property to rearrange terms.}$$
$$= 5x^3y - 2y + 3x \qquad \text{Combine like terms.}$$

We can add the polynomials in a vertical format by writing like terms in a column and adding the like terms, column by column.

$$
\begin{array}{l}
3x^3y + 5x^2 - 2y \\
\underline{2x^3y - 5x^2 \qquad + 3x} \\
5x^3y \qquad\quad - 2y + 3x
\end{array}
$$

Self Check 1   Add: $(4x^2 + 3x - 5) + (3x^2 - 5x + 7)$.

Now Try Exercise 21.

EXAMPLE 2   **Subtracting Polynomials**

Subtract: $(2x^2 + 3y^2) - (x^2 - 2y^2 + 7)$.

SOLUTION   To subtract the polynomials, we remove parentheses and combine like terms.

$$(2x^2 + 3y^2) - (x^2 - 2y^2 + 7)$$
$$= 2x^2 + 3y^2 - x^2 + 2y^2 - 7$$
$$= 2x^2 - x^2 + 3y^2 + 2y^2 - 7 \qquad \text{Use the Commutative Property to rearrange terms.}$$
$$= x^2 + 5y^2 - 7 \qquad \text{Combine like terms.}$$

We can subtract the polynomials in a vertical format by writing like terms in a column and subtracting the like terms, column by column.

$$2x^2 + 3y^2$$
$$\underline{-(x^2 - 2y^2 + 7)}$$
$$x^2 + 5y^2 - 7$$

$2x^2 - x^2 = (2 - 1)x^2$

$3y^2 - (-2)y^2 = 3y^2 + 2y^2 = (3 + 2)y^2$
$0 - 7 = -7$

Self Check 2   Subtract: $(4x^2 + 3x - 5) - (3x^2 - 5x + 7)$.

Now Try Exercise 23.

We can also use the Distributive Property to remove parentheses enclosing several terms that are multiplied by a constant. For example,

$$4(3x^2 - 2x + 6) = 4(3x^2) - 4(2x) + 4(6)$$
$$= 12x^2 - 8x + 24$$

This example suggests that *to add multiples of one polynomial to another, or to subtract multiples of one polynomial from another, we remove parentheses and combine like terms.*

EXAMPLE 3   **Using the Distributive Property and Combining Like Terms**

Simplify: $7x(2y^2 + 13x^2) - 5(xy^2 - 13x^3)$.

SOLUTION $7x(2y^2 + 13x^2) - 5(xy^2 - 13x^3)$

$$= 14xy^2 + 91x^3 - 5xy^2 + 65x^3 \qquad \text{Use the Distributive Property to remove parentheses.}$$
$$= 14xy^2 - 5xy^2 + 91x^3 + 65x^3 \qquad \text{Use the Commutative Property to rearrange terms.}$$
$$= 9xy^2 + 156x^3 \qquad \text{Combine like terms.}$$

Self Check 3   Simplify: $3(2b^2 - 3a^2b) + 2b(b + a^2)$.

Now Try Exercise 30.

3. Multiply Polynomials

To find the product of $3x^2y^3z$ and $5xyz^2$, we proceed as follows:

$$(3x^2y^3z)(5xyz^2) = 3 \cdot x^2 \cdot y^3 \cdot z \cdot 5 \cdot x \cdot y \cdot z^2$$
$$= 3 \cdot 5 \cdot x^2 \cdot x \cdot y^3 \cdot y \cdot z \cdot z^2 \qquad \text{Use the Commutative Property to rearrange terms.}$$
$$= 15x^3y^4z^3$$

This illustrates that *to multiply two monomials, we multiply the coefficients and then multiply the variables.*

To find the product of a monomial and a polynomial, we use the Distributive Property.

$$3xy^2(2xy + x^2 - 7yz) = 3xy^2(2xy) + (3xy^2)(x^2) - (3xy^2)(7yz)$$
$$= 6x^2y^3 + 3x^3y^2 - 21xy^3z$$

This illustrates that *to multiply a polynomial by a monomial, we multiply each term of the polynomial by the monomial.*

To multiply one binomial by another, we use the Distributive Property twice.

EXAMPLE 4   **Multiplying Binomials**

Multiply: **a.** $(x + y)(x + y)$ **b.** $(x - y)(x - y)$ **c.** $(x + y)(x - y)$

SOLUTION   **a.** $(x + y)(x + y) = (x + y)x + (x + y)y$
$$= x^2 + xy + xy + y^2$$
$$= x^2 + 2xy + y^2$$

b. $(x - y)(x - y) = (x - y)x - (x - y)y$
$$= x^2 - xy - xy + y^2$$
$$= x^2 - 2xy + y^2$$

c. $(x + y)(x - y) = (x + y)x - (x + y)y$
$$= x^2 + xy - xy - y^2$$
$$= x^2 - y^2$$

Self Check 4   Multiply: **a.** $(x + 2)(x + 2)$ **b.** $(x - 3)(x - 3)$
c. $(x + 4)(x - 4)$

Now Try Exercise 45.

The products in Example 4 are called **special products**. Because they occur so often, it is worthwhile to learn their forms.

Special Product Formulas $(x + y)^2 = (x + y)(x + y) = x^2 + 2xy + y^2$
$(x - y)^2 = (x - y)(x - y) = x^2 - 2xy + y^2$
$(x + y)(x - y) = x^2 - y^2$

Caution

Remember that $(x + y)^2$ and $(x - y)^2$ have trinomials for their products and that
$$(x + y)^2 \neq x^2 + y^2 \quad \text{and} \quad (x - y)^2 \neq x^2 - y^2$$
For example,
$$(3 + 5)^2 \neq 3^2 + 5^2 \quad \text{and} \quad (3 - 5)^2 \neq 3^2 - 5^2$$
$$8^2 \neq 9 + 25 \qquad\qquad (-2)^2 \neq 9 - 25$$
$$64 \neq 34 \qquad\qquad\qquad 4 \neq -16$$

We can use the **FOIL method** to multiply one binomial by another. FOIL is an acronym for **F**irst terms, **O**uter terms, **I**nner terms, and **L**ast terms. To use this method to multiply $3x - 4$ by $2x + 5$, we write

First terms   Last terms

$$(3x - 4)(2x + 5) = 3x(2x) + 3x(5) - 4(2x) - 4(5)$$

Inner terms

$$= 6x^2 + 15x - 8x - 20$$

Outer terms

$$= 6x^2 + 7x - 20$$

In this example,

- the product of the first terms is $6x^2$,
- the product of the outer terms is $15x$,
- the product of the inner terms is $-8x$, and
- the product of the last terms is -20.

The resulting like terms of the product are then combined.

EXAMPLE 5   **Using the FOIL Method to Multiply Polynomials**

Use the FOIL method to multiply: $\left(\sqrt{3} + x\right)\left(2 - \sqrt{3}x\right)$.

SOLUTION $(\sqrt{3} + x)(2 - \sqrt{3}x) = 2\sqrt{3} - \sqrt{3}\sqrt{3}x + 2x - x\sqrt{3}x$

$$= 2\sqrt{3} - 3x + 2x - \sqrt{3}x^2$$

$$= 2\sqrt{3} - x - \sqrt{3}x^2$$

Self Check 5   Multiply: $\left(2x + \sqrt{3}\right)\left(x - \sqrt{3}\right)$.

Now Try Exercise 63.

To multiply a polynomial with more than two terms by another polynomial, we multiply each term of one polynomial by each term of the other polynomial and combine like terms whenever possible.

EXAMPLE 6   **Multiplying Polynomials**

Multiply: **a.** $(x + y)(x^2 - xy + y^2)$ **b.** $(x + 3)^3$

SOLUTION   **a.** $(x + y)(x^2 - xy + y^2) = x^3 - x^2y + xy^2 + yx^2 - xy^2 + y^3$

$$= x^3 + y^3$$

b. $(x + 3)^3 = (x + 3)(x + 3)^2$

$$= (x + 3)(x^2 + 6x + 9)$$

$$= x^3 + 6x^2 + 9x + 3x^2 + 18x + 27$$

$$= x^3 + 9x^2 + 27x + 27$$

Self Check 6   Multiply: $(x + 2)(2x^2 + 3x - 1)$.

Now Try Exercise 67.

We can use a vertical format to multiply two polynomials, such as the polynomials given in Self Check 6. We first write the polynomials as follows and draw a line beneath them. We then multiply each term of the upper polynomial by each term of the lower polynomial and write the results so that like terms appear in each column. Finally, we combine like terms column by column.

$$2x^2 + 3x - 1$$
$$x + 2$$

$4x^2 + 6x - 2$	Multiply $2x^2 + 3x - 1$ by 2.
$2x^3 + 3x^2 - x$	Multiply $2x^2 + 3x - 1$ by x.
$2x^3 + 7x^2 + 5x - 2$	In each column, combine like terms.

If n is a whole number, the expressions $a^n + 1$ and $2a^n - 3$ are polynomials and we can multiply them as follows:

$$(a^n + 1)(2a^n - 3) = 2a^{2n} - 3a^n + 2a^n - 3$$

$$= 2a^{2n} - a^n - 3 \qquad \text{Combine like terms.}$$

We can also use the methods previously discussed to multiply expressions that are not polynomials, such as $x^{-2} + y$ and $x^2 - y^{-1}$.

$$(x^{-2} + y)(x^2 - y^{-1}) = x^{-2+2} - x^{-2}y^{-1} + x^2y - y^{1-1}$$

$$= x^0 - \frac{1}{x^2 y} + x^2 y - y^0$$

$$= 1 - \frac{1}{x^2 y} + x^2 y - 1 \qquad x^0 = 1 \text{ and } y^0 = 1.$$

$$= x^2 y - \frac{1}{x^2 y}$$

4. Rationalize Denominators

If the denominator of a fraction is a binomial containing square roots, we can use the product formula $(x + y)(x - y)$ to rationalize the denominator. For example, to rationalize the denominator of

$$\frac{6}{\sqrt{7} + 2} \qquad \text{To rationalize a denominator means to change the denominator into a rational number.}$$

we multiply the numerator and denominator by $\sqrt{7} - 2$ and simplify.

$$\frac{6}{\sqrt{7} + 2} = \frac{6(\sqrt{7} - 2)}{(\sqrt{7} + 2)(\sqrt{7} - 2)} \qquad \frac{\sqrt{7} - 2}{\sqrt{7} - 2} = 1$$

$$= \frac{6(\sqrt{7} - 2)}{7 - 4}$$

$$= \frac{6(\sqrt{7} - 2)}{3} \qquad \text{Here the denominator is a rational number.}$$

$$= 2(\sqrt{7} - 2)$$

In this example, we multiplied both the numerator and the denominator of the given fraction by $\sqrt{7} - 2$. This binomial is the same as the denominator of the given fraction $\sqrt{7} + 2$, except for the sign between the terms. Such binomials are called **conjugate binomials** or **radical conjugates**.

Conjugate Binomials   **Conjugate binomials** are binomials that are the same except for the sign between their terms. The conjugate of $a + b$ is $a - b$, and the conjugate of $a - b$ is $a + b$.

EXAMPLE 7   **Rationalizing the Denominator of a Radical Expression**

Rationalize the denominator: $\dfrac{\sqrt{3x} - \sqrt{2}}{\sqrt{3x} + \sqrt{2}}$ $(x > 0)$.

SOLUTION   We multiply the numerator and the denominator by $\sqrt{3x} - \sqrt{2}$ (the conjugate of $\sqrt{3x} + \sqrt{2}$) and simplify.

$$\frac{\sqrt{3x} - \sqrt{2}}{\sqrt{3x} + \sqrt{2}} = \frac{\left(\sqrt{3x} - \sqrt{2}\right)\left(\sqrt{3x} - \sqrt{2}\right)}{\left(\sqrt{3x} + \sqrt{2}\right)\left(\sqrt{3x} - \sqrt{2}\right)} \qquad \frac{\sqrt{3x} - \sqrt{2}}{\sqrt{3x} - \sqrt{2}} = 1$$

$$= \frac{\sqrt{3x}\sqrt{3x} - \sqrt{3x}\sqrt{2} - \sqrt{2}\sqrt{3x} + \sqrt{2}\sqrt{2}}{\left(\sqrt{3x}\right)^2 - \left(\sqrt{2}\right)^2}$$

$$= \frac{3x - \sqrt{6x} - \sqrt{6x} + 2}{3x - 2}$$

$$= \frac{3x - 2\sqrt{6x} + 2}{3x - 2}$$

Self Check 7   Rationalize the denominator: $\dfrac{\sqrt{x} + 2}{\sqrt{x} - 2}$.

Now Try Exercise 89.

In calculus, we often rationalize a numerator.

EXAMPLE 8   **Rationalizing the Numerator of a Radical Expression**

Rationalize the numerator: $\dfrac{\sqrt{x + h} - \sqrt{x}}{h}$.

SOLUTION   To rid the numerator of radicals, we multiply the numerator and the denominator by the conjugate of the numerator and simplify.

$$\frac{\sqrt{x + h} - \sqrt{x}}{h} = \frac{\left(\sqrt{x + h} - \sqrt{x}\right)\left(\sqrt{x + h} + \sqrt{x}\right)}{h\left(\sqrt{x + h} + \sqrt{x}\right)} \qquad \frac{\sqrt{x + h} + \sqrt{x}}{\sqrt{x + h} + \sqrt{x}} = 1$$

$$= \frac{x + h - x}{h\left(\sqrt{x + h} + \sqrt{x}\right)} \qquad \text{Here the numerator has no radicals.}$$

$$= \frac{h}{h\left(\sqrt{x + h} + \sqrt{x}\right)}$$

$$= \frac{1}{\sqrt{x + h} + \sqrt{x}} \qquad \text{Divide out the common factor of } h.$$

Self Check 8   Rationalize the numerator: $\dfrac{\sqrt{4 + h} - 2}{h}$.

Now Try Exercise 99.

5. Divide Polynomials

To divide monomials, we write the quotient as a fraction and simplify by using the rules of exponents. For example,

$$\frac{6x^2y^3}{-2x^3y} = -3x^{2-3}y^{3-1}$$

$$= -3x^{-1}y^2$$

$$= -\frac{3y^2}{x}$$

To divide a polynomial by a monomial, we write the quotient as a fraction, write the fraction as a sum of separate fractions, and simplify each one. For example, to divide $8x^5y^4 + 12x^2y^5 - 16x^2y^3$ by $4x^3y^4$, we proceed as follows:

$$\frac{8x^5y^4 + 12x^2y^5 - 16x^2y^3}{4x^3y^4} = \frac{8x^5y^4}{4x^3y^4} + \frac{12x^2y^5}{4x^3y^4} + \frac{-16x^2y^3}{4x^3y^4}$$

$$= 2x^2 + \frac{3y}{x} - \frac{4}{xy}$$

To divide two polynomials, we can use long division. To illustrate, we consider the division

$$\frac{2x^2 + 11x - 30}{x + 7}$$

which can be written in long division form as

$$x + 7 \overline{)2x^2 + 11x - 30}$$

The binomial $x + 7$ is called the **divisor**, and the trinomial $2x^2 + 11x - 30$ is called the **dividend**. The final answer, called the **quotient**, will appear above the long division symbol.

We begin the division by asking "What monomial, when multiplied by x, gives $2x^2$?" Because $x \cdot 2x = 2x^2$, the answer is $2x$. We place $2x$ in the quotient, multiply each term of the divisor by $2x$, subtract, and bring down the -30.

$$
\begin{array}{r}
2x \\
x + 7 \overline{)2x^2 + 11x - 30} \\
\underline{2x^2 + 14x } \\
-3x - 30
\end{array}
$$

We continue the division by asking "What monomial, when multiplied by x, gives $-3x$?" We place the answer, -3, in the quotient, multiply each term of the divisor by -3, and subtract. This time, there is no number to bring down.

$$
\begin{array}{r}
2x - 3 \\
x + 7 \overline{)2x^2 + 11x - 30} \\
\underline{2x^2 + 14x } \\
-3x - 30 \\
\underline{-3x - 21} \\
-9
\end{array}
$$

Because the degree of the remainder, -9, is less than the degree of the divisor, the division process stops, and we can express the result in the form

$$\text{quotient} + \frac{\text{remainder}}{\text{divisor}}$$

Thus,

$$\frac{2x^2 + 11x - 30}{x + 7} = 2x - 3 + \frac{-9}{x + 7}$$

EXAMPLE 9   **Using Long Division to Divide Polynomials**

Divide $6x^3 - 11$ by $2x + 2$.

SOLUTION   We set up the division, leaving spaces for the missing powers of x in the dividend.

$$2x + 2 \overline{)6x^3 \quad\quad - 11}$$

Comment

In Example 9, we could write the missing powers of x using coefficients of 0.

$$2x + 2 \overline{)6x^3 + 0x^2 + 0x - 11}$$

The division process continues as usual, with the following results:

$$
\begin{array}{r}
3x^2 - 3x + 3 \\
2x + 2 \overline{)6x^3 \quad\quad\quad\quad - 11} \\
\underline{6x^3 + 6x^2} \\
-6x^2 \\
\underline{-6x^2 - 6x} \\
+6x - 11 \\
\underline{+6x + 6} \\
-17
\end{array}
$$

Thus, $\dfrac{6x^3 - 11}{2x + 2} = 3x^2 - 3x + 3 + \dfrac{-17}{2x + 2}$.

Self Check 9   Divide: $3x + 1 \overline{)9x^2 - 1}$.

Now Try Exercise 113.

EXAMPLE 10   **Using Long Division to Divide Polynomials**

Divide $-3x^3 - 3 + x^5 + 4x^2 - x^4$ by $x^2 - 3$.

SOLUTION   The division process works best when the terms in the divisor and dividend are written with their exponents in descending order.

$$
\begin{array}{r}
x^3 - x^2 + 1 \\
x^2 - 3 \overline{)x^5 - x^4 - 3x^3 + 4x^2 - 3} \\
\underline{x^5 \quad\quad - 3x^3} \\
-x^4 \quad\quad + 4x^2 \\
\underline{-x^4 \quad\quad + 3x^2} \\
x^2 - 3 \\
\underline{x^2 - 3} \\
0
\end{array}
$$

Thus, $\dfrac{-3x^3 - 3 + x^5 + 4x^2 - x^4}{x^2 - 3} = x^3 - x^2 + 1$.

Self Check 10   Divide: $x^2 + 1 \overline{)3x^2 - x + 1 - 2x^3 + 3x^4}$.

Now Try Exercise 115.

Self Check Answers   1. $7x^2 - 2x + 2$ 2. $x^2 + 8x - 12$ 3. $8b^2 - 7a^2b$

4. **a.** $x^2 + 4x + 4$ **b.** $x^2 - 6x + 9$ **c.** $x^2 - 16$ 5. $2x^2 - x\sqrt{3} - 3$

6. $2x^3 + 7x^2 + 5x - 2$ 7. $\dfrac{x + 4\sqrt{x} + 4}{x - 4}$ 8. $\dfrac{1}{\sqrt{4 + h} + 2}$

9. $3x - 1$ 10. $3x^2 - 2x + \dfrac{x + 1}{x^2 + 1}$

Exercises **0.4**

Getting Ready

You should be able to complete these vocabulary and concept statements before you proceed to the practice exercises.

Fill in the blanks.

1. A _____ is a real number or the product of a real number and one or more _____.

2. The _____ of a monomial is the sum of the exponents of its _____.

3. A _____ is a polynomial with three terms.

4. A _____ is a polynomial with two terms.

5. A monomial is a polynomial with _____ term.

6. The constant 0 is called the _____ polynomial.

7. Terms with the same variables with the same exponents are called _____ terms.

8. The _____ of a polynomial is the same as the degree of its term of highest degree.

9. To combine like terms, we add their _____ and keep the same _____ and the same exponents.

10. The conjugate of $3\sqrt{x} + 2$ is _____.

Determine whether the given expression is a polynomial. If so, tell whether it is a monomial, a binomial, or a trinomial, and give its degree.

11. $x^2 + 3x + 4$

12. $5xy - x^3$

13. $x^3 + y^{1/2}$

14. $x^{-3} - 5y^{-2}$

15. $4x^2 - \sqrt{5}x^3$

16. x^2y^3

17. $\sqrt{15}$

18. $\dfrac{5}{x} + \dfrac{x}{5} + 5$

19. 0

20. $3y^3 - 4y^2 + 2y + 2$

Practice

Perform the operations and simplify.

21. $(x^3 - 3x^2) + (5x^3 - 8x)$

22. $(2x^4 - 5x^3) + (7x^3 - x^4 + 2x)$

23. $(y^5 + 2y^3 + 7) - (y^5 - 2y^3 - 7)$

24. $(3t^7 - 7t^3 + 3) - (7t^7 - 3t^3 + 7)$

25. $2(x^2 + 3x - 1) - 3(x^2 + 2x - 4) + 4$

26. $5(x^3 - 8x + 3) + 2(3x^2 + 5x) - 7$

27. $8(t^2 - 2t + 5) + 4(t^2 - 3t + 2) - 6(2t^2 - 8)$

28. $-3(x^3 - x) + 2(x^2 + x) + 3(x^3 - 2x)$

29. $y(y^2 - 1) - y^2(y + 2) - y(2y - 2)$

30. $-4a^2(a + 1) + 3a(a^2 - 4) - a^2(a + 2)$

31. $xy(x - 4y) - y(x^2 + 3xy) + xy(2x + 3y)$

32. $3mn(m + 2n) - 6m(3mn + 1) - 2n(4mn - 1)$

33. $2x^2y^3(4xy^4)$

34. $-15a^3b(-2a^2b^3)$

35. $-3m^2n(2mn^2)\left(-\dfrac{mn}{12}\right)$

36. $-\dfrac{3r^2s^3}{5}\left(\dfrac{2r^2s}{3}\right)\left(\dfrac{15rs^2}{2}\right)$

37. $-4rs(r^2 + s^2)$

38. $6u^2v(2uv^2 - y)$

39. $6ab^2c(2ac + 3bc^2 - 4ab^2c)$

40. $-\dfrac{mn^2}{2}(4mn - 6m^2 - 8)$

41. $(a + 2)(a + 2)$ 42. $(y - 5)(y - 5)$

43. $(a - 6)^2$ 44. $(t + 9)^2$

45. $(x + 4)(x - 4)$ 46. $(z + 7)(z - 7)$

47. $(x - 3)(x + 5)$

48. $(z + 4)(z - 6)$

49. $(u + 2)(3u - 2)$

50. $(4x + 1)(2x - 3)$

51. $(5x - 1)(2x + 3)$

52. $(4x - 1)(2x - 7)$

53. $(3a - 2b)^2$

54. $(4a + 5b)(4a - 5b)$

55. $(3m + 4n)(3m - 4n)$

56. $(4r + 3s)^2$

57. $(2y - 4x)(3y - 2x)$

58. $(-2x + 3y)(3x + y)$

59. $(9x - y)(x^2 - 3y)$

60. $(8a^2 + b)(a + 2b)$

61. $(5z + 2t)(z^2 - t)$

62. $(y - 2x^2)(x^2 + 3y)$

63. $\left(\sqrt{5} + 3x\right)\left(2 - \sqrt{5}x\right)$

64. $\left(\sqrt{2} + x\right)\left(3 + \sqrt{2}x\right)$

65. $(3x - 1)^3$

66. $(2x - 3)^3$

67. $(3x + 1)(2x^2 + 4x - 3)$
68. $(2x - 5)(x^2 - 3x + 2)$
69. $(3x + 2y)(2x^2 - 3xy + 4y^2)$
70. $(4r - 3s)(2r^2 + 4rs - 2s^2)$

Multiply the expressions as you would multiply polynomials.

71. $2y^n(3y^n + y^{-n})$

72. $3a^{-n}(2a^n + 3a^{n-1})$
73. $-5x^{2n}y^n(2x^{2n}y^{-n} + 3x^{-2n}y^n)$
74. $-2a^{3n}b^{2n}(5a^{-3n}b - ab^{-2n})$
75. $(x^n + 3)(x^n - 4)$
76. $(a^n - 5)(a^n - 3)$
77. $(2r^n - 7)(3r^n - 2)$
78. $(4z^n + 3)(3z^n + 1)$
79. $x^{1/2}(x^{1/2}y + xy^{1/2})$
80. $ab^{1/2}(a^{1/2}b^{1/2} + b^{1/2})$
81. $(a^{1/2} + b^{1/2})(a^{1/2} - b^{1/2})$
82. $(x^{3/2} + y^{1/2})^2$

Rationalize each denominator.

83. $\dfrac{2}{\sqrt{3} - 1}$

84. $\dfrac{1}{\sqrt{5} + 2}$

85. $\dfrac{3x}{\sqrt{7} + 2}$

86. $\dfrac{14y}{\sqrt{2} - 3}$

87. $\dfrac{x}{x - \sqrt{3}}$

88. $\dfrac{y}{2y + \sqrt{7}}$

89. $\dfrac{y + \sqrt{2}}{y - \sqrt{2}}$

90. $\dfrac{x - \sqrt{3}}{x + \sqrt{3}}$

91. $\dfrac{\sqrt{2} - \sqrt{3}}{1 - \sqrt{3}}$

92. $\dfrac{\sqrt{3} - \sqrt{2}}{1 + \sqrt{2}}$

93. $\dfrac{\sqrt{x} - \sqrt{y}}{\sqrt{x} + \sqrt{y}}$

94. $\dfrac{\sqrt{2x} + y}{\sqrt{2x} - y}$

Rationalize each numerator.

95. $\dfrac{\sqrt{2} + 1}{2}$

96. $\dfrac{\sqrt{x} - 3}{3}$

97. $\dfrac{y - \sqrt{3}}{y + \sqrt{3}}$

98. $\dfrac{\sqrt{a} - \sqrt{b}}{\sqrt{a} + \sqrt{b}}$

99. $\dfrac{\sqrt{x + 3} - \sqrt{x}}{3}$

100. $\dfrac{\sqrt{2 + h} - \sqrt{2}}{h}$

Perform each division and write all answers without using negative exponents.

101. $\dfrac{36a^2b^3}{18ab^6}$

102. $\dfrac{-45r^2s^5t^3}{27r^6s^2t^8}$

103. $\dfrac{16x^6y^4z^9}{-24x^9y^6z^0}$

104. $\dfrac{32m^6n^4p^2}{26m^6n^7p^2}$

105. $\dfrac{5x^3y^2 + 15x^3y^4}{10x^2y^3}$

106. $\dfrac{9m^4n^9 - 6m^3n^4}{12m^3n^3}$

107. $\dfrac{24x^5y^7 - 36x^2y^5 + 12xy}{60x^5y^4}$

108. $\dfrac{9a^3b^4 + 27a^2b^4 - 18a^2b^3}{18a^2b^7}$

Perform each division. If there is a nonzero remainder, write the answer in quotient $+ \frac{\text{remainder}}{\text{divisor}}$ *form.*

109. $x + 3\overline{)3x^2 + 11x + 6}$
110. $3x + 2\overline{)3x^2 + 11x + 6}$

111. $2x - 5\overline{)2x^2 - 19x + 37}$

112. $x - 7\overline{)2x^2 - 19x + 35}$

113. $\dfrac{2x^3 + 1}{x - 1}$

114. $\dfrac{2x^3 - 9x^2 + 13x - 20}{2x - 7}$

115. $x^2 + x - 1\overline{)x^3 - 2x^2 - 4x + 3}$

116. $x^2 - 3\overline{)x^3 - 2x^2 - 4x + 5}$

117. $\dfrac{x^5 - 2x^3 - 3x^2 + 9}{x^3 - 2}$

118. $\dfrac{x^5 - 2x^3 - 3x^2 + 9}{x^3 - 3}$

119. $\dfrac{x^5 - 32}{x - 2}$

120. $\dfrac{x^4 - 1}{x + 1}$

121. $11x - 10 + 6x^2)\overline{36x^4 - 121x^2 + 120 + 72x^3 - 142x}$

122. $x + 6x^2 - 12)\overline{-121x^2 + 72x^3 - 142x + 120 + 36x^4}$

Applications

123. Geometry Find an expression that represents the area of the brick wall.

$(x - 2)$ ft

$(x + 5)$ ft

124. Geometry The area of the triangle shown in the illustration is represented as $(x^2 + 3x - 40)$ square feet. Find an expression that represents its height.

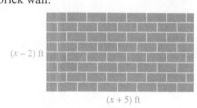

Height

$(x + 8)$ ft

125. Gift Boxes The corners of a 12 in.-by-12 in. piece of cardboard are folded inward and glued to make a box. Write a polynomial that represents the volume of the resulting box.

Crease here and fold inward

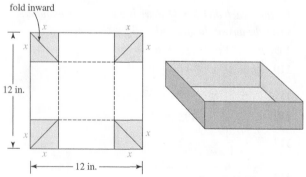

12 in.

12 in.

126. Travel Complete the following table, which shows the rate (mph), time traveled (hr), and distance traveled (mi) by a family on vacation.

r	$\cdot$	t	$=$	d
$3x + 4$				$3x^2 + 19x + 20$

Discovery and Writing

127. Show that a trinomial can be squared by using the formula
$$(a + b + c)^2 = a^2 + b^2 + c^2 + 2ab + 2bc + 2ac.$$

128. Show that $(a + b + c + d)^2 = a^2 + b^2 + c^2 + d^2 + 2ab + 2ac + 2ad + 2bc + 2bd + 2cd$.

129. Explain the FOIL method.

130. Explain how to rationalize the numerator of $\dfrac{\sqrt{x} + 2}{x}$.

131. Explain why $(a + b)^2 \neq a^2 + b^2$.

132. Explain why $\sqrt{a^2 + b^2} \neq \sqrt{a^2} + \sqrt{b^2}$.

Review

Simplify each expression. Assume that all variables represent positive numbers.

133. $9^{3/2}$

134. $\left(\dfrac{8}{125}\right)^{-2/3}$

135. $\left(\dfrac{625x^4}{16y^8}\right)^{3/4}$

136. $\sqrt{80x^4}$

137. $\sqrt[3]{16ab^4} - b\sqrt[3]{54ab}$

138. $x\sqrt[4]{1{,}280x} + \sqrt[4]{80x^5}$

0.5 Factoring Polynomials

In this section, we will learn to

1. Factor out a common monomial.
2. Factor by grouping.
3. Factor the difference of two squares.
4. Factor trinomials.
5. Factor trinomials by grouping.
6. Factor the sum and difference of two cubes.
7. Factor miscellaneous polynomials.

The television network series *CSI: Crime Scene Investigation* and its spinoffs, *CSI: NY* and *CSI: Miami*, are favorite television shows of many people. Their fans enjoy watching a team of forensic scientists uncover the circumstances that led to an unusual death or crime. These mysteries are captivating because many viewers are interested in the field of forensic science.

In this section, we will investigate a mathematics mystery. We will be given a polynomial and asked to unveil or uncover the two or more polynomials that were multiplied together to obtain the given polynomial. The process that we will use to solve this mystery is called *factoring*.

When two or more polynomials are multiplied together, each one is called a **factor** of the resulting product. For example, the factors of $7(x + 2)(x + 3)$ are

$$7, \quad x + 2, \quad \text{and} \quad x + 3$$

The process of writing a polynomial as the product of several factors is called **factoring**.

In this section, we will discuss factoring where the coefficients of the polynomial and the polynomial factors are integers. If a polynomial cannot be factored by using integers only, we call it a **prime polynomial**.

1. Factor Out a Common Monomial

The simplest type of factoring occurs when we see a common monomial factor in each term of the polynomial. In this case, our strategy is to use the Distributive Property and factor out the greatest common factor.

EXAMPLE 1 **Factoring by Removing a Common Monomial**

Factor: $3xy^2 + 6x$.

SOLUTION We note that each term contains a greatest common factor of $3x$:

$$3xy^2 + 6x = 3x(y^2) + 3x(2)$$

We can then use the Distributive Property to factor out the common factor of $3x$:

$$3xy^2 + 6x = 3x(y^2 + 2) \qquad \text{We can check by multiplying: } 3x(y^2 + 2) = 3xy^2 + 6x.$$

Self Check 1 Factor: $4a^2 - 8ab$.

Now Try Exercise 11.

EXAMPLE 2   **Factoring by Removing a Common Monomial**

Factor: $x^2y^2z^2 - xyz$.

SOLUTION   We factor out the greatest common factor of xyz:

$$x^2y^2z^2 - xyz = xyz(xyz) - xyz(1)$$
$$= xyz(xyz - 1) \qquad \text{We can check by multiplying.}$$

The last term in the expression $x^2y^2z^2 - xyz$ has an understood coefficient of 1. When the xyz is factored out, the 1 must be written.

Self Check 2   Factor: $a^2b^2c^2 + a^3b^3c^3$.

Now Try Exercise 13.

2. Factor by Grouping

A strategy that is often helpful when factoring a polynomial with four or more terms is called *grouping*. Terms with common factors are grouped together and then their greatest common factors are factored out using the Distributive Property.

EXAMPLE 3   **Factoring by Grouping**

Factor: $ax + bx + a + b$.

SOLUTION   Although there is no factor common to all four terms, we can factor x out of the first two terms and write the expression as

$$ax + bx + a + b = x(a + b) + (a + b)$$

We can now factor out the common factor of $a + b$.

$$ax + bx + a + b = x(a + b) + (a + b)$$
$$= x(a + b) + 1(a + b)$$
$$= (a + b)(x + 1) \qquad \text{We can check by multiplying.}$$

Self Check 3   Factor: $x^2 + xy + 2x + 2y$.

Now Try Exercise 17.

3. Factor the Difference of Two Squares

A binomial that is the difference of the squares of two quantities factors easily. The strategy used is to write the polynomial as the product of two factors. The first factor is the sum of the quantities and the other factor is the difference of the quantities.

EXAMPLE 4   **Factoring the Difference of Two Squares**

Factor: $49x^2 - 4$.

SOLUTION   We observe that each term is a perfect square:

$$49x^2 - 4 = (7x)^2 - 2^2$$

The difference of the squares of two quantities is the product of two factors. One is the sum of the quantities, and the other is the difference of the quantities. Thus, $49x^2 - 4$ factors as

$$49x^2 - 4 = (7x)^2 - 2^2$$
$$= (7x + 2)(7x - 2) \qquad \text{We can check by multiplying.}$$

Self Check 4   Factor: $9a^2 - 16b^2$.

Now Try Exercise 21.

Example 4 suggests a formula for factoring the difference of two squares.

Factoring the Difference of Two Squares $x^2 - y^2 = (x + y)(x - y)$

EXAMPLE 5   **Factoring the Difference of Two Squares Twice in One Problem**

Factor: $16m^4 - n^4$.

SOLUTION   The binomial $16m^4 - n^4$ can be factored as the difference of two squares:

$$16m^4 - n^4 = (4m^2)^2 - (n^2)^2$$
$$= (4m^2 + n^2)(4m^2 - n^2)$$

Caution

If you are limited to integer coefficients, the sum of two squares **cannot** be factored. For example, $x^2 + y^2$ is a prime polynomial.

The first factor is the sum of two squares and is prime. The second factor is a difference of two squares and can be factored:

$$16m^4 - n^4 = (4m^2 + n^2)[(2m)^2 - n^2]$$
$$= (4m^2 + n^2)(2m + n)(2m - n) \qquad \text{We can check by multiplying.}$$

Self Check 5   Factor: $a^4 - 81b^4$.

Now Try Exercise 23.

EXAMPLE 6   **Removing a Common Factor and Factoring the Difference of Two Squares**

Factor: $18t^2 - 32$.

SOLUTION   We begin by factoring out the common monomial factor of 2.

$$18t^2 - 32 = 2(9t^2 - 16)$$

Since $9t^2 - 16$ is the difference of two squares, it can be factored.

$$18t^2 - 32 = 2(9t^2 - 16)$$
$$= 2(3t + 4)(3t - 4) \qquad \text{We can check by multiplying.}$$

Self Check 6   Factor: $-3x^2 + 12$.

Now Try Exercise 61.

4. Factor Trinomials

Trinomials that are squares of binomials can be factored by using the following formulas.

Factoring Trinomial Squares

(1) $x^2 + 2xy + y^2 = (x + y)(x + y) = (x + y)^2$

(2) $x^2 - 2xy + y^2 = (x - y)(x - y) = (x - y)^2$

For example, to factor $a^2 - 6a + 9$, we note that it can be written in the form

$$a^2 - 2(3a) + 3^2 \quad x = a \text{ and } y = 3$$

which matches the left side of Equation 2 above. Thus,

$$a^2 - 6a + 9 = a^2 - 2(3a) + 3^2$$
$$= (a - 3)(a - 3)$$
$$= (a - 3)^2 \qquad \text{We can check by multiplying.}$$

Factoring trinomials that are not squares of binomials often requires some guesswork. If a trinomial with no common factors is factorable, it will factor into the product of two binomials.

EXAMPLE 7   **Factoring a Trinomial with Leading Coefficient of 1**

Factor: $x^2 + 3x - 10$.

SOLUTION   To factor $x^2 + 3x - 10$, we must find two binomials $x + a$ and $x + b$ such that

$$x^2 + 3x - 10 = (x + a)(x + b)$$

where the product of a and b is -10 and the sum of a and b is 3.

$$ab = -10 \quad \text{and} \quad a + b = 3$$

To find such numbers, we list the possible factorizations of -10:

$$10(-1) \qquad 5(-2) \qquad -10(1) \qquad -5(2)$$

Only in the factorization $5(-2)$ do the factors have a sum of 3. Thus, $a = 5$ and $b = -2$, and

$$x^2 + 3x - 10 = (x + a)(x + b)$$

(3) $\qquad x^2 + 3x - 10 = (x + 5)(x - 2) \qquad \text{We can check by multiplying.}$

Because of the Commutative Property of Multiplication, the order of the factors in Equation 3 is not important. Equation 3 can also be written as

$$x^2 + 3x - 10 = (x - 2)(x + 5)$$

Self Check 7   Factor: $p^2 - 5p - 6$.

Now Try Exercise 29.

EXAMPLE 8   **Factoring a Trinomial with Leading Coefficient not 1**

Factor: $2x^2 - x - 6$.

SOLUTION   Since the first term is $2x^2$, the first terms of the binomial factors must be $2x$ and x:

$$2x^2 - x - 6 = (2x)(x)$$

The product of the last terms must be -6, and the sum of the products of the outer terms and the inner terms must be $-x$. Since the only factorization of -6 that will cause this to happen is $3(-2)$, we have

$$2x^2 - x - 6 = (2x + 3)(x - 2) \qquad \text{We can check by multiplying.}$$

Self Check 8   Factor: $6x^2 - x - 2$.

Now Try Exercise 33.

It is not easy to give specific rules for factoring trinomials, because some guess-work is often necessary. However, the following hints are helpful.

Strategy for Factoring a General Trinomial with Integer Coefficients

1. Write the trinomial in descending powers of one variable.
2. Factor out any greatest common factor, including -1 if that is necessary to make the coefficient of the first term positive.
3. When the sign of the first term of a trinomial is $+$ and the sign of the third term is $+$, the sign between the terms of each binomial factor is the same as the sign of the middle term of the trinomial.

   When the sign of the first term is $+$ and the sign of the third term is $-$, one of the signs between the terms of the binomial factors is $+$ and the other is $-$.
4. Try various combinations of first terms and last terms until you find one that works. If no possibilities work, the trinomial is prime.
5. Check the factorization by multiplication.

EXAMPLE 9   **Factoring a Trinomial Completely**

Factor: $10xy + 24y^2 - 6x^2$.

SOLUTION   We write the trinomial in descending powers of x and then factor out the common factor of -2.

$$10xy + 24y^2 - 6x^2 = -6x^2 + 10xy + 24y^2$$
$$= -2(3x^2 - 5xy - 12y^2)$$

Since the sign of the third term of $3x^2 - 5xy - 12y^2$ is $-$, the signs between the binomial factors will be opposite. Since the first term is $3x^2$, the first terms of the binomial factors must be $3x$ and x:

$$-2(3x^2 - 5xy - 12y^2) = -2(3x)(x)$$

The product of the last terms must be $-12y^2$, and the sum of the outer terms and the inner terms must be $-5xy$. Of the many factorizations of $-12y^2$, only $4y(-3y)$ leads to a middle term of $-5xy$. So we have

$$10xy + 24y^2 - 6x^2 = -6x^2 + 10xy + 24y^2$$
$$= -2(3x^2 - 5xy - 12y^2)$$
$$= -2(3x + 4y)(x - 3y) \qquad \text{We can check by multiplying.}$$

Self Check 9   Factor: $-6x^2 - 15xy - 6y^2$.

Now Try Exercise 69.

5. Factor Trinomials by Grouping

Another way of factoring trinomials involves factoring by grouping. This method can be used to factor trinomials of the form $ax^2 + bx + c$. For example, to factor $6x^2 + 5x - 6$, we note that $a = 6$, $b = 5$, and $c = -6$, and proceed as follows:

1. Find the product ac: $6(-6) = -36$. This number is called the **key number**.
2. Find two factors of the key number (-36) whose sum is $b = 5$. Two such numbers are 9 and -4.

$$9(-4) = -36 \quad \text{and} \quad 9 + (-4) = 5$$

3. Use the factors 9 and -4 as coefficients of two terms to be placed between $6x^2$ and -6.

$$6x^2 + 5x - 6 = 6x^2 + 9x - 4x - 6$$

4. Factor by grouping:

$$6x^2 + 9x - 4x - 6 = 3x(2x + 3) - 2(2x + 3)$$
$$= (2x + 3)(3x - 2) \qquad \text{Factor out } 2x + 3.$$

EXAMPLE 10   **Factoring a Trinomial by Grouping**

Factor: $15x^2 + x - 2$.

SOLUTION   Since $a = 15$ and $c = -2$ in the trinomial, $ac = -30$. We now find factors of -30 whose sum is $b = 1$. Such factors are 6 and -5. We use these factors as coefficients of two terms to be placed between $15x^2$ and -2.

$$15x^2 + 6x - 5x - 2$$

Finally, we factor by grouping.

$$3x(5x + 2) - (5x + 2) = (5x + 2)(3x - 1)$$

Self Check 10   Factor: $15a^2 + 17a - 4$.

Now Try Exercise 39.

We can often factor polynomials with variable exponents. For example, if n is a natural number,

$$a^{2n} - 5a^n - 6 = (a^n + 1)(a^n - 6)$$

because

$$(a^n + 1)(a^n - 6) = a^{2n} - 6a^n + a^n - 6$$
$$= a^{2n} - 5a^n - 6 \qquad \text{Combine like terms.}$$

6. Factor the Sum and Difference of Two Cubes

Two other types of factoring involve binomials that are the sum or the difference of two cubes. Like the difference of two squares, they can be factored by using a formula.

Factoring the Sum and Difference of Two Cubes

$$x^3 + y^3 = (x + y)(x^2 - xy + y^2)$$
$$x^3 - y^3 = (x - y)(x^2 + xy + y^2)$$

EXAMPLE 11 **Factoring the Sum of Two Cubes**

Factor: $27x^6 + 64y^3$.

SOLUTION   We can write this expression as the sum of two cubes and factor it as follows:

$$27x^6 + 64y^3 = (3x^2)^3 + (4y)^3$$
$$= (3x^2 + 4y)[(3x^2)^2 - (3x^2)(4y) + (4y)^2]$$
$$= (3x^2 + 4y)(9x^4 - 12x^2y + 16y^2) \qquad \text{We can check by multiplying.}$$

Self Check 11   Factor: $8a^3 + 1,000b^6$.

Now Try Exercise 41.

EXAMPLE 12 **Factoring the Difference of Two Cubes**

Factor: $x^3 - 8$.

SOLUTION   This binomial can be written as $x^3 - 2^3$, which is the difference of two cubes. Substituting into the formula for the difference of two cubes gives

$$x^3 - 2^3 = (x - 2)(x^2 + 2x + 2^2)$$
$$= (x - 2)(x^2 + 2x + 4) \qquad \text{We can check by multiplying.}$$

Self Check 12   Factor: $p^3 - 64$.

Now Try Exercise 43.

7. Factor Miscellaneous Polynomials

EXAMPLE 13 **Factoring a Miscellaneous Polynomial**

Factor: $x^2 - y^2 + 6x + 9$.

SOLUTION   Here we will factor a trinomial and a difference of two squares.

$$x^2 - y^2 + 6x + 9 = x^2 + 6x + 9 - y^2 \qquad \text{Use the Commutative Property to rearrange the terms.}$$
$$= (x + 3)^2 - y^2 \qquad \text{Factor } x^2 + 6x + 9.$$
$$= (x + 3 + y)(x + 3 - y) \qquad \text{Factor the difference of two squares.}$$

We could try to factor this expression in another way.

$$x^2 - y^2 + 6x + 9 = (x + y)(x - y) + 3(2x + 3) \qquad \text{Factor } x^2 - y^2 \text{ and } 6x + 9.$$

However, we are unable to finish the factorization. If grouping in one way doesn't work, try various other ways.

Self Check 13   Factor: $a^2 + 8a - b^2 + 16$.

Now Try Exercise 97.

EXAMPLE 14   **Factoring a Miscellaneous Trinomial**

Factor: $z^4 - 3z^2 + 1$.

SOLUTION   This trinomial cannot be factored as the product of two binomials, because no combination will give a middle term of $-3z^2$. However, if the middle term were $-2z^2$, the trinomial would be a perfect square, and the factorization would be easy:

$$z^4 - 2z^2 + 1 = (z^2 - 1)(z^2 - 1)$$
$$= (z^2 - 1)^2$$

We can change the middle term in $z^4 - 3z^2 + 1$ to $-2z^2$ by adding z^2 to it. However, to make sure that adding z^2 does not change the value of the trinomial, we must also subtract z^2. We can then proceed as follows.

$$\begin{aligned}
z^4 - 3z^2 + 1 &= z^4 - 3z^2 + z^2 + 1 - z^2 && \text{Add and subtract } z^2. \\
&= z^4 - 2z^2 + 1 - z^2 && \text{Combine } -3z^2 \text{ and } z^2. \\
&= (z^2 - 1)^2 - z^2 && \text{Factor } z^4 - 2z^2 + 1. \\
&= (z^2 - 1 + z)(z^2 - 1 - z) && \text{Factor the difference of two squares.}
\end{aligned}$$

In this type of problem, we will always try to add and subtract a perfect square in hopes of making a perfect-square trinomial that will lead to factoring a difference of two squares.

Self Check 14   Factor: $x^4 + 3x^2 + 4$.

Now Try Exercise 103.

It is helpful to identify the problem type when we must factor polynomials that are given in random order.

Factoring Strategy
1. Factor out all common monomial factors.
2. If an expression has two terms, check whether the problem type is
   a. The difference of two squares:
   $$x^2 - y^2 = (x + y)(x - y)$$
   b. The sum of two cubes:
   $$x^3 + y^3 = (x + y)(x^2 - xy + y^2)$$
   c. The difference of two cubes:
   $$x^3 - y^3 = (x - y)(x^2 + xy + y^2)$$
3. If an expression has three terms, try to factor it as a *trinomial*.
4. If an expression has four or more terms, try factoring by *grouping*.
5. Continue until each individual factor is prime.
6. Check the results by multiplying.

Self Check Answers   1. $4a(a - 2b)$ 2. $a^2b^2c^2(1 + abc)$ 3. $(x + y)(x + 2)$
4. $(3a + 4b)(3a - 4b)$ 5. $(a^2 + 9b^2)(a + 3b)(a - 3b)$
6. $-3(x + 2)(x - 2)$ 7. $(p - 6)(p + 1)$ 8. $(3x - 2)(2x + 1)$
9. $-3(x + 2y)(2x + y)$ 10. $(3a + 4)(5a - 1)$
11. $8(a + 5b^2)(a^2 - 5ab^2 + 25b^4)$ 12. $(p - 4)(p^2 + 4p + 16)$
13. $(a + 4 + b)(a + 4 - b)$ 14. $(x^2 + 2 + x)(x^2 + 2 - x)$

Exercises 0.5

Getting Ready

You should be able to complete these vocabulary and concept statements before you proceed to the practice exercises.

Fill in the blanks.

1. When polynomials are multiplied together, each polynomial is a _____ of the product.
2. If a polynomial cannot be factored using _____ coefficients, it is called a _____ polynomial.

Complete each factoring formula.

3. $ax + bx =$ _____
4. $x^2 - y^2 =$ _____
5. $x^2 + 2xy + y^2 =$ _____
6. $x^2 - 2xy + y^2 =$ _____
7. $x^3 + y^3 =$ _____
8. $x^3 - y^3 =$ _____

Practice

In each expression, factor out the greatest common monomial.

9. $3x - 6$
10. $5y - 15$
11. $8x^2 + 4x^3$
12. $9y^3 + 6y^2$
13. $7x^2y^2 + 14x^3y^2$
14. $25y^2z - 15yz^2$

In each expression, factor by grouping.

15. $a(x + y) + b(x + y)$
16. $b(x - y) + a(x - y)$
17. $4a + b - 12a^2 - 3ab$
18. $x^2 + 4x + xy + 4y$

In each expression, factor the difference of two squares.

19. $4x^2 - 9$
20. $36z^2 - 49$
21. $4 - 9r^2$
22. $16 - 49x^2$
23. $81x^4 - 1$
24. $81 - x^4$
25. $(x + z)^2 - 25$
26. $(x - y)^2 - 9$

In each expression, factor the trinomial.

27. $x^2 + 8x + 16$
28. $a^2 - 12a + 36$
29. $b^2 - 10b + 25$
30. $y^2 + 14y + 49$
31. $m^2 + 4mn + 4n^2$
32. $r^2 - 8rs + 16s^2$

33. $12x^2 - xy - 6y^2$
34. $8x^2 - 10xy - 3y^2$

In each expression, factor the trinomial by grouping.

35. $x^2 + 10x + 21$
36. $x^2 + 7x + 10$
37. $x^2 - 4x - 12$
38. $x^2 - 2x - 63$
39. $6p^2 + 7p - 3$
40. $4q^2 - 19q + 12$

In each expression, factor the sum of two cubes.

41. $t^3 + 343$
42. $r^3 + 8s^3$

In each expression, factor the difference of two cubes.

43. $8z^3 - 27$
44. $125a^3 - 64$

Factor each expression completely. If an expression is prime, so indicate.

45. $3a^2bc + 6ab^2c + 9abc^2$
46. $5x^3y^3z^3 + 25x^2y^2z^2 - 125xyz$
47. $3x^3 + 3x^2 - x - 1$
48. $4x + 6xy - 9y - 6$
49. $2txy + 2ctx - 3ty - 3ct$
50. $2ax + 4ay - bx - 2by$
51. $ax + bx + ay + by + az + bz$
52. $6x^2y^3 + 18xy + 3x^2y^2 + 9x$
53. $x^2 - (y - z)^2$
54. $z^2 - (y + 3)^2$
55. $(x - y)^2 - (x + y)^2$
56. $(2a + 3)^2 - (2a - 3)^2$
57. $x^4 - y^4$
58. $z^4 - 81$
59. $3x^2 - 12$
60. $3x^3y - 3xy$
61. $18xy^2 - 8x$
62. $27x^2 - 12$
63. $x^2 - 2x + 15$
64. $x^2 + x + 2$
65. $-15 + 2a + 24a^2$
66. $-32 - 68x + 9x^2$
67. $6x^2 + 29xy + 35y^2$
68. $10x^2 - 17xy + 6y^2$
69. $12p^2 - 58pq - 70q^2$
70. $3x^2 - 6xy - 9y^2$
71. $-6m^2 + 47mn - 35n^2$
72. $-14r^2 - 11rs + 15s^2$
73. $-6x^3 + 23x^2 + 35x$
74. $-y^3 - y^2 + 90y$

75. $6x^4 - 11x^3 - 35x^2$

76. $12x + 17x^2 - 7x^3$

77. $x^4 + 2x^2 - 15$

78. $x^4 - x^2 - 6$

79. $a^{2n} - 2a^n - 3$

80. $a^{2n} + 6a^n + 8$

81. $6x^{2n} - 7x^n + 2$

82. $9x^{2n} + 9x^n + 2$

83. $4x^{2n} - 9y^{2n}$

84. $8x^{2n} - 2x^n - 3$

85. $10y^{2n} - 11y^n - 6$

86. $16y^{4n} - 25y^{2n}$

87. $2x^3 + 2,000$

88. $3y^3 + 648$

89. $(x + y)^3 - 64$

90. $(x - y)^3 + 27$

91. $64a^6 - y^6$

92. $a^6 + b^6$

93. $a^3 - b^3 + a - b$

94. $(a^2 - y^2) - 5(a + y)$

95. $64x^6 + y^6$

96. $z^2 + 6z + 9 - 225y^2$

97. $x^2 - 6x + 9 - 144y^2$

98. $x^2 + 2x - 9y^2 + 1$

99. $(a + b)^2 - 3(a + b) - 10$

100. $2(a + b)^2 - 5(a + b) - 3$

101. $x^6 + 7x^3 - 8$

102. $x^6 - 13x^4 + 36x^2$

103. $x^4 + x^2 + 1$

104. $x^4 + 3x^2 + 4$

105. $x^4 + 7x^2 + 16$

106. $y^4 + 2y^2 + 9$

107. $4a^4 + 1 + 3a^2$

108. $x^4 + 25 + 6x^2$

109. Candy To find the amount of chocolate used in the outer coating of one of the malted-milk balls shown, we can find the volume V of the chocolate shell using the formula $V = \frac{4}{3}\pi r_1^3 - \frac{4}{3}\pi r_2^3$. Factor the expression on the right side of the formula.

Inner radius r_2

Outer radius r_1

© istockphoto.com/maureenpr

110. Movie Stunts The formula that gives the distance a stuntwoman is above the ground t seconds after she falls over the side of a 144-foot tall building is $f = 144 - 16t^2$. Factor the right side.

144 ft

Discovery and Writing

111. Explain how to factor the difference of two squares.

112. Explain how to factor the difference of two cubes.

113. Explain how to factor $a^2 - b^2 + a + b$.

114. Explain how to factor $x^2 + 2x + 1$.

Factor the indicated monomial from the given expression.

115. $3x + 2; 2$

116. $5x - 3; 5$

117. $x^2 + 2x + 4; 2$

118. $3x^2 - 2x - 5; 3$

119. $a + b; a$

120. $a - b; b$

121. $x + x^{1/2}; x^{1/2}$

122. $x^{3/2} - x^{1/2}; x^{1/2}$

123. $2x + \sqrt{2}y; \sqrt{2}$

124. $\sqrt{3}a - 3b; \sqrt{3}$

125. $ab^{3/2} - a^{3/2}b; ab$

126. $ab^2 + b; b^{-1}$

Factor each expression by grouping three terms and two terms.

127. $x^2 + x - 6 + xy - 2y$

128. $2x^2 + 5x + 2 - xy - 2y$

129. $a^4 + 2a^3 + a^2 + a + 1$

130. $a^4 + a^3 - 2a^2 + a - 1$

Review

131. Which natural number is neither prime nor composite?

132. Graph the interval $[-2,3)$.

133. Simplify: $(x^3x^2)^4$.

134. Simplify: $\dfrac{(a^3)^3(a^2)^4}{(a^2a^3)^3}$.

135. $\left(\dfrac{3x^4x^3}{6x^{-2}x^4}\right)^0$

136. Simplify: $\sqrt{20x^5}$.

137. Simplify: $\sqrt{20x} - \sqrt{125x}$.

138. Rationalize the denominator: $\dfrac{3}{\sqrt[3]{3}}$.

0.6 Rational Expressions

In this section, we will learn to

> **1.** Define rational expressions.
> **2.** Simplify rational expressions.
> **3.** Multiple and divide rational expressions.
> **4.** Add and subtract rational expressions.
> **5.** Simplify complex fractions.

Abercrombie and Fitch (A&F) is a very successful American clothing company founded in 1892 by David Abercrombie and Ezra Fitch. Today the stores are popular shopping destinations for university students wanting to keep up with the latest styles and trends.

Photo by Tim Boyle/Getty Images

Suppose that a clothing manufacturer finds that the cost in dollars of producing x fleece vintage shirts is given by the algebraic expression $13x + 1,000$. The average cost of producing each shirt could be obtained by dividing the production cost, $13x + 1,000$, by the number of shirts produced, x. The algebraic fraction

$$\frac{13x + 1,000}{x}$$

represents the average cost per shirt. We see that the average cost of producing 200 shirts would be $18.

$$\frac{13(200) + 1,000}{200} = 18$$

An understanding of algebraic fractions is important in solving many real-life problems.

1. Define Rational Expressions

If x and y are real numbers, the quotient $\frac{x}{y}$ ($y \neq 0$) is called a **fraction**. The number x is called the **numerator**, and the number y is called the **denominator**.

   Algebraic fractions are quotients of algebraic expressions. If the expressions are polynomials, the fraction is called a **rational expression**. The first two of the following algebraic fractions are rational expressions. The third is not, because the numerator and denominator are not polynomials.

Caution

> Remember that the denominator of a fraction **cannot** be zero.

$$\frac{5y^2 + 2y}{y^2 - 3y - 7} \qquad \frac{8ab^2 - 16c^3}{2x + 3} \qquad \frac{x^{1/2} + 4x}{x^{3/2} - x^{1/2}}$$

We summarize some of the properties of fractions as follows:

Properties of Fractions   If a, b, c, and d are real numbers and no denominators are 0, then

Equality of Fractions

$$\frac{a}{b} = \frac{c}{d} \quad \text{if and only if} \quad ad = bc$$

Fundamental Property of Fractions

$$\frac{ax}{bx} = \frac{a}{b}$$

Multiplication and Division of Fractions

$$\frac{a}{b} \cdot \frac{c}{d} = \frac{ac}{bd} \quad \text{and} \quad \frac{a}{b} \div \frac{c}{d} = \frac{a}{b} \cdot \frac{d}{c} = \frac{ad}{bc}$$

Addition and Subtraction of Fractions

$$\frac{a}{b} + \frac{c}{b} = \frac{a+c}{b} \quad \text{and} \quad \frac{a}{b} - \frac{c}{b} = \frac{a-c}{b}$$

The first two examples illustrate each of the previous properties of fractions.

EXAMPLE 1   Illustrating the Properties of Fractions

Assume that no denominators are 0.

a. $\dfrac{2a}{3} = \dfrac{4a}{6}$ Because $2a(6) = 3(4a)$

b. $\dfrac{6xy}{10xy} = \dfrac{3(2xy)}{5(2xy)}$ Factor the numerator and denominator and divide out the common factors.

$= \dfrac{3}{5}$

Self Check 1   a. Is $\dfrac{3y}{5} = \dfrac{15z}{25}$?   **b.** Simplify: $\dfrac{15a^2b}{25ab^2}$.

Now Try Exercise 9.

EXAMPLE 2   Illustrating the Properties of Fractions

Assume that no denominators are 0.

a. $\dfrac{2r}{7s} \cdot \dfrac{3r}{5s} = \dfrac{2r \cdot 3r}{7s \cdot 5s}$

$= \dfrac{6r^2}{35s^2}$

b. $\dfrac{3mn}{4pq} \div \dfrac{2pq}{7mn} = \dfrac{3mn}{4pq} \cdot \dfrac{7mn}{2pq}$

$= \dfrac{21m^2n^2}{8p^2q^2}$

c. $\dfrac{2ab}{5xy} + \dfrac{ab}{5xy} = \dfrac{2ab + ab}{5xy}$

$= \dfrac{3ab}{5xy}$

d. $\dfrac{6uv^2}{7w^2} - \dfrac{3uv^2}{7w^2} = \dfrac{6uv^2 - 3uv^2}{7w^2}$

$= \dfrac{3uv^2}{7w^2}$

Self Check 2   Perform each operation:

a. $\dfrac{3a}{5b} \cdot \dfrac{2a}{7b}$ b. $\dfrac{2ab}{3rs} \div \dfrac{2rs}{4ab}$ c. $\dfrac{5pq}{3t} + \dfrac{3pq}{3t}$ d. $\dfrac{5mn^2}{3w} - \dfrac{mn^2}{3w}$

Now Try Exercise 19.

To add or subtract rational expressions with unlike denominators, we write each expression as an equivalent expression with a common denominator. We can then add or subtract the expressions. For example,

$$\frac{3x}{5} + \frac{2x}{7} = \frac{3x(7)}{5(7)} + \frac{2x(5)}{7(5)} \qquad\qquad \frac{4a^2}{15} - \frac{3a^2}{10} = \frac{4a^2(2)}{15(2)} - \frac{3a^2(3)}{10(3)}$$

$$= \frac{21x}{35} + \frac{10x}{35} \qquad\qquad\qquad = \frac{8a^2}{30} - \frac{9a^2}{30}$$

$$= \frac{21x + 10x}{35} \qquad\qquad\qquad\quad = \frac{8a^2 - 9a^2}{30}$$

$$= \frac{31x}{35} \qquad\qquad\qquad\qquad\quad = \frac{-a^2}{30}$$

$$\qquad\qquad\qquad\qquad\qquad\qquad\quad = -\frac{a^2}{30}$$

A rational expression is **in lowest terms** if all factors common to the numerator and the denominator have been removed. To **simplify a rational expression** means to write it in lowest terms.

2. Simplify Rational Expressions

To simplify rational expressions, we use the Fundamental Property of Fractions. This enables us to divide out all factors that are common to the numerator and the denominator.

EXAMPLE 3   **Simplifying a Rational Expression**

Simplify: $\dfrac{x^2 - 9}{x^2 - 3x}$ $(x \neq 0, 3)$.

SOLUTION   We factor the difference of two squares in the numerator, factor out x in the denominator, and divide out the common factor of $x - 3$.

$$\frac{x^2 - 9}{x^2 - 3x} = \frac{(x + 3)(x - 3)}{x(x - 3)} \qquad \frac{x - 3}{x - 3} = 1$$

$$= \frac{x + 3}{x}$$

Self Check 3   Simplify: $\dfrac{a^2 - 4a}{a^2 - a - 12}$ $(a \neq 4, -3)$.

Now Try Exercise 23.

We will encounter the following properties of fractions in the next examples.

Properties of Fractions   If a and b represent real numbers and there are no divisions by 0, then

- $\dfrac{a}{1} = a$

- $\dfrac{a}{a} = 1$

- $\dfrac{a}{b} = \dfrac{-a}{-b} = -\dfrac{a}{-b} = -\dfrac{-a}{b}$

- $-\dfrac{a}{b} = \dfrac{a}{-b} = \dfrac{-a}{b} = -\dfrac{-a}{-b}$

EXAMPLE 4   **Simplifying a Rational Expression**

Simplify: $\dfrac{x^2 - 2xy + y^2}{y - x}$ $(x \neq y)$.

SOLUTION   We factor the trinomial in the numerator, factor -1 from the denominator, and divide out the common factor of $x - y$.

$$\frac{x^2 - 2xy + y^2}{y - x} = \frac{(x - y)(x - y)}{-1(x - y)} \qquad \frac{x - y}{x - y} = 1$$

$$= \frac{x - y}{-1}$$

$$= -\frac{x - y}{1}$$

$$= -(x - y)$$

Self Check 4   Simplify: $\dfrac{a^2 - ab - 2b^2}{2b - a}$ $(2b - a \neq 0)$.

Now Try Exercise 25.

EXAMPLE 5   **Simplifying a Rational Expression**

Simplify: $\dfrac{x^2 - 3x + 2}{x^2 - x - 2}$ $(x \neq 2, -1)$.

SOLUTION   We factor the numerator and denominator and divide out the common factor of $x - 2$.

$$\frac{x^2 - 3x + 2}{x^2 - x - 2} = \frac{(x - 1)(x - 2)}{(x + 1)(x - 2)} \qquad \frac{x - 2}{x - 2} = 1$$

$$= \frac{x - 1}{x + 1}$$

Self Check 5   Simplify: $\dfrac{a^2 + 3a - 4}{a^2 + 2a - 3}$ $(a \neq 1, -3)$.

Now Try Exercise 27.

3. Multiply and Divide Rational Expressions

EXAMPLE 6   **Multiplying Rational Expressions**

Multiply: $\dfrac{x^2 - x - 2}{2} \cdot \dfrac{x^2 + 2x - 3}{2}$ $(x \neq 1, -1, 2)$.

SOLUTION To multiply the rational expressions, we multiply the numerators, multiply the denominators, and divide out the common factors.

$$\frac{x^2 - x - 2}{x^2 - 1} \cdot \frac{x^2 + 2x - 3}{x - 2} = \frac{(x^2 - x - 2)(x^2 + 2x - 3)}{(x^2 - 1)(x - 2)}$$

$$= \frac{(x - 2)(x + 1)(x - 1)(x + 3)}{(x + 1)(x - 1)(x - 2)} \qquad \frac{x-2}{x-2} = 1, \frac{x+1}{x+1} = 1, \frac{x-1}{x-1} = 1$$

$$= x + 3$$

Self Check 6 Simplify: $\dfrac{x^2 - 9}{x^2 - x} \cdot \dfrac{x - 1}{x^2 - 3x}$ $(x \neq 0, 1, 3)$.

Now Try Exercise 33.

EXAMPLE 7 Dividing Rational Expressions

Divide: $\dfrac{x^2 - 2x - 3}{x^2 - 4} \div \dfrac{x^2 + 2x - 15}{x^2 + 3x - 10}$ $(x \neq 2, -2, 3, -5)$.

SOLUTION To divide the rational expressions, we multiply by the reciprocal of the second rational expression. We then simplify by factoring the numerator and denominator and dividing out the common factors.

$$\frac{x^2 - 2x - 3}{x^2 - 4} \div \frac{x^2 + 2x - 15}{x^2 + 3x - 10} = \frac{x^2 - 2x - 3}{x^2 - 4} \cdot \frac{x^2 + 3x - 10}{x^2 + 2x - 15}$$

$$= \frac{(x^2 - 2x - 3)(x^2 + 3x - 10)}{(x^2 - 4)(x^2 + 2x - 15)}$$

$$= \frac{(x - 3)(x + 1)(x - 2)(x + 5)}{(x + 2)(x - 2)(x + 5)(x - 3)} \qquad \frac{x-3}{x-3} = 1, \frac{x-2}{x-2} = 1, \frac{x+5}{x+5} = 1$$

$$= \frac{x + 1}{x + 2}$$

Self Check 7 Simplify: $\dfrac{a^2 - a}{a + 2} \div \dfrac{a^2 - 2a}{a^2 - 4}$ $(a \neq 0, 2, -2)$.

Now Try Exercise 39.

EXAMPLE 8 Using Multiplication and Division to Simplify a Rational Expression

Simplify: $\dfrac{2x^2 - 5x - 3}{3x - 1} \cdot \dfrac{3x^2 + 2x - 1}{x^2 - 2x - 3} \div \dfrac{2x^2 + x}{3x}$ $\left(x \neq \dfrac{1}{3}, -1, 3, 0, -\dfrac{1}{2}\right)$.

SOLUTION We can change the division to a multiplication, factor, and simplify.

$$\frac{2x^2 - 5x - 3}{3x - 1} \cdot \frac{3x^2 + 2x - 1}{x^2 - 2x - 3} \div \frac{2x^2 + x}{3x}$$

$$= \frac{2x^2 - 5x - 3}{3x - 1} \cdot \frac{3x^2 + 2x - 1}{x^2 - 2x - 3} \cdot \frac{3x}{2x^2 + x}$$

$$= \frac{(2x^2 - 5x - 3)(3x^2 + 2x - 1)(3x)}{(3x - 1)(x^2 - 2x - 3)(2x^2 + x)}$$

$$= \frac{(x - 3)(2x + 1)(3x - 1)(x + 1)3x}{(3x - 1)(x + 1)(x - 3)x(2x + 1)} \qquad \frac{x-3}{x-3} = 1, \frac{2x+1}{2x+1} = 1, \frac{3x-1}{3x-1} = 1, \frac{x+1}{x+1} = 1, \frac{x}{x} = 1$$

$$= 3$$

Self Check 8 Simplify: $\dfrac{x^2 - 25}{x - 2} \div \dfrac{x^2 - 5x}{x^2 - 2x} \cdot \dfrac{x^2 + 2x}{x^2 + 5x}$ $(x \neq 0, 2, 5, -5)$.

Now Try Exercise 45.

4. Add and Subtract Rational Expressions

To add (or subtract) rational expressions with like denominators, we add (or subtract) the numerators and keep the common denominator.

EXAMPLE 9 **Adding Rational Expression with Like Deonominators**

Add: $\dfrac{2x + 5}{x + 5} + \dfrac{3x + 20}{x + 5}$ $(x \neq -5)$.

SOLUTION $\dfrac{2x + 5}{x + 5} + \dfrac{3x + 20}{x + 5} = \dfrac{5x + 25}{x + 5}$ Add the numerators and keep the common denominator.

$= \dfrac{5(\cancel{x + 5})}{1(\cancel{x + 5})}$ Factor out 5 and divide out the common factor of $x + 5$.

$= 5$

Self Check 9 Add: $\dfrac{3x - 2}{x - 2} + \dfrac{x - 6}{x - 2}$ $(x \neq 2)$.

Now Try Exercise 49.

To add (or subtract) rational expressions with unlike denominators, we must find a common denominator, called the **least** (or lowest) **common denominator (LCD)**. Suppose the unlike denominators of three rational expressions are 12, 20, and 35. To find the LCD, we first find the prime factorization of each number.

$$12 = 4 \cdot 3 \qquad 20 = 4 \cdot 5 \qquad 35 = 5 \cdot 7$$
$$ = 2^2 \cdot 3 \qquad = 2^2 \cdot 5$$

Because the LCD is the smallest number that can be divided by 12, 20, and 35, it must contain factors of 2^2, 3, 5, and 7. Thus, the

$$\text{LCD} = 2^2 \cdot 3 \cdot 5 \cdot 7 = 420$$

That is, 420 is the smallest number that can be divided without remainder by 12, 20, and 35.

When finding an LCD, we always factor each denominator and then create the LCD by using each factor the greatest number of times that it appears in any one denominator. The product of these factors is the LCD.

Comment

Remember to find the *least* common denominator, use each factor the *greatest* number of times that it occurs.

This rule also applies if the unlike denominators of the rational expressions contain variables. Suppose the unlike denominators are $x^2(x - 5)$ and $x(x - 5)^3$. To find the LCD, we use x^2 and $(x - 5)^3$. Thus, the LCD is the product $x^2(x - 5)^3$.

EXAMPLE 10 **Adding Rational Expressions with Unlike Denominators**

Add: $\dfrac{1}{x^2 - 4} + \dfrac{2}{x^2 - 4x + 4}$ $(x \neq 2, -2)$.

SOLUTION   We factor each denominator and find the LCD.

$$x^2 - 4 = (x + 2)(x - 2)$$

$$x^2 - 4x + 4 = (x - 2)(x - 2) = (x - 2)^2$$

The LCD is $(x + 2)(x - 2)^2$. We then write each rational expression with its denominator in factored form, convert each rational expression into an equivalent expression with a denominator of $(x + 2)(x - 2)^2$, add the expressions, and simplify.

$$\frac{1}{x^2 - 4} + \frac{2}{x^2 - 4x + 4} = \frac{1}{(x + 2)(x - 2)} + \frac{2}{(x - 2)(x - 2)}$$

$$= \frac{1(x - 2)}{(x + 2)(x - 2)(x - 2)} + \frac{2(x + 2)}{(x - 2)(x - 2)(x + 2)} \qquad \frac{x - 2}{x - 2} = 1, \frac{x + 2}{x + 2} = 1$$

$$= \frac{1(x - 2) + 2(x + 2)}{(x + 2)(x - 2)(x - 2)}$$

$$= \frac{x - 2 + 2x + 4}{(x + 2)(x - 2)(x - 2)}$$

$$= \frac{3x + 2}{(x + 2)(x - 2)^2}$$

Comment

Always attempt to simplify the final result. In this case, the final fraction is already in lowest terms.

Self Check 10   Add: $\dfrac{3}{x^2 - 6x + 9} + \dfrac{1}{x^2 - 9}$ $(x \neq 3, -3)$.

Now Try Exercise 59.

EXAMPLE 11   **Combining and Simplifying Rational Expressions with Unlike Denominators**

Simplify: $\dfrac{x - 2}{x^2 - 1} - \dfrac{x + 3}{x^2 + 3x + 2} + \dfrac{3}{x^2 + x - 2}$ $(x \neq 1, -1, -2)$.

SOLUTION   We factor the denominators to find the LCD.

$$x^2 - 1 = (x + 1)(x - 1)$$

$$x^2 + 3x + 2 = (x + 2)(x + 1)$$

$$x^2 + x - 2 = (x + 2)(x - 1)$$

The LCD is $(x + 1)(x + 2)(x - 1)$. We now write each rational expression as an equivalent expression with this LCD, and proceed as follows:

$$\frac{x - 2}{x^2 - 1} - \frac{x + 3}{x^2 + 3x + 2} + \frac{3}{x^2 + x - 2}$$

$$= \frac{x - 2}{(x + 1)(x - 1)} - \frac{x + 3}{(x + 1)(x + 2)} + \frac{3}{(x - 1)(x + 2)}$$

$$= \frac{(x - 2)(x + 2)}{(x + 1)(x - 1)(x + 2)} - \frac{(x + 3)(x - 1)}{(x + 1)(x + 2)(x - 1)} + \frac{3(x + 1)}{(x - 1)(x + 2)(x + 1)} \qquad \frac{x + 2}{x + 2} = 1, \frac{x - 1}{x - 1} = 1, \frac{x + 1}{x + 1} = 1$$

$$= \frac{(x^2 - 4) - (x^2 + 2x - 3) + (3x + 3)}{(x + 1)(x + 2)(x - 1)}$$

$$= \frac{x^2 - 4 - x^2 - 2x + 3 + 3x + 3}{(x + 1)(x + 2)(x - 1)}$$

$$= \frac{x + 2}{(x + 1)(x + 2)(x - 1)}$$

$$= \frac{1}{(x + 1)(x - 1)} \qquad \text{Divide out the common factor of } x + 2. \ \frac{x + 2}{x + 2} = 1$$

Self Check 11   Simplify: $\dfrac{4y}{y^2 - 1} - \dfrac{2}{y + 1} + 2$ $(y \neq 1, -1)$.

Now Try Exercise 61.

5. Simplify Complex Fractions

A **complex fraction** is a fraction that has a fraction in its numerator or a fraction in its denominator. There are two methods generally used to simplify complex fractions. These are stated here for you.

Strategies for Simplifying Complex Fractions

Method 1: Multiply the Complex Fraction by 1

- Determine the LCD of all fractions in the complex fraction.
- Multiply both numerator and denominator of the complex fraction by the LCD. Note that when we multiply by $\frac{LCD}{LCD}$ we are multiplying by 1.

Method 2: Simplify the Numerator and Denominator and then Divide

- Simplify the numerator and denominator so that both are single fractions.
- Perform the division by multiplying the numerator by the reciprocal of the denominator.

EXAMPLE 12   **Simplifying Complex Fractions**

Simplify: $\dfrac{\dfrac{1}{x} + \dfrac{1}{y}}{\dfrac{x}{y}}$ $(x, y \neq 0)$.

Method 1: We note that the LCD of the three fractions in the complex fraction is xy. So we multiply the numerator and denominator of the complex fraction by xy and simplify:

$$\dfrac{\dfrac{1}{x} + \dfrac{1}{y}}{\dfrac{x}{y}} = \dfrac{xy\left(\dfrac{1}{x} + \dfrac{1}{y}\right)}{xy\left(\dfrac{x}{y}\right)} = \dfrac{\dfrac{xy}{x} + \dfrac{xy}{y}}{\dfrac{xyx}{y}} = \dfrac{y + x}{x^2}$$

Method 2: We combine the fractions in the numerator of the complex fraction to obtain a single fraction over a single fraction.

$$\dfrac{\dfrac{1}{x} + \dfrac{1}{y}}{\dfrac{x}{y}} = \dfrac{\dfrac{1(y)}{x(y)} + \dfrac{1(x)}{y(x)}}{\dfrac{x}{y}} = \dfrac{\dfrac{y + x}{xy}}{\dfrac{x}{y}}$$

Then we use the fact that any fraction indicates a division:

$$\dfrac{\dfrac{y + x}{xy}}{\dfrac{x}{y}} = \dfrac{y + x}{xy} \div \dfrac{x}{y} = \dfrac{y + x}{xy} \cdot \dfrac{y}{x} = \dfrac{(y + x)y}{xyx} = \dfrac{y + x}{x^2}$$

Self Check 12   Simplify: $\dfrac{\dfrac{1}{x} - \dfrac{1}{y}}{\dfrac{1}{x} + \dfrac{1}{y}}$ $(x, y \neq 0)$.

Now Try Exercise 81.

Self Check Answers   **1. a.** no   **b.** $\dfrac{3a}{5b}$ **2. a.** $\dfrac{6a^2}{35b^2}$ **b.** $\dfrac{4a^2b^2}{3r^2s^2}$ **c.** $\dfrac{8pq}{3t}$ **d.** $\dfrac{4mn^2}{3w}$

3. $\dfrac{a}{a+3}$ **4.** $-(a+b)$ **5.** $\dfrac{a+4}{a+3}$ **6.** $\dfrac{x+3}{x^2}$ **7.** $a - 1$

8. $x + 2$ **9.** 4   **10.** $\dfrac{4x+6}{(x+3)(x-3)^2}$ **11.** $\dfrac{2y}{y-1}$ **12.** $\dfrac{y-x}{y+x}$

Exercises **0.6**

Getting Ready
You should be able to complete these vocabulary and concept statements before you proceed to the practice exercises.

Fill in the blanks.

1. In the fraction $\frac{a}{b}$, a is called the _____.

2. In the fraction $\frac{a}{b}$, b is called the _____.

3. $\frac{a}{b} = \frac{c}{d}$ if and only if _____.

4. The denominator of a fraction can never be _____.

Complete each formula.

5. $\dfrac{a}{b} \cdot \dfrac{c}{d} =$ ____

6. $\dfrac{a}{b} \div \dfrac{c}{d} =$ ____

7. $\dfrac{a}{b} + \dfrac{c}{b} =$ _____

8. $\dfrac{a}{b} - \dfrac{c}{b} =$ _____

Determine whether the fractions are equal. Assume that no denominators are 0.

9. $\dfrac{8x}{3y}, \dfrac{16x}{6y}$

10. $\dfrac{3x^2}{4y^2}, \dfrac{12y^2}{16x^2}$

11. $\dfrac{25xyz}{12ab^2c}, \dfrac{50a^2bc}{24xyz}$

12. $\dfrac{15rs^2}{4rs^2}, \dfrac{37.5a^3}{10a^3}$

Practice
Simplify each rational expression. Assume that no denominators are 0.

13. $\dfrac{7a^2b}{21ab^2}$

14. $\dfrac{35p^3q^2}{49p^4q}$

Perform the operations and simplify, whenever possible. Assume that no denominators are 0.

15. $\dfrac{4x}{7} \cdot \dfrac{2}{5a}$

16. $\dfrac{-5y}{2z} \cdot \dfrac{4}{y^2}$

17. $\dfrac{8m}{5n} \div \dfrac{3m}{10n}$

18. $\dfrac{15p}{8q} \div \dfrac{-5p}{16q^2}$

19. $\dfrac{3z}{5c} + \dfrac{2z}{5c}$

20. $\dfrac{7a}{4b} - \dfrac{3a}{4b}$

21. $\dfrac{15x^2y}{7a^2b^3} - \dfrac{x^2y}{7a^2b^3}$

22. $\dfrac{8rst^2}{15m^4t^2} + \dfrac{7rst^2}{15m^4t^2}$

Simplify each fraction. Assume that no denominators are 0.

23. $\dfrac{2x-4}{x^2-4}$

24. $\dfrac{x^2-16}{x^2-8x+16}$

25. $\dfrac{4-x^2}{x^2-5x+6}$

26. $\dfrac{25-x^2}{x^2+10x+25}$

27. $\dfrac{6x^3+x^2-12x}{4x^3+4x^2-3x}$

28. $\dfrac{6x^4-5x^3-6x^2}{2x^3-7x^2-15x}$

29. $\dfrac{x^3-8}{x^2+ax-2x-2a}$

30. $\dfrac{xy+2x+3y+6}{x^3+27}$

Perform the operations and simplify, whenever possible. Assume that no denominators are 0.

31. $\dfrac{x^2-1}{x} \cdot \dfrac{x^2}{x^2+2x+1}$

32. $\dfrac{y^2 - 2y + 1}{y} \cdot \dfrac{y + 2}{y^2 + y - 2}$

33. $\dfrac{3x^2 + 7x + 2}{x^2 + 2x} \cdot \dfrac{x^2 - x}{3x^2 + x}$

34. $\dfrac{x^2 + x}{2x^2 + 3x} \cdot \dfrac{2x^2 + x - 3}{x^2 - 1}$

35. $\dfrac{x^2 + x}{x - 1} \cdot \dfrac{x^2 - 1}{x + 2}$

36. $\dfrac{x^2 + 5x + 6}{x^2 + 6x + 9} \cdot \dfrac{x + 2}{x^2 - 4}$

37. $\dfrac{2x^2 + 32}{8} \div \dfrac{x^2 + 16}{2}$

38. $\dfrac{x^2 + x - 6}{x^2 - 6x + 9} \div \dfrac{x^2 - 4}{x^2 - 9}$

39. $\dfrac{z^2 + z - 20}{z^2 - 4} \div \dfrac{z^2 - 25}{z - 5}$

40. $\dfrac{ax + bx + a + b}{a^2 + 2ab + b^2} \div \dfrac{x^2 - 1}{x^2 - 2x + 1}$

41. $\dfrac{3x^2 + 5x - 2}{x^3 + 2x^2} \div \dfrac{6x^2 + 13x - 5}{2x^3 + 5x^2}$

42. $\dfrac{x^2 + 13x + 12}{8x^2 - 6x - 5} \div \dfrac{2x^2 - x - 3}{8x^2 - 14x + 5}$

43. $\dfrac{x^2 + 7x + 12}{x^3 - x^2 - 6x} \cdot \dfrac{x^2 - 3x - 10}{x^2 + 2x - 3} \cdot \dfrac{x^3 - 4x^2 + 3x}{x^2 - x - 20}$

44. $\dfrac{x(x - 2) - 3}{x(x + 7) - 3(x - 1)} \cdot \dfrac{x(x + 1) - 2}{x(x - 7) + 3(x + 1)}$

45. $\dfrac{x^2 - 2x - 3}{21x^2 - 50x - 16} \cdot \dfrac{3x - 8}{x - 3} \div \dfrac{x^2 + 6x + 5}{7x^2 - 33x - 10}$

46. $\dfrac{x^3 + 27}{x^2 - 4} \div \left(\dfrac{x^2 + 4x + 3}{x^2 + 2x} \div \dfrac{x^2 + x - 6}{x^2 - 3x + 9} \right)$

47. $\dfrac{3}{x + 3} + \dfrac{x + 2}{x + 3}$

48. $\dfrac{3}{x + 1} + \dfrac{x + 2}{x + 1}$

49. $\dfrac{4x}{x - 1} - \dfrac{4}{x - 1}$

50. $\dfrac{6x}{x - 2} - \dfrac{3}{x - 2}$

51. $\dfrac{2}{5 - x} + \dfrac{1}{x - 5}$

52. $\dfrac{3}{x - 6} - \dfrac{2}{6 - x}$

53. $\dfrac{3}{+ 1} + \dfrac{2}{1}$

54. $\dfrac{3}{x + 4} + \dfrac{x}{x - 4}$

55. $\dfrac{a + 3}{a^2 + 7a + 12} + \dfrac{a}{a^2 - 16}$

56. $\dfrac{a}{a^2 + a - 2} + \dfrac{2}{a^2 - 5a + 4}$

57. $\dfrac{x}{x^2 - 4} - \dfrac{1}{x + 2}$

58. $\dfrac{b^2}{b^2 - 4} - \dfrac{4}{b^2 + 2b}$

59. $\dfrac{3x - 2}{x^2 + 2x + 1} - \dfrac{x}{x^2 - 1}$

60. $\dfrac{2t}{t^2 - 25} - \dfrac{t + 1}{t^2 + 5t}$

61. $\dfrac{2}{y^2 - 1} + 3 + \dfrac{1}{y + 1}$

62. $2 + \dfrac{4}{t^2 - 4} - \dfrac{1}{t - 2}$

63. $\dfrac{1}{x - 2} + \dfrac{3}{x + 2} - \dfrac{3x - 2}{x^2 - 4}$

64. $\dfrac{x}{x - 3} - \dfrac{5}{x + 3} + \dfrac{3(3x - 1)}{x^2 - 9}$

65. $\left(\dfrac{1}{x - 2} + \dfrac{1}{x - 3} \right) \cdot \dfrac{x - 3}{2x}$

66. $\left(\dfrac{1}{x + 1} - \dfrac{1}{x - 2} \right) \div \dfrac{1}{x - 2}$

67. $\dfrac{3x}{x - 4} - \dfrac{x}{x + 4} - \dfrac{3x + 1}{16 - x^2}$

68. $\dfrac{7x}{x - 5} + \dfrac{3x}{5 - x} + \dfrac{3x - 1}{x^2 - 25}$

69. $\dfrac{1}{x^2 + 3x + 2} - \dfrac{2}{x^2 + 4x + 3} + \dfrac{1}{x^2 + 5x + 6}$

70. $\dfrac{-2}{x - y} + \dfrac{2}{x - z} - \dfrac{2z - 2y}{(y - x)(z - x)}$

71. $\dfrac{3x - 2}{x^2 + x - 20} - \dfrac{4x^2 + 2}{x^2 - 25} + \dfrac{3x^2 - 25}{x^2 - 16}$

72. $\dfrac{3x + 2}{8x^2 - 10x - 3} + \dfrac{x + 4}{6x^2 - 11x + 3} - \dfrac{1}{4x + 1}$

Simplify each complex fraction. Assume that no denominators are 0.

73. $\dfrac{\dfrac{3a}{b}}{\dfrac{6ac}{b^2}}$

74. $\dfrac{\dfrac{3t^2}{9x}}{\dfrac{t}{18x}}$

75. $\dfrac{\dfrac{3a^2b}{ab}}{27}$

76. $\dfrac{\dfrac{3u^2v}{4t}}{3uv}$

77. $\dfrac{\dfrac{x-y}{ab}}{\dfrac{y-x}{ab}}$

78. $\dfrac{\dfrac{x^2-5x+6}{2x^2y}}{\dfrac{x^2-9}{2x^2y}}$

79. $\dfrac{\dfrac{1}{x}+\dfrac{1}{y}}{xy}$

80. $\dfrac{xy}{\dfrac{11}{x}+\dfrac{11}{y}}$

81. $\dfrac{\dfrac{1}{x}+\dfrac{1}{y}}{\dfrac{1}{x}-\dfrac{1}{y}}$

82. $\dfrac{\dfrac{1}{x}-\dfrac{1}{y}}{\dfrac{1}{x}+\dfrac{1}{y}}$

83. $\dfrac{\dfrac{3a}{b}-\dfrac{4a^2}{x}}{\dfrac{1}{b}+\dfrac{1}{ax}}$

84. $\dfrac{1-\dfrac{x}{y}}{\dfrac{x^2}{y^2}-1}$

85. $\dfrac{x+1-\dfrac{6}{x}}{x+5+\dfrac{6}{x}}$

86. $\dfrac{2z}{1-\dfrac{3}{z}}$

87. $\dfrac{3xy}{1-\dfrac{1}{xy}}$

88. $\dfrac{x-3+\dfrac{1}{x}}{-\dfrac{1}{x}-x+3}$

89. $\dfrac{3x}{x+\dfrac{1}{x}}$

90. $\dfrac{2x^2+4}{2+\dfrac{4x}{5}}$

91. $\dfrac{\dfrac{x}{x+2}-\dfrac{2}{x-1}}{\dfrac{3}{x+2}+\dfrac{x}{x-1}}$

92. $\dfrac{\dfrac{2x}{x-3}+\dfrac{1}{x-2}}{\dfrac{3}{x-3}-\dfrac{x}{x-2}}$

Write each expression without using negative exponents, and simplify the resulting complex fraction. Assume that no denominators are 0.

93. $\dfrac{1}{1+x^{-1}}$

94. $\dfrac{y^{-1}}{x^{-1}+y^{-1}}$

95. $\dfrac{3(x+2)^{-1}+2(x-1)^{-1}}{(x+2)^{-1}}$

96. $\dfrac{2x(x-3)^{-1}-3(x+2)^{-1}}{(x-3)^{-1}(x+2)^{-1}}$

Applications

97. Engineering The stiffness k of the shaft shown in the illustration is given by the following formula where k_1 and k_2 are the individual stiffnesses of each section. Simplify the complex fraction on the right side of the formula.

$$k = \dfrac{1}{\dfrac{1}{k_1}+\dfrac{1}{k_2}}$$

Section 1   Section 2

98. Electronics The combined resistance R of three resistors with resistances of R_1, R_2, and R_3 is given by the following formula. Simplify the complex fraction on the right side of the formula.

$$R = \dfrac{1}{\dfrac{1}{R_1}+\dfrac{1}{R_2}+\dfrac{1}{R_3}}$$

Discovery and Writing

Simplify each complex fraction. Assume that no denominators are 0.

99. $\dfrac{x}{1+\dfrac{1}{3x^{-1}}}$

100. $\dfrac{ab}{2+\dfrac{3}{2a^{-1}}}$

101. $\dfrac{1}{1+\dfrac{1}{1+\dfrac{1}{x}}}$

102. $\dfrac{y}{2+\dfrac{2}{2+\dfrac{2}{y}}}$

103. Explain why the formula $\dfrac{a}{b}+\dfrac{c}{d}=\dfrac{ad+bc}{bd}$ is valid.

104. Explain why the formula $\dfrac{a}{b}\div\dfrac{c}{d}=\dfrac{a}{b}\cdot\dfrac{d}{c}$ is valid.

105. Explain the Commutative Property of Addition and explain why it is useful.

106. Explain the Distributive Property and explain why it is useful.

Review

Write each expression without using absolute value symbols.

107. $|-6|$

108. $|5-x|$, given that $x<0$

Simplify each expression.

109. $\left(\dfrac{x^3y^{-2}}{x^{-1}y}\right)^{-3}$

110. $(27x^6)^{2/3}$

111. $\sqrt{20}-\sqrt{45}$

112. $2(x^2+4)-3(2x^2+5)$

CHAPTER REVIEW

SECTION 0.1　Sets of Real Numbers

Definitions and Concepts	Examples
Natural numbers: The numbers that we count with.	1, 2, 3, 4, 5, 6, 7, 8, 9, 10, ...
Whole numbers: The natural numbers and 0.	0, 1, 2, 3, 4, 5, 6, 7, 8, 9, 10, ...
Integers: The whole numbers and the negatives of the natural numbers.	... , $-5, -4, -3, -2, -1, 0, 1, 2, 3, 4, 5,$ ...
Rational numbers: $\{x \mid x$ can be written in the form $\frac{a}{b}$ $(b \neq 0)$, where a and b are integers.$\}$	$2 = \dfrac{2}{1}, -5 = -\dfrac{5}{1}, \dfrac{2}{3}, -\dfrac{7}{3}, 0.25 = \dfrac{1}{4}$
All decimals that either terminate or repeat.	$\dfrac{3}{4} = 0.25, \dfrac{13}{5} = 2.6, \dfrac{2}{3} = 0.666 \ldots = 0.\overline{6}, \dfrac{7}{11} = 0.\overline{63}$
Irrational numbers: Nonrational real numbers. All decimals that neither terminate nor repeat.	$\sqrt{2}, -\sqrt{26}, \pi, 0.232232223 \ldots$
Real numbers: Any number that can be expressed as a decimal.	$-6, -\dfrac{9}{13}, 0, \pi, \sqrt{31}, 10.73$
Prime numbers: A natural number greater than 1 that is divisible only by itself and 1.	2, 3, 5, 7, 11, 13, 17, ...
Composite numbers: A natural number greater than 1 that is not prime.	4, 6, 8, 9, 10, 12, 14, 15, ...
Even integers: The integers that are exactly divisible by 2.	..., $-6, -4, -2, 0, 2, 4, 6,$ ...
Odd integers: The integers that are not exactly divisible by 2.	..., $-5, -3, -1, 1, 3, 5,$...
Associative Properties: 　of addition $(a + b) + c = a + (b + c)$	$5 + (4 + 7) = (5 + 4) + 7$
of multiplication $(ab)c = a(bc)$	$(5 \cdot 4) \cdot 7 = 5(4 \cdot 7)$
Commutative Properties: 　of addition $a + b = b + a$	$4 + 7 = 7 + 4 \qquad 1.7 + 2.5 = 2.5 + 1.7$
of multiplication $ab = ba$	$4 \cdot 7 = 7 \cdot 4 \qquad 1.7(2.5) = 2.5(1.7)$
Distributive Property: 　$a(b + c) = ab + ac$	$3(x + 6) = 3x + 3 \cdot 6 \qquad 0.2(y - 10) = 0.2y - 0.2(10)$
Double Negative Rule: 　$-(-a) = a$	$-(-5) = 5 \qquad -(-a) = a$
Open intervals have no endpoints.	$(-3, 2)$
Closed intervals have two endpoints.	$[-3, 2]$
Half-open intervals have one endpoint.	$(-3, 2]$

Definitions and Concepts	Examples
Absolute value: If $x \geq 0$, then $|x| = x$. If $x < 0$, then $|x| = -x$.	$|7| = 7 \quad |3.5| = 3.5 \quad \left\|\dfrac{7}{2}\right\| = \dfrac{7}{2} \quad |0| = 0$ $|-7| = 7 \quad |-3.5| = 3.5 \quad \left\|-\dfrac{7}{2}\right\| = \dfrac{7}{2}$
Distance: The **distance** between points a and b on a number line is $d = |b - a|$.	The distance on the number line between points with coordinates of -3 and 2 is $d = |2 - (-3)| = |5| = 5$.

EXERCISES

Consider the set $\{-6, -3, 0, \frac{1}{2}, 3, \pi, \sqrt{5}, 6, 8\}$*. List the numbers in this set that are*

1. natural numbers.
2. whole numbers.
3. integers.
4. rational numbers.
5. irrational numbers.
6. real numbers.

Consider the set $\{-6, -3, 0, \frac{1}{2}, 3, \pi, \sqrt{5}, 6, 8\}$*. List the numbers in this set that are*

7. prime numbers.
8. composite numbers.
9. even integers.
10. odd integers.

Determine which property of real numbers justifies each statement.

11. $(a + b) + 2 = a + (b + 2)$

12. $a + 7 = 7 + a$

13. $4(2x) = (4 \cdot 2)x$

14. $3(a + b) = 3a + 3b$

15. $(5a)7 = 7(5a)$

16. $(2x + y) + z = (y + 2x) + z$

17. $-(-6) = 6$

Graph each subset of the real numbers:

18. the prime numbers between 10 and 20

19. the even integers from 6 to 14

Graph each interval on the number line.

20. $-3 < x \leq 5$

21. $x \geq 0$ or $x < -1$

22. $(-2, 4]$

23. $(-\infty, 2) \cap (-5, \infty)$

24. $(-\infty, -4) \cup [6, \infty)$

Write each expression without absolute value symbols.

25. $|6|$ 26. $|-25|$

27. $|1 - \sqrt{2}|$ 28. $|\sqrt{3} - 1|$

29. On a number line, find the distance between points with coordinates of -5 and 7.

SECTION **0.2**   Integer Exponents and Scientific Notation

Definitions and Concepts	Examples
Natural-number exponents: $$x^n = \overbrace{x \cdot x \cdot x \cdot \cdots \cdot x}^{n \text{ factors of } x}$$	$$x^5 = x \cdot x \cdot x \cdot x \cdot x$$

Rules of exponents:
If there are no divisions by 0,
  • $x^m x^n = x^{m+n}$ • $(x^m)^n = x^{mn}$
 	
  • $(xy)^n = x^n y^n$ • $\left(\dfrac{x}{y}\right)^n = \dfrac{x^n}{y^n}$
 	
  • $x^0 = 1 \ (x \neq 0)$ • $x^{-n} = \dfrac{1}{x^n}$
 	
  • $\dfrac{x^m}{x^n} = x^{m-n}$ • $\left(\dfrac{x}{y}\right)^{-n} = \left(\dfrac{y}{x}\right)^n$
	$x^2 x^5 = x^{2+5} = x^7$ $(x^2)^7 = x^{2 \cdot 7} = x^{14}$
	
	$(xy)^5 = x^5 y^5$ $\left(\dfrac{x}{y}\right)^5 = \dfrac{x^5}{y^5}$
	
	$6^0 = 1$ $6^{-2} = \dfrac{1}{6^2} = \dfrac{1}{36}$
	
	$\dfrac{x^6}{x^4} = x^{6-4} = x^2$ $\left(\dfrac{x}{6}\right)^{-3} = \left(\dfrac{6}{x}\right)^3 = \dfrac{6^3}{x^3} = \dfrac{216}{x^3}$

Scientific notation: A number is written in **scientific notation** when it is written in the form $N \times 10^n$, where $1 \leq |N| < 10$.	Write each number in scientific notation. $386{,}000 = 3.86 \times 10^5$ $0.0025 = 2.5 \times 10^{-3}$ Write each number in standard form. $7.3 \times 10^3 = 7{,}300$ $5.25 \times 10^{-4} = 0.000525$

EXERCISES

Write each expression without using exponents.

30. $-5a^3$ **31.** $(-5a)^2$

Write each expression using exponents.

32. $3ttt$ **33.** $(-2b)(3b)$

Simplify each expression.

34. $n^2 n^4$ **35.** $(p^3)^2$

36. $(x^3 y^2)^4$ **37.** $\left(\dfrac{a^4}{b^2}\right)^3$

38. $(m^{-3} n^0)^2$ **39.** $\left(\dfrac{p^{-2} q^2}{2}\right)^3$

40. $\dfrac{a^5}{a^8}$ **41.** $\left(\dfrac{a^2}{b^3}\right)^{-2}$

42. $\left(\dfrac{3x^2 y^{-2}}{x^2 y^2}\right)^{-2}$ **43.** $\left(\dfrac{a^{-3} b^2}{ab^{-3}}\right)^{-2}$

44. $\left(\dfrac{-3x^3 y}{xy^3}\right)^{-2}$ **45.** $\left(-\dfrac{2m^{-2} n^0}{4m^2 n^{-1}}\right)^{-3}$

46. If $x = -3$ and $y = 3$, evaluate $-x^2 - xy^2$

Write each number in scientific notation.

47. $6{,}750$ **48.** 0.00023

Write each number in standard notation.

49. 4.8×10^2 **50.** 0.25×10^{-3}

51. Use scientific notation to simplify $\dfrac{(45{,}000)(350{,}000)}{0.000105}$.

SECTION **0.3**   Rational Exponents and Radicals

Definitions and Concepts	Examples
Summary of $a^{1/n}$ definitions: • If $a \geq 0$, then $a^{1/n}$ is the nonnegative number b such that $b^n = a$. • If $a < 0$ and n is odd, then $a^{1/n}$ is the real number b such that $b^n = a$. • If $a < 0$ and n is even, then $a^{1/n}$ is not a real number.	$16^{1/2} = 4$ because $4^2 = 16$ $(-27)^{1/3} = -3$ because $(-3)^3 = -27$ $(-16)^{1/2}$ is not a real number because no real number squared is -16.
Rule for rational exponents: If m and n are positive integers, $\frac{m}{n}$ is in lowest terms, and $a^{1/n}$ is a real number, then $\quad a^{m/n} = (a^{1/n})^m = (a^m)^{1/n}$	$8^{2/3} = (8^{1/3})^2 = 2^2 = 4$ or $(8^2)^{1/3} = 64^{1/3} = 4$
Definition of $\sqrt[n]{a}$: $\quad \sqrt[n]{a} = a^{1/n}$	$\sqrt[3]{125} = 125^{1/3} = 5$
Properties of radicals: If all radicals are real numbers and there are no divisions by 0, then • $\sqrt[n]{ab} = \sqrt[n]{a}\sqrt[n]{b}$ • $\sqrt[n]{\dfrac{a}{b}} = \dfrac{\sqrt[n]{a}}{\sqrt[n]{b}}$ • $\sqrt[m]{\sqrt[n]{a}} = \sqrt[n]{\sqrt[m]{a}} = \sqrt[mn]{a}$	$\sqrt[5]{32x^{10}} = \sqrt[5]{32}\sqrt[5]{x^{10}} = 2x^2$ $\sqrt[4]{\dfrac{x^{12}}{625}} = \dfrac{\sqrt[4]{x^{12}}}{\sqrt[4]{625}} = \dfrac{x^{12/4}}{5} = \dfrac{x^3}{5}$ $\sqrt[3]{\sqrt{64}} = \sqrt[3]{8} = 2 \quad \sqrt{\sqrt[3]{64}} = \sqrt{4} = 2 \quad \sqrt[2 \cdot 3]{64} = \sqrt[6]{64} = 2$

EXERCISES

Simplify each expression, if possible.

52. $121^{1/2}$

53. $\left(\dfrac{27}{125}\right)^{1/3}$

54. $(32x^5)^{1/5}$

55. $(81a^4)^{1/4}$

56. $(-1,000x^6)^{1/3}$

57. $(-25x^2)^{1/2}$

58. $(x^{12}y^2)^{1/2}$

59. $\left(\dfrac{x^{12}}{y^4}\right)^{-1/2}$

60. $\left(\dfrac{-c^{2/3}c^{5/3}}{c^{-2/3}}\right)^{1/3}$

61. $\left(\dfrac{a^{-1/4}a^{3/4}}{a^{9/2}}\right)^{-1/2}$

Simplify each expression.

62. $64^{2/3}$

63. $32^{-3/5}$

64. $\left(\dfrac{16}{81}\right)^{3/4}$

65. $\left(\dfrac{32}{243}\right)^{2/5}$

66. $\left(\dfrac{8}{27}\right)^{-2/3}$

67. $\left(\dfrac{16}{625}\right)^{-3/4}$

68. $(-216x^3)^{2/3}$

69. $\dfrac{p^{a/2}p^{a/3}}{p^{a/6}}$

Simplify each expression.

70. $\sqrt{36}$

71. $-\sqrt{49}$

72. $\sqrt{\dfrac{9}{25}}$

73. $\sqrt[3]{\dfrac{27}{125}}$

74. $\sqrt{x^2y^4}$

75. $\sqrt[3]{x^3}$

76. $\sqrt[4]{\dfrac{m^8n^4}{p^{16}}}$

77. $\sqrt[5]{\dfrac{a^{15}b^{10}}{c^5}}$

Simplify and combine terms.

78. $\sqrt{50} + \sqrt{8}$

79. $\sqrt{12} + \sqrt{3} - \sqrt{27}$

80. $\sqrt[3]{24x^4} - \sqrt[3]{3x^4}$

Rationalize each denominator.

81. $\dfrac{\sqrt{7}}{\sqrt{5}}$

82. $\dfrac{8}{\sqrt{8}}$

83. $\dfrac{1}{\sqrt[3]{2}}$

84. $\dfrac{2}{\sqrt[3]{25}}$

Rationalize each numerator.

85. $\dfrac{\sqrt{2}}{5}$

86. $\dfrac{\sqrt{5}}{5}$

87. $\dfrac{\sqrt{2x}}{3}$

88. $\dfrac{3\sqrt[3]{7x}}{2}$

SECTION 0.4   Polynomials

Definitions and Concepts	Examples
Monomial: A polynomial with one term.	$2,\ 3x,\ 4x^2y,\ -x^3y^2z$
Binomial: A polynomial with two terms.	$2t + 3,\ 3r^2 - 6r,\ 4m + 5n$
Trinomial: A polynomial with three terms.	$3p^2 - 7p + 8,\ 3m^2 + 2n - p$
The **degree of a monomial** is the sum of the exponents on its variables.	The degree of $4x^2y^3$ is $2 + 3 = 5$
The **degree of a polynomial** is the degree of the term in the polynomial with highest degree.	The degree of the first term of $3p^2q^3 - 6p^3q^4 + 9pq^2$ is $2 + 3 = 5$, the degree of the second term is $3 + 4 = 7$, and the degree of the third term is $1 + 2 = 3$. The degree of the polynomial is the largest of these. It is 7.
Multiplying a monomial times a polynomial: $$a(b + c + d + \cdots) = ab + ac + ad + \cdots$$	$3(x + 2) = 3x + 6$ $2x(3x^2 - 2y + 3) = 6x^3 - 4xy + 6x$
Addition and subtraction of polynomials: To add or subtract polynomials, remove parentheses and combine like terms.	Add: $(3x^2 + 5x) + (2x^2 - 2x)$. $$\begin{aligned}(3x^2 + 5x) + (2x^2 - 2x) &= 3x^2 + 5x + 2x^2 - 2x \\ &= 3x^2 + 2x^2 + 5x - 2x \\ &= 5x^2 + 3x\end{aligned}$$ Subtract: $(4a^2 - 5b) - (3a^2 - 7b)$. $$\begin{aligned}(4a^2 - 5b) - (3a^2 - 7b) &= 4a^2 - 5b - 3a^2 + 7b \\ &= 4a^2 - 3a^2 - 5b + 7b \\ &= a^2 + 2b\end{aligned}$$
Special products: $$(x + y)^2 = x^2 + 2xy + y^2$$ $$(x - y)^2 = x^2 - 2xy + y^2$$ $$(x + y)(x - y) = x^2 - y^2$$	$(2m + 3)^2 = 4m^2 + 12m + 9$ $(4t - 3s)^2 = 16t^2 - 24ts + 9s^2$ $(2m + n)(2m - n) = 4m^2 - 2mn + 2mn - n^2 = 4m^2 - n^2$
Multiplying a binomial times a binomial: Use the FOIL method.	$$\begin{aligned}(2a + b)(a - b) &= 2a(a) + 2a(-b) + ba + b(-b) \\ &= 2a^2 - 2ab + ab - b^2 \\ &= 2a^2 - ab - b^2\end{aligned}$$

Definitions and Concepts	Examples
The **conjugate** of $a + b$ is $a - b$.	
To rationalize the denominator of a radical expression, multiply both the numerator and denominator of the rational expression by the conjugate of the denominator.	Rationalize the denominator: $\dfrac{x}{\sqrt{x} + 2}$. $$\dfrac{x}{\sqrt{x} + 2} = \dfrac{x(\sqrt{x} - 2)}{(\sqrt{x} + 2)(\sqrt{x} - 2)}$$ Multiply the numerator and denominator by the conjugate of $\sqrt{x} + 2$. $$= \dfrac{x\sqrt{x} - 2x}{x - 4}$$ Simplify.
Division of polynomials: To divide polynomials, use long division.	Divide: $2x + 3\overline{)6x^3 + 7x^2 - x + 3}$. $$\begin{array}{r} 3x^2 - x + 1 \\ 2x + 3\overline{)6x^3 + 7x^2 - x + 3} \\ \underline{6x^3 + 9x^2} \\ -2x^2 - x \\ \underline{-2x^2 - 3x} \\ +2x + 3 \\ \underline{+2x + 3} \\ 0 \end{array}$$

EXERCISES

Give the degree of each polynomial and tell whether the polynomial is a monomial, a binomial, or a trinomial.

89. $x^3 - 8$

90. $8x - 8x^2 - 8$

91. $\sqrt{3}x^2$

92. $4x^4 - 12x^2 + 1$

Perform the operations and simplify.

93. $2(x + 3) + 3(x - 4)$

94. $3x^2(x - 1) - 2x(x + 3) - x^2(x + 2)$

95. $(3x + 2)(3x + 2)$

96. $(3x + y)(2x - 3y)$

97. $(4a + 2b)(2a - 3b)$

98. $(z + 3)(3z^2 + z - 1)$

99. $(a^n + 2)(a^n - 1)$

100. $\left(\sqrt{2} + x\right)^2$

101. $\left(\sqrt{2} + 1\right)\left(\sqrt{3} + 1\right)$

102. $\left(\sqrt[3]{3} - 2\right)\left(\sqrt[3]{9} + 2\sqrt[3]{3} + 4\right)$

Rationalize each denominator.

103. $\dfrac{2}{\sqrt{3} - 1}$

104. $\dfrac{-2}{\sqrt{3} - \sqrt{2}}$

105. $\dfrac{2x}{\sqrt{x} - 2}$

106. $\dfrac{\sqrt{x} - \sqrt{y}}{\sqrt{x} + \sqrt{y}}$

Rationalize each numerator.

107. $\dfrac{\sqrt{x} + 2}{5}$

108. $\dfrac{1 - \sqrt{a}}{a}$

Perform each division.

109. $\dfrac{3x^2y^2}{6x^3y}$

110. $\dfrac{4a^2b^3 + 6ab^4}{2b^2}$

111. $2x + 3\overline{)2x^3 + 7x^2 + 8x + 3}$

112. $x^2 - 1\overline{)x^5 + x^3 - 2x - 3x^2 - 3}$

SECTION **0.5**   Factoring Polynomials

Definitions and Concepts	Examples
Factoring out a common monomial:	
$\quad ab + ac = a(b + c)$	$3p^3 - 6p^2q + 9p = 3p(p^2 - 2pq + 3)$
Factoring the difference of two squares:	
$\quad x^2 - y^2 = (x + y)(x - y)$	$4x^2 - 9 = (2x + 3)(2x - 3)$
Factoring trinomials:	
$\quad$ • Trinomial squares	
$\qquad x^2 + 2xy + y^2 = (x + y)^2$	$9a^2 + 12ab + 4b^2 = (3a + 2b)(3a + 2b) = (3a + 2b)^2$
$\qquad x^2 - 2xy + y^2 = (x - y)^2$	$r^2 - 4rs + 4s^2 = (r - 2s)(r - 2s) = (r - 2s)^2$
$\quad$ • To factor general trinomials use trial and error or grouping.	$6x^2 - 5x - 6 = (2x - 3)(3x + 2)$
Factoring the sum and difference of two cubes:	
$\quad x^3 + y^3 = (x + y)(x^2 - xy + y^2)$	$r^3 + 8 = (r + 2)(r^2 - 2r + 4)$
$\quad x^3 - y^3 = (x - y)(x^2 + xy + y^2)$	$27a^3 - 8b^3 = (3a - 2b)(9a^2 + 6ab + 4b^2)$

EXERCISES

Factor each expression completely, if possible.

113. $3t^3 - 3t$ **114.** $5r^3 - 5$

115. $6x^2 + 7x - 24$ **116.** $3a^2 + ax - 3a - x$

117. $8x^3 - 125$ **118.** $6x^2 - 20x - 16$

119. $x^2 + 6x + 9 - t^2$ **120.** $3x^2 - 1 + 5x$

121. $8z^3 + 343$ **122.** $1 + 14b + 49b^2$

123. $121z^2 + 4 - 44z$ **124.** $64y^3 - 1,000$

125. $2xy - 4zx - wy + 2zw$ **126.** $x^8 + x^4 + 1$

SECTION **0.6**   Algebraic Fractions

Definitions and Concepts	Examples
Properties of fractions:	
If there are no divisions by 0, then	
$\quad$ • $\dfrac{a}{b} = \dfrac{c}{d}$ if and only if $ad = bc$.	$\dfrac{3x}{4} = \dfrac{6x}{8}$ because $(3x)8$ and $4(6x)$ both equal $24x$.
$\quad$ • $\dfrac{a}{b} = \dfrac{ax}{bx}$	$\dfrac{6x^2}{8x^3} = \dfrac{3 \cdot 2 \cdot x \cdot x}{2 \cdot 4 \cdot x \cdot x \cdot x} = \dfrac{3}{4x}$
$\quad$ • $\dfrac{a}{b} \cdot \dfrac{c}{d} = \dfrac{ac}{bd}$	$\dfrac{3p}{2q} \cdot \dfrac{2p}{6q} = \dfrac{3p \cdot 2p}{2q \cdot 6q} = \dfrac{3p \cdot 2p}{2q \cdot 3 \cdot 2q} = \dfrac{p^2}{2q^2}$
$\quad$ • $\dfrac{a}{b} \div \dfrac{c}{d} = \dfrac{ad}{bc}$	$\dfrac{2t}{3s} \div \dfrac{2t}{6s} = \dfrac{2t}{3s} \cdot \dfrac{6s}{2t} = \dfrac{2t \cdot 6s}{3s \cdot 2t} = \dfrac{2t \cdot 2 \cdot 3s}{3s2t} = 2$

Definitions and Concepts	Examples
• $\dfrac{a}{b} + \dfrac{c}{b} = \dfrac{a+c}{b}$ • $\dfrac{a}{b} - \dfrac{c}{b} = \dfrac{a-c}{b}$	$\dfrac{x}{4} + \dfrac{y}{4} = \dfrac{x+y}{4}$ $\dfrac{3p}{2q} - \dfrac{p}{2q} = \dfrac{3p-p}{2q} = \dfrac{2p}{2q} = \dfrac{p}{q}$
• $a \cdot 1 = a$ • $\dfrac{a}{1} = a$ • $\dfrac{a}{a} = 1$	$7 \cdot 1 = 1$ $\dfrac{7}{1} = 7$ $\dfrac{7}{7} = 1$
• $\dfrac{a}{b} = \dfrac{-a}{-b} = -\dfrac{a}{-b} = -\dfrac{-a}{b}$	$\dfrac{7}{2} = \dfrac{-7}{-2} = -\dfrac{7}{-2} = -\dfrac{-7}{2}$
• $-\dfrac{a}{b} = \dfrac{a}{-b} = \dfrac{-a}{b} = -\dfrac{-a}{-b}$	$\dfrac{7}{2} = \dfrac{7}{-2} = \dfrac{-7}{2} = -\dfrac{-7}{-2}$
Simplifying rational expressions: To simplify a rational expression, factor the numerator and denominator, if possible, and divide out factors that are common to the numerator and denominator.	To simplify $\dfrac{2-x}{2x-4}$, factor -1 from the numerator and 2 from the denominator to get $$\dfrac{2-x}{2x-4} = \dfrac{-1(-2+x)}{2(x-2)} = \dfrac{-1(x-2)}{2(x-2)} = \dfrac{-1}{2} = -\dfrac{1}{2}$$
Adding or subtracting rational expressions: To add or subtract rational expressions with unlike denominators, find the LCD of the expressions, write each expression with a denominator that is the LCD, add or subtract the expressions, and simplify the result, if possible.	$\dfrac{2x}{x+2} - \dfrac{2x}{x-3} = \dfrac{2x(x-3)}{(x+2)(x-3)} - \dfrac{2x(x+2)}{(x-3)(x+2)}$ $= \dfrac{2x(x-3) - 2x(x+2)}{(x+2)(x-3)}$ $= \dfrac{2x^2 - 6x - 2x^2 - 4x}{(x+2)(x-3)}$ $= \dfrac{-10x}{(x+2)(x-3)}$
Complex fractions: To simplify complex fractions, multiply the numerator and denominator of the complex fraction by the LCD of all the fractions.	$\dfrac{1 - \dfrac{y}{2}}{\dfrac{1}{y} + \dfrac{1}{2}} = \dfrac{2y\left(1 - \dfrac{y}{2}\right)}{2y\left(\dfrac{1}{y} + \dfrac{1}{2}\right)} = \dfrac{2y - y^2}{2 + y} = \dfrac{y(2 - y)}{2 + y}$

EXERCISES

Simplify each rational expression.

127. $\dfrac{2-x}{x^2 - 4x + 4}$

128. $\dfrac{a^2 - 9}{a^2 - 6a + 9}$

Perform each operation and simplify. Assume that no denominators are 0.

129. $\dfrac{x^2 - 4x + 4}{x+2} \cdot \dfrac{x^2 + 5x + 6}{x-2}$

130. $\dfrac{2y^2 - 11y + 15}{y^2 - 6y + 8} \cdot \dfrac{y^2 - 2y - 8}{y^2 - y - 6}$

131. $\dfrac{2t^2 + t - 3}{3t^2 - 7t + 4} \div \dfrac{10t + 15}{3t^2 - t - 4}$

132. $\dfrac{p^2 + 7p + 12}{p^3 + 8p^2 + 4p} \div \dfrac{p^2 - 9}{p^2}$

133. $\dfrac{x^2 + x - 6}{x^2 - x - 6} \cdot \dfrac{x^2 - x - 6}{x^2 + x - 2} \div \dfrac{x^2 - 4}{x^2 - 5x + 6}$

134. $\left(\dfrac{2x+6}{x+5} \div \dfrac{2x^2 - 2x - 4}{x^2 - 25}\right) \dfrac{x^2 - x - 2}{x^2 - 2x - 15}$

135. $\dfrac{2}{x-4} + \dfrac{3x}{x+5}$

136. $\dfrac{5x}{x-2} - \dfrac{3x+7}{x+2} + \dfrac{2x+1}{x+2}$

137. $\dfrac{x}{x-1} + \dfrac{x}{x-2} + \dfrac{x}{x-3}$

138. $\dfrac{x}{x+1} - \dfrac{3x+7}{x+2} + \dfrac{2x+1}{x+2}$

139. $\dfrac{3(x+1)}{x} - \dfrac{5(x^2+3)}{x^2} + \dfrac{x}{x+1}$

140. $\dfrac{3x}{x+1} + \dfrac{x^2+4x+3}{x^2+3x+2} - \dfrac{x^2+x-6}{x^2-4}$

Simplify each complex fraction. Assume that no denominators are 0.

141. $\dfrac{\dfrac{5x}{2}}{\dfrac{3x^2}{8}}$

142. $\dfrac{\dfrac{3x}{y}}{\dfrac{6x}{y^2}}$

143. $\dfrac{\dfrac{1}{x} + \dfrac{1}{y}}{x - y}$

144. $\dfrac{x^{-1} + y^{-1}}{y^{-1} - x^{-1}}$

CHAPTER TEST

Consider the set $\left\{-7, -\frac{2}{3}, 0, 1, 3, \sqrt{10}, 4\right\}$.

1. List the numbers in the set that are odd integers.

2. List the numbers in the set that are prime numbers.

Determine which property justifies each statement.

3. $(a + b) + c = (b + a) + c$

4. $a(b + c) = ab + ac$

Graph each interval on a number line.

5. $-4 < x \le 2$

6. $(-\infty, -3) \cup [6, \infty)$

Write each expression without using absolute value symbols.

7. $|-17|$

8. $|x - 7|$, when $x < 0$

Find the distance on a number line between points with the following coordinates.

9. -4 and 12

10. -20 and -12

Simplify each expression. Assume that all variables represent positive numbers, and write all answers without using negative exponents.

11. $x^4 x^5 x^2$

12. $\dfrac{r^2 r^3 s}{r^4 s^2}$

13. $\dfrac{(a^{-1}a^2)^{-2}}{a^{-3}}$

14. $\left(\dfrac{x^0 x^2}{x^{-2}}\right)^6$

Write each number in scientific notation.

15. $450{,}000$

16. 0.000345

Write each number in standard notation.

17. 3.7×10^3

18. 1.2×10^{-3}

Simplify each expression. Assume that all variables represent positive numbers, and write all answers without using negative exponents.

19. $(25a^4)^{1/2}$

20. $\left(\dfrac{36}{81}\right)^{3/2}$

21. $\left(\dfrac{8t^6}{27s^9}\right)^{-2/3}$

22. $\sqrt[3]{27a^6}$

23. $\sqrt{12} + \sqrt{27}$

24. $2\sqrt[3]{3x^4} - 3x\sqrt[3]{24x}$

25. Rationalize the denominator: $\dfrac{x}{\sqrt{x} - 2}$.

26. Rationalize the numerator: $\dfrac{\sqrt{x} - \sqrt{y}}{\sqrt{x} + \sqrt{y}}$.

Perform each operation.

27. $(a^2 + 3) - (2a^2 - 4)$

28. $(3a^3 b^2)(-2a^3 b^4)$

29. $(3x - 4)(2x + 7)$

30. $(a^n + 2)(a^n - 3)$

31. $(x^2 + 4)(x^2 - 4)$

32. $(x^2 - x + 2)(2x - 3)$

33. $x - 3\overline{)6x^2 + x - 23}$

34. $2x - 1\overline{)2x^3 + 3x^2 - 1}$

Factor each polynomial.

35. $3x + 6y$

36. $x^2 - 100$

37. $10t^2 - 19tw + 6w^2$

38. $3a^3 - 648$

39. $x^4 - x^2 - 12$

40. $6x^4 + 11x^2 - 10$

Perform each operation and simplify if possible. Assume that no denominators are 0.

41. $\dfrac{x}{x + 2} + \dfrac{2}{x + 2}$

42. $\dfrac{x}{x + 1} - \dfrac{x}{x - 1}$

43. $\dfrac{x^2 + x - 20}{x^2 - 16} \cdot \dfrac{x^2 - 25}{x - 5}$

44. $\dfrac{x + 2}{x^2 + 2x + 1} \div \dfrac{x^2 - 4}{x + 1}$

Simplify each complex fraction. Assume that no denominators are 0.

45. $\dfrac{\dfrac{1}{a} + \dfrac{1}{b}}{\dfrac{1}{b}}$

46. $\dfrac{x^{-1}}{x^{-1} + y^{-1}}$

The Rectangular Coordinate System and Graphs of Equations

2

CAREERS AND MATHEMATICS: Cartographer

© Stock Connection Blue/Alamy

Cartographers collect, analyze, interpret, and map geographic information about the earth's surface. Their work involves geographical research and compiling data to produce maps. They analyze latitude and longitude, elevation and distance, as well as population density, land-use patterns, precipitation levels, and demographic characteristics. Their maps are prepared in either digital or graphic form, using information provided by geodetic surveys, aerial cameras, satellites, light-imaging detection, and Geographic Information Systems (GIS).

Education and Mathematics Required
- Cartographers usually have a bachelor's degree in cartography, geography, surveying, engineering, forestry, computer science, or a physical science.
- College Algebra, Trigonometry, Calculus I and II, Elementary Statistics, and Spatial Statistics are usually required.

How Cartographers Use Math and Who Employs Them
- Math helps cartographers with map scale, coordinate systems, and map projection. Map scale is the relationship between distances on a map and the corresponding distances on the earth's surface. Coordinate systems are numeric methods of representing locations on the earth's surface. Map projection is a function or transformation that relates coordinates of points on a curved surface to coordinates of points on a plane.
- Most cartographers work with engineering, architectural, and surveying firms. Government agencies hire cartographers to work in highway departments and in areas such as land management, natural resources planning, and national defense.

Career Outlook and Salary
- Employment of cartographers is expected to grow 19 percent from 2008 to 2018.
- The median annual wage in May 2008 was $51,180.

For more information see: www.bls.gov/oco

Mathematical expressions often indicate relationships between two variables. To visualize these relationships, we draw graphs of their equations.

2.1 The Rectangular Coordinate System

In this section, we will learn to

1. Plot points in the rectangular coordinate system.
2. Graph linear equations.
3. Graph vertical and horizontal lines.
4. Solve applications using linear equations.
5. Find the distance between two points.
6. Find the midpoint of a line segment.

We often say that a picture is worth a thousand words. In fact, pictures and graphs are an effective way to present information. For this reason, they appear frequently in newspapers and magazines. For example, the graph shown in Figure 2-1 provides a visual representation of the manatee population in Florida after the year 2003.

From the graph we can note many facts about manatees. Among them are:

- The number of manatees in Florida declined from 2005 to 2007.
- In 2005, the population was about 3,100 animals.
- In this time period, the lowest population of manatees occurred in 2004.

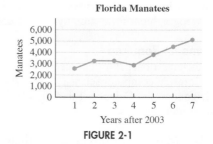

Florida Manatees

FIGURE 2-1

In mathematics, graphs are also an effective way to present information. In this chapter, we will draw graphs of equations containing two variables and then discuss the information that we can derive from graphs.

The solutions of an equation with variables x and y such as $y = -\frac{1}{2}x + 4$ are ordered pairs of real numbers (x, y) that satisfy the equation. To find some ordered pairs that satisfy the equation, we substitute **input values** of x into the equation and find the corresponding **output values** of y. For example, if we substitute 2 for x, we obtain

$$y = -\frac{1}{2}x + 4$$

$$y = -\frac{1}{2}(2) + 4 \qquad \text{Substitute 2 for } x.$$

$$= -1 + 4$$

$$= 3$$

Since $y = 3$ when $x = 2$, the ordered pair $(2, 3)$ is a solution of the equation. The first coordinate, 2, of the ordered pair is usually called the **x-coordinate**. The second coordinate, 3, is usually called the **y-coordinate**. The solution $(2, 3)$ and several other solutions are listed in the table of values shown in Figure 2-2.

Comment

To complete the table of solutions, we first pick values for x. Next we compute each y-value. Then we write each solution as an ordered pair. Note that we choose x-values that are multiples of the denominator, 2. This makes the computations easier when multiplying the x-value by $-\frac{1}{2}$ to find the corresponding y-value.

$y = -\dfrac{1}{2}x + 4$		
x	y	(x, y)
-4	6	$(-4, 6)$
-2	5	$(-2, 5)$
0	4	$(0, 4)$
2	3	$(2, 3)$
4	2	$(4, 2)$

Pick values for x. —→   —— Write each solution as an ordered pair.

Compute each y-value.

FIGURE 2-2

ACCENT ON TECHNOLOGY   ## Generating Table Values

If an equation in x and y is solved for y, we can use a graphing calculator to generate a table of solutions. The instructions in this discussion are for a TI-84 Plus graphing calculator. For details about other brands, please consult the owner's manual.

To construct a table of solutions for $x + 2y = 8$, we first solve the equation for y.

$$x + 2y = 8$$
$$2y = -x + 8 \qquad \text{Subtract } x \text{ from both sides.}$$
$$y = -\frac{1}{2}x + 4 \qquad \text{Divide both sides by 2 and simplify.}$$

- To construct a table of values for $y = -\frac{1}{2}x + 4$, we first enter the equation. We press [Y=] and enter $-(1/2)x + 4$, as shown in Figure 2-3(a).
- Next, we press [2nd] [WINDOW] and enter one value for x on the line labeled TblStart=. In Figure 2-3(b), -4 has been entered on this line. Other values for x that will appear in the table are determined by setting an **increment value** on the line labeled ΔTbl=. In Figure 2-3(b), an increment value of 2 has been entered. This means that each x-value in the table will be 2 units larger than the previous one.
- Finally, we press [2nd] [GRAPH] to obtain the table of values shown in Figure 2-3(c). This table contains all of the solutions listed in Figure 2-2, plus the two additional solutions $(6, 1)$ and $(8, 0)$.

To see other values, we simply scroll up and down the screen by pressing the up and down arrow keys.

(a)   (b)   (c)

FIGURE 2-3

Before we can present the table of solutions shown in Figure 2-2 in graphical form, we need to discuss the rectangular coordinate system.

1. Plot Points in the Rectangular Coordinate System

The **rectangular coordinate system** consists of two perpendicular number lines that divide the plane into four **quadrants,** numbered as shown in Figure 2-4. The horizontal number line is called the *x*-**axis,** and the vertical number line is called the *y*-**axis.** These axes intersect at a point called the **origin,** which is 0 on each axis. The positive direction on the *x*-axis is to the right, the positive direction on the *y*-axis is upward, and the same unit distance is used on both axes, unless otherwise indicated.

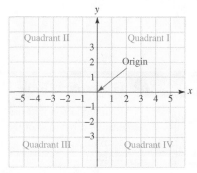

FIGURE 2-4

To plot (or graph) the point associated with the pair $x = 2$ and $y = 3$, denoted as $(2, 3)$, we start at the origin, count 2 units to the right, and then count 3 units up. (See Figure 2-5.) Point *P* (which lies in the first quadrant) is the graph of the ordered pair $(2, 3)$. The ordered pair $(2, 3)$ gives the **coordinates** of point *P*.

To plot point *Q* with coordinates $(-4, 6)$, we start at the origin, count 4 units to the left, and then count 6 units up. Point *Q* lies in the second quadrant. Point *R* with coordinates $(6, -4)$ lies in the fourth quadrant.

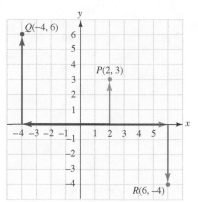

FIGURE 2-5

Caution

The ordered pairs $(-4, 6)$ and $(6, -4)$ represent **different** points. $(-4, 6)$ is in the second quadrant and $(6, -4)$ is in the fourth quadrant.

2. Graph Linear Equations

The **graph of the equation** $y = -\frac{1}{2}x + 4$ is the graph of all points (x, y) on the rectangular coordinate system whose coordinates satisfy the equation. To graph $y = -\frac{1}{2}x + 4$, we plot the pairs listed in the table of solutions shown in Figure 2-6. These points lie on the line shown in the figure. This line is the graph of the equation.

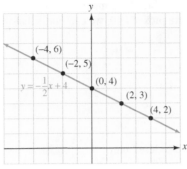

$y = -\frac{1}{2}x + 4$		
x	y	(x, y)
-4	6	$(-4, 6)$
-2	5	$(-2, 5)$
0	4	$(0, 4)$
2	3	$(2, 3)$
4	2	$(4, 2)$

FIGURE 2-6

Comment   When we say that the graph of an equation is a line, we imply two things:

1. Every point with coordinates that satisfy the equation will lie on the line.
2. Every point on the line will have coordinates that satisfy the equation.

When the graph of an equation is a line, we call the equation a **linear equation.** These equations are often written in **standard form** as $Ax + By = C$, where A, B, and C are specific numbers (called **constants**) and x and y are variables. Either A or B can be 0, but A and B cannot both be 0.

Standard Form of an Equation of a Line

The **standard form of an equation of a line** is

$$Ax + By = C$$

where A, B, and C are real numbers and A and B are not both 0.

Here are four examples of linear equations written in standard form.

Linear Equation	Values of A, B, and C
$3x + 2y = 6$	$A = 3, B = 2, C = 6$
$5x - 2y = -10$	$A = 5, B = -2, C = -10$
$2y = 7$	$A = 0, B = 2, C = 7$
$x = -4$	$A = 1, B = 0, C = -4$

EXAMPLE 1   Graphing a Linear Equation

Graph: $x + 2y = 5$.

SOLUTION   We will solve the equation for y and form a table of solutions by picking values for x, substituting them into the equation, and solving for the other variable y. We will plot the points represented in the table of solutions and draw a line through the points.

Solve the equation for y.

$$x + 2y = 5$$
$$x - x + 2y = 5 - x \qquad \text{Subtract } x \text{ from both sides.}$$
$$2y = -x + 5 \qquad \text{Simplify.}$$
$$y = -\frac{1}{2}x + \frac{5}{2} \qquad \text{Divide both sides by 2.}$$

Pick values for x and solve for y.

If we pick $x = 0$, we can find y as follows:

$$y = -\frac{1}{2}x + \frac{5}{2}$$

$$y = -\frac{1}{2}(0) + \frac{5}{2} \qquad \text{Substitute 0 in for } x.$$

$$y = \frac{5}{2} \qquad \text{Simplify.}$$

The ordered pair $\left(0, \frac{5}{2}\right)$ satisfies the equation.

To find another ordered pair, we pick $x = 1$ and find y.

$$y = -\frac{1}{2}x + \frac{5}{2}$$

$$y = -\frac{1}{2}(1) + \frac{5}{2} \qquad \text{Substitute 1 in for } x.$$

$$y = 2 \qquad \text{Simplify.}$$

The ordered pair $(1, 2)$ satisfies the equation.

These pairs and others that satisfy the equation are shown in Figure 2-7. We plot the points and join them with a line to get the graph of the equation.

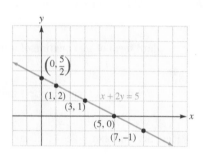

$x + 2y = 5$		
x	y	(x, y)
0	$\frac{5}{2}$	$\left(0, \frac{5}{2}\right)$
1	2	$(1, 2)$
3	1	$(3, 1)$
5	0	$(5, 0)$
7	-1	$(7, -1)$

FIGURE 2-7

Comment

Even though there are infinitely many points that lie on a line, only two are required to graph a line. However, it is a good idea to find a third point as a check.

Self Check 1   Graph: $3x - 2y = 6$.

Now Try Exercise 35.

EXAMPLE 2   **Graphing a Linear Equation**

Graph: $3(y + 2) = 2x - 3$.

SOLUTION   We will solve the equation for y and find ordered pairs (x, y) that satisfy the equation. Then, we will plot the points and graph the line.

Solve the equation for y.

$$3(y + 2) = 2x - 3$$

$$3y + 6 = 2x - 3 \qquad \text{Use the Distributive Property to remove parentheses.}$$

$$3y = 2x - 9 \qquad \text{Subtract 6 from both sides.}$$

$$y = \frac{2}{3}x - 3 \qquad \text{Divide both sides by 3.}$$

Pick values for *x*, solve for *y*.
We now substitute numbers for *x* to find the corresponding values of *y*. If we let *x* = 0 and find *y*, we get

$$y = \frac{2}{3}x - 3$$

$$y = \frac{2}{3}(0) - 3 \qquad \text{Substitute 0 for } x.$$

$$y = -3 \qquad \text{Simplify.}$$

The point (0, −3) lies on the graph.
   If we let *x* = 3, we get

$$y = \frac{2}{3}x - 3$$

$$y = \frac{2}{3}(3) - 3 \qquad \text{Substitute 3 for } x.$$

$$y = 2 - 3 \qquad \text{Simplify.}$$

$$y = -1$$

The point (3, −1) lies on the graph.
   We plot these points and others, as in Figure 2-8, and draw the line that passes through the points.

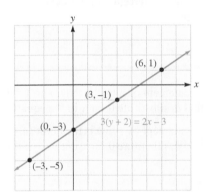

$3(y + 2) = 2x - 3$		
x	*y*	(*x*, *y*)
−3	−5	(−3, −5)
0	−3	(0, −3)
3	−1	(3, −1)
6	1	(6, 1)

FIGURE 2-8

Self Check 2   Graph: $2(x - 1) = 6 - 8y$.

Now Try Exercise 39.

ACCENT ON TECHNOLOGY   **Graphing Equations**

We can graph equations with a graphing calculator. To see a graph, we must choose the minimum and maximum values of the *x*- and *y*-coordinates that will appear on the calculator's window. A window with standard settings of

   Xmin = −10   Xmax = 10   Ymin = −10   Ymax = 10

will produce a graph where the value of *x* is in the interval [−10, 10], and the value of *y* is in the interval [−10, 10].

- To use a graphing calculator to graph $3x + 2y = 12$, we first solve the equation for y.

$$2y = -3x + 12 \qquad \text{Subtract } 3x \text{ from both sides.}$$

$$y = -\frac{3}{2}x + 6 \qquad \text{Divide both sides by 2.}$$

- Next, we press [Y=] and enter the right side of the equation. The screen is shown in Figure 2-9(a).
- We then press [GRAPH] to obtain the graph shown in Figure 2-9(b).

(a)   (b)

FIGURE 2-9

In Figure 2-9, the graph intersects the y-axis at the point $(0, 6)$, which is called the **y-intercept.** It intersects the x-axis at the point $(4, 0)$, which is called the **x-intercept.**

Intercepts of a Line

The **y-intercept** of a line is the point $(0, b)$, where the line intersects the y-axis. To find b, substitute 0 for x in the equation of the line and solve for y.

The **x-intercept** of a line is the point $(a, 0)$, where the line intersects the x-axis. To find a, substitute 0 for y in the equation of the line and solve for x.

EXAMPLE 3   **Graphing a Line by Finding the Intercepts**

Use the x- and y-intercepts to graph the equation $3x + 2y = 12$.

SOLUTION   To find the y-intercept, we substitute 0 for x and solve for y. To find the x-intercept, we substitute 0 for y and solve for x. We will also find a third point as a check and then plot the points and draw the graph.

Find the y-intercept.

To find the y-intercept, we substitute 0 for x and solve for y.

$$3x + 2y = 12$$

$$3(0) + 2y = 12 \qquad \text{Substitute 0 for } x.$$

$$2y = 12 \qquad \text{Simplify.}$$

$$y = 6 \qquad \text{Divide both sides by 2.}$$

The y-intercept is the point $(0, 6)$.

Find the *x*-intercept.

To find the *x*-intercept, we substitute 0 for *y* and solve for *x*.

$$3x + 2y = 12$$

$$3x + 2(0) = 12 \qquad \text{Substitute 0 for } y.$$

$$3x = 12 \qquad \text{Simplify.}$$

$$x = 4 \qquad \text{Divide both sides by 3.}$$

The *x*-intercept is the point $(4, 0)$.

Find a third point as a check.

If we let $x = 2$, we will find that $y = 3$.

$$3x + 2y = 12$$

$$3(2) + 2y = 12 \qquad \text{Substitute 2 for } x.$$

$$6 + 2y = 12 \qquad \text{Simplify.}$$

$$2y = 6 \qquad \text{Subtract 6 from both sides.}$$

$$y = 3 \qquad \text{Divide both sides by 2.}$$

The point $(2, 3)$ satisfies the equation.

We plot each pair (as in Figure 2-10) and join them with a line to get the graph of the equation.

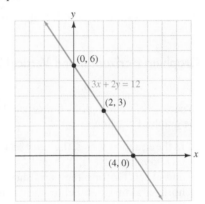

$3x + 2y = 12$		
x	y	(x, y)
0	6	$(0, 6)$
2	3	$(2, 3)$
4	0	$(4, 0)$

FIGURE 2-10

Self Check 3   Graph: $2x - 3y = 12$.

Now Try Exercise 47.

ACCENT ON TECHNOLOGY   **Finding Intercepts Using Zoom and Trace**

We can use the trace feature on a graphing calculator to find the approximate coordinates of any point on a graph. When we press TRACE, a flashing cursor will appear on the screen. The coordinates of the cursor will also appear at the bottom of the screen.

• To find the *y*-intercept of the graph of $2y = -5x - 7$ (or $y = -\frac{5}{2}x - \frac{7}{2}$), we graph the equation, using $[-10, 10]$ for *x* and $[-10, 10]$ for *y*, and press TRACE to get Figure 2-11(a). We see from the figure that the y-intercept is $(0, -3.5)$.

- We can approximate the x-intercept by using the left arrow key and moving the cursor toward the *x*-intercept until we arrive at a point with the coordinates shown in Figure 2-11(b). We see from the graph that the *x*-coordinate of the *x*-intercept is approximately -1.489362.

  To get better results, we can zoom in to get a magnified picture, trace again, and move the cursor to the point with coordinates shown in Figure 2-11(c). Since the *y*-coordinate is almost 0, we now have a good approximation for the *x*-intercept. The *x*-coordinate of the *x*-intercept is approximately -1.382979. We can achieve better results with repeated zooms.

(a)

(b)

(c)

FIGURE 2-11

3. Graph Horizontal and Vertical Lines

In the next example, we will graph a horizontal and a vertical line.

EXAMPLE 4   **Graphing Horizontal and Vertical Lines**

Graph: **a.** $y = 2$ **b.** $x = -3$

SOLUTION   In each case, we will plot a few ordered pairs that satisfy the equation and then draw the graph of the line.

a. In the equation $y = 2$, the value of *y* is always 2. Any value can be used for *x*. If we pick *x*-values of $-3, 0, 2$, and 4, we get the ordered pairs: $(-3, 2), (0, 2), (2, 2),$ and $(4, 2)$. Plotting the pairs shown in Figure 2-12, we see that the graph is a horizontal line, parallel to the *x*-axis and having a *y*-intercept of $(0, 2)$. The line has no *x*-intercept.

b. In the equation $x = -3$, the value of *x* is always -3. Any value can be used for *y*. If we pick *y*-values of $-2, 0, 2$ and 3, we get the ordered pairs: $(-3, -2), (-3, 0), (-3, 2)$ and $(-3, 3)$. After plotting the pairs shown in Figure 2-12, we see that the graph is a vertical line, parallel to the *y*-axis and having an *x*-intercept of $(-3, 0)$. The line has no *y*-intercept.

$y = 2$		
x	y	(x, y)
-3	2	$(-3, 2)$
0	2	$(0, 2)$
2	2	$(2, 2)$
4	2	$(4, 2)$

$x = -3$		
x	y	(x, y)
-3	-2	$(-3, -2)$
-3	0	$(-3, 0)$
-3	2	$(-3, 2)$
-3	3	$(-3, 3)$

FIGURE 2-12

Self Check 4   Graph: **a.** $x = 2$ **b.** $y = -3$

Now Try Exercise 51.

Example 4 suggests the following facts.

Equations of Vertical and Horizontal Lines

If a and b are real numbers, then

- The graph of the equation $x = a$ is a vertical line with x-intercept of $(a, 0)$. If $a = 0$, the line $x = 0$ is the y-axis.
- The graph of the equation $y = b$ is a horizontal line with y-intercept of $(0, b)$. If $b = 0$, the line $y = 0$ is the x-axis.

---

4. Solve Applications Using Linear Equations

EXAMPLE 5   **Solving an Application Problem**

A computer purchased for \$2,750 is expected to depreciate according to the formula $y = -550x + \$2{,}750$, where y is the value of the computer after x years. When will the computer be worth nothing?

SOLUTION   The computer will have no value when its value (y) is 0. To find x when $y = 0$, we substitute 0 for y and solve for x.

$$y = -550x + 2{,}750$$

$$0 = -550x + 2{,}750$$

$$-2{,}750 = -550x \qquad \text{Subtract 2,750 from both sides.}$$

$$5 = x \qquad \text{Divide both sides by } -550.$$

The computer will have no value in 5 years.

Self Check 5   When will the value of the computer be \$1,650?

Now Try Exercise 97.

5. Find the Distance between Two Points

To derive the formula used to find the distance between two points on a rectangular coordinate system, we use **subscript notation** and denote the points as

$$P(x_1, y_1) \qquad \text{Read as "point } P \text{ with coordinates of } x \text{ sub 1 and } y \text{ sub 1."}$$

$$Q(x_2, y_2) \qquad \text{Read as "point } Q \text{ with coordinates of } x \text{ sub 2 and } y \text{ sub 2."}$$

If $P(x_1, y_1)$ and $Q(x_2, y_2)$ are two points in Figure 2-13 and point R has coordinates (x_2, y_1), triangle PQR is a right triangle. By the Pythagorean Theorem, the square of the hypotenuse of right triangle PQR is equal to the sum of the squares of the two legs. Because leg RQ is vertical, the square of its length is $(y_2 - y_1)^2$. Since leg PR is horizontal, the square of its length is $(x_2 - x_1)^2$. Thus, we have

$$(1) \quad d^2 = (x_2 - x_1)^2 + (y_2 - y_1)^2$$

Because equal positive numbers have equal positive square roots, we can take the positive square root of both sides of Equation 1 to obtain the **Distance Formula**.

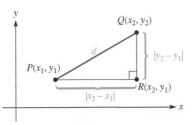

FIGURE 2-13

The Distance Formula   The distance d between points (x_1, y_1) and (x_2, y_2) is given by

$$d = \sqrt{(x_2 - x_1)^2 + (y_2 - y_1)^2}$$

EXAMPLE 6   Finding the Distance between Two Points

Find the distance between $P(-1, -2)$ and $Q(-7, 8)$.

SOLUTION   We use the Distance Formula, $d = \sqrt{(x_2 - x_1)^2 + (y_2 - y_1)^2}$, to find the distance between $P(-1, -2)$ and $Q(-7, 8)$.

If we let $P(-1, -2) = P(x_1, y_1)$ and $Q(-7, 8) = Q(x_2, y_2)$, we can substitute -1 for x_1, -2 for y_1, -7 for x_2, and 8 for y_2 into the formula and simplify.

$$d(PQ) = \sqrt{(x_2 - x_1)^2 + (y_2 - y_1)^2} \qquad \text{Read } d(PQ) \text{ as "the length of segment } PQ."$$

$$d(PQ) = \sqrt{[-7 - (-1)]^2 + [8 - (-2)]^2}$$

$$= \sqrt{(-6)^2 + (10)^2}$$

$$= \sqrt{36 + 100}$$

$$= \sqrt{136}$$

$$= \sqrt{4 \cdot 34}$$

$$= 2\sqrt{34} \qquad\qquad \sqrt{4 \cdot 34} = \sqrt{4}\sqrt{34} = 2\sqrt{34}$$

Self Check 6   Find the distance between $P(-2, -5)$ and $Q(3, 7)$.

Now Try Exercise 73.

6. Find the Midpoint of a Line Segment

If point M in Figure 2-14 lies midway between points $P(x_1, y_1)$ and $Q(x_2, y_2)$, point M is called the **midpoint** of segment PQ. To find the coordinates of M, we find the average of the x-coordinates and the average of the y-coordinates of P and Q.

The Midpoint Formula   The midpoint of the line segment with endpoints at $P(x_1, y_1)$ and $Q(x_2, y_2)$ is the point M with coordinates of

$$M = \left(\frac{x_1 + x_2}{2}, \frac{y_1 + y_2}{2} \right)$$

FIGURE 2-14

You will be asked to prove this formula in Exercise 107 by using the Distance Formula to show that $d(PM) + d(MQ) = d(PQ)$.

EXAMPLE 7   Finding the Midpoint of a Line Segment

Find the midpoint of the segment joining $P(-7, 2)$ and $Q(1, -4)$.

SOLUTION   We use the Midpoint Formula, $M = \left(\dfrac{x_1 + x_2}{2}, \dfrac{y_1 + y_2}{2} \right)$ to find the midpoint of the line segment joining $P(-7, 2)$ and $Q(1, -4)$. To do so, we substitute $P(-7, 2)$ for $P(x_1, y_1)$ and $Q(1, -4)$ for $Q(x_2, y_2)$ into the Midpoint Formula to get

$$x_M = \frac{x_1 + x_2}{2} \quad \text{and} \quad y_M = \frac{y_1 + y_2}{2}$$

$$= \frac{-7 + 1}{2} \qquad\qquad = \frac{2 + (-4)}{2}$$

$$= \frac{-6}{2} \qquad\qquad = \frac{-2}{2}$$

$$= -3 \qquad\qquad = -1$$

The midpoint is $M(-3, -1)$.

Self Check 7   Find the midpoint of the segment joining $P(-7, -8)$ and $Q(-2, 10)$.

Now Try Exercise 83.

EXAMPLE 8   Using Midpoint Formula to Find Coordinates

The midpoint of the segment joining $P(-3, 2)$ and $Q(x_2, y_2)$ is $M(1, 4)$. Find the coordinates of Q.

SOLUTION   We can let $P(x_1, y_1) = P(-3, 2)$ and $M(x_M, y_M) = M(1, 4)$, and then find the coordinates x_2 and y_2 of point $Q(x_2, y_2)$.

$$x_M = \frac{x_1 + x_2}{2} \quad \text{and} \quad y_M = \frac{y_1 + y_2}{2}$$

$$1 = \frac{-3 + x_2}{2} \qquad\qquad 4 = \frac{2 + y_2}{2}$$

$$2 = -3 + x_2 \qquad\qquad 8 = 2 + y_2 \qquad \text{Multiply both sides by 2.}$$

$$5 = x_2 \qquad\qquad 6 = y_2$$

The coordinates of point Q are $(5, 6)$.

Self Check 8   If the midpoint of a segment PQ is $M(2, -5)$ and one endpoint is $Q(6, 9)$, find P.

Now Try Exercise 87.

Self Check Answers

1.   2.   3.   4.

5. 2 years   6. 13   7. $M\left(-\dfrac{9}{2}, 1\right)$ 8. $(-2, -19)$

Exercises 2.1

Getting Ready
You should be able to complete these vocabulary and concept statements before you proceed to the practice exercises.

Fill in the blanks.

1. The coordinate axes divide the plane into four _____.

2. The coordinate axes intersect at the _____.

3. The positive direction on the x-axis is _____.

4. The positive direction on the y-axis is _____.

5. The x-coordinate is the _____ coordinate in an ordered pair.

6. The y-coordinate is the _____ coordinate in an ordered pair.

7. A _____ equation is an equation whose graph is a line.

8. The point where a line intersects the _____ is called the y-intercept.

9. The point where a line intersects the x-axis is called the _____.

10. The graph of the equation $x = a$ will be a _____ line.

11. The graph of the equation $y = b$ will be a _____ line.

12. Complete the Distance Formula:

    $d =$ _____.

13. If a point divides a segment into two equal segments, the point is called the _____ of the segment.

14. The midpoint of the segment joining $P(x_1, y_1)$ and

    $Q(x_2, y_2)$ is _____.

Practice
Refer to the illustration and determine the coordinates of each point.

15. A 16. B
17. C 18. D
19. E 20. F
21. G 22.

Graph each point. Indicate the quadrant in which the point lies, or the axis on which it lies.

23. $(2, 5)$ 24. $(-3, 4)$
25. $(-4, -5)$ 26. $(6, 2)$
27. $(5, 2)$ 28. $(3, -4)$
29. $(4, 0)$ 30. $(0, 2)$

Solve each equation for y and graph the equation. Then check your graph with a graphing calculator.

31. $y - 2x = 7$ 32. $y + 3 = -4x$

33. $y + 5x = 5$ 34. $y - 3x = 6$

35. $6x - 3y = 10$ 36. $4x + 8y - 1 = 0$

37. $3x = 6y - 1$ 38. $2x + 1 = 4y$

39. $2(x + y + 1) = x + 2$ **40.** $5(x + 2) = 3y - x$

Graph each equation.

49. $y = 3$ **50.** $x = -4$

Find the x- and y-intercepts and use them to graph each equation.

41. $x + y = 5$ **42.** $x - y = 3$

51. $3x + 5 = -1$ **52.** $7y - 1 = 6$

43. $2x - y = 4$ **44.** $3x + y = 9$

53. $3(y + 2) = y$ **54.** $4 + 3y = 3(x + y)$

45. $3x + 2y = 6$ **46.** $2x - 3y = 6$

55. $3(y + 2x) = 6x + y$ **56.** $5(y - x) = x + 5y$

47. $4x - 5y = 20$ **48.** $3x - 5y = 15$

 Use a graphing calculator to graph each equation and then find the x-coordinate of the x-intercept to the nearest hundredth.

57. $y = 3.7x - 4.5$ **58.** $y = \dfrac{3}{5}x + \dfrac{5}{4}$

59. $1.5x - 3y = 7$ **60.** $0.3x + y = 7.5$

Find the distance between P and O(0, 0).

61. $P(4, -3)$ **62.** $P(-5, 12)$

63. $P(-3, 2)$ **64.** $P(5, 0)$

65. $P(1, 1)$ **66.** $P(6, -8)$

67. $P\left(\sqrt{3}, 1\right)$ **68.** $P\left(\sqrt{7}, \sqrt{2}\right)$

Find the distance between P and Q.

69. $P(3, 7)$; $Q(6, 3)$

70. $P(4, 9)$; $Q(9, 21)$

71. $P(4, -6)$; $Q(-1, 6)$

72. $P(0, 5)$; $Q(6, -3)$

73. $P(-2, -15)$; $Q(-6, -21)$ **74.** $P(-7, 11)$; $Q(-11, 7)$

75. $P(3, -3)$; $Q(-5, 5)$

76. $P(6, -3)$; $Q(-3, 2)$

77. $P(\pi, -2)$; $Q(\pi, 5)$

78. $P\left(\sqrt{5}, 0\right)$; $Q(0, 2)$

Find the midpoint of the line segment PQ.

79. $P(2, 4)$; $Q(6, 8)$

80. $P(3, -6)$; $Q(-1, -6)$

81. $P(2, -5)$; $Q(-2, 7)$

82. $P(0, 3)$; $Q(-10, -13)$

83. $P(-8, 5)$; $Q(6, -4)$

84. $P(3, -2)$; $Q(2, -3)$

85. $P(0, 0)$; $Q\left(\sqrt{5}, \sqrt{5}\right)$

86. $P\left(\sqrt{3}, 0\right)$; $Q\left(0, -\sqrt{5}\right)$

One endpoint P and the midpoint M of line segment PQ are given. Find the coordinates of the other endpoint, Q.

87. $P(1, 4)$; $M(3, 5)$

88. $P(2, -7)$; $M(-5, 6)$

89. $P(5, -5)$; $M(5, 5)$

90. $P(-7, 3)$; $M(0, 0)$

91. Show that a triangle with vertices at $(13, -2)$, $(9, -8)$, and $(5, -2)$ is isosceles.

92. Show that a triangle with vertices at $(-1, 2)$, $(3, 1)$, and $(4, 5)$ is isosceles.

93. In the illustration, points M and N are the midpoints of AC and BC, respectively. Find the length of MN.

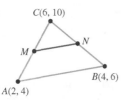

94. In the illustration, points M and N are the midpoints of AC and BC, respectively. Show that $d(MN) = \frac{1}{2}[d(AB)]$.

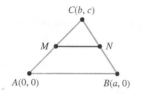

95. In the illustration, point M is the midpoint of the hypotenuse of right triangle AOB. Show that the area of rectangle $OLMN$ is one-half of the area of triangle AOB.

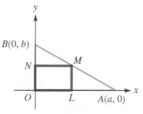

96. Rectangle $ABCD$ in the illustration is twice as long as it is wide, and its sides are parallel to the coordinate axes. If the perimeter is 42, find the coordinates of point C.

Applications

97. House appreciation A house purchased for $225,000 is expected to appreciate according to the formula $y = 17{,}500x + 225{,}000$, where y is the value of the house after x years. Find the value of the house 5 years later.

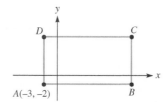

98. Car depreciation A Chevy Cruze car purchased for $17,000 is expected to depreciate according to the formula $y = -1{,}360x + 17{,}000$, where y is the value of the car after x years. When will the car be worthless?

99. Demand equations The number of photo scanners that consumers buy depends on price. The higher the price, the fewer photo scanners people will buy. The equation that relates price to the number of photo scanners sold at that price is called a **demand equation.** If the demand equation for a photo scanner is $p = -\frac{1}{10}q + 170$, where p is the price and q is the number of photo scanners sold at that price, how many photo scanners will be sold at a price of $150?

100. Supply equations The number of television sets that manufacturers produce depends on price. The higher the price, the more TVs manufacturers will produce. The equation that relates price to the number of TVs produced at that price is called a **supply equation.** If the supply equation for a 25-inch TV is $p = \frac{1}{10}q + 130$, where p is the price and q is the number of TVs produced for sale at that price, how many TVs will be produced if the price is $150?

101. Meshing gears The rotational speed V of a large gear (with N teeth) is related to the speed v of the smaller gear (with n teeth) by the equation $V = \frac{nv}{N}$. If the larger gear in the illustration is making 60 revolutions per minute, how fast is the smaller gear spinning?

102. Crime prevention The number n of incidents of family violence requiring police response appears to be related to d, the money spent on crisis intervention, by the equation $n = 430 - 0.005d$. What expenditure would reduce the number of incidents to 350?

103. Navigation See the illustration. An ocean liner is located 23 miles east and 72 miles north of Pigeon Cove Lighthouse, and its home port is 47 miles west and 84 miles south of the lighthouse. How far is the ship from port?

104. Engineering Two holes are to be drilled at locations specified by the engineering drawing shown in the illustration. Find the distance between the centers of the holes.

Discovery and Writing

105. Explain how to graph a line using the intercept method.

106. Explain how to determine the quadrant in which the point $P(a, b)$ lies.

107. In Figure 2-14, show that $d(PM) + d(MQ) = d(PQ)$.

108. Use the result of Exercise 107 to explain why point M is the midpoint of segment PQ.

Review

Graph each interval on the number line.

109. $[-3, 2) \cup (-2, 3]$

110. $(-1, 4) \cap [-2, 2]$

111. $[-3, -2) \cap (2, 3]$

112. $[-4, -3) \cup (2, 3]$

Solve each equation.

113. $\dfrac{3}{y + 6} = \dfrac{4}{y + 4}$

114. $\dfrac{z + 4}{z^2 + z} - \dfrac{z + 1}{z^2 + 2z} = \dfrac{8}{z^2 + 3z + 2}$

2.2 The Slope of a Nonvertical Line

In this section, we will learn to

1. Find the slope of a line.
2. Use slope to solve applications.
3. Find slopes of horizontal and vertical lines.
4. Find slopes of parallel and perpendicular lines.

The world's steepest passenger railway is the Lookout Mountain Incline Railway in Chattanooga, Tennessee. Passengers experience breathtaking views of the city and surrounding mountains as the trolley-style railcars travel up Lookout Mountain. The grade or steepness of the track is 72.7% near the top.

Mathematicians use the term **slope** to represent the measure of the steepness of a line. We will explore the topic of slope in this section because it has many real-life applications.

1. Find the Slope of a Line

Suppose that a college student rents a room for $300 per month, plus a $200 nonrefundable deposit. The table shown in Figure 2-15(b) gives the cost (y) for different numbers of months (x). If we construct a graph from these data, we get the line shown in Figure 2-15(a).

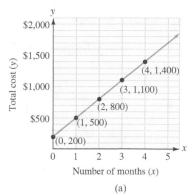

Time in Months	Total Cost
x	y
0	200
1	500
2	800
3	1,100
4	1,400

(a)   (b)

FIGURE 2-15

From the graph, we can see that if x changes from 0 to 1, y changes from 200 to 500. As x changes from 1 to 2, y changes from 500 to 800, and so on. The ratio of the change in y divided by the change in x is the constant 300.

$$\frac{\text{Change in } y}{\text{Change in } x} = \frac{500 - 200}{1 - 0} = \frac{800 - 500}{2 - 1} = \frac{1,100 - 800}{3 - 2} = \frac{1,400 - 1,100}{4 - 3} = \frac{300}{1} = 300$$

The ratio of the change in y divided by the change in x between any two points on any line is always a constant. This constant rate of change is called the **slope** of the line.

The Slope of a Nonvertical Line   The **slope of the nonvertical line** (see Figure 2-16) passing through points $P(x_1, y_1)$ and $Q(x_2, y_2)$ is

$$m = \frac{\text{change in } y}{\text{change in } x} = \frac{y_2 - y_1}{x_2 - x_1} \qquad (x_2 \neq x_1)$$

Comment

Slope is often considered to be a measure of the steepness or tilt of a line. Note that we can use the coordinates of any two points on a line to compute the slope of the line.

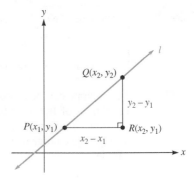

FIGURE 2-16

EXAMPLE 1   **Finding the Slope of a Line Given Two Points**

Find the slope of the line passing through $P(-1, -2)$ and $Q(7, 8)$.

SOLUTION   We will substitute the points $P(-1, -2)$ and $Q(7, 8)$ into the slope formula, $m = \dfrac{\text{change in } y}{\text{change in } x} = \dfrac{y_2 - y_1}{x_2 - x_1}$, to find the slope of the line.

Let $P(x_1, y_1) = P(-1, -2)$ and $Q(x_2, y_2) = Q(7, 8)$. Then we substitute -1 for x_1, -2 for y_1, 7 for x_2, and 8 for y_2 to get

$$m = \frac{\text{change in } y}{\text{change in } x}$$

$$m = \frac{y_2 - y_1}{x_2 - x_1}$$

$$= \frac{8 - (-2)}{7 - (-1)}$$

$$= \frac{10}{8}$$

$$= \frac{5}{4}$$

The slope of the line is $\frac{5}{4}$. See Figure 2-17.

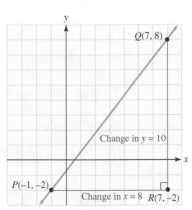

FIGURE 2-17

We would have obtained the same result if we had let $P(x_1, y_1) = P(7, 8)$ and $Q(x_2, y_2) = Q(-1, -2)$.

Self Check 1   Find the slope of the line passing through $P(-3, -4)$ and $Q(5, 9)$.

N   T   **Exercise 13.**

Caution

When calculating slope, always subtract the y-values and the x-values in the same order.

$$m = \frac{y_2 - y_1}{x_2 - x_1} \quad \text{or} \quad m = \frac{y_1 - y_2}{x_1 - x_2}$$

Otherwise, we will obtain an *incorrect* result.

A slope can be a positive real number, 0, or a negative real number. If the denominator of the slope formula is 0, slope is not defined.

The change in y (often denoted as Δy) is the **rise** of the line between points P and Q. The change in x (often denoted as Δx) is the **run.** Using this terminology, we can define slope to be the ratio of the rise to the run:

$$m = \frac{y_2 - y_1}{x_2 - x_1} = \frac{\Delta y}{\Delta x} = \frac{\text{rise}}{\text{run}} \quad (\Delta x \neq 0)$$

EXAMPLE 2   **Finding the Slope of a Line Given Its Equation in Standard Form**

Find the slope of the line determined by $5x + 2y = 10$. (See Figure 2-18.)

SOLUTION   We will find the coordinates of the x- and y-intercepts and substitute into slope formula, $m = \dfrac{\text{change in } y}{\text{change in } x} = \dfrac{y_2 - y_1}{x_2 - x_1}$, to find the slope of the line

$5x + 2y = 10$

FIGURE 2-18

- If $y = 0$, then $x = 2$, and the point $(2, 0)$ lies on the line.
- If $x = 0$, then $y = 5$, and the point $(0, 5)$ lies on the line.

We then find the slope of the line between $P(2, 0)$ and $Q(0, 5)$.

$$m = \frac{\text{change in } y}{\text{change in } x}$$

$$m = \frac{y_2 - y_1}{x_2 - x_1}$$

$$= \frac{5 - 0}{0 - 2}$$

$$= -\frac{5}{2}$$

The slope is $-\frac{5}{2}$.

Self Check 2   Find the slope of the line determined by $3x - 2y = 9$.

Now Try Exercise 27.

2. Use Slope to Solve Applications

EXAMPLE 3   **Using Slope to Solve an Application Problem**

If carpet costs \$25 per square yard plus a delivery charge of \$30, the total cost C of n square yards is given by the formula

Total cost	equals	cost per square yard	times	the number of square yards purchased	plus	the delivery charge.
C	$=$	25	$\cdot$	n	$+$	30

Graph the equation $C = 25n + 30$ and interpret the slope of the line.

SOLUTION   We will complete a table of solutions and graph the equation on a coordinate system with a vertical C-axis and a horizontal n-axis. Figure 2-19 shows a table of ordered pairs and the graph.

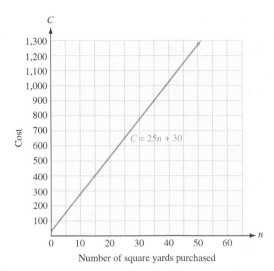

\multicolumn{3}{c}{$C = 25n + 30$}		
n	C	(n, C)
10	280	(10, 280)
20	530	(20, 530)
30	780	(30, 780)
40	1,030	(40, 1,030)
50	1,280	(50, 1,280)

FIGURE 2-19

If we pick the points (30, 780) and (50, 1,280) to find the slope, we have

$$m = \frac{\Delta C}{\Delta n}$$

$$= \frac{C_2 - C_1}{n_2 - n_1}$$

$$= \frac{1,280 - 780}{50 - 30} \qquad \text{Substitute 1,280 for } C_2, 780 \text{ for } C_1, 50 \text{ for } n_2, \text{ and 30 for } n_1.$$

$$= \frac{500}{20}$$

$$= 25$$

The slope of 25 (in dollars/square yard) is the cost per square yard of the carpet. ■

Self Check 3   If the cost of the carpet in Example 3 increases to $35 per square yard, find the slope of the line.

Now Try Exercise 81.

EXAMPLE 4   Solving an Application Problem

It takes a skier 25 minutes to complete the course shown in Figure 2-20. Find his average rate of descent in feet per minute.

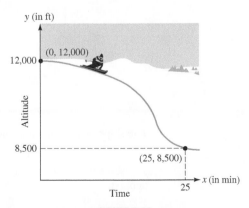

FIGURE 2-20

SOLUTION   To find the average rate of descent, we will find the ratio of the change in altitude to the change in time. To find this ratio, we will calculate the slope of the line passing through the points (0, 12,000) and (25, 8,500).

$$\frac{\text{Average rate}}{\text{of descent}} = \frac{12,000 - 8,500}{0 - 25}$$

$$= \frac{3,500}{-25}$$

$$= -140$$

The average rate of descent is 140 ft/min.

Self Check 4   If it takes the skier 20 minutes to complete the course, find his average rate of descent in feet per minute.

Now Try Exercise 83.

3. Find Slopes of Horizontal and Vertical Lines

If $P(x_1, y_1)$ and $Q(x_2, y_2)$ are points on the horizontal line shown in Figure 2-21(a), then $y_1 = y_2$, and the numerator of the fraction is 0.

$$\frac{y_2 - y_1}{x_2 - x_1} \qquad \text{On a horizontal line, } x_2 \neq x_1.$$

Thus, the value of the fraction is 0, and the slope of the horizontal line is 0.

If $P(x_1, y_1)$ and $Q(x_2, y_2)$ are points on the vertical line shown in Figure 2-21(b), then $x_1 = x_2$, and the denominator of the fraction is 0.

$$\frac{y_2 - y_1}{x_2 - x_1} \qquad \text{On a vertical line, } y_2 \neq y_1.$$

Since the denominator of a fraction cannot be 0, the slope of a vertical line is not defined.

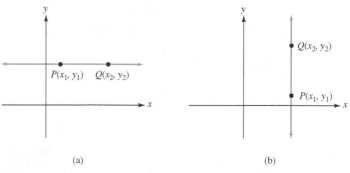

(a)   (b)

FIGURE 2-21

Slopes of Horizontal and Vertical Lines   The slope of a horizontal line (a line with an equation of the form $y = b$) is 0.

The slope of a vertical line (a line with an equation of the form $x = a$) is not defined.

Here are a few facts about slope. See Figure 2-22.

- If a line rises as we follow it from left to right, as in Figure 2-22(a), its slope is positive.
- If a line drops as we follow it from left to right, as in Figure 2-22(b), its slope is negative.
- If a line is horizontal, as in Figure 2-22(c), its slope is 0.
- If a line is vertical, as in Figure 2-22(d), it has no defined slope.

Slope Concepts

Positive slope	Negative slope	Zero slope	Undefined slope
(a)	(b)	(c)	(d)

FIGURE 2-22

4. Find Slopes of Parallel and Perpendicular Lines

To see a relationship between parallel lines and their slopes, we refer to the parallel lines l_1 and l_2 shown in Figure 2-23, with slopes of m_1 and m_2, respectively. Because right triangles ABC and DEF are similar, it follows that

$$m_1 = \frac{\Delta y \text{ of } l_1}{\Delta x \text{ of } l_1} = \frac{\Delta y \text{ of } l_2}{\Delta x \text{ of } l_2} = m_2$$

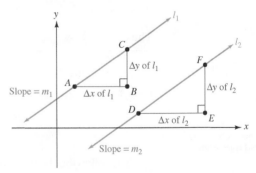

FIGURE 2-23

This shows that if two nonvertical lines are parallel, they have the same slope. It is also true that when two lines have the same slope, they are parallel.

Slopes of Parellel Lines   Nonvertical parallel lines have the same slope, and lines having the same slope are parallel.

Since vertical lines are parallel, lines with undefined slopes are parallel.

EXAMPLE 5   **Solving a Slope Problem Involving Parallel Lines**

The lines in Figure 2-24 are parallel. Find y.

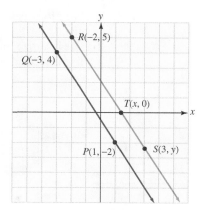

FIGURE 2-24

SOLUTION   Since the lines are parallel, their slopes are equal. To find y, we will find the slope of each line, set them equal, and solve the resulting equation.

Slope of PQ = slope of RS

$$\frac{-2 - 4}{1 - (-3)} = \frac{y - 5}{3 - (-2)}$$

$$\frac{-6}{4} = \frac{y - 5}{5} \qquad \text{Simplify.}$$

$$-30 = 4(y - 5) \qquad \text{Multiply both sides by 20.}$$

$$-30 = 4y - 20 \qquad \text{Remove parentheses and simplify.}$$

$$-10 = 4y \qquad \text{Add 20 to both sides.}$$

$$-\frac{5}{2} = y \qquad \text{Divide both sides by 4 and simplify.}$$

Thus, $y = -\frac{5}{2}$.

Self Check 5   Find x in Figure 2-24.

Now Try Exercise 59.

Comment

If the product of two numbers is -1, the numbers are called **negative reciprocals.**

The following theorem relates perpendicular lines and their slopes.

Slopes of Perpendicular Lines   If two nonvertical lines are perpendicular, the product of their slopes is -1.

If the product of the slopes of two lines is -1, the lines are perpendicular.

PROOF   Suppose l_1 and l_2 are lines with slopes of m_1 and m_2 that intersect at some point. See Figure 2-25. Then superimpose a coordinate system over the lines so that the intersection point is the origin. Let $P(a, b)$ be a point on l_1, and let $Q(c, d)$ be a point on l_2. Neither point P nor point Q can be the origin.

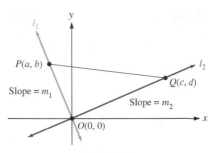

FIGURE 2-25

First, we suppose that l_1 and l_2 are perpendicular. Then triangle POQ is a right triangle with its right angle at O. By the Pythagorean Theorem,

$$d(OP)^2 + d(OQ)^2 = d(PQ)^2$$

$$(a - 0)^2 + (b - 0)^2 + (c - 0)^2 + (d - 0)^2 = (a - c)^2 + (b - d)^2$$

$$a^2 + b^2 + c^2 + d^2 = a^2 - 2ac + c^2 + b^2 - 2bd + d^2$$

$$0 = -2ac - 2bd$$

$$bd = -ac$$

(1) $\dfrac{b}{a} \cdot \dfrac{d}{c} = -1$ Divide both sides by ac.

The coordinates of P are (a, b), and the coordinates of O are $(0, 0)$. Using the definition of slope, we have

$$m_1 = \frac{b - 0}{a - 0} = \frac{b}{a}$$

Similarly, we have

$$m_2 = \frac{d}{c}$$

We substitute m_1 for $\frac{b}{a}$ and m_2 for $\frac{d}{c}$ in Equation 1 to obtain

$$m_1 m_2 = -1$$

Hence, if lines l_1 and l_2 are perpendicular, the product of their slopes is -1.

Conversely, we suppose that the product of the slopes of lines l_1 and l_2 is -1. Because the steps in the previous discussion are reversible, we have $d(OP)^2 + d(OQ)^2 = d(PQ)^2$. By the Pythagorean Theorem, triangle POQ is a right triangle. Thus, l_1 and l_2 are perpendicular. ◼

Comment

It is also true that a horizontal line is perpendicular to a vertical line.

EXAMPLE 6   **Solving a Slope Problem Involving Perpendicular Lines**

Are the lines shown in Figure 2-26 perpendicular?

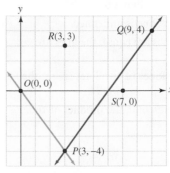

FIGURE 2-26

SOLUTION   We will determine the slopes of the lines and see whether their product is -1.

$$\text{Slope of } OP = \frac{\Delta y}{\Delta x} \qquad\qquad \text{Slope of } PQ = \frac{\Delta y}{\Delta x}$$

$$= \frac{y_2 - y_1}{x_2 - y_1} \qquad\qquad\qquad = \frac{y_2 - y_1}{x_2 - y_1}$$

$$= \frac{-4 - 0}{3 - 0} \qquad\qquad\qquad = \frac{4 - (-4)}{9 - 3}$$

$$= -\frac{4}{3} \qquad\qquad\qquad\qquad = \frac{8}{6}$$

$$\qquad\qquad\qquad\qquad\qquad = \frac{4}{3}$$

Since the product of the slopes is $-\frac{16}{9}$ and not -1, the lines are not perpendicular.

Self Check 6   Is either line in Figure 2-26 perpendicular to the line passing through R and S?

Now Try Exercise 55.

Self Check Answers   **1.** $\frac{13}{8}$ **2.** $\frac{3}{2}$ **3.** 35   **4.** 175 ft/min   **5.** $\frac{4}{3}$ **6.** yes

Exercises **2.2**

Getting Ready
You should be able to complete these vocabulary and concept statements before you proceed to the practice exercises.

Fill in the blanks.

1. The slope of a nonvertical line is defined to be the change in y _____ by the change in x.
2. The change in ___ is often called the rise.
3. The change in x is often called the ____.
4. When computing the slope from the coordinates of two points, always subtract the y-values and the x-values in the _____.
5. The symbol Δy means _____ y.
6. The slope of a _____ line is 0.
7. The slope of a _____ line is undefined.
8. If the slopes of two lines are equal, the lines are _____.
9. If the product of the slopes of two lines is -1, the lines are _____.
10. If two lines are perpendicular, the product of their slopes is ___.

Practice
Find the slope of the line passing through each pair of points, if possible.

11. $P(2, 2)$; $Q(-1, -1)$ **12.** $P(3, -1)$; $Q(5, 3)$

   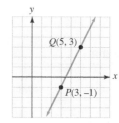

13. $P(-6, 3)$; $Q(6, -2)$ **14.** $P(2, 5)$; $Q(3, 10)$

15. $P(3, -2)$; $Q(-1, 5)$

16. $P(3, 7)$; $Q(6, 16)$

17. $P(8, -7)$; $Q(4, 1)$

18. $P(5, 17)$; $Q(17, 17)$

19. $P(-4, 3)$; $Q(-4, -3)$

20. $P(2, \sqrt{7})$; $Q(\sqrt{7}, 2)$

21. $P\left(\dfrac{3}{2}, \dfrac{2}{3}\right)$; $Q\left(\dfrac{5}{2}, \dfrac{7}{3}\right)$

22. $P\left(-\dfrac{2}{5}, \dfrac{1}{3}\right)$; $Q\left(\dfrac{3}{5}, -\dfrac{5}{3}\right)$

23. $P(a + b, c)$; $Q(b + c, a)$ assume $c \neq a$

24. $P(b, 0)$; $Q(a + b, a)$ assume $a \neq 0$

Find two points on the line and use slope formula to find the slope of the line.

25. $y = 3x + 2$

26. $y = 5x - 8$

27. $5x - 10y = 3$

28. $8y + 2x = 5$

29. $3(y + 2) = 2x - 3$

30. $4(x - 2) = 3y + 2$

31. $3(y + x) = 3(x - 1)$

32. $2x + 5 = 2(y + x)$

Find the slope of the line, if possible.

33. $y = 7$

34. $2y = 5$

35. $x = -\dfrac{1}{2}$

36. $x - 7 = 0$

Determine whether the slope of the line is positive, negative, 0, or undefined.

37.

38.

39.

40.

41.

42.

Determine whether the lines with the given slopes are parallel, perpendicular, or neither.

43. $m_1 = 3$; $m_2 = -\dfrac{1}{3}$

44. $m_1 = \dfrac{2}{3}$; $m_2 = \dfrac{3}{2}$

45. $m_1 = \sqrt{8}$; $m_2 = 2\sqrt{2}$

46. $m_1 = 1$; $m_2 = -1$

47. $m_1 = -\sqrt{2}$; $m_2 = \dfrac{\sqrt{2}}{2}$

48. $m_1 = 2\sqrt{7}$; $m_2 = \sqrt{28}$

49. $m_1 = -0.125$; $m_2 = 8$

50. $m_1 = 0.125$; $m_2 = \dfrac{1}{8}$

51. $m_1 = ab^{-1}$; $m_2 = -a^{-1}b$ $(a \neq 0, b \neq 0)$

52. $m_1 = \left(\dfrac{a}{b}\right)^{-1}$; $m_2 = -\dfrac{b}{a}$ $(a \neq 0, b \neq 0, a \neq b)$

Determine whether the line through the given points and the line through $R(-3, 5)$ and $S(2, 7)$ are parallel, perpendicular, or neither.

53. $P(2, 4)$; $Q(7, 6)$

54. $P(-3, 8)$; $Q(-13, 4)$

55. $P(-4, 6)$; $Q(-2, 1)$

56. $P(0, -9)$; $Q(4, 1)$

57. $P(a, a)$; $Q(3a, 6a)$ $(a \neq 0)$

58. $P(b, b)$; $Q(-b, 6b)$ $(b \neq 0)$

Lines PQ and RS are either parallel or perpendicular. Find x or y.

59. Parallel: $P(-3, 7)$; $Q(2, 9)$; $R(10, -4)$; $S(x, -6)$

60. Parallel: $P(2, -3)$; $Q(5, 7)$; $R(3, -1)$; $S(6, y)$

61. Perpendicular: $P(2, -7)$; $Q(1, 0)$; $R(-9, 5)$; $S(-2, y)$

62. Perpendicular: $P(1, -2)$; $Q(3, 4)$; $R(x, 6)$; $S(6, 5)$

Find the slopes of lines PQ and PR, and determine whether points P, Q, and R lie on the same line.

63. $P(-2, 8)$; $Q(-6, 9)$; $R(2, 5)$

64. $P(1, -1)$; $Q(3, -2)$; $R(-3, 0)$

65. $P(-a, a)$; $Q(0, 0)$; $R(a, -a)$

66. $P(a, a + b)$; $Q(a + b, b)$; $R(a - b, a)$

Determine which, if any, of the three lines PQ, PR, and QR are perpendicular.

67. $P(5, 4)$; $Q(2, -5)$; $R(8, -3)$

68. $P(8, -2)$; $Q(4, 6)$; $R(6, 7)$

69. $P(1, 3)$; $Q(1, 9)$; $R(7, 3)$

70. $P(2, -3)$; $Q(-3, 2)$; $R(3, 8)$

71. $P(0, 0)$; $Q(a, b)$; $R(-b, a)$

72. $P(a, b)$; $Q(-b, a)$; $R(a - b, a + b)$

73. **Right triangles** Show that the points $A(-1, -1)$, $B(-3, 4)$, and $C(4, 1)$ are the vertices of a right triangle.

74. **Right triangles** Show that the points $D(0, 1)$, $E(-1, 3)$, and $F(3, 5)$ are the vertices of a right triangle.

75. **Squares** Show that the points $A(1, -1)$, $B(3, 0)$, $C(2\ 2)$, and $D(0\ 1)$ are the vertices of a square.

76. Squares Show that the points $E(-1, -1)$, $F(3, 0)$, $G(2, 4)$, and $H(-2, 3)$ are the vertices of a square.

77. Parallelograms Show that the points $A(-2, -2)$, $B(3, 3)$, $C(2, 6)$, and $D(-3, 1)$ are the vertices of a parallelogram. (Show that both pairs of opposite sides are parallel.)

78. Trapezoids Show that points $E(1, -2)$, $F(5, 1)$, $G(3, 4)$, and $H(-3, 4)$ are the vertices of a trapezoid. (Show that only one pair of opposite sides is parallel.)

79. Geometry In the illustration, points M and N are midpoints of CB and BA, respectively. Show that MN is parallel to AC.

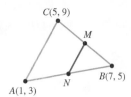

80. Geometry In the illustration, $d(AB) = d(AC)$. Show that AD is perpendicular to BC.

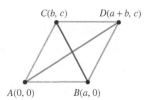

Applications

81. Rate of growth When a college started an aviation program, the administration agreed to predict enrollments using a straight-line method. If the enrollment during the first year was 12, and the enrollment during the fifth year was 26, find the rate of growth per year (the slope of the line). See the illustration.

82. Rate of growth A small business predicts sales according to a straight-line method. If sales were $50,000 in the first year and $110,000 in the third year, find the rate of growth in dollars per year (the slope of the line).

83. Rate of decrease The price of computers has been dropping steadily for the past ten years. If a desktop PC cost $6,700 ten years ago, and the same computing power cost $2,200 three years ago, find the rate of decrease per year. (Assume a straight-line model.)

84. Hospital costs The table shows the changing mean daily cost for a hospital room. For the ten-year period, find the rate of change per year of the portion of the room cost that is absorbed by the hospital.

Year	Total Cost to the Hospital	Amount Passed on to Patient
2000	$459	$212
2005	$670	$295
2010	$812	$307

85. Charting temperature changes The following Fahrenheit temperature readings were recorded over a four-hour period.

Time	12:00	1:00	2:00	3:00	4:00
Temperature	47°	53°	59°	65°	71°

Let t represent the time (in hours), with 12:00 corresponding to $t = 0$. Let T represent the temperature. Plot the points (t, T), and draw the line through those points. Explain the meaning of $\frac{\Delta T}{\Delta t}$.

86. Tracking the Dow The Dow Jones Industrial Averages at the close of trade on three consecutive days were as follows:

Day	Monday	Tuesday	Wednesday
Close	12,981	12,964	12,947

Let d represent the day, with $d = 0$ corresponding to Monday, and let D represent the Dow Jones average. Plot the points (d, D), and draw the graph. Explain the meaning of $\frac{\Delta D}{\Delta d}$.

87. Speed of an airplane A pilot files a flight plan indicating her intention to fly at a constant speed of 590 mph. Write an equation that expresses the distance traveled in terms of the flying time. Then graph the equation and interpret the slope of the line. (*Hint: d = rt.*)

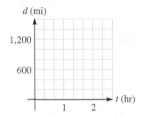

88. Growth of savings A student deposits $25 each month in a Holiday Club account at her bank. The account pays no interest. Write an equation that expresses the amount A in her account in terms of the number of deposits n. Then graph the line, and interpret the slope of the line.

Discovery and Writing

89. Explain why the slope of a vertical line is undefined.

90. Explain how to determine whether two lines are parallel, perpendicular, or neither.

Review

Solve each equation for y and simplify.

91. $3x + 7y = 21$

92. $y - 3 = 5(x + 2)$

93. $\dfrac{x}{5} + \dfrac{y}{2} = 1$

94. $x - 5y = 15$

Factor each expression.

95. $6p^2 + p - 12$

96. $b^3 - 27$

97. $mp + mq + np + nq$

98. $x^4 + x^2 - 2$

2.3 Writing Equations of Lines

In this section, we will learn to

1. Use point-slope form to write an equation of a line.
2. Use slope-intercept form to write an equation of a line.
3. Graph linear equations using the slope and *y*-intercept.
4. Determine whether linear equations represent lines that are parallel, perpendicular, or neither.
5. Write equations of parallel and perpendicular lines.
6. Recognize and use the standard form of the equation of a line.
7. Write an equation of a line that models a real-life problem.
8. Use linear curve fitting to solve problems.

Suppose we purchase a Kawasaki motorcycle for $10,000 and know that it depreciates $1,200 in value each year.

We can use the facts given to write a linear equation that represents the value y of the motorcycle x years after it was purchased. Because the motorcycle's value decreases $1,200 each year, the slope of the line's graph is $-1,200$. Because the purchase price is $10,000, we know that when we let $x = 0$, the value of y will equal 10,000. A linear equation that satisfies these two conditions is $y = -1,200x + 10,000$. This equation represents the straight-line depreciation of the motorcycle.

In this section, we will write equations of lines given specific characteristics or features of the line.

1. Use Point-Slope Form to Write an Equation of a Line

Suppose that line l in Figure 2-27 has a slope of m and passes through the point $P(x_1, y_1)$. If $Q(x, y)$ is any other point on line l, we have

$$m = \frac{y - y_1}{x - x_1}$$

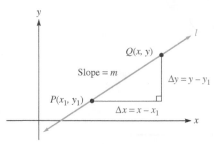

FIGURE 2-27

Comment

$y - y_1 = m(x - x_1)$ is often referred to as **point-slope formula** because we substitute a point and slope into it to write an equation of a line.

If we multiply both sides by $x - x_1$, we have

(1) $y - y_1 = m(x - x_1)$

Since Equation 1 displays the coordinates of the point (x_1, y_1) on the line and the slope m of the line, it is called the **point-slope form** of the equation of a line.

Point-Slope Form of an Equation of a Line

The equation of a line passing through $P(x_1, y_1)$ and with slope m is

$$y - y_1 = m(x - x_1).$$

EXAMPLE 1   **Writing an Equation of the Line with a Given Slope Passing through a Given Point**

Write an equation of the line with slope $-\frac{5}{3}$ and passing through $P(3, -1)$.

SOLUTION   We will substitute $-\frac{5}{3}$ for m, 3 for x_1, and -1 for y_1 in the point-slope form and simplify.

$$y - y_1 = m(x - x_1) \qquad \text{This is the point-slope form.}$$

$$y - (-1) = -\frac{5}{3}(x - 3) \qquad \text{Substitute } -\frac{5}{3} \text{ for } m, 3 \text{ for } x_1, \text{ and } -1 \text{ for } y_1.$$

$$y + 1 = -\frac{5}{3}x + 5 \qquad \text{Remove parentheses.}$$

$$y = -\frac{5}{3}x + 4 \qquad \text{Subtract 1 from both sides.}$$

An equation of the line is $y = -\frac{5}{3}x + 4$.

Self Check 1 Write an equation of the line with slope $-\frac{2}{3}$ and passing through $P(-4, 5)$.

Now Try Exercise 11.

EXAMPLE 2 **Writing an Equation of the Line that Passes through Two Given Points**

Find an equation of the line passing through $P(3, 7)$ and $Q(-5, 3)$.

SOLUTION We will find the slope of the line and then choose either point P or point Q and substitute both the slope and coordinates of the point into the point-slope form.
First we find the slope of the line.

$$m = \frac{y_2 - y_1}{x_2 - x_1} \qquad \text{This is the slope formula.}$$

$$= \frac{3 - 7}{-5 - 3} \qquad \text{Substitute 3 for } y_2, 7 \text{ for } y_1, -5 \text{ for } x_2, \text{ and 3 for } x_1.$$

$$= \frac{-4}{-8}$$

$$= \frac{1}{2}$$

We can choose either point P or point Q and substitute its coordinates into the point-slope form. If we choose $P(3, 7)$, we substitute $\frac{1}{2}$ for m, 3 for x_1, and 7 for y_1.

$$y - y_1 = m(x - x_1) \qquad \text{This is the point-slope form.}$$

$$y - 7 = \frac{1}{2}(x - 3) \qquad \text{Substitute } \frac{1}{2} \text{ for } m, 3 \text{ for } x_1, \text{ and 7 for } y_1.$$

$$y = \frac{1}{2}x - \frac{3}{2} + 7 \qquad \text{Remove parentheses and add 7 to both sides.}$$

$$y = \frac{1}{2}x + \frac{11}{2} \qquad -\frac{3}{2} + 7 = -\frac{3}{2} + \frac{14}{2} = \frac{11}{2}$$

An equation of the line is $y = \frac{1}{2}x + \frac{11}{2}$.

Self Check 2 Find an equation of the line passing through $P(-5, 4)$ and $Q(8, -6)$.

Now Try Exercise 23.

2. Use Slope-Intercept Form to Write an Equation of a Line

Since the y-intercept of the line shown in Figure 2-28 is the point $P(0, b)$, we can write an equation of the line by substituting 0 for x_1 and b for y_1 into the point-slope form and simplifying.

$$y - y_1 = m(x - x_1) \qquad \text{This is the point-slope form.}$$

$$y - b = m(x - 0) \qquad \text{Substitute 0 for } x_1 \text{ and } b \text{ for } y_1.$$

$$y - b = mx \qquad x - 0 = x$$

$$(2) \qquad y = mx + b \qquad \text{Add } b \text{ to both sides.}$$

Slope = m $P(0, b)$

FIGURE 2-28

Because Equation 2 displays the slope m and the y-coordinate b of the y-intercept, it is called the **slope-intercept form** of the equation of a line.

Slope-Intercept Form of an Equation of a line An equation of the line with slope m and y-intercept $(0, b)$ is

$$y = mx + b$$

Three examples of linear equations written in slope-intercept form are shown below.

Comment

Note that when a line is written in slope-intercept form the coefficient of x is the slope and the constant term is the y-coordinate of the y-intercept.

Example	Slope	y-Intercept
$y = 2x + 7$	$m = 2$	$b = 7;\ (0, 7)$
$y = \dfrac{2}{3}x - 5$	$m = \dfrac{2}{3}$	$b = -5;\ (0, -5)$
$y = -4x + \dfrac{1}{5}$	$m = -4$	$b = \dfrac{1}{5};\ \left(0, \dfrac{1}{5}\right)$

EXAMPLE 3   **Using Slope-Intercept Form to Write an Equation of a Line**

Use slope-intercept form to write an equation of the line with slope 4 that passes through $P(5, 9)$.

SOLUTION   Since we know that $m = 4$ and that the ordered pair $(5, 9)$ satisfies the equation, we substitute 4 for m, 5 for x, and 9 for y in the equation $y = mx + b$ and solve for b.

$\quad y = mx + b$ This is the slope-intercept form.

$\quad 9 = 4(5) + b$ Substitute 4 for m, 5 for x, and 9 for y.

$\quad 9 = 20 + b$ Simplify.

$\quad -11 = b$ Subtract 20 from both sides.

Comment

When we are given a point and slope we can determine an equation of the line by substituting into point-slope form or slope-intercept form.

Because $m = 4$ and $b = -11$, an equation is $y = 4x - 11$.

Self Check 3   Use slope-intercept form to write an equation of the line with slope $\frac{7}{3}$ and passing through $(3, 1)$.

Now Try Exercise 37.

3. Graph Linear Equations Using the Slope and y-Intercept.

It is easy to graph a linear equation when it is written in slope-intercept form. For example, to graph $y = \frac{4}{3}x - 2$ we note that $b = -2$ and that the y-intercept is $(0, b) = (0, -2)$. (See Figure 2-29.)

Because the slope is $\frac{\Delta y}{\Delta x} = \frac{4}{3}$, we can locate another point Q on the line by starting at point P and counting 3 units to the right and 4 units up. The change in x from point P to point Q is $\Delta x = 3$, and the corresponding change in y is $\Delta y = 4$. The line joining points P and Q is the graph of the equation.

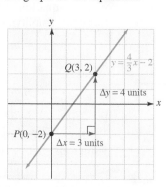

FIGURE 2-29

EXAMPLE 4   **Finding the Slope and y-Intercept of a Line and Graphing the Line**

Find the slope and the y-intercept of the line with equation $3(y + 2) = 6x - 1$ and graph it.

SOLUTION   We will write the equation in the form $y = mx + b$ to find the slope m and the y-intercept $(0, b)$. Then we will use m and b to graph the line.

$$3(y + 2) = 6x - 1$$

$$3y + 6 = 6x - 1 \qquad \text{Remove parentheses.}$$

$$3y = 6x - 7 \qquad \text{Subtract 6 from both sides.}$$

$$y = 2x - \frac{7}{3} \qquad \text{Divide both sides by 3.}$$

The slope of the graph is 2, and the y-intercept is $\left(0, -\frac{7}{3}\right)$. We plot the y-intercept. Then we find a second point on the line by moving 1 unit to the right and 2 units up to the point $\left(1, -\frac{1}{3}\right)$. To get the graph, we draw a line through the two points, as shown in Figure 2-30.

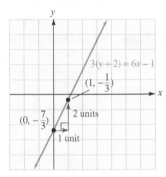

FIGURE 2-30

Self Check 4   Find the slope and the y-intercept of the line with equation $2(x - 3) = -3(y + 5)$. Then graph it.

Now Try Exercise 45.

4. Determine Whether Linear Equations Represent Lines that Are Parallel, Perpendicular, or Neither

EXAMPLE 5   **Determining Whether Lines are Parallel, Perpendicular, or Neither**

Determine whether the lines represented by $4x + 8y = 10$ and $2x = 12 - 4y$ are parallel, perpendicular, or neither.

SOLUTION   We will find the slope of each line and compare their slopes. If their slopes are the same, the lines are parallel. If the product of their slopes is -1, the lines are perpendicular. Otherwise, they are neither parallel nor perpendicular.

We solve each equation for y and write each equation in slope-intercept form.

$$4x + 8y = 10 \qquad\qquad\qquad 2x = 12 - 4y$$

$$8y = -4x + 10 \qquad\qquad 4y = -2x + 12$$

$$y = \frac{-4x}{8} + \frac{10}{8} \qquad\qquad y = \frac{-2x}{4} + \frac{12}{4}$$

$$y = -\frac{1}{2}x + \frac{5}{4} \qquad\qquad y = -\frac{1}{2}x + 3$$

Since the values of b are different, the lines are distinct. Since each slope is $-\frac{1}{2}$, the lines are parallel.

Self Check 5   Are the lines represented by $y = 3x + 2$ and $6x - 2y = 5$ parallel, perpendicular, or neither?

Now Try Exercise 57.

EXAMPLE 6   **Determining Whether Lines are Parallel, Perpendicular, or Neither**

Determine whether the lines represented by $4x + 8y = 10$ and $4x - 2y = 21$ are parallel, perpendicular, or neither.

SOLUTION   We will find the slope of each line and compare their slopes. If their slopes are the same, the lines are parallel. If the product of their slopes is -1, the lines are perpendicular. Otherwise, they are neither parallel nor perpendicular.

We solve each equation for y and write each equation in slope-intercept form.

$$4x + 8y = 10 \qquad\qquad\qquad 4x - 2y = 21$$

$$8y = -4x + 10 \qquad\qquad -2y = -4x + 21$$

$$y = \frac{-4x}{8} + \frac{10}{8} \qquad\qquad y = \frac{-4x}{-2} + \frac{21}{-2}$$

$$y = -\frac{1}{2}x + \frac{5}{4} \qquad\qquad y = 2x - \frac{21}{2}$$

Since the product of their slopes $\left(-\frac{1}{2} \text{ and } 2\right)$ is -1, the lines are perpendicular.

Self Check 6   Are the lines represented by $3x + 2y = 7$ and $y = \frac{2}{3}x + 3$ parallel, perpendicular, or neither?

Now Try Exercise 59.

5. Write Equations of Parallel and Perpendicular Lines

EXAMPLE 7   **Writing an Equation of a Parallel Line**

Write an equation of the line passing through $P(-2, 5)$ and parallel to the line $y = 8x - 3$.

SOLUTION   We will substitute the coordinates of $P(-2, 5)$ and the slope of the line parallel to $y = 8x - 3$ into point-slope form and simplify the results to write an equation of the parallel line.

The slope of the line given by $y = 8x - 3$ is 8, the coefficient of x. Since the graph of the desired equation is to be parallel to the graph of $y = 8x - 3$, its slope must also be 8.

We will substitute -2 for x_1, 5 for y_1, and 8 for m into the point-slope form and simplify.

$$y - y_1 = m(x - x_1)$$

$$y - 5 = 8[x - (-2)] \quad \text{Substitute 5 for } y_1, 8 \text{ for } m, \text{ and } -2 \text{ for } x_1.$$

$$y - 5 = 8(x + 2) \quad -(-2) = 2$$

$$y - 5 = 8x + 16 \quad \text{Use the Distributive Property to remove parentheses.}$$

$$y = 8x + 21 \quad \text{Add 5 to both sides.}$$

An equation of the desired line is $y = 8x + 21$.

Self Check 7   Write an equation of the line passing through $Q(1, 2)$ and parallel to the line $y = 8x - 3$.

Now Try Exercise 67.

EXAMPLE 8   Writing an Equation of a Perpendicular Line

Write an equation of the line passing through $P(-2, 5)$ and perpendicular to the line $y = 8x - 3$.

SOLUTION   We will substitute the coordinates of $P(-2, 5)$ and the slope of the line perpendicular to $y = 8x - 3$ into point-slope form and simplify to write an equation of the parallel line.

Because the slope of the given line is 8, the slope of the desired perpendicular line must be $-\frac{1}{8}$.

We substitute -2 for x_1, 5 for y_1, and $-\frac{1}{8}$ for m into the point-slope form and simplify.

$$y - y_1 = m(x - x_1)$$

$$y - 5 = -\frac{1}{8}[x - (-2)] \quad \text{Substitute 5 for } y_1, -\frac{1}{8} \text{ for } m, \text{ and } -2 \text{ for } x_1.$$

$$y - 5 = -\frac{1}{8}(x + 2) \quad -(-2) = 2$$

$$y = -\frac{1}{8}x - \frac{1}{4} + 5 \quad \text{Remove parentheses and add 5 to both sides.}$$

$$y = -\frac{1}{8}x + \frac{19}{4} \quad -\frac{1}{4} + 5 = -\frac{1}{4} + \frac{20}{4} = \frac{19}{4}$$

An equation of the line is $y = -\frac{1}{8}x + \frac{19}{4}$.

Self Check 8   Write an equation of the line passing through $Q(1, 2)$ and perpendicular to $y = 8x - 3$.

Now Try Exercise 73.

6. Recognize and Use the Standard Form of the Equation of a Line

We have shown that the graph of any equation of the form $y = mx + b$ is a line with slope m and y-intercept $(0, b)$. In Section 2.1, we saw that the graph of any equation of the form $Ax + By = C$ (where A and B are not *both* zero) is also a line. We consider three possibilities.

- If $A \neq 0$ and $B \neq 0$, the equation $Ax + By = C$ can be written in slope-intercept form.

$$Ax + By = C$$

$$By = -Ax + C \qquad \text{Subtract } Ax \text{ from both sides.}$$

$$y = -\frac{A}{B}x + \frac{C}{B} \qquad \text{Divide both sides by } B.$$

This is an equation of a line with slope $-\frac{A}{B}$ and y-intercept $\left(0, \frac{C}{B}\right)$.

- If $A = 0$ and $B \neq 0$, the equation $Ax + By = C$ can be written in the form $y = \frac{C}{B}$. This is an equation of a horizontal line with y-intercept $\left(0, \frac{C}{B}\right)$.

- If $A \neq 0$ and $B = 0$, the equation $Ax + By = C$ can be written in the form $x = \frac{C}{A}$. This is an equation of a vertical line with x-intercept at $\left(\frac{C}{A}, 0\right)$.

Recall that $Ax + By = C$ is called the **standard form of the equation of a line.**

Standard Form of an Equation on a Line

The **standard form of an equation of a line** is

$$Ax + By = C$$

where A, B, and C are real numbers, and both A and B are not zero.

- If $B \neq 0$, the slope of the nonvertical line is $-\frac{A}{B}$ and the y-intercept is $\left(0, \frac{C}{B}\right)$.
- If $B = 0$ the graph is a vertical line with x-intercept of $\left(\frac{C}{A}, 0\right)$.

Comment When writing equations in $Ax + By = C$ form, we usually clear the equation of fractions and make A positive. For example, the equation $-x + \frac{5}{2}y = 2$ can be changed to $2x - 5y = -4$ by multiplying both sides by -2. We will also divide out any common integer factors of A, B, and C. For example, we would write $4x + 8y = 12$ as $x + 2y = 3$.

Comment Sometimes linear equations are written with a constant term of 0 on the right side of the equation. This form is referred to as *general form*. The line $2x - 5y + 3 = 0$ is written in general form.

EXAMPLE 9 **Using Formulas to Find the Slope and *y*-Intercept**

Find the slope and the y-intercept of the graph of $3x - 2y = 5$.

SOLUTION The equation $3x - 2y = 5$ is in standard form, with $A = 3$, $B = -2$, and $C = 5$. We will use $-\frac{A}{B}$ to determine the slope of the line and $\left(0, \frac{C}{B}\right)$ to determine the y-intercept.

The slope of the graph is

$$m = -\frac{A}{B} = -\frac{3}{-2} = \frac{3}{2}$$

and the y-intercept is

$$\left(0, \frac{C}{B}\right) = \left(0, \frac{5}{-2}\right)$$

The slope is $\frac{3}{2}$ and the y-intercept is $\left(0, -\frac{5}{2}\right)$.

Self Check 9   Find the slope and the y-intercept of the graph of $3x - 4y = 12$.

Now Try Exercise 77.

We summarize the various forms of an equation of a line as follows.

Forms of an Equation of a Line	
Standard form	$Ax + By = C$ A and B cannot both be 0.
Slope-intercept form	$y = mx + b$ The slope is m, and the y-intercept is $(0, b)$.
Point-slope form	$y - y_1 = m(x - x_1)$ The slope is m, and the line passes through (x_1, y_1).
A horizontal line	$y = b$ The slope is 0, and the y-intercept is $(0, b)$.
A vertical line	$x = a$ There is no defined slope, and the x-intercept is $(a, 0)$.

7. Write an Equation of the Line that Models a Real-Life Problem

For tax purposes, many businesses use *straight-line depreciation* to find the declining value of aging equipment.

EXAMPLE 10   **Solving an Application Problem**

A business purchases a digital multimedia projector for $1,970 and expects it to last for ten years. It can then be sold as scrap for a *salvage value* of $270.

If y is the value of the projector after x years of use, and y and x are related by the equation of a line,

a. Find an equation of the line.

b. Find the value of the projector after $2\frac{1}{2}$ years.

c. Find the economic meaning of the y-intercept of the line.

d. Find the economic meaning of the slope of the line.

SOLUTION   **a.** We will find the slope and use the point-slope form to write an equation of the line. (See Figure 2-31.)

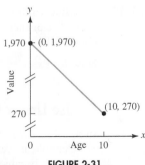

FIGURE 2-31

When the projector is new, its age x is 0, and its value y is $1,970. When the projector is 10 years old, $x = 10$ and $y = 270. Since the line passes through the points $(0, 1,970)$ and $(10, 270)$ the slope of the line is

$$m = \frac{y_2 - y_1}{x_2 - x_1} \qquad \text{This is the slope formula.}$$

$$= \frac{270 - 1,970}{10 - 0} \qquad \text{Substitute 270 for } y_2, \text{ 1,970 for } y_1, \text{ 10 for } x_2, \text{ and 0 for } x_1.$$

$$= \frac{-1,700}{10}$$

$$= -170$$

To find an equation of the line, we substitute -170 for m, 0 for x_1, and 1,970 for y_1 in the point-slope form and simplify.

$$y - y_1 = m(x - x_1)$$

$$y - 1,970 = -170(x - 0)$$

(3) $$y = -170x + 1,970$$

The value y of the projector is related to its age x by the equation $y = -170x + 1,970$.

b. To find the value after $2\frac{1}{2}$ years, we will substitute 2.5 for x in Equation 3 and solve for y.

$$y = -170x + 1,970$$

$$= -170(2.5) + 1,970 \qquad \text{Substitute 2.5 for } x.$$

$$= -425 + 1,970$$

$$= 1,545$$

In $2\frac{1}{2}$ years, the projector will be worth $1,545.

c. The y-intercept of the graph is $(0, b)$, where b is the value of y when $x = 0$.

$$y = -170x + 1,970$$

$$y = -170(0) + 1,970 \qquad \text{Substitute 0 for } x.$$

$$y = 1,970$$

The y-coordinate b of the y-intercept is the value of a 0-year-old projector, which is the projector's original cost, $1,970.

d. Each year, the value decreases by $170, because the slope of the line is -170. The slope of the depreciation line is called the *annual depreciation rate*.

Problems that have an annual appreciation rate can be worked similarly.

Self Check 10   A business purchases a Canon copier for $2,700 and expects it to last for ten years. It can then be sold for $300. Write a straight-line depreciation line for the copier.

Now Try Exercise 91.

8. Use Linear Curve Fitting to Solve Problems

In statistics, the process of using one variable to predict another is called **regression.** For example, if we know a woman's height, we can make a good prediction about her weight, because taller women usually weigh more than shorter women.

Figure 2-32 shows the result of sampling ten women and finding their heights and weights. The graph of the ordered pairs (h, w) is called a **scattergram.**

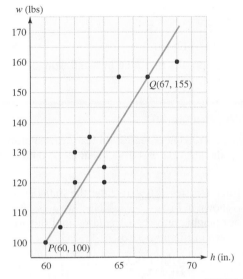

Woman	Height (h) in inches	Weight (w) in pounds
1	60	100
2	61	105
3	62	120
4	62	130
5	63	135
6	64	120
7	64	125
8	65	155
9	67	155
10	69	160

FIGURE 2-32

To write a **prediction equation** (sometimes called a **regression equation**), we must find an equation of the line that comes closer to all of the points in the scattergram than any other possible line. There are statistical methods to find this equation, but we can only approximate it here.

To write an approximation of the regression equation, we place a straightedge on the scattergram shown in Figure 2-32 and draw the line joining two points that seems to best fit all the points. In the figure, line PQ is drawn, where point P has coordinates of $(60, 100)$ and point Q has coordinates of $(67, 155)$.

Our approximation of the regression equation will be an equation of the line passing through points P and Q. To find an equation of this line, we first find its slope.

$$m = \frac{y_2 - y_1}{x_2 - x_1}$$ This is the slope formula.

$$= \frac{155 - 100}{67 - 60}$$ Substitute 155 for y_2, 100 for y_1, 67 for x_2, and 60 for x_1.

$$= \frac{55}{7}$$

We can then use point-slope form to find an equation of the line.

$$y - y_1 = m(x - x_1)$$ This is the point-slope form.

$$y - 100 = \frac{55}{7}(x - 60)$$ Choose $(60, 100)$ for (x_1, y_1).

$$y = \frac{55}{7}x - \frac{3,300}{7} + 100$$ Remove parentheses and add 100 to both sides.

(4) $$y = \frac{55}{7}x - \frac{2,600}{7}$$ Simplify.

Our approximation of the regression equation is $y = \frac{55}{7}x - \frac{2,600}{7}$.

To predict the weight of a woman who is 66 inches tall, for example, we substitute 66 for x in Equation 4 and simplify.

$$y = \frac{55}{7}x - \frac{2,600}{7}$$

$$y = \frac{55}{7}(66) - \frac{2,600}{7}$$

$$y \approx 147.1428571$$

We would predict that a 66-inch-tall woman chosen at random will weigh about 147 pounds.

ACCENT ON TECHNOLOGY   Linear Regression

We can use the linear regression feature on a graphing calculator to find an equation of the line that best fits a given set of data points. We will do that for the data given in Figure 2-32.

- First, we press **STAT** to enter the statistics menu on the calculator. This screen is shown in Figure 2-33(a). Next we press **ENTER** to input our data. We can input our heights into the L1 column and our weights into the L2 column. This is shown in Figure 2-33(b).

(a)

(b)

FIGURE 2-33

- To obtain an equation of the regression line, we press **STAT** and then the right-arrow key once to access the calculate menu. This screen is shown in Figure 2-34(a). To calculate a linear regression equation, we press **4** to select LinReg $(ax + b)$ and then **ENTER** to obtain an equation. The screen is shown in Figure 2-34(b).

(a)

(b)

FIGURE 2-34

Note that the regression line is of the form $y = ax + b$, where a is the slope and b is the y-coordinate of the y-intercept. If we substitute the values shown in Figure 2-34(b) for a and b and round to hundredths, we can write an equation of the line that best fits the data. The regression line is $y = 6.78x - 301.18$.

Self Check Answers   1. $y = -\frac{2}{3}x + \frac{7}{3}$ 2. $y = -\frac{10}{13}x + \frac{2}{13}$ 3. $y = \frac{7}{3}x - 6$ 4. $-\frac{2}{3}, (0, -3)$

5. parallel   **6.** perpendicular   **7.** $y = 8x - 6$ **8.** $y = -\dfrac{1}{8}x + \dfrac{17}{8}$

9. $\dfrac{3}{4}, (0, -3)$ **10.** $y = -240x + 2,700$

Exercises **2.3**

Getting Ready

You should be able to complete these vocabulary and concept statements before you proceed to the practice exercises.

Fill in the blanks.

1. The formula for the point-slope form of a line is

   _____.

2. In the equation $y = mx + b$, ___ is the slope of the graph of the line, and $(0, b)$ is the _____.

3. The equation $y = mx + b$ is called the

   _____ form of the equation of a line.

4. The standard form of an equation of a line is

   _____.

5. The slope of the graph of $Ax + By = C$ is ___.

6. The y-intercept of the graph of $Ax + By = C$ is

   ___.

Practice

Write an equation of the line with the given properties. Your answer should be written in standard form.

7. $m = 2$ passing through $P(2, 4)$

8. $m = -3$ passing through $P(3, 5)$

9. $m = 2$ passing through $P\left(-\tfrac{3}{2}, \tfrac{1}{2}\right)$

10. $m = -6$ passing through $P\left(\tfrac{1}{4}, -2\right)$

11. $m = \tfrac{2}{5}$ passing through $P(-1, 1)$

12. $m = -\tfrac{1}{5}$ passing through $P(-2, -3)$

13. $m = 0$ passing through $P(-6, -3)$

14. $m = 0$ passing through $P(7, 5)$

15. m is undefined passing through $P(-6, -3)$

16. m is undefined passing through $P(6, -1)$

17. $m = \pi$ passing through $P(\pi, 0)$

18. $m = \pi$ passing through $P(0, \pi)$

Find an equation of each line shown. Your answer should be written in standard form.

19.

20.

Write an equation of a line that passes through the two given points. Your answer should be written in slope-intercept form.

21. $P(0, 0), Q(4, 4)$

22. $P(-5, -5), Q(0, 0)$

23. $P(3, 4), Q(0, -3)$

24. $P(4, 0), Q(6, -8)$

Write an equation in slope-intercept form of each line shown.

25.

26.

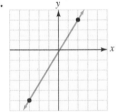

Use slope-intercept form to write an equation of the line with the given properties.

27. $m = 3; b = -2$

28. $m = -\dfrac{1}{3}; b = \dfrac{2}{3}$

29. $m = 5; b = -\dfrac{1}{5}$

30. $m = \sqrt{2}; b = \sqrt{2}$

31. $m = a; b = \dfrac{1}{a}$

32. $m = a; b = 2a$

33. $m = a; b = a$

34. $m = \dfrac{1}{a}; b = a$

Use slope-intercept form to write an equation of a line passing through the given point and having the given slope. Express the answer in standard form.

35. $P(0, 0); m = \dfrac{3}{2}$

36. $P(-3, -7); m = -\dfrac{2}{3}$

37. $P(-3, 5); m = -3$

38. $P(-5, 1); m = 1$

39. $P\left(0, \sqrt{2}\right); m = \sqrt{2}$

40. $P\left(-\sqrt{3}, 0\right); m = 2\sqrt{3}$

Write each equation in slope-intercept form to determine the slope and y-intercept. Then use the slope and y-intercept to graph the line.

41. $x - y = 1$

42. $x + y = 2$

43. $x = \dfrac{3}{2}y - 3$

44. $x = -\dfrac{4}{5}y + 2$

45. $3(y - 4) = -2(x - 3)$

46. $-4(2x + 3) = 3(3y + 8)$

Find the slope and the y-intercept of the lines determined by the given equations.

47. $3x - 2y = 8$

48. $-2x + 4y = 12$

49. $-2(x + 3y) = 5$

50. $5(2x - 3y) = 4$

51. $x = \dfrac{2y - 4}{7}$

52. $3x + 4 = -\dfrac{2(y - 3)}{5}$

Determine whether the graphs of each pair of equations are parallel, perpendicular, or neither.

53. $y = 3x + 4, y = 3x - 7$

54. $y = 4x - 13, y = \dfrac{1}{4}x + 13$

55. $x + y = 2, y = x + 5$

56. $x = y + 2 \; y = x + 3$

57. $y = 3x + 7, 2y = 6x - 9$

58. $2x + 3y = 9, 3x - 2y = 5$

59. $x = 3y + 4, y = -3x + 7$

60. $3x + 6y = 1, y = \dfrac{1}{2}x$

61. $y = 3, x = 4$

62. $y = -3, y = -7$

63. $x = \dfrac{y - 2}{3}, 3(y - 3) + x = 0$

64. $2y = 8, 3(2 + x) = 3(y + 2)$

Write an equation of the line that passes through the given point and is parallel to the given line. Your answer should be written in slope-intercept form.

65. $P(0, 0), y = 4x - 7$

66. $P(0, 0), x = -3y - 12$

67. $P(2, 5), 4x - y = 7$

68. $P(-6, 3), y + 3x = -12$

69. $P(4, -2), x = \dfrac{5}{4}y - 2$

70. $P(1, -5), x = -\dfrac{3}{4}y + 5$

Write an equation of the line that passes through the given point and is perpendicular to the given line. Your answer should be written in slope-intercept form.

71. $P(0, 0), y = 4x - 7$

72. $P(0, 0), x = -3y - 12$

73. $P(2, 5), 4x - y = 7$

74. $P(-6, 3), y + 3x = -12$

75. $P(4, -2), x = \dfrac{5}{4}y - 2$

76. $P(1, -5), x = -\dfrac{3}{4}y + 5$

Use the method of Example 9 to find the slope and the y-intercept of the graph of each equation.

77. $4x + 5y = 20$ **78.** $9x - 12y = 17$

79. $2x + 3y = 12$ **80.** $5x + 6y = 30$

81. Find an equation of the line perpendicular to the line $y = 3$ and passing through the midpoint of the segment joining $(2, 4)$ and $(-6, 10)$.

82. Find an equation of the line parallel to the line $y = -8$ and passing through the midpoint of the segment joining $(-4, 2)$ and $(-2, 8)$.

83. Find an equation of the line parallel to the line $x = 3$ and passing through the midpoint of the seg-

84. Find an equation of the line perpendicular to the line $x = 3$ and passing through the midpoint of the segment joining $(-2, 2)$ and $(4, -8)$.

Applications

In Exercises 85-95, assume straight-line depreciation or straight-line appreciation.

85. **Depreciation** A Toyota Tundra truck was purchased for $24,300. Its salvage value at the end of its 7-year useful life is expected to be $1,900. Find a depreciation equation.

86. **Depreciation** A small business purchases the laptop computer shown. It will be depreciated over a 4-year period, when its salvage value will be $300. Find a depreciation equation.

$2,700

87. **Appreciation** A condominium in San Diego was purchased for $475,000. The owners expect the condominium to double in value in 10 years. Find an appreciation equation.

88. **Appreciation** A house purchased for $112,000 is expected to double in value in 12 years. Find an appreciation equation.

89. **Depreciation** Find a depreciation equation for the TV in the following want ad.

> *For Sale*: 3-year-old 54-inch TV, $1,900 new. Asking $1,190. Call 875-5555. Ask for Mike.

90. **Depreciation** A Bose Wave Radio cost $555 when new and is expected to be worth $80 after 5 years. What will it be worth after 3 years?

91. **Salvage value** A copier cost $1,050 when new and will be depreciated at the rate of $120 per year. If the useful life of the copier is 8 years, find its salvage value.

92. **Rate of depreciation** A ski boat that cost $27,600 when new will have no salvage value after 12 years. Find its annual rate of depreciation.

93. **Value of an antique** An antique table is expected to appreciate $40 each year. If the table will be worth $450 in 2 years, what will it be worth in 13 years?

94. **Value of an antique** An antique clock is expected to be worth $350 after 2 years and $530 after 5 years. What will the clock be worth after 7 years?

95. **Purchase price of real estate** A cottage that was purchased 3 years ago is now appraised at $47,700. If the property has been appreciating $3,500 per year, find its original purchase price.

96. **Computer repair** A computer repair company charges a fixed amount, plus an hourly rate, for a service call. Use the information in the illustration to find the hourly rate

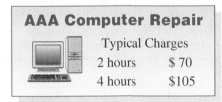

AAA Computer Repair	
Typical Charges	
2 hours	$ 70
4 hours	$105

97. **Automobile repair** An auto repair shop charges an hourly rate, plus the cost of parts. If the cost of labor for a $1\frac{1}{2}$-hour radiator repair is $69, find the cost of labor for a 5-hour transmission overhaul.

98. **Printer charges** A printer charges a fixed setup cost, plus $1 for every 100 copies. If 700 copies cost $52, how much will it cost to print 1,000 copies?

99. **Predicting fires** A local fire department recognizes that city growth and the number of reported fires are related by a linear equation. City records show that 300 fires were reported in a year when the local population was 57,000 persons, and 325 fires were reported in a year when the population was 59,000 persons. How many fires can be expected in the year when the population reaches 100,000 persons?

100. **Estimating the cost of rain gutter** A neighbor tells you that an installer of rain gutter charges $60, plus a dollar amount per foot. If the neighbor paid $435 for the installation of 250 feet of gutter, how much will it cost you to have 300 feet installed?

101. Converting temperatures Water freezes at 32° F, or 0° C. Water boils at 212° F, or 100° C. Find a formula for converting a temperature from degrees Fahrenheit to degrees Celsius.

102. Converting units A speed of 1 mile per hour is equal to 88 feet per minute, and of course, 0 miles per hour is 0 feet per minute. Find an equation for converting a speed x, in miles per hour, to the corresponding speed y, in feet per minute.

103. Smoking The percent y of 18-to-25-year-old smokers in the United States has been declining at a constant rate since 1974. If about 47% of this group smoked in 1974 and about 29% smoked in 1994, find a linear equation that models this decline. If this trend continues, estimate what percent will smoke in 2014.

104. Forensic science Scientists believe there is a linear relationship between the height h (in centimeters) of a male and the length f (in centimeters) of his femur bone. Use the data in the table to find a linear equation that expresses the height h in terms of f. Round all constants to the nearest thousandth. How tall would you expect a man to be if his femur measures 50 cm? Round to the nearest centimeter.

Person	Length of femur (f)	Height (h)
A	62.5 cm	200 cm
B	40.2 cm	150 cm

105. Predicting stock prices The value of the stock of ABC Corporation has been increasing by the same fixed dollar amount each year. The pattern is expected to continue. Let 2010 be the base year corresponding to $x = 0$ with $x = 1, 2, 3, \ldots$ corresponding to later years. ABC stock was selling at $37\frac{1}{2}$ in 2010 and at $45 in 2012. If y represents the price of ABC stock, find the equation $y = mx + b$ that relates x and y, and predict the price in the year 2014.

106. Estimating inventory Inventory of unsold goods showed a surplus of 375 units in January and 264 in April. Assume that the relationship between inventory and time is given by the equation of a line, and estimate the expected inventory in March. Because March lies between January and April, this estimation is called **interpolation.**

107. Oil depletion When a Petroland oil well was first brought on line, it produced 1,900 barrels of crude oil per day. In each later year, owners expect its daily production to drop by 70 barrels. Find the daily production after $3\frac{1}{2}$ years.

108. Waste management The corrosive waste in industrial sewage limits the useful life of the piping in a waste processing plant to 12 years. The piping system was originally worth $137,000, and it will cost the company $33,000 to remove it at the end of its 12-year useful life. Find a depreciation equation.

109. Crickets The table shows the approximate chirping rate at various temperatures for one type of cricket.

Temperature (° F)	Chirps per minute
50	20
60	80
70	115
80	150
100	250

a. Construct a scattergram below.

b. Assume a linear relationship and write a regression equation.

c. Estimate the chirping rate at a temperature of 90° F.

110. Fishing The table shows the lengths and weights of seven muskies captured by the Department of Natural Resources in Catfish Lake in Eagle River, Wisconsin.

Musky	Length (in.)	Weight (lb)
1	26	5
2	27	8
3	29	9
4	33	12
5	35	14
6	36	14
7	38	19

a. Construct a scattergram for the data.

b. Assume a linear relationship and write a regression equation.

c. Estimate the weight of a musky that is 32 inches long.

 111. Use the linear regression feature on a graphing calculator to determine an equation of the line that best fits the data given in Exercise 109. Round to the hundredths.

 112. Use the linear regression feature on a graphing calculator to determine an equation of the line that best fits the data given in Exercise 110. Round to the hundredths.

Discovery and Writing

113. Explain how to find an equation of a line passing through two given points.

114. In straight-line depreciation, explain why the slope of the line is called the *rate of depreciation*.

115. Prove that an equation of a line with x-intercept of $(a, 0)$ and y-intercept of $(0, b)$ can be written in the form

$$\frac{x}{a} + \frac{y}{b} = 1$$

116. Find the x- and y-intercepts of the line $bx + ay = ab$.

Investigate the properties of slope and the y-intercept by experimenting with the following problems.

117. Graph $y = mx + 2$ for several positive values of m. What do you notice?

118. Graph $y = mx + 2$ for several negative values of m. What do you notice?

119. Graph $y = 2x + b$ for several increasing positive values of b. What do you notice?

120. Graph $y = 2x + b$ for several decreasing negative values of b. What do you notice?

121. How will the graph of $y = \frac{1}{2}x + 5$ compare to the graph of $y = \frac{1}{2}x - 5$?

Using Excel to solve a linear regression problem.

122. The following table shows the length of a femur bone and the height for ten Caucasian males.

Length of femur bone (cm)	Height (cm)
x	y
49.3	180.8
47.4	176.7
47.1	176.1
48.5	176.5
45.2	170.6
47.8	176.8
49.4	178.6
49.6	179.6
50.9	185.2
47.8	176.2

a. Enter the data in an Excel spreadsheet. Enter the femur values in Column A and the height values in Column B.

b. To plot the data, click and drag to highlight the two columns, select Insert on the menu bar, and then select Chart. When a window pops up, select XY (Scatter) as the chart type. When you click Finish, a **scattergram** will appear on the spreadsheet.

c. Observe that the points are approximately linear. To draw the regression line, select Chart on the menu bar and select Add Trendline. When the dialog box appears, be sure that the Linear Regression type is selected, and then click OK. The regression line will appear.

d. To find an equation of the regression line, estimate the coordinates of two points on the regression line. Then use the two points to write an equation of the line.

e. Use the equation of the regression line to predict the height of a male whose femur bone measures 46 cm.

Review

Simplify each expression.

123. $x^7 x^3 x^{-5}$

124. $\dfrac{y^3 y^{-4}}{y^{-5}}$

125. $\left(\dfrac{81}{25}\right)^{-3/2}$

126. $\sqrt[3]{27x^7}$

127. $\sqrt{27} - 2\sqrt{12}$

128. $\dfrac{5}{\sqrt{5}}$

129. $\dfrac{5}{\sqrt{x} + 2}$

130. $\left(\sqrt{x} - 2\right)^2$

Functions

3

CAREERS AND MATHEMATICS: Computer Scientist

Benis Arapovic/Shutterstock.com

Computer scientists are highly trained innovative workers who design and invent new technology. They solve complex business, scientific, and general computing problems. Computer scientists conduct research on a variety of topics, including computer hardware, virtual reality, and robotics.

Education and Mathematics Required
- Most are required to possess a Ph.D. in computer science, computer engineering, or a closely related discipline. An aptitude for math is important.
- College Algebra, Trigonometry, Calculus, Linear Algebra, Ordinary Differential Equations, Theory of Analysis, Abstract Algebra, Graph Theory, Numerical Methods, and Combinatorics are math courses required.

How Computer Scientists Use Math and Who Employs Them
- Computer scientists use mathematics as they span a range of topics from theoretical studies of algorithms to the computation of implementing computing systems in hardware and software.
- Many computer scientists are employed by Internet service providers; Web search portals; and data processing, hosting, and related services firms. Others work for government, manufacturers of computer and electronic products, insurance companies, financial institutions, and universities.

Career Outlook and Earnings
- Employment of computer scientists is expected to grow by 24 percent through 2018, which is much faster than the average for all occupations.
- The median annual wages of computer and information scientists is approximately $98,000. Some earn more than $150,000 a year.

For more information see: www.bls.gov/oco

In this chapter, we will discuss one of the most important concepts in mathematics—the concept of a function.

3.1 Functions and Function Notation

In this section, we will learn to

1. Understand the concept of a function.
2. Determine whether an equation represents a function.
3. Find the domain of a function.
4. Evaluate a function.
5. Evaluate the difference quotient for a function.
6. Graph a function by plotting points.
7. Use the Vertical Line Test to identify functions.
8. Use linear functions to model applications.

Correspondences between the elements of two sets is a common occurrence in everyday life. For example,

- To every Motorola cell phone, there corresponds exactly one phone number.
- To every Honda Civic car, there corresponds exactly one vehicle identification number.
- To every case on the television show "Deal or No Deal," there corresponds exactly one amount of money.
- To every item's barcode at the Target store, there corresponds exactly one price.

This table shows the four highest-grossing movies of all time and the year each movie was released.

Movie	Year
Avatar	2009
The Lord of the Rings: The Return of the King	2003
Pirates of the Caribbean: Dead Man's Chest	2006
The Dark Knight	2008

The information shown in the table sets up a correspondence between a movie and the year it was released. Note that for each of the movies, there corresponds exactly one year in which it was released. The phase *there corresponds exactly one* is extremely important in mathematics, and we will use this idea to solve problems.

1. Understand the Concept of a Function

Correspondences in which exactly one quantity corresponds to (or depends on) another quantity according to some specific rule are called **functions.** Equations are frequently used in mathematics to represent functions. For example, the equation $y = x^2 - 1$ sets up a correspondence between two infinite sets of real numbers, x and y, according to the rule *square x and subtract 1.*

Equation: $y = x^2 - 1$

Correspondence: Each real number x determines exactly one real number y.

Rule: Square x and subtract 1.

Since the value of y depends on the number x, we call y the **dependent variable** and x the **independent variable.**

The equation $y = x^2 - 1$ determines what **output value** y will result from each **input value** x. This idea of inputs and outputs is shown in Figure 3-1(a). In the equation $y = x^2 - 1$, if the input x is 2, the output y is

$$y = 2^2 - 1 = 3$$

This is illustrated in Figure 3-1(b).

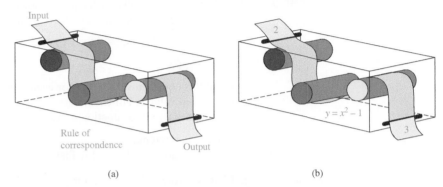

Input

Rule of
correspondence

Output

$y = x^2 - 1$

(a)

(b)

FIGURE 3-1

Comment

The equation $y = x^2 - 1$ also determines the table of ordered pairs, and the graph shown in Figure 3-2. To see how the table determines the correspondence, we find an input in the x-column and read across to find the corresponding output in the y-column. If we select $x = 2$ as an input, we get $y = 3$ for the output.

To see how the graph of $y = x^2 - 1$ determines the correspondence, we draw a vertical and horizontal line through any point (say, point P) on the graph shown in Figure 3-2. Because these lines intersect the x-axis at 2 and the y-axis at 3, the point $P(2, 3)$ associates 3 on the y-axis with 2 on the x-axis.

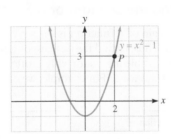

$y = x^2 - 1$		
x	y	(x, y)
-2	3	$(-2, 3)$
-1	0	$(-1, 0)$
0	-1	$(0, -1)$
1	0	$(1, 0)$
2	3	$(2, 3)$

FIGURE 3-2

Any correspondence that assigns exactly one value of y to each number x is called a **function.** We refer to the set of inputs as the **domain** of the function and the set of outputs as the **range** of the function.

Function   A **function** f is a correspondence between a set of input values x and a set of output values y, where to each x-value there corresponds exactly one y-value.

Domain   The set of input values x is called the **domain** of the function.

Range   The set of output values y is called the **range** of the function.

2. Determine Whether an Equation Represents a Function

EXAMPLE 1   **Determining Whether an Equation Represents a Function**

Determine whether the following equations define y to be a function of x.
a. $7x + y = 5$ **b.** $y = |x| + 1$ **c.** $y^2 = x + 2$

SOLUTION   In each case, we will solve each equation for y, if necessary, and determine whether each input value x determines exactly one output value y.

a. First, we solve $7x + y = 5$ for y to get

$$y = 5 - 7x$$

From this equation we see that for each input value x there corresponds exactly one output value y. For example, if $x = 3$, then $y = 5 - 7(3) = -16$. The equation defines y to be a function of x.

b. Since each input number x that we substitute for x determines exactly one output y, the equation $y = |x| + 1$ defines y to be a function of x.

Caution

> Some equations represent functions and some do not. If to some input x in an equation there corresponds more than one output y, the equation will not represent a function.

c. First, we solve $y^2 = x + 2$ for y using the Square Root Property covered in Section 1.3 to get $y = \pm\sqrt{x + 2}$. Note that each input value x for which the function is defined (except -2) gives two outputs y. For example, if $x = 7$, then $y = \pm\sqrt{7 + 2} = \pm\sqrt{9} = \pm 3$. For this reason, the equation does not define y to be a function of x.

Self Check 1   Determine whether each equation defines y to be a function of x.
a. $y = |x|$ **b.** $y = \sqrt{x}$ **c.** $y^2 = 2x$

Now Try Exercise 17.

3.. Find the Domain of a Function

The **domain** of a function is the set of all real numbers x for which the function is defined. Thus, to find the domain of a function we must find the set of numbers that are permissible inputs for x. It is often helpful to determine any restrictions on the input values for x. For example, we consider the information in the following table.

Equation	Restriction	Domain
$y = x^3 - x^2 + x - 5$	There are no restrictions on x because any real number can be cubed, squared and combined with constants.	all real numbers, $(-\infty, \infty)$
$y = \sqrt{x}$	The restriction that x cannot be a negative real number is placed on x because the square root of a negative number is an imaginary number.	$x \geq 0$, the interval $[0, \infty)$
$y = \dfrac{1}{x}$	The restriction that x cannot be 0 is placed on x because division by 0 isn't defined.	$x \neq 0$, $(-\infty, 0) \cup (0, \infty)$

EXAMPLE 2   **Finding the Domain of a Function**

Find the domain of the function defined by each equation:

a. $y = 2x - 5$ **b.** $y = \sqrt{3x - 2}$ **c.** $y = \dfrac{3}{x + 2}$

SOLUTION   We must determine what numbers are permissible inputs for x. This set of numbers is the domain.

a. Any real number that we input for x can be multiplied by 2 and then 5 can be subtracted from the result. Thus, the domain is the interval $(-\infty, \infty)$.

b. Since the radicand must be nonnegative, we have

$$3x - 2 \geq 0$$

$$3x \geq 2 \qquad \text{Add 2 to both sides.}$$

$$x \geq \frac{2}{3} \qquad \text{Divide both sides by 3.}$$

Thus, the domain is the interval $\left[\frac{2}{3}, \infty\right)$.

c. Since the fraction $\frac{3}{x+2}$ is undefined when $x = -2$, -2 is not a permissible input value. Since all other values of x are permissible inputs, the domain is $(-\infty, -2) \cup (-2, \infty)$.

Self Check 2   Find the domain of each function: **a.** $y = |x| + 2$ **b.** $y = \sqrt[3]{x + 2}$

Now Try Exercise 27.

EXAMPLE 3   **Finding the Domain of a Function**

Find the domain of the function defined by the equation $y = \dfrac{1}{x^2 - 5x - 6}$.

SOLUTION   We can factor the denominator to see what values of x will give 0's in the denominator. These values are not in the domain.

$$x^2 - 5x - 6 = 0$$

$$(x - 6)(x + 1) = 0$$

$$x - 6 = 0 \quad \text{or} \quad x + 1 = 0$$

$$x = 6 \qquad\qquad x = -1$$

The domain is $(-\infty, -1) \cup (-1, 6) \cup (6, \infty)$.

Self Check 3   Find the domain of the function defined by the equation $y = \dfrac{2}{x^2 - 16}$.

Now Try Exercise 41.

4. Evaluate a Function

To indicate that y is a function of x, we often use **function notation** and write

$$y = f(x) \qquad \text{Read as "y is a function of x."}$$

The notation $y = f(x)$ provides a way of denoting the value of y (the dependent variable) that corresponds to some input number x (the independent variable). For example, if $y = f(x)$, the value of y that is determined when $x = 2$ is denoted by $f(2)$, read as "f of 2." If $f(x) = 5 - 7x$, we can evaluate $f(2)$ by substituting 2 for x.

$$f(x) = 5 - 7x$$

$$f(2) = 5 - 7(2) \qquad \text{Substitute the input 2 for x.}$$

$$= -9$$

If $x = 2$, then $y = f(2) = -9$.

To evaluate $f(-5)$, we substitute -5 for x.

$$f(x) = 5 - 7x$$

$$f(-5) = 5 - 7(-5) \qquad \text{Substitute the input } -5 \text{ for } x.$$

$$= 40$$

If $x = -5$, then $y = f(-5) = 40$.

Comment   To see why function notation is helpful, consider the following sentences. Note that the second sentence is much more concise.

1. In the function $y = 3x^2 + x - 4$, find the value of y when $x = -3$.

2. In the function $f(x) = 3x^2 + x - 4$, find $f(-3)$.

In this context, the notations y and $f(x)$ both represent the output of a function and can be used interchangeably, but function notation is more concise.

Sometimes functions are denoted by letters other than f. The notations $y = g(x)$ and $y = h(x)$ also denote functions involving the independent variable x.

EXAMPLE 4   **Evaluating a Function**

Let $g(x) = 3x^2 + x - 4$. Find **a.** $g(-3)$ **b.** $g(k)$ **c.** $g(-t^3)$ **d.** $g(k + 1)$

SOLUTION   In each case, we will substitute the input value into the function and simplify.

a. $g(x) = 3x^2 + x - 4$ **b.** $g(x) = 3x^2 + x - 4$

$g(-3) = 3(-3)^2 + (-3) - 4$ $g(k) = 3k^2 + k - 4$

$= 3(9) - 3 - 4$

$= 20$

c. $g(x) = 3x^2 + x - 4$ **d.** $g(x) = 3x^2 + x - 4$

$g(-t^3) = 3(-t^3)^2 + (-t^3) - 4$ $g(k + 1) = 3(k + 1)^2 + (k + 1) - 4$

$= 3t^6 - t^3 - 4$ $= 3(k^2 + 2k + 1) + k + 1 - 4$

$= 3k^2 + 6k + 3 + k + 1 - 4$

$= 3k^2 + 7k$

Self Check 4   Evaluate: **a.** $g(0)$ **b.** $g(2)$ **c.** $g(k - 1)$

Now Try Exercise 49.

ACCENT ON TECHNOLOGY   **Evaluating a Function**

Functions can be easily evaluated on a graphing calculator. There are several ways to do this, but one of the easiest is to use the graph editor and the table. Press $\boxed{\text{Y=}}$ and input $3x^2 + x - 4$ in the graph editor. Next, press $\boxed{\text{2nd}}$ $\boxed{\text{WINDOW}}$ and use the table setup shown on the next page. Then press $\boxed{\text{2nd}}$ $\boxed{\text{GRAPH}}$ and enter values for x. The function values will appear in the table.

(a)   (b)   (c)

FIGURE 3-3

5. Evaluate the Difference Quotient for a Function

The fraction $\frac{f(x + h) - f(x)}{h}$ is called the **difference quotient** and is important in calculus. The difference quotient can be used to find quantities such as the velocity of a guided missile or the rate of change of a company's profit.

EXAMPLE 5   **Finding the Difference Quotient**

If $f(x) = x^2 - 2x - 5$, evaluate $\frac{f(x + h) - f(x)}{h}$.

SOLUTION   We will evaluate the difference quotient in three steps. Find $f(x + h)$. Then subtract $f(x)$. Then divide by h.

Step 1: Find $f(x + h)$.

$$f(x) = x^2 - 2x - 5$$
$$f(x + h) = (x + h)^2 - 2(x + h) - 5 \qquad \text{Substitute } x + h \text{ for } x.$$
$$= x^2 + 2xh + h^2 - 2x - 2h - 5$$

Step 2: Find $f(x + h) - f(x)$. We can use the result from Step 1.

$$f(x + h) - f(x) = x^2 + 2xh + h^2 - 2x - 2h - 5 - (x^2 - 2x - 5) \qquad \text{Subtract } f(x).$$
$$= x^2 + 2xh + h^2 - 2x - 2h - 5 - x^2 + 2x + 5 \qquad \text{Remove parentheses.}$$
$$= 2xh + h^2 - 2h \qquad \text{Combine like terms.}$$

Step 3: Find the difference quotient $\frac{f(x + h) - f(x)}{h}$. We can use the result from Step 2.

$$\frac{f(x + h) - f(x)}{h} = \frac{2xh + h^2 - 2h}{h} \qquad \text{Divide both sides by } h.$$

Comment

After the completion of Step 2, in a polynomial function, when $f(x + h) - f(x)$ is simplified, each term will always include an h. Use that fact to check your work as you progress through the problem.

$$= \frac{h(2x + h - 2)}{h} \qquad \text{In the numerator, factor out } h.$$
$$= 2x + h - 2 \qquad \text{Divide out } h: \frac{h}{h} = 1.$$

Self Check 5   If $f(x) = x^2 + 2$, evaluate $\frac{f(x + h) - f(x)}{h}$.

Now Try Exercise 65.

6. Graph a Function by Plotting Points

If f is a function whose domain and range are sets of real numbers, its graph is the set of all points $(x, f(x))$ in the xy-plane that satisfy the equation $y = f(x)$. For example, the graph of the function $y = f(x) = -7x + 5$ is a line with slope -7 and y-intercept $(0, 5)$. (See Figure 3-4.) If the graph of a function is a nonvertical line, the function is called a **linear function.**

FIGURE 3-4

Graph of a Function   The **graph** of a function f in the xy-plane is the set of all points (x, y) where x is in the domain of f, y is in the range of f, and $y = f(x)$.

EXAMPLE 6   **Graphing a Function by Plotting Points**

Graph the functions.   **a.** $f(x) = -2|x| + 3$ **b.** $f(x) = \sqrt{x - 2}$

SOLUTION   In each case, we will make a table of solutions and plot the points given by the table. Then we will connect the points by drawing a smooth curve through them and obtain the graph of the function.

a. $f(x) = -2|x| + 3$

$f(x) = -2|x| + 3$		
x	$f(x)$	$(x, f(x))$
-2	-1	$(-2, -1)$
-1	1	$(-1, 1)$
0	3	$(0, 3)$
1	1	$(1, 1)$
2	-1	$(2, -1)$

FIGURE 3-5

b. $f(x) = \sqrt{x - 2}$

$f(x) = \sqrt{x - 2}$		
x	$f(x)$	$(x, f(x))$
2	0	$(2, 0)$
6	2	$(6, 2)$
11	3	$(11, 3)$
18	4	$(18, 4)$

FIGURE 3-6

Self Check 6   Graph: $f(x) = |x + 3|$.

Now Try Exercise 83.

Both the **domain** and the **range** of a function can be identified by viewing the graph of the function. The inputs or x-values that correspond to points on the graph of the function can be identified on the x-axis and used to state the domain of the function. The outputs or $f(x)$ values that correspond to points on the graph of the function can be identified on the y-axis and used to state the range of the function. (See Figure 3-7).

(a)   (b)

FIGURE 3-7

From Figure 3-6, we can see that the domain of the function $f(x) = -2|x| + 3$ is the set of all real numbers, and that the range is the set of real numbers that are less than or equal to 3.

From Figure 3-6, we can see that the domain of the function $f(x) = \sqrt{x - 2}$ is the set of all real numbers greater than or equal to 2, and that the range is the set of all real numbers greater than or equal to 0.

In Figure 3-8, we see the graphs of several basic functions.

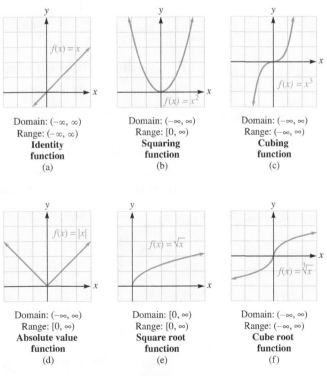

FIGURE 3-8

Graphing the Absolute Value Function

To graph the absolute value function on a graphing calculator, we must call up the function abs(into the graphing window. We press (MATH), then scroll right to NUM as shown below in Figure 3-9.

Press (Y=). Go to (MATH) NUM and press (1). Input (x) and (GRAPH). Use (ZOOM) (4) as the window.

FIGURE 3-9

Graphing the Cube Root Function

We can graph this function on a graphing calculator using the cube root key by selecting (MATH) (4) from the graph window as shown in Figure 3-10. Input (x) and (GRAPH). Use (ZOOM) (4) as the window.

FIGURE 3-10

7. Use the Vertical Line Test to Identify Functions

We can use a **Vertical Line Test** to determine whether a graph represents a function.

Vertical Line Test
- If every vertical line that can be drawn intersects the graph in no more than one point, the graph represents a function. See Figure 3-11(a).

- If a vertical line can be drawn that intersects the graph at more than one point, the graph does not represent a function. See Figure 3-11(b).

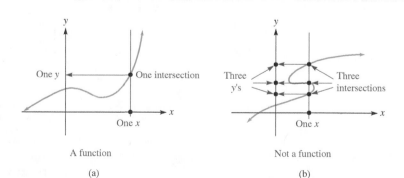

A function   Not a function

(a)   (b)

EXAMPLE 7   **Using the Vertical Line Test to Identify Functions**

Determine which of the following graphs represent functions.

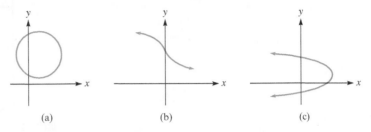

(a)   (b)   (c)

SOLUTION   We will use the Vertical Line Test by drawing several vertical lines through each graph. If every vertical line that intersects the graph does so exactly once, the graph represents a function. Otherwise, the graph does not represent a function.

a. This graph fails the Vertical Line Test, so it does not represent a function.

b. This graph passes the Vertical Line Test, so it does represent a function.

c. This graph fails the Vertical Line Test, so it does not represent a function.

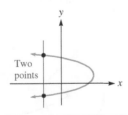

Self Check 7   Does the graph shown in Figure 3-2 represent a function?

Now Try Exercise 97.

Comment

Some graphs represent functions and some do not. Graphs that pass the Vertical Line Test are functions.

Not all equations define functions. For example, the equation $x = |y|$ does not define a function, because two values of y can correspond to one number x. For example, if $x = 2$, then y can be either 2 or -2. The graph of the equation is shown in Figure 3-12. Since the graph does not pass the Vertical Line Test, it does

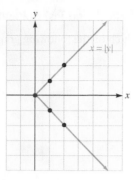

$x = |y|$		
x	y	(x, y)
2	-2	$(2, -2)$
1	-1	$(1, -1)$
0	0	$(0, 0)$
1	1	$(1, 1)$
2	2	$(2, 2)$

FIGURE 3-12

Correspondences between a set of input values x (called the domain) and a set of output values y (called the range), where to each x-value in the domain there corresponds one or more y-values in the range, are called **relations.** Although the graph in Figure 3-12 does not represent a function, it does represent a relation. We note that all functions are relations, but not all relations are functions.

Another way to visualize the definition of function is to consider the diagram shown in Figure 3-13(a). The function f that assigns the element y to the element x is represented by an arrow leaving x and pointing to y. The set of elements in **X** from which arrows originate is the domain of the function. The set of elements in **Y** to which arrows point is the range.

To constitute a function, each element of the domain must determine exactly one y-value in the range. However, the same value of y could correspond to several numbers x. In the function shown in Figure 3-13(b), the single value y corresponds to the three numbers x_1, x_2, and x_3 in the domain.

The correspondence shown in Figure 3-13(c) is not a function, because two values of y correspond to the same number x. However, it is still a relation.

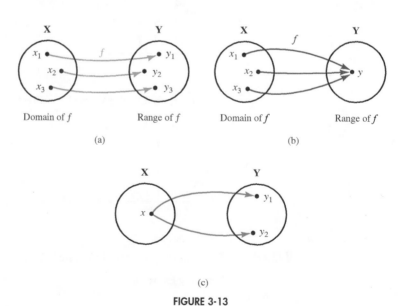

FIGURE 3-13

8. Use Linear Functions to Model Applications

We have seen that the equation of a nonvertical line defines a linear function—an important function in mathematics and its applications.

Linear Functions   A **linear function** is a function determined by an equation of the form

$$f(x) = mx + b \quad \text{or} \quad y = mx + b$$

EXAMPLE 8   Using a Linear Function to Model an Application

Cost of a Fraternity Dance   The cost associated with a fraternity dance is $300 for Country Club rental and $24 for each couple that attends.
a. Write the cost C of the dance in terms of the number of couples x attending.
b. Find the cost if 45 couples attend the dance.

SOLUTION   Use the information stated in the problem to write a linear function that models the application.

a. The cost C for the dance is $24 per couple plus the $300 rental fee. If x couples attend, the cost is $24x$ plus 300. Therefore, the linear cost function is

$$C(x) = 24x + 300$$

b. To find the cost when 45 couples attend, we find C(45).

$$C(x) = 24x + 300$$
$$C(45) = 24(45) + 300 \qquad \text{Substitute 45 for } x.$$
$$= 1{,}080 + 300$$
$$= 1{,}380$$

If 45 couples attend, the cost of the dance is $1,380.

Self Check 8   Find the cost when 60 couples attend.

Now Try Exercise 105.

EXAMPLE 9   Writing a Linear Function that Models an Application

Heart Rates   The target heart rate at which a person should train to get an effective workout is a linear function of his age. For a 20-year-old starting an exercise program, the target heart rate should be 120 beats per minute. For a 40-year-old, it should be 108 beats per minute. Express the target heart rate R as a function of age A.

Nicholas Piccillo/Shutterstock.com

SOLUTION   We will use the information stated in the problem to find the slope of the linear function and write a linear function that models the application.

Since the target heart rate (R) is given to be a linear function of age (A), there are constants m and b such that

$$R = mA + b$$

Since $R = 120$ when $A = 20$, the point $(A_1, R_1) = (20, 120)$ lies on the straight-line graph of this function. Since $R = 108$ when $A = 40$, the point $(A_2, R_2) = (40, 108)$ also lies on that line. The slope of the line is

$$m = \frac{R_2 - R_1}{A_2 - A_1}$$
$$= \frac{108 - 120}{40 - 20} \qquad \text{Substitute 108 for } R_2, \text{ 120 for } R_1, \text{ 40 for } A_2, \text{ and 20 for } A_1.$$
$$= -\frac{12}{20}$$
$$= -\frac{3}{5}$$
$$= -0.6$$

Thus, $m = -0.6$. To determine b, we can substitute -0.6 for m and the coordinates of one point, say $P(20, 120)$, in the equation $R = mA + b$ and solve for b.

$$R = mA + b$$

$$120 = -0.6(20) + b \quad\quad \text{Substitute 120 for } R, \text{ 20 for } b, \text{ and } -0.6 \text{ for } m.$$

$$120 = -12 + b$$

$$132 = b \quad\quad\quad\quad\quad \text{Add 12 to both sides.}$$

If we substitute -0.6 for m and 132 for b in $R = mA + b$, we obtain $R = -0.6A + 132$.

Self Check 9 Find the target heart rate for a 30-year-old person.

Now Try Exercise 111.

Self Check Answers   **1. a.** a function   **b.** a function   **c.** not a function   **2. a.** $(-\infty, \infty)$
b. $(-\infty, \infty)$ **3.** $(-\infty, -4) \cup (-4, 4) \cup (4, \infty)$ **4. a.** -4 **b.** 10
c. $3k^2 - 5k - 2$ **5.** $2x + h$ **6.**   **7.** yes
8. \$1,740   **9.** 114 beats per minute

Exercises **3.1**

Getting Ready
You should be able to complete these vocabulary and concept statements before you proceed to the practice exercises.

Fill in the blanks.

1. A correspondence that assigns exactly one value of y to any number x is called a _____.

2. A correspondence that assigns one or more values of y to any number x is called a _____.

3. The set of input numbers x in a function is called the _____ of the function.

4. The set of all output values y in a function is called the _____ of the function.

5. The statement "y is a function of x" can be written as the equation _____.

6. The graph of a function $y = f(x)$ in the xy-plane is the set of all points _____ that satisfy the equation, where x is in the _____ of f and y is in the _____ of f.

7. In the function of Exercise 5, ___ is called the independent variable.

8. In the function of Exercise 5, y is called the _____ variable.

9. If every _____ line that intersects a graph does so _____, the graph represents a function.

10. A function that can be written in the form $y = mx + b$ is called a _____ function.

Practice
Assume that all variables represent real numbers. Determine whether each equation determines y to be a function of x.

11. $y = x$

12. $y - 2x = 0$

13. $y^2 = x$

14. $|y| = x$

15. $y = x^2$

16. $y - 7 = 7$

17. $y^2 - 4x = 1$

18. $|x - 2| = y$

19. $|x| = |y|$

20. $x = 7$

21. $y = 7$

22. $|x + y| = 7$

Let the function f be defined by the equation $y = f(x)$, where x and $f(x)$ are real numbers. Find the domain of each function.

23. $f(x) = 3x + 5$

24. $f(x) = -5x + 2$

25. $f(x) = x^2 - x + 1$

26. $f(x) = x^3 - 3x + 2$

27. $f(x) = \sqrt{x - 2}$

28. $f(x) = \sqrt{2x + 3}$

29. $f(x) = \sqrt{4 - x}$

30. $f(x) = 3\sqrt{2 - x}$

31. $f(x) = \sqrt{x^2 - 1}$

32. $f(x) = \sqrt{x^2 - 2x - 3}$

33. $f(x) = \sqrt[3]{x + 1}$

34. $f(x) = \sqrt[3]{5 - x}$

35. $f(x) = \dfrac{3}{x + 1}$

36. $f(x) = \dfrac{-7}{x + 3}$

37. $f(x) = \dfrac{x}{x - 3}$

38. $f(x) = \dfrac{x + 2}{x - 1}$

39. $f(x) = \dfrac{x}{x^2 - 4}$

40. $f(x) = \dfrac{2x}{x^2 - 9}$

41. $f(x) = \dfrac{1}{x^2 - 4x - 5}$

42. $f(x) = \dfrac{x}{2x^2 - 16x + 30}$

*Let the function f be defined by y = f(x), where x and f(x)
are real numbers. Find f(2), f(−3), f(k), and f(k² − 1).*

43. $f(x) = 3x - 2$

44. $f(x) = 5x + 7$

45. $f(x) = \dfrac{1}{2}x + 3$

46. $f(x) = \dfrac{2}{3}x + 5$

47. $f(x) = x^2$

48. $f(x) = 3 - x^2$

49. $f(x) = x^2 + 3x - 1$

50. $f(x) = -x^2 - 2x + 1$

51. $f(x) = |x^2 + 1|$

52. $f(x) = |x^2 + x + 4|$

53. $f(x) = \dfrac{2}{x + 4}$

54. $f(x) = \dfrac{3}{x - 5}$

55. $f(x) = \dfrac{1}{x^2 - 1}$

56. $f(x) = \dfrac{3}{x^2 + 3}$

57. $f(x) = \sqrt{x^2 + 1}$

58. $f(x) = \sqrt{x^2 - 1}$

Evaluate the difference quotient for each function f(x).

59. $f(x) = 3x + 1$

60. $f(x) = 5x - 1$

61. $f(x) = x^2 + 1$

62. $f(x) = x^2 - 3$

63. $f(x) = 4x^2 - 6$

64. $f(x) = 5x^2 + 3$

65. $f(x) = x^2 + 3x - 7$

66. $f(x) = x^2 - 5x + 1$

67. $f(x) = 2x^2 - 4x + 2$

68. $f(x) = 3x^2 + 2x - 3$

69. $f(x) = x^3$

70. $f(x) = \dfrac{1}{x}$

*Graph each function. Use the graph to identify the domain
and range of each function.*

71. $f(x) = 2x + 3$

72. $f(x) = 3x + 2$

73. $f(x) = -\dfrac{3}{4}x + 4$

74. $f(x) = \dfrac{1}{2}x - 3$

75. $2x = 3y - 3$

76. $3x = 2(y + 1)$

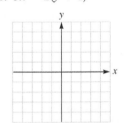

77. $f(x) = x^2 - 4$

78. $f(x) = -x^2 + 3$

79. $f(x) = -x^3 + 2$

80. $f(x) = -x^3 + 1$

81. $f(x) = -|x|$

82. $f(x) = -|x| - 3$

83. $f(x) = |x - 2|$

84. $f(x) = -|x - 2|$

85. $f(x) = \left|\dfrac{1}{2}x + 3\right|$

86. $f(x) = -\left|\dfrac{1}{2}x + 3\right|$

87. $f(x) = -\sqrt{x + 1}$

88. $f(x) = \sqrt{x} + 2$

89. $f(x) = \sqrt{2x - 4}$

90. $f(x) = -\sqrt{2x - 4}$

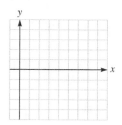

91. $f(x) = \sqrt[3]{x} + 2$

92. $f(x) = -\sqrt[3]{x} + 1$

Draw lines to indicate the domain and range of each function as intervals on the x- and y-axes.

93.

94.

Use the Vertical Line Test to determine whether each graph represents a function.

95.

96.

97.

98.

99.

100.

Use a graphing calculator to graph each function. Then determine the domain and range of the function.

101. $f(x) = |3x + 2|$ **102.** $f(x) = \sqrt{2x - 5}$

103. $f(x) = \sqrt[3]{5x - 1}$ **104.** $f(x) = -\sqrt[3]{3x + 2}$

Applications

105. Cost of *t*-shirts A chapter of Phi Theta Kappa, an honors society for two-year college students, is purchasing *t*-shirts for each of its members. A local company has agreed to make the shirts for $8 each plus a graphic arts fee of $75.

 a. Write a linear function that describes the cost C for the shirts in terms of x, the number of *t*-shirts ordered.

 b. Find the total cost of 85 *t*-shirts.

106. Service projects The Circle "K" Club is planning a service project for children at a local children's home. They plan to rent a "Dora the Explorer Moonwalk" for the event. The cost of the moonwalk will include a $60 delivery fee and $45 for each hour it is used. Express the total bill b in terms of the hours used h.

107. Cell phone plans A grandmother agrees to purchase a cell phone for emergency use only. AT&T now offers such a plan for $9.99 per month and $0.07 for each minute t the phone is used.

 a. Write a linear function that describes the monthly cost C in terms of the time in minutes t the phone is used.

 b. If the grandmother uses her phone for 20 minutes during the first month, what was her bill?

108. Concessions A concessionaire at a football game pays a vendor $40 per game for selling hot dogs at $2.50 each.

 a. Write a linear function that describes the income I the vendor earns for the concessionaire during the game if the vendor sells h hot dogs.

 b. Find the income if the vendor sells 175 hot dogs.

109. Home construction In a proposal to prospective clients, a contractor listed the following costs:

1. Fees, permits, site preparation	$14,000
2. Construction, per square foot	$95

 a. Write a linear function the clients can use to determine the cost C of building a house having f square feet.

 b. Find the cost to build a 2,600-square-foot house.

110. Temperature conversion The Fahrenheit temperature reading (F) is a linear function of the Celsius reading (C). If $C = 0$ when $F = 32$ and the readings are the same at $-40°$, express F as a function of C.

111. Cost of electricity The cost C of electricity in Eagle River is a linear function of x, the number of kilowatt-hours (kwh) used. If the cost of 100 kwh is $17 and the cost of 500 kwh is $57, find an equation that expresses C in terms of x.

112. Water billing The cost C of water is a linear function of n, the number of gallons used. If 1,000 gallons cost $4.70 and 9,000 gallons cost $14.30, express C as a function of n.

113. Coffee locations Suppose that in 2008 there were approximately 6,400 of your coffee company locations. Suppose that in 2012 this number had grown to approximately 13,168. Write a linear function that represents the number of coffee locations n as a function of time t. Let $t = 0$ represent 2008.

114. Cliff divers The cliff divers of Acapulco amaze tourists with their diving skills. The velocity v of a diver is a function of the time t the diver has fallen. If the initial velocity of the diver is 2 feet per second and $v = -66$ feet per second when $t = 2$ seconds, express v as a function t.

115. Exchange rates If fifty U.S. dollars can be exchanged for 69.5550 Euros and 125 U.S. dollars can be exchanged for 173.8875 Euros, write a linear function that represents the number of Euros E in terms of U.S. dollars D.

116. Exchange rates If fifty U.S. dollars can be exchanged for 600.1100 Mexican pesos and 125 U.S. dollars can be exchanged for 1500.275 Mexican pesos, write a linear function that represents the number of Mexican pesos P in terms of U.S. dollars D.

Discovery and Writing

Find all values of x that will make f(x) = 0.

117. $f(x) = 3x + 2$ **118.** $f(x) = -2x - 5$

119. Write a paragraph explaining how to find the domain of a function.

120. Write a paragraph explaining how to find the range of a function.

121. Explain why all functions are relations, but not all relations are functions.

 122. Use a graphing calculator to graph the function $f(x) = \sqrt{x}$, and use TRACE and ZOOM to find $\sqrt{5}$ to three decimal places.

Review
Consider this set: $\{-3, -1, 0, 0.5, \frac{3}{4}, 1, \pi, 7, 8\}$

123. Which numbers are natural numbers?

124. Which numbers are rational numbers?

125. Which numbers are prime numbers?

126. Which numbers are even numbers?

Write each in interval notation.

127.

128. ◄────────(────)──────[──────►
                    -3   5

Graph each union of two intervals.

129. $(-3, 5) \cup [6, \infty)$ **130.** $(-\infty, 0) \cup (0, \infty)$

3.2 Quadratic Functions

In this section, we will learn to

1. Recognize the characteristics of a quadratic function.
2. Find the vertex of a parabola whose equation is in standard form.
3. Graph a quadratic function.
4. Find the vertex of a parabola whose equation is in general form.
5. Use a quadratic function to solve maximum and minimum problems.

Quadratic functions are important because we can use them to model many real-life problems. For example, the path of a basketball jump shot by Shaquille O'Neal and the path of a guided missile can be modeled with quadratic functions. Businesses like Coca Cola and Best Buy can use quadratic functions to help maximize the profit and revenue for the products they produce and sell.

1. Recognize the Characteristics of a Quadratic Function

The linear function $f(x) = mx + b$ $(m \neq 0)$ is a first-degree polynomial function, because its right side is a first-degree polynomial in the variable x. A function defined by a polynomial of second degree is called a **quadratic function.**

Quadratic Function   A **quadratic function** is a second-degree polynomial function in one variable of the form

$$f(x) = ax^2 + bx + c \quad \text{or} \quad y = ax^2 + bx + c,$$

where a, b, and c are real numbers and $a \neq 0$.

Some examples of quadratic functions are

$$f(x) = x^2 - 2x - 3 \quad \text{and} \quad f(x) = -2x^2 - 8x - 3.$$

Quadratic functions can be graphed by plotting points. For example, to graph the function $f(x) = x^2 - 2x - 3$, we plot several points with coordinates that satisfy the equation. We then join them with a smooth curve to obtain the graph shown in Figure 3-14.

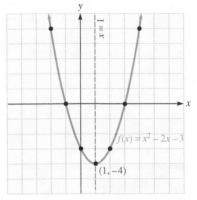

$f(x) = x^2 - 2x - 3$		
x	$f(x)$	$(x, f(x))$
-2	5	$(-2, 5)$
-1	0	$(-1, 0)$
0	-3	$(0, -3)$
1	-4	$(1, -4)$
2	-3	$(2, -3)$
3	0	$(3, 0)$
4	5	$(4, 5)$

Domain: $(-\infty, \infty)$, **Range:** $[-4, \infty)$

FIGURE 3-14

A table of values and the graph of $f(x) = -2x^2 - 8x - 3$ are shown in Figure 3-15.

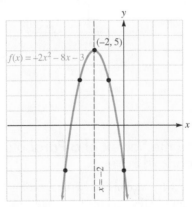

$f(x) = -2x^2 - 8x - 3$		
x	$f(x)$	$(x, f(x))$
-4	-3	$(-4, -3)$
-3	3	$(-3, 3)$
-2	5	$(-2, 5)$
-1	3	$(-1, 3)$
0	-3	$(0, -3)$

Domain: $(-\infty, \infty)$, **Range:** $(-\infty, 5]$

FIGURE 3-15

The graph of a quadratic function is called a **parabola**, a cup-shaped curve that either opens upward $\cup$ or downward $\cap$. The graphs in Figures 3-14 and 3-15 suggest that the graph of a quadratic function has the following characteristics.

Characteristics of Quadratic Functions		
Characteristics	**Examples**	
Equation of a quadratic function $f(x) = ax^2 + bx + c$	$f(x) = x^2 - 2x - 3$	$f(x) = -2x^2 - 8x - 3$
If $a > 0$, the parabola **opens up**. If $a < 0$, the parabola **opens down**.	$a = 1$, opens up	$a = -2$, opens down
The **vertex** is the turning point of the parabola.	Vertex is $(1, -4)$	Vertex is $(-2, 5)$
The **minimum** or **maximum** **point** occurs at the vertex.	$(1, -4)$ is the minimum or lowest point on the graph.	$(-2, 5)$ is the maximum or highest point on the graph.
The **axis of symmetry** is the vertical line that intersects the parabola at the vertex. The parabola is symmetric about this vertical line.	The graph of $x = 1$ is the axis of symmetry.	The graph of $x = -2$ is the axis of symmetry.

ACCENT ON TECHNOLOGY ⟋ Graphing Quadratic Functions

We can use a graphing calculator to graph quadratic functions. If we use window settings of $[-10, 10]$ for x and $[-10, 10]$ for y, the graph of $f(x) = x^2 - 2x - 3$ will look like Figure 3-16(a). The graph of $f(x) = -2x^2 - 8x - 3$ will look like Figure 3-16(b).

(a)   (b)

FIGURE 3-16

2. Find the Vertex of a Parabola Whose Equation Is in Standard Form

In Figure 3-14, we considered the function $f(x) = x^2 - 2x - 3$ with vertex $(1, -4)$. If we complete the square on the right side of the equation we will obtain

$$f(x) = (x^2 - 2x + 1) - 3 - 1 \qquad \text{One-half of } -2 \text{ is } -1, \text{ and } (-1)^2 \text{ is } 1.$$
$$\text{Add 1 and subtract 1 on the right side of the equation.}$$

$$f(x) = (x - 1)(x - 1) - 4 \qquad \text{Factor } x^2 - 2x + 1.$$

$$f(x) = (x - 1)^2 - 4$$

In this factored form, the coordinates of the vertex of the parabola can be read from the equation. The vertex of $f(x) = (x - 1)^2 - 4$ is $(1, -4)$. We call this factored form the **standard form** of an equation of a quadratic function.

Standard Form of an Equation of a Quadratic Function	The graph of a quadratic function

$$y = f(x) = a(x - h)^2 + k \ (a \neq 0)$$

is a parabola with vertex at (h, k). The parabola opens upward when $a > 0$ and downward when $a < 0$. The axis of symmetry of the parabola is the vertical line graph of the equation $x = h$.

EXAMPLE 1   **Finding the Vertex of a Parabola in Standard Form**

Find the vertex of the graph of each quadratic function:
a. $f(x) = 2(x - 3)^2 + 5$ **b.** $f(x) = -3(x + 2)^2 - 4$

SOLUTION   In each case, the equation of the quadratic function is given in standard form. From the equations, we can identify h and k, because the vertex is the point with coordinates (h, k).

a. We identify the values of h and k.

Standard Form: $f(x) = a(x - h)^2 + k$

Given Function: $f(x) = 2(x - 3)^2 + 5$ $h = 3$ and $k = 5.$

Since $h = 3$ and $k = 5$, the vertex is the point with coordinates of $(3, 5)$.

b. We identify the values of h and k.

Standard Form: $f(x) = a(x - h)^2 + k$

Given Function: $f(x) = -3(x + 2)^2 - 4$

$$f(x) = -3[x - (-2)]^2 + (-4)$$ $h = -2$ and $k = -4.$

Since $h = -2$ and $k = -4$, the vertex is the point with coordinates of $(-2, -4)$.

Self Check 1   Find the vertex of the graph of the quadratic function $f(x) = 2(x + 5)^2 - 4$.

Now Try Exercise 19.

3. Graph a Quadratic Function

The easiest way to graph a quadratic function is to follow these steps.

Strategy for Graphing a Quadratic Function	To graph a quadratic function

1. Determine whether the parabola opens upward or downward.
2. Find the vertex of the parabola.
3. Find the x-intercept(s).
4. Find the y-intercept.
5. Identity one additional point on the graph.
6. Draw a smooth curve through the points found in Steps 2–5.

EXAMPLE 2 **Graphing a Quadratic Function Written in Standard Form**

Graph the quadratic function $f(x) = 2(x + 1)^2 - 8$.

SOLUTION We first determine whether the parabola opens upward or downward. Then we will find the vertex and the x- and y-intercepts. Finally, we will find one additional point and draw a smooth curve through the plotted points.

Step 1: Determine whether the parabola opens upward or downward.

Standard Form: $f(x) = a(x - h)^2 + k$

Given Form: $f(x) = 2(x + 1)^2 - 8$

Since $a = 2$ and 2 is positive, the parabola opens upward.

Step 2: Find the vertex of the parabola.

Standard Form: $f(x) = a(x - h)^2 + k$

Given Form: $f(x) = 2(x + 1)^2 - 8$

$f(x) = 2[x - (-1)]^2 + (-8)$

Since $h = -1$ and $k = -8$ the vertex is the point with coordinates of $(-1, -8)$.

Step 3: Find the x-intercept(s).
To find the x-intercepts, we substitute 0 for $f(x)$ and solve for x.

$f(x) = 2(x + 1)^2 - 8$

$0 = 2(x + 1)^2 - 8$ Substitute 0 for $f(x)$.

$8 = 2(x + 1)^2$ Add 8 to both sides of the equation.

$4 = (x + 1)^2$ Divide both sides by 2.

$x + 1 = \pm 2$ Write $(x + 1)^2$ on the left side and use the Square Root Property.

$x = -1 \pm 2$ Subtract 1 from both sides.

$x = 1$ or $x = -3$

The x-intercepts are the points with coordinates of $(1, 0)$ and $(-3, 0)$.

Step 4: Find the y-intercept.
To find the y-intercept, we substitute 0 in for x and solve for y.

$f(x) = 2(x + 1)^2 - 8$

$y = 2(x + 1)^2 - 8$ Substitute y for $f(x)$.

$y = 2(0 + 1)^2 - 8$ Substitute 0 in for x.

$y = 2(1)^2 - 8$

$y = 2 - 8$

$y = -6$

The y-intercept is the point with coordinates of $(0, -6)$.

Step 5: Identify one additional point on the graph.
Because of symmetry, the point $(-2, -6)$ is on the graph.

Step 6: Draw a smooth curve through the points found in Steps 2–5.

We can now draw the graph of the function as shown in Figure 3-17.

FIGURE 3-17

Comment

Sometimes the vertex of the graph of a quadratic function occurs at the origin, $(0, 0)$. In this case, both $h = 0$ and $k = 0$, and the equation of the parabola is of the form $f(x) = a(x - 0)^2 + 0$ or $f(x) = ax^2$ and $a \neq 0$.

Self Check 2   Graph the function: $f(x) = -(x - 2)^2 + 4$.

Now Try Exercise 41.

Comment

The graph of a quadratic function can have one, two, or no x-intercepts. However, it will always have one y-intercept.

4. Find the Vertex of a Parabola Whose Equation Is in General Form

To graph a quadratic function given in the form $f(x) = ax^2 + bx + c$ $(a \neq 0)$, called **general form,** we must find the coordinates of the vertex of the parabola. To do so, we can complete the square on $ax^2 + bx$ to change the equation into standard form $y = a(x - h)^2 + k$. As we have seen, we can read the coordinates (h, k) of the vertex from this form. Once the quadratic function is in standard form, we can graph the function following the steps stated earlier.

EXAMPLE 3   **Finding the Vertex of a Parabola Written in General Form**

Find the vertex of the parabola whose equation is $f(x) = -2x^2 + 12x - 16$.

SOLUTION   We will complete the square on x, write the equation in standard form, and identify h and k, the coordinates of the vertex.

We begin by completing the square on $-2x^2 + 12x$.

$f(x) = -2x^2 + 12x - 16$	Identify a: $a = -2$.
$f(x) = -2(x^2 - 6x) - 16$	Factor $a = -2$ from $-2x^2 + 12x$.
$f(x) = -2(x^2 - 6x + 9 - 9) - 16$	One-half of -6 is -3 and $(-3)^2 = 9$. Add and subtract 9 within the parentheses.
$f(x) = -2(x^2 - 6x + 9) - 2(-9) - 16$	Distribute the multiplication by -2.
$f(x) = -2(x - 3)^2 + 18 - 16$	Factor $x^2 - 6x + 9$ and multiply.
$f(x) = -2(x - 3)^2 + 2$	Simplify.

The equation is now in standard form with $h = 3$ and $k = 2$. Therefore, the vertex is the point with coordinates $(h, k) = (3, 2)$.

Self Check 3   Find the vertex of the graph of $y = 4x^2 - 16x + 19$.

Now Try Exercise 27.

To find formulas for the coordinates of the vertex of a parabola defined by $y = ax^2 + bx + c$ $(a \neq 0)$, we can complete the square on x to write the equation in standard form $(y = a(x - h)^2 + k)$:

$$y = ax^2 + bx + c$$

$$y = a\left(x^2 + \frac{b}{a}x\right) + c \qquad \text{Factor } a \text{ from } ax^2 + bx.$$

$$y = a\left(x^2 + \frac{b}{a}x + \frac{b^2}{4a^2} - \frac{b^2}{4a^2}\right) + c \qquad \text{Add and subtract } \frac{b^2}{4a^2} \text{ within the parentheses.}$$

$$y = a\left(x^2 + \frac{b}{a}x + \frac{b^2}{4a^2}\right) - a\left(\frac{b^2}{4a^2}\right) + c \qquad \text{Distribute the multiplication of } a.$$

$$y = a\left(x + \frac{b}{2a}\right)^2 + c - \frac{b^2}{4a} \qquad \text{Factor } x^2 + \frac{b}{a}x + \frac{b^2}{4a^2} \text{ and simplify } a\left(\frac{b^2}{4a^2}\right).$$

$$y = a\left[x - \left(-\frac{b}{2a}\right)\right]^2 + c - \frac{b^2}{4a} \qquad -\left(\frac{b}{2a}\right) = \frac{b}{2a}$$

Comment

You don't need to memorize the formula for the y-coordinate of the vertex of a parabola. It is usually convenient to find the y-coordinate by substituting $-\frac{b}{2a}$ for x in the function and solving for y.

If we compare the last equation to the form $y = a(x - h)^2 + k$, we see that $h = -\frac{b}{2a}$ and $k = c - \frac{b^2}{4a}$. This result gives the following fact.

Vertex of a Parabola   The graph of the function $y = f(x) = ax^2 + bx + c$ $(a \neq 0)$ is a parabola with vertex at $\left(-\frac{b}{2a}, c - \frac{b^2}{4a}\right)$.

EXAMPLE 4   Graphing a Quadratic Function Written in General Form

Graph the function: $y = f(x) = -2x^2 - 5x + 3$.

SOLUTION   We begin by determining whether the parabola opens upward or downward. Then we find the vertex by using the formula $h = -\frac{b}{2a}$. Next we find the x- and y-intercepts and one additional point and then draw a smooth curve through the plotted points.

Step 1: Determine whether the parabola opens up or downward.
The equation has the form $y = ax^2 + bx + c$, where $a = -2$, $b = -5$, and $c = 3$. Since $a < 0$, the parabola opens downward.

Step 2: Find the vertex.
To find the x-coordinate of the vertex, we substitute the values of a and b into the formula $x = -\frac{b}{2a}$.

$$x = -\frac{b}{2a} = -\frac{-5}{2(-2)} = -\frac{5}{4}$$

The x-coordinate of the vertex is $-\frac{5}{4}$. To find the y-coordinate, we substitute $-\frac{5}{4}$ for x in the equation and solve for y.

$$y = -2x^2 - 5x + 3$$

$$y = -2\left(-\frac{5}{4}\right)^2 - 5\left(-\frac{5}{4}\right) + 3 \qquad \text{Substitute } -\frac{5}{4} \text{ for } x.$$

$$= -2\left(\frac{25}{16}\right) + \frac{25}{4} + 3$$

$$= -\frac{25}{8} + \frac{50}{8} + \frac{24}{8}$$

$$= \frac{49}{8}$$

Since the vertex is the point $\left(-\frac{5}{4}, \frac{49}{8}\right)$, we can plot it on the coordinate system in Figure 3-18(a) and draw the axis of symmetry.

Step 3: Find the x-intercept(s).
To find the x-intercepts, we substitute 0 for y and solve for x.

$$y = -2x^2 - 5x + 3$$

$$0 = -2x^2 - 5x + 3 \qquad \text{Substitute 0 for } y.$$

$$0 = 2x^2 + 5x - 3 \qquad \text{Divide both sides by } -1 \text{ to make the leading coefficient positive.}$$

$$0 = (2x - 1)(x + 3) \qquad \text{Factor the trinomial.}$$

$$2x - 1 = 0 \quad \text{or} \quad x + 3 = 0 \qquad \text{Set each factor equal to 0.}$$

$$x = \frac{1}{2} \quad | \quad x = -3 \qquad \text{Solve each linear equation.}$$

The x-intercepts are $\left(\frac{1}{2}, 0\right)$ and $(-3, 0)$. We plot these intercepts as shown in Figure 3-18(a).

Step 4: Find the y-intercept.
To find the y-intercept, we let $x = 0$ and solve for y.

$$y = -2x^2 - 5x + 3$$

$$= -2(0)^2 - 5(0) + 3 \qquad \text{Substitute 0 for } x.$$

$$= 0 - 0 + 3$$

$$= 3$$

The y-intercept is $(0, 3)$. We plot the intercept as shown in Figure 3-18(a).

Step 5: Plot one additional point.
Because of symmetry, we know that the point $\left(-2\frac{1}{2}, 3\right)$ is on the graph. We plot this point on the coordinate system in Figure 3-18(a).

Step 6: We can now draw the graph of the function, as shown in Figure 3-18(b).

Comment

The y-intercept of a parabola written in the general form $f(x) = ax^2 + bx + c$ $(a \neq 0)$ is the point $(0, c)$. This is because when we substitute 0 for x, y is always c.

(a)

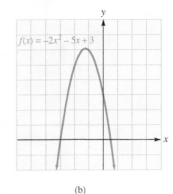

(b)

FIGURE 3-18

Self Check 4   Graph the function: $f(x) = -3x^2 + 7x - 2$.

Now Try Exercise 53.

ACCENT ON TECHNOLOGY   **Finding the Maximum Point or Minimum Point (Vertex) of a Parabola**

We can use a graphing calculator to find the maximum point or minimum point (vertex) of a parabola. Consider the $f(x) = -2x^2 - 5x + 3$ given in Example 4. We will apply the following steps to determine the maximum point or vertex of the parabola.

1. Enter the function.

2. Set a window that shows the function.

3. Graph the function.

4. Go to the CALC menu by pressing [2nd] [TRACE] and select maximum.

5. Use the [TRACE] key to get a left bound.

6. Use the [TRACE] key to get a right bound.

7. Use the [TRACE] key to make a guess.

8. Press [ENTER] and find the maximum point.

FIGURE 3-19

We see that the maximum point or the vertex is $(-1.250001, 6.125)$.

5. Use a Quadratic Function to Solve Maximum and Minimum Problems

EXAMPLE 5   **Using a Quadratic Function to Solve a Maximum Area Problem**

The Montana Dude Rancher's Association has 400 feet of fencing to enclose a rectangular corral. To save money and fencing, the association intends to use the bank of a river as one boundary of the corral, as in Figure 3-20. Find the dimensions that will enclose the largest area.

SOLUTION   We will represent the fenced area with a quadratic function. Since its parabolic graph opens downward, the largest or maximum area will occur at the vertex. We can use the vertex formula to find the vertex.

Step 1: Represent the area with a quadratic function.
Let x represent the width of the fenced area. Then $400 - 2x$ represents the length. Because the area A of a rectangle is the product of the length and the width, we have

$$A = (400 - 2x)x \quad \text{or} \quad A(x) = -2x^2 + 400x$$

FIGURE 3-20

The graph of this area function is a parabola. Since the coefficient of x^2 is negative, the parabola opens downward and its vertex is its highest point. The A-coordinate of the vertex (x, A) represents the maximum area, and the x-coordinate represents the width of the corral that will give the maximum area.

Step 2: Find the vertex of the parabola.
We compare the equations

$$A(x) = -2x^2 + 400x \quad \text{and} \quad y = ax^2 + bx + c$$

to see that $a = -2$, $b = 400$, and $c = 0$. Using the vertex formula, the vertex of the parabola is the point with coordinates

$$\left(-\frac{b}{2a}, c - \frac{b^2}{4a}\right) = \left(-\frac{400}{2(-2)}, 0 - \frac{400^2}{4(-2)}\right) = (100, 20{,}000)$$

Comment   Note that we could have determined the y-coordinate of 20,000 by finding $A(100)$.

$$A(x) = -2x^2 + 400x$$

$$A(100) = -2(100)^2 + 400(100) \qquad \text{Substitute 100 for } x.$$

$$= -2(10{,}000) + 40{,}000$$

$$= -20{,}000 + 40{,}000$$

$$= 20{,}000$$

If the fence runs 100 feet out from the river, 200 feet parallel to the river, and 100 feet back to the river, it will enclose the largest possible area, which is 20,000 square feet. ∎

Self Check 5   Find the largest area possible if the association has 1,200 feet of fencing available.

Now Try Exercise 55.

EXAMPLE 6   **Using a Quadratic Function to Solve a Minimum Cost Problem**

A company that makes and sells water skis has found that the total weekly cost C of producing x water skis is given by the function $C(x) = 0.5x^2 - 210x + 26{,}250$. Find the production level that minimizes the weekly cost and find that weekly minimum cost.

SOLUTION   The weekly cost function $C(x)$ is a quadratic function whose graph is a parabola that opens upward. The minumum value of $C(x)$ occurs at the vertex of the parabola. We will use the vertex formula to find the vertex of the parabola.

Since the coefficient of x^2 is 0.5 (a positive real number), the x-coordinate of the vertex is the production level that will minimize the cost, and the y-coordinate is that minimum cost. We compare the equations

$$C(x) = 0.5x^2 - 210x + 26{,}250 \quad \text{and} \quad y = ax^2 + bx + c$$

to see that $a = 0.5$, $b = -210$, and $c = 26{,}250$. Using the vertex formula, we see that the vertex of the parabola is the point with coordinates

$$\left(-\frac{b}{2a}, c - \frac{b^2}{4a} \right) = \left(-\frac{-210}{2(0.5)}, 26{,}250 - \frac{(-210)^2}{4(0.5)} \right) = (210, 4{,}200)$$

Comment   We can also determine the y-coordinate of 4,200 by finding $C(210)$.

$$C(x) = 0.5x^2 - 210x + 26{,}250$$

$$C(210) = 0.5(210)^2 - 210(210) + 26{,}250 \qquad \text{Substitute 210 for } x.$$

$$= 0.5(44{,}100) - 44{,}100 + 26{,}250$$

$$= 22{,}050 - 17{,}850$$

$$= 4{,}200$$

If the company makes 210 water skis each week, it will minimize its production cost. The minimum weekly cost will be $4,200. ∎

Self Check 6   A company that makes and sells baseball caps has found that the total monthly cost C of producing x caps is given by the function $C(x) = 0.2x^2 - 80x + 9{,}000$. Find the production level that will minimize the monthly cost and find the minimum cost.

Now Try Exercise 67.

Self Check Answers   **1.** $(-5, -4)$ **2.**   **3.** $(2, 3)$ **4.**
5. 180,000 square feet
6. 200, $1,000

Exercises **3.2**

Getting Ready
You should be able to complete these vocabulary and concept statements before you proceed to the practice exercises.

Fill in the blanks.

1. A quadratic function is defined by the equation
   _____ $(a \neq 0)$.
2. The standard form for the equation of a parabola is
   _____ $(a \neq 0)$.
3. The vertex of the parabolic graph of the equation
   $y = 2(x - 3)^2 + 5$ will be at _____.
4. The vertical line that intersects the parabola at its
   vertex is the _____.
5. If the parabola opens _____ the vertex will be a
   minimum point.
6. If the parabola opens _____ the vertex will be a
   maximum point.
7. The x-coordinate of the vertex of the parabolic graph
   of $f(x) = ax^2 + bx + c$ is _____.
8. The y-coordinate of the vertex of the parabolic
   graph of $f(x) = ax^2 + bx + c$ is _____.

Practice
Determine whether the graph of each quadratic function opens upward or downward. State whether a maximum or minimum point occurs at the vertex of the parabola.

9. $f(x) = \frac{1}{2}x^2 + 3$ 10. $f(x) = 2x^2 - 3x$

11. $f(x) = -3(x + 1)^2 + 2$ 12. $f(x) = -5(x - 1)^2 - 1$

13. $f(x) = -2x^2 + 5x - 1$ 14. $f(x) = 2x^2 - 3x + 1$

Find the vertex of each parabola.

15. $y = x^2 - 1$ 16. $y = -x^2 + 2$
17. $f(x) = (x - 3)^2 + 5$ 18. $f(x) = -2(x - 3)^2 + 4$

19. $f(x) = -2(x + 6)^2 - 4$ 20. $f(x) = \frac{1}{3}(x + 1)^2 - 5$

21. $f(x) = \frac{2}{3}(x - 3)^2$ 22. $f(x) = 7(x + 2)^2 + 8$

23. $f(x) = x^2 - 4x + 4$ 24. $y = x^2 - 10x + 25$

25. $y = x^2 + 6x - 3$ 26. $y = -x^2 + 9x - 2$

27. $y = -2x^2 + 12x - 17$ 28. $y = 2x^2 + 16x + 33$

29. $y = 3x^2 - 4x + 5$ 30. $y = -4x^2 + 3x + 4$

31. $y = \frac{1}{2}x^2 + 4x - 3$ 32. $y = -\frac{2}{3}x^2 + 3x - 5$

Graph each quadratic function given in standard form.

33. $f(x) = x^2 - 4$ 34. $f(x) = x^2 + 1$

35. $f(x) = -3x^2 + 6$ 36. $f(x) = -4x^2 + 4$

37. $f(x) = -\frac{1}{2}x^2 + 8$ 38. $f(x) = \frac{1}{2}x^2 - 2$

39. $f(x) = (x - 3)^2 - 1$ 40. $f(x) = (x + 3)^2 - 1$

41. $f(x) = 2(x + 1)^2 - 2$ **42.** $f(x) = -\dfrac{3}{4}(x - 2)^2$

49. $f(x) = x^2 - 4x + 1$ **50.** $f(x) = x^2 - 6x - 7$

 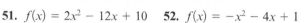

43. $f(x) = -(x + 4)^2 + 1$ **44.** $f(x) = -3(x - 4)^2 + 3$

51. $f(x) = 2x^2 - 12x + 10$ **52.** $f(x) = -x^2 - 4x + 1$

45. $f(x) = -3(x - 2)^2 + 6$ **46.** $f(x) = 2(x - 3)^2 - 4$

53. $f(x) = -3x^2 - 6x - 9$ **54.** $f(x) = -3x^2 - 3x + 18$

Graph each quadratic function given in general form.

47. $f(x) = x^2 + 2x$ **48.** $f(x) = x^2 - 6x$

Applications

55. Police investigations A police officer seals off the scene of an accident using a roll of yellow tape that is 300 feet long. What dimensions should be used to seal off the maximum rectangular area around the collision? Find the maximum area.

56. Maximizing area The rectangular garden shown has a width of x and a perimeter of 100 feet. Find x such that the area of the rectangle is maximum.

100 ft

57. Maximizing storage area A farmer wants to partition a rectangular feed storage area in a corner of his barn, as shown in the illustration. The barn walls form two sides of the stall, and the farmer has 50 feet of partition for the remaining two sides. What dimensions will maximize the area?

50 ft

58. Maximizing grazing area A rancher wishes to enclose a rectangular partitioned corral with 1,800 feet of fencing. (See the illustration.) What dimensions of the corral would enclose the largest possible area? Find the maximum area.

59. Sheet metal fabrication A 24-inch-wide sheet of metal is to be bent into a rectangular trough with the cross section shown in the illustration. Find the dimensions that will maximize the amount of water the trough can hold. That is, find the dimensions that will maximize the cross-sectional area.

Depth

24 in.

Width

60. Landscape design A gardener will use D feet of edging to border a rectangular plot of ground. Show that the maximum area will be enclosed if the rectangle is a square.

61. Architecture A parabolic arch has an equation of $x^2 + 20y - 400 = 0$, where x is measured in feet. Find the maximum height of the arch.

62. Path of a guided missile A guided missile is propelled from the origin of a coordinate system with the x-axis along the ground and the y-axis vertical. Its path, or **trajectory,** is given by the equation $y = 400x - 16x^2$. Find the object's maximum height.

63. Height of a basketball The path of a basketball thrown from the free throw line can be modeled by the quadratic function $f(x) = -0.06x^2 + 1.5x + 6$, where x is the horizontal distance (in feet) from the free throw line and $f(x)$ is the height (in feet) of the ball. Find the maximum height of the basketball.

64. Ballistics A child throws a ball up a hill that makes an angle of 45° with the horizontal. The ball lands 100 feet up the hill. Its trajectory is a parabola with equation $y = -x^2 + ax$ for some number a. Find a.

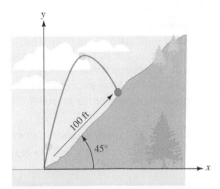

65. Maximizing height A ball is thrown straight up from the top of a building 144 ft. tall with an initial velocity of 64 ft per second. The distance $s(t)$ (in feet) of the ball from the ground is given by $s(t) = 144 + 64t - 16t^2$. Find the maximum height attained by the ball.

66. Flat-panel television sets A wholesaler of appliances finds that she can sell $(2,400 - p)$ flat-panel television sets each week when the price is p dollars. What price will maximize revenue?

67. Digital camera A company that produces and sells digital cameras has determined that the total weekly cost C of producing x digital cameras is given by the function $C(x) = 1.5x^2 - 144x + 5{,}856$. Determine the production level that minimizes the weekly cost for producing the digital cameras and find that weekly minimum cost.

68. Finding mass transit fares The Municipal Transit Authority serves 150,000 commuters daily when the fare is $1.80. Market research has determined that every penny decrease in the fare will result in 1,000 new riders. What fare will maximize revenue?

69. Finding hotel rates A 300-room hotel is two-thirds filled when the nightly room rate is $90. Experience has shown that each $5 increase in cost results in 10 fewer occupied rooms. Find the nightly rate that will maximize income.

70. Selling concert tickets Tickets for a concert are cheaper when purchased in quantity. The first 100 tickets are priced at $10 each, but each additional block of 100 tickets purchased decreases the cost of each ticket by 50¢. How many blocks of tickets should be sold to maximize the revenue?

Use this information: At a time t seconds after an object is tossed vertically upward, it reaches a height s in feet given by the equation $s = 80t - 16t^2$.

71. In how many seconds does the object reach its maximum height?

72. In how many seconds does the object return to the point from which it was thrown?

73. What is the maximum height reached by the object?

74. Show that it takes the same amount of time for the object to reach its maximum height as it does to return from that height to the point from which it was thrown.

Use a graphing calculator to determine the coordinates of the vertex of each parabola. You will have to select appropriate viewing windows.

75. $y = 2x^2 + 9x - 56$

76. $y = 14x - \dfrac{x^2}{5}$

77. $y = (x - 7)(5x + 2)$

78. $y = -x(0.2 + 0.1x)$

Discovery and Writing

Find all values of x that will make $f(x) = 0$.

79. $f(x) = x^2 - 5x + 6$

80. $f(x) = 6x^2 + x - 2$

81. Find the dimensions of the largest rectangle that can be inscribed in the right triangle ABC shown in the illustration.

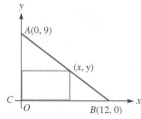

82. Point P lies in the first quadrant and on the line $x + y = 1$ in such a position that the area of triangle OPA is maximum. Find the coordinates of P. (See the illustration.)

83. The sum of two numbers is 6, and the sum of the squares of those two numbers is as small as possible. What are the numbers?

84. What number most exceeds its square?

The maximum or minimum value of a quadratic function can be found automatically by using a computer program, such as Excel.

85. Find the minimum value of the function $f(x) = 2x^2 - 3x - 4$ by using the Solver in Excel. Give the value of x that minimizes the function as well as the minimum value of the function. See Problem 119 in Section 1.3.

86. Find the maximum value of the function $f(x) = -2x^2 + 3x + 4$ by using the Solver in Excel. Give the value of x that maximizes the function as well as the maximum value of the function. See Problem 119 in Section 1.3.

Review

Find $f(a)$ and $f(-a)$.

91. $f(x) = 7$

92. $f(x) = -|x|$

Review

Find $f(a)$ and $f(-a)$.

87. $f(x) = x^2 - 3x$

88. $f(x) = x^3 - 3x$

89. $f(x) = (5 - x)^2$

90. $f(x) = \dfrac{1}{x^2 - 4}$

3.3 Polynomial and Other Functions

In this section, we will learn to

1. Understand the characteristics of polynomial functions.
2. Graph polynomial functions.
3. Determine whether a function is even, odd, or neither.
4. Identify the open intervals on which a function is increasing, decreasing, or constant.
5. Graph piecewise-defined functions.
6. Evaluate and graph the greatest-integer function.

So far, we have discussed two types of polynomial functions—first-degree (or linear) functions, and second-degree (or quadratic) functions. In this section, we will discuss polynomial functions of higher degree.

Polynomial functions can be used to model the path of a roller coaster or to model the fluctuation of gasoline prices over the past few months. Goliath, a hypercoaster, is located in Atlanta at Six Flags over Georgia. It climbs to a height of 200 feet and reaches speeds of nearly 70 mph. It has over 4,400 feet of steel track. Portions of Goliath's tracks can be modeled with a polynomial function.

Polynomial Functions

A **polynomial function in one variable (say, x)** is a function of the form

$$f(x) = a_n x^n + a_{n-1} x^{n-1} + \cdots + a_1 x + a_0$$

where $a_n, a_{n-1}, \ldots, a_1,$ and a_0 are real numbers and n is a whole number.

The **degree of a polynomial function** is the largest power of x that appears in the polynomial.

The table shows three basic polynomial functions that we have already covered:

Name	Function	Degree	Graph
Constant function	$f(x) = 5$	0	Horizontal line
Linear function	$f(x) = 2x - 7$	1	Nonvertical line
Quadratic function	$f(x) = -2x^2 + 4x - 5$	2	Parabola

Here are two examples of higher-degree polynomial functions, along with their graphs.

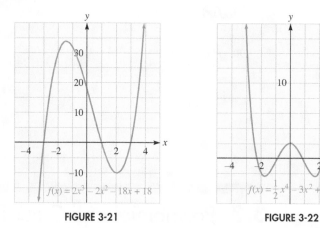

FIGURE 3-21   FIGURE 3-22

1. Understand the Characteristics of Polynomial Functions

There are several basic characteristics common to all polynomial functions. We will list several of them.

1: The graphs of polynomial functions are smooth and continuous curves.

Like the graphs of linear and quadratic functions, the graphs of higher-degree polynomial functions are smooth continuous curves. Because their graphs are smooth, they have no cusps or corners. Because they are continuous, their graphs have no breaks or holes. They can always be drawn without lifting the pencil from the paper.

- The graph of a polynomial function

Graph of a polynomial
function

FIGURE 3-23

- The graphs of two functions that are **not** polynomial functions

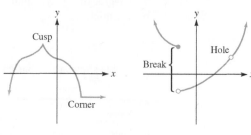

Not the graph of a polynomial   Not the graph of a polynomial
function   function

FIGURE 3-24

2: Many polynomial functions have graphs similar to the graphs of $f(x) = x$, $f(x) = x^2$, and $f(x) = x^3$.

Many polynomial functions are of the form $f(x) = x^n$, and several of their graphs are shown in Figure 3-25. Note that when n is even, the graph has the same general shape as $y = x^2$. When n is odd and greater than 1, the graph has the same general shape as $y = x^3$. However, the graphs are flatter at the origin and steeper as n becomes large.

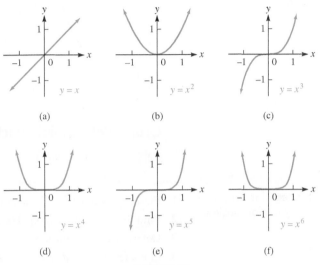

(a)   (b)   (c)

(d)   (e)   (f)

FIGURE 3-25

3: The end behavior of the graph of a polynomial function is similar to the graph of its term with highest degree.

The ends of the graph of any polynomial function will be similar to the graph of its term with the highest power of x, because when n becomes large, the other terms become relatively insignificant.

Consider the polynomial function $f(x) = x^3 + x^2 - 2x$. The end behavior of its graph will be similar to the ends of the graph of its leading term x^3. In Figure 3-25 (c), we see that the graph of $y = x^3$ falls on the far left and rises on the far right. Therefore, the graph of $f(x)$ will also fall on the far left and rise on the far right. See Figure 3-26.

FIGURE 3-26

4: Polynomial functions can be symmetric about the y-axis or the origin.

In Section 2.4, we learned that a graph is symmetric about the y-axis if the graph of $y = f(x)$ has the same y-coordinate when the function is evaluated at x or at $-x$.

Thus, a function is symmetric about the y-axis if $f(x) = f(-x)$ for all values of x that are in the domain of the function. See Figure 3-27(a). Also recall that a graph is symmetric about the origin if the point $(-x, -f(x))$ lies on the graph whenever $(x, f(x))$ does. In this case, $f(-x) = -f(x)$. See Figure 3-27(b).

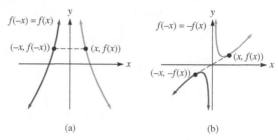

(a)   (b)

FIGURE 3-27

2. Graph Polynomial Functions

To graph polynomial functions, we can use the following steps.

Strategy for Graphing Polynomial Functions

1. Find any symmetries of the graph.
2. Find the x- and y-intercepts of the graph.
3. Determine where the graph is above and below the x-axis.
4. Plot a few points, if necessary, and draw the graph as a smooth continuous curve.

EXAMPLE 1   **Graphing a Polynomial Function of Degree 3**

Graph the function: $f(x) = x^3 - 4x$.

SOLUTION   We will use the four steps stated above to graph the polynomial function.

Step 1: Find any symmetries of the graph.
To test for symmetry about the y-axis, we check to see whether $f(x) = f(-x)$. To test for symmetry about the origin, we check to see whether $f(-x) = -f(x)$.

$$f(x) = x^3 - 4x$$

$$f(-x) = (-x)^3 - 4(-x) \qquad \text{Substitute } -x \text{ for } x.$$

$$f(-x) = -x^3 + 4x \qquad \text{Simplify.}$$

Since $f(x) \neq f(-x)$, there is no symmetry about the y-axis. However, since $f(-x) = -f(x)$, there is symmetry about the origin.

Step 2: Find the x- and y-intercepts of the graph.
To find the x-intercepts, we let $f(x) = 0$ and solve for x.

$$x^3 - 4x = 0$$

$$x(x^2 - 4) = 0 \qquad \text{Factor out } x.$$

$$x(x + 2)(x - 2) = 0 \qquad \text{Factor } x^2 - 4.$$

$$x = 0 \quad \text{or} \quad x + 2 = 0 \quad \text{or} \quad x - 2 = 0 \qquad \text{Set each factor equal to 0.}$$
$$x = -2 \qquad\qquad x = 2$$

The x-intercepts are $(0, 0)$, $(-2, 0)$, and $(2, 0)$. If we let $x = 0$ and solve for $f(x)$, we see that the y-intercept is also $(0, 0)$.

Step 3: Determine where the graph is above or below the x-axis.

To determine where the graph is above or below the x-axis, we plot the solutions of $x^3 - 4x = 0$ (the x-coordinates of the x-intercepts) on a number line and establish the four intervals shown in Figure 3-28. We then test a number from each interval to determine the sign of $f(x)$. (For a review of this process, see Example 7 in Section 1.7.)

FIGURE 3-28

Comment

Note that the far right and far left ends of the graph are similar to the ends of the graph of $f(x) = x^3$, which is the leading term of the function $f(x) = x^3 - 4x$ or the term with highest degree. On the far right the graph rises and on the far left the graph falls.

Step 4: Plot a few points and draw the graph as a smooth continuous curve.

We now plot the intercepts and one additional point. In the previous step we found that $f(1) = -3$. This will be the additional point we plot $(1, -3)$. Making use of our knowledge of symmetry and where the graph is above and below the x-axis we now draw the graph as shown in Figure 3-29(a). A calculator graph, using the standard viewing window, is shown in Figure 3-29(b).

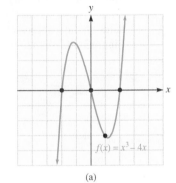

$f(x) = x^3 - 4x$		
x	$f(x)$	$(x, f(x))$
-2	0	$(-2, 0)$
0	0	$(0, 0)$
1	-3	$(1, -3)$
2	0	$(2, 0)$

(a)

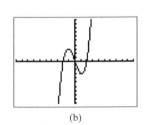

(b)

FIGURE 3-29

Self Check 1   Graph: $f(x) = x^3 - 9x$.

Now Try Exercise 13.

The peak and valley of the graph shown in Figure 3-29 are called **turning points.** In calculus, such points are called **local minima** and **local maxima.** Although we cannot find these points without using calculus, we can approximate them by plotting points or by using the ⬛TRACE feature on a graphing calculator. We can also use the CALC Minimum and CALC Maximum features on a graphing calculator to find these local extrema.

Note that Figure 3-29 shows the graph of a third-degree polynomial and the graph has two turning points. This suggests the following result from calculus that helps us understand the shape of many polynomial graphs.

Number of Turning Points   If $f(x)$ is a polynomial function of nth degree, then the graph of $f(x)$ will have $n - 1$, or fewer, turning points.

EXAMPLE 2   **Graphing a Polynomial Function of Degree 4**

Graph the function: $f(x) = x^4 - 5x^2 + 4$.

SOLUTION   We will use the four steps for graphing a polynomial function.

Step 1: Find any symmetries of the graph.
Because x appears with only even exponents, $f(x) = f(-x)$, and the graph is symmetric about the y-axis. The graph is not symmetric about the origin.

Step 2: Find the x- and y-intercepts of the graph.
To find the x-intercepts, we let $f(x) = 0$ and solve for x.

$$x^4 - 5x^2 + 4 = 0$$

$$(x^2 - 4)(x^2 - 1) = 0$$

$$(x + 2)(x - 2)(x + 1)(x - 1) = 0$$

$$x + 2 = 0 \quad \text{or} \quad x - 2 = 0 \quad \text{or} \quad x + 1 = 0 \quad \text{or} \quad x - 1 = 0$$

$$x = -2 \quad | \quad x = 2 \quad | \quad x = -1 \quad | \quad x = 1$$

The x-intercepts are $(-2, 0)$, $(2, 0)$, $(-1, 0)$, and $(1, 0)$. To find the y-intercept, we let $x = 0$ and see that the y-intercept is $(0, 4)$.

Step 3: Determine where the graph is above or below the x-axis.
To determine where the graph is above or below the x-axis, we plot the x-coordinates of the x-intercepts on a number line and establish the five intervals shown in Figure 3-30. We then test a number from each interval to determine the sign of $f(x)$.

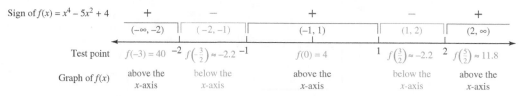

Sign of $f(x) = x^4 - 5x^2 + 4$

	$+$	$-$	$+$	$-$	$+$
	$(-\infty, -2)$	$(-2, -1)$	$(-1, 1)$	$(1, 2)$	$(2, \infty)$
Test point	$f(-3) = 40$ -2	$f\left(\frac{3}{2}\right) \approx -2.2$ -1	$f(0) = 4$	1 $f\left(\frac{3}{2}\right) \approx -2.2$ 2	$f\left(\frac{5}{2}\right) \approx 11.8$
Graph of $f(x)$	above the x-axis	below the x-axis	above the x-axis	below the x-axis	above the x-axis

FIGURE 3-30

Comment

Note that the far right and far left ends of the graph are similar to the ends of the graph of $f(x) = x^4$, which is the leading term of the function $f(x) = x^4 - 5x^2 + 4$ or the term with highest degree. On the far right and far left the graph rises. Also note that the graph has three turning points.

Step 4: Plot a few points and draw the graph as a smooth continuous curve.
We can now plot the intercepts and use our knowledge of symmetry and where the graph is above and below the x-axis to draw the graph, as shown in Figure 3-31(a). A calculator graph, using the standard viewing window, is shown in Figure 3-31(b).

$f(x) = x^4 - 5x^2 + 4$		
x	$f(x)$	$(x, f(x))$
-2	0	$(-2, 0)$
-1	0	$(-1, 0)$
0	4	$(0, 4)$
1	0	$(1, 0)$
$\frac{3}{2}$	$-\frac{35}{16}$	$\left(\frac{3}{2}, -\frac{35}{16}\right)$
2	0	$(2, 0)$

(a)

(b)

FIGURE 3-31

Self Check 2   Graph: $f(x) = x^4 - 10x^2 + 9$.

Now Try Exercise 19.

3. Determine Whether a Function Is Even, Odd, or Neither

Functions can be classified as being even, odd, or neither even nor odd. These definitions are given next.

Even Function A function is an **even function** if $f(-x) = f(x)$ for all x in the domain of f.

Even functions are symmetric about the y-axis.

Odd Function A function is an **odd function** if $f(-x) = f(x)$ for all x in the domain of f.

Odd functions are symmetric about the origin.

Since the graph of the function $f(x) = x^3 - 4x$ in Example 1 is symmetric about the origin, it represents an odd function. Since the graph of the function $f(x) = x^4 - 5x + 4$ in Example 2 is symmetric about the y-axis, it represents an even function. If $f(x)$ does not have either of these symmetries, it is neither even nor odd.

EXAMPLE 3 **Determining Whether a Function Is Even, Odd, or Neither**

Determine whether each function is even, odd, or neither:
a. $f(x) = x^2 + 1$ **b.** $f(x) = x^3$

SOLUTION To check whether the function is an even function, we find $f(-x)$ and see whether $f(-x) = f(x)$. To check whether the function is an odd function, we find $f(-x)$ and see whether $f(-x) = -f(x)$.

a. $f(-x) = (-x)^2 + 1 = x^2 + 1 = f(x)$

Since $f(-x) = f(x)$, the function is an even function.

The graph of $f(x) = x^2 + 1$ is shown in Figure 3-32. We see that the graph is symmetric about the y-axis.

b. $f(-x) = (-x)^3 = -x^3 = -f(x)$

Since $f(-x) \neq f(x)$, the function is not an even function.

However, the function is an odd function, because $f(-x) = -f(x)$.

The graph of $f(x) = x^3$ is shown in Figure 3-33. Note that the graph is symmetric about the origin.

FIGURE 3-32

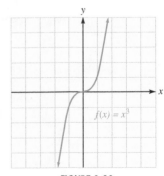

FIGURE 3-33

Self Check 3   Classify each function as even, odd, or neither: **a.** $f(x) = x^3 + x$
b. $f(x) = x^2 + 4$

Now Try Exercise 23.

4. Identify the Open Intervals on Which a Function Is Increasing, Decreasing, or Constant

If we trace the graph of a function from left to right and the values $f(x)$ increase as shown in Figure 3-34(a), we say that the function is an **increasing function.** If the values $f(x)$ decrease as in Figure 3-34(b), we say that the function is a **decreasing function.** If the values $f(x)$ remain unchanged as x increases, we say that the function is a **constant function.**

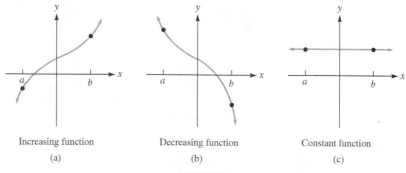

Increasing function   Decreasing function   Constant function
        (a)   (b)   (c)

FIGURE 3-34

As we would expect, when we trace the graphs of some functions from left to right, there will be intervals where the function increases, intervals where the function decreases, and intervals where the function is constant. We will always state these intervals as open intervals because of the following definition.

Increasing on an Open Interval   A function f is **increasing on an open interval** (a, b) if for any x_1 and x_2 in (a, b), where $x_1 < x_2$, then $f(x_1) < f(x_2)$.

Decreasing on an Open Interval   A function f is **decreasing on an open interval** (a, b) if for any x_1 and x_2 in (a, b), where $x_1 < x_2$, then $f(x_1) > f(x_2)$.

Constant on an Open Interval   A function f is **constant on an open interval** (a, b) if for any x_1 and x_2 in (a, b), $f(x_1) = f(x_2)$.

EXAMPLE 4   **Identify the Open Intervals Where a Function Increases or Decreases**

Use the graph of the polynomial function shown to determine the intervals on which the function is increasing or decreasing.

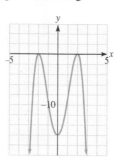

SOLUTION   We trace the graph of the function from left to right and identify the open intervals on which $f(x)$ values increase and where they decrease. We see from the graph shown in Figure 3-35 that the values of $f(x)$ increase on the open intervals $(-\infty, -2)$ and $(0, 2)$. They decrease on the open intervals $(-2, 0)$ and $(2, \infty)$. Hence, the function is increasing on $(-\infty, -2) \cup (0, 2)$ and is decreasing on $(-2, 0) \cup (2, \infty)$. ∎

Self Check 4   Use the graph shown in Figure 3-35 to identify the open intervals, if any, on which the function is constant.

Now Try Exercise 41.

Comment

Intervals on which a function is increasing, decreasing, or constant are open intervals. We use interval notation and x-values to write the open intervals. Note that y-values are not used.

5. Graph Piecewise-Defined Functions

Some functions, called **piecewise-defined functions,** are defined by using different equations for different intervals in their domains. To illustrate, we will graph the piecewise-defined function f given by

$$f(x) = \begin{cases} -2 & \text{if } x \le 0 \\ x + 1 & \text{if } x > 0 \end{cases}$$

To evaluate this piecewise-defined function, we must determine which part of the function's definition to use.

- If $x \le 0$, we use the top part of the definition and the corresponding value of $f(x)$ is -2. Some examples are:

$$f(-2) = -2, \quad f(-1) = -2, \quad \text{and} \quad f(0) = -2$$

In the interval $(-\infty, 0]$, the function value is always -2 and the graph is the horizontal line $y = -2$.

- If $x > 0$, we use the bottom part of the definition and the corresponding value of $f(x)$ is $x + 1$. Some examples are:

$$f(1) = 1 + 1 = 2 \text{ and } f(2) = 2 + 1 = 3$$

In the interval $(0, \infty)$, the graph of the function is the line $f(x) = x + 1$. This is a linear function with slope $m = 1$ and y-intercept $(0, b) = (0, 1)$.

The graph of this piecewise-defined function appears in Figure 3-36.

Comment

Note that when $x = 0$, we have $f(x) = -2$. For this reason, the point $(0, -2)$ is shown as a closed point and the point $(0, 1)$ is shown as an open point.

FIGURE 3-36

EXAMPLE 5   **Graphing a Piecewise-Defined Function**

Graph the function: $f(x) = \begin{cases} -x & \text{if } x < 0 \\ x^2 & \text{if } 0 \le x \le 1. \end{cases}$

SOLUTION   This piecewise-defined function is defined in three parts. We will graph each part of the function. That is, we will graph $f(x) = -x$ in the interval $(-\infty, 0)$, $f(x) = x^2$ in the interval $[0, 1]$, and $f(x) = 1$ in the interval $(1, \infty)$.

If $x < 0$, the value of $f(x)$ is determined by the equation $f(x) = -x$. We graph the line with slope $m = -1$ and y-intercept $(0, b) = (0, 0)$ in the interval $(-\infty, 0)$. In the interval $(-\infty, 0)$, the function is decreasing.

If $0 \leq x \leq 1$, the value of $f(x)$ is x^2. We graph the parabola in the interval $[0, 1]$. In the open interval $(0,1)$ the function is increasing.

If $x > 1$, the value of $f(x)$ is 1. In the open interval $(1, \infty)$, the function is constant and its graph is the same as the graph of $y = 1$.

The graph of the piecewise function appears in Figure 3-37.

$$f(x) = \begin{cases} -x & \text{if } x < 0 \\ x^2 & \text{if } 0 \leq x \leq 1 \\ 1 & \text{if } x > 1 \end{cases}$$

FIGURE 3-37

Self Check 5   Graph: $f(x) = \begin{cases} 2x & \text{if } x \leq 0 \\ x - 1 & \text{if } x > 0 \end{cases}$.

Now Try Exercise 57.

ACCENT ON TECHNOLOGY   **Piecewise-Defined Functions**

Piecewise-defined functions can be graphed on a calculator. We will graph the piecewise-defined function $f(x) = \begin{cases} -x & \text{if } x < 0 \\ x^2 & \text{if } 0 \leq x \leq 1 \\ 1 & \text{if } x > 1 \end{cases}$ given in Example 5.

- The inequality symbols are found by pressing [2nd] [MATH] (TEST) shown in Figure 3-38(a).
- The "and" command is found in the LOGIC menu which is accessed via the TEST menu. See Figure 3-38(b).
- When graphing these functions, place the calculator in DOT mode. See Figure 3-38(c).
- Enter the function as shown in Figure 3-38(d). Note that the use of parentheses is essential. A viewing window of $[-5, 5]$ for x and $[-3, 3]$ for y is used here.

The graph of the function is shown in Figure 3-38(e).

(a)

(b)

(c)

FIGURE 3-38

(d)   (e)

FIGURE 3-38 (Continued)

6. Evaluate and Graph the Greatest-Integer Function

The **greatest-integer function** is important in many business applications and in the field of computer science. This function is determined by the equation $f(x) = [x]$, where the value of $f(x)$ that corresponds to x is the greatest integer that is less than or equal to x.

Comment

Recall that the set of integers is $\{\ldots, -2, -1, 0, 1, 2, \ldots\}$.

For example,

$$f(2.71) = [2.71] = 2$$
$$f(23.5) = [23.5] = 23$$
$$f(10) = [10] = 10$$
$$f(\pi) = [\pi] = 3$$
$$f(-2.5) = [-2.5] = -3$$

EXAMPLE 6   **Graphing the Greatest-Integer Function**

Graph: $f(x) = [x]$.

SOLUTION   We will list several intervals and determine the corresponding values of the greatest-integer function. Then we will use these values to graph the function.

$[0, 1)$ $f(x) = [x] = 0$ For numbers from 0 to 1 (not including 1), the greatest integer in the interval is 0.

$[1, 2)$ $f(x) = [x] = 1$ For numbers from 1 to 2 (not including 2), the greatest integer in the interval is 1.

$[2, 3)$ $f(x) = [x] = 2$ For numbers from 2 to 3 (not including 3), the greatest integer in the interval is 2.

Within each interval, the values of y are constant, but they jump by 1 at integer values of x. The graph is shown in Figure 3-39. From the graph, we can see that the domain of the greatest integer function is the interval $(-\infty, \infty)$. The range is the set of integers.

FIGURE 3-39

Self Check 6   Find **a.** $[7.61]$ and **b.** $[-3.75]$.

Now Try Exercise 63.

Since the greatest-integer function is made up of a series of horizontal line segments, it is an example of a group of functions called **step functions.**

EXAMPLE 7   Graphing a Step Function Occurring in an Application

To print business forms, a printing company charges customers $10 for the order, plus $20 for each box containing 200 forms. The printing company counts any portion of a box as a full box. Graph this step function.

SOLUTION   To graph the step function, we will determine the cost for printing various amounts of boxes of forms. Then we will graph our result.

If we order the forms and then change our minds before the forms are printed, the cost will be $10. Thus, the ordered pair (0, 10) will be on the graph.

If we purchase up to one full box, the cost will be $10 for the order and $20 for the printing, for a total of $30. Thus, the ordered pair (1, 30) will be on the graph.

The cost for $1\frac{1}{2}$ boxes will be the same as the cost for 2 full boxes, or $50. Thus, the ordered pairs (1.5, 50) and (2, 50) are on the graph.

The complete graph is shown in Figure 3-40.

FIGURE 3-40

Self Check 7   Find the cost of $4\frac{1}{2}$ boxes.

Now Try Exercise 69.

Self Check Answers   **1.**

$f(x) = x^3 - 9x$

2.

$f(x) = x^4 - 10x^2 + 9$

3. a. odd   **b.** even

4. no intervals   **5.**

$f(x) = \begin{cases} 2x & \text{if } x \le 0 \\ x - 1 & \text{if } x > 0 \end{cases}$

6. a. 7   **b.** -4 **7.** $110

Exercises **3.3**

Getting Ready

You should be able to complete these vocabulary and con-cept statements before you proceed to the practice exercises.

Fill in the blanks.

1. The degree of the function $y = f(x) = x^4 - 3$ is ___.
2. Peaks and valleys on a polynomial graph are called _____ points.
3. The graph of a nth degree polynomial function can have at most _____ turning points.
4. If the graph of a function is symmetric about the _____, it is called an even function.
5. If the graph of a function is symmetric about the origin, it is called an ____ function.
6. If the values of $f(x)$ get larger as x increases on an interval, we say that the function is _____ on the open interval.
7. _____ functions are defined by different equations for different intervals in their domains.
8. If the values of $f(x)$ get smaller as x increases on an interval, we say that the function is _____ on the open interval.
9. $\lceil 3.69 \rceil =$ ___.
10. If the values of $f(x)$ do not change as x increases on an interval, we say that the function is _____ on the open interval.

Practice

Graph each polynomial function.

11. $f(x) = x^3 - 9x$

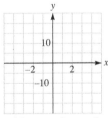

12. $f(x) = x^3 - 16x$

13. $f(x) = -x^3 - 4x^2$

14. $f(x) = x^3 - x$

15. $f(x) = x^3 + x^2$

16. $f(x) = -x^3 + 1$

17. $f(x) = x^3 - x^2 - 4x + 4$

18. $f(x) = 4x^3 - 4x^2 - x + 1$

19. $f(x) = x^4 - 2x^2 + 1$

20. $f(x) = x^4 - 5x^2 + 4$

21. $f(x) = -x^4 + 5x^2 - 4$

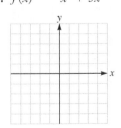

22. $f(x) = x(x - 3)(x - 2)(x + 1)$

Determine whether each function is even, odd, or neither.

23. $f(x) = x^4 + x^2$ **24.** $f(x) = x^3 - 2x$

25. $f(x) = x^3 + x^2$ **26.** $f(x) = x^6 - x^2$

27. $f(x) = x^5 + x^3$ **28.** $f(x) = x^3 - x^2$

29. $f(x) = 2x^3 - 3x$ **30.** $f(x) = 4x^2 - 5$

Determine whether each function is even, odd, or neither.

31.

32.

33.

34.

35.

36.

State the open intervals where each function is increasing, decreasing, or constant.

37.

38.

39.

40.

41.

42.

43. $f(x) = x^2 - 4x + 4$

44. $f(x) = 4 - x^2$

Evaluate each piecewise-defined function.

45. $f(x) = \begin{cases} 2x + 2 & \text{if } x < 0 \\ 3 & \text{if } x \geq 0 \end{cases}$

   a. $f(-2)$ **b.** $f(0)$

46. $f(x) = \begin{cases} x - 2 & \text{if } x < 1 \\ x^2 & \text{if } x \geq 1 \end{cases}$

   a. $f(1)$ **b.** $f(5)$

47. $f(x) = \begin{cases} 2 & \text{if } x < 0 \\ 2 - x & \text{if } 0 \leq x < 2 \\ x + 1 & \text{if } x \geq 2 \end{cases}$

   a. $f(-1)$ **b.** $f(1)$ **c.** $f(2)$

48. $f(x) = \begin{cases} 2x & \text{if } x < 0 \\ 3 - x & \text{if } 0 \leq x < 2 \\ |x| & \text{if } x \geq 2 \end{cases}$

   a. $f(-0.5)$ **b.** $f(0)$ **c.** $f(2)$

Graph each piecewise-defined function.

49. $f(x) = \begin{cases} x + 2 & \text{if } x < 0 \\ 2 & \text{if } x \geq 0 \end{cases}$

50. $f(x) = \begin{cases} 2x & \text{if } x < 0 \\ -2x & \text{if } x \geq 0 \end{cases}$

51. $f(x) = \begin{cases} x & \text{if } x \leq 0 \\ 2 & \text{if } x > 0 \end{cases}$

52. $f(x) = \begin{cases} -x & \text{if } x < 0 \\ \dfrac{1}{2}x & \text{if } x > 0 \end{cases}$

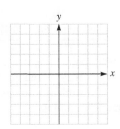

53. $f(x) = \begin{cases} -4 - x & \text{if } x < 1 \\ 3 & \text{if } x \geq 1 \end{cases}$

54. $f(x) = \begin{cases} -5 - x & \text{if } x < 1 \\ -3 & \text{if } x \geq 1 \end{cases}$

55. $f(x) = \begin{cases} -x & \text{if } x < 0 \\ x^2 & \text{if } x \geq 0 \end{cases}$

56. $f(x) = \begin{cases} |x| & \text{if } x < 0 \\ \sqrt{x} & \text{if } x \geq 0 \end{cases}$

57. $f(x) = \begin{cases} 0 & \text{if } x < 0 \\ x^2 & \text{if } 0 \le x \le 2 \\ 4 - 2x & \text{if } x > 2 \end{cases}$

58. $f(x) = \begin{cases} 2 & \text{if } x < 0 \\ 2 - x & \text{if } 0 \le x < 2 \\ x & \text{if } x \ge 2 \end{cases}$

Evalute each function at the indicated x-values.

59. $f(x) = [\![x]\!]$ **a.** $f(3)$ **b.** $f(-4)$ **c.** $f(-2.3)$

60. $f(x) = [\![3x]\!]$ **a.** $f(4)$ **b.** $f(-2)$ **c.** $f(-1.2)$

61. $f(x) = [\![x + 3]\!]$ **a.** $f(-1)$ **b.** $f\left(\dfrac{2}{3}\right)$ **c.** $f(1.3)$

62. $f(x) = [\![4x]\!] - 1$ **a.** $f(-3)$ **b.** $f(0)$ **c.** $f(\pi)$

Graph each function.

63. $y = [\![2x]\!]$

64. $y = \left[\!\!\left[\dfrac{1}{3}x + 3\right]\!\!\right]$

65. $y = [\![x]\!] - 1$

66. $y = [\![x + 2]\!]$

Applications

67. Grading scales A mathematics instructor assigns letter grades according to the following scale.

From	Up to but less than	Grade
60%	70%	D
70%	80%	C
80%	90%	B
90%	100% (including 100%)	A

Graph the ordered pairs (p, g), where p represents the percent and g represents the grade. Find the final semester grade of a student who has test scores of 67%, 73%, 84%, 87%, and 93%.

68. Calculating grades See Exercise 67 and find the final semester grade of a student who has test scores of 53%, 65%, 64%, 73%, 89%, and 82%.

69. Renting a jeep A rental company charges $20 to rent a Jeep Wrangler for one day, plus $4 for every 100 miles (or portion of 100 miles) that it is driven. Graph the ordered pairs (m, C), where m represents the miles driven and C represents the cost. Find the cost if the Jeep is driven 275 miles in one day.

70. Riding in a taxi A taxicab company charges $3 for a trip up to 1 mile, and $2 for every extra mile (or portion of a mile). Graph the ordered pairs (m, C), where m represents the miles traveled and C represents the cost. Find the cost to ride $10\frac{1}{4}$ miles.

71. Computer communications An on-line information service charges for connect time at a rate of $12 per hour, computed for every minute or fraction of a minute. Graph the points (t, C), where C is the cost of t minutes of connect time. Find the cost of $7\frac{1}{2}$ minutes.

72. iPad repair There is a charge of $30, plus $40 per hour (or fraction of an hour), to repair an iPad. Graph the points (t, C), where t is the time it takes to do the job and C is the cost. If it takes 4 hours to repair the iPad, how much did it cost?

73. Rounding numbers Measurements are rarely exact; they are often *rounded* to an appropriate precision. Graph the points (x, y), where y is the result of rounding the number x to the nearest ten.

74. Signum function Computer programmers often use the following function, denoted by $y = \text{sgn } x$. Graph this function and find its domain and range.

$$y = \begin{cases} -1 & \text{if } x < 0 \\ 0 & \text{if } x = 0 \\ 1 & \text{if } x > 0 \end{cases}$$

75. Graph the function defined by $y = \frac{|x|}{x}$ and compare it to the graph in Exercise 74. Are the graphs the same?

76. Graph: $y = x + |x|$.

Discovery and Writing

Use a graphing calculator to explore the properties of graphs of polynomial functions. Write a paragraph summarizing your observations.

77. Graph the function $y = x^2 + ax$ for several values of a. How does the graph change?

78. Graph the function $y = x^3 + ax$ for several values of a. How does the graph change?

79. Graph the function $y = (x - a)(x - b)$ for several values of a and b. What is the relationship between the x-intercepts and the equation?

80. Use the insight you gained in Exercise 79 to factor $x^3 - 3x^2 - 4x + 12$.

Review

81. If $f(x) = 3x + 2$, find $f(x + 1)$ and $f(x) + 1$.

82. If $f(x) = x^2$, find $f(x - 2)$ and $f(x) - 2$.

83. If $f(x) = \dfrac{3x + 1}{5}$, find $f(x - 3)$ and $f(x) - 3$.

84. If $f(x) = 8$, find $f(x + 8)$ and $f(x) + 8$.

85. Solve: $2x^2 - 3 = x$.

86. Solve: $4x^2 = 24x - 37$.

3.4 Transformations of the Graphs of Functions

In this section, we will learn to

1. Use vertical translations to graph functions.
2. Use horizontal translations to graph functions.
3. Graph functions using two translations.
4. Use reflections about the x- and y-axes to graph functions.
5. Use vertical stretching and shrinking to graph functions.
6. Use horizontal stretching and shrinking to graph functions.
7. Graph functions using a combination of transformations.

We can often transform the graph of a function into the graph of another function by shifting the graph vertically or horizontally. Also, we can reflect a graph about the x- or y-axis, and stretch or shrink a graph horizontally or vertically to transform the graph of a function into the graph of another function. In this section, we will graph new functions from known ones using these methods.

Consider a white water rafting trip on the Ocoee River in Tennessee. Suppose one company charges a group of students $20 for each hour on the river, plus $100 for a guide and equipment. The cost of the rafting trip can be represented by the function

$$C_1(t) = 20t + 100$$

where $C_1(t)$ represents the cost in dollars to raft t hours on the river.

If the company increases its charge for the guide and equipment to $150, the new cost function can be represented by

$$C_2(t) = 20t + 150$$

The graphs of the two cost functions are shown in Figure 3-41.

FIGURE 3-41

Note that if we shift the graph of $C_1(t)$ 50 units vertically, we obtain the graph of $C_2(t)$. This shift is called a *translation*.

As we continue our study of translations, it will be helpful to review the graphs of the basic functions that are shown in Figure 3-8 in Section 3.1. In this section, the graphs of $f(x) = x^2$, $f(x) = x^3$, $f(x) = |x|$, $f(x) = \sqrt{x}$, and $f(x) = \sqrt[3]{x}$ will be translated and stretched in various ways.

1. Use Vertical Translations to Graph Functions

The graphs of functions can be identical except for their position in the xy-plane. For example, Figure 3-42 shows the graph of $y = x^2 + k$ for three values of k. If $k = 0$, we have the graph of $y = x^2$. The graph of $y = x^2 + 2$ is identical to the graph of $y = x^2$, except that it is shifted 2 units upward. The graph of $y = x^2 - 3$ is identical to the graph of $y = x^2$, except that it is shifted 3 units downward. These shifts are called **vertical translations.**

$y = x^2$		
x	y	(x, y)
-2	4	$(-2, 4)$
-1	1	$(-1, 1)$
0	0	$(0, 0)$
1	1	$(1, 1)$
2	4	$(2, 4)$

$y = x^2 + 2$		
x	y	(x, y)
-2	6	$(-2, 6)$
-1	3	$(-1, 3)$
0	2	$(0, 2)$
1	3	$(1, 3)$
2	6	$(2, 6)$

$y = x^2 - 3$		
x	y	(x, y)
-2	1	$(-2, 1)$
-1	-2	$(-1, -2)$
0	-3	$(0, -3)$
1	-2	$(1, -2)$
2	1	$(2, 1)$

FIGURE 3-42

In general, we can make the following observations:

Vertical Translations   If f is a function and k is a positive number, then

- The graph of $y = f(x) + k$ is identical to the graph of $y = f(x)$ except that it is translated k units upward.

- The graph of $y = f(x) - k$ is identical to the graph of $y = f(x)$ except that it is translated k units downward.

EXAMPLE 1   Using Vertical Translations to Graph Functions

Graph each function: **a.** $g(x) = |x| - 2$ **b.** $h(x) = |x| + 3$

SOLUTION   We will use vertical translations of $f(x) = |x|$ to graph each function.

a. The graph of $g(x) = |x| - 2$ is identical to the graph of $f(x) = |x|$, except that it is translated 2 units downward. It is translated downward because 2 is subtracted from $|x|$. The graph of $g(x)$ is shown in Figure 3-43(a).

b. The graph of $h(x) = |x| + 3$ is identical to the graph of $f(x) = |x|$, except that it is translated 3 units upward. It is translated upward because 3 is added to $|x|$. The graph of $h(x)$ is shown in Figure 3-43(b).

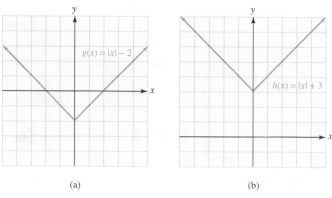

(a)   (b)

FIGURE 3-43

Self Check 1   *Fill in the blanks:* The graph of $g(x) = x^2 + 3$ is identical to the graph of $f(x) = x^2$, except that it is translated ___ units _____ . The graph of $h(x) = x^2 - 4$ is identical to the graph of $f(x) = x^2$, except that it is translated ___ units _____ .

Now Try Exercise 27.

2. Use Horizontal Translations to Graph Functions

Comment

The graphs of the functions shown in Figure 3-44 are exactly the graphs we would expect based on our previous knowledge of quadratic functions.

Figure 3-44 shows the graph of $y = (x + k)^2$ for three values of k. If $k = 0$, we have the graph of $y = x^2$. The graph of $y = (x - 2)^2$ is identical to the graph of $y = x^2$, except that it is shifted 2 units to the right. The graph of $y = (x + 3)^2$ is identical to the graph of $y = x^2$, except that it is shifted 3 units to the left. These shifts are called **horizontal translations**.

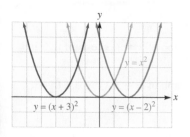

$y = x^2$		
x	y	(x, y)
-2	4	$(-2, 4)$
-1	1	$(-1, 1)$
0	0	$(0, 0)$
1	1	$(1, 1)$
2	4	$(2, 4)$

$y = (x - 2)^2$		
x	y	(x, y)
0	4	$(0, 4)$
1	1	$(1, 1)$
2	0	$(2, 0)$
3	1	$(3, 1)$
4	4	$(4, 4)$

$y = (x + 3)^2$		
x	y	(x, y)
-5	4	$(-5, 4)$
-4	1	$(-4, 1)$
-3	0	$(-3, 0)$
-2	1	$(-2, 1)$
-1	4	$(-1, 4)$

FIGURE 3-44

In general, we can make the following observations.

Horizontal Translations

If f is a function and k is a positive number, then

- The graph of $y = f(x - k)$ is identical to the graph of $y = f(x)$ except that it is translated k units to the right.

- The graph of $y = f(x + k)$ is identical to the graph of $y = f(x)$ except that it is translated k units to the left.

EXAMPLE 2   **Using Horizontal Translations to Graph Functions**

Graph each function: **a.** $g(x) = |x - 4|$ **b.** $h(x) = |x + 2|$

SOLUTION   We will use horizontal translations of the graph of $f(x) = |x|$ to graph each function.

a. The graph of $g(x) = |x - 4|$ is identical to the graph of $f(x) = |x|$, except that it is translated 4 units to the right. It is translated 4 units to the right because within the absolute value symbols 4 is subtracted from x. The graph of $g(x)$ is shown in Figure 3-45(a).

b. The graph of $h(x) = |x + 2|$ is identical to the graph of $f(x) = |x|$, except that it is translated 2 units to the left. It is translated 2 units to the left because within the absolute value symbols 2 is added to x. The graph of $h(x)$ is shown in Figure 3-45(b).

(a)   (b)

FIGURE 3-45

Self Check 2   *Fill in the blanks:* The graph of $g(x) = (x - 3)^2$ is identical to the graph of $f(x) = x^2$ except that it is translated ___ units to the _____. The graph of $h(x) = (x + 2)^2$ is identical to the graph of $f(x) = x^2$ except that it is translated ___ units to the _____.

Now Try Exercise 29.

Caution   When using horizontal translations to graph a function, it is easy to shift the function in the *wrong* direction.

- If we see a positive constant subtracted from x, we have the tendency to shift the graph left. This is **incorrect.**

- If we see a positive constant added to x, we have the tendency to shift the graph right. This too is **incorrect.**

We should avoid making these common errors.

3. Graph Functions Using Two Translations

Sometimes we can obtain a graph by using both a horizontal and a vertical translation.

EXAMPLE 3 **Using a Horizontal and a Vertical Translation to Graph a Function**

Graph each function:
a. $g(x) = (x - 5)^3 + 4$ **b.** $h(x) = (x + 2)^2 - 2$

SOLUTION By inspection, we see that the function in part **a** involves two translations of $f(x) = x^3$ and the function in part **b** involves two translations of $f(x) = x^2$. We will perform the horizontal translation first, followed by a vertical translation to obtain the graph of each function.

a. The graph of $g(x) = (x - 5)^3 + 4$ is identical to the graph of $f(x) = x^3$, except that it is translated 5 units to the right and 4 units upward, as shown in Figure 3-46(a).

b. The graph of $h(x) = (x + 2)^2 - 2$ is identical to the graph of $f(x) = x^2$, except that it is translated 2 units to the left and 2 units downward, as shown in Figure 3-46(b).

(a)

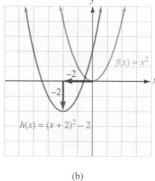

(b)

FIGURE 3-46

Self Check 3   *Fill in the blanks:* The graph of $g(x) = |x - 4| + 5$ is identical to the graph of $f(x) = |x|$, except that it is translated ___ units to the _____ and ___ units _____.

Now Try Exercise 31.

ACCENT ON TECHNOLOGY   **Translations of Functions**

We can use a graphing calculator to help understand translations of functions. Compare the graph of each function listed to the graph of $f(x) = \sqrt{x}$.

   a. $g(x) = \sqrt{x} - 4$ **b.** $h(x) = \sqrt{x + 2}$ **c.** $k(x) = \sqrt{x - 2} + 3$

a. Graph the functions $f(x) = \sqrt{x}$ and $g(x) = \sqrt{x} - 4$ on the same screen using the window shown in Figure 3-47(a). From these graphs, we can see that the graph of g is obtained by shifting the graph of f downward 4 units.

b. Graph the functions $f(x) = \sqrt{x}$ and $h(x) = \sqrt{x + 2}$ on the same screen using the window shown in Figure 3-47(b). From these graphs, we can see that the graph of h is obtained by shifting the graph of f to the left 2 units.

c. Graph the functions $f(x) = \sqrt{x}$ and $k(x) = \sqrt{x-2} + 3$ on the same screen using the window shown in Figure 3-47(c). From these graphs, we can see that the graph of k is obtained by shifting the graph of f right 2 units and upward 3 units.

Comment

To make the graph of $f(x) = \sqrt{x}$ appear bold, scroll to the left of Y₁ and press ENTER.

(a) Vertical shift downward 4 units. The graph of $f(x) = \sqrt{x}$ is the bold graph.

  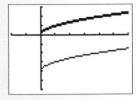

(b) Horizontal shift left 2 units. The graph of $f(x) = \sqrt{x}$ is the bold graph.

  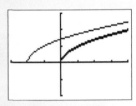

(c) Horizontal shift 2 units right and vertical shift 3 units upward. The graph of $f(x) = \sqrt{x}$ is the bold graph.

FIGURE 3-47

4. Use Reflections about the x- and y- Axes to Graph Functions

Figure 3-48(a) shows that the graph of $y = -\sqrt{x}$ is identical to the graph of $y = \sqrt{x}$ except that it is reflected about the x-axis. Figure 3-48(b) shows that the graph of $y = \sqrt{-x}$ is identical to the graph of $y = \sqrt{x}$ except that it is reflected about the y-axis.

$y = -\sqrt{x}$		
x	y	(x, y)
0	0	$(0, 0)$
1	-1	$(1, -1)$
4	-2	$(4, -2)$

(a)

$y = \sqrt{-x}$		
x	y	(x, y)
0	0	$(0, 0)$
-1	1	$(-1, 1)$
-4	2	$(-4, 2)$

(b)

FIGURE 3-48

In general, we can make the following observations.

Reflections   If f is a function, then

- The graph of $y = -f(x)$ is identical to the graph of $f(x)$ except that it is reflected about the x-axis.

- The graph of $y = f(-x)$ is identical to the graph of $f(x)$ except that it is reflected about the y-axis.

EXAMPLE 4   **Using Reflections to Graph Functions**

Graph each function: **a.** $g(x) = -|x + 1|$ **b.** $h(x) = |-x + 1|$

SOLUTION   By inspection, we see that the function given in part **a** involves a reflection about the x-axis and the function given in part **b** involves a reflection about the y-axis. We will use reflections to draw the graph of each function.

a. The graph of $g(x) = -|x + 1|$ is identical to the graph of $f(x) = |x + 1|$, except that it is reflected about the x-axis. This is because $g(x) = -f(x)$. The graphs of both functions are shown in Figure 3-49(a).

b. The graph of $h(x) = |-x + 1|$ is identical to the graph of $f(x) = |x + 1|$, except that it is reflected about the y-axis. This is because $f(-x) = h(x)$. The graphs of both functions are shown in Figure 3-49(b).

Comment

It is often helpful to think of a reflection as a mirror image of the graph about the x- or y-axis.

(a)

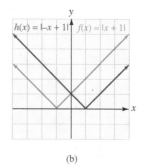

(b)

FIGURE 3-49

Self Check 4   *Fill in the blanks:* The graph of $g(x) = -\sqrt[3]{x}$ is identical to the graph of $f(x) = \sqrt[3]{x}$, except that it is reflected about the _____ axis. The graph of $h(x) = \sqrt{-x} - 4$ is identical to the graph of $f(x) = \sqrt{x} - 4$, except that it is reflected about the _____ axis.

Now Try Exercise 51.

5. Use Vertical Stretching and Shrinking to Graph Functions

Figure 3-50 shows the graphs of $y = x^2$, $y = 3x^2$, and $y = \frac{1}{3}x^2$.

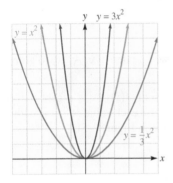

$y = x^2$		
x	y	(x, y)
-2	4	$(-2, 4)$
-1	1	$(-1, 1)$
0	0	$(0, 0)$
1	1	$(1, 1)$
2	4	$(2, 4)$

$y = 3x^2$		
x	y	(x, y)
-2	12	$(-2, 12)$
-1	3	$(-1, 3)$
0	0	$(0, 0)$
1	3	$(1, 3)$
2	12	$(2, 12)$

$y = \dfrac{1}{3}x^2$		
x	y	(x, y)
-2	$\dfrac{4}{3}$	$\left(-2, \dfrac{4}{3}\right)$
-1	$\dfrac{1}{3}$	$\left(-1, \dfrac{1}{3}\right)$
0	0	$(0, 0)$
1	$\dfrac{1}{3}$	$\left(1, \dfrac{1}{3}\right)$
2	$\dfrac{4}{3}$	$\left(2, \dfrac{4}{3}\right)$

FIGURE 3-50

Because each value of $y = 3x^2$ is 3 times greater than the corresponding value of $y = x^2$, its graph is stretched vertically by a factor of 3. Because each value of $y = \frac{1}{3}x^2$ is 3 times smaller than the corresponding value of $y = x^2$, its graph shrinks vertically by a factor of $\frac{1}{3}$.

In general, we can make the following observations.

Vertical Stretching and Shrinking   If f is a function and $k > 1$, then

- The graph of $y = kf(x)$ can be obtained by stretching the graph of $y = f(x)$ vertically by multiplying each value of $f(x)$ by k.

If f is a function and $0 < k < 1$, then

- The graph of $y = kf(x)$ can be obtained by shrinking the graph of $y = f(x)$ vertically by multiplying each value of $f(x)$ by k.

EXAMPLE 5   Graphing a Function by Vertical Stretching or Shrinking

Graph each function: **a.** $g(x) = 2|x|$ **b.** $h(x) = \dfrac{1}{2}|x|$

SOLUTION   We will vertically stretch or vertically shrink the basic function $f(x) = |x|$ to graph each of the given functions.

a. The graph of $g(x) = 2|x|$ is identical to the graph of $f(x) = |x|$ except that it is vertically stretched by a factor of 2. This is because each value of $|x|$ is multiplied by 2. The graphs of both functions are shown in Figure 3-51.

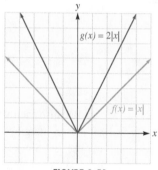

FIGURE 3-51

b. The graph of $g(x) = \frac{1}{2}|x|$ is identical to the graph of $f(x) = |x|$ except that it is vertically shrunk by a factor of $\frac{1}{2}$. This is because each value of $|x|$ is multiplied by $\frac{1}{2}$. The graphs of both functions are shown in Figure 3-52.

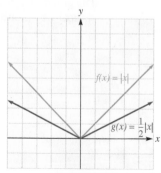

FIGURE 3-52

Comment

Note that vertically stretching the graph of a function narrows the graph of the function. Vertically shrinking the graph of a function widens the graph.

Self Check 5   *Fill in the blanks:* The graph of $g(x) = 5x^3$ is identical to the graph of $f(x) = x^3$, except that it is vertically _____ by a factor of ___. The graph of $h(x) = \frac{1}{5}x^3$ is identical to the graph $f(x) = x^3$, except that it is vertically _____ by a factor of ___.

Now Try Exercise 57.

6. Use Horizontal Stretching and Shrinking to Graph Functions

Functions can also be graphed by using horizontal stretchings and shrinkings.

Horizontal Stretching and Shrinking   If f is a function and $k > 1$, then

• The graph of $y = f(kx)$ can be obtained by shrinking the graph of $y = f(x)$ horizontally by multiplying each x-value of $f(x)$ by $\frac{1}{k}$.

If f is a function and $0 < k < 1$, then

• The graph of $y = f(kx)$ can be obtained by stretching the graph of $y = f(x)$ horizontally by multiplying each x-value of $f(x)$ by $\frac{1}{k}$.

Because we multiply each x-value of $f(x)$ by k to obtain the graph of $y = f(kx)$, the graphs are horizontally stretched or shrunk by a factor of $\frac{1}{k}$.

EXAMPLE 6   **Graphing a Function by Horizontally Shrinking or Stretching**

Graph $y = (3x)^2 - 1$ using the graph of the function $y = x^2 - 1$.

SOLUTION   Since $3 > 1$, the graph of $y = (3x)^2 - 1$ can be obtained by shrinking the graph of $y = x^2 - 1$ horizontally by multiplying each x-coordinate of $y = x^2 - 1$ by $\frac{1}{3}$.

First, we complete the table of solutions for $y = x^2 - 1$, shown in Figure 3-53. Next, we multiply each x-value in the table by $\frac{1}{3}$ to obtain the table of solutions for $y = (3x)^2 - 1$, also shown in Figure 3-53.

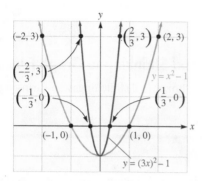

$y = x^2 - 1$		
x	y	(x, y)
-2	3	$(-2, 3)$
-1	0	$(-1, 0)$
0	-1	$(0, -1)$
1	0	$(1, 0)$
2	3	$(2, 3)$

$y = (3x)^2 - 1$		
x	y	(x, y)
$-\dfrac{2}{3}$	3	$\left(-\dfrac{2}{3}, 3\right)$
$-\dfrac{1}{3}$	0	$\left(-\dfrac{1}{3}, 0\right)$
0	-1	$(0, -1)$
$\dfrac{1}{3}$	0	$\left(\dfrac{1}{3}, 0\right)$
$\dfrac{2}{3}$	3	$\left(\dfrac{2}{3}, 3\right)$

FIGURE 3-53

We now draw each graph as shown in Figure 3-53.

Self Check 6   *Fill in the blank:* The graph of $g(x) = \left(\frac{1}{3}x\right)^2 - 1$ is identical to the graph of $f(x) = x^2 - 1$, except that it is horizontally _____ by a factor of __.

Now Try Exercise 63.

We can summarize the ideas in this section as follows.

Summary of Transformations   If f is a function and k represents a positive number, then

The graph of	***can be obtained by graphing*** $y = f(x)$ ***and***
$y = f(x) + k$	translating the graph k units upward.
$y = f(x) - k$	translating the graph k units downward.
$y = f(x + k)$	translating the graph k units to the left.
$y = f(x - k)$	translating the graph k units to the right.
$y = -f(x)$	reflecting the graph about the x-axis.
$y = f(-x)$	reflecting the graph about the y-axis.
$y = kf(x)$ $k > 1$	stretching the graph vertically by multiplying each value of $f(x)$ by k.
$y = kf(x)$ $0 < k < 1$	shrinking the graph vertically by multiplying each value $f(x)$ by k.
$y = f(kx)$ $k > 1$	shrinking the graph horizontally by multiplying each x-value of $f(x)$ by $\frac{1}{k}$.
$y = f(kx)$ $0 < k < 1$	stretching the graph horizontally by multiplying each x-value of $f(x)$ by $\frac{1}{k}$.

EXAMPLE 7   Applying Transformations of Graphs

Figure 3-54 shows the graph of $y = f(x)$. Use this graph and a translation to sketch the graph of **a.** $y = f(x) + 2$ **b.** $y = f(x - 2)$ **c.** $y = 2f(x)$

FIGURE 3-54

SOLUTION   We will use the summary of transformations in the section given earlier to graph each function.

a. The graph of $y = f(x) + 2$ is identical to the graph of $y = f(x)$, except that it is translated 2 units upward. See Figure 3-55(a).

b. The graph of $y = f(x - 2)$ is identical to the graph of $y = f(x)$, except that it is translated 2 units to the right. See Figure 3-55(b).

c. The graph of $y = 2f(x)$ is identical to the graph of $y = f(x)$, except that it is stretched vertically by multiplying each y-value of $f(x)$ by 2. See Figure 3-55(c).

(a)   (b)   (c)

FIGURE 3-55

Self Check 7   Use Figure 3-50 and a reflection to sketch the graph of **a.** $y = -f(x)$
b. $y = f(-x)$

Now Try Exercise 79.

7. Graph Functions Using a Combination of Transformations

To graph functions involving a combination of transformations, we must apply each translation or stretching to the function.

Strategy for Graphing Using a Sequence of Transformations   To graph a function using a combination of transformations, perform the transformations in the following order:

1. horizontal translation
2. stretching or shrinking
3. reflection
4. vertical translation

EXAMPLE 8   **Graphing a Function by Using a Combination of Transformations**

Use the function $f(x) = |x|$ to graph $g(x) = 3|x - 2| + 4$.

SOLUTION   We will graph $g(x) = 3|x - 2| + 4$ by applying three transformations to the basic function $f(x) = |x|$:

Step 1: Translate $f(x) = |x|$ horizontally 2 units to the right.

Step 2: Vertically stretch the graph by a factor of 3.

Step 3: Translate the graph vertically 4 units upward.

Step 1: Translate $f(x) = |x|$ horizontally 2 units to the right to obtain the graph of $y = |x - 2|$.

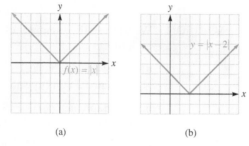

(a)   (b)

FIGURE 3-56

Step 2: Vertically stretch the graph of $y = |x - 2|$ by a factor of 3 to obtain the graph of $y = 3|x - 2|$.

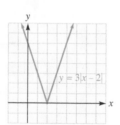

FIGURE 3-57

Step 3: Translate the graph of $y = 3|x - 2|$ vertically 4 units upward to obtain the graph of $g(x) = 3|x - 2| + 4$.

FIGURE 3-58

Self Check 8   Use the graph of the function $f(x) = x^3$ to graph $g(x) = \frac{1}{3}(x + 1)^3 - 2$.

Now Try Exercise 69.

Self Check Answers   **1.** 3, upward; 4, downward   **2.** 3, right; 2, left   **3.** 4, right; 5, upward

4. x; y **5.** stretched, 5; shrunk, $\dfrac{1}{5}$ **6.** stretched, 3

7. a.   **b.**   **8.**

Exercises **3.4**

Getting Ready

You should be able to complete these vocabulary and concept statements before you proceed to the practice exercises.

Fill in the blanks.

1. The graph of $y = f(x) + 5$ is identical to the graph of $y = f(x)$ except that it is translated 5 units _____.

2. The graph of _____ is identical to the graph of $y = f(x)$ except that it is translated 7 units downward.

3. The graph of $y = f(x - 3)$ is identical to the graph of $y = f(x)$ except that it is translated 3 units _____.

4. The graph of $y = f(x + 2)$ is identical to the graph of $y = f(x)$ except that it is translated 2 units _____.

5. To draw the graph of $y = (x + 2)^2 - 3$, translate the graph of $y = x^2$ ___ units to the left and 3 units _____.

6. To draw the graph of $y = (x - 3)^3 + 1$, translate the graph of $y = x^3$ 3 units to the ____ and 1 unit _____.

7. The graph of $y = f(-x)$ is a reflection of the graph of $y = f(x)$ about the ____.

8. The graph of _____ is a reflection of the graph of $y = f(x)$ about the x-axis.

9. The graph of $y = f(4x)$ shrinks the graph of $y = f(x)$ _____ by multiplying each x-value of $f(x)$ by $\frac{1}{4}$.

10. The graph of $y = 8f(x)$ stretches the graph of $y = f(x)$ _____ by a factor of 8.

Practice

The graph of each function is a translation of the graph of $f(x) = x^2$. Graph each function.

11. $g(x) = x^2 - 2$ **12.** $g(x) = (x - 2)^2$

13. $g(x) = (x + 3)^2$ **14.** $g(x) = x^2 + 3$

15. $h(x) = (x + 1)^2 + 2$ **16.** $h(x) = (x - 3)^2 - 1$

17. $h(x) = \left(x + \dfrac{1}{2}\right)^2 - \dfrac{1}{2}$

18. $h(x) = \left(x - \dfrac{3}{2}\right)^2 + \dfrac{5}{2}$

The graph of each function is a translation of the graph of $f(x) = x^3$. Graph each function.

19. $g(x) = x^3 + 1$

20. $g(x) = x^3 - 3$

21. $g(x) = (x - 2)^3$

22. $g(x) = (x + 3)^3$

23. $h(x) = (x - 2)^3 - 3$

24. $h(x) = (x + 1)^3 + 4$

25. $y + 2 = x^3$

26. $y - 7 = (x - 5)^3$

The graph of each function is a translation of the graph of $f(x) = |x|$. Graph each function.

27. $g(x) = |x| + 2$

28. $g(x) = |x| - 2$

29. $g(x) = |x - 5|$

30. $g(x) = |x + 4|$

31. $f(x) = |x + 2| - 1$

32. $h(x) = |x - 3| + 3$

The graph of each function is a translation of the graph of $f(x) = \sqrt{x}$. Graph each function.

33. $g(x) = \sqrt{x} + 1$

34. $g(x) = \sqrt{x} - 3$

35. $g(x) = \sqrt{x + 2}$

36. $g(x) = \sqrt{x - 4}$

37. $h(x) = \sqrt{x - 2} - 1$

38. $h(x) = \sqrt{x + 2} + 3$

47. $h(x) = -x^3$

48. $f(x) = -|x|$

The graph of each function is a translation of the graph of $f(x) = \sqrt[3]{x}.$ *Graph each function.*

39. $g(x) = \sqrt[3]{x} - 4$

40. $g(x) = \sqrt[3]{x} + 3$

49. $f(x) = -\sqrt{x}$

50. $g(x) = \sqrt[3]{-x}$

41. $g(x) = \sqrt[3]{x - 2}$

42. $g(x) = \sqrt[3]{x + 5}$

51. $f(x) = |-x|$

52. $g(x) = (-x)^2$

The graph of each function is a vertical stretching or shrinking of the graph of $y = x^2,$ $y = x^3,$ *or* $y = |x|.$ *Graph each function.*

53. $f(x) = 2x^2$

54. $g(x) = \frac{1}{2}x^2$

43. $h(x) = \sqrt[3]{x + 1} - 1$

44. $h(x) = \sqrt[3]{x - 1} - 1$

55. $h(x) = -3x^2$

56. $f(x) = -\frac{1}{3}x^2$

The graph of each function is a reflection of the graph of $y = x^2,$ $y = x^3,$ $y = |x|,$ $y = \sqrt{x},$ *or* $y = \sqrt[3]{x}.$ *Graph each function.*

45. $f(x) = -x^2$

46. $g(x) = (-x)^3$

57. $f(x) = \frac{1}{2}x^3$

58. $g(x) = 2x^3$

59. $h(x) = -3|x|$

60. $f(x) = \frac{1}{3}|x|$

The graph of each function is a horizontal stretching or shrinking of the graph of y = x² or y = x³. Graph each function.

61. $f(x) = \left(\frac{1}{2}x\right)^3$

62. $f(x) = (2x)^3$

63. $f(x) = (2x)^2$

64. $f(x) = (-2x)^3$

Graph each function using a combination of transformations applied to the graph of a basic function.

65. $g(x) = 3(x + 2)^2 - 1$

66. $g(x) = -\frac{1}{3}(x + 1)^2 + 1$

67. $h(x) = -2|x| + 3$

68. $f(x) = -2|x + 3|$

69. $f(x) = 2|x - 2| + 1$

70. $f(x) = -3|x + 5| - 2$

71. $f(x) = 2\sqrt{x} + 3$
    $(x \geq 0)$

72. $g(x) = 2\sqrt{x + 3}$
    $(x \geq -3)$

73. $h(x) = 2\sqrt{x - 2} + 1$
    $(x \geq 2)$

74. $h(x) = \frac{1}{2}\sqrt{x + 5} - 2$
    $(x \geq -5)$

75. $g(x) = -2(x + 2)^3 - 1$

76. $g(x) = \frac{1}{3}(x + 1)^3 - 1$

77. $f(x) = 2\sqrt[3]{x} + 4$

78. $f(x) = -2\sqrt[3]{x} + 1$

85. $y = 2f(-x)$

86. $y = f(x + 1) - 2$

Use the following graph and a translation, stretching, or reflection to sketch the graph of each function.

79. $y = f(x) + 1$

80. $y = f(x + 1)$

81. $y = 2f(x)$

82. $y = f\left(\dfrac{x}{2}\right)$

83. $y = f(x - 2) + 1$

84. $y = -f(x)$

Discovery and Writing

Use a graphing calculator to perform each experiment. Write a brief paragraph describing your findings.

87. Investigate the translations of the graph of a function by graphing the parabola $y = (x - k)^2 + k$ for several values of k. What do you observe about successive positions of the vertex?

88. Investigate the translations of the graph of a function by graphing the parabola $y = (x - k)^2 + k^2$ for several values of k. What do you observe about successive positions of the vertex?

89. Investigate the horizontal stretching of the graph of a function by graphing $y = \sqrt{ax}$ for several values of a. What do you observe?

90. Investigate the vertical stretching of the graph of a function by graphing $y = b\sqrt{x}$ for several values of b. What do you observe? Are these graphs different from the graphs in Exercise 89?

Write a paragraph using your own words.

91. Explain why the effect of vertically stretching a graph by a factor of -1 is to reflect the graph about the x-axis.

92. Explain why the effect of horizontally stretching a graph by a factor of -1 is to reflect the graph about the y-axis.

Review

Simplify each function.

93. $\dfrac{x^2 + x - 6}{x^2 + 5x + 6}$

94. $\dfrac{2x^2 + 3x}{2x^2 + x - 3}$

Find the domain of each function. Use interval notation to write each answer.

95. $f(x) = \dfrac{x + 7}{x - 3}$

96. $f(x) = \dfrac{x^2 + 1}{x^2 + 3x + 2}$

Perform each division and write the answer in quotient $+ \frac{\text{remainder}}{\text{divider}}$ form.

97. $\dfrac{x^2 + 3x}{x + 1}$

98. $\dfrac{x^2 + 3}{x + 1}$

Exponential and Logarithmic Functions

4

CAREERS AND MATHEMATICS: Epidemiologists

Kiselev Andrey Valerevich/Shutterstock.com

Epidemiologists investigate and describe the determinants and distribution of disease, disability, and other health outcomes. They also develop means for prevention and control. *Applied epidemiologists* typically work for state health agencies and are responsible for responding to disease outbreaks and determining the cause and method of containment. *Research epidemiologists* work in laboratories studying ways to prevent future outbreaks. This career can be quite rewarding, both mentally and financially. Epidemiologists spend a lot of time saving lives and finding solutions for better health.

Education and Mathematics Required
- Applied epidemiologists are generally required to have a master's degree from a school of public health. Research epidemiologists may need a Ph.D. or medical degree, depending on their area of work.
- College Algebra, Trigonometry, Calculus, Applied Data Analysis, Survey and Research Methods, Mathematical Statistics, and Biostatistics are required math courses.

How Epidemiologists Use Math and Who Employs Them
- Epidemiologists use mathematical models when they are tracking the progress of an infectious disease. The SIR model consists of three variables: S (for susceptible), I (for infectious), and R (for recovered). It is used for infectious diseases such as measles, mumps, and rubella.
- Government agencies employ 57%; hospitals employ 12%; colleges and universities employ 11%, and 9% are employed in areas of scientific research and developmental services like the American Cancer Society.

Career Outlook and Earnings
- Employment growth is projected to be 15% over the 2008–2018 decade, which is faster than average. This is due to an increased threat of bioterrorism and rare but infectious diseases, such as West Nile Virus or Avian flu.
- The median annual income is $61,700, with the top 10% of salaries at $92,610.

For more information see: www.bls.gov/oco

In this chapter, we will discuss exponential functions, which are often used in banking, ecology, and science. We will also discuss logarithmic functions, which are applied in chemistry, geology, and environmental science.

4.1   Exponential Functions and Their Graphs

In this section, we will learn to

1. Approximate and simplify exponential expressions.
2. Graph exponential functions.
3. Solve compound interest problems.
4. Define e and graph base-e exponential functions.
5. Use transformations to graph exponential functions.

Extreme water slides, called "plunge" or "plummet" slides, are fearsome water slides because of their heights. With near vertical drops, the slides are designed to allow riders to reach the greatest possible speeds. Summit Plummet at Blizzard Beach, a part of Walt Disney World Resort in Florida, stands 120 ft tall. On this slide, riders can achieve speeds up to 55 mph.

The shapes of extreme water slides can be modeled using *exponential functions*, the topic of this section.

Exponential functions are also important in business. Consider the graph shown in Figure 4-1. It shows the balance in a bank account in which $5,000 was invested in 1990 at 8%, compounded monthly. The graph shows that in the year 2015, the value of the account will be approximately $38,000, and in the year 2030, the value will be approximately $121,000.

The curve in Figure 4-1 is the graph of an exponential function. From the graph, we can see that the longer the money is kept on deposit, the more rapidly it will grow.

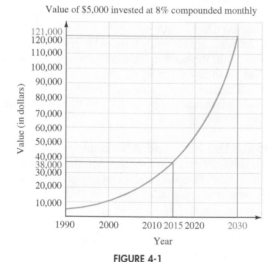

Value of $5,000 invested at 8% compounded monthly

FIGURE 4-1

Before we can discuss exponential functions, we must define irrational exponents.

1. Approximate and Simplify Exponential Expressions

We have discussed expressions of the form b^x, where x is a rational number.

- 5^2 means "the square of 5."
- $4^{1/3}$ means "the cube root of 4."
- $6^{-2/5} = \frac{1}{6^{2/5}}$ means "the reciprocal of the fifth root of 6^2."

To understand exponential functions and their graphs requires that we give meaning to b^x when x is an irrational number. Consider the expression

$3^{\sqrt{2}}$ where $\sqrt{2}$ is the irrational number 1.414213562 ...

We can use closer and closer approximations as shown below. Since $\sqrt{2}$ is an irrational number, we will use a calculator to find the approximations.

$3^{\sqrt{2}} \approx 3^{1.4} \approx 4.655536722$

$3^{\sqrt{2}} \approx 3^{1.41} \approx 4.706965002$

$3^{\sqrt{2}} \approx 3^{1.414} \approx 4.727695035$

$3^{\sqrt{2}} \approx 3^{1.4142} \approx 4.72873393$

Since the exponents of the expressions in the list are getting closer to $\sqrt{2}$, the values of the expressions are getting closer to the value of $3^{\sqrt{2}}$.

On a scientific calculator, there is an exponential key, usually y^x. On a graphing calculator, we can use the ⌃ key.

EXAMPLE 1 **Approximating Exponential Expressions**

Approximate each expression correct to 4 decimals.

a. $4^{2/3}$ **b.** $5^{-\sqrt{3}}$ **c.** $\left(\dfrac{4}{7}\right)^{\pi}$

SOLUTION We will use a calculator.

a. $4^{\wedge}(2/3) \approx 2.5198$ Enter 2/3 in parentheses.

b. $5^{\wedge}\left(-\sqrt{3}\right) \approx 0.0616$ Enter $-\sqrt{3}$ in parentheses.

c. $(4/7)^{\wedge}\pi \approx 0.1724$ Enter the base, 4/7, in parentheses.

Figure 4-2 shows the graphing calculator screen that was used to find the values.

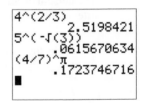

FIGURE 4-2

Self Check 1 Approximate each expression correct to 4 decimals.

a. $5^{3/5}$ **b.** $-3^{\sqrt{6}}$ **c.** $7^{-2.356}$

Now Try Exercise 15.

If b is a positive number and x is a real number, the expression b^x always represents a positive number. It is also true that the familiar properties of exponents hold for irrational exponents.

EXAMPLE 2 **Simplifying Expressions with Irrational Exponents**

Simplify each expression:

a. $\left(3^{\sqrt{2}}\right)^{\sqrt{2}}$

b. $a^{\sqrt{8}} \cdot a^{\sqrt{2}}$

SOLUTION   We will use properties of exponents to simplify each expression.

a. $\left(3^{\sqrt{2}}\right)^{\sqrt{2}} = 3^{\sqrt{2}\sqrt{2}}$ Keep the base and multiply the exponents.

$\qquad\qquad\quad = 3^2$ $\sqrt{2}\sqrt{2} = \sqrt{4} = 2$

$\qquad\qquad\quad = 9$

b. $a^{\sqrt{8}} \cdot a^{\sqrt{2}} = a^{\sqrt{8}+\sqrt{2}}$ Keep the base and add the exponents.

$\qquad\qquad\quad = a^{2\sqrt{2}+\sqrt{2}}$ $\sqrt{8} = \sqrt{4}\sqrt{2} = 2\sqrt{2}$

$\qquad\qquad\quad = a^{3\sqrt{2}}$ $2\sqrt{2} + \sqrt{2} = 3\sqrt{2}$

Self Check 2   Simplify: **a.** $\left(2^{\sqrt{3}}\right)^{\sqrt{12}}$ **b.** $x^{\sqrt{20}} \cdot x^{\sqrt{5}}$

Now Try Exercise 19.

2. Graph Exponential Functions

If $b > 0$ and $b \neq 1$, the function $y = b^x$ defines a function, because for each input x, there is exactly one output y. Since x can be any real number, the domain of the function is the set of real numbers. Since the base b of the expression b^x is positive, y is always positive, and the range is the set of positive numbers. Since b^x is an exponential expression, the function is called an **exponential function.**

We make the restriction that $b > 0$ to exclude any imaginary numbers that might result from taking even roots of negative numbers. The restriction that $b \neq 1$ excludes the constant function $f(x) = 1^x$, in which $f(x) = 1$ for every real number x.

Exponential Functions ·   An **exponential function with base b** is defined by the equation

$$f(x) = b^x \quad \text{or} \quad y = b^x \qquad (b > 0, b \neq 1, \text{ and } x \text{ is a real number})$$

The **domain of any exponential function** is the interval $(-\infty, \infty)$. The **range** is the interval $(0, \infty)$.

Since the domain and range of $f(x) = b^x$ are sets of real numbers, we can graph exponential functions. For example, to graph

$$f(x) = 2^x$$

we find several points $(x, f(x))$ whose coordinates satisfy the equation, plot the points, and join them with a smooth curve, as in Figure 4-3(a). To graph the function

$$f(x) = \left(\frac{1}{2}\right)^x$$

we find several points $(x, f(x))$ whose coordinates satisfy the equation, plot the points, and join them with a smooth curve, as shown in Figure 4-3(b) on the next page.

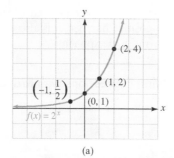

	$f(x) = 2^x$	
x	$f(x)$	$(x, f(x))$
-1	$\dfrac{1}{2}$	$\left(-1, \dfrac{1}{2}\right)$
0	1	$(0, 1)$
1	2	$(1, 2)$
2	4	$(2, 4)$

(a)

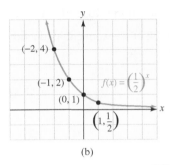

FIGURE 4-3

By looking at the graphs in Figure 4-3, we can see that the domain of each function is the interval $(-\infty, \infty)$ and that the range is the interval $(0, \infty)$.

EXAMPLE 3 **Graphing an Exponential Function**

Graph: $f(x) = 4^x$.

SOLUTION We will find several points (x, y) that satisfy the equation, plot the points, and join them with a smooth curve, as in Figure 4-4.

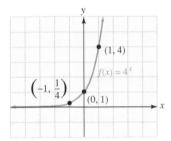

FIGURE 4-4

Self Check 3 Graph: $f(x) = \left(\dfrac{1}{4}\right)^x$.

Now Try Exercise 29.

The graph of $f(x) = 4^x$ in Example 3 has the following properties:

1. It passes through the point $(0, 1)$.
2. It passes through the point $(1, 4)$.
3. It approaches the x-axis. The x-axis is a horizontal asymptote.
4. The domain is the interval $(-\infty, \infty)$, and the range is the interval $(0, \infty)$.

This example illustrates the following properties of exponential functions.

Properties of Exponential Functions

- The **domain of the exponential function** $f(x) = b^x$ is $(-\infty, \infty)$, the set of real numbers.

- The **range** is $(0, \infty)$, the set of positive real numbers.

- The graph has a y-intercept at $(0, 1)$.

- The x-axis is a horizontal asymptote of the graph.

- The graph of $f(x) = b^x$ passes through the point $(1, b)$.

<hr />

EXAMPLE 4   **Determining the Base of an Exponential Function**

The graph of an exponential function of the form $f(x) = b^x$ is shown in Figure 4-5. Find the value of b.

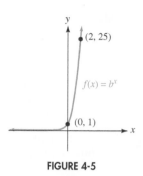

FIGURE 4-5

SOLUTION   We note that the graph passes through the point $(0, 1)$, a property of exponential functions of this form. Since the graph also passes through the point $(2, 25)$, we can find the base b by substituting 2 for x and 25 for $f(2)$ in the equation $f(x) = b^x$ and solving for b.

$$f(x) = b^x$$

$$f(2) = b^2$$

$$25 = b^2$$

$$5 = b \qquad b \text{ must be positive.}$$

The base b is 5. Note that the points $(0, 1)$ and $(2, 25)$ satisfy the equation $f(x) = 5^x$.

<hr />

Self Check 4   Can a graph passing through $(0, 2)$ and $\left(1, \dfrac{3}{2}\right)$ be the graph of $f(x) = b^x$?

Now Try Exercise 45.

In Figure 4-3(a) (where $b = 2$ and $2 > 1$), the values of y increase as the values of x increase. Since the graph rises as we move to the right, the function is an increasing function. Such a function is said to model *exponential growth*.

In Figure 4-3(b) where $\left(b = \dfrac{1}{2} \text{ and } 0 < \dfrac{1}{2} < 1\right)$, the values of y decrease as the values of x increase. Since the graph drops as we move to the right, the function is a decreasing function. Such a function is said to model *exponential decay*. Two additional properties are stated here.

Additional Properties of Exponential Functions   If $b > 1$, then $f(x) = b^x$ is an **increasing function.** This function models **exponential growth.**

Increasing function

If $0 < b < 1$, then $f(x) = b^x$ is a **decreasing function.** This function models **exponential decay.**

$f(x) = b^x$
$0 < b < 1$

$(0, 1)$ $(1, b)$

Decreasing function

Comment   Recall that $b^{-x} = \frac{1}{b^x} = \left(\frac{1}{b}\right)^x$. If $b > 1$, any function of the form $f(x) = b^{-x}$ models exponential decay, because $0 < \frac{1}{b} < 1$.

An exponential function $f(x) = b^x$ is either increasing (for $b > 1$) or decreasing (for $0 < b < 1$). Because different real numbers x always determine different values of b^x, an exponential function is one-to-one.

One-to-One Property of Exponential Functions   An exponential function defined by $f(x) = b^x$ or $y = b^x$, where $b > 0$ and $b \neq 1$, is one-to-one. This implies that

1. If $b^r = b^s$, then $r = s$.
2. If $r \neq s$, then $b^r \neq b^s$.

ACCENT ON TECHNOLOGY   **Graphing Exponential Functions**

When using a graphing calculator to draw the graphs of exponential functions, use care entering the function. Proper use of parentheses is critical to obtaining the correct graph. Since we know the shape of an exponential function, it is usually easy to find a good window for the graph. For any function in the form $f(x) = b^x$, where $b > 1$, the graph will be steeper as the base increases. The opposite is true if the base is between 0 and 1. Several graphs are shown below along with a window that works well with these basic functions.

FIGURE 4-6

3. Solve Compound Interest Problems

Banks pay **interest** for using their customers' money. Interest is calculated as a percent of the amount on deposit in an account and is paid annually (once a year), quarterly (four times per year), monthly, or daily. Interest left on deposit in a bank account will also earn interest. Such accounts are said to earn **compound interest.**

Compound Interest Formula   If P dollars are deposited in an account earning interest at an annual rate r, compounded n times each year, the amount A in the account after t years is given by

$$A = P\left(1 + \frac{r}{n}\right)^{nt}$$

EXAMPLE 5   **Solving a Compound Interest Problem**

The parents of a newborn child invest $8,000 in a plan that earns 9% interest, compounded quarterly. If the money is left untouched, how much will the child have in the account in 55 years?

SOLUTION   We will substitute 8,000 for P, 0.09 for r, and 55 for t in the formula for compound interest. Because quarterly compounding means four times per year, we will substitute 4 for n.

$$A = P\left(1 + \frac{r}{n}\right)^{nt}$$

$$A = 8,000\left(1 + \frac{0.09}{4}\right)^{4 \cdot 55}$$

$$= 8,000(1.0225)^{220}$$

$$\approx 1,069,103.266 \qquad \text{Use a calculator.}$$

In 55 years, the account will be worth $1,069,103.27.

Self Check 5   Would $20,000 invested at 7% interest, compounded monthly, have provided more income at age 55?

Now Try Exercise 81.

In financial calculations, the initial amount deposited is often called the **present value,** denoted by PV. The amount to which the account will grow is called the **future value,** denoted by FV. The interest rate for each compounding period is called the **periodic interest rate,** i, and the number of times interest is compounded is the **number of compounding periods,** n. Using these definitions, an alternate formula for compound interest is as follows.

$$FV = PV(1 + i)^n$$

To use this formula to solve Example 5, we proceed as follows:

$$FV = PV(1 + i)^n$$

$$FV = 8,000(1 + 0.0225)^{220} \qquad i = \frac{0.09}{4} = 0.0225 \text{ and } n = 4(55) = 220.$$

$$= 8,000(1.0225)^{220}$$

$$\approx 1,069,103.266 \qquad \text{Use a calculator.}$$

4. Define e and Graph Base-e Exponential Functions

In mathematical models of natural events, the number

$$e = 2.71828182845904 \ldots$$

often appears as the base of an exponential function. We can introduce this number by considering the compound interest formula

$$A = P\left(1 + \frac{r}{n}\right)^{nt}$$ A is the amount, P is the initial deposit, r is the annual rate, n is the number of compoundings per year, and t is the time in years.

and allowing n to become very large. To see what happens, we let $n = rx$, where x is another variable.

$$A = P\left(1 + \frac{r}{n}\right)^{nt}$$

$$A = P\left(1 + \frac{r}{rx}\right)^{rxt}$$ Substitute rx for n.

$$A = P\left(1 + \frac{1}{x}\right)^{rxt}$$ Simplify $\frac{r}{rx}$.

$$A = P\left[\left(1 + \frac{1}{x}\right)^{x}\right]^{rt}$$ Remember that $(a^m)^n = a^{mn}$.

Since all variables in this formula are positive, r is a constant rate, and $n = rx$, it follows that as n becomes large, so does x. What happens to the value of A as n becomes large will depend on the value of $\left(1 + \frac{1}{x}\right)^{x}$ as x becomes large. Some results calculated for increasing values of x appear in the table shown.

x	$\left(1 + \dfrac{1}{x}\right)^{x}$
1	2
10	2.5937425
100	2.7048138
1,000	2.7169239
1,000,000	2.7182805
1,000,000,000	2.7182818

From the table, we can see that as x increases, the value of $\left(1 + \frac{1}{x}\right)^{x}$ approaches the value of e, and the formula

$$A = P\left[\left(1 + \frac{1}{x}\right)^{x}\right]^{rt}$$

becomes

$$A = Pe^{rt}$$ Substitute e for $\left(1 + \frac{1}{x}\right)^{x}$.

When the amount invested grows exponentially according to the formula $A = Pe^{rt}$, we say that interest is **compounded continuously.**

Continuous Compound Interest Formula   If P dollars are deposited in an account earning interest at an annual rate r, compounded continuously, the amount A after t years is given by the formula

$$A = Pe^{rt}$$

EXAMPLE 6   **Solving a Continuous Compound Interest Problem**

If the parents of the newborn child in Example 5 had invested $8,000 at an annual rate of 9%, compounded continuously, how much would the child have in the account in 55 years?

SOLUTION   We will substitute $8,000 for P, 0.09 for r, and 55 for t in the continuous compound interest formula $A = Pe^{rt}$.

$$A = Pe^{rt}$$

$$A = 8,000e^{(0.09)(55)}$$

$$= 8,000e^{4.95}$$

$$\approx 1,129,399.711 \qquad \text{Use a calculator.}$$

In 55 years, the balance will be $1,129,399.71, which is $60,296.44 more than the amount earned with quarterly compounding.

Self Check 6   Find the balance in 60 years.

Now Try Exercise 89.

To graph the exponential function $f(x) = e^x$, we plot several points and join them with a smooth curve [as in Figure 4-7(a)] or use a graphing calculator [as in Figure 4-7(b)].

$f(x) = e^x$		
x	$f(x)$	$(x, f(x))$
-1	0.37	$(-1, 0.37)$
0	1	$(0, 1)$
1	2.72	$(1, 2.72)$
2	7.39	$(2, 7.39)$

(a)

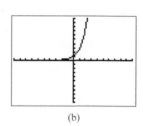

(b)

FIGURE 4-7

Comment   The graph of $f(x) = e^x$ is very important in mathematics and should be memorized.

5. Use Transformations to Graph Exponential Functions

In Section 3.4, translations, reflections, and stretchings were applied to functions. These may also be applied to the graphs of exponential functions. A summary of these transformations, when $k > 0$, is shown in the table.

Equation	Transformations of the Graph of $f(x) = b^x$
$y = b^x + k$	Translates the graph of $f(x) = b^x$ upward k units
$y = b^x - k$	Translates the graph of $f(x) = b^x$ downward k units
$y = b^{x-k}$	Translates the graph of $f(x) = b^x$ to the right k units
$y = b^{x+k}$	Translates the graph of $f(x) = b^x$ to the left k units
$y = -b^x$	Reflects the graph of $f(x) = b^x$ about the x-axis
$y = b^{-x}$	Reflects the graph of $f(x) = b^x$ about the y-axis
$y = kb^x$	• Vertically stretches the graph of $f(x) = b^x$ if $k > 1$ • Vertically shrinks the graph of $f(x) = b^x$ if $0 < k < 1$
$y = b^{kx}$	• Horizontally stretches the graph of $f(x) = b^x$ if $0 < k < 1$ • Horizontally shrinks the graph of $f(x) = b^x$ if $k > 1$

EXAMPLE 7   Using Translations to Graph an Exponential Function

On one set of axes, graph $f(x) = 2^x$ and $g(x) = 2^x + 3$.

SOLUTION   The graph of $g(x) = 2^x + 3$ is identical to the graph of $f(x) = 2^x$, except that it is translated 3 units upward. (See Figure 4-8.)

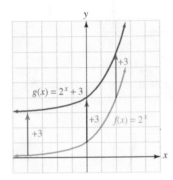

$f(x) = 2^x$		
x	$f(x)$	$(x, f(x))$
-4	$\dfrac{1}{16}$	$\left(-4, \dfrac{1}{16}\right)$
0	1	$(0, 1)$
2	4	$(2, 4)$

$g(x) = 2^x + 3$		
x	$g(x)$	$(x, g(x))$
-4	$3\dfrac{1}{16}$	$\left(-4, 3\dfrac{1}{16}\right)$
0	4	$(0, 4)$
2	7	$(2, 7)$

FIGURE 4-8

Self Check 7   On one set of axes, graph $f(x) = 2^x$ and $g(x) = 2^x - 2$.

Now Try Exercise 53.

EXAMPLE 8   Using Translations to Graph an Exponential Function with Base e

On one set of axes, graph $f(x) = e^x$ and $g(x) = e^{x-3}$.

SOLUTION   The graph of $g(x) = e^{x-3}$ is identical to the graph of $f(x) = e^x$, except that it is translated 3 units to the right. (See Figure 4-9.)

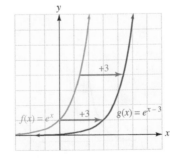

$f(x) = e^x$		
x	$f(x)$	$(x, f(x))$
-1	0.37	$(-1, 0.37)$
0	1	$(0, 1)$
1	2.72	$(1, 2.72)$
2	7.39	$(2, 7.39)$

$g(x) = e^{x-3}$		
x	$g(x)$	$(x, g(x))$
2	0.37	$(2, 0.37)$
3	1	$(3, 1)$
4	2.72	$(4, 2.72)$
5	7.39	$(5, 7.39)$

FIGURE 4-9

Self Check 8   On one set of axes, graph $f(x) = e^x$ and $g(x) = e^{x+2}$.

Now Try Exercise 61.

We can use a graphing calculator to graph exponential functions that are vertically or horizontally stretched or shrunk.

ACCENT ON TECHNOLOGY   **Graphing Exponential Functions**

Some exponential functions are very difficult to graph by hand. A graphing calculator can be used.

- To graph the exponential function $f(x) = 2(3^{x/2})$, we enter the right side of the equation after $Y_1 =$. The display will show the equation $Y_1 = 2(3^{\wedge}(X/2))$. If we use [WINDOW] settings of $[-10, 10]$ for x and $[-2, 18]$ for y and press [GRAPH], we will obtain the graph shown in Figure 4-10.

FIGURE 4-10

- To graph the exponential function $f(x) = 3e^{-x/2}$, we enter the right side of the equation $Y_1 =$. The display will show the equation $Y_1 = 3e^{\wedge}(-x/2)$. If we use [WINDOW] settings of $[-10, 10]$ for x and $[-2, 18]$ for y and press [GRAPH], we will obtain the graph shown in Figure 4-11.

FIGURE 4-11

Self Check Answers   **1. a.** 2.6265   **b.** -14.7470 **c.** 0.0102   **2. a.** 64   **b.** $x^{3\sqrt{5}}$
3.   **4.** no   **5.** no   **6.** $1,771,251.33

7.   **8.**

Exercises **4.1**

Getting Ready

You should be able to complete these vocabulary and concept statements before you proceed to the practice exercises.

Fill in the blanks.

1. If $b > 0$ and $b \neq 1$, $y = b^x$ represents an
   _____ function.

2. If $f(x) = b^x$ represents an increasing function, then
   $b > \underline{\ }$.

3. In interval notation, the domain of the exponential
   function $f(x) = b^x$ is _____.

4. The number b is called the _____ of the exponential
   function $y = b^x$.

5. The range of the exponential function $f(x) = b^x$ is
   _____.

6. The graphs of all exponential functions $y = b^x$ have
   the same ___-intercept, the point _____.

7. If $b > 0$ and $b \neq 1$, the graph of $y = b^x$ approaches
   the x-axis, which is called a horizontal _____ of
   the curve.

8. If $f(x) = b^x$ represents a decreasing function, then
   $\underline{\ } < b < \underline{\ }$.

9. If $b > 1$, then $y = b^x$ defines a (an) _____ function.

10. The graph of an exponential function $y = b^x$ always
    passes through the points $(0, 1)$ and _____.

11. To two decimal places, the value of e is _____.

12. The continuous compound interest formula is $A =$
    _____.

13. Since $e > 1$, the base-e exponential function is a
    (an) _____ function.

14. The graph of the exponential function $y = e^x$ passes
    through the points $(0, 1)$ and _____.

Practice

 Use a calculator to find each value to four decimal places.

15. $4^{\sqrt{3}}$ 16. $5^{\sqrt{2}}$

17. 7^{π} 18. $3^{-\pi}$

Simplify each expression.

19. $5^{\sqrt{2}}5^{\sqrt{2}}$ 20. $\left(5^{\sqrt{2}}\right)^{\sqrt{2}}$

21. $\left(a^{\sqrt{8}}\right)^{\sqrt{2}}$ 22. $a^{\sqrt{12}}a^{\sqrt{3}}$

**Find $f(0)$ and $f(2)$ for each of the given exponential
functions.**

23. $f(x) = 5^x$ 24. $f(x) = 4^{-x}$

25. $f(x) = \left(\dfrac{1}{3}\right)^{-x}$ 26. $f(x) = \left(\dfrac{1}{4}\right)^{x}$

Graph each exponential function.

27. $f(x) = 3^x$

28. $f(x) = 5^x$

29. $f(x) = \left(\dfrac{1}{5}\right)^x$

30. $f(x) = \left(\dfrac{1}{3}\right)^x$

31. $f(x) = \left(\dfrac{3}{4}\right)^x$

32. $f(x) = \left(\dfrac{4}{3}\right)^x$

33. $f(x) = (1.5)^x$

34. $f(x) = (0.3)^x$

35. $f(x) = 3^{-x}$

36. $f(x) = -5^x$

37. $f(x) = -\left(\dfrac{1}{5}\right)^x$

38. $f(x) = \left(\dfrac{1}{3}\right)^{-x}$

49.

50.

Determine whether the graph could represent an exponential function of the form $f(x) = b^x$.

39.

40.

Graph each function by using transformations. **Do not use a graphing calculator.**

51. $f(x) = 3^x - 1$

52. $f(x) = 2^x + 3$

41.

42.

53. $f(x) = 2^x + 1$

54. $f(x) = 4^x - 4$

Find the value of b, if any, that would cause the graph of $y = b^x$ to look like the graph indicated.

43.

44.

55. $f(x) = 3^{x-1}$

56. $f(x) = 2^{x+3}$

45.

46.

57. $f(x) = 3^{x+1}$

58. $f(x) = 2^{x-3}$

47.

48.

59. $f(x) = e^x - 4$

60. $f(x) = e^x + 2$

69. $f(x) = 2^{-x} - 3$

70. $f(x) = 4^{-x} + 4$

61. $f(x) = e^{x-2}$

62. $f(x) = e^{x+3}$

71. $f(x) = -e^x + 2$

72. $f(x) = e^{-x} + 3$

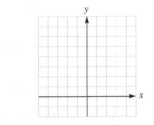

63. $f(x) = 2^{x+1} - 2$

64. $f(x) = 3^{x-1} + 2$

Use a graphing calculator to graph each function.

73. $f(x) = 5(2^x)$

74. $f(x) = 2(5^x)$

75. $f(x) = 3^{-x}$

76. $f(x) = 2^{-x}$

65. $y = 3^{x-2} + 1$

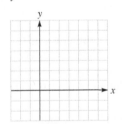

66. $y = 3^{x+2} - 1$

77. $f(x) = 2e^x$

78. $f(x) = 3e^{-x}$

79. $f(x) = 5e^{-0.5x}$

80. $f(x) = -3e^{2x}$

67. $f(x) = -3^x + 1$

68. $f(x) = -2^x - 3$

Applications

*In Exercises **81–84**, assume that there are no deposits or withdrawals.*

81. Compound interest An initial deposit of $10,000 earns 8% interest, compounded quarterly. How much will be in the account in 10 years?

82. Compound interest An initial deposit of $1,000 earns 9% interest, compounded monthly. How much will be in the account in $4\frac{1}{2}$ years?

83. Comparing interest rates How much more interest could $500 earn in 5 years, compounded semi-annually (two times a year), if the annual interest rate were $5\frac{1}{2}\%$ instead of 5%?

84. Comparing savings plans Which institution in the ads provides the better investment?

> ### *Fidelity Savings & Loan*
> Earn 5.25%
> compounded monthly

> ### Union Trust
> Money Market Account
> paying 5.35%
> compounded annually

85. Compound interest If $1 had been invested on July 4, 1776, at 5% interest, compounded annually, what would it be worth on July 4, 2076?

86. 360/365 method Some financial institutions pay daily interest, compounded by the 360/365 method, using the following formula. Using this method, what will an initial investment of $1,000 be worth in 5 years, assuming a 7% annual interest rate?

$$A = A_0\left(1 + \frac{r}{360}\right)^{365t} \quad (t \text{ is in years})$$

87. Carrying charges A college student takes advantage of the ad shown and buys a bedroom set for $1,100. He plans to pay the $1,100 plus interest when his income tax refund comes in 8 months. At that time, what will he need to pay?

> ### BUY NOW, PAY LATER!
> Only $1\frac{3}{4}\%$ interest per month.

88. Credit card interest A bank credit card charges interest at the rate of 21% per year, compounded monthly. If a senior in college charges $1,500 to pay for college expenses and intends to pay it in one year, what will she have to pay?

89. Continuous compound interest An initial investment of $5,000 earns 8.2% interest, compounded continuously. What will the investment be worth in 12 years?

90. Continuous compound interest An initial investment of $2,000 earns 8% interest, compounded continuously. What will the investment be worth in 15 years?

91. Comparison of compounding methods An initial deposit of $5,000 grows at an annual rate of 8.5% for 5 years. Compare the final balances resulting from continuous compounding and annual compounding.

92. Comparison of compounding methods An initial deposit of $30,000 grows at an annual rate of 8% for 20 years. Compare the final balances resulting from continuous compounding and annual compounding.

93. Frequency of compounding $10,000 is invested in each of two accounts, both paying 6% annual interest. In the first account, interest compounds quarterly, and in the second account, interest compounds daily. Find the difference between the accounts after 20 years.

94. Determining an initial deposit An account now contains $11,180 and has been accumulating interest at a 7% annual rate, compounded continuously, for 7 years. Find the initial deposit.

95. Saving for college In 20 years, a father wants to accumulate $40,000 to pay for his daughter's college expenses. If he can get 6% interest, compounded quarterly, how much must he invest now to achieve his goal?

96. Saving for college In Problem 95, how much should he invest to achieve his goal if he can get 6% interest, compounded continuously?

97. Population of a city The population $P(t)$ of a small city can be approximated by the exponential function, $P(t) = 1,200e^{0.2t}$, where t represents time in years. What will be the population of the city in 12 years? Round to a whole number.

98. Amount of drug present The amount of a drug $A(t)$, in mg, present in the bloodstream t hours after being intravenously administered can be approximated by the exponential function, $A(t) = -1,000e^{-0.3t} + 1,250$. How much of the drug is present in the bloodstream after 14 hours? Round to a whole number.

Discovery and Writing

99. Financial planning To have $P available in n years, $A can be invested now in an account paying interest at an annual rate r, compounded annually. Show that

$$A = P(1 + r)^{-n}$$

100. If $2^{t+4} = k2^t$, find k.

101. If $5^{3t} = k^t$, find k.

102. a. If $e^{t+3} = ke^t$, find k.

   b. If $e^{3t} = k^t$, find k.

Review
Factor each expression completely.

103. $x^2 + 9x^4$

104. $x^2 - 9x^4$

105. $x^2 + x - 12$

106. $x^3 + 27$

4.2 Applications of Exponential Functions

In this section, we will learn to

1. Solve radioactive decay problems.

2. Solve oceanography problems.

3. Solve Malthusian population growth problems.

4. Solve epidemiology problems.

Flu kills an estimated 36,000 Americans each year and results is a much larger number of hospitalizations. The influenza virus replicates quickly and can rapidly infect a population. The most effective method of preventing the virus infection and its severe complications is a flu vaccination.

An event that changes with time, such as the spread of the influenza virus, can by modeled by an exponential function. In this section, we will see several important applications of these functions: radioactive decay, oceanography, population growth, and epidemiology.

A mathematical description of an observed event is called a **model** of that event. Many real-world occurrences change with time and can be modeled by exponential functions of the form

$$y = f(t) = ab^{kt} \qquad \text{Remember that } ab^{kt} \text{ means } a(b^{kt}).$$

where a, b, and k are constants and t represents time. If f is an increasing function, we say that y *grows exponentially.* If f is a decreasing function, we say that y *decays exponentially.*

1. Solve Radioactive Decay Problems

The atomic structure of a radioactive material changes as the material emits radiation. Uranium, for example, changes (decays) into thorium, then into radium, and eventually into lead.

Experiments have determined the time it takes for one-half of a sample of a given radioactive element to decompose. That time is a constant, called the element's **half-life.** The amount present decays exponentially according to this formula.

Radioactive Decay Formula   The amount A of radioactive material present at time t is given by

$$A = A_0 2^{-t/h}$$

where A_0 is the amount that was present initially (at $t = 0$) and h is the material's half-life.

EXAMPLE 1   **Solving a Radioactive Decay Problem**

The half-life of radium is approximately 1,600 years. How much of a 1-gram sample will remain after 1,000 years?

SOLUTION   In this example, $A_0 = 1$, $h = 1,600$, and $t = 1,000$. We substitute these values into the formula for radioactive decay and simplify.

$$A = A_0 2^{-t/h}$$

$$A = 1 \cdot 2^{-1,000/1,600}$$

$$\approx 0.648419777 \qquad \text{Use a calculator.}$$

After 1,000 years, approximately 0.65 gram of radium will remain.

Self Check 1   After 800 years, how much radium will remain?

Now Try Exercise 3.

2. Solve Oceanography Problems

Intensity of Light Formula   The intensity I of light (in lumens) at a distance x meters below the surface of a body of water decreases exponentially according to the formula

$$I = I_0 k^x$$

where I_0 is the intensity of light above the water and k is a constant that depends on the clarity of the water.

Comment   A lumen is a unit of standard measurement that describes how much light is contained in a certain area. The lumen is part of the photometry group which measures different aspects of light.

EXAMPLE 2   **Solving an Intensity of Light Problem**

At one location in the Atlantic Ocean, the intensity of light above water I_0 is 12 lumens and $k = 0.6$. Find the intensity of light at a depth of 5 meters.

SOLUTION   We will substitute 12 for I_0, 0.6 for k, and 5 for x into the formula for light intensity and then simplify.

$$I = I_0 k^x$$

$$I = 12(0.6)^5$$

$$I = 0.93312$$

At a depth of 5 meters, the intensity of the light is slightly less than 1 lumen.

Self Check 2   Find the intensity at a depth of 10 meters.

Now Try Exercise 11.

3. Solve Malthusian Population Growth Problems

An equation based on the exponential function provides a model for **population growth.** One such model, called the **Malthusian model of population growth,** assumes a constant birth rate and a constant death rate. In this model, the population P grows exponentially according to the following formula.

Malthusian Model of Population Growth

If b is the annual birth rate, d is the annual death rate, t is the time (in years), P_0 is the initial population at $t = 0$, and P is the current population, then

$$P = P_0 e^{kt}$$

where $k = b - d$ is the **annual growth rate,** the difference between the annual birth rate and death rate.

EXAMPLE 3   **Using the Malthusian Model to Predict Population Growth**

The population of the United States is approximately 300 million people. Assuming that the annual birth rate is 19 per 1,000 and the annual death rate is 7 per 1,000, what does the Malthusian model predict the U.S. population will be in 50 years?

SOLUTION   We can use the stated information to write the Malthusian model for U.S. population. We will then substitute into the model to predict the population in 50 years. Since k is the difference between the birth and death rates, we have

$$k = b - d$$

$$k = \frac{19}{1,000} - \frac{7}{1,000} \qquad \text{Substitute } \frac{19}{1,000} \text{ for } b \text{ and } \frac{7}{1,000} \text{ for } d.$$

$$k = 0.019 - 0.007$$

$$= 0.012$$

We can now substitute 300,000,000 for P_0, 50 for t, and 0.012 for k in the formula for the Malthusian model of population growth and simplify.

$$P = P_0 e^{kt}$$

$$P = (300,000,000) e^{(0.012)(50)}$$

$$= (300,000,000) e^{0.6}$$

$$\approx 546,635,640.1 \qquad \text{Use a calculator.}$$

After 50 years, the U.S. population will exceed 546 million people.

Self Check 3   Find the population in 100 years.

Now Try Exercise 23.

The English economist Thomas Robert Malthus (1766–1834) pioneered in population study. He believed that poverty and starvation were unavoidable, because the human population tends to grow exponentially, whereas the food supply tends to grow linearly.

EXAMPLE 4   **Using a Graphing Calculator to Solve a Population Problem**

Suppose that a country with a population of 1,000 people is growing exponentially according to the formula

$$P = 1,000e^{0.02t}$$

where t is in years. Furthermore, assume that the food supply, measured in adequate food per day per person, is growing linearly according to the formula

$$y = 30.625x + 2,000$$

In how many years will the population outstrip the food supply?

SOLUTION   We can use a graphing calculator with WINDOW settings of $[0,100]$ for x and $[0,10,000]$ for y. After graphing the functions as shown in Figure 4-12, we find the point where the two graphs intersect. We can see that the food supply will be adequate for about 72 years. At that time, the population of approximately 4,200 people will begin to have problems, assuming all conditions remain static.

FIGURE 4-12

Self Check 4   In 80 years, what is the approximate number of people per day that will not have adequate food?

Now Try Exercise 43.

4. Solve Epidemiology Problems

Many infectious diseases, including some caused by viruses, spread most rapidly when they first infect a population, but then more slowly as the number of uninfected individuals decreases. These situations are often modeled by a function, called a *logistic function*.

Logistic Epidemiology Model   The size P of an infected population at any time t in years is given by the logistic function

$$P = \frac{M}{1 + \left(\dfrac{M}{P_0} - 1\right)e^{-kt}}$$

where P_0 is the infected population size at $t = 0$, k is a constant determined by how contagious the virus is in a given environment, and M is the theoretical maximum size of the population P.

EXAMPLE 5   **Solving an Epidemiology Problem**

In a city with a population of 1,200,000, there are currently 1,000 cases of infection with HIV. If the spread of the disease is projected by the formula

$$P = \frac{1,200,000}{1 + (1,200 - 1)e^{-0.4t}}$$

how many people will be infected in 3 years?

SOLUTION   We can substitute 3 for t in the logistic formula and calculate P.

$$P = \frac{1,200,000}{1 + (1,200 - 1)e^{-0.4t}}$$

$$P = \frac{1,200,000}{1 + (1,199)e^{-0.4(3)}}$$

$$\approx 3,313.710094$$

In 3 years, approximately 3,300 people are expected to be infected.   ∎

Self Check 5   How many will be infected in 10 years?

Now Try Exercise 35.

ACCENT ON TECHNOLOGY   **Exponential Regression**

The table below shows the cooling temperatures of a hot cup of coffee after it is made.

Time in minutes	Temperature °F
0	179.5
5	168.7
8	158.1
11	149.2
15	141.7
18	134.6
22	125.4
25	123.5
30	116.3
34	113.2
38	109.1
42	105.7
45	102.2
50	100.5

graphx/Shutterstock.com

We can use a graphing calculator to determine an exponential regression model function that best fits or represents the given data.

- **Step 1:** Enter the data into lists in the calculator. Press `STAT` and then choose 1:Edit to access the list window and then enter the values. Enter the x-values (time in minutes) into L1 and the y-values (temperature) into LIST 2. See Figure 4-13(a).
- **Step 2:** Set a window to fit the data. See Figure 4-13(b).
- **Step 3:** Create a scatter plot of the data. To do so, select STAT PLOT, located above the `Y=` button, and turn Plot 1 on. See Figure 4-14(c). Press `GRAPH` to see the scatter plot. See Figure 4-13(d).

FIGURE 4-13

- **Step 4:** To determine the exponential regression function, we Press `STAT` and scroll right to the CALC menu. We scroll downward to 0:ExpReg and press `ENTER` twice. This gives the equation. See Figure 4-14 (a) and (b). The function is $y = 171.4617283 \cdot (0.9882469577)^x$.
- **Step 5:** To graph the exponential function, we first press `Y=`, then we press `VARS` and scroll downward to 5: Statistics and press `ENTER`. Finally, we select EQ, then press `ENTER` and `GRAPH`. See Figure 4-14(c), (d), (e) and (f).

FIGURE 4-14

Self Check Answers   1. about 0.71 g   2. 0.073 lumen   3. over 996 million   4. About 503   5. about 52,000

Exercises **4.2**

Getting Ready

You should be able to complete these vocabulary and concept statements before you proceed to the practice exercises.

Fill in the blanks.

1. The Malthusian model assumes a constant _____ rate and a constant _____ rate.

2. The Malthusian prediction is pessimistic, because a _____ grows exponentially, but food supplies grow _____.

Applications

Use a calculator to help solve each problem.

3. **Tritium decay** Tritium, a radioactive isotope of hydrogen, has a half-life of 12.4 years. Of an initial sample of 50 grams, how much will remain after 100 years?

4. **Chernobyl** In April 1986, the world's worst nuclear power disaster occurred at Chernobyl in the former USSR. An explosion released about 1,000 kilograms of radioactive cesium-137 (^{137}Cs) into the atmosphere. If the half-life of ^{137}Cs is 30.17 years, how much will remain in the atmosphere in 100 years?

5. **Chernobyl** Refer to Exercise 4. How much ^{137}Cs will remain in 200 years?

6. **Carbon-14 decay** The half-life of radioactive carbon-14 is 5,700 years. How much of an initial sample will remain after 3,000 years?

7. **Plutonium decay** One of the isotopes of plutonium, ^{237}Pu, decays with a half-life of 40 days. How much of an initial sample will remain after 60 days?

8. **Comparing radioactive decay** One isotope of holmium, ^{162}Ho, has a half-life of 22 minutes. The half-life of a second isotope, ^{164}Ho, is 37 minutes. Starting with a sample containing equal amounts, find the ratio of the amounts of ^{162}Ho to ^{164}Ho after one hour.

9. **Drug absorption in smokers** The biological half-life of the asthma medication theophylline is 4.5 hours for smokers. Find the amount of the drug retained in a smoker's system 12 hours after a dose of 1 unit is taken.

10. **Drug absorption in nonsmokers** For a nonsmoker, the biological half-life of theophylline is 8 hours. Find the amount of the drug retained in a nonsmoker's system 12 hours after taking a one-unit dose.

11. **Oceanography** The intensity I of light (in lumens) at a distance x meters below the surface is given by $I = I_0 k^x$, where I_0 is the intensity at the surface and k depends on the clarity of the water. At one location in the Arctic Ocean, $I_0 = 8$ lumens and $k = 0.5$. Find the intensity at a depth of 2 meters.

12. **Oceanography** At one location in the Atlantic Ocean, $I_0 = 14$ lumens and $k = 0.7$. Find the intensity of light at a depth of 12 meters. (See Exercise 11.)

13. **Oceanography** At a depth of 3 meters at one location in the Pacific Ocean, the intensity I of light is 1 lumen and $k = 0.5$. Find the intensity I_0 of light at the surface.

14. **Oceanography** At a depth of 2 meters at one location off the coast of Belize, the intensity I of light is 2 lumens and $k = 0.2$. Find the intensity I_0 of light at the surface.

15. **Bluegill population** A Wisconsin lake is stocked with 10,000 bluegill. The population is expected to grow exponentially according to the model $P = P_0 2^{t/2}$. How many bluegill will be in the lake in 5 years?

© Istockphoto.com/Dirk Nelson

16. **Community growth** The population of Eagle River is growing exponentially according to the model $P = 375(1.3)^t$, where t is measured in years from the present date. Find the population in 3 years.

17. **Newton's Law of Cooling** Some hot water, initially at 100°C, is placed in a room with a temperature of 40°C. The temperature T of the water after t hours is given by $T = 40 + 60(0.75)^t$. Find the temperature in $3\frac{1}{2}$ hours.

18. **Bacterial cultures** A colony of 6 million bacteria is growing in a culture medium. The population P after t hours is given by the formula $P = (6 \times 10^6)(2.3)^t$. Find the population after 4 hours.

19. **Population growth** The growth of a town's population is modeled by $P = 173e^{0.03t}$. How large will the population be when $t = 20$?

20. **Population decline** The decline of a city's population is modeled by $P = 1.2 \times 10^6 e^{-0.008t}$. How large will the population be when $t = 30$?

21. **Epidemics** The spread of hoof and mouth disease through a herd of cattle can be modeled by the formula $P = P_0e^{0.27t}$, where P is the size of the infected population, P_0 is the infected population size at $t = 0$, and t is in days. If a rancher does not act quickly to treat two cases, how many cattle will have the disease in one week?

22. **Alcohol absorption** In one individual, the percent of alcohol absorbed into the bloodstream after drinking two glasses of wine is given by the following formula. Find the percent of alcohol absorbed into the blood after $\frac{1}{2}$ hour.

$$P = 0.3(1 - e^{-0.05t}) \text{ where } t \text{ is in minutes}$$

23. **World population growth** The population of the Earth is approximately 6 billion people and is growing at an annual rate of 1.9%. Assuming a Malthusian growth model, find the world population in 30 years.

24. **World population growth** See Exercise 23. Assuming a Malthusian growth model, find the world population in 40 years.

25. **World population growth** See Exercise 23. By what factor will the current population of the Earth increase in 50 years?

26. **World population growth** See Exercise 23. By what factor will the current population of the Earth increase in 100 years?

27. **Drug absorption** The percent P of the drug triazolam (a drug for treating insomnia) remaining in a person's bloodstream after t hours is given by $P = e^{-0.3t}$. What percent will remain in the bloodstream after 24 hours?

28. **Medicine** The concentration x of a certain drug in an organ after t minutes is given by $x = 0.08(1 - e^{-0.1t})$. Find the concentration of the drug in $\frac{1}{2}$ hour.

29. **Medicine** Refer to Exercise 28. Find the initial concentration of the drug (*Hint:* when $t = 0$).

30. **Spreading the news** Suppose the function

$$N = P(1 - e^{-0.1t})$$

is used to model the length of time t (in hours) it takes for N people living in a town with population P to hear a news flash. How many people in a town of 50,000 will hear the news between 1 and 2 hours after it happened?

31. **Spreading the news** How many people in the town described in Problem 30 will not have heard the news after 10 hours?

32. **Epidemics** Refer to Example 5. How many people will be infected with HIV in 5 years?

33. **Epidemics** Refer to Example 5. How many people will be infected with HIV in 8 years?

34. **Epidemics** In a city with a population of 450,000, there are currently 1,000 cases of hepatitis. If the spread of the disease is projected by the following logistic function, how many people will contract the hepatitis virus after 6 years?

$$P = \frac{450,000}{1 + (450 - 1)e^{-0.2t}}$$

35. **Epidemics** In an Indonesian city with a population of 55,000, there are currently 100 cases of the avian bird flu. If the spread of the disease is projected by the following formula, how many people will contract the bird flu after 2 years?

$$P = \frac{55,000}{1 + (550 - 1)e^{-0.8t}}$$

36. **Life expectancy** The life expectancy l of white females can be estimated by using the function $l = 78.5(1.001)^x$, where x is the current age. Find the life expectancy of a white female who is currently 50 years old. Give the answer to the nearest tenth.

37. **Oceanography** The width w (in millimeters) of successive growth spirals of the sea shell *Catapulus voluto,* shown in the illustration, is given by the function $w = 1.54e^{0.503n}$, where n is the spiral number. To the nearest tenth of a millimeter, find the width of the fifth spiral.

38. **Skydiving** Before the parachute opens, the velocity v (in meters per second) of a skydiver is given by $v = 50(1 - e^{-0.2t})$. Find the initial velocity.

39. **Skydiving** Refer to Exercise 38 and find the velocity after 20 seconds.

40. **Free-falling objects** After t seconds, a certain falling object has a velocity v given by $v = 50(1 - e^{-0.3t})$. Which is falling faster after 2 seconds, this object or the skydiver in Exercise 38?

41. **Population growth** In 1999, the male population of the United States was about 133 million, and the female population was about 139 million. Assuming a Malthusian growth model with a 1% annual growth rate, how many more females than males will there be in 20 years?

42. **Population growth** See Exercise 41. How many more females than males will there be in 50 years?

 Use a graphing calculator to solve each problem.

43. In Example 4, suppose that better farming methods change the formula for food growth to $y = 31x + 2,000$. How long will the food supply be adequate?

44. In Example 4, suppose that a birth control program changed the formula for population growth to $P = 1,000e^{0.01t}$. How long will the food supply be adequate?

Discovery and Writing

45. The value of e can be calculated to any degree of accuracy by adding the first several terms of the following list. The more terms that are added, the closer the sum will be to e. Add the first six numbers in the following list. To how many decimal places is the sum accurate?

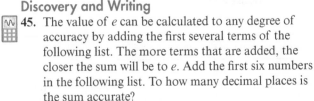

$$1, 1, \frac{1}{2}, \frac{1}{2 \cdot 3}, \frac{1}{2 \cdot 3 \cdot 4}, \frac{1}{2 \cdot 3 \cdot 4 \cdot 5}, \cdots$$

46. Graph the function defined by the equation $f(x) = \frac{e^x + e^{-x}}{2}$ from $x = -2$ to $x = 2$. The graph will look like a parabola, but it is not. The graph, called a **catenary**, is important in the design of power distribution networks, because it represents the shape of a uniform flexible cable whose ends are suspended from the same height. The function is called the **hyperbolic cosine function.**

47. Graph the following logistic function, first discussed in Example 5. Use WINDOW settings of $[0, 20]$ for x and $[0, 1,500,000]$ for y.

$$P = \frac{1,200,000}{1 + (1,199)e^{-0.4t}}$$

48. Use the TRACE capabilities of your graphing calculator to explore the logistic function of Example 5 and Exercise 47. As time passes, what value does P approach? How many years does it take for 20% of the population to become infected? For 80%?

Review
Find the value of x that makes each statement true.

49. $2^3 = x$

50. $3^x = 9$

51. $x^3 = 27$

52. $3^{-2} = x$

53. $x^{-3} = \frac{1}{8}$

54. $3^x = \frac{1}{3}$ -1

55. $9^{1/2} = x$

56. $x^{1/3} = 3$

4.3 Logarithmic Functions and Their Graphs

In this section, we will learn to

1. Evaluate logarithms.
2. Evaluate common logarithms.
3. Evaluate natural logarithms.
4. Graph logarithmic functions.
5. Use transformations to graph logarithmic functions.

Guests aboard the Royal Caribbean's cruise ship *Freedom of the Seas* can now "hang ten" while out to sea. The flowrider surf simulator allows riders to body board surf against a wave-like water flow of 34,000 gallons per minute.

It is important that water in the flowrider has the proper pH value. For example, if it is too acidic, the water will make our eyes and nose burn, and it will make our skin get dry and itchy. The pH of the water is one of the most important factors in pool water balance and should be tested frequently. To calculate pH, we need to understand *logarithms*, the topic of this section. As we continue through this chapter, we will see several real-life applications of logarithms.

Since exponential functions are one-to-one functions, each one has an inverse. For example, to find the inverse of the function $y = 3^x$, we interchange the positions of x and y to obtain $x = 3^y$. The graphs of these two functions are shown in Figure 4-15(a).

To find the inverse of the function $y = \left(\frac{1}{3}\right)^x$, we again interchange the positions of x and y to obtain $x = \left(\frac{1}{3}\right)^y$. The graphs of these two functions are shown in Figure 4-15(b).

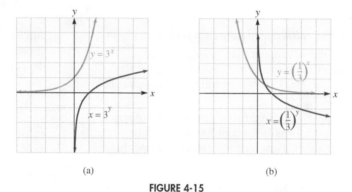

(a)   (b)

FIGURE 4-15

Comment   The graphs of the functions are inverses and therefore symmetric about the line $y = x$.

In general, the inverse of the function $y = b^x$ is $x = b^y$. When $b > 1$, their graphs appear as shown in Figure 4-16(a). When $0 < b < 1$, their graphs appear as shown in Figure 4-16(b).

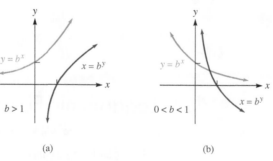

(a)   (b)

FIGURE 4-16

1. Evaluate Logarithms

Since an exponential function defined by $y = b^x$ is one-to-one, it has an inverse function that is defined by the equation $x = b^y$. To express this inverse function in the form $y = f^{-1}(x)$, we must solve the equation $x = b^y$ for y. To do this, we need the following definition.

Logarithmic Functions

If $b > 0$ and $b \neq 1$, the **logarithmic function with base b** is defined by

$$y = \log_b x \qquad \text{if and only if} \qquad x = b^y$$

The **domain of the logarithmic function** is the interval $(0, \infty)$. The **range** is the interval $(-\infty, \infty)$. The logarithmic function is also denoted as $f(x) = \log_b x$.

Caution

Since the domain of the logarithmic function is the set of positive numbers, the logarithm of 0 and the logarithm of a negative number are **undefined** in the set of real numbers.

The range of the logarithmic function is the set of real numbers, because the value of y in the equation $x = b^y$ can be any real number. The domain is the set of positive numbers, because the value of x in the equation $x = b^y$ $(b > 0)$ is always positive.

Since the function $y = \log_b x$ is the inverse of the one-to-one exponential function $y = b^x$, the logarithmic function is also one-to-one.

The expression $x = b^y$ is said to be written in *exponential form.* The equivalent expression $y = \log_b x$ is said to be written in *logarithmic form.* To translate from one form to the other, it is helpful to keep track of the base and the exponent.

Exponential Form	*Logarithmic Form*
$x = b^y$	$y = \log_b x$
Base Exponent	Exponent Base

Comment

In general, we usually write $b^y = x$ instead of writing $x = b^y$. Both are acceptable. Also, many students prefer writing $\log_b x = y$ instead of writing $y = \log_b x$. This too is acceptable.

EXAMPLE 1   Converting from Exponential Form to Logarithmic Form

Write each equation in logarithmic form.

a. $2^6 = 64$ **b.** $27^{\frac{1}{3}} = \sqrt[3]{27} = 3$ **c.** $6^{-2} = \dfrac{1}{36}$

SOLUTION   For each part, we can use the definition of the logarithm of a number.

a. $2^6 = 64$	is equivalent to	$\log_2 64 = 6$
b. $27^{\frac{1}{3}} = \sqrt[3]{27} = 3$	is equivalent to	$\log_{27} 3 = \frac{1}{3}$
c. $6^{-2} = \frac{1}{36}$	is equivalent to	$\log_6 \frac{1}{36} = -2$

Self Check 1   Write $13^{-2} = \dfrac{1}{169}$ in logarithmic form.

Now Try Exercise 21.

EXAMPLE 2   Converting from Logarithmic Form to Exponential Form

Write each equation in exponential form.

a. $\log_5 125 = 3$ **b.** $\log_{64} 8 = \dfrac{1}{2}$ **c.** $\log_{\frac{1}{4}} 16 = -2$

SOLUTION   For each part, we can use the definition of the logarithm of a number ($b > 0$).

a. $\log_5 125 = 3$	is equivalent to	$5^3 = 125$
b. $\log_{64} 8 = \frac{1}{2}$	is equivalent to	$64^{\frac{1}{2}} = 8$
c. $\log_{\frac{1}{4}} 16 = -2$	is equivalent to	$\left(\frac{1}{4}\right)^{-2} = 16$

Self Check 2   Write $\log_5 625 = 4$ in exponential form.

Now Try Exercise 29.

The definition of a logarithm can be used to find the values of many logarithms. Several examples are shown in the table.

Examples of the Values of Logarithms
$\log_5 25 = 2$ because 2 is the exponent to which 5 is raised to get 25: $5^2 = 25$
$\log_7 1 = 0$ because 0 is the exponent to which 7 is raised to get 1: $7^0 = 1$
$\log_{16} 4 = \dfrac{1}{2}$ because $\dfrac{1}{2}$ is the exponent to which 16 is raised to get 4: $16^{1/2} = \sqrt{16} = 4$
$\log_2 \dfrac{1}{8} = -3$ because -3 is the exponent to which 2 is raised to get $\dfrac{1}{8}$: $2^{-3} = \dfrac{1}{8}$

In each of these examples, the logarithm of a number is an exponent. In fact,

$\log_b x$ *is the exponent to which b is raised to get x.*

To express this as an equation, we write $b^{\log_b x} = x$

EXAMPLE 3   **Finding an Unknown Term in a Logarithmic Equation**

Find y in each equation: **a.** $\log_2 8 = y$ **b.** $\log_5 1 = y$ **c.** $\log_7 \dfrac{1}{49} = y$

SOLUTION   For each part, we can use the definition of the logarithm of a number to find y.

a. $\log_2 8 = y$ is equivalent to $2^y = 8$. Since $2^3 = 8$, we have $2^y = 2^3$ and $y = 3$.

b. $\log_5 1 = y$ is equivalent to $5^y = 1$. Since $5^0 = 1$, we have $5^y = 5^0$ and $y = 0$.

c. $\log_7 \frac{1}{49} = y$ is equivalent to $7^y = \frac{1}{49}$. Since $7^{-2} = \frac{1}{49}$, we have $7^y = 7^{-2}$ and $y = -2$.

Self Check 3   Find y in each equation:

a. $\log_3 9 = y$ **b.** $\log_2 16 = y$ **c.** $\log_5 \dfrac{1}{25} = y$

Now Try Exercise 35.

EXAMPLE 4   **Finding an Unknown Term in a Logarithmic Equation**

Find a in each equation: **a.** $\log_a 32 = 5$ **b.** $\log_9 a = -\dfrac{1}{2}$ **c.** $\log_9 3 = a$.

SOLUTION   For each part, we will use the definition of the logarithm of a number to find a.

a. $\log_a 32 = 5$ is equivalent to $a^5 = 32$. Since $2^5 = 32$, we have $a^5 = 2^5$ and $a = 2$.

b. $\log_9 a = -\frac{1}{2}$ is equivalent to $9^{-1/2} = a$. Since $9^{-1/2} = \frac{1}{3}$, it follows that $a = \frac{1}{3}$.

c. $\log_9 3 = a$ is equivalent to $9^a = 3$. Since $3 = 9^{1/2}$, we have $9^a = 9^{1/2}$ and $a = \frac{1}{2}$.

Self Check 4   Find d in each equation:

a. $\log_4 \dfrac{1}{16} = d$ **b.** $\log_d 36 = 2$ **c.** $\log_8 d = -\dfrac{1}{3}$

Now Try Exercise 49.

2. Evaluate Common Logarithms

Many applications use base-10 logarithms (also called **common logarithms**). When the base b is not indicated in the notation log x, we assume that $b = 10$:

$$\log x \qquad \text{means} \qquad \log_{10} x$$

Because base-10 logarithms appear so often, you should become familiar with the following base-10 logarithms:

Examples of Common Logarithms		
$\log_{10}\dfrac{1}{100} = -2$	because	$10^{-2} = \dfrac{1}{100}$
$\log_{10}\dfrac{1}{10} = -1$	because	$10^{-1} = \dfrac{1}{10}$
$\log_{10} 1 = 0$	because	$10^0 = 1$
$\log_{10} 10 = 1$	because	$10^1 = 10$
$\log_{10} 100 = 2$	because	$10^2 = 100$
$\log_{10} 1{,}000 = 3$	because	$10^3 = 1{,}000$

In general, we have

$$\log_{10} 10^x = x$$

ACCENT ON TECHNOLOGY   **Approximating Base-10 Logarithms**

We can use the [LOG] key on a graphing calculator to evaluate base-10 logarithms. Figure 4-17 shows the evaluation of log 2.34 and demonstrates that **a logarithm is an exponent**. Notice that the logarithm is evaluated, and then the answer is used as the exponent of 10 to get 2.34. Remember: log 2.34 is the exponent of 10 that will yield 2.34.

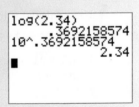

```
log(2.34)
        .3692158574
10^.3692158574
             2.34
■
```

FIGURE 4-17

EXAMPLE 5   **Using a Calculator to Solve a Common Logarithmic Equation**

Find x in the equation log $x = 0.7482$ to four decimal places.

SOLUTION   We can use the definition of the common logarithm and a calculator to find x.

The equation log $x = 0.7482$ is equivalent to $10^{0.7482} = x$.

Therefore we have $x = 10^{0.7482} \approx 5.6002$.

Self Check 5   Solve: log $x = 1.87737$. Give the result to four decimal places.

Now Try Exercise 81.

3. Evaluate Natural Logarithms

We have seen the importance of the number e in mathematical models of events in nature. Base-e logarithms are just as important. They are called **natural logarithms** or **Napierian logarithms** after John Napier (1550–1617). They are usually written as $\ln x$, rather than $\log_e x$:

> $\ln x$ means $\log_e x$

Like all logarithmic functions, the domain of $f(x) = \ln x$ is the interval $(0, \infty)$, and the range is the interval $(-\infty, \infty)$.

To estimate the base-e logarithms of numbers, we can use a calculator. Scientific and graphing calculators have a natural logarithm key $\boxed{\text{LN}}$, which is used like the $\boxed{\text{LOG}}$ key.

ACCENT ON TECHNOLOGY   **Approximating Natural Logarithms**

We can use the $\boxed{\text{LN}}$ key on a graphing calculator to evaluate base-e logarithms. Figure 4-18 shows the evaluation of $\ln 2.34$ and demonstrates that **a logarithm is an exponent**. Notice that the logarithm is evaluated, and then the answer is used as the exponent of e to get 2.34. Remember: $\ln 2.34$ is the exponent of e that will yield 2.34.

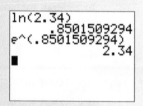

```
ln(2.34)
            .8501509294
e^(.8501509294)
                   2.34
■
```

FIGURE 4-18

EXAMPLE 6   **Using a Calculator to Approximate Natural Logarithms**

Use a calculator to find   **a.** $\ln 17.32$ **b.** $\ln(\log 0.05)$

SOLUTION   **a.** $\ln 17.32 \approx 2.851861903$, which means $e^{2.851861903} \approx 17.32$

b. $\ln(\log 0.05)$ has no value because $\log(0.05) < 0$. Our calculator gives an error message.

Self Check 6   Find each value to four decimal places:

a. $\ln \pi$ **b.** $\ln\left(\log \dfrac{1}{3}\right)$

Now Try Exercise 75.

EXAMPLE 7   **Using a Calculator to Solve Natural Logarithmic Equations**

Solve each equation and give the result to four decimal places:

a. $\ln x = 1.335$ **b.** $\ln x = \log 5.5$

SOLUTION   We will write the equation in exponential form and use our calculator to find x.

a. The equation $\ln x = 1.335$ is equivalent to $e^{1.335} = x$. We will use a calculator to evaluate the expression. $x = e^{1.335} \approx 3.8000$.

b. The equation $\ln x = \log 5.5$ is equivalent to $e^{\log 5.5} = x$. Using a calculator, we find $x = e^{\log 5.5} \approx 2.0967$.

Self Check 7 Solve each equation and give each result to four decimal places:

a. $\ln x = 1.9344$ **b.** $\log x = \ln 3.2$

Now Try Exercise 85.

4. Graph Logarithmic Functions

To draw the graph of a logarithmic function, we will use the fact that a logarithmic function is the inverse of an exponential function.

To graph the logarithmic function $y = f(x) = \log_2 x$, we calculate and plot several points with coordinates (x, y) that satisfy the equivalent equation $x = 2^y$. After joining these points with a smooth curve, we have the graph shown in Figure 4-19.

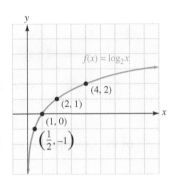

$f(x) = \log_2 x$		
x	$f(x)$	$(x, f(x))$
$\dfrac{1}{4}$	-2	$\left(\dfrac{1}{4}, -2\right)$
$\dfrac{1}{2}$	-1	$\left(\dfrac{1}{2}, -1\right)$
1	0	$(1, 0)$
2	1	$(2, 1)$
4	2	$(4, 2)$
8	3	$(8, 3)$

FIGURE 4-19

EXAMPLE 8 **Graphing a Logarithmic Function**

Graph: $y = f(x) = \log_{1/2} x$.

SOLUTION To graph $y = f(x) = \log_{1/2} x$. we calculate and plot several points with coordinates (x, y) that satisfy the equation $x = \left(\dfrac{1}{2}\right)^y$. After joining these points with a smooth curve, we have the graph shown in Figure 4-20.

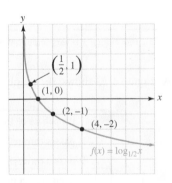

$f(x) = \log_{1/2} x$		
x	$f(x)$	$(x, f(x))$
$\dfrac{1}{4}$	2	$\left(\dfrac{1}{4}, 2\right)$
$\dfrac{1}{2}$	1	$\left(\dfrac{1}{2}, 1\right)$
1	0	$(1, 0)$
2	-1	$(2, -1)$
4	-2	$(4, -2)$
8	-3	$(8, -3)$

FIGURE 4-20

Self Check 8 Graph: $y = f(x) = \log_6 x$.

Now Try Exercise 105.

The graphs of all logarithmic functions are similar to those in Figure 4-21. If $b > 1$, the logarithmic function is an increasing function, as in Figure 4-21(a). If $0 < b < 1$, the logarithmic function is a decreasing function, as in Figure 4-21(b). We also know that the exponential function $f(x) = b^x$ and the logarithmic function $f(x) = \log_b x$ are inverse functions and therefore symmetric about the line $y = x$, as in Figure 4-21(c) and (d).

(a)   (b)   (c)   (d)

FIGURE 4-21

To graph, $f(x) = \log_{10} x$, we can plot points that satisfy the equation $x = 10^y$ and join them with a smooth curve, as shown in Figure 4-22.

The Graph of the Common Logarithm Function $f(x) = \log_{10} x$

$f(x) = \log x$		
x	$f(x)$	$(x, f(x))$
$\dfrac{1}{100}$	-2	$\left(\dfrac{1}{100}, -2\right)$
$\dfrac{1}{10}$	-1	$\left(\dfrac{1}{10}, -1\right)$
1	0	$(1, 0)$
10	1	$(10, 1)$
100	2	$(100, 2)$

FIGURE 4-22

Comment The function $f(x) = \log_{10} x$ is very important and its graph should be memorized.

As Figure 4-22 shows, the graph of $f(x) = \log_b x$ has these properties:

Properties of the Graph of $f(x) = \log_b x$
1. It passes through the point $(1, 0)$.
2. It passes through the point $(b, 1)$.
3. The y-axis is a vertical asymptote.
4. The domain is $(0, \infty)$, and the range is $(-\infty, \infty)$.

To graph $f(x) = \ln x$, we can plot points that satisfy the equation $x = e^y$ and join them with a smooth curve, as shown in Figure 4-23.

The Graph of the Natural Logarithm Function $f(x) = \ln x$

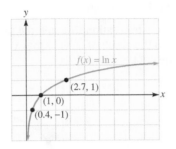

$f(x) = \ln x$		
x	$f(x)$	$(x, f(x))$
$\dfrac{1}{e} \approx 0.4$	-1	$(0.4, -1)$
1.0	0	$(1, 0)$
$e \approx 2.7$	1	$(2.7, 1)$
$e^2 \approx 7.4$	2	$(7.4, 2)$

FIGURE 4-23

Comment

The function $y = \ln x$ is very important and its graph should be memorized. The functions $y = e^x$ and $y = \ln x$ are inverses.

From the definition of logarithm, we know that

$$y = \ln x \quad \text{if and only if} \quad x = e^y \qquad \text{Remember that } \ln x = \log_e x.$$

Thus, $\ln e = 1$ because $e^1 = e$. This is an important property of the natural logarithm function. Two other important properties follow from the fact that $y = \ln x$ and $y = e^x$ are inverses:

$$\ln e^x = x \quad \text{and} \quad e^{\ln x} = x.$$

These two properties and examples are shown in the table:

Properties Involving e and ln	Examples
$\ln e^x = x$	$\ln e^8 = 8$
	$\ln e^{-5x} = -5x$
	$\ln e^{3x+2} = 3x + 2$
$e^{\ln x} = x$	$e^{\ln 4} = 4$
	$e^{\ln(7x)} = 7x$
	$e^{\ln(9x-2)} = 9x - 2$

5. Use Transformations to Graph Logarithmic Functions

The graphs of many functions involving logarithms are transformations of the basic logarithmic graphs. A summary of these are shown in the table for $k > 0$.

Equation	Transformations of the Graph of $f(x) = \log_b x$
$y = \log_b x + k$	Translates the graph of $f(x) = \log_b x$ upward k units
$y = \log_b x - k$	Translates the graph of $f(x) = \log_b x$ downward k units
$y = \log_b(x - k)$	Translates the graph of $f(x) = \log_b x$ to the right k units
$y = \log_b(x + k)$	Translates the graph of $f(x) = \log_b x$ to the left k units
$y = -\log_b x$	Reflects the graph of $f(x) = \log_b x$ about the x-axis
$y = \log_b(-x)$	Reflects the graph of $f(x) = \log_b x$ about the y-axis
$y = k \log_b x$	• Vertically stretches the graph of $y = \log_b x$ if $k > 1$ • Vertically shrinks the graph of $y = \log_b x$ if $0 < k < 1$
$y = \log_b(kx)$	• Horizontally stretches the graph of $y = \log_b x$ if $0 < k < 1$ • Horizontally shrinks the graph of $y = \log_b x$ if $k > 1$

EXAMPLE 9   **Using a Translation to Graph a Logarithmic Function**

Graph: $g(x) = 3 + \log_2 x$.

SOLUTION   We can use a translation to graph the function. The graph of $g(x) = 3 + \log_2 x$ is identical to the graph of $f(x) = \log_2 x$, except that it is translated 3 units upward. See Figure 4-24.

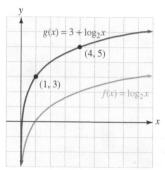

FIGURE 4-24

Self Check 9   Graph: $g(x) = -2 + \log_3 x$.

Now Try Exercise 111.

EXAMPLE 10   **Using a Translation to Graph a Logarithmic Function**

Graph: $g(x) = \log_{1/2}(x - 1)$.

SOLUTION   We can use a translation to graph the function. The graph of $g(x) = \log_{1/2}(x - 1)$ is identical to the graph of $f(x) = \log_{1/2} x$, except that it is translated 1 unit to the right. See Figure 4-25.

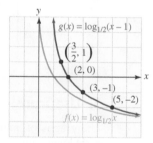

FIGURE 4-25

Self Check 10   Graph: $g(x) = \log_{1/3}(x + 2)$.

Now Try Exercise 113.

Many graphs of logarithmic functions involve translations of the graph of $f(x) = \ln x$. Consider the calculator graphs of the functions $f(x) = \ln x$, $g(x) = 2 + \ln x$, and $h(x) = -2 + \ln x$.

FIGURE 4-26

The graph of $f(x) = \ln x$ is the middle graph shown.

The graph of $g(x) = 2 + \ln x$ is 2 units above the graph of $f(x) = \ln x$.

The graph of $h(x) = -2 + \ln x$ is 2 units below the graph of $f(x) = \ln x$.

Figure 4-27 shows a calculator graph of the functions $f(x) = \ln x$, $g(x) = \ln(x + 2)$, and $h(x) = \ln(x - 2)$.

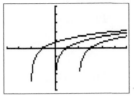

The graph of $f(x) = \ln x$ is the middle graph shown.

The graph of $g(x) = \ln(x + 2)$ is 2 units to the left of the graph of $f(x) = \ln x$.

The graph of $h(x) = \ln(x - 2)$ is 2 units to the right of the graph of $f(x) = \ln x$.

FIGURE 4-27

ACCENT ON TECHNOLOGY   **Graphing Logarithmic Functions**

Graphing calculators can be used to graph logarithmic functions. However, the only bases that are built in are 10 and e. There is a way to graph logarithmic functions in other bases, but it involves changing the base. We will cover that in Section 4.5. In most applications either common logarithms or natural logarithms are used. When we are graphing logarithmic functions on a graphing calculator, we need to be aware of the domain so that we can set a proper window.

- Graph: $f(x) = -2 + \log_{10}\left(\frac{1}{2}x\right)$.

  To graph the function, we enter the right-hand side of the equation and use WINDOW settings of $[-1, 5]$ for x and $[-5, 1]$ for y. The graph is shown in Figure 4-28.

FIGURE 4-28

- Notice that the graph in Figure 4-28 appears to stop on the left and not continue toward negative infinity. That is a result of how the calculator plots points as it approaches the vertical asymptote.

Self Check Answers   **1.** $\log_{13}\dfrac{1}{169} = -2$ **2.** $5^4 = 625$ **3. a.** 2 **b.** 4 **c.** -2

4. a. -2 **b.** 6 **c.** $\dfrac{1}{2}$ **5.** 75.3998   **6. a.** 1.1447 **b.** no value

7. a. 6.9199 **b.** 14.5596

8.

9.

10.

Exercises **4.3**

Getting Ready
You should be able to complete these vocabulary and con-cept statements before you proceed to the practice exercises.

Fill in the blanks.

1. The equation $y = \log_b x$ is equivalent to _____.
2. The domain of a logarithmic function is the interval _____.
3. The _____ of a logarithmic function is the interval $(-\infty, \infty)$.
4. $b^{\log_b x} = $ ___.
5. Because the exponential function is one-to-one, it has an _____ function.
6. The inverse of an exponential function is called a _____ function.
7. $\log_b x$ is the _____ to which b is raised to get x.
8. The y-axis is an _____ of a graph of $f(x) = \log_b x$.
9. The graph of $f(x) = \log_b x$ passes through the points _____ and _____.
10. $\log_{10} 10^x = $ ___.
11. $\ln x$ means _____.
12. The domain of the function $f(x) = \ln x$ is the interval _____.
13. The range of the function $f(x) = \ln x$ is the interval _____.
14. The graph of $f(x) = \ln x$ has the _____ as an asymptote
15. In the expression $\log x$, the base is understood to be ___.
16. In the expression $\ln x$, the base is understood to be ___.

Practice
Write each equation in logarithmic form.

17. $8^2 = 64$
18. $10^3 = 1,000$
19. $4^{-2} = \dfrac{1}{16}$
20. $3^{-4} = \dfrac{1}{81}$
21. $\left(\dfrac{1}{2}\right)^{-5} = 32$
22. $\left(\dfrac{1}{3}\right)^{-3} = 27$
23. $x^y = z$
24. $m^n = p$

Write each equation in exponential form.

25. $\log_3 81 = 4$
26. $\log_7 7 = 1$
27. $\log_{1/2} \dfrac{1}{} = 3$
28. $\log_{1/5} 1 = 0$

29. $\log_4 \dfrac{1}{64} = -3$
30. $\log_6 \dfrac{1}{36} = -2$
31. $\log_\pi \pi = 1$
32. $\log_7 \dfrac{1}{49} = -2$

Find each value of x.

33. $\log_2 8 = x$
34. $\log_3 9 = x$
35. $\log_4 \dfrac{1}{64} = x$
36. $\log_6 216 = x$
37. $\log_{1/2} \dfrac{1}{8} = x$
38. $\log_{1/3} \dfrac{1}{81} = x$
39. $\log_9 3 = x$
40. $\log_{125} 5 = x$
41. $\log_{1/2} 8 = x$
42. $\log_{1/2} 16 = x$
43. $\log_8 x = 2$
44. $\log_7 x = 0$
45. $\log_7 x = 1$
46. $\log_2 x = 8$
47. $\log_{25} x = \dfrac{1}{2}$
48. $\log_4 x = \dfrac{1}{2}$
49. $\log_5 x = -2$
50. $\log_3 x = -4$
51. $\log_{36} x = -\dfrac{1}{2}$
52. $\log_{27} x = -\dfrac{1}{3}$
53. $\log_x 5^3 = 3$
54. $\log_x 5 = 1$
55. $\log_x \dfrac{9}{4} = 2$
56. $\log_x \dfrac{\sqrt{3}}{3} = \dfrac{1}{2}$
57. $\log_x \dfrac{1}{64} = -3$
58. $\log_x \dfrac{1}{100} = -2$
59. $\log_x \dfrac{9}{4} = -2$
60. $\log_x \dfrac{\sqrt{3}}{3} = -\dfrac{1}{2}$
61. $2^{\log_2 5} = x$
62. $3^{\log_3 4} = x$
63. $x^{\log_4 6} = 6$
64. $x^{\log_3 8} = 8$

📊 *Use a calculator to find each value to four decimal places.*

65. $\log 3.25$
66. $\log 0.57$
67. $\log 0.00467$
68. $\log 375.876$
69. $\ln 45.7$
70. $\ln 0.005$
71. $\ln \dfrac{2}{3}$
72. $\ln \dfrac{12}{7}$
73. $\ln 35.15$
74. $\ln 0.675$
75. $\ln 7.896$
76. $\ln 0.00465$
77. $\log(\ln 1.7)$
78. $\ln(\log 9.8)$
79. $\ln(\log 0.1)$
80. $\log(\ln 0.01)$

Use a calculator to find y to four decimal places, if possible.

81. $\log y = 1.4023$

82. $\log y = 0.926$

83. $\log y = -3.71$

84. $\log y = \log \pi$

85. $\ln y = 1.4023$

86. $\ln y = 2.6490$

87. $\ln y = 4.24$

88. $\ln y = 0.926$

89. $\ln y = -3.71$

90. $\ln y = -0.28$

91. $\log y = \ln 8$

92. $\ln y = \log 7$

Find each value without using a calculator.

93. $\log 10,000$

94. $\log 1,000,000$

95. $\log 0.001$

96. $\log \dfrac{1}{100,000}$

97. $e^{(\ln 7)}$

98. $e^{(\ln 9)}$

99. $\ln(e^4)$

100. $\ln(e^{-6})$

Find the value of b, if any, that would cause the graph of $y = \log_b x$ to look like the graph shown.

101.

102.

103.

104.

Graph each function.

105. $f(x) = \log_3 x$

106. $f(x) = \log_4 x$

107. $f(x) = \log_{1/3} x$

108. $f(x) = \log_{1/4} x$

109. $f(x) = -\log_5 x$

110. $f(x) = -\log_2 x$

111. $f(x) = 2 + \log_2 x$

112. $f(x) = \log_2(x - 1)$

113. $f(x) = \log_3(x + 2)$

114. $f(x) = -3 + \log_3 x$

115. $f(x) = 3 + \log_3(x + 1)$

116. $f(x) = -3 + \log_3(x + 1)$

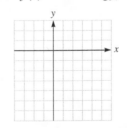

117. $f(x) = -3 + \ln x$

118. $f(x) = \ln(x + 1)$

119. $f(x) = \ln(x - 4)$

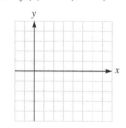

120. $f(x) = 2 + \ln x$

121. $f(x) = 1 - \ln x$

122. $f(x) = 2 - \ln x$

Use a graphing calculator to graph each function.

123. $f(x) = \log(3x)$

124. $f(x) = \log\left(\dfrac{x}{3}\right)$

125. $f(x) = \log(-x)$

126. $f(x) = -\log x$

127. $f(x) = \ln\left(\dfrac{1}{2}x\right)$

128. $f(x) = \ln x^2$

129. $f(x) = \ln(-x)$

130. $f(x) = \ln(3x)$

Discovery and Writing

131. Consider the following graphs. Which is larger, a or b, and why?

132. Consider the following graphs. Which is larger, a or b, and why?

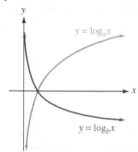

133. Pick two numbers and add their logarithms. Then find the logarithm of the product of those two numbers. What do you observe? Does it work for three numbers?

134. If $\log_a b = 7$, find $\log_b a$.

Review

Find the vertex of each parabola.

135. $y = x^2 + 7x + 3$

136. $y = 3x^2 - 8x - 1$

137. Fencing a pasture A farmer will use 3,400 feet of fencing to enclose and divide the pasture shown in the illustration. What dimensions will enclose the greatest area?

138. Selling appliances When the price is p dollars, an appliance dealer can sell $(2,200 - p)$ refrigerators. What price will maximize his revenue?

139. Write an equation of a line passing through the origin and parallel to the line $y = 5x - 8$.

140. Write an equation of a line passing through $(3, 2)$ and perpendicular to the line $y = \frac{2}{3}x - 12$.

4.4 Applications of Logarithmic Functions

In this section, we will learn to

1. Use logarithms to solve electrical engineering problems.

2. Use logarithms to solve geology problems.

3. Use logarithms to solve charging battery problems.

4. Use logarithms to solve population growth problems.

5. Use logarithms to solve isothermal expansion problems.

Earthquakes are one of the deadliest natural disasters that can occur. In 2004, an earthquake in the Indian Ocean triggered a series of tsunamis killing more than 225,000 people in eleven countries. Indonesia, Sri Lanka, Thailand, and India were hit the hardest. The earthquake was the second largest ever recorded and had a magnitude between 9.1 and 9.3 on the Richter scale. In 2010, a 7.0 catastrophic earthquake hit 16 miles west of Port-au-Prince, Haiti's capital, affecting more than 3 million people.

© Istockphoto.com/Claudia Dewald

In 2011, a massive earthquake of magnitude 9.0 hit off the coast of Japan, killing thousands and affecting Japan's nuclear reactors and triggering a nuclear crisis.

The intensity of an earthquake is based on a logarithmic function, the topic of this section. We will also use logarithmic functions to solve problems in engineering, geology, social science, and physics.

1. Use Logarithms to Solve Electrical Engineering Problems

© Istockphoto.com/Dragan Trifunovic

Electronic engineers use common logarithms to measure the voltage gain of devices such as amplifiers or the length of a transmission line. The unit of gain, called the **decibel,** is defined by a logarithmic function.

Decibel Voltage Gain   If E_O is the output voltage of a device and E_I is the input voltage, the **decibel voltage gain** is given by

$$\text{dB gain} = 20 \log \frac{E_O}{E_I}$$

___

EXAMPLE 1   **Finding the Decibel Gain of an Amplifier**

Find the dB gain of an amplifier if its input is 0.5 volt and its output is 40 volts.

SOLUTION   We can find the decibel voltage gain by substituting the given values into the dB gain formula.

$$\text{dB voltage gain} = 20 \log \frac{E_O}{E_I}$$

$$\text{dB voltage gain} = 20 \log \frac{40}{0.5} \qquad \text{Substitute 40 for } E_O \text{ and 0.5 for } E_I.$$

$$= 20 \log 80$$

$$\approx 38.06179974 \qquad \text{Use a calculator.}$$

To the nearest decibel, the db gain is 38 decibels. ∎

Self Check 1   Find the dB gain if the input is 0.7 volt.

Now Try Exercise 7.

2. Use Logarithms to Solve Geology Problems

Seismologists measure the intensity of earthquakes on the **Richter scale,** which is based on a logarithmic function.

Haiti's Presidential Palace after
2010 earthquake

Richter Scale   If R is the intensity of an earthquake, A is the amplitude (measured in micrometers), and P is the period (the time of one oscillation of the Earth's surface, measured in seconds), then

$$R = \log \frac{A}{P}$$

___

EXAMPLE 2   **Finding the Intensity of an Earthquake**

Find the intensity of an earthquake with amplitude of 5,000 micrometers $\left(\frac{1}{2} \text{ centimeter}\right)$ and a period of 0.07 second.

SOLUTION   We substitute 5,000 for A and 0.07 for P in the Richter scale formula and simplify.

$$R = \log \frac{A}{P}$$

$$R = \log \frac{5,000}{0.07}$$

$$\approx \log 71,428.57143 \qquad \text{Use a calculator.}$$

$$\approx 4.853871964$$

To the nearest tenth, the earthquake measures 4.9 on the Richter scale.

Self Check 2   Find the intensity of an aftershock with the same period but one-half of the amplitude.

Now Try Exercise 13.

3. Use Logarithms to Solve Charging Battery Problems

A battery charges at a rate that depends on how close it is to being fully charged—it charges fastest when it is most discharged. The formula that determines the time required to charge a battery to a certain level is based on a natural logarithmic function.

Charging Batteries   If M is the theoretical maximum charge that a battery can hold and k is a positive constant that depends on the battery and the charger, the length of time t (in minutes) required to charge the battery to a given level C is given by

$$t = -\frac{1}{k} \ln\left(1 - \frac{C}{M}\right)$$

EXAMPLE 3   **Solving a Charging Battery Problem**

How long will it take to bring a fully discharged battery to 90% of full charge? Assume that $k = 0.025$ and that time is measured in minutes.

SOLUTION   90% of full charge means 90% of M. We can substitute $0.90M$ for C and 0.025 for k in the formula for charging batteries to find t.

$$t = -\frac{1}{k} \ln\left(1 - \frac{C}{M}\right)$$

$$t = -\frac{1}{0.025} \ln\left(1 - \frac{0.90M}{M}\right)$$

$$= -40 \ln(1 - 0.9)$$

$$= -40 \ln(0.1)$$

$$\approx 92.10340372 \qquad \text{Use a calculator.}$$

The battery will reach 90% charge in about 92 minutes.

Self Check 3   How long will it take this battery to reach 80% of full charge?

Now Try Exercise 19.

4. Use Logarithms to Solve Population Growth Problems

If a population grows exponentially at a certain annual rate, the time required for the population to double is called the **doubling time** and is given by the following formula. You will be asked to prove this formula in Exercise 112 in Section 4.6.

Population Doubling Time If r is the annual growth rate and t is the time (in years) required for a population to double, then

$$t = \frac{\ln 2}{r}$$

EXAMPLE 4 Finding the Doubling Time of a Population

The population of the Earth is growing at the approximate rate of 2% per year. If this rate continues, how long will it take the population to double?

SOLUTION Because the population is growing at the rate of 2% per year, we can substitute 0.02 for r in the formula for doubling time and simplify.

$$t = \frac{\ln 2}{r}$$

$$t = \frac{\ln 2}{0.02}$$

$$\approx 34.65735903$$

It will take about 35 years for the Earth's population to double.

Self Check 4 If the world population's annual growth rate could be reduced to 1.5% per year, what would be the doubling time?

Now Try Exercise 21.

5. Use Logarithms to Solve Isothermal Expansion Problems

When energy is added to a gas, its temperature and volume could increase. In **isothermal expansion,** the temperature remains constant—only the volume changes. The energy required is calculated as follows.

Isothermal Expansion If the temperature T is constant, the energy E required to increase the volume of 1 mole of gas from an initial volume V_i to a final volume V_f is given by

$$E = RT \ln\left(\frac{V_f}{V_i}\right)$$

E is measured in joules and T in Kelvins. R is the universal gas constant, which is 8.314 joules/mole/K.

EXAMPLE 5   **Solving an Isothermal Expansion Problem**

Find the amount of energy that must be supplied to triple the volume of 1 mole of gas at a constant temperature of 300 K.

SOLUTION   We substitute 8.314 for R and 300 for T in the formula. Since the final volume is to be three times the initial volume, we also substitute $3V_i$ for V_f.

$$E = RT \ln\left(\frac{V_f}{V_i}\right)$$

$$E = (8.314)(300)\ln\left(\frac{3V_i}{V_i}\right)$$

$$= 2{,}492.2 \ln 3$$

$$\approx 2{,}740.15877$$

Approximately 2,740 joules of energy must be added to triple the volume.   ∎

Self Check 5   What energy is required to double the volume?

Now Try Exercise 25.

Self Check Answers   **1.** about 35 decibels   **2.** about 4.6   **3.** about 64 min   **4.** about 46 years
5. 1,729 joules

Exercises **4.4**

Getting Ready
You should be able to complete these vocabulary and concept statements before you proceed to the practice exercises.

Fill in the blanks.

1. dB gain = _____

2. The intensity of an earthquake is measured by the
   formula $R =$ _____.

3. The formula for charging batteries is

   _____.

4. If a population grows exponentially at a rate r, the time it will take for the population to double is given

   by the formula $t =$ _____.

5. The formula for isothermal expansion is

   _____.

6. The logarithm of a negative number is _____.

Applications
Use a calculator to solve each problem.

7. **Gain of an amplifier** An amplifier produces an output of 17 volts when the input signal is 0.03 volt.

8. **Transmission lines** A 4.9-volt input to a long transmission line decreases to 4.7 volts at the other end. Find the decibel voltage loss.

9. **Gain of an amplifier** Find the dB gain of an amplifier whose input voltage is 0.71 volt and whose output voltage is 20 volts.

10. **Gain of an amplifier** Find the dB gain of an amplifier whose output voltage is 2.8 volts and whose input voltage is 0.05 volt.

11. **dB gain** Find the dB gain of the amplifier shown below.

12. **dB gain** Find the dB gain of the amplifier shown below.

13. **Earthquakes** An earthquake has an amplitude of 5,000 micrometers and a period of 0.2 second. Find its measure on the Richter scale.

14. **Earthquakes** An earthquake has an amplitude of 8,000 micrometers and a period of 0.008 second. Find its measure on the Richter scale.

15. **Earthquakes** An earthquake with a period of $\frac{1}{4}$ second has an amplitude of 2,500 micrometers. Find its measure on the Richter scale.

16. **Earthquakes** An earthquake has a period of $\frac{1}{2}$ second and an amplitude of 5 cm. Find its measure on the Richter scale. (*Hint:* 1 cm = 10,000 micrometers)

17. **Earthquakes** An earthquake measuring between 3.5 and 5.4 on the Richter scale is often felt but rarely causes damage. Suppose an earthquake in Northern California has an amplitude of 6,000 micrometers and a period of 0.3 second. Is it likely to cause damage?

18. **Earthquakes** An earthquake measuring between 7 and 7.9 on the Richter scale is a major earthquake and can cause serious damage over larger areas. Suppose an earthquake in Chile has an amplitude of 198.5 cm and a period of 0.1 second. Would it cause serious damage over large areas? (*Hint:* 1 cm = 10,000 micrometers)

19. **Battery charge** If $k = 0.116$, how long will it take a battery to reach a 90% charge? Assume that the battery was fully discharged when it began charging.

20. **Battery charge** If $k = 0.201$, how long will it take a battery to reach a 40% charge? Assume that the battery was fully discharged when it began charging.

21. **Population growth** A town's population grows at the rate of 12% per year. If this growth rate remains constant, how long will it take the population to double?

22. **Fish population growth** One thousand bass were stocked in Catfish Lake in Eagle River, Wisconsin, a lake with no bass population. If the population of bass is expected to grow at a rate of 25% per year, how long will it take the population to double?

23. **Population growth** A population growing at an annual rate r will triple in a time t given by the formula $t = \frac{\ln 3}{r}$. How long will it take the population of the town in Exercise 21 to triple?

24. **Fish population growth** How long would it take the fish population in Exercise 22 to triple?

25. **Isothermal expansion** One mole of gas expands isothermally to triple its volume. If the gas temperature is 400 K, what energy is absorbed?

26. **Isothermal expansion** One mole of gas expands isothermally to double its volume. If the gas temperature is 300K, what energy is absorbed?

If an investment is growing continuously for t years, its annual growth rate r is given by the following formula, where P is the current value and P_0 is the amount originally invested.

$$r = \frac{1}{t} \ln \frac{P}{P_0}$$

27. **Investing** AOL's stock grew continuously from 1992–1999. An investment of $10,400 in the stock in 1992 was worth $10,400,000 in 1999. Find AOL's average annual growth rate during this period.

28. **Investing** A $5,000 investment in Dell Computer in 1995 was worth $237,000 in 1999. It grew continuously during this time period. Find the average annual growth rate of the stock.

29. **Depreciation** In business, equipment is often depreciated using the double declining-balance method. In this method, a piece of equipment with a life expectancy of N years, costing C, will depreciate to a value of V in n years, where n is given by the following formula.

$$n = \frac{\log V - \log C}{\log\left(1 - \dfrac{2}{N}\right)}$$

If a computer that cost $37,000 has a life expectancy of 5 years and has depreciated to a value of $8,000, how old is it?

30. **Depreciation** A word processor worth $470 when new had a life expectancy of 12 years. If it is now worth $189, how old is it? (See Exercise 29.)

31. **Annuities** If P is invested at the end of each year in an annuity earning interest at an annual rate r, the amount in the account will be A after n years, where

$$n = \frac{\log\left[\dfrac{Ar}{P} + 1\right]}{\log(1 + r)}$$

If $1,000 is invested each year in an annuity earning 12% annual interest, when will the account be worth $20,000?

32. Annuities If \$5,000 is invested each year in an annuity earning 8% annual interest, when will the account be worth \$50,000? (See Exercise 31.)

33. Breakdown voltage The coaxial power cable shown has a central wire with radius $R_1 = 0.25$ centimeter. It is insulated from a surrounding shield with inside radius $R_2 = 2$ centimeters. The maximum voltage the cable can withstand is called the **breakdown voltage** V of the insulation. V is given by the formula

$$V = ER_1 \ln \frac{R_2}{R_1}$$

where E is the **dielectric strength** of the insulation. If $E = 400,000$ volts/centimeter, find V.

34. Breakdown voltage In Exercise 33, if the inside diameter of the shield were doubled, what voltage could the cable withstand?

35. Suppose you graph the function $f(x) = \ln x$ on a coordinate grid with a unit distance of 1 centimeter on the x- and y-axes. How far out must you go on the x-axis so that $f(x) = 12$? Give your result to the nearest mile.

36. Suppose you graph the function $f(x) = \log x$ on a coordinate grid with a unit distance of 1 centimeter on the x- and y-axes. How far out must you go on the x-axis so that $f(x) = 12$? Give the result to the nearest mile. Why is this result so much larger than the result in Exercise 35?

Discovery and Writing

37. One form of the logistic function is given by the following equation. Explain how you would find the y-intercept of its graph.

$$y = \frac{1}{1 + e^{-2x}}$$

38. Graph the function $y = \ln|x|$. Explain why the graph looks the way it does.

Review

Write an equation of the required line.

39. Having a slope of 7 and a y-intercept of 3

40. Parallel to the line $3x + 2y = 9$ and passing through the point $(-3, 5)$

41. A vertical line passing through $(2, 3)$

42. A horizontal line passing through $(2, 3)$

Simplify each expression.

43. $\dfrac{2(x + 2) - 1}{4x^2 - 9}$

44. $\dfrac{x + 1}{x} + \dfrac{x - 1}{x + 1}$

45. $\dfrac{x^2 + 3x + 2}{3x + 9} \cdot \dfrac{x + 3}{x^2 - 4}$

46. $\dfrac{1 + \dfrac{y}{x}}{\dfrac{y}{x} - 1}$

4.5 Properties of Logarithms

In this section, we will learn to

1. Use properties of logarithms to simplify expressions.

2. Use the Change-of-Base Formula.

3. Use logarithms to solve pH problems.

4. Use logarithms to solve problems in electronics.

5. Use logarithms to solve physiology problems.

Rolling Stone magazine lists the rock band U2 at number 22 in their list of the top 100 artists of all time. The Irish band is noted for lead singer Bono's vocals and their anthem-like sound.

Attending a U2 rock concert or cranking up a car stereo and playing U2's song "With or Without You" is an enjoyable activity. Music is an important part of our pop culture. Since many students prefer their music loud, the loudness of sound and its intensity are interesting concepts. In this section, we will see that loudness of sound and the intensity of sound are related by a formula involving the natural logarithmic function.

1. Use Properties of Logarithms to Simplify Expressions

Since logarithms are exponents, the properties of exponents have counterparts in the theory of logarithms. We begin with four basic properties.

Properties of Logarithms If b is a positive number and $b \neq 1$, then

1. $\log_b 1 = 0$ 2. $\log_b b = 1$
3. $\log_b b^x = x$ 4. $b^{\log_b x} = x$ $(x > 0)$

Properties 1 through 4 follow directly from the definition of logarithm.

1. $\log_b 1 = 0$, because $b^0 = 1$.
2. $\log_b b = 1$, because $b^1 = b$.
3. $\log_b b^x = x$, because $b^x = b^x$.
4. $b^{\log_b x} = x$, because $\log_b x$ is the exponent to which b is raised to get x.

Properties 3 and 4 also indicate that the composition of the exponential and logarithmic functions (in both directions) is the identity function. This is expected, because the exponential and logarithmic functions with the same base are inverse functions.

EXAMPLE 1 **Using Properties of Logarithms to Simplify Expressions**

Simplify each expression: **a.** $\log_3 1$ **b.** $\log_4 4$ **c.** $\log_7 7^3$ **d.** $b^{\log_b 3}$

SOLUTION We can simplify each expression using the properties of logariathms.

a. By Property 1, $\log_3 1 = 0$, because $3^0 = 1$.

b. By Property 2, $\log_4 4 = 1$, because $4^1 = 4$.

c. By Property 3, $\log_7 7^3 = 3$, because $7^3 = 7^3$.

d. By Property 4, $b^{\log_b 3} = 3$, because $\log_b 3$ is the power to which b is raised to get 3.

Self Check 1 Simplify: **a.** $\log_4 1$ **b.** $\log_3 3$ **c.** $\log_2 2^4$ **d.** $5^{\log_5 2}$

Now Try Exercise 13.

The four properties also hold for natural logarithms.

1. $\ln 1 = 0$, because $e^0 = 1$.
2. $\ln e = 1$, because $e^1 = e$.
3. $\ln e^x = x$, because $e^x = e^x$.
4. $e^{\ln x} = x$, because $\ln x$ is the exponent to which e is raised to get x.

The next two properties state that

The logarithm of a product is the sum of the logarithms.
The logarithm of a quotient is the difference of the logarithms.

The Logarithm of a Product and a Difference	If M, N, and b are positive numbers and $b \neq 1$, then

5. $\log_b MN = \log_b M + \log_b N$ **6.** $\log_b \dfrac{M}{N} = \log_b M - \log_b N$

Property 5 is known as the **Product Rule**.
Property 6 is known as the **Quotient Rule**.

PROOF   To prove Property 5, we let $x = \log_b M$ and $y = \log_b N$ and use the definition of logarithm to write each equation in exponential form.

$$M = b^x \qquad \text{and} \qquad N = b^y$$

Then $MN = b^x b^y$ and a property of exponents gives

$$MN = b^{x+y} \qquad b^x b^y = b^{x+y}; \text{ keep the base and add the exponents.}$$

We write this exponential equation in logarithmic form as

$$\log_b MN = x + y$$

Substituting the values of x and y completes the proof.

$$\log_b MN = \log_b M + \log_b N$$

The proof of Property 6 is similar. You will be asked to do it in an Exercise 111. ∎

Caution

> By Property 5 of logarithms, the logarithm of a *product* is equal to the *sum* of the logarithms. The logarithm of a product is **not** the product of the logarithms:
>
> $$\log_b MN = (\log_b M)(\log_b N)$$

Caution

> The logarithm of a sum or a difference usually does **not** simplify. In general,
>
> $$\log_b(M + N) = \log_b M + \log_b N$$
>
> and
>
> $$\log_b(M - N) = \log_b M - \log_b N$$

Caution

> By Property 6, the logarithm of a *quotient* is equal to the *difference* of the logarithms. The logarithm of a quotient is **not** the quotient of the logarithms:
>
> $$\log_b \frac{M}{N} = \frac{\log_b M}{\log_b N}$$

Properties 5 and 6 also hold for natural logarithms.

5. $\ln MN = \ln M + \ln N$ Product Rule

6. $\ln \dfrac{M}{N} = \ln M - \ln N$ Quotient Rule

EXAMPLE 2   **Using the Product and Quotient Rules**

Assume that x, y, z, and b are positive numbers and $b \neq 1$. Write each expression in terms of the logarithms of x, y, and z: **a.** $\log_b xyz$ **b.** $\ln \dfrac{x}{yz}$

SOLUTION   We can use the properties of logarithms to write each logarithm as the sum or difference of several logarithms.

a. $\log_b xyz = \log_b(xy)z$

$\qquad\qquad = \log_b(xy) + \log_b z$ The log of a product is the sum of the logs.

$\qquad\qquad = \log_b x + \log_b y + \log_b z$ The log of a product is the sum of the logs.

b. $\ln \dfrac{x}{yz} = \ln x - \ln(yz)$ The ln of a quotient is the difference of the natural logs.

$\qquad\qquad = \ln x - (\ln y + \ln z)$ The ln of a product is the sum of the natural logs.

$\qquad\qquad = \ln x - \ln y - \ln z$ Remove parentheses.

Self Check 2   Write the expression in terms of the logarithms of x, y, and z: $\log_b \dfrac{xy}{z}$

Now Try Exercise 27.

ACCENT ON TECHNOLOGY   **Product and Quotient Rules**

A graphing calculator can be used to verify the Product and Quotient Rules.

- Using the Product Rule, we can write the expression

  $\ln(75 \cdot 20) = \ln 75 + \ln 20$

  Using a graphing calculator, we can verify that these two are equal as shown in Figure 4-29.

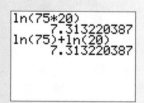

FIGURE 4-29

- Using the Quotient Rule, we can write the expression

  $\log \dfrac{240}{13} = \log 240 - \log 13.$

  Using a graphing calculator, we can verify that these two are equal as shown in Figure 4-30.

FIGURE 4-30

Two more properties state that

The logarithm of a power is the power times the logarithm.

If the logarithms of two numbers are equal, the numbers are equal.

More Properties of Logarithms   If M and b are positive numbers and $b \neq 1$, then

7. $\log_b M^p = p \log_b M$ **8.** If $\log_b x = \log_b y$, then $x = y$.

Property 7 is known as the **Power Rule**.
Property 8 is known as the **One-to-One Property**.

PROOF   To prove Property 7, we let $x = \log_b M$, write the expression in exponential form, and raise both sides to the pth power:

$$M = b^x$$

$$(M)^p = (b^x)^p \qquad \text{Raise both sides to the } p\text{th power.}$$

$$M^p = b^{px} \qquad \text{Keep the base and multiply the exponents.}$$

Using the definition of logarithm gives

$$\log_b M^p = px$$

Substituting the value for x completes the proof.

$$\log_b M^p = p \log_b M$$

Property 8 follows from the fact that the logarithmic function is a one-to-one function. Property 8 will be important in the next section when we solve logarithmic equations.

Properties 7 and 8 also hold for natural logarithms.

7. $\ln M^p = p \ln M$ Power Rule
8. If $\ln x = \ln y$, then $x = y$.

We can use the properties of logarithms to write a logarithm as the sum or difference of several logarithms.

EXAMPLE 3   **Using the Power Rule and Expanding a Logarithmic Expression**

Assume that x, y, z, and b are positive numbers and $b \neq 1$. Write each expression in terms of the logarithms of x, y, and z:

a. $\log_b(x^3 y^2 z)$ **b.** $\ln \dfrac{y^2 \sqrt{z}}{x}$

SOLUTION   We can use the properties of logarithms to write each logarithm as the sum or difference of several logarithms.

a. $\log_b(x^3 y^2 z) = \log_b x^3 + \log_b y^2 + \log_b z$ The log of a product is the sum of the logs.

$\qquad\qquad\qquad = 3 \log_b x + 2 \log_b y + \log_b z$ The log of a power is the power times the log.

b. $\ln \dfrac{y^2 \sqrt{z}}{x} = \ln\left(y^2 \sqrt{z}\right) - \ln x$ The ln of a quotient is the difference of the natural logs.

$\qquad\qquad\qquad = \ln y^2 + \ln z^{1/2} - \ln z$ The ln of a product is the sum of the natural logs: $\sqrt{z} = z^{1/2}$.

$\qquad\qquad\qquad = 2 \ln y + \dfrac{1}{2} \ln z - \ln z$ The ln of a power is the power times the ln.

Self Check 3   Write the expression in terms of the logarithms of x, y, and z: $\log_b \sqrt[3]{\dfrac{x^2 y}{z}}$.

Now Try Exercise 35.

Applying the Power Rule

The development of calculators has made computations extremely easy and accurate, but hand-held calculators have a limit to the size of numbers they can display and evaluate.

- For example, if we were to try to calculate $\log 12^{1000}$, see Figure 4-31(a), we would most likely get an overflow error message as shown in Figure 4-31(b). However, by applying the Power Rule, the number can be evaluated with our calculator as shown in Figure 4-31(c).

(a)   (b)   (c)

FIGURE 4-31

We can use the properties of logarithms to combine several logarithms into one logarithm.

EXAMPLE 4   **Combining Logarithmic Expressions**

Assume that x, y, z, and b are positive numbers and $b \neq 1$. Write each expression as one logarithm:

a. $2 \log_b x + \dfrac{1}{3} \log_b y$ **b.** $\dfrac{1}{2} \log_b(x - 2) - \log_b y + 3 \log_b z$

SOLUTION   We can use the properties of logarithms to combine several logarithms into one logarithm.

a. $2 \log_b x + \dfrac{1}{3} \log_b y = \log_b x^2 + \log_b y^{1/3}$ A power times a log is the log of the power.

$\qquad\qquad\qquad\qquad = \log_b(x^2 y^{1/3})$ The sum of two logs is the log of the product.

$\qquad\qquad\qquad\qquad = \log_b\!\left(x^2 \sqrt[3]{y}\right)$

b. $\dfrac{1}{2} \log_b(x - 2) - \log_b y + 3 \log_b z$

$\qquad = \log_b(x - 2)^{1/2} - \log_b y + \log_b z^3$ A power times a log is the log of the power.

$\qquad = \log_b \dfrac{(x - 2)^{1/2}}{y} + \log_b z^3$ The difference of two logs is the log of the quotient.

$\qquad = \log_b \dfrac{z^3 \sqrt{x - 2}}{y}$ The sum of two logs is the log of the product.

Self Check 4   Write as one logarithm: $2 \ln x + \dfrac{1}{2} \ln y - 3 \ln(x - y)$.

Now Try Exercise 45.

We summarize the eight properties of logarithms and natural logarithms as follows.

Summary of the Properties of Logarithms

If b, M, and N are positive numbers and $b \neq 1$, then

1. $\log_b 1 = 0$
2. $\log_b b = 1$
3. $\log_b b^x = x$
4. $b^{\log_b x} = x$
5. $\log_b MN = \log_b M + \log_b N$
6. $\log_b \dfrac{M}{N} = \log_b M - \log_b N$
7. $\log_b M^p = p \log_b M$
8. If $\log_b x = \log_b y$, then $x = y$.

1. $\ln 1 = 0$
2. $\ln e = 1$
3. $\ln e^x = x$
4. $e^{\ln x} = x$
5. $\ln MN = \ln M + \ln N$
6. $\ln \dfrac{M}{N} = \ln M - \ln N$
7. $\ln M^p = p \ln M$
8. If $\ln x = \ln y$, then $x = y$.

EXAMPLE 5   **Using Properties of Logarithms to Find Approximations**

Given that $\log_{10} 2 \approx 0.3010$ and $\log_{10} 3 \approx 0.4771$, find approximations for

a. $\log_{10} 18$ **b.** $\log_{10} 2.5$

SOLUTION   We will use the properties of logarithms to write each expression in terms of known logarithms. Then, we can substitute the values of the known logarithms and simplify.

a. $\log_{10} 18 = \log_{10}(2 \cdot 3^2)$

$\qquad\qquad = \log_{10} 2 + \log_{10} 3^2$ The log of a product is the sum of the logs.

$\qquad\qquad = \log_{10} 2 + 2 \log_{10} 3$ The log of a power is the power times the log.

$\qquad\qquad \approx 0.3010 + 2(0.4771)$

$\qquad\qquad \approx 1.2552$

b. $\log_{10} 2.5 = \log_{10}\left(\dfrac{5}{2}\right)$

$\qquad\qquad = \log_{10} 5 - \log_{10} 2$ The log of a quotient is the difference of the logs.

$\qquad\qquad = \log_{10} \dfrac{10}{2} - \log_{10} 2$ Write 5 as $\dfrac{10}{2}$.

$\qquad\qquad = \log_{10} 10 - \log_{10} 2 - \log_{10} 2$ The log of a quotient is the difference of the logs.

$\qquad\qquad = 1 - 2 \log_{10} 2$ $\log_{10} 10 = 1$

$\qquad\qquad \approx 1 - 2(0.3010)$

$\qquad\qquad \approx 0.3980$

Self Check 5   Use the information given in Example 5 to find an approximation for $\log_{10} 0.75$.

Now Try Exercise 77.

Comment   In Example 5, it is important to note that we can use logarithmic values that are not stated in the problem. For example, $\log 10 = 1$, $\log 100 = 2$, and $\log 1000 = 3$.

2. Use the Change-of-Base Formula

We have seen how to use a calculator to find base-10 and base-e logarithms. To use a calculator to find logarithms with different bases, such as $\log_7 63$, we can divide the base-10 (or base-e) logarithm of 63 by the base-10 (or base-e) logarithm of 7.

$$\log_7 63 = \frac{\log 63}{\log 7} \qquad \log_7 63 = \frac{\ln 63}{\ln 7}$$

$$\approx 2.129150068 \qquad\qquad \approx 2.129150068$$

To check the result, we verify that $7^{2.129150063} \approx 63$. This example suggests that if we know the base-a logarithm of a number, we can find its logarithm to some other base b.

Change-of-Base Formula If a, b, and x are positive numbers and $a \neq 1$ and $b \neq 1$, then

$$\log_b x = \frac{\log_a x}{\log_a b}$$

To prove this formula, we begin with the equation $\log_b x = y$.

$$y = \log_b x$$

$$x = b^y \qquad \text{Change the equation from logarithmic to exponential form.}$$

$$\log_a x = \log_a b^y \qquad \text{Take the base-}a\text{ logarithm of both sides.}$$

$$\log_a x = y \log_a b \qquad \text{The log of a power is the power times the log.}$$

$$y = \frac{\log_a x}{\log_a b} \qquad \text{Divide both sides by } \log_a b.$$

$$\log_b x = \frac{\log_a x}{\log_a b} \qquad \text{Refer to the first equation and substitute } \log_b x \text{ for } y.$$

Caution

$\dfrac{\log_a x}{\log_a b}$ means that one logarithm is to be divided by the other. They are **not** to be subtracted.

If we know logarithms to base a (for example, $a = 10$), we can find the logarithm of x to a new base b by dividing the base-a logarithm of x by the base-a logarithm of b.

EXAMPLE 6 **Using the Change-of-Base Formula**

Use the Change-of-Base Formula to find $\log_3 5$.

SOLUTION We can substitute 3 for b, 10 for a, and 5 for x into the Change-of-Base Formula and simplify.

$$\log_b x = \frac{\log_a x}{\log_a b}$$

$$\log_3 5 = \frac{\log_{10} 5}{\log_{10} 3} \qquad \text{Divide the base-10 logarithm of 5 by the base-10 logarithm of 3.}$$

$$\approx 1.464973521$$

To four decimal places, $\log_3 5 = 1.4650$.

Self Check 6 Find $\log_5 3$ to four decimal places.

Now Try Exercise 89.

ACCENT ON TECHNOLOGY   **Using the Change-of-Base Formula to Graph a Logarithmic Function**

We can use the Change-of-Base Formula to graph logarithmic functions that do not have a base of 10. Consider the function

$$f(x) = \log_4(x + 1)$$

- Since the base of the function $f(x) = \log_4(x + 1)$ is 4, to graph this function on a calculator, we use the Change-of-Base Formula and rewrite the function as

$$f(x) = \log_4(x + 1) = \frac{\log(x + 1)}{\log 4}$$

We enter the function as shown in Figure 4-32(a). We can also use the natural logarithm function if we prefer.
- The domain of this function is $(-1, \infty)$, so there will be a vertical asymptote of $x = -1$. This will help us set our WINDOW. We then GRAPH the function. See Figures 4-32(b) and (c).
- Notice that the graph appears to "stop" at $x = -1$, but that is not the case. We can have the calculator evaluate the function at a value very close to $x = -1$ to verify this. Notice in Figure 4-32(d) that the point on the graph is not shown, but the value is indicated.

FIGURE 4-32

We can use properties of logarithms to solve many problems.

3. Use Logarithms to Solve pH Problems

The more acidic a chemical solution, the greater the concentration of hydrogen ions. Chemists measure this concentration indirectly by the **pH scale,** or the **hydrogen ion index.**

pH of a Solution   If $[H^+]$ is the hydrogen ion concentration in gram-ions per liter, then

$$pH = -\log[H^+]$$

Since pure water has approximately 10^{-7} gram-ions per liter, its pH is

$$\text{pH} = -\log[\text{H}^+]$$
$$\text{pH} = -\log 10^{-7}$$
$$= -(-7)\log 10 \qquad \text{\small The log of a power is the power times the log.}$$
$$= -(-7) \cdot 1 \qquad \text{\small Use Property 2 of logarithms: } \log_b b = 1.$$
$$= 7$$

EXAMPLE 7   **Solving an Application Involving pH**

Seawater has a pH of approximately 8.5. Find its hydrogen ion concentration.

SOLUTION   We can substitute 8.5 for pH and solve the equation $\text{pH} = -\log[\text{H}^+]$ for $[\text{H}^+]$.

$$8.5 = -\log[\text{H}^+]$$
$$-8.5 = \log[\text{H}^+]$$
$$[\text{H}^+] = 10^{-8.5} \qquad \text{\small Change the equation from logarithmic form to exponential form.}$$

We can then use a calculator to find that $[\text{H}^+] \approx 3.2 \times 10^{-9}$ gram-ions per liter. ∎

Self Check 7   The pH of a solution is 5.7. Find the hydrogen ion concentration.

Now Try Exercise 101.

4. Use Logarithms to Solve Problems in Electronics

Recall that if E_O is the output voltage of a device and E_I is the input voltage, the decibel voltage gain is given by

$$(1) \quad \text{dB gain} = 20 \log \frac{E_O}{E_I}$$

If input and output are measured in watts instead of volts, a different formula is needed.

EXAMPLE 8   **Finding an Alternate Formula for Voltage Gain**

Show that an alternate formula for dB voltage gain is

$$\text{dB gain} = 10 \log \frac{P_O}{P_I}$$

where P_I is the power input and P_O is the power output.

SOLUTION   Power is directly proportional to the square of the voltage. So for some constant k,

$$P_I = k(E_I)^2 \qquad \text{and} \qquad P_O = k(E_O)^2$$

and

$$\frac{P_O}{P_I} = \frac{k(E_O)^2}{k(E_I)^2} = \left(\frac{E_O}{E_I}\right)^2$$

We raise both sides to the $\frac{1}{2}$ power to get

$$\frac{E_O}{E_I} = \left(\frac{P_O}{P_I}\right)^{1/2}$$

which we substitute into Equation (1) for dB gain.

$$\text{dB gain} = 20 \log \frac{E_O}{E_I}$$

$$= 20 \log \left(\frac{P_O}{P_I}\right)^{1/2}$$

$$= 20 \cdot \frac{1}{2} \log \frac{P_O}{P_I} \qquad \text{The log of a power is the power times the log.}$$

$$\text{dB gain} = 10 \log \frac{P_O}{P_I} \qquad \text{Simplify.}$$

Self Check 8   Find the dB gain of a device to the nearest hundredth when $P_O = 30$ watts and $P_I = 2$ watts.

Now Try Exercise 103.

5. Use Logarithms to Solve Physiology Problems

In physiology, experiments suggest that the relationship between the loudness and the intensity of sound is a logarithmic one known as the Weber–Fechner Law.

Weber–Fechner Law   If L is the apparent loudness of a sound and I is the intensity, then

$$L = k \ln I$$

EXAMPLE 9   **Using the Weber-Fechner Law**

What increase in the intensity of a sound is necessary to cause a doubling of the apparent loudness?

SOLUTION   We use the formula $L = k \ln I$. To double the apparent loudness, we multiply both sides of the equation by 2 and use Property 7 of logarithms.

$$L = k \ln I$$

$$2L = 2k \ln I$$

$$= k \ln I^2$$

To double the apparent loudness, we must square the intensity.

Self Check 9   What increase is necessary to triple the apparent loudness?

Now Try Exercise 105.

Self Check Answers   **1. a.** 0   **b.** 1   **c.** 4   **d.** 2   **2.** $\log_b x + \log_b y - \log_b z$

3. $\frac{1}{3}(2 \log_b x + \log_b y - \log_b z)$ **4.** $\ln \frac{x^2 \sqrt{y}}{(x-y)^3}$

5. -0.1249 **6.** 0.6826 **7.** 2×10^{-6} .**8.** 11.76 decibels

9. Cube the intensity.

Exercises **4.5**

Getting Ready

You should be able to complete these vocabulary and concept statements before you proceed to the practice exercises.

Fill in the blanks.

1. $\log_b 1 = $ ___
2. $\log_b b = $ ___
3. $\log_b MN = \log_b$ ___ $+ \log_b$ ___
4. $b^{\log_b x} = $ ___
5. If $\log_b x = \log_b y$, then ___ $= $ ___.
6. $\log_b \dfrac{M}{N} = \log_b M$ ___ $\log_b N$
7. $\log_b x^p = p \cdot \log_b$ ___
8. $\log_b b^x = $ ___
9. $\log_b(A + B)$ ___ $\log_b A + \log_b B$
10. $\log_b A + \log_b B$ ___ $\log_b AB$

Simplify each expression.

11. $\log_4 1 = $ ___
12. $\log_4 4 = $ ___
13. $\log_4 4^7 = $ ___
14. $4^{\log_4 8} = $ ___
15. $5^{\log_5 10} = $ ___
16. $\log_5 5^2 = $ ___
17. $\log_5 5 = $ ___
18. $\log_5 1 = $ ___

Practice

Use a calculator to verify each equation.

19. $\log[(3.7)(2.9)] = \log 3.7 + \log 2.9$
20. $\ln \dfrac{9.3}{2.1} = \ln 9.3 - \ln 2.1$
21. $\ln(3.7)^3 = 3 \ln 3.7$
22. $\log\sqrt{14.1} = \dfrac{1}{2}\log 14.1$
23. $\log 3.2 = \dfrac{\ln 3.2}{\ln 10}$
24. $\ln 9.7 = \dfrac{\log 9.7}{\log e}$

Assume that x, y, z, and b are positive numbers and $b \ne 1$. Use the properties of logarithms to write each expression in terms of the logarithms of x, y, and z.

25. $\log_b 2xy$
26. $\log_b 3xz$
27. $\log_b \dfrac{2x}{y}$
28. $\log_b \dfrac{x}{yz}$
29. $\log_b x^2 y^3$
30. $\log_b x^3 y^2 z$
31. $\log_b(xy)^{1/3}$
32. $\log_b x^{1/2} y^3$
33. $\log_b x\sqrt{z}$
34. $\log_b \sqrt{xy}$
35. $\log_b \dfrac{\sqrt[3]{x}}{\sqrt[3]{yz}}$
36. $\log_b \sqrt[4]{\dfrac{x^3 y^2}{z^4}}$
37. $\ln x^7 y^8$
38. $\ln \dfrac{4x}{y}$
39. $\ln \dfrac{x}{y^4 z}$
40. $\ln x\sqrt{y}$

Assume that x, y, z, and b are positive numbers and $b \ne 1$. Use the properties of logarithms to write each expression as the logarithm of one quantity.

41. $\log_b(x + 1) - \log_b x$
42. $\log_b x + \log_b(x + 2) - \log_b 8$
43. $2 \log_b x + \dfrac{1}{3} \log_b y$
44. $-2 \log_b x - 3 \log_b y + \log_b z$
45. $-3 \log_b x - 2 \log_b y + \dfrac{1}{2} \log_b z$
46. $3 \log_b(x + 1) - 2 \log_b(x + 2) + \log_b x$
47. $\log_b\left(\dfrac{x}{z} + x\right) - \log_b\left(\dfrac{y}{z} + y\right)$
48. $\log_b(xy + y^2) - \log_b(xz + yz) + \log_b z$
49. $\ln x + \ln(x + 5) - \ln 9$
50. $5 \ln x + \dfrac{1}{5} \ln y$
51. $-6 \ln x - 2 \ln y + \ln z$
52. $-2 \ln x - 3 \ln y + \dfrac{1}{3} \ln z$

Determine whether each statement is true or false.

53. $\log_b ab = \log_b a + 1$
54. $\log_b \dfrac{1}{a} = -\log_b a$
55. $\log_b 0 = 1$
56. $\log_b 2 = \log_2 b$
57. $\log_b(x + y) \ne \log_b x + \log_b y$

58. $\log_b xy = (\log_b x)(\log_b y)$

59. If $\log_a b = c$, then $\log_b a = c$.

60. If $\log_a b = c$, then $\log_b a = \dfrac{1}{c}$.

61. $\log_7 7^7 = 7$

62. $7^{\log_7 7} = 7$

63. $\log_b(-x) = -\log_b x$

64. If $\log_b a = c$, then $\log_b a^p = pc$.

65. $\dfrac{\log_b A}{\log_b B} = \log_b A - \log_b B$

66. $\log_b(A - B) = \dfrac{\log_b A}{\log_b B}$

67. $\log_b \dfrac{1}{5} = -\log_b 5$

68. $3\log_b\sqrt[3]{a} = \log_b a$

69. $\dfrac{1}{3}\log_b a^3 = \log_b a$

70. $\log_{4/3} y = -\log_{3/4} y$

71. $\log_b y + \log_{1/b} y = 0$

72. $\log_{10} 10^3 = 3(10^{\log_{10} 3})$

73. $\ln xy = (\ln x)(\ln y)$

74. $\dfrac{\ln A}{\ln B} = \ln A - \ln B$

75. $\dfrac{1}{5}\ln a^5 = \ln a$

76. $\ln y = -\ln\dfrac{1}{y}$

Given that $\log_{10} 4 \approx 0.6021$, $\log_{10} 7 \approx 0.8451$, *and* $\log_{10} 9 \approx 0.9542$, *use these values and the properties of logarithms to approximate each value. Do not use a calculator.*

77. $\log_{10} 28$

78. $\log_{10} \dfrac{7}{4}$

79. $\log_{10} 2.25$

80. $\log_{10} 36$

81. $\log_{10} \dfrac{63}{4}$

82. $\log_{10} \dfrac{4}{63}$

83. $\log_{10} 252$

84. $\log_{10} 49$

85. $\log_{10} 112$

86. $\log_{10} 324$

87. $\log_{10} \dfrac{144}{49}$

88. $\log_{10} \dfrac{324}{63}$

Use a calculator and the Change-of-Base Formula to find each logarithm. Round to four decimal places.

89. $\log_3 7$

90. $\log_7 3$

91. $\log_\pi 3$

92. $\log_3 \pi$

93. $\log_3 8$

94. $\log_5 10$

95. $\log_{\sqrt{2}} \sqrt{5}$

96. $\log_\pi e$

Applications

97. pH of water slide The water in the Abyss, a water slide at the Atlantis Resort in the Bahamas, has a hydrogen ion concentration of 6.3×10^{-8} gram-ions per liter. Find the pH.

98. pH of swimming pool The ideal pH for a swimming pool is 7.2, the same pH as our eyes. The swimming pool at the local YMCA has a hydrogen ion concentration of 1.6×10^{-7} gram-ions per liter. Find the pH of the pool. Is this ideal?

99. pH of a solution Find the pH of a solution with a hydrogen ion concentration of 1.7×10^{-5} gram-ions per liter.

100. pH of calcium hydroxide Find the hydrogen ion concentration of a saturated solution of calcium hydroxide whose pH is 13.2.

101. pH of apples The pH of apples can range from 2.9 to 3.3. Find the range in the hydrogen ion concentration.

Mazzzur/Shutterstock.com

102. pH of sour pickles The hydrogen ion concentration of sour pickles is 6.31×10^{-4}. Find the pH.

© iStockphoto.com/James McQuillan

103. dB gain An amplifier produces a 40-watt output with a $\frac{1}{2}$-watt input. Find the dB gain.

104. dB loss Losses in a long telephone line reduce a 12-watt input signal to an output of 3 watts. Find the dB gain. (Because it is a loss, the "gain" will be negative.)

105. Weber–Fechner Law What increase in intensity is necessary to quadruple the loudness?

106. Weber–Fechner Law What decrease in intensity is necessary to make a sound half as loud?

107. Isothermal expansion If a certain amount E of energy is added to one mole of a gas, it expands from an initial volume of 1 liter to a final volume V without changing its temperature according to the formula

$$E = 8{,}300 \ln V$$

Find the volume if twice that energy is added to the gas.

108. Richter scale By what factor must the amplitude of an earthquake change to increase its severity by 1 point on the Richter scale? Assume that the period remains constant. The Richter scale is given by

$$R = \log \frac{A}{P}$$

where A is the amplitude and P the period of the tremor.

Discovery and Writing

109. Simplify: $3^{4\log_3 2} + 5^{\frac{1}{2}\log_5 25}$

110. Find the value of $a - b$:

$$5\log x + \frac{1}{3}\log y - \frac{1}{2}\log x - \frac{5}{6}\log y = \log(x^a y^b)$$

111. Prove Property 6 of logarithms:

$$\log_b \frac{M}{N} = \log_b M - \log_b N$$

112. Show that $-\log_b x = \log_{1/b} x$.

113. Show that $e^{x \ln a} = a^x$.

114. Show that $e^{\ln x} = x$.

115. Show that $\ln(e^x) = x$.

116. If $\log_b 3x = 1 + \log_b x$, find b.

117. Explain why $\ln(\log 0.9)$ is undefined.

118. Explain why $\log_b(\ln 1)$ is undefined.

In Exercises 119–120, A and B both are negative. Thus, AB and $\frac{A}{B}$ are positive, and $\log AB$ and $\log \frac{A}{B}$ are defined.

119. Is it still true that $\log AB = \log A + \log B$? Explain.

120. Is it still true that $\log \frac{A}{B} = \log A - \log B$? Explain.

Review

Determine whether each equation defines a function.

121. $y = 3x - 1$

122. $y = \dfrac{x + 3}{x - 1}$

123. $y^2 = 4x$

124. $y = 4x^2$

Find the domain of each function.

125. $f(x) = x^2 - 4$

126. $f(x) = \dfrac{1}{x^2 - 4}$

127. $f(x) = \sqrt{x^2 + 4}$

128. $f(x) = \sqrt{x^2 - 4}$

4.6 Exponential and Logarithmic Equations

In this section, we will learn to

1. Use like bases to solve exponential equations.
2. Use logarithms to solve exponential equations.
3. Solve logarithmic equations.
4. Solve carbon-14 dating problems.
5. Solve population growth problems.

Coffee is one of the most popular beverages worldwide. Suppose we visit a coffee shop and order a white chocolate mocha. After blending smooth white chocolate with rich espresso and steamed milk and topping it with whipped cream, the coffee is served to us at a temperature of 180°F.

Suppose the exponential function $T = 70 + 110e^{-0.2t}$ models the temperature T of the mocha after t minutes. If we are interested in determining how long it will take for the temperature of the coffee to reach 80°F, we would substitute 80 in for

T and solve the resulting equation $80 = 70 + 110e^{-0.2t}$ for t. This equation is called an *exponential equation* because the variable t occurs as an exponent.

In this section, we will learn to solve exponential equations. When we complete Exercise 105, we will see that it takes the mocha approximately 12 minutes to reach a temperature of 80°F. We will also learn to solve *logarithmic equations* in this section.

An **exponential equation** is an equation with a variable in one of its exponents. Some examples of exponential equations are

$$3^x = 5 \qquad e^{2x} = 7 \qquad 6^{x-3} = 2^x \qquad 3^{2x+1} - 10(3^x) + 3 = 0$$

A **logarithmic equation** is an equation with logarithmic expressions that contain a variable. Some examples of logarithmic equations are

$$\log 2x = 25 \qquad \ln x - \ln(x - 12) = 24 \qquad \log x = \log \frac{1}{x} + 4$$

1. Use Like Bases to Solve Exponential Equations

Some exponential equations can be solved by using like bases.

One-to-One Property of Exponents	If $b^x = b^y$ and $b \neq 1$, $b \neq 0$, then $x = y$. That is, equal quantities with like bases have equal exponents.

EXAMPLE 1   Using Like Bases to Solve an Exponential Equation

Solve: $4^{x+3} = 8^{2x}$.

SOLUTION   We will use like bases to solve the exponential equation.

$$4^{x+3} = 8^{2x}$$
$$(2^2)^{x+3} = (2^3)^{2x} \qquad \text{Write 4 as } 2^2 \text{ and 8 as } 2^3.$$
$$2^{2(x+3)} = 2^{6x} \qquad \text{Multiply exponents.}$$
$$2(x + 3) = 6x \qquad \text{Equal quantities with like bases have equal exponents.}$$
$$2x + 6 = 6x \qquad \text{Use the Distributive Property.}$$
$$-4x = -6 \qquad \text{Subtract 6 and } 6x \text{ from both sides.}$$
$$x = \frac{3}{2} \qquad \text{Divide both sides by } -4 \text{ and simplify.}$$

Self Check 1   Solve: $3^{3x-5} = 81$.

Now Try Exercise 13.

EXAMPLE 2   Using Like Bases to Solve an Exponential Equation

Solve: $2^{x^2+2x} = \frac{1}{2}$.

SOLUTION   Since $\frac{1}{2} = 2^{-1}$, we can write the equation in the form $2^{x^2+2x} = 2^{-1}$ and use like bases to solve the equation.

Because equal quantities with like bases have equal exponents, we have

$$x^2 + 2x = -1$$

$x^2 + 2x + 1 = 0$	Add 1 to both sides.
$(x + 1)(x + 1) = 0$	Factor the trinomial.
$x + 1 = 0$ or $x + 1 = 0$	Set each factor equal to 0.
$x = -1$ $x = -1$	

Verify that -1 satisfies the equation.

Self Check 2   Solve: $3^{x^2+2x} = 27$.

Now Try Exercise 19.

ACCENT ON TECHNOLOGY   **Verifying Solutions of an Exponential Equation**

We can verify that -1 satisfies the equation shown in Example 2 by using the TABLE feature on a graphing calculator.

- Enter each side of the equation as shown in Figure 4-33.
- Go to TABLE and enter $x = -1$. Notice in Figure 4-33 that the y-values are exactly the same. This confirms that $x = -1$ is a solution.

Plot1 Plot2 Plot3		X	Y₁	Y₂
\Y₁⊟2^(X^2+2X)		-1	.5	.5
\Y₂⊟1/2				
\Y₃=				
\Y₄=				
\Y₅=				
\Y₆=				
\Y₇=		X=		

FIGURE 4-33

EXAMPLE 3   **Using Like Bases to Solve an Exponential Equation**

Solve: $e^{6x^2} = e^{-x+1}$.

SOLUTION   We can use like bases to solve the exponential equation.
Because equal quantities with like bases have equal exponents, we have

$$6x^2 = -x + 1$$

$6x^2 + x - 1 = 0$	Add $x - 1$ to both sides.
$(3x - 1)(2x + 1) = 0$	Factor the trinomial.
$3x - 1 = 0$ or $2x + 1 = 0$	Set each factor equal to 0.
$x = \dfrac{1}{3}$ $x = -\dfrac{1}{2}$	Solve each equation.

Verify that $\frac{1}{3}$ and $-\frac{1}{2}$ satisfy the equation.

Self Check 3   Solve: $e^{4x^2} = e^{24}$.

Now Try Exercise 23.

2. Use Logarithms to Solve Exponential Equations

If the bases of the terms in an exponential equation are not equal, as is often the case, we use logarithms to solve the equation.

Since logarithmic functions are one-to-one, we can take the logarithm of both sides of an equation. This allows us to use the properties of logarithms to help solve the equation. A logarithm of any base may be used, but it is most efficient to use natural logarithms or common logarithms because a calculator is often needed to get an approximate answer. A strategy for solving exponential equations with different bases is given next.

Strategy for Solving Exponential Equations with Different Bases

To solve an exponential equation we can follow these steps:

Step 1: Isolate the exponential expression.

Step 2: Take the same logarithm of both sides.

Step 3: Simplify using the rules of logarithms.

Step 4: Solve for the variable.

When using the strategy given, please keep the following things in mind:

- If the equation contains base e, it is most efficient to use natural logarithms because

  $\ln e^x = x$

- If the equation contains base 10, it is most efficient to use common logarithms because

  $\log 10^x = x$

- If the equation contains exponential terms with bases other than base e or 10, use either natural logarithms or common logarithms.

EXAMPLE 4   **Using Logarithms to Solve an Exponential Equation with Different Bases**

Solve the exponential equation: $3^x = 5$.

SOLUTION   We will use the strategy outlined above to solve the exponential equation. First, we note that the exponential expression 3^x is isolated. Since logarithms of equal numbers are equal, we can take the common logarithm of each side of the equation. We can then use the Power Rule and move the variable x from its position as an exponent to a position as a coefficient and solve the equation.

$$3^x = 5$$

$$\log 3^x = \log 5 \qquad \text{Take the common logarithm of each side.}$$

$$x \log 3 = \log 5 \qquad \text{The log of a power is the power times the log.}$$

$$(1) \qquad x = \frac{\log 5}{\log 3} \qquad \text{Divide both sides by log 3.}$$

$$\approx 1.464973521 \qquad \text{Use a calculator.}$$

To four decimal places, $x = 1.4650$.

Self Check 4   Solve $5^x = 3$ to four decimal places.

Now Try Exercise 27.

Caution

A careless reading of Equation 1 leads to a common error. The right side of the equation calls for a division, **not** a subtraction.

$$\frac{\log 5}{\log 3} \quad \text{means} \quad (\log 5) \div (\log 3)$$

It is the expression $\log \frac{5}{3}$ that means $\log 5 - \log 3$.

EXAMPLE 5 Using Logarithms to Solve an Exponential Equation with Different Bases

Solve the exponential equation: $6^{x-3} = 2^x$.

SOLUTION We will use logarithms to solve the exponential equation and apply the strategy stated earlier.

$$6^{x-3} = 2^x$$

$\log 6^{x-3} = \log 2^x$ Take the common logarithm of each side.

$(x - 3)\log 6 = x \log 2$ The log of a power is the power times the log.

$x \log 6 - 3 \log 6 = x \log 2$ Use the Distributive Property.

$x \log 6 - x \log 2 = 3 \log 6$ Add 3 log 6 and subtract x log 2 from both sides.

$x(\log 6 - \log 2) = 3 \log 6$ Factor out x on the left-hand side.

$$x = \frac{3 \log 6}{\log 6 - \log 2}$$ Divide both sides by log 6 − log 2.

$x \approx 4.892789261$ Use a calculator.

To four decimal places, $x = 4.8928$.

Self Check 5 Solve: $5^{x+3} = 3^x$.

Now Try Exercise 29.

Comment We can use common logarithms or natural logarithms to solve many exponential equations. In Examples 4 and 5, we took the common logarithm of both sides of an equation to solve the equation. We could just as well have taken the natural logarithm of both sides and obtained the same decimal result.

In the next example, we will take the natural logarithm of both sides of an exponential equation. However, before we do, it is a good idea to review the following properties of natural logarithms.

Natural Logarithm Properties
$\ln 1 = 0$ $\ln e = 1$ $\ln e^x = x$
Product Rule: $\ln MN = \ln M + \ln N$
Quotient Rule: $\ln \dfrac{M}{N} = \ln M - \ln N$
Power Rule: $\ln M^p = p \ln M$

EXAMPLE 6 Using Natural Logarithms to Solve Exponential Equations

Use natural logarithms to solve **a.** $e^x - 7 = 0$ **b.** $4^{x+3} = 8^{2x}$

SOLUTION   For each problem, we will use the strategy stated earlier. We will isolate the exponential expression, take the natural logarithm of both sides, simplify using the natural logarithms properties, and solve for x.

a. $e^x - 7 = 0$

$$e^x - 7 + 7 = 0 + 7 \qquad \text{Isolate the exponential expression. Add 7 to both sides.}$$

$$e^x = 7$$

$$\ln e^x = \ln 7 \qquad \text{Take the natural logarithm of both sides.}$$

$$x = \ln 7 \qquad \text{Substitute } x \text{ for } \ln e^x : \ln e^x = x \,.$$

$$x \approx 1.95 \qquad \text{Use a calculator and round to two decimal places.}$$

b. $4^{x+3} = 8^{2x}$

$$\ln 4^{x+3} = \ln 8^{2x} \qquad \text{Take the natural logarithm of both sides.}$$

$$(x + 3)\ln 4 = (2x)\ln 8 \qquad \text{The log of a power is the power times the log.}$$

$$x \ln 4 + 3 \ln 4 = 2x \ln 8 \qquad \text{Use the Distributive Property on the left side.}$$

$$x \ln 4 - 2x \ln 8 = -3 \ln 4 \qquad \text{Subtract } 2x \ln 8 \text{ and } 3 \ln 4 \text{ from both sides.}$$

$$x(\ln 4 - 2 \ln 8) = -3 \ln 4 \qquad \text{Factor out } x \text{ on the left-hand side.}$$

$$x = \frac{-3 \ln 4}{\ln 4 - 2 \ln 8} \qquad \text{Divide both sides by } \ln 4 - 2 \ln 8.$$

$$x = 1.5 \qquad \text{Use a calculator.}$$

Comment

As we see in Example 6a, if an exponential equation has a term with a base of e, then taking the natural logarithm of both sides is a good choice.

Comment

Note that the exponential equations in Examples 1 and 6b are identical and the answers are the same. As we see, sometimes we can use like bases or logarithms to solve the same equation.

Self Check 6   Use natural logarithms to solve: **a.** $3e^x = 12$ **b.** $8^{x+1} = 4^{2x}$

Now Try Exercise 39.

ACCENT ON TECHNOLOGY   **Finding Approximate Solutions to an Exponential Equation**

If only a decimal approximation of a solution is needed, a graphing calculator can be used to solve exponential equations. Our strategy is to graph each side of the equation and then find the point of intersection.

We will use a graphing calculator to solve the exponential equation
$$\sqrt{3}^{\,x} = 2^{\pi x - 3}.$$

• Enter each side of the equation in the graph menu and find the point of intersection. We see in the figure below that the solution is $x \approx 1.2770786$.

(a)   (b)   (c)

(d)   (e)   (f)

FIGURE 4-34

3. Solve Logarithmic Equations

We can use the One-to-One Property of logarithms to change some logarithmic equations into algebraic equations that we can solve. Here's a reminder of that property.

One-to-One Property of Logarithms	If $\log_b x = \log_b y$, then $x = y$. That is, logarithms of equal numbers are equal.

EXAMPLE 7 **Using the One-to-One Property of Logarithms to Solve a Logarithmic Equation**

Solve: $\log_5(3x + 2) = \log_5(2x - 3)$.

SOLUTION We will use the property of logarithms stated above to solve the equation. Then we will check our solutions.

$$\log_5(3x + 2) = \log_5(2x - 3)$$

$$3x + 2 = 2x - 3 \qquad \text{If the logs of two numbers are equal, the numbers are equal.}$$

$$x = -5 \qquad \text{Subtract } 2x \text{ and } 2 \text{ from both sides.}$$

Check: $$\log_5(3x + 2) = \log_5(2x - 3)$$

$$\log_5[3(-5) + 2] \overset{?}{=} \log_5[2(-5) - 3]$$

$$\log_5(-13) \overset{?}{=} \log_5(-13)$$

Since the logarithm of a negative number does not exist, -5 is extraneous and must be discarded. The equation has no roots.

Self Check 7 Solve: $\log_3(5x + 2) = \log_3(6x + 1)$.

Now Try Exercise 57.

Comment It is incorrect to state that the logarithms in Example 7 are canceled. The logarithms aren't canceled; the One-to-One Property is used.

Caution

> Example 7 illustrates that we **must** check the solutions of a logarithmic equation. If we fail to do so, we risk having incorrect answers.

EXAMPLE 8 **Solving a Logarithmic Equation Using the Properties of Logarithms**

Solve: $\log x + \log(x - 3) = 1$.

SOLUTION We will first combine the two logarithms as a single logarithm. Next, we will use the definition of logarithm to write the equation in exponential form. Finally, we will solve the equation and check the solutions.

$$\log x + \log(x - 3) = 1$$

$$\log x(x - 3) = 1 \qquad \text{The sum of two logs is the log of a product.}$$

$$x(x - 3) = 10^1 \qquad \text{Use the definition of logarithms to change the equation to exponential form.}$$

$$x^2 - 3x - 10 = 0 \qquad \text{Remove parentheses and subtract 10 from both sides.}$$

$$(x + 2)(x - 5) = 0 \qquad \text{Factor the trinomial.}$$

$$x + 2 = 0 \quad \text{or} \quad x - 5 = 0$$

$$x = -2 \qquad \qquad x = 5$$

Check: The number -2 is not a solution, because it does not satisfy the equation (a negative number does not have a logarithm). We check the remaining number, 5.

$$\log x + \log(x - 3) = 1$$

$$\log 5 + \log(5 - 3) \stackrel{?}{=} 1 \qquad \text{Substitute 5 for } x.$$

$$\log 5 + \log 2 \stackrel{?}{=} 1$$

$$\log 10 \stackrel{?}{=} 1 \qquad \text{The sum of two logs is the log of a product.}$$

$$1 = 1 \qquad \log_b b = 1$$

Since 5 does check, it is a root.

Self Check 8   Solve: $\log x + \log(x - 15) = 2$.

Now Try Exercise 61.

EXAMPLE 9   **Solving Logarithmic Equations**

Solve: $\ln(2x + 5) - \ln(x + 5) = \ln \dfrac{5}{3}$.

SOLUTION   First, we combine the two logarithms on the left. Then we will use the One-to-One Property and solve for x.

$$\ln(2x + 5) - \ln(x + 5) = \ln \frac{5}{3}$$

$$\ln \frac{2x + 5}{x + 5} = \ln \frac{5}{3} \qquad \text{Use the Quotient Rule and combine logs.}$$

$$\frac{2x + 5}{x + 5} = \frac{5}{3} \qquad \text{Use the One-to-One Property of logs.}$$

$$3(2x + 5) = 5(x + 5) \qquad \text{Multiply both sides by } 3(x + 5).$$

$$6x + 15 = 5x + 25$$

$$x = 10$$

Check: The solution $x = 10$ checks as we see here.

$$\ln(2x + 5) - \ln(x + 5) \stackrel{?}{=} \ln \frac{5}{3}$$

$$\ln[2(10) + 5] - \ln[(10) + 5] \stackrel{?}{=} \ln \frac{5}{3} \qquad \text{Substitute 10 in for } x.$$

$$\ln 25 - \ln 15 \stackrel{?}{=} \ln \frac{5}{3}$$

$$\ln \frac{25}{15} \stackrel{?}{=} \ln \frac{5}{3} \qquad \text{Use the Quotient Rule.}$$

$$\ln \frac{5}{3} = \ln \frac{5}{3} \qquad \text{This is a true statement.}$$

Self Check 9   Solve: $\log_7(2x + 2) - \log_7(x + 6) = \log_7 \dfrac{4}{3}$.

Now Try Exercise 69.

EXAMPLE 10   **Solving Logarithmic Equations**

Solve **a.** $\ln x = 5$ **b.** $\dfrac{\ln(5x - 6)}{\ln x} = 2$

SOLUTION   For part (a), we will write the natural logarithm as $\log_e x = 5$ and use the definition of logarithm to solve the equation. For part (b), we will multiply both sides by $\ln x$ and then use properties of logarithms to write an algebraic equation. We will then solve the equation. We must verify the solutions to both parts.

a. $\ln x = 5$

   $\log_e x = 5$ Rewrite using the definition of natural logarithm.

   $x = e^5$ Write in exponential form.

Verify that e^5 satisfies the solution.

b. We multiply both sides of $\dfrac{\ln(5x - 6)}{\ln x} = 2$ by $\ln x$ to get

   $\ln(5x - 6) = 2 \ln x$

and apply the Power Rule of logarithms to get

   $\ln(5x - 6) = \ln x^2$

By the property of logarithms stated above $5x - 6 = x^2$, because they have equal logarithms. So

$$x^2 = 5x - 6$$

$$x^2 - 5x + 6 = 0$$

$$(x - 3)(x - 2) = 0$$

$$x - 3 = 0 \quad \text{or} \quad x - 2 = 0$$

$$x = 3 \quad | \quad x = 2$$

Verify that both 2 and 3 satisfy the equation.

Self Check 10   Solve: **a.** $6 \ln x = 12$ **b.** $\dfrac{\ln(8x - 15)}{\ln x} = 2$

Now Try Exercise 79.

The strategy we used to solve a logarithmic equation was dependent upon the nature of the equation. A summary of these strategies appears here.

Summary of Strategies Used to Solve Logarithmic Equations

1. For logarithmic equations containing one logarithm, we can use the definition of the logarithm. We write the logarithm in exponential form and then solve for the variable.

   Note: This strategy can be used to solve the following logarithmic equations.

   $$\log_3(x + 5) = 2, \log(x^2 - 4) = 5, \ln(4x) = 7$$

2. For more complicated logarithmic equations, we can combine and isolate the logarithmic expressions. We can then use the definition of the logarithm and write the logarithm in exponential form to solve for the variable.

Note: This strategy can be used to solve the following logarithmic equations.

$$\log(x) + \log(x - 1) = 3,\ \log_5(3x + 2) - \log_5(2x - 3) = 2,$$
$$\ln x - \ln(x + 3) = 4$$

3. We can use the One-to-One Property of logarithms for logarithmic equations of the form $\log_b x = \log_b y$.

Note: This strategy can be used to solve the following logarithmic equations.

$$\log(5x - 6) = \log x^2,\ \ln(2x - 7) = \ln(3x + 5)$$

4. For other types of logarithmic equations, we sometimes combine logarithms on one or both sides and then use the One-to-One Property of logarithms to solve the equations.

Note: This strategy can be used to solve the following logarithmic equations.

$$\ln(x^2) + \ln(x - 3) = \ln(x + 4),\ \log_4 x - \log_4(x + 2) = \log_4 5 + \log_4(3x)$$

ACCENT ON TECHNOLOGY　**Finding Approximate Solutions to a Logarithmic Equation**

We can use a graphing calculator to approximate the solutions of a logarithmic equation.

Consider the log equation $\ln x^2 + \ln(x - 3) = \ln(x + 4)$.

- Enter each side of the equation in the graph menu, and then find the point of intersection. We see that in Figure 4-35 that $x \approx 3.5891327$. Use ⌜ZOOM⌟ and select ZDecimal to graph.

FIGURE 4-35

4. Solve Carbon-14 Dating Problems

When a living organism dies, the oxygen/carbon dioxide cycle common to all living things ceases; then carbon-14, a radioactive isotope with a half-life of 5,700 years, is no longer absorbed. By measuring the amount of carbon-14 present in ancient objects, archaeologists can estimate the object's age.

The Shroud of Turin, the piece of linen long believed to have been wrapped around Jesus's body after the crucifixion, is much older than the date suggested by radiocarbon tests, according to new microchemical research. Published in the current issue of *Thermochimica Acta*, a chemistry peer-reviewed scientific journal, the study dismisses the results of the 1988 carbon-14 dating. At that time, three reputable laboratories in Oxford, Zurich, and Tucson, Ariz., concluded that the cloth on which the smudged outline of the body of a man is indelibly impressed was a medieval fake dating from 1260 to 1390 and not the burial cloth wrapped around the body of Christ.

AP Photo/Barrie M. Schwortz

The amount A of radioactive material present at time t is given by the model

$$A = A_0 2^{-t/h}$$

where A_0 is the amount present initially and h is the half-life of the material.

EXAMPLE 11   Solving a Carbon-14 Dating Problem

An archeologist finds a wooden statue in the tomb of an ancient Egyptian ruler. If the statue contains two-thirds of its original carbon-14 content, how old is it?

SOLUTION   To find the time t when $A = \frac{2}{3}A_0$, we substitute $\frac{2A_0}{3}$ for A and 5,700 for h in the radioactive decay formula and solve for t:

$$A = A_0 2^{-t/h}$$

$$\frac{2A_0}{3} = A_0 2^{-t/5,700}$$

$$1 = \frac{3}{2}\left(2^{-t/5,700}\right) \qquad \text{Divide both sides by } A_0 \text{ and multiply both sides by } \frac{3}{2}.$$

$$\log 1 = \log \frac{3}{2}\left(2^{-t/5,700}\right) \qquad \text{Take the common logarithm of each side.}$$

$$0 = \log \frac{3}{2} + \log 2^{-t/5,700} \qquad \text{The log of a product is the sum of the logs.}$$

$$-\log \frac{3}{2} = -\frac{t}{5,700}\log 2 \qquad \text{Subtract } \log \frac{3}{2} \text{ from both sides and use the Power Rule of logarithms.}$$

$$5,700\left(\frac{\log \frac{3}{2}}{\log 2}\right) = t \qquad \text{Multiply both sides by } -\frac{5,700}{\log 2}.$$

$$t \approx 3,334.286254 \qquad \text{Use a calculator.}$$

The wooden statue is approximately 3,300 years old.

Self Check 11   How old is an artifact that has 60% of its original carbon-14 content?

Now Try Exercise 95.

5. Solve Population Growth Problems

When there is sufficient food and space, populations of living organisms tend to increase exponentially according to the Malthusian growth model

$$P = P_0 e^{kt}$$

where P_0 is the initial population at $t = 0$ and k depends on the rate of growth.

EXAMPLE 12   **Solving a Population Growth Problem**

Streptococcus bacteria in a laboratory culture increased from an initial population of 500 to 1,500 in 3 hours. Find the time it will take for the population to reach 10,000.

SOLUTION   We will apply the following two steps to solve the problem:

Step 1: Substitute 1,500 for P, 500 for P_0, and 3 for t into the Malthusian growth model and find k.

Step 2: Substitute 10,000 for P, 500 for P_0, and the value of k found in Step 1 into the model and use logarithms to solve for t.

1. Substitute 1,500 for P, 500 for P_0, and 3 for t into the Malthusian growth model and find k:

$$P = P_0 e^{kt}$$

$$1{,}500 = 500(e^{k3}) \qquad \text{Substitute 1,500 for } P \text{, 500 for } P_0 \text{, and 3 for } t.$$

$$3 = e^{3k} \qquad \text{Divide both sides by 500.}$$

$$3k = \ln 3 \qquad \text{Take the natural log of both sides.}$$

$$k = \frac{\ln 3}{3} \qquad \text{Divide both sides by 3.}$$

2. To find out when the population will reach 10,000, we substitute 10,000 for P, 500 for P_0, and $\frac{\ln 3}{3}$ for k in the equation $P = P_0 e^{kt}$, and solve for t:

$$P = P_0 e^{kt}$$

$$10{,}000 = 500 e^{\left(\frac{\ln 3}{3}\right)t}$$

$$20 = e^{\left(\frac{\ln 3}{3}\right)t} \qquad \text{Divide both sides by 500.}$$

$$\ln(20) = \ln\left[e^{\left(\frac{\ln 3}{3}\right)t}\right] \qquad \text{Take the natural log of both sides.}$$

$$\ln(20) = \frac{\ln 3}{3}t \qquad \text{Simplify the right side using the natural log property } \ln(e^x) = x.$$

$$t = \frac{3\ln 20}{\ln 3} \qquad \text{Multiply both sides by } \frac{3}{\ln 3}.$$

$$\approx 8.180499084 \qquad \text{Use a calculator.}$$

The culture will reach 10,000 bacteria in a little more than 8 hours.

Self Check 12   If the population increases from 1,000 to 3,000 in 3 hours, how long will it take to reach 20,000?

Now Try Exercise 103.

Self Check Answers   **1.** 3   **2.** 1, −3   **3.** ±$\sqrt{6}$ **4.** $x = 0.6826$ **5.** −9.4520
   6. a. ln 4   **b.** 3   **7.** 1   **8.** 20; −5 is extraneous   **9.** 9
   10. a. e^2 **b.** 3, 5   **11.** about 4,200 years   **12.** about 8 hr

Exercises **4.6**

Getting Ready

You should be able to complete these vocabulary and concept statements before you proceed to the practice exercises.

Fill in the blanks.

1. An equation with a variable in its exponent is called a(n) _____ equation.
2. An equation with a logarithmic expression that contains a variable is a(n) _____ equation.
3. The formula for carbon dating is $A =$ _____.
4. The formula for population growth is $P =$ _____.

Practice

Solve each exponential equation using like bases.

5. $2^{3x+2} = 16^x$
6. $32^{x+2} = 2^{7x+12}$
7. $27^{x+1} = 3^{2x+1}$
8. $3^{x-1} = 9^{2x}$
9. $5^{4x+1} = 25^{-x-2}$
10. $5^{2x+1} = 125^x$
11. $4^{x-2} = 8^x$
12. $16^{x+1} = 8^{2x+1}$
13. $81^{2x} = 27^{2x-5}$
14. $625^{x-9} = 125^{x-12}$
15. $2^{x^2-2x} = 8$
16. $5^{x^2+3x} = 625$
17. $36^{x^2} = 216^{x^2-3}$
18. $25^{x^2-5x} = 3{,}125^{4x}$
19. $7^{x^2+3x} = \dfrac{1}{49}$
20. $3^{x^2+4x} = \dfrac{1}{81}$
21. $e^{-x+6} = e^x$
22. $e^{2x+1} = e^{3x-11}$
23. $e^{x^2-1} = e^{24}$
24. $e^{x^2+7x} = \dfrac{1}{e^{12}}$

Solve each exponential equation using logarithms. Give the answer in decimal form, rounding to four decimal places.

25. $4^x = 5$
26. $7^x = 12$
27. $13^{x-1} = 2$
28. $5^{x+1} = 3$
29. $2^{x+1} = 3^x$
30. $5^{x-3} = 3^{2x}$
31. $2^x = 3^x$
32. $3^{2x} = 4^x$
33. $7^{x^2} = 10$
34. $8^{x^2} = 11$
35. $8^{x^2} = 9^x$
36. $5^{x^2} = 2^{5x}$

Find the exact solution to each exponential equation.

37. $e^x = 10$
38. $8e^x = 16$
39. $4e^{2x} = 24$
40. $2e^{5x} = 18$

Solve each equation. If an answer is not exact, give the answer in decimal form. Round to four decimal places.

41. $4^{x+2} - 4^x = 15$ (*Hint:* $4^{x+2} = 4^x 4^2$.)
42. $3^{x+3} + 3^x = 84$ (*Hint:* $3^{x+3} = 3^x 3^3$.)
43. $2(3^x) = 6^{2x}$
44. $2(3^{x+1}) = 3(2^{x-1})$
45. $2^{2x} - 10(2^x) + 16 = 0$ (*Hint:* Let $y = 2^x$.)
46. $3^{2x} - 10(3^x) + 9 = 0$ (*Hint:* Let $y = 3^x$.)
47. $2^{2x+1} - 2^x = 1$ (*Hint:* $2^{a+b} = 2^a 2^b$.)
48. $3^{2x+1} - 10(3^x) + 3 = 0$ (*Hint:* $3^{a+b} = 3^a 3^b$.)

Solve each logarithmic equation. Use the definition of logarithm or the definition of natural logarithm.

49. $\log x^2 = 2$
50. $\log x^3 = 3$
51. $\log \dfrac{4x + 1}{2x + 9} = 0$
52. $\log \dfrac{5x + 2}{2(x + 7)} = 0$
53. $\ln x = 6$
54. $\ln x = 3$
55. $\ln(2x - 7) = 4$
56. $\ln(3x - 5) = 7$

Solve each logarithmic equation.

57. $\log(2x - 3) = \log(x + 4)$
58. $\log(3x + 5) - \log(2x + 6) = 0$
59. $\log x + \log(x - 48) = 2$
60. $\log x + \log(x + 9) = 1$
61. $\log x + \log(x - 15) = 2$
62. $\log x + \log(x + 21) = 2$
63. $\log(x + 90) = 3 - \log x$
64. $\log(x - 3) - \log(6) = 2$
65. $\log(5{,}000) - \log(x - 2) = 3$
66. $\log(2x - 3) - \log(x - 1) = 0$
67. $\log_7 x + \log_7(x - 5) = \log_7 6$
68. $\ln x + \ln(x - 2) = \ln 120$
69. $\ln 15 - \ln(x - 2) = \ln x$
70. $\ln 10 - \ln(x - 3) = \ln x$
71. $\log_6 8 - \log_6 x = \log_6(x - 2)$
72. $\log(x - 6) - \log(x - 2) = \log \dfrac{5}{x}$

73. $\log(x - 1) - \log 6 = \log(x - 2) - \log x$

74. $\log x^2 = (\log x)^2$

75. $\log(\log x) = 1$

76. $\log_3(\log_3 x) = 1$

77. $\dfrac{\log(3x - 4)}{\log x} = 2$

78. $\dfrac{\ln(8x - 7)}{\ln x} = 2$

79. $\dfrac{\ln(5x + 6)}{2} = \ln x$

80. $\dfrac{1}{2} \log(4x + 5) = \log x$

81. $\log_3 x = \log_3\left(\dfrac{1}{x}\right) + 4$

82. $\log_5(7 + x) + \log_5(8 - x) - \log_5 2 = 2$

83. $2 \log_2 x = 3 + \log_2(x - 2)$

84. $2 \log_3 x - \log_3(x - 4) = 2 + \log_3 2$

85. $\ln(7y + 1) = 2 \ln(y + 3) - \ln 2$

86. $2 \log(y + 2) = \log(y + 2) - \log 12$

Use a graphing calculator to solve each equation. If an answer is not exact, give the result to the nearest hundredth.

87. $\log x + \log(x - 15) = 2$

88. $\log x + \log(x + 3) = 1$

89. $2^{x+1} = 7$

90. $\ln(2x + 5) - \ln 3 = \ln(x - 1)$

Applications

Use a calculator to help solve each problem.

91. Tritium decay The half-life of tritium is 12.4 years. How long will it take for 25% of a sample of tritium to decompose?

92. Radioactive decay In 2 years, 20% of a radioactive element decays. Find its half-life.

93. Thorium decay An isotope of thorium, ^{227}Th, has a half-life of 18.4 days. How long will it take 80% of the sample to decompose?

94. Lead decay An isotope of lead, ^{201}Pb, has a half-life of 8.4 hours. How many hours ago was there 30% more of the substance?

95. Carbon-14 dating A cloth fragment is found in an ancient tomb. It contains 70% of the carbon-14 that it is assumed to have had initially. How old is the cloth?

96. Carbon-14 dating Only 25% of the carbon-14 in a wooden bowl remains. How old is the bowl?

97. Compound interest If $500 is deposited in an account paying 8.5% annual interest, compounded semiannually, how long will it take for the account to increase to $800?

98. Continuous compound interest In Exercise 97, how long will it take if the interest is compounded continuously?

99. Compound interest If $1,300 is deposited in a savings account paying 9% interest, compounded quarterly, how long will it take the account to increase to $2,100?

100. Compound interest A sum of $5,000 deposited in an account grows to $7,000 in 5 years. Assuming annual compounding, what interest rate is being paid?

101. Rule of Seventy A rule of thumb for finding how long it takes an investment to double is called the **Rule of Seventy.** To apply the rule, divide 70 by the interest rate (expressed as a percent). At 5%, it takes $\dfrac{70}{5} = 14$ years to double the investment. At 7%, it takes $\dfrac{70}{7} = 10$ years. Explain why this formula works.

102. Oceanography The intensity I of a light a distance x meters beneath the surface of a lake decreases exponentially. If the light intensity at 6 meters is 70% of the intensity at the surface, at what depth will the intensity be 20%?

103. Bacterial growth A staphylococcus bacterial culture grows according to the formula $P = P_0 a^t$. If it takes 5 days for the culture to triple in size, how long will it take to double in size?

104. Rodent control The rodent population in a city is currently estimated at 30,000. If it is expected to double every 5 years, when will the population reach 1 million?

105. Temperature of coffee Refer to the section opener and find the time it takes for the white chocolate mocha to reach a temperature of 80°F.

106. Time of death The exponential function $T(t) = 17e^{-0.0626t} + 20$ models the temperature T in °C of a person's body t hours after death. If a dead body is discovered at 8:30 a.m. and the body's temperature is 30°C, what was the person's approximate time of death?

107. Newton's Law of Cooling Water whose temperature is at 100°C is left to cool in a room where the temperature is 60°C. After 3 minutes, the water temperature is 90°. If the water temperature T is a function of time t given by $T = 60 + 40e^{kt}$, find k.

108. Newton's Law of Cooling Refer to Exercise 107 and find the time for the water temperature to reach 70°C.

109. Newton's Law of Cooling A block of steel, initially at $0°C$, is placed in an oven heated to $300°C$. After 5 minutes, the temperature of the steel is $100°C$. If the steel temperature T is a function of time t given by $T = 300 - 300e^{kt}$, find the value of k.

110. Newton's Law of Cooling Refer to Exercise 109 and find the time for the steel temperature to reach $200°C$.

Discovery and Writing

111. Explain why it is necessary to check the solutions of a logarithmic equation.

112. Use the population growth formula to show that the doubling time for population growth is given by $t = \frac{\ln 2}{r}$.

113. Use the population growth formula to show that the tripling time for population growth is given by $t = \frac{\ln 3}{r}$.

114. Can you solve $x = \log x$ algebraically? Can you find an approximate solution?

Find x.

115. $\log_2(\log_5(\log_7 x)) = 2$

116. $\log_8 \left[16\sqrt[3]{4,096} \right]^{\frac{1}{6}} = x$

Review

Find the inverse of the function defined by each equation.

117. $y = 3x + 2$

118. $y = \dfrac{1}{x - 3}$

Let $f(x) = 5x - 1$ and $g(x) = x^2$. Find each value.

119. $(f \circ g)(2)$

120. $(g \circ f)(2)$

121. $(f \circ g)(x)$

122. $(g \circ f)(x)$

Appendix I: A Proof of the Binomial Theorem

The Binomial Theorem can be proved for positive-integer exponents using mathematical induction.

The Binomial Theorem If n is a positive integer, then

$$(a + b)^n = a^n + \frac{n!}{1!(n - 1)!}a^{n-1}b^1 + \frac{n!}{2!(n - 2)!}a^{n-2}b^2 + \cdots$$

$$+ \frac{n!}{r!(n - r)!}a^{n-r}b^r + \cdots + b^n$$

PROOF As in all induction proofs, there are two parts.

Part 1: Substituting the number 1 for n on both sides of the equation, we have

$$(a + b)^1 = a^1 + \frac{1!}{1!(1 - 1)!}a^{1-1}b^1$$

$$a + b = a + a^0 b$$

$$a + b = a + b$$

and the theorem is true when $n = 1$. Part 1 is complete.

Part 2: We write expressions for two general terms in the statement of the induction hypothesis. We assume that the theorem is true for $n = k$:

$$(a + b)^k = a^k + \frac{k!}{1!(k - 1)!}a^{k-1}b + \frac{k!}{2!(k - 2)!}a^{k-2}b^2 + \cdots$$

$$+ \frac{k!}{(r - 1)!(k - r + 1)!}a^{k-r+1}b^{r-1}$$

$$+ \frac{k!}{r!(k - r)!}a^{k-r}b^r + \cdots + b^k$$

We multiply both sides of this equation by $a + b$ and hope to obtain a similar equation in which the quantity $k + 1$ replaces all of the n values in the Binomial Theorem:

$$(a + b)^k(a + b)$$

$$= (a + b)\left[a^k + \frac{k!}{1!(k - 1)!}a^{k-1}b + \frac{k!}{2!(k - 2)!}a^{k-2}b^2 + \cdots \right.$$

$$\left. + \frac{k!}{(r - 1)!(k - r + 1)!}a^{k-r+1}b^{r-1} + \frac{k!}{r!(k - r)!}a^{k-r}b^r + \cdots + b^k \right]$$

We distribute the multiplication first by a and then by b:

$$(a + b)^{k+1} = \left[a^{k+1} + \frac{k!}{1!(k - 1)!}a^k b + \frac{k!}{2!(k - 2)!}a^{k-1}b^2 + \cdots \right.$$

$$\left. + \frac{k!}{(r - 1)!(k - r + 1)!}a^{k-r+2}b^{r-1} + \frac{k!}{r!(k - r)!}a^{k-r+1}b^r + \cdots + ab^k \right]$$

$$+ \left[a^k b + \frac{k!}{1!(k - 1)!}a^{k-1}b^2 + \frac{k!}{2!(k - 2)!}a^{k-2}b^3 + \cdots \right.$$

$$\left. + \frac{k!}{(r - 1)!(k - r + 1)!}a^{k-r+1}b^r + \frac{k!}{r!(k - r)!}a^{k-r}b^{r+1} + \cdots + b^{k+1} \right]$$

Combining like terms, we have

$$(a + b)^{k+1} = a^{k+1} + \left[\frac{k!}{1!(k-1)!} + 1 \right] a^k b$$

$$+ \left[\frac{k!}{2!(k-2)!} + \frac{k!}{1!(k-1)!} \right] a^{k-1} b^2 + \cdots$$

$$+ \left[\frac{k!}{r!(k-r)!} + \frac{k!}{(r-1)!(k-r+1)!} \right] a^{k-r+1} b^r + \cdots + b^{k+1}$$

These results may be written as

$$(a + b)^{k+1} = a^{k+1} + \frac{(k+1)!}{1!(k+1-1)!} a^{(k+1)-1} b + \frac{(k+1)!}{2!(k+1-2)!} a^{(k+1)-2} b^2$$

$$+ \cdots + \frac{(k+1)!}{r!(k+1-r)!} a^{(k+1)-r} b^r + \cdots + b^{k+1}$$

This formula has precisely the same form as the Binomial Theorem, with the quantity $k + 1$ replacing all of the original n values. Therefore, the truth of the theorem for $n = k$ implies the truth of the theorem for $n = k + 1$. Because both parts of the axiom of mathematical induction are verified, the theorem is proved. ∎

Appendix II: Tables

Table A Powers and Roots

n	n^2	$\sqrt{n}$	n^3	$\sqrt[3]{n}$	n	n^2	$\sqrt{n}$	n^3	$\sqrt[3]{n}$
1	1	1.000	1	1.000	51	2,601	7.141	132,651	3.708
2	4	1.414	8	1.260	52	2,704	7.211	140,608	3.733
3	9	1.732	27	1.442	53	2,809	7.280	148,877	3.756
4	16	2.000	64	1.587	54	2,916	7.348	157,464	3.780
5	25	2.236	125	1.710	55	3,025	7.416	166,375	3.803
6	36	2.449	216	1.817	56	3,136	7.483	175,616	3.826
7	49	2.646	343	1.913	57	3,249	7.550	185,193	3.849
8	64	2.828	512	2.000	58	3,364	7.616	195,112	3.871
9	81	3.000	729	2.080	59	3,481	7.681	205,379	3.893
10	100	3.162	1,000	2.154	60	3,600	7.746	216,000	3.915
11	121	3.317	1,331	2.224	61	3,721	7.810	226,981	3.936
12	144	3.464	1,728	2.289	62	3,844	7.874	238,328	3.958
13	169	3.606	2,197	2.351	63	3,969	7.937	250,047	3.979
14	196	3.742	2,744	2.410	64	4,096	8.000	262,144	4.000
15	225	3.873	3,375	2.466	65	4,225	8.062	274,625	4.021
16	256	4.000	4,096	2.520	66	4,356	8.124	287,496	4.041
17	289	4.123	4,913	2.571	67	4,489	8.185	300,763	4.062
18	324	4.243	5,832	2.621	68	4,624	8.246	314,432	4.082
19	361	4.359	6,859	2.668	69	4,761	8.307	328,509	4.102
20	400	4.472	8,000	2.714	70	4,900	8.367	343,000	4.121
21	441	4.583	9,261	2.759	71	5,041	8.426	357,911	4.141
22	484	4.690	10,648	2.802	72	5,184	8.485	373,248	4.160
23	529	4.796	12,167	2.844	73	5,329	8.544	389,017	4.179
24	576	4.899	13,824	2.884	74	5,476	8.602	405,224	4.198
25	625	5.000	15,625	2.924	75	5,625	8.660	421,875	4.217
26	676	5.099	17,576	2.962	76	5,776	8.718	438,976	4.236
27	729	5.196	19,683	3.000	77	5,929	8.775	456,533	4.254
28	784	5.292	21,952	3.037	78	6,084	8.832	474,552	4.273
29	841	5.385	24,389	3.072	79	6,241	8.888	493,039	4.291
30	900	5.477	27,000	3.107	80	6,400	8.944	512,000	4.309
31	961	5.568	29,791	3.141	81	6,561	9.000	531,441	4.327
32	1,024	5.657	32,768	3.175	82	6,724	9.055	551,368	4.344
33	1,089	5.745	35,937	3.208	83	6,889	9.110	571,787	4.362
34	1,156	5.831	39,304	3.240	84	7,056	9.165	592,704	4.380
35	1,225	5.916	42,875	3.271	85	7,225	9.220	614,125	4.397
36	1,296	6.000	46,656	3.302	86	7,396	9.274	636,056	4.414
37	1,369	6.083	50,653	3.332	87	7,569	9.327	658,503	4.431
38	1,444	6.164	54,872	3.362	88	7,744	9.381	681,472	4.448
39	1,521	6.245	59,319	3.391	89	7,921	9.434	704,969	4.465
40	1,600	6.325	64,000	3.420	90	8,100	9.487	729,000	4.481
41	1,681	6.403	68,921	3.448	91	8,281	9.539	753,571	4.498
42	1,764	6.481	74,088	3.476	92	8,464	9.592	778,688	4.514
43	1,849	6.557	79,507	3.503	93	8,649	9.644	804,357	4.531
44	1,936	6.633	85,184	3.530	94	8,836	9.695	830,584	4.547
45	2,025	6.708	91,125	3.557	95	9,025	9.747	857,375	4.563
46	2,116	6.782	97,336	3.583	96	9,216	9.798	884,736	4.579
47	2,209	6.856	103,823	3.609	97	9,409	9.849	912,673	4.595
48	2,304	6.928	110,592	3.634	98	9,604	9.899	941,192	4.610
49	2,401	7.000	117,649	3.659	99	9,801	9.950	970,299	4.626
50	2,500	7.071	125,000	3.684	100	10,000	10.000	1,000,000	4.642

Table B (continued)

N	0	1	2	3	4	5	6	7	8	9
5.5	.7404	.7412	.7419	.7427	.7435	.7443	.7451	.7459	.7466	.7474
5.6	.7482	.7490	.7497	.7505	.7513	.7520	.7528	.7536	.7543	.7551
5.7	.7559	.7566	.7574	.7582	.7589	.7597	.7604	.7612	.7619	.7627
5.8	.7634	.7642	.7649	.7657	.7664	.7672	.7679	.7686	.7694	.7701
5.9	.7709	.7716	.7723	.7731	.7738	.7745	.7752	.7760	.7767	.7774
6.0	.7782	.7789	.7796	.7803	.7810	.7818	.7825	.7832	.7839	.7846
6.1	.7853	.7860	.7868	.7875	.7882	.7889	.7896	.7903	.7910	.7917
6.2	.7924	.7931	.7938	.7945	.7952	.7959	.7966	.7973	.7980	.7987
6.3	.7993	.8000	.8007	.8014	.8021	.8028	.8035	.8041	.8048	.8055
6.4	.8062	.8069	.8075	.8082	.8089	.8096	.8102	.8109	.8116	.8122
6.5	.8129	.8136	.8142	.8149	.8156	.8162	.8169	.8176	.8182	.8189
6.6	.8195	.8202	.8209	.8215	.8222	.8228	.8235	.8241	.8248	.8254
6.7	.8261	.8267	.8274	.8280	.8287	.8293	.8299	.8306	.8312	.8319
6.8	.8325	.8331	.8338	.8344	.8351	.8357	.8363	.8370	.8376	.8382
6.9	.8388	.8395	.8401	.8407	.8414	.8420	.8426	.8432	.8439	.8445
7.0	.8451	.8457	.8463	.8470	.8476	.8482	.8488	.8494	.8500	.8506
7.1	.8513	.8519	.8525	.8531	.8537	.8543	.8549	.8555	.8561	.8567
7.2	.8573	.8579	.8585	.8591	.8597	.8603	.8609	.8615	.8621	.8627
7.3	.8633	.8639	.8645	.8651	.8657	.8663	.8669	.8675	.8681	.8686
7.4	.8692	.8698	.8704	.8710	.8716	.8722	.8727	.8733	.8739	.8745
7.5	.8751	.8756	.8762	.8768	.8774	.8779	.8785	.8791	.8797	.8802
7.6	.8808	.8814	.8820	.8825	.8831	.8837	.8842	.8848	.8854	.8859
7.7	.8865	.8871	.8876	.8882	.8887	.8893	.8899	.8904	.8910	.8915
7.8	.8921	.8927	.8932	.8938	.8943	.8949	.8954	.8960	.8965	.8971
7.9	.8976	.8982	.8987	.8993	.8998	.9004	.9009	.9015	.9020	.9025
8.0	.9031	.9036	.9042	.9047	.9053	.9058	.9063	.9069	.9074	.9079
8.1	.9085	.9090	.9096	.9101	.9106	.9112	.9117	.9122	.9128	.9133
8.2	.9138	.9143	.9149	.9154	.9159	.9165	.9170	.9175	.9180	.9186
8.3	.9191	.9196	.9201	.9206	.9212	.9217	.9222	.9227	.9232	.9238
8.4	.9243	.9248	.9253	.9258	.9263	.9269	.9274	.9279	.9284	.9289
8.5	.9294	.9299	.9304	.9309	.9315	.9320	.9325	.9330	.9335	.9340
8.6	.9345	.9350	.9355	.9360	.9365	.9370	.9375	.9380	.9385	.9390
8.7	.9395	.9400	.9405	.9410	.9415	.9420	.9425	.9430	.9435	.9440
8.8	.9445	.9450	.9455	.9460	.9465	.9469	.9474	.9479	.9484	.9489
8.9	.9494	.9499	.9504	.9509	.9513	.9518	.9523	.9528	.9533	.9538
9.0	.9542	.9547	.9552	.9557	.9562	.9566	.9571	.9576	.9581	.9586
9.1	.9590	.9595	.9600	.9605	.9609	.9614	.9619	.9624	.9628	.9633
9.2	.9638	.9643	.9647	.9652	.9657	.9661	.9666	.9671	.9675	.9680
9.3	.9685	.9689	.9694	.9699	.9703	.9708	.9713	.9717	.9722	.9727
9.4	.9731	.9736	.9741	.9745	.9750	.9754	.9759	.9763	.9768	.9773
9.5	.9777	.9782	.9786	.9791	.9795	.9800	.9805	.9809	.9814	.9818
9.6	.9823	.9827	.9832	.9836	.9841	.9845	.9850	.9854	.9859	.9863
9.7	.9868	.9872	.9877	.9881	.9886	.9890	.9894	.9899	.9903	.9908
9.8	.9912	.9917	.9921	.9926	.9930	.9934	.9939	.9943	.9948	.9952
9.9	.9956	.9961	.9965	.9969	.9974	.9978	.9983	.9987	.9991	.9996

Table B   Base-10 Logarithms

N	0	1	2	3	4	5	6	7	8	9
1.0	.0000	.0043	.0086	.0128	.0170	.0212	.0253	.0294	.0334	.0374
1.1	.0414	.0453	.0492	.0531	.0569	.0607	.0645	.0682	.0719	.0755
1.2	.0792	.0828	.0864	.0899	.0934	.0969	.1004	.1038	.1072	.1106
1.3	.1139	.1173	.1206	.1239	.1271	.1303	.1335	.1367	.1399	.1430
1.4	.1461	.1492	.1523	.1553	.1584	.1614	.1644	.1673	.1703	.1732
1.5	.1761	.1790	.1818	.1847	.1875	.1903	.1931	.1959	.1987	.2014
1.6	.2041	.2068	.2095	.2122	.2148	.2175	.2201	.2227	.2253	.2279
1.7	.2304	.2330	.2355	.2380	.2405	.2430	.2455	.2480	.2504	.2529
1.8	.2553	.2577	.2601	.2625	.2648	.2672	.2695	.2718	.2742	.2765
1.9	.2788	.2810	.2833	.2856	.2878	.2900	.2923	.2945	.2967	.2989
2.0	.3010	.3032	.3054	.3075	.3096	.3118	.3139	.3160	.3181	.3201
2.1	.3222	.3243	.3263	.3284	.3304	.3324	.3345	.3365	.3385	.3404
2.2	.3424	.3444	.3464	.3483	.3502	.3522	.3541	.3560	.3579	.3598
2.3	.3617	.3636	.3655	.3674	.3692	.3711	.3729	.3747	.3766	.3784
2.4	.3802	.3820	.3838	.3856	.3874	.3892	.3909	.3927	.3945	.3962
2.5	.3979	.3997	.4014	.4031	.4048	.4065	.4082	.4099	.4116	.4133
2.6	.4150	.4166	.4183	.4200	.4216	.4232	.4249	.4265	.4281	.4298
2.7	.4314	.4330	.4346	.4362	.4378	.4393	.4409	.4425	.4440	.4456
2.8	.4472	.4487	.4502	.4518	.4533	.4548	.4564	.4579	.4594	.4609
2.9	.4624	.4639	.4654	.4669	.4683	.4698	.4713	.4728	.4742	.4757
3.0	.4771	.4786	.4800	.4814	.4829	.4843	.4857	.4871	.4886	.4900
3.1	.4914	.4928	.4942	.4955	.4969	.4983	.4997	.5011	.5024	.5038
3.2	.5051	.5065	.5079	.5092	.5105	.5119	.5132	.5145	.5159	.5172
3.3	.5185	.5198	.5211	.5224	.5237	.5250	.5263	.5276	.5289	.5302
3.4	.5315	.5328	.5340	.5353	.5366	.5378	.5391	.5403	.5416	.5428
3.5	.5441	.5453	.5465	.5478	.5490	.5502	.5514	.5527	.5539	.5551
3.6	.5563	.5575	.5587	.5599	.5611	.5623	.5635	.5647	.5658	.5670
3.7	.5682	.5694	.5705	.5717	.5729	.5740	.5752	.5763	.5775	.5786
3.8	.5798	.5809	.5821	.5832	.5843	.5855	.5866	.5877	.5888	.5899
3.9	.5911	.5922	.5933	.5944	.5955	.5966	.5977	.5988	.5999	.6010
4.0	.6021	.6031	.6042	.6053	.6064	.6075	.6085	.6096	.6107	.6117
4.1	.6128	.6138	.6149	.6160	.6170	.6180	.6191	.6201	.6212	.6222
4.2	.6232	.6243	.6253	.6263	.6274	.6284	.6294	.6304	.6314	.6325
4.3	.6335	.6345	.6355	.6365	.6375	.6385	.6395	.6405	.6415	.6425
4.4	.6435	.6444	.6454	.6464	.6474	.6484	.6493	.6503	.6513	.6522
4.5	.6532	.6542	.6551	.6561	.6571	.6580	.6590	.6599	.6609	.6618
4.6	.6628	.6637	.6646	.6656	.6665	.6675	.6684	.6693	.6702	.6712
4.7	.6721	.6730	.6739	.6749	.6758	.6767	.6776	.6785	.6794	.6803
4.8	.6812	.6821	.6830	.6839	.6848	.6857	.6866	.6875	.6884	.6893
4.9	.6902	.6911	.6920	.6928	.6937	.6946	.6955	.6964	.6972	.6981
5.0	.6990	.6998	.7007	.7016	.7024	.7033	.7042	.7050	.7059	.7067
5.1	.7076	.7084	.7093	.7101	.7110	.7118	.7126	.7135	.7143	.7152
5.2	.7160	.7168	.7177	.7185	.7193	.7202	.7210	.7218	.7226	.7235
5.3	.7243	.7251	.7259	.7267	.7275	.7284	.7292	.7300	.7308	.7316
5.4	.7324	.7332	.7340	.7348	.7356	.7364	.7372	.7380	.7388	.7396

Table C Base-e Logarithms

N	0	1	2	3	4	5	6	7	8	9
1.0	.0000	.0100	.0198	.0296	.0392	.0488	.0583	.0677	.0770	.0862
1.1	.0953	.1044	.1133	.1222	.1310	.1398	.1484	.1570	.1655	.1740
1.2	.1823	.1906	.1989	.2070	.2151	.2231	.2311	.2390	.2469	.2546
1.3	.2624	.2700	.2776	.2852	.2927	.3001	.3075	.3148	.3221	.3293
1.4	.3365	.3436	.3507	.3577	.3646	.3716	.3784	.3853	.3920	.3988
1.5	.4055	.4121	.4187	.4253	.4318	.4383	.4447	.4511	.4574	.4637
1.6	.4700	.4762	.4824	.4886	.4947	.5008	.5068	.5128	.5188	.5247
1.7	.5306	.5365	.5423	.5481	.5539	.5596	.5653	.5710	.5766	.5822
1.8	.5878	.5933	.5988	.6043	.6098	.6152	.6206	.6259	.6313	.6366
1.9	.6419	.6471	.6523	.6575	.6627	.6678	.6729	.6780	.6831	.6881
2.0	.6931	.6981	.7031	.7080	.7129	.7178	.7227	.7275	.7324	.7372
2.1	.7419	.7467	.7514	.7561	.7608	.7655	.7701	.7747	.7793	.7839
2.2	.7885	.7930	.7975	.8020	.8065	.8109	.8154	.8198	.8242	.8286
2.3	.8329	.8372	.8416	.8459	.8502	.8544	.8587	.8629	.8671	.8713
2.4	.8755	.8796	.8838	.8879	.8920	.8961	.9002	.9042	.9083	.9123
2.5	.9163	.9203	.9243	.9282	.9322	.9361	.9400	.9439	.9478	.9517
2.6	.9555	.9594	.9632	.9670	.9708	.9746	.9783	.9821	.9858	.9895
2.7	.9933	.9969	1.0006	.0043	.0080	.0116	.0152	.0188	.0225	.0260
2.8	1.0296	.0332	.0367	.0403	.0438	.0473	.0508	.0543	.0578	.0613
2.9	.0647	.0682	.0716	.0750	.0784	.0818	.0852	.0886	.0919	.0953
3.0	1.0986	.1019	.1053	.1086	.1119	.1151	.1184	.1217	.1249	.1282
3.1	.1314	.1346	.1378	.1410	.1442	.1474	.1506	.1537	.1569	.1600
3.2	.1632	.1663	.1694	.1725	.1756	.1787	.1817	.1848	.1878	.1909
3.3	.1939	.1969	.2000	.2030	.2060	.2090	.2119	.2149	.2179	.2208
3.4	.2238	.2267	.2296	.2326	.2355	.2384	.2413	.2442	.2470	.2499
3.5	1.2528	.2556	.2585	.2613	.2641	.2669	.2698	.2726	.2754	.2782
3.6	.2809	.2837	.2865	.2892	.2920	.2947	.2975	.3002	.3029	.3056
3.7	.3083	.3110	.3137	.3164	.3191	.3218	.3244	.3271	.3297	.3324
3.8	.3350	.3376	.3403	.3429	.3455	.3481	.3507	.3533	.3558	.3584
3.9	.3610	.3635	.3661	.3686	.3712	.3737	.3762	.3788	.3813	.3838
4.0	1.3863	.3888	.3913	.3938	.3962	.3987	.4012	.4036	.4061	.4085
4.1	.4110	.4134	.4159	.4183	.4207	.4231	.4255	.4279	.4303	.4327
4.2	.4351	.4375	.4398	.4422	.4446	.4469	.4493	.4516	.4540	.4563
4.3	.4586	.4609	.4633	.4656	.4679	.4702	.4725	.4748	.4770	.4793
4.4	.4816	.4839	.4861	.4884	.4907	.4929	.4951	.4974	.4996	.5019
4.5	1.5041	.5063	.5085	.5107	.5129	.5151	.5173	.5195	.5217	.5239
4.6	.5261	.5282	.5304	.5326	.5347	.5369	.5390	.5412	.5433	.5454
4.7	.5476	.5497	.5518	.5539	.5560	.5581	.5602	.5623	.5644	.5665
4.8	.5686	.5707	.5728	.5748	.5769	.5790	.5810	.5831	.5851	.5872
4.9	.5892	.5913	.5933	.5953	.5974	.5994	.6014	.6034	.6054	.6074
5.0	1.6094	.6114	.6134	.6154	.6174	.6194	.6214	.6233	.6253	.6273
5.1	.6292	.6312	.6332	.6351	.6371	.6390	.6409	.6429	.6448	.6467
5.2	.6487	.6506	.6525	.6544	.6563	.6582	.6601	.6620	.6639	.6658
5.3	.6677	.6696	.6715	.6734	.6752	.6771	.6790	.6808	.6827	.6845
5.4	.6864	.6882	.6901	.6919	.6938	.6956	.6974	.6993	.7011	.7029

Table C (continued)

N	0	1	2	3	4	5	6	7	8	9
5.5	1.7047	.7066	.7084	.7102	.7120	.7138	.7156	.7174	.7192	.7210
5.6	.7228	.7246	.7263	.7281	.7299	.7317	.7334	.7352	.7370	.7387
5.7	.7405	.7422	.7440	.7457	.7475	.7492	.7509	.7527	.7544	.7561
5.8	.7579	.7596	.7613	.7630	.7647	.7664	.7681	.7699	.7716	.7733
5.9	.7750	.7766	.7783	.7800	.7817	.7834	.7851	.7867	.7884	.7901
6.0	1.7918	.7934	.7951	.7967	.7984	.8001	.8017	.8034	.8050	.8066
6.1	.8083	.8099	.8116	.8132	.8148	.8165	.8181	.8197	.8213	.8229
6.2	.8245	.8262	.8278	.8294	.8310	.8326	.8342	.8358	.8374	.8390
6.3	.8405	.8421	.8437	.8453	.8469	.8485	.8500	.8516	.8532	.8547
6.4	.8563	.8579	.8594	.8610	.8625	.8641	.8656	.8672	.8687	.8703
6.5	1.8718	.8733	.8749	.8764	.8779	.8795	.8810	.8825	.8840	.8856
6.6	.8871	.8886	.8901	.8916	.8931	.8946	.8961	.8976	.8991	.9006
6.7	.9021	.9036	.9051	.9066	.9081	.9095	.9110	.9125	.9140	.9155
6.8	.9169	.9184	.9199	.9213	.9228	.9242	.9257	.9272	.9286	.9301
6.9	.9315	.9330	.9344	.9359	.9373	.9387	.9402	.9416	.9430	.9445
7.0	1.9459	.9473	.9488	.9502	.9516	.9530	.9544	.9559	.9573	.9587
7.1	.9601	.9615	.9629	.9643	.9657	.9671	.9685	.9699	.9713	.9727
7.2	.9741	.9755	.9769	.9782	.9796	.9810	.9824	.9838	.9851	.9865
7.3	.9879	.9892	.9906	.9920	.9933	.9947	.9961	.9974	.9988	2.0001
7.4	2.0015	.0028	.0042	.0055	.0069	.0082	.0096	.0109	.0122	.0136
7.5	2.0149	.0162	.0176	.0189	.0202	.0215	.0229	.0242	.0255	.0268
7.6	.0281	.0295	.0308	.0321	.0334	.0347	.0360	.0373	.0386	.0399
7.7	.0412	.0425	.0438	.0451	.0464	.0477	.0490	.0503	.0516	.0528
7.8	.0541	.0554	.0567	.0580	.0592	.0605	.0618	.0631	.0643	.0656
7.9	.0669	.0681	.0694	.0707	.0719	.0732	.0744	.0757	.0769	.0782
8.0	2.0794	.0807	.0819	.0832	.0844	.0857	.0869	.0882	.0894	.0906
8.1	.0919	.0931	.0943	.0956	.0968	.0980	.0992	.1005	.1017	.1029
8.2	.1041	.1054	.1066	.1078	.1090	.1102	.1114	.1126	.1138	.1150
8.3	.1163	.1175	.1187	.1199	.1211	.1223	.1235	.1247	.1258	.1270
8.4	.1282	.1294	.1306	.1318	.1330	.1342	.1353	.1365	.1377	.1389
8.5	2.1401	.1412	.1424	.1436	.1448	.1459	.1471	.1483	.1494	.1506
8.6	.1518	.1529	.1541	.1552	.1564	.1576	.1587	.1599	.1610	.1622
8.7	.1633	.1645	.1656	.1668	.1679	.1691	.1702	.1713	.1725	.1736
8.8	.1748	.1759	.1770	.1782	.1793	.1804	.1815	.1827	.1838	.1849
8.9	.1861	.1872	.1883	.1894	.1905	.1917	.1928	.1939	.1950	.1961
9.0	2.1972	.1983	.1994	.2006	.2017	.2028	.2039	.2050	.2061	.2072
9.1	.2083	.2094	.2105	.2116	.2127	.2138	.2148	.2159	.2170	.2181
9.2	.2192	.2203	.2214	.2225	.2235	.2246	.2257	.2268	.2279	.2289
9.3	.2300	.2311	.2322	.2332	.2343	.2354	.2364	.2375	.2386	.2396
9.4	.2407	.2418	.2428	.2439	.2450	.2460	.2471	.2481	.2492	.2502
9.5	2.2513	.2523	.2534	.2544	.2555	.2565	.2576	.2586	.2597	.2607
9.6	.2618	.2628	.2638	.2649	.2659	.2670	.2680	.2690	.2701	.2711
9.7	.2721	.2732	.2742	.2752	.2762	.2773	.2783	.2793	.2803	.2814
9.8	.2824	.2834	.2844	.2854	.2865	.2875	.2885	.2895	.2905	.2915
9.9	.2925	.2935	.2946	.2956	.2966	.2976	.2986	.2996	.3006	.3016

Answers to Selected Exercises

Section 0.1

1. set **3.** union **5.** decimal **7.** 2 **9.** composite
11. decimals **13.** negative **5.** $x + (y + z)$
17. $5m + 5 \cdot 2$ **19.** interval **21.** two **23.** positive
25. true **27.** false **29.** true **31.** {a, b, c, d, e, f, g}
33. {a, c, e} **35.** terminates **37.** repeats
39. 1, 2, 6, 7 **41.** $-5, -4, 0, 1, 2, 6, 7$ **43.** $\sqrt{2}$
45. 6 **47.** $-5, 1, 7$

49.

51.

53.

55.

57. $(2, \infty)$

59. $(0, 5)$

61. $(-4, \infty)$

63. $[-2, 2)$

65. $(-\infty, 5]$

67. $(-5, 0]$

69. $[-2, 3]$

71. $[2, 6]$

73. $(-5, \infty) \cap (-\infty, 4)$

75. $[-8, \infty) \cap (-\infty, -3]$

77. $(-\infty, -2) \cup (2, \infty)$

79. $(-\infty, -1] \cup [3, \infty)$

81. 13 **83.** 0 **85.** -8 **87.** -32 **89.** $5 - \pi$
91. 0 **93.** $x + 1$ **95.** $-(x - 4)$ **97.** 5 **99.** 5
101. natural numbers **103.** integers

Section 0.2

1. factor **3.** $3, 2x$ **5.** scientific, integer **7.** x^{m+n}
9. $x^n y^n$ **11.** 1 **13.** 169 **15.** -25
17. $4 \cdot x \cdot x \cdot x$ **19.** $(-5x)(-5x)(-5x)(-5x)$
21. $-8 \cdot x \cdot x \cdot x \cdot x$ **23.** $7x^3$ **25.** x^2 **27.** $-27t^3$
29. $x^3 y^2$ **31.** 10.648 **33.** -0.0625 **35.** x^5 **37.** z^6
39. y^{21} **41.** z^{26} **43.** a^{14} **45.** $27x^3$ **47.** $x^6 y^3$
49. $\dfrac{a^6}{b^3}$ **51.** 1 **53.** 1 **55.** $\dfrac{1}{z^4}$ **57.** $\dfrac{1}{y^5}$ **59.** x^2

61. x^4 **63.** a^4 **65.** x **67.** $\dfrac{m^9}{n^6}$ **69.** $\dfrac{1}{a^9}$ **71.** $\dfrac{a^{12}}{b^4}$

73. $\dfrac{1}{r^4}$ **75.** $\dfrac{x^{32}}{y^{16}}$ **77.** $\dfrac{9x^{10}}{25y^2}$ **79.** $\dfrac{4y^{12}}{x^{20}}$ **81.** $\dfrac{64z^7}{25y^6}$

83. -50 **85.** 4 **87.** -8 **89.** 216 **91.** -12

93. 20 **95.** $\dfrac{3}{64}$ **97.** 3.72×10^5 **99.** -1.77×10^8

101. 7×10^{-3} **103.** -6.93×10^{-7} **105.** 1×10^{12}
107. 937,000 **109.** 0.0000221 **111.** 3.2
113. -0.0032 **115.** 1.17×10^4 **117.** 7×10^4
119. 5.3×10^{19} **121.** 1.986×10^4 meters per min
123. 1.67248×10^{-15} g **125.** 9.3×10^7 mi, 1.48×10^8 mi
127. polar radius: 6.356750×10^3 km;
equatorial radius: 6.378135×10^3 km
129. x^{n+2} **131.** x^{m-1} **133.** x^{m+4}
137. **139.** $5 - \pi$

Section 0.3

1. 0 **3.** not **5.** $a^{1/n}$ **7.** $\sqrt[n]{ab}$ **9.** $\neq$ **11.** 3
13. $\dfrac{1}{5}$ **15.** -3 **17.** 10 **19.** $-\dfrac{3}{2}$
21. not a real number **23.** $4|a|$ **25.** $2|a|$
27. $-2a$ **29.** $-6b^2$ **31.** $\dfrac{4a^2}{5|b|}$ **33.** $-\dfrac{10x^2}{3y}$
35. 8 **37.** -64 **39.** -100 **41.** $\dfrac{1}{8}$ **43.** $\dfrac{1}{512}$
45. $-\dfrac{1}{27}$ **47.** $\dfrac{32}{243}$ **49.** $\dfrac{16}{9}$ **51.** $10s^2$ **53.** $\dfrac{1}{2y^2 z}$
55. $x^6 y^3$ **57.** $\dfrac{1}{r^6 s^{12}}$ **59.** $\dfrac{4a^4}{25b^6}$ **61.** $\dfrac{100s^8}{9r^4}$ **63.** a
65. 7 **67.** 5 **69.** -5 **71.** $-\dfrac{1}{5}$ **73.** $6|x|$
75. $3y^2$ **77.** $2y$ **79.** $\dfrac{|x|y^2}{|z^3|}$ **81.** $\sqrt{2}$ **83.** $17x\sqrt{2}$
85. $2y^2\sqrt{3y}$ **87.** $12\sqrt[3]{3}$ **89.** $6z\sqrt[4]{3z}$ **91.** $6x\sqrt{2y}$
93. 0 **95.** $\sqrt{3}$ **97.** $\dfrac{2\sqrt{x}}{x}$ **99.** $\sqrt[3]{4}$ **101.** $\sqrt[3]{5a^2}$
103. $\dfrac{2b\sqrt[4]{27a^2}}{3a}$ **105.** $\dfrac{u\sqrt[3]{6uv^2}}{3v}$ **107.** $\dfrac{1}{2\sqrt{5}}$ **109.** $\dfrac{1}{\sqrt[3]{3}}$
111. $\dfrac{b}{32a\sqrt[5]{2b^2}}$ **113.** $\dfrac{2\sqrt{3}}{9}$ **115.** $-\dfrac{\sqrt{2x}}{8}$ **117.** $\sqrt{3}$
119. $\sqrt[5]{4x^3}$ **121.** $\sqrt[6]{32}$ **123.** $\dfrac{\sqrt[4]{12}}{2}$ **129.** $(-2, 5]$
131. -5 **133.** 6.17×10^8

Section 0.4

1. monomial, variables **3.** trinomial **5.** one **7.** like
9. coefficients, variables **11.** yes, trinomial, 2nd degree

13. no   **15.** yes, binomial, 3rd degree   **17.** yes, monomial, 0th degree   **19.** yes, monomial, no defined degree

21. $6x^3 - 3x^2 - 8x$ **23.** $4y^3 + 14$ **25.** $-x^2 + 14$

27. $-28t + 96$ **29.** $-4y^2 + y$ **31.** $2x^2y - 4xy^2$

33. $8x^3y^7$ **35.** $\dfrac{m^4n^4}{2}$ **37.** $-4r^3s - 4rs^3$

39. $12a^2b^2c^2 + 18ab^3c^3 - 24a^2b^4c^2$ **41.** $a^2 + 4a + 4$

43. $a^2 - 12a + 36$ **45.** $x^2 - 16$ **47.** $x^2 + 2x - 15$

49. $3u^2 + 4u - 4$ **51.** $10x^2 + 13x - 3$

53. $9a^2 - 12ab + 4b^2$ **55.** $9m^2 - 16n^2$

57. $6y^2 - 16xy + 8x^2$ **59.** $9x^3 - x^2y - 27xy + 3y^2$

61. $5z^3 - 5tz + 2tz^2 - 2t^2$ **63.** $-3\sqrt{5}x^2 + x + 2\sqrt{5}$

65. $27x^3 - 27x^2 + 9x - 1$ **67.** $6x^3 + 14x^2 - 5x - 3$

69. $6x^3 - 5x^2y + 6xy^2 + 8y^3$ **71.** $6y^{2n} + 2$

73. $-10x^{4n} - 15y^{2n}$ **75.** $x^{2n} - x^n - 12$

77. $6r^{2n} - 25r^n + 14$ **79.** $xy + x^{3/2}y^{1/2}$

81. $a - b$ **83.** $\sqrt{3} + 1$ **85.** $x\left(\sqrt{7} - 2\right)$

87. $\dfrac{x\left(x + \sqrt{3}\right)}{x^2 - 3}$ **89.** $\dfrac{\left(y + \sqrt{2}\right)^2}{y^2 - 2}$

91. $\dfrac{\sqrt{3} + 3 - \sqrt{2} - \sqrt{6}}{2}$ **93.** $\dfrac{x - 2\sqrt{xy} + y}{x - y}$

95. $\dfrac{1}{2\left(\sqrt{2} - 1\right)}$ **97.** $\dfrac{y^2 - 3}{y^2 + 2y\sqrt{3} + 3}$

99. $\dfrac{1}{\sqrt{x + 3} + \sqrt{x}}$ **101.** $\dfrac{2a}{b^3}$ **103.** $-\dfrac{2z^9}{3x^3y^2}$

105. $\dfrac{x}{2y} + \dfrac{3xy}{2}$ **107.** $\dfrac{2y^3}{5} - \dfrac{3y}{5x^3} + \dfrac{1}{5x^4y^3}$ **109.** $3x + 2$

111. $x - 7 + \dfrac{2}{2x - 5}$ **113.** $2x^2 + 2x + 2 + \dfrac{3}{x - 1}$

115. $x - 3$ **117.** $x^2 - 2 + \dfrac{-x^2 + 5}{x^3 - 2}$

119. $x^4 + 2x^3 + 4x^2 + 8x + 16$ **121.** $6x^2 + x - 12$

123. $(x^2 + 3x - 10)$ ft^2 **125.** $(4x^3 - 48x^2 + 144x)$ in.^{3}

133. 27   **135.** $\dfrac{125x^3}{8y^6}$ **137.** $-b\sqrt[3]{2ab}$

Section 0.5

1. factor   **3.** $x(a + b)$ **5.** $(x + y)^2$

7. $(x + y)(x^2 - xy + y^2)$ **9.** $3(x - 2)$ **11.** $4x^2(2 + x)$

13. $7x^2y^2(1 + 2x)$ **15.** $(x + y)(a + b)$

17. $(4a + b)(1 - 3a)$ **19.** $(2x + 3)(2x - 3)$

21. $(2 + 3r)(2 - 3r)$ **23.** $(9x^2 + 1)(3x + 1)(3x - 1)$

25. $(x + z + 5)(x + z - 5)$ **27.** $(x + 4)^2$

29. $(b - 5)^2$ **31.** $(m + 2n)^2$

33. $(4x - 3y)(3x + 2y)$ **35.** $(x + 7)(x + 3)$

37. $(x - 6)(x + 2)$ **39.** $(2p + 3)(3p - 1)$

41. $(t + 7)(t^2 - 7t + 49)$ **43.** $(2z - 3)(4z^2 + 6z + 9)$

45. $3abc(a + 2b + 3c)$ **47.** $(x + 1)(3x^2 - 1)$

49. $t(y + c)(2x - 3)$ **51.** $(a + b)(x + y + z)$

53. $(x + y - z)(x - y + z)$ **55.** $-4xy$

57. $(x^2 + y^2)(x + y)(x - y)$ **59.** $3(x + 2)(x - 2)$

61. $2x(3y + 2)(3y - 2)$ **63.** prime

65. $(6a + 5)(4a - 3)$ **67.** $(3x + 7y)(2x + 5y)$

69. $2(6p - 35q)(p + q)$ **71.** $-(6m - 5n)(m - 7n)$

73. $-x(6x + 7)(x - 5)$ **75.** $x^2(2x - 7)(3x + 5)$

77. $(x^2 + 5)(x^2 - 3)$ **79.** $(a^n - 3)(a^n + 1)$

81. $(3x^n - 2)(2x^n - 1)$ **83.** $(2x^n + 3y^n)(2x^n - 3y^n)$

85. $(5y^n + 2)(2y^n - 3)$ **87.** $2(x + 10)(x^2 - 10x + 100)$

89. $(x + y - 4)(x^2 + 2xy + y^2 + 4x + 4y + 16)$

91. $(2a + y)(2a - y)(4a^2 - 2ay + y^2)(4a^2 + 2ay + y^2)$

93. $(a - b)(a^2 + ab + b^2 + 1)$

95. $(4x^2 + y^2)(16x^4 - 4x^2y^2 + y^4)$

97. $(x - 3 + 12y)(x - 3 - 12y)$

99. $(a + b - 5)(a + b + 2)$

101. $(x + 2)(x^2 - 2x + 4)(x - 1)(x^2 + x + 1)$

103. $(x^2 + 1 + x)(x^2 + 1 - x)$

105. $(x^2 + x + 4)(x^2 - x + 4)$

107. $(2a^2 + a + 1)(2a^2 - a + 1)$

109. $\dfrac{4}{3}\pi(r_1 - r_2)(r_1^2 + r_1r_2 + r_2^2)$ **115.** $2\left(\dfrac{3}{2}x + 1\right)$

117. $2\left(\dfrac{1}{2}x^2 + x + 2\right)$ **119.** $a\left(1 + \dfrac{b}{a}\right)$ **121.** $x^{1/2}(x^{1/2} + 1)$

123. $\sqrt{2}\left(\sqrt{2}x + y\right)$ **125.** $ab(b^{1/2} - a^{1/2})$

127. $(x - 2)(x + 3 + y)$ **129.** $(a + 1)(a^3 + a^2 + 1)$

131. 1   **133.** x^{20} **135.** 1   **137.** $-3\sqrt{5x}$

Section 0.6

1. numerator   **3.** $ad = bc$ **5.** $\dfrac{ac}{bd}$ **7.** $\dfrac{a + c}{b}$

9. equal   **11.** not equal   **13.** $\dfrac{a}{3b}$ **15.** $\dfrac{8x}{35a}$

17. $\dfrac{16}{3}$ **19.** $\dfrac{z}{c}$ **21.** $\dfrac{2x^2y}{a^2b^3}$ **23.** $\dfrac{2}{x + 2}$

25. $-\dfrac{x + 2}{x - 3}$ **27.** $\dfrac{3x - 4}{2x - 1}$ **29.** $\dfrac{x^2 + 2x + 4}{x + a}$

31. $\dfrac{x(x - 1)}{x + 1}$ **33.** $\dfrac{x - 1}{x}$ **35.** $\dfrac{x(x + 1)^2}{x + 2}$

37. $\dfrac{1}{2}$ **39.** $\dfrac{z - 4}{(z + 2)(z - 2)}$ **41.** 1   **43.** 1

45. $\dfrac{x - 5}{x + 5}$ **47.** $\dfrac{x + 5}{x + 3}$ **49.** 4   **51.** $\dfrac{-1}{x - 5}$

53. $\dfrac{5x - 1}{(x + 1)(x - 1)}$ **55.** $\dfrac{2(a - 2)}{(a + 4)(a - 4)}$

57. $\dfrac{2}{(x + 2)(x - 2)}$ **59.** $\dfrac{2(x^2 - 3x + 1)}{(x + 1)^2(x - 1)}$

61. $\dfrac{3y - 2}{y - 1}$ **63.** $\dfrac{1}{x + 2}$ **65.** $\dfrac{2x - 5}{2x(x - 2)}$

67. $\dfrac{2x^2 + 19x + 1}{(x + 4)(x - 4)}$ **69.** 0

71. $\dfrac{-x^4 + 3x^3 - 43x^2 - 58x + 697}{(x + 5)(x - 5)(x + 4)(x - 4)}$ **73.** $\dfrac{b}{2c}$

75. $81a$ **77.** -1 **79.** $\dfrac{y + x}{x^2y^2}$ **81.** $\dfrac{y + x}{y - x}$

83. $\dfrac{a^2(3x - 4ab)}{ax + b}$ **85.** $\dfrac{x - 2}{x + 2}$ **87.** $\dfrac{3x^2y^2}{xy - 1}$

89. $\dfrac{3x^2}{x^2 + 1}$ **91.** $\dfrac{x^2 - 3x - 4}{x^2 + 5x - 3}$ **93.** $\dfrac{x}{x + 1}$

95. $\dfrac{5x + 1}{x - 1}$ **97.** $\dfrac{k_1k_2}{k_2 + k_1}$ **99.** $\dfrac{3x}{3 + x}$

101. $\dfrac{x + 1}{2x + 1}$ **107.** 6   **109.** $\dfrac{y^9}{x^{12}}$ **111.** $-\sqrt{5}$

Chapter Review

1. 3, 6, 8   **2.** 0, 3, 6, 8   **3.** $-6, -3, 0, 3, 6, 8$

4. $-6, -3, 0, \frac{1}{2}, 3, 6, 8$ **5.** $\pi, \sqrt{5}$

6. $-6, -3, 0, \frac{1}{2}, 3, \pi, \sqrt{5}, 6, 8$ **7.** 3   **8.** 6, 8

9. $-6, 0, 6, 8$ **10.** $-3, 3$

11. Associative Property of Addition

12. Commutative Property of Addition

13. Associative Property of Multiplication

14. Distributive Property

15. Commutative Property of Multiplication

16. Commutative Property of Addition

17. Double Negative Rule

18.

19.

20.   **21.**

22.   **23.**

24.

25. 6   **26.** 25   **27.** $\sqrt{2} - 1$ **28.** $\sqrt{3} - 1$

29. 12   **30.** $-5aaa$ **31.** $(-5a)(-5a)$ **32.** $3t^3$

33. $-6b^2$ **34.** n^6 **35.** p^6 **36.** $x^{12}y^8$

37. $\dfrac{a^{12}}{b^6}$ **38.** $\dfrac{1}{m^6}$ **39.** $\dfrac{q^6}{8p^6}$ **40.** $\dfrac{1}{a^3}$ **41.** $\dfrac{b^6}{a^4}$

42. $\dfrac{y^8}{9}$ **43.** $\dfrac{a^8}{b^{10}}$ **44.** $\dfrac{y^4}{9x^4}$ **45.** $-\dfrac{8m^{12}}{n^3}$

46. 18   **47.** 6.75×10^3 **48.** 2.3×10^{-4}

49. 480   **50.** 0.00025   **51.** 1.5×10^{14} **52.** 11

53. $\dfrac{3}{5}$ **54.** $2x$ **55.** $3|a|$ **56.** $-10x^2$

57. not a real number   **58.** $x^6|y|$ **59.** $\dfrac{y^2}{x^6}$

60. $-c$ **61.** a^2 **62.** 16   **63.** $\dfrac{1}{8}$ **64.** $\dfrac{8}{27}$ **65.** $\dfrac{4}{9}$

66. $\dfrac{9}{4}$ **67.** $\dfrac{125}{8}$ **68.** $36x^2$ **69.** $p^{2a/3}$ **70.** 6

71. -7 **72.** $\dfrac{3}{5}$ **73.** $\dfrac{3}{5}$ **74.** $|x|y^2$ **75.** x

76. $\dfrac{m^2|n|}{p^4}$ **77.** $\dfrac{a^3b^2}{c}$ **78.** $7\sqrt{2}$ **79.** 0   **80.** $x\sqrt[3]{3x}$

81. $\dfrac{\sqrt{35}}{5}$ **82.** $2\sqrt{2}$ **83.** $\dfrac{\sqrt[3]{4}}{2}$ **84.** $\dfrac{2\sqrt[3]{5}}{5}$

85. $\dfrac{2}{5\sqrt{2}}$ **86.** $\dfrac{1}{\sqrt{5}}$ **87.** $\dfrac{2x}{3\sqrt{2x}}$ **88.** $\dfrac{21x}{2\sqrt[3]{49x^2}}$

89. 3rd degree, binomial   **90.** 2nd degree, trinomial

91. 2nd degree, monomial   **92.** 4th degree, trinomial

93. $5x - 6$ **94.** $2x^3 - 7x^2 - 6x$ **95.** $9x^2 + 12x + 4$

96. $6x^2 - 7xy - 3y^2$ **97.** $8a^2 - 8ab - 6b^2$

98. $3z^3 + 10z^2 + 2z - 3$ **99.** $a^{2n} + a^n - 2$

100. $2 + 2x\sqrt{2} + x^2$ **101.** $\sqrt{6} + \sqrt{2} + \sqrt{3} + 1$

102. -5 **103.** $\sqrt{3} + 1$ **104.** $-2\left(\sqrt{3} + \sqrt{2}\right)$

105. $\dfrac{2x\left(\sqrt{x} + 2\right)}{x - 4}$ **106.** $\dfrac{x - 2\sqrt{xy} + y}{x - y}$

107. $\dfrac{x - 4}{5\left(\sqrt{x} - 2\right)}$ **108.** $\dfrac{1 - a}{a\left(1 + \sqrt{a}\right)}$ **109.** $\dfrac{y}{2x}$

110. $2a^2b + 3ab^2$ **111.** $x^2 + 2x + 1$

112. $x^3 + 2x - 3 - \dfrac{6}{x^2 - 1}$ **113.** $3t(t + 1)(t - 1)$

114. $5(r - 1)(r^2 + r + 1)$ **115.** $(3x + 8)(2x - 3)$

116. $(3a + x)(a - 1)$ **117.** $(2x - 5)(4x^2 + 10x + 25)$

118. $2(3x + 2)(x - 4)$ **119.** $(x + 3 + t)(x + 3 - t)$

120. prime   **121.** $(2z + 7)(4z^2 - 14z + 49)$

122. $(7b + 1)^2$ **123.** $(11z - 2)^2$

124. $8(2y - 5)(4y^2 + 10y + 25)$ **125.** $(y - 2z)(2x - w)$

126. $(x^2 + 1 + x)(x^2 + 1 - x)(x^4 + 1 - x^2)$

127. $\dfrac{-1}{x - 2}$ **128.** $\dfrac{a + 3}{a - 3}$ **129.** $(x - 2)(x + 3)$

130. $\dfrac{2y - 5}{y - 2}$ **131.** $\dfrac{t + 1}{5}$ **132.** $\dfrac{p(p + 4)}{(p^2 + 8p + 4)(p - 3)}$

133. $\dfrac{(x - 2)(x + 3)(x - 3)}{(x - 1)(x + 2)^2}$ **134.** 1

135. $\dfrac{3x^2 - 10x + 10}{(x - 4)(x + 5)}$ **136.** $\dfrac{2(2x^2 + 3x + 6)}{(x + 2)(x - 2)}$

137. $\dfrac{3x^3 - 12x^2 + 11x}{(x - 1)(x - 2)(x - 3)}$ **138.** $\dfrac{-5x - 6}{(x + 1)(x + 2)}$

139. $\dfrac{-x^3 + x^2 - 12x - 15}{x^2(x + 1)}$ **140.** $\dfrac{3x}{x + 1}$

141. $\dfrac{20}{3x}$ **142.** $\dfrac{y}{2}$ **143.** $\dfrac{y + x}{xy(x - y)}$ **144.** $\dfrac{y + x}{x - y}$

Chapter Test

1. $-7, 1, 3$ **2.** 3   **3.** Commutative Property of Addition   **4.** Distributive Property

5.   **6.**

7. 17   **8.** $-(x - 7)$ **9.** 16   **10.** 8   **11.** x^{11}

12. $\dfrac{r}{s}$ **13.** a **14.** x^{24} **15.** 4.5×10^5

16. 3.45×10^{-4} **17.** 3,700   **18.** 0.0012

19. $5a^2$ **20.** $\dfrac{216}{729}$ **21.** $\dfrac{9s^6}{4t^4}$ **22.** $3a^2$

23. $5\sqrt{3}$ **24.** $-4x\sqrt[3]{3x}$ **25.** $\dfrac{x\left(\sqrt{x} + 2\right)}{x - 4}$

26. $\dfrac{x - y}{x + 2\sqrt{xy} + y}$ **27.** $-a^2 + 7$ **28.** $-6a^6b^6$

29. $6x^2 + 13x - 28$ **30.** $a^{2n} - a^n - 6$ **31.** $x^4 - 16$

32. $2x^3 - 5x^2 + 7x - 6$ **33.** $6x + 19 + \dfrac{34}{x - 3}$

34. $x^2 + 2x + 1$ **35.** $3(x + 2y)$ **36.** $(x + 10)(x - 10)$

37. $(5t - 2w)(2t - 3w)$ **38.** $3(a - 6)(a^2 + 6a + 36)$

39. $(x + 2)(x - 2)(x^2 + 3)$ **40.** $(3x^2 - 2)(2x^2 + 5)$

41. 1   **42.** $\dfrac{-2x}{(x + 1)(x - 1)}$ **43.** $\dfrac{(x + 5)^2}{x + 4}$

44. $\dfrac{1}{(x + 1)(x - 2)}$ **45.** $\dfrac{b + a}{a}$ **46.** $\dfrac{y}{y + x}$

Section 1.1
1. root; solution 3. no 5. linear 7. one 9. no restrictions 11. $x \neq 0$ 13. $x \neq 3$ or -2
15. $x \neq 3, 4,$ or -4 17. 5; conditional equation
19. no solution; contradiction 21. 7; conditional equation
23. no solution; contradiction 25. all real numbers; identity
27. 6; conditional equation 29. all real numbers; identity
31. 1 33. 6 35. $\frac{5}{2}$ 37. 9 39. 10 41. -3
43. 3 45. $\frac{21}{19}$ 47. $-\frac{14}{11}$ 49. 2 51. all real numbers
53. 4 55. -4 57. no solution 59. 17
61. $-\frac{2}{5}$ 63. $\frac{2}{3}$ 65. 3 67. 5 69. no solution
71. 2 73. $p = \frac{k}{2.2}$ 75. $w = \frac{P-2l}{2}$ 77. $r^2 = \frac{3V}{\pi h}$
79. $s = \frac{f(P_n - L)}{i}$ 81. $m = \frac{r^2 F}{Mg}$ 83. $y = b\left(1 - \frac{x}{a}\right)$
85. $r = \frac{r_1 r_2}{r_1 + r_2}$ 87. $n = \frac{l - a + d}{d}$ 89. $n = \frac{360}{180 - a}$
91. $r_1 = \frac{-Rr_2 r_3}{Rr_3 + Rr_2 - r_2 r_3}$ 95. $5|x|$ 97. $\frac{4y^4}{25x^2}$
99. $5|y|$ 101. $\frac{|ab^3|}{z^2}$

Section 1.2
1. add 3. amount 5. rate; time 7. 84 9. 94
11. 7 13. 10 ft by 36 ft 15. $2\frac{1}{2}$ ft 17. 20 ft by 8 ft
19. 20 ft 21. $10,000 at 7%, $12,000 at 6%
23. $29,100 25. 327 27. $79.95 29. 200 units
31. 21 33. $2\frac{6}{11}$ days 35. $1\frac{1}{3}$ hr 37. $21\frac{1}{9}$ hr
39. 10 oz 41. 1 liter 43. $\frac{1}{15}$ liter 45. about 4.5 gal
47. 4 liters 49. 50 lb 51. 30 gal 53. 39 mph going; 65 mph returning 55. $2\frac{1}{2}$ hr 57. 50 sec 59. 12 mph
61. 600 lb barley; 1,637 lb oats; 163 lb soybean meal
63. about 11.2 mm 67. $(x + 7)(x - 9)$
69. $(3x - 5)(3x + 1)$ 71. $(x + 3)^2$
73. $(x + 2)(x^2 - 2x + 4)$

Section 1.3
1. $ax^2 + bx + c = 0$ 3. $\sqrt{c}; -\sqrt{c}$
5. rational numbers 7. $3, -2$ 9. $12, -12$
11. $2, -\frac{5}{2}$ 13. $2, \frac{3}{5}$ 15. $\frac{3}{5}, -\frac{5}{3}$ 17. $\frac{3}{2}, \frac{1}{2}$
19. $3, -3$ 21. $5\sqrt{2}, -5\sqrt{2}$ 23. $2\sqrt{5}, -2\sqrt{5}$
25. $\frac{\sqrt{7}}{2}, -\frac{\sqrt{7}}{2}$ 27. $\frac{\sqrt{26}}{2}, -\frac{\sqrt{26}}{2}$ 29. $3, -1$
31. $-1 + 2\sqrt{2}, -1 - 2\sqrt{2}$ 33. $\frac{-1 + 3\sqrt{3}}{2}, \frac{-1 - 3\sqrt{3}}{2}$
35. $x^2 + 6x + 9$ 37. $x^2 - 4x + 4$ 39. $a^2 + 5a + \frac{25}{4}$
41. $r^2 - 11r + \frac{121}{4}$ 43. $y^2 + \frac{3}{4}y + \frac{9}{64}$ 45. $q^2 - \frac{1}{5}q + \frac{1}{100}$

47. 5, 3 49. $-6 \pm 2\sqrt{7}$ 51. $\frac{-5 \pm \sqrt{5}}{2}$
53. $\frac{10 \pm \sqrt{2}}{2}$ 55. $\frac{-2 \pm \sqrt{7}}{3}$ 57. $\frac{3 \pm \sqrt{17}}{4}$
59. $\pm 2\sqrt{3}$ 61. 0, 25 63. $3, -\frac{5}{2}$ 65. $\frac{-5 \pm \sqrt{13}}{6}$
67. $\frac{-7 \pm 3\sqrt{5}}{2}$ 69. $\frac{-3 \pm \sqrt{6}}{3}$ 71. $\frac{-1 \pm \sqrt{61}}{10}$
73. $t = \pm\frac{\sqrt{2hg}}{g}$ 75. $t = \frac{8 \pm \sqrt{64 - h}}{4}$
77. $y = \pm\frac{b\sqrt{a^2 - x^2}}{a}$ 79. $a = \pm\frac{bx\sqrt{b^2 + y^2}}{b^2 + y^2}$
81. $x = \frac{-y \pm y\sqrt{5}}{2}$ 83. one repeated rational root
85. no real roots 87. two different rational roots
89. two different irrational roots 91. yes 93. 2, 10
95. $3, -4$ 97. $\frac{3}{2}, -\frac{1}{4}$ 99. $\frac{1}{2}, -\frac{4}{3}$ 101. $\frac{5}{6}, -\frac{2}{5}$
103. $1, -1$ 105. $-\frac{1}{2}, 5$ 107. -2 109. $3, -\frac{8}{11}$
111. $\frac{7 \pm \sqrt{145}}{4}$ 121. $2x^2 - 8x$ 123. 12m
125. $3x\sqrt{2x}$

Section 1.4
1. $A = lw$ 3. 4 ft by 8 ft 5. 72 ft by 160 ft 7. 9 cm
9. width: $7\frac{1}{4}$ ft; length: $13\frac{3}{4}$ ft 11. 2 in. 13. 4 m
15. 10 m and 24 m 17. 40.1 in. by 22.6 in.
19. 20 mph going and 10 mph returning 21. 7 hr
23. 25 sec 25. about 9.5 sec 27. 1.6 sec 29. 10¢
31. 1,440 33. Morgan at 7%; Chloe at 8% 35. 10
37. 4 hr 39. about 9.5 hr 41. 221 43. 24.3 ft
45. 1.70 in. 47. No 49. $\frac{x - 6}{x(x - 3)}$ 51. $\frac{x + 3}{x(x + 2)}$
53. $\frac{y + x}{y - x}$

Section 1.5
1. imaginary 3. imaginary 5. $2 - 5i$ 7. real
9. $12i$ 11. $-4\sqrt{6}i$ 13. $\frac{5\sqrt{2}}{3}i$ 15. $-\frac{7\sqrt{6}}{4}i$
17. $x = 3; y = 5$ 19. $x = \frac{2}{3}; y = -\frac{2}{9}$ 21. $5 - 6i$
23. $-2 - 10i$ 25. $4 + 10i$ 27. $1 - i$
29. $-15 - 25i$ 31. $56 + 28i$ 33. $-9 + 19i$
35. $-5 + 12i$ 37. $52 - 56i$ 39. $-6 + 17i$
41. $0 + i$ 43. $0 + \frac{4}{3}i$ 45. $\frac{2}{5} - \frac{1}{5}i$ 47. $\frac{1}{25} + \frac{7}{25}i$
49. $\frac{1}{2} + \frac{1}{2}i$ 51. $-\frac{7}{13} - \frac{22}{13}i$ 53. $-\frac{12}{17} + \frac{11}{34}i$
55. $\frac{6 + \sqrt{3}}{10} + \frac{3\sqrt{3} - 2}{10}i$ 57. i 59. -1
61. $-i$ 63. 1 65. -1 67. -1 69. i 71. 4
73. 5 75. $\sqrt{13}$ 77. $7\sqrt{2}$ 79. $\frac{\sqrt{2}}{2}$ 81. 6

83. $\sqrt{2}$ **85.** $\dfrac{3\sqrt{5}}{5}$ **87.** 1   **89.** $\pm 13i$

91. $\pm 3\sqrt{6}i$ **93.** $\pm 3\sqrt{5}i$ **95.** $\pm\dfrac{\sqrt{7}}{3}i$

97. $\pm\dfrac{\sqrt{30}}{2}i$ **99.** $-1\pm 2\sqrt{3}i$ **101.** $-\dfrac{1}{5}\pm\dfrac{2\sqrt{2}}{5}i$

103. $-5\pm 2\sqrt{3}i$ **105.** $-\dfrac{11}{2}\pm\dfrac{5\sqrt{3}}{2}i$

107. $1\pm\dfrac{\sqrt{5}}{3}i$ **109.** $\dfrac{7}{2}\pm\dfrac{\sqrt{11}}{2}i$ **111.** $-1\pm i$

113. $-2\pm i$ **115.** $1\pm 2i$ **117.** $\dfrac{1}{3}\pm\dfrac{1}{3}i$

119. $(x+2i)(x-2i)$ **121.** $(5p+6qi)(5p-6qi)$
123. $2(y+2zi)(y-2zi)$ **125.** $2(5m+ni)(5m-ni)$
127. $21+12i$ **129.** $6.2-0.7i$ **137.** $4x^2\sqrt{2}$
139. $x-4\sqrt{x+1}+5$ **141.** $\sqrt{5}+1$

Section 1.6

1. equal   **3.** extraneous   **5.** $0,-5,-4$ **7.** $0,\dfrac{4}{3},-\dfrac{1}{2}$

9. $5,-5,1,-1$ **11.** $6,-6,1,-1$

13. $3\sqrt{2},-3\sqrt{2},\sqrt{5},-\sqrt{5}$ **15.** $0,1$ **17.** $\dfrac{1}{8},-8$

19. $1,144$ **21.** $\dfrac{1}{64}$ **23.** $\dfrac{1}{9}$ **25.** 27   **27.** $-\dfrac{1}{3}$

29. 2   **31.** $-\dfrac{3}{2},-\dfrac{5}{2}$ **33.** 9   **35.** 20   **37.** 2

39. 2   **41.** $3,4$ **43.** $\dfrac{1}{5},-1$ **45.** $3,5$ **47.** $-2,1$

49. $2,-\dfrac{5}{2}$ **51.** $0,4$ **53.** -2 **55.** no solution

57. 3   **59.** 1   **61.** 400 ft   **63.** 8 ft
65. about \$3,109
69.
71. $[3,\infty)$ **73.** $[-2,1)$
75. $(-\infty,1)\cup[2,\infty)$

Section 1.7

1. right   **3.** $a<c$ **5.** $b-c$ **7.** $>$ **9.** linear
11. equivalent
13. $(-\infty,1)$ **15.** $[1,\infty)$
17. $(-\infty,1)$ **19.** $[1,\infty)$
21. $(-\infty,3]$ **23.** $(-10/3,\infty)$
25. $(5,\infty)$ **27.** $[14,\infty)$
29. $(-\infty,15/4]$ **31.** $(-44/41,\infty)$

33. $(6,9]$ **35.** $(8,22]$
37. $[-11,4]$ **39.** $[5,21]$
41. $(-\infty,0)$ **43.** $(0,\infty)$
45. $(3,14/3)$ **47.** $(2,\infty)$
49. $(-4,5/6)$ **51.** $[-2,\infty)$
53. $(-4,-3)$ **55.** $(-\infty,2]\cup[3,\infty)$
57. $(-3,-2)$ **59.** $(-\infty,-1/2]\cup[-1/3,\infty)$
61. $(1/3,1/2)$ **63.** $(-\infty,-3/2]\cup[1,\infty)$
65. $(-\infty,-\sqrt{3}]\cup[\sqrt{3},\infty)$ **67.** $(-\sqrt{11},\sqrt{11})$
69. $(-3,2)$ **71.** $(-\infty,-1)\cup(-1,0)\cup(1,\infty)$
73. $(-\infty,-3)\cup(-3,-2]\cup(2,\infty)$
75. $(-\infty,-2)\cup(-2,-1/3)\cup(1/2,\infty)$ **77.** $(0,3/2)$
79. $(-\infty,0)\cup(3/2,\infty)$ **81.** $(-\infty,2)\cup[13/5,\infty)$
83. $(-\infty,-\sqrt{7})\cup(-1,1)\cup(\sqrt{7},\infty)$ **85.** 19 min   **87.** 12
89. $p\le \$1,124.12$ **91.** $a>\$50,000$
93. anything over \$1,800   **95.** $16\dfrac{2}{3}$ cm $< s <$ 20 cm
97. $40+2w<P<60+2w$ **101.** $0,-2,2$ **103.** 2
105. All are real.

Section 1.8

1. x **3.** $x=k$ or $x=-k$ **5.** $-k<x<k$
7. $x\le -k$ or $x\ge k$ **9.** 7   **11.** 0   **13.** 2
15. $\pi-2$ **17.** $x-5$ **19.** x^3 if $x\ge 0$; $-x^3$ if $x<0$
21. $0,-4$ **23.** $2,-\dfrac{4}{3}$ **25.** $\dfrac{14}{3},-2$ **27.** $7,-3$

29. no solution   **31.** 5   **33.** $\dfrac{2}{7},2$ **35.** $x\ge 0$

37. $-\dfrac{3}{2}$ **39.** $0,-6$ **41.** 0   **43.** $\dfrac{3}{5},3$

45. $-\dfrac{3}{13}, \dfrac{9}{5}$

47.

$(-3, 9)$

49.

$(-\infty, -9) \cup (3, \infty)$

51.

$(-\infty, -7] \cup [3, \infty)$

53.

$[-13/3, 1]$

55. $(-\infty, -3) \cup (-3, \infty)$

57.

$(-1, 1/5)$

59. $(-\infty, -7/9) \cup (13/9, \infty)$

61.

$(-5, 7)$

63. $(-2, -1/2) \cup (-1/2, 1)$

65. $(-7/3, -2/3) \cup (4/3, 3)$

67. $(-7, -1) \cup (11, 17)$

69. $(-18, -6) \cup (10, 22)$

71. $(-10, -7] \cup [5, 8)$

73. $\left[-\dfrac{1}{2}, \infty\right)$ **75.** $(-\infty, 0)$ **77.** $\left(-\infty, -\dfrac{1}{2}\right)$

79. $[0, \infty)$ **81.** $70° \le t \le 86°$ **83.** $|c - 0.6°| \le 0.5°$

85. $|h - 55| < 17$ **87. a.** 26.45%, 24.76%
b. It is less than or equal to 1%.   **95.** 3.725×10^4
97. 523,000   **99.** $-4xy$

Chapter Review
1. no restrictions   **2.** $x \ne 0$ **3.** $x \ne 1$

4. $x \ne 2, x \ne 3$ **5.** $\dfrac{16}{27}$; conditional equation

6. -14; conditional equation   **7.** $\dfrac{16}{5}$; conditional equation

8. no solution; contradiction   **9.** 7; conditional equation
10. all real numbers; identity   **11.** 7; conditional equation
12. $\dfrac{1}{3}$; conditional equation   **13.** -2; conditional equation

14. 0; conditional equation   **15.** $F = \dfrac{9}{5}C + 32$

16. $f = \dfrac{is}{P_n - l}$ **17.** $f_1 = \dfrac{ff_2}{f_2 - f}$ **18.** $l = \dfrac{a - S + Sr}{r}$

19. 60%   **20.** 22.5 ft by 27.5 ft   **21.** 3 hr   **22.** 0.5 hr

23. 1.5 liters   **24.** about 3.9 hr   **25.** $5\dfrac{1}{7}$ hr   **26.** $3\dfrac{1}{3}$ oz

27. $4,500 at 11%; $5,500 at 14%   **28.** 10   **29.** $2, -\dfrac{3}{2}$

30. $\dfrac{1}{4}, -\dfrac{4}{3}$ **31.** $0, \dfrac{8}{5}$ **32.** $\dfrac{2}{3}, \dfrac{4}{9}$ **33.** $\pm 2\sqrt{2}$

34. $\pm\sqrt{5}$ **35.** $\dfrac{5 \pm 4\sqrt{2}}{4}$ **36.** $\dfrac{7 \pm 3\sqrt{5}}{5}$ **37.** 3, 5

38. $-4, -2$ **39.** $\dfrac{1 \pm \sqrt{21}}{10}$ **40.** $0, \dfrac{1}{5}$ **41.** $2, -7$

42. $9, -\dfrac{2}{3}$ **43.** $\dfrac{-1 \pm \sqrt{21}}{10}$ **44.** $-1 \pm \sqrt{6}$ **45.** 1

46. two different rational numbers   **47.** $\dfrac{1}{3}$ **48.** 10, 2

49. $-\dfrac{5}{2}$ **50.** $\dfrac{8}{5}, 5$ **51.** either 95 by 110 yd or 55 by
190 yd   **52.** 320 mph for prop plane; 440 mph for jet plane
53. 1 sec   **54.** $1\dfrac{1}{2}$ ft   **55.** $-2 - i$ **56.** $-2 - 5i$
57. $5 - 2i$ **58.** $21 - 9i$ **59.** $0 - 3i$ **60.** $0 - 2i$
61. $\dfrac{3}{2} - \dfrac{3}{2}i$ **62.** $-\dfrac{2}{5} + \dfrac{4}{5}i$ **63.** $\dfrac{4}{5} + \dfrac{3}{5}i$ **64.** $\dfrac{1}{2} - \dfrac{5}{2}i$
65. $0 + i$ **66.** $0 - i$ **67.** $\sqrt{10} + 0i$ **68.** $1 + 0i$
69. $\dfrac{1}{3} \pm \dfrac{\sqrt{2}}{3}i$ **70.** $\dfrac{1}{3} \pm \dfrac{\sqrt{11}}{3}i$ **71.** $2, -3$
72. $4, -2$ **73.** $1, 1, -1, -1$ **74.** $1, -1, 6, -6$ **75.** 9
76. $8, -27$ **77.** 5   **78.** 0   **79.** $4, -4$
80. no solution   **81.** $(-\infty, 7)$

82. $[-1/5, \infty)$

83. $(-\infty, 5/3)$

84. $(-\infty, -12/7)$

85. $[-3, 5)$

86. $(2, \infty)$

87. $(-\infty, -2) \cup (4, \infty)$

88. $(-4, 1)$

89. $(-1, 3)$

90. $(-\infty, -3/2) \cup (1, \infty)$

91. $(-\infty, -2] \cup (3, \infty)$

92. $(-4, 1]$

93. $[-2, 1] \cup (3, \infty)$

94. $(-\infty, 0) \cup (5/2, \infty)$

95. $5, -7$ **96.** 0   **97.** $-\dfrac{4}{3}, -6$ **98.** $-\dfrac{3}{8}, \dfrac{3}{10}$
99. $(-6, 0)$ **100.** $(-\infty, 2] \cup [8/3, \infty)$

101. $(-5, 1)$

102. $(-\infty, -29) \cup (35, \infty)$

103. $(-7/2, -2) \cup (-1, 1/2)$

104. $(-1, 4/3) \cup (4/3, 11/3)$

Chapter Test
1. $x \ne 0, x \ne 1$ **2.** $x \ne \dfrac{2}{3}$ **3.** $\dfrac{5}{2}$ **4.** 37

5. $x = \mu + z\sigma$ **6.** $a = \dfrac{bc}{c + b}$ **7.** 87.5   **8.** $14,000

9. $\frac{1}{2}, \frac{3}{2}$ **10.** $\frac{3}{2}, -4$ **11.** $x = \dfrac{-b \pm \sqrt{b^2 - 4ac}}{2a}$

12. $\dfrac{5 \pm \sqrt{133}}{6}$ **13.** $5, -3$ **14.** 8 sec   **15.** $7 - 12i$

16. $-23 - 43i$ **17.** $\dfrac{4}{5} + \dfrac{2}{5}i$ **18.** $0 + i$ **19.** i

20. 1 **21.** 13 **22.** $\dfrac{\sqrt{10}}{10}$ **23.** $2, -2, 3, -3$

24. $1, -\dfrac{1}{32}$ **25.** 139 **26.** -1

27.

28.

29. $[3, 4)$

30. $(2, \infty)$

31. $(-\infty, -1] \cup [8, \infty)$

32. $[-2, 1)$

33. $2, -\dfrac{10}{3}$ **34.** 0

35. $(-\infty, 3/2) \cup (7/2, \infty)$

36. $[-9, 6]$

Cumulative Review

1. $-2, 0, 2, 6$ **2.** $2, 5, 11$
3. $[-4, 7)$

4. $(-\infty, 0) \cup [2, \infty)$

5. Comm. Prop. of Addition   **6.** Transitive Prop.   **7.** $9a^2$

8. $81a^2$ **9.** a^6b^4 **10.** $\dfrac{9y^2}{x^4}$ **11.** $\dfrac{x^4}{16y^2}$ **12.** $\dfrac{4y^{10}}{9x^6}$

13. a^3b^3 **14.** abc^2 **15.** $\sqrt{3}$ **16.** $\dfrac{\sqrt[3]{2x^2}}{x}$

17. $\dfrac{3(y + \sqrt{3})}{y^2 - 3}$ **18.** $\dfrac{3x(\sqrt{x} + 1)}{x - 1}$ **19.** $5\sqrt{3} - 3\sqrt{5}$

20. $3\sqrt{2}$ **21.** $5 - 2\sqrt{6}$ **22.** 4 **23.** $-8x + 8$
24. $9x^4 - 4x^3$ **25.** $6x^2 + 11x - 35$ **26.** $z^3 + z^2 + 4$

27. $2x^2 - x + 1$ **28.** $3x^2 + 1 - \dfrac{x}{x^2 + 2}$ **29.** $3t(t - 2)$

30. $(3x + 2)(x - 4)$ **31.** $(x + 1)^2(x - 1)^2(x^2 + 1)^2$

32. $(x + 1)(x^2 - x + 1)(x - 1)(x^2 + x + 1)$ **33.** $\dfrac{x - 5}{x + 5}$

34. $(2x + 1)(x + 2)$ **35.** $\dfrac{5x^2 + 17x - 6}{(x + 3)(x - 3)}$

36. $\dfrac{-x^2 + x + 7}{(x + 2)(x + 3)}$ **37.** $b + a$ **38.** $-\dfrac{1}{xy}$

39. $0, 10$ **40.** 34 **41.** $R = \dfrac{R_1 R_2}{R_1 + R_2}$

42. $r = \dfrac{a - S}{1 - S}$ or $r = \dfrac{S - a}{S - l}$

43. either 8 ft by 24 ft or 12 ft by 16 ft   **44.** $\$8,000$

45. $\dfrac{3}{5} + \dfrac{4}{5}i$ **46.** $\dfrac{3}{2} - \dfrac{1}{2}i$ **47.** 5 **48.** $0 + 10i$

49. 3 **50.** $2, -2, 3, -3$ **51.** $2, 7$ **52.** $64, 729$
53. $\left(-\infty, \dfrac{11}{5}\right]$ **54.** $(-\infty, 3) \cup (5, \infty)$

55. $[-3, -1] \cup (2, \infty)$ **56.** $(-\infty, -3) \cup (0, 3)$

57. $(-\infty, -1] \cup [4, \infty)$ **58.** $\left(\dfrac{1}{3}, 3\right)$

Section 2.1
1. quadrants   **3.** to the right   **5.** first   **7.** linear
9. x-intercept   **11.** horizontal   **13.** midpoint
15. $A(2, 3)$ **17.** $C(-2, -3)$ **19.** $E(0, 0)$
21. $G(-5, -5)$ **23.** QI   **25.** QIII   **27.** QI
29. x-axis
31.

33.

35.

37.

39.

41.

43.

45.

47.

49.

51.

53.

55.

57. 1.22   **59.** 4.67   **61.** 5   **63.** $\sqrt{13}$ **65.** $\sqrt{2}$
67. 2   **69.** 5   **71.** 13   **73.** $2\sqrt{13}$ **75.** $8\sqrt{2}$
77. 7   **79.** $(4, 6)$ **81.** $(0, 1)$ **83.** $\left(-1, \dfrac{1}{2}\right)$
85. $\left(\dfrac{\sqrt{5}}{2}, \dfrac{\sqrt{5}}{2}\right)$ **87.** $(5, 6)$ **89.** $(5, 15)$
93. $\sqrt{2}$ units   **97.** \$312,500   **99.** 200   **101.** 100 rpm
103. approx. 171 mi   **109.**

111. no graph; the intersection is the empty set   **113.** -12

Section 2.2
1. divided   **3.** run   **5.** the change in   **7.** vertical
9. perpendicular   **11.** 1   **13.** $-\dfrac{5}{12}$ **15.** $-\dfrac{7}{4}$
17. -2 **19.** undefined   **21.** $\dfrac{5}{3}$ **23.** -1 **25.** 3
27. $\dfrac{1}{2}$ **29.** $\dfrac{2}{3}$ **31.** 0   **33.** 0   **35.** undefined
37. negative   **39.** positive   **41.** undefined
43. perpendicular   **45.** parallel   **47.** perpendicular
49. perpendicular   **51.** perpendicular   **53.** parallel
55. perpendicular   **57.** neither   **59.** 5   **61.** 6
63. not on same line   **65.** on same line
67. No two are perpendicular.   **69.** PQ and PR are
perpendicular.   **71.** PQ and PR are perpendicular.
81. 3.5 students per yr   **83.** \$642.86 per year

85. $\dfrac{\Delta T}{\Delta t}$ is the hourly rate of change in temperature.

87. The slope is the speed of the plane.

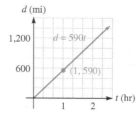

91. $y = -\dfrac{3}{7}x + 3$ **93.** $y = -\dfrac{2}{5}x + 2$
95. $(2p + 3)(3p - 4)$ **97.** $(m + n)(p + q)$

Section 2.3
1. $y - y_1 = m(x - x_1)$ **3.** slope-intercept   **5.** $-\dfrac{A}{B}$
7. $2x - y = 0$ **9.** $4x - 2y = -7$ **11.** $2x - 5y = -7$
13. $y = -3$ **15.** $x = -6$ **17.** $\pi x - y = \pi^2$
19. $2x - 3y = -11$ **21.** $y = x$ **23.** $y = \dfrac{7}{3}x - 3$
25. $y = -\dfrac{9}{5}x + \dfrac{2}{5}$ **27.** $y = 3x - 2$ **29.** $y = 5x - \dfrac{1}{5}$
31. $y = ax + \dfrac{1}{a}$ **33.** $y = ax + a$ **35.** $3x - 2y = 0$
37. $3x + y = -4$ **39.** $\sqrt{2}x - y = -\sqrt{2}$
41. $1, (0, -1)$ **43.** $\dfrac{2}{3}, (0, 2)$

   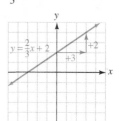

45. $-\dfrac{2}{3}, (0, 6)$ **47.** $\dfrac{3}{2}, (0, -4)$

49. $-\dfrac{1}{3}, \left(0, -\dfrac{5}{6}\right)$ **51.** $\dfrac{7}{2}, (0, 2)$ **53.** parallel
55. perpendicular   **57.** parallel   **59.** perpendicular
61. perpendicular   **63.** perpendicular   **65.** $y = 4x$

67. $y = 4x - 3$ **69.** $y = \dfrac{4}{5}x - \dfrac{26}{5}$ **71.** $y = -\dfrac{1}{4}x$

73. $y = -\dfrac{1}{4}x + \dfrac{11}{2}$ **75.** $y = -\dfrac{5}{4}x + 3$

77. $m = -\dfrac{4}{5}; (0, 4)$ **79.** $m = -\dfrac{2}{3}; (0, 4)$ **81.** $x = -2$

83. $x = 5$ **85.** $y = -3{,}200x + 24{,}300$

87. $y = 47{,}500x + 475{,}000$ **89.** $y = -\dfrac{710}{3}x + 1{,}900$

91. \$90   **93.** \$890   **95.** \$37,200   **97.** \$230

99. about 838   **101.** $C = \dfrac{5}{9}(F - 32)$

103. $y = -\dfrac{9}{10}x + 47; 11\%$ **105.** $y = 3.75x + 37.5; \$52\dfrac{1}{2}$

107. 1,655 barrels per day

109. a. Chirps/min

b. $y = \dfrac{23}{5}x - 210$ (answers may vary)

c. 204 (answers may vary)   **111.** $y = 4.44x - 196.62$

123. x^5 **125.** $\dfrac{125}{729}$ **127.** $-\sqrt{3}$ **129.** $\dfrac{5\left(\sqrt{x} - 2\right)}{x - 4}$

Section 2.4

1. x-intercept   **3.** axis of symmetry   **5.** x-axis
7. circle; center   **9.** $x^2 + y^2 = r^2$

11. $(-2, 0), (2, 0); (0, -4)$ **13.** $(0, 0), \left(\dfrac{1}{2}, 0\right); (0, 0)$

15. $(-1, 0), (5, 0); (0, -5)$ **17.** $(1, 0), (-2, 0); (0, -2)$
19. $(-3, 0), (0, 0), (3, 0); (0, 0)$ **21.** $(-1, 0), (1, 0); (0, -1)$
23.

25.

27.

29.

31. about the y-axis   **33.** about the x-axis
35. about the x-axis, the y-axis, and the origin
37. about the y-axis   **39.** none   **41.** about the x-axis
43. about the y-axis   **45.** about the x-axis
47.

49.

51.

53.

55.

57.

59.

61.

63. $(0, 0); 10$ **65.** $(0, 5); 7$ **67.** $(-6, 0); \dfrac{1}{2}$
69. $(4, 1); 3$ **71.** $\left(\dfrac{1}{4}, -2\right); 3\sqrt{5}$ **73.** $x^2 + y^2 = 25$

75. $x^2 + (y + 6)^2 = 36$ **77.** $(x - 8)^2 + y^2 = \dfrac{1}{25}$

79. $(x + 2)^2 + (y - 12)^2 = 169$ **81.** $x^2 + y^2 - 1 = 0$
83. $x^2 + y^2 - 12x - 16y + 84 = 0$
85. $x^2 + y^2 - 6x + 8y + 23 = 0$
87. $x^2 + y^2 - 6x - 6y - 7 = 0$
89. $x^2 + y^2 + 6x - 8y = 0$ **91.** $(x - 3)^2 + (y + 2)^2 = 9$
93. $(x - 5)^2 + (y - 6)^2 = 4$ **95.** $(x - 2)^2 + (y - 4)^2 = 9$
97.

99.

101.

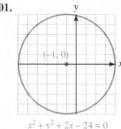

$x^2 + y^2 + 2x - 24 = 0$

103.

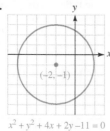

$x^2 + y^2 + 4x + 2y - 11 = 0$

5–8.

105.

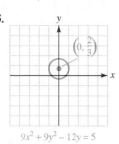

$9x^2 + 9y^2 - 12y = 5$

107.

$4x^2 + 4y^2 - 4x + 8y + 1 = 0$

109. $(0.25, 0.88)$

111. $(0.50, 7.25)$

113. ± 2.65

115. 1.44

117. 4 sec   **119.**

121. $x^2 + y^2 = 36$ **123.** $x^2 + (y - 35)^2 = 900$
125. $x^2 + y^2 - 14x - 8y + 40 = 0$ **127.** $(-3, 2)$
129. a single point   **131.** 6   **133.** -1 **135.** 20 oz

Section 2.5

1. quotient   **3.** means   **5.** extremes; means
7. inverse   **9.** joint   **11.** 14   **13.** $2, -3$ **15.** 18
17. $\dfrac{1}{2}$ **19.** 1,000   **21.** 1   **23.** $\dfrac{21}{4}$ **25.** 6   **27.** -8
29. direct variation   **31.** neither   **33.** 202, 172, 136
35. about 2 gal   **37.** $14\dfrac{6}{11}$ ft^3 **39.** 3 sec   **41.** $\sqrt{2}$ m
43. 15 lumens   **45.** It is multiplied by 18.
47. The force is multiplied by $\dfrac{9}{4}$.   **49.** $\dfrac{\sqrt{3}}{4}$
57. $\dfrac{3x + 5}{(x + 2)(x + 1)}$ **59.** $\dfrac{(x + 4)(x + 1)}{x - 1}$ **61.** $-\dfrac{1}{x}$

Chapter Review

1. $(2, 0)$ **2.** $(-2, 1)$ **3.** $(0, -1)$ **4.** $(3, -1)$

9.

10.

11.

12.

13.

14.

15.

16.

17. $12,150   **18.** $332,500   **19.** 10   **20.** $4\sqrt{2}$
21. 2   **22.** $2\sqrt{2}|a|$ **23.** $(0, 3)$ **24.** $\left(-6, \dfrac{15}{2}\right)$
25. $\left(\sqrt{3}, 8\right)$ **26.** $(0, 0)$ **27.** -6 **28.** 2   **29.** -1
30. 1   **31.** 3   **32.** 5   **33.** 0   **34.** undefined
35. negative   **36.** positive   **37.** perpendicular
38. neither   **39.** $y = 7$ **40.** $x = 3$ **41.** 200 ft/min
42. $48,750 per year   **43.** $7x + 5y = 0$
44. $4x + y = -7$ **45.** $x + 5y = -3$ **46.** $2x + y = 9$
47. $y = \dfrac{2}{3}x + 3$ **48.** $y = -\dfrac{3}{2}x - 5$

49.

50.

84. $(5, -1); 3$ **85.** $x^2 + y^2 = 49$ **86.** $(x - 3)^2 + y^2 = \dfrac{1}{25}$

87. $(x + 2)^2 + (y - 12)^2 = 25$ **88.** $\left(x - \dfrac{2}{7}\right)^2 + (y - 5)^2 = 81$

89. $(x + 3)^2 + (y - 4)^2 = 144$ or $x^2 + y^2 + 6x - 8y - 119 = 0$

90. $\left(x + \dfrac{1}{2}\right)^2 + \left(y - \dfrac{5}{2}\right)^2 = \dfrac{121}{2}$ or $x^2 + y^2 + x - 5y - 54 = 0$

91. $(x + 3)^2 + (y - 2)^2 = 9$
92. $(x - 2)^2 + (y - 4)^2 = 25$

51. $\dfrac{3}{2}, (0, -5)$ **52.** $-\dfrac{1}{2}, (0, -2)$ **53.** $\dfrac{3}{2}, (0, -5)$

54. $-\dfrac{1}{2}, (0, -2)$ **55.** $-\dfrac{5}{2}, \left(0, \dfrac{7}{2}\right)$ **56.** $\dfrac{3}{4}, \left(0, -\dfrac{7}{2}\right)$

57. $y = 17$ **58.** $x = -5$ **59.** $y = \dfrac{3}{4}x - \dfrac{3}{2}$

60. $y = -7x + 47$ **61.** $y = 3x + 5$

62. $y = \dfrac{1}{7}x - 3$ **63.** parallel **64.** perpendicular

65. $(0, 0), \left(\dfrac{1}{2}, 0\right); (0, 0)$ **66.** $(12, 0), (-2, 0); (0, -24)$

67. about the x-axis **68.** about the y-axis
69. about the y-axis **70.** none
71.

72. $y = x^3 - 2$

93.

94.

95.

96.
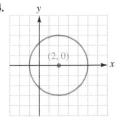

97. $3.32, -3.32$ **98.** $-1, 0, 1$ **99.** $1.73, -1.73, 1, -1$
100. $4.19, -1.19$ **101.** $x = 2, x = 5$ **102.** $x = -5, x = 5$
103. $\dfrac{9}{5}$ lb **104.** $\dfrac{25}{9}$ **105.** $333\dfrac{1}{3}$ cc **106.** 1
107. about 117 ohms **108.** \$385
109. 140 hr

73.

74.
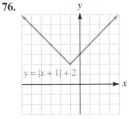

Chapter Test
1. QII **2.** y-axis
3.

4.

75.

76.

77.
78.

79.
80.

5.

6.

81. $(0, 0); 8$ **82.** $(0, 6); 10$ **83.** $(-7, 0); \dfrac{1}{2}$

7.

8.

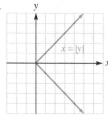

9. $\sqrt{41}$ **10.** approximately 4.44   **11.** $(0, 0)$

12. $\left(\sqrt{2}, 2\sqrt{2}\right)$ **13.** $-\dfrac{5}{4}$ **14.** $\dfrac{\sqrt{3}}{3}$ **15.** neither

16. perpendicular   **17.** $y = 2x - 11$ **18.** $y = 3x + \dfrac{1}{2}$

19. $y = 2x + 5$ **20.** $y = -\dfrac{1}{2}x + 5$ **21.** $y = 2x - \dfrac{11}{2}$

22. $x = 3$ **23.** $(-4, 0), (0, 0), (4, 0); (0, 0)$
24. $(4, 0); (0, 4)$ **25.** about the x-axis
26. about the y-axis

27.

28.

29.

30.

31. $(x - 5)^2 + (y - 7)^2 = 64$ **32.** $(x - 2)^2 + (y - 4)^2 = 32$
33.

34.

35. $y = kz^2$ **36.** $w = krs^2$ **37.** $P = \dfrac{35}{2}$ **38.** $x = \dfrac{27}{32}$

39. $x = 2.65$ **40.** $x = 5.85$

Section 3.1

1. function   **3.** domain   **5.** $y = f(x)$ **7.** x
9. vertical; once   **11.** function   **13.** not a function
15. function   **17.** not a function   **19.** not a function
21. function   **23.** domain: $(-\infty, \infty)$ **25.** domain: $(-\infty, \infty)$
27. domain: $[2, \infty)$ **29.** domain: $(-\infty, 4]$
31. domain: $(-\infty, -1] \cup [1, \infty)$ **33.** domain: $(-\infty, -\infty)$
35. domain: $(-\infty, -1) \cup (-1, \infty)$

37. domain: $(-\infty, 3) \cup (3, \infty)$
39. domain: $(-\infty, -2) \cup (-2, 2) \cup (2, \infty)$
41. domain: $(-\infty, -1) \cup (-1, 5) \cup (5, \infty)$
43. $4; -11; 3k - 2; 3k^2 - 5$ **45.** $4; \dfrac{3}{2}; \dfrac{1}{2}k + 3; \dfrac{1}{2}k^2 + \dfrac{5}{2}$
47. $4; 9; k^2; k^4 - 2k^2 + 1$ **49.** $9; -1; k^2 + 3k - 1;$
$k^4 + k^2 - 3$ **51.** $5; 10; k^2 + 1; k^4 - 2k^2 + 2$
53. $\dfrac{1}{3}; 2; \dfrac{2}{k + 4}; \dfrac{2}{k^2 + 3}$ **55.** $\dfrac{1}{3}; \dfrac{1}{8}; \dfrac{1}{k^2 - 1}; \dfrac{1}{k^4 - 2k^2}$
57. $\sqrt{5}; \sqrt{10}; \sqrt{k^2 + 1}; \sqrt{k^4 - 2k^2 + 2}$ **59.** 3
61. $2x + h$ **63.** $8x + 4h$ **65.** $2x + h + 3$
67. $4x + 2h - 4$ **69.** $3x^2 + 3xh + h^2$
71.

73.

domain: $(-\infty, \infty)$
range: $(-\infty, \infty)$

domain: $(-\infty, \infty)$
range: $(-\infty, \infty)$

75.

77.

domain: $(-\infty, \infty)$
range: $(-\infty, \infty)$

domain: $(-\infty, \infty)$
range: $[-4, \infty]$

79.

81.

domain: $(-\infty, \infty)$
range: $(-\infty, \infty)$

domain: $(-\infty, \infty)$
range: $(-\infty, 0]$

83.

85.

domain: $(-\infty, \infty)$
range: $[0, \infty)$

domain: $(-\infty, \infty)$
range: $[0, \infty)$

87.

domain: $[-1, \infty)$
range: $(-\infty, 0]$

89.

domain: $[2, \infty)$
range: $[0, \infty)$

91.

domain: $(-\infty, \infty)$
range: $(-\infty, \infty)$

93.

domain: $(-\infty, \infty)$
range: $(-\infty, \infty)$

95. function   **97.** function   **99.** function

101.

domain: $(-\infty, \infty)$;
range: $[0, \infty)$

103.

domain: $(-\infty, \infty)$;
range: $(-\infty, \infty)$

105. a. $C(x) = 8x + 75$ **b.** $755
107. a. $C(t) = 0.07t + 9.99$ **b.** $11.39
109. a. $C(f) = 95f + 14{,}000$ **b.** $261,000
111. $C(x) = 0.10x + 7$ **113.** $n(t) = 1{,}692t + 6{,}400$

115. $E(D) = 1.3911D$ **117.** $-\dfrac{2}{3}$ **123.** 1, 7, 8   **125.** 7

127. $(-4, 7]$ **129.**

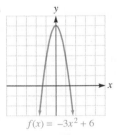

Section 3.2

1. $f(x) = ax^2 + bx + c$ **3.** $(3, 5)$ **5.** upward

7. $-\dfrac{b}{2a}$ **9.** upward; minimum

11. downward; maximum   **13.** downward; maximum
15. $(0, -1)$ **17.** $(3, 5)$ **19.** $(-6, -4)$ **21.** $(3, 0)$
23. $(2, 0)$ **25.** $(-3, -12)$ **27.** $(3, 1)$

29. $\left(\dfrac{2}{3}, \dfrac{11}{3}\right)$ **31.** $(-4, -11)$

33.

35.

37.

$f(x) = -\dfrac{1}{2}x^2 + 8$

39.

$f(x) = (x - 3)^2 - 1$

41.

$f(x) = 2(x + 1)^2 - 2$

43.

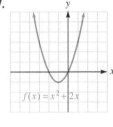

$f(x) = -(x + 4)^2 + 1$

45.

$f(x) = -3(x - 2)^2 + 6$

47.

$f(x) = x^2 + 2x$

49.

$f(x) = x^2 + 4x + 1$

51.

$f(x) = 2x^2 - 12x + 10$

53.

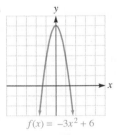

$f(x) = -3x^2 - 6x - 9$

55. 75 ft by 75 ft, 5,625 ft^2

57. 25 ft by 25 ft   **59.** $w = 12$ in.; $d = 6$ in.   **61.** 20 ft
63. 15.4 ft   **65.** 208 ft
67. 48 digital cameras; minimum cost $2,400   **69.** $95

71. $\dfrac{5}{2}$ sec   **73.** 100 ft   **75.** $(-2.25, -66.13)$

77. $(3.3, -68.5)$ **79.** 2, 3   **81.** 6 by $4\dfrac{1}{2}$ units

83. Both numbers are 3.   **87.** $a^2 - 3a; a^2 + 3a$
89. $(5 - a)^2; (5 + a)^2$ **91.** 7; 7

Section 3.3

1. 4   **3.** $n - 1$ **5.** odd   **7.** piecewise-defined   **9.** 3

11.

$f(x) = x^3 - 9x$

13.

$f(x) = -x^3 - 4x^2$

15.

$f(x) = x^3 + x^2$

17.

$f(x) = x^3 - x^2 - 4x + 4$

19.

$f(x) = x^4 - 2x^2 + 1$

21.

$f(x) = -x^4 + 5x^2 - 4$

23. even   **25.** neither   **27.** odd   **29.** odd
31. even   **33.** odd   **35.** neither
37. decreasing on $(-\infty, 0)$; increasing on $(0, \infty)$
39. increasing on $(-\infty, 0)$; decreasing for $(0, \infty)$
41. decreasing on $(-\infty, -2)$; constant on $(-2, 2)$; increasing on
$(2, \infty)$ **43.** decreasing on $(-\infty, 2)$; increasing on $(2, \infty)$
45. a. -2 **b.** 3   **47. a.** 2   **b.** 1   **c.** 3

49.

$f(x) = \begin{cases} x + 2 & \text{if } x < 0 \\ 2 & \text{if } x \geq 0 \end{cases}$

51.

$f(x) = \begin{cases} x & \text{if } x \leq 0 \\ 2 & \text{if } x > 0 \end{cases}$

53.

$f(x) = \begin{cases} -4 - x & \text{if } x < 1 \\ 3 & \text{if } x \geq 1 \end{cases}$

55.

$f(x) = \begin{cases} -x & \text{if } x < 0 \\ x^2 & \text{if } x \geq 0 \end{cases}$

57.

$f(x) = \begin{cases} 0 & \text{if } x < 0 \\ x^2 & \text{if } 0 \leq x \leq 2 \\ 4 - 2x & \text{if } x > 2 \end{cases}$

59. a. 3   **b.** -4
c. -3 **61. a.** 2   **b.** 3
c. 4

63.

$y = [\![2x]\!]$

65.

$y = [\![x]\!] - 1$

67. B

69. $32

71. $1.60

73.

75. no; this is not defined at $x = 0$

81. $3x + 5$; $3x + 3$ **83.** $\dfrac{3x - 8}{5}$; $\dfrac{3x + 1}{5} - 3$ or $\dfrac{3x - 14}{5}$

85. $-1, \dfrac{3}{2}$

Section 3.4

1. upward   **3.** to the right   **5.** 2; downward   **7.** y-axis
9. horizontally

11.

13.

15.

17.

19.

21.

23.

25.

27.

29.

31.

33.

35.

37.

39.

41.

43.

45.

47.

49.

51.

53.

55.

$h(x) = -3x^2$

57.

$f(x) = \frac{1}{2}x^3$

83.

$y = f(x-2) + 1$

85.

$y = 2f(-x)$

93. $\dfrac{x-2}{x+2}$ **95.** $(-\infty, 3) \cup (3, \infty)$ **97.** $x + 2 + \dfrac{-2}{x+1}$

Section 3.5

1. asymptote   **3.** vertical   **5.** x-intercept   **7.** same
9. horizontal; vertical   **11.** vertical asymptote: $x = 2$;
horizontal asymptote: $y = 1$; domain: $(-\infty, 2) \cup (2, \infty)$; range:
$(-\infty, 1) \cup (1, \infty)$ **13.** 20 hr   **15.** 12 hr   **17.** \$5,555.56
19. \$50,000   **21.** $(-\infty, 2) \cup (2, \infty)$
23. $(-\infty, -5) \cup (-5, 5) \cup (5, \infty)$
25. $(-\infty, -1) \cup (-1, 0) \cup (0, 1) \cup (1, \infty)$ **27.** $(-\infty, \infty)$
29. $x = 3$ **31.** $x = 1, x = -1$ **33.** $x = -2, x = 3$
35. none   **37.** $y = 2$ **39.** $y = \dfrac{1}{2}$ **41.** $y = 0$
43. none   **45.** $y = x - 3$ **47.** $y = 2x + 3$
49. $y = x + 2$

59.

$h(x) = -3|x|$

61.

$f(x) = \left(\frac{1}{2}x\right)^3$

51.

$y = \dfrac{1}{x-2}$

53.

$y = \dfrac{x}{x-1}$

63.

$f(x) = (2x)^2$

65.

$g(x) = 3(x+2)^2 - 1$

55.

$f(x) = \dfrac{x+1}{x+2}$

57.

$f(x) = \dfrac{2x-1}{x-1}$

67.

$h(x) = -2|x| + 3$

69.

$f(x) = 2|x-2| + 1$

71.

$f(x) = 2\sqrt{x} + 3$

73.

$h(x) = 2\sqrt{x-2} + 1$

59.

$g(x) = \dfrac{x^2 - 9}{x^2 - 4}$

61.

$g(x) = \dfrac{x^2 - x - 2}{x^2 - 4x + 3}$

75.

$g(x) = -2(x+2)^3 - 1$

77.

$f(x) = 2\sqrt[3]{x} + 4$

79.
$y = f(x) + 1$

81.

$y = 2f(x)$

63.

$y = \dfrac{x^2 + 2x - 3}{x^3 - 4x}$

65.

$y = \dfrac{x^2 - 9}{x^2}$

67.

$f(x) = \dfrac{x}{(x+3)^2}$

69.

$f(x) = \dfrac{x+1}{x^2(x-2)}$

71.

$y = \dfrac{x}{x^2 + 1}$

73.

$y = \dfrac{3x^2}{x^2 + 1}$

75.

$y = x - 1$

$h(x) = \dfrac{x^2 - 2x - 8}{x - 1}$

77.

$y = x + 1$ (2,8)

$f(x) = \dfrac{x^3 + x^2 + 6x}{x^2 - 1}$

79.

$f(x) = \dfrac{x^2}{x}$

81.

$f(x) = \dfrac{x^3 + x}{x}$

83.

$f(x) = \dfrac{x^2 - 2x + 1}{x - 1}$

85.

$f(x) = \dfrac{x^3 - 1}{x - 1}$

87. a. $C(x) = 3.25x + 700$ **b.** \$2,325

c. $\overline{C}(x) = \dfrac{3.25x + 700}{x}$ **d.** \$4.65   **e.** \$3.95   **f.** \$3.60

89. a. $C(n) = 0.095n + 8.50$ **b.** $\overline{C}(n) = \dfrac{0.095n + 8.50}{n}$

c. 10.5¢   **101.** $3x^2 + x$ **103.** $10x^2 + 29x + 10$
105. 3   5

Section 3.6
1. $f(x) + g(x)$ **3.** $f(x)g(x)$ **5.** intersection
7. $g(f(x))$ **9.** commutative
11. $(f + g)(x) = 5x - 1$; $(-\infty, \infty)$
13. $(f \cdot g)(x) = 6x^2 - x - 2$; $(-\infty, \infty)$
15. $(f - g)(x) = x + 1$; $(-\infty, \infty)$
17. $(f/g)(x) = \dfrac{x^2 + x}{x^2 - 1} = \dfrac{x}{x - 1}$; $(-\infty, -1) \cup (-1, 1) \cup (1, \infty)$
19. $(f + g)(x) = x^2 + \sqrt{x} - 7$; $[0, \infty)$
21. $(f/g)(x) = \dfrac{x^2 - 7}{\sqrt{x}}$; $(0, \infty)$ **23.** 7   **25.** 1   **27.** 12
29. undefined   **31.** $f(x) = 3x^2$; $g(x) = 2x$
33. $f(x) = 3x^2$; $g(x) = x^2 - 1$ **35.** $f(x) = 3x^3$; $g(x) = -x$
37. $f(x) = x + 9$; $g(x) = x - 2$ **39.** 11   **41.** -17
43. 190   **45.** 145   **47.** $(-\infty, \infty)$; $(f \circ g)(x) = 3x + 3$
49. $(-\infty, \infty)$; $(f \circ f)(x) = 9x$ **51.** $(-\infty, \infty)$; $(g \circ f)(x) = 2x^2$
53. $(-\infty, \infty)$; $(g \circ g)(x) = 4x$
55. $[-1, \infty)$; $(f \circ g)(x) = \sqrt{x + 1}$
57. $[0, \infty)$; $(f \circ f)(x) = \sqrt[4]{x}$ **59.** $[-1, \infty)$; $(g \circ f)(x) = x$
61. $(-\infty, \infty)$; $(g \circ g)(x) = x^4 - 2x^2$
63. $(-\infty, 2) \cup (2, 3) \cup (3, \infty)$; $(f \circ g)(x) = \dfrac{x - 2}{3 - x}$
65. $(-\infty, 1) \cup (1, 2) \cup (2, \infty)$; $(f \circ f)(x) = \dfrac{x - 1}{2 - x}$
67. $f(x) = x - 2$; $g(x) = 3x$
69. $f(x) = x - 2$; $g(x) = x^2$
71. $f(x) = x^2$; $g(x) = x - 2$
73. $f(x) = \sqrt{x}$; $g(x) = x + 2$
75. $f(x) = x + 2$; $g(x) = \sqrt{x}$
77. $f(x) = x$; $g(x) = x$ **79.** 0   **81.** 0   **83.** 1
85. 1   **87.** 8   **89.** 9
91. a. $(R - C)(x) = 260x - 60{,}000$ **b.** \$70,000
93. $A(t) = \dfrac{9}{4}\pi t^2$; 101,787.6 square inches   **95.** $P = 4\sqrt{A}$
105. $y = \dfrac{x + 7}{3}$ **107.** $y = \dfrac{3x}{1 - x}$

Section 3.7
1. one-to-one   **3.** identity   **5.** one-to-one
7. not one-to-one   **9.** not one-to-one
11. not one-to-one   **13.** not one-to-one   **15.** one-to-one
17. one-to-one   **19.** not a function
25. $f^{-1}(x) = \dfrac{1}{3}x$ **27.** $f^{-1}(x) = \dfrac{x - 2}{3}$
29. $f^{-1}(x) = \sqrt[3]{x} - 2$ **31.** $f^{-1}(x) = x^5$
33. $f^{-1}(x) = \dfrac{1}{x} - 3$ **35.** $f^{-1}(x) = \dfrac{1}{2x}$
37.

$f(x) = 5x$
$f^{-1}(x) = \dfrac{1}{5}x$

39.

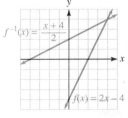

$f^{-1}(x) = \dfrac{x + 4}{2}$
$f(x) = 2x - 4$

41.

$y - x = 2$
$f^{-1}(x) = x + 2$
$x + y = 2$
$f(x) = x - 2$

43.

$2x + y = 4$
$f(x) = 4 - 2x$
$2y + x = 4$
$f^{-1}(x) = \dfrac{4 - x}{2}$

45.

$f^{-1}(x) = x^3 + 4$
$f(x) = \sqrt[3]{x - 4}$

47.

$f^{-1}(x) = \sqrt[3]{x} + 6$
$f(x) = (x - 6)^3$

49.

$f(x) = f^{-1}(x) = \dfrac{1}{2x}$

51.

$f(x) = f^{-1}(x) = \dfrac{x + 1}{x - 1}$

53. $f^{-1}(x) = -\sqrt{x + 3}$ $(x \geq -3)$
55. $f^{-1}(x) = \sqrt[4]{x + 8}$ $(x \geq -8)$
57. $f^{-1}(x) = \sqrt{4 - x^2}$ $(0 \leq x \leq 2)$
59. domain: $(-\infty, 2) \cup (2, \infty)$; range: $(-\infty, 1) \cup (1, \infty)$
61. domain: $(-\infty, 0) \cup (0, \infty)$; range: $(-\infty, -2) \cup (-2, \infty)$
63. a. $f(x) = 0.75x + 8.50$ **b.** $\$11.50$

c. $f^{-1}(x) = \dfrac{x - 8.50}{0.75}$ **d.** 2   **67.** 0   **69.** $a \geq 0$

71. 8   **73.** 4   **75.** $\dfrac{5}{4}$ **77.** $\dfrac{1}{7}$

Chapter Review

1. function   **2.** function   **3.** not a function   **4.** function
5. domain: $(-\infty, \infty)$ **6.** domain: $(-\infty, 5] \cup [5, \infty)$
7. domain: $[1, \infty)$ **8.** domain: $(-\infty, \infty)$ **9.** 8; -17; $5k - 2$
10. -2; $-\dfrac{3}{4}$; $\dfrac{6}{k - 5}$ **11.** 0; 5; $|k - 2|$ **12.** $\dfrac{1}{7}$; $\dfrac{1}{2}$; $\dfrac{k^2 - 3}{k^2 + 3}$
13. 5   **14.** $4x + 2h - 7$
15.

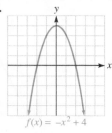

$f(x) = -x^2 + 4$

domain: $(-\infty, \infty)$
range: $(-\infty, 4]$

16.

$f(x) = 3|x - 2|$

domain: $(-\infty, \infty)$
range: $[0, \infty)$

17. function   **18.** not a function   **19. a.** $I(h) = 3.5h - 50$
b. $\$650$ **20.** $C(x) = 0.15x + 5$ **21.** upward; minimum
22. downward; maximum   **23.** $(1, 6)$ **24.** $(-4, -5)$
25. $(-3, -13)$ **26.** $\left(\dfrac{1}{2}, -8\right)$

27.

$f(x) = (x - 2)^2 - 3$
$(2, -3)$

28.

$f(x) = -(x - 4)^2 + 4$
$(4, 4)$

29.

$y = x^2 - x$
$\left(\dfrac{1}{2}, -\dfrac{1}{4}\right)$

30.

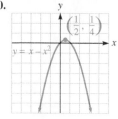

$\left(\dfrac{1}{2}, \dfrac{1}{4}\right)$
$y = x - x^2$

31.

$y = x^2 - 3x - 4$
$\left(\dfrac{3}{2}, -\dfrac{25}{4}\right)$

32.

$y = 3x^2 - 8x - 3$
$\left(\dfrac{4}{3}, -\dfrac{25}{3}\right)$

33. 300 units   **34.** Both numbers are $\dfrac{1}{2}$.
35. 350 ft by 350 ft; 122,500 ft^2
36. 50 digital cameras; minimum cost $\$1,100$
37.

$y = x^3 - x$

odd function

38.

$y = x^2 - 4x$

neither even nor odd

39.

$y = x^3 - x^2$

neither even nor odd

40.

$y = 1 - x^4$

even function

41. a. 2   **b.** 9   **42. a.** $\dfrac{1}{2}$ **b.** 3

43.

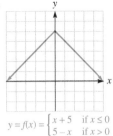

$$y = f(x) = \begin{cases} x+5 & \text{if } x \le 0 \\ 5-x & \text{if } x > 0 \end{cases}$$

increasing on $(-\infty, 0)$;
decreasing on $(0, \infty)$

45. 3   **46.** -1

47.

$f(x) = [\![x]\!] + 2$

49. \$44   **50.** \$26

51.

$g(x) = x^2 + 5$

$f(x) = x^2$

53.

$g(x) = \sqrt{x+2}+3$

$(-2, 3)$

$f(x) = \sqrt{x}$

55.

$f(x) = x^3$ $g(x) = \frac{1}{3}x^3$

57.

$g(x) = -|x-4|+3$

44.

$$y = f(x) = \begin{cases} x+3 & \text{if } x \le 0 \\ 3 & \text{if } x > 0 \end{cases}$$

increasing on $(-\infty, 0)$;
constant on $(0, \infty)$

48.

$f(x) = [\![x-1]\!]$

52.

$f(x) = x^3$

$g(x) = (x-7)^3$

54.

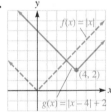

$f(x) = |x|$

$(4, 2)$

$g(x) = |x-4|+2$

56.

$f(x) = x^3$

$g(x) = (-5x)^3$

58.

$g(x) = \frac{1}{4}|x-4|+1$

59.

$g(x) = 3\sqrt{x+3}+2$

61.

$f(x) = \sqrt{-x}+3$

60.

$g(x) = \frac{1}{3}(x+3)^3+2$

62.

$g(x) = 2\sqrt[3]{x}-5$

63. $(-\infty, -5) \cup (-5, 5) \cup (5, \infty)$ **64.** $(-\infty, \infty)$
65. $x = 1, x = -1$ **66.** $x = -7$ **67.** $x = 2, x = -3$
68. $x = 4, x = -1$ **69.** $y = \dfrac{1}{2}$ **70.** $y = -5$
71. $y = 0$ **72.** none   **73.** $y = 2x + 3$ **74.** none

75.

$f(x) = \dfrac{2x}{x-4}$

76.

$f(x) = \dfrac{-4x}{x+4}$

77.

$f(x) = \dfrac{x}{(x-1)^2}$

78.

$f(x) = \dfrac{(x-1)^2}{x}$

79.

$f(x) = \dfrac{x^2-x-2}{x^2+x-2}$

80.

$f(x) = \dfrac{x^3+x}{x^2-4}$

81. $(f+g)(x) = x^2 + 2x$; domain: $(-\infty, \infty)$
82. $(f \cdot g)(x) = 2x^3 + x^2 - 2x - 1$; domain: $(-\infty, \infty)$
83. $(f-g)(x) = x^2 - 2x - 2$; domain: $(-\infty, \infty)$
84. $(f/g)(x) = \dfrac{f(x)}{g(x)} = \dfrac{x^2-1}{2x+1}$; domain: $\left(-\infty, -\dfrac{1}{2}\right) \cup \left(-\dfrac{1}{2}, \infty\right)$
85. 10   **86.** 60   **87.** 21   **88.** undefined
89. $(f \circ g)(x) = f(g(x)) = 4x^2 + 4x$; domain: $(-\infty, \infty)$
90. $(g \circ f)(x) = g(f(x)) = 2x^2 - 1$; domain: $(-\infty, \infty)$

91. 20   **92.** -2 **93.** $f(x) = x^2$; $g(x) = x - 5$

94. $f(x) = x^3$; $g(x) = x + 6$ **95.** not one-to-one

96. one-to-one   **97.** one-to-one   **98.** not one-to-one

101. $f^{-1}(x) = \dfrac{x + 1}{7}$ **102.** $f^{-1}(x) = 2 - \dfrac{1}{x}$

103. $f^{-1}(x) = \dfrac{x}{x + 1}$ **104.** $f^{-1}(x) = \sqrt[3]{\dfrac{3}{x}} = \dfrac{\sqrt[3]{3x^2}}{x}$

105. $f^{-1}(x) = \dfrac{x + 5}{2}$ **106.** $\left(-\infty, \dfrac{2}{5}\right) \cup \left(\dfrac{2}{5}, \infty\right)$

21.

22.

23. $(f + g)(x) = f(x) + g(x) = x^2 + 3x + 2$

24. $(g \circ f)(x) = g(f(x)) = 9x^2 + 2$

25. $(f/g)(x) = \dfrac{f(x)}{g(x)} = \dfrac{3x}{x^2 + 2}$

26. $(f \circ g)(x) = f(g(x)) = 3x^2 + 6$

27. $f^{-1}(x) = \dfrac{x + 1}{x - 1}$ **28.** $f^{-1}(x) = \sqrt[3]{x} + 3$

29. range: $(-\infty, -2) \cup (-2, \infty)$

30. range: $(-\infty, 3) \cup (3, \infty)$

Chapter Test

1. domain: $(-\infty, 5) \cup (5, \infty)$ **2.** domain: $[-3, \infty)$

3. $\dfrac{1}{2}, 2$ **4.** $\sqrt{6}, 3$ **5.** $(7, -3)$ **6.** $(1, -4)$

7. $(4, -10)$ **8.** $(-2, 9)$

9.

10.

11. $\dfrac{25}{8}$ sec   **12.** $\dfrac{625}{4}$ ft   **13.** 10 ft   **14.** 110 ft

15.

16.

17. vertical asymptotes: $x = -3$ and $x = 3$; horizontal asymptote: $y = 0$

18. vertical asymptote: $x = 3$; horizontal asymptote: none; slant asymptote: $y = x - 2$

19.

20.

Cumulative Review

1.

2.

3. $\sqrt{41}$; $\left(\dfrac{1}{2}, \dfrac{3}{2}\right)$; $-\dfrac{4}{5}$ **4.** $2\sqrt{29}$; $(-2, 5)$; $\dfrac{2}{5}$

5. $y = -2x - 1$ **6.** $y = \dfrac{7}{2}x - \dfrac{11}{4}$ **7.** $y = \dfrac{3}{5}x + 6$

8. $y = -4x$

9.

10.

11.

12.

13. $x = 1$, $x = 10$ **14.** $x = 2$, $x = 8$ **15.** \$62.50

16. $\dfrac{25}{4}$ **17.** function   **18.** function   **19.** function

20. not a function   **21.** domain: $(-\infty, \infty)$

22. domain: $(-\infty, -2) \cup (-2, \infty)$ **23.** domain: $[2, \infty)$

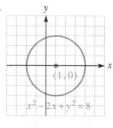

24. domain: $[-4, \infty)$ **25.** $\left(-\dfrac{5}{2}, -\dfrac{49}{4}\right)$ **26.** $\left(\dfrac{5}{2}, \dfrac{49}{4}\right)$

27.

28.

29.

30.

31.

32. $f(x) = \dfrac{x^2 - 1}{x^2 - 9}$

33. $(f + g)(x) = f(x) + g(x) = x^2 + 3x - 3$
domain: $(-\infty, \infty)$
34. $(f - g)(x) = f(x) - g(x) = -x^2 + 3x - 5$
domain: $(-\infty, \infty)$
35. $(f \cdot g)(x) = f(x) \cdot g(x) = 3x^3 - 4x^2 + 3x - 4$
domain: $(-\infty, \infty)$
36. $(f/g)(x) = \dfrac{f(x)}{g(x)} = \dfrac{3x - 4}{x^2 + 1}$ domain: $(-\infty, \infty)$
37. $(f \circ g)(2) = 11$ **38.** $(g \circ f)(2) = 5$
39. $(f \circ g)(x) = 3x^2 - 1$ **40.** $(g \circ f)(x) = 9x^2 - 24x + 17$
41. $f^{-1}(x) = \dfrac{x - 2}{3}$ **42.** $f^{-1}(x) = \dfrac{1}{x} + 3$
43. $f^{-1}(x) = \sqrt{x - 5}$ **44.** $f^{-1}(x) = \dfrac{x + 1}{3}$
45. $y = kwz$ **46.** $y = \dfrac{kx}{t^2}$

Section 4.1
1. exponential   **3.** $(-\infty, \infty)$ **5.** $(0, \infty)$ **7.** asymptote
9. increasing   **11.** 2.72   **13.** increasing   **15.** 11.0357
17. 451.8079   **19.** $5^{2\sqrt{2}} = 25^{\sqrt{2}}$ **21.** a^4 **23.** 1, 25
25. 1, 9

27.

29.

31.

33.

35.

37.

39. yes   **41.** no   **43.** $b = \dfrac{1}{2}$ **45.** no value of b
47. $b = 2$ **49.** $b = e$

51.

53.

55.

57.

59.

61.

63.

65.

67.

69.

103. $b = 2$

105.

107.

71.

73.

109.

111.

75.

77.

79.

113.

115.

81. \$22,080.40   **83.** \$15.79   **85.** \$2,273,996.13
87. \$1,263.77   **89.** \$13,375.68   **91.** \$7,647.95
from continuous compounding, \$7,518.28 from annual
compounding   **93.** \$291.27   **95.** \$12,155.61
97. 13,228   **101.** 125   **103.** $x^2(1 + 9x^2)$
105. $(x + 4)(x - 3)$

117.

119.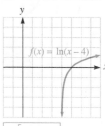

Section 4.2
1. birth; death   **3.** 0.1868 g   **5.** about 10 kg
7. about 35.4%   **9.** 0.1575 unit   **11.** 2 lumens
13. 8 lumens   **15.** about 56,570   **17.** 61.9°C
19. 315   **21.** 13   **23.** 10.6 billion   **25.** 2.6
27. about 0.07%   **29.** 0   **31.** 18,394
33. about 24,060   **35.** about 492   **37.** 19.0 mm
39. 49 mps   **41.** about 7 million   **43.** about 72.2 years
49. 8   **51.** 3   **53.** 2   **55.** 3

121.

123.

Section 4.3
1. $x = b^y$ **3.** range   **5.** inverse   **7.** exponent
9. $(b, 1); (1, 0)$ **11.** $\log_e x$ **13.** $(-\infty, \infty)$ **15.** 10
17. $\log_8 64 = 2$ **19.** $\log_4 \dfrac{1}{16} = -2$ **21.** $\log_{1/2} 32 = -5$

23. $\log_x z = y$ **25.** $3^4 = 81$ **27.** $\left(\dfrac{1}{2}\right)^3 = \dfrac{1}{8}$

29. $4^{-3} = \dfrac{1}{64}$ **31.** $\pi^1 = \pi$ **33.** 3   **35.** -3 **37.** 3

39. $\dfrac{1}{2}$ **41.** -3 **43.** 64   **45.** 7   **47.** 5   **49.** $\dfrac{1}{25}$

51. $\dfrac{1}{6}$ **53.** 5   **55.** $\dfrac{3}{2}$ **57.** 4   **59.** $\dfrac{2}{3}$ **61.** 5

63. 4   **65.** 0.5119   **67.** -2.3307 **69.** 3.8221
71. -0.4055 **73.** 3.5596   **75.** 2.0664   **77.** -0.2752
79. undefined   **81.** 25.2522   **83.** 1.9498×10^{-4}
85. 4.0645   **87.** 69.4079   **89.** 0.0245   **91.** 120.0719
93. 4   **95.** -3 **97.** 7   **99.** 4   **101.** $b = 2$

125.

127.

129.

131. b is larger.   **135.** $\left(-\dfrac{7}{2}, -\dfrac{37}{4}\right)$

137. 425 ft by 850 ft   **139.** $y = 5x$

Section 4.4
1. $20 \log \dfrac{E_0}{E_I}$ **3.** $t = -\dfrac{1}{k} \ln\left(1 - \dfrac{C}{M}\right)$

5. $E = RT \ln\left(\dfrac{V_f}{V_i}\right)$ **7.** 55 dB   **9.** 29 dB   **11.** 49.5 dB

13. 4.4   **15.** 4   **17.** no   **19.** 19.8 min
21. about 5.8 yr   **23.** about 9.2 yr
25. about 3,654 joules   **27.** about 99% per year
29. 3 yr old   **31.** about 10.8 yr   **33.** about 208,000 V
35. 1 mi   **39.** $y = 7x + 3$ **41.** $x = 2$
43. $\dfrac{1}{2x - 3}$ **45.** $\dfrac{x + 1}{3(x - 2)}$

Section 4.5

1. 0   **3.** $M; N$ **5.** $x; y$ **7.** x **9.** $\neq$ **11.** 0
13. 7   **15.** 10   **17.** 1   **25.** $\log_b 2 + \log_b x + \log_b y$
27. $\log_b 2 + \log_b x - \log_b y$ **29.** $2 \log_b x + 3 \log_b y$
31. $\dfrac{1}{3}(\log_b x + \log_b y)$ **33.** $\log_b x + \dfrac{1}{2} \log_b z$
35. $\dfrac{1}{3} \log_b x - \dfrac{1}{3} \log_b y - \dfrac{1}{3} \log_b z$ **37.** $7 \ln x + 8 \ln y$
39. $\ln x - 4 \ln y - \ln z$ **41.** $\log_b \dfrac{x + 1}{x}$
43. $\log_b x^2 \sqrt[3]{y}$ **45.** $\log_b \dfrac{\sqrt{z}}{x^3 y^2}$ **47.** $\log_b \dfrac{\dfrac{x}{z} + x}{\dfrac{y}{z} + y} = \log_b \dfrac{x}{y}$
49. $\ln \dfrac{x(x + 5)}{9}$ **51.** $\ln \dfrac{z}{x^6 y^2}$ **53.** true   **55.** false
57. true   **59.** false   **61.** true   **63.** false   **65.** false
67. true   **69.** true   **71.** true   **73.** false   **75.** true
77. 1.4472   **79.** 0.3521   **81.** 1.1972   **83.** 2.4014
85. 2.0493   **87.** 0.4682   **89.** 1.7712   **91.** 0.9597
93. 1.8928   **95.** 2.3219   **97.** 7.20   **99.** 4.77
101. from 5.01×10^{-4} to 1.26×10^{-3} **103.** 19 dB
105. The original intensity must be raised to the 4th power.
107. The volume V is squared.   **121.** yes   **123.** no
125. $(-\infty, \infty)$ **127.** $(-\infty, \infty)$

Section 4.6

1. exponential   **3.** $A_0 2^{-t/h}$ **5.** 2   **7.** -2 **9.** $-\dfrac{5}{6}$
11. -4 **13.** $-\dfrac{15}{2}$ **15.** 3, -1 **17.** ± 3
19. $-2, -1$ **21.** 3   **23.** ± 5 **25.** 1.1610
27. 1.2702   **29.** 1.7095   **31.** 0   **33.** ± 1.0878
35. 0, 1.0566   **37.** $\ln 10$ **39.** $\dfrac{1}{2} \ln 6$ **41.** 0
43. 0.2789   **45.** 1, 3   **47.** 0   **49.** 10, -10 **51.** 4
53. e^6 **55.** $\dfrac{1}{2}(e^4 + 7)$ **57.** 7   **59.** 50   **61.** 20
63. 10   **65.** 7   **67.** 6   **69.** 5   **71.** 4   **73.** 3, 4
75. 10^{10} **77.** no solution   **79.** 6   **81.** 9   **83.** 4
85. 7, 1   **87.** 20   **89.** 1.81   **91.** about 5.1 yr
93. about 42.7 days   **95.** about 2,900 yr
97. about 5.6 yr   **99.** about 5.4 yr
101. because $\ln 2 \approx 0.70$ **103.** about 3.2 days
105. about 12 min   **107.** $k = \dfrac{\ln 0.75}{3}$ **109.** $\dfrac{\ln\left(\dfrac{2}{3}\right)}{5}$
117. $f^{-1}(x) = \dfrac{x - 2}{3}$ **119.** 19   **121.** $5x^2 - 1$

Chapter Review

1. $5^{2\sqrt{2}}$ **2.** $2^{\sqrt{10}}$
3.   **4.**

5. $p = 1, q = 7$ **6.** domain: $(-\infty, \infty)$; range: $(0, \infty)$
7.   **8.**

9.   **10.**

11.   **12.**

13. $2,189,703.45   **14.** $2,324,767.37   **15.** $\dfrac{2}{3}$
16. 0.19 lumen   **17.** about 635,000,000   **18.** about 2,708
19. $(0, \infty)$; $(-\infty, \infty)$ **20.** $(0, \infty)$; $(-\infty, \infty)$ **21.** 2
22. $-\dfrac{1}{2}$ **23.** 0   **24.** -2 **25.** $\dfrac{1}{2}$ **26.** $\dfrac{1}{3}$ **27.** 32
28. 9   **29.** 8   **30.** -1 **31.** $\dfrac{1}{8}$ **32.** 2   **33.** 4
34. 2   **35.** 10   **36.** $\dfrac{1}{25}$ **37.** 5   **38.** 3
39.   **40.**

41.

42.

11.

12.

43. 6.1137   **44.** -0.1111 **45.** 10.3398   **46.** 2.5715

47.

48.

13. $2 \log a + \log b + 3 \log c$ **14.** $\frac{1}{2}(\ln a - 2 \ln b - \ln c)$

15. $\log \dfrac{b\sqrt{a + 2}}{c^2}$ **16.** $\ln \dfrac{\sqrt[3]{\dfrac{a}{b^2}}}{c}$ **17.** 1.3801

18. 0.4259   **19.** $\dfrac{\log 3}{\log 7}$ or $\dfrac{\ln 3}{\ln 7}$ **20.** $\dfrac{\log e}{\log \pi}$ or $\dfrac{1}{\ln \pi}$

21. true   **22.** false   **23.** 6.4   **24.** 46 dB   **25.** $-1, 3$

26. $\dfrac{\log 3}{\log 3 - 2} \approx -0.3133$ **27.** $\ln 9 \approx 2.1972$ **28.** 1

29. 10   **30.** 9

49. 12   **50.** $14x$ **51.** 53 dB   **52.** 4.4   **53.** $9\dfrac{1}{2}$ min

54. 23 yr   **55.** 2,017 joules   **56.** 0   **57.** 1   **58.** 3

59. 4   **60.** 4   **61.** 0   **62.** 7   **63.** 3   **64.** 4

65. 9   **66.** $2 \log_b x + 3 \log_b y - 4 \log_b z$

67. $\dfrac{1}{2}(\log_8 x - \log_8 y - 2 \log_8 z)$

68. $4 \ln x - 5 \ln y - 6 \ln z$ **69.** $\dfrac{1}{3}(\ln x + \ln y + \ln z)$

70. $\log_b \dfrac{x^3 z^7}{y^5}$ **71.** $\log_b \dfrac{\sqrt{xy^3}}{z^7}$ **72.** $\ln \dfrac{x^4}{y^5 z^6}$

73. $\ln \dfrac{y^3 \sqrt{x}}{\sqrt[3]{z}}$ **74.** 3.36   **75.** 1.56   **76.** 2.64

77. -6.72 **78.** 1.7604

79. about 7.94×10^{-4} gram-ions per liter   **80.** $k \ln 2$ less

81. $-\dfrac{5}{4}$ **82.** $-1, -3$ **83.** 2   **84.** $3, -3$

85. $\dfrac{\log 7}{\log 3} \approx 1.7712$ **86.** $\dfrac{\log 3}{\log 3 - \log 2} \approx 2.7095$

87. $\ln 8 \approx 2.0794$ **88.** $\ln 7 \approx 1.9459$ **89.** -3

90. 8   **91.** 25, 4   **92.** 4   **93.** 2   **94.** 4, 3   **95.** 6

96. 31   **97.** $\dfrac{\ln 9}{\ln 2} \approx 3.1699$ **98.** no solution

99. $e^7 \approx 1{,}096.6332$ **100.** $\dfrac{e}{e - 1} \approx 1.5820$ **101.** 1

102. about 3,300 yr

Chapter Test

1.

2.

3. $\dfrac{3}{64}$ g   **4.** $1{,}060.90   **5.** $4{,}451.08   **6.** 3

7. -3 **8.** 17   **9.** 2   **10.** -3

Section 5.1

1. whole   **3.** any   **5.** factor

7. $4x^2 + 2x + 1 + \dfrac{2}{x - 1}$

9. $2x^3 - 3x^2 + 8x - 1 + \dfrac{-3}{x + 2}$

11. -1 **13.** 9   **15.** 3   **17.** -3 **19.** 69

21. 70,249   **23.** 128.3085938   **25.** true   **27.** true

29. false   **31.** true   **33.** $(x - 1)(3x^2 + x - 5) - 9$

35. $(x - 3)(3x^2 + 7x + 15) + 41$

37. $(x + 1)(3x^2 - 5x - 1) - 3$

39. $(x + 3)(3x^2 - 11x + 27) - 85$

41. $x^2 + 2x + 3$ **43.** $7x^2 - 10x + 5 + \dfrac{-4}{x + 1}$

45. $4x^3 + 9x^2 + 27x + 80 + \dfrac{245}{x - 3}$

47. $3x^4 + 12x^3 + 48x^2 + 192x$ **49.** 47   **51.** -569

53. $-1 - 6i$ **55.** $\dfrac{15}{8}$ **57.** 5   **59.** 0   **61.** 384

63. $-28 - 16i$ **65.** $16 + 2i$ **67.** $40 - 40i$

69. $\{-1, -5, 3\}$ **71.** $\left\{-\dfrac{1}{2}, 3, -3\right\}$

73. $\left\{2, 2 + \sqrt{5}, 2 - \sqrt{5}\right\}$

75. $\left\{-3, 3 + \sqrt{10}i, 3 - \sqrt{10}i\right\}$

77. $\left\{1, 1, \sqrt{3}, -\sqrt{3}\right\}$ **79.** $\{2, 3, i, -i\}$

81. $P(x) = x^2 - 9x + 20$ **83.** $P(x) = x^3 - 3x^2 + 3x - 1$

85. $P(x) = x^3 - 11x^2 + 38x - 40$

87. $P(x) = x^4 - 3x^2 + 2$

89. $P(x) = x^3 - \sqrt{2}x^2 + x - \sqrt{2}$

91. $P(x) = x^3 - 2x^2 + 2x$ **93.** 0   **97.** QIV   **99.** QI

101. 10   **103.** 1

Section 5.2

1. zero   **3.** conjugate   **5.** 0   **7.** 2
9. lower bound   **11.** 10   **13.** 4   **15.** 4   **17.** 4, 4
19. 5, 5   **21.** $x^2 + 4 = 0$ **23.** $x^2 - 6x + 10 = 0$
25. $x^3 - 3x^2 + x - 3 = 0$
27. $x^3 - 6x^2 + 13x - 10 = 0$
29. $x^4 - 5x^3 + 7x^2 - 5x + 6 = 0$
31. $x^4 - 2x^3 + 3x^2 - 2x + 2 = 0$
33. $x^2 - 4xi - 4 = 0$
35. 0 or 2 positive; 1 negative; 0 or 2 nonreal
37. 0 positive; 1 or 3 negative; 0 or 2 nonreal
39. 0 positive; 0 negative; 4 nonreal
41. 1 positive; 1 negative; 2 nonreal
43. 0 positive; 0 negative; 10 nonreal
45. 0 positive; 0 negative; 8 nonreal; yes
47. 1 positive; 1 negative; 2 nonreal   **49.** $(-2, 4)$
51. $(-1, 1)$ **53.** $(-4, 6)$ **55.** $(-4, 3)$ **57.** $(-2, 4)$
63. k units to the right   **65.** reflected about the y-axis
67. stretched vertically by a factor of k

Section 5.3

1. -7 **3.** root   **5.** $\pm 1, \pm 2, \pm 3, \pm 4, \pm 6, \pm 12$
7. $\pm 1, \pm 2, \pm 3, \pm 6, \pm\dfrac{1}{2}, \pm\dfrac{3}{2}$
9. $\pm 1, \pm 2, \pm 5, \pm 10, \pm\dfrac{1}{2}, \pm\dfrac{5}{2}, \pm\dfrac{1}{4}, \pm\dfrac{5}{4}$
11. $1, -1, 5$ **13.** $1, 2, -1$ **15.** $1, 2, -2$ **17.** $3, -3, 2$
19. $1, -1, \dfrac{1}{2}$ **21.** $-1, -1, \dfrac{1}{3}$ **23.** $\dfrac{3}{2}, \dfrac{2}{3}, -\dfrac{3}{5}$
25. $\dfrac{2}{3}, -\dfrac{3}{5}, 4$ **27.** $\dfrac{3}{2}, \dfrac{2}{3}, \dfrac{5}{4}$ **29.** $1, 2, 3, 4$ **31.** $2, -5$
33. $1, -1, \dfrac{1}{2}, \dfrac{3}{2}$ **35.** $-2, \dfrac{5}{2}$ **37.** $\dfrac{1}{3}, -\dfrac{1}{2}$
39. $1, -1, 2, -2, -3$ **41.** $3, \dfrac{1}{2}, -\dfrac{1}{2}$
43. $0, 2, 2, 2, -2, -2, -2$ **45.** $3, \sqrt{2}, -\sqrt{2}$
47. $\dfrac{1}{2}, i, -i$ **49.** $2, -2, 1 + \sqrt{5}, 1 - \sqrt{5}$
51. $\dfrac{1}{2}, -1, 3i, -3i$ **53.** $1, 1, 1, 5i, -5i$
55. $\dfrac{3}{2}, 1, -1, 2i, -2i$ **57.** $3, 1 - i$ **59.** $3, -3, 1 - i$
61. $-\dfrac{2}{3}, 3, -1$ **63.** $\dfrac{1}{2}, \dfrac{1}{2}, \dfrac{1}{2}, 1, 1$ **65.** 10, 20, 60 ohms
67. 13 in.   **69.** 1, 5, and 9 miles
73. $(3, 7)$ or approx. $(1.54, 13.63)$ **75.** $6ab^2\sqrt{2abc}$
77. $8a\sqrt{2b}$ **79.** $\sqrt{3} + 1$

Section 5.4

1. $P(a)$ and $P(b)$ **3.** x_l and x_r
9. $P(-2) = 3; P(-1) = -2$ The signs of the results are opposites.
11. $P(4) = -40; P(5) = 30$ The signs of the results are opposites.
13. $P(1) = 8; P(2) = -1$ The signs of the results are opposites.

15. $P(2) = -72; P(3) = 154$ The signs of the results are opposites.
17. $P(0) = 10; P(1) = -60$ The signs of the results are opposites.
19. 1.7   **21.** -2.2 **23.** 1.7   **25.** -1.2 **27.** $-2.2, 2.2$
29. 1, 2; The Bisection Method fails to find the solution 2.
31. yes   **33.** $(0.83, 0.56), (-0.83, -0.56)$
37. vertical: $x = 2, x = -2$; horizontal: $y = 0$; slant: none
39. vertical: $x = 2$; horizontal: none; slant: $y = x + 2$

Chapter Review

1. 1   **2.** 66   **3.** 241   **4.** 34   **5.** false   **6.** false
7. true   **8.** true   **9.** $3x^3 + 9x^2 + 29x + 90 + \dfrac{277}{x - 3}$
10. $2x^3 + 4x^2 + 5x + 13 + \dfrac{25}{x - 2}$
11. $5x^4 - 14x^3 + 31x^2 - 64x + 129 + \dfrac{-259}{x + 2}$
12. $4x^4 - 2x^3 + x^2 + 2x + \dfrac{1}{x + 1}$ **13.** 151   **14.** -113
15. $\dfrac{13}{8}$ **16.** $-1 - 6i$ **17.** $\left\{3, \dfrac{1}{2}, -2\right\}$
18. $\left\{-2, -2, \sqrt{5}, -\sqrt{5}\right\}$
19. $P(x) = 2x^3 - 5x^2 - x + 6$
20. $P(x) = 2x^3 + 3x^2 - 8x + 3$
21. $P(x) = x^4 + 3x^3 - 9x^2 + 3x - 10$
22. $P(x) = x^4 + x^3 - 5x^2 + x - 6$ **23.** 6   **24.** 6
25. 65   **26.** 1,984   **27.** 4, 4   **28.** 40, 40   **29.** 5, 5
30. 3, 3   **31.** $2 - i$ **32.** i
33. $x^3 - 4x^2 + x - 4 = 0$ **34.** $x^3 + 5x^2 + x + 5 = 0$
35. 0 or 2 positive; 0 or 2 negative; 0, 2, or 4 nonreal
36. 1 or 3 positive; 1 negative; 0 or 2 nonreal
37. 1 positive; 0, 2, or 4 negative; 0, 2, or 4 nonreal
38. 1 or 3 positive; 0 or 2 negative; 2, 4, or 6 nonreal
39. 0 positive; 0 negative; 4 nonreal
40. 0 positive; 1 negative; 6 nonreal
41. $(-1, 2)$ **42.** $(-5, 2)$ **43.** $\pm 1, \pm 2, \pm 3, \pm 6, \pm\dfrac{1}{2}, \pm\dfrac{3}{2}$
44. $\pm 1, \pm 2, \pm 5, \pm 10, \pm\dfrac{1}{2}, \pm\dfrac{5}{2}, \pm\dfrac{1}{4}, \pm\dfrac{5}{4}$ **45.** 1, 4, 5
46. $1, -1, 8$ **47.** $-5, -\dfrac{3}{2}, -2$ **48.** $\dfrac{1}{3}$
49. $2, -2, \dfrac{3}{2}, -\dfrac{3}{2}$ **50.** $4, 4, -2, -\dfrac{1}{2}$ **51.** $\dfrac{1}{3}, 4i, -4i$
52. $2, -2, 1 + \sqrt{6}, 1 - \sqrt{6}$ **53.** $P(-1) = -9; P(0) = 18$
54. $P(1) = -8; P(2) = 21$ **55.** 4.2   **56.** 2.5
57. 1.67   **58.** 0.67
59. 10 m by 6 m; 12 m by 5 m; 15 m by 4 m   **60.** 17.27 ft

Chapter Test

1. yes   **2.** 1   **3.** -30 **4.** no
5. $(x - 2)(2x^2 + x - 2) - 5$
6. $(x + 1)(2x^2 - 5x + 1) - 2$ **7.** $2x + 3$ **8.** $3x^2 + x$
9. 5   **10.** -28 **11.** $\dfrac{11}{3}$ **12.** $6 - 3i$
13. $P(x) = x^3 - 4x^2 - 5x$ **14.** $P(x) = x^4 - 2x^2 - 3$
15. $x^3 - 2x^2 + x - 2 = 0$ **16.** $x^3 - 5x^2 + 9x - 5 = 0$
17. 3, 3   **18.** $3 + 2i$

19. 1 or 3 positive; 0 or 2 negative; 0, 2, or 4 nonreal
20. 1 positive; 0 or 2 negative; 0 or 2 nonreal   **21.** $(-3, 3)$
22. $(-1, 6)$

23. $\pm 1, \pm 2, \pm 4, \pm 8$ **24.** $\pm 1, \pm 2, \pm \dfrac{1}{5}, \pm \dfrac{2}{5}$

25. $2, -3, -\dfrac{1}{2}$ **26.** $2, i, -i$ **27.** $2, -3, 3i, -3i$

28. $1, -1, -2, 2i, -2i$ **29.** no   **30.** 3.3

Cumulative Review

1.

2.

3.

4.

5. 6   **6.** -3 **7.** 3   **8.** 2
9. $\log a + \log b + \log c$ **10.** $2 \log a + \log b - \log c$

11. $\dfrac{1}{2}(\log a + \log b - 3 \log c)$ **12.** $\dfrac{1}{2} \ln a + \ln b - \ln c$

13. $\ln \dfrac{a^3}{b^3}$ **14.** $\log \dfrac{\sqrt{ab^3}}{\sqrt[3]{c^2}}$ **15.** $x = \dfrac{\log 8}{\log 3} - 1$

16. $x = -1$ **17.** $x = 500$ **18.** $x = \sqrt{11}$ **19.** 9
20. -36 **21.** 4   **22.** $2 - i$ **23.** a factor
24. not a factor   **25.** a factor   **26.** a factor   **27.** 12
28. 2,000   **29.** 2 or 0 positive; 2 or 0 negative; 4, 2, or 0
nonreal   **30.** 1 positive; 3 or 1 negative; 2 or 0 nonreal
31. $-1, -3, 3$ **32.** $-1, 1, 2$

Section 6.1

1. system   **3.** consistent   **5.** independent
7. consistent   **9.** dependent   **11.** is
13.

15.

17.

19.

21. $(2.2, -4.7)$ **23.** $(1.7, 0.3)$ **25.** $(-1, -2)$

27. $(3, -2)$ **29.** $\left(\dfrac{1}{2}, \dfrac{1}{3}\right)$ **31.** no solution; inconsistent

system   **33.** dependent equations; a general solution is
$(x, 3x - 6)$ **35.** $(3, 1)$ **37.** $(3, 2)$ **39.** $(-3, 0)$

41. $\left(1, -\dfrac{1}{2}\right)$ **43.** dependent equations; a general solution

is $(x, 5 - 2x)$ **45.** no solution; inconsistent system

47. $(4, -7)$ **49.** $(2, -3)$ **51.** $(9, -1)$ **53.** $(1, 2, 0)$

55. $\left(0, -\dfrac{1}{3}, -\dfrac{1}{3}\right)$ **57.** $(1, 2, -1)$ **59.** $(1, 0, 5)$

61. no solution; inconsistent system   **63.** $(0, 1, 0)$

65. $\left(\dfrac{2}{3}, \dfrac{1}{4}, \dfrac{1}{2}\right)$ **67.** $\left(\dfrac{1}{2}, \dfrac{1}{2}, \dfrac{1}{2}\right)$

69. dependent equations; a general solution is $(x, 2 - x, 1)$
71. hamburger $2; fries $1
73. 225 acres of corn; 125 acres of soybeans   **75.** 8 kph
77. 40 g and 20 g   **79.** 10 ft
81. $E(x) = 43.53x + 742.72$, $R(x) = 89.95x$; 16 pairs/day
83. 15 hr cooking hamburgers, 10 hr pumping gas, 5 hr
janitorial   **85.** 1.05 million in 0–14 group, 1.56 million in
15–49 group, 0.39 million in 50-and-older group
87. $30°, 50°, 100°$
95.

97. 8   **99.** $\log x - 2 \log y - \log z$ **101.** $\log \dfrac{xy^3}{\sqrt{z}}$

Section 6.2

1. matrix   **3.** coefficient   **5.** equation
7. row equivalent   **9.** interchanged
11. adding, multiple   **13.** $(2, 3)$ **15.** $(7, 6)$
17. $(1, 2, 3)$ **19.** $(1, 1, 3)$ **21.** row echelon form
23. reduced row echelon form   **25.** $(2, -1)$
27. $(-2, 0)$ **29.** $(3, 1)$
31. no solution; inconsistent system   **33.** $(0, -7)$
35. $(1, 0, 2)$ **37.** $(2, -2, 1)$ **39.** $(1, 1, 2)$

41. dependent equations; a general solution is
$\left(x, -x + \dfrac{7}{2}, -\dfrac{3}{2}\right)$ **43.** no solution; inconsistent system

45. $(13, 3)$ **47.** $(-13, 7, -2)$ **49.** $(10, 3)$

51. $(0, 0)$ **53.** $(3, 1, -2)$ **55.** $\left(\dfrac{1}{4}, 1, \dfrac{1}{4}\right)$

57. $(1, 2, 1, 1)$ **59.** $(1, 2, 0, 1)$ **61.** $\left(\dfrac{9}{4}, -3, \dfrac{3}{4}\right)$

63. $\left(0, \dfrac{20}{3}, -\dfrac{1}{3}\right)$ **65.** dependent equations; a general

solution is $\left(x, \dfrac{1}{2}x - 3, 0\right)$ **67.** $(1, -3)$

69. dependent equations; a general solution is
$\left(\dfrac{8}{7} + \dfrac{1}{7}z, \dfrac{10}{7} - \dfrac{4}{7}z, z\right)$ **71.** dependent equations; a general
solution is $(1 + z, -z, -1 - z, z)$

73. no solution; inconsistent system   **75.** 1,300 mi
77. Dictionaries 4.5 in; atlases 3.5 in; thesauruses 4 in
79. 2 niacin, 4 zinc, 6 vitamin C
85. $x = \pm 2; y = \pm 1; z = \pm 3$ **87.** $y = mx + b$
89. equal   **91.** $y = 2x + 7$ **93.** $x = 2$

Section 6.3
1. i, j **3.** corresponding   **5.** columns, rows
7. additive identity   **9.** $x = 2, y = 5$ **11.** $x = 1, y = 2$

13. $\begin{bmatrix} -1 & 2 & 1 \\ -6 & 0 & 0 \end{bmatrix}$ **15.** $\begin{bmatrix} -5 & 2 & -7 \\ 5 & 0 & -3 \\ 2 & -3 & 5 \end{bmatrix}$

17. $\begin{bmatrix} -6 & 5 & 0 \\ 1 & -1 & 0 \end{bmatrix}$ **19.** $\begin{bmatrix} 15 & -15 \\ 0 & -10 \end{bmatrix}$

21. $\begin{bmatrix} 25 & 75 & -10 \\ -10 & -25 & 5 \end{bmatrix}$ **23.** $\begin{bmatrix} 18 & -1 & -4 \\ -35 & 0 & -1 \end{bmatrix}$

25. $\begin{bmatrix} 2 & -2 \\ 3 & 10 \end{bmatrix}$ **27.** $\begin{bmatrix} -22 & -22 \\ -105 & 126 \end{bmatrix}$

29. $\begin{bmatrix} 4 & 2 & 10 \\ 5 & -2 & 4 \\ 2 & -2 & 1 \end{bmatrix}$ **31.** $\begin{bmatrix} 4 & -5 & -6 \\ -8 & 10 & 12 \\ -12 & 15 & 18 \end{bmatrix}$

33. not possible   **35.** $\begin{bmatrix} 16 \\ 12 \\ 12 \end{bmatrix}$ **37.** not possible

39. $\begin{bmatrix} -36.29 \\ 16.2 \\ -19.26 \end{bmatrix}$ **41.** $\begin{bmatrix} -16.11 & 4.71 & 33.64 \\ -19.6 & 20.35 & 6.4 \\ -100.6 & 72.82 & 62.71 \end{bmatrix}$

47. $\begin{bmatrix} 4 & 5 \\ -7 & -1 \end{bmatrix}$ **49.** not possible

51. $\begin{bmatrix} 24 & 16 \\ 39 & 26 \end{bmatrix}$ **53.** $\begin{bmatrix} 47 \\ 81 \end{bmatrix}$

55. $QC = \begin{bmatrix} 2,000 \\ 1,700 \end{bmatrix}$ The cost to Supplier 1 is \$2,000.
The cost to Supplier 2 is \$1,700.

57. $QP = \begin{bmatrix} 584.50 \\ 709.25 \\ 1,036.75 \end{bmatrix}$ Adult males spent \$584.50.
Adult females spent \$709.25.
Children spent \$1,036.75.

59. $\begin{bmatrix} 1 & 1 & 0 \\ 0 & 1 & 1 \\ 1 & 0 & 0 \end{bmatrix}$

61. $A^2 = \begin{bmatrix} 5 & 1 & 2 & 2 \\ 1 & 5 & 2 & 2 \\ 2 & 2 & 6 & 0 \\ 2 & 2 & 0 & 4 \end{bmatrix}$ indicates the number of ways two cities can be linked with exactly one intermediate city to relay messages.

63. No; if $A = \begin{bmatrix} 1 & 1 \\ 1 & 1 \end{bmatrix}$ and $B = \begin{bmatrix} 1 & 0 \\ 0 & 0 \end{bmatrix}$, then $(AB)^2 \neq A^2B^2$.

65. Let $A = \begin{bmatrix} 1 & 2 \\ 1 & 2 \end{bmatrix}$ and $B = \begin{bmatrix} 2 & 2 \\ -1 & -1 \end{bmatrix}$. Neither is the zero
matrix, yet $AB = 0$.

67. $6x^2 - 4x - 8$ **69.** $\dfrac{x + 1}{x - 1}$ **71.** $a = \dfrac{2s}{n} - l$

Section 6.4
1. $AB = BA = I$ **3.** $[I \mid A^{-1}]$ **5.** $\begin{bmatrix} 3 & 4 \\ 2 & 3 \end{bmatrix}$

7. $\begin{bmatrix} 5 & -7 \\ -2 & 3 \end{bmatrix}$ **9.** $\begin{bmatrix} -2 & 3 & -3 \\ -5 & 7 & -6 \\ 1 & -1 & 1 \end{bmatrix}$

11. $\begin{bmatrix} 4 & 1 & -3 \\ -5 & -1 & 4 \\ -1 & -1 & 1 \end{bmatrix}$ **13.** no inverse

15. $\begin{bmatrix} 1 & -2 & 1 \\ 0 & 1 & -2 \\ 0 & 0 & 1 \end{bmatrix}$ **17.** no inverse

19. $\begin{bmatrix} 1 & -2 & 1 & 0 \\ 0 & 1 & -2 & 1 \\ 0 & 0 & 1 & -2 \\ 0 & 0 & 0 & 1 \end{bmatrix}$ **21.** $\begin{bmatrix} 8 & -2 & -6 \\ -5 & 2 & 4 \\ 2 & 0 & -2 \end{bmatrix}$

23. $\begin{bmatrix} -2.5 & 5 & 3 & 5.5 \\ 5.5 & -8 & -6 & -9.5 \\ -1 & 3 & 1 & 3 \\ -5.5 & 9 & 6 & 10.5 \end{bmatrix}$

25. $x = 23, y = 17$ **27.** $x = 0, y = 0$
29. $x = 1, y = 2, z = 2$ **31.** $x = 54, y = -37, z = -49$
33. $x = 2, y = 1$ **35.** $x = 1, y = 2, z = 1$
37. 2 of model A, 3 of model B   **39.** hi   **41.** no

45. $X = \begin{bmatrix} 0 \\ 0 \\ 0 \end{bmatrix}$ **51.** $(-\infty, -2) \cup (-2, 2) \cup (2, \infty)$

53. $(-\infty, \infty)$ **55.** $[0, \infty)$ **57.** $(-\infty, \infty)$

Section 6.5
1. $|A|$, $\det(A)$ **3.** 0   **5.** 0   **7.** 8   **9.** 1
11. -42 **13.** 13   **15.** 42   **17.** 13   **19.** -54
21. -7 **23.** 86   **25.** -2 **27.** 2   **29.** 120
31. true   **33.** false   **35.** 3   **37.** 3   **39.** $(1, 2)$
41. $(3, 0)$ **43.** $(1, 0, 1)$ **45.** $(1, -1, 2)$ **47.** $(6, 6, 12)$
49. $\left(\dfrac{5}{6}, \dfrac{2}{3}, \dfrac{1}{2}, \dfrac{5}{2}\right)$ **51.** $3x - 2y = 0$ **53.** $6x + 7y = 9$
55. 30 sq. units   **57.** 73 sq. units   **63.** 8   **65.** -1
67. \$5,000 in HiTech, \$8,000 in SaveTel, \$7,000 in OilCo
69. 10   **71.** 24   **73.** 8
77. domain: $n \times n$ matrices; range: all real numbers
79. yes   **81.** 21.468   **83.** $(x - 1)(x + 4)$

85. $x(3x + 1)(3x - 1)$ **87.** $\dfrac{4x - 5}{(x - 2)(2x - 1)}$

89. $\dfrac{x^2 + 2x + 1}{x(x^2 + 1)}$

Section 6.6

1. first-degree; second-degree   **3.** $\dfrac{1}{x} + \dfrac{2}{x - 1}$

5. $\dfrac{5}{x} - \dfrac{3}{x - 3}$ **7.** $\dfrac{1}{x + 1} + \dfrac{2}{x - 1}$ **9.** $\dfrac{2}{x} - \dfrac{2}{x - 2}$

11. $\dfrac{1}{x - 3} - \dfrac{3}{x + 2}$ **13.** $\dfrac{8}{x + 3} - \dfrac{5}{x - 1}$

15. $\dfrac{5}{2x - 3} + \dfrac{2}{x - 5}$ **17.** $\dfrac{2}{x} + \dfrac{3}{x - 1} - \dfrac{1}{x + 1}$

19. $\dfrac{1}{x} + \dfrac{1}{x^2 + 3}$ **21.** $\dfrac{3}{x + 1} + \dfrac{2}{x^2 + 2x + 3}$

23. $\dfrac{3}{x} + \dfrac{2}{x + 1} + \dfrac{1}{(x + 1)^2}$ **25.** $\dfrac{1}{x} + \dfrac{2}{x^2} - \dfrac{3}{x - 1}$

27. $\dfrac{2}{x} + \dfrac{1}{x - 3} + \dfrac{2}{(x - 3)^2}$ **29.** $\dfrac{1}{x - 1} - \dfrac{4}{(x - 1)^3}$

31. $\dfrac{1}{x} + \dfrac{1}{x^2} + \dfrac{2}{x^2 + x + 1}$ **33.** $\dfrac{3}{x} + \dfrac{4}{x^2} + \dfrac{x + 1}{x^2 + 1}$

35. $-\dfrac{1}{x + 1} - \dfrac{3}{x^2 + 2}$ **37.** $\dfrac{x + 1}{x^2 + 2} + \dfrac{2}{x^2 + x + 2}$

39. $\dfrac{1}{x} + \dfrac{x}{x^2 + 2x + 5} + \dfrac{x + 2}{(x^2 + 2x + 5)^2}$

41. $x - 3 - \dfrac{1}{x + 1} + \dfrac{8}{x + 2}$ **43.** $1 + \dfrac{2}{3x + 1} + \dfrac{1}{x^2 + 1}$

45. $1 + \dfrac{1}{x} + \dfrac{x}{x^2 + x + 1}$ **47.** $2 + \dfrac{1}{x} + \dfrac{3}{x - 1} + \dfrac{2}{x^2 + 1}$

49. No, it's the sum of two cubes.   **51.** $2|a|\sqrt{2ab}$

53. $3x^2\sqrt{2x}$ **55.** $x = 9$

Section 6.7

1. half-plane; boundary   **3.** is not

5.

7.

9.

11.

13.

15.

17.

19.

21.

23.

25.

27.

29.

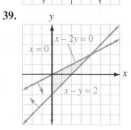

31.

33.

35.

37.

39.

41.

43.

45. $\begin{cases} 6s + 4l \le 60 \\ s \ge 0 \\ l \ge 0 \end{cases}$ **53.** one; one   **55.** 0

Section 6.8

1. constraints   **3.** objective   **5.** $P = 12$ at $(0, 4)$

7. $P = \dfrac{13}{6}$ at $\left(\dfrac{5}{3}, \dfrac{4}{3}\right)$ **9.** $P = \dfrac{18}{7}$ at $\left(\dfrac{3}{7}, \dfrac{12}{7}\right)$

11. $P = 3$ at $(1, 0)$ **13.** $P = 0$ at $(0, 0)$

15. $P = 0$ at $(0, 0)$ **17.** $P = -12$ at $(-2, 0)$

19. $P = -2$ at the edge joining $(1, 2)$ and $(-1, 0)$

21. 3 tables, 12 chairs; \$1,260

23. 30 IBMs, 30 Apple; \$2,700

25. 15 DVRs, 30 TVs; \$1,560

27. \$150,000 in stocks, \$50,000 in bonds; \$17,000

29. 2 buses, 2 trucks; \$1,100

33. $\begin{bmatrix} 1 & 0 & 0 \\ 0 & 1 & 0 \\ 0 & 0 & 1 \\ 0 & 0 & 0 \end{bmatrix}$ **35.** $\left(\dfrac{1}{3} - 3y, y, -\dfrac{1}{3}\right)$

Chapter Review

1.

2.

3.

4.
a general solution is $\left(x, -\dfrac{3}{2}x + 3\right)$

5.

6. $x = 2, y = -1$ **7.** $x = 0, y = -3$ **8.** $x = 1, y = 1$

9. dependent equations; a general solution is $(x, 3x - 4)$

10. no solution; inconsistent system   **11.** $x = -3, y = 2$

12. $x = -2, y = 5$ **13.** $x = 2, y = -1$

14. no solution; inconsistent system   **15.** dependent

equations; a general solution is $(x, 3x - 4)$

16. $x = 1, y = 0, z = 1$ **17.** $x = 1, y = 1, z = -1$

18. $x = 0, y = 1, z = 2$ **19.** \$10,400

20. 900 adult tickets, 450 senior tickets, 450 children's tickets

21. $x = 1, y = 1$ **22.** dependent equations; a general

solution is $(x, 3x + 4)$ **23.** $x = 3, y = 1, z = -2$

24. $x = -10, y = 1, z = 10$

25. no solution; inconsistent system

26. $x = -4, y = 3$ **27.** $\begin{bmatrix} 1 & 3 & 4 \\ 4 & 0 & 2 \end{bmatrix}$

28. $\begin{bmatrix} 2 & 5 & 4 \\ -2 & -6 & 6 \\ -4 & 5 & -3 \end{bmatrix}$ **29.** $\begin{bmatrix} 4 & -1 \\ -7 & -7 \end{bmatrix}$

30. $\begin{bmatrix} -17 & 19 \\ 10 & -12 \end{bmatrix}$ **31.** $[5]$ **32.** $\begin{bmatrix} 2 & -1 & 1 & 3 \\ 4 & -2 & 2 & 6 \\ 2 & -1 & 1 & 3 \\ 10 & -5 & 5 & 15 \end{bmatrix}$

33. not possible   **34.** $[-24]$ **35.** $\begin{bmatrix} 0 \\ -6 \end{bmatrix}$

36. $\begin{bmatrix} 5 & -3 \\ -3 & 2 \end{bmatrix}$ **37.** $\begin{bmatrix} 1 & 0 & 0 \\ -\dfrac{3}{2} & \dfrac{1}{2} & \dfrac{1}{2} \\ 1 & -\dfrac{1}{2} & 0 \end{bmatrix}$

38. $\begin{bmatrix} 9 & 16 & -56 \\ -3 & -5 & 18 \\ -1 & -2 & 7 \end{bmatrix}$ **39.** No inverse exists.

40. No inverse exists.   **41.** $x = 1, y = 2, z = -1$

42. $w = 1, x = 1, y = 0, z = -1$ **43.** -7 **44.** -6

45. 3   **46.** -25 **47.** $x = 1, y = -2$

48. $x = 1, y = 0, z = -2$ **49.** $x = 1, y = -1, z = 3$

50. $w = 1, x = 0, y = -1, z = 2$ **51.** 21   **52.** 7

53. $\dfrac{3}{x} + \dfrac{4}{x + 1}$ **54.** $\dfrac{3}{x} + \dfrac{2}{x^2} + \dfrac{x - 1}{x^2 + 1}$

55. $\dfrac{1}{x} - \dfrac{1}{x^2 + x + 5}$ **56.** $\dfrac{1}{x + 1} - \dfrac{2}{(x + 1)^2} + \dfrac{2}{(x + 1)^3}$

57.

58.

59.

60.

61. $P = 6$ at $(3,0)$ **62.** $P = 12$ at $(0, -4)$

63. $P = 2$ at $(1,1)$ **64.** $P = 3$ at $\left(-\dfrac{2}{3}, \dfrac{5}{3}\right)$

65. 1,000 bags of x, 1,400 bags of y

Chapter Test

1.

2.

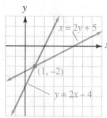

3. $x = 1, y = -3$ **4.** $x = 3, y = 5$

5. 6 liters of 20% solution, 4 liters of 45% solution

6. CD World 100 units, Ace 25 units, Hi-Fi 50 units

7. $x = 2, y = 1$ **8.** $x = 1, y = 2, z = 1$

9. $x = 1, y = 0, z = -2$

10. $x = -\dfrac{2}{5}y + \dfrac{7}{5},\ z = -\dfrac{8}{5}y - \dfrac{7}{5},\ y = $ any number

11. $\begin{bmatrix} 16 & -14 & 20 \\ 0 & -6 & -13 \end{bmatrix}$ **12.** $[-1]$ **13.** $\begin{bmatrix} -\dfrac{7}{3} & \dfrac{19}{3} \\ \dfrac{2}{3} & -\dfrac{5}{3} \end{bmatrix}$

14. $\begin{bmatrix} -13 & -3 & 14 \\ 4 & 1 & -4 \\ 12 & 3 & -13 \end{bmatrix}$ **15.** $x = \dfrac{17}{3}, y = -\dfrac{4}{3}$

16. $x = -36, y = 11, z = 34$ **17.** -12 **18.** -24

19. $-\dfrac{5}{4}$ **20.** 1   **21.** $\dfrac{3}{2x - 3} + \dfrac{1}{x + 1}$

22. $\dfrac{1}{x} + \dfrac{2x + 1}{x^2 + 2}$

23.

24.

25. $P = 7$ at $(1, 2)$ **26.** $P = -8$ at $(8, 0)$

Section 7.1

1. $2, -5, 3$ **3.** $0, 0, \sqrt{5}$ **5.** to the left

7. downward   **9.** directrix, focus   **11.** circle

13. parabola   **15.** $x^2 + y^2 = 49,\ x^2 + y^2 - 49 = 0$

17. $(x - 2)^2 + (y + 2)^2 = 17,\ x^2 + y^2 - 4x + 4y - 9 = 0$

19. $(x - 1)^2 + (y + 2)^2 = 36,\ x^2 + y^2 - 2x + 4y - 31 = 0$

21.

23.

25. $(0, 0), (0, 3), y = -3$ **27.** $(0, 3), (5, 3), x = -5$

29. $(-2, 1), (-2, -5), y = 7$ **31.** $x^2 = 12y$

33. $y^2 = -12x$ **35.** $(x - 3)^2 = -12(y - 5)$

37. $(x - 3)^2 = -28(y - 5)$ **39.** $x^2 = -4(y - 2)$

41. $(y + 5)^2 = 8(x - 1)$

43. $(y - 2)^2 = -2(x - 2)$ or $(x - 2)^2 = -2(y - 2)$

45. $(x + 4)^2 = -\dfrac{16}{3}(y - 6)$ or $(y - 6)^2 = \dfrac{9}{4}(x + 4)$

47. $(y - 8)^2 = -4(x - 6)$ **49.** $(x - 3)^2 = \dfrac{1}{2}(y - 1)$

51.

$y = x^2 + 4x + 5$
or
$y - 1 = (x + 2)^2$

53.

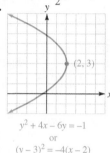

$y^2 + 4x - 6y = -1$
or
$(y - 3)^2 = -4(x - 2)$

55.

$y^2 - 4y = 4x - 8$
or
$(y - 2)^2 = 4(x - 1)$

57.

$y^2 - 4y = -8x + 20$
or
$(y - 2)^2 = -8(x - 3)$

59.

$x^2 - 6y + 22 = -4x$
or
$(x + 2)^2 = 6(y - 3)$

61.

$4x^2 - 4x + 32y = 47$
or
$\left(x - \dfrac{1}{2}\right)^2 = -8\left(y - \dfrac{3}{2}\right)$

63.

65. yes   **67.** 60 mi   **69.** $(x - 4)^2 + y^2 = 16$

71. $(x - 7)^2 + y^2 = 9$ **73.** 2 ft   **75.** $x^2 = -\dfrac{45}{2}y$

77. 1 ft   **79.** 300 ft   **81.** about 12.6 cm

83. about 520 ft   **85.** $0x^2 + 0xy + y^2 - 8x - 4y + 12 = 0$

87. $x^2 + (y - 3)^2 = 25$ **89.** $y = x^2 + 4x + 3$ **93.** 4

95. $\dfrac{49}{4}$ **97.** $x = 1, -5$ **99.** $x = -2, 9$

Section 7.2

1. sum, constant   **3.** vertices   **5.** $a, 0; -a, 0$

7. 26-in string; thumbtacks 24 in. apart   **9.** circle

11. parabola   **13.** ellipse   **15.** $\dfrac{x^2}{16} + \dfrac{y^2}{9} = 1$

17. $\dfrac{x^2}{25} + \dfrac{y^2}{16} = 1$ **19.** $\dfrac{9x^2}{16} + \dfrac{9y^2}{25} = 1$

21. $\dfrac{x^2}{7} + \dfrac{y^2}{16} = 1$ **23.** $\dfrac{(x-3)^2}{4} + \dfrac{(y-4)^2}{9} = 1$

25. $\dfrac{(x-3)^2}{9} + \dfrac{(y-4)^2}{4} = 1$

27. $\dfrac{(x-3)^2}{41} + \dfrac{(y-4)^2}{16} = 1$ **29.** $\dfrac{x^2}{36} + \dfrac{(y-4)^2}{20} = 1$

31. $\dfrac{x^2}{100} + \dfrac{y^2}{64} = 1$

33.

35.

37.

39.

41. $\dfrac{x^2}{4} + \dfrac{(y-1)^2}{16} = 1$ **43.** $\dfrac{(x+1)^2}{4} + \dfrac{(y+2)^2}{9} = 1$

45.

47.

49.   **51.** $\dfrac{x^2}{900} + \dfrac{y^2}{400} = 1$

53. $\dfrac{x^2}{2,500} + \dfrac{y^2}{900} = 1$; 36 m   **55.** about 20.8 in.

57. 199,395 mi   **63.** $\dfrac{x^2}{9} + \dfrac{y^2}{8} = 1$

67. 4 of the 75 planets shown have eccentricity 0.

69. $\begin{bmatrix} 1 & 3 \\ 1 & 1 \\ -3 & 1 \end{bmatrix}$ **71.** $\begin{bmatrix} -2 & 4 \\ 2 & 2 \\ -4 & 5 \end{bmatrix}$

Section 7.3

1. difference, constant   **3.** $a, 0; -a, 0$ **5.** transverse axis

7. circle   **9.** parabola   **11.** ellipse   **13.** hyperbola

15. $\dfrac{x^2}{25} - \dfrac{y^2}{24} = 1$ **17.** $\dfrac{(x-2)^2}{4} - \dfrac{(y-4)^2}{9} = 1$

19. $\dfrac{(y-3)^2}{9} - \dfrac{(x-5)^2}{9} = 1$ **21.** $\dfrac{y^2}{9} - \dfrac{x^2}{16} = 1$

23. $\dfrac{(x-1)^2}{4} - \dfrac{(y-4)^2}{32} = 1$ **25.** $\dfrac{x^2}{10} - \dfrac{3y^2}{20} = 1$

27. 24 sq. units   **29.** 12 sq. units

31. $\dfrac{(x+2)^2}{4} - \dfrac{4(y+4)^2}{81} = 1$ or $\dfrac{(y+4)^2}{4} - \dfrac{4(x+2)^2}{81} = 1$

33. $\dfrac{x^2}{36} - \dfrac{16y^2}{25} = 1$

35.   **37.**

$4x^2 - 3y^2 = 36$

39.   **41.**

$y^2 - x^2 = 1$ $\dfrac{(x+2)^2}{9} - \dfrac{y^2}{4} = 1$

43.   **45.**

$4(y-2)^2 - 9(x+1)^2 = 36$ $4x^2 - 2y^2 + 8x - 8y = 8$

47.   **49.**

$-xy = 6$

$y^2 - 4x^2 + 6y + 32x = 59$

51. $\dfrac{(x-3)^2}{9} - \dfrac{(y-1)^2}{16} = 1$ **53.** $4x^2 - 5y^2 - 60y = 0$

55.   **57.** 24   **59.** 3 units

61. hyperbola; $\dfrac{x^2}{144} - \dfrac{y^2}{25} = 1$

63. hyperbola; $\dfrac{x^2}{36} - \dfrac{y^2}{64} = 1$

69. $f^{-1}(x) = \dfrac{x + 2}{3}$ **71.** $f^{-1}(x) = \dfrac{2x}{5 - x}$

73. $f(g(x)) = (x + 1)^4 + 1$

75. $f(f(x)) = (x^2 + 1)^2 + 1$

Section 7.4

1. graphs

3.

5.

7.

9.

11.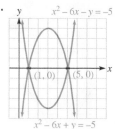

13. $(1, 2), (-1, 0)$ **15.** $(1, 0.67), (-1, -0.67)$

17. $(3, 0), (0, 5)$ **19.** $(1, 1)$ **21.** $(1, 2), (2, 1)$

23. $(-2, 3), (2, 3)$ **25.** $\left(\sqrt{5}, 5\right), \left(-\sqrt{5}, 5\right)$

27. $\left(\sqrt{3}, 0\right), \left(-\sqrt{3}, 0\right)$

29. $(2, 4), (2, -4), (-2, 4), (-2, -4)$

31. $\left(-\sqrt{15}, 5\right), \left(\sqrt{15}, 5\right), (-2, -6), (2, -6)$

33. $(0, -4), (-3, 5), (3, 5)$

35. $(-2, 3), (2, 3), (-2, -3), (2, -3)$

37. $(3, 3)$ **39.** $(6, 2), (-6, -2), \left(\sqrt{42}, 0\right), \left(-\sqrt{42}, 0\right)$

41. $\left(\dfrac{1}{2}, \dfrac{1}{3}\right), \left(\dfrac{1}{3}, \dfrac{1}{2}\right)$ **43.** 7 cm by 9 cm

45. 80 ft by 100 ft or 50 ft by 160 ft

47. either $750 at 9% or $900 at 7.5%

49. $(30, 3)$ **51.** yes at $(-2, 4)$ and $(1, 1)$

53. about 23 mi

61. vertical: $x = 1$; horizontal: $y = 3$

63. vertical: $x = 1$, $x = -1$; horizontal: $y = 0$

65. y-axis   **67.** origin

Chapter Review

1. $x^2 + y^2 = 16$ **2.** $x^2 + y^2 = 100$

3. $(x - 3)^2 + (y + 2)^2 = 25$ **4.** $(x + 2)^2 + (y - 4)^2 = 25$

5. $(x - 5)^2 + (y - 10)^2 = 85$

6. $(x - 2)^2 + (y - 2)^2 = 89$ **7.** $(x - 3)^2 + (y + 2)^2 = 16$

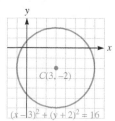

8. $(x + 2)^2 + (y - 5)^2 = 16$ **9.** $y^2 = -2x$

10. $x^2 = 16y$ **11.** $(x + 2)^2 = -\dfrac{4}{11}(y - 3)$

12.   **13.**

14. $\dfrac{x^2}{36} + \dfrac{y^2}{16} = 1$ **15.** $\dfrac{x^2}{4} + \dfrac{y^2}{25} = 1$

16. $\dfrac{(x + 2)^2}{16} + \dfrac{(y - 3)^2}{9} = 1$

17. $(x - 2)^2 + \dfrac{(y + 1)^2}{4} = 1$

18. $\dfrac{x^2}{4} - \dfrac{y^2}{12} = 1$ **19.** $\dfrac{y^2}{9} - \dfrac{x^2}{16} = 1$ **20.** $\dfrac{x^2}{9} - \dfrac{(y - 3)^2}{16} = 1$

21. $\dfrac{y^2}{9} - \dfrac{(x - 3)^2}{16} = 1$ **22.** $y = \pm\dfrac{4}{5}x$

23. $\dfrac{(x-1)^2}{4} - \dfrac{(y+2)^2}{9} = 1$

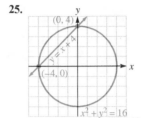

$9x^2 - 4y^2 - 16y - 18x = 43$

24.

25.

26.

27.

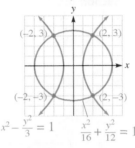

28. $(-4, 2), (-4, -2), (4, 2), (4, -2)$

29. $(0, 4), \left(2\sqrt{3}, -2\right)$ **30.** $(-2, 3), (-2, -3), (2, 3), (2, -3)$

Chapter Test

1. $(x-2)^2 + (y-3)^2 = 9$ **2.** $(x-2)^2 + (y-3)^2 = 41$
3. $(x-2)^2 + (y+5)^2 = 169$
4.

5. $(x-3)^2 = 16(y-2)$ **6.** $(y+6)^2 = -4(x-4)$
7. $(x-2)^2 = \dfrac{4}{3}(y+3)$ or $(y+3)^2 = -\dfrac{9}{2}(x-2)$
8.

9. $\dfrac{x^2}{100} + \dfrac{y^2}{64} = 1$ **10.** $\dfrac{x^2}{169} + \dfrac{y^2}{144} = 1$

11. $\dfrac{(x-2)^2}{4} + \dfrac{(y-3)^2}{36} = 1$ **12.**

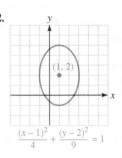

$\dfrac{(x-1)^2}{4} + \dfrac{(y-2)^2}{9} = 1$

13. $\dfrac{x^2}{25} - \dfrac{y^2}{144} = 1$ **14.** $\dfrac{x^2}{36} - \dfrac{4y^2}{25} = 1$
15. $\dfrac{(x-2)^2}{64} - \dfrac{(y+1)^2}{36} = 1$
16.

$\dfrac{(y-2)^2}{2} - \dfrac{x^2}{8} = 1$

17. $\left(\sqrt{7}, 4\right), \left(-\sqrt{7}, 4\right)$
18. $\left(3\sqrt{2}, 3\right), \left(-3\sqrt{2}, 3\right), \left(3\sqrt{2}, -3\right), \left(-3\sqrt{2}, -3\right)$
19. $(y-2)^2 = 6(x+3)$; parabola
20. $\dfrac{(x-1)^2}{3} + \dfrac{(y+2)^2}{2} = 1$; ellipse

Cumulative Review

1. 16 **2.** $\dfrac{1}{2}$ **3.** y^2 **4.** $x^{17/12}$ **5.** $x^{4/3} - x^{2/3}$

6. $\dfrac{1}{x} + 2 + x$ **7.** $-3x$ **8.** $4t\sqrt{3t}$ **9.** $4x$

10. $x + 3$ **11.** $7\sqrt{2}$ **12.** $-12\sqrt[4]{2} + 10\sqrt[4]{3}$

13. $-18\sqrt{6}$ **14.** $\dfrac{5\sqrt[3]{x^2}}{x}$ **15.** $\dfrac{x + 3\sqrt{x} + 2}{x - 1}$

16. $\sqrt{xy}$ **17.** 2, 7 **18.** $\dfrac{1}{4}$ **19.** $1, -\dfrac{3}{2}$

20. $\dfrac{-2 \pm \sqrt{7}}{3}$ **21.** $7 + 2i$ **22.** $-5 - 7i$

23. $13 + 0i$ **24.** $12 - 6i$ **25.** $-12 - 10i$

26. $\dfrac{3}{2} + \dfrac{1}{2}i$ **27.** $\sqrt{13}$ **28.** $\sqrt{61}$ **29.** -2

30. $\left(1, \dfrac{1}{2}\right)$ **31.** $(-\infty, -2) \cup (3, \infty)$ **32.** $[-2, 3]$

33. 5 **34.** 27 **35.** $12x^2 - 12x + 5$ **36.** $6x^2 + 3$
37. $2^y = x$ **38.** $\log_3 a = b$ **39.** 5 **40.** 3

41. $\dfrac{1}{27}$ **42.** 1 **43.** $y = 2^x$ **44.** x

45. 1.9912 **46.** 0.301 **47.** 1.6902 **48.** 0.1461

49. $\dfrac{2\log 2}{\log 3 - \log 2}$ **50.** 16 **51.** $\$2{,}848.31$

52. 1.16056   **53.** (2, 1)   **54.** (1, 1)   **55.** (2, −2)
56. (3, 1)   **57.** −1   **58.** −1   **59.** (−1, −1, 3)
60. (1, 1, 1)

Section 8.1

1. power   **3.** first   **5.** $7 \cdot 6 \cdot 5 \cdot 4 \cdot 3 \cdot 2 \cdot 1$
7. $(n-1)!$ **9.** 120   **11.** 4,320   **13.** 1,440
15. $\dfrac{1}{1,320}$ **17.** $\dfrac{5}{3}$ **19.** 18,564
21. $a^5 + 5a^4b + 10a^3b^2 + 10a^2b^3 + 5ab^4 + b^5$
23. $x^3 - 3x^2y + 3xy^2 - y^3$ **25.** $a^3 + 3a^2b + 3ab^2 + b^3$
27. $a^5 - 5a^4b + 10a^3b^2 - 10a^2b^3 + 5ab^4 - b^5$
29. $8x^3 + 12x^2y + 6xy^2 + y^3$
31. $x^3 - 6x^2y + 12xy^2 - 8y^3$
33. $16x^4 + 96x^3y + 216x^2y^2 + 216xy^3 + 81y^4$
35. $x^4 - 8x^3y + 24x^2y^2 - 32xy^3 + 16y^4$
37. $x^5 - 15x^4y + 90x^3y^2 - 270x^2y^3 + 405xy^4 - 243y^5$
39. $\dfrac{x^4}{16} + \dfrac{x^3y}{2} + \dfrac{3x^2y^2}{2} + 2xy^3 + y^4$ **41.** $6a^2b^2$
43. $35a^3b^4$ **45.** $-b^5$ **47.** $2,380a^{13}b^4$ **49.** $-4\sqrt{2}a^3$
51. $1,134a^5b^4$ **53.** $\dfrac{3x^2y^2}{2}$ **55.** $-\dfrac{55r^2s^9}{2,048}$
57. $\dfrac{n!}{3!(n-3)!}a^{n-3}b^3$ **59.** $\dfrac{n!}{(r-1)!(n-r+1)!}a^{n-r+1}b^{r-1}$
63. −252   **71.** $3xyz^2(x^2yz^2 - 2z^3 + 5x)$
73. $(a^2 + b^2)(a + b)(a - b)$ **75.** $\dfrac{3+x}{3-x}$

Section 8.2

1. domain   **3.** series   **5.** infinite
7. Summation notation   **9.** 6   **11.** $5c$
13. 0, 10, 30, 60, 100, 150   **15.** 21   **17.** $a + 4d$
19. 15   **21.** 15   **23.** 15   **25.** $\dfrac{242}{243}$ **27.** 35
29. 3, 7, 15, 31   **31.** $-4, -2, -1, -\dfrac{1}{2}$ **33.** k, k^2, k^4, k^8
35. $8, \dfrac{16}{k}, \dfrac{32}{k^2}, \dfrac{64}{k^3}$ **37.** an alternating infinite series
39. not an alternating infinite series   **41.** 30   **43.** −50
45. 40   **47.** 500   **49.** $\dfrac{7}{12}$ **51.** 160   **53.** 3,725
59. 6 cm   **61.** 26 ft

Section 8.3

1. $(n-1)$ **3.** infinite   **5.** $a_n = a + (n-1)d$
7. Arithmetic means   **9.** 1, 3, 5, 7, 9, 11
11. $5, \dfrac{7}{2}, 2, \dfrac{1}{2}, -1, -\dfrac{5}{2}$ **13.** $9, \dfrac{23}{2}, 14, \dfrac{33}{2}, 19, \dfrac{43}{2}$
15. 318   **17.** 6   **19.** 370   **21.** 44   **23.** $\dfrac{25}{2}, 15, \dfrac{35}{2}$
25. $-\dfrac{82}{15}, -\dfrac{59}{15}, -\dfrac{12}{5}, -\dfrac{13}{15}$ **27.** 285   **29.** 555
31. $157\dfrac{1}{2}$ **33.** 20,100   **35.** 1080°; 1800°   **37.** $460
39. $1,587,500   **41.** 80 ft   **43.** 210   **49.** 6   **51.** −1
53. $1, -1, i, -i$

Section 8.4

1. r^{n-1} **3.** ar^{n-1} **5.** infinite   **7.** Geometric means
9. 10, 20, 40, 80   **11.** $-2, -6, -18, -54$
13. $3, 3\sqrt{2}, 6, 6\sqrt{2}$ **15.** 2, 6, 18, 54   **17.** 256
19. −162   **21.** $10\sqrt[4]{2}, 10\sqrt[4]{4}$ or $10\sqrt{2}, 10\sqrt[4]{8}$
23. 8, 32, 128, 512   **25.** 124   **27.** −29,524
29. $\dfrac{1,995}{32}$ **31.** 18   **33.** 8   **35.** $\dfrac{5}{9}$ **37.** $\dfrac{25}{99}$
39. 23   **41.** 12.96 ft, 400 ft   **43.** 5.13 m
45. $69.82   **47.** about $\dfrac{1}{3}C$ **49.** about 1.03×10^{20}
51. $180,176.87   **53.** $2,001.60   **55.** $2,013.62
57. $264,094.58   **59.** 5,000   **61.** 1.8447×10^{19} grains
63. no   **65.** $5 - 3i$ **67.** $10 + 0i$ **69.** $\dfrac{1}{5} + \dfrac{8}{5}i$
71. $0 - i$

Section 8.5

1. two   **3.** $n = k + 1$
5. $5 = 5; 15 = 15; 30 = 30; 50 = 50$
7. $7 = 7; 17 = 17; 30 = 30; 46 = 46$
29. no
37. a. 1   **b.** 3   **c.** 7   **d.** 15
39.   **41.**

Section 8.6

1. 24   **3.** $\dfrac{n!}{(n-r)!}$ **5.** 1   **7.** $\dfrac{n!}{r!(n-r)!}$ **9.** 1
11. $\dfrac{n!}{a!b!\cdots}$ **13.** 840   **15.** 35   **17.** 120   **19.** 5
21. 1   **23.** 1,200   **25.** 40   **27.** 2,278   **29.** 144
31. 8,000,000   **33.** 240   **35.** 6   **37.** 40,320
39. 14,400   **41.** 24,360   **43.** 5,040   **45.** 48
47. 96   **49.** 210   **51.** 24   **53.** 5,040   **55.** 60
57. 2,721,600   **59.** 1,120   **61.** 59,400   **63.** 272
65. 28   **67.** 252   **69.** 142,506   **71.** 66   **73.** 256
75. 56   **83.** 2   **85.** 4   **87.** true   **89.** true

Section 8.7

1. experiment   **3.** $\dfrac{n(E)}{n(S)}$
5. $\{(1, H), (2, H), (3, H), (4, H), (5, H), (6, H), (1, T), (2, T),$ $(3, T), (4, T), (5, T), (6, T)\}$ **7.** $\{$a, b, c, d, e, f, g, h, i, j, k, l, m, n, o, p, q, r, s, t, u, v, w, x, y, z$\}$ **9.** $\dfrac{1}{6}$ **11.** $\dfrac{2}{3}$
13. $\dfrac{19}{42}$ **15.** $\dfrac{13}{42}$ **17.** $\dfrac{3}{8}$ **19.** 0   **21.** $\dfrac{1}{12}$
23. $\dfrac{1}{169}$ **25.** $\dfrac{5}{12}$ **27.** about 6.3×10^{-12} **29.** 0
31. $\dfrac{3}{13}$ **33.** $\dfrac{1}{6}$ **35.** $\dfrac{1}{8}$ **37.** $\dfrac{5}{16}$

39. {SSSS, SSSF, SSFS, SFSS, FSSS, SSFF, SFSF, FSSF, SFFS, FSFS, FFSS, SFFF, FSFF, FFSF, FFFS, FFFF}

41. $\dfrac{1}{4}$ **43.** $\dfrac{1}{4}$ **45.** 1   **47.** $\dfrac{32}{119}$ **49.** $\dfrac{1}{3}$

51. 0.18   **53.** 0.14   **55.** about 33%   **57.** no

59. $-10, 4$ **61.** $(-4, 10)$

Chapter Review

1. 720   **2.** 30,240   **3.** 8   **4.** $\dfrac{280}{3}$

5. $x^3 + 3x^2y + 3xy^2 + y^3$

6. $p^4 + 4p^3q + 6p^2q^2 + 4pq^3 + q^4$

7. $a^5 - 5a^4b + 10a^3b^2 - 10a^2b^3 + 5ab^4 - b^5$

8. $8a^3 - 12a^2b + 6ab^2 - b^3$ **9.** $56a^5b^3$ **10.** $80x^3y^2$

11. $84x^3y^6$ **12.** $439,040x^3$ **13.** 63   **14.** 9

15. 5, 17, 53, 161   **16.** $-2, 8, 128, 32,768$ **17.** 90

18. 60   **19.** 1,718   **20.** -360 **21.** 117   **22.** 281

23. -92 **24.** $-\dfrac{135}{2}$ **25.** $\dfrac{7}{2}, 5, \dfrac{13}{2}$

26. 25, 40, 55, 70, 85   **27.** 3,320   **28.** 5,780

29. $-5,220$ **30.** $-1,540$ **31.** $\dfrac{1}{729}$ **32.** 13,122

33. $\dfrac{9}{16,384}$ **34.** $\dfrac{8}{15,625}$ **35.** $2\sqrt{2}, 4, 4\sqrt{2}$

36. $4, -8, 16, -32$ **37.** 16   **38.** $\dfrac{3,280}{27}$ **39.** 6,560

40. $\dfrac{2,295}{128}$ **41.** $\dfrac{520,832}{78,125}$ **42.** $\dfrac{3,280}{3}$ **43.** $16\sqrt{2}$

44. $\dfrac{2}{3}$ **45.** $\dfrac{3}{25}$ **46.** no sum   **47.** 1   **48.** $\dfrac{1}{3}$

49. 1   **50.** $\dfrac{17}{99}$ **51.** $\dfrac{5}{11}$ **52.** \$4,775.81

53. 6,516; 3,134   **54.** \$3,486.78

55. $1 = 1; 9 = 9; 36 = 36; 100 = 100$

57. 6,720   **58.** 35   **59.** 1   **60.** 4,050   **61.** 564,480

62. 840   **63.** 21   **64.** 66   **65.** 120   **66.** $\dfrac{56}{1,287}$

67. $\dfrac{1}{6}$ **68.** $\dfrac{33}{66,640}$ **69.** 20,160   **70.** 90,720

72. 24   **73.** $\dfrac{1}{108,290}$ **74.** $\dfrac{108,289}{108,290}$

75. about 6.3×10^{-12} **76.** $\dfrac{60}{143}$ **77.** $\dfrac{1}{2}$ **78.** $\dfrac{7}{13}$

79. $\dfrac{1}{2,598,960}$ **80.** $\dfrac{33}{16,660}$ **81.** $\dfrac{15}{16}$

Chapter Test

1. 144   **2.** 384   **3.** $10x^4y$ **4.** $112a^2b^6$ **5.** 27

6. -36 **7.** 155   **8.** -130 **9.** 9, 14, 19

10. $-6, -18$ **11.** 255.75   **12.** about 9

13. about \$0.42C **14.** about \$1.46C **16.** 800,000

17. 42   **18.** 24   **19.** 28   **20.** 1   **21.** 576

22. 120   **23.** 60   **24.** {(H, H, H), (H, H, T), (H, T, H), (H, T, T), (T, H, H), (T, H, T), (T, T, H), (T, T, T)}

25. $\dfrac{1}{6}$ **26.** $\dfrac{2}{13}$ **27.** $\dfrac{33}{66,640}$ **28.** $\dfrac{1}{9}$ **29.** $\dfrac{87}{245}$

30. $\dfrac{12}{19}$

Index

Title: Finite Mathematics

Authors: Waner/Costenoble

6th Edition

Preface

Finite Mathematics, sixth edition, is intended for a one- or two-term course for students majoring in business, the social sciences, or the liberal arts. Like the earlier editions, the sixth edition of *Finite Mathematics* is designed to address the challenge of generating enthusiasm and mathematical sophistication in an audience that is often underprepared and lacks motivation for traditional mathematics courses. We meet this challenge by focusing on real-life applications and topics of current interest that students can relate to, by presenting mathematical concepts intuitively and thoroughly, and by employing a writing style that is informal, engaging, and occasionally even humorous.

The sixth edition goes further than earlier editions in implementing support for a wide range of instructional paradigms: from traditional face-to-face courses to online distance learning courses, from settings incorporating little or no technology to courses taught in computerized classrooms, and from classes in which a single form of technology is used exclusively to those incorporating several technologies. We fully support three forms of technology in this text: TI-83/84 Plus graphing calculators, spreadsheets, and powerful online utilities we have created for the book. In particular, our comprehensive support for spreadsheet technology, both in the text and online, is highly relevant for students who are studying business and economics, where skill with spreadsheets may be vital to their future careers.

Our Approach to Pedagogy

Real-World Orientation We are confident that you will appreciate the diversity, breadth, and abundance of examples and exercises included in this edition. A large number of these are based on real, referenced data from business, economics, the life sciences, and the social sciences. Examples and exercises based on dated information have generally been replaced by more current versions; applications based on unique or historically interesting data have been kept.

Adapting real data for pedagogical use can be tricky; available data can be numerically complex, intimidating for students, or incomplete. We have modified and streamlined many of the real-world applications, rendering them as tractable as any "made-up" application. At the same time, we have been careful to strike a pedagogically sound balance between applications based on real data and more traditional "generic" applications. Thus, the density and selection of real data–based applications has been tailored to the pedagogical goals and appropriate difficulty level for each section.

Readability We would like students to read this book. We would like students to *enjoy* reading this book. Thus, we have written the book in a conversational and student-oriented style, and have made frequent use of question-and-answer dialogues to encourage the development of the student's mathematical curiosity and intuition. We hope that this text will give the student insight into how a mathematician develops and thinks about mathematical ideas and their applications.

Rigor We feel that mathematical rigor need not be antithetical to the kind of applied focus and conceptual approach that are earmarks of this book. We have worked hard to ensure that we are always mathematically honest without being unnecessarily formal. Sometimes we do this through the question-and-answer dialogues and sometimes through the "Before we go on . . ." discussions that follow examples, but always in manner designed to provoke the interest of the student.

Five Elements of Mathematical Pedagogy to Address Different Learning Styles The "Rule of Four" is a common theme in many texts. Implementing this approach, we discuss many of the central concepts **numerically**, **graphically**, and **algebraically** and clearly delineate these distinctions. The fourth element, **verbal communication** of mathematical concepts, is emphasized through our discussions on translating English sentences into mathematical statements and in our extensive Communication and Reasoning exercises at the end of each section. A fifth element, **interactivity**, is implemented through expanded use of question-and-answer dialogues but is seen most dramatically in the student Website. Using this resource, students can interact with the material in several ways: through interactive tutorials in the form of games, chapter summaries, and chapter review exercises, all in reference to concepts and examples covered in sections and with online utilities that automate a variety of tasks, from graphing to regression and matrix algebra.

Exercise Sets Our comprehensive collection of exercises provides a wealth of material that can be used to challenge students at almost every level of preparation and includes everything from straightforward drill exercises to interesting and rather challenging applications. The exercise sets have been carefully graded to move from straightforward basic exercises and exercises that are similar to examples in the text to more interesting and advanced ones, marked as "more advanced" for easy reference. There are also several much more difficult exercises, designated as "challenging." We have also included, in virtually every section of every chapter, interesting applications based on real data, Communication and Reasoning exercises that help students articulate mathematical concepts and recognize common errors, and exercises ideal for the use of technology.

Many of the scenarios used in application examples and exercises are revisited several times throughout the book. Thus, for instance, students will find themselves using a variety of techniques, from solving systems of equations to linear programming to analyze the same application. Reusing scenarios and important functions provides unifying threads and shows students the complex texture of real-life problems.

New to This Edition

Content

- Chapter 1 (page 39): We now include, in Section 1.1, careful discussion of the common practice of representing functions as equations and vice versa; for instance, a cost equation like $C = 10x + 50$ can be thought of as defining a cost *function* $C(x) = 10x + 50$. Instead of rejecting this practice, we encourage the student to see this connection between functions and equations and to be able to switch from one interpretation to the other.

  Our discussion of functions and models in Section 1.2 now includes a careful discussion of the algebra of functions presented through the context of important applications rather than as an abstract concept. Thus, the student will see from the outset *why* we want to talk about sums, products, etc. of functions rather than simply *how* to manipulate them.

- Chapter 2 (page 125): The Mathematics of Finance is now Chapter 2 of the text because the discussion of many important topics in finance relates directly to the first discussions of compound interest and other mathematical models in Chapter 1. Note that our discussion of the Mathematics of Finance does not require the use of logarithmic functions to solve for exponents analytically but instead focuses on numerical solution using the technologies we discuss. However, the use of logarithms is presented as an option for students and instructors who prefer to use them.

- **Case Studies:** A number of the Case Studies at the ends of the chapters have been extensively revised, using updated real data, and continue to reflect topics of current interest, such as subprime mortgages, hybrid car production, and the diet problem (in linear programming).

Current Topics in the Applications

- We have added and updated numerous real data exercises and examples based on topics that are either of intense current interest or of general interest to contemporary students, including Facebook, XBoxes, iPhones, iPads, foreclosure rates, the housing crisis, subprime mortgages, stock market gyrations, shorting the stock market, and even travel to Cancun. (Also see the list, in the inside back cover, of the corporations we reference in the applications.)

Exercises

- We have expanded the chapter review exercise sets to be more representative of the material within the chapter. Note that all the applications in the chapter review exercises revolve around the fictitious online bookseller, *OHaganBooks.com,* and the various—often amusing—travails of *OHaganBooks.com* CEO John O'Hagan and his business associate Marjory Duffin.

- We have added many new conceptual Communication and Reasoning exercises, including many dealing with common student errors and misconceptions.

End-of-Chapter Technology Guides

- Our end-of-chapter detailed Technology Guides now discuss the use of spreadsheets in general rather than focusing exclusively on Microsoft® Excel, thus enabling readers to use any of the several alternatives now available, such as Google's online Google Sheets®, Open Office®, and Apple's Numbers®.

Continuing Features

Case Study   Projecting Market Share

You are the sales director at *Selular*, a cellphone provider, and things are not looking good for your company: The recently launched *iClone* competitor is beginning to chip away at Selular's market share. Particularly disturbing are rumors of fierce brand loyalty by iClone customers, with several bloggers suggesting that iClone retains close to 100% of their customers. Worse, you will shortly be presenting a sales report to the board of directors, and the CEO has "suggested" that your report include 2-, 5-, and 10-year projections of Selular's market share given the recent impact on the market by iClone, and also a "worst-case" scenario projecting what would happen if iClone customers are so loyal that none of them ever switch services.

- **Case Studies** Each chapter ends with a section entitled "Case Study," an extended application that uses and illustrates the central ideas of the chapter, focusing on the development of mathematical models appropriate to the topics. These applications are ideal for assignment as projects, and to this end we have included groups of exercises at the end of each.

- **Before We Go On** Most examples are followed by supplementary discussions, which may include a check on the answer, a discussion of the feasibility and significance of a solution, or an in-depth look at what the solution means.

- **Quick Examples** Most definition boxes include quick, straightforward examples that a student can use to solidify each new concept.

- **Question-and-Answer Dialogue** We frequently use informal question-and-answer dialogues that anticipate the kinds of questions that may occur to the student and also guide the student through the development of new concepts.

> **Q** : *Why a row and a column instead of, say, two rows?*
>
> **A** : It's rather a long story, but mathematicians found that it works best this way . . .

- **Marginal Technology Notes** We give brief marginal technology notes to outline the use of graphing calculator, spreadsheet, and Website technology in appropriate examples. When necessary, the reader is referred to more detailed discussion in the end-of-chapter Technology Guides.

- **End-of-Chapter Technology Guides** We continue to include detailed TI-83/84 Plus and Spreadsheet Guides at the end of each chapter. These Guides are referenced liberally in marginal technology notes at appropriate points in the chapter, so instructors and students can easily use this material or not, as they prefer. Groups of exercises for which the use of technology is suggested or required appear throughout the exercise sets.

TI-83/84 Plus **Technology Guide**

Section 3.1

Example 1 (page 177) Find all solutions (x, y) of the following system of two equations:

$$x + y = 3$$
$$x - y = 1.$$

Solution with Technology

You can use a graphing calculator to draw the graphs of the two equations on the same set of axes and to check the solution. First, solve the equations for y, obtaining $y = -x + 3$ and $y = x - 1$. On the TI-83/84 Plus:

1. Set
$$Y_1 = -X + 3$$
$$Y_2 = X - 1$$

SPREADSHEET **Technology Guide**

Section 3.1

Example 1 (page 177) Find all solutions (x, y) of the following system of two equations:

$$x + y = 3$$
$$x - y = 1.$$

Solution with Technology

You can use a spreadsheet to draw the graphs of the two equations on the same set of axes, and to check the solution.

1. Solve the equations for y, obtaining $y = -x + 3$ and $y = x - 1$.

- **Communication and Reasoning Exercises for Writing and Discussion** These are exercises designed to broaden the student's grasp of the mathematical concepts and develop modeling skills. They include exercises in which the student is asked to provide his or her own examples to illustrate a point or design an application with a given solution. They also include "fill in the blank" type exercises, exercises that invite discussion and debate, and exercises in which the student must identify common errors. These exercises often have no single correct answer.

Supplemental Material

For Instructors and Students

Enhanced WebAssign®

Content

Exclusively from Cengage Learning, Enhanced WebAssign® combines the exceptional mathematics content in Waner and Costenoble's text with the most powerful online homework solution, WebAssign. Enhanced WebAssign engages students with immediate feedback, rich tutorial content, videos, animations, and an interactive eBook, helping students to develop a deeper conceptual understanding of the subject matter. The interactive eBook contains helpful search, highlighting, and note-taking features.

Instructors can build online assignments by selecting from thousands of text-specific problems, supplemented if desired with problems from any Cengage Learning textbook. Flexible assignment options give instructors the ability to choose how feedback and tutorial content is released to students as well as the ability to release assignments conditionally based on students' prerequisite assignment scores. Increase student engagement, improve course outcomes, and experience the superior service offered through CourseCare. Visit us at http://webassign.net/cengage or www.cengage.com/ewa to learn more.

Service

Your adoption of Enhanced WebAssign® includes CourseCare, Cengage Learning's industry leading service and training program designed to ensure that you have everything that you need to make the most of your use of Enhanced WebAssign. CourseCare provides one-on-one service, from finding the right solutions for your course to training and support. A team of Cengage representatives, including Digital Solutions Managers and Coordinators as well as Service and Training Consultants, assists you every step of the way. For additional information about CourseCare, please visit www.cengage.com/coursecare.

Our Enhanced WebAssign training program provides a comprehensive curriculum of beginner, intermediate, and advanced sessions, designed to get you started and effectively integrate Enhanced WebAssign into your course. We offer a flexible online and recorded training program designed to accommodate your busy schedule. Whether you are using Enhanced WebAssign for the first time or an experienced user, there is a training option to meet your needs.

www.WanerMath.com

The authors' Website, accessible through www.WanerMath.com and linked within Enhanced WebAssign, has been evolving for more than a decade and has been receiving increasingly more recognition. Students, raised in an environment in which computers permeate both work and play, now use the Internet to engage with the material in an active way. The following features of the authors' Website are fully integrated with the text and can be used as a personalized study resource as well as a valuable teaching aid for instructors:

- *Interactive tutorials* on almost all topics, with guided exercises, which also can be used in classroom instruction or in distance learning courses

- *More challenging game versions of tutorials* with randomized questions that complement the traditional interactive tutorials and can be used as in-class quizzes

- *Detailed interactive chapter summaries* that review basic definitions and problem-solving techniques and can act as pre-test study tools

- *Downloadable Excel tutorials* keyed to examples given in the text

- *Online utilities for use in solving many of the technology-based application exercises*. The utilities, for instructor use in class and student use out of class, include a function grapher and evaluator, regression tools, a matrix algebra tool, linear programming tools, and a line entry calculator that calculates permutations and combinations and expands multinomial expressions.

- *Chapter true-false quizzes* with feedback for many incorrect answers

- *Supplemental topics* including interactive text and exercise sets for selected topics not found in the printed texts

- *Spanish versions* of chapter summaries, tutorials, game tutorials, and utilities

For Students

Student Solutions Manual *by Waner and Costenoble*
ISBN: 9781285085586
The student solutions manual provides worked-out solutions to the odd-numbered exercises in the text, plus problem-solving strategies and additional algebra steps and review for selected problems.

   To access this and other course materials and companion resources, please visit **www.cengagebrain.com**. At the CengageBrain.com home page, search for the ISBN of your title (from the back cover of your book) using the search box at the top of the page. This will take you to the product page where free companion resources can be found.

For Instructors

Complete Solution Manual *by Waner and Costenoble*
ISBN: 9781285085593
The instructor's solutions manual provides worked-out solutions to all of the exercises in the text.

Solution Builder *by Waner and Costenoble*
ISBN: 9781285085609
This time-saving resource offers fully worked instructor solutions to all exercises in the text in customizable online format. Adopting instructors can sign up for access at www.cengage.com/solutionbuilder.

PowerLecture™ with ExamView® *by Waner and Costenoble*
ISBN: 9781285085654
This CD-ROM provides the instructor with dynamic media tools for teaching, including Microsoft® PowerPoint® lecture slides, figures from the book, and the Test Bank. You can create, deliver, and customize tests (both print and online) in minutes with ExamView® Computerized Testing, which includes Test Bank items in electronic format. In addition, you can easily build solution sets for homework or exams by linking to Solution Builder's online solutions manual.

Instructor's Edition
ISBN: 9781133934790

www.WanerMath.com
The Instructor's Resource Page at www.WanerMath.com features an expanded collection of instructor resources, including an updated corrections page, an expanding set of author-created teaching videos for use in distance learning courses, and a utility that automatically updates homework exercise sets from the fifth edition to the sixth.

Acknowledgments

This project would not have been possible without the contributions and suggestions of numerous colleagues, students, and friends. We are particularly grateful to our colleagues at Hofstra and elsewhere who used and gave us useful feedback on previous editions. We are also grateful to everyone at Cengage Learning for their encouragement and guidance throughout the project. Specifically, we would like to thank Richard Stratton and Jay Campbell for their unflagging enthusiasm and Alison Eigel Zade for whipping the book into shape.

We would also like to thank our accuracy checker, Jerrold Grossman, and the numerous reviewers who provided many helpful suggestions that have shaped the development of this book.

Igor Fulman, *Arizona State University*

Tom Rosenwinkel, *Concordia University Texas*

Kim Ricketts, *Northwest-Shoals Community College*

Elaine Fitt, *Bucks County Community College*

Xian Wu, *University of South Carolina*

Catherine Remus, *University of Tennessee*

Hugh Cornell, *University of North Florida*

Upasana Kashyap, *The Citadel*

Laura Urbanski, *Northern Kentucky University*

Stefan Waner
Steven R. Costenoble

O

Precalculus Review

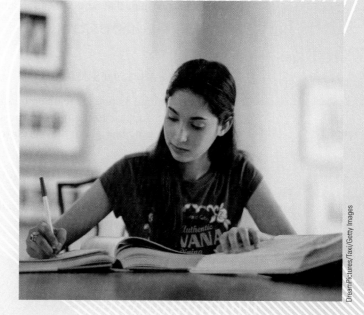

DreamPictures/Taxi/Getty Images

Website
www.WanerMath.com

- At the Website you will find section-by-section interactive tutorials for further study and practice.

1

Introduction

In this chapter we review some topics from algebra that you need to know to get the most out of this book. This chapter can be used either as a refresher course or as a reference.

There is one crucial fact you must always keep in mind: The letters used in algebraic expressions stand for numbers. All the rules of algebra are just facts about the arithmetic of numbers. If you are not sure whether some algebraic manipulation you are about to do is legitimate, try it first with numbers. If it doesn't work with numbers, it doesn't work.

0.1   Real Numbers

The **real numbers** are the numbers that can be written in decimal notation, including those that require an infinite decimal expansion. The set of real numbers includes all integers, positive and negative; all fractions; and the irrational numbers, those with decimal expansions that never repeat. Examples of irrational numbers are

$$\sqrt{2} = 1.414213562373\ldots$$

and

$$\pi = 3.141592653589\ldots$$

Figure 1

It is very useful to picture the real numbers as points on a line. As shown in Figure 1, larger numbers appear to the right, in the sense that if $a < b$ then the point corresponding to b is to the right of the one corresponding to a.

Intervals

Some subsets of the set of real numbers, called **intervals**, show up quite often and so we have a compact notation for them.

Interval Notation

Here is a list of types of intervals along with examples.

	Interval	Description	Picture	Example
Closed	$[a, b]$	Set of numbers x with $a \leq x \leq b$	(includes end points)	$[0, 10]$
Open	(a, b)	Set of numbers x with $a < x < b$	(excludes end points)	$(-1, 5)$
Half-Open	$(a, b]$	Set of numbers x with $a < x \leq b$		$(-3, 1]$
	$[a, b)$	Set of numbers x with $a \leq x < b$		$[0, 5)$

Infinite	$[a, +\infty)$	Set of numbers x with $a \le x$	←——•————————→ a	$[10, +\infty)$
	$(a, +\infty)$	Set of numbers x with $a < x$	←——○————————→ a	$(-3, +\infty)$
	$(-\infty, b]$	Set of numbers x with $x \le b$	←————————•——→ b	$(-\infty, -3]$
	$(-\infty, b)$	Set of numbers x with $x < b$	←————————○——→ b	$(-\infty, 10)$
	$(-\infty, +\infty)$	Set of all real numbers	←——————————→	$(-\infty, +\infty)$

Operations

There are five important operations on real numbers: addition, subtraction, multiplication, division, and exponentiation. "Exponentiation" means raising a real number to a power; for instance, $3^2 = 3 \cdot 3 = 9$; $2^3 = 2 \cdot 2 \cdot 2 = 8$.

A note on technology: Most graphing calculators and spreadsheets use an asterisk * for multiplication and a caret sign ^ for exponentiation. Thus, for instance, 3×5 is entered as `3*5`, $3x$ as `3*x`, and 3^2 as `3^2`.

When we write an expression involving two or more operations, like

$$2 \cdot 3 + 4$$

or

$$\frac{2 \cdot 3^2 - 5}{4 - (-1)}$$

we need to agree on the order in which to do the operations. Does $2 \cdot 3 + 4$ mean $(2 \cdot 3) + 4 = 10$ or $2 \cdot (3 + 4) = 14$? We all agree to use the following rules for the order in which we do the operations.

Standard Order of Operations

Parentheses and Fraction Bars   First, calculate the values of all expressions inside parentheses or brackets, working from the innermost parentheses out, before using them in other operations. In a fraction, calculate the numerator and denominator separately before doing the division.

Quick Examples

1. $6(2 + [3 - 5] - 4) = 6(2 + (-2) - 4) = 6(-4) = -24$

2. $\dfrac{(4 - 2)}{3(-2 + 1)} = \dfrac{2}{3(-1)} = \dfrac{2}{-3} = -\dfrac{2}{3}$

3. $3/(2 + 4) = \dfrac{3}{2 + 4} = \dfrac{3}{6} = \dfrac{1}{2}$

4. $(x + 4x)/(y + 3y) = 5x/(4y)$

Exponents   Next, perform exponentiation.

Quick Examples

$\left.\begin{array}{l} \textbf{1. } 2 + 4^2 = 2 + 16 = 18 \\ \textbf{2. } (2 + 4)^2 = 6^2 = 36 \end{array}\right\}$ Note the difference.

$\textbf{3. } 2\left(\dfrac{3}{4-5}\right)^2 = 2\left(\dfrac{3}{-1}\right)^2 = 2(-3)^2 = 2 \times 9 = 18$

$\textbf{4. } 2(1 + 1/10)^2 = 2(1.1)^2 = 2 \times 1.21 = 2.42$

Multiplication and Division   Next, do all multiplications and divisions, from left to right.

Quick Examples

$\textbf{1. } 2(3 - 5)/4 \cdot 2 = 2(-2)/4 \cdot 2$ Parentheses first

$\qquad\qquad\qquad = -4/4 \cdot 2$ Left-most product

$\qquad\qquad\qquad = -1 \cdot 2 = -2$ Multiplications and divisions, left to right

$\textbf{2. } 2(1 + 1/10)^2 \times 2/10 = 2(1.1)^2 \times 2/10$ Parentheses first

$\qquad\qquad\qquad\qquad = 2 \times 1.21 \times 2/10$ Exponent

$\qquad\qquad\qquad\qquad = 4.84/10 = 0.484$ Multiplications and divisions, left to right

$\textbf{3. } 4\dfrac{2(4 - 2)}{3(-2 \cdot 5)} = 4\dfrac{2(2)}{3(-10)} = 4\dfrac{4}{-30} = \dfrac{16}{-30} = -\dfrac{8}{15}$

Addition and Subtraction   Last, do all additions and subtractions, from left to right.

Quick Examples

$\textbf{1. } 2(3 - 5)^2 + 6 - 1 = 2(-2)^2 + 6 - 1 = 2(4) + 6 - 1$

$\qquad\qquad\qquad\qquad = 8 + 6 - 1 = 13$

$\textbf{2. } \left(\dfrac{1}{2}\right)^2 - (-1)^2 + 4 = \dfrac{1}{4} - 1 + 4 = -\dfrac{3}{4} + 4 = \dfrac{13}{4}$

$\left.\begin{array}{l} \textbf{3. } 3/2 + 4 = 1.5 + 4 = 5.5 \\ \textbf{4. } 3/(2 + 4) = 3/6 = 1/2 = 0.5 \end{array}\right\}$ Note the difference.

$\textbf{5. } 4/2^2 + (4/2)^2 = 4/2^2 + 2^2 = 4/4 + 4 = 1 + 4 = 5$

▣ Entering Formulas

Any good calculator or spreadsheet will respect the standard order of operations. However, we must be careful with division and exponentiation and use parentheses as necessary. The following table gives some examples of simple mathematical expressions and their equivalents in the functional format used in most graphing calculators, spreadsheets, and computer programs.

Mathematical Expression	*Formula*	*Comments*
$\dfrac{2}{3-x}$	`2/(3-x)`	Note the use of parentheses instead of the fraction bar. If we omit the parentheses, we get the expression shown next.
$\dfrac{2}{3}-x$	`2/3-x`	The calculator follows the usual order of operations.
$\dfrac{2}{3\times 5}$	`2/(3*5)`	Putting the denominator in parentheses ensures that the multiplication is carried out first. The asterisk is usually used for multiplication in graphing calculators and computers.
$\dfrac{2}{x}\times 5$	`(2/x)*5`	Putting the fraction in parentheses ensures that it is calculated first. Some calculators will interpret $2/3*5$ as $\dfrac{2}{3\times 5}$, but $2/3(5)$ as $\dfrac{2}{3}\times 5$.
$\dfrac{2-3}{4+5}$	`(2-3)/(4+5)`	Note once again the use of parentheses in place of the fraction bar.
2^3	`2^3`	The caret $^\wedge$ is commonly used to denote exponentiation.
2^{3-x}	`2^(3-x)`	Be careful to use parentheses to tell the calculator where the exponent ends. Enclose the *entire exponent* in parentheses.
2^3-x	`2^3-x`	Without parentheses, the calculator will follow the usual order of operations: exponentiation and then subtraction.
3×2^{-4}	`3*2^(-4)`	On some calculators, the negation key is separate from the minus key.
$2^{-4\times 3}\times 5$	`2^(-4*3)*5`	Note once again how parentheses enclose the entire exponent.
$100\left(1+\dfrac{0.05}{12}\right)^{60}$	`100*(1+0.05/12)^60`	This is a typical calculation for compound interest.
$PV\left(1+\dfrac{r}{m}\right)^{mt}$	`PV*(1+r/m)^(m*t)`	This is the compound interest formula. *PV* is understood to be a single number (present value) and not the product of P and V (or else we would have used `P*V`).
$\dfrac{2^{3-2}\times 5}{y-x}$	`2^(3-2)*5/(y-x)` or `(2^(3-2)*5)/(y-x)`	Notice again the use of parentheses to hold the denominator together. We could also have enclosed the numerator in parentheses, although this is optional. (Why?)
$\dfrac{2^y+1}{2-4^{3x}}$	`(2^y+1)/(2-4^(3*x))`	Here, it is necessary to enclose both the numerator and the denominator in parentheses.
$2^y+\dfrac{1}{2}-4^{3x}$	`2^y+1/2-4^(3*x)`	This is the effect of leaving out the parentheses around the numerator and denominator in the previous expression.

Accuracy and Rounding

When we use a calculator or computer, the results of our calculations are often given to far more decimal places than are useful. For example, suppose we are told that a square has an area of 2.0 square feet and we are asked how long its sides are. Each side is the square root of the area, which the calculator tells us is

$$\sqrt{2} \approx 1.414213562$$

However, the measurement of 2.0 square feet is probably accurate to only two digits, so our estimate of the lengths of the sides can be no more accurate than that. Therefore, we round the answer to two digits:

$$\text{Length of one side} \approx 1.4 \text{ feet}$$

The digits that follow 1.4 are meaningless. The following guide makes these ideas more precise.

Significant Digits, Decimal Places, and Rounding

The number of **significant digits** in a decimal representation of a number is the number of digits that are not leading zeros after the decimal point (as in .0005) or trailing zeros before the decimal point (as in 5,400,000). We say that a value is **accurate to n significant digits** if only the first n significant digits are meaningful.

When to Round
After doing a computation in which all the quantities are accurate to no more than n significant digits, round the final result to n significant digits.

Quick Examples

1. 0.00067 has two significant digits.   The 000 before 67 are leading zeros.

2. 0.000670 has three significant digits.   The 0 after 67 is significant.

3. 5,400,000 has two or more significant digits.   We can't say how many of the zeros are trailing.[1]

4. 5,400,001 has 7 significant digits.   The string of zeros is not trailing.

5. Rounding 63,918 to three significant digits gives 63,900.

6. Rounding 63,958 to three significant digits gives 64,000.

7. $\pi = 3.141592653...$ $\frac{22}{7} = 3.142857142...$ Therefore, $\frac{22}{7}$ is an approximation of π that is accurate to only three significant digits (3.14).

8. $4.02(1 + 0.02)^{1.4} \approx 4.13$ We rounded to three significant digits.

---

[1] If we obtained 5,400,000 by rounding 5,401,011, then it has three significant digits because the zero after the 4 is significant. On the other hand, if we obtained it by rounding 5,411,234, then it has only two significant digits. The use of scientific notation avoids this ambiguity: 5.40×10^6 (or 5.40 E6 on a calculator or computer) is accurate to three digits and 5.4×10^6 is accurate to two.

One more point, though: If, in a long calculation, you round the intermediate results, your final answer may be even less accurate than you think. As a general rule,

When calculating, don't round intermediate results. Rather, use the most accurate results obtainable or have your calculator or computer store them for you.

When you are done with the calculation, *then* round your answer to the appropriate number of digits of accuracy.

0.1 EXERCISES

Calculate each expression in Exercises 1–24, giving the answer as a whole number or a fraction in lowest terms.

1. $2(4 + (-1))(2 \cdot -4)$

2. $3 + ([4 - 2] \cdot 9)$

3. $20/(3*4)-1$

4. $2-(3*4)/10$

5. $\dfrac{3 + ([3 + (-5)])}{3 - 2 \times 2}$

6. $\dfrac{12 - (1 - 4)}{2(5 - 1) \cdot 2 - 1}$

7. $(2-5*(-1))/1-2*(-1)$

8. $2-5*(-1)/(1-2*(-1))$

9. $2 \cdot (-1)^2/2$

10. $2 + 4 \cdot 3^2$

11. $2 \cdot 4^2 + 1$

12. $1 - 3 \cdot (-2)^2 \times 2$

13. 3^2+2^2+1

14. $2^(2^2-2)$

15. $\dfrac{3 - 2(-3)^2}{-6(4 - 1)^2}$

16. $\dfrac{1 - 2(1 - 4)^2}{2(5 - 1)^2 \cdot 2}$

17. $10*(1+1/10)^3$

18. $121/(1+1/10)^2$

19. $3\left(\dfrac{-2 \cdot 3^2}{-(4 - 1)^2}\right)$

20. $-\left(\dfrac{8(1 - 4)^2}{-9(5 - 1)^2}\right)$

21. $3\left(1 - \left(-\dfrac{1}{2}\right)^2\right)^2 + 1$

22. $3\left(\dfrac{1}{9} - \left(\dfrac{2}{3}\right)^2\right)^2 + 1$

23. $(1/2)^2-1/2^2$

24. $2/(1^2)-(2/1)^2$

Convert each expression in Exercises 25–50 into its technology formula equivalent as in the table in the text.

25. $3 \times (2 - 5)$

26. $4 + \dfrac{5}{9}$

27. $\dfrac{3}{2 - 5}$

28. $\dfrac{4 - 1}{3}$

29. $\dfrac{3 - 1}{8 + 6}$

30. $3 + \dfrac{3}{2 - 9}$

31. $3 - \dfrac{4 + 7}{8}$

32. $\dfrac{4 \times 2}{\left(\frac{2}{3}\right)}$

33. $\dfrac{2}{3 + x} - xy^2$

34. $3 + \dfrac{3 + x}{xy}$

35. $3.1x^3 - 4x^{-2} - \dfrac{60}{x^2 - 1}$

36. $2.1x^{-3} - x^{-1} + \dfrac{x^2 - 3}{2}$

37. $\dfrac{\left(\frac{2}{3}\right)}{5}$

38. $\dfrac{2}{\left(\frac{3}{5}\right)}$

39. $3^{4-5} \times 6$

40. $\dfrac{2}{3 + 5^{7-9}}$

41. $3\left(1 + \dfrac{4}{100}\right)^{-3}$

42. $3\left(\dfrac{1 + 4}{100}\right)^{-3}$

43. $3^{2x-1} + 4^x - 1$

44. $2^{x^2} - (2^{2x})^2$

45. 2^{2x^2-x+1}

46. $2^{2x^2-x} + 1$

47. $\dfrac{4e^{-2x}}{2 - 3e^{-2x}}$

48. $\dfrac{e^{2x} + e^{-2x}}{e^{2x} - e^{-2x}}$

49. $3\left(1 - \left(-\dfrac{1}{2}\right)^2\right)^2 + 1$

50. $3\left(\dfrac{1}{9} - \left(\dfrac{2}{3}\right)^2\right)^2 + 1$

0.2 Exponents and Radicals

In Section 1 we discussed exponentiation, or "raising to a power"; for example, $2^3 = 2 \cdot 2 \cdot 2$. In this section we discuss the algebra of exponentials more fully. First, we look at *integer* exponents: cases in which the powers are positive or negative whole numbers.

Integer Exponents

Positive Integer Exponents

If a is any real number and n is any positive integer, then by a^n we mean the quantity $a \cdot a \cdots \cdot a$ (n times); thus, $a^1 = a$, $a^2 = a \cdot a$, $a^5 = a \cdot a \cdot a \cdot a \cdot a$. In the expression a^n the number n is called the **exponent**, and the number a is called the **base**.

Quick Examples

$$3^2 = 9 \qquad\qquad 2^3 = 8$$

$$0^{34} = 0 \qquad\quad (-1)^5 = -1$$

$$10^3 = 1{,}000 \qquad 10^5 = 100{,}000$$

Negative Integer Exponents

If a is any real number *other than zero* and n is any positive integer, then we define

$$a^{-n} = \frac{1}{a^n} = \frac{1}{a \cdot a \cdots \cdot a} \ (n \text{ times})$$

Quick Examples

$$2^{-3} = \frac{1}{2^3} = \frac{1}{8} \qquad\qquad 1^{-27} = \frac{1}{1^{27}} = 1$$

$$x^{-1} = \frac{1}{x^1} = \frac{1}{x} \qquad\qquad (-3)^{-2} = \frac{1}{(-3)^2} = \frac{1}{9}$$

$$y^7 y^{-2} = y^7 \frac{1}{y^2} = y^5 \qquad 0^{-2} \text{ is not defined}$$

Zero Exponent

If a is any real number other than zero, then we define

$$a^0 = 1$$

Quick Examples

$$3^0 = 1 \qquad\qquad\qquad 1{,}000{,}000^0 = 1$$

$$0^0 \text{ is not defined}$$

When combining exponential expressions, we use the following identities.

Exponent Identity	**Quick Examples**
1. $a^m a^n = a^{m+n}$	$2^3 2^2 = 2^{3+2} = 2^5 = 32$
	$x^3 x^{-4} = x^{3-4} = x^{-1} = \dfrac{1}{x}$
	$\dfrac{x^3}{x^{-2}} = x^3 \dfrac{1}{x^{-2}} = x^3 x^2 = x^5$
2. $\dfrac{a^m}{a^n} = a^{m-n}$ if $a \neq 0$	$\dfrac{4^3}{4^2} = 4^{3-2} = 4^1 = 4$
	$\dfrac{x^3}{x^{-2}} = x^{3-(-2)} = x^5$
	$\dfrac{3^2}{3^4} = 3^{2-4} = 3^{-2} = \dfrac{1}{9}$
3. $(a^n)^m = a^{nm}$	$(3^2)^2 = 3^4 = 81$
	$(2^x)^2 = 2^{2x}$
4. $(ab)^n = a^n b^n$	$(4 \cdot 2)^2 = 4^2 2^2 = 64$
	$(-2y)^4 = (-2)^4 y^4 = 16y^4$
5. $\left(\dfrac{a}{b}\right)^n = \dfrac{a^n}{b^n}$ if $b \neq 0$	$\left(\dfrac{4}{3}\right)^2 = \dfrac{4^2}{3^2} = \dfrac{16}{9}$
	$\left(\dfrac{x}{-y}\right)^3 = \dfrac{x^3}{(-y)^3} = -\dfrac{x^3}{y^3}$

Caution

- In the first two identities, the bases of the expressions must be the same. For example, the first gives $3^2 3^4 = 3^6$, but does *not* apply to $3^2 4^2$.
- People sometimes invent their own identities, such as $a^m + a^n = a^{m+n}$, which is wrong! (Try it with $a = m = n = 1$.) If you wind up with something like $2^3 + 2^4$, you are stuck with it; there are no identities around to simplify it further. (You can factor out 2^3, but whether or not that is a simplification depends on what you are going to do with the expression next.)

EXAMPLE 1 Combining the Identities

$$\dfrac{(x^2)^3}{x^3} = \dfrac{x^6}{x^3} \qquad \text{By (3)}$$

$$= x^{6-3} \qquad \text{By (2)}$$

$$= x^3$$

$$\dfrac{(x^4 y)^3}{y} = \dfrac{(x^4)^3 y^3}{y} \qquad \text{By (4)}$$

$$= \dfrac{x^{12} y^3}{y} \qquad \text{By (3)}$$

$$= x^{12} y^{3-1} \qquad \text{By (2)}$$

$$= x^{12} y^2$$

EXAMPLE 2 **Eliminating Negative Exponents**

Simplify the following and express the answer using no negative exponents.

a. $\dfrac{x^4 y^{-3}}{x^5 y^2}$ **b.** $\left(\dfrac{x^{-1}}{x^2 y}\right)^5$

Solution

a. $\dfrac{x^4 y^{-3}}{x^5 y^2} = x^{4-5} y^{-3-2} = x^{-1} y^{-5} = \dfrac{1}{x y^5}$

b. $\left(\dfrac{x^{-1}}{x^2 y}\right)^5 = \dfrac{(x^{-1})^5}{(x^2 y)^5} = \dfrac{x^{-5}}{x^{10} y^5} = \dfrac{1}{x^{15} y^5}$

Radicals

If a is any non-negative real number, then its **square root** is the non-negative number whose square is a. For example, the square root of 16 is 4, because $4^2 = 16$. We write the square root of n as $\sqrt{n}$. (Roots are also referred to as **radicals**.) It is important to remember that $\sqrt{n}$ is never negative. Thus, for instance, $\sqrt{9}$ is 3, and not -3, even though $(-3)^2 = 9$. If we want to speak of the "negative square root" of 9, we write it as $-\sqrt{9} = -3$. If we want to write both square roots at once, we write $\pm\sqrt{9} = \pm 3$.

The **cube root** of a real number a is the number whose cube is a. The cube root of a is written as $\sqrt[3]{a}$ so that, for example, $\sqrt[3]{8} = 2$ (because $2^3 = 8$). Note that we can take the cube root of any number, positive, negative, or zero. For instance, the cube root of -8 is $\sqrt[3]{-8} = -2$ because $(-2)^3 = -8$. Unlike square roots, the cube root of a number may be negative. In fact, the cube root of a always has the same sign as a.

Higher roots are defined similarly. The **fourth root** of the *non-negative* number a is defined as the non-negative number whose fourth power is a, and written $\sqrt[4]{a}$. The **fifth root** of any number a is the number whose fifth power is a, and so on.

Note We cannot take an even-numbered root of a negative number, but we can take an odd-numbered root of any number. Even roots are always positive, whereas odd roots have the same sign as the number we start with. ■

EXAMPLE 3 *n*th **Roots**

$\sqrt{4} = 2$	Because $2^2 = 4$
$\sqrt{16} = 4$	Because $4^2 = 16$
$\sqrt{1} = 1$	Because $1^2 = 1$
If $x \geq 0$, then $\sqrt{x^2} = x$	Because $x^2 = x^2$
$\sqrt{2} \approx 1.414213562$	$\sqrt{2}$ is not a whole number.
$\sqrt{1+1} = \sqrt{2} \approx 1.414213562$	First add, then take the square root.[2]
$\sqrt{9+16} = \sqrt{25} = 5$	Contrast with $\sqrt{9} + \sqrt{16} = 3 + 4 = 7$.

---

[2]In general, $\sqrt{a+b}$ means the square root of the *quantity* $(a+b)$. The radical sign acts as a pair of parentheses or a fraction bar, telling us to evaluate what is inside before taking the root. (See the Caution on the next page.)

$$\frac{1}{\sqrt{2}} = \frac{\sqrt{2}}{2}$$ Multiply top and bottom by $\sqrt{2}$.

$$\sqrt[3]{27} = 3$$ Because $3^3 = 27$

$$\sqrt[3]{-64} = -4$$ Because $(-4)^3 = -64$

$$\sqrt[4]{16} = 2$$ Because $2^4 = 16$

$\sqrt[4]{-16}$ is not defined   Even-numbered root of a negative number

$\sqrt[5]{-1} = -1$, since $(-1)^5 = -1$ Odd-numbered root of a negative number

$\sqrt[n]{-1} = -1$ if n is any odd number

Q: *In the example we saw that $\sqrt{x^2} = x$ if x is non-negative. What happens if x is negative?*

A: If x is negative, then x^2 is positive, and so $\sqrt{x^2}$ is still defined as the non-negative number whose square is x^2. This number must be $|x|$, the **absolute value of x**, which is the non-negative number with the same size as x. For instance, $|-3| = 3$, while $|3| = 3$, and $|0| = 0$. It follows that

$$\sqrt{x^2} = |x|$$

for every real number x, positive or negative. For instance,

$$\sqrt{(-3)^2} = \sqrt{9} = 3 = |-3|$$

and $\sqrt{3^2} = \sqrt{9} = 3 = |3|$.

In general, we find that

$$\sqrt[n]{x^n} = x \text{ if } n \text{ is odd, and } \sqrt[n]{x^n} = |x| \text{ if } n \text{ is even.}$$

We use the following identities to evaluate radicals of products and quotients.

Radicals of Products and Quotients

If a and b are any real numbers (non-negative in the case of even-numbered roots), then

$$\sqrt[n]{ab} = \sqrt[n]{a}\,\sqrt[n]{b}$$ Radical of a product = Product of radicals

$$\sqrt[n]{\frac{a}{b}} = \frac{\sqrt[n]{a}}{\sqrt[n]{b}} \quad \text{if } b \neq 0$$ Radical of a quotient = Quotient of radicals

Notes

- The first rule is similar to the rule $(a \cdot b)^2 = a^2 b^2$ for the square of a product, and the second rule is similar to the rule $\left(\dfrac{a}{b}\right)^2 = \dfrac{a^2}{b^2}$ for the square of a quotient.

- *Caution* There is no corresponding identity for addition:

$$\sqrt{a+b} \text{ is } not \text{ equal to } \sqrt{a} + \sqrt{b}$$

(Consider $a = b = 1$, for example.) Equating these expressions is a common error, so be careful! ■

Quick Examples

1. $\sqrt{9 \cdot 4} = \sqrt{9}\sqrt{4} = 3 \times 2 = 6$ Alternatively, $\sqrt{9 \cdot 4} = \sqrt{36} = 6$

2. $\sqrt{\dfrac{9}{4}} = \dfrac{\sqrt{9}}{\sqrt{4}} = \dfrac{3}{2}$

3. $\dfrac{\sqrt{2}}{\sqrt{5}} = \dfrac{\sqrt{2}\sqrt{5}}{\sqrt{5}\sqrt{5}} = \dfrac{\sqrt{10}}{5}$

4. $\sqrt{4(3 + 13)} = \sqrt{4(16)} = \sqrt{4}\sqrt{16} = 2 \times 4 = 8$

5. $\sqrt[3]{-216} = \sqrt[3]{(-27)8} = \sqrt[3]{-27}\sqrt[3]{8} = (-3)2 = -6$

6. $\sqrt{x^3} = \sqrt{x^2 \cdot x} = \sqrt{x^2}\sqrt{x} = x\sqrt{x}$ if $x \geq 0$

7. $\sqrt{\dfrac{x^2 + y^2}{z^2}} = \dfrac{\sqrt{x^2 + y^2}}{\sqrt{z^2}} = \dfrac{\sqrt{x^2 + y^2}}{|z|}$ We can't simplify the numerator any further.

Rational Exponents

We already know what we mean by expressions such as x^4 and a^{-6}. The next step is to make sense of *rational* exponents: exponents of the form p/q with p and q integers as in $a^{1/2}$ and $3^{-2/3}$.

Q: *What should we mean by $a^{1/2}$?*

A: The overriding concern here is that all the exponent identities should remain true. In this case the identity to look at is the one that says that $(a^m)^n = a^{mn}$. This identity tells us that

$$(a^{1/2})^2 = a^1 = a.$$

That is, $a^{1/2}$, when squared, gives us a. But that must mean that $a^{1/2}$ is the *square root* of a, or

$$a^{1/2} = \sqrt{a}.$$

A similar argument tells us that, if q is any positive whole number, then

$$a^{1/q} = \sqrt[q]{a}, \text{ the } q\text{th root of } a.$$

Notice that if a is negative, this makes sense only for q odd. To avoid this problem, we usually stick to positive a.

Q: *If p and q are integers (q positive), what should we mean by $a^{p/q}$?*

A: By the exponent identities, $a^{p/q}$ should equal both $(a^p)^{1/q}$ and $(a^{1/q})^p$. The first is the qth root of a^p, and the second is the pth power of $a^{1/q}$, which gives us the following.

Conversion Between Rational Exponents and Radicals

If a is any non-negative number, then

$$a^{p/q} = \sqrt[q]{a^p} = \left(\sqrt[q]{a}\right)^p.$$

Using exponents   Using radicals

In particular,

$$a^{1/q} = \sqrt[q]{a}, \text{ the } q\text{th root of } a.$$

Notes

- If a is negative, all of this makes sense only if q is odd.
- All of the exponent identities continue to work when we allow rational exponents p/q. In other words, we are free to use all the exponent identities even though the exponents are not integers. ∎

Quick Examples

1. $4^{3/2} = (\sqrt{4})^3 = 2^3 = 8$
2. $8^{2/3} = (\sqrt[3]{8})^2 = 2^2 = 4$
3. $9^{-3/2} = \dfrac{1}{9^{3/2}} = \dfrac{1}{(\sqrt{9})^3} = \dfrac{1}{3^3} = \dfrac{1}{27}$
4. $\dfrac{\sqrt{3}}{\sqrt[3]{3}} = \dfrac{3^{1/2}}{3^{1/3}} = 3^{1/2-1/3} = 3^{1/6} = \sqrt[6]{3}$
5. $2^2 2^{7/2} = 2^2 2^{3+1/2} = 2^2 2^3 2^{1/2} = 2^5 2^{1/2} = 2^5 \sqrt{2}$

EXAMPLE 4 Simplifying Algebraic Expressions

Simplify the following.

a. $\dfrac{(x^3)^{5/3}}{x^3}$ **b.** $\sqrt[4]{a^6}$ **c.** $\dfrac{(xy)^{-3}y^{-3/2}}{x^{-2}\sqrt{y}}$

Solution

a. $\dfrac{(x^3)^{5/3}}{x^3} = \dfrac{x^5}{x^3} = x^2$

b. $\sqrt[4]{a^6} = a^{6/4} = a^{3/2} = a \cdot a^{1/2} = a\sqrt{a}$

c. $\dfrac{(xy)^{-3}y^{-3/2}}{x^{-2}\sqrt{y}} = \dfrac{x^{-3}y^{-3}y^{-3/2}}{x^{-2}y^{1/2}} = \dfrac{1}{x^{-2+3}y^{1/2+3+3/2}} = \dfrac{1}{xy^5}$

Converting Between Rational, Radical, and Exponent Form

In calculus we must often convert algebraic expressions involving powers of x, such as $\dfrac{3}{2x^2}$, into expressions in which x does not appear in the denominator, such as $\dfrac{3}{2}x^{-2}$. Also, we must often convert expressions with radicals, such as $\dfrac{1}{\sqrt{1+x^2}}$, into expressions with no radicals and all powers in the numerator, such as $(1 + x^2)^{-1/2}$. In these cases, we are converting from **rational form** or **radical form** to **exponent form.**

Rational Form

An expression is in **rational form** if it is written with positive exponents only.

Quick Examples

1. $\dfrac{2}{3x^2}$ is in rational form.

2. $\dfrac{2x^{-1}}{3}$ is not in rational form because the exponent of x is negative.

3. $\dfrac{x}{6} + \dfrac{6}{x}$ is in rational form.

Radical Form

An expression is in **radical form** if it is written with integer powers and roots only.

Quick Examples

1. $\dfrac{2}{5\sqrt[3]{x}} + \dfrac{2}{x}$ is in radical form.

2. $\dfrac{2x^{-1/3}}{5} + 2x^{-1}$ is not in radical form because $x^{-1/3}$ appears.

3. $\dfrac{1}{\sqrt{1 + x^2}}$ is in radical form, but $(1 + x^2)^{-1/2}$ is not.

Exponent Form

An expression is in **exponent form** if there are no radicals and all powers of unknowns occur in the numerator. We write such expressions as sums or differences of terms of the form

$$\text{Constant} \times (\text{Expression with } x)^p \qquad \text{As in } \frac{1}{3}x^{-3/2}$$

Quick Examples

1. $\dfrac{2}{3}x^4 - 3x^{-1/3}$ is in exponent form.

2. $\dfrac{x}{6} + \dfrac{6}{x}$ is not in exponent form because the second expression has x in the denominator.

3. $\sqrt[3]{x}$ is not in exponent form because it has a radical.

4. $(1 + x^2)^{-1/2}$ is in exponent form, but $\dfrac{1}{\sqrt{1 + x^2}}$ is not.

EXAMPLE 5 **Converting from One Form to Another**

Convert the following to rational form:

a. $\dfrac{1}{2}x^{-2} + \dfrac{4}{3}x^{-5}$

b. $\dfrac{2}{\sqrt{x}} - \dfrac{2}{x^{-4}}$

Convert the following to radical form:

c. $\dfrac{1}{2}x^{-1/2} + \dfrac{4}{3}x^{-5/4}$

d. $\dfrac{(3+x)^{-1/3}}{5}$

Convert the following to exponent form:

e. $\dfrac{3}{4x^2} - \dfrac{x}{6} + \dfrac{6}{x} + \dfrac{4}{3\sqrt{x}}$

f. $\dfrac{2}{(x+1)^2} - \dfrac{3}{4\sqrt[5]{2x-1}}$

Solution For (a) and (b), we eliminate negative exponents as we did in Example 2:

a. $\dfrac{1}{2}x^{-2} + \dfrac{4}{3}x^{-5} = \dfrac{1}{2}\cdot\dfrac{1}{x^2} + \dfrac{4}{3}\cdot\dfrac{1}{x^5} = \dfrac{1}{2x^2} + \dfrac{4}{3x^5}$

b. $\dfrac{2}{\sqrt{x}} - \dfrac{2}{x^{-4}} = \dfrac{2}{\sqrt{x}} - 2x^4$

For (c) and (d), we rewrite all terms with fractional exponents as radicals:

c. $\dfrac{1}{2}x^{-1/2} + \dfrac{4}{3}x^{-5/4} = \dfrac{1}{2}\cdot\dfrac{1}{x^{1/2}} + \dfrac{4}{3}\cdot\dfrac{1}{x^{5/4}}$

$= \dfrac{1}{2}\cdot\dfrac{1}{\sqrt{x}} + \dfrac{4}{3}\cdot\dfrac{1}{\sqrt[4]{x^5}} = \dfrac{1}{2\sqrt{x}} + \dfrac{4}{3\sqrt[4]{x^5}}$

d. $\dfrac{(3+x)^{-1/3}}{5} = \dfrac{1}{5(3+x)^{1/3}} = \dfrac{1}{5\sqrt[3]{3+x}}$

For (e) and (f), we eliminate any radicals and move all expressions involving x to the numerator:

e. $\dfrac{3}{4x^2} - \dfrac{x}{6} + \dfrac{6}{x} + \dfrac{4}{3\sqrt{x}} = \dfrac{3}{4}x^{-2} - \dfrac{1}{6}x + 6x^{-1} + \dfrac{4}{3x^{1/2}}$

$= \dfrac{3}{4}x^{-2} - \dfrac{1}{6}x + 6x^{-1} + \dfrac{4}{3}x^{-1/2}$

f. $\dfrac{2}{(x+1)^2} - \dfrac{3}{4\sqrt[5]{2x-1}} = 2(x+1)^{-2} - \dfrac{3}{4(2x-1)^{1/5}}$

$= 2(x+1)^{-2} - \dfrac{3}{4}(2x-1)^{-1/5}$

Solving Equations with Exponents

EXAMPLE 6 **Solving Equations**

Solve the following equations:

a. $x^3 + 8 = 0$ **b.** $x^2 - \dfrac{1}{2} = 0$ **c.** $x^{3/2} - 64 = 0$

Solution

a. Subtracting 8 from both sides gives $x^3 = -8$. Taking the cube root of both sides gives $x = -2$.

b. Adding $\frac{1}{2}$ to both sides gives $x^2 = \frac{1}{2}$. Thus, $x = \pm\sqrt{\frac{1}{2}} = \pm\frac{1}{\sqrt{2}}$.

c. Adding 64 to both sides gives $x^{3/2} = 64$. Taking the reciprocal (2/3) power of both sides gives

$$(x^{3/2})^{2/3} = 64^{2/3}$$

$$x^1 = \left(\sqrt[3]{64}\right)^2 = 4^2 = 16$$

so $\qquad x = 16.$

0.2 EXERCISES

Evaluate the expressions in Exercises 1–16.

1. 3^3 **2.** $(-2)^3$ **3.** $-(2 \cdot 3)^2$ **4.** $(4 \cdot 2)^2$

5. $\left(\dfrac{-2}{3}\right)^2$ **6.** $\left(\dfrac{3}{2}\right)^3$ **7.** $(-2)^{-3}$ **8.** -2^{-3}

9. $\left(\dfrac{1}{4}\right)^{-2}$ **10.** $\left(\dfrac{-2}{3}\right)^{-2}$ **11.** $2 \cdot 3^0$ **12.** $3 \cdot (-2)^0$

13. $2^3\, 2^2$ **14.** $3^2 3$ **15.** $2^2 2^{-1} 2^4 2^{-4}$ **16.** $5^2 5^{-3} 5^2 5^{-2}$

Simplify each expression in Exercises 17–30, expressing your answer in rational form.

17. $x^3 x^2$ **18.** $x^4 x^{-1}$ **19.** $-x^2 x^{-3} y$ **20.** $-xy^{-1}x^{-1}$

21. $\dfrac{x^3}{x^4}$ **22.** $\dfrac{y^5}{y^3}$ **23.** $\dfrac{x^2 y^2}{x^{-1} y}$ **24.** $\dfrac{x^{-1} y}{x^2 y^2}$

25. $\dfrac{(xy^{-1}z^3)^2}{x^2 yz^2}$ **26.** $\dfrac{x^2 yz^2}{(xyz^{-1})^{-1}}$ **27.** $\left(\dfrac{xy^{-2}z}{x^{-1}z}\right)^3$

28. $\left(\dfrac{x^2 y^{-1}z^0}{xyz}\right)^2$ **29.** $\left(\dfrac{x^{-1}y^{-2}z^2}{xy}\right)^{-2}$ **30.** $\left(\dfrac{xy^{-2}}{x^2 y^{-1}z}\right)^{-3}$

Convert the expressions in Exercises 31–36 to rational form.

31. $3x^{-4}$ **32.** $\dfrac{1}{2}x^{-4}$ **33.** $\dfrac{3}{4}x^{-2/3}$

34. $\dfrac{4}{5}y^{-3/4}$ **35.** $1 - \dfrac{0.3}{x^{-2}} - \dfrac{6}{5}x^{-1}$ **36.** $\dfrac{1}{3x^{-4}} + \dfrac{0.1x^{-2}}{3}$

Evaluate the expressions in Exercises 37–56, rounding your answer to four significant digits where necessary.

37. $\sqrt{4}$ **38.** $\sqrt{5}$ **39.** $\sqrt{\dfrac{1}{4}}$

40. $\sqrt{\dfrac{1}{9}}$ **41.** $\sqrt{\dfrac{16}{9}}$ **42.** $\sqrt{\dfrac{9}{4}}$

43. $\dfrac{\sqrt{4}}{5}$ **44.** $\dfrac{6}{\sqrt{25}}$ **45.** $\sqrt{9} + \sqrt{16}$

46. $\sqrt{25} - \sqrt{16}$ **47.** $\sqrt{9 + 16}$ **48.** $\sqrt{25 - 16}$

49. $\sqrt[3]{8 - 27}$ **50.** $\sqrt[4]{81 - 16}$ **51.** $\sqrt[3]{27/8}$

52. $\sqrt[3]{8 \times 64}$ **53.** $\sqrt{(-2)^2}$ **54.** $\sqrt{(-1)^2}$

55. $\sqrt{\dfrac{1}{4}(1 + 15)}$ **56.** $\sqrt{\dfrac{1}{9}(3 + 33)}$

Simplify the expressions in Exercises 57–64, given that x, y, z, a, b, and c are positive real numbers.

57. $\sqrt{a^2 b^2}$ **58.** $\sqrt{\dfrac{a^2}{b^2}}$ **59.** $\sqrt{(x + 9)^2}$

60. $(\sqrt{x + 9})^2$ **61.** $\sqrt[3]{x^3(a^3 + b^3)}$ **62.** $\sqrt[4]{\dfrac{x^4}{a^4 b^4}}$

63. $\sqrt{\dfrac{4xy^3}{x^2 y}}$ **64.** $\sqrt{\dfrac{4(x^2 + y^2)}{c^2}}$

Convert the expressions in Exercises 65–84 to exponent form.

65. $\sqrt{3}$ **66.** $\sqrt{8}$ **67.** $\sqrt{x^3}$

68. $\sqrt[3]{x^2}$ **69.** $\sqrt[3]{xy^2}$ **70.** $\sqrt{x^2 y}$

71. $\dfrac{x^2}{\sqrt{x}}$ **72.** $\dfrac{x}{\sqrt{x}}$ **73.** $\dfrac{3}{5x^2}$

74. $\dfrac{2}{5x^{-3}}$ **75.** $\dfrac{3x^{-1.2}}{2} - \dfrac{1}{3x^{2.1}}$ **76.** $\dfrac{2}{3x^{-1.2}} - \dfrac{x^{2.1}}{3}$

77. $\dfrac{2x}{3} - \dfrac{x^{0.1}}{2} + \dfrac{4}{3x^{1.1}}$ **78.** $\dfrac{4x^2}{3} + \dfrac{x^{3/2}}{6} - \dfrac{2}{3x^2}$

79. $\dfrac{3\sqrt{x}}{4} - \dfrac{5}{3\sqrt{x}} + \dfrac{4}{3x\sqrt{x}}$ **80.** $\dfrac{3}{5\sqrt{x}} - \dfrac{5\sqrt{x}}{8} + \dfrac{7}{2\sqrt[3]{x}}$

81. $\dfrac{3\sqrt[5]{x^2}}{4} - \dfrac{7}{2\sqrt{x^3}}$ **82.** $\dfrac{1}{8x\sqrt{x}} - \dfrac{2}{3\sqrt[5]{x^3}}$

83. $\dfrac{1}{(x^2 + 1)^3} - \dfrac{3}{4\sqrt[3]{(x^2 + 1)}}$ **84.** $\dfrac{2}{3(x^2 + 1)^{-3}} - \dfrac{3\sqrt[3]{(x^2 + 1)^7}}{4}$

Convert the expressions in Exercises 85–96 to radical form.

85. $2^{2/3}$ **86.** $3^{4/5}$ **87.** $x^{4/3}$ **88.** $y^{7/4}$

89. $(x^{1/2}y^{1/3})^{1/5}$ **90.** $x^{-1/3}y^{3/2}$ **91.** $-\dfrac{3}{2}x^{-1/4}$ **92.** $\dfrac{4}{5}x^{3/2}$

93. $0.2x^{-2/3} + \dfrac{3}{7x^{-1/2}}$ **94.** $\dfrac{3.1}{x^{-4/3}} - \dfrac{11}{7}x^{-1/7}$

95. $\dfrac{3}{4(1-x)^{5/2}}$ **96.** $\dfrac{9}{4(1-x)^{-7/3}}$

Simplify the expressions in Exercises 97–106.

97. $4^{-1/2}4^{7/2}$ **98.** $2^{1/a}/2^{2/a}$ **99.** $3^{2/3}3^{-1/6}$

100. $2^{1/3}2^{-1}2^{2/3}2^{-1/3}$ **101.** $\dfrac{x^{3/2}}{x^{5/2}}$ **102.** $\dfrac{y^{5/4}}{y^{3/4}}$

103. $\dfrac{x^{1/2}y^2}{x^{-1/2}y}$ **104.** $\dfrac{x^{-1/2}y}{x^2y^{3/2}}$

105. $\left(\dfrac{x}{y}\right)^{1/3}\left(\dfrac{y}{x}\right)^{2/3}$ **106.** $\left(\dfrac{x}{y}\right)^{-1/3}\left(\dfrac{y}{x}\right)^{1/3}$

Solve each equation in Exercises 107–120 for x, rounding your answer to four significant digits where necessary.

107. $x^2 - 16 = 0$ **108.** $x^2 - 1 = 0$

109. $x^2 - \dfrac{4}{9} = 0$ **110.** $x^2 - \dfrac{1}{10} = 0$

111. $x^2 - (1+2x)^2 = 0$ **112.** $x^2 - (2-3x)^2 = 0$

113. $x^5 + 32 = 0$ **114.** $x^4 - 81 = 0$

115. $x^{1/2} - 4 = 0$ **116.** $x^{1/3} - 2 = 0$

117. $1 - \dfrac{1}{x^2} = 0$ **118.** $\dfrac{2}{x^3} - \dfrac{6}{x^4} = 0$

119. $(x-4)^{-1/3} = 2$ **120.** $(x-4)^{2/3} + 1 = 5$

0.3 Multiplying and Factoring Algebraic Expressions

Multiplying Algebraic Expressions

Distributive Law

The **distributive law** for real numbers states that

$$a(b \pm c) = ab \pm ac$$
$$(a \pm b)c = ac \pm bc$$

for any real numbers a, b, and c.

Quick Examples

1. $2(x-3)$ is *not* equal to $2x - 3$ but is equal to $2x - 2(3) = 2x - 6$.
2. $x(x+1) = x^2 + x$
3. $2x(3x - 4) = 6x^2 - 8x$
4. $(x - 4)x^2 = x^3 - 4x^2$
5. $(x+2)(x+3) = (x+2)x + (x+2)3$
   $$= (x^2 + 2x) + (3x + 6) = x^2 + 5x + 6$$
6. $(x+2)(x-3) = (x+2)x - (x+2)3$
   $$= (x^2 + 2x) - (3x + 6) = x^2 - x - 6$$

There is a quicker way of expanding expressions like the last two, called the "FOIL" method (First, Outer, Inner, Last). Consider, for instance, the expression $(x+1)(x-2)$. The FOIL method says: Take the product of the first terms: $x \cdot x = x^2$, the product of the outer terms: $x \cdot (-2) = -2x$, the product of the inner terms: $1 \cdot x = x$, and the product of the last terms: $1 \cdot (-2) = -2$, and then add them all up, getting $x^2 - 2x + x - 2 = x^2 - x - 2$.

EXAMPLE 1 FOIL

a. $(x-2)(2x+5) = 2x^2 + 5x - 4x - 10 = 2x^2 + x - 10$

$$\uparrow\qquad\uparrow\qquad\uparrow\qquad\uparrow$$

$$\text{First}\quad\text{Outer}\ \ \text{Inner}\ \ \text{Last}$$

b. $(x^2+1)(x-4) = x^3 - 4x^2 + x - 4$

c. $(a-b)(a+b) = a^2 + ab - ab - b^2 = a^2 - b^2$

d. $(a+b)^2 = (a+b)(a+b) = a^2 + ab + ab + b^2 = a^2 + 2ab + b^2$

e. $(a-b)^2 = (a-b)(a-b) = a^2 - ab - ab + b^2 = a^2 - 2ab + b^2$

The last three are particularly important and are worth memorizing.

Special Formulas

$$(a-b)(a+b) = a^2 - b^2 \qquad \text{Difference of two squares}$$

$$(a+b)^2 = a^2 + 2ab + b^2 \qquad \text{Square of a sum}$$

$$(a-b)^2 = a^2 - 2ab + b^2 \qquad \text{Square of a difference}$$

Quick Examples

1. $(2-x)(2+x) = 4 - x^2$

2. $(1+a)(1-a) = 1 - a^2$

3. $(x+3)^2 = x^2 + 6x + 9$

4. $(4-x)^2 = 16 - 8x + x^2$

Here are some longer examples that require the distributive law.

EXAMPLE 2 Multiplying Algebraic Expressions

a. $(x+1)(x^2+3x-4) = (x+1)x^2 + (x+1)3x - (x+1)4$

$$= (x^3 + x^2) + (3x^2 + 3x) - (4x + 4)$$

$$= x^3 + 4x^2 - x - 4$$

b. $\left(x^2 - \dfrac{1}{x} + 1\right)(2x+5) = \left(x^2 - \dfrac{1}{x} + 1\right)2x + \left(x^2 - \dfrac{1}{x} + 1\right)5$

$$= (2x^3 - 2 + 2x) + \left(5x^2 - \dfrac{5}{x} + 5\right)$$

$$= 2x^3 + 5x^2 + 2x + 3 - \dfrac{5}{x}$$

c. $(x-y)(x-y)(x-y) = (x^2 - 2xy + y^2)(x-y)$

$$= (x^2 - 2xy + y^2)x - (x^2 - 2xy + y^2)y$$

$$= (x^3 - 2x^2y + xy^2) - (x^2y - 2xy^2 + y^3)$$

$$= x^3 - 3x^2y + 3xy^2 - y^3$$

Factoring Algebraic Expressions

We can think of factoring as applying the distributive law in reverse—for example,

$$2x^2 + x = x(2x + 1),$$

which can be checked by using the distributive law. Factoring is an art that you will learn with experience and the help of a few useful techniques.

Factoring Using a Common Factor

To use this technique, locate a **common factor**—a term that occurs as a factor in each of the expressions being added or subtracted (for example, x is a common factor in $2x^2 + x$, because it is a factor of both $2x^2$ and x). Once you have located a common factor, "factor it out" by applying the distributive law.

Quick Examples

1. $2x^3 - x^2 + x$ has x as a common factor, so
$$2x^3 - x^2 + x = x(2x^2 - x + 1)$$

2. $2x^2 + 4x$ has $2x$ as a common factor, so
$$2x^2 + 4x = 2x(x + 2)$$

3. $2x^2y + xy^2 - x^2y^2$ has xy as a common factor, so
$$2x^2y + xy^2 - x^2y^2 = xy(2x + y - xy)$$

4. $(x^2 + 1)(x + 2) - (x^2 + 1)(x + 3)$ has $x^2 + 1$ as a common factor, so
$$(x^2 + 1)(x + 2) - (x^2 + 1)(x + 3) = (x^2 + 1)[(x + 2) - (x + 3)]$$
$$= (x^2 + 1)(x + 2 - x - 3)$$
$$= (x^2 + 1)(-1) = -(x^2 + 1)$$

5. $12x(x^2 - 1)^5(x^3 + 1)^6 + 18x^2(x^2 - 1)^6(x^3 + 1)^5$ has $6x(x^2 - 1)^5(x^3 + 1)^5$ as a common factor, so
$$12x(x^2 - 1)^5(x^3 + 1)^6 + 18x^2(x^2 - 1)^6(x^3 + 1)^5$$
$$= 6x(x^2 - 1)^5(x^3 + 1)^5[2(x^3 + 1) + 3x(x^2 - 1)]$$
$$= 6x(x^2 - 1)^5(x^3 + 1)^5(2x^3 + 2 + 3x^3 - 3x)$$
$$= 6x(x^2 - 1)^5(x^3 + 1)^5(5x^3 - 3x + 2)$$

We would also like to be able to reverse calculations such as $(x + 2)(2x - 5) = 2x^2 - x - 10$. That is, starting with the expression $2x^2 - x - 10$, we would like to **factor** it to get the expression $(x + 2)(2x - 5)$. An expression of the form $ax^2 + bx + c$, where a, b, and c are real numbers, is called a **quadratic** expression in x. Thus, given a quadratic expression $ax^2 + bx + c$, we would like to write it in the form $(dx + e)(fx + g)$ for some real numbers $d, e, f,$ and g. There are some quadratics, such as $x^2 + x + 1$, that cannot be factored in this form at all. Here, we consider only quadratics that do factor, and in such a way that the numbers $d, e, f,$ and g are integers (whole numbers; other cases are discussed in Section 5). The usual technique of factoring such quadratics is a "trial and error" approach.

Factoring Quadratics by Trial and Error

To factor the quadratic $ax^2 + bx + c$, factor ax^2 as $(a_1x)(a_2x)$ (with a_1 positive) and c as c_1c_2, and then check whether or not $ax^2 + bx + c = (a_1x \pm c_1)(a_2x \pm c_2)$. If not, try other factorizations of ax^2 and c.

Quick Examples

1. To factor $x^2 - 6x + 5$, first factor x^2 as $(x)(x)$, and 5 as $(5)(1)$:

$$(x + 5)(x + 1) = x^2 + 6x + 5. \qquad \text{No good}$$
$$(x - 5)(x - 1) = x^2 - 6x + 5. \qquad \text{Desired factorization}$$

2. To factor $x^2 - 4x - 12$, first factor x^2 as $(x)(x)$, and -12 as $(1)(-12)$, $(2)(-6)$, or $(3)(-4)$. Trying them one by one gives

$$(x + 1)(x - 12) = x^2 - 11x - 12. \qquad \text{No good}$$
$$(x - 1)(x + 12) = x^2 + 11x - 12. \qquad \text{No good}$$
$$(x + 2)(x - 6) = x^2 - 4x - 12. \qquad \text{Desired factorization}$$

3. To factor $4x^2 - 25$, we can follow the above procedure, or recognize $4x^2 - 25$ as the difference of two squares:

$$4x^2 - 25 = (2x)^2 - 5^2 = (2x - 5)(2x + 5).$$

Note: Not all quadratic expressions factor. In Section 5 we look at a test that tells us whether or not a given quadratic factors.

Here are examples requiring either a little more work or a little more thought.

EXAMPLE 3 Factoring Quadratics

Factor the following: **a.** $4x^2 - 5x - 6$ **b.** $x^4 - 5x^2 + 6$

Solution

a. Possible factorizations of $4x^2$ are $(2x)(2x)$ or $(x)(4x)$. Possible factorizations of -6 are $(1)(-6)$, $(2)(-3)$. We now systematically try out all the possibilities until we come up with the correct one.

$$
\begin{array}{lll}
(2x)(2x) \text{ and } (1)(-6): & (2x + 1)(2x - 6) = 4x^2 - 10x - 6 & \text{No good} \\
(2x)(2x) \text{ and } (2)(-3): & (2x + 2)(2x - 3) = 4x^2 - 2x - 6 & \text{No good} \\
(x)(4x) \text{ and } (1)(-6): & (x + 1)(4x - 6) = 4x^2 - 2x - 6 & \text{No good} \\
(x)(4x) \text{ and } (2)(-3): & (x + 2)(4x - 3) = 4x^2 + 5x - 6 & \text{Almost!} \\
\text{Change signs:} & (x - 2)(4x + 3) = 4x^2 - 5x - 6 & \text{Correct}
\end{array}
$$

b. The expression $x^4 - 5x^2 + 6$ is not a quadratic, you say? Correct. It's a quartic (a fourth degree expression). However, it looks rather like a quadratic. In fact, it is quadratic *in* x^2, meaning that it is

$$(x^2)^2 - 5(x^2) + 6 = y^2 - 5y + 6$$

where $y = x^2$. The quadratic $y^2 - 5y + 6$ factors as

$$y^2 - 5y + 6 = (y - 3)(y - 2)$$

so

$$x^4 - 5x^2 + 6 = (x^2 - 3)(x^2 - 2)$$

This is a sometimes useful technique.

Our last example is here to remind you why we should want to factor polynomials in the first place. We shall return to this in Section 5.

EXAMPLE 4 Solving a Quadratic Equation by Factoring

Solve the equation $3x^2 + 4x - 4 = 0$.

Solution We first factor the left-hand side to get

$$(3x - 2)(x + 2) = 0.$$

Thus, the product of the two quantities $(3x - 2)$ and $(x + 2)$ is zero. Now, if a product of two numbers is zero, one of the two must be zero. In other words, either $3x - 2 = 0$, giving $x = \frac{2}{3}$, or $x + 2 = 0$, giving $x = -2$. Thus, there are two solutions: $x = \frac{2}{3}$ and $x = -2$.

0.3 EXERCISES

Expand each expression in Exercises 1–22.

1. $x(4x + 6)$

2. $(4y - 2)y$

3. $(2x - y)y$

4. $x(3x + y)$

5. $(x + 1)(x - 3)$

6. $(y + 3)(y + 4)$

7. $(2y + 3)(y + 5)$

8. $(2x - 2)(3x - 4)$

9. $(2x - 3)^2$

10. $(3x + 1)^2$

11. $\left(x + \dfrac{1}{x}\right)^2$

12. $\left(y - \dfrac{1}{y}\right)^2$

13. $(2x - 3)(2x + 3)$

14. $(4 + 2x)(4 - 2x)$

15. $\left(y - \dfrac{1}{y}\right)\left(y + \dfrac{1}{y}\right)$

16. $(x - x^2)(x + x^2)$

17. $(x^2 + x - 1)(2x + 4)$

18. $(3x + 1)(2x^2 - x + 1)$

19. $(x^2 - 2x + 1)^2$

20. $(x + y - xy)^2$

21. $(y^3 + 2y^2 + y)(y^2 + 2y - 1)$

22. $(x^3 - 2x^2 + 4)(3x^2 - x + 2)$

In Exercises 23–30, factor each expression and simplify as much as possible.

23. $(x + 1)(x + 2) + (x + 1)(x + 3)$

24. $(x + 1)(x + 2)^2 + (x + 1)^2(x + 2)$

25. $(x^2 + 1)^5(x + 3)^4 + (x^2 + 1)^6(x + 3)^3$

26. $10x(x^2 + 1)^4(x^3 + 1)^5 + 15x^2(x^2 + 1)^5(x^3 + 1)^4$

27. $(x^3 + 1)\sqrt{x + 1} - (x^3 + 1)^2\sqrt{x + 1}$

28. $(x^2 + 1)\sqrt{x + 1} - \sqrt{(x + 1)^3}$

29. $\sqrt{(x + 1)^3} + \sqrt{(x + 1)^5}$

30. $(x^2 + 1)\sqrt[3]{(x + 1)^4} - \sqrt[3]{(x + 1)^7}$

*In Exercises 31–48, **(a)** factor the given expression; **(b)** set the expression equal to zero and solve for the unknown (x in the odd-numbered exercises and y in the even-numbered exercises).*

31. $2x + 3x^2$

32. $y^2 - 4y$

33. $6x^3 - 2x^2$

34. $3y^3 - 9y^2$

35. $x^2 - 8x + 7$

36. $y^2 + 6y + 8$

37. $x^2 + x - 12$

38. $y^2 + y - 6$

39. $2x^2 - 3x - 2$

40. $3y^2 - 8y - 3$

41. $6x^2 + 13x + 6$

42. $6y^2 + 17y + 12$

43. $12x^2 + x - 6$

44. $20y^2 + 7y - 3$

45. $x^2 + 4xy + 4y^2$

46. $4y^2 - 4xy + x^2$

47. $x^4 - 5x^2 + 4$

48. $y^4 + 2y^2 - 3$

0.4   Rational Expressions

Rational Expression

A **rational expression** is an algebraic expression of the form $\dfrac{P}{Q}$, where P and Q are simpler expressions (usually polynomials) and the denominator Q is not zero.

Quick Examples

1. $\dfrac{x^2 - 3x}{x}$ $\qquad$ $P = x^2 - 3x,\ Q = x$

2. $\dfrac{x + \frac{1}{x} + 1}{2x^2 y + 1}$ $\qquad$ $P = x + \dfrac{1}{x} + 1,\ Q = 2x^2 y + 1$

3. $3xy - x^2$ $\qquad$ $P = 3xy - x^2,\ Q = 1$

Algebra of Rational Expressions

We manipulate rational expressions in the same way that we manipulate fractions, using the following rules:

Algebraic Rule	**Quick Example**
Product: $\dfrac{P}{Q} \cdot \dfrac{R}{S} = \dfrac{PR}{QS}$	$\dfrac{x+1}{x} \cdot \dfrac{x-1}{2x+1} = \dfrac{(x+1)(x-1)}{x(2x+1)} = \dfrac{x^2-1}{2x^2+x}$
Sum: $\dfrac{P}{Q} + \dfrac{R}{S} = \dfrac{PS + RQ}{QS}$	$\dfrac{2x-1}{3x+2} + \dfrac{1}{x} = \dfrac{(2x-1)x + 1(3x+2)}{x(3x+2)}$ $= \dfrac{2x^2 + 2x + 2}{3x^2 + 2x}$
Difference: $\dfrac{P}{Q} - \dfrac{R}{S} = \dfrac{PS - RQ}{QS}$	$\dfrac{x}{3x+2} - \dfrac{x-4}{x} = \dfrac{x^2 - (x-4)(3x+2)}{x(3x+2)}$ $= \dfrac{-2x^2 + 10x + 8}{3x^2 + 2x}$
Reciprocal: $\dfrac{1}{\left(\frac{P}{Q}\right)} = \dfrac{Q}{P}$	$\dfrac{1}{\left(\frac{2xy}{3x-1}\right)} = \dfrac{3x-1}{2xy}$
Quotient: $\dfrac{\left(\frac{P}{Q}\right)}{\left(\frac{R}{S}\right)} = \dfrac{P}{Q} \cdot \dfrac{S}{R} = \dfrac{PS}{QR}$	$\dfrac{\left(\frac{x}{x-1}\right)}{\left(\frac{y-1}{y}\right)} = \dfrac{xy}{(x-1)(y-1)} = \dfrac{xy}{xy - x - y + 1}$
Cancellation: $\dfrac{P\cancel{R}}{Q\cancel{R}} = \dfrac{P}{Q}$	$\dfrac{(x-1)(xy+4)}{(x^2y-8)(x-1)} = \dfrac{xy+4}{x^2y-8}$

Caution Cancellation of summands is *invalid*. For instance,

$$\frac{\cancel{x} + (2xy^2 - y)}{\cancel{x} + 4y} = \frac{(2xy^2 - y)}{4y} \quad \text{✗ } \textbf{\textit{WRONG!}} \quad \text{Do } not \text{ cancel a summand.}$$

$$\frac{\cancel{x}(2xy^2 - y)}{4\cancel{x}y} = \frac{(2xy^2 - y)}{4y} \quad \text{✔ } \textbf{\textit{CORRECT}} \quad \text{Do cancel a factor.}$$

Here are some examples that require several algebraic operations.

EXAMPLE 1 Simplifying Rational Expressions

a. $\dfrac{\left(\frac{1}{x+y} - \frac{1}{x}\right)}{y} = \dfrac{\left(\frac{x - (x+y)}{x(x+y)}\right)}{y} = \dfrac{\left(\frac{-y}{x(x+y)}\right)}{y} = \dfrac{-y}{xy(x+y)} = -\dfrac{1}{x(x+y)}$

b. $\dfrac{(x+1)(x+2)^2 - (x+1)^2(x+2)}{(x+2)^4} = \dfrac{(x+1)(x+2)[(x+2) - (x+1)]}{(x+2)^4}$

$= \dfrac{(x+1)(x+2)(x+2-x-1)}{(x+2)^4} = \dfrac{(x+1)(x+2)}{(x+2)^4} = \dfrac{x+1}{(x+2)^3}$

c. $\dfrac{2x\sqrt{x+1} - \frac{x^2}{\sqrt{x+1}}}{x+1} = \dfrac{\left(\frac{2x(\sqrt{x+1})^2 - x^2}{\sqrt{x+1}}\right)}{x+1} = \dfrac{2x(x+1) - x^2}{(x+1)\sqrt{x+1}}$

$= \dfrac{2x^2 + 2x - x^2}{(x+1)\sqrt{x+1}} = \dfrac{x^2 + 2x}{\sqrt{(x+1)^3}} = \dfrac{x(x+2)}{\sqrt{(x+1)^3}}$

0.4 EXERCISES

Rewrite each expression in Exercises 1–16 as a single rational expression, simplified as much as possible.

1. $\dfrac{x-4}{x+1} \cdot \dfrac{2x+1}{x-1}$

2. $\dfrac{2x-3}{x-2} \cdot \dfrac{x+3}{x+1}$

3. $\dfrac{x-4}{x+1} + \dfrac{2x+1}{x-1}$

4. $\dfrac{2x-3}{x-2} + \dfrac{x+3}{x+1}$

5. $\dfrac{x^2}{x+1} - \dfrac{x-1}{x+1}$

6. $\dfrac{x^2-1}{x-2} - \dfrac{1}{x-1}$

7. $\dfrac{1}{\left(\frac{x}{x-1}\right)} + x - 1$

8. $\dfrac{2}{\left(\frac{x-2}{x^2}\right)} - \dfrac{1}{x-2}$

9. $\dfrac{1}{x}\left[\dfrac{x-3}{xy} + \dfrac{1}{y}\right]$

10. $\dfrac{y^2}{x}\left[\dfrac{2x-3}{y} + \dfrac{x}{y}\right]$

11. $\dfrac{(x+1)^2(x+2)^3 - (x+1)^3(x+2)^2}{(x+2)^6}$

12. $\dfrac{6x(x^2+1)^2(x^3+2)^3 - 9x^2(x^2+1)^3(x^3+2)^2}{(x^3+2)^6}$

13. $\dfrac{(x^2-1)\sqrt{x^2+1} - \frac{x^4}{\sqrt{x^2+1}}}{x^2+1}$

14. $\dfrac{x\sqrt{x^3-1} - \frac{3x^4}{\sqrt{x^3-1}}}{x^3-1}$

15. $\dfrac{\frac{1}{(x+y)^2} - \frac{1}{x^2}}{y}$

16. $\dfrac{\frac{1}{(x+y)^3} - \frac{1}{x^3}}{y}$

0.5 Solving Polynomial Equations

Polynomial Equation

A **polynomial equation** in one unknown is an equation that can be written in the form

$$ax^n + bx^{n-1} + \cdots + rx + s = 0$$

where $a, b, \ldots, r$, and s are constants.

We call the largest exponent of x appearing in a nonzero term of a polynomial the **degree** of that polynomial.

Quick Examples

1. $3x + 1 = 0$ has degree 1 because the largest power of x that occurs is $x = x^1$. Degree 1 equations are called **linear** equations.
2. $x^2 - x - 1 = 0$ has degree 2 because the largest power of x that occurs is x^2. Degree 2 equations are also called **quadratic equations**, or just **quadratics**.
3. $x^3 = 2x^2 + 1$ is a degree 3 polynomial (or **cubic**) in disguise. It can be rewritten as $x^3 - 2x^2 - 1 = 0$, which is in the standard form for a degree 3 equation.
4. $x^4 - x = 0$ has degree 4. It is called a **quartic**.

Now comes the question: How do we solve these equations for x? This question was asked by mathematicians as early as 1600 BCE. Let's look at these equations one degree at a time.

Solution of Linear Equations

By definition, a linear equation can be written in the form

$$ax + b = 0. \qquad \text{\small a and b are fixed numbers with $a \neq 0$.}$$

Solving this is a nice mental exercise: Subtract b from both sides and then divide by a, getting $x = -b/a$. Don't bother memorizing this formula; just go ahead and solve linear equations as they arise. If you feel you need practice, see the exercises at the end of the section.

Solution of Quadratic Equations

By definition, a quadratic equation has the form

$$ax^2 + bx + c = 0. \qquad \text{\small a, b, and c are fixed numbers and $a \neq 0$.[3]}$$

---

[3]What happens if $a = 0$?

The solutions of this equation are also called the **roots** of $ax^2 + bx + c$. We're assuming that you saw quadratic equations somewhere in high school but may be a little hazy about the details of their solution. There are two ways of solving these equations—one works sometimes, and the other works every time.

Solving Quadratic Equations by Factoring (works sometimes)

If we can factor[4] a quadratic equation $ax^2 + bx + c = 0$, we can solve the equation by setting each factor equal to zero.

Quick Examples

1. $x^2 + 7x + 10 = 0$

   $(x + 5)(x + 2) = 0$ Factor the left-hand side.

   $x + 5 = 0$ or $x + 2 = 0$ If a product is zero, one or both factors is zero.

   Solutions: $x = -5$ and $x = -2$

2. $2x^2 - 5x - 12 = 0$

   $(2x + 3)(x - 4) = 0$ Factor the left-hand side.

   $2x + 3 = 0$ or $x - 4 = 0$

   Solutions: $x = -3/2$ and $x = 4$

Test for Factoring

The quadratic $ax^2 + bx + c$, with a, b, and c being integers (whole numbers), factors into an expression of the form $(rx + s)(tx + u)$ with r, s, t, and u integers precisely when the quantity $b^2 - 4ac$ is a perfect square. (That is, it is the square of an integer.) If this happens, we say that the quadratic **factors over the integers**.

Quick Examples

1. $x^2 + x + 1$ has $a = 1$, $b = 1$, and $c = 1$, so $b^2 - 4ac = -3$, which is not a perfect square. Therefore, this quadratic does not factor over the integers.

2. $2x^2 - 5x - 12$ has $a = 2$, $b = -5$, and $c = -12$, so $b^2 - 4ac = 121$. Because $121 = 11^2$, this quadratic does factor over the integers. (We factored it above.)

Solving Quadratic Equations with the Quadratic Formula (works every time)

The solutions of the general quadratic $ax^2 + bx + c = 0$ ($a \neq 0$) are given by

$$x = \frac{-b \pm \sqrt{b^2 - 4ac}}{2a}.$$

---

[4]See the section on factoring for a review of how to factor quadratics.

We call the quantity $\Delta = b^2 - 4ac$ the **discriminant** of the quadratic (Δ is the Greek letter delta), and we have the following general rules:

• If Δ is positive, there are two distinct real solutions.

• If Δ is zero, there is only one real solution: $x = -\dfrac{b}{2a}$. (Why?)

• If Δ is negative, there are no real solutions.

Quick Examples

1. $2x^2 - 5x - 12 = 0$ has $a = 2$, $b = -5$, and $c = -12$.

$$x = \frac{-b \pm \sqrt{b^2 - 4ac}}{2a} = \frac{5 \pm \sqrt{25 + 96}}{4} = \frac{5 \pm \sqrt{121}}{4} = \frac{5 \pm 11}{4}$$

$$= \frac{16}{4} \text{ or } -\frac{6}{4} = 4 \text{ or } -3/2 \qquad \Delta \text{ is positive in this example.}$$

2. $4x^2 = 12x - 9$ can be rewritten as $4x^2 - 12x + 9 = 0$, which has $a = 4$, $b = -12$, and $c = 9$.

$$x = \frac{-b \pm \sqrt{b^2 - 4ac}}{2a} = \frac{12 \pm \sqrt{144 - 144}}{8} = \frac{12 \pm 0}{8} = \frac{12}{8} = \frac{3}{2}$$

Δ is zero in this example.

3. $x^2 + 2x - 1 = 0$ has $a = 1$, $b = 2$, and $c = -1$.

$$x = \frac{-b \pm \sqrt{b^2 - 4ac}}{2a} = \frac{-2 \pm \sqrt{8}}{2} = \frac{-2 \pm 2\sqrt{2}}{2} = -1 \pm \sqrt{2}$$

The two solutions are $x = -1 + \sqrt{2} = 0.414\ldots$ and $x = -1 - \sqrt{2} = -2.414\ldots$ Δ is positive in this example.

4. $x^2 + x + 1 = 0$ has $a = 1$, $b = 1$, and $c = 1$. Because $\Delta = -3$ is negative, there are no real solutions. Δ is negative in this example.

Q: *This is all very useful, but where does the quadratic formula come from?*

A: To see where it comes from, we will solve a general quadratic equation using "brute force." Start with the general quadratic equation.

$$ax^2 + bx + c = 0.$$

First, divide out the nonzero number a to get

$$x^2 + \frac{bx}{a} + \frac{c}{a} = 0.$$

Now we **complete the square:** Add and subtract the quantity $\dfrac{b^2}{4a^2}$ to get

$$x^2 + \frac{bx}{a} + \frac{b^2}{4a^2} - \frac{b^2}{4a^2} + \frac{c}{a} = 0.$$

We do this to get the first three terms to factor as a perfect square:

$$\left(x + \frac{b}{2a}\right)^2 - \frac{b^2}{4a^2} + \frac{c}{a} = 0.$$

(Check this by multiplying out.) Adding $\dfrac{b^2}{4a^2} - \dfrac{c}{a}$ to both sides gives:

$$\left(x + \frac{b}{2a}\right)^2 = \frac{b^2}{4a^2} - \frac{c}{a} = \frac{b^2 - 4ac}{4a^2}.$$

Taking square roots gives

$$x + \frac{b}{2a} = \frac{\pm\sqrt{b^2 - 4ac}}{2a}.$$

Finally, adding $-\dfrac{b}{2a}$ to both sides yields the result:

$$x = -\frac{b}{2a} + \frac{\pm\sqrt{b^2 - 4ac}}{2a}$$

or

$$x = \frac{-b \pm \sqrt{b^2 - 4ac}}{2a}.$$

Solution of Cubic Equations

By definition, a cubic equation can be written in the form

$$ax^3 + bx^2 + cx + d = 0. \qquad \text{a, b, c, and d are fixed numbers and $a \neq 0$.}$$

Now we get into something of a bind. Although there is a perfectly respectable formula for the solutions, it is very complicated and involves the use of complex numbers rather heavily.[5] So we discuss instead a much simpler method that *sometimes* works nicely. Here is the method in a nutshell.

Solving Cubics by Finding One Factor

Start with a given cubic equation $ax^3 + bx^2 + cx + d = 0$.

Step 1 By trial and error, find one solution $x = s$. If a, b, c, and d are integers, the only possible *rational* solutions[6] are those of the form $s = \pm(\text{factor of } d)/(\text{factor of } a)$.

Step 2 It will now be possible to factor the cubic as

$$ax^3 + bx^2 + cx + d = (x - s)(ax^2 + ex + f) = 0$$

To find $ax^2 + ex + f$, divide the cubic by $x - s$, using long division.[7]

Step 3 The factored equation says that either $x - s = 0$ or $ax^2 + ex + f = 0$. We already know that s is a solution, and now we see that the other solutions are the roots of the quadratic. Note that this quadratic may or may not have any real solutions, as usual.

---

[5]It was when this formula was discovered in the 16th century that complex numbers were first taken seriously. Although we would like to show you the formula, it is too large to fit in this footnote.

[6]There may be *irrational* solutions, however; for example, $x^3 - 2 = 0$ has the single solution $x = \sqrt[3]{2}$.

[7]Alternatively, use "synthetic division," a shortcut that would take us too far afield to describe.

> ### Quick Example
>
> To solve the cubic $x^3 - x^2 + x - 1 = 0$, we first find a single solution. Here, $a = 1$ and $d = -1$. Because the only factors of ± 1 are ± 1, the only possible rational solutions are $x = \pm 1$. By substitution, we see that $x = 1$ is a solution. Thus, $(x - 1)$ is a factor. Dividing by $(x - 1)$ yields the quotient $(x^2 + 1)$. Thus,
>
> $$x^3 - x^2 + x - 1 = (x - 1)(x^2 + 1) = 0$$
>
> so that either $x - 1 = 0$ or $x^2 + 1 = 0$.
>
> Because the discriminant of the quadratic $x^2 + 1$ is negative, we don't get any real solutions from $x^2 + 1 = 0$, so the only real solution is $x = 1$.

Possible Outcomes When Solving a Cubic Equation

If you consider all the cases, there are three possible outcomes when solving a cubic equation:

1. One real solution (as in the Quick Example above)
2. Two real solutions (try, for example, $x^3 + x^2 - x - 1 = 0$)
3. Three real solutions (see the next example)

EXAMPLE 1 Solving a Cubic

Solve the cubic $2x^3 - 3x^2 - 17x + 30 = 0$.

Solution First we look for a single solution. Here, $a = 2$ and $d = 30$. The factors of a are ± 1 and ± 2, and the factors of d are ± 1, ± 2, ± 3, ± 5, ± 6, ± 10, ± 15, and ± 30. This gives us a large number of possible ratios: ± 1, ± 2, ± 3, ± 5, ± 6, ± 10, ± 15, ± 30, $\pm 1/2$, $\pm 3/2$, $\pm 5/2$, $\pm 15/2$. Undaunted, we first try $x = 1$ and $x = -1$, getting nowhere. So we move on to $x = 2$, and we hit the jackpot, because substituting $x = 2$ gives $16 - 12 - 34 + 30 = 0$. Thus, $(x - 2)$ is a factor. Dividing yields the quotient $2x^2 + x - 15$. Here is the calculation:

$$
\begin{array}{r}
2x^2 + x - 15 \\
x - 2 \overline{\smash{\big)}\ 2x^3 - 3x^2 - 17x + 30} \\
\underline{2x^3 - 4x^2} \\
x^2 - 17x \\
\underline{x^2 - 2x} \\
-15x + 30 \\
\underline{-15x + 30} \\
0.
\end{array}
$$

Thus,

$$2x^3 - 3x^2 - 17x + 30 = (x - 2)(2x^2 + x - 15) = 0.$$

Setting the factors equal to zero gives either $x - 2 = 0$ or $2x^2 + x - 15 = 0$. We could solve the quadratic using the quadratic formula, but, luckily, we notice that it factors as

$$2x^2 + x - 15 = (x + 3)(2x - 5).$$

Thus, the solutions are $x = 2$, $x = -3$ and $x = 5/2$.

Solution of Higher-Order Polynomial Equations

Logically speaking, our next step should be a discussion of quartics, then quintics (fifth degree equations), and so on forever. Well, we've got to stop somewhere, and cubics may be as good a place as any. On the other hand, since we've gotten so far, we ought to at least tell you what is known about higher order polynomials.

Quartics Just as in the case of cubics, there is a formula to find the solutions of quartics.[8]

Quintics and Beyond All good things must come to an end, we're afraid. It turns out that there is no "quintic formula." In other words, there is no single algebraic formula or collection of algebraic formulas that gives the solutions to all quintics. This question was settled by the Norwegian mathematician Niels Henrik Abel in 1824 after almost 300 years of controversy about this question. (In fact, several notable mathematicians had previously claimed to have devised formulas for solving the quintic, but these were all shot down by other mathematicians—this being one of the favorite pastimes of practitioners of our art.) The same negative answer applies to polynomial equations of degree 6 and higher. It's not that these equations don't have solutions; it's just that they can't be found using algebraic formulas.[9] However, there are certain special classes of polynomial equations that can be solved with algebraic methods. The way of identifying such equations was discovered around 1829 by the French mathematician Évariste Galois.[10]

---

[8]See, for example, *First Course in the Theory of Equations* by L. E. Dickson (New York: Wiley, 1922), or *Modern Algebra* by B. L. van der Waerden (New York: Frederick Ungar, 1953).

[9]What we mean by an "algebraic formula" is a formula in the coefficients using the operations of addition, subtraction, multiplication, division, and the taking of radicals. Mathematicians call the use of such formulas in solving polynomial equations "solution by radicals." If you were a math major, you would eventually go on to study this under the heading of Galois theory.

[10]Both Abel (1802–1829) and Galois (1811–1832) died young. Abel died of tuberculosis at the age of 26, while Galois was killed in a duel at the age of 20.

0.5   EXERCISES

Solve the equations in Exercises 1–12 for x (mentally, if possible).

1. $x + 1 = 0$

2. $x - 3 = 1$

3. $-x + 5 = 0$

4. $2x + 4 = 1$

5. $4x - 5 = 8$

6. $\dfrac{3}{4}x + 1 = 0$

7. $7x + 55 = 98$

8. $3x + 1 = x$

9. $x + 1 = 2x + 2$

10. $x + 1 = 3x + 1$

11. $ax + b = c$ $(a \neq 0)$

12. $x - 1 = cx + d$ $(c \neq 1)$

By any method, determine all possible real solutions of each equation in Exercises 13–30. Check your answers by substitution.

13. $2x^2 + 7x - 4 = 0$

14. $x^2 + x + 1 = 0$

15. $x^2 - x + 1 = 0$

16. $2x^2 - 4x + 3 = 0$

17. $2x^2 - 5 = 0$

18. $3x^2 - 1 = 0$

19. $-x^2 - 2x - 1 = 0$

20. $2x^2 - x - 3 = 0$

21. $\frac{1}{2}x^2 - x - \frac{3}{2} = 0$

22. $-\frac{1}{2}x^2 - \frac{1}{2}x + 1 = 0$

23. $x^2 - x = 1$

24. $16x^2 = -24x - 9$

25. $x = 2 - \frac{1}{x}$

26. $x + 4 = \frac{1}{x - 2}$

27. $x^4 - 10x^2 + 9 = 0$

28. $x^4 - 2x^2 + 1 = 0$

29. $x^4 + x^2 - 1 = 0$

30. $x^3 + 2x^2 + x = 0$

33. $x^3 + 4x^2 + 4x + 3 = 0$

34. $y^3 + 64 = 0$

35. $x^3 - 1 = 0$

36. $x^3 - 27 = 0$

37. $y^3 + 3y^2 + 3y + 2 = 0$

38. $y^3 - 2y^2 - 2y - 3 = 0$

39. $x^3 - x^2 - 5x + 5 = 0$

40. $x^3 - x^2 - 3x + 3 = 0$

41. $2x^6 - x^4 - 2x^2 + 1 = 0$

42. $3x^6 - x^4 - 12x^2 + 4 = 0$

43. $(x^2 + 3x + 2)(x^2 - 5x + 6) = 0$

44. $(x^2 - 4x + 4)^2(x^2 + 6x + 5)^3 = 0$

Find all possible real solutions of each equation in Exercises 31–44.

31. $x^3 + 6x^2 + 11x + 6 = 0$

32. $x^3 - 6x^2 + 12x - 8 = 0$

0.6 Solving Miscellaneous Equations

Equations often arise in calculus that are not polynomial equations of low degree. Many of these complicated-looking equations can be solved easily if you remember the following, which we used in the previous section:

Solving an Equation of the Form $P \cdot Q = 0$

If a product is equal to 0, then at least one of the factors must be 0. That is, if $P \cdot Q = 0$, then either $P = 0$ or $Q = 0$.

Quick Examples

1. $x^5 - 4x^3 = 0$

$\quad x^3(x^2 - 4) = 0$ Factor the left-hand side.

$\quad$ Either $x^3 = 0$ or $x^2 - 4 = 0$ Either $P = 0$ or $Q = 0$.

$\quad x = 0, 2$ or -2.   Solve the individual equations.

2. $(x^2 - 1)(x + 2) + (x^2 - 1)(x + 4) = 0$

$\quad (x^2 - 1)[(x + 2) + (x + 4)] = 0$ Factor the left-hand side.

$\quad (x^2 - 1)(2x + 6) = 0$

$\quad$ Either $x^2 - 1 = 0$ or $2x + 6 = 0$ Either $P = 0$ or $Q = 0$.

$\quad x = -3, -1,$ or 1.   Solve the individual equations.

EXAMPLE 1 Solving by Factoring

Solve $12x(x^2 - 4)^5(x^2 + 2)^6 + 12x(x^2 - 4)^6(x^2 + 2)^5 = 0$.

Solution

Again, we start by factoring the left-hand side:

$$12x(x^2 - 4)^5(x^2 + 2)^6 + 12x(x^2 - 4)^6(x^2 + 2)^5$$
$$= 12x(x^2 - 4)^5(x^2 + 2)^5[(x^2 + 2) + (x^2 - 4)]$$
$$= 12x(x^2 - 4)^5(x^2 + 2)^5(2x^2 - 2)$$
$$= 24x(x^2 - 4)^5(x^2 + 2)^5(x^2 - 1).$$

Setting this equal to 0, we get:

$$24x(x^2 - 4)^5(x^2 + 2)^5(x^2 - 1) = 0,$$

which means that at least one of the factors of this product must be zero. Now it certainly cannot be the 24, but it could be the x: $x = 0$ is one solution. It could also be that

$$(x^2 - 4)^5 = 0$$

or

$$x^2 - 4 = 0,$$

which has solutions $x = \pm 2$. Could it be that $(x^2 + 2)^5 = 0$? If so, then $x^2 + 2 = 0$, but this is impossible because $x^2 + 2 \geq 2$, no matter what x is. Finally, it could be that $x^2 - 1 = 0$, which has solutions $x = \pm 1$. This gives us five solutions to the original equation:

$$x = -2, -1, 0, 1, \text{ or } 2.$$

EXAMPLE 2 Solving by Factoring

Solve $(x^2 - 1)(x^2 - 4) = 10$.

Solution Watch out! You may be tempted to say that $x^2 - 1 = 10$ or $x^2 - 4 = 10$, but this does not follow. If two numbers multiply to give you 10, what must they be? There are lots of possibilities: 2 and 5, 1 and 10, $-500{,}000$ and -0.00002 are just a few. The fact that the left-hand side is factored is nearly useless to us if we want to solve this equation. What we will have to do is multiply out, bring the 10 over to the left, and hope that we can factor what we get. Here goes:

$$x^4 - 5x^2 + 4 = 10$$
$$x^4 - 5x^2 - 6 = 0$$
$$(x^2 - 6)(x^2 + 1) = 0$$

(Here we used a sometimes useful trick that we mentioned in Section 3: We treated x^2 like x and x^4 like x^2, so factoring $x^4 - 5x^2 - 6$ is essentially the same as factoring $x^2 - 5x - 6$.) *Now* we are allowed to say that one of the factors must be 0: $x^2 - 6 = 0$ has solutions $x = \pm\sqrt{6} = \pm 2.449\ldots$ and $x^2 + 1 = 0$ has no real solutions. Therefore, we get exactly two solutions, $x = \pm\sqrt{6} = \pm 2.449\ldots$.

To solve equations involving rational expressions, the following rule is very useful.

Solving an Equation of the Form $P/Q = 0$

If $\dfrac{P}{Q} = 0$, then $P = 0$.

How else could a fraction equal 0? If that is not convincing, multiply both sides by Q (which cannot be 0 if the quotient is defined).

Quick Example

$$\frac{(x + 1)(x + 2)^2 - (x + 1)^2(x + 2)}{(x + 2)^4} = 0$$

$(x + 1)(x + 2)^2 - (x + 1)^2(x + 2) = 0$ If $\frac{P}{Q} = 0$, then $P = 0$.

$(x + 1)(x + 2)[(x + 2) - (x + 1)] = 0$ Factor.

$(x + 1)(x + 2)(1) = 0$

Either $x + 1 = 0$ or $x + 2 = 0$,

$x = -1$ or $x = -2$

$x = -1$ $x = -2$ does not make sense in the original equation: it makes the denominator 0. So it is not a solution and $x = -1$ is the only solution.

EXAMPLE 3 Solving a Rational Equation

Solve $1 - \dfrac{1}{x^2} = 0$.

Solution Write 1 as $\frac{1}{1}$, so that we now have a difference of two rational expressions:

$$\frac{1}{1} - \frac{1}{x^2} = 0.$$

To combine these we can put both over a common denominator of x^2, which gives

$$\frac{x^2 - 1}{x^2} = 0.$$

Now we can set the numerator, $x^2 - 1$, equal to zero. Thus,

$$x^2 - 1 = 0$$

so

$$(x - 1)(x + 1) = 0,$$

giving $x = \pm 1$.

➡ **Before we go on...** This equation could also have been solved by writing

$$1 = \frac{1}{x^2}$$

and then multiplying both sides by x^2. ∎

EXAMPLE 4 **Another Rational Equation**

Solve $\dfrac{2x-1}{x} + \dfrac{3}{x-2} = 0$.

Solution We *could* first perform the addition on the left and then set the top equal to 0, but here is another approach. Subtracting the second expression from both sides gives

$$\frac{2x-1}{x} = \frac{-3}{x-2}.$$

Cross-multiplying [multiplying both sides by both denominators—that is, by $x(x-2)$] now gives

$$(2x-1)(x-2) = -3x$$

so

$$2x^2 - 5x + 2 = -3x.$$

Adding $3x$ to both sides gives the quadratic equation

$$2x^2 - 2x + 1 = 0.$$

The discriminant is $(-2)^2 - 4 \cdot 2 \cdot 1 = -4 < 0$, so we conclude that there is no real solution.

➡ **Before we go on...** Notice that when we said that $(2x-1)(x-2) = -3x$, we were *not* allowed to conclude that $2x - 1 = -3x$ or $x - 2 = -3x$. ∎

EXAMPLE 5 **A Rational Equation with Radicals**

Solve $\dfrac{\left(2x\sqrt{x+1} - \dfrac{x^2}{\sqrt{x+1}}\right)}{x+1} = 0$.

Solution Setting the top equal to 0 gives

$$2x\sqrt{x+1} - \frac{x^2}{\sqrt{x+1}} = 0.$$

This still involves fractions. To get rid of the fractions, we could put everything over a common denominator ($\sqrt{x+1}$) and then set the top equal to 0, or we could multiply the whole equation by that common denominator in the first place to clear fractions. If we do the second, we get

$$2x(x+1) - x^2 = 0$$
$$2x^2 + 2x - x^2 = 0$$
$$x^2 + 2x = 0.$$

Factoring,

$$x(x+2) = 0$$

so either $x = 0$ or $x + 2 = 0$, giving us $x = 0$ or $x = -2$. Again, one of these is not really a solution. The problem is that $x = -2$ cannot be substituted into $\sqrt{x+1}$, because we would then have to take the square root of -1, and we are not allowing ourselves to do that. Therefore, $x = 0$ is the only solution.

0.6   EXERCISES

Solve the following equations:

1. $x^4 - 3x^3 = 0$

2. $x^6 - 9x^4 = 0$

3. $x^4 - 4x^2 = -4$

4. $x^4 - x^2 = 6$

5. $(x + 1)(x + 2) + (x + 1)(x + 3) = 0$

6. $(x + 1)(x + 2)^2 + (x + 1)^2(x + 2) = 0$

7. $(x^2 + 1)^5(x + 3)^4 + (x^2 + 1)^6(x + 3)^3 = 0$

8. $10x(x^2 + 1)^4(x^3 + 1)^5 - 10x^2(x^2 + 1)^5(x^3 + 1)^4 = 0$

9. $(x^3 + 1)\sqrt{x + 1} - (x^3 + 1)^2\sqrt{x + 1} = 0$

10. $(x^2 + 1)\sqrt{x + 1} - \sqrt{(x + 1)^3} = 0$

11. $\sqrt{(x + 1)^3} + \sqrt{(x + 1)^5} = 0$

12. $(x^2 + 1)\sqrt[3]{(x + 1)^4} - \sqrt[3]{(x + 1)^7} = 0$

13. $(x + 1)^2(2x + 3) - (x + 1)(2x + 3)^2 = 0$

14. $(x^2 - 1)^2(x + 2)^3 - (x^2 - 1)^3(x + 2)^2 = 0$

15. $\dfrac{(x + 1)^2(x + 2)^3 - (x + 1)^3(x + 2)^2}{(x + 2)^6} = 0$

16. $\dfrac{6x(x^2 + 1)^2(x^2 + 2)^4 - 8x(x^2 + 1)^3(x^2 + 2)^3}{(x^2 + 2)^8} = 0$

17. $\dfrac{2(x^2 - 1)\sqrt{x^2 + 1} - \dfrac{x^4}{\sqrt{x^2 + 1}}}{x^2 + 1} = 0$

18. $\dfrac{4x\sqrt{x^3 - 1} - \dfrac{3x^4}{\sqrt{x^3 - 1}}}{x^3 - 1} = 0$

19. $x - \dfrac{1}{x} = 0$

20. $1 - \dfrac{4}{x^2} = 0$

21. $\dfrac{1}{x} - \dfrac{9}{x^3} = 0$

22. $\dfrac{1}{x^2} - \dfrac{1}{x + 1} = 0$

23. $\dfrac{x - 4}{x + 1} - \dfrac{x}{x - 1} = 0$

24. $\dfrac{2x - 3}{x - 1} - \dfrac{2x + 3}{x + 1} = 0$

25. $\dfrac{x + 4}{x + 1} + \dfrac{x + 4}{3x} = 0$

26. $\dfrac{2x - 3}{x} - \dfrac{2x - 3}{x + 1} = 0$

0.7   The Coordinate Plane

Q: *Just what is the xy-plane?*

A: The *xy*-plane is an infinite flat surface with two perpendicular lines, usually labeled the **x-axis** and **y-axis**. These axes are calibrated as shown in Figure 2. (Notice also how the plane is divided into four **quadrants**.)

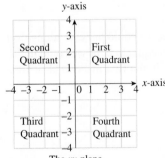

The *xy*-plane

Figure 2

Thus, the *xy*-plane is nothing more than a very large—in fact, infinitely large—flat surface. The purpose of the axes is to allow us to locate specific positions, or **points**, on the plane, with the use of **coordinates**. (If Captain Picard wants to have himself beamed to a specific location, he must supply its coordinates, or he's in trouble.)

Q: *So how do we use coordinates to locate points?*

A: The rule is simple. Each point in the plane has two coordinates, an **x-coordinate** and a **y-coordinate**. These can be determined in two ways:

1. The *x*-coordinate measures a point's distance to the right or left of the *y*-axis. It is positive if the point is to the right of the axis, negative if it is to the left of the axis, and 0 if it is on the axis. The *y*-coordinate measures a point's distance above or below the *x*-axis. It is positive if the point is above the axis, negative if it is below the axis, and 0 if it is on the axis. Briefly, the *x*-coordinate tells us the *horizontal* position (distance left or right), and the *y*-coordinate tells us the *vertical* position (height).

2. Given a point P, we get its x-coordinate by drawing a vertical line from P and seeing where it intersects the x-axis. Similarly, we get the y-coordinate by extending a horizontal line from P and seeing where it intersects the y-axis.

This way of assigning coordinates to points in the plane is often called the system of **Cartesian** coordinates, in honor of the mathematician and philosopher René Descartes (1596–1650), who was the first to use them extensively.

Here are a few examples to help you review coordinates.

EXAMPLE 1 Coordinates of Points

a. Find the coordinates of the indicated points. (See Figure 3. The grid lines are placed at intervals of one unit.)

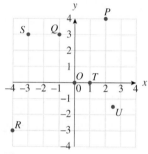

Figure 3

b. Locate the following points in the xy-plane.

$$A(2, 3),\ B(-4, 2),\ C(3, -2.5),\ D(0, -3),\ E(3.5, 0),\ F(-2.5, -1.5)$$

Solution

a. Taking them in alphabetical order, we start with the origin O. This point has height zero and is also zero units to the right of the y-axis, so its coordinates are $(0, 0)$. Turning to P, dropping a vertical line gives $x = 2$ and extending a horizontal line gives $y = 4$. Thus, P has coordinates $(2, 4)$. For practice, determine the coordinates of the remaining points, and check your work against the list that follows:

$$Q(-1, 3),\ R(-4, -3),\ S(-3, 3),\ T(1, 0),\ U(2.5, -1.5)$$

b. In order to locate the given points, we start at the origin $(0, 0)$, and proceed as follows. (See Figure 4.)

To locate A, we move 2 units to the right and 3 up, as shown.

To locate B, we move -4 units to the right (that is, 4 to the *left*) and 2 up, as shown.

To locate C, we move 3 units right and 2.5 down.

We locate the remaining points in a similar way.

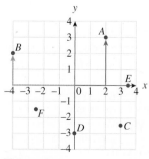

Figure 4

The Graph of an Equation

One of the more surprising developments of mathematics was the realization that equations, which are algebraic objects, can be represented by graphs, which are geometric objects. The kinds of equations that we have in mind are equations in x and y, such as

$$y = 4x - 1, \quad 2x^2 - y = 0, \quad y = 3x^2 + 1, \quad y = \sqrt{x - 1}.$$

The **graph** of an equation in the two variables x and y consists of all points (x, y) in the plane whose coordinates are solutions of the equation.

EXAMPLE 2 Graph of an Equation

Obtain the graph of the equation $y - x^2 = 0$.

Solution We can solve the equation for y to obtain $y = x^2$. Solutions can then be obtained by choosing values for x and then computing y by squaring the value of x, as shown in the following table:

x	-3	-2	-1	0	1	2	3
$y = x^2$	9	4	1	0	1	4	9

Plotting these points (x, y) gives the following picture (left side of Figure 5), suggesting the graph on the right in Figure 5.

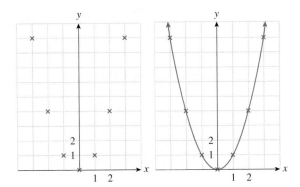

Figure 5

Distance

The distance between two points in the xy-plane can be expressed as a function of their coordinates, as follows:

Distance Formula

The distance between the points $P(x_1, y_1)$ and $Q(x_2, y_2)$ is

$$d = \sqrt{(x_2 - x_1)^2 + (y_2 - y_1)^2} = \sqrt{(\Delta x)^2 + (\Delta y)^2}.$$

Derivation

The distance d is shown in the figure below.

By the Pythagorean theorem applied to the right triangle shown, we get

$$d^2 = (x_2 - x_1)^2 + (y_2 - y_1)^2.$$

Taking square roots (d is a distance, so we take the positive square root), we get the distance formula. Notice that if we switch x_1 with x_2 or y_1 with y_2, we get the same result.

Quick Examples

1. The distance between the points $(3, -2)$ and $(-1, 1)$ is
$$d = \sqrt{(-1-3)^2 + (1+2)^2} = \sqrt{25} = 5.$$

2. The distance from (x, y) to the origin $(0, 0)$ is
$$d = \sqrt{(x-0)^2 + (y-0)^2} = \sqrt{x^2 + y^2}. \qquad \text{Distance to the origin}$$

The set of all points (x, y) whose distance from the origin $(0, 0)$ is a fixed quantity r is a circle centered at the origin with radius r. From the second Quick Example, we get the following equation for the circle centered at the origin with radius r:

$$\sqrt{x^2 + y^2} = r. \qquad \text{Distance from the origin} = r.$$

Squaring both sides gives the following equation:

Equation of the Circle of Radius r Centered at the Origin

$$x^2 + y^2 = r^2$$

Quick Examples

1. The circle of radius 1 centered at the origin has equation $x^2 + y^2 = 1$.

2. The circle of radius 2 centered at the origin has equation $x^2 + y^2 = 4$.

0.7 EXERCISES

1. Referring to the following figure, determine the coordinates of the indicated points as accurately as you can.

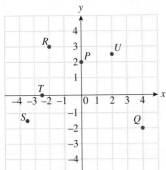

2. Referring to the following figure, determine the coordinates of the indicated points as accurately as you can.

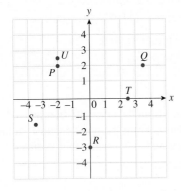

3. Graph the following points.

$P(4, 4)$, $Q(4, -4)$, $R(3, 0)$, $S(4, 0.5)$, $T(0.5, 2.5)$, $U(-2, 0)$, $V(-4, 4)$

4. Graph the following points.

$P(4, -2)$, $Q(2, -4)$, $R(1, -3)$, $S(-4, 2)$, $T(2, -1)$, $U(-2, 0)$, $V(-4, -4)$

Sketch the graphs of the equations in Exercises 5–12.

5. $x + y = 1$

6. $y - x = -1$

7. $2y - x^2 = 1$

8. $2y + \sqrt{x} = 1$

9. $xy = 4$

10. $x^2 y = -1$

11. $xy = x^2 + 1$

12. $xy = 2x^3 + 1$

In Exercises 13–16, find the distance between the given pairs of points.

13. $(1, -1)$ and $(2, -2)$

14. $(1, 0)$ and $(6, 1)$

15. $(a, 0)$ and $(0, b)$

16. (a, a) and (b, b)

17. Find the value of k such that $(1, k)$ is equidistant from $(0, 0)$ and $(2, 1)$.

18. Find the value of k such that (k, k) is equidistant from $(-1, 0)$ and $(0, 2)$.

19. Describe the set of points (x, y) such that $x^2 + y^2 = 9$.

20. Describe the set of points (x, y) such that $x^2 + y^2 = 0$.

1

Functions and Applications

WW Website
www.WanerMath.com
At the Website you will find:

- Section-by-section tutorials, including game tutorials with randomized quizzes

- A detailed chapter summary

- A true/false quiz

- Additional review exercises

- Graphers, Excel tutorials, and other resources

- The following extra topic:

  New Functions from Old: Scaled and Shifted Functions

Case Study Modeling Spending on Internet Advertising

You are the new director of *Impact Advertising Inc.'s* Internet division, which has enjoyed a steady 0.25% of the Internet advertising market. You have drawn up an ambitious proposal to expand your division in light of your anticipation that Internet advertising will continue to skyrocket. The VP in charge of Financial Affairs feels that current projections (based on a linear model) do not warrant the level of expansion you propose. **How can you persuade the VP that those projections do not fit the data convincingly?**

Jeff Titcomb/Photographer's Choice / Getty Images

39

Introduction

To analyze recent trends in spending on Internet advertising and to make reasonable projections, we need a mathematical model of this spending. Where do we start? To apply mathematics to real-world situations like this, we need a good understanding of basic mathematical concepts. Perhaps the most fundamental of these concepts is that of a function: a relationship that shows how one quantity depends on another. Functions may be described numerically and, often, algebraically. They can also be described graphically—a viewpoint that is extremely useful.

The simplest functions—the ones with the simplest formulas and the simplest graphs—are linear functions. Because of their simplicity, they are also among the most useful functions and can often be used to model real-world situations, at least over short periods of time. In discussing linear functions, we will meet the concepts of slope and rate of change, which are the starting point of the mathematics of change.

In the last section of this chapter, we discuss *simple linear regression*: construction of linear functions that best fit given collections of data. Regression is used extensively in applied mathematics, statistics, and quantitative methods in business. The inclusion of regression utilities in computer spreadsheets like Excel® makes this powerful mathematical tool readily available for anyone to use.

algebra Review

For this chapter, you should be familiar with real numbers and intervals. To review this material, see **Chapter 0.**

1.1 Functions from the Numerical, Algebraic, and Graphical Viewpoints

The following table gives the approximate number of Facebook users at various times since its establishment early in 2004.[1]

Year t (Since start of 2004)	0	1	2	3	4	5	6
Facebook Members n (Millions)	0	1	5.5	12	58	150	450

Let's write $n(0)$ for the number of members (in millions) at time $t = 0$, $n(1)$ for the number at time $t = 1$, and so on (we read $n(0)$ as "n of 0"). Thus, $n(0) = 0$, $n(1) = 1$, $n(2) = 5.5, \ldots, n(6) = 450$. In general, we write $n(t)$ for the number of members (in millions) at time t. We call n a **function** of the variable t, meaning that for each value of t between 0 and 6, n gives us a single corresponding number $n(t)$ (the number of members at that time).

In general, we think of a function as a way of producing new objects from old ones. The functions we deal with in this text produce new numbers from old numbers. The numbers we have in mind are the *real* numbers, including not only positive and negative integers and fractions but also numbers like $\sqrt{2}$ or π. (See Chapter 0 for more on real numbers.) For this reason, the functions we use are called **real-valued functions of a real variable**. For example, the function n takes the year since the start of 2004 as input and returns the number of Facebook members as output (Figure 1).

Year
t

n

$n(t)$
Members

Figure 1

[1]Sources: www.facebook.com, www.insidefacebook.com.

The variable t is called the **independent variable**, while n is called the **dependent variable** as its value depends on t. A function may be specified in several different ways. Here, we have specified the function n **numerically** by giving the values of the function for a number of values of the independent variable, as in the preceding table.

Q : *For which values of t does it make sense to ask for n(t)? In other words, for which years t is the function n defined?*

A : Because $n(t)$ refers to the number of members from the start of 2004 to the start of 2010, $n(t)$ is defined when t is any number between 0 and 6, that is, when $0 \le t \le 6$. Using interval notation (see Chapter 0), we can say that $n(t)$ is defined when t is in the interval [0, 6].

The set of values of the independent variable for which a function is defined is called its **domain** and is a necessary part of the definition of the function. Notice that the preceding table gives the value of $n(t)$ at only some of the infinitely many possible values in the domain [0, 6]. The domain of a function is not always specified explicitly; if no domain is specified for the function f, we take the domain to be the largest set of numbers x for which $f(x)$ makes sense. This "largest possible domain" is sometimes called the **natural domain**.

The previous Facebook data can also be represented on a graph by plotting the given pairs of numbers $(t, n(t))$ in the xy-plane. (See Figure 2. We have connected successive points by line segments.) In general, the **graph** of a function f consists of all points $(x, f(x))$ in the plane with x in the domain of f.

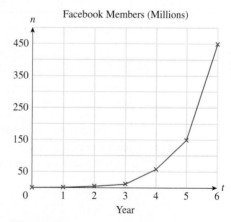

Figure 2

In Figure 2 we specified the function n **graphically** by using a graph to display its values. Suppose now that we had only the graph without the table of data. We could use the graph to find approximate values of n. For instance, to find $n(5)$ from the graph, we do the following:

1. Find the desired value of t at the bottom of the graph ($t = 5$ in this case).

2. Estimate the height (n-coordinate) of the corresponding point on the graph (around 150 in this case).

Thus, $n(5) \approx 150$ million members.*

✱ In a graphically defined function, we can never know the y-coordinates of points exactly; no matter how accurately a graph is drawn, we can obtain only *approximate* values of the coordinates of points. That is why we have been using the word *estimate* rather than *calculate* and why we say $n(5) \approx 150$ rather than $n(5) = 150$.

In some cases we may be able to use an algebraic formula to calculate the function, and we say that the function is specified **algebraically**. These are not the only ways in which a function can be specified; for instance, it could also be specified **verbally**, as in "Let $n(t)$ be the number of Facebook members, in millions, t years since the start of 2004."[*] Notice that any function can be represented graphically by plotting the points $(x, f(x))$ for a number of values of x in its domain.

Here is a summary of the terms we have just introduced.

[*] Specifying a function verbally in this way is useful for understanding what the function is doing, but it gives no numerical information.

Functions

A **real-valued function** f of a **real-valued variable** x assigns to each real number x in a specified set of numbers, called the **domain** of f, a unique real number $f(x)$, read "f of x." The variable x is called the **independent variable**, and f is called the **dependent variable**. A function is usually specified **numerically** using a table of values, **graphically** using a graph, or **algebraically** using a formula. The **graph of a function** consists of all points $(x, f(x))$ in the plane with x in the domain of f.

Quick Examples

1. **A function specified numerically:** Take $c(t)$ to be the world emission of carbon dioxide in year t since 2000, represented by the following table:[2]

t (Year Since 2000)	$c(t)$ (Billion Metric Tons of CO_2)
0	24
5	28
10	31
15	33
20	36
25	38
30	41

The domain of c is [0, 30], the independent variable is t, the number of years since 2000, and the dependent variable is c, the world production of carbon dioxide in a given year. Some values of c are:

$c(0) = 24$ 24 billion metric tons of CO_2 were produced in 2000.

$c(10) = 31$ 31 billion metric tons of CO_2 were produced in 2010.

$c(30) = 41$ 41 billion metric tons of CO_2 were projected to be produced in 2030.

[2]Figures for 2015 and later are projections. Source: Energy Information Administration (EIA) (www.eia.doe.gov)

Graph of c: Plotting the pairs $(t, c(t))$ gives the following graph:

2. A function specified graphically: Take $m(t)$ to be the median U.S. home price in thousands of dollars, t years since 2000, as represented by the following graph:[3]

The domain of m is $[0, 14]$, the independent variable is t, the number of years since 2000, and the dependent variable is m, the median U.S. home price in thousands of dollars. Some values of m are:

$m(2) \approx 180$ The median home price in 2002 was about $180,000.

$m(10) \approx 210.$ The median home price in 2010 was about $210,000.

3. A function specified algebraically: Let $f(x) = \frac{1}{x}$. The function f is specified algebraically. The independent variable is x and the dependent variable is f. The natural domain of f consists of all real numbers except zero because $f(x)$ makes sense for all values of x other than $x = 0$. Some specific values of f are

$$f(2) = \frac{1}{2} \qquad f(3) = \frac{1}{3} \qquad f(-1) = \frac{1}{-1} = -1$$

$f(0)$ is not defined because 0 is not in the domain of f.

---

[3]Source for data through end of 2010: www.zillow.com/local-info.

4. The graph of a function: Let $f(x) = x^2$, with domain the set of all real numbers. To draw the graph of f, first choose some convenient values of x in the domain and compute the corresponding y-coordinates $f(x)$:

x	-3	-2	-1	0	1	2	3
$f(x) = x^2$	9	4	1	0	1	4	9

Plotting these points $(x, f(x))$ gives the picture on the left, suggesting the graph on the right.*

✱ If you plot more points, you will find that they lie on a smooth curve as shown. That is why we did not use line segments to connect the points.

(This particular curve happens to be called a **parabola**, and its lowest point, at the origin, is called its **vertex**.)

EXAMPLE 1 **iPod Sales**

The total number of iPods sold by Apple up to the end of year x can be approximated by

$$f(x) = 4x^2 + 16x + 2 \text{ million iPods } (0 \leq x \leq 6),$$

where $x = 0$ represents 2003.[4]

a. What is the domain of f? Compute $f(0)$, $f(2)$, $f(4)$, and $f(6)$. What do these answers tell you about iPod sales? Is $f(-1)$ defined?

b. Compute $f(a)$, $f(-b)$, $f(a + h)$, and $f(a) + h$ assuming that the quantities a, $-b$, and $a + h$ are in the domain of f.

c. Sketch the graph of f. Does the shape of the curve suggest that iPod sales were accelerating or decelerating?

Solution

a. The domain of f is the set of numbers x with $0 \leq x \leq 6$—that is, the interval $[0, 6]$. If we substitute 0 for x in the formula for $f(x)$, we get

$$f(0) = 4(0)^2 + 16(0) + 2 = 2.$$ By the end of 2003 approximately 2 million iPods had been sold.

---

[4]Source for data: Apple quarterly earnings reports at www.apple.com/investor/.

Similarly,

$$f(2) = 4(2)^2 + 16(2) + 2 = 50$$ By the end of 2005 approximately 50 million iPods had been sold.

$$f(4) = 4(4)^2 + 16(4) + 2 = 130$$ By the end of 2007 approximately 130 million iPods had been sold.

$$f(6) = 4(6)^2 + 16(6) + 2 = 242.$$ By the end of 2009 approximately 242 million iPods had been sold.

As -1 is not in the domain of f, $f(-1)$ is not defined.

b. To find $f(a)$ we substitute a for x in the formula for $f(x)$ to get

$$f(a) = 4a^2 + 16a + 2.$$ Substitute a for x.

Similarly,

$$f(-b) = 4(-b)^2 + 16(-b) + 2$$ Substitute $-b$ for x.
$$= 4b^2 - 16b + 2$$ $(-b)^2 = b^2$

$$f(a + h) = 4(a + h)^2 + 16(a + h) + 2$$ Substitute $(a + h)$ for x.
$$= 4(a^2 + 2ah + h^2) + 16a + 16h + 2$$ Expand.
$$= 4a^2 + 8ah + 4h^2 + 16a + 16h + 2$$

$$f(a) + h = 4a^2 + 16a + 2 + h.$$ Add h to $f(a)$.

Note how we placed parentheses around the quantities at which we evaluated the function. If we tried to do without any of these parentheses we would likely get an error:

Correct expression: $f(a + h) = 4(a + h)^2 + 16(a + h) + 2.$ ✓

NOT $4a + h^2 + 16a + h + 2x$

Also notice the distinction between $f(a + h)$ and $f(a) + h$: To find $f(a + h)$, we replace x by the quantity $(a + h)$; to find $f(a) + h$ we add h to $f(a)$.

c. To draw the graph of f we plot points of the form $(x, f(x))$ for several values of x in the domain of f. Let us use the values we computed in part (a):

x	0	2	4	6
$f(x) = 4x^2 + 16x + 2$	2	50	130	242

Graphing these points gives the graph shown in Figure 3, suggesting the curve shown on the right.

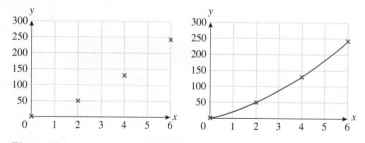

Figure 3

The graph becomes more steep as we move from left to right, suggesting that iPod sales were accelerating.

---

using Technology

See the Technology Guides at the end of the chapter for detailed instructions on how to obtain the table of values and graph in Example 1 using a TI-83/84 Plus or Excel. Here is an outline:

TI-83/84 Plus
Table of values:
Y₁=4X^2+16X+2
2ND TABLE .
Graph: WINDOW ;
Xmin = 0, Xmax = 6
ZOOM 0 .
[More details on page 114.]

Spreadsheet
Table of values: Headings x and $f(x)$ in A1–B1; x-values 0, 2, 4, 6 in A2–A5.
=4*A2^2+16*A2+2
in B2; copy down through B5.
Graph: Highlight A1 through B5 and insert a Scatter chart. [More details on page 119.]

 Website
www.WanerMath.com
Go to the Function Evaluator and Grapher under Online Utilities, and enter
4x^2+16x+2
for y_1. To obtain a table of values, enter the x-values 0, 1, 2, 3 in the Evaluator box, and press "Evaluate" at the top of the box. Graph: Set Xmin = 0, Xmax = 6, and press "Plot Graphs".

⇒ **Before we go on...** The following table compares the value of f in Example 1 with the actual sales figures:

x	0	2	4	6
$f(x) = 4x^2 + 16x + 2$	2	50	130	242
Actual iPod Sales (Millions)	2	32	141	240

The actual figures are only stated here for (some) integer values of x; for instance, $x = 4$ gives the total sales up to the end of 2007. But what were, for instance, the sales through June of 2008 ($x = 4.5$)? This is where our formula comes in handy: We can use the formula for f to **interpolate**—that is, to find sales at values of x other than those between values that are stated:

$$f(4.5) = 4(4.5)^2 + 16(4.5) + 2 = 155 \text{ million iPods.}$$

We can also use the formula to **extrapolate**—that is, to predict sales at values of x *outside* the domain—say, for $x = 6.5$ (that is, sales through June 2009):

$$f(6.5) = 4(6.5)^2 + 16(6.5) + 2 = 275 \text{ million iPods.}$$

As a general rule, extrapolation is far less reliable than interpolation: Predicting the future from current data is difficult, especially given the vagaries of the marketplace.

We call the algebraic function f an **algebraic model** of iPod sales because it uses an algebraic formula to model—or mathematically represent (approximately)—the annual sales. The particular kind of algebraic model we used is called a **quadratic model**. (See the end of this section for the names of some commonly used models.) ∎

Functions and Equations

Instead of using the usual "function notation" to specify a function, as in, say,

$$f(x) = 4x^2 + 16x + 2, \qquad \text{Function notation}$$

we could have specified it by an equation by replacing $f(x)$ by y:

$$y = 4x^2 + 16x + 2 \qquad \text{Equation notation}$$

(the choice of the letter y is a convention, but any letter will do).

Technically, $y = 4x^2 + 16x + 2$ is an equation and not a function. However, an equation of this type, $y = $ *Expression in x*, can be thought of as "specifying y as a function of x." When we specify a function in this way, the variable x is the independent variable and y is the dependent variable.

We could also write the above function as $f = 4x^2 + 16x + 2$, in which case the dependent variable would be f.

Quick Example

* We will discuss cost functions more fully in the next section.

If the cost to manufacture x items is given by the "cost function"* C specified by

$$C(x) = 40x + 2{,}000, \qquad \text{Cost function}$$

we could instead write

$$C = 40x + 2{,}000 \qquad \text{Cost equation}$$

and think of C, the cost, as a function of x.

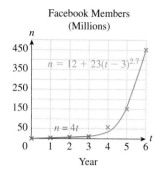

Figure 4

Function notation and equation notation, sometimes using the same letter for the function name and the dependent variable, are often used interchangeably. It is important to be able to switch back and forth between function notation and equation notation, and we shall do so when it is convenient.

Look again at the graph of the number of Facebook users in Figure 2. From year 0 through year 3 the membership appears to increase more-or-less linearly (that is, the graph is almost a straight line), but then curves upward quite sharply from year 3 to year 6. This behavior can be modeled by using two different functions: one for the interval [0, 3] and another for the interval [3, 6] (see Figure 4).

A function specified by two or more different formulas like this is called a **piecewise-defined function**.

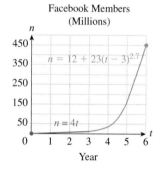

Figure 5

EXAMPLE 2 **A Piecewise-Defined Function: Facebook Membership**

The number $n(t)$ of Facebook members can be approximated by the following function of time t in years ($t = 0$ represents January 2004):

$$n(t) = \begin{cases} 4t & \text{if } 0 \le t \le 3 \\ 12 + 23(t-3)^{2.7} & \text{if } 3 < t \le 6 \end{cases} \quad \text{million members.}$$

What was the approximate membership of Facebook in January 2005, January 2007, and June 2009? Sketch the graph of n by plotting several points.

Solution We evaluate the given function at the corresponding values of t:

Jan. 2005 ($t = 1$):　$n(1) = 4(1) = 4$　　　Use the first formula because $0 \le t \le 3$.

Jan. 2007 ($t = 3$):　$n(3) = 4(3) = 12$　　　Use the first formula because $0 \le t \le 3$.

June 2009 ($t = 5.5$): $n(5.5) = 12 + 23(5.5 - 3)^{2.7} \approx 285$.　Use the second formula because $3 < t \le 6$.

Thus, the number of Facebook members was approximately 4 million in January 2005, 12 million in January 2007, and 285 million in June 2009.

To sketch the graph of n we use a table of rounded values of $n(t)$ (some of which we have already calculated above), plot the points, and connect them to sketch the graph:

t	0	1	2	3	4	5	6
$n(t)$	0	4	8	12	35	161	459

First Formula　　　　　Second Formula

The graph (Figure 5) has the following features:

1. The first formula (the line) is used for $0 \le t \le 3$.

2. The second formula (ascending curve) is used for $3 < t \le 6$.

3. The domain is [0, 6], so the graph is cut off at $t = 0$ and $t = 6$.

4. The heavy solid dots at the ends indicate the endpoints of the domain.

☰ using Technology

See the Technology Guides at the end of the chapter for detailed instructions on how to obtain the table of values and graph in Example 2 using a TI-83/84 Plus or Excel. Here is an outline:

TI-83/84 Plus
Table of values:
$Y_1 = (X \le 3) * (4X) + (X > 3) *$
$(12 + 23 * \text{abs}(X-3)^\wedge 2.7)$
2ND TABLE .
Graph: WINDOW ; Xmin = 0,
Xmax = 6; ZOOM 0 .
[More details on page 114.]

Spreadsheet
Table of values: Headings t and $n(t)$ in A1–B1; t-values 0, 1, . . . , 6 in A2–A8.
$= (A2 <= 3) * (4 * A2) + (A2 > 3) *$
$(12 + 23 * \text{abs}(A2-3)^\wedge 2.7)$
in B2; copy down through B8.
Graph: Highlight A1 through B8 and insert a Scatter chart.
[More details on page 120.]

EXAMPLE 3 **More Complicated Piecewise-Defined Functions**

Let f be the function specified by

$$f(x) = \begin{cases} -1 & \text{if } -4 \le x < -1 \\ x & \text{if } -1 \le x \le 1 \\ x^2 - 1 & \text{if } 1 < x \le 2 \end{cases}.$$

a. What is the domain of f? Find $f(-2)$, $f(-1)$, $f(0)$, $f(1)$, and $f(2)$.

b. Sketch the graph of f.

Solution

a. The domain of f is $[-4, 2]$, because $f(x)$ is specified only when $-4 \le x \le 2$.

$$f(-2) = -1 \qquad \text{We used the first formula because } -4 \le x < -1.$$
$$f(-1) = -1 \qquad \text{We used the second formula because } -1 \le x \le 1.$$
$$f(0) = 0 \qquad \text{We used the second formula because } -1 \le x \le 1.$$
$$f(1) = 1 \qquad \text{We used the second formula because } -1 \le x \le 1.$$
$$f(2) = 2^2 - 1 = 3 \qquad \text{We used the third formula because } 1 < x \le 2.$$

b. To sketch the graph by hand, we first sketch the three graphs $y = -1$, $y = x$, and $y = x^2 - 1$, and then use the appropriate portion of each (Figure 6).

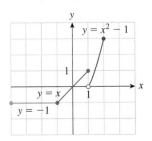

Figure 6

Note that solid dots indicate points on the graph, whereas the open dots indicate points not on the graph. For example, when $x = 1$, the inequalities in the formula tell us that we are to use the middle formula (x) rather than the bottom one ($x^2 - 1$). Thus, $f(1) = 1$, not 0, so we place a solid dot at $(1, 1)$ and an open dot at $(1, 0)$.

Vertical Line Test

Every point in the graph of a function has the form $(x, f(x))$ for some x in the domain of f. Because f assigns a *single* value $f(x)$ to each value of x in the domain, it follows that, in the graph of f, there should be only one y corresponding to any such value of x—namely, $y = f(x)$. In other words, *the graph of a function cannot contain two or more points with the same x-coordinate—that is, two or more points on the same vertical line*. On the other hand, a vertical line at a value of x not in the domain will not contain any points in the graph. This gives us the following rule.

Vertical-Line Test

For a graph to be the graph of a function, every vertical line must intersect the graph in *at most* one point.

Quick Examples

As illustrated below, only graph B passes the vertical line test, so only graph B is the graph of a function.

Table 1 lists some common types of functions that are often used to model real world situations.

Table 1 A Compendium of Functions and Their Graphs

Type of Function	*Examples*	
Linear $f(x) = mx + b$ m, b constant Graphs of linear functions are straight lines. The quantity m is the **slope** of the line; the quantity b is the **y-intercept** of the line. [See Section 1.3.] Technology formulas:	$y = x$ x	$y = -2x + 2$ $-2*x+2$
Quadratic $f(x) = ax^2 + bx + c$ a, b, c constant $(a \neq 0)$ Graphs of quadratic functions are called **parabolas**. Technology formulas:	$y = x^2$ x^2	$y = -2x^2 + 2x + 4$ $-2*x^2+2*x+4$
Cubic $f(x) = ax^3 + bx^2 + cx + d$ a, b, c, d constant $(a \neq 0)$ Technology formulas:	$y = x^3$ x^3	$y = -x^3 + 3x^2 + 1$ $-x^3+3*x^2+1$
Polynomial $f(x) = ax^n + bx^{n-1} + \ldots + rx + s$ $a, b, \ldots, r, s$ constant (includes all of the above functions) Technology formula:	All the above, and $$f(x) = x^6 - 2x^5 - 2x^4 + 4x^2$$ x^6-2x^5-2x^4+4x^2	

Table 1 (*Continued*)

Type of Function	Examples
Exponential $f(x) = Ab^x$ A, b constant $(b > 0$ and $b \neq 1)$ The y-coordinate is multiplied by b every time x increases by 1.	$y = 2^x$ $\qquad\qquad$ $y = 4(0.5)^x$ y is doubled every time x increases by 1. $\qquad$ y is halved every time x increases by 1.
Technology formulas:	`2^x` $\qquad\qquad$ `4*0.5^x`
Rational $f(x) = \dfrac{P(x)}{Q(x)};$ $P(x)$ and $Q(x)$ polynomials The graph of $y = 1/x$ is a **hyperbola**. The domain excludes zero because $1/0$ is not defined.	$y = \dfrac{1}{x}$ $\qquad\qquad$ $y = \dfrac{x}{x - 1}$
Technology formulas:	`1/x` $\qquad\qquad$ `x/(x-1)`
Absolute value For x positive or zero, the graph of $y = |x|$ is the same as that of $y = x$. For x negative or zero, it is the same as that of $y = -x$.	$y = |x|$ $\qquad\qquad$ $y = |2x + 2|$
Technology formulas:	`abs(x)` $\qquad\qquad$ `abs(2*x+2)`
Square Root The domain of $y = \sqrt{x}$ must be restricted to the nonnegative numbers, because the square root of a negative number is not real. Its graph is the top half of a horizontally oriented parabola.	$y = \sqrt{x}$ $\qquad\qquad$ $y = \sqrt{4x - 2}$
Technology formulas:	`x^0.5 or √(x)` $\qquad$ `(4*x-2)^0.5 or √(4*x-2)`

Go to the Website and follow the path

Online Text

→ New Functions from Old: Scaled and Shifted Functions

where you will find complete online interactive text, examples, and exercises on scaling and translating the graph of a function by changing the formula.

Functions and models other than linear ones are called **nonlinear**.

1.1   EXERCISES

▼ more advanced   ◆ challenging
T indicates exercises that should be solved using technology

In Exercises 1–4, evaluate or estimate each expression based on the following table. HINT [See Quick Example 1 on page 42.]

x	-3	-2	-1	0	1	2	3
$f(x)$	1	2	4	2	1	0.5	0.25

1. a. $f(0)$ **b.** $f(2)$ **2. a.** $f(-1)$ **b.** $f(1)$
3. a. $f(2) - f(-2)$ **b.** $f(-1)f(-2)$ **c.** $-2f(-1)$
4. a. $f(1) - f(-1)$ **b.** $f(1)f(-2)$ **c.** $3f(-2)$

In Exercises 5–8, use the graph of the function f to find approximations of the given values. HINT [See Example 1.]

5.

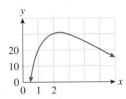

a. $f(1)$ **b.** $f(2)$
c. $f(3)$ **d.** $f(5)$
e. $f(3) - f(2)$

6.

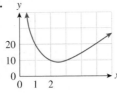

a. $f(1)$ **b.** $f(2)$
c. $f(3)$ **d.** $f(5)$
e. $f(3) - f(2)$

7.

a. $f(-3)$ **b.** $f(0)$
c. $f(1)$ **d.** $f(2)$
e. $\dfrac{f(2) - f(1)}{2 - 1}$

8.

a. $f(-2)$ **b.** $f(0)$
c. $f(1)$ **d.** $f(3)$
e. $\dfrac{f(3) - f(1)}{3 - 1}$

In Exercises 9–12, say whether or not $f(x)$ is defined for the given values of x. If it is defined, give its value. HINT [See Quick Example 3 on page 43.]

9. $f(x) = x - \dfrac{1}{x^2}$, with domain $(0, +\infty)$
   a. $x = 4$ **b.** $x = 0$ **c.** $x = -1$

10. $f(x) = \dfrac{2}{x} - x^2$, with domain $[2, +\infty)$
   a. $x = 4$ **b.** $x = 0$ **c.** $x = 1$

11. $f(x) = \sqrt{x + 10}$, with domain $[-10, 0)$
   a. $x = 0$ **b.** $x = 9$ **c.** $x = -10$

12. $f(x) = \sqrt{9 - x^2}$, with domain $(-3, 3)$
   a. $x = 0$ **b.** $x = 3$ **c.** $x = -3$

13. Given $f(x) = 4x - 3$, find **a.** $f(-1)$ **b.** $f(0)$
   c. $f(1)$ **d.** $f(y)$ **e.** $f(a + b)$ HINT [See Example 1.]

14. Given $f(x) = -3x + 4$, find
   a. $f(-1)$ **b.** $f(0)$ **c.** $f(1)$ **d.** $f(y)$ **e.** $f(a + b)$

15. Given $f(x) = x^2 + 2x + 3$, find
   a. $f(0)$ **b.** $f(1)$ **c.** $f(-1)$ **d.** $f(-3)$
   e. $f(a)$ **f.** $f(x + h)$ HINT [See Example 1.]

16. Given $g(x) = 2x^2 - x + 1$, find
   a. $g(0)$ **b.** $g(-1)$ **c.** $g(r)$ **d.** $g(x + h)$

17. Given $g(s) = s^2 + \dfrac{1}{s}$, find
   a. $g(1)$ **b.** $g(-1)$ **c.** $g(4)$ **d.** $g(x)$ **e.** $g(s + h)$
   f. $g(s + h) - g(s)$

18. Given $h(r) = \dfrac{1}{r + 4}$, find
   a. $h(0)$ **b.** $h(-3)$ **c.** $h(-5)$ **d.** $h(x^2)$
   e. $h(x^2 + 1)$ **f.** $h(x^2) + 1$

In Exercises 19–24, graph the given functions. Give the technology formula and use technology to check your graph. We suggest that you become familiar with these graphs in addition to those in Table 1. HINT [See Quick Example 4 on page 44.]

19. $f(x) = -x^3$ (domain $(-\infty, +\infty)$)
20. $f(x) = x^3$ (domain $[0, +\infty)$)
21. $f(x) = x^4$ (domain $(-\infty, +\infty)$)
22. $f(x) = \sqrt[3]{x}$ (domain $(-\infty, +\infty)$)
23. $f(x) = \dfrac{1}{x^2}$ $(x \neq 0)$ **24.** $f(x) = x + \dfrac{1}{x}$ $(x \neq 0)$

In Exercises 25 and 26, match the functions to the graphs. Using technology to draw the graphs is suggested, but not required.

25. T **a.** $f(x) = x$ $(-1 \leq x \leq 1)$
   b. $f(x) = -x$ $(-1 \leq x \leq 1)$
   c. $f(x) = \sqrt{x}$ $(0 < x < 4)$
   d. $f(x) = x + \dfrac{1}{x} - 2$ $(0 < x < 4)$
   e. $f(x) = |x|$ $(-1 \leq x \leq 1)$
   f. $f(x) = x - 1$ $(-1 \leq x \leq 1)$

(I)

(II)

(III)

(IV)

(V)

(VI)

26. ▢ **a.** $f(x) = -x + 4$ $(0 < x \le 4)$
   b. $f(x) = 2 - |x|$ $(-2 < x \le 2)$
   c. $f(x) = \sqrt{x + 2}$ $(-2 < x \le 2)$
   d. $f(x) = -x^2 + 2$ $(-2 < x \le 2)$
   e. $f(x) = \dfrac{1}{x} - 1$ $(0 < x \le 4)$
   f. $f(x) = x^2 - 1$ $(-2 < x \le 2)$

(I)

(II)

(III)

(IV)

(V)

(VI)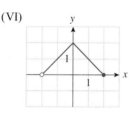

▢ In Exercises 27–30, first give the technology formula for the given function and then use technology to evaluate the function for the given values of x (when defined there).

27. ▢ $f(x) = 0.1x^2 - 4x + 5$; $x = 0, 1, \ldots, 10$

28. ▢ $g(x) = 0.4x^2 - 6x - 0.1$; $x = -5, -4, \ldots, 4, 5$

29. ▢ $h(x) = \dfrac{x^2 - 1}{x^2 + 1}$; $x = 0.5, 1.5, 2.5, \ldots, 10.5$ (Round all answers to four decimal places.)

30. ▢ $r(x) = \dfrac{2x^2 + 1}{2x^2 - 1}$; $x = -1, 0, 1, \ldots, 9$ (Round all answers to four decimal places.)

In Exercises 31–36, sketch the graph of the given function, evaluate the given expressions, and then use technology to duplicate the graphs. Give the technology formula. HINT [See Example 2.]

31. $f(x) = \begin{cases} x & \text{if } -4 \le x < 0 \\ 2 & \text{if } 0 \le x \le 4 \end{cases}$
   a. $f(-1)$ **b.** $f(0)$ **c.** $f(1)$

32. $f(x) = \begin{cases} -1 & \text{if } -4 \le x \le 0 \\ x & \text{if } 0 < x \le 4 \end{cases}$
   a. $f(-1)$ **b.** $f(0)$ **c.** $f(1)$

33. $f(x) = \begin{cases} x^2 & \text{if } -2 < x \le 0 \\ 1/x & \text{if } 0 < x \le 4 \end{cases}$
   a. $f(-1)$ **b.** $f(0)$ **c.** $f(1)$

34. $f(x) = \begin{cases} -x^2 & \text{if } -2 < x \le 0 \\ \sqrt{x} & \text{if } 0 < x < 4 \end{cases}$
   a. $f(-1)$ **b.** $f(0)$ **c.** $f(1)$

35. $f(x) = \begin{cases} x & \text{if } -1 < x \le 0 \\ x + 1 & \text{if } 0 < x \le 2 \\ x & \text{if } 2 < x \le 4 \end{cases}$
   a. $f(0)$ **b.** $f(1)$ **c.** $f(2)$ **d.** $f(3)$ HINT [See Example 3.]

36. $f(x) = \begin{cases} -x & \text{if } -1 < x < 0 \\ x - 2 & \text{if } 0 \le x \le 2 \\ -x & \text{if } 2 < x \le 4 \end{cases}$
   a. $f(0)$ **b.** $f(1)$ **c.** $f(2)$ **d.** $f(3)$

In Exercises 37–40, find and simplify **(a)** $f(x + h) - f(x)$
(b) $\dfrac{f(x + h) - f(x)}{h}$

37. ▼ $f(x) = x^2$

38. ▼ $f(x) = 3x - 1$

39. ▼ $f(x) = 2 - x^2$

40. ▼ $f(x) = x^2 + x$

APPLICATIONS

41. *Petrochemical Sales: Mexico* The following table shows annual petrochemical sales in Mexico by **Pemex**, Mexico's national oil company, for 2005–2010 ($t = 0$ represents 2005):[5]

Year t (Year since 2005)	0	1	2	3	4	5
Petrochemical Sales s (Billion metric tons)	3.7	3.8	4.0	4.1	4.0	4.1

   a. Find $s(1)$, $s(4)$, and $s(5)$. Interpret your answers.
   b. What is the domain of s?
   c. Represent s graphically and use your graph to estimate $s(1.5)$. Interpret your answer. HINT [See Quick Example 1 on page 42.]

[5]2010 figure is a projection based on data through May 2010. Source: www.pemex.com (July 2010).

42. *Petrochemical Production: Mexico* The following table shows annual petrochemical production in Mexico by **Pemex**, Mexico's national oil company, for 2005–2010 ($t = 0$ represents 2005):[6]

Year t (Year since 2005)	0	1	2	3	4	5
Petrochemical Production p (Billion metric tons)	10.8	11.0	11.8	12.0	12.0	13.3

a. Find $p(0)$, $p(2)$, and $p(4)$. Interpret your answers.
b. What is the domain of p?
c. Represent p graphically and use your graph to estimate $p(2.5)$. Interpret your answer. HINT [See Quick Example 1 on page 42]

Housing Starts *Exercises 43–46 refer to the following graph, which shows the number f(t) of housing starts in the U.S. each year from 2000 through 2010 (t = 0 represents 2000, and f(t) is the number of housing starts in year t in thousands of units).*[7]

Housing starts (Thousands)

43. Estimate $f(4)$, $f(5)$, and $f(7.5)$. Interpret your answers.

44. Estimate $f(3)$, $f(6)$, and $f(8.5)$. Interpret your answers.

45. Which has the larger magnitude: $f(5) - f(0)$ or $f(8) - f(0)$? Interpret the answer.

46. Which has the larger magnitude: $f(5) - f(0)$ or $f(9) - f(7)$? Interpret the answer.

47. *Airline Net Income* The following graph shows the approximate annual after-tax net income $P(t)$, in millions of dollars, of **Continental Airlines** for 2005–2009 ($t = 0$ represents 2005):[8]

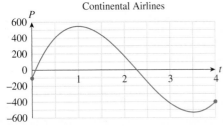

Continental Airlines

a. Estimate $P(0)$, $P(4)$, and $P(1.5)$ to the nearest 100. Interpret your answers.

b. At which of the following values of t is $P(t)$ *increasing* most rapidly: 0, 0.5, 1, 2.5, 3.5? Interpret the result.
c. At which of the following values of t is $P(t)$ *decreasing* most rapidly: 0, 0.5, 1, 2.5, 3.5? Interpret the result.

48. *Airline Net Income* The following graph shows the approximate annual after-tax net income $P(t)$, in millions of dollars, of **Delta Air Lines** for 2005–2009 ($t = 0$ represents 2005):[9]

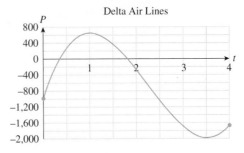

Delta Air Lines

a. Estimate $P(0)$, $P(1)$, and $P(3.5)$ to the nearest 100. Interpret your answers.

b. At which of the following values of t is $P(t)$ *increasing* most rapidly: 0, 0.5, 1, 2.5, 3.5? Interpret the result.

c. At which of the following values of t is $P(t)$ *decreasing* most rapidly: 0, 0.5, 1, 2.5, 3.5? Interpret the result.

49. *Trade with China* The value of U.S. trade with China from 1994 through 2004 can be approximated by
$$C(t) = 3t^2 - 7t + 50 \text{ billion dollars}$$
(t is time in years since 1994).[10]

a. Find an appropriate domain of C. Is $t \geq 0$ an appropriate domain? Why or why not?
b. Compute $C(10)$. What does the answer say about trade with China?

50. *Scientific Research* The number of research articles in *Physical Review* that were written by researchers in the United States from 1983 through 2003 can be approximated by
$$A(t) = -0.01\,t^2 + 0.24t + 3.4 \text{ hundred articles}$$
(t is time in years since 1983).[11]

a. Find an appropriate domain of A. Is $t \leq 20$ an appropriate domain? Why or why not?
b. Compute $A(10)$. What does the answer say about the number of research articles?

51. ▪ *Acquisition of Language* The percentage $p(t)$ of children who can speak in at least single words by the age of t months can be approximated by the equation[12]
$$p(t) = 100\left(1 - \frac{12{,}200}{t^{4.48}}\right) \quad (t \geq 8.5).$$

[6]*Ibid.*

[7]Sources for data: www.census.gov, www.forecast-chart.com

[8]"Net income" is an accounting term for profit (see Section 1.2). Model is the authors'. Source for data: Company reports.

[9]*Ibid.*

[10]Based on a regression by the authors. Source for data: U.S. Census Bureau/*New York Times*, September 23, 2004, p. C1.

[11]Based on a regression by the authors. Source for data: The American Physical Society/*New York Times*, May 3, 2003, p. A1.

[12]The model is the authors' and is based on data presented in the article *The Emergence of Intelligence* by William H. Calvin, *Scientific American*, October, 1994, pp. 101–107.

a. Give a technology formula for p.
b. Graph p for $8.5 \le t \le 20$ and $0 \le p \le 100$.
c. Create a table of values of p for $t = 9, 10, \ldots, 20$ (rounding answers to one decimal place).
d. What percentage of children can speak in at least single words by the age of 12 months?
e. By what age are 90% or more children speaking in at least single words?

52. ▣ *Acquisition of Language* The percentage $p(t)$ of children who can speak in sentences of five or more words by the age of t months can be approximated by the equation[13]

$$p(t) = 100 \left(1 - \frac{5.27 \times 10^{17}}{t^{12}}\right) \quad (t \ge 30).$$

a. Give a technology formula for p.
b. Graph p for $30 \le t \le 45$ and $0 \le p \le 100$.
c. Create a table of values of p for $t = 30, 31, \ldots, 40$ (rounding answers to one decimal place).
d. What percentage of children can speak in sentences of five or more words by the age of 36 months?
e. By what age are 75% or more children speaking in sentences of five or more words?

53. ▼ *Processor Speeds* The processor speed, in megahertz (MHz), of Intel processors during the period 1980–2010 could be approximated by the following function of time t in years since the start of 1980:[14]

$$v(t) = \begin{cases} 8(1.22)^t & \text{if } 0 \le t < 16 \\ 400t - 6{,}200 & \text{if } 16 \le t < 25 \\ 3{,}800 & \text{if } 25 \le t \le 30 \end{cases}$$

a. Evaluate $v(10)$, $v(16)$, and $v(28)$ and interpret the results.
b. Write down a technology formula for v.
c. ▣ Use technology to sketch the graph of v and to generate a table of values for $v(t)$ with $t = 0, 2, \ldots, 30$. (Round values to two significant digits.)
d. When, to the nearest year, did processor speeds reach 3 gigahertz (1 gigahertz = 1,000 megahertz) according to the model?

54. ▼ *Processor Speeds* The processor speed, in megahertz (MHz), of Intel processors during the period 1970–2000 could be approximated by the following function of time t in years since the start of 1970:[15]

$$v(t) = \begin{cases} 0.12t^2 + 0.04t + 0.2 & \text{if } 0 \le t < 12 \\ 1.1(1.22)^t & \text{if } 12 \le t < 26 \\ 400t - 10{,}200 & \text{if } 26 \le t \le 30 \end{cases}$$

a. Evaluate $v(2)$, $v(12)$, and $v(28)$ and interpret the results.
b. Write down a technology formula for v.
c. ▣ Use technology to sketch the graph of v and to generate a table of values for $v(t)$ with $t = 0, 2, \ldots, 30$. (Round values to two significant digits.)

[13]*Ibid.*

[14]Based on the fastest processors produced by Intel. Source for data: www.intel.com.

[15]*Ibid.*

d. When, to the nearest year, did processor speeds reach 500 megahertz?

55. ▼ *Income Taxes* The U.S. Federal income tax is a function of taxable income. Write $T(x)$ for the tax owed on a taxable income of x dollars. For tax year 2010, the function T for a single taxpayer was specified as follows:

If your taxable income was			*of the amount*
	But not		
Over...	*over...*	*Your tax is*	*over...*
$0	8,375	.... 10%	$0
8,375	34,000	$837.50 + 15%	$8,375
34,000	82,400	4,663.25 + 25%	$34,000
82,400	171,850	16,763.25 + 28%	$82,400
171,850	373,650	41,809.25 + 33%	$171,850
373,650	....	108,403.25 + 35%	$373,650

a. Represent T as a piecewise-defined function of income x. HINT [Each row of the table defines a formula with a condition.]
b. Use your function to compute the tax owed by a single taxpayer on a taxable income of $36,000.

56. ▼ *Income Taxes* Repeat Exercise 55 using the following information for tax year 2009.

If your taxable income was			*of the amount*
	But not		
Over...	*over...*	*Your tax is*	*over...*
$0	8,350	.... 10%	$0
8,350	33,950	$835.00 + 15%	$8,350
33,950	82,250	4,675.00 + 25%	$33,950
82,250	171,550	16,750.00 + 28%	$82,250
171,550	372,950	41,754.00 + 33%	$171,550
372,950	....	108,216.00 + 35%	$372,950

COMMUNICATION AND REASONING EXERCISES

57. Complete the following sentence: If the market price m of gold varies with time t, then the independent variable is ____ and the dependent variable is ____.

58. Complete the following sentence: If weekly profit P is specified as a function of selling price s, then the independent variable is ____ and the dependent variable is ____.

59. Complete the following: The function notation for the equation $y = 4x^2 - 2$ is ____.

60. Complete the following: The equation notation for $C(t) = -0.34t^2 + 0.1t$ is ____.

61. True or false? Every graphically specified function can also be specified numerically. Explain.

62. True or false? Every algebraically specified function can also be specified graphically. Explain.

63. True or false? Every numerically specified function with domain [0, 10] can also be specified algebraically. Explain.

64. True or false? Every graphically specified function can also be specified algebraically. Explain.

65. ▼ True or false? Every function can be specified numerically. Explain.

66. ▼ Which supplies more information about a situation: a numerical model or an algebraic model?

67. ▼ Why is the following assertion false? "If $f(x) = x^2 - 1$, then $f(x + h) = x^2 + h - 1$."

68. ▼ Why is the following assertion false? "If $f(2) = 2$ and $f(4) = 4$, then $f(3) = 3$."

69. How do the graphs of two functions differ if they are specified by the same formula but have different domains?

70. How do the graphs of two functions f and g differ if $g(x) = f(x) + 10$? (Try an example.)

71. ▼ How do the graphs of two functions f and g differ if $g(x) = f(x - 5)$? (Try an example.)

72. ▼ How do the graphs of two functions f and g differ if $g(x) = f(-x)$? (Try an example.)

1.2   Functions and Models

The functions we used in Examples 1 and 2 in Section 1.1 are **mathematical models** of real-life situations, because they model, or represent, situations in mathematical terms.

Mathematical Modeling

To mathematically model a situation means to represent it in mathematical terms. The particular representation used is called a **mathematical model** of the situation. Mathematical models do not always represent a situation perfectly or completely. Some (like Example 1 of Section 1.1) represent a situation only approximately, whereas others represent only some aspects of the situation.

Quick Examples

1. The temperature is now 10°F and increasing by 20° per hour.

   Model: $T(t) = 10 + 20t$ (t = time in hours, T = temperature)

2. I invest $1,000 at 5% interest compounded quarterly. Find the value of the investment after t years.

   Model: $A(t) = 1,000 \left(1 + \dfrac{0.05}{4}\right)^{4t}$ (This is the compound interest formula we will study in Example 6.)

3. I am fencing a rectangular area whose perimeter is 100 ft. Find the area as a function of the width x.

   Model: Take y to be the length, so the perimeter is
   $$100 = x + y + x + y = 2(x + y).$$
   This gives
   $$x + y = 50.$$
   Thus the length is $y = 50 - x$, and the area is
   $$A = xy = x(50 - x).$$

4. You work 8 hours a day Monday through Friday, 5 hours on Saturday, and have Sunday off. Model the number of hours you work as a function of the day of the week n, with $n = 1$ being Sunday.

Model: Take $f(n)$ to be the number of hours you work on the nth day of the week, so

$$f(n) = \begin{cases} 0 & \text{if } n = 1 \\ 8 & \text{if } 2 \le n \le 6 \\ 5 & \text{if } n = 7 \end{cases}.$$

Note that the domain of f is $\{1, 2, 3, 4, 5, 6, 7\}$—a discrete set rather than a continuous interval of the real line.

5. The function

$$f(x) = 4x^2 + 16x + 2 \text{ million iPods sold } (x = \text{years since 2003})$$

in Example 1 of Section 1.1 is a model of iPod sales.

6. The function

$$n(t) = \begin{cases} 4t & \text{if } 0 \le t \le 3 \\ 12 + 23(t - 3)^{2.7} & \text{if } 3 < t \le 6 \end{cases} \text{ million members}$$

(t = years since January 2004) in Example 2 of Section 1.1 is a model of Facebook membership.

Types of Models

Quick Examples 1–4 are **analytical models**, obtained by analyzing the situation being modeled, whereas Quick Examples 5 and 6 are **curve-fitting models**, obtained by finding mathematical formulas that approximate observed data. All the models except for Quick Example 4 are **continuous models**, defined by functions whose domains are intervals of the real line, whereas Quick Example 4 is a **discrete model** as its domain is a discrete set, as mentioned above. Discrete models are used extensively in probability and statistics.

Cost, Revenue, and Profit Models

EXAMPLE 1 Modeling Cost: Cost Function

As of August 2010, Yellow Cab Chicago's rates amounted to $2.05 on entering the cab plus $1.80 for each mile.[16]

a. Find the cost C of an x-mile trip.

b. Use your answer to calculate the cost of a 40-mile trip.

c. What is the cost of the second mile? What is the cost of the tenth mile?

d. Graph C as a function of x.

---

[16] According to their Web site at www.yellowcabchicago.com.

Solution

a. We are being asked to find how the cost C depends on the length x of the trip, or to find C as a function of x. Here is the cost in a few cases:

Cost of a 1-mile trip: $C = 1.80(1) + 2.05 = 3.85$ 1 mile at $1.80 per mile plus $2.05

Cost of a 2-mile trip: $C = 1.80(2) + 2.05 = 5.65$ 2 miles at $1.80 per mile plus $2.05

Cost of a 3-mile trip: $C = 1.80(3) + 2.05 = 7.45$ 3 miles at $1.80 per mile plus $2.05

Do you see the pattern? The cost of an x-mile trip is given by the linear function

$$C(x) = 1.80x + 2.05.$$

Notice that the cost function is a sum of two terms: The **variable cost** $1.80x$, which depends on x, and the **fixed cost** 2.05, which is independent of x:

$$\text{Cost} = \text{Variable Cost} + \text{Fixed Cost}.$$

The quantity 1.80 by itself is the incremental cost per mile; you might recognize it as the *slope* of the given linear function. In this context we call 1.80 the **marginal cost**. You might recognize the fixed cost 2.05 as the C-*intercept* of the given linear function.

b. We can use the formula for the cost function to calculate the cost of a 40-mile trip as

$$C(40) = 1.80(40) + 2.05 = \$74.05.$$

c. To calculate the cost of the second mile, we *could* proceed as follows:

Find the cost of a 1-mile trip: $C(1) = 1.80(1) + 2.05 = \$3.85$.

Find the cost of a 2-mile trip: $C(2) = 1.80(2) + 2.05 = \$5.65$.

Therefore, the cost of the second mile is $\$5.65 - \$3.85 = \$1.80$.

But notice that this is just the marginal cost. In fact, the marginal cost is the cost of each additional mile, so we could have done this more simply:

$$\text{Cost of second mile} = \text{Cost of tenth mile} = \text{Marginal cost} = \$1.80.$$

Figure 7

d. Figure 7 shows the graph of the cost function, which we can interpret as a *cost vs. miles* graph. The fixed cost is the starting height on the left, while the marginal cost is the slope of the line: It rises 1.80 units per unit of x. (See Section 1.3 for a discussion of properties of straight lines.)

➡ **Before we go on...** The cost function in Example 1 is an example of an *analytical model:* We derived the form of the cost function from a knowledge of the cost per mile and the fixed cost.

As we discussed in Section 1.1, we can specify the cost function in Example 1 using equation notation:

$$C = 1.80x + 2.05.$$ Equation notation

Here, the independent variable is x, and the dependent variable is C. (This is the notation we have used in Figure 7. Remember that we will often switch between function and equation notation when it is convenient to do so.) ∎

Here is a summary of some terms we used in Example 1, along with an introduction to some new terms:

Cost, Revenue, and Profit Functions

A **cost function** specifies the cost C as a function of the number of items x. Thus, $C(x)$ is the cost of x items, and has the form

$$\text{Cost} = \text{Variable cost} + \text{Fixed cost}$$

where the variable cost is a function of x and the fixed cost is a constant. A cost function of the form

$$C(x) = mx + b$$

is called a **linear cost function**; the variable cost is mx and the fixed cost is b. The slope m, the **marginal cost**, measures the incremental cost per item.

The **revenue**, or **net sales**, resulting from one or more business transactions is the total income received. If $R(x)$ is the revenue from selling x items at a price of m each, then R is the linear function $R(x) = mx$ and the selling price m can also be called the **marginal revenue**.

The **profit**, or **net income**, on the other hand, is what remains of the revenue when costs are subtracted. If the profit depends linearly on the number of items, the slope m is called the **marginal profit**. Profit, revenue, and cost are related by the following formula.

$$\text{Profit} = \text{Revenue} - \text{Cost}$$
$$P(x) = R(x) - C(x).^*$$

If the profit is negative, say −$500, we refer to a **loss** (of $500 in this case). To **break even** means to make neither a profit nor a loss. Thus, breakeven occurs when $P = 0$, or

$$R(x) = C(x). \qquad \text{Breakeven}$$

The **break-even point** is the number of items x at which breakeven occurs.

* We say that the profit function P is the **difference** between the revenue and cost functions, and express this fact as a formula about functions: $P = R - C$. (We will discuss this further when we talk about the algebra of functions at the end of this section.)

Quick Example

If the daily cost (including operating costs) of manufacturing x T-shirts is $C(x) = 8x + 100$, and the revenue obtained by selling x T-shirts is $R(x) = 10x$, then the daily profit resulting from the manufacture and sale of x T-shirts is

$$P(x) = R(x) - C(x) = 10x - (8x + 100) = 2x - 100.$$

Breakeven occurs when $P(x) = 0$, or $x = 50$.

EXAMPLE 2 Cost, Revenue, and Profit

The annual operating cost of *YSport* Fitness gym is estimated to be

$$C(x) = 100{,}000 + 160x - 0.2x^2 \text{ dollars} \qquad (0 \le x \le 400),$$

where x is the number of members. Annual revenue from membership averages $800 per member. What is the variable cost? What is the fixed cost? What is the profit function? How many members must *YSport* have to make a profit? What will happen if it has fewer members? If it has more?

Solution The variable cost is the part of the cost function that depends on x:

$$\text{Variable cost} = 160x - 0.2x^2.$$

The fixed cost is the constant term:

$$\text{Fixed cost} = 100,000.$$

The annual revenue *YSport* obtains from a single member is $800. So, if it has x members, it earns an annual revenue of

$$R(x) = 800x.$$

For the profit, we use the formula

$$
\begin{aligned}
P(x) &= R(x) - C(x) & &\text{Formula for profit} \\
&= 800x - (100,000 + 160x - 0.2x^2) & &\text{Substitute } R(x) \text{ and } C(x). \\
&= -100,000 + 640x + 0.2x^2.
\end{aligned}
$$

To make a profit, *YSport* needs to do better than break even, so let us find the break-even point: the value of x such that $P(x) = 0$. All we have to do is set $P(x) = 0$ and solve for x:

$$-100,000 + 640x + 0.2x^2 = 0.$$

Notice that we have a quadratic equation $ax^2 + bx + c = 0$ with $a = 0.2$, $b = 640$, and $c = -100,000$. Its solution is given by the quadratic formula:

using Technology

Excel has a feature called "Goal Seek," which can be used to find the point of intersection of the cost and revenue graphs numerically rather than graphically. See the downloadable Excel tutorial for this section at the Website.

$$
\begin{aligned}
x &= \frac{-b \pm \sqrt{b^2 - 4ac}}{2a} = \frac{-640 \pm \sqrt{640^2 + 4(0.2)(100,000)}}{2(0.2)} \\
&\approx \frac{-640 \pm 699.71}{2(0.2)} \\
&\approx 149.3 \text{ or } -3,349.3.
\end{aligned}
$$

We reject the negative solution (as the domain is $[0, 400]$) and conclude that $x \approx 149.3$ members. To make a profit, should *YSport* have 149 members or 150 members? To decide, take a look at Figure 8, which shows two graphs: On the left we see the graph of revenue and cost, and on the right we see the graph of the profit function.

Cost: $C(x) = 100,000 + 160x - 0.2x^2$
Revenue: $R(x) = 800x$
Breakeven occurs at the point of intersection
of the graphs of revenue and cost.

Profit: $P(x) = -100,000 + 640x + 0.2x^2$
Breakeven occurs when $P(x) = 0$

Figure 8

For values of x less than the break-even point of 149.3, $P(x)$ is negative, so the company will have a loss. For values of x greater than the break-even point, $P(x)$ is positive, so the company will make a profit. Thus, *YSport Fitness* needs at least 150 members to make a profit. (Note that we rounded 149.3 up to 150 in this case.)

Demand and Supply Models

The demand for a commodity usually goes down as its price goes up. It is traditional to use the letter q for the (quantity of) demand, as measured, for example, in sales. Consider the following example.

EXAMPLE 3 Demand: Private Schools

The demand for private schools in Michigan depends on the tuition cost and can be approximated by

$$q = 77.8p^{-0.11} \text{ thousand students} \qquad (200 \le p \le 2{,}200), \qquad \text{Demand curve}$$

where p is the net tuition cost in dollars.[17]

a. Use technology to plot the demand function.

b. What is the effect on demand if the tuition cost is increased from \$1,000 to \$1,500?

Solution

a. The demand function is given by $q(p) = 77.8p^{-0.11}$. Its graph is known as a **demand curve** (Figure 9).

b. The demand at tuition costs of \$1,000 and \$1,500 is

$$q(1{,}000) = 77.8(1{,}000)^{-0.11} \approx 36.4 \text{ thousand students}$$
$$q(1{,}500) = 77.8(1{,}500)^{-0.11} \approx 34.8 \text{ thousand students.}$$

The change in demand is therefore

$$q(1{,}500) - q(1{,}000) \approx 34.8 - 36.4 = -1.6 \text{ thousand students.}$$

Technology Formula:
```
y = 77.8x^(-0.11)
```

Figure 9

We have seen that a demand function gives the number of items consumers are willing to buy at a given price, and a higher price generally results in a lower demand. However, as the price rises, suppliers will be more inclined to produce these items (as opposed to spending their time and money on other products), so supply will generally rise. A **supply function** gives q, the number of items suppliers are willing to make available for sale*, as a function of p, the price per item.

✱ Although a bit confusing at first, it is traditional to use the same letter q for the quantity of supply and the quantity of demand, particularly when we want to compare them, as in the next example.

Demand, Supply, and Equilibrium Price

A **demand equation** or **demand function** expresses demand q (the number of items demanded) as a function of the unit price p (the price per item). A **supply equation** or **supply function** expresses supply q (the number of items a supplier is willing to make available) as a function of the unit price p (the price per item). It is usually the case that demand decreases and supply increases as the unit price increases.

---

[17] The tuition cost is net cost: tuition minus tax credit. The model is based on data in "The Universal Tuition Tax Credit: A Proposal to Advance Personal Choice in Education," Patrick L. Anderson, Richard McLellan, J.D., Joseph P. Overton, J.D., Gary Wolfram, Ph.D., Mackinac Center for Public Policy, www.mackinac.org/

Demand and supply are said to be in **equilibrium** when demand equals supply. The corresponding values of p and q are called the **equilibrium price** and **equilibrium demand**. To find the equilibrium price, determine the unit price p where the demand and supply curves cross (sometimes we can determine this value analytically by setting demand equal to supply and solving for p). To find the equilibrium demand, evaluate the demand (or supply) function at the equilibrium price.

Quick Example

If the demand for your exclusive T-shirts is $q = -20p + 800$ shirts sold per day and the supply is $q = 10p - 100$ shirts per day, then the equilibrium point is obtained when demand = supply:

$$-20p + 800 = 10p - 100$$
$$30p = 900, \text{ giving } p = \$30.$$

The equilibrium price is therefore \$30 and the equilibrium demand is $q = -20(30) + 800 = 200$ shirts per day. What happens at prices other than the equilibrium price is discussed in Example 4.

Note In economics it is customary to plot the independent variable (price) on the vertical axis and the dependent variable (demand or supply) on the horizontal axis, but in this book we follow the usual mathematical convention for all graphs and plot the independent variable on the horizontal axis.

EXAMPLE 4 Demand, Supply, and Equilibrium Price

Continuing with Example 3, suppose that private school institutions are willing to create private schools to accommodate

$$q = 30.4 + 0.006p \text{ thousand students} \qquad (200 \le p \le 2{,}200) \qquad \text{Supply curve}$$

who pay a net tuition of p dollars.

a. Graph the demand curve of Example 3 and the supply curve given here on the same set of axes. Use your graph to estimate, to the nearest \$100, the tuition at which the demand equals the supply. Approximately how many students will be accommodated at that price, known as the **equilibrium price**?

b. What happens if the tuition is higher than the equilibrium price? What happens if it is lower?

c. Estimate the shortage or surplus of openings at private schools if tuition is set at \$1,200.

Solution

a. Figure 10 shows the graphs of demand $q = 77.8p^{-0.11}$ and supply $q = 30.4 + 0.006p$. (See the margin note for a brief description of how to plot them.)

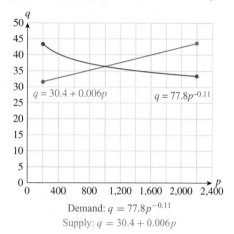

Demand: $q = 77.8p^{-0.11}$
Supply: $q = 30.4 + 0.006p$

Figure 10

using Technology

See the Technology Guides at the end of the chapter for detailed instructions on how to obtain the table of values and graph in Example 4 using a TI-83/84 Plus or Excel. Here is an outline:

TI-83/84 Plus
Graphs:
Y_1=77.8*X^(-0.11)
Y_2=30.4+0.006*X
2ND TABLE Graph:
Xmin = 200, Xmax = 2200;
ZOOM 0 [More details on page 115.]

Spreadsheet
Headings p, Demand, Supply in A1–C1; p-values 200, 300, ..., 2200 in A2-A22.
=77.8*A2^(-0.11) in B2
=30.4+0.006*A2 in C2
Copy down through C22.
Highlight A1–C22; insert Scatter chart. [More details on page 120.]

Ⓦ Website
www.WanerMath.com
Go to the Function Evaluator and Grapher under Online Utilities, and enter
77.8*x^(-0.11) for y_1 and
30.4+0.006*x for y_2.
Graph: Set Xmin = 200, Xmax = 2200, and press "Plot Graphs".

The lines cross close to $p = \$1{,}000$, so we conclude that demand = supply when $p \approx \$1{,}000$ (to the nearest \$100). This is the (approximate) equilibrium tuition price. At that price, we can estimate the demand or supply at around

Demand: $q = 77.8(1{,}000)^{-0.11} \approx 36.4$

Supply: $q = 30.4 + 0.006(1{,}000) = 36.4$ Demand = Supply at equilibrium

or 36,400 students.

b. Take a look at Figure 11, which shows what happens if schools charge more or less than the equilibrium price.

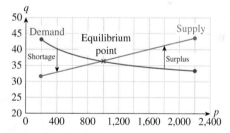

Figure 11

If tuition is, say, \$1,800, then the supply will be larger than demand and there will be a surplus of available openings at private schools. Similarly, if tuition is less—say \$400—then the supply will be less than the demand, and there will be a shortage of available openings.

c. The discussion in part (b) shows that if tuition is set at \$1,200 there will be a surplus of available openings. To estimate that number, we calculate the projected demand and supply when $p = \$1{,}200$:

Demand: $q = 77.8(1{,}200)^{-0.11} \approx 35.7$ thousand seats

Supply: $q = 30.4 + 0.006(1{,}200) = 37.6$ thousand seats

Surplus = Supply − Demand $\approx 37.6 - 35.7 = 1.9$ thousand seats.

So, there would be a surplus of around 1,900 available seats.

➡ **Before we go on...** We just saw in Example 4 that if tuition is less than the equilibrium price there will be a shortage. If schools were to raise their tuition toward the equilibrium, they would create and fill more openings and increase revenue, because it is the supply equation—and not the demand equation—that determines what one can sell below the equilibrium price. On the other hand, if they were to charge more than the equilibrium price, they will be left with a possibly costly surplus of unused openings (and will want to lower tuition to reduce the surplus). Prices tend to move toward the equilibrium, so supply tends to equal demand. When supply equals demand, we say that the market **clears**. ∎

Modeling Change over Time

Things around us change with time. Thus, there are many quantities, such as your income or the temperature in Honolulu, that are natural to think of as functions of time. Example 1 on page 44 (on iPod sales) and Example 2 on page 47 (on Facebook membership) in Section 1.1 are models of change over time. Both of those models are curve-fitting models: We used algebraic functions to approximate observed data.

Note We usually use the independent variable t to denote time (in seconds, hours, days, years, etc.). If a quantity q changes with time, then we can regard q as a function of t. ∎

In the next example we are asked to select from among several curve-fitting models for given data.

ⓘ EXAMPLE 5 Model Selection: Sales

The following table shows annual sales, in billions of dollars, by Nike from 2005 through 2010:[18]

Year	2005	2006	2007	2008	2009	2010
Sales ($ billion)	13.5	15	16.5	18.5	19	19

Take t to be the number of years since 2005, and consider the following four models:

(1) $s(t) = 14 + 1.2t$ Linear model

(2) $s(t) = 13 + 2.2t - 0.2t^2$ Quadratic model

(3) $s(t) = 14(1.07^t)$ Exponential model

(4) $s(t) = \dfrac{19.5}{1 + 0.48(1.8^{-t})}$ Logistic model

a. Which models fit the data significantly better than the rest?

b. Of the models you selected in part (a), which gives the most reasonable prediction for 2013?

---

[18]Figures are rounded. Source: http://invest.nike.com.

Solution

a. The following table shows the original data together with the values, rounded to the nearest 0.5, for all four models:

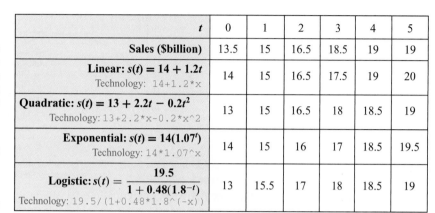

	t	0	1	2	3	4	5
Sales ($billion)		13.5	15	16.5	18.5	19	19
Linear: $s(t) = 14 + 1.2t$ Technology: `14+1.2*x`		14	15	16.5	17.5	19	20
Quadratic: $s(t) = 13 + 2.2t - 0.2t^2$ Technology: `13+2.2*x-0.2*x^2`		13	15	16.5	18	18.5	19
Exponential: $s(t) = 14(1.07^t)$ Technology: `14*1.07^x`		14	15	16	17	18.5	19.5
Logistic: $s(t) = \dfrac{19.5}{1 + 0.48(1.8^{-t})}$ Technology: `19.5/(1+0.48*1.8^(-x))`		13	15.5	17	18	18.5	19

Notice that all the models give values that seem reasonably close to the actual sales values. However, the quadratic and logistic curves seem to model their behavior more accurately than the others (see Figure 12).

using Technology

See the Technology Guides at the end of the chapter for detailed instructions on how to obtain the table and graphs in Example 5 using a TI-83/84 Plus or Excel. Here is an outline:

TI-83/84 Plus
STAT EDIT; enter the values of t in L_1, and $r(t)$ in L_2.
Plotting the points: ZOOM 9
Adding a curve:
Turn on Plot1 in Y= screen. Then (for the second curve)
Y_1=13+2.2*X-0.2*X^2
Press GRAPH [More details on page 115.]

Spreadsheet
Table of values: Headings t, Sales, $s(t)$ in A1–C1;
t-values in A2-A7; sales values in B2–B7. Formula in C2:
=13+2.2*A2-0.2*A2^2
(second model)
Copy down through C7
Graph: Highlight A1–C7; insert Scatter chart. [More details on page 121.]

Website
www.WanerMath.com
In the Function Evaluator and Grapher utility, enter the data and model(s) as shown below. Set xMin = 0, xMax = 5 and press "Plot Graphs".

Linear: $s(t) = 14 + 1.2t$

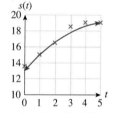

Quadratic: $s(t) = 13 + 2.2t - 0.2t^2$

Exponential: $s(t) = 14(1.07^t)$

Logistic: $s(t) = \dfrac{19.5}{1 + 0.48(1.8^{-t})}$

Figure 12

We therefore conclude that the quadratic and logistic models fit the data significantly better than the others.

b. Although the quadratic and logistic models both appear to fit the data well, they do not both extrapolate to give reasonable predictions for 2013:

$$\text{Quadratic Model: } s(8) = 13 + 2.2(8) - 0.2(8)^2 = 17.8$$

$$\text{Logistic Model: } s(8) = \frac{19.5}{1 + 0.48(1.8^{-8})} \approx 19.4.$$

Notice that the quadratic model predicts a significant *decline* in sales whereas the logistic model predicts a more reasonable modest increase. This discrepancy can be seen quite dramatically in Figure 13.

Figure 13

We now derive an analytical model of change over time based on the idea of **compound interest**. Suppose you invest $500 (the **present value**) in an investment account with an annual yield of 15%, and the interest is reinvested at the end of every year (we say that the interest is **compounded** or **reinvested** once a year). Let t represent the number of years since you made the initial $500 investment. Each year, the investment is worth 115% (or 1.15 times) of its value the previous year. The **future value** A of your investment changes over time t, so we think of A as a function of t. The following table illustrates how we can calculate the future value for several values of t:

t	0	1	2	3
Future Value $A(t)$	500	575	661.25	760.44
A		$500(1.15)$	$500(1.15)^2$	$500(1.15)^3$
		$\times 1.15$	$\times 1.15$	$\times 1.15$

Thus, $A(t) = 500(1.15)^t$. A traditional way to write this formula is

$$A(t) = P(1 + r)^t,$$

where P is the present value ($P = 500$) and r is the annual interest rate ($r = 0.15$).

If, instead of compounding the interest once a year, we compound it every three months (four times a year), we would earn one quarter of the interest ($r/4$ of the current investment) every three months. Because this would happen $4t$ times in t years, the formula for the future value becomes

$$A(t) = P\left(1 + \frac{r}{4}\right)^{4t}.$$

Compound Interest

If an amount (**present value**) P is invested for t years at an annual rate of r, and if the interest is compounded (reinvested) m times per year, then the **future value** A is

$$A(t) = P\left(1 + \frac{r}{m}\right)^{mt}.$$

A special case is **interest compounded once a year**:

$$A(t) = P(1 + r)^t.$$

> **Quick Example**
>
> If \$2,000 is invested for two and a half years in a mutual fund with an annual yield of 12.6% and the earnings are reinvested each month, then $P = 2{,}000$, $r = 0.126$, $m = 12$, and $t = 2.5$, which gives
>
> $$A(2.5) = 2{,}000\left(1 + \frac{0.126}{12}\right)^{12 \times 2.5} \qquad \texttt{2000*(1+0.126/12)\^(12*2.5)}$$
>
> $$= 2{,}000(1.0105)^{30} = \$2{,}736.02.$$

EXAMPLE 6 Compound Interest: Investments

Consider the scenario in the preceding Quick Example: You invest \$2,000 in a mutual fund with an annual yield of 12.6% and the interest is reinvested each month.

a. Find the associated exponential model.

b. 🔲 Use a table of values to estimate the year during which the value of your investment reaches \$5,000.

c. Use a graph to confirm your answer in part (b).

Solution

a. Apply the formula

$$A(t) = P\left(1 + \frac{r}{m}\right)^{mt}$$

with $P = 2{,}000$, $r = 0.126$, and $m = 12$. We get

$$A(t) = 2{,}000\left(1 + \frac{0.126}{12}\right)^{12t}$$

$$= 2{,}000(1.0105)^{12t}. \qquad \texttt{2000*(1+0.126/12)\^(12*t)}$$

This is the exponential model. (What would happen if we left out the last set of parentheses in the technology formula?)

b. We need to find the value of t for which $A(t) = \$5{,}000$, so we need to solve the equation

$$5{,}000 = 2{,}000(1.0105)^{12t}.$$

Logarithms can be used to solve this equation algebraically, but we can answer the question numerically using a graphing calculator, a spreadsheet, or the Function Evaluator and Grapher utility at the Website. Just enter the model and compute the balance at the end of several years. Here are examples of tables obtained using three forms of technology:

 using Technology

TI-83/84 Plus
Y₁=2000(1+0.126/12)^
(12X)
2ND TABLE

Spreadsheet
Headings *t* and *A* in A1–B1;
t-values 0–11 in A2–A13.
=2000*(1+0.126/12)^
(12*A2)
in B2; copy down through B13.

 Website
www.WanerMath.com
Go to the Function Evaluator and Grapher under Online Utilities, and enter
2000(1+0.126/12)^(12x)
for *y*₁. Scroll down to the Evaluator, enter the values 0–11 under *x*-values and press "Evaluate."

TI-83/84 Plus

$Y_1 = 5451.50618802$

	A	B
1	t	A
2	0	$ 2,000.00
3	1	$ 2,267.07
4	2	$ 2,569.81
5	3	$ 2,912.98
6	4	$ 3,301.97
7	5	$ 3,742.91
8	6	$ 4,242.72
9	7	$ 4,809.29
10	8	$ 5,451.51
11	9	$ 6,179.49

Excel

x-Values	y_1-Values
3	2912.98
4	3301.97
5	3742.91
6	4242.72
7	4809.29
8	5451.51

Website

Because the balance first exceeds $5,000 at $t = 8$ (the end of year 8), your investment has reached $5,000 during year 8.

c. Figure 14 shows the graph of $A(t) = 2,000(1.0105)^{12t}$ together with the horizontal line $y = 5,000$. The graphs cross between $t = 7$ and $t = 8$, confirming that year 8 is the first year during which the value of the investment reaches $5,000.

The compound interest examples we saw above are instances of **exponential growth:** a quantity whose magnitude is an increasing exponential function of time. The decay of unstable radioactive isotopes provides instances of **exponential decay:** a quantity whose magnitude is a *decreasing* exponential function of time. For example, carbon 14, an unstable isotope of carbon, decays exponentially to nitrogen. Because carbon 14 decay is extremely slow, it has important applications in the dating of fossils.

Graph with y-axis labeled y showing values 2,000 to 8,000, x-axis labeled t from 0 to 10, with horizontal line $y = 5,000$

Technology formula:
2000*1.0105^(12*x)

Figure 14

EXAMPLE 7 **Exponential Decay: Carbon Dating**

The amount of carbon 14 remaining in a sample that originally contained A grams is approximately

$$C(t) = A(0.999879)^t,$$

where t is time in years.

a. What percentage of the original amount remains after one year? After two years?

b. Graph the function C for a sample originally containing 50 g of carbon 14, and use your graph to estimate how long, to the nearest 1,000 years, it takes for half the original carbon 14 to decay.

c. A fossilized plant unearthed in an archaeological dig contains 0.50 g of carbon 14 and is known to be 50,000 years old. How much carbon 14 did the plant originally contain?

Solution

Notice that the given model is exponential as it has the form $f(t) = Ab^t$. (See page 51.)

a. At the start of the first year, $t = 0$, so there are

$$C(0) = A(0.999879)^0 = A \text{ grams.}$$

At the end of the first year, $t = 1$, so there are

$$C(1) = A(0.999879)^1 = 0.999879A \text{ grams;}$$

Technology formula:
`50*0.999879^x`

Figure 15

that is, 99.9879% of the original amount remains. After the second year, the amount remaining is

$$C(2) = A(0.999879)^2 \approx 0.999758A \text{ grams,}$$

or about 99.9758% of the original sample.

b. For a sample originally containing 50 g of carbon 14, $A = 50$, so $C(t) = 50(0.999879)^t$. Its graph is shown in Figure 15. We have also plotted the line $y = 25$ on the same graph. The graphs intersect at the point where the original sample has decayed to 25 g: about $t = 6{,}000$ years.

c. We are given the following information: $C = 0.50$, $A =$ the unknown, and $t = 50{,}000$. Substituting gives

$$0.50 = A(0.999879)^{50,000}.$$

Solving for A gives

$$A = \frac{0.5}{0.999879^{50,000}} \approx 212 \text{ grams.}$$

Thus, the plant originally contained 212 g of carbon 14.

➡ **Before we go on...**

The formula we used for A in Example 7(c) has the form

$$A(t) = \frac{C}{0.999879^t},$$

which gives the original amount of carbon 14 t years ago in terms of the amount C that is left now. A similar formula can be used in finance to find the present value, given the future value. ■

Algebra of Functions

If you look back at some of the functions considered in this section, you will notice that we frequently constructed them by combining simpler or previously constructed functions. For instance:

Quick Example 3 on page 56:	Area = Width × Length: $A(x) = x(50 - x)$
Example 1:	Cost = Variable Cost + Fixed Cost: $C(x) = 1.80x + 2.05$
Quick Example on page 59:	Profit = Revenue − Cost: $P(x) = 10x - (8x + 100)$.

Let us look a little more deeply at each of the above examples:

Area Example: $A(x) =$ Width × Length $= x(50 - x)$:
Think of the width and length as separate functions of x:

$$\text{Width: } W(x) = x; \qquad \text{Length: } L(x) = 50 - x$$

so that

$$A(x) = W(x)L(x). \qquad \text{Area = Width × Length}$$

We say that the area function A is the **product of the functions** W and L, and we write

$$A = WL. \qquad \text{\small A is the product of the functions W and L.}$$

To calculate $A(x)$, we multiply $W(x)$ by $L(x)$.

Cost Example: $C(x) = $ Variable Cost + Fixed Cost $= 1.80x + 2.05$:
Think of the variable and fixed costs as separate functions of x:

✱ *F* is called a constant function
as its value, 2.05, is the same
for every value of *x*.

$$\text{Variable Cost: } V(x) = 1.80x; \qquad \text{Fixed Cost: } F(x) = 2.05*$$

so that

$$C(x) = V(x) + F(x). \qquad \text{Cost} = \text{Variable Cost} + \text{Fixed Cost}$$

We say that the cost function C is the **sum of the functions V and F**, and we write

$$C = V + F. \qquad \text{C is the sum of the functions V and F.}$$

To calculate $C(x)$, we add $V(x)$ to $F(x)$.

Profit Example: $P(x) = $ Revenue $-$ Cost $= 10x - (8x + 100)$:
Think of the revenue and cost as separate functions of x:

$$\text{Revenue: } R(x) = 10x; \qquad \text{Cost: } C(x) = 8x + 100$$

so that

$$P(x) = R(x) - C(x). \qquad \text{Profit} = \text{Revenue} - \text{Cost}$$

We say that the profit function P is the **difference between the functions R and C**, and we write

$$P = R - C. \qquad \text{P is the difference of the functions R and C.}$$

To calculate $P(x)$, we subtract $C(x)$ from $R(x)$.

Algebra of Functions

If f and g are real-valued functions of the real variable x, then we define their **sum s, difference d, product p,** and **quotient q** as follows:

$s = f + g$ is the function specified by $s(x) = f(x) + g(x)$.

$d = f - g$ is the function specified by $d(x) = f(x) - g(x)$.

$p = fg$ is the function specified by $p(x) = f(x)g(x)$.

$q = \dfrac{f}{g}$ is the function specified by $q(x) = \dfrac{f(x)}{g(x)}$.

Also, if f is as above and c is a constant (real number), then we define the associated **constant multiple m of f** by

$m = cf$ is the function specified by $m(x) = cf(x)$.

Note on Domains

In order for any of the expressions $f(x) + g(x)$, $f(x) - g(x)$, $f(x)g(x)$, or $f(x)/g(x)$ to make sense, x must be simultaneously in the domains of both f and g. Further, for the quotient, the denominator $g(x)$ cannot be zero. Thus, we specify the domains of these functions as follows:

Domain of $f + g$, $f - g$, and fg: All real numbers x simultaneously in the domains of f and g

Domain of f/g: All real numbers x simultaneously in the domains of f and g such that $g(x) \neq 0$

Domain of cf: Same as the domain of f

Quick Examples

1. If $f(x) = x^2 - 1$ and $g(x) = \sqrt{x}$ with domain $[0, +\infty)$, then the sum s of f and g has domain $[0, +\infty)$ and is specified by
$s(x) = f(x) + g(x) = x^2 - 1 + \sqrt{x}$.

2. If $f(x) = x^2 - 1$ and $c = 3$, then the associated constant multiple m of f is specified by $m(x) = 3f(x) = 3(x^2 - 1)$.

3. If there are $N = 1,000t$ Mars shuttle passengers in year t who pay a total cost of $C = 40,000 + 800t$ million dollars, then the cost per passenger is given by the quotient of the two functions,

$$\text{Cost per passenger} = q(t) = \frac{C(t)}{N(t)}$$

$$= \frac{40,000 + 800t}{1,000t} \text{ million dollars per passenger.}$$

The largest possible domain of C/N is $(0, +\infty)$, as the quotient is not defined if $t = 0$.

1.2 EXERCISES

▼ more advanced   ◆ challenging
⊤ indicates exercises that should be solved using technology

Exercises 1–8 are based on the following functions:

$f(x) = x^2 + 1$ *with domain all real numbers*
$g(x) = x - 1$ *with domain all real numbers*
$h(x) = x + 4$ *with domain $x \geq 10$*
$u(x) = \sqrt{x + 10}$ *with domain $[-10, 0)$*
$v(x) = \sqrt{10 - x}$ *with domain $[0, 10]$*

In each exercise, **a.** *write a formula for the indicated function,* **b.** *give its domain, and* **c.** *specify its value at the given point a, if defined.*

1. $s = f + g$; $a = -3$
2. $d = g - f$; $a = -1$
3. $p = gu$; $a = -6$
4. $p = hv$; $a = 1$
5. $q = \dfrac{v}{g}$; $a = 1$
6. $q = \dfrac{g}{v}$; $a = 1$
7. $m = 5f$; $a = 1$
8. $m = 3u$; $a = -1$

APPLICATIONS

9. **Resources** You now have 200 music files on your hard drive, and this number is increasing by 10 music files each day. Find a mathematical model for this situation. HINT [See Quick Example 1 on page 56.]

10. **Resources** The amount of free space left on your hard drive is now 50 gigabytes (GB) and is decreasing by 5 GB/month. Find a mathematical model for this situation.

11. **Soccer** My rectangular soccer field site has a length equal to twice its width. Find its area in terms of its length x. HINT [See Quick Example 3 on page 56.]

12. **Cabbage** My rectangular cabbage patch has a total area of 100 sq. ft. Find its perimeter in terms of the width x.

13. **Vegetables** I want to fence in a square vegetable patch. The fencing for the east and west sides costs $4 per foot, and the fencing for the north and south sides costs only $2 per foot. Find the total cost of the fencing as a function of the length of a side x.

14. **Orchids** My square orchid garden abuts my house so that the house itself forms the northern boundary. The fencing for the southern boundary costs $4 per foot, and the fencing for the east and west sides costs $2 per foot. Find the total cost of the fencing as a function of the length of a side x.

15. **Study** You study math 4 hours a day Sunday through Thursday, and take the rest of the week off. Model the number of hours h you study math as a function of the day of the week n (with $n = 1$ being Sunday). HINT [See Quick Example 4 on page 57.]

16. **Recreation** You spend 5 hours per day on Saturdays and Sundays watching movies, but only two hours per day during the

week. Model the number of hours h you watch movies as a function of the day of the week n (with $n = 1$ being Sunday).

17. *Cost* A piano manufacturer has a daily fixed cost of $1,200 and a marginal cost of $1,500 per piano. Find the cost $C(x)$ of manufacturing x pianos in one day. Use your function to answer the following questions:

a. On a given day, what is the cost of manufacturing 3 pianos?
b. What is the cost of manufacturing the 3rd piano that day?
c. What is the cost of manufacturing the 11th piano that day?
d. What is the variable cost? What is the fixed cost? What is the marginal cost?
e. Graph C as a function of x. HINT [See Example 1.]

18. *Cost* The cost of renting tuxes for the Choral Society's formal is $20 down, plus $88 per tux. Express the cost C as a function of x, the number of tuxedos rented. Use your function to answer the following questions.

a. What is the cost of renting 2 tuxes?
b. What is the cost of the 2nd tux?
c. What is the cost of the 4,098th tux?
d. What is the variable cost? What is the fixed cost? What is the marginal cost?
e. Graph C as a function of x.

19. *Break-Even Analysis* Your college newspaper, *The Collegiate Investigator*, has fixed production costs of $70 per edition and marginal printing and distribution costs of 40¢ per copy. *The Collegiate Investigator* sells for 50¢ per copy.

a. Write down the associated cost, revenue, and profit functions. HINT [See Examples 1 and 2.]
b. What profit (or loss) results from the sale of 500 copies of *The Collegiate Investigator*?
c. How many copies should be sold in order to break even?

20. *Break-Even Analysis* The Audubon Society at Enormous State University (ESU) is planning its annual fund-raising "Eat-a-thon." The society will charge students 50¢ per serving of pasta. The only expenses the society will incur are the cost of the pasta, estimated at 15¢ per serving, and the $350 cost of renting the facility for the evening.

a. Write down the associated cost, revenue, and profit functions.
b. How many servings of pasta must the Audubon Society sell in order to break even?
c. What profit (or loss) results from the sale of 1,500 servings of pasta?

21. *Break-Even Analysis* Gymnast Clothing manufactures expensive hockey jerseys for sale to college bookstores in runs of up to 200. Its cost (in dollars) for a run of x hockey jerseys is
$$C(x) = 2,000 + 10x + 0.2x^2 \quad (0 \le x \le 200).$$
Gymnast Clothing sells the jerseys at $100 each. Find the revenue and profit functions. How many should Gymnast Clothing manufacture to make a profit? HINT [See Example 2.]

22. *Break-Even Analysis* Gymnast Clothing also manufactures expensive soccer cleats for sale to college bookstores in runs of up to 500. Its cost (in dollars) for a run of x pairs of cleats is
$$C(x) = 3,000 + 8x + 0.1x^2 \quad (0 \le x \le 500).$$
Gymnast Clothing sells the cleats at $120 per pair. Find the revenue and profit functions. How many should Gymnast Clothing manufacture to make a profit?

23. *Break-Even Analysis: School Construction Costs* The cost, in millions of dollars, of building a two-story high school in New York State was estimated to be
$$C(x) = 1.7 + 0.12x - 0.0001x^2 \quad (20 \le x \le 400),$$
where x is the number of thousands of square feet.[19] Suppose that you are contemplating building a for-profit two-story high school and estimate that your total revenue will be $0.1 million dollars per thousand square feet. What is the profit function? What size school should you build in order to break even?

24. *Break-Even Analysis: School Construction Costs* The cost, in millions of dollars, of building a three-story high school in New York State was estimated to be
$$C(x) = 1.7 + 0.14x - 0.0001x^2 \quad (20 \le x \le 400),$$
where x is the number of thousands of square feet.[20] Suppose that you are contemplating building a for-profit three-story high school and estimate that your total revenue will be $0.2 million dollars per thousand square feet. What is the profit function? What size school should you build in order to break even?

25. ▼ *Profit Analysis—Aviation* The hourly operating cost of a Boeing 747-100, which seats up to 405 passengers, is estimated to be $5,132.[21] If an airline charges each passenger a fare of $100 per hour of flight, find the hourly profit P it earns operating a 747-100 as a function of the number of passengers x. (Be sure to specify the domain.) What is the least number of passengers it must carry in order to make a profit? HINT [The cost function is constant (Variable cost = 0).]

26. ▼ *Profit Analysis—Aviation* The hourly operating cost of a McDonnell Douglas DC 10-10, which seats up to 295 passengers, is estimated to be $3,885.[22] If an airline charges each passenger a fare of $100 per hour of flight, find the hourly profit P it earns operating a DC10-10 as a function of the number of passengers x. (Be sure to specify the domain.) What is the least number of passengers it must carry in order to make a profit? HINT [The cost function is constant (Variable cost = 0).]

27. ▼ *Break-Even Analysis (based on a question from a CPA exam)* The Oliver Company plans to market a new product. Based on its market studies, Oliver estimates that it can sell up to 5,500 units in 2005. The selling price will be $2 per unit. Variable costs are estimated to be 40% of total revenue. Fixed costs are estimated to be $6,000 for 2005. How many units should the company sell to break even?

---

[19]The model is the authors'. Source for data: *Project Labor Agreements and Public Construction Cost in New York State,* Paul Bachman and David Tuerck, Beacon Hill Institute at Suffolk University, April 2006, www.beaconhill.org.
[20]*Ibid.*
[21]In 1992. Source: Air Transportation Association of America.
[22]*Ibid.*

28. ▼ *Break-Even Analysis (based on a question from a CPA exam)* The Metropolitan Company sells its latest product at a unit price of $5. Variable costs are estimated to be 30% of the total revenue, while fixed costs amount to $7,000 per month. How many units should the company sell per month in order to break even, assuming that it can sell up to 5,000 units per month at the planned price?

29. ◆ *Break-Even Analysis (from a CPA exam)* Given the following notations, write a formula for the break-even sales level.

SP = Selling price per unit
FC = Total fixed cost
VC = Variable cost per unit

30. ◆ *Break-Even Analysis (based on a question from a CPA exam)* Given the following notation, give a formula for the total fixed cost.

SP = Selling price per unit
VC = Variable cost per unit
BE = Break even sales level in units

31. ◆ *Break-Even Analysis—Organized Crime* The organized crime boss and perfume king Butch (Stinky) Rose has daily overheads (bribes to corrupt officials, motel photographers, wages for hit men, explosives, and so on) amounting to $20,000 per day. On the other hand, he has a substantial income from his counterfeit perfume racket: He buys imitation French perfume (Chanel № 22.5) at $20 per gram, pays an additional $30 per 100 grams for transportation, and sells it via his street thugs for $600 per gram. Specify Stinky's profit function, $P(x)$, where x is the quantity (in grams) of perfume he buys and sells, and use your answer to calculate how much perfume should pass through his hands per day in order that he break even.

32. ◆ *Break-Even Analysis—Disorganized Crime* Butch (Stinky) Rose's counterfeit Chanel № 22.5 racket has run into difficulties; it seems that the *authentic* Chanel № 22.5 perfume is selling for less than his counterfeit perfume. However, he has managed to reduce his fixed costs to zero, and his overall costs are now $400 per gram plus $30 per gram transportation costs and commission. (The perfume's smell is easily detected by specially trained Chanel Hounds, and this necessitates elaborate packaging measures.) He therefore decides to sell it for $420 per gram in order to undercut the competition. Specify Stinky's profit function, $P(x)$, where x is the quantity (in grams) of perfume he buys and sells, and use your answer to calculate how much perfume should pass through his hands per day in order that he break even. Interpret your answer.

33. *Demand for Monorail Service, Las Vegas* The demand for monorail service in Las Vegas can be approximated by

$$q(p) = 64p^{-0.76} \text{ thousand rides per day } \quad (3 \le p \le 5),$$

where p is the cost per ride in dollars.[23]

a. Graph the demand function.
b. What is the result on demand if the cost per ride is increased from $3.00 to $3.50? HINT [See Example 3.]

34. *Demand for Monorail Service, Mars* The demand for monorail service on the Utarek monorail, which links the three urbynes (or districts) of Utarek, Mars, can be approximated by

$$q(p) = 30p^{-0.49} \text{ million rides per day } \quad (3 \le p \le 5),$$

where p is the cost per ride in zonars ($\bar{\bar{Z}}$).[24]

a. Graph the demand function.
b. What is the result on demand if the cost per ride is decreased from $\bar{\bar{Z}}5.00$ to $\bar{\bar{Z}}3.50$?

35. ▼ *Demand: Smart Phones* The worldwide demand for smart phones may be modeled by

$$q(p) = 0.0009p^2 - 0.63p + 245 \text{ million units sold annually} \quad (50 \le p \le 150),$$

where p is the unit price in dollars.[25]

a. Graph the demand function.
b. Use the demand function to estimate, to the nearest million units, worldwide sales of smart phones if the price is $60.
c. Extrapolate the demand function to estimate, to the nearest million units, worldwide sales of smart phones if the price is $20.
d. Model the worldwide annual revenue from the sale of smart phones as a function of unit price, and use your model to estimate, to the nearest billion dollars, worldwide annual revenue when the price is set at $60.
HINT [Revenue = Price × Quantity = p · q(p)]

36. ▼ *Demand: Smart Phones* (See Exercise 35.) Here is another model for worldwide demand for smart phones:

$$q(p) = 700p^{-0.284} \text{ million units sold annually} \quad (50 \le p \le 150),$$

where p is the unit price in dollars.[26]

a. Graph the demand function.
b. Use the demand function to estimate, to the nearest million units, worldwide sales of smart phones if the price is $70.
c. Extrapolate the demand function to estimate, to the nearest million units, worldwide sales of smart phones if the price is $180.
d. Model the worldwide annual revenue from the sale of smart phones as a function of unit price, and use your model to estimate, to the nearest billion dollars, worldwide annual revenue when the price is set at $70.
HINT [Revenue = Price × Quantity = p · q(p)]

---

[23]Source: *New York Times*, February 10, 2007, p. A9.

[24]The zonar ($\bar{\bar{Z}}$) is the official currency in the city-state of Utarek, Mars (formerly www.Marsnext.com, a now extinct virtual society).

[25]The model is the authors' based on data available in 2010. Sources for Data: www.businessweek.com, http://techcrunch.com.

[26]*Ibid.*

37. *Equilibrium Price* The demand for your hand-made skateboards, in weekly sales, is $q = -3p + 700$ if the selling price is $\$p$. You are prepared to supply $q = 2p - 500$ per week at the price $\$p$. At what price should you sell your skateboards so that there is neither a shortage nor a surplus? HINT [See Quick Example on page 62.]

38. *Equilibrium Price* The demand for your factory-made skateboards, in weekly sales, is $q = -5p + 50$ if the selling price is $\$p$. If you are selling them at that price, you can obtain $q = 3p - 30$ per week from the factory. At what price should you sell your skateboards so that there is neither a shortage nor a surplus?

39. *Equilibrium Price: Cell Phones* Worldwide quarterly sales of Nokia® cell phones were approximately $q = -p + 156$ million phones when the wholesale price[27] was $\$p$.

a. If Nokia was prepared to supply $q = 4p - 394$ million phones per quarter at a wholesale price of $\$p$, what would have been the equilibrium price?

b. The actual wholesale price was $\$105$ in the fourth quarter of 2004. Estimate the projected shortage or surplus at that price. HINT [See Quick Example on page 62 and also Example 4.]

40. *Equilibrium Price: Cell Phones* Worldwide annual sales of all cell phones were approximately $-10p + 1,600$ million phones when the wholesale price[28] was $\$p$.

a. If manufacturers were prepared to supply $q = 14p - 800$ million phones per year at a wholesale price of $\$p$, what would have been the equilibrium price?

b. The actual wholesale price was projected to be $\$80$ in the fourth quarter of 2008. Estimate the projected shortage or surplus at that price.

41. 🔲 *Equilibrium Price: Las Vegas Monorail Service* The demand for monorail service in Las Vegas could be approximated by

$$q = 64p^{-0.76} \quad \text{thousand rides per day,}$$

where p was the fare the Las Vegas Monorail Company charges in dollars.[29] Assume the company was prepared to provide service for

$$q = 2.5p + 15.5 \quad \text{thousand rides per day}$$

at a fare of $\$p$.

a. Graph the demand and supply equations, and use your graph to estimate the equilibrium price (to the nearest 50¢).

b. Estimate, to the nearest 10 rides, the shortage or surplus of monorail service at the December 2005 fare of $\$5$ per ride.

42. 🔲 *Equilibrium Price: Mars Monorail Service* The demand for monorail service in the three urbynes (or districts) of Utarek, Mars can be approximated by

$$q = 31p^{-0.49} \text{ million rides per day,}$$

where p is the fare the Utarek Monorail Cooperative charges in zonars ($\bar{\bar{Z}}$).[30] Assume the cooperative is prepared to provide service for

$$q = 2.5p + 17.5 \text{ million rides per day}$$

at a fare of $\bar{\bar{Z}}p$.

a. Graph the demand and supply equations, and use your graph to estimate the equilibrium price (to the nearest 0.50 zonars).

b. Estimate the shortage or surplus of monorail service at the December 2085 fare of $\bar{\bar{Z}}1$ per ride.

43. ▼ *Toxic Waste Treatment* The cost of treating waste by removing PCPs goes up rapidly as the quantity of PCPs removed goes up. Here is a possible model:

$$C(q) = 2,000 + 100q^2,$$

where q is the reduction in toxicity (in pounds of PCPs removed per day) and $C(q)$ is the daily cost (in dollars) of this reduction.

a. Find the cost of removing 10 pounds of PCPs per day.

b. Government subsidies for toxic waste cleanup amount to

$$S(q) = 500q,$$

where q is as above and $S(q)$ is the daily dollar subsidy. The *net cost* function is given by $N = C - S$. Give a formula for $N(q)$ and interpret your answer.

c. Find $N(20)$ and interpret your answer.

44. ▼ *Dental Plans* A company pays for its employees' dental coverage at an annual cost C given by

$$C(q) = 1,000 + 100\sqrt{q},$$

where q is the number of employees covered and $C(q)$ is the annual cost in dollars.

a. If the company has 100 employees, find its annual outlay for dental coverage.

b. Assume that the government subsidizes coverage by an annual dollar amount of

$$S(q) = 200q.$$

The *net cost* function is given by $N = C - S$. Give a formula for $N(q)$ and interpret your answer.

c. Find $N(100)$ and interpret your answer.

---

[27]Source: Embedded.com/Company reports December, 2004.

[28]Wholesale price projections are the authors'. Source for sales prediction: I-Stat/NDR December, 2004.

[29]The model is the authors'. Source for data: *New York Times,* February 10, 2007, p. A9.

[30]The official currency of Utarek, Mars. (See the footnote to Exercise 34.)

45. *Spending on Corrections in the 1990s* The following table shows the annual spending by all states in the United States on corrections ($t = 0$ represents the year 1990):[31]

Year (t)	0	2	4	6	7
Spending ($ billion)	16	18	22	28	30

a. Which of the following functions best fits the given data? (Warning: None of them fits exactly, but one fits more closely than the others.) HINT [See Example 5.]

(A) $S(t) = -0.2t^2 + t + 16$
(B) $S(t) = 0.2t^2 + t + 16$
(C) $S(t) = t + 16$

b. Use your answer to part (a) to "predict" spending on corrections in 1998, assuming that the trend continued.

46. *Spending on Corrections in the 1990s* Repeat Exercise 45, this time choosing from the following functions:

(A) $S(t) = 16 + 2t$
(B) $S(t) = 16 + t + 0.5t^2$
(C) $S(t) = 16 + t - 0.5t^2$

47. *Soccer Gear* The East Coast College soccer team is planning to buy new gear for its road trip to California. The cost per shirt depends on the number of shirts the team orders as shown in the following table:

x (Shirts ordered)	5	25	40	100	125
$A(x)$ (Cost/shirt, $)	22.91	21.81	21.25	21.25	22.31

a. Which of the following functions best models the data?

(A) $A(x) = 0.005x + 20.75$
(B) $A(x) = 0.01x + 20 + \dfrac{25}{x}$
(C) $A(x) = 0.0005x^2 - 0.07x + 23.25$
(D) $A(x) = 25.5(1.08)^{(x-5)}$

b. ⬛ Graph the model you chose in part (a) for $10 \le x \le 100$. Use your graph to estimate the lowest cost per shirt and the number of shirts the team should order to obtain the lowest price per shirt.

48. *Hockey Gear* The South Coast College hockey team wants to purchase wool hats for its road trip to Alaska. The cost per hat depends on the number of hats the team orders as shown in the following table:

x (Hats ordered)	5	25	40	100	125
$A(x)$ (Cost/hat, $)	25.50	23.50	24.63	30.25	32.70

a. Which of the following functions best models the data?

(A) $A(x) = 0.05x + 20.75$
(B) $A(x) = 0.1x + 20 + \dfrac{25}{x}$

(C) $A(x) = 0.0008x^2 - 0.07x + 23.25$
(D) $A(x) = 25.5(1.08)^{(x-5)}$

b. ⬛ Graph the model you chose in part (a) with $5 \le x \le 30$. Use your graph to estimate the lowest cost per hat and the number of hats the team should order to obtain the lowest price per hat.

Cost: Hard Drive Storage *Exercises 49 and 50 are based on the following data showing how the approximate retail cost of a gigabyte of hard drive storage has fallen since 2000:*[32]

t (Year since 2000)	$c(t)$ (Cost per Gigabyte ($))
0	7.5
2	2.5
4	1.2
6	0.6
8	0.2
10	0.1
12	0.06

49. ⬛ **a.** Graph each of the following models together with the data points above and use your graph to decide which two of the models best fit the data: HINT [See Example 5 and accompanying technology note.]

(A) $c(t) = 6.3(0.67)^t$
(B) $c(t) = 0.093t^2 - 1.6t + 6.7$
(C) $c(t) = 4.75 - 0.50t$
(D) $c(t) = \dfrac{12.8}{t^{1.7} + 1.7}$

b. Of the two models you chose in part (a), which predicts the lower price in 2020? What price does that model predict?

50. ⬛ **a.** Graph each of the following models together with the data points above and use your graph to decide which three of the models best fit the given data:

(A) $c(t) = \dfrac{15}{1 + 2^t}$
(B) $c(t) = (7.32)0.59^t + 0.10$
(C) $c(t) = 0.00085(t - 9.6)^4$
(D) $c(t) = 7.5 - 0.82t$

b. One of the three best-fit models in part (a) gives an unreasonable prediction for the price in 2020. Which is it, what price does it predict, and why is the prediction unreasonable?

[31]Data are rounded. Source: National Association of State Budget Officers/*New York Times*, February 28, 1999, p. A1.

[32]2012 price is estimated. Source for data: Historical Notes about the Cost of Hard Drive Storage Space http://ns1758.ca/winch/winchest.html.

51. *Value of Euro* The following table shows the approximate value V of one euro in U.S. dollars during three months in 2010. ($t = 1$ represents January, 2010.)[33]

t (Month)	1	5	6
V (Value in $)	1.42	1.26	1.22

Which of the following kinds of models would best fit the given data? Explain your choice of model. (A, a, b, c, and m are constants.)

(A) Linear: $V(t) = mt + b$
(B) Quadratic: $V(t) = at^2 + bt + c$
(C) Exponential: $V(t) = Ab^t$

52. *Value of Yen* The following table shows the approximate value V of one yen in U.S. dollars during three months in 2010. ($t = 1$ represents January, 2010.)[34]

t (Month)	1	4	10
V (Value in $)	0.0110	0.0107	0.0122

Which of the following kinds of models would best fit the given data? Explain your choice of model. (A, a, b, c, and m are constants.)

(A) Linear: $V(t) = mt + b$
(B) Quadratic: $V(t) = at^2 + bt + c$
(C) Exponential: $V(t) = Ab^t$

53. *Petrochemical Sales: Mexico* The following table shows annual petrochemial sales in Mexico by Pemex, Mexico's national oil company, for 2005–2010 ($t = 0$ represents 2005).[35]

Year t (Year since 2005)	0	2	3	4
Petrochemical Sales s (Billion metric tons)	3.7	4.0	4.1	4.0

Which of the following kinds of models would best fit the given data? Explain your choice of model. (A, a, b, and c are constants.)

(A) $s(t) = Ab^t$ ($b > 1$)
(B) $s(t) = Ab^t$ ($b < 1$)

(C) $s(t) = at^2 + bt + c$ ($a > 0$)
(D) $s(t) = at^2 + bt + c$ ($a < 0$)

54. *Petrochemical Production: Mexico* The following table shows annual petrochemical production in Mexico by Pemex, Mexico's national oil company, for 2005–2010 ($t = 0$ represents 2005):[36]

Year t (Year since 2005)	1	3	5
Petrochemical Production p (Billion metric tons)	11.0	12.0	13.3

Which of the following kinds of models would best fit the given data? Explain your choice of model. (A, a, b, c, and m are constants.)

(A) $s(t) = Ab^t$ ($b > 1$)
(B) $s(t) = Ab^t$ ($b < 1$)
(C) $s(t) = mt + b$ ($m > 0$)
(D) $s(t) = at^2 + bt + c$ ($a < 0$)

55. *Investments* In November 2010, E*Trade Financial was offering only 0.3% interest on its online savings accounts, with interest reinvested monthly.[37] Find the associated exponential model for the value of a $5,000 deposit after t years. Assuming this rate of return continued for seven years, how much would a deposit of $5,000 in November 2010 be worth in November 2017? (Answer to the nearest $1.) HINT [See Quick Example on page 67.]

56. *Investments* In November 2010, ING Direct was offering 2.4% interest on its Orange Savings Account, with interest reinvested quarterly.[38] Find the associated exponential model for the value of a $4,000 deposit after t years. Assuming this rate of return continued for eight years, how much would a deposit of $4,000 in November 2010 be worth in November 2018? (Answer to the nearest $1.)

57. ▧ *Investments* Refer to Exercise 55. In November of which year will an investment of $5,000 made in November of 2010 first exceed $5,200? HINT [See Example 6.]

58. ▧ *Investments* Refer to Exercise 56. In November of which year will an investment of $4,000 made in November of 2010 first exceed $5,200?

59. *Carbon Dating* A fossil originally contained 104 grams of carbon 14. Refer to the formula for $C(t)$ in Example 7 and estimate the amount of carbon 14 left in the sample after 10,000 years, 20,000 years, and 30,000 years. HINT [See Example 7.]

---

[33]Source: www.exchange-rates.org.

[34]*Ibid.*

[35]2010 figure is a projection based on data through May 2010. Source: www.pemex.com (July 2010)

[36]*Ibid.*

[37]Interest rate based on annual percentage yield. Source: https://us. etrade.com, November 2010.

[38]Interest rate based on annual percentage yield. Source: http://home. ingdirect.com, November 2010.

60. *Carbon Dating* A fossil contains 4.06 grams of carbon 14. Refer to the formula for $A(t)$ at the end of Example 7, and estimate the amount of carbon 14 in the sample 10,000 years, 20,000 years, and 30,000 years ago.

61. *Carbon Dating* A fossil contains 4.06 grams of carbon 14. It is estimated that the fossil originally contained 46 grams of carbon 14. By calculating the amount left after 5,000 years, 10,000 years, . . . , 35,000 years, estimate the age of the sample to the nearest 5,000 years. (Refer to the formula for $C(t)$ in Example 7.)

62. *Carbon Dating* A fossil contains 2.8 grams of carbon 14. It is estimated that the fossil originally contained 104 grams of carbon 14. By calculating the amount 5,000 years, 10,000 years, . . . , 35,000 years ago, estimate the age of the sample to the nearest 5,000 years. (Refer to the formula for $C(t)$ at the end of Example 7.)

63. *Radium Decay* The amount of radium 226 remaining in a sample that originally contained A grams is approximately

$$C(t) = A(0.999567)^t$$

where t is time in years.

a. Find, to the nearest whole number, the percentage of radium 226 left in an originally pure sample after 1,000 years, 2,000 years, and 3,000 years.

b. Use a graph to estimate, to the nearest 100 years, when one half of a sample of 100 grams will have decayed.

64. *Iodine Decay* The amount of iodine 131 remaining in a sample that originally contained A grams is approximately

$$C(t) = A(0.9175)^t$$

where t is time in days.

a. Find, to the nearest whole number, the percentage of iodine 131 left in an originally pure sample after 2 days, 4 days, and 6 days.

b. Use a graph to estimate, to the nearest day, when one half of a sample of 100 g will have decayed.

COMMUNICATION AND REASONING EXERCISES

65. If the population of the lunar station at Clavius has a population of $P = 200 + 30t$, where t is time in years since the station was established, then the population is increasing by _____ per year.

66. My bank balance can be modeled by $B(t) = 5,000 - 200t$ dollars, where t is time in days since I opened the account. The balance on my account is _____ by $200 per day.

67. Classify the following model as analytical or curve-fitting, and give a reason for your choice: The price of gold was $700 on Monday, $710 on Tuesday, and $700 on Wednesday. Therefore, the price can be modeled by $p(t) = -10t^2 + 20t + 700$ where t is the day since Monday.

68. Classify the following model as analytical or curve-fitting, and give a reason for your choice: The width of a small animated square on my computer screen is currently 10 mm and is growing by 2 mm per second. Therefore, its area can be modeled by $a(t) = (10 + 2t)^2$ square mm where t is time in seconds.

69. Fill in the missing information for the following *analytical model* (answers may vary): _____. Therefore, the cost of downloading a movie can be modeled by $c(t) = 4 - 0.2t$, where t is time in months since January.

70. Repeat Exercise 69, but this time regard the given model as a *curve-fitting model*.

71. Fill in the blanks: In a linear cost function, the _____ cost is x times the _____ cost.

72. Complete the following sentence: In a linear cost function, the marginal cost is the _____.

73. ▼ We said on page 61 that the demand for a commodity generally goes down as the price goes up. Assume that the demand for a certain commodity goes up as the price goes up. Is it still possible for there to be an equilibrium price? Explain with the aid of a demand and supply graph.

74. ▼ What would happen to the price of a certain commodity if the demand was always greater than the supply? Illustrate with a demand and supply graph.

75. You have a set of data points showing the sales of videos on your Web site versus time that are closely approximated by two different mathematical models. Give one criterion that would lead you to choose one over the other. (Answers may vary.)

76. Would it ever be reasonable to use a quadratic model $s(t) = at^2 + bt + c$ to predict long-term sales if a is negative? Explain.

77. If f and g are functions with $f(x) \geq g(x)$ for every x, what can you say about the values of the function $f - g$?

78. If f and g are functions with $f(x) > g(x) > 0$ for every x, what can you say about the values of the function $\frac{f}{g}$?

79. If f is measured in books, and g is measured in people, what are the units of measurement of the function $\frac{f}{g}$?

80. If f and g are linear functions, then what can you say about $f - g$?

1.3 **Linear Functions and Models**

Linear functions are among the simplest functions and are perhaps the most useful of all mathematical functions.

> ### Linear Function
>
> A **linear function** is one that can be written in the form
>
> **Quick Example**
>
> $$f(x) = mx + b \qquad \text{Function form} \qquad\qquad f(x) = 3x - 1$$
>
> or
>
> $$y = mx + b \qquad \text{Equation form} \qquad\qquad y = 3x - 1$$
>
> where m and b are fixed numbers. (The names m and b are traditional.*)

✳ Actually, *c* is sometimes instead of *b*. As for *m*, there has even been some research into the question of its origin, but no one knows exactly why the letter *m* is used.

Linear Functions from the Numerical and Graphical Point of View

The following table shows values of $y = 3x - 1$ ($m = 3, b = -1$) for some values of x:

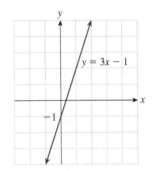

Figure 16

x	-4	-3	-2	-1	0	1	2	3	4
y	-13	-10	-7	-4	-1	2	5	8	11

Its graph is shown in Figure 16.

Looking first at the table, notice that setting $x = 0$ gives $y = -1$, the value of b.

> *Numerically, b is the value of y when x = 0.*

On the graph, the corresponding point $(0, -1)$ is the point where the graph crosses the y-axis, and we say that $b = -1$ is the **y-intercept** of the graph (Figure 17).

What about m? Looking once again at the table, notice that y increases by $m = 3$ units for every increase of 1 unit in x. This is caused by the term $3x$ in the formula: for every increase of 1 in x we get an increase of $3 \times 1 = 3$ in y.

> *Numerically, y increases by m units for every 1-unit increase of x.*

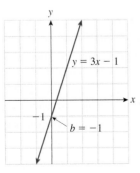

y-intercept $= b = -1$
Graphically, b is the y-intercept of the graph.

Figure 17

Likewise, for every increase of 2 in x we get an increase of $3 \times 2 = 6$ in y. In general, if x increases by some amount, y will increase by three times that amount. We write:

Change in $y = 3 \times$ Change in x.

The Change in a Quantity: Delta Notation

If a quantity q changes from q_1 to q_2, the **change in q** is just the difference:

$$\text{Change in } q = \text{Second value} - \text{First value}$$
$$= q_2 - q_1.$$

Mathematicians traditionally use Δ (delta, the Greek equivalent of the Roman letter D) to stand for change, and write the change in q as Δq.

$$\Delta q = \text{Change in } q = q_2 - q_1$$

> ### Quick Examples
>
> 1. If x is changed from 1 to 3, we write
>
> $$\Delta x = \text{Second value} - \text{First value} = 3 - 1 = 2.$$
>
> 2. Looking at our linear function, we see that, when x changes from 1 to 3, y changes from 2 to 8. So,
>
> $$\Delta y = \text{Second value} - \text{First value} = 8 - 2 = 6.$$

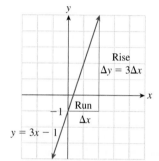

$y = 3x - 1$

Using delta notation, we can now write, for our linear function,

$$\Delta y = 3\Delta x \qquad \text{Change in } y = 3 \times \text{Change in } x.$$

or

$$\frac{\Delta y}{\Delta x} = 3.$$

Because the value of y increases by exactly 3 units for every increase of 1 unit in x, the graph is a straight line rising by 3 units for every 1 unit we go to the right. We say that we have a **rise** of 3 units for each **run** of 1 unit. Because the value of y changes by $\Delta y = 3\Delta x$ units for every change of Δx units in x, in general we have a rise of $\Delta y = 3\Delta x$ units for each run of Δx units (Figure 18). Thus, we have a rise of 6 for a run of 2, a rise of 9 for a run of 3, and so on. So, $m = 3$ is a measure of the steepness of the line; we call m the **slope of the line**:

$$\text{Slope} = m = \frac{\Delta y}{\Delta x} = \frac{\text{Rise}}{\text{Run}}.$$

In general (replace the number 3 by a general number m), we can say the following.

Slope $= m = 3$
Graphically, m is the slope of the graph.

Figure 18

The Roles of *m* and *b* in the Linear Function *f(x)* = *mx* + *b*

Role of *m*

Numerically If $y = mx + b$, then y changes by m units for every 1-unit change in x. A change of Δx units in x results in a change of $\Delta y = m\,\Delta x$ units in y. Thus,

$$m = \frac{\Delta y}{\Delta x} = \frac{\text{Change in } y}{\text{Change in } x}.$$

Graphically m is the slope of the line $y = mx + b$:

$$m = \frac{\Delta y}{\Delta x} = \frac{\text{Rise}}{\text{Run}} = \text{Slope.}$$

For positive m, the graph rises m units for every 1-unit move to the right, and rises $\Delta y = m\Delta x$ units for every Δx units moved to the right. For negative m, the graph drops $|m|$ units for every 1-unit move to the right, and drops $|m|\Delta x$ units for every Δx units moved to the right.

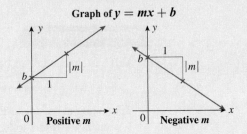

Graph of $y = mx + b$

Positive m Negative m

Role of *b*

Numerically When $x = 0$, $y = b$.

Graphically b is the y-intercept of the line $y = mx + b$.

Quick Examples

1. $f(x) = 2x + 1$ has slope $m = 2$ and y-intercept $b = 1$. To sketch the graph, we start at the y-intercept $b = 1$ on the y-axis, and then move 1 unit to the right and up $m = 2$ units to arrive at a second point on the graph. Now connect the two points to obtain the graph on the left.

2. The line $y = -1.5x + 3.5$ has slope $m = -1.5$ and y-intercept $b = 3.5$. Because the slope is negative, the graph (above right) goes *down* 1.5 units for every 1 unit it moves to the right.

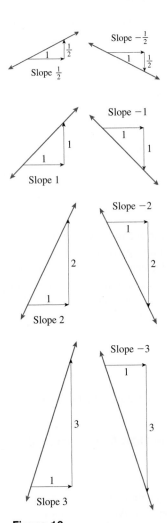

Figure 19

It helps to be able to picture what different slopes look like, as in Figure 19. Notice that the larger the absolute value of the slope, the steeper is the line.

using Technology

See the Technology Guides at the end of the chapter for detailed instructions on how to obtain a table with the successive quotients $m = \Delta y / \Delta x$ for the functions f and g in Example 1 using a TI-83/84 Plus or Excel. These tables show at a glance that f is not linear. Here is an outline:

TI-83/84 Plus

$\boxed{\text{STAT}}$ EDIT; Enter values of x and $f(x)$ in lists L_1 and L_2.
Highlight the heading L_3 then enter the following formula (including the quotes)
`"ΔList(L₂)/ΔList(L₁)"`
[More details on page 116.]

Spreadsheet

Enter headings x, $f(x)$, Df/Dx in cells A1–C1, and the corresponding values from one of the tables in cells A2–B8. Enter
`=(B3-B2)/(A3-A2)`
in cell C2, and copy down through C8.
[More details on page 122.]

EXAMPLE 1 Recognizing Linear Data Numerically and Graphically

Which of the following two tables gives the values of a linear function? What is the formula for that function?

x	0	2	4	6	8	10	12
$f(x)$	3	-1	-3	-6	-8	-13	-15

x	0	2	4	6	8	10	12
$g(x)$	3	-1	-5	-9	-13	-17	-21

Solution The function f cannot be linear: If it were, we would have $\Delta f = m \Delta x$ for some fixed number m. However, although the change in x between successive entries in the table is $\Delta x = 2$ each time, the change in f is not the same each time. Thus, the ratio $\Delta f / \Delta x$ is not the same for every successive pair of points.

On the other hand, the ratio $\Delta g / \Delta x$ is the same each time, namely,

$$\frac{\Delta g}{\Delta x} = \frac{-4}{2} = -2$$

as we see in the following table:

Δx		$2-0=2$	$4-2=2$	$6-4=2$	$8-6=2$	$10-8=2$	$12-10=2$
x	0	2	4	6	8	10	12
$g(x)$	3	-1	-5	-9	-13	-17	-21
Δg		$-1-3$ $=-4$	$-5-(-1)$ $=-4$	$-9-(-5)$ $=-4$	$-13-(-9)$ $=-4$	$-17-(-13)$ $=-4$	$-21-(-17)$ $=-4$

Thus, g is linear with slope $m = -2$. By the table, $g(0) = 3$, hence $b = 3$. Thus,

$$g(x) = -2x + 3. \qquad \text{Check that this formula gives the values in the table.}$$

If you graph the points in the tables defining f and g above, it becomes easy to see that g is linear and f is not; the points of g lie on a straight line (with slope -2), whereas the points of f do not lie on a straight line (Figure 20).

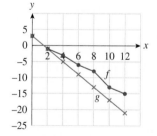

Figure 20

Finding a Linear Equation from Data

If we happen to know the slope and y-intercept of a line, writing down its equation is straightforward. For example, if we know that the slope is 3 and the y-intercept is -1, then the equation is $y = 3x - 1$. Sadly, the information we are given is seldom so convenient. For instance, we may know the slope and a point other than the *y*-intercept, two points on the line, or other information. We therefore need to know how to use the information we are given to obtain the slope and the intercept.

Computing the Slope

We can always determine the slope of a line if we are given two (or more) points on the line, because any two points—say (x_1, y_1) and (x_2, y_2)—determine the line, and hence its slope. To compute the slope when given two points, recall the formula

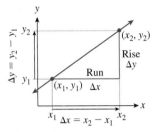

Figure 21

$$\text{Slope} = m = \frac{\text{Rise}}{\text{Run}} = \frac{\Delta y}{\Delta x}.$$

To find its slope, we need a run Δx and corresponding rise Δy. In Figure 21, we see that we can use $\Delta x = x_2 - x_1$, the change in the *x*-coordinate from the first point to the second, as our run, and $\Delta y = y_2 - y_1$, the change in the *y*-coordinate, as our rise. The resulting formula for computing the slope is given in the box.

Computing the Slope of a Line

We can compute the slope m of the line through the points (x_1, y_1) and (x_2, y_2) using

$$m = \frac{\Delta y}{\Delta x} = \frac{y_2 - y_1}{x_2 - x_1}.$$

Quick Examples

1. The slope of the line through $(x_1, y_1) = (1, 3)$ and $(x_2, y_2) = (5, 11)$ is

$$m = \frac{\Delta y}{\Delta x} = \frac{y_2 - y_1}{x_2 - x_1} = \frac{11 - 3}{5 - 1} = \frac{8}{4} = 2.$$

Notice that we can use the points in the reverse order: If we take $(x_1, y_1) = (5, 11)$ and $(x_2, y_2) = (1, 3)$, we obtain the same answer:

$$m = \frac{\Delta y}{\Delta x} = \frac{y_2 - y_1}{x_2 - x_1} = \frac{3 - 11}{1 - 5} = \frac{-8}{-4} = 2.$$

2. The slope of the line through $(x_1, y_1) = (1, 2)$ and $(x_2, y_2) = (2, 1)$ is

$$m = \frac{\Delta y}{\Delta x} = \frac{y_2 - y_1}{x_2 - x_1} = \frac{1 - 2}{2 - 1} = \frac{-1}{1} = -1.$$

3. The slope of the line through $(2, 3)$ and $(-1, 3)$ is

$$m = \frac{\Delta y}{\Delta x} = \frac{y_2 - y_1}{x_2 - x_1} = \frac{3 - 3}{-1 - 2} = \frac{0}{-3} = 0.$$

A line of slope 0 has zero rise, so is a *horizontal* line, as shown in Figure 22.

4. The line through $(3, 2)$ and $(3, -1)$ has slope

$$m = \frac{\Delta y}{\Delta x} = \frac{y_2 - y_1}{x_2 - x_1} = \frac{-1 - 2}{3 - 3} = \frac{-3}{0},$$

which is undefined. The line passing through these points is *vertical*, as shown in Figure 23.

Figure 22

Vertical lines have undefined slope.

Figure 23

Computing the *y*-Intercept

Once we know the slope m of a line, and also the coordinates of a point (x_1, y_1), then we can calculate its y-intercept b as follows: The equation of the line must be

$$y = mx + b,$$

where b is as yet unknown. To determine b we use the fact that the line must pass through the point (x_1, y_1), so that (x_1, y_1) satisfies the equation $y = mx + b$. In other words,

$$y_1 = mx_1 + b.$$

Solving for b gives

$$b = y_1 - mx_1.$$

In summary:

Computing the *y*-Intercept of a Line

The y-intercept of the line passing through (x_1, y_1) with slope m is

$$b = y_1 - mx_1.$$

Quick Example

The line through $(2, 3)$ with slope 4 has

$$b = y_1 - mx_1 = 3 - (4)(2) = -5.$$

Its equation is therefore

$$y = mx + b = 4x - 5.$$

EXAMPLE 2 Finding Linear Equations

Find equations for the following straight lines.

a. Through the points $(1, 2)$ and $(3, -1)$
b. Through $(2, -2)$ and parallel to the line $3x + 4y = 5$
c. Horizontal and through $(-9, 5)$
d. Vertical and through $(-9, 5)$

Solution

a. To write down the equation of the line, we need the slope m and the y-intercept b.

• **Slope** Because we are given two points on the line, we can use the slope formula:

$$m = \frac{y_2 - y_1}{x_2 - x_1} = \frac{-1 - 2}{3 - 1} = -\frac{3}{2}.$$

• **Intercept** We now have the slope of the line, $m = -3/2$, and also a point—we have two to choose from, so let us choose $(x_1, y_1) = (1, 2)$. We can now use the formula for the y-intercept:

$$b = y_1 - mx_1 = 2 - \left(-\frac{3}{2}\right)(1) = \frac{7}{2}.$$

Thus, the equation of the line is

$$y = -\frac{3}{2}x + \frac{7}{2}. \qquad y = mx + b$$

b. Proceeding as before,

• **Slope** We are not given two points on the line, but we are given a parallel line. We use the fact that *parallel lines have the same slope*. (Why?) We can find the slope of $3x + 4y = 5$ by solving for y and then looking at the coefficient of x:

$$y = -\frac{3}{4}x + \frac{5}{4} \qquad \text{To find the slope, solve for } y.$$

so the slope is $-3/4$.

• **Intercept** We now have the slope of the line, $m = -3/4$, and also a point $(x_1, y_1) = (2, -2)$. We can now use the formula for the y-intercept:

$$b = y_1 - mx_1 = -2 - \left(-\frac{3}{4}\right)(2) = -\frac{1}{2}.$$

Thus, the equation of the line is

$$y = -\frac{3}{4}x - \frac{1}{2}. \qquad y = mx + b$$

c. We are given a point: $(-9, 5)$. Furthermore, we are told that the line is horizontal, which tells us that the slope is $m = 0$. Therefore, all that remains is the calculation of the y-intercept:

$$b = y_1 - mx_1 = 5 - (0)(-9) = 5$$

so the equation of the line is

$$y = 5. \qquad y = mx + b$$

d. We are given a point: $(-9, 5)$. This time, we are told that the line is vertical, which means that the slope is undefined. Thus, we can't express the equation of the line in the form $y = mx + b$. (This formula makes sense only when the slope m of the line is defined.) What can we do? Well, here are some points on the desired line:

$$(-9, 1), (-9, 2), (-9, 3), \ldots$$

so $x = -9$ and $y = $ *anything*. If we simply say that $x = -9$, then these points are all solutions, so the equation is $x = -9$.

Applications: Linear Models

Using linear functions to describe or approximate relationships in the real world is called **linear modeling**.

Figure 24

Figure 25

Recall from Section 1.2 that a **cost function** specifies the cost C as a function of the number of items x.

EXAMPLE 3 Linear Cost Function from Data

The manager of the FrozenAir Refrigerator factory notices that on Monday it cost the company a total of $25,000 to build 30 refrigerators and on Tuesday it cost $30,000 to build 40 refrigerators. Find a linear cost function based on this information. What is the daily fixed cost, and what is the marginal cost?

Solution We are seeking the cost C as a linear function of x, the number of refrigerators sold:

$$C = mx + b.$$

We are told that $C = 25,000$ when $x = 30$, and this amounts to being told that $(30, 25{,}000)$ is a point on the graph of the cost function. Similarly, $(40, 30{,}000)$ is another point on the line (Figure 24).

We can use the two points on the line to construct the linear cost equation:

- **Slope** $m = \dfrac{C_2 - C_1}{x_2 - x_1} = \dfrac{30{,}000 - 25{,}000}{40 - 30} = 500$ C plays the role of y.

- **Intercept** $b = C_1 - mx_1 = 25{,}000 - (500)(30) = 10{,}000$.   We used the point $(x_1, C_1) = (30, 25{,}000)$.

The linear cost function is therefore

$$C(x) = 500x + 10{,}000.$$

Because $m = 500$ and $b = 10{,}000$ the factory's fixed cost is $10,000 each day, and its marginal cost is $500 per refrigerator. (See page 59 in Section 1.2.) These are illustrated in Figure 25.

⮕ **Before we go on...**   Recall that, in general, the slope m measures the number of units of change in y per 1-unit change in x, so it is measured in units of y per unit of x:

Units of Slope = Units of y per unit of x.

In Example 3, y is the cost C, measured in dollars, and x is the number of items, measured in refrigerators. Hence,

Units of Slope = Units of y per Unit of x = Dollars per refrigerator.

The y-intercept b, being a value of y, is measured in the same units as y. In Example 3, b is measured in dollars. ∎

In Section 1.2 we saw that a **demand function** specifies the demand q as a function of the price p per item.

EXAMPLE 4 Linear Demand Function from Data

You run a small supermarket and must determine how much to charge for Hot'n'Spicy brand baked beans. The following chart shows weekly sales figures (the demand) for Hot'n'Spicy at two different prices.

Price/Can	$0.50	$0.75
Demand (cans sold/week)	400	350

using Technology
To obtain the cost equation for Example 3 with technology, apply the Technology note for Example 2(a) to the given points (30, 25,000) and (40, 30,000) on the graph of the cost equation.

a. Model these data with a linear demand function. (See Example 4 in Section 1.2.)

b. How do we interpret the slope and q-intercept of the demand function?

Solution

a. Recall that a demand equation—or demand function—expresses demand q (in this case, the number of cans of beans sold per week) as a function of the unit price p (in this case, price per can). We model the demand using the two points we are given: $(0.50, 400)$ and $(0.75, 350)$.

$$\textit{Slope:} \quad m = \frac{q_2 - q_1}{p_2 - p_1} = \frac{350 - 400}{0.75 - 0.50} = \frac{-50}{0.25} = -200$$

$$\textit{Intercept:} \quad b = q_1 - mp_1 = 400 - (-200)(0.50) = 500$$

So, the demand equation is

$$q = -200p + 500. \qquad q = mp + b$$

b. The key to interpreting the slope in a demand equation is to recall (see the "Before we go on" note at the end of Example 3) that we measure the slope in *units of y per unit of x*. Here, $m = -200$, and the units of m are units of q per unit of p, or the number of cans sold per dollar change in the price. Because m is negative, we see that the number of cans sold decreases as the price increases. We conclude that the weekly sales will drop by 200 cans per \$1 increase in the price.

To interpret the q-intercept, recall that it gives the q-coordinate when $p = 0$. Hence it is the number of cans the supermarket can "sell" every week if it were to give them away.*

using Technology

To obtain the demand equation for Example 4 with technology, apply the Technology note for Example 2(a) to the given points (0.50, 400) and (0.75, 350) on the graph of the demand equation.

* Does this seem realistic? Demand is not always unlimited if items were given away. For instance, campus newspapers are sometimes given away, and yet piles of them are often left untaken. Also see the "Before we go on" discussion at the end of this example.

➡ **Before we go on...**

Q : *Just how reliable is the linear model used in Example 4?*

A : The *actual* demand graph could in principle be obtained by tabulating demand figures for a large number of different prices. If the resulting points were plotted on the *pq* plane, they would probably suggest a curve and not a straight line. However, if you looked at a small enough portion of any curve, you could closely *approximate* it by a straight line. In other words, *over a small range of values of p, a linear model is accurate*. Linear models of real-world situations are generally reliable only for small ranges of the variables. (This point will come up again in some of the exercises.)

■

The next example illustrates modeling change over time t with a linear function of t.

EXAMPLE 5 Modeling Change Over Time: Growth of Sales

The worldwide market for portable navigation devices was expected to grow from 50 million units in 2007 to around 530 million units in 2015.[39]

---

[39]Sales were expected to grow to more than 500 million in 2015 according to a January 2008 press release by Telematics Research Group. Source: www.telematicsresearch.com.

a. Use this information to model annual worldwide sales of portable navigation devices as a linear function of time t in years since 2007. What is the significance of the slope?

b. Use the model to predict when annual sales of mobile navigation devices will reach 440 million units.

Solution

a. Since we are interested in worldwide sales s of portable navigation devices as a function of time, we take time t to be the independent coordinate (playing the role of x) and the annual sales s, in million of units, to be the dependent coordinate (in the role of y). Notice that 2007 corresponds to $t = 0$ and 2015 corresponds to $t = 8$, so we are given the coordinates of two points on the graph of sales s as a function of time t: $(0, 50)$ and $(8, 530)$. We model the sales using these two points:

$$m = \frac{s_2 - s_1}{t_2 - t_1} = \frac{530 - 50}{8 - 0} = \frac{480}{8} = 60$$
$$b = s_1 - mt_1 = 50 - (60)(0) = 50$$

So, $s = 60t + 50$ million units. $s = mt + b$

The slope m is measured in units of s per unit of t; that is, millions of devices per year, and is thus the *rate of change of annual sales*. To say that $m = 60$ is to say that annual sales are increasing at a rate of 60 million devices per year.

b. Our model of annual sales as a function of time is

$$s = 60t + 50 \text{ million units.}$$

Annual sales of mobile portable devices will reach 440 million when $s = 440$, or

$$440 = 60t + 50$$

Solving for t, $60t = 440 - 50 = 390$

$$t = \frac{390}{60} = 6.5 \text{ years},$$

which is midway through 2013. Thus annual sales are expected to reach 440 million midway through 2013.

using Technology

To use technology to obtain s as a function of t in Example 5, apply the Technology note for Example 2(a) to the points (0, 50) and (8, 530) on its graph.

EXAMPLE 6 **Velocity**

You are driving down the Ohio Turnpike, watching the mileage markers to stay awake. Measuring time in hours after you see the 20-mile marker, you see the following markers each half hour:

Time (h)	0	0.5	1	1.5	2
Marker (mi)	20	47	74	101	128

Find your location s as a function of t, the number of hours you have been driving. (The number s is also called your **position** or **displacement**.)

Solution

If we plot the location s versus the time t, the five markers listed give us the graph in Figure 26. These points appear to lie along a straight line. We can verify this by

Figure 26

calculating how far you traveled in each half hour. In the first half hour, you traveled $47 - 20 = 27$ miles. In the second half hour you traveled $74 - 47 = 27$ miles also. In fact, you traveled exactly 27 miles each half hour. The points we plotted lie on a straight line that rises 27 units for every 0.5 unit we go to the right, for a slope of $27/0.5 = 54$.

To get the equation of that line, notice that we have the s-intercept, which is the starting marker of 20. Thus, the equation of s as a function of time t is

$$s(t) = 54t + 20. \qquad \text{We used } s \text{ in place of } y \text{ and } t \text{ in place of } x.$$

using Technology

To use technology to obtain s as a function of t in Example 6, apply the Technology note for Example 2(a) to the points $(0, 20)$ and $(1, 74)$ on its graph.

Notice the significance of the slope: For every hour you travel, you drive a distance of 54 miles. In other words, you are traveling at a constant velocity of 54 mph. We have uncovered a very important principle:

In the graph of displacement versus time, velocity is given by the slope.

Linear Change over Time

If a quantity q is a linear function of time t,

$$q = mt + b,$$

then the slope m measures the **rate of change** of q, and b is the quantity at time $t = 0$, the **initial quantity**. If q represents the position of a moving object, then the rate of change is also called the **velocity**.

Units of *m* and *b*

The units of measurement of m are units of q per unit of time; for instance, if q is income in dollars and t is time in years, then the rate of change m is measured in dollars per year.

The units of b are units of q; for instance, if q is income in dollars and t is time in years, then b is measured in dollars.

Quick Example

If the accumulated revenue from sales of your video game software is given by $R = 2,000t + 500$ dollars, where t is time in years from now, then you have earned \$500 in revenue so far, and the accumulated revenue is increasing at a rate of \$2,000 per year.

Examples 3–6 share the following common theme.

General Linear Models

If $y = mx + b$ is a linear model of changing quantities x and y, then the slope m is the rate at which y is increasing per unit increase in x, and the y-intercept b is the value of y that corresponds to $x = 0$.

Units of *m* and *b*

The slope m is measured in units of y per unit of x, and the intercept b is measured in units of y.

Quick Example

If the number n of spectators at a soccer game is related to the number g of goals your team has scored so far by the equation $n = 20g + 4$, then you can expect 4 spectators if no goals have been scored and 20 additional spectators per additional goal scored.

FAQs

What to Use as _x_ and _y_, and How to Interpret a Linear Model

Q: *In a problem where I must find a linear relationship between two quantities, which quantity do I use as x and which do I use as y?*

A: The key is to decide which of the two quantities is the independent variable, and which is the dependent variable. Then use the independent variable as _x_ and the dependent variable as _y_. In other words, _y_ depends on _x_.

Here are examples of phrases that convey this information, usually of the form *Find y [dependent variable] in terms of x [independent variable]:*

- Find the cost in terms of the number of items. $y = $ Cost, $x = $ # Items
- How does color depend on wavelength? $y = $ Color, $x = $ Wavelength

If no information is conveyed about which variable is intended to be independent, then you can use whichever is convenient.

Q: *How do I interpret a general linear model y = mx + b?*

A: The key to interpreting a linear model is to remember the units we use to measure _m_ and _b_:

> The slope _m_ is measured in units of _y_ per unit of _x_; the intercept _b_ is measured in units of _y_.

For instance, if $y = 4.3x + 8.1$ and you know that x is measured in feet and y in kilograms, then you can already say, "y is 8.1 kilograms when $x = 0$ feet, and increases at a rate of 4.3 kilograms per foot" without knowing anything more about the situation!

1.3 EXERCISES

▼ more advanced   ◆ challenging
T indicates exercises that should be solved using technology

In Exercises 1–6, a table of values for a linear function is given. Fill in the missing value and calculate m in each case.

1.

x	-1	0	1
y	5	8	

2.

x	-1	0	1
y	-1	-3	

3.

x	2	3	5
y	-1	-2	

4.

x	2	4	5
y	-1	-2	

5.

x	-2	0	2
y	4		10

6.

x	0	3	6
y	-1		-5

In Exercises 7–10, first find f(0), if not supplied, and then find the equation of the given linear function.

7.

x	-2	0	2	4
f(x)	-1	-2	-3	-4

8.

x	-6	-3	0	3
f(x)	1	2	3	4

9.

x	-4	-3	-2	-1
f(x)	-1	-2	-3	-4

10.

x	1	2	3	4
f(x)	4	6	8	10

In each of Exercises 11–14, decide which of the two given functions is linear and find its equation. HINT [See Example 1.]

11.

x	0	1	2	3	4
f(x)	6	10	14	18	22
g(x)	8	10	12	16	22

12.

x	-10	0	10	20	30
f(x)	-1.5	0	1.5	2.5	3.5
g(x)	-9	-4	1	6	11

13.

x	0	3	6	10	15
f(x)	0	3	5	7	9
g(x)	-1	5	11	19	29

14.

x	0	3	5	6	9
f(x)	2	6	9	12	15
g(x)	-1	8	14	17	26

In Exercises 15–24, find the slope of the given line, if it is defined.

15. $y = -\dfrac{3}{2}x - 4$ **16.** $y = \dfrac{2x}{3} + 4$

17. $y = \dfrac{x+1}{6}$ **18.** $y = -\dfrac{2x-1}{3}$

19. $3x + 1 = 0$ **20.** $8x - 2y = 1$

21. $3y + 1 = 0$ **22.** $2x + 3 = 0$

23. $4x + 3y = 7$ **24.** $2y + 3 = 0$

In Exercises 25–38, graph the given equation. HINT [See Quick Examples on page 80.]

25. $y = 2x - 1$ **26.** $y = x - 3$

27. $y = -\frac{2}{3}x + 2$ **28.** $y = -\frac{1}{2}x + 3$

29. $y + \frac{1}{4}x = -4$ **30.** $y - \frac{1}{4}x = -2$

31. $7x - 2y = 7$ **32.** $2x - 3y = 1$

33. $3x = 8$ **34.** $2x = -7$

35. $6y = 9$ **36.** $3y = 4$

37. $2x = 3y$ **38.** $3x = -2y$

In Exercises 39–58, calculate the slope, if defined, of the straight line through the given pair of points. Try to do as many as you can without writing anything down except the answer. HINT [See Quick Examples on page 82.]

39. $(0, 0)$ and $(1, 2)$ **40.** $(0, 0)$ and $(-1, 2)$

41. $(-1, -2)$ and $(0, 0)$ **42.** $(2, 1)$ and $(0, 0)$

43. $(4, 3)$ and $(5, 1)$ **44.** $(4, 3)$ and $(4, 1)$

45. $(1, -1)$ and $(1, -2)$ **46.** $(-2, 2)$ and $(-1, -1)$

47. $(2, 3.5)$ and $(4, 6.5)$ **48.** $(10, -3.5)$ and $(0, -1.5)$

49. $(300, 20.2)$ and $(400, 11.2)$

50. $(1, -20.2)$ and $(2, 3.2)$

51. $(0, 1)$ and $\left(-\frac{1}{2}, \frac{3}{4}\right)$

52. $\left(\frac{1}{2}, 1\right)$ and $\left(-\frac{1}{2}, \frac{3}{4}\right)$

53. (a, b) and (c, d) $(a \neq c)$

54. (a, b) and (c, b) $(a \neq c)$

55. (a, b) and (a, d) $(b \neq d)$

56. (a, b) and $(-a, -b)$ $(a \neq 0)$

57. $(-a, b)$ and $(a, -b)$ $(a \neq 0)$

58. (a, b) and (b, a) $(a \neq b)$

59. In the following figure, estimate the slopes of all line segments.

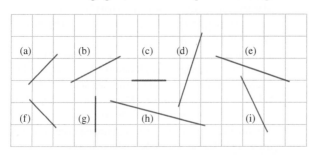

60. In the following figure, estimate the slopes of all line segments.

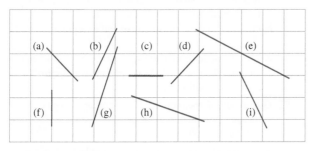

In Exercises 61–78, find a linear equation whose graph is the straight line with the given properties. HINT [See Example 2.]

61. Through $(1, 3)$ with slope 3

62. Through $(2, 1)$ with slope 2

63. Through $(1, -\frac{3}{4})$ with slope $\frac{1}{4}$

64. Through $(0, -\frac{1}{3})$ with slope $\frac{1}{3}$

65. Through $(20, -3.5)$ and increasing at a rate of 10 units of y per unit of x

66. Through $(3.5, -10)$ and increasing at a rate of 1 unit of y per 2 units of x

67. Through $(2, -4)$ and $(1, 1)$

68. Through $(1, -4)$ and $(-1, -1)$

69. Through $(1, -0.75)$ and $(0.5, 0.75)$

70. Through $(0.5, -0.75)$ and $(1, -3.75)$

71. Through $(6, 6)$ and parallel to the line $x + y = 4$

72. Through $(1/3, -1)$ and parallel to the line $3x - 4y = 8$

73. Through $(0.5, 5)$ and parallel to the line $4x - 2y = 11$

74. Through $(1/3, 0)$ and parallel to the line $6x - 2y = 11$

75. ▼ Through $(0, 0)$ and (p, q) $(p \neq 0)$

76. ▼ Through (p, q) parallel to $y = rx + s$

77. ▼ Through (p, q) and (r, q) $(p \neq r)$

78. ▼ Through (p, q) and (r, s) $(p \neq r)$

APPLICATIONS

79. *Cost* The RideEm Bicycles factory can produce 100 bicycles in a day at a total cost of $10,500 and it can produce 120 bicycles in a day at a total cost of $11,000. What are the company's daily fixed costs, and what is the marginal cost per bicycle? HINT [See Example 3.]

80. *Cost* A soft-drink manufacturer can produce 1,000 cases of soda in a week at a total cost of $6,000, and 1,500 cases of soda at a total cost of $8,500. Find the manufacturer's weekly fixed costs and marginal cost per case of soda.

81. *Cost: iPhones* If it costs Apple $1,900 to manufacture 10 iPhone 4s per hour and $3,780 to manufacture 20 per hour at a particular plant,[40] obtain the corresponding linear cost function. What was the cost to manufacture each additional iPhone? Use the cost function to estimate the cost of manufacturing 40 iPhones in an hour.

82. *Cost: Kinects* If it costs Microsoft $1,230 to manufacture 8 Kinects per hour for the Xbox 360 and $2,430 to manufacture 16 per hour at a particular plant,[41] obtain the corresponding linear cost function. What was the cost to manufacture each additional Kinect? Use the cost function to estimate the cost of manufacturing 30 Kinects in an hour.

83. *Demand* Sales figures show that your company sold 1,960 pen sets each week when they were priced at $1/pen set and 1,800 pen sets each week when they were priced at $5/pen set. What is the linear demand function for your pen sets? HINT [See Example 4.]

84. *Demand* A large department store is prepared to buy 3,950 of your tie-dye shower curtains per month for $5 each, but only 3,700 shower curtains per month for $10 each. What is the linear demand function for your tie-dye shower curtains?

85. *Demand for Cell Phones* The following table shows worldwide sales of cell phones by Nokia and their average wholesale prices in the first quarters of 2009 and 2010:[42]

Quarter	Q1 2009	Q1 2010
Wholesale Price ($)	85	81
Sales (millions)	103	111

a. Use the data to obtain a linear demand function for (Nokia) cell phones, and use your demand equation to predict sales if Nokia lowered the price further to $75.

b. Fill in the blanks: For every ____ increase in price, sales of cell phones decrease by ___ units.

---

[40]Based on marginal cost data at www.isuppli.com.

[41]Based on marginal cost data provided by a "highly-positioned, trusted source." www.develop-online.net.

[42]Data are approximate. Source: www.nokia.com.

86. *Demand for Smart Phones* The following table shows worldwide sales of smart phones and their average whole-sale prices in 2009 and 2010:[43]

Quarter	*Q1 2009*	*Q1 2010*
Wholesale Price ($)	162	152
Sales (millions)	174	213

a. Use the data to obtain a linear demand function for smart phones, and use your demand equation to predict sales to the nearest million phones if the price was set at $155.

b. Fill in the blanks: For every _____ increase in price, sales of smart phones decrease by ___ units.

87. *Demand for Monorail Service, Las Vegas* In 2005, the Las Vegas monorail charged $3 per ride and had an average ridership of about 28,000 per day. In December 2005 the Las Vegas Monorail Company raised the fare to $5 per ride, and average ridership in 2006 plunged to around 19,000 per day.[44]

a. Use the given information to find a linear demand equation.

b. Give the units of measurement and interpretation of the slope.

c. What would have been the effect on ridership of raising the fare to $6 per ride?

88. *Demand for Monorail Service, Mars* The Utarek monorail, which links the three urbynes (or districts) of Utarek, Mars, charged $\overline{\overline{Z}}5$ per ride[45] and sold about 14 million rides per day. When the Utarek City Council lowered the fare to $\overline{\overline{Z}}3$ per ride, the number of rides increased to 18 million per day.

a. Use the given information to find a linear demand equation.

b. Give the units of measurement and interpretation of the slope.

c. What would have been the effect on ridership of raising the fare to $\overline{\overline{Z}}10$ per ride?

89. *Pasta Imports in the 90s* During the period 1990–2001, U.S. imports of pasta increased from 290 million pounds in 1990 ($t = 0$) by an average of 40 million pounds/year.[46]

a. Use this information to express y, the annual U.S. imports of pasta (in millions of pounds), as a linear function of t, the number of years since 1990.

b. Use your model to estimate U.S. pasta imports in 2005, assuming the import trend continued.

90. *Mercury Imports in the 10s* During the period 2210–2220, Martian imports of mercury (from the planet of that name) increased from 550 million kg in 2210 ($t = 0$) by an average of 60 million kg/year.

a. Use this information to express y, the annual Martian imports of mercury (in millions of kilograms), as a linear function of t, the number of years since 2210.

b. Use your model to estimate Martian mercury imports in 2230, assuming the import trend continued.

91. *Net Income* The net income of Amazon.com increased from $10 billion in 2006 to $25 billion in 2009.[47]

a. Use this information to find a linear model for Amazon's net income N (in billions of dollars) as a function of time t in years since 2000.

b. Give the units of measurement and interpretation of the slope.

c. Use the model from part (a) to estimate the 2008 net income. (The actual 2008 net income was approximately $19 billion.)

92. *Operating Expenses* The operating expenses of Amazon.com increased from $2.0 billion in 2006 to $4.4 billion in 2009.[48]

a. Use this information to find a linear model for Amazon's operating expenses E (in billions of dollars) as a function of time t in years since 2000.

b. Give the units of measurement and interpretation of the slope.

c. Use the model from part (a) to estimate the 2007 operating expenses. (The actual 2007 operating expenses were approximately $2.5 billion.)

93. *Velocity* The position of a model train, in feet along a railroad track, is given by

$$s(t) = 2.5t + 10$$

after t seconds.

a. How fast is the train moving?

b. Where is the train after 4 seconds?

c. When will it be 25 feet along the track?

94. *Velocity* The height of a falling sheet of paper, in feet from the ground, is given by

$$s(t) = -1.8t + 9$$

after t seconds.

a. What is the velocity of the sheet of paper?

b. How high is it after 4 seconds?

c. When will it reach the ground?

95. ▼ *Fast Cars* A police car was traveling down Ocean Park-way in a high-speed chase from Jones Beach. It was at Jones Beach at exactly 10 pm ($t = 10$) and was at Oak Beach, 13 miles from Jones Beach, at exactly 10:06 pm.

a. How fast was the police car traveling? HINT [See Example 6.]

b. How far was the police car from Jones Beach at time t?

---

[43]Data are approximate. Sources: www.techcrunch.com, www.businessweek.com.

[44]Source: *New York Times,* February 10, 2007, p. A9.

[45]The zonar ($\overline{\overline{Z}}$) is the official currency in the city-state of Utarek, Mars (formerly www.Marsnext.com, a now extinct virtual society).

[46]Data are rounded. Sources: Department of Commerce/*New York Times,* September 5, 1995, p. D4; International Trade Administration, March 31, 2002, www.ita.doc.gov/.

[47]Recall that "net income" is another term for "profit." Source: www.wikinvest.com.

[48]*Ibid.*

96. ▼ *Fast Cars* The car that was being pursued by the police in Exercise 95 was at Jones Beach at exactly 9:54 pm ($t = 9.9$) and passed Oak Beach (13 miles from Jones Beach) at exactly 10:06 pm, where it was overtaken by the police.

a. How fast was the car traveling? HINT [See Example 6.]
b. How far was the car from Jones Beach at time t?

97. *Textbook Sizes* The second edition of *Applied Calculus* by Waner and Costenoble was 585 pages long. By the time we got to the fifth edition, the book had grown to 750 pages.

a. Use this information to obtain the page length L as a linear function of the edition number n.
b. What are the units of measurement of the slope? What does the slope tell you about the length of *Applied Calculus*?
c. At this rate, by which edition will the book have grown to over 1,500 pages?

98. *Textbook Sizes* The second edition of *Finite Mathematics* by Waner and Costenoble was 603 pages long. By the time we got to the fifth edition, the book had grown to 690 pages.

a. Use this information to obtain the page length L as a linear function of the edition number n.
b. What are the units of measurement of the slope? What does the slope tell you about the length of *Finite Mathematics*?
c. At this rate, by which edition will the book have grown to over 1,000 pages?

99. *Fahrenheit and Celsius* In the Fahrenheit temperature scale, water freezes at 32°F and boils at 212°F. In the Celsius scale, water freezes at 0°C and boils at 100°C. Further, the Fahrenheit temperature F and the Celsius temperature C are related by a linear equation. Find F in terms of C. Use your equation to find the Fahrenheit temperatures corresponding to 30°C, 22°C, -10°C, and -14°C, to the nearest degree.

100. *Fahrenheit and Celsius* Use the information about Celsius and Fahrenheit given in Exercise 99 to obtain a linear equation for C in terms of F, and use your equation to find the Celsius temperatures corresponding to 104°F, 77°F, 14°F, and -40°F, to the nearest degree.

Airline Net Income Exercises 101 and 102 are based on the following table, which compares the net incomes, in millions of dollars, of American Airlines, Continental Airlines, and Southwest Airlines:[49]

Year	2005	2006	2007	2008	2009	2010
American Airlines	-850	250	450	$-2,100$	$-1,450$	-300
Continental Airlines	-50	350	450	-600	-300	150
Southwest Airlines	550	500	650	200	100	300

101. a. Use the 2005 and 2009 data to obtain American's net income A as a linear function of Continental's net income C. (Use millions of dollars for all units.)

b. How far off is your model in estimating American's net income based on Continental's 2007 income?
c. What does the slope of the linear function from part (a) suggest about the net income of these two airlines?

102. a. Use the 2006 and 2010 data to obtain Continental's net income C as a linear function of Southwest's net income S. (Use millions of dollars for all units.)
b. How far off is your model in estimating Continental's net income based on Southwest's 2008 income?
c. What does the slope of the linear function from part (a) suggest about the net income of these two airlines?

103. ▼ *Income* The well-known romance novelist Celestine A. Lafleur (a.k.a. Bertha Snodgrass) has decided to sell the screen rights to her latest book, *Henrietta's Heaving Heart*, to Boxoffice Success Productions for $50,000. In addition, the contract ensures Ms. Lafleur royalties of 5% of the net profits.[50] Express her income I as a function of the net profit N, and determine the net profit necessary to bring her an income of $100,000. What is her marginal income (share of each dollar of net profit)?

104. ▼ *Income* Due to the enormous success of the movie *Henrietta's Heaving Heart* based on a novel by Celestine A. Lafleur (see Exercise 103), Boxoffice Success Productions decides to film the sequel, *Henrietta, Oh Henrietta*. At this point, Bertha Snodgrass (whose novels now top the best seller lists) feels she is in a position to demand $100,000 for the screen rights and royalties of 8% of the net profits. Express her income I as a function of the net profit N and determine the net profit necessary to bring her an income of $1,000,000. What is her marginal income (share of each dollar of net profit)?

105. *Processor Speeds* The processor speed, in megahertz (MHz), of Intel processors during the period 1996–2010 could be approximated by the following function of time t in years since the start of 1990:[51]

$$v(t) = \begin{cases} 400t - 2{,}200 & \text{if } 6 \le t < 15 \\ 3{,}800 & \text{if } 15 \le t \le 20. \end{cases}$$

How fast and in what direction was processor speed changing in 2000?

106. *Processor Speeds* The processor speed, in megahertz (MHz), of Intel processors during the period 1970–2000 could be approximated by the following function of time t in years since the start of 1970:[52]

$$v(t) = \begin{cases} 3t & \text{if } 0 \le t < 20 \\ 174t - 3{,}420 & \text{if } 20 \le t \le 30. \end{cases}$$

How fast and in what direction was processor speed changing in 1995?

---

[49]Data are rounded. 2010 net incomes projected based on first three quarters. Source: www.wikinvest.com.

[50]Percentages of net profit are commonly called "monkey points." Few movies ever make a net profit on paper, and anyone with any clout in the business gets a share of the *gross*, not the net.
[51]A rough model based on the fastest processors produced by Intel. Source: www.intel.com.
[52]*Ibid.*

Superbowl Advertising

Exercises 107 and 108 are based on the following graph and data from Wikipedia showing the increasing cost of a 30-second television ad during the Super Bowl.[53]

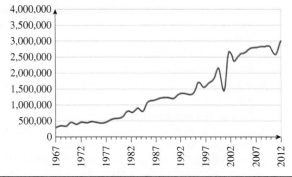

Year	1970	1980	1990	2000	2010
Cost (Thousands of $)	78	222	700	1,100	2,500

107. ▼ Take t to be the number of years since 1970 and y to be the cost, in thousands of dollars, of a Super Bowl ad.

  a. Model the 1970 and 1990 data with a linear equation.
  b. Model the 1990 and 2010 data with a linear equation.
  c. Use the results of parts (a) and (b) to obtain a piecewise linear model of the cost of a Super Bowl ad during 1970–2010.
  d. Use your model to estimate the cost in 2004. Is your answer in rough agreement with the graph? Explain any discrepancy.

108 ▼ Take t to be the number of years since 1980 and y to be the cost, in thousands of dollars, of a Super Bowl ad.

  a. Model the 1980 and 2000 data with a linear equation.
  b. Model the 2000 and 2010 data with a linear equation.
  c. Use the results of parts (a) and (b) to obtain a piecewise linear model of the cost of a Super Bowl ad during 1980–2010.
  d. Use your model to estimate the cost in 1992. Is your answer in rough agreement with the graph? Explain any discrepancy.

109. ▼ *Employment in Mexico* The number of workers employed in manufacturing jobs in Mexico was 3 million in 1995, rose to 4.1 million in 2000, and then dropped to 3.5 million in 2004.[54] Model this number N as a piecewise-linear function of the time t in years since 1995, and use your model to estimate the number of manufacturing jobs in Mexico in 2002. (Take the units of N to be millions.)

110. ▼ *Mortgage Delinquencies* The percentage of borrowers in the highest risk category who were delinquent on their payments decreased from 9.7% in 2001 to 4.3% in 2004 and

then shot up to 10.3% in 2007.[55] Model this percentage P as a piecewise-linear function of the time t in years since 2001, and use your model to estimate the percentage of delinquent borrowers in 2006.

COMMUNICATION AND REASONING EXERCISES

111. How would you test a table of values of x and y to see if it comes from a linear function?

112. You have ascertained that a table of values of x and y corresponds to a linear function. How do you find an equation for that linear function?

113. To what linear function of x does the linear equation $ax + by = c$ $(b \neq 0)$ correspond? Why did we specify $b \neq 0$?

114. Complete the following. The slope of the line with equation $y = mx + b$ is the number of units that _____ increases per unit increase in _____.

115. Complete the following. If, in a straight line, y is increasing three times as fast as x, then its _____ is _____.

116. Suppose that y is decreasing at a rate of 4 units per 3-unit increase of x. What can we say about the slope of the linear relationship between x and y? What can we say about the intercept?

117. If y and x are related by the linear expression $y = mx + b$, how will y change as x changes if m is positive? negative? zero?

118. Your friend April tells you that $y = f(x)$ has the property that, whenever x is changed by Δx, the corresponding change in y is $\Delta y = -\Delta x$. What can you tell her about f?

119. 🅣 ▼ Consider the following worksheet:

◆	A	B	C	D
1	x	y	m	b
2		1	2 =(B3-B2)/(A3-A2)	=B2-C2*A2
3		3	-1 Slope	Intercept

What is the effect on the slope of increasing the y-coordinate of the second point (the point whose coordinates are in Row 3)? Explain.

120. 🅣 ▼ Referring to the worksheet in Exercise 119, what is the effect on the slope of increasing the x-coordinate of the second point (the point whose coordinates are in row 3)? Explain.

121. If y is measured in bootlags[56] and x is measured in zonars[57], and $y = mx + b$, then m is measured in _____ and b is measured in _____.

---

[53]Source: http//en.wikipedia.org/wiki/Super_Bowl_advertising.

[54]Source: *New York Times*, Februrary 18, 2007, p. WK4.

[55]The 2007 figure was projected from data through October 2006. Source: *New York Times*, Februrary 18, 2007, p. BU9.

[56]An ancient Martian unit of length; one bootlag is the mean distance from a Martian's foreleg to its rearleg.

[57]The official currency of Utarek, Mars. (See the footnote to Exercise 88.)

122. If the slope in a linear relationship is measured in miles per dollar, then the independent variable is measured in _____ and the dependent variable is measured in _____.

123. If a quantity is changing linearly with time, and it increases by 10 units in the first day, what can you say about its behavior in the third day?

124. The quantities Q and T are related by a linear equation of the form

$$Q = mT + b.$$

When $T = 0$, Q is positive, but decreases to a negative quantity when T is 10. What are the signs of m and b? Explain your answers.

125. ▼ The velocity of an object is given by $v = 0.1t + 20$ m/sec, where t is time in seconds. The object is

(A) moving with fixed speed **(B)** accelerating
(C) decelerating **(D)** impossible to say from the given information

126. ▼ The position of an object is given by $x = 0.2t - 4$, where t is time in seconds. The object is

(A) moving with fixed speed **(B)** accelerating
(C) decelerating **(D)** impossible to say from the given information

127. If f and g are linear functions with slope m and n respectively, then what can you say about $f + g$?

128. If f and g are linear functions, then is $\frac{f}{g}$ linear? Explain.

129. Give examples of nonlinear functions f and g whose product is linear.

130. Give examples of nonlinear functions f and g whose quotient is linear (on a suitable domain).

131. ▼ Suppose the cost function is $C(x) = mx + b$ (with m and b positive), the revenue function is $R(x) = kx \ (k > m)$, and the number of items is increased from the break-even quantity. Does this result in a loss, a profit, or is it impossible to say? Explain your answer.

132. ▼ You have been constructing a demand equation, and you obtained a (correct) expression of the form $p = mq + b$, whereas you would have preferred one of the form $q = mp + b$. Should you simply switch p and q in the answer, should you start again from scratch, using p in the role of x and q in the role of y, or should you solve your demand equation for q? Give reasons for your decision.

1.4 Linear Regression

We have seen how to find a linear model given two data points: We find the equation of the line that passes through them. However, we often have more than two data points, and they will rarely all lie on a single straight line, but may often come close to doing so. The problem is to find the line coming *closest* to passing through all of the points.

Suppose, for example, that we are conducting research for a company interested in expanding into Mexico. Of interest to us would be current and projected growth in that country's economy. The following table shows past and projected per capita gross domestic product (GDP)[58] of Mexico for 2000–2014.[59]

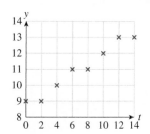

Figure 27(a)

Year t ($t = 0$ represents 2000)	0	2	4	6	8	10	12	14
Per Capita GDP y ($1,000)	9	9	10	11	11	12	13	13

A plot of these data suggests a roughly linear growth of the GDP (Figure 27(a)). These points suggest a roughly linear relationship between t and y, although they clearly do not all lie on a single straight line. Figure 27(b) shows the points together with several lines, some fitting better than others. Can we precisely measure which lines fit better than others? For instance, which of the two lines labeled as "good" fits in Figure 27(b) models the data more accurately? We begin by considering, for each value of t, the difference between the actual GDP (the **observed value**) and the GDP

Figure 27(b)

---

[58]The GDP is a measure of the total market value of all goods and services produced within a country.

[59]Data are approximate and/or projected. Sources: CIA World Factbook/www.indexmundi.com, www.economist.com.

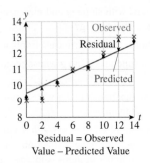

Residual = Observed
Value − Predicted Value

Figure 28

✳ Why not add the absolute values of the residuals instead? Mathematically, using the squares rather than the absolute values results in a simpler and more elegant solution. Further, using the squares always results in a *single* best-fit line in cases where the *x*-coordinates are all different, whereas this is not the case if we use absolute values.

predicted by a linear equation (the **predicted value**). The difference between the predicted value and the observed value is called the **residual**.

Residual = Observed Value − Predicted Value

On the graph, the residuals measure the vertical distances between the (observed) data points and the line (Figure 28) and they tell us how far the linear model is from predicting the actual GDP.

The more accurate our model, the smaller the residuals should be. We can combine all the residuals into a single measure of accuracy by adding their *squares*. (We square the residuals in part to make them all positive.✳) The sum of the squares of the residuals is called the **sum-of-squares error**, **SSE**. Smaller values of SSE indicate more accurate models.

Here are some definitions and formulas for what we have been discussing.

Observed and Predicted Values

Suppose we are given a collection of data points $(x_1, y_1), \ldots, (x_n, y_n)$. The n quantities $y_1, y_2, \ldots, y_n$ are called the **observed *y*-values**. If we model these data with a linear equation

$$\hat{y} = mx + b, \qquad \hat{y} \text{ stands for "estimated } y\text{" or "predicted } y\text{."}$$

then the *y*-values we get by substituting the given *x*-values into the equation are called the **predicted *y*-values**:

$$\hat{y}_1 = mx_1 + b \qquad \text{Substitute } x_1 \text{ for } x.$$
$$\hat{y}_2 = mx_2 + b \qquad \text{Substitute } x_2 \text{ for } x.$$
$$\ldots$$
$$\hat{y}_n = mx_n + b. \qquad \text{Substitute } x_n \text{ for } x.$$

Quick Example

Consider the three data points (0, 2), (2, 5), and (3, 6). The observed *y*-values are $y_1 = 2$, $y_2 = 5$, and $y_3 = 6$. If we model these data with the equation $\hat{y} = x + 2.5$, then the predicted values are:

$$\hat{y}_1 = x_1 + 2.5 = 0 + 2.5 = 2.5$$
$$\hat{y}_2 = x_2 + 2.5 = 2 + 2.5 = 4.5$$
$$\hat{y}_3 = x_3 + 2.5 = 3 + 2.5 = 5.5.$$

Residuals and Sum-of-Squares Error (SSE)

If we model a collection of data $(x_1, y_1), \ldots, (x_n, y_n)$ with a linear equation $\hat{y} = mx + b$, then the **residuals** are the n quantities (Observed Value − Predicted Value):

$$(y_1 - \hat{y}_1), (y_2 - \hat{y}_2), \ldots, (y_n - \hat{y}_n).$$

The **sum-of-squares error (SSE)** is the sum of the squares of the residuals:

$$\text{SSE} = (y_1 - \hat{y}_1)^2 + (y_2 - \hat{y}_2)^2 + \cdots + (y_n - \hat{y}_n)^2.$$

> ### Quick Example
>
> For the data and linear approximation given above, the residuals are:
>
> $$y_1 - \hat{y}_1 = 2 - 2.5 = -0.5$$
> $$y_2 - \hat{y}_2 = 5 - 4.5 = 0.5$$
> $$y_3 - \hat{y}_3 = 6 - 5.5 = 0.5$$
>
> and so SSE $= (-0.5)^2 + (0.5)^2 + (0.5)^2 = 0.75$.

EXAMPLE 1 **Computing SSE**

Using the data above on the GDP in Mexico, compute SSE for the linear models $y = 0.5t + 8$ and $y = 0.25t + 9$. Which model is the better fit?

Solution We begin by creating a table showing the values of t, the observed (given) values of y, and the values predicted by the first model.

using Technology

See the Technology Guides at the end of the chapter for detailed instructions on how to obtain the tables and graphs in Example 1 using a TI-83/84 Plus or a spreadsheet. Here is an outline:

TI-83/84 Plus

STAT EDIT

Values of t in L$_1$, and y in L$_2$. Predicted y: Highlight L$_3$. Enter
`0.5*L₁+8`
Squares of residuals: Highlight L$_4$. Enter
`(L₂-L₃)^2`
SSE: Home screen `sum(L₄)`
Graph: `Y₁=0.5X+8`
Y = screen: Turn on Plot 1 ZOOM
(STAT) [More details on page 117.]

Spreadsheet

Headings t, y, y-hat, Residual^2, m, b, and SSE in A1–F1.
t-values in A2–A9, y-values in B2–B9; 0.25 for m and 9 for b in E2–F2
Predicted y: `=$E$2*A2+$F$2` in C2 and copy down to C9.
Squares of residuals: `= (B2-C2)^2` in D2 and copy down to D9.
SSE: `=SUM(D2:D9)` in G2
Graph: Highlight A1–C9. Insert a Scatter chart.
[More details on page 122.]

Year t	Observed y	Predicted $\hat{y} = 0.5t + 8$
0	9	8
2	9	9
4	10	10
6	11	11
8	11	12
10	12	13
12	13	14
14	13	15

We now add two new columns for the residuals and their squares.

Year t	Observed y	Predicted $\hat{y} = 0.5t + 8$	Residual $y - \hat{y}$	Residual^2 $(y - \hat{y})^2$
0	9	8	$9 - 8 = 1$	$1^2 = 1$
2	9	9	$9 - 9 = 0$	$0^2 = 0$
4	10	10	$10 - 10 = 0$	$0^2 = 0$
6	11	11	$11 - 11 = 0$	$0^2 = 0$
8	11	12	$11 - 12 = -1$	$(-1)^2 = 1$
10	12	13	$12 - 13 = -1$	$(-1)^2 = 1$
12	13	14	$13 - 14 = -1$	$(-1)^2 = 1$
14	13	15	$13 - 15 = -2$	$(-2)^2 = 4$

SSE, the sum of the squares of the residuals, is then the sum of the entries in the last column,

$$SSE = 8.$$

Repeating the process using the second model, $0.25t + 9$, yields the following table:

Year t	Observed y	Predicted $\hat{y} = 0.25t + 9$	Residual $y - \hat{y}$	Residual^2 $(y - \hat{y})^2$
0	9	9	$9 - 9 = 0$	$0^2 = 0$
2	9	9.5	$9 - 9.5 = -0.5$	$(-0.5)^2 = 0.25$
4	10	10	$10 - 10 = 0$	$0^2 = 0$
6	11	10.5	$11 - 10.5 = 0.5$	$0.5^2 = 0.25$
8	11	11	$11 - 11 = 0$	$0^2 = 0$
10	12	11.5	$12 - 11.5 = 0.5$	$0.5^2 = 0.25$
12	13	12	$13 - 12 = 1$	$1^2 = 1$
14	13	12.5	$13 - 12.5 = 0.5$	$0.5^2 = 0.25$

This time, SSE $= 2$ and so the second model is a better fit.

Figure 29 shows the data points and the two linear models in question.

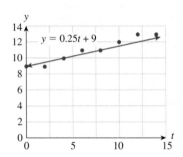

Figure 29

➡ Before we go on...

Q : *It seems clear from the figure that the second model in Example 1 gives a better fit. Why bother to compute SSE to tell me this?*

A : The difference between the two models we chose is so great that it is clear from the graphs which is the better fit. However, if we used a third model with $m = 0.25$ and $b = 9.1$, then its graph would be almost indistinguishable from that of the second, but a slightly better fit as measured by SSE $= 1.68$.

Among all possible lines, there ought to be one with the least possible value of SSE—that is, the greatest possible accuracy as a model. The line (and there is only one such line) that minimizes the sum of the squares of the residuals is called the **regression line**, the **least-squares line**, or the **best-fit line**.

To find the regression line, we need a way to find values of m and b that give the smallest possible value of SSE. As an example, let us take the second linear model in the example above. We said in the "Before we go on" discussion that increasing b from 9 to 9.1 had the desirable effect of decreasing SSE from 2 to 1.68. We could then increase m to 0.26, further reducing SSE to 1.328. Imagine this as a kind of game: Alternately alter the values of m and b by small amounts until SSE is as small as you can make it. This works, but is extremely tedious and time-consuming.

Fortunately, there is an algebraic way to find the regression line. Here is the calculation. To justify it rigorously requires calculus of several variables or linear algebra.

Regression Line

The **regression line** (**least squares line, best-fit line**) associated with the points $(x_1, y_1), (x_2, y_2), \ldots, (x_n, y_n)$ is the line that gives the minimum SSE. The regression line is

$$y = mx + b,$$

where m and b are computed as follows:

$$m = \frac{n\left(\sum xy\right) - \left(\sum x\right)\left(\sum y\right)}{n\left(\sum x^2\right) - \left(\sum x\right)^2}$$

$$b = \frac{\sum y - m\left(\sum x\right)}{n}$$

$n =$ number of data points.

The quantities m and b are called the **regression coefficients**.

Here, "$\sum$" means "the sum of." Thus, for example,

$$\sum x = \text{Sum of the } x\text{-values} = x_1 + x_2 + \cdots + x_n$$
$$\sum xy = \text{Sum of products} = x_1 y_1 + x_2 y_2 + \cdots + x_n y_n$$
$$\sum x^2 = \text{Sum of the squares of the } x\text{-values} = x_1{}^2 + x_2{}^2 + \cdots + x_n{}^2.$$

On the other hand,

$$\left(\sum x\right)^2 = \text{Square of } \sum x = \text{Square of the sum of the } x\text{-values.}$$

EXAMPLE 2 Per Capita Gross Domestic Product in Mexico

In Example 1 we considered the following data on the per capita gross domestic product (GDP) of Mexico:

Year x ($x = 0$ represents 2000)	0	2	4	6	8	10	12	14
Per Capita GDP y ($1,000)	9	9	10	11	11	12	13	13

Find the best-fit linear model for these data and use the model to predict the per capita GDP in Mexico in 2016.

using Technology

See the Technology Guides at the end of the chapter for detailed instructions on how to obtain the regression line and graph in Example 2 using a TI-83/84 Plus or a spreadsheet. Here is an outline:

TI-83/84 Plus
STAT EDIT
Values of x in L_1, and y in L_2.
Regression equation: STAT CALC
option #4: LinReg(ax+b)
Graph: Y= VARS 5 EQ 1,
then ZOOM 9
[More details on page 118.]

Spreadsheet
x-values in A2–A9, y-values in B2–B9
Graph: Highlight A2–B9. Insert a Scatter Chart.
Regression line: Add a linear trend-line. [More details on page 123.]

Website
www.WanerMath.com
The following two utilities will calculate and plot regression lines (link to either from Math Tools for Chapter 1):

Simple Regression

Function Evaluator and Grapher

Solution Let's organize our work in the form of a table, where the original data are entered in the first two columns and the bottom row contains the column sums.

x	y	xy	x^2
0	9	0	0
2	9	18	4
4	10	40	16
6	11	66	36
8	11	88	64
10	12	120	100
12	13	156	144
14	13	182	196
$\sum$ (**Sum**) 56	88	670	560

Because there are $n = 8$ data points, we get

$$m = \frac{n\left(\sum xy\right) - \left(\sum x\right)\left(\sum y\right)}{n\left(\sum x^2\right) - \left(\sum x\right)^2} = \frac{8(670) - (56)(88)}{8(560) - (56)^2} \approx 0.321$$

and

$$b = \frac{\sum y - m\left(\sum x\right)}{n} \approx \frac{88 - (0.321)(56)}{8} \approx 8.75.$$

So, the regression line is

$$y = 0.321x + 8.75.$$

To predict the per capita GDP in Mexico in 2016 we substitute $x = 16$ and get $y \approx 14$, or $\$14,000$ per capita.

Figure 30 shows the data points and the regression line (which has SSE ≈ 0.643; a lot lower than in Example 1).

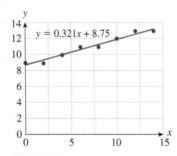

Figure 30

Coefficient of Correlation

If all the data points do not lie on one straight line, we would like to be able to measure how closely they can be approximated by a straight line. Recall that SSE measures the sum of the squares of the deviations from the regression line; therefore it constitutes a measurement of what is called "goodness of fit." (For instance, if SSE $= 0$, then all the points lie on a straight line.) However, SSE depends on the units we use to measure y, and also on the number of data points (the more data points we use, the larger SSE tends to be). Thus, while we can (and do) use SSE to compare the goodness of fit of two lines to the same data, we cannot use it to compare the goodness of fit of one line to one set of data with that of another to a different set of data.

To remove this dependency, statisticians have found a related quantity that can be used to compare the goodness of fit of lines to different sets of data. This quantity, called the **coefficient of correlation** or **correlation coefficient**, and usually denoted r, is between -1 and 1. The closer r is to -1 or 1, the better the fit. For an *exact* fit, we would have $r = -1$ (for a line with negative slope) or $r = 1$ (for a line with positive slope). For a bad fit, we would have r close to 0. Figure 31 shows several collections of data points with least-squares lines and the corresponding values of r.

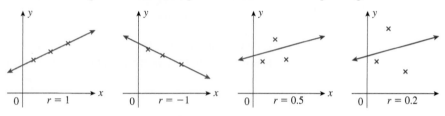

Figure 31

Correlation Coefficient

The coefficient of correlation of the n data points $(x_1, y_1), (x_2, y_2), \ldots, (x_n, y_n)$ is

$$r = \frac{n\left(\sum xy\right) - \left(\sum x\right)\left(\sum y\right)}{\sqrt{n\left(\sum x^2\right) - \left(\sum x\right)^2} \cdot \sqrt{n\left(\sum y^2\right) - \left(\sum y\right)^2}}.$$

It measures how closely the data points $(x_1, y_1), (x_2, y_2), \ldots, (x_n, y_n)$ fit the regression line. (The value r^2 is sometimes called the **coefficient of determination**.)

Interpretation

- If r is positive, the regression line has positive slope; if r is negative, the regression line has negative slope.

- If $r = 1$ or -1, then all the data points lie exactly on the regression line; if it is close to ± 1, then all the data points are close to the regression line.

- On the other hand, if r is not close to ± 1, then the data points are not close to the regression line, so the fit is not a good one. As a general rule of thumb, a value of $|r|$ less than around 0.8 indicates a poor fit of the data to the regression line.

using Technology

See the Technology Guides at the end of the chapter for detailed instructions on how to obtain the correlation coefficient in Example 3 using a TI-83/84 Plus or a spreadsheet. Here is an outline:

TI-83/84 Plus

2ND CATALOG DiagnosticOn
Then STAT CALC option #4:
LinReg(ax+b) [More details on page 119.]

Spreadsheet
Add a trendline and select the option to "Display R-squared value on chart."
[More details and other alternatives on page 124.]

Website
www.WanerMath.com
The following two utilities will show regression lines and also r^2 (link to either from Math Tools for Chapter 1):

   Simple Regression

   Function Evaluator and Grapher

EXAMPLE 3 Computing the Coefficient of Correlation

Find the correlation coefficient for the data in Example 2. Is the regression line a good fit?

Solution The formula for r requires $\sum x, \sum x^2, \sum xy, \sum y$, and $\sum y^2$. We have all of these except for $\sum y^2$, which we find in a new column as shown.

x	y	xy	x^2	y^2
0	9	0	0	81
2	9	18	4	81
4	10	40	16	100
6	11	66	36	121
8	11	88	64	121
10	12	120	100	144
12	13	156	144	169
14	13	182	196	169
$\sum$ (**Sum**) 56	88	670	560	986

Substituting these values into the formula, we get

$$r = \frac{n\left(\sum xy\right) - \left(\sum x\right)\left(\sum y\right)}{\sqrt{n\left(\sum x^2\right) - \left(\sum x\right)^2} \cdot \sqrt{n\left(\sum y^2\right) - \left(\sum y\right)^2}}$$

$$= \frac{8(670) - (56)(88)}{\sqrt{8(560) - 56^2} \cdot \sqrt{8(986) - 88^2}}$$

$$\approx 0.982.$$

As r is close to 1, the fit is a fairly good one; that is, the original points lie nearly along a straight line, as can be confirmed from the graph in Example 2.

1.4 EXERCISES

▼ more advanced   ◆ challenging
T indicates exercises that should be solved using technology

In Exercises 1–4, compute the sum-of-squares error (SSE) by hand for the given set of data and linear model. HINT [See Example 1.]

1. $(1, 1), (2, 2), (3, 4); y = x - 1$

2. $(0, 1), (1, 1), (2, 2); y = x + 1$

3. $(0, -1), (1, 3), (4, 6), (5, 0); y = -x + 2$

4. $(2, 4), (6, 8), (8, 12), (10, 0); y = 2x - 8$

T *In Exercises 5–8, use technology to compute the sum-of-squares error (SSE) for the given set of data and linear models. Indicate which linear model gives the better fit.*

5. $(1, 1), (2, 2), (3, 4);$ **a.** $y = 1.5x - 1$ **b.** $y = 2x - 1.5$

6. $(0, 1), (1, 1), (2, 2);$ **a.** $y = 0.4x + 1.1$ **b.** $y = 0.5x + 0.9$

7. $(0, -1), (1, 3), (4, 6), (5, 0);$ **a.** $y = 0.3x + 1.1$
    b. $y = 0.4x + 0.9$

8. $(2, 4), (6, 8), (8, 12), (10, 0);$ **a.** $y = -0.1x + 7$
    b. $y = -0.2x + 6$

Find the regression line associated with each set of points in Exercises 9–12. Graph the data and the best-fit line. (Round all coefficients to 4 decimal places.) HINT [See Example 2.]

9. $(1, 1), (2, 2), (3, 4)$

10. $(0, 1), (1, 1), (2, 2)$

11. $(0, -1), (1, 3), (3, 6), (4, 1)$

12. $(2, 4), (4, 8), (8, 12), (10, 0)$

In the next two exercises, use correlation coefficients to determine which of the given sets of data is best fit by its associated regression line and which is fit worst. Is it a perfect fit for any of the data sets? HINT [See Example 3.]

13. a. $\{(1, 3), (2, 4), (5, 6)\}$
    b. $\{(0, -1), (2, 1), (3, 4)\}$
    c. $\{(4, -3), (5, 5), (0, 0)\}$

14. a. $\{(1, 3), (-2, 9), (2, 1)\}$
    b. $\{(0, 1), (1, 0), (2, 1)\}$
    c. $\{(0, 0), (5, -5), (2, -2.1)\}$

APPLICATIONS

15. *Mobile Broadband Subscriptions* The following table shows the number of mobile broadband subscribers worldwide (x is the number of years since 2000):[60]

Year x	2	6	10
Subscribers y (Millions)	0	70	900

Complete the following table and obtain the associated regression line. (Round coefficients to one decimal place.) HINT [See Example 3.]

x	y	xy	x^2
2	0		
6	70		
10	900		
$\sum$ (**Sum**)			

Use your regression equation to project the number in 2012.

16. *Investment in Gold* Following are approximate values of the Amex Gold BUGS Index ($x = 0$ represents 2000):[61]

Year x	0	5	10
Index y	50	200	500

---

[60]Data are rounded (2010 figure is estimated). Source: International Telecommunication Union www.itu.int/ITU-D/ict/statistics/at_glance/KeyTelecom.html.

[61]BUGS stands for "basket of unhedged gold stocks." Figures are approximate. Source: www.google.com/finance.

Complete the following table and obtain the associated regression line. (Round coefficients to the nearest whole number.) HINT [See Example 3.]

x	y	xy	x^2
0	50		
5	200		
10	500		
$\sum$ (Sum)			

Use your regression equation to project the index in 2011.

17. E-Commerce The following chart shows second quarter total retail e-commerce sales in the U.S. in 2000, 2005, and 2010 ($t = 0$ represents 2000):[62]

Year t	0	5	10
Sales ($ billion) y	6	20	40

Find the regression line (round coefficients to one decimal place) and use it to estimate second quarter retail e-commerce sales in 2006. (The actual figure was approximately $25 billion.)

18. Net Sales The following table show the reported net sales by Nokia in the third quarters of 2008, 2009, and 2010 ($t = 0$ represents the third quarter of 2008):[63]

Year t	0	1	2
Net Sales (€ billion) y	12	10	10

Find the regression line (round coefficients to one decimal place) and use it to "predict" Nokia's net income in the third quarter of 2011. (The actual figure was approximately €9.0 billion.)

19. Oil Recovery The Texas Bureau of Economic Geology published a study on the economic impact of using carbon dioxide enhanced oil recovery (EOR) technology to extract additional oil from fields that have reached the end of their conventional economic life. The following table gives the approximate number of jobs for the citizens of Texas that would be created at various levels of recovery.[64]

Percent Recovery (%)	20	40	80	100
Jobs Created (Millions)	3	6	9	15

Find the regression line and use it to estimate the number of jobs that would be created at a recovery level of 50%.

20. Oil Recovery (Refer to Exercise 19.) The following table gives the approximate economic value associated with various levels of oil recovery in Texas.[65]

Percent Recovery (%)	10	40	50	80
Economic Value ($ billions)	200	900	1,000	2,000

Find the regression line and use it to estimate the economic value associated with a recovery level of 70%.

21. Profit: Amazon.com The following table shows Amazon.com's approximate net sales (revenue) and net income (profit) in the period 2006–2009:[66]

Net Sales ($ billions)	10	15	20	25
Net Income ($ millions)	200	500	600	900

a. Use this information to find a linear regression model for Amazon's net income I (in millions of dollars) as a function of net sales S (in billions of dollars).
b. Give the units of measurement and interpretation of the slope.
c. What, according to the model, would Amazon.com need to earn in net sales in order for its net income to be $1 billion? (Round answer to the nearest $ billion.)
d. Plot the data and regression line. Based on the graph, would you say that the linear model is reasonable? Why?

22. Operating Expenses: Amazon.com The following table shows Amazon.com's approximate net sales (revenue) and operating expenses in 2006–2009:[67]

Net Sales ($ billions)	10	15	20	25
Operating Expenses ($ billions)	2	2.5	3	4.5

a. Use this information to find a linear regression model for Amazon's operating expenses E (in billions of dollars) as a function of net sales S (in billions of dollars).
b. Give the units of measurement and interpretation of the slope.
c. What, according to the model, would Amazon.com need to earn in net sales in order for its operating expenses to be $5 billion? (Round answer to the nearest $ billion.)
d. Plot the data and regression line. Based on the graph, would you say that the linear model is reasonable? Why?

---

[62]Figures are rounded. Source: U.S. Census Bureau www.census.gov

[63]Data are approximate. Source: www.nokia.com.

[64]Source: "CO2–Enhanced Oil Recovery Resource Potential in Texas: Potential Positive Economic Impacts," Texas Bureau of Economic Geology, April 2004, www.rrc.state.tx.us/tepc/CO2-EOR_white_paper.pdf.

[65]Ibid.

[66]Figures are approximate. Source: www.wikinvest.com.

[67]Ibid.

23. 🖳 ***Textbook Sizes*** The following table shows the numbers of pages in previous editions of *Applied Calculus* by Waner and Costenoble:

Edition n	2	3	4	5
Number of Pages L	585	656	694	748

a. With the edition number as the independent variable, use technology to obtain a regression line and a plot of the points together with the regression line. (Round coefficients to two decimal places.)

b. Interpret the slope of the regression line.

24. 🖳 ***Textbook Sizes*** Repeat Exercise 23 using the following corresponding table for *Finite Mathematics* by Waner and Costenoble:

Edition n	2	3	4	5
Number of Pages L	603	608	676	692

25. 🖳 ***Soybean Production: Cerrados*** The following table shows soybean production, in millions of tons, in Brazil's *Cerrados* region, as a function of the cultivated area, in millions of acres.[68]

Area (millions of acres)	25	30	32	40	52
Production (millions of tons)	15	25	30	40	60

a. Use technology to obtain the regression line and to show a plot of the points together with the regression line. (Round coefficients to two decimal places.)

b. Interpret the slope of the regression line.

26. 🖳 ***Soybean Production: U.S.*** The following table shows soybean production, in millions of tons, in the U.S. as a function of the cultivated area, in millions of acres.[69]

Area (millions of acres)	30	42	69	59	74	74
Production (millions of tons)	20	33	55	57	83	88

a. Use technology to obtain the regression line and to show a plot of the points together with the regression line. (Round coefficients to two decimal places.)

b. Interpret the slope of the regression line.

27. 🖳 ***Airline Profits and the Price of Oil*** A common perception is that airline profits are strongly correlated with the price of oil. Following are annual net incomes of **Continental Airlines** together with the approximate price of oil in the period 2005–2010:[70]

Year	2005	2006	2007	2008	2009	2010
Price of Oil ($ per barrel)	56	63	67	92	54	71
Continental Net Income ($ million)	−70	370	430	−590	−280	150

a. Use technology to obtain a regression line showing Continental's net income as a function of the price of oil, and also the coefficient of correlation r.

b. What does the value of r suggest about the relationship of Continental's net income to the price of oil?

c. Support your answer to part (b) with a plot of the data and regression line.

28. 🖳 ***Airline Profits and the Price of Oil*** Repeat Exercise 27 using the following corresponding data for **American Airlines:**[71]

Year	2005	2006	2007	2008	2009	2010
Price of Oil ($ per barrel)	56	63	67	92	54	71
American Net Income ($ million)	−850	250	450	−2,100	−1,450	−700

🖳 ***Doctorates in Mexico*** Exercises 29–32 are based on the following table showing the annual number of PhD graduates in Mexico in various fields.[72]

	Natural Sciences	Engineering	Social Sciences
1990	84	8	98
1995	107	55	161
2000	174	247	222
2005	515	371	584
2010	979	578	1,230

29. a. With $x =$ the number of natural science doctorates and $y =$ the number of engineering doctorates, use technology to obtain the regression equation and graph the associated points and regression line. (Round coefficients to three significant digits.)

b. What does the slope tell you about the relationship between the number of natural science doctorates and the number of engineering doctorates?

c. Use technology to obtain the coefficient of correlation r. Does the value of r suggest a strong correlation between x and y?

d. Judging from the graph, would you say that a linear relationship between x and y is appropriate? Why?

30. a. With $x =$ the number of natural science doctorates and $y =$ the number of social science doctorates, use technology to obtain the regression equation and graph the associated points and regression line. (Round coefficients to three significant digits.)

---

[68]Source: Brazil Agriculture Ministry/*New York Times*, December 12, 2004, p. N32.

[69]Data are approximate. Source for data: L. David Roper, June 2010, *Crop Production in the World & the United States*, www.roperld.com/science/cropsworld&us.htm.

[70]Figures are rounded and oil prices are inflation adjusted. Sources: www.wikinvest.com, www.inflationdata.com.

[71]*Ibid.*

[72]2010 data is estimated. Source: Instituto Nacional de Estadística y Geografía www.inegi.org.mx.

b. What does the slope tell you about the relationship between the number of natural science doctorates and the number of social science doctorates?

c. Use technology to obtain the coefficient of correlation r. Does the value of r suggest a strong correlation between x and y?

d. Judging from the graph, would you say that a linear relationship between x and y is appropriate? Why?

31. ▼ **a.** Use technology to obtain the regression equation and the coefficient of correlation r for the number of natural science doctorates as a function of time t in years since 1990, and graph the associated points and regression line. (Round coefficients to three significant digits.)

b. What does the slope tell you about the number of natural science doctorates?

c. Judging from the graph, would you say that the number of natural science doctorates is increasing at a faster and faster rate, a slower and slower rate, or neither? Why?

d. If r had been equal to 1, could you have drawn the same conclusion as in part (c)? Explain.

32. ▼ **a.** Use technology to obtain the regression equation and the coefficient of correlation r for the number of engineering doctorates as a function of time t in years since 1990, and graph the associated points and regression line. (Round coefficients to three significant digits.)

b. What does the slope tell you about the number of engineering doctorates?

c. Judging from the graph, would you say that the number of engineering doctorates is increasing at a faster and faster rate, a slower and slower rate, or neither? Why?

d. If r had been close to 0, could you have drawn the same conclusion as in part (c)? Explain.

33. ▣ ▼ *NY City Housing Costs: Downtown* The following table shows the average price of a two-bedroom apartment in downtown New York City from 1994 to 2004 ($t = 0$ represents 1994).[73]

Year t	0	2	4	6	8	10
Price p ($ million)	0.38	0.40	0.60	0.95	1.20	1.60

a. Use technology to obtain the linear regression line and correlation coefficient r, with all coefficients rounded to two decimal places, and plot the regression line and the given points.

b. Does the graph suggest that a non-linear relationship between t and p would be more appropriate than a linear one? Why?

c. Use technology to obtain the residuals. What can you say about the residuals in support of the claim in part (b)?

34. ▣ ▼ *Fiber Optic Connections* The following table shows the number of fiber optic cable connections to homes in the U.S. from 2000 to 2004 ($t = 0$ represents 2000):[74]

Year t	0	1	2	3	4
Connections c (Thousands)	0	10	25	65	150

a. Use technology to obtain the linear regression line and correlation coefficient r, with all coefficients rounded to two decimal places, and plot the regression line and the given points.

b. Does the graph suggest that a non-linear relationship between t and c would be more appropriate than a linear one? Why?

c. Use technology to obtain the residuals. What can you say about the residuals in support of the claim in part (b)?

COMMUNICATION AND REASONING EXERCISES

35. Why is the regression line associated with the two points (a, b) and (c, d) the same as the line that passes through both? (Assume that $a \neq c$.)

36. What is the smallest possible sum-of-squares error if the given points happen to lie on a straight line? Why?

37. If the points $(x_1, y_1), (x_2, y_2), \ldots, (x_n, y_n)$ lie on a straight line, what can you say about the regression line associated with these points?

38. If all but one of the points $(x_1, y_1), (x_2, y_2), \ldots, (x_n, y_n)$ lie on a straight line, must the regression line pass through all but one of these points?

39. ▼ Verify that the regression line for the points $(0, 0)$, $(-a, a)$, and (a, a) has slope 0. What is the value of r? (Assume that $a \neq 0$.)

40. ▼ Verify that the regression line for the points $(0, a)$, $(0, -a)$, and $(a, 0)$ has slope 0. What is the value of r? (Assume that $a \neq 0$.)

41. ▼ Must the regression line pass through at least one of the data points? Illustrate your answer with an example.

42. ▼ Why must care be taken when using mathematical models to extrapolate?

43. ▼ Your friend Imogen tells you that if r for a collection of data points is more than 0.9, then the most appropriate relationship between the variables is a linear one. Explain why she is wrong by referring to one of the exercises.

44. ▼ Your other friend Mervyn tells you that if r for a collection of data points has an absolute value less than 0.8, then the most appropriate relationship between the variables is a quadratic and not a linear one. Explain why *he* is wrong.

---

[73]Data are rounded and 2004 figure is an estimate. Source: Miller Samuel/*New York Times*, March 28, 2004, p. RE 11.

[74]Source: Render, Vanderslice & Associates/*New York Times*, October 11, 2004, p. C1.

CHAPTER 1 REVIEW

KEY CONCEPTS

REVIEW EXERCISES

In Exercises 1–4, use the graph of the function f to find approximations of the given values.

1.

a. $f(-2)$ **b.** $f(0)$
c. $f(2)$ **d.** $f(2) - f(-2)$

2.

a. $f(-2)$ **b.** $f(0)$
c. $f(2)$ **d.** $f(2) - f(-2)$

3.

a. $f(-1)$ **b.** $f(0)$
c. $f(1)$ **d.** $f(1) - f(-1)$

4.

a. $f(-1)$ **b.** $f(0)$
c. $f(1)$ **d.** $f(1) - f(-1)$

In Exercises 5–8, graph the given function or equation.

5. $y = -2x + 5$ **6.** $2x - 3y = 12$

7. $y = \begin{cases} \frac{1}{2}x & \text{if } -1 \le x \le 1 \\ x - 1 & \text{if } 1 < x \le 3 \end{cases}$

8. $f(x) = 4x - x^2$ with domain $[0, 4]$

In Exercises 9–14, decide whether the specified values come from a linear, quadratic, exponential, or absolute value function.

9.

x	−2	0	1	2	4
$f(x)$	4	2	1	0	2

10.

x	−2	0	1	2	4
$g(x)$	−5	−3	−2	−1	1

11.

x	−2	0	1	2	4
$h(x)$	1.5	1	0.75	0.5	0

12.

x	−2	0	1	2	4
$k(x)$	0.25	1	2	4	16

13.

x	−2	0	1	2	4
$u(x)$	0	4	3	0	−12

14.

x	−2	0	1	2	4
w(x)	32	8	4	2	0.5

Year t	0	1	2	3	4	5
Cost C(t)	$5.42	$5.10	$5.00	$5.12	$5.40	$5.88

In Exercises 15–22, find the equation of the specified line.

15. Through $(3, 2)$ with slope -3

16. Through $(-2, 4)$ with slope -1

17. Through $(1, -3)$ and $(5, 2)$

18. Through $(-1, 2)$ and $(1, 0)$

19. Through $(1, 2)$ parallel to $x - 2y = 2$

20. Through $(-3, 1)$ parallel to $-2x - 4y = 5$

21. With slope 4 crossing $2x - 3y = 6$ at its x-intercept

22. With slope $1/2$ crossing $3x + y = 6$ at its x-intercept

In Exercises 23 and 24, determine which of the given lines better fits the given points.

23. $(-1, 1), (1, 2), (2, 0); y = -x/2 + 1$ or $y = -x/4 + 1$

24. $(-2, -1), (-1, 1), (0, 1), (1, 2), (2, 4), (3, 3); y = x + 1$ or $y = x/2 + 1$

In Exercises 25 and 26, find the line that best fits the given points and compute the correlation coefficient.

25. $(-1, 1), (1, 2), (2, 0)$

26. $(-2, -1), (-1, 1), (0, 1), (1, 2), (2, 4), (3, 3)$

APPLICATIONS: OHaganBooks.com

27. *Web Site Traffic* John Sean O'Hagan is CEO of the online bookstore OHaganBooks.com and notices that, since the establishment of the company Web site six years ago ($t = 0$), the number of visitors to the site has grown quite dramatically, as indicated by the following table:

Year t	0	1	2	3	4	5	6
Web site Traffic V(t) (visits/day)	100	300	1,000	3,300	10,500	33,600	107,400

a. Graph the function V as a function of time t. Which of the following types of function seem to fit the curve best: linear, quadratic, or exponential?

b. Compute the ratios $\dfrac{V(1)}{V(0)}, \dfrac{V(2)}{V(1)}, \ldots,$ and $\dfrac{V(6)}{V(5)}$. What do you notice?

c. Use the result of part (b) to predict Web site traffic next year (to the nearest 100).

28. *Publishing Costs* Marjory Maureen Duffin is CEO of publisher Duffin House, a major supplier of paperback titles to OHaganBooks.com. She notices that publishing costs over the past five years have varied considerably as indicated by the following table, which shows the average cost to the company of publishing a paperback novel (t is time in years, and the current year is $t = 5$):

a. Graph the function C as a function of time t. Which of the following types of function seem to fit the curve best: linear, quadratic, or exponential?

b. Compute the differences $C(1) - C(0), C(2) - C(1), \ldots,$ and $C(5) - C(4)$, rounded to one decimal place. What do you notice?

c. Use the result of part (b) to predict the cost of producing a paperback novel next year.

29. *Web Site Stability* John O'Hagan is considering upgrading the Web server equipment at OHaganBooks.com because of frequent crashes. The tech services manager has been monitoring the frequency of crashes as a function of Web site traffic (measured in thousands of visits per day) and has obtained the following model:

$$c(x) = \begin{cases} 0.03x + 2 & \text{if } 0 \le x \le 50 \\ 0.05x + 1 & \text{if } x > 50 \end{cases}$$

where $c(x)$ is the average number of crashes in a day in which there are x thousand visitors.

a. On average, how many times will the Web site crash on a day when there are 10,000 visits? 50,000 visits? 100,000 visits?

b. What does the coefficient 0.03 tell you about the Web site's stability?

c. Last Friday, the Web site went down 8 times. Estimate the number of visits that day.

30. *Book Sales* As OHaganBooks.com has grown in popularity, the sales manager has been monitoring book sales as a function of the Web site traffic (measured in thousands of visits per day) and has obtained the following model:

$$s(x) = \begin{cases} 1.55x & \text{if } 0 \le x \le 100 \\ 1.75x - 20 & \text{if } 100 < x \le 250 \end{cases}$$

where $s(x)$ is the average number of books sold in a day in which there are x thousand visitors.

a. On average, how many books per day does the model predict OHaganBooks.com will sell when it has 60,000 visits in a day? 100,000 visits in a day? 160,000 visits in a day?

b. What does the coefficient 1.75 tell you about book sales?

c. According to the model, approximately how many visitors per day will be needed in order to sell an average of 300 books per day?

31. *New Users* The number of registered users at OHaganBooks. com has increased substantially over the past few months. The following table shows the number of new users registering each month for the past six months:

Month t	1	2	3	4	5	6
New Users (thousands)	12.5	37.5	62.5	72.0	74.5	75.0

a. Which of the following models best approximates the data?

(A) $n(t) = \dfrac{300}{4 + 100(5^{-t})}$ **(B)** $n(t) = 13.3t + 8.0$

(C) $n(t) = -2.3t^2 + 30.0t - 3.3$

(D) $n(t) = 7(3^{0.5t})$

b. What do each of the above models predict for the number of new users in the next few months: rising, falling, or leveling off?

32. Purchases OHaganBooks.com has been promoting a number of books published at Duffin House. The following table shows the number of books purchased each month from Duffin House for the past five months:

Month t	1	2	3	4	5
Purchases (books)	1,330	520	520	1,340	2,980

a. Which of the following models best approximates the data?

(A) $n(t) = \dfrac{3,000}{1 + 12(2^{-t})}$ **(B)** $n(t) = \dfrac{2,000}{4.2 - 0.7t}$

(C) $n(t) = 300(1.6^t)$

(D) $n(t) = 100(4.1t^2 - 20.4t + 29.5)$

b. What do each of the above models predict for the number of new users in the next few months: rising, falling, leveling off, or something else?

33. Internet Advertising Several months ago. John O'Hagan investigated the effect on the popularity of OHaganBooks.com of placing banner ads at well-known Internet portals. The following model was obtained from available data:

$$v(c) = -0.000005c^2 + 0.085c + 1,750 \text{ new visits per day}$$

where c is the monthly expenditure on banner ads.

a. John O'Hagan is considering increasing expenditure on banner ads from the current level of $5,000 to $6,000 per month. What will be the resulting effect on Web site popularity?

b. According to the model, would the Web site popularity continue to grow at the same rate if he continued to raise expenditure on advertising $1,000 each month? Explain.

c. Does this model give a reasonable prediction of traffic at expenditures larger than $8,500 per month? Why?

34. Production Costs Over at Duffin House, Marjory Duffin is trying to decide on the size of the print runs for the best-selling new fantasy novel *Larry Plotter and the Simplex Method*. The following model shows a calculation of the total cost to produce a million copies of the novel, based on an analysis of setup and storage costs:

$$c(n) = 0.0008n^2 - 72n + 2,000,000 \text{ dollars}$$

where n is the print run size (the number of books printed in each run).

a. What would be the effect on cost if the run size was increased from 20,000 to 30,000?

b. Would increasing the run size in further steps of 10,000 result in the same changes in the total cost? Explain.

c. What approximate run size would you recommend that Marjoy Duffin use for a minimum cost?

35. Internet Advertising When OHaganBooks.com actually went ahead and increased Internet advertising from $5,000 per month to $6,000 per month (see Exercise 33) it was noticed that the number of new visits increased from an estimated 2,050 per day to 2,100 per day. Use this information to construct a linear model giving the average number v of new visits per day as a function of the monthly advertising expenditure c.

a. What is the model?

b. Based on the model, how many new visits per day could be anticipated if OHaganBooks.com budgets $7,000 per month for Internet advertising?

c. The goal is to eventually increase the number of new visits to 2,500 per day. Based on the model, how much should be spent on Internet advertising in order to accomplish this?

36. Production Costs When Duffin House printed a million copies of *Larry Plotter and the Simplex Method* (see Exercise 34), it used print runs of 20,000, which cost the company $880,000. For the sequel, *Larry Plotter and the Simplex Method, Phase 2* it used print runs of 40,000 which cost the company $550,000. Use this information to construct a linear model giving the production cost c as a function of the run size n.

a. What is the model?

b. Based on the model, what would print runs of 25,000 have cost the company?

c. Marjory Duffin has decided to budget $418,000 for production of the next book in the *Simplex Method* series. Based on the model, how large should the print runs be to accomplish this?

37. Recreation John O'Hagan has just returned from a sales convention at Puerto Vallarta, Mexico where, in order to win a bet he made with Marjory Duffin (Duffin House was also at the convention), he went bungee jumping at a nearby mountain retreat. The bungee cord he used had the property that a person weighing 70 kg would drop a total distance of 74.5 meters, while a 90 kg person would drop 93.5 meters. Express the distance d a jumper drops as a linear function of the jumper's weight w. John OHagan dropped 90 m. What was his approximate weight?

38. Crickets The mountain retreat near Puerto Vallarta was so quiet at night that all one could hear was the chirping of the snowy tree crickets. These crickets behave in a rather interesting way: The rate at which they chirp depends linearly on the temperature. Early in the evening, John O'Hagan counted 140 chirps/minute and noticed that the temperature was 80°F. Later in the evening the temperature dropped to 75°F, and the chirping slowed down to 120 chirps/minute. Express the temperature T as a function of the rate of chirping r. The temperature that night dropped to a low of 65°F. At approximately what rate were the crickets chirping at that point?

39. Break-Even Analysis OHaganBooks.com has recently decided to start selling music albums online through a service it calls *o'Tunes*.[75] Users pay a fee to download an entire music album. Composer royalties and copyright fees cost an average of $5.50 per album, and the cost of operating and maintaining *o'Tunes* amounts to $500 per week. The company is currently charging customers $9.50 per album.

   a. What are the associated (weekly) cost, revenue, and profit functions?

   b. How many albums must be sold per week in order to make a profit?

   c. If the charge is lowered to $8.00 per album, how many albums must be sold per week in order to make a profit?

40. Break-Even Analysis OHaganBooks.com also generates revenue through its *o'Books* e-book service. Author royalties and copyright fees cost the company an average of $4 per novel, and the monthly cost of operating and maintaining the service amounts to $900 per month. The company is currently charging readers $5.50 per novel.

   a. What are the associated cost, revenue, and profit functions?

   b. How many novels must be sold per month in order to break even?

   c. If the charge is lowered to $5.00 per novel, how many books must be sold in order to break even?

41. Demand and Profit In order to generate a profit from its new *o'Tunes* service, OHaganBooks.com needs to know how the demand for music albums depends on the price it charges. During the first week of the service, it was charging $7 per album, and sold 500. Raising the price to $9.50 had the effect of lowering demand to 300 albums per week.

   a. Use the given data to construct a linear demand equation.

   b. Use the demand equation you constructed in part (a) to estimate the demand if the price was raised to $12 per album.

_____
[75] The (highly original) name was suggested to John O'Hagan by Marjory Duffin over cocktails one evening.

c. Using the information on cost given in Exercise 39, determine which of the three prices ($7, $9.50 and $12) would result in the largest weekly profit, and the size of that profit.

42. Demand and Profit In order to generate a profit from its *o'Books* e-book service, OHaganBooks.com needs to know how the demand for novels depends on the price it charges. During the first month of the service, it was charging $10 per novel, and sold 350. Lowering the price to $5.50 per novel had the effect of increasing demand to 620 novels per month.

   a. Use the given data to construct a linear demand equation.

   b. Use the demand equation you constructed in part (a) to estimate the demand if the price was raised to $15 per novel.

   c. Using the information on cost given in Exercise 40, determine which of the three prices ($5.50, $10 and $15) would result in the largest profit, and the size of that profit.

43. Demand OHaganBooks.com has tried selling music albums on *o'Tunes* at a variety of prices, with the following results:

Price	$8.00	$8.50	$10	$11.50
Demand (Weekly sales)	440	380	250	180

   a. Use the given data to obtain a linear regression model of demand.

   b. Use the demand model you constructed in part (a) to estimate the demand if the company charged $10.50 per album. (Round the answer to the nearest album.)

44. Demand OHaganBooks.com has tried selling novels through *o'Books* at a variety of prices, with the following results:

Price	$5.50	$10	$11.50	$12
Demand (Monthly sales)	620	350	350	300

   a. Use the given data to obtain a linear regression model of demand.

   b. Use the demand model you constructed in part (a) to estimate the demand if the company charged $8 per novel. (Round the answer to the nearest novel.)

Case Study   **Modeling Spending on Internet Advertising**

You are the new director of Impact Advertising Inc.'s Internet division, which has enjoyed a steady 0.25% of the Internet advertising market. You have drawn up an ambitious proposal to expand your division in light of your anticipation that Internet advertising will continue to skyrocket. However, upper management sees things differently and, based on the following email, does not seem likely to approve the budget for your proposal.

Jeff Titcomb/Photographer's Choice / Getty Images

TO: JCheddar@impact.com (J. R. Cheddar)
CC: CVODoylePres@impact.com (C. V. O'Doyle, CEO)
FROM: SGLombardoVP@impact.com (S. G. Lombardo, VP Financial Affairs)
SUBJECT: Your Expansion Proposal
DATE: May 30, 2014

Hi John:

Your proposal reflects exactly the kind of ambitious planning and optimism we like to see in our new upper management personnel. Your presentation last week was most impressive, and obviously reflected a great deal of hard work and preparation.

I am in full agreement with you that Internet advertising is on the increase. Indeed, our Market Research department informs me that, based on a regression of the most recently available data, Internet advertising revenue in the United States will continue to grow at a rate of approximately $2.7 billion per year. This translates into approximately $6.75 million in increased revenues per year for Impact, given our 0.25% market share. This rate of expansion is exactly what our planned 2015 budget anticipates. Your proposal, on the other hand, would require a budget of approximately *twice* the 2015 budget allocation, even though your proposal provides no hard evidence to justify this degree of financial backing.

At this stage, therefore, I am sorry to say that I am inclined not to approve the funding for your project, although I would be happy to discuss this further with you. I plan to present my final decision on the 2015 budget at next week's divisional meeting.

Regards, Sylvia

Refusing to admit defeat, you contact the Market Research department and request the details of their projections on Internet advertising. They fax you the following information:[76]

Year	2007	2008	2009	2010	2011	2012	2013	2014
Internet Advertising Revenue ($ Billion)	21.2	23.4	22.7	25.8	28.5	32.6	36	40.5

Regression Model: $y = 2.744x + 19.233$ (x = time in years since 2007)

Correlation Coefficient: $r = 0.970$

Now you see where the VP got that $2.7 billion figure: The slope of the regression equation is close to 2.7, indicating a rate of increase of about $2.7 billion per year. Also, the correlation coefficient is very high—an indication that the linear model fits the data well. In view of this strong evidence, it seems difficult to argue that revenues will increase by significantly more than the projected $2.7 billion per year. To get a

_____
[76]The 2011–2014 figures are projections by eMarketer. Source: www.eMarketer.com.

Internet Advertising Revenue
($ billions)

Year since 2007

Figure 32

✻ Note that this *r* is *not* the linear correlation coefficient we defined on page 101; what this *r* measures is how closely the *quadratic* regression model fits the data.

Internet Advertising Revenue
($ billions)

Year since 2007

Figure 33

† The number of degrees of freedom in a regression model is 1 less than the number of coefficients. For a linear model, it is 1 (there are two coefficients: the slope *m* and the intercept *b*), and for a quadratic model it is 2. For a detailed discussion, consult a text on regression analysis.

better picture of what's going on, you decide to graph the data together with the regression line in your spreadsheet. What you get is shown in Figure 32. You immediately notice that the data points seem to suggest a curve, and not a straight line. Then again, perhaps the suggestion of a curve is an illusion. Thus there are, you surmise, two possible interpretations of the data:

1. (Your first impression) As a function of time, Internet advertising revenue is nonlinear, and is in fact accelerating (the rate of change is increasing), so a linear model is inappropriate.

2. (Devil's advocate) Internet advertising revenue *is* a linear function of time; the fact that the points do not lie on the regression line is simply a consequence of random factors that do not reflect a long-term trend, such as world events, mergers and acquisitions, short-term fluctuations in economy or the stock market, etc.

You suspect that the VP will probably opt for the second interpretation and discount the graphical evidence of accelerating growth by claiming that it is an illusion: a "statistical fluctuation." That is, of course, a possibility, but you wonder how likely it really is.

For the sake of comparison, you decide to try a regression based on the simplest nonlinear model you can think of—a quadratic function.

$$y = ax^2 + bx + c$$

Your spreadsheet allows you to fit such a function with a click of the mouse. The result is the following.

$$y = 0.3208x^2 + 0.4982x + 21.479 \quad (x = \text{number of years since 2007})$$
$$r = 0.996 \qquad \text{See Note.}^✻$$

Figure 33 shows the graph of the regression function together with the original data.

Aha! The fit is visually far better, and the correlation coefficient is even higher! Further, the quadratic model predicts 2015 revenue as

$$y = 0.3208(8)^2 + 0.4982(8) + 21.479 \approx \$46.0 \text{ billion,}$$

which is \$5.5 billion above the 2014 spending figure in the table above. Given Impact Advertising's 0.25% market share, this translates into an increase in revenues of \$13.75 million, which is about double the estimate predicted by the linear model!

You quickly draft an email to Lombardo, and are about to click "Send" when you decide, as a precaution, to check with a colleague who is knowledgeable in statistics. He tells you to be cautious: The value of *r* will always tend to increase if you pass from a linear model to a quadratic one because of the increase in "degrees of freedom."† A good way to test whether a quadratic model is more appropriate than a linear one is to compute a statistic called the "*p*-value" associated with the coefficient of x^2. A low value of *p* indicates a high degree of confidence that the coefficient of x^2 cannot be zero (see below). Notice that if the coefficient of x^2 *is* zero, then you have a linear model.

You can, your colleague explains, obtain the *p*-value using your spreadsheet as follows (the method we describe here works on all the popular spreadsheets, including *Excel, Google Docs,* and *Open Office Calc*).

First, set up the data in columns, with an extra column for the values of x^2:

◇	A	B	C
1	y	x	x^2
2	21.2	0	0
3	23.4	1	1
4	22.7	2	4
5	25.8	3	9
6	28.5	4	16
7	32.6	5	25
8	36	6	36
9	40.5	7	49

Then, highlight a vacant 5×3 block (the block E1:G5 say), type the formula =LINEST(A2:A9,B2:C9,,TRUE), and press Cntl+Shift+Enter (not just Enter!). You will see a table of statistics like the following:

◇	E	F	G
1	=LINEST(A2:A9,B2:C9,,TRUE)		
2			
3			
4			
5			

↓

Cntl+Shift+Enter

◇	E	F	G
1	0.32083333	0.49821429	21.4791667
2	0.05808804	0.42288732	0.63366572
3	0.99157395	0.75290706	#N/A
4	294.198816	5	#N/A
5	333.544405	2.83434524	#N/A

(Notice the coefficients of the quadratic model in the first row.) The p-value is then obtained by the formula =TDIST(ABS(E1/E2),F4,2), which you can compute in any vacant cell. You should get $p \approx 0.00267$.

Q: *What does p actually measure?*

A: *Roughly speaking, $1 - p \approx 0.997733$ gives the degree of confidence you can have (99.7733%) in asserting that the coefficient of x^2 is not zero. (Technically, p is the probability—allowing for random fluctuation in the data—that, if the coefficient of x^2 were in fact zero, the ratio E1/E2 could be as large as it is.)*

In short, you can go ahead and send your email with almost 100% confidence!

EXERCISES

Suppose you are given the following data for the spending on Internet advertising in a hypothetical country in which Impact Advertising also has a 0.25% share of the market.

Year	2010	2011	2012	2013	2014	2015	2016
Spending on Advertising ($ Billion)	0	0.3	1.5	2.6	3.4	4.3	5.0

1. Obtain a linear regression model and the correlation coefficient r. (Take t to be time in years since 2010.) According to the model, at what rate is spending on Internet Advertising increasing in this country? How does this translate to annual revenues for Impact Advertising?

2. Use a spreadsheet or other technology to graph the data together with the best-fit line. Does the graph suggest a quadratic model (parabola)?

3. Test your impression in the preceding exercise by using technology to fit a quadratic function and graphing the resulting curve together with the data. Does the graph suggest that the quadratic model is appropriate?

4. Perform a regression analysis using the quadratic model and find the associated p-value. What does it tell you about the appropriateness of a quadratic model?

TI-83/84 Plus   Technology Guide

Section 1.1

Example 1(a) and (c) (page 44)   The total number of iPods sold by Apple up to the end of year x can be approximated by $f(x) = 4x^2 + 16x + 2$ million iPods ($0 \le x \le 6$), where $x = 0$ represents 2003. Compute $f(0)$, $f(2)$, $f(4)$, and $f(6)$, and obtain the graph of f.

Solution with Technology

You can use the Y= screen to enter an algebraically defined function.

1. Enter the function in the Y= screen, as

    Y₁ = 4X^2+16X+2

or   Y₁ = 4X²+16X+2

(See Chapter 0 for a discussion of technology formulas.)

2. To evaluate $f(0)$, for example, enter Y₁(0) in the Home screen to evaluate the function Y₁ at 0. Alternatively, you can use the table feature: After entering the function under Y₁, press 2ND TBLSET, and set Indpnt to Ask. (You do this once and for all; it will permit you to specify values for x in the table screen.) Then, press 2ND TABLE, and you will be able to evaluate the function at several values of x. Below (top) is a table showing the values requested:

3. To obtain the graph above press WINDOW, set Xmin = 0, Xmax = 6 (the range of x-values we are interested in), Ymin = 0, Ymax = 300 (we estimated Ymin and Ymax from the corresponding set of y-values in the table) and press GRAPH to obtain the curve. Alternatively, you can avoid having to estimate Ymin and Ymax by pressing ZoomFit (ZOOM 0), which automatically sets Ymin and Ymax to the smallest and greatest values of y in the specified range for x.

Example 2 (page 47)   The number $n(t)$ of Facebook members can be approximated by the following function of time t in years ($t = 0$ represents January 2004):

$$n(t) = \begin{cases} 4t & \text{if } 0 \le t \le 3 \\ 12 + 23(t - 3)^{2.7} & \text{if } 3 < t \le 6 \end{cases}$$
$$\text{million members.}$$

Obtain a table showing the values $n(t)$ for $t = 0, \ldots, 6$ and also obtain the graph of n.

Solution with Technology

You can enter a piecewise-defined function using the logical inequality operators $<$, $>$, $\le$, and $\ge$, which are found by pressing 2ND TEST :

1. Enter the function n in the Y= screen as:

    Y₁=(X≤3)*(4X)+(X>3)*(12+23*abs(X-
              3)^2.7)

When x is less than or equal to 3, the logical expression (X≤3) evaluates to 1 because it is true, and the expression (X>3) evaluates to 0 because it is false. The value of the function is therefore given by the expression (4X). When x is greater than 3, the expression (X≤3) evaluates to 0 while the expression (X>3) evaluates to 1, so the value of the function is given by the expression (12+23*abs(X-3)^2.7). (The reason we use the abs in the formula is to prevent an error in evaluating $(x - 3)^{2.7}$ when $x < 3$; even though we don't use that formula when $x < 3$, we are in fact evaluating it and multiplying it by zero.)

2. As in Example 1, use the Table feature to compute several values of the function at once by pressing 2ND TABLE .

3. To obtain the graph, we proceed as in Example 1: Press WINDOW, set Xmin = 0, Xmax = 6 (the range of x-values we are interested in), Ymin = 0, Ymax = 500 (see the y-values in the table) and press GRAPH.

Section 1.2

Example 4(a) (page 62)   The demand and supply curves for private schools in Michigan are $q = 77.8p^{-0.11}$ and $q = 30.4 + 0.006p$ thousand students, respectively ($200 \leq p \leq 2{,}200$), where p is the net tuition cost in dollars. Graph the demand and supply curves on the same set of axes. Use your graph to estimate, to the nearest \$100, the tuition at which the demand equals the supply (equilibrium price). Approximately how many students will be accommodated at that price?

Solution with Technology

To obtain the graphs of demand and supply:

1. Enter $Y_1=77.8*X^{\wedge}(-0.11)$ and $Y_2=30.4+ 0.006*X$ in the "Y=" screen.
2. Press WINDOW, enter Xmin = 200, Xmax = 2200, Ymin = 0, Ymax = 50 and press GRAPH for the graph shown below:

3. To estimate the equilibrium price, press TRACE and use the arrow keys to follow the curve to the approximate point of intersection (around X = 1008) as shown below.

4. For a more accurate estimate, zoom in by pressing ZOOM and selecting Option 1 ZBox.
5. Move the curser to a point slightly above and to the left of the intersection, press ENTER, and then move the curser to a point slightly below and to the right and press ENTER again to obtain a box.

6. Now press ENTER again for a zoomed-in view of the intersection.
7. You can now use TRACE to obtain the intersection coordinates more accurately: X ≈ 1,000, representing a tuition cost of \$1,000. The associated demand is the Y-coordinate: around 36.4 thousand students.

Example 5(a) (page 64)   The following table shows annual sales, in billions of dollars, by *Nike* from 2005 through 2010 ($t = 0$ represents 2005):

t	0	1	2	3	4	5
Sales (\$ billion)	13.5	15	16.5	18.5	19	19

Consider the following four models:

(1) $s(t) = 14 + 1.2t$ — Linear model

(2) $s(t) = 13 + 2.2t - 0.2t^2$ — Quadratic model

(3) $s(t) = 14(1.07^t)$ — Exponential model

(4) $s(t) = \dfrac{19.5}{1 + 0.48(1.8^{-t})}$ — Logistic model

a. Which models fit the data significantly better than the rest?
b. Of the models you selected in part (a), which gives the most reasonable prediction for 2013?

Solution with Technology

1. First enter the actual revenue data in the stat list editor ($\boxed{\text{STAT}}$ EDIT) with the values of t in L_1, and the values of $s(t)$ in L_2.

2. Now go to the Y= window and turn Plot1 on by selecting it and pressing $\boxed{\text{ENTER}}$. (You can also turn it on in the $\boxed{\text{2ND}}$ STAT PLOT screen.) Then press ZoomStat ($\boxed{\text{ZOOM}}$ $\boxed{9}$) to obtain a plot of the points (above).

3. To see any of the four curves plotted along with the points, enter its formula in the Y= screen (for instance, $Y_1=13+2.2x-0.2X^2$ for the second model) and press $\boxed{\text{GRAPH}}$ (figure on top below).

4. To see the extrapolation of the curve to 2013, just change Xmax to 8 (in the $\boxed{\text{WINDOW}}$ screen) and press $\boxed{\text{GRAPH}}$ again (lower figure above).

5. Now change Y_1 to see similar graphs for the remaining curves.

6. When you are done, turn Plot1 off again so that the points you entered do not show up in other graphs.

Section 1.3

Example 1 (page 81)   Which of the following two tables gives the values of a linear function? What is the formula for that function?

x	0	2	4	6	8	10	12
$f(x)$	3	-1	-3	-6	-8	-13	-15

x	0	2	4	6	8	10	12
$g(x)$	3	-1	-5	-9	-13	-17	-21

Solution with Technology

We can use the "List" feature in the TI-83/84 Plus to automatically compute the successive quotients $m = \Delta y/\Delta x$ for either f or g as follows:

1. Use the stat list editor ($\boxed{\text{STAT}}$ EDIT) to enter the values of x and $f(x)$ in the first two columns, called L_1 and L_2, as shown in the screenshot below. (If there is already data in a column you want to use, you can clear it by highlighting the column heading (e.g., L_1) using the arrow key, and pressing $\boxed{\text{CLEAR}}$ $\boxed{\text{ENTER}}$.)

2. Highlight the heading L_3 by using the arrow keys, and enter the following formula (with the quotes, as explained below):

"ΔList(L_2)/ΔList(L_1)"   ΔList is found under $\boxed{\text{2ND}}$ $\boxed{\text{LIST}}$ OPS. L_1 is $\boxed{\text{2ND}}$ $\boxed{1}$

The "ΔList" function computes the differences between successive elements of a list, returning a list with one less element. The formula above then computes the quotients $\Delta y/\Delta x$ in the list L_3 as shown in the following screenshot. As you can see in the third column, $f(x)$ is not linear.

3. To redo the computation for $g(x)$, all you need to do is edit the values of L_2 in the stat list editor. By putting quotes around the formula we used for L_3, we told the calculator to remember the formula, so it automatically recalculates the values.

Example 2(a) (page 83)   Find the equation of the line through the points $(1, 2)$ and $(3, -1)$.

Solution with Technology

1. Enter the coordinates of the given points in the stat list editor (STAT EDIT) with the values of x in L_1, and the values of y in L_2.

2. To compute the slope, enter the following formula in the Home screen:

$$(L_2(2)-L_2(1))/(L_1(2)-L_1(1)) \rightarrow M$$

L_1 and L_2 are under 2ND LIST and the arrow is STO

3. Then, to compute the y-intercept, enter

$$L_2(1)-M*L_1(1)$$

Section 1.4

Example 1(a) (page 97)   Using the data on the per capita GDP in Mexico given at the beginning of Section 1.4, compute SSE, the sum-of-squares error, for the linear models $y = 0.5t + 8$ and $y = 0.25t + 9$, and graph the data with the given models.

Solution with Technology

We can use the "List" feature in the TI-83/84 Plus to automate the computation of SSE.

1. Use the stat list editor (STAT EDIT) to enter the given data in the lists L_1 and L_2, as shown in the first screenshot below. (If there is already data in a column you want to use, you can clear it by highlighting the column heading (e.g., L_1) using the arrow key, and pressing CLEAR ENTER.)

2. To compute the predicted values, highlight the heading L_3 using the arrow keys, and enter the following formula for the predicted values (figure on the top below):

$$0.5*L_1+8 \qquad L_1 \text{ is } 2\text{ND} \boxed{1}$$

Pressing ENTER again will fill column 3 with the predicted values (below bottom). Note that only seven of the eight data points can be seen on the screen at one time.

3. Highlight the heading L_4 and enter the following formula (including the quotes):

$$"(L_2-L_3)^2" \qquad \text{Squaring the residuals}$$

4. Pressing ENTER will fill L_4 with the squares of the residuals. (Putting quotes around the formula will allow us to easily check the second model, as we shall see.)

5. To compute SSE, the sum of the entries in L_4, go to the home screen and enter sum(L_4) (see below; "sum" is under 2ND LIST MATH.)

6. To check the second model, go back to the List screen, highlight the heading L_3, enter the formula for the second model, 0.25*L_1+9, and press ENTER. Because we put quotes around the formula for the residuals in L_4, the TI-83/84 Plus will remember the formula and automatically recalculate the values (below top). On the home screen we can again calculate sum(L_4) to get SSE for the second model (below bottom).

The second model gives a much smaller SSE, so is the better fit.

7. You can also use the TI-83/84 Plus to plot both the original data points and the two lines (see below). Turn Plot1 on in the STAT PLOT window, obtained by pressing 2ND STAT PLOT. To show the lines, enter them in the "Y=" screen as usual. To obtain a convenient window showing all the points and the lines, press ZOOM and choose 9: ZoomStat.

Example 2 (page 99)   Use the data on the per capita GDP in Mexico to find the best-fit linear model.

Solution with Technology

1. Enter the data in the TI-83/84 Plus using the List feature, putting the x-coordinates in L_1 and the y-coordinates in L_2, just as in Example 1.

2. Press STAT, select CALC, and choose #4: LinReg(ax+b). Pressing ENTER will cause the equation of the regression line to be displayed in the home screen:

So, the regression line is $y \approx 0.321x + 8.75$.

3. To graph the regression line without having to enter it by hand in the "Y=" screen, press Y=, clear the contents of Y_1, press VARS, choose #5: Statistics, select EQ, and then choose #1:RegEQ. The regression equation will then be entered under Y_1.

4. To simultaneously show the data points, press 2ND STATPLOT and turn Plot1 on as in Example 1. To obtain a convenient window showing all the points and the line (see below), press ZOOM and choose #9: ZoomStat.

Example 3 (page 101) Find the correlation coefficient for the data in Example 2.

Solution with Technology

To find the correlation coefficient using a TI-83/84 Plus you need to tell the calculator to show you the coefficient at the same time that it shows you the regression line.

1. Press 2ND CATALOG and select DiagnosticOn from the list. The command will be pasted to the home screen, and you should then press ENTER to execute the command.

2. Once you have done this, the "LinReg(ax+b)" command (see the discussion for Example 2) will show you not only a and b, but r and r^2 as well:

SPREADSHEET Technology Guide

Section 1.1

Example 1(a) and (c) (page 44) The total number of iPods sold by Apple up to the end of year x can be approximated by $f(x) = 4x^2 + 16x + 2$ million iPods ($0 \leq x \leq 6$), where $x = 0$ represents 2003. Compute $f(0)$, $f(2)$, $f(4)$, and $f(6)$, and obtain the graph of f.

Solution with Technology

To create a table of values of f using a spreadsheet:

1. Set up two columns: one for the values of x and one for the values of $f(x)$. Then enter the sequence of values 0, 2, 4, 6 in the x column as shown.

◇	A	B
1	x	f(x)
2	0	
3	2	
4	4	
5	6	

2. Now we enter a formula for $f(x)$ in cell B2 (below). The technology formula is 4*x^2+16*x+2. To use this formula in a spreadsheet, we modify it slightly:

=4*A2^2+16*A2+2   Spreadsheet version of tech
formula

Notice that we have preceded the Excel formula by an equals sign (=) and replaced each occurrence of x by the name of the cell holding the value of x (cell A2 in this case).

◇	A	B	C
1	x	f(x)	
2		0	=4*A2^2+16*A2+2
3		2	
4		4	
5		6	

Note Instead of typing in the name of the cell "A2" each time, you can simply click on the cell A2, and "A2" will be automatically inserted. ∎

3. Now highlight cell B2 and drag the **fill handle** (the little square at the lower right-hand corner of the selection) down until you reach Row 5 as shown below on the top, to obtain the result shown on the bottom.

◇	A	B	C
1	x	f(x)	
2		0	=4*A2^2+16*A2+2
3		2	
4		4	
5		6	

◇	A	B
1	x	f(x)
2		0	2
3		2	50
4		4	130
5		6	242

4. To graph the data, highlight A1 through B5, and insert a "Scatter chart" (the exact method of doing this depends on the specific version of the spreadsheet program). When choosing the style of the chart,

choose a style that shows points connected by lines (if possible) to obtain a graph something like the following:

Example 2 (page 47) The number $n(t)$ of Facebook members can be approximated by the following function of time t in years ($t = 0$ represents January 2004):

$$n(t) = \begin{cases} 4t & \text{if } 0 \le t \le 3 \\ 12 + 23(t-3)^{2.7} & \text{if } 3 < t \le 6 \end{cases} \text{ million members.}$$

Obtain a table showing the values $n(t)$ for $t = 0, \ldots, 6$ and also obtain the graph of n.

Solution with Technology

We can generate a table of values of $n(t)$ for $t = 0, 1, \ldots, 6$ as follows:

1. Set up two columns; one for the values of t and one for the values of $n(t)$, and enter the values 0, 1, .., 6 in the t column as shown in the first screenshot below:

2. We must now enter the formula for n in cell B2. The following formula defines the function n in Excel:

```
=(x<=3)*(4*x)+(x>3)*(12+23*abs
(x-3)^2.7)
```

When x is less than or equal to 3, the logical expression $(x \le 3)$ evaluates to 1 because it is true, and the expression $(x > 3)$ evaluates to 0 because it is false. The value of the function is therefore given by the expression $(4*x)$. When x is greater than 3, the expression $(x \le 3)$ evaluates to 0 while the expression $(x > 3)$ evaluates to 1, so the value of the function is given by the expression $(12+23*abs$ $(x-3)^2.7)$. (The reason we use the abs in the formula is to prevent an error in evaluating $(x - 3)^{2.7}$ when $x < 3$; even though we don't use that formula

when $x < 3$, we are in fact evaluating it and multiplying it by zero.) We therefore enter the formula

```
=(A2<=3)*(4*A2)+(A2>3)*(12+23
*ABS(A2-3)^2.7)
```

in cell B2 and then copy down to cell B8 (below top) to obtain the result shown on the bottom:

◇	A	B	C	D	E
1	t	n(t)			
2	0	=(A2<=3)*(4*A2)+(A2>3)*(12+23*ABS(A2-3)^2.7)			
3	1				
4	2				
5	3				
6	4				
7	5				
8	6				

◇	A	B
1	t	n(t)
2	0	0
3	1	4
4	2	8
5	3	12
6	4	35
7	5	161.454
8	6	458.638

3. To graph the data, highlight A1 through B8, and insert a "Scatter chart" as in Example 1 to obtain the result shown below:

Section 1.2

Example 4(a) (page 62) The demand and supply curves for private schools in Michigan are $q = 77.8p^{-0.11}$ and $q = 30.4 + 0.006p$ thousand students, respectively ($200 \le p \le 2{,}200$), where p is the net tuition cost in dollars. Graph the demand and supply curves on the same set of axes. Use your graph to estimate, to the nearest \$100, the tuition at which the demand equals the supply (equilibrium price). Approximately how many students will be accommodated at that price?

Solution with Technology

To obtain the graphs of demand and supply:

1. Enter the headings p, Demand, and Supply in cells A1–C1 and the p-values 200, 300, . . . , 2,200 in A2–A22.

2. Next, enter the formulas for the demand and supply functions in cells B2 and C2.

Demand: `=77.8*A2^(-0.11)`　　in cell B2

Supply: `=30.4+0.006*A2`　　in cell C2

3. To graph the data, highlight A1 through C22, and insert a Scatter chart:

4. If you place the cursor as close as you can get to the intersection point (or just look at the table of values), you will see that the curves cross close to $p = \$1{,}000$ (to the nearest \$100).

5. To more accurately determine where the curves cross, you can narrow down the range of values shown on the x-axis by changing the p-values to 990, 991, ..., 1010.

Example 5(a) (page 64) The following table shows annual sales, in billions of dollars, by *Nike* from 2005 through 2010 ($t = 0$ represents 2005):

t	0	1	2	3	4	5
Sales ($ billion)	13.5	15	16.5	18.5	19	19

Consider the following four models:

(1) $s(t) = 14t + 1.2t$　　Linear model

(2) $s(t) = 13 + 2.2t - 0.2t^2$　　Quadratic model

(3) $s(t) = 14(1.07^t)$　　Exponential model

(4) $s(t) = \dfrac{19.5}{1 + 0.48(1.8^{-t})}$　　Logistic model

a. Which models fit the data significantly better than the rest?

b. Of the models you selected in part (a), which gives the most reasonable prediction for 2013?

Solution with Technology

1. First create a scatter plot of the given data by tabulating the data as shown below, and selecting the Insert tab and choosing a "Scatter" chart:

2. In column C use the formula for the model you are interested in seeing; for example, model (2): `=13+2.2*A2-0.2*A2^2`

3. To adjust the graph to include the graph of the model you have added, you need to change the graph data from \$A\$2:\$B\$7 to \$A\$2:\$C\$7 so as to include column C. In Excel you can obtain this by right-clicking on the graph to select "Source Data". In OpenOffice, double-click on the graph and then right-click it to choose "Data Ranges". In Excel, you can also click once on the graph—the effect will be to outline the data you have graphed in columns A and B—and then use the fill handle at the bottom of Column B to extend the selection to Column C as shown:

The graph will now include markers showing the values of both the actual sales and the model you inserted in Column C.

4. Right-click on any of the markers corresponding to column B in the graph (in OpenOffice you would first double-click on the graph), select "Format data series" to add lines connecting the points and remove the markers. The effect will be as shown below, with the model represented by a curve and the actual data points represented by dots:

TECHNOLOGY GUIDE

5. To see the extrapolation of the curve to 2013, add the values 6, 7, 8 to Column A. The values of $s(t)$ may automatically be computed in Column C as you type, depending on the spreadsheet. If not, you will need to copy the formula in column C down to C10. (Do not touch Column B, as that contains the observed data up through $t = 5$ only.) Click on the graph, and use the fill handle at the base of Column C to include the new data in the graph:

6. To see the plots for the remaining curves, change the formula in Column B (and don't forget to copy the new formula down to cell C10 when you do so).

Section **1.3**

Example 1 (page 81)   Which of the following two tables gives the values of a linear function? What is the formula for that function?

x	0	2	4	6	8	10	12
$f(x)$	3	-1	-3	-6	-8	-13	-15

x	0	2	4	6	8	10	12
$g(x)$	3	-1	-5	-9	-13	-17	-21

Solution with Technology

1. The following worksheet shows how you can compute the successive quotients $m = \Delta y / \Delta x$, and hence check whether a given set of data shows a linear relationship, in which case all the quotients will be the same. (The shading indicates that the formula is to be copied down only as far as cell C7. Why not cell C8?)

2. Here are the results for both f and g.

Example 2(a) (page 83)   Find the equation of the line through the points $(1, 2)$ and $(3, -1)$.

Solution with Technology

1. Enter the x- and y-coordinates in columns A and B, as shown below on the left.

	A	B
1	x	y
2	1	2
3	3	-1

	A	B	C	D
1	x	y	m	b
2	1	2	=(B3-B2)/(A3-A2)	=B2-C2*A2
3	3	-1	Slope	Intercept

2. Add the headings m and b in C1-D1, and then the formulas for the slope and intercept in C2-D2, as shown above on the right. The result will be as shown below:

	A	B	C	D
1	x	y	m	b
2	1	2	-1.5	3.5
3	3	-1	Slope	Intercept

Section **1.4**

Example 1(a) (page 97)   Using the data on the per capita GDP in Mexico given at the beginning of Section 1.4, compute SSE, the sum-of-squares error, for the linear models $y = 0.5t + 8$ and $y = 0.25t + 9$, and graph the data with the given models.

Solution with Technology

1. Begin by setting up your worksheet with the observed data in two columns, t and y, and the predicted data for the first model in the third.

	A	B	C	D	E	F
1	t	y (Observed)	y (Predicted)		m	b
2	0	9	=$E$2*A2+$F$2		0.5	8
3	2	9				
4	4	10				
5	6	11				
6	8	11				
7	10	12				
8	12	13				
9	14	13				

2. Notice that, instead of using the numerical equation for the first model in column C, we used absolute references to the cells containing the slope m and the intercept b. This way, we can switch from one linear model to the next by changing only m and b in cells E2 and F2. (We have deliberately left column D empty in anticipation of the next step.)

3. In column D we compute the squares of the residuals using the Excel formula $=(B2-C2)^2$.

4. We now compute SSE in cell F4 by summing the entries in column D:

5. Here is the completed spreadsheet:

6. Changing m to 0.25 and b to 9 gives the sum of squares error for the second model, SSE = 2.

7. To plot both the original data points and each of the two lines, use a scatter plot to graph the data in columns A through C in each of the last two worksheets above.

$$y = 0.5t + 8 \qquad\qquad y = 0.25t + 9$$

Example 2 (page 99)   Use the data on the per capita GDP in Mexico to find the best-fit linear model.

Solution with Technology

Here are two spreadsheet shortcuts for linear regression; one graphical and one based on a spreadsheet formula:

Using a Trendline

1. Start with the original data and insert a scatter plot (below left and right).

2. Insert a "linear trendline", choosing the option to display the equation on the chart. The method for doing so varies from spreadsheet to spreadsheet.[77] In Excel, you can right-click on one of the points in the graph and choose "Add Trendline" (in OpenOffice you would first double-click on the graph). Then, under "Trendline Options", select "Display Equation on chart". The procedure for OpenOffice is almost identical, but you first need to double-click on the graph. The result is shown below.

Using a Formula

1. Enter your data as above, and select a block of unused cells two wide and one tall; for example, C2:D2. Then enter the formula

```
=LINEST(B2:B9,A2:A9)
```

---

[77]At the time of this writing, Google Docs has no trendline feature for its spreadsheet, so you would need to use the formula method.

as shown on the left. Then press Control-Shift-Enter. The result should appear as on the right, with m and b appearing in cells C2 and D2 as shown:

Example 3 (page 101)   Find the correlation coefficient for the data in Example 2.

Solution with Technology

1. When you add a trendline to a chart you can select the option "Display R-squared value on chart" to show the value of r^2 on the chart (it is common to examine r^2, which takes on values between 0 and 1, instead of r).

2. Alternatively, the LINEST function we used above in 2 can be used to display quite a few statistics about a best-fit line, including r^2. Instead of selecting a block of cells two wide and one tall as we did in Example 2, we select one two wide and *five* tall. We now enter the requisite LINEST formula with two additional arguments set to "TRUE" as shown, and press Control-Shift-Enter:

The values of m and b appear in cells C2 and D2 as before, and the value of r^2 in cell C4. (Among the other numbers shown is SSE in cell D6. For the meanings of the remaining numbers shown, do a Web search for "LINEST"; you will see numerous articles, including many that explain all the terms. A good course in statistics wouldn't hurt, either.)

2

The Mathematics of Finance

Case Study Adjustable Rate and Subprime Mortgages

Mr. and Mrs. Wong have an appointment tomorrow with you, their investment counselor, to discuss their plan to purchase a $400,000 house in Orlando, Florida. Their combined annual income is $80,000 per year, which they estimate will increase by 4% annually over the foreseeable future, and they are considering three different specialty 30-year mortgages:

Hybrid: The interest is fixed at a low introductory rate of 4% for 5 years.

Interest-Only: During the first 5 years, the rate is set at 4.2% and no principal is paid.

Negative Amortization: During the first 5 years, the rate is set at 4.7% based on a principal of 60% of the purchase price of the home.

How would you advise them?

Andy Dean Photography/Shutterstock

Website

www.WanerMath.com

At the Website you will find:

- A detailed chapter summary

- A true/false quiz

- A time value of money utility

- Excel tutorials for every section

Introduction

A knowledge of the mathematics of investments and loans is important not only for business majors but also for everyone who deals with money, which is all of us. This chapter is largely about *interest*: interest paid by an investment, interest paid on a loan, and variations on these.

We focus on three forms of investment: investments that pay simple interest, investments in which interest is compounded, and annuities. An investment that pays *simple interest* periodically gives interest directly to the investor, perhaps in the form of a monthly check. If instead, the interest is reinvested, the interest is *compounded*, and the value of the account grows as the interest is added. An *annuity* is an investment earning compound interest into which periodic payments are made or from which periodic withdrawals are made; in the case of periodic payments, such an investment is more commonly called a *sinking fund*. From the point of view of the lender, a loan is a kind of annuity.

We also look at bonds, the primary financial instrument used by companies and governments to raise money. Although bonds nominally pay simple interest, determining their worth, particularly in the secondary market, requires an annuity calculation.

2.1 Simple Interest

You deposit $1,000, called the **principal** or **present value**, into a savings account. The bank pays you 5% interest, in the form of a check, each year. How much interest will you earn each year? Because the bank pays you 5% interest each year, your annual (or yearly) interest will be 5% of $1,000, or $1,000 \times 0.05 = \$50$.

Generalizing this calculation, call the present value PV and the interest rate (expressed as a decimal) r. Then INT, the annual interest paid to you, is given by*

$$INT = PVr.$$

If the investment is made for a period of t years, then the total interest accumulated is t times this amount, which gives us the following:

* Multiletter variables like PV and INT used here may be unusual in a math textbook but are almost universally used in finance textbooks, calculators (such as the TI-83/84 Plus), and such places as study guides for the finance portion of the Society of Actuaries exams. Just watch out for expressions like PVr, which is the product of two things, PV and r, not three.

Simple Interest

The **simple interest** on an investment (or loan) of PV dollars at an annual interest rate of r for a period of t years is

$$INT = PVrt.$$

Quick Example

The simple interest over a period of 4 years on a $5,000 investment earning 8% per year is

$$INT = PVrt$$
$$= (5,000)(0.08)(4) = \$1,600.$$

Given your $1,000 investment at 5% simple interest, how much money will you have after 2 years? To find the answer, we need to add the accumulated interest to the principal to get the **future value** (FV) of your deposit.

$$FV = PV + INT = \$1,000 + (1,000)(0.05)(2) = \$1,100$$

In general, we can compute the future value as follows:

$$FV = PV + INT = PV + PVrt = PV(1 + rt).$$

Future Value for Simple Interest

The **future value** of an investment of PV dollars at an annual simple interest rate of r for a period of t years is

$$FV = PV(1 + rt).$$

Quick Examples

1. The value, at the end of 4 years, of a $5,000 investment earning 8% simple interest per year is

$$FV = PV(1 + rt)$$
$$= 5,000[1 + (0.08)(4)] = \$6,600.$$

2. Writing the future value in Quick Example 1 as a function of time, we get

$$FV = 5,000(1 + 0.08t)$$
$$= 5,000 + 400t,$$

which is a linear function of time t. The intercept is $PV = \$5,000$, and the slope is the annual interest, $400 per year.

In general: *Simple interest growth is a linear function of time, with intercept given by the present value and slope given by annual interest.*

EXAMPLE 1 **Savings Accounts**

In November 2011, the Bank of Montreal was paying 1.30% interest on savings accounts.[1] If the interest is paid as simple interest, find the future value of a $2,000 deposit in 6 years. What is the total interest paid over the period?

---

[1]Source: Canoe Money (http://money.canoe.ca/rates/savings.html)

Solution We use the future value formula:

$$FV = PV(1 + rt)$$
$$= 2,000[1 + (0.013)(6)] = 2,000[1.078] = \$2,156.$$

The total interest paid is given by the simple interest formula:

$$INT = PVrt$$
$$= (2,000)(0.013)(6) = \$156.$$

Note To find the interest paid, we could also have computed

$$INT = FV - PV = 2,156 - 2,000 = \$156. \quad \blacksquare$$

➡ **Before we go on...** In the preceding example, we could look at the future value as a function of time:

$$FV = 2,000(1 + 0.013t) = 2,000 + 26t.$$

Thus, the future value is growing linearly at a rate of $26 per year. ■

EXAMPLE 2 **Bridge Loans**

When "trading up," homeowners sometimes have to buy a new house before they sell their old house. One way to cover the costs of the new house until they get the proceeds from selling the old house is to take out a short-term *bridge loan*. Suppose a bank charges 12% simple annual interest on such a loan. How much will be owed at the maturation (the end) of a 90-day bridge loan of $90,000?

Solution We use the future value formula

$$FV = PV(1 + rt)$$

with $t = 90/365$, the fraction of a year represented by 90 days:

$$FV = 90,000[1 + (0.12)(90/365)]$$
$$= \$92,663.01.$$

(We will always round our answers to the nearest cent after calculation. Be careful not to round intermediate results.)

➡ **Before we go on...** Many banks use 360 days for this calculation rather than 365, which makes a "year" for the purposes of the loan slightly shorter than a calendar year. The effect is to increase the amount owed:

$$FV = 90,000[1 + (0.12)(90/360)] = \$92,700 \qquad \blacksquare$$

One of the primary ways companies and governments raise money is by selling **bonds**. At its most straightforward, a corporate bond promises to pay simple interest, usually twice a year, for a length of time until it **matures**, at which point it returns the original investment to the investor (U.S. Treasury notes and bonds are similar). Things get more complicated when the selling price is negotiable, as we will see later in this chapter.

EXAMPLE 3 Corporate Bonds

The Megabucks Corporation is issuing 10-year bonds paying an annual rate of 6.5%. If you buy $10,000 worth of bonds, how much interest will you earn every 6 months, and how much interest will you earn over the life of the bonds?

Solution Using the simple interest formula, every 6 months you will receive

$$INT = PVrt$$

$$= (10,000)(0.065)\left(\frac{1}{2}\right) = \$325.$$

Over the 10-year life of the bonds, you will earn

$$INT = PVrt$$

$$= (10,000)(0.065)(10) = \$6,500$$

in interest. So, at the end of 10 years, when your original investment is returned to you, your $10,000 will have turned into $16,500.

We often want to turn an interest calculation around: Rather than starting with the present value and finding the future value, there are times when we know the future value and need to determine the present value. Solving the future value formula for PV gives us the following.

Present Value for Simple Interest

The present value of an investment at an annual simple interest rate of r for a period of t years, with future value FV, is

$$PV = \frac{FV}{1 + rt}.$$

Quick Example

If an investment earns 5% simple interest and will be worth $1,000 in 4 years, then its present value (its initial value) is

$$PV = \frac{FV}{1 + rt}$$

$$= \frac{1,000}{1 + (0.05)(4)} = \$833.33.$$

Here is a typical example. U.S. Treasury bills (T-bills) are short-term investments (up to 1 year) that pay you a set amount after a period of time; what you pay to buy a T-bill depends on the interest rate.

EXAMPLE 4 Treasury Bills

A U.S. Treasury bill paying $10,000 after 6 months earns 3.67% simple annual interest. How much did it cost to buy?

Solution The future value of the T-bill is $10,000; the price we paid is its present value. We know that

$$FV = \$10,000$$

$$r = 0.0367$$

and

$$t = 0.5.$$

Substituting into the present value formula, we have

$$PV = \frac{10,000}{1 + (0.0367)(0.5)} = 9,819.81$$

so we paid $9,819.81 for the T-bill.

➡ **Before we go on...** The simplest way to find the interest earned on the T-bill is by subtraction:

$$INT = FV - PV = 10,000 - 9,819.81 = \$180.19.$$

So, after 6 months we received back $10,000, which is our original investment plus $180.19 in interest. ∎

Here is some additional terminology on Treasury bills:

Treasury Bills (T-Bills): Maturity Value, Discount Rate, and Yield

The **maturity value** of a T-bill is the amount of money it will pay at the end of its life, that is, upon **maturity**.

Quick Example

A 1-year $10,000 T-bill has a maturity value of $10,000, and so will pay you $10,000 after one year.

The cost of a T-bill is generally less than its maturity value.* In other words, a T-bill will generally sell at a *discount*, and the **discount rate** is the *annualized* percentage of this discount; that is, the percentage is adjusted to give an annual percentage. (See Quick Examples 2 and 3.)

Quick Examples

1. A 1-year $10,000 T-bill with a discount rate of 5% will sell for 5% less than its maturity value of $10,000, that is, for $9,500.
2. A 6-month $10,000 T-bill with a discount rate of 5% will sell at an actual discount of half of that—2.5% less than its maturity value, or $9,750—because 6 months is half of a year.
3. A 3-month $10,000 T-bill with a discount rate of 5% will sell at an actual discount of a fourth of that: 1.25% less than its maturity value, or $9,875.

The annual **yield** of a T-bill is the simple annual interest rate an investor earns when the T-bill matures, as calculated in the next example.

*An exception occurred during the financial meltdown of 2008, when T-bills were heavily in demand as "safe haven" investments and were sometimes selling at—or even above—their maturity values.

EXAMPLE 5 Treasury Bills

A T-bill paying $10,000 after 6 months sells at a discount rate of 3.6%. What does it sell for? What is the annual yield?

Solution The (annualized) discount rate is 3.6%; so, for a 6-month bill, the actual discount will be half of that: $3.6\%/2 = 1.8\%$ below its maturity value. This makes the selling price

$$10,000 - (0.018)(10,000) = \$9,820. \quad \text{\small Maturity value − Discount}$$

To find the annual yield, note that the present value of the investment is the price the investor pays, $9,820, and the future value is its maturity value, $10,000 six months later. So,

$$PV = \$9,820 \qquad FV = \$10,000 \qquad t = 0.5$$

and we wish to find the annual interest rate r. Substituting in the future value formula, we get

$$FV = PV(1 + rt)$$
$$10,000 = 9,820(1 + 0.5r)$$

so

$$1 + 0.5r = 10,000/9,820$$

and

$$r = (10,000/9,820 - 1)/0.5 \approx 0.0367.$$

Thus, the T-bill is paying 3.67% simple annual interest, so we say that its annual yield is 3.67%.

➡ **Before we go on...** The T-bill in Example 5 is the same one as in Example 4 (with a bit of rounding). The yield and the discount rate are two different ways of telling what the investment pays. One of the Communication and Reasoning Exercises asks you to find a formula for the yield in terms of the discount rate. ■

Fees on loans can also be thought of as a form of interest.

EXAMPLE 6 Tax Refunds

You are expecting a tax refund of $800. Because it may take up to 6 weeks to get the refund, your tax preparation firm offers, for a fee of $40, to give you an "interest-free" loan of $800 to be paid back with the refund check. If we think of the fee as interest, what simple annual interest rate is the firm actually charging?

Solution If we view the $40 as interest, then the future value of the loan (the value of the loan to the firm, or the total you will pay the firm) is $840. Thus, we have

$$FV = 840$$
$$PV = 800$$
$$t = 6/52 \qquad \text{\small Using 52 weeks in a year}$$

and we wish to find r. Substituting, we get

$$FV = PV(1 + rt)$$

$$840 = 800(1 + 6r/52) = 800 + \frac{4{,}800r}{52}$$

so

$$\frac{4{,}800r}{52} = 840 - 800 = 40$$

$$r = \frac{40 \times 52}{4{,}800} \approx 0.43.$$

In other words, the firm is charging you 43% annual interest! Save your money and wait 6 weeks for your refund.

2.1   EXERCISES

▼ more advanced   ◆ challenging
T indicates exercises that should be solved using technology

In Exercises 1–6, compute the simple interest for the specified period and the future value at the end of the period. Round all answers to the nearest cent. HINT [See Example 1.]

1. $2,000 is invested for 1 year at 6% per year.

2. $1,000 is invested for 10 years at 4% per year.

3. $20,200 is invested for 6 months at 5% per year.

4. $10,100 is invested for 3 months at 11% per year.

5. You borrow $10,000 for 10 months at 3% per year.

6. You borrow $6,000 for 5 months at 9% per year.

In Exercises 7–12, find the present value of the given investment. HINT [See the Quick Example on page 129.]

7. An investment earns 2% per year and is worth $10,000 after 5 years.

8. An investment earns 5% per year and is worth $20,000 after 2 years.

9. An investment earns 7% per year and is worth $1,000 after 6 months.

10. An investment earns 10% per year and is worth $5,000 after 3 months.

11. An investment earns 3% per year and is worth $15,000 after 15 months.

12. An investment earns 6% per year and is worth $30,000 after 20 months.

APPLICATIONS

In Exercises 13–30, compute the specified quantity. Round all answers to the nearest month, the nearest cent, or the nearest 0.001%, as appropriate.

13. *Simple Loans* You take out a 6-month, $5,000 loan at 8% simple interest. How much would you owe at the end of the 6 months? HINT [See Example 2.]

14. *Simple Loans* You take out a 15-month, $10,000 loan at 11% simple interest. How much would you owe at the end of the 15 months? HINT [See Example 2.]

15. *Savings* How much would you have to deposit in an account earning 4.5% simple interest if you wanted to have $1,000 after 6 years? HINT [See Example 4.]

16. *Simple Loans* Your total payment on a 4-year loan, which charged 9.5% simple interest, amounted to $30,360. How much did you originally borrow? HINT [See Example 4.]

17. *Bonds* A 5-year bond costs $1,000 and will pay a total of $250 interest over its lifetime. What is its annual interest rate? HINT [See Example 3.]

18. *Bonds* A 4-year bond costs $10,000 and will pay a total of $2,800 in interest over its lifetime. What is its annual interest rate? HINT [See Example 3.]

19. *Treasury Bills* In December 2008 (in the midst of the financial crisis) a $5,000 6-month T-bill was selling at a discount rate of only 0.25%.[2] What was its simple annual yield? HINT [See Example 5.]

20. *Treasury Bills* In December 2008 (in the midst of the financial crisis) a $15,000 3-month T-bill was selling at a discount rate of only 0.06%.[3] What was its simple annual yield? HINT [See Example 5.]

21. ▼ *Simple Loans* A $4,000 loan, taken now, with a simple interest rate of 8% per year, will require a total repayment of $4,640. When will the loan mature?

22. ▼ *Simple Loans* The simple interest on a $1,000 loan at 8% per year amounted to $640. When did the loan mature?

---

[2]Discount rate on December 29, 2008. Source: U.S. Treasury (www.ustreas.gov/offices/domestic-finance/debt-management/interest-rate/daily_treas_bill_rates.shtml).

[3]*Ibid.*

23. ▼ *Treasury Bills* At auction on August 18, 2005, 6-month T-bills were sold at a discount of 3.705%.[4] What was the simple annual yield? HINT [See Example 5.]

24. ▼ *Treasury Bills* At auction on August 18, 2005, 3-month T-bills were sold at a discount of 3.470%.[5] What was the simple annual yield? HINT [See Example 5.]

25. ▼ *Fees* You are expecting a tax refund of $1,000 in 4 weeks. A tax preparer offers you a $1,000 loan for a fee of $50 to be repaid by your refund check when it arrives in 4 weeks. Thinking of the fee as interest, what annual simple interest rate would you be paying on this loan? HINT [See Example 6.]

26. ▼ *Fees* You are expecting a tax refund of $1,500 in 3 weeks. A tax preparer offers you a $1,500 loan for a fee of $60 to be repaid by your refund check when it arrives in 3 weeks. Thinking of the fee as interest, what annual simple interest rate would you be paying on this loan?

27. ▼ *Fees* You take out a 2-year, $5,000 loan at 9% simple annual interest. The lender charges you a $100 fee. Thinking of the fee as additional interest, what is the actual annual interest rate you will pay?

28. ▼ *Fees* You take out a 3-year, $7,000 loan at 8% simple annual interest. The lender charges you a $100 fee. Thinking of the fee as additional interest, what is the actual annual interest rate you will pay?

29. ▼ *Layaway Fees* Layaway plans allow you, for a fee, to pay for an item over a period of time and then receive the item when you finish paying for it. In November 2011, Senator Charles E. Schumer of New York warned that the holiday layaway programs recently reinstated by several popular retailers were, when you took the fees into account, charging interest at a rate significantly higher than the highest credit card rates.[6] Suppose that you bought a $69 item on November 15 on layaway, with the final payment due December 15, and that the retailer charged you a $5 service fee. Thinking of the fee as interest, what simple interest rate would you be paying for this layaway plan?

30. ▼ *Layaway Fees* Referring to Exercise 29, suppose that you bought a $99 item on October 15 on layaway, with the final payment due December 15, and that the retailer charged you a $10 service fee. Thinking of the fee as interest, what simple interest rate would you be paying for this layaway plan?

Stock Investments Exercises 31–36 are based on the following chart, which shows monthly figures for Apple Computer, Inc. stock in 2010.[7]

Marked are the following points on the chart:

Jan. 10	Feb. 10	Mar. 10	Apr. 10	May 10	June 10
211.98	195.46	218.95	235.97	235.86	255.96
July 10	Aug. 10	Sep. 10	Oct. 10	Nov. 10	Dec. 10
246.94	260.09	258.77	294.07	317.13	317.44

31. Calculate to the nearest 0.01% your annual percentage return (on a simple interest basis) if you had bought Apple stock in June and sold in December.

32. Calculate to the nearest 0.01% your annual percentage return (on a simple interest basis) if you had bought Apple stock in February and sold in June.

33. ▼ Suppose you bought Apple stock in April. If you later sold at one of the marked dates on the chart, which of those dates would have given you the largest annual return (on a simple interest basis), and what would that return have been?

34. ▼ Suppose you bought Apple stock in May. If you later sold at one of the marked dates on the chart, which of those dates would have given you the largest annual return (on a simple interest basis), and what would that return have been?

35. ▼ Did Apple's stock undergo simple interest change in the period January through May? (Give a reason for your answer.)

36. ▼ If Apple's stock had undergone simple interest change from April to June at the same simple rate as from March to April, what would the price have been in June?

Population Exercises 37–42 are based on the following graph, which shows the population of San Diego County from 1950 to 2000.[8]

[4]Source: The Bureau of the Public Debt's Web site: www.publicdebt.treas.gov.

[5]*Ibid.*

[6]Source: November 14, 2011 press release from the office of Senator Charles E. Schumer (http://schumer.senate.gov/Newsroom/releases.cfm)

[7]Source: Yahoo! Finance (http://finance.yahoo.com).

[8]Source: Census Bureau/*New York Times*, April 2, 2002, p. F3.

37. At what annual (simple interest) rate did the population of San Diego County increase from 1950 to 2000?

38. At what annual (simple interest) rate did the population of San Diego County increase from 1950 to 1990?

39. ▼ If you used your answer to Exercise 37 as the annual (simple interest) rate at which the population was growing since 1950, what would you predict the San Diego County population to be in 2010?

40. ▼ If you used your answer to Exercise 38 as the annual (simple interest) rate at which the population was growing since 1950, what would you predict the San Diego County population to be in 2010?

41. ▼ Use your answer to Exercise 37 to give a linear model for the population of San Diego County from 1950 to 2000. Draw the graph of your model over that period of time.

42. ▼ Use your answer to Exercise 38 to give a linear model for the population of San Diego County from 1950 to 2000. Draw the graph of your model over that period of time.

COMMUNICATION AND REASONING EXERCISES

43. One or more of the following three graphs represents the future value of an investment earning simple interest. Which one(s)? Give the reason for your choice(s).

(A)

(B)

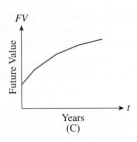

(C)

44. Given that $FV = 5t + 400$, for what interest rate is this the equation of future value (in dollars) as a function of time t (in years)?

45. ▼ *Interpreting the News* You hear the following on your local radio station's business news: "The economy last year grew by 1%. This was the second year in a row in which the economy showed a 1% growth." Because the rate of growth was the same two years in a row, this represents simple interest growth, right? Explain your answer.

46. ▼ *Interpreting the News* You hear the following on your local radio station's business news: "The economy last year grew by 1%. This was the second year in a row in which the economy showed a 1% growth." This means that, in dollar terms, the economy grew more last year than the year before. Why?

47. ▼ Explain why simple interest is not the appropriate way to measure interest on a savings account that pays interest directly into your account.

48. ▼ Suppose that a one-year T-bill sells at a discount rate d. Find a formula, in terms of d, for the simple annual interest rate r the bill will pay.

2.2 Compound Interest

You deposit $1,000 into a savings account. The bank pays you 5% interest, which it deposits into your account, or **reinvests**, at the end of each year. At the end of 5 years, how much money will you have accumulated? Let us compute the amount you have at the end of each year. At the end of the first year, the bank will pay you simple interest of 5% on your $1,000, which gives you

$$PV(1 + rt) = 1,000(1 + 0.05)$$
$$= \$1,050.$$

At the end of the second year, the bank will pay you another 5% interest, but this time computed on the total in your account, which is $1,050. Thus, you will have a total of

$$1,050(1 + 0.05) = \$1,102.50.$$

If you were being paid simple interest on your original $1,000, you would have only $1,100 at the end of the second year. The extra $2.50 is the interest earned on the $50 interest added to your account at the end of the first year. Having interest earn interest is called **compounding** the interest. We could continue like this until the end of the fifth year, but notice what we are doing: Each year we are multiplying by $1 + 0.05$. So, at the end of 5 years, you will have

$$1,000(1 + 0.05)^5 \approx \$1,276.28.$$

It is interesting to compare this to the amount you would have if the bank paid you simple interest:

$$1,000(1 + 0.05 \times 5) = \$1,250.00.$$

The extra $26.28 is again the effect of compounding the interest.

Banks often pay interest more often than once a year. Paying interest quarterly (four times per year) or monthly is common. If your bank pays interest monthly, how much will your $1,000 deposit be worth after 5 years? The bank will not pay you 5% interest every month, but will give you 1/12 of that,* or 5/12% interest each month. Thus, instead of multiplying by $1 + 0.05$ every year, we should multiply by $1 + 0.05/12$ each month. Because there are $5 \times 12 = 60$ months in 5 years, the total amount you will have at the end of 5 years is

$$1,000 \left(1 + \frac{0.05}{12}\right)^{60} \approx \$1,283.36.$$

* This is approximate. They will actually give you 31/365 of the 5% at the end of January and so on, but it's simpler and reasonably accurate to call it 1/12.

Compare this to the $1,276.28 you would get if the bank paid the interest every year. You earn an extra $7.08 if the interest is paid monthly because interest gets into your account and starts earning interest earlier. The amount of time between interest payments is called the **compounding period**.

The following table summarizes the results above.

Time in Years	Amount with Simple Interest	Amount with Annual Compounding	Amount with Monthly Compounding
0	$1,000	$1,000	$1,000
1	$1,000(1 + 0.05)$ $= \$1,050$	$1,000(1 + 0.05)$ $= \$1,050$	$1,000(1 + 0.05/12)^{12}$ $= \$1,051.16$
2	$1,000(1 + 0.05 \times 2)$ $= \$1,100$	$1,000(1 + 0.05)^2$ $= \$1,102.50$	$1,000(1 + 0.05/12)^{24}$ $= \$1,104.94$
5	$1,000(1 + 0.05 \times 5)$ $= \$1,250$	$1,000(1 + 0.05)^5$ $= \$1,276.28$	$1,000(1 + 0.05/12)^{60}$ $= \$1,283.36$

The preceding calculations generalize easily to give the general formula for future value when interest is compounded.

Future Value for Compound Interest

The future value of an investment of PV dollars earning interest at an annual rate of r compounded (reinvested) m times per year for a period of t years is

$$FV = PV\left(1 + \frac{r}{m}\right)^{mt}$$

or

$$FV = PV(1 + i)^n,$$

where $i = r/m$ is the interest paid each compounding period and $n = mt$ is the total number of compounding periods.

Quick Examples

1. To find the future value after 5 years of a $10,000 investment earning 6% interest, with interest reinvested every month, we set $PV = 10,000$, $r = 0.06, m = 12$, and $t = 5$. Thus,

$$FV = PV\left(1 + \frac{r}{m}\right)^{mt} = 10,000\left(1 + \frac{0.06}{12}\right)^{60} \approx \$13,488.50.$$

2. Writing the future value in Quick Example 1 as a function of time, we get

$$FV = 10,000\left(1 + \frac{0.06}{12}\right)^{12t}$$
$$= 10,000(1.005)^{12t},$$

which is an **exponential** function of time t.

In general: *Compound interest growth is an exponential function of time.*

using Technology

All three technologies discussed in this book have built-in mathematics of finance capabilities. See the Technology Guides at the end of the chapter for details on using a TI-83/84 Plus or a spreadsheet to do the calculations in Example 1. [Details: TI-83/84 Plus: page 166, Spreadsheet: page 170]

Website
www.WanerMath.com
→ On Line Utilities
→ Time Value of Money Utility

This utility is similar to the TVM Solver on the TI-83/84 Plus. To compute the future value, enter the values shown, and press "Compute" next to FV.

(For an explanation of the terms, see the Technology Guide for the TI-83/84 Plus.)

EXAMPLE 1 Savings Accounts

In November 2011, the Bank of Montreal was paying 1.30% interest on savings accounts.[9] If the interest is compounded quarterly, find the future value of a $2,000 deposit in 6 years. What is the total interest paid over the period?

Solution We use the future value formula with $m = 4$:

$$FV = PV\left(1 + \frac{r}{m}\right)^{mt}$$
$$= 2,000\left(1 + \frac{0.0130}{4}\right)^{4 \times 6} \approx \$2,161.97.$$

The total interest paid is

$$INT = FV - PV = 2,161.97 - 2,000 = \$161.97.$$

---

[9]Source: Canoe Money (http://money.canoe.ca/rates/savings.html)

Example 1 illustrates the concept of the **time value of money**: A given amount of money received now will usually be worth a different amount to us than the same amount received some time in the future. In the example above, we can say that $2,000 received now is worth the same as $2,161.97 received 6 years from now, because if we receive $2,000 now, we can turn it into $2,161.97 by the end of 6 years.

We often want to know, for some amount of money in the future, what is the equivalent value at present. As we did for simple interest, we can solve the future value formula for the present value and obtain the following formula.

Present Value for Compound Interest

The present value of an investment earning interest at an annual rate of r compounded m times per year for a period of t years, with future value FV, is

$$PV = \frac{FV}{\left(1 + \frac{r}{m}\right)^{mt}}$$

or

$$PV = \frac{FV}{(1 + i)^n} = FV(1 + i)^{-n},$$

where $i = r/m$ is the interest paid each compounding period and $n = mt$ is the total number of compounding periods.

Quick Example

To find the amount we need to invest in an investment earning 12% per year, compounded annually, so that we will have $1 million in 20 years, use $FV = \$1,000,000$, $r = 0.12$, $m = 1$, and $t = 20$:

$$PV = \frac{FV}{\left(1 + \frac{r}{m}\right)^{mt}} = \frac{1,000,000}{(1 + 0.12)^{20}} \approx \$103,666.77.$$

Put another way, $1,000,000 20 years from now is worth only $103,666.77 to us now, if we have a 12% investment available.

In the preceding section, we mentioned that a bond pays interest until it reaches maturity, at which point it pays you back an amount called its **maturity value** or **par value**. The two parts, the interest and the maturity value, can be separated and sold and traded by themselves. A **zero coupon bond** is a form of corporate bond that pays no interest during its life but, like U.S. Treasury bills, promises to pay you the maturity value when it reaches maturity. Zero coupon bonds are often created by removing or *stripping* the interest coupons from an ordinary bond, so are also known as **strips**. Zero coupon bonds sell for less than their maturity value, and the return on the investment is the difference between what the investor pays and the maturity value. Although no interest is actually paid, we measure the return on investment by thinking of the interest rate that would make the selling price (the present value) grow to become the maturity value (the future value).*

* The IRS refers to this kind of interest as **original issue discount (OID)** and taxes it as if it were interest actually paid to you each year.

✳ The return investors look for depends on a number of factors, including risk (the chance that the
company will go bankrupt and
you will lose your investment);
the higher the risk, the higher the
return. U.S. Treasuries are considered risk free because the
federal government has never
defaulted on its debts. On the
other hand, so-called junk bonds
are high-risk investments (below
investment grade) and have cor-
respondingly high yields.

using Technology

See the Technology Guides at the
end of the chapter for details on
using TVM Solver on the TI-83/84
Plus or the built-in finance functions
in spreadsheets to do the calculations in Example 2. [Details: TI-83/84
Plus: page 166, Spreadsheet:
page 171]

Website
www.WanerMath.com

→ On Line Utilities

→ Time Value of Money Utility

This utility is similar to the TVM
Solver on the TI-83/84 Plus. To
compute the present value, enter
the values shown, and press
"Compute" next to PV.

EXAMPLE 2 Zero Coupon Bonds

Megabucks Corporation is issuing 10-year zero coupon bonds. How much would you
pay for bonds with a maturity value of $10,000 if you wish to get a return of 6.5%
compounded annually?✳

Solution As we said earlier, we think of a zero coupon bond as if it were an account
earning (compound) interest. We are asked to calculate the amount you will pay for
the bond—the present value *PV*. We have

$$FV = \$10,000$$
$$r = 0.065$$
$$t = 10$$
$$m = 1.$$

We can now use the present value formula:

$$PV = \frac{FV}{\left(1 + \frac{r}{m}\right)^{mt}}$$

$$PV = \frac{10,000}{\left(1 + \frac{0.065}{1}\right)^{10 \times 1}} \approx \$5,327.26.$$

Thus, you should pay $5,327.26 to get a return of 6.5% annually.

➡ **Before we go on...** Particularly in financial applications, you will hear the word
"discounted" in place of "compounded" when discussing present value. Thus, the
result of Example 2 might be phrased, "The present value of $10,000 to be
received 10 years from now, with an interest rate of 6.5% discounted annually, is
$5,327.26." ∎

Time value of money calculations are often done to take into account inflation,
which behaves like compound interest. Suppose, for example, that inflation is running at 5% per year. Then prices will increase by 5% each year, so if *PV* represents
the price now, the price one year from now will be 5% higher, or $PV(1 + 0.05)$. The
price a year from then will be 5% higher still, or $PV(1 + 0.05)^2$. Thus, the effects of
inflation are compounded just as reinvested interest is.

EXAMPLE 3 Inflation

Inflation in East Avalon is 5% per year. TruVision television sets cost $200 today.
How much will a comparable set cost 2 years from now?

Solution To find the price of a television set 2 years from now, we compute the
future value of $200 at an inflation rate of 5% compounded yearly:

$$FV = 200(1 + 0.05)^2 = \$220.50.$$

EXAMPLE 4 **Constant Dollars**

Inflation in North Avalon is 6% per year. Which is really more expensive, a car costing $20,000 today or one costing $22,000 in 3 years?

Solution We cannot compare the two costs directly because inflation makes $1 today worth more (it buys more) than a dollar 3 years from now. We need the two prices expressed in comparable terms, so we convert to **constant dollars**. We take the car costing $22,000 three years from now and ask what it would cost in today's dollars. In other words, we convert the future value of $22,000 to its present value:

$$PV = FV(1+i)^{-n}$$
$$= 22,000(1+0.06)^{-3}$$
$$\approx \$18,471.62.$$

Thus, the car costing $22,000 in 3 years actually costs less, after adjusting for inflation, than the one costing $20,000 now.

➡ **Before we go on...** In the presence of inflation, the only way to compare prices at different times is to convert all prices to constant dollars. We pick some fixed time and compute future or present values as appropriate to determine what things would have cost at that time. ■

There are some other interesting calculations related to compound interest, besides present and future values.

EXAMPLE 5 **Effective Interest Rate**

You have just won $1 million in the lottery and are deciding what to do with it during the next year before you move to the South Pacific. Bank Ten offers 10% interest, compounded annually, while Bank Nine offers 9.8% compounded monthly. In which should you deposit your money?

Solution Let's calculate the future value of your $1 million after one year in each of the banks:

$$\text{Bank Ten:} \quad FV = 1(1+0.10)^1 = \$1.1 \text{ million}$$

$$\text{Bank Nine:} \quad FV = 1\left(1 + \frac{0.098}{12}\right)^{12} = \$1.1025 \text{ million}.$$

Bank Nine turns out to be better: It will pay you a total of $102,500 in interest over the year, whereas Bank Ten will pay only $100,000 in interest.

Another way of looking at the calculation in Example 5 is that Bank Nine gave you a total of 10.25% interest on your investment over the year. We call 10.25% the **effective interest rate** of the investment (also referred to as the **annual percentage**

yield, or **APY** in the banking industry); the stated 9.8% is called the **nominal** interest rate. In general, to best compare two different investments, it is wisest to compare their *effective*—rather than nominal—interest rates.

Notice that we got 10.25% by computing

$$\left(1 + \frac{0.098}{12}\right)^{12} = 1.1025$$

and then subtracting 1 to get 0.1025, or 10.25%. Generalizing, we get the following formula.

Effective Interest Rate

The effective interest rate r_{eff} of an investment paying a nominal interest rate of r_{nom} compounded m times per year is

$$r_{\text{eff}} = \left(1 + \frac{r_{\text{nom}}}{m}\right)^{m} - 1.$$

To compare rates of investments with different compounding periods, always compare the effective interest rates rather than the nominal rates.

Quick Example

To calculate the effective interest rate of an investment that pays 8% per year, with interest reinvested monthly, set $r_{\text{nom}} = 0.08$ and $m = 12$, to obtain

$$r_{\text{eff}} = \left(1 + \frac{0.08}{12}\right)^{12} - 1 \approx 0.0830, \text{ or } 8.30\%.$$

EXAMPLE 6 **How Long to Invest**

You have $5,000 to invest at 6% interest compounded monthly. How long will it take for your investment to grow to $6,000?

Solution If we use the future value formula, we already have the values

$$FV = 6,000$$
$$PV = 5,000$$
$$r = 0.06$$
$$m = 12.$$

Substituting, we get

$$6,000 = 5,000 \left(1 + \frac{0.06}{12}\right)^{12t}.$$

using Technology

See the Technology Guides at the end of the chapter for details on using TVM Solver on the TI-83/84 Plus or the built-in finance functions in spreadsheets to do the calculations in Example 6. [Details: TI-83/84 Plus: page 167, Spreadsheet: page 171]

 Website
www.WanerMath.com
→ On Line Utilities
→ Time Value of Money Utility

This utility is similar to the TVM Solver on the TI-83/84 Plus. To compute the time needed, enter the values shown, and press "Compute" next to t.

If you are familiar with logarithms, you can solve explicitly for t as follows:

$$\left(1+\frac{0.06}{12}\right)^{12t}=\frac{6,000}{5,000}=1.2$$

$$\log\left(1+\frac{0.06}{12}\right)^{12t}=\log 1.2$$

$$12t\log\left(1+\frac{0.06}{12}\right)=\log 1.2$$

$$t=\frac{\log 1.2}{12\log\left(1+\frac{0.06}{12}\right)}\approx 3.046\approx 3 \text{ years.}$$

Another approach is to use a bit of trial and error to find the answer. Let's see what the future value is after 2, 3, and 4 years:

$$5,000\left(1+\frac{0.06}{12}\right)^{12\times 2}=5,635.80 \quad \text{Future value after 2 years}$$

$$5,000\left(1+\frac{0.06}{12}\right)^{12\times 3}=5,983.40 \quad \text{Future value after 3 years}$$

$$5,000\left(1+\frac{0.06}{12}\right)^{12\times 4}=6,352.45. \quad \text{Future value after 4 years}$$

From these calculations, it looks as if the answer should be a bit more than 3 years, but is certainly between 3 and 4 years. We could try 3.5 years next and then narrow it down systematically until we have a pretty good approximation of the correct answer.

Graphing calculators and spreadsheets give us alternative methods of solution.

FAQs

Recognizing When to Use Compound Interest and the Meaning of Present Value

Q: *How do I distinguish a problem that calls for compound interest from one that calls for simple interest?*

A: Study the scenario to ascertain whether the interest is being withdrawn as it is earned or reinvested (deposited back into the account). If the interest is being withdrawn, the problem is calling for simple interest because the interest is not itself earning interest. If it is being reinvested, the problem is calling for compound interest.

Q: *How do I distinguish present value from future value in a problem?*

A: The present value always refers to the value of an investment before any interest is included (or, in the case of a depreciating investment, before any depreciation takes place). As an example, the future value of a bond is its maturity value. The value of $1 today in constant 2010 dollars is its present value (even though 2010 is in the past).

2.2 EXERCISES

▼ more advanced ◆ challenging
T indicates exercises that should be solved using technology

In Exercises 1–8, calculate, to the nearest cent, the future value of an investment of $10,000 at the stated interest rate after the stated amount of time. HINT [See Example 1.]

1. 3% per year, compounded annually, after 10 years

2. 4% per year, compounded annually, after 8 years

3. 2.5% per year, compounded quarterly (4 times/year), after 5 years

4. 1.5% per year, compounded weekly (52 times/year), after 5 years

5. 6.5% per year, compounded daily (assume 365 days/year), after 10 years

6. 11.2% per year, compounded monthly, after 12 years

7. 0.2% per month, compounded monthly, after 10 years

8. 0.45% per month, compounded monthly, after 20 years

In Exercises 9–14, calculate, to the nearest cent, the present value of an investment that will be worth $1,000 at the stated interest rate after the stated amount of time. HINT [See Example 2.]

9. 10 years, at 5% per year, compounded annually

10. 5 years, at 6% per year, compounded annually

11. 5 years, at 4.2% per year, compounded weekly (assume 52 weeks per year)

12. 10 years, at 5.3% per year, compounded quarterly

13. 4 years, depreciating 5% each year

14. 5 years, depreciating 4% each year

In Exercises 15–20, find the effective annual interest rates of the given annual interest rates. Round your answers to the nearest 0.01%. HINT [See Quick Example on page 140.]

15. 5% compounded quarterly

16. 5% compounded monthly

17. 10% compounded monthly

18. 10% compounded daily (assume 365 days per year)

19. 10% compounded hourly (assume 365 days per year)

20. 10% compounded every minute (assume 365 days per year)

APPLICATIONS

21. *Savings* You deposit $1,000 in an account at the *Lifelong Trust Savings and Loan* that pays 6% interest compounded quarterly. By how much will your deposit have grown after 4 years?

22. *Investments* You invest $10,000 in *Rapid Growth Funds*, which appreciate by 2% per year, with yields reinvested quarterly. By how much will your investment have grown after 5 years?

23. *Depreciation* During 2008, the S&P 500 index depreciated by 37.6%.[10] Assuming that this trend had continued, how much would a $3,000 investment in an S&P index fund have been worth after 3 years?

24. *Depreciation* During 2008, the NASDAQ Composite Index depreciated by 42%.[11] Assuming that this trend had continued, how much would a $5,000 investment in a NASDAQ Composite Index fund have been worth after 4 years?

25. *Bonds* You want to buy a 10-year zero coupon bond with a maturity value of $5,000 and a yield of 5.5% annually. How much will you pay?

26. *Bonds* You want to buy a 15-year zero coupon bond with a maturity value of $10,000 and a yield of 6.25% annually. How much will you pay?

27. ▼ *Investments* When I was considering what to do with my $10,000 Lottery winnings, my broker suggested I invest half of it in gold, the value of which was growing by 10% per year, and the other half in certificates of deposit (CDs), which were yielding 5% per year, compounded every 6 months. Assuming that these rates are sustained, how much will my investment be worth in 10 years?

28. ▼ *Investments* When I was considering what to do with the $10,000 proceeds from my sale of technology stock, my broker suggested I invest half of it in municipal bonds, whose value was growing by 6% per year, and the other half in CDs, which were yielding 3% per year, compounded every 2 months. Assuming that these interest rates are sustained, how much will my investment be worth in 10 years?

29. ▼ *Depreciation* During a prolonged recession, property values on Long Island depreciated by 2% every 6 months. If my house cost $200,000 originally, how much was it worth 5 years later?

30. ▼ *Depreciation* Stocks in the health industry depreciated by 5.1% in the first 9 months of 1993.[12] Assuming that this trend continued, how much would a $40,000 investment be worth in 9 years? HINT [Nine years corresponds to 12 nine-month periods.]

31. ▼ *Retirement Planning* I want to be earning an annual salary of $100,000 when I retire in 15 years. I have been offered a job that guarantees an annual salary increase of 4% per year, and the starting salary is negotiable. What salary should I request in order to meet my goal?

---

[10]Source: http://finance.google.com.

[11]*Ibid.*

[12]Source: *New York Times*, October 9, 1993, p. 37.

32. ▼ *Retirement Planning* I want to be earning an annual salary of $80,000 when I retire in 10 years. I have been offered a job that guarantees an annual salary increase of 5% per year, and the starting salary is negotiable. What salary should I request in order to meet my goal?

33. ▼ *Present Value* Determine the amount of money, to the nearest dollar, you must invest at 6% per year, compounded annually, so that you will be a millionaire in 30 years.

34. ▼ *Present Value* Determine the amount of money, to the nearest dollar, you must invest now at 7% per year, compounded annually, so that you will be a millionaire in 40 years.

35. ▼ *Stocks* Six years ago, I invested some money in *Dracubunny Toy Co.* stock, acting on the advice of a "friend." As things turned out, the value of the stock decreased by 5% every 4 months, and I discovered yesterday (to my horror) that my investment was worth only $297.91. How much did I originally invest?

36. ▼ *Sales* My recent marketing idea, the *Miracle Algae Growing Kit*, has been remarkably successful, with monthly sales growing by 6% every 6 months over the past 5 years. Assuming that I sold 100 kits the first month, how many kits did I sell in the first month of this year?

37. ▼ *Inflation* Inflation has been running 2% per year. A car now costs $30,000. How much would it have cost 5 years ago? HINT [See Example 3.]

38. ▼ *Inflation* (Compare Exercise 37.) Inflation has been running 1% every 6 months. A car now costs $30,000. How much would it have cost 5 years ago?

39. ▼ *Inflation* Housing prices have been rising 6% per year. A house now costs $200,000. What would it have cost 10 years ago?

40. ▼ *Inflation* (Compare Exercise 39.) Housing prices have been rising 0.5% each month. A house now costs $200,000. What would it have cost 10 years ago? HINT [See Example 4.]

41. ▼ *Constant Dollars* Inflation is running 3% per year when you deposit $1,000 in an account earning interest of 5% per year compounded annually. In *constant dollars*, how much money will you have 2 years from now? HINT [First calculate the value of your account in 2 years' time, and then find its present value based on the inflation rate.]

42. ▼ *Constant Dollars* Inflation is running 1% per month when you deposit $10,000 in an account earning 8% compounded monthly. In *constant dollars*, how much money will you have 2 years from now? HINT [See Exercise 41.]

43. ▼ *Investments* You are offered two investments. One promises to earn 12% compounded annually. The other will earn 11.9% compounded monthly. Which is the better investment? HINT [See Example 5.]

44. ▼ *Investments* You are offered three investments. The first promises to earn 15% compounded annually, the second will earn 14.5% compounded quarterly, and the third will earn 14% compounded monthly. Which is the best investment? HINT [See Example 5.]

45. ▼ *History* Legend has it that a band of Lenape Indians known as the "Manhatta" sold Manhattan Island to the Dutch in 1626 for $24. In 2011, the total value of Manhattan real estate was estimated to be $314,119 million.[13] Suppose that the Lenape had instead taken that $24 and invested it at 6.3% compounded annually (a relatively conservative investment goal). Could they then have bought back the island in 2011?

46. ▼ *History* Repeat Exercise 45, assuming that the Lenape had invested the $24 at 6.2% compounded annually.

Inflation Exercises 47–54 are based on the following table, which shows the 2008 annual inflation rates in several Latin American countries.[14] Assume that the rates shown continue indefinitely.

Country	Argentina	Brazil	Bolivia	Nicaragua	Venezuela	Mexico	Uruguay
Currency	Peso	Real	Boliviano	Gold cordoba	Bolivar	Peso	Peso
Inflation Rate (%)	9.2	6.3	15.1	13.8	25.7	5.0	8.5

47. If an item in Brazil now costs 100 reals, what do you expect it to cost 5 years from now? (Answer to the nearest real.)

48. If an item in Argentina now costs 1,000 pesos, what do you expect it to cost 5 years from now? (Answer to the nearest peso.)

49. If an item in Bolivia will cost 1,000 bolivianos in 10 years, what does it cost now? (Answer to the nearest boliviano.)

50. If an item in Mexico will cost 20,000 pesos in 10 years, what does it cost now? (Answer to the nearest peso.)

51. ▼ You wish to invest 1,000 bolivars in Venezuela at 8% annually, compounded twice a year. Find the value of your investment in 10 years, expressing the answer in constant bolivars. (Answer to the nearest bolivar.)

52. ▼ You wish to invest 1,000 pesos in Uruguay at 8% annually, compounded twice a year. Find the value of your investment in 10 years, expressing the answer in constant pesos. (Answer to the nearest peso.)

53. ▼ Which is the better investment: an investment in Mexico yielding 5.3% per year, compounded annually, or an investment in Nicaragua yielding 14% per year, compounded every 6 months? Support your answer with figures that show the future value of an investment of 1 unit of currency in constant units.

[13]Source: FY12 Tentative Assessment Roll summary, New York City Department of Finance, January 14, 2011 (www.nyc.gov/finance)

[14]Sources: www.bloomberg.com, www.csmonitor.com, www.indexmundi.com.

54. ▼ Which is the better investment: an investment in Argentina yielding 10% per year, compounded annually, or an investment in Uruguay, yielding 9% per year, compounded every 6 months? Support your answer with figures that show the future value of an investment of 1 unit of currency in constant units.

Stock Investments *Exercises 55–60 are based on the following chart, which shows monthly figures for* **Apple Computer, Inc.** *stock in 2010.*[15]

Marked are the following points on the chart:

Jan. 10	Feb. 10	Mar. 10	Apr. 10	May 10	June 10
211.98	195.46	218.95	235.97	235.86	255.96
July 10	Aug. 10	Sep. 10	Oct. 10	Nov. 10	Dec. 10
246.94	260.09	258.77	294.07	317.13	317.44

55. ▼ Calculate to the nearest 0.01% your annual percentage return (assuming annual compounding) if you had bought Apple stock in June and sold in December.

56. ▼ Calculate to the nearest 0.01% your annual percentage return (assuming annual compounding) if you had bought Apple stock in February and sold in June.

57. ▼ Suppose you bought Apple stock in April. If you later sold at one of the marked dates on the chart, which of those dates would have given you the largest annual return (assuming annual compounding), and what would that return have been?

58. ▼ Suppose you bought Apple stock in May. If you later sold at one of the marked dates on the chart, which of those dates would have given you the largest annual return (assuming annual compounding), and what would that return have been?

59. ▼ Did Apple's stock undergo compound interest change in the period January through May? (Give a reason for your answer.)

60. ▼ If Apple's stock had undergone compound interest change from April to June at the same monthly rate as from March to April, what would the price have been in June?

61. ▮ ▼ ***Competing Investments*** I just purchased $5,000 worth of municipal funds that are expected to yield 5.4% per year, compounded every 6 months. My friend has just purchased $6,000 worth of CDs that will earn 4.8% per year,

compounded every 6 months. Determine when, to the nearest year, the value of my investment will be the same as hers, and what this value will be. **HINT** [You can either graph the values of both investments or make tables of the values of both investments.]

62. ▮ ▼ ***Investments*** Determine when, to the nearest year, $3,000 invested at 5% per year, compounded daily, will be worth $10,000.

63. ▮ ▼ ***Epidemics*** At the start of 1985, the incidence of AIDS was doubling every 6 months and 40,000 cases had been reported in the United States. Assuming this trend would have continued, determine when, to the nearest tenth of a year, the number of cases would have reached 1 million.

64. ▮ ▼ ***Depreciation*** My investment in *Genetic Splicing, Inc.*, is now worth $4,354 and is depreciating by 5% every 6 months. For some reason, I am reluctant to sell the stock and swallow my losses. Determine when, to the nearest year, my investment will drop below $50.

65. ◆ ***Bonds*** Once purchased, bonds can be sold in the secondary market. The value of a bond depends on the prevailing interest rates, which vary over time. Suppose that in January 2020, you buy a 30-year zero-coupon U.S. Treasury bond with a maturity value of $100,000 and a yield of 15% annually.
  a. How much do you pay for the bond?
  b. In January 2037, your bond has 13 years remaining until maturity. Rates on U.S. Treasury bonds of comparable length are now about 4.75%. If you sell your bond to an investor looking for a return of 4.75% annually, how much money do you receive?
  c. Using your answers to parts (a) and (b), what was the annual yield (assuming annual compounding) on your 17-year investment?

66. ◆ ***Bonds*** Suppose that in January 2040, you buy a 30-year zero-coupon U.S. Treasury bond with a maturity value of $100,000 and a yield of 5% annually.
  a. How much do you pay for the bond?
  b. Suppose that, 15 years later, interest rates have risen again, to 12%. If you sell your bond to an investor looking for a return of 12%, how much money will you receive?
  c. Using your answers to parts (a) and (b), what will be the annual yield (assuming annual compounding) on your 15-year investment?

COMMUNICATION AND REASONING EXERCISES

67. Why is the graph of the future value of a compound interest investment as a function of time not a straight line (assuming a nonzero rate of interest)?

68. An investment that earns 10% (compound interest) every year is the same as an investment that earns 5% (compound interest) every 6 months, right?

69. ▼ If a bacteria culture is currently 0.01 g and increases in size by 10% each day, then its growth is linear, right?

70. ▼ At what point is the future value of a compound interest investment the same as the future value of a simple interest investment at the same annual rate of interest?

[15]Source: Yahoo! Finance (http://finance.yahoo.com).

71. ▼ If two equal investments have the same effective interest rate and you graph the future value as a function of time for each of them, are the graphs necessarily the same? Explain your answer.

72. ▼ For what kind of compound interest investments is the effective rate the same as the nominal rate? Explain your answer.

73. ▼ For what kind of compound interest investments is the effective rate greater than the nominal rate? When is it smaller? Explain your answer.

74. ▼ If an investment appreciates by 10% per year for 5 years (compounded annually) and then depreciates by 10% per year (compounded annually) for 5 more years, will it have the same value as it had originally? Explain your answer.

75. ▼ You can choose between two investments that mature at different times in the future. If you knew the rate of inflation, how would you decide which is the better investment?

76. ▼ If you knew the various inflation rates for the years 2000 through 2011, how would you convert $100 in 2012 dollars to 2000 dollars?

77. 🅣 ▼ On the same set of axes, graph the future value of a $100 investment earning 10% per year as a function of time over a 20-year period, compounded once a year, 10 times a year, 100 times a year, 1,000 times a year, and 10,000 times a year. What do you notice?

78. 🅣 ▼ By graphing the future value of a $100 investment that is depreciating by 1% each year, convince yourself that, eventually, the future value will be less than $1.

2.3 Annuities, Loans, and Bonds

* Defined-contribution pension plans have largely replaced the defined-benefit pensions that were once the norm in private industry. In a defined-benefit plan, the size of your pension is guaranteed; it is typically a percentage of your final working salary. In a defined-contribution plan, the size of your pension depends on how well your investments do.

A typical defined-contribution pension fund works as follows*: Every month while you work, you and your employer deposit a certain amount of money in an account. This money earns (compound) interest from the time it is deposited. When you retire, the account continues to earn interest, but you may then start withdrawing money at a rate calculated to reduce the account to zero after some number of years. This account is an example of an **annuity**, an account earning interest into which you make periodic deposits or from which you make periodic withdrawals. In common usage, the term "annuity" is used for an account from which you make withdrawals. There are various terms used for accounts into which you make payments, based on their purpose. Examples include **savings account**, **pension fund**, and **sinking fund**. A sinking fund is generally used by businesses or governments to accumulate money to pay off an anticipated debt, but we'll use the term to refer to any account into which you make periodic payments.

Sinking Funds

Suppose you make a payment of $100 at the end of every month into an account earning 3.6% interest per year, compounded monthly. This means that your investment is earning $3.6\%/12 = 0.3\%$ per month. We write $i = 0.036/12 = 0.003$. What will be the value of the investment at the end of 2 years (24 months)?

Think of the deposits separately. Each earns interest from the time it is deposited, and the total accumulated after 2 years is the sum of these deposits and the interest they earn. In other words, the accumulated value is the sum of the future values of the deposits, taking into account how long each deposit sits in the account. Figure 1 shows a timeline with the deposits and the contribution of each to the final value. For example, the very last deposit (at the end of month 24) has no time to earn interest, so it contributes only $100. The very first deposit, which earns interest for 23 months, by the future value formula for compound interest contributes $100(1 + 0.003)^{23}$ to the total. Adding together all of the future values gives us the total future value:

$$FV = 100 + 100(1 + 0.003) + 100(1 + 0.003)^2 + \cdots + 100(1 + 0.003)^{23}$$
$$= 100[1 + (1 + 0.003) + (1 + 0.003)^2 + \cdots + (1 + 0.003)^{23}]$$

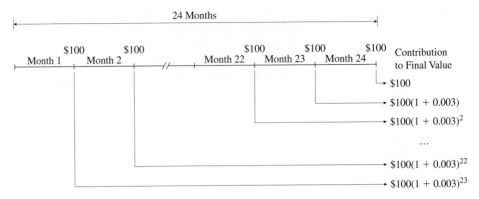

Figure 1

* It is called a **geometric series**.

† The quickest way to convince yourself that this formula is correct is to multiply out $(x-1)(1+x+x^2+\cdots+x^{n-1})$ and see that you get x^n-1. You should also try substituting some numbers. For example, $1+3+3^2=13=(3^3-1)/(3-1)$.

Fortunately, this sort of sum is well-known (to mathematicians, anyway*) and there is a convenient formula for its value†:

$$1+x+x^2+\cdots+x^{n-1}=\frac{x^n-1}{x-1}.$$

In our case, with $x=1+0.003$, this formula allows us to calculate the future value:

$$FV=100\frac{(1+0.003)^{24}-1}{(1+0.003)-1}=100\frac{(1.003)^{24}-1}{0.003}\approx\$2{,}484.65.$$

It is now easy to generalize this calculation.

Future Value of a Sinking Fund

A **sinking fund** is an account earning compound interest into which you make periodic deposits. Suppose that the account has an annual rate of r compounded m times per year, so that $i=r/m$ is the interest rate per compounding period. If you make a payment of PMT at the end of each period, then the future value after t years, or $n=mt$ periods, will be

$$FV=PMT\frac{(1+i)^n-1}{i}.$$

Quick Example

At the end of each month you deposit $50 into an account earning 2% annual interest compounded monthly. To find the future value after 5 years, we use $i=0.02/12$ and $n=12\times5=60$ compounding periods, so

$$FV=50\frac{(1+0.02/12)^{60}-1}{0.02/12}=\$3{,}152.37.$$

using Technology

To automate the computations in Example 1 using a graphing calculator or a spreadsheet, see the Technology Guides at the end of the chapter. Outline:

EXAMPLE 1 Retirement Account

Your retirement account has $5,000 in it and earns 5% interest per year compounded monthly. Every month for the next 10 years you will deposit $100 into the account. How much money will there be in the account at the end of those 10 years?

TI-83/84 Plus

APPS 1:Finance, then
1:TVM Solver
N = 120, I% = 5, PV = -5000,
PMT = -100, P/Y = 12, C/Y = 12
With cursor on FV line, ALPHA
SOLVE [More details on page 167.]

Spreadsheet

=FV(5/12,10*12,-100,-5000)
[More details on page 171.]

 Website

www.WanerMath.com
 → On Line Utilities
 → Time Value of Money Utility
Enter the values shown, and press
"Compute" next to FV.

Solution This is a sinking fund with $PMT = \$100$, $r = 0.05$, $m = 12$, so $i = 0.05/12$, and $n = 12 \times 10 = 120$. Ignoring for the moment the $5,000 already in the account, your payments have the following future value:

$$FV = PMT\frac{(1+i)^n - 1}{i}$$
$$= 100\frac{(1 + 0.05/12)^{120} - 1}{0.05/12}$$
$$\approx \$15,528.23.$$

What about the $5,000 that was already in the account? That sits there and earns interest, so we need to find its future value as well, using the compound interest formula:

$$FV = PV(1 + i)^n$$
$$= 5,000(1 + 0.05/12)^{120}$$
$$= \$8,235.05.$$

Hence, the total amount in the account at the end of 10 years will be

$$\$15,528.23 + 8,235.05 = \$23,763.28.$$

Sometimes we know what we want the future value to be and need to determine the payments necessary to achieve that goal. We can simply solve the future value formula for the payment.

Payment Formula for a Sinking Fund

Suppose that an account has an annual rate of r compounded m times per year, so that $i = r/m$ is the interest rate per compounding period. If you want to accumulate a total of FV in the account after t years, or $n = mt$ periods, by making payments of PMT at the end of each period, then each payment must be

$$PMT = FV\frac{i}{(1+i)^n - 1}.$$

EXAMPLE 2 Education Fund

using Technology

To automate the computations in Example 2 using a graphing calculator or a spreadsheet, see the Technology Guides at the end of the chapter. Outline:

TI-83/84 Plus

APPS 1:Finance, then
1:TVM Solver
N = 68, I% = 4, PV = 0,
FV = 100000, P/Y = 4, C/Y = 4
With cursor on PMT line,
ALPHA SOLVE
[More details on page 167.]

Tony and Maria have just had a son, José Phillipe. They establish an account to accumulate money for his college education, in which they would like to have $100,000 after 17 years. If the account pays 4% interest per year compounded quarterly, and they make deposits at the end of every quarter, how large must each deposit be for them to reach their goal?

Solution This is a sinking fund with $FV = \$100,000$, $m = 4$, $n = 4 \times 17 = 68$, and $r = 0.04$, so $i = 0.04/4 = 0.01$. From the payment formula, we get

$$PMT = 100,000\frac{0.01}{(1 + 0.01)^{68} - 1} \approx \$1,033.89.$$

So, Tony and Maria must deposit $1,033.89 every quarter in order to meet their goal.

Annuities

Suppose we deposit an amount PV now in an account earning 3.6% interest per year, compounded monthly. Starting 1 month from now, the bank will send us monthly payments of $100. What must PV be so that the account will be drawn down to $0 in exactly 2 years?

As before, we write $i = r/m = 0.036/12 = 0.003$, and we have $PMT = 100$. The first payment of $100 will be made 1 month from now, so its present value is

$$\frac{PMT}{(1+i)^n} = \frac{100}{1+0.003} = 100(1+0.003)^{-1} \approx \$99.70.$$

In other words, that much of the original PV goes toward funding the first payment. The second payment, 2 months from now, has a present value of

$$\frac{PMT}{(1+i)^n} = \frac{100}{(1+0.003)^2} = 100(1+0.003)^{-2} \approx \$99.40.$$

That much of the original PV funds the second payment. This continues for 2 years, at which point we receive the last payment, which has a present value of

$$\frac{PMT}{(1+i)^n} = \frac{100}{(1+0.003)^{24}} = 100(1+0.003)^{-24} \approx \$93.06$$

and that exhausts the account. Figure 2 shows a timeline with the payments and the present value of each.

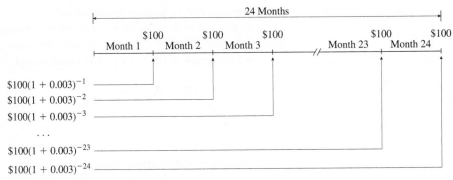

Figure 2

Because PV must be the sum of these present values, we get

$$PV = 100(1+0.003)^{-1} + 100(1+0.003)^{-2} + \cdots + 100(1+0.003)^{-24}$$
$$= 100[(1+0.003)^{-1} + (1+0.003)^{-2} + \cdots + (1+0.003)^{-24}].$$

We can again find a simpler formula for this sum:

$$x^{-1} + x^{-2} + \cdots + x^{-n} = \frac{1}{x^n}(x^{n-1} + x^{n-2} + \cdots + 1)$$
$$= \frac{1}{x^n} \cdot \frac{x^n - 1}{x - 1} = \frac{1 - x^{-n}}{x - 1}.$$

So, in our case,

$$PV = 100\frac{1 - (1 + 0.003)^{-24}}{(1 + 0.003) - 1}$$

or

$$PV = 100\frac{1 - (1.003)^{-24}}{0.003} \approx \$2{,}312.29.$$

If we deposit $2,312.29 initially and the bank sends us $100 per month for 2 years, our account will be exhausted at the end of that time.

Generalizing, we get the following formula:

Present Value of an Annuity

An **annuity** is an account earning compound interest from which periodic withdrawals are made. Suppose that the account has an annual rate of r compounded m times per year, so that $i = r/m$ is the interest rate per compounding period. Suppose also that the account starts with a balance of PV. If you receive a payment of PMT at the end of each compounding period, and the account is down to $0 after t years, or $n = mt$ periods, then

$$PV = PMT\frac{1 - (1 + i)^{-n}}{i}.$$

Quick Example

At the end of each month you want to withdraw $50 from an account earning 2% annual interest compounded monthly. If you want the account to last for 5 years (60 compounding periods), it must have the following amount to begin with:

$$PV = 50\frac{1 - (1 + 0.02/12)^{-60}}{0.02/12} = \$2{,}852.62.$$

Note If you make your withdrawals at the end of each compounding period, as we've discussed so far, you have an **ordinary annuity**. If, instead, you make withdrawals at the beginning of each compounding period, you have an **annuity due**. Because each payment occurs one period earlier, there is one less period in which to earn interest, hence the present value must be larger by a factor of $(1 + i)$ to fund each payment. So, the present value formula for an annuity due is

$$PV = PMT(1 + i)\frac{1 - (1 + i)^{-n}}{i}.$$

In this book, we will concentrate on ordinary annuities. ∎

EXAMPLE 3 Trust Fund

You wish to establish a trust fund from which your niece can withdraw $2,000 every 6 months for 15 years, at the end of which time she will receive the remaining money in the trust, which you would like to be $10,000. The trust will be invested at 7% per year compounded every 6 months. How large should the trust be?

using Technology

To automate the computations in Example 3 using a graphing calculator or a spreadsheet, see the Technology Guides at the end of the chapter. Outline:

TI-83/84 Plus
APPS 1:Finance, then
1:TVM Solver
N = 30, I% = 7, PMT = 2000,
FV = 10000, P/Y = 2, C/Y = 2
With cursor on PV line.
ALPHA SOLVE
[More details on page 168.]

Spreadsheet
=PV(7/2,15*2,2000,10000)
[More details on page 172.]

 Website
www.WanerMath.com
→ On Line Utilities
→ Time Value of Money Utility
Enter the values shown, and press "Compute" next to PV.

FV =	10000	Compute
PV =		Compute
PMT =	2000	Compute
r =	7%	Compute
m =	2	Compute
t =	15	Compute
	Clear All	

Solution We view this account as having two parts, one funding the semiannual payments and the other funding the $10,000 lump sum at the end. The amount of money necessary to fund the semiannual payments is the present value of an annuity, with $PMT = 2,000$, $r = 0.07$, and $m = 2$, so $i = 0.07/2 = 0.035$, and $n = 2 \times 15 = 30$. Substituting gives

$$PV = 2,000\frac{1 - (1 + 0.035)^{-30}}{0.035}$$
$$= \$36,784.09.$$

To fund the lump sum of $10,000 after 15 years, we need the present value of $10,000 under compound interest:

$$PV = 10,000(1 + 0.035)^{-30}$$
$$= \$3,562.78.$$

Thus the trust should start with $36,784.09 + 3,562.78 = \$40,346.87$.

Sometimes we know how much money we begin with and for how long we want to make withdrawals. We then want to determine the amount of money we can withdraw each period. For this, we simply solve the present value formula for the payment.

Payment Formula for an Ordinary Annuity

Suppose that an account has an annual rate of r compounded m times per year, so that $i = r/m$ is the interest rate per compounding period. Suppose also that the account starts with a balance of PV. If you want to receive a payment of PMT at the end of each compounding period, and the account is down to $0 after t years, or $n = mt$ periods, then

$$PMT = PV\frac{i}{1 - (1 + i)^{-n}}.$$

EXAMPLE 4 **Education Fund**

Tony and Maria (see Example 2), having accumulated $100,000 for José Phillipe's college education, would now like to make quarterly withdrawals over the next 4 years. How much money can they withdraw each quarter in order to draw down the account to zero at the end of the 4 years? (Recall that the account pays 4% interest compounded quarterly.)

Solution Now Tony and Maria's account is acting as an annuity with a present value of $100,000. So, $PV = \$100,000$, $r = 0.04$, and $m = 4$, giving $i = 0.04/4 = 0.01$, and $n = 4 \times 4 = 16$. We use the payment formula to get

$$PMT = 100,000\frac{0.01}{1 - (1 + 0.01)^{-16}} \approx \$6,794.46.$$

So, they can withdraw $6,794.46 each quarter for 4 years, at the end of which time their account balance will be 0.

EXAMPLE 5 **Saving for Retirement**

Jane Q. Employee has just started her new job with *Big Conglomerate, Inc.*, and is already looking forward to retirement. BCI offers her as a pension plan an annuity that is guaranteed to earn 6% annual interest compounded monthly. She plans to work for 40 years before retiring and would then like to be able to draw an income of $7,000 per month for 20 years. How much do she and BCI together have to deposit per month into the fund to accomplish this?

Solution Here we have the situation we described at the beginning of the section: a sinking fund accumulating money to be used later as an annuity. We know the desired payment out of the annuity, so we work backward. The first thing we need to do is calculate the present value of the annuity required to make the pension payments. We use the annuity present value formula with $PMT = 7,000$, $i = r/m = 0.06/12 = 0.005$ and $n = 12 \times 20 = 240$.

$$PV = PMT\frac{1 - (1 + i)^{-n}}{i}$$

$$= 7,000\frac{1 - (1 + 0.005)^{-240}}{0.005} \approx \$977,065.40$$

This is the total that must be accumulated in the sinking fund during the 40 years she plans to work. In other words, this is the *future* value, *FV*, of the sinking fund. (Thus, the present value in the first step of our calculation is the future value in the second step.) To determine the payments necessary to accumulate this amount, we use the sinking fund payment formula with $FV = 977,065.40$, $i = 0.005$, and $n = 12 \times 40 = 480$.

$$PMT = FV\frac{i}{(1 + i)^n - 1}$$

$$= 977,065.40\frac{0.005}{1.005^{480} - 1}$$

$$\approx \$490.62$$

So, if she and BCI collectively deposit $490.62 per month into her retirement fund, she can retire with the income she desires.

Installment Loans

In a typical installment loan, such as a car loan or a home mortgage, we borrow an amount of money and then pay it back with interest by making fixed payments (usually every month) over some number of years. From the point of view of the lender, this is an annuity. Thus, loan calculations are identical to annuity calculations.

EXAMPLE 6 **Home Mortgages**

Marc and Mira are buying a house, and have taken out a 30-year, $90,000 mortgage at 8% interest per year. What will their monthly payments be?

Solution From the bank's point of view, a mortgage is an annuity. In this case, the present value is $PV = \$90,000$, $r = 0.08$, $m = 12$, and $n = 12 \times 30 = 360$. To find the payments, we use the payment formula:

$$PMT = 90,000\frac{0.08/12}{1 - (1 + 0.08/12)^{-360}} \approx \$660.39.$$

The word "mortgage" comes from the French for "dead pledge." The process of paying off a loan is called **amortizing** the loan, meaning to kill the debt owed.

EXAMPLE 7 Amortization Schedule

Continuing Example 6: Mortgage interest is tax deductible, so it is important to know how much of a year's mortgage payments represents interest. How much interest will Marc and Mira pay in the first year of their mortgage?

Solution Let us calculate how much of each month's payment is interest and how much goes to reducing the outstanding principal. At the end of the first month Marc and Mira must pay 1 month's interest on $90,000, which is

$$\$90,000 \times \frac{0.08}{12} = \$600.$$

The remainder of their first monthly payment, $660.39 − 600 = $60.39, goes to reducing the principal. Thus, in the second month the outstanding principal is $90,000 − 60.39 = $89,939.61, and part of their second monthly payment will be for the interest on this amount, which is

$$\$89,939.61 \times \frac{0.08}{12} \approx \$599.60.$$

The remaining $660.39 − $599.60 = $60.79 goes to further reduce the principal. If we continue this calculation for the 12 months of the first year, we get the beginning of the mortgage's **amortization schedule**.

using Technology

To automate the construction of the amortization schedule in Example 7 using a graphing calculator or a spreadsheet, see the Technology Guides at the end of the chapter. [Details: TI-83/84 Plus: page 169, Spreadsheet: page 173]

Month	*Interest Payment*	*Payment on Principal*	*Outstanding Principal*
0			$90,000.00
1	$600.00	$60.39	89,939.61
2	599.60	60.79	89,878.82
3	599.19	61.20	89,817.62
4	598.78	61.61	89,756.01
5	598.37	62.02	89,693.99
6	597.96	62.43	89,631.56
7	597.54	62.85	89,568.71
8	597.12	63.27	89,505.44
9	596.70	63.69	89,441.75
10	596.28	64.11	89,377.64
11	595.85	64.54	89,313.10
12	595.42	64.97	89,248.13
Total	$7,172.81	$751.87	

As we can see from the totals at the bottom of the columns, Marc and Mira will pay a total of $7,172.81 in interest in the first year.

Bonds

Suppose that a corporation offers a 10-year bond paying 6.5% with payments every 6 months. As we saw in Example 3 of Section 2.1, this means that if we pay $10,000 for bonds with a maturity value of $10,000, we will receive $6.5/2 = 3.25\%$ of $10,000, or $325, every 6 months for 10 years, at the end of which time the corporation will give us the original $10,000 back. But bonds are rarely sold at their maturity value. Rather, they are auctioned off and sold at a price the bond market determines they are worth.

For example, suppose that bond traders are looking for an investment that has a **rate of return** or **yield** of 7% rather than the stated 6.5% (sometimes called the **coupon interest rate** to distinguish it from the rate of return). How much would they be willing to pay for the bonds above with a maturity value of $10,000? Think of the bonds as an investment that will pay the owner $325 every 6 months for 10 years, and will pay an additional $10,000 on maturity at the end of the 10 years. We can treat the $325 payments as if they come from an annuity and determine how much an investor would pay for such an annuity if it earned 7% compounded semiannually. Separately, we determine the present value of an investment worth $10,000 ten years from now, if it earned 7% compounded semiannually. For the first calculation, we use the annuity present value formula, with $i = 0.07/2$ and $n = 2 \times 10 = 20$.

$$PV = PMT\frac{1 - (1 + i)^{-n}}{i}$$

$$= 325\frac{1 - (1 + 0.07/2)^{-20}}{0.07/2}$$

$$= \$4{,}619.03$$

For the second calculation, we use the present value formula for compound interest:

$$PV = 10{,}000(1 + 0.07/2)^{-20}$$

$$= \$5{,}025.66.$$

Thus, an investor looking for a 7% return will be willing to pay $4,619.03 for the semiannual payments of $325 and $5,025.66 for the $10,000 payment at the end of 10 years, for a total of $4,619.03 + 5,025.66 = \$9,644.69$ for the $10,000 bond.

EXAMPLE 8 Bonds

Suppose that bond traders are looking for only a 6% yield on their investment. How much would they pay per $10,000 for the 10-year bonds above, which have a coupon interest rate of 6.5% and pay interest every 6 months?

Solution We redo the calculation with $r = 0.06$. For the annuity calculation we now get

$$PV = 325\frac{1 - (1 + 0.06/2)^{-20}}{0.06/2} = \$4{,}835.18.$$

For the compound interest calculation we get

$$PV = 10{,}000(1 + 0.06/2)^{-20} = \$5{,}536.76.$$

Thus, traders would be willing to pay a total of $4,835.18 + 5,536.76 = \$10,371.94$ for bonds with a maturity value of $10,000.

➡️ **Before we go on...** Notice how the selling price of the bonds behaves as the desired yield changes. As desired yield goes up, the price of the bonds goes down, and as desired yield goes down, the price of the bonds goes up. When the desired yield equals the coupon interest rate, the selling price will equal the maturity value. Therefore, when the yield is higher than the coupon interest rate, the price of the bond will be below its maturity value, and when the yield is lower than the coupon interest rate, the price will be above the maturity value.

As we've mentioned before, the desired yield depends on many factors, but it generally moves up and down with prevailing interest rates. And interest rates have historically gone up and down cyclically. The effect on the value of bonds can be quite dramatic (see Exercises 65 and 66 in the preceding section). Because bonds can be sold again once bought, someone who buys bonds while interest rates are high and then resells them when interest rates decline can make a healthy profit. ■

 using Technology

To automate the computations in Example 9 using a graphing calculator or a spreadsheet, see the Technology Guides at the end of the chapter. Outline:

TI-83/84 Plus
APPS 1:Finance, then
1:TVM Solver
N = 40, PV = −9800, PMT = 250,
FV = 10000, P/Y = 2, C/Y = 2
With cursor on I% line, ALPHA
SOLVE
[More details on page 170.]

Spreadsheet
=RATE(20*2,250,−9800,
10000)*2
[More details on page 174.]

Website
www.WanerMath.com
→ On Line Utilities
→ Time Value of Money Utility
Enter the values shown, and press "Compute" next to r.

EXAMPLE 9 Rate of Return on a Bond

Suppose that a 5%, 20-year bond sells for $9,800 per $10,000 maturity value. What rate of return will investors get?

Solution Assuming the usual semiannual payments, we know the following about the annuity calculation:

$$PMT = 0.05 \times 10,000/2 = 250$$
$$n = 20 \times 2 = 40.$$

What we do not know is r or i, the annual or semiannual rate of return, respectively. So, we write

$$PV = 250\frac{1 - (1 + i)^{-40}}{i}.$$

For the compound interest calculation, we know $FV = 10,000$ and $n = 40$ again, so we write

$$PV = 10,000(1 + i)^{-40}.$$

Adding these together should give the selling price of $9,800:

$$250\frac{1 - (1 + i)^{-40}}{i} + 10,000(1 + i)^{-40} = 9,800.$$

This equation cannot be solved for i directly. The best we can do by hand is a sort of trial-and-error approach, substituting a few values for i in the left-hand side of the above equation to get an estimate; we use the fact that, because the selling price is below the maturity value, r must be larger than 0.05, so i must be more than 0.025:

i	0.025	0.03	0.035
$250 \dfrac{1 - (1 + i)^{-40}}{i} + 10,000(1 + i)^{-40}$	10,000	8,844	7,864

Since we want the value to be 9,800, we see that the correct answer is somewhere between $i = 0.025$ and $i = 0.03$. Let us try the value midway between 0.025 and 0.03; namely $i = 0.0275$.

i	0.025	0.0275	0.03
$250 \dfrac{1 - (1 + i)^{-40}}{i} + 10,000(1 + i)^{-40}$	10,000	9,398	8,844

Now we know that the correct value of i is somewhere between 0.025 and 0.0275, so we can choose for our next estimate of i the number midway between them: 0.02625. We could continue in this fashion to obtain i as accurately as we like. In fact, $i \approx 0.02581$, corresponding to an annual rate of return of approximately 5.162%.

FAQs

Which Formula to Use

Q: *We have retirement accounts, trust funds, loans, bonds, and so on. Some are sinking funds, others are annuities. How do we distinguish among them, so we can tell which formula to use?*

A: In general, remember that a sinking fund is an interest-bearing fund into which payments are made, while an annuity is an interest-bearing fund from which money is withdrawn. Here is a list of some of the accounts we have discussed in this section:

- *Retirement Accounts* A retirement account is a sinking fund while payments are being made into the account (prior to retirement) and an annuity while a pension is being withdrawn (after retirement).
- *Education Funds* These are similar to retirement accounts.
- *Trust Funds* A trust fund is an annuity if periodic withdrawals are made.
- *Installment Loans* We think of an installment loan as an investment a bank makes in the lender. In this way, the lender's payments can be viewed as the bank's withdrawals, and so a loan is an annuity.
- *Bonds* A bond pays regular fixed amounts until it matures, at which time it pays its maturity value. We think of the bond as an annuity coupled with a compound interest investment funding the payment of the maturity value. We can then determine its present value based on the current market interest rate.

From a mathematical point of view, sinking funds and annuities are really the same thing. See the Communication and Reasoning Exercises for more about this.

2.3 EXERCISES

▼ more advanced   ◆ challenging

T indicates exercises that should be solved using technology

Find the amount accumulated in the sinking funds in Exercises 1–6. (Assume end-of-period deposits and compounding at the same intervals as deposits.) HINT [See Example 1.]

1. $100 deposited monthly for 10 years at 5% per year

2. $150 deposited monthly for 20 years at 3% per year

3. $1,000 deposited quarterly for 20 years at 7% per year

4. $2,000 deposited quarterly for 10 years at 7% per year

5. ▼ $100 deposited monthly for 10 years at 5% per year in an account containing $5,000 at the start

6. ▼ $150 deposited monthly for 20 years at 3% per year in an account containing $10,000 at the start

Find the periodic payments necessary to accumulate the amounts given in Exercises 7–12 in a sinking fund. (Assume end-of-period deposits and compounding at the same intervals as deposits.) HINT [See Example 2.]

7. $10,000 in a fund paying 5% per year, with monthly payments for 5 years

8. $20,000 in a fund paying 3% per year, with monthly payments for 10 years

9. $75,000 in a fund paying 6% per year, with quarterly payments for 20 years

10. $100,000 in a fund paying 7% per year, with quarterly payments for 20 years

11. ▼ $20,000 in a fund paying 5% per year, with monthly payments for 5 years, if the fund contains $10,000 at the start

12. ▼ $30,000 in a fund paying 3% per year, with monthly payments for 10 years, if the fund contains $10,000 at the start

Find the present value of the annuity necessary to fund the withdrawals given in Exercises 13–18. (Assume end-of-period withdrawals and compounding at the same intervals as withdrawals.) HINT [See Example 3.]

13. $500 per month for 20 years, if the annuity earns 3% per year

14. $1,000 per month for 15 years, if the annuity earns 5% per year

15. $1,500 per quarter for 20 years, if the annuity earns 6% per year

16. $2,000 per quarter for 20 years, if the annuity earns 4% per year

17. ▼ $500 per month for 20 years, if the annuity earns 3% per year and if there is to be $10,000 left in the annuity at the end of the 20 years

18. ▼ $1,000 per month for 15 years, if the annuity earns 5% per year and if there is to be $20,000 left in the annuity at the end of the 15 years

Find the periodic withdrawals for the annuities given in Exercises 19–24. (Assume end-of-period withdrawals and compounding at the same intervals as withdrawals.) HINT [See Example 4.]

19. $100,000 at 3%, paid out monthly for 20 years

20. $150,000 at 5%, paid out monthly for 15 years

21. $75,000 at 4%, paid out quarterly for 20 years

22. $200,000 at 6%, paid out quarterly for 15 years

23. ▼ $100,000 at 3%, paid out monthly for 20 years, leaving $10,000 in the account at the end of the 20 years

24. ▼ $150,000 at 5%, paid out monthly for 15 years, leaving $20,000 in the account at the end of the 15 years

Determine the periodic payments on the loans given in Exercises 25–28. HINT [See Example 6.]

25. $10,000 borrowed at 9% for 4 years, with monthly payments

26. $20,000 borrowed at 8% for 5 years, with monthly payments

27. $100,000 borrowed at 5% for 20 years, with quarterly payments

28. $1,000,000 borrowed at 4% for 10 years, with quarterly payments

Determine the selling price, per $1,000 maturity value, of the bonds[16] in Exercises 29–34. (Assume twice-yearly interest payments.) HINT [See Example 8.]

29. ▼ 10 year, 4.875% bond, with a yield of 4.880%

30. ▼ 30 year, 5.375% bond, with a yield of 5.460%

31. ▼ 2 year, 3.625% bond, with a yield of 3.705%

32. ▼ 5 year, 4.375% bond, with a yield of 4.475%

33. ▼ 10 year, 5.5% bond, with a yield of 6.643%

34. ▼ 10 year, 6.25% bond, with a yield of 33.409%

▮ *Determine the yield on the bonds[17] in Exercises 35–40. (Assume twice-yearly interest payments.)* HINT [See Example 9.]

35. ▼ 5 year, 3.5% bond, selling for $994.69 per $1,000 maturity value

36. ▼ 10 year, 3.375% bond, selling for $991.20 per $1,000 maturity value

37. ▼ 2 year, 3% bond, selling for $998.86 per $1,000 maturity value

38. ▼ 5 year, 4.625% bond, selling for $998.45 per $1,000 maturity value

39. ▼ 5 year, 4.25% bond, selling for $923.81 per $1,000 maturity value

40. ▼ 5 year 3.6% bond, selling for $216.96 per $1,000 maturity value

APPLICATIONS

41. *Car Loans* While shopping for a car loan, you get the following offers: Solid Savings & Loan is willing to loan you $10,000 at 9% interest for 4 years. Fifth Federal Bank & Trust will loan you the $10,000 at 7% interest for 3 years. Both require monthly payments. You can afford to pay $250 per month. Which loan, if either, can you take?

42. *Business Loans* You need to take out a loan of $20,000 to start up your T-shirt business. You have two possibilities: One bank is offering a 10% loan for 5 years, and another is offering a 9% loan for 4 years. Which will have the lower monthly payments? On which will you end up paying more interest total?

43. ▼ *Pensions* Your pension plan is an annuity with a guaranteed return of 3% per year (compounded monthly). You would like to retire with a pension of $5,000 per month for 20 years. If you work 40 years before retiring, how much must you and your employer deposit each month into the fund? HINT [See Example 5.]

44. ▼ *Pensions* Meg's pension plan is an annuity with a guaranteed return of 5% per year (compounded quarterly). She would like to retire with a pension of $12,000 per quarter for 25 years. If she works 45 years before retiring, how much money must she and her employer deposit each quarter? HINT [See Example 5.]

45. ▼ *Pensions* Your pension plan is an annuity with a guaranteed return of 4% per year (compounded quarterly). You can afford to put $1,200 per quarter into the fund, and you will work for 40 years before retiring. After you retire, you will

---

[16]The first four are actual U.S. Treasury notes and bonds auctioned in 2001 and 2002. The last two are, respectively, a Spanish and a Greek government bond auctioned November 17, 2011, during the Eurozone crisis. Sources: The Bureau of the Public Debt's Web site (www.publicdebt.treas.gov) and The Wall Street Journal's Web site (www.wsj.com).

[17]*Ibid.*

be paid a quarterly pension based on a 25-year payout. How much will you receive each quarter?

46. ▼ *Pensions* Jennifer's pension plan is an annuity with a guaranteed return of 5% per year (compounded monthly). She can afford to put $300 per month into the fund, and she will work for 45 years before retiring. If her pension is then paid out monthly based on a 20-year payout, how much will she receive per month?

Note: In Exercises 47–52 we suggest the use of the finance functions in the TI-83/84 Plus or amortization tables in a spreadsheet.

47. ⊤ ▼ *Mortgages* You take out a 15-year mortgage for $50,000, at 8%, to be paid off monthly. Construct an amortization table showing how much you will pay in interest each year, and how much goes toward paying off the principal. HINT [See Example 7.]

48. ⊤ ▼ *Mortgages* You take out a 30-year mortgage for $95,000 at 9.75%, to be paid off monthly. If you sell your house after 15 years, how much will you still owe on the mortgage? HINT [See Example 7.]

49. ⊤ ▼ *Mortgages* This exercise describes a popular kind of mortgage. You take out a $75,000, 30-year mortgage. For the first 5 years the interest rate is held at 5%, but for the remaining 25 years it rises to 9.5%. The payments for the first 5 years are calculated as if the 5% rate were going to remain in effect for all 30 years, and then the payments for the last 25 years are calculated to amortize the debt remaining at the end of the fifth year. What are your monthly payments for the first 5 years, and what are they for the last 25 years?

50. ⊤ ▼ *Adjustable Rate Mortgages* You take out an adjustable rate mortgage for $100,000 for 20 years. For the first 5 years, the rate is 4%. It then rises to 7% for the next 10 years, and then 9% for the last 5 years. What are your monthly payments in the first 5 years, the next 10 years, and the last 5 years? (Assume that each time the rate changes, the payments are recalculated to amortize the remaining debt if the interest rate were to remain constant for the remaining life of the mortgage.)

51. ⊤ ▼ *Refinancing* Your original mortgage was a $96,000, 30-year 9.75% mortgage. After 4 years you refinance the remaining principal for 30 years at 6.875%. What was your original monthly payment? What is your new monthly payment? How much will you save in interest over the course of the loan by refinancing?

52. ⊤ ▼ *Refinancing* Kara and Michael take out a $120,000, 30-year, 10% mortgage. After 3 years they refinance the remaining principal with a 15-year, 6.5% loan. What were their original monthly payments? What is their new monthly payment? How much did they save in interest over the course of the loan by refinancing?

53. ⊤ ▼ *Fees* You take out a 2-year, $5,000 loan at 9% interest with monthly payments. The lender charges you a $100 fee that can be paid off, interest free, in equal monthly installments over the life of the loan. Thinking of the fee as additional interest, what is the actual annual interest rate you will pay?

54. ⊤ ▼ *Fees* You take out a 3-year, $7,000 loan at 8% interest with monthly payments. The lender charges you a $100 fee that can be paid off, interest free, in equal monthly installments over the life of the loan. Thinking of the fee as additional interest, what is the actual annual interest rate you will pay?

55. ⊤ ▼ *Savings* You wish to accumulate $100,000 through monthly payments of $500. If you can earn interest at an annual rate of 4% compounded monthly, how long (to the nearest year) will it take to accomplish your goal?

56. ⊤ ▼ *Retirement* Alonzo plans to retire as soon as he has accumulated $250,000 through quarterly payments of $2,500. If Alonzo invests this money at 5.4% interest, compounded quarterly, when (to the nearest year) can he retire?

57. ⊤ ▼ *Loans* You have a $2,000 credit card debt, and you plan to pay it off through monthly payments of $50. If you are being charged 15% interest per year, how long (to the nearest 0.5 years) will it take you to repay your debt?

58. ⊤ ▼ *Loans* You owe $2,000 on your credit card, which charges you 15% interest. Determine, to the nearest 1¢, the minimum monthly payment that will allow you to eventually repay your debt.

59. ⊤ ▼ *Savings* You are depositing $100 per month in an account that pays 4.5% interest per year (compounded monthly) while your friend Lucinda is depositing $75 per month in an account that earns 6.5% interest per year (compounded monthly). When, to the nearest year, will her balance exceed yours?

60. ⊤ ▼ *Car Leasing* You can lease a $15,000 car for $300 per month. For how long (to the nearest year) should you lease the car so that your monthly payments are lower than if you were purchasing it with an 8%-per-year loan?

COMMUNICATION AND REASONING EXERCISES

61. Your cousin Simon claims that you have wasted your time studying annuities: If you wish to retire on an income of $1,000 per month for 20 years, you need to save $1,000 per month for 20 years, period. Explain why he is wrong.

62. ▼ Your other cousin Cecilia claims that you will earn more interest by depositing $10,000 through smaller more frequent payments than through larger less frequent payments. Is she correct? Give a reason for your answer.

63. ▼ A real estate broker tells you that doubling the period of a mortgage halves the monthly payments. Is he correct? Support your answer by means of an example.

64. ▼ Another real estate broker tells you that doubling the size of a mortgage doubles the monthly payments. Is he correct? Support your answer by means of an example.

65. ◆ Consider the formula for the future value of a sinking fund with given payments. Show algebraically that the present value of that future value is the same as the present value of the annuity required to fund the same payments.

66. ◆ Give a non-algebraic justification for the result from the preceding exercise.

CHAPTER 2 REVIEW

KEY CONCEPTS

 Website www.WanerMath.com

Go to the Website at www.WanerMath .com to find a comprehensive and interactive Web-based summary of Chapter 2.

2.1 Simple Interest
Simple interest *p. 126*
Future value *p. 127*
Bond, maturity *p. 128*
Present value *p. 129*
Treasury bills (T-bills); maturity value, discount rate, yield *p. 130*

2.2 Compound Interest
Compound interest *p. 134*
Future value for compound interest *p. 135*
Present value for compound interest *p. 137*
Zero coupon bond or strip *p. 137*
Inflation, constant dollars *pp. 138–139*
Effective interest rate, annual percentage yield (APY) *p. 139*

2.3 Annuities, Loans, and Bonds
Annuity, sinking fund *p. 145*
Future value of a sinking fund *p. 146*
Payment formula for a sinking fund *p. 147*
Present value of an annuity *p. 149*
Ordinary annuity, annuity due *p. 149*
Payment formula for an annuity *p. 150*
Installment loan *p. 151*
Amortization schedule *p. 152*
Bond *p. 153*

REVIEW EXERCISES

In each of Exercises 1–6, find the future value of the investment.

1. $6,000 for 5 years at 4.75% simple annual interest

2. $10,000 for 2.5 years at 5.25% simple annual interest

3. $6,000 for 5 years at 4.75% compounded monthly

4. $10,000 for 2.5 years at 5.25% compounded semiannually

5. $100 deposited at the end of each month for 5 years, at 4.75% interest compounded monthly

6. $2,000 deposited at the end of each half-year for 2.5 years, at 5.25% interest compounded semiannually

In each of Exercises 7–12, find the present value of the investment.

7. Worth $6,000 after 5 years at 4.75% simple annual interest

8. Worth $10,000 after 2.5 years at 5.25% simple annual interest

9. Worth $6,000 after 5 years at 4.75% compounded monthly

10. Worth $10,000 after 2.5 years at 5.25% compounded semiannually

11. Funding $100 withdrawals at the end of each month for 5 years, at 4.75% interest compounded monthly

12. Funding $2,000 withdrawals at the end of each half-year for 2.5 years, at 5.25% interest compounded semiannually

In each of Exercises 13–18, find the amounts indicated.

13. The monthly deposits necessary to accumulate $12,000 after 5 years in an account earning 4.75% compounded monthly

14. The semiannual deposits necessary to accumulate $20,000 after 2.5 years in an account earning 5.25% compounded semiannually

15. The monthly withdrawals possible over 5 years from an account earning 4.75% compounded monthly and starting with $6,000

16. The semiannual withdrawals possible over 2.5 years from an account earning 5.25% compounded semiannually and starting with $10,000

17. The monthly payments necessary on a 5-year loan of $10,000 at 4.75%

18. The semiannual payments necessary on a 2.5-year loan of $15,000 at 5.25%

19. How much would you pay for a $10,000, 5-year, 6% bond if you want a return of 7%? (Assume that the bond pays interest every 6 months.)

20. How much would you pay for a $10,000, 5-year, 6% bond if you want a return of 5%? (Assume that the bond pays interest every 6 months.)

21. ▉ A $10,000, 7-year, 5% bond sells for $9,800. What return does it give you? (Assume that the bond pays interest every 6 months.)

22. ▉ A $10,000, 7-year, 5% bond sells for $10,200. What return does it give you? (Assume that the bond pays interest every 6 months.)

In each of Exercises 23–28, find the time requested, to the nearest 0.1 year.

23. The time it would take $6,000 to grow to $10,000 at 4.75% simple annual interest

24. The time it would take $10,000 to grow to $15,000 at 5.25% simple annual interest

25. ▉ The time it would take $6,000 to grow to $10,000 at 4.75% interest compounded monthly

26. ▉ The time it would take $10,000 to grow to $15,000 at 5.25% interest compounded semiannually

27. ▉ The time it would take to accumulate $10,000 by depositing $100 at the end of each month in an account earning 4.75% interest compounded monthly

28. ▉ The time it would take to accumulate $15,000 by depositing $2,000 at the end of each half-year in an account earning 5.25% compounded semiannually

APPLICATIONS

Stock Investments Exercises 29–34 are based on the following table, which shows some values of ABCromD (ABCD) stock:

Dec. 2002	Aug. 2004	Mar. 2005	May 2005	Aug. 2005	Dec. 2005
3.28	16.31	33.95	21.00	30.47	7.44
Jan. 2007	Mar. 2008	Oct. 2008	Nov. 2009	Feb. 2010	Aug. 2010
12.36	7.07	11.44	33.53	44.86	45.74

29. Marjory Duffin purchased ABCD stock in December 2002 and sold it in August 2010. Calculate her annual return on a simple interest basis to the nearest 0.01%.

30. John O'Hagan purchased ABCD stock in March 2005 and sold it in January 2007. Calculate his annual return on a simple interest basis to the nearest 0.01%.

31. Suppose Marjory Duffin had bought ABCD stock in January 2007. If she had later sold at one of the dates in the table, which of those dates would have given her the largest annual return on a simple interest basis, and what would that return have been?

32. Suppose John O'Hagan had purchased ABCD stock in August 2004. If he had later sold at one of the dates in the table, which of those dates would have given him the largest annual loss on a simple interest basis, and what would that loss have been?

33. Did ABCD stock undergo simple interest increase in the period December 2002 through March 2005? (Give a reason for your answer.)

34. If ABCD stock underwent simple interest increase from February 2010 through August 2010 and into 2011, what would the price have been in December 2011?

35. *Revenue* Total Online revenues at OHaganBooks.com during 1999, its first year of operation, amounted to $150,000. After December, 1999, revenues increased by a steady 20% each year. Track OHaganBooks.com's revenues for the subsequent 5 years, assuming that this rate of growth continued. During which year did the revenue surpass $300,000?

36. *Net Income* Unfortunately, the picture for net income was not so bright: The company lost $20,000 in the fourth quarter of 1999. However, the quarterly loss decreased at an annual rate of 15%. How much did the company lose during the third quarter of 2001?

37. *Stocks* In order to finance anticipated expansion, CEO John O'Hagan is considering making a public offering of OHaganBooks.com shares at $3.00 a share. O'Hagan is not sure how many shares to offer, but would like the shares to reach a total market value of at least $500,000 6 months after the initial offering. He estimates that the value of the stock will double in the first day of trading, and then appreciate at around 8% per month for the first 6 months. How many shares of stock should the company offer?

38. *Stocks* Unfortunately, renewed panic about the Monaco debt crisis cause the U.S. stock market to plunge on the very first day of OHaganBooks.com's initial public offering (IPO) of 600,000 shares at $3.00 per share, and the shares ended the trading day 60% lower. Subsequently, as the Monaco debt crisis worsened, the stock depreciated by 10% per week during the subsequent 5 weeks. What was the total market value of the stocks at the end of 5 weeks?

39. *Loans* OHaganBooks.com is seeking a $250,000 loan to finance its continuing losses. One of the best deals available is offered by Industrial Bank, which offers a 10-year 9.5% loan. What would the monthly payments be for this loan?

40. *Loans* (See Exercise 39.) Expansion Loans offers an 8-year 6.5% loan. What would the monthly payments be for the $250,000 loan from Expansion?

41. *Loans* (See Exercise 39.) OHaganBooks.com can afford to pay only $3,000 per month to service its debt. What, to the nearest dollar, is the largest amount the company can borrow from Industrial Bank?

42. *Loans* (See Exercise 40.) OHaganBooks.com can afford to pay only $3,000 per month to service its debt. What, to the nearest dollar, is the largest amount the company can borrow from Expansion Loans?

43. *Loans* (See Exercise 39.) What interest rate would Industrial Bank have to offer in order to meet the company's loan requirements at a price (no more than $3,000 per month) it can afford?

44. *Loans* (See Exercise 40.) What interest rate would Expansion Loans have to offer in order to meet the company's loan requirements at a price (no more than $3,000 per month) it can afford?

Retirement Planning OHaganBooks.com has just introduced a retirement package for the employees. Under the annuity plan operated by Sleepy Hollow, the monthly contribution by the company on behalf of each employee is $800. Each employee can then supplement that amount through payroll deductions. The current rate of return of Sleepy Hollow's retirement fund is 7.3%. Use this information in Exercises 45–52.

45. Jane Callahan, the Web site developer at OHaganBooks.com, plans to retire in 10 years. She contributes $1,000 per month to the plan (in addition to the company contribution of $800). Currently, there is $50,000 in her retirement annuity. How much (to the nearest dollar) will it be worth when she retires?

46. Percy Egan, the assistant Web site developer at OHaganBooks.com, plans to retire in 8 years. He contributes $950 per month to the plan (in addition to the company contribution of $800). Currently, there is $60,000 in his retirement annuity. How much (to the nearest dollar) will it be worth when he retires?

47. When she retires, how much of Jane Callahan's retirement fund will have resulted from the company contribution? (See Exercise 45. The company did not contribute toward the $50,000 Callahan now has.)

48. When he retires, how much of Percy Egan's retirement fund will have resulted from the company contribution? (See Exercise 46. The company began contributing $800 per month to his retirement fund when he was hired 5 years ago. Assume the rate of return from Sleepy Hollow has been unchanged.)

49. (See Exercise 45.) Jane Callahan actually wants to retire with $500,000. How much should she contribute each month to the annuity?

50. (See Exercise 46.) Percy Egan actually wants to retire with $600,000. How much should he contribute each month to the annuity?

51. (See Exercise 45.) On second thought, Callahan wants to be in a position to draw at least $5,000 per month for 30 years after her retirement. She feels she can invest the proceeds of her retirement annuity at 8.7% per year in perpetuity. Given the information in Exercise 45, how much will she need to contribute to the plan starting now?

52. (See Exercise 46.) On second thought, Egan wants to be in a position to draw at least $6,000 per month for 25 years after

his retirement. He feels he can invest the proceeds of his retirement annuity at 7.8% per year in perpetuity. Given the information in Exercise 46, how much will he need to contribute to the plan starting now?

Actually, Jane Callahan is quite pleased with herself; 1 year ago she purchased a $50,000 government bond paying 7.2% per year (with interest paid every 6 months) and maturing in 10 years, and interest rates have come down since then.

53. The current interest rate on 10-year government bonds is 6.3%. If she were to auction the bond at the current interest rate, how much would she get?

54. If she holds on to the bond for 6 more months and the interest rate drops to 6%, how much will the bond be worth then?

55. ☐ Jane suspects that interest rates will come down further during the next 6 months. If she hopes to auction the bond for $54,000 in 6 months' time, what will the interest rate need to be at that time?

56. ☐ If, in 6 months' time, the bond is auctioned for only $52,000, what will the interest rate be at that time?

Case Study   Adjustable Rate and Subprime Mortgages

Andy Dean Photography/Shutterstock

The term **subprime mortgage** refers to mortgages given to home buyers with a heightened perceived risk of default, as when, for instance, the price of the home being purchased is higher than the borrower can reasonably afford. Such loans are typically **adjustable rate** loans, meaning that the lending rate varies through the duration of the loan.* Subprime adjustable rate loans typically start at artificially low "teaser rates" that the borrower can afford, but then increase significantly over the life of the mortgage. The U.S. real estate bubble of 2000–2005 led to a frenzy of subprime lending, the rationale being that a borrower having trouble meeting mortgage payments could either sell the property at a profit or re-finance the loan, or the lending institution could earn a hefty profit by repossessing the property in the event of foreclosure.

* In an adjustable rate mortgage, the payments are recalculated each time the interest rate changes, based on the assumption that the new interest rate will be unchanged for the remaining life of the loan. We say that the loan is **re-amortized** at the new rate.

Mr. and Mrs. Wong have an appointment tomorrow with you, their investment counselor, to discuss their plan to purchase a $400,000 house in Orlando, Florida. They have saved $20,000 for a down payment, so want to take out a $380,000 mortgage. Their combined annual income is $80,000 per year, which they estimate will increase by 4% annually over the foreseeable future, and they are considering three different specialty 30-year mortgages:

Hybrid: The interest is fixed at a low introductory rate of 4% for 5 years, and then adjusts annually to 5% over the U.S. federal funds rate.†

† The U.S. federal funds rate is the rate banks charge each other for loans and is often used to set rates for other loans. Manipulating this rate is one way the U.S. Federal Reserve regulates the money supply.

Interest-Only: During the first 5 years, the rate is set at 4.2% and no principal is paid. After that time, the mortgage adjusts annually to 5% over the U.S. federal funds rate.

Negative Amortization: During the first 5 years, the rate is set at 4.7% based on a principal of 60% of the purchase price of the home, with the result that the balance on the principal actually grows during this period. After that time, the mortgage adjusts annually to 5% over the U.S. federal funds rate.

Source: Board of Governors of the Federal Reserve System (www.federalreserve.gov)

Figure 3

You decide that you should create an Excel worksheet that will compute the monthly payments for the three types of loan. Of course, you have no way of predicting what the U.S. federal funds rate will be in over the next 30 years (see Figure 3 for historical values), so you decide to include three scenarios for the federal funds rate in each case:

Scenario 1: Federal funds rate is 4.25% in year 6 and then increases by 0.25% per year.

Scenario 2: Federal funds rate is steady at 4% during the term of the loan.

Scenario 3: Federal funds rate is 15% in year 6 and then decreases by 0.25% per year.

Each worksheet will show month-by-month payments for the specific type of loan. Typically, to be affordable, payments should not exceed 28% of gross monthly income, so you will tabulate that quantity as well.

Hybrid Loan: You begin to create your worksheet by estimating 28% of the Wongs' monthly income, assuming a 4% increase each year (the income is computed using the compound interest formula for annual compounding):

	A	B	C	D	E	F	G	H
1	**Year**	**28% of Monthly Income**		**Interest Rate**			**Monthly Payment**	
2			**Scenario 1**	**Scenario 2**	**Scenario 3**	**Scenario 1**	**Scenario 2**	**Scenario 3**
3	1	=0.28*80000*(1.04)^(A3-1)/12						
4	2							
5	3							
30	28							
31	29							
32	30							

The next sheet shows the result, as well as the formulas for computing the interest rate in each scenario.

	A	B	C	D	E	F	G	H
1	Year	28% of Monthly Income		Interest Rate			Monthly Payment	
2			Scenario 1	Scenario 2	Scenario 3	Scenario 1	Scenario 2	Scenario 3
3	1	$1,866.67	4	4	4			
4	2	$1,941.33	4	4	4			
5	3	$2,018.99	4	4	4			
6	4	$2,099.75	4	4	4			
7	5	$2,183.74	4	4	4			
8	6	$2,271.09	9.25	9	15			
9	7	$2,361.93	=C8+0.25	=D8	=E8-0.25			
10	8	$2,456.41						
30	28	$5,382.29						
31	29	$5,597.58						
32	30	$5,821.48						

To compute the monthly payment, you decide to use the built-in function PMT, which has the format

$$PMT(i, n, PV, [FV], [type]),$$

where i = interest per period, n = total number of periods of the loan, PV = present value, FV = future value (optional); the *type*, also optional, is 0 or omitted if payments are at the end of each period, and 1 if at the start of each period. The present value will be the outstanding principal owed on the home each time the rate is changed and so that too will need to be known. During the first 5 years we can use as the present value the original cost of the home, but each year thereafter, the loan is re-amortized at the new interest rate, and so the outstanding principal will need to be computed. Although Excel has a built-in function that calculates payment on the principal, it returns only the payment for a single period (month), so without creating a month-by-month amortization table it would be difficult to use this function to track the outstanding principal. On the other hand, the total outstanding principal at any point in time can be computed using the future value formula FV. You decide to add three more columns to your Excel worksheet to show the principal outstanding at the start of each year. Here is the spreadsheet with the formulas for the payments and outstanding principal for the first 5 years.

	A	B	C	D	E	F	G	H	I	J	K
1	Year	28% of Monthly Income		Interest Rate		Monthly Payment			Balance on Principal		
2			Scenario 1	Scenario 2	Scenario 3	Scenario 1	Scenario 2	Scenario 3	Scenario 1	Scenario 2	Scenario 3
3	1	$1,866.67	4	4	4	=-PMT(C3/1200,360,I$3)			$380,000.00	$380,000.00	$380,000.00
4	2	$1,941.33	4	4	4				=FV(C3/1200,12*$A3,F3,-I$3)		
5	3	$2,018.99	4	4	4						
6	4	$2,099.75	4	4	4						
7	5	$2,183.74	4	4	4						
8	6	$2,271.09	9.25	9	15						
9	7	$2,361.93	9.5	9	14.75						
10	8	$2,456.41	9.75	9	14.5						

The two formulas will each be copied across to the adjacent two cells for the other scenarios. A few things to notice: The negative sign before *PMT* converts the negative quantity returned by *PMT* to a positive amount. The dollar sign in I$3 in the *PMT* formula fixes the present value for each year at the original cost of the home for the first 5 years, during which payments are computed as for a fixed rate loan. In the formula for the balance on principal at the start of each year, the number of periods is the total number of months up through the preceding year, and the present value is the same initial price of the home each year during the 5-year fixed rate period.

The next sheet shows the calculated results for the fixed-rate period, and the new formulas to be added for the adjustable rate period starting with the sixth year.

	C	D	E	F	G	H	I	J	K
1	Interest Rate				Monthly Payment			Balance on Principal	
2	Scenario 1	Scenario 2	Scenario 3	Scenario 1	Scenario 2	Scenario 3	Scenario 1	Scenario 2	Scenario 3
3	4	4	4	$1,814.18	$1,814.18	$1,814.18	$380,000.00	$380,000.00	$380,000.00
4	4	4	4	$1,814.18	$1,814.18	$1,814.18	$373,308.06	$373,308.06	$373,308.06
5	4	4	4	$1,814.18	$1,814.18	$1,814.18	$366,343.48	$366,343.48	$366,343.48
6	4	4	4	$1,814.18	$1,814.18	$1,814.18	$359,095.16	$359,095.16	$359,095.16
7	4	4	4	$1,814.18	$1,814.18	$1,814.18	$351,551.52	$351,551.52	$351,551.52
8	9.25	9	15	=-PMT(C8/1200,360-12*$A7,I8)			=FV(C7/1200,12,F7,-I7)		
9	9.5	9	14.75						
10	9.75	9	14.5						

Notice the changes: The loan is re-amortized each year starting with year 6, and the payment calculation needs to take into account the reduced, remaining lifetime of the loan each time. You now copy these formulas across for the remaining two scenarios, and then copy all six formulas down the remaining rows to complete the calculation. Following is a portion of the complete worksheet showing, in red, those years during which the monthly payment will exceed 28% of the gross monthly income.

	A	B	C	D	E	F	G	H	I	J	K
1	Year	28% of Monthly Income	Interest Rate				Monthly Payment			Balance on Principal	
2			Scenario 1	Scenario 2	Scenario 3	Scenario 1	Scenario 2	Scenario 3	Scenario 1	Scenario 2	Scenario 3
3	1	$1,866.67	4	4	4	$1,814.18	$1,814.18	$1,814.18	$380,000.00	$380,000.00	$380,000.00
4	2	$1,941.33	4	4	4	$1,814.18	$1,814.18	$1,814.18	$373,308.06	$373,308.06	$373,308.06
5	3	$2,018.99	4	4	4	$1,814.18	$1,814.18	$1,814.18	$366,343.48	$366,343.48	$366,343.48
6	4	$2,099.75	4	4	4	$1,814.18	$1,814.18	$1,814.18	$359,095.16	$359,095.16	$359,095.16
7	5	$2,183.74	4	4	4	$1,814.18	$1,814.18	$1,814.18	$351,551.52	$351,551.52	$351,551.52
8	6	$2,271.09	9.25	9	15	$2,943.39	$2,884.32	$4,402.22	$343,700.55	$343,700.55	$343,700.55
9	7	$2,361.93	9.5	9	14.75	$3,001.60	$2,884.32	$4,336.46	$340,018.68	$339,866.12	$342,337.80
10	8	$2,456.41	9.75	9	14.5	$3,058.89	$2,884.32	$4,271.84	$336,135.05	$335,671.99	$340,686.40
11	9	$2,554.66	10	9	14.25	$3,115.17	$2,884.32	$4,208.48	$332,020.97	$331,084.43	$338,694.96
12	10	$2,656.85	10.25	9	14	$3,170.39	$2,884.32	$4,146.53	$327,643.98	$326,066.52	$336,305.10
13	11	$2,763.12	10.5	9	13.75	$3,224.44	$2,884.32	$4,086.13	$322,967.19	$320,577.89	$333,450.89
14	12	$2,873.65	10.75	9	13.5	$3,277.24	$2,884.32	$4,027.41	$317,948.51	$314,574.40	$330,058.36
15	13	$2,988.59	11	9	13.25	$3,328.70	$2,884.32	$3,970.53	$312,539.70	$308,007.73	$326,045.01
16	14	$3,108.14	11.25	9	13	$3,378.71	$2,884.32	$3,915.64	$306,685.30	$300,825.07	$321,319.42
17	15	$3,232.46	11.5	9	12.75	$3,427.16	$2,884.32	$3,862.89	$300,321.34	$292,968.62	$315,780.91
18	16	$3,361.76	11.75	9	12.5	$3,473.93	$2,884.32	$3,812.43	$293,373.72	$284,375.19	$309,319.29
19	17	$3,496.23	12	9	12.25	$3,518.89	$2,884.32	$3,764.40	$285,756.40	$274,975.63	$301,814.76
20	18	$3,636.08	12.25	9	12	$3,561.90	$2,884.32	$3,718.94	$277,369.15	$264,694.33	$293,137.86
21	19	$3,781.52	12.5	9	11.75	$3,602.81	$2,884.32	$3,676.20	$268,094.83	$253,448.57	$283,149.60
22	20	$3,932.79	12.75	9	11.5	$3,641.47	$2,884.32	$3,636.32	$257,796.15	$241,147.88	$271,701.73

In the third scenario, the Wongs' payments would more than double at the start of the sixth year, and remain above what they can reasonably afford for 13 more years. Even if the Fed rate were to remain at the low rate of 4%, the monthly payments would still jump to above what the Wongs can afford at the start of the sixth year.

Interest-Only Loan: Here, the only change in the worksheet constructed previously is the computation of the payments for the first 5 years; because the loan is interest-only during this period, the monthly payment is computed as simple interest at 4.2% on the $380,000 loan for a 30-year period:

$$INT = PVr = 380,000 \times .042/12 = \$1,330.00$$

The formula you could use in the spreadsheet in cell F3 is =C3/1200*I$3, and then copy this across and down the entire block of payments for the first 5 years. The rest of the spreadsheet (including the balance on principal) will adjust itself accordingly with the formulas you had for the hybrid loan. Below is a portion of the result, with a lot more red than in the hybrid loan case!

	A	B	C	D	E	F	G	H	I	J	K
		28% of Monthly Income	**Interest Rate**			**Monthly Payment**			**Balance on Principal**		
1	**Year**										
2			Scenario 1	Scenario 2	Scenario 3	Scenario 1	Scenario 2	Scenario 3	Scenario 1	Scenario 2	Scenario 3
3	1	$1,866.67	4.2	4.2	4.2	$1,330.00	$1,330.00	$1,330.00	$380,000.00	$380,000.00	$380,000.00
4	2	$1,941.33	4.2	4.2	4.2	$1,330.00	$1,330.00	$1,330.00	$380,000.00	$380,000.00	$380,000.00
5	3	$2,018.99	4.2	4.2	4.2	$1,330.00	$1,330.00	$1,330.00	$380,000.00	$380,000.00	$380,000.00
6	4	$2,099.75	4.2	4.2	4.2	$1,330.00	$1,330.00	$1,330.00	$380,000.00	$380,000.00	$380,000.00
7	5	$2,183.74	4.2	4.2	4.2	$1,330.00	$1,330.00	$1,330.00	$380,000.00	$380,000.00	$380,000.00
8	6	$2,271.09	9.25	9	15	$3,254.25	$3,188.95	$4,867.16	$380,000.00	$380,000.00	$380,000.00
9	7	$2,361.93	9.5	9	14.75	$3,318.61	$3,188.95	$4,794.45	$375,929.28	$375,760.60	$378,493.33
10	8	$2,456.41	9.75	9	14.5	$3,381.95	$3,188.95	$4,723.00	$371,635.48	$371,123.52	$376,667.51
11	9	$2,554.66	10	9	14.25	$3,444.18	$3,188.95	$4,652.96	$367,086.90	$366,051.44	$374,465.75
12	10	$2,656.85	10.25	9	14	$3,505.22	$3,188.95	$4,584.46	$362,247.64	$360,503.57	$371,823.49
13	11	$2,763.12	10.5	9	13.75	$3,564.98	$3,188.95	$4,517.68	$357,076.92	$354,435.28	$368,667.84
14	12	$2,873.65	10.75	9	13.5	$3,623.37	$3,188.95	$4,452.76	$351,528.19	$347,797.73	$364,917.01
15	13	$2,988.59	11	9	13.25	$3,680.26	$3,188.95	$4,389.88	$345,548.14	$340,537.54	$360,479.80
16	14	$3,108.14	11.25	9	13	$3,735.55	$3,188.95	$4,329.19	$339,075.44	$332,596.29	$355,255.12
17	15	$3,232.46	11.5	9	12.75	$3,789.12	$3,188.95	$4,270.87	$332,039.35	$323,910.09	$349,131.66
18	16	$3,361.76	11.75	9	12.5	$3,840.82	$3,188.95	$4,215.07	$324,357.97	$314,409.07	$341,987.61
19	17	$3,496.23	12	9	12.25	$3,890.53	$3,188.95	$4,161.97	$315,936.16	$304,016.79	$333,690.51
20	18	$3,636.08	12.25	9	12	$3,938.08	$3,188.95	$4,111.71	$306,663.10	$292,649.65	$324,097.21
21	19	$3,781.52	12.5	9	11.75	$3,983.32	$3,188.95	$4,064.46	$296,409.28	$280,216.18	$313,054.05
22	20	$3,932.79	12.75	9	11.5	$4,026.06	$3,188.95	$4,020.37	$285,022.93	$266,616.37	$300,397.13
23	21	$4,090.10	13	9	11.25	$4,066.11	$3,188.95	$3,979.57	$272,325.66	$251,740.81	$285,952.80
24	22	$4,253.70	13.25	9	11	$4,103.29	$3,188.95	$3,942.23	$258,107.21	$235,469.81	$269,538.33

In all three scenarios, this type of mortgage is worse for the Wongs than the hybrid loan; in particular, their payments in Scenario 3 would jump to more than double what they can afford at the start of the sixth year.

Negative Amortization Loan: Again, the only change in the worksheet is the computation of the payments for the first 5 years. This time, the loan amortizes negatively during the initial 5-year period, so the payment formula in this period is adjusted to reflect this

=-PMT(C3/1200,360,I$3*0.6).

	A	B	C	D	E	F	G	H	I	J	K
1	Year	28% of Monthly Income		Interest Rate				Monthly Payment		Balance on Principal	
2			Scenario 1	Scenario 2	Scenario 3	Scenario 1	Scenario 2	Scenario 3	Scenario 1	Scenario 2	Scenario 3
3	1	$1,866.67	4.7	4.7	4.7	$1,182.49	$1,182.49	$1,182.49	$380,000.00	$380,000.00	$380,000.00
4	2	$1,941.33	4.7	4.7	4.7	$1,182.49	$1,182.49	$1,182.49	$383,750.17	$383,750.17	$383,750.17
5	3	$2,018.99	4.7	4.7	4.7	$1,182.49	$1,182.49	$1,182.49	$387,680.45	$387,680.45	$387,680.45
6	4	$2,099.75	4.7	4.7	4.7	$1,182.49	$1,182.49	$1,182.49	$391,799.48	$391,799.48	$391,799.48
7	5	$2,183.74	4.7	4.7	4.7	$1,182.49	$1,182.49	$1,182.49	$396,116.32	$396,116.32	$396,116.32
8	6	$2,271.09	9.25	9	15	$3,431.01	$3,362.16	$5,131.53	$400,640.49	$400,640.49	$400,640.49
9	7	$2,361.93	9.5	9	14.75	$3,498.87	$3,362.16	$5,054.87	$396,348.66	$396,170.82	$399,051.98
10	8	$2,456.41	9.75	9	14.5	$3,565.64	$3,362.16	$4,979.54	$391,821.64	$391,281.87	$397,127.00
11	9	$2,554.66	10	9	14.25	$3,631.26	$3,362.16	$4,905.69	$387,025.99	$385,934.29	$394,805.64
12	10	$2,656.85	10.25	9	14	$3,695.62	$3,362.16	$4,833.48	$381,923.88	$380,085.08	$392,019.86
13	11	$2,763.12	10.5	9	13.75	$3,758.62	$3,362.16	$4,763.06	$376,472.30	$373,687.17	$388,692.80
14	12	$2,873.65	10.75	9	13.5	$3,820.18	$3,362.16	$4,694.62	$370,622.18	$366,689.09	$384,738.24
15	13	$2,988.59	11	9	13.25	$3,880.16	$3,362.16	$4,628.32	$364,317.31	$359,034.55	$380,060.01
16	14	$3,108.14	11.25	9	13	$3,938.46	$3,362.16	$4,564.34	$357,493.03	$350,661.95	$374,551.54
17	15	$3,232.46	11.5	9	12.75	$3,994.93	$3,362.16	$4,502.85	$350,074.77	$341,503.95	$368,095.48
18	16	$3,361.76	11.75	9	12.5	$4,049.45	$3,362.16	$4,444.02	$341,976.15	$331,486.86	$360,563.39
19	17	$3,496.23	12	9	12.25	$4,101.85	$3,362.16	$4,388.03	$333,096.90	$320,530.10	$351,815.60
20	18	$3,636.08	12.25	9	12	$4,151.99	$3,362.16	$4,335.05	$323,320.15	$308,545.52	$341,701.22
21	19	$3,781.52	12.5	9	11.75	$4,199.68	$3,362.16	$4,285.23	$312,509.37	$295,436.71	$330,058.23
22	20	$3,932.79	12.75	9	11.5	$4,244.74	$3,362.16	$4,238.74	$300,504.55	$281,098.20	$316,713.83
23	21	$4,090.10	13	9	11.25	$4,286.97	$3,362.16	$4,195.73	$287,117.60	$265,414.64	$301,484.92
24	22	$4,253.70	13.25	9	11	$4,326.17	$3,362.16	$4,156.36	$272,126.84	$248,259.85	$284,178.86
25	23	$4,423.85	13.5	9	10.75	$4,362.10	$3,362.16	$4,120.77	$255,270.30	$229,495.82	$264,594.34
26	24	$4,600.80	13.75	9	10.5	$4,394.53	$3,362.16	$4,089.09	$236,237.47	$208,971.60	$242,522.55

Clearly the Wongs should steer clear of this type of loan in order to be able to continue to afford making payments!

In short, it seems unlikely that the Wongs will be able to afford payments on any of the three mortgages in question, and you decide to advise them to either seek a less expensive home or wait until their income has appreciated to enable them to afford a home of this price.

EXERCISES

1. ⊤ In the case of a hybrid loan, what would the federal funds rate have to be in Scenario 2 to ensure that the Wongs can afford to make all payments?

2. ⊤ Repeat the preceding exercise in the case of an interest-only loan.

3. ⊤ Repeat the preceding exercise in the case of a negative-amortization loan.

4. ⊤ What home price, to the nearest $5,000, could the Wongs afford if they took out a hybrid loan, regardless of scenario? HINT [Adjust the original value of the loan on your spreadsheet to obtain the desired result.]

5. ⊤ What home price, to the nearest $5,000, could the Wongs afford if they took out a negative-amortization loan, regardless of scenario? HINT [Adjust the original value of the loan on your spreadsheet to obtain the desired result.]

6. ⊤ How long would the Wongs need to wait before they could afford to purchase a $400,000 home, assuming that their income continues to increase as above, they still have $20,000 for a down payment, and the mortgage offers remain the same?

TECHNOLOGY GUIDE

TI-83/84 Plus   Technology Guide

Section 2.2

Example 1 (page 136)   In November 2011, the Bank of Montreal was paying 1.30% interest on savings accounts. If the interest is compounded quarterly, find the future value of a $2,000 deposit in 6 years. What is the total interest paid over the period?

Solution with Technology

We could calculate the future value using the TI-83/84 Plus by entering

        2000(1+0.0130/4)^(4*6)

However, the TI-83/84 Plus has this and other useful calculations built into its TVM (Time Value of Money) Solver.

1. Press ⌊APPS⌋ then choose item 1:Finance... and then choose item 1:TVM Solver.... This brings up the TVM Solver window.

The second screen shows the values you should enter for this example. The various variables are:

N	Number of compounding periods
I%	Annual interest rate, as percent, not decimal

PV	Negative of present value
PMT	Payment per period (0 in this section)
FV	Future value
P/Y	Payments per year
C/Y	Compounding periods per year
PMT:	Not used in this section

Several things to notice:

- *I%* is the *annual* interest rate, corresponding to *r*, not *i*, in the compound interest formula.

- The present value, *PV*, is entered as a negative number. In general, when using the TVM Solver, any amount of money you give to someone else (such as the $2,000 you deposit in the bank) will be a negative number, whereas any amount of money someone gives to you (such as the future value of your deposit, which the bank will give back to you) will be a positive number.

- *PMT* is not used in this example (it will be used in the next section) and should be 0.

- *FV* is the future value, which we shall compute in a moment; it doesn't matter what you enter now.

- *P/Y* and *C/Y* stand for payments per year and compounding periods per year, respectively: They should both be set to the number of compounding periods per year for compound interest problems (setting *P/Y* automatically sets *C/Y* to the same value).

- *PMT*: *END* or *BEGIN* is not used in this example and it doesn't matter which you select.

2. To compute the future value, use the up or down arrow to put the cursor on the *FV* line, then press ⌊ALPHA⌋ ⌊SOLVE⌋.

Example 2 (page 138)   Megabucks Corporation is issuing 10-year zero coupon bonds. How much would you pay for bonds with a maturity value of $10,000 if you wish to get a return of 6.5% compounded annually?

Solution with Technology

To compute the present value using a TI-83/84 Plus:

1. Enter the numbers shown below (top) in the TVM Solver window.
2. Put the cursor on the PV line, and press ALPHA SOLVE.

```
N=10
I%=6.5
PV=■
PMT=0
FV=10000
P/Y=1
C/Y=1
PMT:END BEGIN
```

```
N=10
 I%=6.5
•PV=-5327.260355
PMT=0
FV=10000
P/Y=1
C/Y=1
PMT:END BEGIN
```

Why is the present value given as negative?

Example 6 (page 141)   You have $5,000 to invest at 6% interest compounded monthly. How long will it take for your investment to grow to $6,000?

Solution with Technology

1. Enter the numbers shown below (top) in the TVM Solver window.
2. Put the cursor on the N line, and press ALPHA SOLVE.

```
N=■
I%=6
PV=-5000
PMT=0
FV=6000
P/Y=12
C/Y=12
PMT:END BEGIN
```

```
•N=36.55539636
 I%=6
PV=-5000
PMT=0
FV=6000
P/Y=12
C/Y=12
PMT:END BEGIN
```

Recall that I% is the annual interest rate, corresponding to r in the formula, but N is the number of compounding

periods, so number of months in this example. Thus, you will need to invest your money for about 36.5 months, or just over 3 years, before it grows to $6,000.

Section 2.3

Example 1 (page 146)   Your retirement account has $5,000 in it and earns 5% interest per year compounded monthly. Every month for the next 10 years, you will deposit $100 into the account. How much money will there be in the account at the end of those 10 years?

Solution with Technology

We can use the TVM Solver in the TI-83/84 Plus to calculate future values like these:

1. The TVM Solver allows you to put the $5,000 already in the account as the present value of the account. Following the TI-83/84 Plus's usual convention, set PV to the *negative* of the present value because this is money you paid into the account.
2. Likewise, set PMT to −100 since you are paying $100 each month.
3. Set the number of payment and compounding periods to 12 per year.
4. Set the payments to be made at the end of each period.
5. With the cursor on the FV line, press ALPHA SOLVE to find the future value.

Example 2 (page 147)   Tony and Maria have just had a son, José Phillipe. They establish an account to accumulate money for his college education. They would like to have $100,000 in this account after 17 years. If the account pays 4% interest per year compounded quarterly, and they make deposits at the end of every quarter, how large must each deposit be for them to reach their goal?

Solution with Technology

1. In the TVM Solver in the TI-83/84 Plus, enter the values shown below.

2. Solve for *PMT*.

Why is *PMT* negative?

Example 3 (page 149) You wish to establish a trust fund from which your niece can withdraw $2,000 every 6 months for 15 years, at which time she will receive the remaining money in the trust, which you would like to be $10,000. The trust will be invested at 7% per year compounded every 6 months. How large should the trust be?

Solution with Technology

1. In the TVM Solver in the TI-83/84 Plus, enter the values shown below.

2. Solve for *PV*.

The payment and future value are positive because you (or your niece) will be receiving these amounts from the investment.

Note We have assumed that your niece receives the withdrawals at the end of each compounding period, so that the trust fund is an ordinary annuity. If, instead, she receives the payments at the beginning of each compounding period, it is an annuity due. You switch between the two types of annuity by changing PMT: END at the bottom to PMT: BEGIN. ∎

As mentioned in the text, the present value must be higher to fund payments at the beginning of each period, because the money in the account has less time to earn interest.

Example 4 (page 150) Tony and Maria (see Example 2), having accumulated $100,000 for José Phillipe's college education, would now like to make quarterly withdrawals over the next 4 years. How much money can they withdraw each quarter in order to draw down the account to zero at the end of the 4 years? (Recall that the account pays 4% interest compounded quarterly.)

Solution with Technology

1. Enter the values shown below in the TI-83/84 Plus TVM Solver.

2. Solve for *PMT*.

The present value is negative because Tony and Maria do not possess it; the bank does.

Example 7 (page 152) Marc and Mira are buying a house and have taken out a 30-year, $90,000 mortgage at 8% interest per year. Mortgage interest is tax deductible, so it is important to know how much of a year's mortgage payments represents interest. How much interest will Marc and Mira pay in the first year of their mortgage?

Solution with Technology

The TI-83/84 Plus has built-in functions to compute the values in an amortization schedule.

1. First, use the TVM Solver to find the monthly payment.

```
N=360
I%=8
PV=90000
•PMT=-660.38811…
FV=0
P/Y=12
C/Y=12
PMT:END BEGIN
```

Three functions correspond to the last three columns of the amortization schedule given in the text: ΣInt, ΣPrn, and bal, (found in the Finance menu accessed through APPS). They all require that the values of I%, PV, and PMT be entered or calculated ahead of time; calculating the payment in the TVM Solver in Step 1 accomplishes this.

2. Use ΣInt($m,n,2$) to compute the sum of the interest payments from payment m through payment n. For example,

ΣInt(1,12,2)

will return −7,172.81, the total paid in interest in the first year, which answers the question asked in this example. (The last argument, 2, tells the calculator to round all intermediate calculations to two decimal places—that is, the nearest cent—as would the mortgage lender.)

3. Use ΣPrn($m,n,2$) to compute the sum of the payments on principal from payment m through payment n. For example,

ΣPrn(1,12,2)

will return −751.87, the total paid on the principal in the first year.

4. Finally, bal($n,2$) finds the balance of the principal outstanding after n payments. For example,

bal(12,2)

will return the value 89,248.13, the balance remaining at the end of one year.

5. To construct an amortization schedule as in the text, make sure that FUNC is selected in the MODE window; then enter the functions in the Y= window as shown below.

6. Press 2ND TBLSET and enter the values shown here.

```
TABLE SETUP
 TblStart=0
 ΔTbl=1
Indpnt: Auto Ask
Depend: Auto Ask
```

7. Press 2ND TABLE, to get the table shown here.

The column labeled X gives the month, the column labeled Y_1 gives the interest payment for each month, the column labeled Y_2 gives the payment on principal for each month, and the column labeled Y_3 (use the right arrow button to make it visible) gives the outstanding principal.

8. To see later months, use the down arrow. As you can see, some of the values will be rounded in the table, but by selecting a value (as the outstanding principal at the end of the first month is selected in the second screen) you can see its exact value at the bottom of the screen.

Example 9 (page 154) Suppose that a 5%, 20-year bond sells for $9,800 per $10,000 maturity value. What rate of return will investors get?

Solution with Technology

We can use the TVM Solver in the TI-83/84 Plus to find the interest rate just as we use it to find any other one of the variables.

1. Enter the values shown in the TVM Solver window.

2. Solve for *I%*. (Recall that *I%* is the annual interest rate, corresponding to *r* in the formula.)

Thus, at $9,800 per $10,000 maturity value, these bonds yield 5.162% compounded semiannually.

SPREADSHEET   Technology Guide

Section 2.2

Example 1 (page 136) In November 2011, the Bank of Montreal was paying 1.30% interest on savings accounts. If the interest is compounded quarterly, find the future value of a $2,000 deposit in 6 years. What is the total interest paid over the period?

Solution with Technology

You can either compute compound interest directly or use financial functions built into your spreadsheet. The following worksheet has more than we need for this example, but will be useful for other examples in this and the next section.

	A	B	C	D
1		Entered	Calculated	
2	Rate	1.30%		
3	Years	6		
4	Payment	$0.00		
5	Present Value	-$2,000.00		
6	Future Value		=FV(B2/B7,B3*B7,B4,B5)	
7	Periods per year	4		

For this example the payment amount in B4 should be 0 (we shall use it in the next section).

1. Enter the other numbers as shown. As with other technologies, like the TVM Solver in the TI-83/84 Plus calculator, money that you pay to others (such as the $2,000 you deposit in the bank) should be entered as negative, whereas money that is paid to you is positive.

2. The formula entered in C6 uses the built-in FV function to calculate the future value based on the entries in column B. This formula has the following format:

$$=\text{FV}(i, n, PMT, PV)$$

i = interest per period   We use B2/B7 for the interest.

n = number of periods   We use B3*B7 for the number of periods.

PMT = payment per period   The payment is 0 (cell B4).

PV = present value   The present value is in cell B5.

Instead of using the built-in FV function, we could use

$$=\text{-B5}*(1+\text{B2}/\text{B7})\text{^}(\text{B3}*\text{B7})$$

based on the future value formula for compound interest. After calculation the result will appear in cell C6.

	A	B	C	D
1		Entered	Calculated	
2	Rate	1.30%		
3	Years	6		
4	Payment	$0.00		
5	Present Value	-$2,000.00		
6	Future Value		$2,161.97	
7	Periods per year	4		

Note that we have formatted the cells B4:C6 as currency with two decimal places. If you change the values in column B, the future value in column C will be automatically recalculated.

Example 2 (page 138)   Megabucks Corporation is issuing 10-year zero coupon bonds. How much would you pay for bonds with a maturity value of $10,000 if you wish to get a return of 6.5% compounded annually?

Solution with Technology

You can compute present value in your spreadsheet using the PV worksheet function. The following worksheet is similar to the one in the preceding example, except that we have entered a formula for computing the present value from the entered values.

	A	B	C	D
1		Entered	Calculated	
2	Rate	6.50%		
3	Years	10		
4	Payment	$0.00		
5	Present Value		=PV(B2/B7,B3*B7,B4,B6)	
6	Future Value	$10,000.00		
7	Periods per year	1		

The next worksheet shows the calculated value.

	A	B	C	D
1		Entered	Calculated	
2	Rate	6.50%		
3	Years	10		
4	Payment	$0.00		
5	Present Value		-$5,327.26	
6	Future Value	$10,000.00		
7	Periods per year	1		

Why is the present value negative?

Example 6 (page 141)   You have $5,000 to invest at 6% interest compounded monthly. How long will it take for your investment to grow to $6,000?

Solution with Technology

You can compute the requisite length of an investment in your spreadsheet using the NPER worksheet function. The following worksheets show the calculation.

	A	B	C	D
1		Entered	Calculated	
2	Rate	6.00%		
3	Years		=NPER(B2/B7,B4,B5,B6)/B7	
4	Payment	$0.00		
5	Present Value	-$5,000.00		
6	Future Value	$6,000.00		
7	Periods per year	12		

	A	B	C	D
1		Entered	Calculated	
2	Rate	6.00%		
3	Years		3.04628303	
4	Payment	$0.00		
5	Present Value	-$5,000.00		
6	Future Value	$6,000.00		
7	Periods per year	12		

The NPER function computes the number of compounding periods, months in this case, so we divide by B7, the number of periods per year, to calculate the number of years, which appears as 3.046. So, you need to invest your money for just over 3 years for it to grow to $6,000.

Section 2.3

Example 1 (page 146)   Your retirement account has $5,000 in it and earns 5% interest per year compounded monthly. Every month for the next 10 years you will deposit $100 into the account. How much money will there be in the account at the end of those 10 years?

Solution with Technology

We can use exactly the same worksheet that we used in Example 1 in the preceding section. In fact, we included the "Payment" row in that worksheet just for this purpose.

	A	B	C	D
1		Entered	Calculated	
2	Rate	5.00%		
3	Years	10		
4	Payment	-$100.00		
5	Present Value	-$5,000.00		
6	Future Value		=FV(B2/B7,B3*B7,B4,B5)	
7	Periods per year	12		

	A	B	C	D
1		Entered	Calculated	
2	Rate	5.00%		
3	Years	10		
4	Payment	-$100.00		
5	Present Value	-$5,000.00		
6	Future Value		$23,763.28	
7	Periods per year	12		

Note that the FV function allows us to enter, as the last argument, the amount of money already in the account. Following the usual convention, we enter the present value and the payment as *negative*, because these are amounts you pay into the account.

Example 2 (page 147)

Tony and Maria have just had a son, José Phillipe. They establish an account to accumulate money for his college education, in which they would like to have $100,000 after 17 years. If the account pays 4% interest per year compounded quarterly, and they make deposits at the end of every quarter, how large must each deposit be for them to reach their goal?

Solution with Technology

Use the following worksheet, in which the PMT worksheet function is used to calculate the required payments.

	A	B	C	D
1		Entered	Calculated	
2	Rate	4.00%		
3	Years	17		
4	Payment		=PMT(B2/B7,B3*B7,B5,B6)	
5	Present Value	$0.00		
6	Future Value	$100,000.00		
7	Periods per year	4		

	A	B	C	D
1		Entered	Calculated	
2	Rate	4.00%		
3	Years	17		
4	Payment		-$1,033.89	
5	Present Value	$0.00		
6	Future Value	$100,000.00		
7	Periods per year	4		

Why is the payment negative?

Example 3 (page 149)

You wish to establish a trust fund from which your niece can withdraw $2,000 every 6 months for 15 years, at which time she will receive the remaining money in the trust, which you would like to be $10,000. The trust will be invested at 7% per year compounded every 6 months. How large should the trust be?

Solution with Technology

You can use the same worksheet as in Example 2 in Section 2.2.

	A	B	C	D
1		Entered	Calculated	
2	Rate	7.00%		
3	Years	15		
4	Payment	$2,000.00		
5	Present Value		=PV(B2/B7,B3*B7,B4,B6)	
6	Future Value	$10,000.00		
7	Periods per year	2		

	A	B	C	D
1		Entered	Calculated	
2	Rate	7.00%		
3	Years	15		
4	Payment	$2,000.00		
5	Present Value		-$40,346.87	
6	Future Value	$10,000.00		
7	Periods per year	2		

The payment and future value are positive because you (or your niece) will be receiving these amounts from the investment.

Note We have assumed that your niece receives the withdrawals at the end of each compounding period, so that the trust fund is an ordinary annuity. If, instead, she receives the payments at the beginning of each compounding period, it is an annuity due. You switch to an annuity due by adding an optional last argument of 1 to the PV function (and similarly for the other finance functions in spreadsheets).

	A	B	C	D
1		Entered	Calculated	
2	Rate	7.00%		
3	Years	15		
4	Payment	$2,000.00		
5	Present Value		=PV(B2/B7,B3*B7,B4,B6,1)	
6	Future Value	$10,000.00		
7	Periods per year	2		

	A	B	C	D
1		Entered	Calculated	
2	Rate	7.00%		
3	Years	15		
4	Payment	$2,000.00		
5	Present Value		-$41,634.32	
6	Future Value	$10,000.00		
7	Periods per year	2		

As mentioned in the text, the present value must be higher to fund payments at the beginning of each period, because the money in the account has less time to earn interest. ∎

Example 4 (page 150)

Tony and Maria (see Example 2), having accumulated $100,000 for José Phillipe's college education, would now like to make quarterly withdrawals over the next 4 years. How much money can they withdraw each quarter in order to draw down the account to zero at the end of the four years? (Recall that the account pays 4% interest compounded quarterly.)

Solution with Technology

You can use the same worksheet as in Example 2.

	A	B	C	D
1		Entered	Calculated	
2	Rate	4.00%		
3	Years	4		
4	Payment		=PMT(B2/B7,B3*B7,B5,B6)	
5	Present Value	-$100,000.00		
6	Future Value	$0.00		
7	Periods per year	4		

	A	B	C	D
1		Entered	Calculated	
2	Rate	4.00%		
3	Years	4		
4	Payment		$6,794.46	
5	Present Value	-$100,000.00		
6	Future Value	$0.00		
7	Periods per year	4		

The present value is negative since Tony and Maria do not possess it; the bank does.

Example 7 (page 152)   Marc and Mira are buying a house and have taken out a 30-year, $90,000 mortgage at 8% interest per year. Mortgage interest is tax deductible, so it is important to know how much of a year's mortgage payments represents interest. How much interest will Marc and Mira pay in the first year of their mortgage?

Solution with Technology

We construct an amortization schedule with which we can answer the question.

1. Begin with the worksheet below.

	A	B	C	D	E	F	G	H
1	Month	Interest Payment	Payment on Principal	Outstanding Principal				
2	0			$90,000.00	Rate	8%		
3					Years	30		
4					Payment	=DOLLAR(-PMT(F2/12,F3*12,D2))		

	A	B	C	D	E	F
1	Month	Interest Payment	Payment on Principal	Outstanding Principal		
2	0			$90,000.00	Rate	8%
3					Years	30
4					Payment	$660.39

Note the formula for the monthly payment:

    =DOLLAR(-PMT(F2/12,F3*12,D2))

The function DOLLAR rounds the payment to the nearest cent, as the bank would.

2. Calculate the interest owed at the end of the first month using the formula

    =DOLLAR(D2*F$2/12)

in cell B3.

3. The payment on the principal is the remaining part of the payment, so enter

    =F$4-B3

in cell C3.

4. Calculate the outstanding principal by subtracting the payment on the principal from the previous outstanding principal, by entering

    =D2-C3

in cell D3.

5. Copy the formulas in cells B3, C3, and D3 into the cells below them to continue the table.

	A	B	C	D	E	F
1	Month	Interest Payment	Payment on Principal	Outstanding Principal		
2	0			$90,000.00	Rate	8%
3	1	$600.00	$60.39	$89,939.61	Years	30
4	2				Payment	$660.39
5	3					
6	4					
7	5					
8	6					
9	7					
10	8					
11	9					
12	10					
13	11					
14	12					

The result should be something like the following:

	A	B	C	D	E	F
1	Month	Interest Payment	Payment on Principal	Outstanding Principal		
2	0			$90,000.00	Rate	8%
3	1	$600.00	$60.39	$89,939.61	Years	30
4	2	$599.60	$60.79	$89,878.82	Payment	$660.39
5	3	$599.19	$61.20	$89,817.62		
6	4	$598.78	$61.61	$89,756.01		
7	5	$598.37	$62.02	$89,693.99		
8	6	$597.96	$62.43	$89,631.56		
9	7	$597.54	$62.85	$89,568.71		
10	8	$597.12	$63.27	$89,505.44		
11	9	$596.70	$63.69	$89,441.75		
12	10	$596.28	$64.11	$89,377.64		
13	11	$595.85	$64.54	$89,313.10		
14	12	$595.42	$64.97	$89,248.13		

6. Adding the calculated interest payments gives us the total interest paid in the first year: $7,172.81.

Note Spreadsheets have built-in functions that compute the interest payment (IPMT) or the payment on the principle (PPMT) in a given period. We could also have used the built-in future value function (FV) to calculate the outstanding principal each month. The main problem with using these functions is that, in a sense, they are too accurate. They do not take into account the fact that payments and interest are rounded to the nearest cent. Over time, this rounding causes the actual value of the outstanding principal to differ from what the FV

TECHNOLOGY GUIDE

function would tell us. In fact, because the actual payment is rounded slightly upward (to $660.39 from 660.38811...), the principal is reduced slightly faster than necessary and a last payment of $660.39 would be $2.95 larger than needed to clear out the debt. The lender would reduce the last payment by $2.95 for this reason; Marc and Mira will pay only $657.44 for their final payment. This is common: The last payment on an installment loan is usually slightly larger or smaller than the others, to compensate for the rounding of the monthly payment amount. ∎

Example 9 (page 154)   Suppose that a 5%, 20-year bond sells for $9,800 per $10,000 maturity value. What rate of return will investors get?

Solution with Technology

Use the following worksheet, in which the RATE worksheet function is used to calculate the interest rate.

	A	B	C	D
1		Entered	Calculated	
2	Rate		=RATE(B3*B7,B4,B5,B6)*B7	
3	Years	20		
4	Payment	$250.00		
5	Present Value	-$9,800.00		
6	Future Value	$10,000.00		
7	Periods per year	2		

	A	B	C	D
1		Entered	Calculated	
2	Rate		5.162%	
3	Years	20		
4	Payment	$250.00		
5	Present Value	-$9,800.00		
6	Future Value	$10,000.00		
7	Periods per year	2		

3

Systems of Linear Equations and Matrices

Website

www.WanerMath.com

At the Website you will find:

- Section-by-section tutorials, including game tutorials with randomized quizzes

- A detailed chapter summary

- A true/false quiz

- Additional review exercises

- Graphers, Excel tutorials, TI-83/84 Plus programs

- A Web page that pivots and does row operations

- An Excel worksheet that pivots and does row operations

Case Study Hybrid Cars—Optimizing the Degree of Hybridization

You are involved in new model development at a major automobile company. The company is planning to introduce two new plug-in hybrid electric vehicles: the subcompact "Green Town Hopper" and the midsize "Electra Supreme," and your department must decide on the degree of hybridization (DOH) for each of these models that will result in the largest reduction in gasoline consumption. The data you have available show the gasoline saving for only three values of the DOH. **How do you estimate the optimal value?**

Oleksiy Maksymenko/Alamy

Introduction

In Chapter 1 we studied single functions and equations. In this chapter we seek solutions to **systems** of two or more equations. For example, suppose we need to *find two numbers whose sum is* 3 *and whose difference is* 1. In other words, we need to find two numbers x and y such that $x + y = 3$ and $x - y = 1$. The only solution turns out to be $x = 2$ and $y = 1$, a solution you might easily guess. But, how do we know that this is the only solution, and how do we find solutions systematically? When we restrict ourselves to systems of *linear* equations, there is a very elegant method for determining the number of solutions and finding them all. Moreover, as we will see, many real-world applications give rise to just such systems of linear equations.

We begin in Section 3.1 with systems of two linear equations in two unknowns and some of their applications. In Section 3.2 we study a powerful matrix method, called *row reduction*, for solving systems of linear equations in any number of unknowns. In Section 3.3 we look at more applications.

Computers have been used for many years to solve the large systems of equations that arise in the real world. You probably already have access to devices that will do the row operations used in row reduction. Many graphing calculators can do them, as can spreadsheets and various special-purpose applications, including utilities available at the Website. Using such a device or program makes the calculations quicker and helps avoid arithmetic mistakes. Then there are programs (and calculators) into which you simply feed the system of equations and out pop the solutions. We can think of what we do in this chapter as looking inside the "black box" of such a program. More important, we talk about how, starting from a real-world problem, to get the system of equations to solve in the first place. No computer will do this conversion for us yet.

3.1 Systems of Two Equations in Two Unknowns

Suppose you have $3 in your pocket to spend on snacks and a drink. If x represents the amount you'll spend on snacks and y represents the amount you'll spend on a drink, you can say that $x + y = 3$. On the other hand, if for some reason you want to spend $1 more on snacks than on your drink, you can also say that $x - y = 1$. These are simple examples of **linear equations in two unknowns**.

Linear Equations in Two Unknowns

A **linear equation in two unknowns** is an equation that can be written in the form

$$ax + by = c$$

with a, b, and c being real numbers. The number a is called the **coefficient of x** and b is called the **coefficient of y**. A **solution** of an equation consists of a pair of numbers: a value for x and a value for y that satisfy the equation.

Quick Example

In the linear equation $3x - y = 15$, the coefficients are $a = 3$ and $b = -1$. The point $(x, y) = (5, 0)$ is a solution, because $3(5) - (0) = 15$.

In fact, a single linear equation such as $3x - y = 15$ has infinitely many solutions: We could solve for $y = 3x - 15$ and then, for every value of x we choose, we can get the corresponding value of y, giving a solution (x, y). As we saw in Chapter 1, these solutions are the points on a straight line, the *graph* of the equation.

In this section we are concerned with pairs (x, y) that are solutions of *two* linear equations at the same time. For example, $(2, 1)$ is a solution of both of the equations $x + y = 3$ and $x - y = 1$, because substituting $x = 2$ and $y = 1$ into these equations gives $2 + 1 = 3$ (true) and $2 - 1 = 1$ (also true), respectively. So, in the simple example we began with, you could spend \$2 on snacks and \$1 on a drink.

In the following set of examples, you will see how to graphically and algebraically solve a system of two linear equations in two unknowns. Then we'll return to some more interesting applications.

EXAMPLE 1 Two Ways of Solving a System: Graphically and Algebraically

Find all solutions (x, y) of the following system of two equations:

$$x + y = 3$$
$$x - y = 1.$$

Solution We will see how to find the solution(s) in two ways: graphically and algebraically. Remember that a solution is a pair (x, y) that simultaneously satisfies *both* equations.

Method 1: Graphical We already know that the solutions of a single linear equation are the points on its graph, which is a straight line. For a point to represent a solution of two linear equations, it must lie simultaneously on both of the corresponding lines. In other words, it must be a point where the two lines cross, or intersect. A look at Figure 1 should convince us that the lines cross only at the point $(2, 1)$, so this is the only possible solution.

Method 2: Algebraic In the algebraic approach, we try to combine the equations in such a way as to eliminate one variable. In this case, notice that if we add the left-hand sides of the equations, the terms with y are eliminated. So, we add the first equation to the second (that is, add the left-hand sides and add the right-hand sides*):

$$
\begin{array}{r}
x + y = 3 \\
x - y = 1 \\
\hline
2x + 0 = 4 \\
2x = 4 \\
x = 2.
\end{array}
$$

Now that we know that x has to be 2, we can substitute back into either equation to find y. Choosing the first equation (it doesn't matter which we choose), we have

$$2 + y = 3$$
$$y = 3 - 2$$
$$= 1.$$

We have found that the only possible solution is $x = 2$ and $y = 1$, or

$$(x, y) = (2, 1).$$

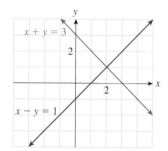

Figure 1

✱ We can add these equations because when we add equal amounts to both sides of an equation, the results are equal. That is, if $A = B$ and $C = D$, then $A + C = B + D$.

using Technology

See the Technology Guides at the end of the chapter for details on the graphical solution of Example 1 using a TI-83/84 Plus or a spreadsheet. Here is an outline:

TI-83/84 Plus

Y_1=-X+3 Y_2=X-1

Graph: WINDOW ; Xmin = −4,
Xmax = 4; ZOOM 0
Trace to estimate the point of intersection.
[More details on page 225.]

Spreadsheet

Headings *x*, *y*1, and *y*2 in A1–C1, *x*-values −4, 4 in A2, A3
=-A2+3 and =A2-1 in B1 and C1; copy down to B2–C2
Graph the data in columns A–C with a line-segment scatter plot. To see a closer view change the values in A2–A3.
[More details on page 227.]

 Website

www.WanerMath.com

→ On Line Utilities

→ Function Evaluator and Grapher

Enter -x+3 for y_1 and x-1 for y_2. Set Xmin = −4, Xmax = 4 and press "Plot Graphs."
Click on the graph and use the trace arrows below to estimate the point of intersection.

Before we go on... There is another way we could find the solution in Example 1 algebraically: First we solve our two equations for *y* to obtain

$$y = -x + 3$$
$$y = x - 1$$

and then we equate the right-hand sides to get

$$-x + 3 = x - 1,$$

which we solve to find $x = 2$. The value for *y* is then found by substituting $x = 2$ in either equation.

Q: *So why don't we solve all systems of equations this way?*

A: The elimination method extends more easily to systems with more equations and unknowns. It is the basis for the matrix method of solving systems—a method we discuss in Section 3.2. So, we shall use it exclusively for the rest of this section. ∎

Example 2 illustrates the drawbacks of the graphical method.

EXAMPLE 2 Solving a System: Algebraically vs. Graphically

Solve the system

$$3x + 5y = 0$$
$$2x + 7y = 1.$$

Solution

Method 1: Graphical First, solve for *y*, obtaining $y = -\frac{3}{5}x$ and $y = -\frac{2}{7}x + \frac{1}{7}$. Graphing these equations, we get Figure 2. The lines appear to intersect slightly above and to the left of the origin. Redrawing with a finer scale (or zooming in using graphing technology), we can get the graph in Figure 3.

If we look carefully at Figure 3, we see that the graphs intersect near (−0.45, 0.27). Is the point of intersection *exactly* (−0.45, 0.27)? (Substitute these values into the equations to find out.) In fact, it is impossible to find the exact solution of this system graphically, but we now have a ballpark answer that we can use to help check the following algebraic solution.

Method 2: Algebraic We first see that adding the equations is not going to eliminate either *x* or *y*. Notice, however, that if we multiply (both sides of) the first equation by 2 and the second by −3, the coefficients of *x* will become 6 and −6. *Then* if we add them, *x* will be eliminated. So we proceed as follows:

$$2(3x + 5y) = 2(0)$$
$$-3(2x + 7y) = -3(1)$$

gives

$$6x + 10y = 0$$
$$-6x - 21y = -3.$$

Adding these equations, we get

$$-11y = -3$$

so that

$$y = \frac{3}{11} = 0.\overline{27}.$$

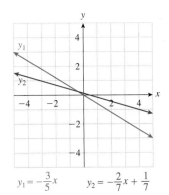

$$y_1 = -\frac{3}{5}x \qquad y_2 = -\frac{2}{7}x + \frac{1}{7}$$

Figure 2

Graphs of y_1 and y_2 with $-1 \le x \le 0$

Figure 3

Substituting $y = \dfrac{3}{11}$ in the first equation gives

$$3x + 5\left(\frac{3}{11}\right) = 0$$

$$3x = -\frac{15}{11}$$

$$x = -\frac{5}{11} = -0.\overline{45}.$$

The solution is $(x, y) = \left(-\frac{5}{11}, \frac{3}{11}\right) = (-0.\overline{45}, 0.\overline{27})$.

Notice that the algebraic method gives us the exact solution that we could not find with the graphical method. Still, we can check that the graph and our algebraic solution agree to the accuracy with which we can read the graph. To be absolutely sure that our answer is correct, we should check it:

$$3\left(-\frac{5}{11}\right) + 5\left(\frac{3}{11}\right) = -\frac{15}{11} + \frac{15}{11} = 0 \qquad ✔$$

$$2\left(-\frac{5}{11}\right) + 7\left(\frac{3}{11}\right) = -\frac{10}{11} + \frac{21}{11} = 1. \qquad ✔$$

Get in the habit of checking your answers.

➡ **Before we go on...**

Q: *In solving the system in Example 2 algebraically, we multiplied (both sides of) the equations by numbers. How does that affect their graphs?*

A: Multiplying both sides of an equation by a nonzero number has no effect on its solutions, so the graph (which represents the set of all solutions) is unchanged. ∎

Before doing some more examples, let's summarize what we've said about solving systems of equations.

Graphical Method for Solving a System of Two Equations in Two Unknowns

Graph both equations on the same graph. (For example, solve each for y to find the slope and y-intercept.) A point of intersection gives the solution to the system. To find the point, you may need to adjust the range of x-values you use. To find the point accurately you may need to use a smaller range (or zoom in if using technology).

Algebraic Method for Solving a System of Two Equations in Two Unknowns

Multiply each equation by a nonzero number so that the coefficients of x are the same in absolute value but opposite in sign. Add the two equations to eliminate x; this gives an equation in y that we can solve to find its value. Substitute this value of y into one of the original equations to find the value of x. (Note that we could eliminate y first instead of x if it's more convenient.)

Sometimes, something appears to go wrong with these methods. The following examples show what can happen.

EXAMPLE 3 **Inconsistent System**

Solve the system

$$x - 3y = 5$$
$$-2x + 6y = 8.$$

Solution To eliminate x, we multiply the first equation by 2 and then add:

$$2x - 6y = 10$$
$$-2x + 6y = 8.$$

Adding gives

$$0 = 18.$$

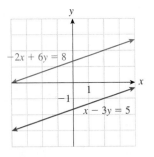

But this is absurd! This calculation shows that if we had two numbers x and y that satisfied both equations, it would be true that $0 = 18$. As 0 is *not* equal to 18, there can be no such numbers x and y. In other words, *the system has no solutions*, and is called an **inconsistent system**.

In slope-intercept form these lines are $y = \frac{1}{3}x - \frac{5}{3}$ and $y = \frac{1}{3}x + \frac{4}{3}$. Notice that they have the same slope but different y-intercepts. This means that they are parallel, but different lines. Plotting them confirms this fact (Figure 4).

Because they are parallel, they do not intersect. A solution must be a point of intersection, so we again conclude that there is no solution.

Figure 4

EXAMPLE 4 **Redundant System**

Solve the system

$$x + \ y = 2$$
$$2x + 2y = 4.$$

Solution Multiplying the first equation by -2 gives

$$-2x - 2y = -4$$
$$2x + 2y = 4.$$

Adding gives the not-very-enlightening result

$$0 = 0.$$

Now what has happened? Looking back at the original system, we note that the second equation is really the first equation in disguise. (It is the first equation multiplied by 2.) Put another way, if we solve both equations for y, we find that, in slope-intercept form, both equations become the same:

$$y = -x + 2.$$

The second equation gives us the same information as the first, so we say that this is a **redundant**, or **dependent system**. In other words, we really have only one equation in two unknowns. From Chapter 1, we know that a single linear equation in two unknowns has infinitely many solutions, one for each value of x. (Recall that to get the corresponding solution for y, we solve the equation for y and substitute the x-value.) The entire set of solutions can be summarized as follows:

x is arbitrary

$y = 2 - x$.   Solve the first equation for y.

This set of solutions is called the **general solution** because it includes all possible solutions. When we write the general solution this way, we say that we have a **parameterized solution** and that x is the **parameter**.

We can also write the general solution as

$(x, 2 - x)$ x arbitrary.

Different choices of the parameter x lead to different **particular solutions**. For instance, choosing $x = 3$ gives the particular solution

$(x, y) = (3, -1)$.

Because there are infinitely many values of x from which to choose, there are infinitely many solutions.

What does this system of equations look like graphically? The two equations are really the same, so their graphs are identical, each being the line with x-intercept 2 and y-intercept 2. The "two" lines intersect at every point, so there is a solution for each point on the common line. In other words, we have a "whole line of solutions" (Figure 5).

We could also have solved the first equation for x instead and used y as a parameter, obtaining another form of the general solution:

$(2 - y, y)$ y arbitrary.   Alternate form of the general solution

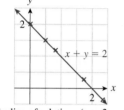

The line of solutions ($y = 2 - x$) and some particular solutions

Figure 5

We summarize the three possible outcomes we have encountered.

Possible Outcomes for a System of Two Linear Equations in Two Unknowns

1. **A single (or *unique*) solution** This happens when the lines corresponding to the two equations are distinct and not parallel so that they intersect at a single point. (See Example 1.)

2. **No solution** This happens when the two lines are parallel. We say that the system is **inconsistent**. (See Example 3.)

3. **An infinite number of solutions** This occurs when the two equations represent the same straight line, and we say that such a system is **redundant**, or **dependent**. In this case, we can represent the solutions by choosing one variable arbitrarily and solving for the other. (See Example 4.)

In cases 1 and 3, we say that the system of equations is **consistent** because it has at least one solution.

You should think about straight lines and convince yourself that these are the only three possibilities.

APPLICATIONS

EXAMPLE 5 Blending

Acme Baby Foods mixes two strengths of apple juice. One quart of Beginner's juice is made from 30 fluid ounces of water and 2 fluid ounces of apple juice concentrate. One quart of Advanced juice is made from 20 fluid ounces of water and 12 fluid ounces of concentrate. Every day Acme has available 30,000 fluid ounces of water and 3,600 fluid ounces of concentrate. If the company wants to use all the water and concentrate, how many quarts of each type of juice should it mix?

Solution In all applications we follow the same general strategy.

1. **Identify and label the unknowns.** What are we asked to find? To answer this question, it is common to respond by saying, "The unknowns are Beginner's juice and Advanced juice." Quite frankly, this is a baffling statement. Just what is unknown about juice? We need to be more precise:

   The unknowns are (1) *the **number of quarts** of Beginner's juice and* (2) *the **number of quarts** of Advanced juice made each day.*

   So, we label the unknowns as follows: Let

   $$x = \text{number of quarts of Beginner's juice made each day}$$
   $$y = \text{number of quarts of Advanced juice made each day.}$$

2. **Use the information given to set up equations in the unknowns.** This step is trickier, and the strategy varies from problem to problem. Here, the amount of juice the company can make is constrained by the fact that they have limited amounts of water and concentrate. This example shows a kind of application we will often see, and it is helpful in these problems to use a table to record the amounts of the resources used.

	Beginner's (x)	Advanced (y)	Available
Water (fl oz)	30	20	30,000
Concentrate (fl oz)	2	12	3,600

We can now set up an equation for each of the items listed in the left column of the table.

Water: We read across the first row. If Acme mixes x quarts of Beginner's juice, each quart using 30 fluid ounces of water, and y quarts of Advanced juice, each using 20 fluid ounces of water, it will use a total of $30x + 20y$ fluid ounces of water. But we are told that the total has to be 30,000 fluid ounces. Thus, $30x + 20y = 30,000$. This is our first equation.

Concentrate: We read across the second row. If Acme mixes x quarts of Beginner's juice, each using 2 fluid ounces of concentrate, and y quarts of Advanced juice, each using 12 fluid ounces of concentrate, it will use a total of $2x + 12y$ fluid ounces of concentrate. But we are told that the total has to be 3,600 fluid ounces. Thus, $2x + 12y = 3,600$.

Now we have two equations:

$$30x + 20y = 30,000$$
$$2x + 12y = 3,600.$$

To make the numbers easier to work with, let's divide (both sides of) the first equation by 10 and the second by 2:

$$3x + 2y = 3,000$$
$$x + 6y = 1,800.$$

using Technology to Check Your Answer

Website
www.WanerMath.com

→ Math Tools for Chapter 3
→ Pivot and Gauss-Jordan Tool

To check Example 5 enter the coefficients of x and y and the right-hand sides of the two equations as shown (no commas in numbers!):

x1	x2	x3
30	20	30000
2	12	3600

Then press "Reduce Completely". The answer will appear in the last column. (In the next section we will see how this works.)

We can now eliminate x by multiplying the second equation by -3 and adding:

$$
\begin{aligned}
3x + 2y &= 3{,}000 \\
-3x - 18y &= -5{,}400 \\
\hline
-16y &= -2{,}400.
\end{aligned}
$$

So, $y = 2{,}400/16 = 150$. Substituting this into the equation $x + 6y = 1{,}800$ gives $x + 900 = 1{,}800$, and so $x = 900$. The solution is $(x, y) = (900, 150)$. In other words, the company should mix 900 quarts of Beginner's juice and 150 quarts of Advanced juice.

EXAMPLE 6 **Blending**

A medieval alchemist's love potion calls for a number of eyes of newt and toes of frog, the total being 20, but with twice as many newt eyes as frog toes. How many of each is required?

Solution As in the preceding example, the first step is to identify and label the unknowns. Let

$$x = \text{number of newt eyes}$$
$$y = \text{number of frog toes.}$$

As for the second step—setting up the equations—a table is less appropriate here than in the preceding example. Instead, we translate each phrase of the problem into an equation. The first sentence tells us that the total number of eyes and toes is 20. Thus,

$$x + y = 20.$$

The end of the first sentence gives us more information, but the phrase "twice as many newt eyes as frog toes" is a little tricky: does it mean that $2x = y$ or that $x = 2y$? We can decide which by rewording the statement using the phrases "the *number of* newt eyes," which is x, and "the *number of* frog toes," which is y. Rephrased, the statement reads:

*The **number of** newt eyes is twice the **number of** frog toes.*

(Notice how the word "twice" is forced into a different place.) With this rephrasing, we can translate directly into algebra:

$$x = 2y.$$

In standard form ($ax + by = c$), this equation reads

$$x - 2y = 0.$$

Thus, we have the two equations:

$$
\begin{aligned}
x + y &= 20 \\
x - 2y &= 0.
\end{aligned}
$$

To eliminate x, we multiply the second equation by -1 and then add:

$$
\begin{aligned}
x + y &= 20 \\
-x + 2y &= 0.
\end{aligned}
$$

We'll leave it to you to finish solving the system and find that $x = 13\frac{1}{3}$ and $y = 6\frac{2}{3}$.

So, the recipe calls for exactly $13\frac{1}{3}$ eyes of newt and $6\frac{2}{3}$ toes of frog. The alchemist needs a very sharp scalpel and a very accurate balance (not to mention a very strong stomach).

We saw in Chapter 1 that the *equilibrium price* of an item (the price at which supply equals demand) and the *break-even point* (the number of items that must be sold to break even) can both be described as the intersection points of two graphs. If the graphs are straight lines, what we need to do to find the intersection is solve a system of two linear equations in two unknowns, as illustrated in the following problem.

EXAMPLE 7 **Equilibrium Price**

The demand for refrigerators in West Podunk is given by

$$q = -\frac{p}{10} + 100,$$

where q is the number of refrigerators that the citizens will buy each year if the refrigerators are priced at p dollars each. The supply is

$$q = \frac{p}{20} + 25,$$

where now q is the number of refrigerators the manufacturers will be willing to ship into town each year if they are priced at p dollars each. Find the equilibrium price and the number of refrigerators that will be sold at that price.

Solution Figure 6 shows the demand and supply curves. The equilibrium price occurs at the point where these two lines cross, which is where demand equals supply. The graph suggests that the equilibrium price is $500, and zooming in confirms this.

To solve this system algebraically, first write both equations in standard form:

$$\frac{p}{10} + q = 100$$

$$-\frac{p}{20} + q = 25.$$

We can clear fractions and also prepare to eliminate p if we multiply the first equation by 10 and the second by 20:

$$p + 10q = 1{,}000$$

$$-p + 20q = 500,$$

and so:

$$30q = 1{,}500$$

$$q = 50.$$

Substituting this value of q into either equation gives us $p = 500$. Thus, the equilibrium price is $500, and 50 refrigerators will be sold at this price.

We could also have solved this system of equations by setting the two expressions for q (the supply and the demand) equal to each other:

$$-p/10 + 100 = p/20 + 25$$

and then solving for p. (See the **Before we go on** discussion at the end of Example 1.)

Supply: $q = \dfrac{p}{20} + 25$

Demand: $q = -\dfrac{p}{10} + 100$

Figure 6

> **FAQs**
>
> **Setting Up the Equations**
>
> **Q**: *Looking through these examples, I notice that in some, we can tabulate the information given and read off the equations (as in Example 5), whereas in others (like Example 6), we have to reword each sentence to turn it into an equation. How do I know what approach to use?*
>
> **A**: There is no hard-and-fast rule, and indeed some applications might call for a bit of each approach. However, it is generally not hard to see when it would be useful to tabulate values: Lists of the numbers of ingredients or components generally lend themselves to tabulation, whereas phrases like "twice as many of these as those" generally require direct translation into equations (after rewording if necessary).

3.1 EXERCISES

▼ more advanced   ◆ challenging
 T indicates exercises that should be solved using technology

In Exercises 1–14, find all solutions of the given system of equations and check your answer graphically. HINT [See Examples 1–4.]

1. $x - y = 0$
$x + y = 4$

2. $x - y = 0$
$x + y = -6$

3. $x + y = 4$
$x - y = 2$

4. $2x + y = 2$
$-2x + y = 2$

5. $3x - 2y = 6$
$2x - 3y = -6$

6. $2x + 3y = 5$
$3x + 2y = 5$

7. $0.5x + 0.1y = 0.7$
$0.2x - 0.2y = 0.6$

8. $-0.3x + 0.5y = 0.1$
$0.1x - 0.1y = 0.4$

9. $\dfrac{x}{3} - \dfrac{y}{2} = 1$
$\dfrac{x}{4} + y = -2$

10. $-\dfrac{2x}{3} + \dfrac{y}{2} = -\dfrac{1}{6}$
$\dfrac{x}{4} - y = -\dfrac{3}{4}$

11. $2x + 3y = 1$
$-x - \dfrac{3y}{2} = -\dfrac{1}{2}$

12. $2x - 3y = 1$
$6x - 9y = 3$

13. $2x + 3y = 2$
$-x - \dfrac{3y}{2} = -\dfrac{1}{2}$

14. $2x - 3y = 2$
$6x - 9y = 3$

T *In Exercises 15–24, use technology to obtain approximate solutions graphically. All solutions should be accurate to one decimal place. (Zoom in for improved accuracy.)*

15. $2x + 8y = 10$
$x + y = 5$

16. $2x - y = 3$
$x + 3y = 5$

17. $3.1x - 4.5y = 6$
$4.5x + 1.1y = 0$

18. $0.2x + 4.5y = 1$
$1.5x + 1.1y = 2$

19. $10.2x + 14y = 213$
$4.5x + 1.1y = 448$

20. $100x + 4.5y = 540$
$1.05x + 1.1y = 0$

21. ▼ Find the intersection of the line through $(0, 1)$ and $(4.2, 2)$ and the line through $(2.1, 3)$ and $(5.2, 0)$.

22. ▼ Find the intersection of the line through $(2.1, 3)$ and $(4, 2)$ and the line through $(3.2, 2)$ and $(5.1, 3)$.

23. ▼ Find the intersection of the line through $(0, 0)$ and $(5.5, 3)$ and the line through $(5, 0)$ and $(0, 6)$.

24. ▼ Find the intersection of the line through $(4.3, 0)$ and $(0, 5)$ and the line through $(2.1, 2.2)$ and $(5.2, 1)$.

APPLICATIONS

25. *Resource Allocation* You manage an ice cream factory that makes two flavors: Creamy Vanilla and Continental Mocha. Into each quart of Creamy Vanilla go 2 eggs and 3 cups of cream. Into each quart of Continental Mocha go 1 egg and 3 cups of cream. You have in stock 500 eggs and 900 cups of cream. How many quarts of each flavor should you make in order to use up all the eggs and cream? HINT [See Example 5.]

26. *Class Scheduling* Enormous State University's Math Department offers two courses: Finite Math and Applied Calculus. Each section of Finite Math has 60 students, and each section of Applied Calculus has 50. The department will offer a total of 110 sections in a semester, and 6,000 students would like to take a math course. How many sections of each course should the department offer in order to fill all sections and accommodate all of the students? HINT [See Example 5.]

27. *Nutrition* Gerber Products' Gerber Mixed Cereal for Baby contains, in each serving, 60 calories and 11 grams of carbohydrates. Gerber Mango Tropical Fruit Dessert contains, in each serving, 80 calories and 21 grams of carbohydrates.[1] If you want to provide your child with 200 calories and 43 grams of carbohydrates, how many servings of each should you use?

28. *Nutrition* Anthony Altino is mixing food for his young daughter and would like the meal to supply 1 gram of protein and 5 milligrams of iron. He is mixing together cereal, with 0.5 grams of protein and 1 milligram of iron per ounce,

---

[1]Source: Nutrition information supplied with the products.

and fruit, with 0.2 grams of protein and 2 milligrams of iron per ounce. What mixture will provide the desired nutrition?

29. *Nutrition* One serving of Campbell Soup Company's Campbell's® Pork & Beans contains 5 grams of protein and 21 grams of carbohydrates.[2] A typical slice of white bread provides 2 grams of protein and 11 grams of carbohydrates per slice. The U.S. RDA (Recommended Daily Allowance) is 60 grams of protein each day.[3]

   a. I am planning a meal of "beans on toast" and wish to have it supply one-half of the RDA for protein and 139 grams of carbohydrates. How should I prepare my meal?

   b. Is it possible to have my meal supply the same amount of protein as in part (a) but only 100 g of carbohydrates?

30. *Nutrition* One serving of Campbell Soup Company's Campbell's® Pork & Beans contains 5 grams of protein and 21 grams of carbohydrates.[4] A typical slice of "lite" rye bread contains 4 grams of protein and 12 grams of carbohydrates.

   a. I am planning a meal of "beans on toast" and wish to have it supply one-third of the U.S. RDA for protein (see the preceding exercise) and 80 grams of carbohydrates. How should I prepare my meal?

   b. Is it possible to have my meal supply the same amount of protein as in part (a) but only 60 grams of carbohydrates?

Protein Supplements Exercises 31–34 are based on the following data on three popular protein supplements. (Figures shown correspond to a single serving.)[5]

	Protein (g)	Carbohydrates (g)	Sodium (mg)	Cost ($)
Designer Whey® (Next)	18	2	80	0.50
Muscle Milk® (Cytosport)	32	16	240	1.60
Pure Whey Protein Stack® (Champion)	24	3	100	0.60

31. You are thinking of combining Designer Whey and Muscle Milk to obtain a 7-day supply that provides exactly 280 grams of protein and 56 grams of carbohydrates. How many servings of each supplement should you combine in order to meet your requirements? What will it cost?

32. You are thinking of combining Muscle Milk and Pure Whey Protein Stack to obtain a supply that provides exactly 640 grams of protein and 3,200 mg of sodium. How many servings of each supplement should you combine in order to meet your requirements? What will it cost?

33. ▼ You have a mixture of Designer Whey and Pure Whey Protein Stack that costs a total of $14 and supplies exactly

540 g of protein. How many grams of carbohydrates does it supply?

34. ▼ You have a mixture of Designer Whey and Muscle Milk that costs a total of $14 and supplies exactly 104 g of carbohydrates. How many grams of protein does it supply?

35. *Investments: Tech Stocks* In July 2011, Apple (AAPL) stock increased from $350 to $400 per share, and Google (GOOG) stock increased from $500 to $600 per share.[6] If you invested a total of $22,000 in these stocks at the beginning of the month and sold them for $26,000 at the end of the month, how many shares of each stock did you buy?

36. *Investments: Energy Stocks* In the two-month period June 1–July 31, 2011, Hess Corp. (HES) stock decreased from $80 to $70 per share, and Exxon Mobil (XOM) stock decreased from $83 to $80 per share.[7] If you invested a total of $19,000 in these stocks at the beginning of June and sold them for $18,100 at the end of July, how many shares of each stock did you buy?

37. ▼ *Investments: Financial Stocks* In August 2011, Bank of Hawaii (BOH) stock cost $45 per share and yielded 4% per year in dividends, while JPMorgan Chase (JPM) stock cost $40 per share and yielded 2.5% per year in dividends.[8] If you invested a total of $25,000 in these stocks and earned $760 in dividends in a year, how many shares of each stock did you purchase? (Assume the dividend rate was unchanged for the year.)

38. ▼ *Investments: Utility Stocks* In April 2011, Consolidated Edison (ED) stock cost $50 per share and yielded 5% per year in dividends, while National Grid (NGG) stock cost $50 per share and yielded 6% per year in dividends.[9] If you invested a total of $45,000 in these stocks and earned $2,400 in dividends in a year, how many shares of each stock did you purchase? (Assume the dividend rate was unchanged for the year.)

39. *Voting* An appropriations bill passes the U.S. House of Representatives with 49 more members voting in favor than against. If all 435 members of the House vote for or against the bill, how many voted in favor and how many voted against?

40. *Voting* The U.S. Senate has 100 members. For a bill to pass with a supermajority, at least twice as many senators must vote in favor of the bill as vote against it. If all 100 senators vote in favor of or against a bill, how many must vote in favor for it to pass with a supermajority?

41. *Intramural Sports* The best sports dorm on campus, Lombardi House, has won a total of 12 games this semester. Some of these games were soccer games, and the others were football games. According to the rules of the university, each win in a soccer game earns the winning house 2 points, whereas each win in a football game earns them 4 points. If the total number of points Lombardi House earned was 38, how many of each type of game did they win?

---

[2]According to the label information on a 16 oz. can.

[3]Recommended Daily Allowance for a person weighing 75 kg (165 lb)

[4]*Ibid.*

[5]Source: Nutritional information supplied by the manufacturers (www.netrition.com). Cost per serving is approximate and varies.

[6]Approximate stock prices at or close to the dates cited. Source: http://finance.google.com.

[7]*Ibid.*

[8]Stock prices and yields are approximate. Source: http://finance.google.com.

[9]*Ibid.*

42. *Law* Enormous State University's campus publication, *The Campus Inquirer*, ran a total of 10 exposés five years ago, dealing with alleged recruiting violations by the football team and with theft by the student treasurer of the film society. Each exposé dealing with recruiting violations resulted in a $4 million libel suit, and the treasurer of the film society sued the paper for $3 million as a result of each exposé concerning his alleged theft. Unfortunately for *The Campus Inquirer*, all the lawsuits were successful, and the paper wound up being ordered to pay $37 million in damages. (It closed down shortly thereafter.) How many of each type of exposé did the paper run?

43. *Purchasing* *(from the GMAT)* Elena purchased brand X pens for $4.00 apiece and brand Y pens for $2.80 apiece. If Elena purchased a total of 12 of these pens for $42.00, how many brand X pens did she purchase?

44. *Purchasing* *(based on a question from the GMAT)* Earl is ordering supplies. Yellow paper costs $5.00 per ream while white paper costs $6.50 per ream. He would like to order 100 reams total, and has a budget of $560. How many reams of each color should he order?

45. *Equilibrium Price* The demand and supply functions for pet chias are, respectively, $q = -60p + 150$ and $q = 80p - 60$, where p is the price in dollars. At what price should the chias be marked so that there is neither a surplus nor a shortage of chias? HINT [See Example 7.]

46. *Equilibrium Price* The demand and supply functions for your college newspaper are, respectively, $q = -10,000p + 2,000$ and $q = 4,000p + 600$, where p is the price in dollars. At what price should the newspapers be sold so that there is neither a surplus nor a shortage of papers? HINT [See Example 7.]

47. *Supply and Demand* *(from the GRE Economics Test)* The demand curve for widgets is given by $D = 85 - 5P$, and the supply curve is given by $S = 25 + 5P$, where P is the price of widgets. When the widget market is in equilibrium, what is the quantity of widgets bought and sold?

48. *Supply and Demand* *(from the GRE Economics Test)* In the market for soybeans, the demand and supply functions are $Q_D = 100 - 10P$ and $Q_S = 20 + 5P$, where Q_D is quantity demanded, Q_S is quantity supplied, and P is price in dollars. If the government sets a price floor of $7, what will be the resulting surplus or shortage?

49. *Equilibrium Price* In June 2001, the retail price of a 25-kg bag of cornmeal was $8 in Zambia; by December, the price had risen to $11. The result was that one retailer reported a drop in sales from 15 bags/day to 3 bags/day.[10] Assume that the retailer is prepared to sell 3 bags/day at $8 and 15 bags/day at $11. Find linear demand and supply equations and then compute the retailer's equilibrium price.

50. *Equilibrium Price* At the start of December 2001, the retail price of a 25 kg bag of cornmeal was $10 in Zambia, while by the end of the month, the price had fallen to $6.[11] The result was that one retailer reported an increase in sales from 3 bags/day to 5 bags/day. Assume that the retailer is prepared to sell 18 bags/day at $8 and 12 bags/day at $6. Obtain linear demand and supply equations, and hence compute the retailer's equilibrium price.

51. *Pollution* Joe Slo, a college sophomore, neglected to wash his dirty laundry for 6 weeks. By the end of that time, his roommate had had enough and tossed Joe's dirty socks and T-shirts into the trash, counting a total of 44 items. (A pair of dirty socks counts as one item.) The roommate noticed that there were three times as many pairs of dirty socks as T-shirts. How many of each item did he throw out?

52. *Diet* The local sushi bar serves 1-ounce pieces of raw salmon (consisting of 50% protein) and $1\frac{1}{4}$-ounce pieces of raw tuna (40% protein). A customer's total intake of protein amounts to $1\frac{1}{2}$ ounces after consuming a total of three pieces. How many of each did the customer consume? (Fractions of pieces are permitted.)

53. ▼ **Management** *(from the GMAT)* A manager has $6,000 budgeted for raises for four full-time and two part-time employees. Each of the full-time employees receives the same raise, which is twice the raise that each of the part-time employees receives. What is the amount of the raise that each full-time employee receives?

54. ▼ **Publishing** *(from the GMAT)* There were 36,000 hardback copies of a certain novel sold before the paperback version was issued. From the time the first paperback copy was sold until the last copy of the novel was sold, nine times as many paperback copies as hardback copies were sold. If a total of 441,000 copies of the novel were sold in all, how many paperback copies were sold?

COMMUNICATION AND REASONING EXERCISES

55. A system of three equations in two unknowns corresponds to three lines in the plane. Describe how these lines might be positioned if the system has a unique solution.

56. A system of three equations in two unknowns corresponds to three lines in the plane. Describe several ways that these lines might be positioned if the system has no solutions.

57. Both the supply and demand equations for a certain product have negative slope. Can there be an equilibrium price? Explain.

58. You are solving a system of equations with x representing the number of rocks and y representing the number of pebbles. The solution is $(200, -10)$. What do you conclude?

59. ▼ Referring to Exercise 25, suppose that the solution of the corresponding system of equations was 198.7 gallons of vanilla and 100.89 gallons of mocha. If your factory can produce only whole numbers of gallons, would you recommend rounding the answers to the nearest whole number? Explain.

60. ▼ Referring to Exercise 25 but using different data, suppose that the general solution of the corresponding system of equations was $(200 - y, y)$, where $x = $ number of gallons of vanilla, and $y = $ number of gallons of mocha. Your factory can

---

[10]The prices quoted are approximate. (Actual prices varied from retailer to retailer.) Source: *New York Times,* December 24, 2001, p. A4.
[11]*Ibid.*

produce only whole numbers of gallons. There are infinitely many ways of making the ice cream, mixes, right? Explain.

61. ▼ Select one: Multiplying both sides of a linear equation by a nonzero constant results in a linear equation whose graph is

(A) parallel to   **(B)** the same as

(C) not always parallel to   **(D)** not the same as

the graph of the original equation.

62. ▼ Select one: If the addition or subtraction of two linear equations results in the equation $3 = 3$, then the graphs of those equations are

(A) equal.   **(B)** parallel.

(C) perpendicular.   **(D)** none of the above.

63. ▼ Select one: If the addition or subtraction of two linear equations results in the equation $0 = 3$, then the graphs of those equations are

(A) equal.   **(B)** parallel.

(C) perpendicular.   **(D)** not parallel.

64. ▼ Select one: If adding two linear equations gives $x = 3$, and subtracting them gives $y = 3$, then the graphs of those equations are

(A) equal.   **(B)** parallel.

(C) perpendicular.   **(D)** not parallel.

65. ▼ Invent an interesting application that leads to a system of two equations in two unknowns with a unique solution.

66. ▼ Invent an interesting application that leads to a system of two equations in two unknowns with no solution.

67. ◆ How likely do you think it is that a "random" system of two equations in two unknowns has a unique solution? Give some justification for your answer.

68. ◆ How likely do you think it is that a "random" system of three equations in two unknowns has a unique solution? Give some justification for your answer.

3.2 # Using Matrices to Solve Systems of Equations

In this section we describe a systematic method for solving systems of equations that makes solving large systems of equations in any number of unknowns straightforward. Although this method may seem a little cumbersome at first, it will prove *immensely* useful in this and the next several chapters. First, some terminology:

Linear Equation

A linear equation in the n variables $x_1, x_2, \ldots, x_n$ has the form

$$a_1 x_1 + \cdots + a_n x_n = b. \qquad (a_1, a_2, \ldots, a_n, b \text{ constants})$$

The numbers $a_1, a_2, \ldots, a_n$ are called the **coefficients**, and the number b is called the **constant term**, or **right-hand side**.

Quick Examples

1. $3x - 5y = 0$ Linear equation in x and y
Coefficients: 3, −5 Constant term: 0

2. $x + 2y - z = 6$ Linear equation in x, y, z
Coefficients: 1, 2, −1 Constant term: 6

3. $30x_1 + 18x_2 + x_3 + x_4 = 19$ Linear equation in x_1, x_2, x_3, x_4
Coefficients: 30, 18, 1, 1 Constant term: 19

Note When the number of variables is small, we will almost always use $x, y, z, \ldots$ (as in Quick Examples 1 and 2) rather than $x_1, x_2, x_3, \ldots$ as the names of the variables. ■

Notice that a linear equation in any number of unknowns (for example, $2x - y = 3$) is entirely determined by its coefficients and its constant term. In other words, if we were simply given the row of numbers

$$[2 \quad -1 \quad 3]$$

we could easily reconstruct the original linear equation by multiplying the first number by x, the second by y, and inserting a plus sign and an equals sign, as follows:

$$2 \cdot x + (-1) \cdot y = 3$$

or $2x - y = 3.$

Similarly, the equation

$$-4x + 2y = 0$$

is represented by the row

$$[-4 \quad 2 \quad 0].$$

and the equation

$$-3y = \frac{1}{4}$$

is represented by

$$\left[0 \quad -3 \quad \frac{1}{4}\right].$$

As the last example shows, the first number is always the coefficient of x and the second is the coefficient of y. If an x or a y is missing, we write a zero for its coefficient. We shall call such a row the **coefficient row** of an equation.

If we have a system of equations, for example the system

$$\begin{aligned} 2x - y &= 3 \\ -x + 2y &= -4, \end{aligned}$$

we can put the coefficient rows together like this:

$$\begin{bmatrix} 2 & -1 & 3 \\ -1 & 2 & -4 \end{bmatrix}.$$

We call this the **augmented matrix** of the system of equations. The term "augmented" means that we have included the right-hand sides 3 and -4. We will often drop the word "augmented" and simply refer to the matrix of the system. A **matrix** (plural: **matrices**) is nothing more than a rectangular array of numbers as above.

Matrix, Augmented Matrix

A **matrix** is a rectangular array of numbers. The **augmented matrix** of a system of linear equations is the matrix whose rows are the coefficient rows of the equations.

Quick Example

The augmented matrix of the system

$$\begin{aligned} x + y &= 3 \\ x - y &= 1 \end{aligned}$$

is $\begin{bmatrix} 1 & 1 & 3 \\ 1 & -1 & 1 \end{bmatrix}.$

We'll be studying matrices in more detail in Chapter 4.

Q : *What good are coefficient rows and matrices?*

A : Think about what we do when we multiply both sides of an equation by a number. For example, consider multiplying both sides of the equation $2x - y = 3$ by -2 to get $-4x + 2y = -6$. All we are really doing is multiplying the coefficients and the right-hand side by -2. This corresponds to *multiplying the row* $[2 \ -1 \ 3]$ *by* -2, that is, multiplying every number in the row by -2. We shall see that any manipulation we want to do with equations can be done instead with rows, and this fact leads to a method of solving equations that is systematic and generalizes easily to larger systems.

Here is the same operation both in the language of equations and the language of rows. (We refer to the equation here as *Equation* 1, or simply E_1 for short, and to the row as *Row* 1, or R_1.)

	Equation	Row
	E_1: $\quad 2x - \ \ y = 3$	$[\ 2 \quad -1 \quad \ 3]\quad R_1$
Multiply by -2:	$(-2)E_1$: $-4x + 2y = -6$	$[-4 \quad \ 2 \ -6]\quad (-2)R_1$

Multiplying both sides of an equation by the number a corresponds to multiplying the coefficient row by a.

Now look at what we do when we add two equations:

	Equation	Row
	E_1: $2x - \ \ y = 3$	$[\ \ 2 \quad -1 \quad \ \ 3]\quad R_1$
	E_2: $-x + 2y = -4$	$[-1 \quad \ \ 2 \ -4]\quad R_2$
Add:	$E_1 + E_2$: $\ x + \ \ y = -1$	$[\ \ 1 \quad \ \ 1 \ -1]\quad R_1 + R_2$

All we are really doing is *adding the corresponding entries in the rows*, or *adding the rows*. In other words,

Adding two equations corresponds to adding their coefficient rows.

In short, the manipulations of equations that we saw in the preceding section can be done more easily with rows in a matrix because we don't have to carry x, y, and other unnecessary notation along with us; x and y can always be inserted at the end if desired.

The manipulations we are talking about are known as **row operations**. In particular, we use three **elementary row operations**.

* We are using the term *elementary row operations* a little more freely than most books. Some mathematicians insist that $a = 1$ in an operation of Type 2, but the less restrictive version is very useful.

† Multiplying an equation or row by zero gives us the not very surprising result $0 = 0$. In fact, we lose any information that the equation provided, which usually means that the resulting system has more solutions than the original system.

Elementary Row Operations*

Type 1: Replacing R_i by $a R_i$ (where $a \neq 0$)†
In words: multiplying or dividing a row by a nonzero number.

Type 2: Replacing R_i by $a R_i \pm b R_j$ (where $a \neq 0$)
Multiplying a row by a nonzero number and adding or subtracting a multiple of another row.

using Technology

See the Technology Guides at the end of the chapter to see how to do row operations using a TI-83/84 Plus or a spreadsheet.

 Website

www.WanerMath.com

→ Math Tools for Chapter 3

→ Pivot and Gauss-Jordan Tool

Enter the matrix in columns $x1$, $x2$, $x3$, …. To do a row operation, type the instruction(s) next to the row(s) you are changing as shown, and press "Do Row Ops" once.

Type 3: Switching the order of the rows

This corresponds to switching the order in which we write the equations; occasionally this will be convenient.

For Types 1 and 2, we write the instruction for the row operation *next to the row we wish to replace.* (See the Quick Examples below.)

Quick Examples

Type 1: $\begin{bmatrix} 1 & 3 & -4 \\ 0 & 4 & 2 \end{bmatrix} 3R_2 \rightarrow \begin{bmatrix} 1 & 3 & -4 \\ 0 & 12 & 6 \end{bmatrix}$ Replace R_2 by $3R_2$.

Type 2: $\begin{bmatrix} 1 & 3 & -4 \\ 0 & 4 & 2 \end{bmatrix} 4R_1 - 3R_2 \rightarrow \begin{bmatrix} 4 & 0 & -22 \\ 0 & 4 & 2 \end{bmatrix}$ Replace R_1 by $4R_1 - 3R_2$.

Type 3: $\begin{bmatrix} 1 & 3 & -4 \\ 0 & 4 & 2 \\ 1 & 2 & 3 \end{bmatrix} R_1 \leftrightarrow R_2 \rightarrow \begin{bmatrix} 0 & 4 & 2 \\ 1 & 3 & -4 \\ 1 & 2 & 3 \end{bmatrix}$ Switch R_1 and R_2.

One very important fact about the elementary row operations is that they do not change the solutions of the corresponding system of equations. In other words, the new system of equations that we get by applying any one of these operations will have exactly the same solutions as the original system: It is easy to see that numbers that make the original equations true will also make the new equations true, because each of the elementary row operations corresponds to a valid operation on the original equations. That any solution of the new system is a solution of the old system follows from the fact that these row operations are *invertible:* The effects of a row operation can be reversed by applying another row operation, called its **inverse**. Here are some examples of this invertibility. (Try them out in the above Quick Examples.)

Operation	*Inverse Operation*
Replace R_2 by $3R_2$.	Replace R_2 by $\frac{1}{3}R_2$.
Replace R_1 by $4R_1 - 3R_2$.	Replace R_1 by $\frac{1}{4}R_1 + \frac{3}{4}R_2$.
Switch R_1 and R_2.	Switch R_1 and R_2.

Our objective, then, is to use row operations to change the system we are given into one with exactly the same set of solutions in which it is easy to see what the solutions are.

Solving Systems of Equations by Using Row Operations

Now we put rows to work for us in solving systems of equations. Let's start with a complicated-looking system of equations:

$$-\frac{2x}{3} + \frac{y}{2} = -3$$
$$\frac{x}{4} - y = \frac{11}{4}.$$

We begin by writing the matrix of the system:

$$\begin{bmatrix} -\frac{2}{3} & \frac{1}{2} & -3 \\ \frac{1}{4} & -1 & \frac{11}{4} \end{bmatrix}.$$

Now what do we do with this matrix?

Step 1 *Clear the fractions and/or decimals (if any) using operations of Type* **1.** To clear the fractions, we multiply the first row by 6 and the second row by 4. We record the operations by writing the symbolic form of an operation next to the row it will change, as follows.

$$\begin{bmatrix} -\frac{2}{3} & \frac{1}{2} & -3 \\ \frac{1}{4} & -1 & \frac{11}{4} \end{bmatrix} \begin{matrix} 6R_1 \\ 4R_2 \end{matrix}$$

By this we mean that we will replace the first row by $6R_1$ and the second by $4R_2$. Doing these operations gives

$$\begin{bmatrix} -4 & 3 & -18 \\ 1 & -4 & 11 \end{bmatrix}.$$

Step 2 *Designate the first nonzero entry in the first row as the* **pivot.** In this case we designate the entry -4 in the first row as the "pivot" by putting a box around it:

$$\begin{bmatrix} \boxed{-4} & 3 & -18 \\ 1 & -4 & 11 \end{bmatrix}. \quad \leftarrow \text{Pivot row}$$
$$\uparrow$$
$$\text{Pivot column}$$

Q: *What is a "pivot"?*

A: A **pivot** is an entry in a matrix that is used to "clear a column." (See Step 3.) In this procedure, we will always select the first nonzero entry of a row as our pivot. In Chapter 5, when we study the simplex method, we will select our pivots differently.

Step 3 *Use the pivot to clear its column using operations of Type* **2.** By **clearing a column**, we mean changing the matrix so that the pivot is the only nonzero number in its column. The procedure of clearing a column using a designated pivot is also called **pivoting**.

$$\begin{bmatrix} \boxed{-4} & 3 & -18 \\ 0 & \# & \# \end{bmatrix} \leftarrow \text{Desired row 2 (the "\#"s stand for as yet unknown numbers)}$$
$$\uparrow$$
$$\text{Cleared pivot column}$$

We want to replace R_2 by a row of the form $aR_2 \pm bR_1$ to get a zero in column 1. Moreover—and this will be important when we discuss the simplex method in Chapter 5—*we are going to choose positive values for both a and b.*[*] We need to choose a and b so that we get the desired cancellation. We can do this quite mechanically as follows:

a. Write the name of the row you need to change on the left and that of the pivot row on the right.

$$\begin{matrix} R_2 & R_1 \\ \uparrow & \uparrow \\ \text{Row to change} & \text{Pivot row} \end{matrix}$$

[*] Thus, the only place a negative sign may appear is between aR_2 and bR_1 as indicated in the formula $aR_2 \pm bR_1$.

b. Focus on the pivot column, $\begin{bmatrix} -4 \\ 1 \end{bmatrix}$. Multiply each row by the *absolute value* of the entry currently in the other. (We are not permitting a or b to be negative.)

$$4R_2 \qquad\qquad 1R_1$$
$$\uparrow \qquad\qquad\quad \uparrow$$
$$\text{From Row 1} \qquad \text{From Row 2}$$

The effect is to make the two entries in the pivot column numerically the same. Sometimes, you can accomplish this by using smaller values of a and b.

c. If the entries in the pivot column have opposite signs, insert a plus $(+)$. If they have the same sign, insert a minus $(-)$. Here, we get the instruction

$$4R_2 + 1R_1,$$

or simply $4R_2 + R_1$.

d. Write the operation next to the row you want to change, and then replace that row using the operation:

$$\begin{bmatrix} \boxed{-4} & 3 & -18 \\ 1 & -4 & 11 \end{bmatrix} \, 4R_2 + 1R_1 \; \rightarrow \; \begin{bmatrix} -4 & 3 & -18 \\ 0 & -13 & 26 \end{bmatrix}.$$

We have cleared the pivot column and completed Step 3.

✱ We are deviating somewhat from the traditional procedure here. It is traditionally recommended first to divide the pivot row by the pivot, turning the pivot into a 1. This allows us to use $a = 1$, but usually results in fractions. The procedure we use here is easier for hand calculations and, we feel, mathematically more elegant, because it eliminates the need to introduce fractions. See the end of this section for an example done using the traditional procedure.

Note In general, the row operation you use should always have the following form✱:

$$a R_c \qquad \pm \qquad b R_p$$
$$\uparrow \qquad\qquad\qquad \uparrow$$
$$\text{Row to change} \qquad\quad \text{Pivot row}$$

with a and b both positive. ∎

The next step is one that can be performed at any time.

Simplification Step (Optional) *If, at any stage of the process, all the numbers in a row are multiples of an integer, divide by that integer*—a Type 1 operation.

This is an optional but extremely helpful step: It makes the numbers smaller and easier to work with. In our case, the entries in R_2 are divisible by 13, so we divide that row by 13. (Alternatively, we could divide by -13. Try it.)

$$\begin{bmatrix} -4 & 3 & -18 \\ 0 & -13 & 26 \end{bmatrix} \, \tfrac{1}{13}R_2 \; \rightarrow \; \begin{bmatrix} -4 & 3 & -18 \\ 0 & -1 & 2 \end{bmatrix}$$

Step 4 *Select the first nonzero number in the second row as the pivot, and clear its column.* Here we have combined two steps in one: selecting the new pivot and clearing the column (pivoting). The pivot is shown below, as well as the desired result when the column has been cleared:

$$\begin{bmatrix} -4 & 3 & -18 \\ 0 & \boxed{-1} & 2 \end{bmatrix} \; \rightarrow \; \begin{bmatrix} \# & 0 & \# \\ 0 & -1 & 2 \end{bmatrix}. \;\leftarrow \text{desired row}$$
$$\qquad\quad \uparrow \qquad\qquad\qquad\quad \uparrow$$
$$\quad \text{Pivot column} \qquad\qquad \text{Cleared pivot column}$$

We now wish to get a 0 in place of the 3 in the pivot column. Let's run once again through the mechanical steps to get the row operation that accomplishes this.

a. Write the name of the row you need to change on the left and that of the pivot row on the right:

$$R_1 \qquad\qquad R_2$$
$$\uparrow \qquad\qquad\quad \uparrow$$
$$\text{Row to change} \qquad \text{Pivot row}$$

b. Focus on the pivot column, $\begin{bmatrix} 3 \\ -1 \end{bmatrix}$. Multiply each row by the absolute value of the entry currently in the other:

$$1R_1 \qquad\qquad 3R_2$$
$$\uparrow \qquad\qquad\quad \uparrow$$
$$\text{From Row 2} \qquad \text{From Row 1}$$

c. If the entries in the pivot column have opposite signs, insert a plus (+). If they have the same sign, insert a minus (−). Here, we get the instruction

$$1R_1 + 3R_2.$$

d. Write the operation next to the row you want to change and then replace that row using the operation.

$$\begin{bmatrix} -4 & 3 & -18 \\ 0 & \boxed{-1} & 2 \end{bmatrix} \begin{array}{c} R_1 + 3R_2 \\ \\ \end{array} \rightarrow \begin{bmatrix} -4 & 0 & -12 \\ 0 & -1 & 2 \end{bmatrix}$$

Now we are essentially done, except for one last step.

Final Step *Using operations of Type* **1**, *turn each pivot (the first nonzero entry in each row) into a* **1.** We can accomplish this by dividing the first row by −4 and multiplying the second row by −1:

$$\begin{bmatrix} -4 & 0 & -12 \\ 0 & -1 & 2 \end{bmatrix} \begin{array}{c} -\frac{1}{4}R_1 \\ -R_2 \end{array} \rightarrow \begin{bmatrix} 1 & 0 & 3 \\ 0 & 1 & -2 \end{bmatrix}.$$

The matrix now has the following nice form:

$$\begin{bmatrix} \boxed{1} & 0 & \# \\ 0 & \boxed{1} & \# \end{bmatrix}.$$

(This is the form we will always obtain with two equations in two unknowns when there is a unique solution.) This form is nice because, when we translate back into equations, we get

$$1x + 0y = 3$$
$$0x + 1y = -2.$$

In other words,

$$x = 3 \text{ and } y = -2$$

and so we have found the solution, which we can also write as $(x, y) = (3, -2)$.

The procedure we've just demonstrated is called **Gauss-Jordan* reduction** or **row reduction.** It may seem too complicated a way to solve a system of two equations in two unknowns, and it is. However, for systems with more equations and more unknowns, it is very efficient.

In Example 1 below we use row reduction to solve a system of linear equations in *three* unknowns: x, y, and z. Just as for a system in two unknowns, a **solution** of a system in any number of unknowns consists of values for each of the variables that, when substituted, satisfy all of the equations in the system. Again, just as for a system in two unknowns, any system of linear equations in any number of unknowns has either no solution, exactly one solution, or infinitely many solutions. There are no other possibilities.

✱ Gauss-Jordan reduction is named after Carl Friedrich Gauss (1777–1855) and Wilhelm Jordan (1842–1899). Gauss was one of the great mathematicians, making fundamental contributions to number theory, analysis, probability, and statistics, as well as many fields of science. Gauss also made contributions to a method of solving systems of equations that has become known as "Gaussian elimination," even though this method had been described by Isaac Newton in 1707 and, independently, had been known to the Chinese more than 2,000 years ago. (See *Mathematicians of Gaussian Elimination,* Notices of the American Mathematical Society, June/July 2011, for a history of Gaussian elimination.) The method we are showing you here, Gauss-Jordan reduction, is Jordan's variation of Gaussian elimination, first published in 1887.

Solving a system in three unknowns graphically would require the graphing of planes (flat surfaces) in three dimensions. (The graph of a linear equation in three unknowns is a flat surface.) The use of row reduction makes three-dimensional graphing unnecessary.

EXAMPLE 1 Solving a System by Gauss-Jordan Reduction

Solve the system

$$x - y + 5z = -6$$
$$3x + 3y - z = 10$$
$$x + 3y + 2z = 5.$$

Solution The augmented matrix for this system is

$$\begin{bmatrix} 1 & -1 & 5 & -6 \\ 3 & 3 & -1 & 10 \\ 1 & 3 & 2 & 5 \end{bmatrix}.$$

Note that the columns correspond to x, y, z, and the right-hand side, respectively. We begin by selecting the pivot in the first row and clearing its column. Remember that clearing the column means that we turn *all* other numbers in the column into zeros. Thus, to clear the column of the first pivot, we need to change two rows, setting up the row operations in exactly the same way as above.

$$\begin{bmatrix} \boxed{1} & -1 & 5 & -6 \\ 3 & 3 & -1 & 10 \\ 1 & 3 & 2 & 5 \end{bmatrix} \begin{matrix} \\ R_2 - 3R_1 \rightarrow \\ R_3 - R_1 \end{matrix} \begin{bmatrix} 1 & -1 & 5 & -6 \\ 0 & 6 & -16 & 28 \\ 0 & 4 & -3 & 11 \end{bmatrix}$$

Notice that both row operations have the required form

$$aR_c \pm bR_1$$

$\qquad\quad\uparrow\qquad\quad\uparrow$
Row to change   Pivot row

with a and b both positive.

Now we use the optional simplification step to simplify R_2:

$$\begin{bmatrix} 1 & -1 & 5 & -6 \\ 0 & 6 & -16 & 28 \\ 0 & 4 & -3 & 11 \end{bmatrix} \tfrac{1}{2}R_2 \rightarrow \begin{bmatrix} 1 & -1 & 5 & -6 \\ 0 & 3 & -8 & 14 \\ 0 & 4 & -3 & 11 \end{bmatrix}.$$

Next, we select the pivot in the second row and clear its column:

$$\begin{bmatrix} 1 & -1 & 5 & -6 \\ 0 & \boxed{3} & -8 & 14 \\ 0 & 4 & -3 & 11 \end{bmatrix} \begin{matrix} 3R_1 + R_2 \\ \rightarrow \\ 3R_3 - 4R_2 \end{matrix} \begin{bmatrix} 3 & 0 & 7 & -4 \\ 0 & 3 & -8 & 14 \\ 0 & 0 & 23 & -23 \end{bmatrix}.$$

R_1 and R_3 are to be changed.
R_2 is the pivot row.

We simplify R_3.

$$\begin{bmatrix} 3 & 0 & 7 & -4 \\ 0 & 3 & -8 & 14 \\ 0 & 0 & 23 & -23 \end{bmatrix} \tfrac{1}{23}R_3 \rightarrow \begin{bmatrix} 3 & 0 & 7 & -4 \\ 0 & 3 & -8 & 14 \\ 0 & 0 & 1 & -1 \end{bmatrix}$$

using Technology

See the Technology Guides at the end of the chapter to see how to use a TI-83/84 Plus or a spreadsheet to solve this system of equations.

Website
www.WanerMath.com

Everything for Finite Math

→ Math Tools for Chapter 3

→ Pivot and Gauss-Jordan Tool

Enter the augmented matrix in columns x1, x2, x3, ... At each step, type in the row operations exactly as written above next to the rows to which they apply. For example, for the first step type:
R2-3R1 next to Row 2, and
R3-R1 next to Row 3.
Press "Do Row Ops" once, and then "Clear Row Ops" to prepare for the next step.
For the last step, type
(1/3)R1 next to Row 1, and
(1/3)R2 next to Row 2.
Press "Do Row Ops" once.
The utility also does other things, such as automatic pivoting and complete reduction in one step. Use these features to check your work.

Now we select the pivot in the third row and clear its column:

$$\begin{bmatrix} 3 & 0 & 7 & -4 \\ 0 & 3 & -8 & 14 \\ 0 & 0 & \boxed{1} & -1 \end{bmatrix} \begin{matrix} R_1 - 7R_3 \\ R_2 + 8R_3 \end{matrix} \rightarrow \begin{bmatrix} 3 & 0 & 0 & 3 \\ 0 & 3 & 0 & 6 \\ 0 & 0 & 1 & -1 \end{bmatrix}.$$

R_1 and R_2 are to be changed.
R_3 is the pivot row.

Finally, we turn all the pivots into 1s:

$$\begin{bmatrix} 3 & 0 & 0 & 3 \\ 0 & 3 & 0 & 6 \\ 0 & 0 & 1 & -1 \end{bmatrix} \begin{matrix} \frac{1}{3}R_1 \\ \frac{1}{3}R_2 \end{matrix} \rightarrow \begin{bmatrix} 1 & 0 & 0 & 1 \\ 0 & 1 & 0 & 2 \\ 0 & 0 & 1 & -1 \end{bmatrix}.$$

The matrix is now reduced to a simple form, so we translate back into equations to obtain the solution:

$$x = 1, \ y = 2, \ z = -1, \text{ or } (x, y, z) = (1, 2, -1).$$

Notice the form of the very last matrix in the example:

$$\begin{bmatrix} 1 & 0 & 0 & \# \\ 0 & 1 & 0 & \# \\ 0 & 0 & 1 & \# \end{bmatrix}.$$

The 1s are on the **(main) diagonal** of the matrix; the goal in Gauss-Jordan reduction is to reduce our matrix to this form. If we can do so, then we can easily read off the solution, as we saw in Example 1. However, as we will see in several examples in this section, it is not always possible to achieve this ideal state. After Example 6, we will give a form that is always possible to achieve.

EXAMPLE 2   Solving a System by Gauss-Jordan Reduction

Solve the system:

$$2x + \ y + 3z = 1$$
$$4x + 2y + 4z = 4$$
$$x + 2y + \ z = 4.$$

Solution

$$\begin{bmatrix} \boxed{2} & 1 & 3 & 1 \\ 4 & 2 & 4 & 4 \\ 1 & 2 & 1 & 4 \end{bmatrix} \begin{matrix} \\ R_2 - 2R_1 \\ 2R_3 - R_1 \end{matrix} \rightarrow \begin{bmatrix} 2 & 1 & 3 & 1 \\ 0 & 0 & -2 & 2 \\ 0 & 3 & -1 & 7 \end{bmatrix}$$

Now we have a slight problem: The number in the position where we would like to have a pivot—the second column of the second row—is a zero and thus cannot be a pivot. There are two ways out of this problem. One is to move on to the third column and pivot on the -2. Another is to switch the order of the second and third rows so that we can use the 3 as a pivot. We will do the latter.

$$\begin{bmatrix} 2 & 1 & 3 & 1 \\ 0 & 0 & -2 & 2 \\ 0 & 3 & -1 & 7 \end{bmatrix} \begin{matrix} \\ \\ R_2 \leftrightarrow R_3 \end{matrix} \rightarrow \begin{bmatrix} 2 & 1 & 3 & 1 \\ 0 & \boxed{3} & -1 & 7 \\ 0 & 0 & -2 & 2 \end{bmatrix} \begin{matrix} 3R_1 - R_2 \\ \\ \end{matrix}$$

$$\rightarrow \begin{bmatrix} 6 & 0 & 10 & -4 \\ 0 & 3 & -1 & 7 \\ 0 & 0 & -2 & 2 \end{bmatrix} \begin{matrix} \\ \\ -\frac{1}{2}R_3 \end{matrix} \rightarrow \begin{bmatrix} 6 & 0 & 10 & -4 \\ 0 & 3 & -1 & 7 \\ 0 & 0 & \boxed{1} & -1 \end{bmatrix} \begin{matrix} R_1 - 10R_3 \\ R_2 + R_3 \\ \end{matrix}$$

$$\rightarrow \begin{bmatrix} 6 & 0 & 0 & 6 \\ 0 & 3 & 0 & 6 \\ 0 & 0 & 1 & -1 \end{bmatrix} \begin{matrix} \frac{1}{6}R_1 \\ \frac{1}{3}R_2 \\ \end{matrix} \rightarrow \begin{bmatrix} 1 & 0 & 0 & 1 \\ 0 & 1 & 0 & 2 \\ 0 & 0 & 1 & -1 \end{bmatrix}$$

Thus, the solution is $(x, y, z) = (1, 2, -1)$, as you can check in the original system.

EXAMPLE 3 Inconsistent System

Solve the system:

$$\begin{aligned} x + y + z &= 1 \\ 2x - y + z &= 0 \\ 4x + y + 3z &= 3. \end{aligned}$$

Solution

$$\begin{bmatrix} \boxed{1} & 1 & 1 & 1 \\ 2 & -1 & 1 & 0 \\ 4 & 1 & 3 & 3 \end{bmatrix} \begin{matrix} \\ R_2 - 2R_1 \\ R_3 - 4R_1 \end{matrix} \rightarrow \begin{bmatrix} 1 & 1 & 1 & 1 \\ 0 & \boxed{-3} & -1 & -2 \\ 0 & -3 & -1 & -1 \end{bmatrix} \begin{matrix} 3R_1 + R_2 \\ \\ R_3 - R_2 \end{matrix}$$

$$\rightarrow \begin{bmatrix} 3 & 0 & 2 & 1 \\ 0 & -3 & -1 & -2 \\ 0 & 0 & 0 & 1 \end{bmatrix}$$

Stop. That last row translates into $0 = 1$, which is nonsense, and so, as in Example 3 in Section 3.1, we can say that this system has no solution. We also say, as we did for systems with only two unknowns, that a system with no solution is **inconsistent**. A system with at least one solution is **consistent**.

➡ **Before we go on...**

Q: *How, exactly, does the nonsensical equation $0 = 1$ tell us that there is no solution of the system in Example 3?*

A: Here is an argument similar to that in Example 3 in Section 3.1: If there *were* three numbers x, y, and z satisfying the original system of equations, then manipulating the equations according to the instructions in the row operations above leads us to conclude that $0 = 1$. Because 0 is *not* equal to 1, there can be no such numbers x, y, and z. ∎

EXAMPLE 4 Infinitely Many Solutions

Solve the system:

$$\begin{aligned} x + y + z &= 1 \\ \frac{1}{4}x - \frac{1}{2}y + \frac{3}{4}z &= 0 \\ x + 7y - 3z &= 3. \end{aligned}$$

Solution

$$\begin{bmatrix} 1 & 1 & 1 & 1 \\ \frac{1}{4} & -\frac{1}{2} & \frac{3}{4} & 0 \\ 1 & 7 & -3 & 3 \end{bmatrix} \begin{matrix} \\ 4R_2 \\ \\ \end{matrix} \rightarrow \begin{bmatrix} \boxed{1} & 1 & 1 & 1 \\ 1 & -2 & 3 & 0 \\ 1 & 7 & -3 & 3 \end{bmatrix} \begin{matrix} \\ R_2 - R_1 \\ R_3 - R_1 \end{matrix}$$

$$\rightarrow \begin{bmatrix} 1 & 1 & 1 & 1 \\ 0 & -3 & 2 & -1 \\ 0 & 6 & -4 & 2 \end{bmatrix} \begin{matrix} \\ \\ \frac{1}{2}R_3 \end{matrix} \rightarrow \begin{bmatrix} 1 & 1 & 1 & 1 \\ 0 & \boxed{-3} & 2 & -1 \\ 0 & 3 & -2 & 1 \end{bmatrix} \begin{matrix} 3R_1 + R_2 \\ \\ R_3 + R_2 \end{matrix}$$

$$\rightarrow \begin{bmatrix} 3 & 0 & 5 & 2 \\ 0 & -3 & 2 & -1 \\ 0 & 0 & 0 & 0 \end{bmatrix}$$

There are no nonzero entries in the third row, so there can be no pivot in the third row. We skip to the final step and turn the pivots we did find into 1s.

$$\begin{bmatrix} 3 & 0 & 5 & 2 \\ 0 & -3 & 2 & -1 \\ 0 & 0 & 0 & 0 \end{bmatrix} \begin{matrix} \frac{1}{3}R_1 \\ -\frac{1}{3}R_2 \\ \end{matrix} \rightarrow \begin{bmatrix} 1 & 0 & \frac{5}{3} & \frac{2}{3} \\ 0 & 1 & -\frac{2}{3} & \frac{1}{3} \\ 0 & 0 & 0 & 0 \end{bmatrix}$$

Now we translate back into equations and obtain:

$$x \;\;\;\; + \tfrac{5}{3}z = \tfrac{2}{3}$$
$$y - \tfrac{2}{3}z = \tfrac{1}{3}$$
$$0 = 0.$$

But how does this help us find a solution? The last equation doesn't tell us anything useful, so we ignore it. The thing to notice about the other equations is that we can easily solve the first equation for x and the second for y, obtaining

$$x = \tfrac{2}{3} - \tfrac{5}{3}z$$
$$y = \tfrac{1}{3} + \tfrac{2}{3}z.$$

This is the solution! We can choose z to be any number and get corresponding values for x and y from the formulas above. This gives us infinitely many different solutions. Thus, the general solution (see Example 4 in Section 3.1) is

$$x = \tfrac{2}{3} - \tfrac{5}{3}z$$
$$y = \tfrac{1}{3} + \tfrac{2}{3}z \qquad\qquad\qquad \text{General solution}$$
$$z \text{ is arbitrary.}$$

We can also write the general solution as

$$\left(\tfrac{2}{3} - \tfrac{5}{3}z, \tfrac{1}{3} + \tfrac{2}{3}z, z\right) z \text{ arbitrary.} \qquad\qquad \text{General solution}$$

This general solution has z as the parameter. Specific choices of values for the parameter z give particular solutions. For example, the choice $z = 6$ gives the particular solution

$$x = \tfrac{2}{3} - \tfrac{5}{3}(6) = -\tfrac{28}{3}$$
$$y = \tfrac{1}{3} + \tfrac{2}{3}(6) = \tfrac{13}{3} \qquad\qquad\qquad \text{Particular solution}$$
$$z = 6,$$

while the choice $z = 0$ gives the particular solution $(x, \; y, \; z) = \left(\tfrac{2}{3}, \tfrac{1}{3}, 0\right)$.

Note that, unlike the system given in the preceding example, the system given in this example does have solutions, and is thus *consistent*.

➡ **Before we go on...** Why were there infinitely many solutions to Example 4? The reason is that the third equation was really a combination of the first and second equations to begin with, so we effectively had only two equations in three unknowns.* Choosing a specific value for z (say, $z = 6$) has the effect of supplying the "missing" equation. ∎

✱ In fact, you can check that the third equation, E_3, is equal to $3E_1 - 8E_2$. Thus, the third equation could have been left out because it conveys no more information than the first two. The process of row reduction always eliminates such a redundancy by creating a row of zeros.

Q : *How do we know when there are infinitely many solutions?*

A : When there are solutions (we have a consistent system, unlike the one in Example 3), and when the matrix we arrive at by row reduction has fewer pivots than there are unknowns. In Example 4 we had three unknowns but only two pivots.

Q : *How do we know which variables to use as parameters in a parameterized solution?*

A : The variables to use as parameters are those in the columns without pivots. In Example 4 there were pivots in the x and y columns, but no pivot in the z column, and it was z that we used as a parameter.

EXAMPLE 5 Four Unknowns

Solve the system:

$$
\begin{aligned}
x + 3y + 2z - \quad w &= 6 \\
2x + 6y + 6z + \quad 3w &= 16 \\
x + 3y - 2z - 11w &= -2 \\
2x + 6y + 8z + \quad 8w &= 20.
\end{aligned}
$$

Solution

$$
\begin{bmatrix}
\boxed{1} & 3 & 2 & -1 & 6 \\
2 & 6 & 6 & 3 & 16 \\
1 & 3 & -2 & -11 & -2 \\
2 & 6 & 8 & 8 & 20
\end{bmatrix}
\begin{matrix}
\\ R_2 - 2R_1 \\ R_3 - R_1 \\ R_4 - 2R_1
\end{matrix}
\rightarrow
\begin{bmatrix}
1 & 3 & 2 & -1 & 6 \\
0 & 0 & 2 & 5 & 4 \\
0 & 0 & -4 & -10 & -8 \\
0 & 0 & 4 & 10 & 8
\end{bmatrix}
$$

There is no pivot available in the second column, so we move on to the third column.

$$
\begin{bmatrix}
1 & 3 & 2 & -1 & 6 \\
0 & 0 & \boxed{2} & 5 & 4 \\
0 & 0 & -4 & -10 & -8 \\
0 & 0 & 4 & 10 & 8
\end{bmatrix}
\begin{matrix}
R_1 - R_2 \\ \\ R_3 + 2R_2 \\ R_4 - 2R_2
\end{matrix}
\rightarrow
\begin{bmatrix}
1 & 3 & 0 & -6 & 2 \\
0 & 0 & 2 & 5 & 4 \\
0 & 0 & 0 & 0 & 0 \\
0 & 0 & 0 & 0 & 0
\end{bmatrix}
\begin{matrix}
\\ \frac{1}{2}R_2 \\ \\ \\
\end{matrix}
$$

$$
\rightarrow
\begin{bmatrix}
1 & 3 & 0 & -6 & 2 \\
0 & 0 & 1 & \frac{5}{2} & 2 \\
0 & 0 & 0 & 0 & 0 \\
0 & 0 & 0 & 0 & 0
\end{bmatrix}
$$

Translating back into equations, we get:

$$
\begin{aligned}
x + 3y - 6w &= 2 \\
z + \tfrac{5}{2}w &= 2.
\end{aligned}
$$

(We have not written down the equations corresponding to the last two rows, each of which is $0 = 0$.) There are no pivots in the y or w columns, so we use these two variables as parameters. We bring them over to the right-hand sides of the equations above and write the general solution as

$$x = 2 - 3y + 6w$$

y is arbitrary

$$z = 2 - \tfrac{5}{2}w$$

w is arbitrary

or

$$(x, y, z, w) = (2 - 3y + 6w, y, 2 - 5w/2, w) \ y, w \text{ arbitrary}.$$

➡ **Before we go on...** In Examples 4 and 5, you might have noticed an interesting phenomenon: If at any time in the process, two rows are equal or one is a multiple of the other, then one of those rows (eventually) becomes all zero. ■

Up to this point, we have always been given as many equations as there are unknowns. However, we shall see in the next section that some applications lead to systems where the number of equations is not the same as the number of unknowns. As the following example illustrates, such systems can be handled the same way as any other.

EXAMPLE 6 Number of Equations ≠ Number of Unknowns

Solve the system:

$$
\begin{aligned}
x + \ y &= 1 \\
13x - 26y &= -11 \\
26x - 13y &= 2.
\end{aligned}
$$

Solution We proceed exactly as before and ignore the fact that there is one more equation than unknown.

$$
\begin{bmatrix}
\boxed{1} & 1 & 1 \\
13 & -26 & -11 \\
26 & -13 & 2
\end{bmatrix}
\begin{matrix}
 \\
R_2 - 13R_1 \\
R_3 - 26R_1
\end{matrix}
\rightarrow
\begin{bmatrix}
1 & 1 & 1 \\
0 & -39 & -24 \\
0 & -39 & -24
\end{bmatrix}
\begin{matrix}
 \\
\tfrac{1}{3}R_2 \\
\tfrac{1}{3}R_3
\end{matrix}
$$

$$
\rightarrow
\begin{bmatrix}
1 & 1 & 1 \\
0 & \boxed{-13} & -8 \\
0 & -13 & -8
\end{bmatrix}
\begin{matrix}
13R_1 + R_2 \\
 \\
R_3 - R_2
\end{matrix}
\rightarrow
\begin{bmatrix}
13 & 0 & 5 \\
0 & -13 & -8 \\
0 & 0 & 0
\end{bmatrix}
\begin{matrix}
\tfrac{1}{13}R_1 \\
-\tfrac{1}{13}R_2 \\

\end{matrix}
$$

$$
\rightarrow
\begin{bmatrix}
1 & 0 & \tfrac{5}{13} \\
0 & 1 & \tfrac{8}{13} \\
0 & 0 & 0
\end{bmatrix}
$$

Thus, the solution is $(x, y) = \left(\tfrac{5}{13}, \tfrac{8}{13}\right)$.

If, instead of a row of zeros, we had obtained, say, [0 0 6] in the last row, we would immediately have concluded that the system was inconsistent.

The fact that we wound up with a row of zeros indicates that one of the equations was actually a combination of the other two; you can check that the third equation can be obtained by multiplying the first equation by 13 and adding the result to the second. Because the third equation therefore tells us nothing that we don't already know from the first two, we call the system of equations **redundant**, or **dependent.** (Compare Example 4 in Section 3.1.)

➡ **Before we go on...** Example 5 above is another example of a redundant system; we could have started with the following smaller system of two equations in four unknowns

$$x + 3y + 2z - w = 6$$
$$2x + 6y + 6z + 3w = 16$$

and obtained the same general solution as we did with the larger system. Verify this by solving the smaller system. ∎

The preceding examples illustrated that we cannot always reduce a matrix to the form shown before Example 2, with pivots going all the way down the diagonal. What we *can* always do is reduce a matrix to the following form:

Reduced Row Echelon Form

A matrix is said to be in **reduced row echelon form** or to be **row-reduced** if it satisfies the following properties.

P1. The first nonzero entry in each row (called the **leading entry** of that row) is a 1.

P2. The columns of the leading entries are **clear** (i.e., they contain zeros in all positions other than that of the leading entry).

P3. The leading entry in each row is to the right of the leading entry in the row above, and any rows of zeros are at the bottom.

Quick Examples

$$\begin{bmatrix} 1 & 0 & 0 & 2 \\ 0 & 1 & 0 & 4 \\ 0 & 0 & 1 & -3 \end{bmatrix}, \begin{bmatrix} 0 & 1 & -3 \\ 0 & 0 & 0 \end{bmatrix}, \text{ and } \begin{bmatrix} 1 & 0 & 0 & -2 \\ 0 & 0 & 1 & 4 \\ 0 & 0 & 0 & 0 \end{bmatrix} \text{ are row-reduced.}$$

$$\begin{bmatrix} 1 & 1 & 0 & 2 \\ 0 & 1 & 0 & 4 \\ 0 & 0 & 1 & -3 \end{bmatrix}, \begin{bmatrix} 0 & 1 & -3 \\ 0 & 0 & 1 \end{bmatrix}, \text{ and } \begin{bmatrix} 0 & 0 & 1 & 4 \\ 1 & 0 & 0 & -2 \\ 0 & 0 & 0 & 0 \end{bmatrix} \text{ are not row-reduced.}$$

You should check in the examples we did that the final matrices were all in reduced row echelon form.

It is an interesting and useful fact, though not easy to prove, that any two people who start with the same matrix and row-reduce it will reach exactly the same row-reduced matrix, even if they use different row operations.

The Traditional Gauss-Jordan Method (Optional)

In the version of the Gauss-Jordan method we have presented, we eliminated fractions and decimals in the first step and then worked with integer matrices, partly to make hand computation easier and partly for mathematical elegance. However, complicated fractions and decimals present no difficulty when we use technology. The following example illustrates the more traditional approach to Gauss-Jordan reduction used in many of the computer programs that solve the huge systems of equations that arise in practice.*

✱ Actually, for reasons of efficiency and accuracy, the methods used in commercial programs are closer to the method presented above. To learn more, consult a text on numerical methods.

EXAMPLE 7 Solving a System with the Traditional Gauss-Jordan Method

Solve the following system using the traditional Gauss-Jordan method:

$$2x + y + 3z = 5$$
$$3x + 2y + 4z = 7$$
$$2x + y + 5z = 10.$$

Solution We make two changes in our method. First, there is no need to get rid of decimals (because computers and calculators can handle decimals as easily as they can integers). Second, after selecting a pivot, *divide the pivot row by the pivot value, turning the pivot into a* 1. It is easier to determine the row operations that will clear the pivot column if the pivot is a 1.

If we use technology to solve this system of equations, the sequence of matrices might look like this:

 using Technology

Website
www.WanerMath.com

Follow

→ Everything for Finite Math
→ Math Tools for Chapter 3

to find the following resources:
- An online Web page that pivots and does row operations automatically
- A TI-83/84 Plus program that pivots and does other row operations
- An Excel worksheet that pivots and does row operations automatically

$$\begin{bmatrix} \boxed{2} & 1 & 3 & 5 \\ 3 & 2 & 4 & 7 \\ 2 & 1 & 5 & 10 \end{bmatrix} \begin{matrix} \frac{1}{2}R_1 \\ \\ \\ \end{matrix} \rightarrow \begin{bmatrix} \boxed{1} & 0.5 & 1.5 & 2.5 \\ 3 & 2 & 4 & 7 \\ 2 & 1 & 5 & 10 \end{bmatrix} \begin{matrix} \\ R_2 - 3R_1 \\ R_3 - 2R_1 \end{matrix}$$

$$\rightarrow \begin{bmatrix} 1 & 0.5 & 1.5 & 2.5 \\ 0 & \boxed{0.5} & -0.5 & -0.5 \\ 0 & 0 & 2 & 5 \end{bmatrix} \begin{matrix} \\ 2R_2 \\ \\ \end{matrix} \rightarrow \begin{bmatrix} 1 & 0.5 & 1.5 & 2.5 \\ 0 & \boxed{1} & -1 & -1 \\ 0 & 0 & 2 & 5 \end{bmatrix} \begin{matrix} R_1 - 0.5R_2 \\ \\ \\ \end{matrix}$$

$$\rightarrow \begin{bmatrix} 1 & 0 & 2 & 3 \\ 0 & 1 & -1 & -1 \\ 0 & 0 & \boxed{2} & 5 \end{bmatrix} \begin{matrix} \\ \\ \frac{1}{2}R_3 \end{matrix} \rightarrow \begin{bmatrix} 1 & 0 & 2 & 3 \\ 0 & 1 & -1 & -1 \\ 0 & 0 & \boxed{1} & 2.5 \end{bmatrix} \begin{matrix} R_1 - 2R_3 \\ R_2 + R_3 \\ \\ \end{matrix}$$

$$\rightarrow \begin{bmatrix} 1 & 0 & 0 & -2 \\ 0 & 1 & 0 & 1.5 \\ 0 & 0 & 1 & 2.5 \end{bmatrix}.$$

The solution is $(x, y, z) = (-2, 1.5, 2.5)$.

Q: *The solution to Example 7 looked quite easy. Why didn't we use the traditional method from the start like the other textbooks?*

A: It looked easy because we deliberately chose an example that leads to simple decimals. In all but the most contrived examples, the decimals or fractions involved get very complicated very quickly.

FAQs

Getting Unstuck, Going Round in Circles, and Knowing When to Stop

Q : *Help! I have been doing row operations on this matrix for half an hour. I have filled two pages, and I am getting nowhere. What do I do?*

A : Here is a way of keeping track of where you are *at any stage of the process* and also deciding what to do next.

Starting at the top row of your current matrix:

1. Scan along the row until you get to the leading entry: the first nonzero entry. If there is none—that is, the row is all zero—go to the next row.
2. Having located the leading entry, scan up and down its *column*. If its column is not clear (that is, it contains other nonzero entries), use your leading entry as a pivot to clear its column as in the examples in this section.
3. Now go to the next row and start again at Step 1.

When you have scanned all the rows and find that all the columns of the leading entries are clear, it means you are done (except possibly for reordering the rows so that the leading entries go from left to right as you read down the matrix, and zero rows are at the bottom).

Q : *No good. I have been following these instructions, but every time I try to clear a column, I unclear a column I had already cleared. What is going on?*

A : Are you using *leading entries* as pivots? Also, are you *using the pivot* to clear its column? That is, are your row operations all of the following form?

$$aR_c \pm bR_p$$

$$\uparrow \qquad \uparrow$$

Row to change   Pivot row

The instruction next to the row you are changing should involve only that row and the pivot row, even though you might be tempted to use some other row instead.

Q : *Must I continue until I get a matrix that has 1s down the leading diagonal and 0s above and below?*

A : Not necessarily. You are completely done when your matrix is row-reduced: Each leading entry is a 1, the column of each leading entry is clear, and the leading entries go from left to right. You are done *pivoting* when the column of each leading entry is clear. After that, all that remains is to turn each pivot into a 1 (the "Final Step") and, if necessary, rearrange the rows.

3.2 EXERCISES

▼ more advanced   ◆ challenging
T indicates exercises that should be solved using technology

In Exercises 1–42, use Gauss-Jordan row reduction to solve the given systems of equation. We suggest doing some by hand, and others using technology. HINT [See Examples 1–6.]

1. $x + y = 4$
  $x - y = 2$

2. $2x + y = 2$
  $-2x + y = 2$

3. $3x - 2y = 6$
  $2x - 3y = -6$

4. $2x + 3y = 5$
  $3x + 2y = 5$

5. $2x + 3y = 1$
  $-x - \dfrac{3y}{2} = -\dfrac{1}{2}$

6. $2x - 3y = 1$
  $6x - 9y = 3$

7. $2x + 3y = 2$

$-x - \dfrac{3y}{2} = -\dfrac{1}{2}$

8. $2x - 3y = 2$

$6x - 9y = 3$

9. $x + y = 1$

$3x - y = 0$

$x - 3y = -2$

10. $x + y = 1$

$3x - 2y = -1$

$5x - y = \dfrac{1}{5}$

11. $x + y = 0$

$3x - y = 1$

$x - y = -1$

12. $x + 2y = 1$

$3x - 2y = -2$

$5x - y = \dfrac{1}{5}$

13. $0.5x + 0.1y = 1.7$

$0.1x - 0.1y = 0.3$

$x + y = \dfrac{11}{3}$

14. $-0.3x + 0.5y = 0.1$

$x - y = 4$

$\dfrac{x}{17} + \dfrac{y}{17} = 1$

15. $-x + 2y - z = 0$

$-x - y + 2z = 0$

$2x \qquad - z = 4$

16. $x + 2y \qquad = 4$

$y - z = 0$

$x + 3y - 2z = 5$

17. $x + y + 6z = -1$

$\dfrac{1}{3}x - \dfrac{1}{3}y + \dfrac{2}{3}z = 1$

$\dfrac{1}{2}x \qquad + z = 0$

18. $x - \dfrac{1}{2}y \qquad = 0$

$\dfrac{1}{3}x + \dfrac{1}{3}y + \dfrac{1}{3}z = 2$

$\dfrac{1}{2}x \qquad - \dfrac{1}{2}z = -1$

19. $-\dfrac{1}{2}x + y - \dfrac{1}{2}z = 0$

$-\dfrac{1}{2}x - \dfrac{1}{2}y + z = 0$

$x - \dfrac{1}{2}y - \dfrac{1}{2}z = 0$

20. $x - \dfrac{1}{2}y \qquad = 0$

$\dfrac{1}{2}x - \dfrac{1}{2}z = -1$

$3x - y - z = -2$

21. $x + y + 2z = -1$

$2x + 2y + 2z = 2$

$\dfrac{3}{5}x + \dfrac{3}{5}y + \dfrac{3}{5}z = \dfrac{2}{5}$

22. $x + y - z = -2$

$x - y - 7z = 0$

$\dfrac{2}{7}x \qquad - \dfrac{8}{7}z = 14$

23. $-0.5x + 0.5y + 0.5z = 1.5$

$4.2x + 2.1y + 2.1z = 0$

$0.2x \qquad + 0.2z = 0$

24. $0.25x - 0.5y \qquad = 0$

$0.2x + 0.2y - 0.2z = -0.6$

$0.5x - 1.5y + z = 0.5$

25. $2x - y + z = 4$

$3x - y + z = 5$

26. $3x - y - z = 0$

$x + y + z = 4$

27. $0.75x - 0.75y - z = 4$

$x - y + 4z = 0$

28. $2x - y + z = 4$

$-x + 0.5y - 0.5z = 1.5$

29. ▼ $3x + y - z = 12$

30. ▼ $x + y - 3z = 21$

(Yes: One equation in three unknowns!)

31. ▼ $\quad x + \quad y + 2z = -1$

$2x + \quad 2y + 2z = 2$

$0.75x + 0.75y + \quad z = 0.25$

$-x \qquad - 2z = 21$

32. ▼ $\quad x + \quad y - \quad z = -2$

$x - \quad y - \quad 7z = 0$

$0.75x - 0.5y + 0.25z = 14$

$x + \quad y + \quad z = 4$

33. ▼ $x + y + 5z \qquad = 1$

$y + 2z + w = 1$

$x + 3y + 7z + 2w = 2$

$x + y + 5z + w = 1$

34. ▼ $x + y \qquad + 4w = 1$

$2x - 2y - 3z + 2w = -1$

$4y + 6z + w = 4$

$2x + 4y + 9z \qquad = 6$

35. ▼ $x + y + 5z \qquad = 1$

$y + 2z + w = 1$

$x + y + 5z + w = 1$

$x + 2y + 7z + 2w = 2$

36. ▼ $x + y + \qquad 4w = 1$

$2x - 2y - 3z + 2w = -1$

$4y + 6z + w = 4$

$3x + 3y + 3z + 7w = 4$

37. ▼ $x - 2y + z - 4w = 1$

$x + 3y + 7z + 2w = 2$

$2x + y + 8z - 2w = 3$

38. ▼ $x - 3y - 2z - w = 1$

$x + 3y + z + 2w = 2$

$2x \qquad - z + w = 3$

39. ▼ $x + y + z + u + v = 15$

$y - z + u - v = -2$

$z + u + v = 12$

$u - v = -1$

$v = 5$

40. ▼ $x - y + z - u + v = 1$

$y + z + u + v = 2$

$z - u + v = 1$

$u + v = 1$

$v = 1$

41. ▼ $x - y + z - u + v = 0$

$y - z + u - v = -2$

$x \qquad - 2v = -2$

$2x - y + z - u - 3v = -2$

$4x - y + z - u - 7v = -6$

42. ▼ $x + y + z + u + v = 15$

$y + z + u + v = 3$

$x + 2y + 2z + 2u + 2v = 18$

$x - y - z - u - v = 9$

$x - 2y - 2z - 2u - 2v = 6$

T *In Exercises 43–46, use technology to solve the systems of equations. Express all solutions as fractions.*

43. $\begin{aligned} x + 2y - z + w &= 30 \\ 2x \quad\quad - z + 2w &= 30 \\ x + 3y + 3z - 4w &= 2 \\ 2x - 9y \quad\quad + w &= 4 \end{aligned}$

44. $\begin{aligned} 4x - 2y + z + w &= 20 \\ 3y + 3z - 4w &= 2 \\ 2x + 4y \quad\quad - w &= 4 \\ x + 3y + 3z \quad &= 2 \end{aligned}$

45. $\begin{aligned} x + 2y + 3z + 4w + 5t &= 6 \\ 2x + 3y + 4z + 5w + t &= 5 \\ 3x + 4y + 5z + w + 2t &= 4 \\ 4x + 5y + z + 2w + 3t &= 3 \\ 5x + y + 2z + 3w + 4t &= 2 \end{aligned}$

46. $\begin{aligned} x - 2y + 3z - 4w \quad &= 0 \\ -2x + 3y - 4z + \quad t &= 0 \\ 3x - 4y \quad + w - 2t &= 0 \\ -4x \quad + z - 2w + 3t &= 0 \\ y - 2z + 3w - 4t &= 1 \end{aligned}$

T *In Exercises 47–50, use technology to solve the systems of equations. Express all solutions as decimals, rounded to one decimal place.*

47. $\begin{aligned} 1.6x + 2.4y - 3.2z &= 4.4 \\ 5.1x - 6.3y + 0.6z &= -3.2 \\ 4.2x + 3.5y + 4.9z &= 10.1 \end{aligned}$

48. $\begin{aligned} 2.1x + 0.7y - 1.4z &= -2.3 \\ 3.5x - 4.2y - 4.9z &= 3.3 \\ 1.1x + 2.2y - 3.3z &= -10.2 \end{aligned}$

49. $\begin{aligned} -0.2x + 0.3y + 0.4z - \quad t &= 4.5 \\ 2.2x + 1.1y - 4.7z + 2t &= 8.3 \\ 9.2y \quad\quad - 1.3t &= 0 \\ 3.4x \quad + 0.5z - 3.4t &= 0.1 \end{aligned}$

50. $\begin{aligned} 1.2x - 0.3y + 0.4z - 2t &= 4.5 \\ 1.9x \quad\quad - 0.5z - 3.4t &= 0.2 \\ 12.1y \quad\quad - 1.3t &= 0 \\ 3x + 2y - 1.1z \quad &= 9 \end{aligned}$

COMMUNICATION AND REASONING EXERCISES

51. What is meant by a pivot? What does pivoting do?

52. Give instructions to check whether or not a matrix is row-reduced.

53. You are row-reducing a matrix and have chosen a -6 as a pivot in Row 4. Directly above the pivot, in Row 1, is a 15. What row operation can you use to clear the 15?

54. You are row-reducing a matrix and have chosen a -4 as a pivot in Row 2. Directly below the pivot, in Row 4, is a -6. What row operation can you use to clear the -6?

55. In the matrix of a system of linear equations, suppose that two of the rows are equal. What can you say about the row-reduced form of the matrix?

56. In the matrix of a system of linear equations, suppose that one of the rows is a multiple of another. What can you say about the row-reduced form of the matrix?

57. ▼ Your friend Frans tells you that the system of linear equations you are solving cannot have a unique solution because the reduced matrix has a row of zeros. Comment on his claim.

58. ▼ Your other friend Hans tells you that because he is solving a consistent system of five linear equations in six unknowns, he will get infinitely many solutions. Comment on his claim.

59. ▼ If the reduced matrix of a consistent system of linear equations has five rows, three of which are zero, and five columns, how many parameters does the general solution contain?

60. ▼ If the reduced matrix of a consistent system of linear equations has five rows, two of which are zero, and seven columns, how many parameters does the general solution contain?

61. ▼ Suppose a system of equations has a unique solution. What must be true of the number of pivots in the reduced matrix of the system? Why?

62. ▼ Suppose a system has infinitely many solutions. What must be true of the number of pivots in the reduced matrix of the system? Why?

63. ▼ Give an example of a system of three linear equations with the general solution $x = 1$, $y = 1 + z$, z arbitrary. (Check your system by solving it.)

64. ▼ Give an example of a system of three linear equations with the general solution $x = y - 1$, y arbitrary, $z = y$. (Check your system by solving it.)

65. ◆ A system of linear equations is called **homogeneous** if the right-hand side of each equation in the system is 0. If a homogeneous system has a unique solution, what can you say about that solution? Why?

66. ◆ A certain homogeneous system of linear equations in three unknowns (see the preceding exercise) has a solution $(1, 2, 0)$. Is this solution unique? Explain.

67. ◆ Can a homogeneous system (see Exercise 65) of linear equations be inconsistent? Explain.

68. ◆ Can a non-homogeneous system (see Exercise 65) of linear equations have the zero solution? Explain.

Applications of Systems of Linear Equations

> ✱ See the discussion at the end of the first example below.

In the examples and the exercises of this section, we consider scenarios that lead to systems of linear equations in three or more unknowns. Some of these applications will strike you as a little idealized or even contrived compared with the kinds of problems you might encounter in the real world.✱ One reason is that we will not have tools to handle more realistic versions of these applications until we have studied linear programming in Chapter 5.

In each example that follows, we set up the problem as a linear system and then give the solution; the emphasis in this section is on modeling a scenario by a system of linear equations and then interpreting the solution that results, rather than on obtaining the solution. For practice, you should do the row reduction necessary to get the solution.

EXAMPLE 1 Resource Allocation

The Arctic Juice Company makes three juice blends: PineOrange, using 2 quarts of pineapple juice and 2 quarts of orange juice per gallon; PineKiwi, using 3 quarts of pineapple juice and 1 quart of kiwi juice per gallon; and OrangeKiwi, using 3 quarts of orange juice and 1 quart of kiwi juice per gallon. Each day the company has 800 quarts of pineapple juice, 650 quarts of orange juice, and 350 quarts of kiwi juice available. How many gallons of each blend should it make each day if it wants to use up all of the supplies?

Solution We take the same steps to understand the problem that we took in Section 3.1. The first step is to identify and label the unknowns. Looking at the question asked in the last sentence, we see that we should label the unknowns like this:

x = number of gallons of PineOrange made each day

y = number of gallons of PineKiwi made each day

z = number of gallons of OrangeKiwi made each day.

Next, we can organize the information we are given in a table:

	PineOrange (x)	*PineKiwi (y)*	*OrangeKiwi (z)*	*Total Available*
Pineapple Juice (qt)	2	3	0	800
Orange Juice (qt)	2	0	3	650
Kiwi Juice (qt)	0	1	1	350

Notice how we have arranged the table; we have placed headings corresponding to the unknowns along the top, rather than down the side, and we have added a heading for the available totals. This gives us a table that is essentially the matrix of the system of linear equations we are looking for. (However, read the caution in the **Before we go on** section.)

using Technology

Website
www.WanerMath.com
Everything for Finite Math
→ Math Tools for Chapter 3
→ Pivot and Gauss-Jordan Tool

Once you have set up the system of equations, you can obtain the solution in a single step using the Pivot and Gauss-Jordan Tool at the Website:

Enter the augmented matrix of the system as shown, and press "Reduce Completely". You can then use the reduced matrix to write down the unique solution or general solution as discussed in Section 3.2.

Now we read across each row of the table. The fact that we want to use exactly the amount of each juice that is available leads to the following three equations:

$$2x + 3y \qquad = 800$$
$$2x \qquad + 3z = 650$$
$$y + z = 350.$$

The solution of this system is $(x, y, z) = (100, 200, 150)$, so Arctic Juice should make 100 gallons of PineOrange, 200 gallons of PineKiwi, and 150 gallons of OrangeKiwi each day.

➡ **Before we go on…**
Caution

We do not recommend relying on the coincidence that the table we created to organize the information in Example 1 happened to be the matrix of the system; it is too easy to set up the table "sideways" and get the wrong matrix. You should always write down the system of equations *and be sure you understand each equation*. For example, the equation $2x + 3y = 800$ in Example 1 indicates that the number of quarts of pineapple juice that will be used ($2x + 3y$) is equal to the amount available (800 quarts). By thinking of the reason for each equation, you can check that you have the correct system. If you have the wrong system of equations to begin with, solving it won't help you.

Q : *Just how realistic is the scenario in Example 1?*

A : This is a very unrealistic scenario, for several reasons:

1. Isn't it odd that we happened to end up with exactly the same number of equations as unknowns? Real scenarios are rarely so considerate. If there had been four equations, there would in all likelihood have been no solution at all. However, we need to understand these idealized problems before we can tackle the real world.

2. Even if a real-world scenario does give the same number of equations as unknowns, there is still no guarantee that there will be a unique solution consisting of positive values. What, for instance, would we have done in this example if x had turned out to be negative?

3. The requirement that we use exactly all the ingredients would be an unreasonable constraint in real life. When we discuss linear programming, we will be able to substitute the more reasonable constraint that you use no more than is available, and we will add the more reasonable objective that you maximize profit. ■

EXAMPLE 2 **Aircraft Purchases:** Airbus **and** Boeing

A new airline has recently purchased a fleet of Airbus A330-300s, Boeing 767-200ERs, and Boeing Dreamliner 787-9s to meet an estimated demand for 4,800 seats. The A330-300s seat 320 passengers and cost \$200 million each, the 767-200ERs each seat 250 passengers and cost \$125 million each, while the Dreamliner 787-9s seat 275 passengers and cost \$200 million each.[12] The total cost of the fleet, which had twice as many Dreamliners as 767s, was \$3,100 million. How many of each type of aircraft did the company purchase?

---

[12]The prices are approximate 2008 prices. Prices and seating capacities found at the companies' Web sites and in Wikipedia.

Solution We label the unknowns as follows:

$$x = \text{number of Airbus A330-300s}$$
$$y = \text{number of Boeing 767-200ERs}$$
$$z = \text{number of Boeing Dreamliner 787-9s.}$$

We must now set up the equations. We can organize some (but not all) of the given information in a table:

	A330-300	**767-200ER**	**787-9 Dreamliner**	**Total**
Capacity	320	250	275	4,800
Cost ($ million)	200	125	200	3,100

Reading across, we get the equations expressing the facts that the airline needed to seat 4,800 passengers and that it spent $3,100 million:

$$320x + 250y + 275z = 4{,}800$$
$$200x + 125y + 200z = 3{,}100.$$

There is an additional piece of information we have not yet used: the airline bought twice as many Dreamliners as 767s. As we said in Section 3.1, it is easiest to translate a statement like this into an equation if we first reword it using the phrase "the number of." Thus, we say: "The number of Dreamliners ordered was twice the number of 767s ordered," or

$$z = 2y$$
$$2y - z = 0.$$

We now have a system of three equations in three unknowns:

$$320x + 250y + 275z = 4{,}800$$
$$200x + 125y + 200z = 3{,}100$$
$$2y - \quad z = 0.$$

Solving the system, we get the solution $(x, y, z) = (5, 4, 8)$. Thus, the airline ordered five A330-300s, four 767-200ERs, and eight Dreamliner 787-9s.

EXAMPLE 3 Traffic Flow

Traffic through downtown Urbanville flows through the one-way system shown in Figure 7.

Traffic counting devices installed in the road (shown as boxes) count 200 cars entering town from the west each hour, 150 leaving town on the north each hour, and 50 leaving town on the south each hour.

a. From this information, is it possible to determine how many cars drive along Allen, Baker, and Coal streets every hour?

b. What is the maximum possible traffic flow along Baker Street?

c. What is the minimum possible traffic along Allen Street?

d. What is the maximum possible traffic flow along Coal Street?

Figure 7

Solution

a. Our unknowns are:

x = number of cars per hour on Allen Street

y = number of cars per hour on Baker Street

z = number of cars per hour on Coal Street.

Assuming that, at each intersection, cars do not fall into a pit or materialize out of thin air, the number of cars entering each intersection has to equal the number exiting. For example, at the intersection of Allen and Baker Streets there are 200 cars entering and $x + y$ cars exiting:

$$\text{Traffic in} = \text{Traffic out}$$
$$200 = x + y.$$

At the intersection of Allen and Coal Streets, we get:

$$\text{Traffic in} = \text{Traffic out}$$
$$x = z + 150$$

and at the intersection of Baker and Coal Streets, we get:

$$\text{Traffic in} = \text{Traffic out}$$
$$y + z = 50.$$

We now have the following system of equations:

$$
\begin{aligned}
x + y \quad &= 200 \\
x \quad -z &= 150 \\
y + z &= 50.
\end{aligned}
$$

If we solve this system using the methods of the preceding section, we find that it has infinitely many solutions. The general solution is:

$$
\begin{aligned}
x &= z + 150 \\
y &= -z + 50 \\
z &\text{ is arbitrary.}
\end{aligned}
$$

Because we do not have a unique solution, it is *not* possible to determine how many cars drive along Allen, Baker and Coal Streets every hour.

b. The traffic flow along Baker Street is measured by y. From the general solution,

$$y = -z + 50$$

where z is arbitrary. How arbitrary is z? It makes no sense for any of the variables x, y, or z to be negative in this scenario, so $z \geq 0$. Therefore, the largest possible value y can have is

$$y = -0 + 50 = 50 \text{ cars per hour.}$$

c. The traffic flow along Allen Street is measured by x. From the general solution,

$$x = z + 150,$$

where $z \geq 0$, as we saw in part (b). Therefore, the smallest possible value x can have is

$$x = 0 + 150 = 150 \text{ cars per hour.}$$

d. The traffic flow along Coal Street is measured by z. Referring to the general solution, we see that z shows up in the expressions for both x and y:

$$x = z + 150$$
$$y = -z + 50.$$

In the first of these equations, there is nothing preventing z from being as big as we like; the larger we make z, the larger x becomes. However, the second equation places a limit on how large z can be: If $z > 50$, then y is negative, which is impossible. Therefore, the largest value z can take is 50 cars per hour.

From the discussion above, we see that z is not completely arbitrary: We must have $z \geq 0$ and $z \leq 50$. Thus, z has to satisfy $0 \leq z \leq 50$ for us to get a realistic answer.

➡ **Before we go on...** Here are some questions to think about in Example 3: If you wanted to nail down x, y, and z to see where the cars are really going, how would you do it with only one more traffic counter? Would it make sense for z to be fractional? What if you interpreted x, y, and z as *average* numbers of cars per hour over a long period of time?

Traffic flow is only one kind of flow in which we might be interested. Water and electricity flows are others. In each case, to analyze the flow, we use the fact that the amount entering an intersection must equal the amount leaving it. ■

EXAMPLE 4 **Transportation**

A car rental company has four locations in the city: Southwest, Northeast, Southeast, and Northwest. The Northwest location has 20 more cars than it needs, and the Northeast location has 15 more cars than it needs. The Southwest location needs 10 more cars than it has, and the Southeast location needs 25 more cars than it has. It costs $10 (in salary and gas) to have an employee drive a car from Northwest to Southwest. It costs $20 to drive a car from Northwest to Southeast. It costs $5 to drive a car from Northeast to Southwest, and it costs $10 to drive a car from Northeast to Southeast. If the company will spend a total of $475 rearranging its cars, how many cars will it drive from each of Northwest and Northeast to each of Southwest and Southeast?

Solution

Figure 8 shows a diagram of this situation. Each arrow represents a route along which the rental company can drive cars. At each location is written the number of extra cars the location has or the number it needs. Along each route is written the cost of driving a car along that route.

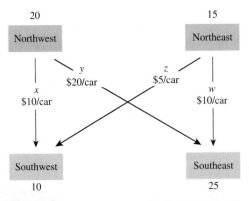

Figure 8

The unknowns are the number of cars the company will drive along each route, so we have the following four unknowns, as indicated in the figure:

$$x = \text{number of cars driven from Northwest to Southwest}$$
$$y = \text{number of cars driven from Northwest to Southeast}$$
$$z = \text{number of cars driven from Northeast to Southwest}$$
$$w = \text{number of cars driven from Northeast to Southeast.}$$

Consider the Northwest location. It has 20 more cars than it needs, so the total number of cars being driven out of Northwest should be 20. This gives us the equation

$$x + y = 20.$$

Similarly, the total number of cars being driven out of Northeast should be 15, so

$$z + w = 15.$$

Considering the number of cars needed at the Southwest and Southeast locations, we get the following two equations as well:

$$x + z = 10$$
$$y + w = 25.$$

There is one more equation that we should write down, the equation that says that the company will spend $475:

$$10x + 20y + 5z + 10w = 475.$$

Thus, we have the following system of five equations in four unknowns:

$$
\begin{aligned}
x + \quad y \qquad\qquad\qquad &= 20 \\
z + \quad w &= 15 \\
x \qquad\quad + z \qquad\qquad &= 10 \\
y \qquad + \quad w &= 25 \\
10x + 20y + 5z + 10w &= 475
\end{aligned}
$$

Solving this system, we find that $(x, y, z, w) = (5, 15, 5, 10)$. In words, the company will drive 5 cars from Northwest to Southwest, 15 from Northwest to Southeast, 5 from Northeast to Southwest, and 10 from Northeast to Southeast.

⮕ **Before we go on...** A very reasonable question to ask in Example 4 is, Can the company rearrange its cars for less than $475? Even better, what is the least possible cost? In general, a question asking for the optimal cost may require the techniques of linear programming, which we will discuss in Chapter 5. However, in this case we can approach the problem directly. If we remove the equation that says that the total cost is $475 and solve the system consisting of the other four equations, we find that there are infinitely many solutions and that the general solution may be written as

$$x = w - 5$$
$$y = 25 - w$$
$$z = 15 - w$$
$$w \text{ is arbitrary.}$$

This allows us to write the total cost as a function of w:

$$\text{Cost} = 10x + 20y + 5z + 10w = 10(w - 5) + 20(25 - w) + 5(15 - w) + 10w$$
$$= 525 - 5w.$$

So, the larger we make w, the smaller the total cost will be. The largest we can make w is 15 (why?), and if we do so we get $(x, y, z, w) = (10, 10, 0, 15)$ and a total cost of $450. ■

3.3 EXERCISES

▼ more advanced   ◆ challenging
🔟 indicates exercises that should be solved using technology

APPLICATIONS

1. *Resource Allocation* You manage an ice cream factory that makes three flavors: Creamy Vanilla, Continental Mocha, and Succulent Strawberry. Into each batch of Creamy Vanilla go 2 eggs, 1 cup of milk, and 2 cups of cream. Into each batch of Continental Mocha go 1 egg, 1 cup of milk, and 2 cups of cream, while into each batch of Succulent Strawberry go 1 egg, 2 cups of milk, and 1 cup of cream. You have in stock 350 eggs, 350 cups of milk, and 400 cups of cream. How many batches of each flavor should you make in order to use up all of your ingredients? HINT [See Example 1.]

2. *Resource Allocation* You own a hamburger franchise and are planning to shut down operations for the day, but you are left with 13 bread rolls, 19 defrosted beef patties, and 15 opened cheese slices. Rather than throw them out, you decide to use them to make burgers that you will sell at a discount. Plain burgers each require 1 beef patty and 1 bread roll, double cheeseburgers each require 2 beef patties, 1 bread roll, and 2 slices of cheese, while regular cheeseburgers each require 1 beef patty, 1 bread roll, and 1 slice of cheese. How many of each should you make? HINT [See Example 1.]

3. *Resource Allocation* Urban Community College is planning to offer courses in Finite Math, Applied Calculus, and Computer Methods. Each section of Finite Math has 40 students and earns the college $40,000 in revenue. Each section of Applied Calculus has 40 students and earns the college $60,000, while each section of Computer Methods has 10 students and earns the college $20,000. Assuming the college wishes to offer a total of six sections, to accommodate 210 students, and to bring in $260,000 in revenues, how many sections of each course should it offer? HINT [See Example 2.]

4. *Resource Allocation* The Enormous State University History Department offers three courses, Ancient, Medieval, and Modern History, and the chairperson is trying to decide how many sections of each to offer this semester. The department is allowed to offer 45 sections total, there are 5,000 students who would like to take a course, and there are 60 professors to teach them. Sections of Ancient History have 100 students each, sections of Medieval History hold 50 students each, and sections of Modern History have 200 students each. Modern History sections are taught by a team of 2 professors, while Ancient and Medieval History need only 1 professor per section. How many sections of each course should the chair schedule in order to offer all the sections that they are allowed to, accommodate all of the students, and give one teaching assignment to each professor? HINT [See Example 2.]

5. *Latin Music Sales (Digital)* In 2010, total revenues from digital sales of regional (Mexican/Tejano), pop/rock, and tropical (salsa/merengue/cumbia/bachata) Latin music in the U.S. amounted to $46 million. Regional music brought in fives times as much as tropical music and $9 million more than pop/rock music.[13] How much revenue was earned from digital sales in each of the three categories?

6. *Latin Music Sales (Digital)* In 2009, total revenues from digital sales of pop/rock, tropical (salsa/merengue/cumbia/bachata), and urban (reggaeton) Latin music in the U.S. amounted to $28 million. Tropical music brought in twice as much as urban music, and pop/rock music brought in $10 million more than the others combined.[14] How much revenue was earned from digital sales in each of the three categories?

7. *Purchasing Aircraft* In Example 2 we saw that Airbus A330-300s seat 320 passengers and cost $200 million each, Boeing 767-200ERs seat 250 passengers and cost $125 million each, while Boeing Dreamliner 787-9s seat 275 passengers and cost $200 million each. You are the purchasing manager of an airline company and have a spending goal of $2,900 million for the purchase of new aircraft to seat a total of 4,480 passengers. Your company has a policy of supporting U.S. industries, and you have been instructed to buy twice as many Dreamliners as Airbus A330-300s. Given the selection of three aircraft, how many of each should you order?

8. *Purchasing Aircraft* Refer to Exercise 7. René DuFleur has just been appointed the new CEO of your airline, and you

---

[13]Revenues are based on suggested list prices, and rounded to the nearest $1 million. Source: Recording Industry Association of America http://riaa.org
[14]*Ibid.*

have received instructions that the company policy is now to purchase 25% more Airbus A330-300s than Boeing 767-200ERs (that is, 1.25 times as many Airbus A330-300s as 767-200ERs). Further, the desired seating capacity has been revised downward to 2,600 passengers, and the cost target to $1,500 million. Given the selection of three aircraft, how many of each should you order?

9. *Supply* A bagel store orders cream cheese from three suppliers, Cheesy Cream Corp. (CCC), Super Smooth & Sons (SSS), and Bagel's Best Friend Co. (BBF). One month, the total order of cheese came to 100 tons (they do a booming trade). The costs were $80, $50, and $65 per ton from the three suppliers, respectively, with total cost amounting to $5,990. Given that the store ordered the same amount from CCC and BBF, how many tons of cream cheese were ordered from each supplier?

10. *Supply* Refer to Exercise 9. The bagel store's outlay for cream cheese the following month was $2,310, when it purchased a total of 36 tons. Two more tons of cream cheese came from Bagel's Best Friend Co. than from Super Smooth & Sons. How many tons of cream cheese came from each supplier?

11. *Pest Control* Aragorn the Great has boasted to his hordes of followers that many a notorious villain has fallen to his awesome sword: His total of 560 victims consists of evil sorcerers, trolls, and orcs. These he has slain with a total of 620 mighty thrusts of his sword; evil sorcerers and trolls each requiring two thrusts (to the chest) and orcs each requiring one thrust (to the neck). When asked about the number of trolls he has slain, he replies, "I, the mighty Aragorn, despise trolls five times as much as I despise evil sorcerers. Accordingly, five times as many trolls as evil sorcerers have fallen to my sword!" How many of each type of villain has he slain?

12. *Manufacturing Perfume* The Fancy French Perfume Company recently had its secret formula divulged. It turned out that it was using, as the three ingredients, rose oil, oil of fermented prunes, and alcohol. Moreover, each 22-ounce econo-size bottle contained 4 more ounces of alcohol than oil of fermented prunes, while the amount of alcohol was equal to the combined volume of the other two ingredients. How much of each ingredient did it use in an econo-size bottle?[15]
HINT [The answer is the brand-name of a famous eau de cologne.]

13. ▼ *Donations* The Enormous State University Good Works Society recently raised funds for three worthwhile causes: the Math Professors' Benevolent Fund (MPBF), the Society of Computer Nerds (SCN), and the NY Jets. Because the society's members are closet jocks, the society donated twice as much to the NY Jets as to the MPBF, and equal amounts to the first two funds (it is unable to distinguish between mathematicians and nerds). Further, for every $1 it gave to the MPBF, it decided to keep $1 for itself; for every $1 it gave to the SCN, it kept $2, and for every $1 to the Jets, it also kept $2. The treasurer of the Society, Johnny Treasure, was required to itemize all donations for the Dean of Students, but discovered to his consternation that he had lost

the receipts! The only information available to him was that the society's bank account had swelled by $4,200. How much did the society donate to each cause?

14. ▼ *Tenure* Professor Walt is up for tenure, and wishes to submit a portfolio of written student evaluations as evidence of his good teaching. He begins by grouping all the evaluations into four categories: good reviews, bad reviews (a typical one being "GET RID OF WALT! THE MAN CAN'T TEACH!"), mediocre reviews (such as "I suppose he's OK, given the general quality of teaching at this college"), and reviews left blank. When he tallies up the piles, Walt gets a little worried: There are 280 more bad reviews than good ones and only half as many blank reviews as bad ones. The good reviews and blank reviews together total 170. On an impulse, he decides to even up the piles a little by removing 280 of the bad reviews, and this leaves him with a total of 400 reviews of all types. How many of each category of reviews were there originally?

🔲 *Airline Costs* *Exercises 15 and 16 are based on the following table, which shows the amount spent by four U.S. airlines to fly one available seat one mile in the second quarter of 2011.*[16] *Set up each system and then solve using technology.*
HINT [See the technology note accompanying Example 1.]

Airline	American	Continental	Delta	Southwest
Cost	13.1¢	13.0¢	14.4¢	12.5¢

15. ▼ Suppose that, on a 3,000-mile New York–Los Angeles flight, Continental, American, and Southwest flew a total of 210 empty seats, costing them a total of $81,270. If Continental had three times as many empty seats as American, how many empty seats did each of these three airlines carry on its flight?

16. ▼ Suppose that, on a 2,000-mile Miami–Memphis flight, Continental, Delta, and Southwest flew a total of 200 empty seats, costing them a total of $54,300. If Delta had twice as many empty seats as Southwest, how many empty seats did each of these three airlines carry on its flight?

Investing: Inverse Mutual Funds *Inverse mutual funds, sometimes referred to as "bear market" or "short" funds, seek to deliver the opposite of the performance of the index or category they track, and can thus be used by traders to bet against the stock market. Exercises 17 and 18 are based on the following table, which shows the performance of three such funds as of August 12, 2011.*[17]

	Year-to-date Loss
SHPIX (Short Smallcap Profund)	6%
RYURX (Rydex Inverse S&P 500)	5%
RYIHX (Rydex Inverse High Yield)	7%

---

[15]Most perfumes consist of 10 to 20% perfume oils dissolved in alcohol. This may or may not be reflected in this company's formula.

[16]Costs are rounded to the nearest 0.1¢. Source: Company financial statements, obtained from their respective Web sites. The cost per available seat-mile (CASM) is a widely used operating statistic in the airline industry.

[17]Based on prices at the close of the stock market on August 12, 2011. YTD losses rounded to the nearest percentage point. Source: www.fidelity.com.

17. You invested a total of $9,000 in the three funds at the beginning of 2011, including an equal amount in RYURX and RYIHX. Your year-to-date loss from the first two funds amounted to $400. How much did you invest in each of the three funds?

18. You invested a total of $6,000 in the three funds at the beginning of 2011, including an equal amount in SHPIX and RYURX. Your total year-to-date loss amounted to $360. How much did you invest in each of the three funds?

Investing: Lesser-Known Stocks *Exercises 19 and 20 are based on the following information about the stocks of* KT Corporation, International Flavors & Fragrances, *and* Quality Systems.[18]

	Price	*Dividend Yield*
KT (KT Corporation)	$16	7%
IFF (International Flavors & Fragrances)	56	2
QSII (Quality Systems)	80	2

19. ▼ You invested a total of $8,400 in shares of the three stocks at the given prices, and expected to earn $248 in annual dividends. If you purchased a total of 200 shares, how many shares of each stock did you purchase?

20. ▼ You invested a total of $11,200 in shares of the three stocks at the given prices, and expected to earn $304 in annual dividends. If you purchased a total of 250 shares, how many shares of each stock did you purchase?

21. ■ *Internet Audience* At the end of 2003, the four companies with the largest number of home Internet users in the United States were Microsoft, Time Warner, Yahoo, and Google, with a combined audience of 284 million users.[19] Taking x to be the Microsoft audience in millions, y the Time Warner audience in millions, z the Yahoo audience in millions, and u the Google audience in millions, it was observed that

$$z - u = 3(x - y) + 6$$
$$x + y = 50 + z + u$$
and $x - y + z - u = 42.$

How large was the audience of each of the four companies in November 2003?

22. ■ *Internet Audience* At the end of 2003, the four organizations ranking 5 through 8 in home Internet users in the United States were eBay, the U.S. government, Amazon, and Lycos, with a combined audience of 112 million users.[20] Taking x to be the eBay audience in millions, y the U.S. Government audience in millions, z the Amazon

audience in millions, and u the Lycos audience in millions, it was observed that

$$y - z = z - u$$
$$x - y = 3(y - u) + 5$$
and $x - y + z - u = 12.$

How large was the audience of each of the four companies in November 2003?

23. ▼ ***Market Share: Homeowners Insurance*** The three market leaders in homeowners insurance in Missouri are State Farm, American Family Insurance Group, and Allstate. Based on data from 2007, two relationships between the Missouri homeowners insurance percentage market shares are found to be

$$x = 1 + y + z$$
$$z = 16 - 0.2w,$$

where x, y, z, and w are, respectively, the percentages of the market held by State Farm, American Family, Allstate, and other companies.[21] Given that the four groups account for the entire market, obtain a third equation relating x, y, z, and w, and solve the associated system of three linear equations to show how the market shares of State Farm, American Family, and Allstate depend on the share held by other companies. Which of the three companies' market share is most impacted by the share held by other companies?

24. ▼ ***Market Share: Auto Insurance*** Repeat the preceding exercise using the following relationships among the auto insurance percentage market shares:

$$x = -40 + 5y + z$$
$$z = 3 - 2y + w.$$

25. ***Inventory Control*** Red Bookstore wants to ship books from its warehouses in Brooklyn and Queens to its stores, one on Long Island and one in Manhattan. Its warehouse in Brooklyn has 1,000 books and its warehouse in Queens has 2,000. Each store orders 1,500 books. It costs $5 to ship each book from Brooklyn to Long Island and $1 to ship each book from Brooklyn to Manhattan. It costs $4 to ship each book from Queens to Long Island and $2 to ship each book from Queens to Manhattan.

a. If Red has a transportation budget of $9,000 and is willing to spend all of it, how many books should Red ship from each warehouse to each store in order to fill all the orders?

b. Is there a way of doing this for less money?
HINT [See Example 4.]

26. ***Inventory Control*** The Tubular Ride Boogie Board Company has manufacturing plants in Tucson, AZ and Toronto, Ontario. You have been given the job of coordinating distribution of the latest model, the Gladiator, to outlets in Honolulu and Venice Beach. The Tucson plant, when operating at full capacity, can manufacture 620 Gladiator boards per week, while the

---

[18]Yields rounded to the nearest percentage point and stock prices at the close of the stock market on August 12, 2011 rounded to the nearest $1. Source: www.google.com/finance.

[19]Source: Nielsen/NetRatings www.nielsen-netratings.com/ January 1, 2004.

[20]*Ibid.*

[21]Source: Missouri Dept. of Insurance (www.insurance.mo.gov).

Toronto plant, beset by labor disputes, can produce only 410 boards per week. The outlet in Honolulu orders 500 Gladiator boards per week, while Venice Beach orders 530 boards per week. Transportation costs are as follows:

Tucson to Honolulu: $10 per board; Tucson to Venice Beach: $5 per board.

Toronto to Honolulu: $20 per board; Toronto to Venice Beach: $10 per board.

a. Assuming that you wish to fill all orders and assure full capacity production at both plants, is it possible to meet a total transportation budget of $10,200? If so, how many Gladiator boards are shipped from each manufacturing plant to each distribution outlet?

b. Is there a way of doing this for less money? HINT [See Example 4.]

27. ▼ Tourism in the 1990s In the 1990s, significant numbers of tourists traveled from North America and Europe to Australia and South Africa. In 1998, a total of 1,390,000 of these tourists visited Australia, while 1,140,000 of them visited South Africa. Further, 630,000 of them came from North America and 1,900,000 of them came from Europe.[22] (Assume no single tourist visited both destinations or traveled from both North America and Europe.)

a. The given information is not sufficient to determine the number of tourists from each region to each destination. Why?

b. If you were given the additional information that a total of 2,530,000 tourists traveled from these two regions to these two destinations, would you now be able to determine the number of tourists from each region to each destination? If so, what are these numbers?

c. If you were given the additional information that the same number of people from Europe visited South Africa as visited Australia, would you now be able to determine the number of tourists from each region to each destination? If so, what are these numbers?

28. ▼ Tourism in the 1990s In the 1990s, significant numbers of tourists traveled from North America and Asia to Australia and South Africa. In 1998, a total of 2,230,000 of these tourists visited Australia, while 390,000 of them visited South Africa. Also, 630,000 of these tourists came from North America, and a total of 2,620,000 tourists traveled from these two regions to these two destinations.[23] (Assume no single tourist visited both destinations or traveled from both North America and Asia.)

a. The given information is not sufficient to determine the number of tourists from each region to each destination. Why?

b. If you were given the additional information that a total of 1,990,000 tourists came from Asia, would you now be

able to determine the number of tourists from each region to each destination? If so, what are these numbers?

c. If you were given the additional information that 200,000 tourists visited South Africa from Asia, would you now be able to determine the number of tourists from each region to each destination? If so, what are these numbers?

29. ▼ Alcohol The following table shows some data from a 2000 study on substance use among 10th graders in the United States and Europe.[24]

	Used Alcohol	Alcohol-Free	Totals
U.S.	x	y	14,000
Europe	z	w	95,000
Totals	63,550	45,450	

a. The table leads to a linear system of four equations in four unknowns. What is the system? Does it have a unique solution? What does this indicate about the given and the missing data?

b. ▣ Given that the number of U.S. 10th graders who were alcohol-free was 50% more than the number who had used alcohol, find the missing data.

30. ▼ Tobacco The following table shows some data from the same study cited in Exercise 30.[25]

	Smoked Cigarettes	Cigarette-Free	Totals
U.S.	x	y	14,000
Europe	z	w	95,000
Totals		70,210	109,000

a. The table leads to a linear system of four equations in four unknowns. What is the system? Does it have a unique solution? What does this indicate about the missing data?

b. ▣ Given that 31,510 more European 10th graders smoked cigarettes than U.S. 10th graders, find the missing data.

31. Traffic Flow One-way traffic through Enormous State University is shown in the figure, where the numbers indicate daily counts of vehicles.

[22]Figures are rounded to the nearest 10,000. Sources: South African Dept. of Environmental Affairs and Tourism; Australia Tourist Commission/*New York Times*, January 15, 2000, p. C1.

[23]*Ibid.*

[24]"Used Alcohol" indicates consumption of alcohol at least once in the past 30 days. Source: Council of Europe/University of Michigan. "Monitoring the Future"/*New York Times*, February 21, 2001, p. A10.

[25]"Smoked Cigarettes" indicates that at least one cigarette was smoked in the past 30 days. Source: *Ibid.*

a. Is it possible to determine the daily flow of traffic along each of the three streets from the information given? If your answer is *yes*, what is the traffic flow along each street? If your answer is *no*, what additional information would suffice?

b. Is a flow of 60 vehicles per day along Southwest Lane consistent with the information given?

c. What is the minimum traffic flow possible along Northwest Lane consistent with the information given? HINT [See Example 3.]

32. *Traffic Flow* The traffic through downtown East Podunk flows through the one-way system shown below.

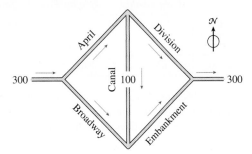

Traffic counters find that 300 vehicles enter town from the west each hour, and 300 leave town toward the east each hour. Also, 100 cars drive down Canal Street each hour.

a. Write down the general solution of the associated system of linear equations. Is it possible to determine the number of vehicles on each street per hour?

b. On which street could you put another traffic counter in order to determine the flow completely?

c. What is the minimum traffic flow along April Street consistent with the information given? HINT [See Example 3.]

33. *Traffic Flow* The traffic through downtown Johannesburg follows the one-way system shown below, with traffic movement recorded at incoming and outgoing streets (in cars per minute) as shown.

a. Set up and solve a system of equations to solve for the traffic flow along the middle sections of the four streets.

b. Is there sufficient information to calculate the traffic along the middle section of Jeppe Street? If so, what is it; if not, why not?

c. Given that 400 cars per minute flow down the middle section of Bree Street, how many cars per minute flow down the middle section of Simmons?

d. What is the minimum traffic flow along the middle section of Harrison Street?

e. Is there an upper limit to the possible traffic down Simmons Street consistent with the information given? Explain.

34. *Traffic Flow* Town of Hempstead officials were planning to make Hempstead Turnpike and the surrounding streets into one-way streets to prepare for the opening of Hofstra USA. In an experiment, they restricted traffic flow along the streets near Hofstra as shown in the diagram. The numbers show traffic flow per minute and the arrows indicate the direction of traffic.

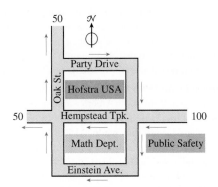

a. Set up and solve the associated traffic flow problem with the following unknowns:
x = traffic per minute along the middle stretch of Oak St.,
y = traffic per minute along the middle stretch of Hempstead Tpk.,
z = traffic per minute along Einstein Ave., and
u = traffic per minute along Party Drive.

b. If 20 cars per minute drive along Party Drive, what is the traffic like along the middle stretch of Oak Street?

c. If 20 vehicles per minute drive along Einstein Ave., and 90 vehicles per minute drive down the middle stretch of Hempstead Tpk., how many cars per minute drive along the middle stretch of Oak Street?

d. If Einstein Avenue is deserted, what is the minimum traffic along the middle stretch of Hempstead Tpk.?

35. ▼ *Traffic Management* The Outer Village Town Council has decided to convert its (rather quiet) main street, Broadway, to a one-way street, but is not sure of the direction of most of the traffic. The accompanying diagram illustrates the downtown area of Outer Village, as well as the *net* traffic flow along the intersecting streets (in vehicles per day). (There are no one-way streets; a net traffic flow in a certain direction is defined as the traffic flow in that direction minus the flow in the opposite direction.)

a. Is the given information sufficient to determine the net traffic flow along the three portions of Broadway shown? If your answer is *yes,* give the traffic flow along each stretch. If your answer is *no,* what additional information would suffice? HINT [For the direction of net traffic flow, choose either east or west. If a corresponding value is negative, it indicates net flow in the opposite direction.]

b. Assuming that there is little traffic (less than 160 vehicles per day) east of Fleet Street, in what direction is the net flow of traffic along the remaining stretches of Broadway?

36. ▼ *Electric Current* Electric current measures (in **amperes** or **amps**) the flow of electrons through wires. Like traffic flow, the current entering an intersection of wires must equal the current leaving it.[26] Here is an electrical circuit known as a **Wheatstone bridge.**

a. If the currents in two of the wires are 10 amps and 5 amps as shown, determine the currents in the unlabeled wires in terms of suitable parameters.

b. In which wire should you measure the current in order to know all of the currents exactly?

37. ▼ *Econometrics* (*from the GRE Economics Test*) This and the next exercise are based on the following simplified model of the determination of the money stock.

$$M = C + D$$
$$C = 0.2D$$
$$R = 0.1D$$
$$H = R + C$$

where

$$M = \text{money stock}$$
$$C = \text{currency in circulation}$$
$$R = \text{bank reserves}$$
$$D = \text{deposits of the public}$$
$$H = \text{high-powered money}$$

If the money stock were $120 billion, what would bank reserves have to be?

38. ▼ *Econometrics* (*from the GRE Economics Test*) With the model in the previous exercise, if H were equal to $42 billion, what would M equal?

CAT Scans CAT (*Computerized Axial Tomographic*) scans are used to map the exact location of interior features of the human body. CAT scan technology is based on the following principles: (1) different components of the human body (water, gray matter, bone, etc.) absorb X-rays to different extents; and (2) to measure the X-ray absorption by a specific region of, say, the brain, it suffices to pass a

number of line-shaped pencil beams of X-rays through the brain at different angles and measure the total absorption for each beam, which is the sum of the absorptions of the regions through which it passes. The accompanying diagram illustrates a simple example. (The number in each region shows its absorption, and the number on each X-ray beam shows the total absorption for that beam.)[27]

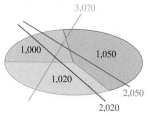

In Exercises 39–44, use the table and the given X-ray absorption diagrams to identify the composition of each of the regions marked by a letter.

Type	Air	Water	Gray Matter	Tumor	Blood	Bone
Absorption	0	1,000	1,020	1,030	1,050	2,000

39.

40.

41.

42.

---

[26]This is known as **Kirchhoff's current law,** named after Gustav Robert Kirchhoff (1824–1887). Kirchhoff made important contributions to the fields of geometric optics, electromagnetic radiation, and electrical network theory.

[27]Based on a COMAP article *Geometry, New Tools for New Technologies,* by J. Malkevitch, Video Applications Library, COMAP, 1992. The absorptions are actually calibrated on a logarithmic scale. In real applications, the size of the regions is very small, and very large numbers of beams must be used.

43. ▼ Identify the composition of site x.

(The horizontal and slanted beams each pass through five regions.)

44. ▼ Identify the composition of site x.

(The horizontal and slanted beams each pass through five regions.)

45. ◆ *Voting* In the 75th Congress (1937–1939) the U.S. House of Representatives had 333 Democrats, 89 Republicans, and 13 members of other parties. Suppose that a bill passed the House with 31 more votes in favor than against, with 10 times as many Democrats voting for the bill as Republicans, and with 36 more non-Democrats voting against the bill than for it. If every member voted either for the bill or against it, how many Democrats, how many Republicans, and how many members of other parties voted in favor of the bill?

46. ◆ *Voting* In the 75th Congress (1937–1939) there were in the Senate 75 Democrats, 17 Republicans, and 4 members of other parties. Suppose that a bill passed the Senate with 16 more votes in favor than against, with three times as many Democrats voting in favor as non-Democrats voting in favor, and 32 more Democrats voting in favor than Republicans voting in favor. If every member voted either for the bill or against it, how many Democrats, how many Republicans, and how many members of other parties voted in favor of the bill?

47. ◆ *Investments* Things have not been going too well here at Accurate Accounting, Inc. since we hired Todd Smiley. He has a tendency to lose important documents, especially around April, when tax returns of our business clients are due. Today Smiley accidentally shredded Colossal Conglomerate Corp.'s investment records. We must therefore reconstruct them based on the information he can gather. Todd recalls that the company earned an $8 million return on investments totaling $65 million last year. After a few frantic telephone calls to sources in Colossal, he learned that Colossal had made investments in four companies last year: X, Y, Z, and W. (For reasons of confidentiality, we are withholding their names.) Investments in company X earned 15% last year, investments in Y depreciated by 20% last year, investments in Z neither appreciated nor

depreciated last year, while investments in W earned 20% last year. Smiley was also told that Colossal invested twice as much in company X as in company Z, and three times as much in company W as in company Z. Does Smiley have sufficient information to piece together Colossal's investment portfolio before its tax return is due next week? If so, what does the investment portfolio look like?

48. ◆ *Investments* Things are going from bad to worse here at Accurate Accounting, Inc.! Colossal Conglomerate Corp.'s tax return is due tomorrow and the accountant Todd Smiley seems to have no idea how Colossal earned a return of $8 million on a $65 million investment last year. It appears that, although the returns from companies X, Y, Z, and W were as listed in Exercise 47, the rest of the information there was wrong. What Smiley is now being told is that Colossal only invested in companies X, Y, and Z and that the investment in X amounted to $30 million. His sources in Colossal still maintain that twice as much was invested in company X as in company Z. What should Smiley do?

COMMUNICATION AND REASONING EXERCISES

49. Are Exercises 1 and 2 realistic in their expectation of using up all the ingredients? What does your answer have to do with the solution(s) of the associated system of equations?

50. Suppose that you obtained a solution for Exercise 3 or 4 consisting of positive values that were not all whole numbers. What would such a solution signify about the situation in the exercise? Should you round these values to the nearest whole numbers?

In Exercises 51–56, x, y and z represent the weights of the three ingredients X, Y, and Z in a gasoline blend. Say which of the following is represented by a linear equation in x, y, and z, and give a form of the equation when it is:

51. The blend consists of 100 pounds of ingredient X.

52. The blend is free of ingredient X.

53. The blend contains 30% ingredient Y by weight.

54. The weight of ingredient X is the product of the weights of ingredients Y and Z.

55. There is at least 30% ingredient Y by weight.

56. There is twice as much ingredient X by weight as Y and Z combined.

57. Make up an entertaining word problem leading to the following system of equations.
$$\begin{aligned} 10x + 20y + 10z &= 100 \\ 5x + 15y &= 50 \\ x + y + z &= 10 \end{aligned}$$

58. Make up an entertaining word problem leading to the following system of equations.
$$\begin{aligned} 10x + 20y &= 300 \\ 10z + 20w &= 400 \\ 20x + 10z &= 400 \\ 10y + 20w &= 300 \end{aligned}$$

CHAPTER 3 REVIEW

KEY CONCEPTS

Website www.WanerMath.com
Go to the Website at www.WanerMath
.com to find a comprehensive and
interactive Web-based summary
of Chapter 3.

3.1 Systems of Two Equations in Two Unknowns

Linear equation in two unknowns *p. 176*
Coefficient *p. 176*
Solution of an equation in two
unknowns *p. 176*
Graphical method for solving a system
of two linear equations *p. 179*

Algebraic method for solving a system
of two linear equations *p. 179*
Redundant or dependent system *p. 180*
Possible outcomes for a system of two
linear equations *p. 181*
Consistent system *p. 181*

3.2 Using Matrices to Solve Systems of Equations

Linear equation (in any number of
unknowns) *p. 188*
Matrix *p. 189*

Augmented matrix of a system of linear
equations *p. 189*
Elementary row operations *p. 190*
Pivot *p. 192*
Clearing a column; pivoting *p. 192*
Gauss-Jordan or row reduction *p. 194*
Reduced row echelon form *p. 201*

3.3 Applications of Systems of Linear Equations

Resource allocation *p. 206*
(Traffic) flow *p. 208*
Transportation *p. 210*

REVIEW EXERCISES

In each of Exercises 1–6, graph the equations and determine how many solutions the system has, if any.

1. $x + 2y = 4$
$2x - y = 1$

2. $0.2x - 0.1y = 0.3$
$0.2x + 0.2y = 0.4$

3. $\frac{1}{2}x - \frac{3}{4}y = 0$
$6x - 9y = 0$

4. $2x + 3y = 2$
$-x - 3y/2 = 1/2$

5. $x + y = 1$
$2x + y = 0.3$
$3x + 2y = \frac{13}{10}$

6. $3x + 0.5y = 0.1$
$6x + y = 0.2$
$\frac{3x}{10} - 0.05y = 0.01$

Solve each of the systems of linear equations in Exercises 7–18.

7. $x + 2y = 4$
$2x - y = 1$

8. $0.2x - 0.1y = 0.3$
$0.2x + 0.2y = 0.4$

9. $\frac{1}{2}x - \frac{3}{4}y = 0$
$6x - 9y = 0$

10. $2x + 3y = 2$
$-x - 3y/2 = 1/2$

11. $x + y = 1$
$2x + y = 0.3$
$3x + 2y = \frac{13}{10}$

12. $3x + 0.5y = 0.1$
$6x + y = 0.2$
$\frac{3x}{10} - 0.05y = 0.01$

13. $x + 2y = -3$
$x - z = 0$
$x + 3y - 2z = -2$

14. $x - y + z = 2$
$7x + y - z = 6$
$x - \frac{1}{2}y + \frac{1}{3}z = 1$
$x + y + z = 6$

15. $x - \frac{1}{2}y + z = 0$
$\frac{1}{2}x - \frac{1}{2}z = -1$
$\frac{3}{2}x - \frac{1}{2}y + \frac{1}{2}z = -1$

16. $x + y - 2z = -1$
$-2x - 2y + 4z = 2$
$0.75x + 0.75y - 1.5z = -0.75$

17. $x = \frac{1}{2}y$
$\frac{1}{2}x = -\frac{1}{2}z + 2$
$z = -3x + y$

18. $x - y + z = 1$
$y - z + w = 1$
$x + z - w = 1$
$2x + z = 3$

Exercises 19–22 are based on the following equation relating the Fahrenheit and Celsius (or centigrade) temperature scales:

$$5F - 9C = 160,$$

where F is the Fahrenheit temperature of an object and C is its Celsius temperature.

19. What temperature should an object be if its Fahrenheit and Celsius temperatures are the same?

20. What temperature should an object be if its Celsius temperature is half its Fahrenheit temperature?

21. Is it possible for the Fahrenheit temperature of an object to be 1.8 times its Celsius temperature? Explain.

22. Is it possible for the Fahrenheit temperature of an object to be 30° more than 1.8 times its Celsius temperature? Explain.

In Exercises 23–28, let x, y, z, and w represent the population in millions of four cities A, B, C, and D, respectively. Express the given statement as an equation in x, y, z, and w. If the equation is linear, say so and express it in the standard form $ax + by + cz + dw = k$.

23. The total population of the four cities is 10 million people.

24. City A has three times as many people as cities B and C combined.

25. City D is actually a ghost town; there are no people living in it.

26. The population of City A is the sum of the squares of the populations of the other three cities.

27. City C has 30% more people than City B.

28. City C has 30% fewer people than City B.

APPLICATIONS: OHaganBooks.com

Purchasing You are the buyer for *OHaganBooks.com* and are considering increasing stocks of romance and horror novels at the new *OHaganBooks.com* warehouse in Texas. You have offers from two publishers: *Duffin House* and *Higgins Press*. *Duffin* offers a package of 5 horror novels and 5 romance novels for $50, and *Higgins* offers a package of 5 horror and 11 romance novels for $15. Exercises 29–32 deal with your purchasing options given these offers.

29. How many packages should you purchase from each publisher to get exactly 4,500 horror novels and 6,600 romance novels?

30. You want to spend a total of $50,000 on books and have promised to buy twice as many packages from Duffin as from Higgins. How many packages should you purchase from each publisher?

31. The accountant tells you that the company can actually afford to spend a total of $90,000 on romance and horror books. She also reminds you that you had signed an agreement to spend twice as much money for books from Duffin as from Higgins. How many packages should you purchase from each publisher?

32. Upon revising her records, the accountant now tells you that the company can afford to spend a total of only $60,000 on romance and horror books, and that it is company policy to spend the same amount of money at both publishers. How many packages should you purchase from each publisher?

33. *Equilibrium* The demand per year for *Finite Math the OHagan Way* is given by $q = -1,000p + 140,000$, where p is the price per book in dollars. The supply is given by $q = 2,000p + 20,000$. Find the price at which supply and demand balance.

34. *Equilibrium* OHaganbooks.com CEO John O'Hagan announces to a stunned audience at the annual board meeting that he is considering expanding into the jumbo jet airline manufacturing business. The demand per year for jumbo jets is given by $q = -2p + 18$ where p is the price per jet in millions of dollars. The supply is given by $q = 3p + 3$. Find the price the envisioned O'Hagan jumbo jet division should charge to balance supply and demand.

35. *Feeding Schedules* Billy-Sean O'Hagan is John O'Hagan's son and a freshman in college. Billy's 36-gallon tropical fish tank contains three types of carnivorous creatures: baby sharks, piranhas and squids, and he feeds them three types of delicacies: goldfish, angelfish and butterfly fish. Each baby shark can consume 1 goldfish, 2 angelfish, and 2 butterfly fish per day; each piranha can consume 1 goldfish and 3 butterfly fish per day (the piranhas are rather large as a result of their diet); while each squid can consume 1 goldfish and 1 angelfish per day. After a trip to the local pet store, he was able to feed his creatures to capacity, and noticed that 21 goldfish, 21 angelfish, and 35 butterfly fish were eaten. How many of each type of creature does he have?

36. *Resource Allocation* Duffin House is planning its annual Song Festival, when it will serve three kinds of delicacies: granola treats, nutty granola treats, and nuttiest granola treats. The following table shows the ingredients required (in ounces) for a single serving of each delicacy, as well as the total amount of each ingredient available.

	Granola	Nutty Granola	Nuttiest Granola	Total Available
Toasted Oats	1	1	5	1,500
Almonds	4	8	8	10,000
Raisins	2	4	8	4,000

The Song Festival planners at Duffin House would like to use up all the ingredients. Is this possible? If so, how many servings of each kind of delicacy can they make?

37. *Web Site Traffic* OHaganBooks.com has two principal competitors: JungleBooks.com and FarmerBooks.com. Combined Web site traffic at the three sites is estimated at 10,000 hits per day. Only 10% of the hits at OHaganBooks.com result in orders, whereas JungleBooks.com and FarmerBooks.com report that 20% of the hits at their sites result in book orders. Together, the three sites process 1,500 book orders per day. FarmerBooks.com appears to be the most successful of the three, and gets as many book orders as the other two combined. What is the traffic (in hits per day) at each of the sites?

38. *Sales* As the buyer at OHaganBooks.com you are planning to increase stocks of books about music, and have been monitoring worldwide sales. Last year, worldwide sales of books about rock, rap, and classical music amounted to $5.8 billion. Books on rock music brought in twice as much revenue as books on rap music and they brought in 900% the revenue of books on classical music. How much revenue was earned in each of the three categories of books?

39. *Investing in Stocks* Billy-Sean O'Hagan is the treasurer at his college fraternity, which recently earned $12,400 in its annual carwash fundraiser. Billy-Sean decided to invest all the proceeds in the purchase of three computer stocks: HAL, POM, and WELL.

	Price per Share	Dividend Yield
HAL	$100	0.5%
POM	$20	1.50%
WELL	$25	0%

If the investment was expected to earn $56 in annual dividends, and he purchased a total of 200 shares, how many shares of each stock did he purchase?

40. *Initial Public Offerings (IPOs)* Duffin House, Higgins Press, and Sickle Publications all went public on the same day recently. John O'Hagan had the opportunity to participate in all three initial public offerings (partly because he and Marjory Duffin are good friends). He made a considerable profit when he sold all of the stock two days later on the open market. The following table shows the purchase price and percentage yield on the investment in each company.

	Purchase Price per Share	Yield
Duffin House (DHS)	$8	20%
Higgins Press (HPR)	$10	15%
Sickle Publications (SPUB)	$15	15%

He invested $20,000 in a total of 2,000 shares, and made a $3,400 profit from the transactions. How many shares in each company did he purchase?

41. *Degree Requirements* During his lunch break, John O'Hagan decides to devote some time to assisting his son Billy-Sean, who is having a terrible time coming up with a college course schedule. One reason for this is the very complicated Bulletin of Suburban State University. It reads as follows:

> *All candidates for the degree of Bachelor of Science at SSU must take a total of 124 credits from the Sciences, Fine Arts, Liberal Arts, and Mathematics,[28] including an equal number of Science and Fine Arts credits, and twice as many Mathematics credits as Science credits and Fine Arts credits combined, but with Liberal Arts credits exceeding Mathematics credits by exactly one-third of the number of Fine Arts credits.*

What are all the possible degree programs for Billy-Sean?

42. *Degree Requirements* Having finally decided on his degree program, Billy-Sean learns that the Suburban State University Senate (under pressure from the English Department) has revised the Bulletin to include a "Verbal Expression" component in place of the Fine Arts requirement in all programs (including the sciences):

> *All candidates for the degree of Bachelor of Science at SSU must take a total of 120 credits from the Liberal Arts, Sciences, Verbal Expression, and Mathematics, including an equal number of Science and Liberal Arts credits, and twice as many Verbal Expression credits as Science credits and Liberal Arts credits combined, but with Liberal Arts credits exceeding Mathematics credits by one quarter of the number of Verbal Expression Credits.*

What are now the possible degree programs for Billy-Sean?

---

[28]Strictly speaking, mathematics is not a science; it is the Queen of the Sciences, although we like to think of it as the Mother of all Sciences.

43. *Network Traffic* All book orders received at the Order Department at OHaganBooks.com are transmitted through a small computer network to the Shipping Department. The following diagram shows the network (which uses two intermediate computers as routers), together with some of the average daily traffic measured in book orders.

OD = Order department
SD = Shipping department

a. Set up a system of linear equations in which the unknowns give the average traffic along the paths labeled x, y, z, w, and find the general solution.
b. What is the minimum volume of traffic along y?
c. What is the maximum volume of traffic along w?
d. If there is no traffic along z, find the volume of traffic along all the paths.
e. If there is the same volume of traffic along y and z, what is the volume of traffic along w?

44. *Business Retreats* Marjory Duffin is planning a joint business retreat for Duffin House and OHaganBooks.com at Laguna Surf City, but is concerned about traffic conditions (she feels that too many cars tend to spoil the ambiance of a seaside retreat). She managed to obtain the following map from the Laguna Surf City Engineering Department (all the streets are one-way as indicated). The counters show traffic every five minutes.

a. Set up and solve the associated system of linear equations. *Be sure to give the general solution.*
(Take x = traffic along North Beach Way, y = traffic along South Beach Way, z = traffic along Beach View

St., u = traffic along Lagoon Drive and v = traffic along Dock Road.)

b. Assuming that all roads are one-way in the directions shown, what, if any, is the maximum possible traffic along Lagoon Drive?

c. The Laguna Surf City Traffic Department is considering opening up Beach View Street to two-way traffic, but an environmentalist group is concerned that this will result in increased traffic on Lagoon Drive. What, if any, is the maximum possible traffic along Lagoon Drive assuming that Beach View Street is two-way and the traffic counter readings are as shown?

45. *Shipping* On the same day that the sales department at Duffin House received an order for 600 packages from the OHaganBooks.com Texas headquarters, it received an additional order for 200 packages from FantasyBooks.com, based in California. Duffin House has warehouses in New York and Illinois. The Illinois warehouse is closing down and must clear all 300 packages it has in stock. Shipping costs per package of books are as follows:

New York to Texas: $20   New York to California: $50
Illinois to Texas: $30   Illinois to California: $40

Is it possible to fill both orders and clear the Illinois warehouse at a cost of $22,000? If so, how many packages should be sent from each warehouse to each online bookstore?

46. *Transportation Scheduling* Duffin House is about to start a promotional blitz for its new book, *Physics for the Liberal Arts*. The company has 20 salespeople stationed in Chicago and 10 in Denver, and would like to fly 15 to sales fairs at each of Los Angeles and New York. A round-trip plane flight from Chicago to LA costs $200; from Chicago to NY costs $150; from Denver to LA costs $400; and from Denver to NY costs $200. For tax reasons, Duffin House needs to budget exactly $6,500 for the total cost of the plane flights. How many salespeople should the company fly from each of Chicago and Denver to each of LA and NY?

Case Study — Hybrid Cars—Optimizing the Degree of Hybridization

You are involved in new model development at a major automobile company. The company is planning to introduce two new plug-in hybrid electric vehicles: the subcompact "Green Town Hopper" and the midsize "Electra Supreme," and your department must decide on the degree of hybridization (DOH) for each of these models that will result in the largest reduction in gasoline consumption. (The DOH of a vehicle is defined as the ratio of electric motor power to the total power, and typically ranges from 10% to 50%. For example, a model with a 20% DOH has an electric motor that delivers 20% of the total power of the vehicle.)

The tables below show the benefit for each of the two models, measured as the estimated reduction in annual gasoline consumption, as well as an estimate of retail cost increment, for various DOH percentages[29]: (The retail cost increment estimate is given by the formula $5,000 + 50(DOH - 10)$ for the Green Town Hopper and $7,000 + 50(DOH - 10)$ for the Electra Supreme.)

Green Town Hopper

DOH (%)	10	20	50
Reduction in Annual Consumption (gals)	180	230	200
Retail Cost Increment ($)	5,000	5,500	7,000

Electra Supreme

DOH (%)	10	20	50
Reduction in Annual Consumption (gals)	220	270	260
Retail Cost Increment ($)	7,000	7,500	9,000

---

[29]The figures are approximate and based on data for two actual vehicles as presented in a 2006 paper entitled *Cost-Benefit Analysis of Plug-In Hybrid Electric Vehicle Technology* by A. Simpson. Source: National Renewable Energy Laboratory, U.S. Department of Energy (www.nrel.gov).

Green Town Hopper

Electra Supreme

Figure 9

Notice that increasing the DOH toward 50% results in a decreased benefit. This is due in part to the need to increase the weight of the batteries while keeping the vehicle performance at a desirable level, thus necessitating a more powerful gasoline engine. The *optimum* DOH is the percentage that gives the largest reduction in gasoline consumption, and this is what you need to determine. Since the optimum DOH may not be 20%, you would like to create a mathematical model to compute the reduction R in gas consumption as a function of the DOH x. Your first inclination is to try linear equations—that is, an equation of the form

$$R = ax + b \quad (a \text{ and } b \text{ constants}),$$

but you quickly discover that the data simply won't fit, no matter what the choice of the constants. The reason for this can be seen graphically by plotting R versus x (Figure 9). In neither case do the three points lie on a straight line. In fact, the data are not even *close* to being linear. Thus, you will need curves to model these data. After giving the matter further thought, you remember something your mathematics instructor once said: The simplest curve passing through any three points not all on the same line is a parabola. Since you are looking for a simple model of the data, you decide to try a parabola. A general parabola has the equation

$$R = ax^2 + bx + c,$$

where a, b, and c are constants. The problem now is: What are a, b, and c? You decide to try substituting the values of R and x for the Green Town Hopper into the general equation, and you get the following:

$$x = 10, R = 180 \quad \text{gives} \quad 180 = 100a + 10b + c$$
$$x = 20, R = 230 \quad \text{gives} \quad 230 = 400a + 20b + c$$
$$x = 50, R = 200 \quad \text{gives} \quad 200 = 2{,}500a + 50b + c.$$

Now you notice that you have three linear equations in three unknowns! You solve the system:

$$a = -0.15, b = 9.5, c = 100.$$

Thus your reduction equation for the Green Town Hopper becomes

$$R = -0.15x^2 + 9.5x + 100.$$

For the Electra Supreme, you get

$$x = 10, R = 220: \quad 220 = 100a + 10b + c$$
$$x = 20, R = 270: \quad 270 = 400a + 20b + c$$
$$x = 50, R = 260: \quad 260 = 2{,}500a + 50b + c.$$

$$a = -0.1\bar{3}, b = 9, c = 143.\bar{3}$$

and so

$$R = -0.1\bar{3}x^2 + 9x + 143.\bar{3}.$$

Figure 10 shows the parabolas superimposed on the data points. You can now estimate a value for the optimal DOH as the value of x that gives the largest benefit R.

Green Town Hopper

Electra Supreme

Figure 10

Recalling that the x-coordinate of the vertex of the parabola $y = ax^2 + bx + c$ is $x = -\frac{b}{2a}$, you obtain the following estimates:

Green Town Hopper: Optimal DOH $= -\dfrac{9.5}{2(-0.15)} \approx 31.67\%$

Electra Supreme: Optimal DOH $= -\dfrac{9}{2(-0.1\overline{3})} \approx 33.75\%.$

You can now use the formulas given earlier to estimate the resulting reductions in gasoline consumption and increases in cost:

Green Town Hopper:

Reduction in gasoline consumption $= R \approx -0.15(31.67)^2 + 9.5(31.67) + 100$
$$\approx 250.4 \text{ gals/year}$$

Retail Cost Increment $\approx 5{,}000 + 50(31.67 - 10) \approx \$6{,}080$

Electra Supreme:

Reduction in gasoline consumption $= R = -0.1\overline{3}(33.75)^2 + 9(33.75) + 143.\overline{3}$
$$\approx 295.2 \text{ gals/year}$$

Retail Cost Increment $\approx 7{,}000 + 50(33.75 - 10) \approx \$8{,}190.$

You thus submit the following estimates: The optimal degree of hybridization for the Green Town Hopper is about 31.67% and will result in a reduction in gasoline consumption of 250.4 gals/year and a retail cost increment of around $6,080. The optimal degree of hybridization for the Electra Supreme is about 33.75% and will result in a reduction in gasoline consumption of 295.2 gals/year and a retail cost increment of around $8,190.

EXERCISES

1. Repeat the computations above for the "Earth Suburban" using the following data:

Earth Suburban

DOH (%)	10	20	50
Reduction in Annual Consumption (gals)	240	330	300
Retail Cost Increment ($)	9,000	9,500	11,000

Retail cost increment $= 9{,}000 + 50(DOH - 10)$

2. ▮ Repeat the analysis for the Green Town Hopper, but this time take x to be the cost increment, in thousands of dollars. (The curve of benefit versus cost is referred to as a *cost-benefit* curve.) What value of DOH corresponds to the optimal cost? What do you notice? Comment on the answer.

3. ▮ Repeat the analysis for the Electra Supreme, but this time use the optimal values, DOH $= 33.8$, Reduction $= 295.2$ gals/year in place of the 20% data. What do you notice?

4. Find the equation of the parabola that passes through the points $(1, 2)$, $(2, 9)$, and $(3, 19)$.

5. Is there a parabola that passes through the points $(1, 2)$, $(2, 9)$, and $(3, 16)$?

6. Is there a parabola that passes though the points $(1, 2)$, $(2, 9)$, $(3, 19)$, and $(-1, 2)$?

7. ▮ You submit your recommendations to your manager, and she tells you, "Thank you very much, but we have additional data for the Green Town Hopper: A 30% DOH results in a saving of 255 gals/year. Please resubmit your recommendations taking this into account by tomorrow." HINT [You now have four data points on each graph, so try a general cubic instead: $R = ax^3 + bx^2 + cx + d.$ Use a graph to estimate the optimal DOH.]

TI-83/84 Plus **Technology Guide**

Section 3.1

Example 1 (page 177) Find all solutions (x, y) of the following system of two equations:

$$x + y = 3$$
$$x - y = 1.$$

Solution with Technology

You can use a graphing calculator to draw the graphs of the two equations on the same set of axes and to check the solution. First, solve the equations for y, obtaining $y = -x + 3$ and $y = x - 1$. On the TI-83/84 Plus:

1. Set

    Y₁=-X+3
    Y₂=X-1

2. Decide on the range of x-values you want to use. As in Figure 1, let us choose the range $[-4, 4]$.[30]

3. In the WINDOW menu set Xmin $= -4$ and Xmax $= 4$.

4. Press ZOOM and select Zoomfit to set the y range.

You can now zoom in for a more accurate view by choosing a smaller x-range that includes the point of intersection, like $[1.5, 2.5]$, and using Zoomfit again. You can also use the trace feature to see the coordinates of points near the point of intersection.

To check that $(2, 1)$ is the correct solution, use the table feature to compare the two values of y corresponding to $x = 2$:

1. Press 2ND TABLE.

2. Set X $= 2$, and compare the corresponding values of Y₁ and Y₂; they should each be 1.

Q : *How accurate is the answer shown using the trace feature?*

A : That depends. We can increase the accuracy up to a point by zooming in on the point of intersection of the two graphs. But there is a limit to this: Most graphing calculators are capable of giving an answer correct to about 13 decimal places. This means, for instance, that, in the eyes of the TI-83/84 Plus, 2.000 000 000 000 1 is exactly the same as 2 (subtracting them yields 0). It follows that if you attempt to use a window so narrow that you need approximately 13 significant digits to distinguish the left and right edges, you will run into accuracy problems.

Section 3.2

Row Operations with a TI-83/84 Plus Start by entering the matrix into [A] using MATRIX EDIT. You can then do row operations on [A] using the following instructions (*row, *row+, and rowSwap are found in the MATRIX MATH menu).

---

[30]How did we come up with this interval? Trial and error. You might need to try several intervals before finding one that gives a graph showing the point of intersection clearly.

TECHNOLOGY GUIDE

Row Operation	TI-83/84 Plus Instruction (Matrix name is [A])
$R_i \to kR_i$	`*row(k,[A],i)→[A]`
Example: $R_2 \to 3R_2$	`*row(3,[A],2)→[A]`
$R_i \to R_i + kR_j$	`*row+(k,[A],j,i)→[A]`
Examples: $R_1 \to R_1 - 3R_2$	`*row+(-3,[A],2,1)→[A]`
$R_1 \to 4R_1 - 3R_2$	`*row(4,[A],1)→[A]` `*row+(-3,[A],2,1)→[A]`
Swap R_i and R_j	`rowSwap([A],i,j)→[A]`
Example: Swap R_1 and R_2	`rowSwap([A],1,2)→[A]`

Example 1 (page 195)   Solve the system:

$$x - y + 5z = -6$$
$$3x + 3y - z = 10$$
$$x + 3y + 2z = 5.$$

Solution with Technology

1. Begin by entering the matrix into [A] using MATRX EDIT. Only three columns can be seen at a time; you can see the rest of the matrix by scrolling left or right.

2. Now perform the operations given in Example 1:

```
*row+(-4,[A],2,3
)→[A]
   [[3 0 7  -4 ]
    [0 3 -8 14 ]
    [0 0 23 -23]]
■
```

```
*row(1/23,[A],3)
→[A]
   [[3 0 7  -4]
    [0 3 -8 14]
    [0 0 1  -1]]
■
```

```
*row+(-7,[A],3,1
)→[A]
   [[3 0 0   3 ]
    [0 3 -8 14]
    [0 0 1  -1]]
■
```

```
*row+(8,[A],3,2)
→[A]
   [[3 0 0 3 ]
    [0 3 0 6 ]
    [0 0 1 -1]]
■
```

```
*row(1/3,[A],1)→
[A]
   [[1 0 0 1 ]
    [0 3 0 6 ]
    [0 0 1 -1]]
■
```

```
*row(1/3,[A],2)→
[A]
   [[1 0 0 1 ]
    [0 1 0 2 ]
    [0 0 1 -1]]
■
```

As in Example 1, we can now read the solution from the right-hand column: $x = 1$, $y = 2$, $z = -1$.

Note The TI-83/84 Plus has a function, `rref`, that gives the reduced row echelon form of a matrix in one step. (See the text for the definition of reduced row echelon form.) Internally it uses a variation of Gauss-Jordan reduction to do this. ∎

SPREADSHEET Technology Guide

Section 3.1

Example 1 (page 177) Find all solutions (x, y) of the following system of two equations:

$$x + y = 3$$
$$x - y = 1.$$

Solution with Technology

You can use a spreadsheet to draw the graphs of the two equations on the same set of axes, and to check the solution.

1. Solve the equations for y, obtaining $y = -x + 3$ and $y = x - 1$.

2. To graph these lines we can use the following simple worksheet:

The two values of x give the x-coordinates of the two points we will use as endpoints of the lines. (We have—somewhat arbitrarily—chosen the range $[-4, 4]$ for x.) The formula for the first line, $y = -x + 3$, is in cell B2, and the formula for the second line, $y = x - 1$, is in C2.

3. Copy these two cells as shown to yield the following result:

	A	B	C
1	x	y1	y2
2	-4	7	-5
3	4	-1	3

4. For the graph, select all nine cells and create a scatter graph with line segments joining the data points. Instruct the spreadsheet to insert a chart and select the "scatter" option. In the same dialogue box, select the option that shows points connected by lines. If you are using Excel, press "Next" to bring up a new dialogue box called "Data Type," where you should make sure that the "Series in Columns" option is selected,

telling the program that the x- and y-coordinates are arranged vertically, down columns. (Other spreadsheet programs have corresponding options you may need to set.) Your graph should appear as shown below.

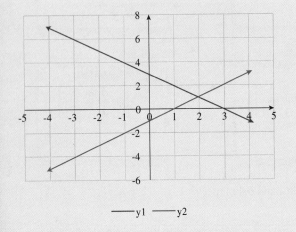

——— y1   ——— y2

To zoom in:

1. First decide on a new x-range, say, $[1, 3]$.

2. Change the value in cell A2 to 1 and the value in cell A3 to 3, and the spreadsheet will automatically update the y-values and the graph.*

To check that $(2, 1)$ is the correct solution:

1. Enter the value 2 in cell A4 in your spreadsheet.

2. Copy the formulas in B3 and C3 down to row 4 to obtain the corresponding values of y.

	A	B	C
1	x	y1	y2
2	-4	7	-5
3	4	-1	3
4	2	1	1

Because the values of y agree, we have verified that $(2, 1)$ is a solution of both equations.

Section **3.2**

Row Operations with a Spreadsheet   To a spreadsheet, a block of data with one or more rows or columns is an **array**, and a spreadsheet has built in the capability to handle arrays in much the same way as it handles single cells. Consider the following example:

$$\begin{bmatrix} 1 & 3 & -4 \\ 0 & 4 & 2 \end{bmatrix} 3R_2 \rightarrow \begin{bmatrix} 1 & 3 & -4 \\ 0 & 12 & 6 \end{bmatrix}.$$ Replace R_2 by $3R_2$.

1. Enter the original matrix in a convenient location, say the cells A1 through C2.

2. To get the first row of the new matrix, which is simply a copy of the first row of the old matrix, decide where you want to place the new matrix, and highlight *the whole row of the new matrix,* say A4:C4.

3. Enter the formula =A1:C1 (the easiest way to do this is to type "=" and then use the mouse to select cells A1 through C1, i.e., the first row of the old matrix).

Enter formula for new first row.   Press Control-Shift-Enter.

* **NOTE** Your spreadsheet will set the y-range of the graph automatically, and the range it chooses may not always be satisfactory. It may sometimes be necessary to "narrow down" the range of one or both axes (in Excel, double-click on the axis in question).

4. Press **Control-Shift-Enter** (instead of "Enter" alone) and the whole row will be copied.[31] Pressing Control-Shift-Enter tells the spreadsheet that your formula is an *array formula,* one that returns an array rather than a single number. Once entered, the spreadsheet will show an array formula enclosed in "curly braces." (Note that you must also use Control-Shift-Enter to delete any array you create: Select the block you wish to delete and press Delete followed by Control-Shift-Enter.)

5. Similarly, to get the second row, select cells A5 through C5, where the new second row will go, enter the formula $=3*A2:C2$, and press Control-Shift-Enter. (Again, the easiest way to enter the formula is to type "$=3*$" and then select the cells A2 through C2 using the mouse.)

Enter formula for new second row.   Press Control-Shift-Enter.

We can perform the following operation in a similar way:

$$\begin{bmatrix} 1 & 3 & -4 \\ 0 & 4 & 2 \end{bmatrix} \xrightarrow{4R_1 - 3R_2} \begin{bmatrix} 4 & 0 & -22 \\ 0 & 4 & 2 \end{bmatrix}.$$ Replace R_1 by $4R_1 - 3R_2$.

(To easily enter the formula for $4R_1 - 3R_2$, type "$=4*$", select the first row A1:C1 using the mouse, type "$-3*$", and then select the second row A2:C2 using the mouse.)

Example 1 (page 195)   Solve the system:

$$x - y + 5z = -6$$
$$3x + 3y - z = 10$$
$$x + 3y + 2z = 5.$$

---

[31] Note that on a Mac, Command-Enter and Command-Shift-Enter have the same effect as Control-Shift-Enter.

Solution with Technology

Here is the complete row reduction as it would appear in a spreadsheet.

	A	B	C	D	E
1	1	-1	5	-6	
2	3	3	-1	10	R2 - 3R1
3	1	3	2	5	R3 - R1
4					
5	=A1:D1				
6	=A2:D2-3*A1:D1				
7	=A3:D3-A1:D1				

	A	B	C	D	E
1	1	-1	5	-6	
2	3	3	-1	10	R2 - 3R1
3	1	3	2	5	R3 - R1
4					
5	1	-1	5	-6	
6	0	6	-16	28	(1/2)R2
7	0	4	-3	11	
8					
9	=A5:D5				
10	=(1/2)*A6:D6				
11	=A7:D7				

	A	B	C	D	E
8					
9	1	-1	5	-6	3R1 + R2
10	0	3	-8	14	
11	0	4	-3	11	3R3 - 4R2
12					
13	=3*A9:D9+A10:D10				
14	=A10:D10				
15	=3*A11:D11-4*A10:D10				

	A	B	C	D	E
12					
13	3	0	7	-4	
14	0	3	-8	14	
15	0	0	23	-23	(1/23)R3
16					
17	=A13:D13				
18	=A14:D14				
19	=(1/23)*A15:D15				

	A	B	C	D	E
16					
17	3	0	7	-4	R1 - 7R3
18	0	3	-8	14	R2 + 8R3
19	0	0	1	-1	
20					
21	=A17:D17-7*A19:D19				
22	=A18:D18+8*A19:D19				
23	=A19:D19				

	A	B	C	D	E
20					
21	3	0	0	3	(1/3)R1
22	0	3	0	6	(1/3)R2
23	0	0	1	-1	
24					
25	=(1/3)*A21:D21				
26	=(1/3)*A22:D22				
27	=A23:D23				

	A	B	C	D
24				
25	1	0	0	1
26	0	1	0	2
27	0	0	1	-1

As in Example 1, we can now read the solution from the right hand column: $x = 1, y = 2, z = -1$. What do you notice if you change the entries in cells D1, D2, and D3?

4

Matrix Algebra and Applications

Website

www.WanerMath.com

At the Website you will find:

- Section-by-section tutorials

- A detailed chapter summary

- A true/false quiz

- Additional review exercises

- A matrix algebra utility

- A game theory utility

- The following optional extra sections:

  Determinants

  Using Determinants to Solve Systems: Cramer's Rule

Case Study Predicting Market Share

You are the sales director at *Selular*, a cellphone provider, and things are not looking good for your company: The recently launched *iClone* competitor is beginning to chip away at *Selular's* market share. Particularly disturbing are rumors of fierce brand loyalty by *iClone* customers, with several bloggers suggesting that *iClone* retains close to 100% of their customers. Worse, you will shortly be presenting a sales report to the board of directors, and the CEO has "suggested" that your report include 2-, 5-, and 10-year projections of *Selular's* market share given the recent impact on the market by *iClone*, and also a "worst-case" scenario projecting what would happen if *iClone* customers are so loyal that none of them ever switch services. You have results from two market surveys, taken one quarter apart, of the major cellphone providers, which shows the current market shares and the percentages of subscribers who switched from one service to another during the quarter. **How should you respond?**

GOH CHAI HIN/AFP/Newscom

231

Introduction

We used matrices in Chapter 3 simply to organize our work. It is time we examined them as interesting objects in their own right. There is much that we can do with matrices besides row operations: We can add, subtract, multiply, and even, in a sense, "divide" matrices. We use these operations to study game theory and input-output models in this chapter, and Markov chains in a later chapter.

Many calculators, spreadsheets, and other computer programs can do these matrix operations, which is a big help in doing calculations. However, we need to know how these operations are defined to see why they are useful and to understand which to use in any particular application.

4.1 Matrix Addition and Scalar Multiplication

Let's start by formally defining what a matrix is and introducing some basic terms.

Matrix, Dimension, and Entries

An **_m_ × _n_ matrix** A is a rectangular array of real numbers with m rows and n columns. We refer to m and n as the **dimensions** of the matrix. The numbers that appear in the matrix are called its **entries**. We customarily use capital letters $A, B, C, \ldots$ for the names of matrices.

Quick Examples

1. $A = \begin{bmatrix} 2 & 0 & 1 \\ 33 & -22 & 0 \end{bmatrix}$ is a 2 × 3 matrix because it has two rows and three columns.

2. $B = \begin{bmatrix} 2 & 3 \\ 10 & 44 \\ -1 & 3 \\ 8 & 3 \end{bmatrix}$ is a 4 × 2 matrix because it has four rows and two columns.*

   The entries of A are 2, 0, 1, 33, −22, and 0. The entries of B are the numbers 2, 3, 10, 44, −1, 3, 8, and 3.

✳ Remember that the number of rows is given first and the number of columns second. An easy way to remember this is to think of the acronym "RC" for "Row then Column."

Referring to the Entries of a Matrix

There is a systematic way of referring to particular entries in a matrix. If i and j are numbers, then the entry in the ith row and jth column of the matrix A is called the **_ij_th entry** of A. We usually write this entry as a_{ij} or A_{ij}. (If the matrix was called B, we would write its ijth entry as b_{ij} or B_{ij}.) Notice that this follows the "RC" convention: The row number is specified first and the column number second.

With $A = \begin{bmatrix} 2 & 0 & 1 \\ 33 & -22 & 0 \end{bmatrix}$,

$a_{13} = 1$ First row, third column

$a_{21} = 33.$ Second row, first column

According to the labeling convention, the entries of the matrix A above are

$$A = \begin{bmatrix} a_{11} & a_{12} & a_{13} \\ a_{21} & a_{22} & a_{23} \end{bmatrix}.$$

In general, the $m \times n$ matrix A has its entries labeled as follows:

$$A = \begin{bmatrix} a_{11} & a_{12} & a_{13} & \cdots & a_{1n} \\ a_{21} & a_{22} & a_{23} & \cdots & a_{2n} \\ \vdots & \vdots & \vdots & \ddots & \vdots \\ a_{m1} & a_{m2} & a_{m3} & \cdots & a_{mn} \end{bmatrix}.$$

We say that two matrices A and B are **equal** if they have the same dimensions and the corresponding entries are equal. Note that a 3×4 matrix can never equal a 3×5 matrix because they do not have the same dimensions.

EXAMPLE 1 Matrix Equality

Let $A = \begin{bmatrix} 7 & 9 & x \\ 0 & -1 & y+1 \end{bmatrix}$ and $B = \begin{bmatrix} 7 & 9 & 0 \\ 0 & -1 & 11 \end{bmatrix}$. Find the values of x and y such that $A = B$.

Solution For the two matrices to be equal, we must have corresponding entries equal, so

$$\begin{aligned} x &= 0 & a_{13} = b_{13} \\ y + 1 &= 11 \quad \text{or} \quad y = 10. & a_{23} = b_{23} \end{aligned}$$

➡ **Before we go on...** Note in Example 1 that the matrix equation

$$\begin{bmatrix} 7 & 9 & x \\ 0 & -1 & y+1 \end{bmatrix} = \begin{bmatrix} 7 & 9 & 0 \\ 0 & -1 & 11 \end{bmatrix}$$

is really six equations in one: $7 = 7, 9 = 9, x = 0, 0 = 0, -1 = -1$, and $y + 1 = 11$. We used only the two that were interesting. ∎

Row Matrix, Column Matrix, and Square Matrix

A matrix with a single row is called a **row matrix**, or **row vector**. A matrix with a single column is called a **column matrix** or **column vector**. A matrix with the same number of rows as columns is called a **square matrix**.

Quick Examples

The 1×5 matrix $C = \begin{bmatrix} 3 & -4 & 0 & 1 & -11 \end{bmatrix}$ is a row matrix.

The 4×1 matrix $D = \begin{bmatrix} 2 \\ 10 \\ -1 \\ 8 \end{bmatrix}$ is a column matrix.

The 3×3 matrix $E = \begin{bmatrix} 1 & -2 & 0 \\ 0 & 1 & 4 \\ -4 & 32 & 1 \end{bmatrix}$ is a square matrix.

Matrix Addition and Subtraction

The first matrix operations we discuss are matrix addition and subtraction. The rules for these operations are simple.

Matrix Addition and Subtraction

Two matrices can be added (or subtracted) if and only if they have the same dimensions. To add (or subtract) two matrices of the same dimensions, we add (or subtract) the corresponding entries. More formally, if A and B are $m \times n$ matrices, then $A + B$ and $A - B$ are the $m \times n$ matrices whose entries are given by:

$$(A + B)_{ij} = A_{ij} + B_{ij} \qquad ij\text{th entry of the sum} = \text{sum of the } ij\text{th entries}$$
$$(A - B)_{ij} = A_{ij} - B_{ij}. \qquad ij\text{th entry of the difference} = \text{difference of the } ij\text{th entries}$$

Visualizing Matrix Addition

$$\begin{bmatrix} 2 & -3 \\ 1 & 0 \end{bmatrix} + \begin{bmatrix} 1 & 1 \\ -2 & 1 \end{bmatrix} = \begin{bmatrix} 3 & -2 \\ -1 & 1 \end{bmatrix}$$

Quick Examples

1. $\begin{bmatrix} 2 & -3 \\ 1 & 0 \\ -1 & 3 \end{bmatrix} + \begin{bmatrix} 9 & -5 \\ 0 & 13 \\ -1 & 3 \end{bmatrix} = \begin{bmatrix} 11 & -8 \\ 1 & 13 \\ -2 & 6 \end{bmatrix}$ Corresponding entries added

2. $\begin{bmatrix} 2 & -3 \\ 1 & 0 \\ -1 & 3 \end{bmatrix} - \begin{bmatrix} 9 & -5 \\ 0 & 13 \\ -1 & 3 \end{bmatrix} = \begin{bmatrix} -7 & 2 \\ 1 & -13 \\ 0 & 0 \end{bmatrix}$ Corresponding entries subtracted

Technology can be used to enter, add, and subtract matrices. Here is an outline (see the Technology Guides at the end of the chapter for additional details on using a TI-83/84 Plus or a spreadsheet):

TI-83/84 Plus
Entering a matrix: `MATRX`; EDIT
Select a name, `ENTER`; type in the entries.
Adding two matrices:
Home Screen: `[A]+[B]`
(Use `MATRX`; NAMES to enter them on the home screen.)
[More details on page 304.]

Spreadsheet
Entering a matrix: Type entries in a convenient block of cells.
Adding two matrices: Highlight block where you want the answer to appear.
Type "="; highlight first matrix; type "+"; highlight second matrix; press Control+Shift+Enter
[More details on page 307.]

 Website
www.WanerMath.com
   Student Home
      → On Line Utilities
      → Matrix Algebra Tool

Enter matrices as shown (use a single letter for the name).

```
Enter your matrices here.
J = [20, 15
10, 12
8, 4]

F = [23, 12,
8, 12
4, 5]
```

To compute their difference, type `F-J` in the formula box and press "Compute". (You can enter multiple formulas separated by commas in the formula box. For instance, `F+J`, `F-J` will compute both the sum and the difference. *Note:* The utility is case sensitive, so be consistent.)

EXAMPLE 2 Sales

The A-Plus auto parts store chain has two outlets, one in Vancouver and one in Quebec. Among other things, it sells wiper blades, windshield cleaning fluid, and floor mats. The monthly sales of these items at the two stores for two months are given in the following tables:

January Sales

	Vancouver	Quebec
Wiper Blades	20	15
Cleaning Fluid (bottles)	10	12
Floor Mats	8	4

February Sales

	Vancouver	Quebec
Wiper Blades	23	12
Cleaning Fluid (bottles)	8	12
Floor Mats	4	5

Use matrix arithmetic to calculate the change in sales of each product in each store from January to February.

Solution The tables suggest two matrices:

$$J = \begin{bmatrix} 20 & 15 \\ 10 & 12 \\ 8 & 4 \end{bmatrix} \quad \text{and} \quad F = \begin{bmatrix} 23 & 12 \\ 8 & 12 \\ 4 & 5 \end{bmatrix}.$$

To compute the change in sales of each product for both stores, we want to subtract corresponding entries in these two matrices. In other words, we want to compute the difference of the two matrices:

$$F - J = \begin{bmatrix} 23 & 12 \\ 8 & 12 \\ 4 & 5 \end{bmatrix} - \begin{bmatrix} 20 & 15 \\ 10 & 12 \\ 8 & 4 \end{bmatrix} = \begin{bmatrix} 3 & -3 \\ -2 & 0 \\ -4 & 1 \end{bmatrix}.$$

Thus, the change in sales of each product is the following:

	Vancouver	Quebec
Wiper Blades	3	−3
Cleaning Fluid (bottles)	−2	0
Floor Mats	−4	1

Scalar Multiplication

A matrix A can be added to itself because the expression $A + A$ is the sum of two matrices that have the same dimensions. When we compute $A + A$, we end up doubling every entry in A. So we can think of the expression $2A$ as telling us to *multiply every element in A by 2.*

In general, to multiply a matrix by a number, multiply every entry in the matrix by that number. For example,

$$6 \begin{bmatrix} \frac{5}{2} & -3 \\ 1 & 0 \\ -1 & \frac{5}{6} \end{bmatrix} = \begin{bmatrix} 15 & -18 \\ 6 & 0 \\ -6 & 5 \end{bmatrix}.$$

It is traditional when talking about matrices to call individual numbers **scalars**. For this reason, we call the operation of multiplying a matrix by a number **scalar multiplication**.

EXAMPLE 3 Sales

The revenue generated by sales in the Vancouver and Quebec branches of the A-Plus auto parts store (see Example 2) was as follows:

January Sales in Canadian Dollars

	Vancouver	Quebec
Wiper Blades	140.00	105.00
Cleaning Fluid	30.00	36.00
Floor Mats	96.00	48.00

If the Canadian dollar was worth $0.65 U.S. at the time, compute the revenue in U.S. dollars.

Solution We need to multiply each revenue figure by 0.65. Let A be the matrix of revenue figures in Canadian dollars:

$$A = \begin{bmatrix} 140.00 & 105.00 \\ 30.00 & 36.00 \\ 96.00 & 48.00 \end{bmatrix}.$$

The revenue figures in U.S. dollars are then given by the scalar multiple

$$0.65A = 0.65 \begin{bmatrix} 140.00 & 105.00 \\ 30.00 & 36.00 \\ 96.00 & 48.00 \end{bmatrix} = \begin{bmatrix} 91.00 & 68.25 \\ 19.50 & 23.40 \\ 62.40 & 31.20 \end{bmatrix}.$$

In other words, in U.S. dollars, $91 worth of wiper blades was sold in Vancouver, $68.25 worth of wiper blades was sold in Quebec, and so on.

Formally, scalar multiplication is defined as follows:

Scalar Multiplication

If A is an $m \times n$ matrix and c is a real number, then cA is the $m \times n$ matrix obtained by multiplying all the entries of A by c. (We usually use lowercase letters $c, d, e, \ldots$ to denote scalars.) Thus, the ijth entry of cA is given by

$$(cA)_{ij} = c(A_{ij}).$$

In words, this rule is: To get the ijth entry of cA, multiply the ijth entry of A by c.

EXAMPLE 4 Combining Operations

Let $A = \begin{bmatrix} 2 & -1 & 0 \\ 3 & 5 & -3 \end{bmatrix}$, $B = \begin{bmatrix} 1 & 3 & -1 \\ 5 & -6 & 0 \end{bmatrix}$, and $C = \begin{bmatrix} x & y & w \\ z & t+1 & 3 \end{bmatrix}$.

Evaluate the following: $4A$, xB, and $A + 3C$.

Solution First, we find $4A$ by multiplying each entry of A by 4:

$$4A = 4 \begin{bmatrix} 2 & -1 & 0 \\ 3 & 5 & -3 \end{bmatrix} = \begin{bmatrix} 8 & -4 & 0 \\ 12 & 20 & -12 \end{bmatrix}.$$

Similarly, we find xB by multiplying each entry of B by x:

$$xB = x \begin{bmatrix} 1 & 3 & -1 \\ 5 & -6 & 0 \end{bmatrix} = \begin{bmatrix} x & 3x & -x \\ 5x & -6x & 0 \end{bmatrix}.$$

We get $A + 3C$ in two steps as follows:

$$A + 3C = \begin{bmatrix} 2 & -1 & 0 \\ 3 & 5 & -3 \end{bmatrix} + 3 \begin{bmatrix} x & y & w \\ z & t+1 & 3 \end{bmatrix}$$

$$= \begin{bmatrix} 2 & -1 & 0 \\ 3 & 5 & -3 \end{bmatrix} + \begin{bmatrix} 3x & 3y & 3w \\ 3z & 3t+3 & 9 \end{bmatrix}$$

$$= \begin{bmatrix} 2+3x & -1+3y & 3w \\ 3+3z & 3t+8 & 6 \end{bmatrix}.$$

Addition and scalar multiplication of matrices have nice properties, reminiscent of the properties of addition and multiplication of real numbers. Before we state them, we need to introduce some more notation.

If A is any matrix, then $-A$ is the matrix $(-1)A$. In other words, $-A$ is A multiplied by the scalar -1. This amounts to changing the signs of all the entries in A. For example,

$$-\begin{bmatrix} 4 & -2 & 0 \\ 6 & 10 & -6 \end{bmatrix} = \begin{bmatrix} -4 & 2 & 0 \\ -6 & -10 & 6 \end{bmatrix}.$$

For any two matrices A and B, $A - B$ is the same as $A + (-B)$. (Why?)

Also, a **zero matrix** is a matrix all of whose entries are zero. Thus, for example, the 2×3 zero matrix is

$$O = \begin{bmatrix} 0 & 0 & 0 \\ 0 & 0 & 0 \end{bmatrix}.$$

Now we state the most important properties of the operations that we have been talking about:

Properties of Matrix Addition and Scalar Multiplication

If A, B, and C are any $m \times n$ matrices and if O is the zero $m \times n$ matrix, then the following hold:

$A + (B + C) = (A + B) + C$	*Associative law*
$A + B = B + A$	*Commutative law*
$A + O = O + A = A$	*Additive identity law*
$A + (-A) = O = (-A) + A$	*Additive inverse law*
$c(A + B) = cA + cB$	*Distributive law*
$(c + d)A = cA + dA$	*Distributive law*
$1A = A$	*Scalar unit*
$0A = O$	*Scalar zero*

These properties would be obvious if we were talking about addition and multiplication of *numbers*, but here we are talking about addition and multiplication of *matrices*. We are using "+" to mean something new: matrix addition. There is no reason why matrix addition has to obey *all* the properties of addition of numbers. It happens that it does obey many of them, which is why it is convenient to call it *addition* in the first place. This means that we can manipulate equations involving matrices in much the same way that we manipulate equations involving numbers. One word of caution: We haven't yet discussed how to multiply matrices, and it probably isn't what you think. It will turn out that multiplication of matrices does *not* obey all the same properties as multiplication of numbers.

Transposition

We mention one more operation on matrices:

Transposition

If A is an $m \times n$ matrix, then its **transpose** is the $n \times m$ matrix obtained by writing its rows as columns, so that the ith row of the original matrix becomes the ith column of the transpose. We denote the transpose of the matrix A by A^T.

Visualizing Transposition

$$\begin{bmatrix} 2 & -3 \\ 1 & 0 \\ 5 & 1 \end{bmatrix} \quad \begin{bmatrix} 2 & 1 & 5 \\ -3 & 0 & 1 \end{bmatrix}$$

Quick Examples

1. Let $A = \begin{bmatrix} 2 & 0 & 1 & 0 \\ 33 & -22 & 0 & 5 \\ 1 & -1 & 2 & -2 \end{bmatrix}$. Then $A^T = \begin{bmatrix} 2 & 33 & 1 \\ 0 & -22 & -1 \\ 1 & 0 & 2 \\ 0 & 5 & -2 \end{bmatrix}$.

   3×4 matrix $\qquad$ 4×3 matrix

2. $\begin{bmatrix} -1 & 1 & 2 \end{bmatrix}^T = \begin{bmatrix} -1 \\ 1 \\ 2 \end{bmatrix}$.

   1×3 matrix $\qquad$ 3×1 matrix

using Technology

Technology can be used to compute transposes like Quick Example 1 on the right:

TI-83/84 Plus
Enter the matrix [A] using
MATRX ; EDIT
Home Screen: [A] ^{T}
(The symbol ^{T} is found in
MATRX ; MATH.)

Spreadsheet
Enter the matrix A in a convenient 3×4 block of cells (e.g., A1–D3). Highlight a 4×3 block for the answer (e.g., A5–C8).
Type =TRANSPOSE(A1:D3)
Press Control+Shift+Enter

 Website
www.WanerMath.com
    Student Home
        → On Line Utilities
        → Matrix Algebra Tool
Enter the matrix A as shown.

| Enter your matrices here. |
| A = [2, 0, 1, 0 |
| 33, -22, 0, 5 |
| 1, -1, 2, -2] |

Type A^T in the formula box and press "Compute".

Properties of Transposition

If A and B are $m \times n$ matrices, then the following hold:

$$(A + B)^T = A^T + B^T$$
$$(cA)^T = c(A^T)$$
$$(A^T)^T = A.$$

To see why the laws of transposition are true, let us consider the first one: $(A + B)^T = A^T + B^T$. The left-hand side is the transpose of $A + B$, and so is obtained by first adding A and B, and then writing the rows as columns. This is the same as first writing the rows of A and B individually as columns before adding, which gives the right-hand side. Similar arguments can be used to establish the other laws of transposition.

4.1 EXERCISES

▼ more advanced   ◆ challenging
⊤ indicates exercises that should be solved using technology

In each of Exercises 1–10, find the dimensions of the given matrix and identify the given entry.

1. $A = [1 \quad 5 \quad 0 \quad \frac{1}{4}]; a_{13}$ 2. $B = [44 \quad 55]; b_{12}$

3. $C = \begin{bmatrix} \frac{5}{2} \\ 1 \\ -2 \\ 8 \end{bmatrix}; C_{11}$ 4. $D = \begin{bmatrix} 15 & -18 \\ 6 & 0 \\ -6 & 5 \\ 48 & 18 \end{bmatrix}; d_{31}$

5. $E = \begin{bmatrix} e_{11} & e_{12} & e_{13} & \cdots & e_{1q} \\ e_{21} & e_{22} & e_{23} & \cdots & e_{2q} \\ \vdots & \vdots & \vdots & \ddots & \vdots \\ e_{p1} & e_{p2} & e_{p3} & \cdots & e_{pq} \end{bmatrix}; E_{22}$

6. $A = \begin{bmatrix} 2 & -1 & 0 \\ 3 & 5 & -3 \end{bmatrix}; A_{21}$ 7. $B = \begin{bmatrix} 1 & 3 \\ 5 & -6 \end{bmatrix}; b_{12}$

8. $C = \begin{bmatrix} x & y & w & e \\ z & t+1 & 3 & 0 \end{bmatrix}; C_{23}$

9. $D = [d_1 \quad d_2 \quad \cdots \quad d_n]; D_{1r}$ (any r)

10. $E = [d \quad d \quad d \quad d]; E_{1r}$ (any r)

11. Solve for $x, y, z,$ and w. **HINT** [See Example 1.]
$$\begin{bmatrix} x+y & y+z \\ z+w & w \end{bmatrix} = \begin{bmatrix} 3 & 5 \\ 7 & 4 \end{bmatrix}$$

12. Solve for $x, y, z,$ and w. **HINT** [See Example 1.]
$$\begin{bmatrix} x-y & x-z \\ y-w & w \end{bmatrix} = \begin{bmatrix} 0 & 0 \\ 0 & 6 \end{bmatrix}$$

In Exercises 13–20, evaluate the given expression. Take
$$A = \begin{bmatrix} 0 & -1 \\ 1 & 0 \\ -1 & 2 \end{bmatrix}, B = \begin{bmatrix} 0.25 & -1 \\ 0 & 0.5 \\ -1 & 3 \end{bmatrix}, \text{ and}$$
$$C = \begin{bmatrix} 1 & -1 \\ 1 & 1 \\ -1 & -1 \end{bmatrix}.$$

HINT [See Example 4 and Quick Examples page 234.]

13. $A + B$ 14. $A - C$
15. $A + B - C$ 16. $12B$
17. $2A - C$ 18. $2A + 0.5C$
19. $2A^T$ 20. $A^T + 3C^T$

In Exercises 21–28, evaluate the given expression. Take
$$A = \begin{bmatrix} 1 & -1 & 0 \\ 0 & 2 & -1 \end{bmatrix}, B = \begin{bmatrix} 3 & 0 & -1 \\ 5 & -1 & 1 \end{bmatrix}, \text{ and}$$
$$C = \begin{bmatrix} x & 1 & w \\ z & r & 4 \end{bmatrix}.$$

HINT [See Example 4 and Quick Examples page 234.]

21. $A + B$ 22. $B - C$
23. $A - B + C$ 24. $\frac{1}{2}B$
25. $2A - B$ 26. $2A - 4C$
27. $3B^T$ 28. $2A^T - C^T$

⊤ *Use technology in Exercises 29–36.*
$$\text{Let } A = \begin{bmatrix} 1.5 & -2.35 & 5.6 \\ 44.2 & 0 & 12.2 \end{bmatrix}, B = \begin{bmatrix} 1.4 & 7.8 \\ 5.4 & 0 \\ 5.6 & 6.6 \end{bmatrix},$$
$$C = \begin{bmatrix} 10 & 20 & 30 \\ -10 & -20 & -30 \end{bmatrix}.$$

29. $A - C$ 30. $C - A$
31. $1.1B$ 32. $-0.2B$
33. $A^T + 4.2B$ 34. $(A + 2.3C)^T$
35. $(2.1A - 2.3C)^T$ 36. $(A - C)^T - B$

APPLICATIONS

37. ***Sales*** The following table shows the number of Mac computers, iPods, and iPhones sold, in millions of units, in the first quarter (Q1) of 2009, and the changes over the previous year in each of 2010 Q1 and 2011 Q1.[1]

	Macs	**iPods**	**iPhones**
Q1 2009	2.5	22.7	4.4
Change in 2010	0.8	−1.7	4.3
Change in 2011	0.8	−1.6	7.5

Use matrix algebra to find the sales of Macs, iPods, and iPhones in Q1 2010 and Q1 2011. **HINT** [See Example 2.]

---

[1] Apple's first quarter ends at the end of December on the preceding year. Source for data: Apple company reports (www.apple.com/investor).

38. *Home Prices* The following table shows median home prices, in thousands of dollars, in four regions of the U.S. in December 2010, as well as the month-over-month changes for the subsequent two months.[2]

	Northeast	Midwest	South	West
Dec. 2010	238	140	149	205
Change in Jan. 2011	-2	-13	-13	-14
Change in Feb. 2011	-6	-5	-1	-1

Use matrix algebra to find the median home price in each region in January and February 2011. HINT [See Example 2.]

39. *Inventory* The *Left Coast Bookstore* chain has two stores, one in San Francisco and one in Los Angeles. It stocks three kinds of book: hardcover, softcover, and plastic (for infants). At the beginning of January, the central computer showed the following books in stock:

	Hard	Soft	Plastic
San Francisco	1,000	2,000	5,000
Los Angeles	1,000	5,000	2,000

Suppose its sales in January were as follows: 700 hardcover books, 1,300 softcover books, and 2,000 plastic books sold in San Francisco, and 400 hardcover, 300 softcover, and 500 plastic books sold in Los Angeles. Write these sales figures in the form of a matrix, and then show how matrix algebra can be used to compute the inventory remaining in each store at the end of January.

40. *Inventory* The *Left Coast Bookstore* chain discussed in Exercise 39 actually maintained the same sales figures for the first 6 months of the year. Each month, the chain restocked the stores from its warehouse by shipping 600 hardcover, 1,500 softcover, and 1,500 plastic books to San Francisco and 500 hardcover, 500 softcover, and 500 plastic books to Los Angeles.

   a. Use matrix operations to determine the total sales over the 6 months, broken down by store and type of book.

   b. Use matrix operations to determine the inventory in each store at the end of June.

41. *Profit* Annual revenues and production costs at *Luddington's Wellington Boots & Co.* are shown in the following spreadsheet.

	A	B	C	D
1	**Revenue**			
2		2004	2005	2006
3	**Full Boots**	$10,000	$9,000	$11,000
4	**Half Boots**	$8,000	$7,200	$8,800
5	**Sandals**	$4,000	$5,000	$6,000
6				
7	**Production Costs**			
8		2004	2005	2006
9	**Full Boots**	$2,000	$1,800	$2,200
10	**Half Boots**	$2,400	$1,440	$1,760
11	**Sandals**	$1,200	$1,500	$2,000

Use matrix algebra to compute the profits from each sector each year.

42. *Revenue* The following spreadsheet gives annual production costs and profits at *Gauss-Jordan Sneakers, Inc.*

	A	B	C	D
1	**Production Costs**			
2		2004	2005	2006
3	**Gauss Grip**	$1,800	$2,200	$2,400
4	**Air Gauss**	$1,400	$1,700	$1,200
5	**Gauss Gel**	$1,500	$2,000	$1,300
6				
7	**Profit**			
8		2004	2005	2006
9	**Gauss Grip**	$10,000	$14,000	$16,000
10	**Air Gauss**	$8,000	$12,000	$14,000
11	**Gauss Gel**	$9,000	$14,000	$12,000

Use matrix algebra to compute the revenues from each sector each year.

43. *Population Movement* In 2000 the U.S. population, broken down by regions, was 53.6 million in the Northeast, 64.4 million in the Midwest, 100.2 million in the South, and 63.2 million in the West.[3] In 2010 the population was 55.3 million in the Northeast, 66.9 million in the Midwest, 114.6 million in the South, and 71.9 million in the West. Set up the population figures for each year as a row vector, and then show how to use matrix operations to find the net increase or decrease of population in each region from 2000 to 2010. Assuming the same population growth from 2010 to 2020 as from 2000 to 2010, use matrix operations to predict the population in each region in 2020.

44. *Population Movement* In 1990 the U.S. population, broken down by regions, was 50.8 million in the Northeast, 59.7 million in the Midwest, 85.4 million in the South, and 52.8 million in the West.[4] Between 1990 and 2000, the population in the Northeast grew by 2.8 million, the population in the Midwest grew by 4.7 million, the population in the South grew by 14.8 million, and the population in the West grew by 10.4 million. Set up the population figures for 1990 and the growth figures for the decade as row vectors. Assuming the same population growth from 2000 to 2010 as from 1990 to 2000, use matrix operations to estimate the population in each region in 2010. Compare the predicted 2010 population in the Northeast with the actual population given in the preceding exercise.

Foreclosures *Exercises 45–48 are based on the following table, which shows the numbers of foreclosures in three states in April through August of 2011.[5]*

	April	May	June	July	Aug.
California	55,900	51,900	54,100	56,200	59,400
Florida	19,600	19,200	23,800	22,400	23,600
Texas	8,800	9,100	9,300	10,600	10,100

Use matrix algebra to compute the profits from each sector each year.

---

[2]Source for data: Census Bureau (www.census.gov).

[3]Source: U.S. Census Bureau http://2010.census.gov/2010census/data/apportionment-pop-text.php.

[4]*Ibid.*

[5]Figures are rounded. Source: www.realtytrac.com.

45. Use matrix algebra to determine the total number of fore-closures in each of the given months.

46. Use matrix algebra to determine the total number of foreclosures in each of the given states during the entire period shown.

47. Use matrix algebra to determine in which month the difference between the number of foreclosures in California and in Florida was greatest.

48. Use matrix algebra to determine in which region the difference between the number of foreclosures in April and August was greatest.

49. ▼ *Inventory Microbucks Computer Company* makes two computers, the Pomegranate II and the Pomegranate Classic, at two different factories. The Pom II requires 2 processor chips, 16 memory chips, and 20 vacuum tubes, while the Pom Classic requires 1 processor chip, 4 memory chips, and 40 vacuum tubes. Microbucks has in stock at the beginning of the year 500 processor chips, 5,000 memory chips, and 10,000 vacuum tubes at the Pom II factory, and 200 processor chips, 2,000 memory chips, and 20,000 vacuum tubes at the Pom Classic factory. It manufactures 50 Pom IIs and 50 Pom Classics each month.

a. Find the company's inventory of parts after 2 months, using matrix operations.

b. When (if ever) will the company run out of one of the parts?

50. ▼ *Inventory Microbucks Computer Company*, besides having the stock mentioned in Exercise 49, gets shipments of parts every month in the amounts of 100 processor chips, 1,000 memory chips, and 3,000 vacuum tubes at the Pom II factory, and 50 processor chips, 1,000 memory chips, and 2,000 vacuum tubes at the Pom Classic factory.

a. What will the company's inventory of parts be after 6 months?

b. When (if ever) will the company run out of one of the parts?

51. ▼ *Tourism in the 1990s* The following table gives the number of people (in thousands) who visited Australia and South Africa in 1998[6]:

	To	Australia	South Africa
From	**North America**	440	190
	Europe	950	950
	Asia	1,790	200

It was predicted that in 2008, 20,000 fewer people from North America would visit Australia and 40,000 more would visit South Africa, 50,000 more people from Europe would visit each of Australia and South Africa, and 100,000 more people from Asia would visit South Africa, but there would be no change in the number visiting Australia.

a. Represent the changes predicted in 2008 in the form of a matrix, and use matrix algebra to predict the number

of visitors from the three regions to Australia and South Africa in 2008.

b. Take A to be the 3×2 matrix whose entries are the 1998 tourism figures and take B to be the 3×2 matrix whose entries are the 2008 tourism figures. Give a formula (in terms of A and B) that predicts the average of the numbers of visitors from the three regions to Australia and South Africa in 1998 and 2008. Compute its value.

52. ▼ *Tourism in the 1990s* Referring to the 1998 tourism figures given in the preceding exercise, assume that the following (fictitious) figures represent the corresponding numbers from 1988.

	To	Australia	South Africa
From	**North America**	500	100
	Europe	900	800
	Asia	1,400	50

Take A to be the 3×2 matrix whose entries are the 1998 tourism figures and take B to be the 3×2 matrix whose entries are the 1988 tourism figures.

a. Compute the matrix $A - B$. What does this matrix represent?

b. Assuming that the changes in tourism over 1988–1998 are repeated in 1998–2008, give a formula (in terms of A and B) that predicts the number of visitors from the three regions to Australia and South Africa in 2008.

COMMUNICATION AND REASONING EXERCISES

53. Is it possible for a 2×3 matrix to equal a 3×2 matrix? Explain.

54. If A and B are 2×3 matrices and $A = B$, what can you say about $A - B$? Explain.

55. What does it mean when we say that $(A + B)_{ij} = A_{ij} + B_{ij}$?

56. What does it mean when we say that $(cA)_{ij} = c(A_{ij})$?

57. What would a 5×5 matrix A look like if $A_{ii} = 0$ for every i?

58. What would a matrix A look like if $A_{ij} = 0$ whenever $i \neq j$?

59. ▼ Give a formula for the ijth entry of the transpose of a matrix A.

60. ▼ A matrix is **symmetric** if it is equal to its transpose. Give an example of **a.** a nonzero 2×2 symmetric matrix and **b.** a nonzero 3×3 symmetric matrix.

61. ▼ A matrix is **skew-symmetric** or **antisymmetric** if it is equal to the negative of its transpose. Give an example of **a.** a nonzero 2×2 skew-symmetric matrix and **b.** a nonzero 3×3 skew-symmetric matrix.

62. ▼ Referring to Exercises 60 and 61, what can be said about a matrix that is both symmetric and skew-symmetric?

63. ▼ Why is matrix addition associative?

64. Describe a scenario (possibly based on one of the preceding examples or exercises) in which you might wish to compute $A - 2B$ for certain matrices A and B.

65. Describe a scenario (possibly based on one of the preceding examples or exercises) in which you might wish to compute $A + B - C$ for certain matrices A, B, and C.

---

[6]Figures are rounded to the nearest 10,000. Sources: South African Dept. of Environmental Affairs and Tourism; Australia Tourist Commission/*New York Times*, January 15, 2000, p. C1.

4.2 Matrix Multiplication

Suppose we download 3 movies at $10 each and 5 Chopin albums at $8 each. We calculate our total cost by computing the products' price × quantity and adding:

$$\text{Cost} = 10 \times 3 + 8 \times 5 = \$70.$$

Let us instead put the prices in a row vector

$$P = [10 \quad 8] \qquad \text{The price matrix}$$

and the quantities purchased in a column vector,

$$Q = \begin{bmatrix} 3 \\ 5 \end{bmatrix}. \qquad \text{The quantity matrix}$$

Q: *Why a row and a column instead of, say, two rows?*

A: It's rather a long story, but mathematicians found that it works best this way . . .

Because P represents the prices of the items we are purchasing and Q represents the quantities, it would be useful if the product PQ represented the total cost, a *single number* (which we can think of as a 1×1 matrix). For this to work, PQ should be calculated the same way we calculated the total cost:

$$PQ = [10 \quad 8]\begin{bmatrix} 3 \\ 5 \end{bmatrix} = [10 \times 3 + 8 \times 5] = [70].$$

Notice that we obtain the answer by multiplying each entry in P (going from left to right) by the corresponding entry in Q (going from top to bottom) and then adding the results.

The Product *Row* × *Column*

The **product** AB of a row matrix A and a column matrix B is a 1×1 matrix. The length of the row in A must match the length of the column in B for the product to be defined. To find the product, multiply each entry in A (going from left to right) by the corresponding entry in B (going from top to bottom) and then add the results.

Visualizing Matrix Multiplication

$$\begin{bmatrix} 2 \\ 10 \\ -1 \end{bmatrix}$$

$$[2 \quad 4 \quad 1]$$

2×2	$= 4$	Product of first entries $= 4$
4×10	$= 40$	Product of second entries $= 40$
$1 \times (-1)$	$= \underline{-1}$	Product of third entries $= -1$
	43	Sum of products $= 43$

Quick Examples

1. $[2 \quad 1]\begin{bmatrix} -3 \\ 1 \end{bmatrix} = [2 \times (-3) + 1 \times 1] = [-6 + 1] = [-5]$

2. $[2 \quad 4 \quad 1]\begin{bmatrix} 2 \\ 10 \\ -1 \end{bmatrix} = [2 \times 2 + 4 \times 10 + 1 \times (-1)] = [4 + 40 + (-1)]$

$$= [43]$$

Notes

1. In the discussion so far, *the row is on the left and the column is on the right* (RC again). (Later we will consider products where the column matrix is on the left and the row matrix is on the right.)

2. The row size has to match the column size. This means that, if we have a 1×3 row on the left, then the column on the right must be 3×1 in order for the product to make sense. For example, the product

$$[a \quad b \quad c] \begin{bmatrix} x \\ y \end{bmatrix}$$

is not defined. ∎

EXAMPLE 1 Revenue

The A-Plus auto parts store mentioned in examples in the previous section had the following sales in its Vancouver store:

	Vancouver
Wiper Blades	20
Cleaning Fluid (bottles)	10
Floor Mats	8

The store sells wiper blades for $7.00 each, cleaning fluid for $3.00 per bottle, and floor mats for $12.00 each. Use matrix multiplication to find the total revenue generated by sales of these items.

Solution We need to multiply each sales figure by the corresponding price and then add the resulting revenue figures. We represent the sales by a column vector, as suggested by the table:

$$Q = \begin{bmatrix} 20 \\ 10 \\ 8 \end{bmatrix}.$$

We put the selling prices in a row vector:

$$P = [\,7.00 \quad 3.00 \quad 12.00\,].$$

We can now compute the total revenue as the product

$$R = PQ = [\,7.00 \quad 3.00 \quad 12.00\,] \begin{bmatrix} 20 \\ 10 \\ 8 \end{bmatrix}$$

$$= [140.00 + 30.00 + 96.00] = [266.00].$$

So, the sale of these items generated a total revenue of $266.00.

Note We could also have written the quantity sold as a row vector (which would be Q^T) and the prices as a column vector (which would be P^T) and then multiplied them in the opposite order ($Q^T P^T$). Try this. ∎

EXAMPLE 2 **Relationship with Linear Equations**

a. Represent the matrix equation

$$[2 \quad -4 \quad 1]\begin{bmatrix} x \\ y \\ z \end{bmatrix} = [5]$$

as an ordinary equation.

b. Represent the linear equation $3x + y - z + 2w = 8$ as a matrix equation.

Solution

a. If we perform the multiplication on the left, we get the 1×1 matrix $[2x - 4y + z]$. Thus the equation may be rewritten as

$$[2x - 4y + z] = [5]. \quad \text{1 × 1 matrix on the left = 1 × 1 matrix on the right}$$

Saying that these two 1×1 matrices are equal means that their entries are equal, so we get the equation

$$2x - 4y + z = 5.$$

b. This is the reverse of part (a):

$$[3 \quad 1 \quad -1 \quad 2]\begin{bmatrix} x \\ y \\ z \\ w \end{bmatrix} = [8].$$

➡ **Before we go on...** The row matrix $[3 \quad 1 \quad -1 \quad 2]$ in Example 2 is the row of **coefficients** of the original equation. (See Section 3.1.) ∎

Now to the general case of matrix multiplication:

The Product of Two Matrices: General Case

In general, for matrices A and B, we can take the product AB only if the number of columns of A equals the number of rows of B (so that we can multiply the rows of A by the columns of B as above). The product AB is then obtained by taking its ijth entry to be

ijth entry of AB = Row i of $A \times$ Column j of B.   As defined above

Quick Examples

(R stands for row; C stands for column.)

1.
$$R_1 \to [2 \quad 0 \quad -1 \quad 3]\begin{matrix} C_1 & C_2 & C_3 \\ \downarrow & \downarrow & \downarrow \end{matrix}\begin{bmatrix} 1 & 1 & -8 \\ 1 & -6 & 0 \\ 0 & 5 & 2 \\ -3 & 8 & 1 \end{bmatrix} = [R_1 \times C_1 \quad R_1 \times C_2 \quad R_1 \times C_3]$$
$$= [-7 \quad 21 \quad -15]$$

2.
$$\begin{matrix} R_1 \to \\ R_2 \to \end{matrix}\begin{bmatrix} 1 & -1 \\ 0 & 2 \end{bmatrix}\begin{matrix} C_1 & C_2 \\ \downarrow & \downarrow \end{matrix}\begin{bmatrix} 3 & 0 \\ 5 & -1 \end{bmatrix} = \begin{bmatrix} R_1 \times C_1 & R_1 \times C_2 \\ R_2 \times C_1 & R_2 \times C_2 \end{bmatrix} = \begin{bmatrix} -2 & 1 \\ 10 & -2 \end{bmatrix}$$

In matrix multiplication we always take

Rows on the left × Columns on the right.

Look at the dimensions in the two Quick Examples on the previous page.

$$\underset{\downarrow\ \ \downarrow}{\text{Match}} \qquad \underset{\downarrow\ \ \downarrow}{\text{Match}}$$

$$(1 \times 4)(4 \times 3) \to 1 \times 3 \qquad (2 \times 2)(2 \times 2) \to 2 \times 2$$

The fact that the number of columns in the left-hand matrix equals the number of rows in the right-hand matrix amounts to saying that the middle two numbers must match as above. If we "cancel" the middle matching numbers, we are left with the dimensions of the product.

Before continuing with examples, we state the rule for matrix multiplication formally.

Multiplication of Matrices: Formal Definition

If A is an $m \times n$ matrix and B is an $n \times k$ matrix, then the product AB is the $m \times k$ matrix whose ijth entry is the product

$$\overset{\text{Row } i \text{ of } A \times \text{Column } j \text{ of } B}{}$$

$$(AB)_{ij} = [a_{i1}\ a_{i2}\ a_{i3}\ldots a_{in}]\begin{bmatrix} b_{1j} \\ b_{2j} \\ b_{3j} \\ \vdots \\ b_{nj} \end{bmatrix} = a_{i1}b_{1j} + a_{i2}b_{2j} + a_{i3}b_{3j} + \cdots + a_{in}b_{nj}.$$

EXAMPLE 3 **Matrix Product**

Calculate:

a. $\begin{bmatrix} 2 & 0 & -1 & 3 \\ 1 & -1 & 2 & -2 \end{bmatrix}\begin{bmatrix} 1 & 1 & -8 \\ 1 & 0 & 0 \\ 0 & 5 & 2 \\ -2 & 8 & -1 \end{bmatrix}$ **b.** $\begin{bmatrix} -3 \\ 1 \end{bmatrix}[2\ \ 1]$

Solution

a. Before we start the calculation, we check that the dimensions of the matrices match up.

$$\underset{2 \times 4 \qquad\quad 4 \times 3}{\overset{\text{Match}}{\nearrow\ \searrow}}$$

$$\begin{bmatrix} 2 & 0 & -1 & 3 \\ 1 & -1 & 2 & -2 \end{bmatrix}\begin{bmatrix} 1 & 1 & -8 \\ 1 & 0 & 0 \\ 0 & 5 & 2 \\ -2 & 8 & -1 \end{bmatrix}$$

Technology can be used to multiply the matrices in Example 3. Here is an outline for part (a) (see the Technology Guides at the end of the chapter for additional details on using a TI-83/84 Plus or a spreadsheet):

TI-83/84 Plus
Enter the matrices A and B using `MATRX`; EDIT
Home Screen: `[A]*[B]`
[More details on page 304.]

Spreadsheet
Enter the matrices in convenient blocks of cells (e.g., A1–D2 and F1–H4).
Highlight a 2×3 block for the answer.
Type `=MMULT(A1:D2,F1:H4)`
Press Control+Shift+Enter
[More details on page 308.]

Website
www.WanerMath.com
Student Home
→ On Line Utilities
→ Matrix Algebra Tool
Enter matrices as shown:

```
Enter your matrices here.
A = [2, 0, -1, 3
1, -1, 2, -2]

B = [1, 1, -8
1, 0, 0
0, 5, 2
-2, 8, -1]
```

Type `A*B` in the formula box and press "Compute". If you try to multiply two matrices whose product is not defined, you will get an error alert box telling you that.

The product of the two matrices is defined, and the product will be a 2×3 matrix (we remove the matching 4s: $(2 \times 4)(4 \times 3) \to 2 \times 3$). To calculate the product, we follow the previous prescription:

$$
\begin{array}{c}
 \; C_1 \; C_2 \; C_3 \\
 \; \downarrow \; \downarrow \; \downarrow
\end{array}
$$

$$
\begin{array}{c} R_1 \to \\ R_2 \to \end{array}
\begin{bmatrix} 2 & 0 & -1 & 3 \\ 1 & -1 & 2 & -2 \end{bmatrix}
\begin{bmatrix} 1 & 1 & -8 \\ 1 & 0 & 0 \\ 0 & 5 & 2 \\ -2 & 8 & -1 \end{bmatrix}
=
\begin{bmatrix} R_1 \times C_1 & R_1 \times C_2 & R_1 \times C_3 \\ R_2 \times C_1 & R_2 \times C_2 & R_2 \times C_3 \end{bmatrix}
$$

$$
= \begin{bmatrix} -4 & 21 & -21 \\ 4 & -5 & -2 \end{bmatrix}.
$$

b. The dimensions of the two matrices given are 2×1 and 1×2. Because the 1s match, the product is defined, and the result will be a 2×2 matrix.

$$
\begin{array}{c} \; C_1 \; C_2 \\ \; \downarrow \; \downarrow \end{array}
$$

$$
\begin{array}{c} R_1 \to \\ R_2 \to \end{array}
\begin{bmatrix} -3 \\ 1 \end{bmatrix}
\begin{bmatrix} 2 & 1 \end{bmatrix}
=
\begin{bmatrix} R_1 \times C_1 & R_1 \times C_2 \\ R_2 \times C_1 & R_2 \times C_2 \end{bmatrix}
=
\begin{bmatrix} -6 & -3 \\ 2 & 1 \end{bmatrix}.
$$

Note In part (a) we *cannot* multiply the matrices in the opposite order—the dimensions do not match. We say simply that the product in the opposite order is **not defined**. In part (b) we *can* multiply the matrices in the opposite order, but we would get a 1×1 matrix if we did so. Thus, order is important when multiplying matrices. In general, if AB is defined, then BA need not even be defined. If BA is also defined, it may not have the same dimensions as AB. And even if AB and BA have the same dimensions, they may have different entries. (See the next example.) ■

EXAMPLE 4   *AB* versus *BA*

Let $A = \begin{bmatrix} 1 & -1 \\ 0 & 2 \end{bmatrix}$ and $B = \begin{bmatrix} 3 & 0 \\ 5 & -1 \end{bmatrix}$. Find AB and BA.

Solution Note first that A and B are both 2×2 matrices, so the products AB and BA are both defined and are both 2×2 matrices—unlike the case in Example 3(b). We first calculate AB:

$$
AB = \begin{bmatrix} 1 & -1 \\ 0 & 2 \end{bmatrix} \begin{bmatrix} 3 & 0 \\ 5 & -1 \end{bmatrix} = \begin{bmatrix} -2 & 1 \\ 10 & -2 \end{bmatrix}.
$$

Now let's calculate BA:

$$
BA = \begin{bmatrix} 3 & 0 \\ 5 & -1 \end{bmatrix} \begin{bmatrix} 1 & -1 \\ 0 & 2 \end{bmatrix} = \begin{bmatrix} 3 & -3 \\ 5 & -7 \end{bmatrix}.
$$

Notice that BA has no resemblance to AB! Thus, we have discovered that, even for square matrices:

Matrix multiplication is not commutative.

In other words, $AB \neq BA$ in general, even when AB and BA both exist and have the same dimensions. (There are instances when $AB = BA$ for particular matrices A and B, but this is an exception, not the rule.)

EXAMPLE 5 **Revenue**

January sales at the A-Plus auto parts stores in Vancouver and Quebec are given in the following table.

	Vancouver	Quebec
Wiper Blades	20	15
Cleaning Fluid (bottles)	10	12
Floor Mats	8	4

The usual selling prices for these items are $7.00 each for wiper blades, $3.00 per bottle for cleaning fluid, and $12.00 each for floor mats. The discount prices for A-Plus Club members are $6.00 each for wiper blades, $2.00 per bottle for cleaning fluid, and $10.00 each for floor mats. Use matrix multiplication to compute the total revenue at each store, assuming first that all items were sold at the usual prices, and then that they were all sold at the discount prices.

Solution We can do all of the requested calculations at once with a single matrix multiplication. Consider the following two labeled matrices.

$$Q = \begin{matrix} & \mathbf{V} & \mathbf{Q} \\ \mathbf{Wb} \\ \mathbf{Cf} \\ \mathbf{Fm} \end{matrix} \begin{bmatrix} 20 & 15 \\ 10 & 12 \\ 8 & 4 \end{bmatrix}$$

$$P = \begin{matrix} & \mathbf{Wb} & \mathbf{Cf} & \mathbf{Fm} \\ \mathbf{Usual} \\ \mathbf{Discount} \end{matrix} \begin{bmatrix} 7.00 & 3.00 & 12.00 \\ 6.00 & 2.00 & 10.00 \end{bmatrix}$$

The first matrix records the quantities sold, while the second records the sales prices under the two assumptions. To compute the revenue at both stores under the two different assumptions, we calculate $R = PQ$.

$$R = PQ = \begin{bmatrix} 7.00 & 3.00 & 12.00 \\ 6.00 & 2.00 & 10.00 \end{bmatrix} \begin{bmatrix} 20 & 15 \\ 10 & 12 \\ 8 & 4 \end{bmatrix}$$

$$= \begin{bmatrix} 266.00 & 189.00 \\ 220.00 & 154.00 \end{bmatrix}$$

We can label this matrix as follows:

$$R = \begin{matrix} & \mathbf{V} & \mathbf{Q} \\ \mathbf{Usual} \\ \mathbf{Discount} \end{matrix} \begin{bmatrix} 266.00 & 189.00 \\ 220.00 & 154.00 \end{bmatrix}.$$

In other words, if the items were sold at the usual price, then Vancouver had a revenue of $266 while Quebec had a revenue of $189, and so on.

➡ **Before we go on...** In Example 5 we were able to calculate PQ because the dimensions matched correctly: $(2 \times 3)(3 \times 2) \rightarrow 2 \times 2$. We could also have multiplied them in the opposite order and gotten a 3×3 matrix. Would the product QP be meaningful? In an application like this, not only do the dimensions have to match, but also the *labels* have to match for the result to be meaningful. The labels on the three columns of P are the parts that were sold, and these are also the labels on the three rows of Q. Therefore, we can "cancel labels" at the same time that we cancel the dimensions in the product. However, the labels on the two columns of Q do not match the labels on the two rows of P, and there is no useful interpretation of the product QP in this situation. ∎

There are very special square matrices of every size: $1 \times 1, 2 \times 2, 3 \times 3$, and so on, called the **identity** matrices.

Identity Matrix

The $n \times n$ identity matrix I is the matrix with 1s down the **main diagonal** (the diagonal starting at the top left) and 0s everywhere else. In symbols,

$$I_{ii} = 1, \quad \text{and}$$

$$I_{ij} = 0 \quad \text{if } i \neq j.$$

Quick Examples

1. 1×1 identity matrix $I = [1]$

2. 2×2 identity matrix $I = \begin{bmatrix} 1 & 0 \\ 0 & 1 \end{bmatrix}$

3. 3×3 identity matrix $I = \begin{bmatrix} 1 & 0 & 0 \\ 0 & 1 & 0 \\ 0 & 0 & 1 \end{bmatrix}$

4. 4×4 identity matrix $I = \begin{bmatrix} 1 & 0 & 0 & 0 \\ 0 & 1 & 0 & 0 \\ 0 & 0 & 1 & 0 \\ 0 & 0 & 0 & 1 \end{bmatrix}$

Note Identity matrices are always square matrices, meaning that they have the same number of rows as columns. There is no such thing, for example, as the "2×4 identity matrix."

The next example shows why I is interesting. ∎

EXAMPLE 6 Identity Matrix

Evaluate the products AI and IA, where $A = \begin{bmatrix} a & b & c \\ d & e & f \\ g & h & i \end{bmatrix}$ and I is the 3×3 identity matrix.

Solution

First notice that A is arbitrary; it could be any 3×3 matrix.

$$AI = \begin{bmatrix} a & b & c \\ d & e & f \\ g & h & i \end{bmatrix} \begin{bmatrix} 1 & 0 & 0 \\ 0 & 1 & 0 \\ 0 & 0 & 1 \end{bmatrix} = \begin{bmatrix} a & b & c \\ d & e & f \\ g & h & i \end{bmatrix}$$

using Technology

Technology can be used to obtain an identity matrix as in Example 6. Here is an outline (see the Technology Guides at the end of the chapter for additional details on using a TI-83/84 Plus or a spreadsheet):

TI-83/84 Plus
3×3 identity matrix: `identity(3)`
Obtained from MATRX ; MATH
[More details on page 305.]

Spreadsheet
Click on a cell for the top left corner (e.g., B1).
Type `=IF(ROW(B1)-ROW($B$1)=COLUMN(B1)-COLUMN($B$1),1,0)`
Copy across and down.
[More details on page 308.]

Website
www.WanerMath.com
  Student Home
    → On Line Utilities
    → Matrix Algebra Tool

Just use `I` in the formula box to refer to the identity matrix of any dimension. The program will choose the correct dimension in the context of the formula. For example, if A is a 3×3 matrix, then the expression `I-A` uses the 3×3 identity matrix for I.

and

$$IA = \begin{bmatrix} 1 & 0 & 0 \\ 0 & 1 & 0 \\ 0 & 0 & 1 \end{bmatrix} \begin{bmatrix} a & b & c \\ d & e & f \\ g & h & i \end{bmatrix} = \begin{bmatrix} a & b & c \\ d & e & f \\ g & h & i \end{bmatrix}.$$

In both cases, the answer is the matrix A we started with. In symbols,

$$AI = A$$

and

$$IA = A$$

no matter which 3×3 matrix A you start with. Now this should remind you of a familiar fact from arithmetic:

$$a \cdot 1 = a$$

and

$$1 \cdot a = a.$$

That is why we call the matrix I the 3×3 *identity* matrix, because it appears to play the same role for 3×3 matrices that the identity 1 does for numbers.

➡ **Before we go on...** Try a similar calculation using 2×2 matrices: Let $A = \begin{bmatrix} a & b \\ c & d \end{bmatrix}$, let I be the 2×2 identity matrix, and check that $AI = IA = A$. In fact, the equation

$$AI = IA = A$$

works for square matrices of every dimension. It is also interesting to notice that $AI = A$ if I is the 2×2 identity matrix and A is any 3×2 matrix (try one). In fact, if I is any identity matrix, then $AI = A$ whenever the product is defined, and $IA = A$ whenever this product is defined. ■

We can now add to the list of properties we gave for matrix arithmetic at the end of Section 4.1 by writing down properties of matrix multiplication. In stating these properties, we shall assume that all matrix products we write are defined—that is, that the matrices have correctly matching dimensions. The first eight properties are the ones we've already seen; the rest are new.

Properties of Matrix Addition and Multiplication

If A, B, and C are matrices, if O is a zero matrix, and if I is an identity matrix, then the following hold:

$A + (B + C) = (A + B) + C$	*Additive associative law*
$A + B = B + A$	*Additive commutative law*
$A + O = O + A = A$	*Additive identity law*
$A + (-A) = O = (-A) + A$	*Additive inverse law*
$c(A + B) = cA + cB$	*Distributive law*
$(c + d)A = cA + dA$	*Distributive law*
$1A = A$	*Scalar unit*

$$
\begin{array}{ll}
0A = O & \textit{Scalar zero} \\
A(BC) = (AB)C & \textit{Multiplicative associative law} \\
c(AB) = (cA)B & \textit{Multiplicative associative law} \\
c(dA) = (cd)A & \textit{Multiplicative associative law} \\
AI = IA = A & \textit{Multiplicative identity law} \\
A(B + C) = AB + AC & \textit{Distributive law} \\
(A + B)C = AC + BC & \textit{Distributive law} \\
OA = AO = O & \textit{Multiplication by zero matrix}
\end{array}
$$

Note that we have not included a multiplicative commutative law for matrices, because the equation $AB = BA$ does not hold in general. In other words, matrix multiplication is *not* exactly like multiplication of numbers. (You have to be a little careful because it is easy to apply the commutative law without realizing it.)

We should also say a bit more about transposition. Transposition and multiplication have an interesting relationship. We write down the properties of transposition again, adding one new one.

Properties of Transposition

$$
(A + B)^T = A^T + B^T
$$
$$
(cA)^T = c(A^T)
$$
$$
(AB)^T = B^T A^T
$$

Notice the change in order in the last one. The order is crucial.

Quick Examples

1. $\left(\begin{bmatrix} 1 & -1 \\ 0 & 2 \end{bmatrix} \begin{bmatrix} 3 & 0 \\ 5 & -1 \end{bmatrix} \right)^T = \begin{bmatrix} -2 & 1 \\ 10 & -2 \end{bmatrix}^T = \begin{bmatrix} -2 & 10 \\ 1 & -2 \end{bmatrix}$ $(AB)^T$

2. $\begin{bmatrix} 3 & 0 \\ 5 & -1 \end{bmatrix}^T \begin{bmatrix} 1 & -1 \\ 0 & 2 \end{bmatrix}^T = \begin{bmatrix} 3 & 5 \\ 0 & -1 \end{bmatrix} \begin{bmatrix} 1 & 0 \\ -1 & 2 \end{bmatrix} = \begin{bmatrix} -2 & 10 \\ 1 & -2 \end{bmatrix}$ $B^T A^T$

3. $\begin{bmatrix} 1 & -1 \\ 0 & 2 \end{bmatrix}^T \begin{bmatrix} 3 & 0 \\ 5 & -1 \end{bmatrix}^T = \begin{bmatrix} 1 & 0 \\ -1 & 2 \end{bmatrix} \begin{bmatrix} 3 & 5 \\ 0 & -1 \end{bmatrix} = \begin{bmatrix} 3 & 5 \\ -3 & -7 \end{bmatrix}$ $A^T B^T$

These properties give you a glimpse of the field of mathematics known as **abstract algebra**. Algebraists study operations like these that resemble the operations on numbers but differ in some way, such as the lack of commutativity for multiplication seen here.

We end this section with more on the relationship between linear equations and matrix equations, which is one of the important applications of matrix multiplication.

EXAMPLE 7 Matrix Form of a System of Linear Equations

a. If

$$
A = \begin{bmatrix} 1 & -2 & 3 \\ 2 & 0 & -1 \\ -3 & 1 & 1 \end{bmatrix}, \ X = \begin{bmatrix} x \\ y \\ z \end{bmatrix}, \ \text{and } B = \begin{bmatrix} 3 \\ -1 \\ 0 \end{bmatrix},
$$

rewrite the matrix equation $AX = B$ as a system of linear equations.

b. Express the following system of equations as a matrix equation of the form $AX = B$:

$$2x + y = 3$$
$$4x - y = -1.$$

Solution

a. The matrix equation $AX = B$ is

$$\begin{bmatrix} 1 & -2 & 3 \\ 2 & 0 & -1 \\ -3 & 1 & 1 \end{bmatrix} \begin{bmatrix} x \\ y \\ z \end{bmatrix} = \begin{bmatrix} 3 \\ -1 \\ 0 \end{bmatrix}.$$

As in Example 2(a), we first evaluate the left-hand side and then set it equal to the right-hand side.

$$\begin{bmatrix} 1 & -2 & 3 \\ 2 & 0 & -1 \\ -3 & 1 & 1 \end{bmatrix} \begin{bmatrix} x \\ y \\ z \end{bmatrix} = \begin{bmatrix} x - 2y + 3z \\ 2x - z \\ -3x + y + z \end{bmatrix}$$

$$\begin{bmatrix} x - 2y + 3z \\ 2x - z \\ -3x + y + z \end{bmatrix} = \begin{bmatrix} 3 \\ -1 \\ 0 \end{bmatrix}$$

Because these two matrices are equal, their corresponding entries must be equal.

$$x - 2y + 3z = 3$$
$$2x \quad - z = -1$$
$$-3x + y + z = 0$$

In other words, the matrix equation $AX = B$ is equivalent to this system of linear equations. Notice that the coefficients of the left-hand sides of these equations are the entries of the matrix A. We call A the **coefficient matrix** of the system of equations. The entries of X are the unknowns and the entries of B are the right-hand sides 3, -1, and 0.

b. As we saw in part (a), the coefficient matrix A has entries equal to the coefficients of the left-hand sides of the equations. Thus,

$$A = \begin{bmatrix} 2 & 1 \\ 4 & -1 \end{bmatrix}.$$

X is the column matrix consisting of the unknowns, while B is the column matrix consisting of the right-hand sides of the equations, so

$$X = \begin{bmatrix} x \\ y \end{bmatrix} \quad \text{and} \quad B = \begin{bmatrix} 3 \\ -1 \end{bmatrix}.$$

The system of equations can be rewritten as the matrix equation $AX = B$ with this A, X, and B.

This translation of systems of linear equations into matrix equations is really the first step in the method of solving linear equations discussed in Chapter 3. There we worked with the **augmented matrix** of the system, which is simply A with B adjoined as an extra column.

Q: *When we write a system of equations as $AX = B$, couldn't we solve for the unknown X by dividing both sides by A?*

A: If we interpret division as multiplication by the inverse (for example, $2 \div 3 = 2 \times 3^{-1}$), we shall see in the next section that *certain* systems of the form $AX = B$ can be solved in this way, by multiplying both sides by A^{-1}. We first need to discuss what we mean by A^{-1} and how to calculate it.

4.2   EXERCISES

▼ more advanced   ◆ challenging
⊤ indicates exercises that should be solved using technology

In Exercises 1–28, compute the products. Some of these may be undefined. Exercises marked ⊤ *should be done using technology. The others should be done two ways: by hand and by using technology where possible.* HINT [See Example 3.]

1. $[\,1 \quad 3 \quad -1\,]\begin{bmatrix} 9 \\ 1 \\ -1 \end{bmatrix}$

2. $[\,4 \quad 0 \quad -1\,]\begin{bmatrix} -4 \\ 1 \\ 8 \end{bmatrix}$

3. $\begin{bmatrix} -1 & \frac{1}{2} \end{bmatrix}\begin{bmatrix} -\frac{1}{3} \\ 1 \end{bmatrix}$

4. $[\,-1 \quad 1\,]\begin{bmatrix} \frac{3}{4} \\ \frac{1}{4} \end{bmatrix}$

5. $[\,0 \quad -2 \quad 1\,]\begin{bmatrix} x \\ y \\ z \end{bmatrix}$

6. $[\,4 \quad -1 \quad 1\,]\begin{bmatrix} -x \\ x \\ y \end{bmatrix}$

7. $[\,1 \quad 3 \quad 2\,]\begin{bmatrix} 1 \\ -1 \end{bmatrix}$

8. $[\,3 \quad 2\,][\,1 \quad -2\,]$

9. $[\,-1 \quad 1\,]\begin{bmatrix} -3 & 1 & 4 & 3 \\ 0 & 1 & -2 & 1 \end{bmatrix}$

10. $[\,2 \quad -1\,]\begin{bmatrix} -3 & 1 & 4 & 3 \\ 4 & 0 & 1 & 3 \end{bmatrix}$

11. $[\,1 \quad -1 \quad 2 \quad 3\,]\begin{bmatrix} -1 & 2 & 0 \\ 2 & -1 & 0 \\ 0 & 5 & 2 \\ -1 & 8 & 1 \end{bmatrix}$

12. $[\,0 \quad 1 \quad -1 \quad 2\,]\begin{bmatrix} 1 & -2 & 1 \\ 0 & 1 & 3 \\ 6 & 0 & 2 \\ -1 & -2 & 11 \end{bmatrix}$

13. $\begin{bmatrix} 1 & 0 & -1 \\ 1 & 1 & 2 \end{bmatrix}\begin{bmatrix} 0 & 1 & -1 \\ 1 & 0 & 1 \\ 4 & 8 & 0 \end{bmatrix}$

14. $\begin{bmatrix} 0 & 1 & -1 \\ 3 & 1 & -1 \end{bmatrix}\begin{bmatrix} 1 & 1 \\ 4 & 2 \\ 0 & 1 \end{bmatrix}$

15. $\begin{bmatrix} 1 & 0 \\ 1 & -1 \end{bmatrix}\begin{bmatrix} 0 & 1 \\ 0 & 1 \end{bmatrix}$

16. $\begin{bmatrix} 1 & -1 \\ 1 & -1 \end{bmatrix}\begin{bmatrix} 3 & -3 \\ 5 & -7 \end{bmatrix}$

17. $\begin{bmatrix} 0 & 1 \\ 0 & 1 \end{bmatrix}\begin{bmatrix} 1 & 0 \\ 1 & -1 \end{bmatrix}$

18. $\begin{bmatrix} 3 & -3 \\ 5 & -7 \end{bmatrix}\begin{bmatrix} 1 & -1 \\ 1 & -1 \end{bmatrix}$

19. $\begin{bmatrix} 1 & -1 \\ 1 & -1 \end{bmatrix}\begin{bmatrix} 2 & 3 \\ 2 & 3 \end{bmatrix}$

20. $\begin{bmatrix} 0 & 1 \\ 1 & 0 \end{bmatrix}\begin{bmatrix} 3 & -3 \\ 2 & -1 \end{bmatrix}$

21. $\begin{bmatrix} 1 & -1 \\ -1 & 1 \end{bmatrix}\begin{bmatrix} 2 & 3 \\ 2 & 3 \\ 1 & 1 \end{bmatrix}$

22. $\begin{bmatrix} 0 & 1 & -1 \\ 0 & -1 & 1 \end{bmatrix}\begin{bmatrix} 3 & -3 \\ 2 & -1 \end{bmatrix}$

23. $\begin{bmatrix} 1 & 0 & -1 \\ 2 & -2 & 1 \\ 0 & 0 & 1 \end{bmatrix}\begin{bmatrix} 1 & -1 & 4 \\ 1 & 1 & 0 \\ 0 & 4 & 1 \end{bmatrix}$

24. $\begin{bmatrix} 1 & 2 & 0 \\ 4 & -1 & 1 \\ 1 & 0 & 1 \end{bmatrix}\begin{bmatrix} 1 & 2 & -4 \\ 4 & 1 & 0 \\ 0 & -2 & 1 \end{bmatrix}$

25. $\begin{bmatrix} 1 & 0 & 1 & 0 \\ -1 & 1 & 0 & 1 \\ -2 & 0 & 1 & 4 \\ 0 & -1 & 0 & 1 \end{bmatrix}\begin{bmatrix} 1 \\ -3 \\ 2 \\ 0 \end{bmatrix}$

26. $\begin{bmatrix} 1 & 1 & -7 & 0 \\ -1 & 0 & 2 & 4 \\ -1 & 0 & -2 & 1 \\ 1 & -1 & 1 & 1 \end{bmatrix}\begin{bmatrix} 1 \\ -3 \\ 2 \\ 1 \end{bmatrix}$

27. ⊤ $\begin{bmatrix} 1.1 & 2.3 & 3.4 & -1.2 \\ 3.4 & 4.4 & 2.3 & 1.1 \\ 2.3 & 0 & -2.2 & 1.1 \\ 1.2 & 1.3 & 1.1 & 1.1 \end{bmatrix}\begin{bmatrix} -2.1 & 0 & -3.3 \\ -3.4 & -4.8 & -4.2 \\ 3.4 & 5.6 & 1 \\ 1 & 2.2 & 9.8 \end{bmatrix}$

28. ⊤ $\begin{bmatrix} 1.2 & 2.3 & 3.4 & 4.5 \\ 3.3 & 4.4 & 5.5 & 6.6 \\ 2.3 & -4.3 & -2.2 & 1.1 \\ 2.2 & -1.2 & -1 & 1.1 \end{bmatrix}\begin{bmatrix} 9.8 & 1 & -1.1 \\ 8.8 & 2 & -2.2 \\ 7.7 & 3 & -3.3 \\ 6.6 & 4 & -4.4 \end{bmatrix}$

29. Find[7] $A^2 = A \cdot A$, $A^3 = A \cdot A \cdot A$, A^4, and A^{100}, given that

$$A = \begin{bmatrix} 0 & 1 & 1 & 1 \\ 0 & 0 & 1 & 1 \\ 0 & 0 & 0 & 1 \\ 0 & 0 & 0 & 0 \end{bmatrix}.$$

30. Repeat the preceding exercise with $A = \begin{bmatrix} 0 & 2 & 0 & -1 \\ 0 & 0 & 2 & 0 \\ 0 & 0 & 0 & 2 \\ 0 & 0 & 0 & 0 \end{bmatrix}$.

Exercises 31–38 should be done two ways: by hand and by using technology where possible.

Let

$$A = \begin{bmatrix} 0 & -1 & 0 & 1 \\ 10 & 0 & 1 & 0 \end{bmatrix}, \quad B = \begin{bmatrix} 0 & -1 \\ 1 & 1 \\ -1 & 3 \\ 5 & 0 \end{bmatrix}, \quad C = \begin{bmatrix} 1 & -1 \\ 1 & 1 \\ 1 & 1 \\ 1 & 1 \end{bmatrix}.$$

Evaluate:

31. AB **32.** AC **33.** $A(B - C)$ **34.** $(B - C)A$

Let $A = \begin{bmatrix} 1 & -1 \\ 0 & 2 \\ 0 & -2 \end{bmatrix}$, $B = \begin{bmatrix} 3 & 0 & -1 \\ 5 & -1 & 1 \end{bmatrix}$, $C = \begin{bmatrix} x & 1 & w \\ z & r & 4 \end{bmatrix}$.

Evaluate:

35. AB **36.** AC **37.** $A(B + C)$ **38.** $(B + C)A$

In Exercises 39–44, calculate (a) $P^2 = P \cdot P$ (b) $P^4 = P^2 \cdot P^2$ and (c) P^8. (Round all entries to four decimal places.) (d) Without computing it explicitly, find $P^{1,000}$.

39. ▼ $P = \begin{bmatrix} 0.2 & 0.8 \\ 0.2 & 0.8 \end{bmatrix}$ **40.** ▼ $P = \begin{bmatrix} 0.1 & 0.1 \\ 0.9 & 0.9 \end{bmatrix}$

41. ▼ $P = \begin{bmatrix} 0.1 & 0.9 \\ 0 & 1 \end{bmatrix}$ **42.** ▼ $P = \begin{bmatrix} 1 & 0 \\ 0.8 & 0.2 \end{bmatrix}$

43. ▼ $P = \begin{bmatrix} 0.3 & 0.3 & 0.4 \\ 0.3 & 0.3 & 0.4 \\ 0.3 & 0.3 & 0.4 \end{bmatrix}$

What do you notice about the rows of P? Compare with Exercise 39 and state a general result about square matrices that these two exercises seem to suggest.

44. ▼ $P = \begin{bmatrix} -0.3 & -0.3 & -0.3 \\ 0.9 & 0.9 & 0.9 \\ 0.4 & 0.4 & 0.4 \end{bmatrix}$

What do you notice about the columns of P? Compare with Exercise 40 and state a general result about square matrices that these two exercises seem to suggest.

In Exercises 45–48, translate the given matrix equations into systems of linear equations. HINT [See Example 7.]

45. $\begin{bmatrix} 2 & -1 & 4 \\ -4 & \frac{3}{4} & \frac{1}{3} \\ -3 & 0 & 0 \end{bmatrix} \begin{bmatrix} x \\ y \\ z \end{bmatrix} = \begin{bmatrix} 3 \\ -1 \\ 0 \end{bmatrix}$

46. $\begin{bmatrix} 1 & -1 & 4 \\ -\frac{1}{3} & -3 & \frac{1}{3} \\ 3 & 0 & 1 \end{bmatrix} \begin{bmatrix} x \\ y \\ z \end{bmatrix} = \begin{bmatrix} -3 \\ -1 \\ 2 \end{bmatrix}$

47. $\begin{bmatrix} 1 & -1 & 0 & 1 \\ 1 & 1 & 2 & 4 \end{bmatrix} \begin{bmatrix} x \\ y \\ z \\ w \end{bmatrix} = \begin{bmatrix} -1 \\ 2 \end{bmatrix}$

48. $\begin{bmatrix} 0 & 1 & 6 & 1 \\ 1 & -5 & 0 & 0 \end{bmatrix} \begin{bmatrix} x \\ y \\ z \\ w \end{bmatrix} = \begin{bmatrix} -2 \\ 9 \end{bmatrix}$

In Exercises 49–52, translate the given systems of equations into matrix form. HINT [See Example 7.]

49. $x - y = 4$
$\quad\ 2x - y = 0$

50. $2x + y = 7$
$\quad\ -x\quad\ = 9$

51. $x + y - z = 8$
$\quad\ 2x + y + z = 4$
$\quad\ \dfrac{3x}{4} \quad + \dfrac{z}{2} = 1$

52. $x + y + 2z = -2$
$\quad\ 4x + 2y - z = -8$
$\quad\ \dfrac{x}{2} - \dfrac{y}{3} \quad = 4$

APPLICATIONS

53. *Revenue* Your T-shirt operation is doing a booming trade. Last week you sold 50 tie-dye shirts for $15 each, 40 Suburban State University Crew shirts for $10 each, and 30 Lacrosse T-shirts for $12 each. Use matrix operations to calculate your total revenue for the week. HINT [See Example 1.]

54. *Revenue* Karen Sandberg, your competitor in Suburban State U's T-shirt market, has apparently been undercutting your prices and outperforming you in sales. Last week she sold 100 tie-dye shirts for $10 each, 50 (low quality) Crew shirts at $5 apiece, and 70 Lacrosse T-shirts for $8 each. Use matrix operations to calculate her total revenue for the week. HINT [See Example 1.]

55. *Real Estate* The following table shows the cost of 1,000 square feet of "business executive"-grade residential real estate in three cities at the end of 2011[8] together with the quantity your development company intends to purchase in each city.

	London	New York	Mumbai
Cost ($ millions)	1.15	0.80	0.50
Quantity Purchased (thousands of square feet)	10	20	10

Use matrix multiplication to estimate the total cost of the purchase.

---

[7] $A \cdot A \cdot A$ is $A(A \cdot A)$, or the equivalent $(A \cdot A)A$ by the associative law. Similarly, $A \cdot A \cdot A \cdot A = A(A \cdot A \cdot A) = (A \cdot A \cdot A)A = (A \cdot A)(A \cdot A)$; it doesn't matter where we place parentheses.

[8] Source: *Insights, World Cities Review* World Press, Savallis, Autumn 2011.

56. *Real Estate* Repeat Exercise 55 using the following table for Hong Kong, Paris, and Tokyo:[9]

	Hong Kong	**Paris**	**Tokyo**
Cost ($ millions)	2.10	1.15	1.30
Quantity Purchased (thousands of square feet)	10	30	5

Use matrix multiplication to estimate the total cost of the purchase.

57. *Revenue* Recall the *Left Coast Bookstore* chain from the preceding section. In January, it sold 700 hardcover books, 1,300 softcover books, and 2,000 plastic books in San Francisco; it sold 400 hardcover, 300 softcover, and 500 plastic books in Los Angeles. Now, hardcover books sell for $30 each, softcover books sell for $10 each, and plastic books sell for $15 each. Write a column matrix with the price data and show how matrix multiplication (using the sales and price data matrices) may be used to compute the total revenue at the two stores. HINT [See Example 5.]

58. *Profit* Refer back to Exercise 57, and now suppose that each hardcover book costs the stores $10, each softcover book costs $5, and each plastic book costs $10. Use matrix operations to compute the total *profit* at each store in January. HINT [See Example 5.]

T *Income* *Exercises 59–62 are based on the following spreadsheet, which shows the projected 2020 and 2030 U.S. male and female population in various age groups, as well as per capita incomes.*[10]

	A	B	C	D	E	F
1			2020 Population		2030 population	
2	Age	Mean Income ($1000)	Female (Millions)	Male (Millions)	Female (Millions)	Male (Millions)
3	15 to 24	14	23	24	25	26
4	25 to 44	42	43	43	45	46
5	45 to 64	48	43	41	42	41
6	65 to 84	29	31	20	40	31

59. Use matrix algebra to estimate the total income for females in 2020. (Round the answer to two significant digits.)

60. Use matrix algebra to estimate the total income for males in 2030. (Round the answer to two significant digits.)

61. Give a single matrix formula that expresses the difference in total income between males and females in 2020, and compute its value, rounded to two significant digits.

62. Give a single matrix formula that expresses the total income in 2030, and compute its value, rounded to two significant digits.

63. *Cheese Production* The total amount of cheese, in billions of pounds, produced in the 13 western and 12 north central U.S. states in 1999 and 2000 was as follows:[11]

	1999	**2000**
Western States	2.7	3.0
North Central States	3.9	4.0

Thinking of this table as a (labeled) 2×2 matrix P, compute the matrix product $[-1 \quad 1]P$. What does this product represent?

64. *Milk Production* The total amount of milk, in billions of pounds, produced in the 13 western and 12 north central U.S. states in 1999 and 2000 was as follows.[12]

	1999	**2000**
Western States	56	60
North Central States	57	59

Thinking of this table as a (labeled) 2×2 matrix P, compute the matrix product $P \begin{bmatrix} -1 \\ 1 \end{bmatrix}$. What does this product represent?

Foreclosures *Exercises 65–70 are based on the following table, which shows the numbers of foreclosures in three states during three months of 2011.*[13]

	June	**July**	**Aug.**
California	54,100	56,200	59,400
Florida	23,800	22,400	23,600
Texas	9,300	10,600	10,100

65. Each month, your law firm handles 10% of all foreclosures in California, 5% of all foreclosures in Florida, and 20% of all foreclosures in Texas. Use matrix multiplication to compute the total number of foreclosures handled by your firm in each of the months shown.

66. Your law firm handled 10% of all foreclosures in each state in June, 30% of all foreclosures in July, and 20% of all foreclosures in August 2011. Use matrix multiplication to compute the total number of foreclosures handled by your firm in each of the states shown.

67. Let A be the 3×3 matrix whose entries are the figures in the table, and let $B = [1 \quad 1 \quad 0]$. What does the matrix BA represent?

68. Let A be the 3×3 matrix whose entries are the figures in the table, and let $B = [1 \quad 1 \quad 0]^T$. What does the matrix AB represent?

[9]*Ibid.*

[10]The population figures are Census Bureau estimates, and the income figures are 2007 mean per capita incomes. All figures are approximate. Source: U.S. Census Bureau (www.census.gov).

[11]Figures are approximate. Source: Department of Agriculture/*New York Times*, June 28, 2001, p. C1.

[12]*Ibid.*

[13]Figures are rounded. Source: www.realtytrac.com.

69. ▼ Write a matrix product whose computation gives the total number by which the combined foreclosures for all three months in California and Texas exceeded the foreclosures in Florida. Calculate the product.

70. ▼ Write a matrix product whose computation gives the total number by which combined foreclosures in August exceeded foreclosures in June. Calculate the product.

71. ▼ *Costs* Microbucks Computer Co. makes two computers, the Pomegranate II and the Pomegranate Classic. The Pom II requires 2 processor chips, 16 memory chips, and 20 vacuum tubes, while the Pom Classic requires 1 processor chip, 4 memory chips, and 40 vacuum tubes. There are two companies that can supply these parts: Motorel can supply them at $100 per processor chip, $50 per memory chip, and $10 per vacuum tube, while Intola can supply them at $150 per processor chip, $40 per memory chip, and $15 per vacuum tube. Write down all of this data in two matrices, one showing the parts required for each model computer, and the other showing the prices for each part from each supplier. Then show how matrix multiplication allows you to compute the total cost for parts for each model when parts are bought from either supplier.

72. ▼ *Profits* Refer back to Exercise 71. It actually costs Motorel only $25 to make each processor chip, $10 for each memory chip, and $5 for each vacuum tube. It costs Intola $50 per processor chip, $10 per memory chip, and $7 per vacuum tube. Use matrix operations to find the total profit Motorel and Intola would make on each model.

73. ▼ *Tourism in the 1990s* The following table gives the number of people (in thousands) who visited Australia and South Africa in 1998.[14]

	To	**Australia**	**South Africa**
From	**North America**	440	190
	Europe	950	950
	Asia	1,790	200

You estimate that 5% of all visitors to Australia and 4% of all visitors to South Africa decide to settle there permanently. Take A to be the 3×2 matrix whose entries are the 1998 tourism figures in the above table and take

$$B = \begin{bmatrix} 0.05 \\ 0.04 \end{bmatrix} \quad \text{and} \quad C = \begin{bmatrix} 0.05 & 0 \\ 0 & 0.04 \end{bmatrix}.$$

Compute the products AB and AC. What do the entries in these matrices represent?

74. ▼ *Tourism in the 1990s* Referring to the tourism figures in the preceding exercise, you estimate that from 1998 to 2018, tourism from North America to each of Australia and South Africa will have increased by 20%, tourism from Europe by 30%, and tourism from Asia by 10%. Take A to be the 3×2 matrix whose entries are the 1998 tourism figures and take

$$B = \begin{bmatrix} 1.2 & 1.3 & 1.1 \end{bmatrix} \quad \text{and} \quad C = \begin{bmatrix} 1.2 & 0 & 0 \\ 0 & 1.3 & 0 \\ 0 & 0 & 1.1 \end{bmatrix}.$$

Compute the products BA and CA. What do the entries in these matrices represent?

75. 🔢▼ *Population Movement* In 2008, the population of the U.S., broken down by regions, was 54.1 million in the Northeast, 65.7 million in the Midwest, 112.9 million in the South, and 70.3 million in the West. The table below shows the population movement during the period 2008–2009. (Thus, 99.23% of the population in the Northeast stayed there, while 0.16% of the population in the Northeast moved to the Midwest, and so on.)[15]

	To	**Northeast**	**Midwest**	**South**	**West**
From	**Northeast**	0.9923	0.0016	0.0042	0.0019
	Midwest	0.0018	0.9896	0.0047	0.0039
	South	0.0056	0.0059	0.9827	0.0058
	West	0.0024	0.0033	0.0044	0.9899

Set up the 2008 population figures as a row vector. Then use matrix multiplication to estimate the population in each region in 2009. (Round all answers to the nearest 0.1 million.)

76. 🔢▼ *Population Movement* Assume that the percentages given in the preceding exercise also describe the population movements from 2009 to 2010. Use two matrix multiplications to estimate from the data in the preceding exercise the population in each region in 2010.

COMMUNICATION AND REASONING EXERCISES

77. Give an example of two matrices A and B such that AB is defined but BA is not defined.

78. Give an example of two matrices A and B of different dimensions such that both AB and BA are defined.

79. Compare addition and multiplication of 1×1 matrices to the arithmetic of numbers.

80. In comparing the algebra of 1×1 matrices, as discussed so far, to the algebra of real numbers (see Exercise 79), what important difference do you find?

81. Comment on the following claim: Every matrix equation represents a system of equations.

---

[14]Figures are rounded to the nearest 10,000. Sources: South African Dept. of Environmental Affairs and Tourism; Australia Tourist Commission/*New York Times*, January 15, 2000, p. C1.

[15]Note that this exercise ignores migration into or out of the country. Source: U.S. Census Bureau, Current Population Survey, 2009 Annual Social and Economic Supplement.

82. When is it true that both AB and BA are defined, even though neither A nor B is a square matrix?

83. ▼ Find a scenario in which it would be useful to "multiply" two row vectors according to the rule

$$[a \quad b \quad c][d \quad e \quad f] = [ad \quad be \quad cf].$$

84. ▼ Make up an application whose solution reads as follows.

$$\text{"Total revenue} = [10 \quad 100 \quad 30] \begin{bmatrix} 10 & 0 & 3 \\ 1 & 2 & 0 \\ 0 & 1 & 40 \end{bmatrix}.\text{"}$$

85. ▼ What happens in a spreadsheet if, instead of using the function MMULT, you use "ordinary multiplication" as shown here?

	A	B	C	D	E	F	G
1	2	0	7		1	1	-8
2	1	-1	0		1	0	0
3	-2	1	1		0	5	2
4							
5	=A1:C3*E1:G3						
6							
7							

86. ▼ Define the *naïve product* $A \square B$ of two $m \times n$ matrices A and B by

$$(A \square B)_{ij} = A_{ij} B_{ij}.$$

(This is how someone who has never seen matrix multiplication before might think to multiply matrices.) Referring to Example 1 in this section, compute and comment on the meaning of $P \square (Q^T)$.

4.3 Matrix Inversion

Now that we've discussed matrix addition, subtraction, and multiplication, you may well be wondering about matrix *division*. In the realm of real numbers, division can be thought of as a form of multiplication: Dividing 3 by 7 is the same as multiplying 3 by 1/7, the inverse of 7. In symbols, $3 \div 7 = 3 \times (1/7)$, or 3×7^{-1}. In order to imitate division of real numbers in the realm of matrices, we need to discuss the multiplicative **inverse,** A^{-1}, of a matrix A.

Note Because multiplication of real numbers is commutative, we can write, for example, $\frac{3}{7}$ as either 3×7^{-1} or $7^{-1} \times 3$. In the realm of matrices, multiplication is not commutative, so from now on we shall *never* talk about "division" of matrices (by "$\frac{B}{A}$" should we mean $A^{-1}B$ or BA^{-1}?). ∎

Before we try to find the inverse of a matrix, we must first know exactly what we *mean* by the inverse. Recall that the inverse of a number a is the number, often written a^{-1}, with the property that $a^{-1} \cdot a = a \cdot a^{-1} = 1$. For example, the inverse of 76 is the number $76^{-1} = 1/76$, because $(1/76) \cdot 76 = 76 \cdot (1/76) = 1$. This is the number calculated by the x^{-1} button found on most calculators. Not all numbers have an inverse. For example—and this is the only example—the number 0 has no inverse, because you cannot get 1 by multiplying 0 by anything.

The inverse of a matrix is defined similarly. To make life easier, we shall restrict attention to **square** matrices, matrices that have the same number of rows as columns.*

✳ Nonsquare matrices *cannot* have inverses in the sense that we are talking about here. This is not a trivial fact to prove.

Inverse of a Matrix

The **inverse** of an $n \times n$ matrix A is that $n \times n$ matrix A^{-1} which, when multiplied by A on either side, yields the $n \times n$ identity matrix I. Thus,

$$AA^{-1} = A^{-1}A = I.$$

If A has an inverse, it is said to be **invertible**. Otherwise, it is said to be **singular**.

> **Quick Examples**
>
> **1.** The inverse of the 1×1 matrix $[3]$ is $[1/3]$, because $[3][1/3] = [1] = [1/3][3]$.
>
> **2.** The inverse of the $n \times n$ identity matrix I is I itself, because $I \times I = I$. Thus, $I^{-1} = I$.
>
> **3.** The inverse of the 2×2 matrix $A = \begin{bmatrix} 1 & -1 \\ -1 & -1 \end{bmatrix}$ is $A^{-1} = \begin{bmatrix} \frac{1}{2} & -\frac{1}{2} \\ -\frac{1}{2} & -\frac{1}{2} \end{bmatrix}$,
>
> because $\begin{bmatrix} 1 & -1 \\ -1 & -1 \end{bmatrix} \begin{bmatrix} \frac{1}{2} & -\frac{1}{2} \\ -\frac{1}{2} & -\frac{1}{2} \end{bmatrix} = \begin{bmatrix} 1 & 0 \\ 0 & 1 \end{bmatrix}$ $AA^{-1} = I$
>
> and $\begin{bmatrix} \frac{1}{2} & -\frac{1}{2} \\ -\frac{1}{2} & -\frac{1}{2} \end{bmatrix} \begin{bmatrix} 1 & -1 \\ -1 & -1 \end{bmatrix} = \begin{bmatrix} 1 & 0 \\ 0 & 1 \end{bmatrix}$. $A^{-1}A = I$

Notes

1. It is possible to show that if A and B are square matrices with $AB = I$, then it must also be true that $BA = I$. In other words, once we have checked that $AB = I$, we know that B is the inverse of A. The second check, that $BA = I$, is unnecessary.

2. If B is the inverse of A, then we can also say that A is the inverse of B (why?). Thus, we sometimes refer to such a pair of matrices as an **inverse pair** of matrices. ∎

EXAMPLE 1 Singular Matrix

Can $A = \begin{bmatrix} 1 & 1 \\ 0 & 0 \end{bmatrix}$ have an inverse?

Solution No. To see why not, notice that both entries in the second row of AB will be 0, no matter what B is. So AB cannot equal I, no matter what B is. Hence, A is singular.

➡ **Before we go on...** If you think about it, you can write down many similar examples of singular matrices. There is only one number with no multiplicative inverse (0), but there are many matrices having no inverses. ∎

Finding the Inverse of a Square Matrix

Q : *In the box, it was stated that the inverse of* $\begin{bmatrix} 1 & -1 \\ -1 & -1 \end{bmatrix}$ *is* $\begin{bmatrix} \frac{1}{2} & -\frac{1}{2} \\ -\frac{1}{2} & -\frac{1}{2} \end{bmatrix}$. *How was that obtained?*

A : We can think of the problem of finding A^{-1} as a problem of finding four unknowns, the four unknown entries of A^{-1}:

$$A^{-1} = \begin{bmatrix} x & y \\ z & w \end{bmatrix}.$$

These unknowns must satisfy the equation $AA^{-1} = I$, or

$$\begin{bmatrix} 1 & -1 \\ -1 & -1 \end{bmatrix} \begin{bmatrix} x & y \\ z & w \end{bmatrix} = \begin{bmatrix} 1 & 0 \\ 0 & 1 \end{bmatrix}.$$

If we were to try to find the first column of A^{-1}, consisting of x and z, we would have to solve

$$\begin{bmatrix} 1 & -1 \\ -1 & -1 \end{bmatrix} \begin{bmatrix} x \\ z \end{bmatrix} = \begin{bmatrix} 1 \\ 0 \end{bmatrix}$$

or

$$x - z = 1$$
$$-x - z = 0.$$

To solve this system by Gauss-Jordan reduction, we would row-reduce the augmented matrix, which is A with the column $\begin{bmatrix} 1 \\ 0 \end{bmatrix}$ adjoined.

$$\begin{bmatrix} 1 & -1 & | & 1 \\ -1 & -1 & | & 0 \end{bmatrix} \rightarrow \begin{bmatrix} 1 & 0 & | & x \\ 0 & 1 & | & z \end{bmatrix}$$

To find the second column of A^{-1} we would similarly row-reduce the augmented matrix obtained by tacking on to A the second column of the identity matrix.

$$\begin{bmatrix} 1 & -1 & | & 0 \\ -1 & -1 & | & 1 \end{bmatrix} \rightarrow \begin{bmatrix} 1 & 0 & | & y \\ 0 & 1 & | & w \end{bmatrix}$$

The row operations used in doing these two reductions would be exactly the same. We could do both reductions simultaneously by "doubly augmenting" A, putting both columns of the identity matrix to the right of A.

$$\begin{bmatrix} 1 & -1 & | & 1 & 0 \\ -1 & -1 & | & 0 & 1 \end{bmatrix} \rightarrow \begin{bmatrix} 1 & 0 & | & x & y \\ 0 & 1 & | & z & w \end{bmatrix}$$

We carry out this reduction in the following example.

EXAMPLE 2 Computing Matrix Inverse

Find the inverse of each matrix.

a. $P = \begin{bmatrix} 1 & -1 \\ -1 & -1 \end{bmatrix}$ **b.** $Q = \begin{bmatrix} 1 & 0 & 1 \\ 2 & -2 & -1 \\ 3 & 0 & 0 \end{bmatrix}$

Solution

a. As described above, we put the matrix P on the left and the identity matrix I on the right to get a 2×4 matrix.

$$\begin{bmatrix} 1 & -1 & | & 1 & 0 \\ -1 & -1 & | & 0 & 1 \end{bmatrix}$$
$$\quad\;\; P \qquad\quad I$$

We now row-reduce the whole matrix:

$$\begin{bmatrix} 1 & -1 & 1 & 0 \\ -1 & -1 & 0 & 1 \end{bmatrix} \begin{matrix} \\ R_2 + R_1 \end{matrix} \rightarrow \begin{bmatrix} 1 & -1 & 1 & 0 \\ 0 & -2 & 1 & 1 \end{bmatrix} \begin{matrix} 2R_1 - R_2 \\ \\ \end{matrix} \rightarrow$$

$$\begin{bmatrix} 2 & 0 & 1 & -1 \\ 0 & -2 & 1 & 1 \end{bmatrix} \begin{matrix} \frac{1}{2}R_1 \\ -\frac{1}{2}R_2 \end{matrix} \rightarrow \begin{bmatrix} 1 & 0 & | & \frac{1}{2} & -\frac{1}{2} \\ 0 & 1 & | & -\frac{1}{2} & -\frac{1}{2} \end{bmatrix}.$$
$$\qquad\qquad\qquad\qquad\qquad\qquad\quad I \qquad\;\; P^{-1}$$

We have now solved the systems of linear equations that define the entries of P^{-1}. Thus,

$$P^{-1} = \begin{bmatrix} \frac{1}{2} & -\frac{1}{2} \\ -\frac{1}{2} & -\frac{1}{2} \end{bmatrix}.$$

b. The procedure to find the inverse of a 3 × 3 matrix (or larger) is just the same as for a 2 × 2 matrix. We place Q on the left and the identity matrix (now 3 × 3) on the right, and reduce.

$$
\begin{array}{cc} Q & I \end{array}
$$

$$
\left[\begin{array}{ccc|ccc} 1 & 0 & 1 & 1 & 0 & 0 \\ 2 & -2 & -1 & 0 & 1 & 0 \\ 3 & 0 & 0 & 0 & 0 & 1 \end{array}\right] \begin{array}{c} \\ R_2 - 2R_1 \\ R_3 - 3R_1 \end{array} \rightarrow \left[\begin{array}{ccc|ccc} 1 & 0 & 1 & 1 & 0 & 0 \\ 0 & -2 & -3 & -2 & 1 & 0 \\ 0 & 0 & -3 & -3 & 0 & 1 \end{array}\right] \begin{array}{c} 3R_1 + R_3 \\ R_2 - R_3 \\ \\ \end{array} \rightarrow
$$

$$
\left[\begin{array}{ccc|ccc} 3 & 0 & 0 & 0 & 0 & 1 \\ 0 & -2 & 0 & 1 & 1 & -1 \\ 0 & 0 & -3 & -3 & 0 & 1 \end{array}\right] \begin{array}{c} \frac{1}{3}R_1 \\ -\frac{1}{2}R_2 \\ -\frac{1}{3}R_3 \end{array} \rightarrow \left[\begin{array}{ccc|ccc} 1 & 0 & 0 & 0 & 0 & \frac{1}{3} \\ 0 & 1 & 0 & -\frac{1}{2} & -\frac{1}{2} & \frac{1}{2} \\ 0 & 0 & 1 & 1 & 0 & -\frac{1}{3} \end{array}\right].
$$

$$
\begin{array}{cc} \qquad\qquad I & \qquad Q^{-1} \end{array}
$$

Thus,

$$
Q^{-1} = \begin{bmatrix} 0 & 0 & \frac{1}{3} \\ -\frac{1}{2} & -\frac{1}{2} & \frac{1}{2} \\ 1 & 0 & -\frac{1}{3} \end{bmatrix}.
$$

We have already checked that P^{-1} is the inverse of P. You should also check that Q^{-1} is the inverse of Q.

The method we used in Example 2 can be summarized as follows:

Inverting an *n* × *n* Matrix

In order to determine whether an $n \times n$ matrix A is invertible or not, and to find A^{-1} if it does exist, follow this procedure:

1. Write down the $n \times 2n$ matrix $[A\,|\,I]$ (this is A with the $n \times n$ identity matrix set next to it).

2. Row-reduce $[A\,|\,I]$.

3. If the reduced form is $[I\,|\,B]$ (i.e., has the identity matrix in the left part), then A is invertible and $B = A^{-1}$. If you cannot obtain I in the left part, then A is singular. (See Example 3.)

Although there is a general formula for the inverse of a matrix, it is not a simple one. In fact, using the formula for anything larger than a 3 × 3 matrix is so inefficient that the row-reduction procedure is the method of choice even for computers. However, the general formula is very simple for the special case of 2 × 2 matrices:

Formula for the Inverse of a 2 × 2 Matrix

The inverse of a 2 × 2 matrix is

$$
\begin{bmatrix} a & b \\ c & d \end{bmatrix}^{-1} = \frac{1}{ad - bc} \begin{bmatrix} d & -b \\ -c & a \end{bmatrix}, \quad \text{provided } ad - bc \neq 0.
$$

If the quantity $ad - bc$ is zero, then the matrix is singular (noninvertible). The quantity $ad - bc$ is called the **determinant** of the matrix $\begin{bmatrix} a & b \\ c & d \end{bmatrix}$.

Quick Examples

1. $\begin{bmatrix} 1 & 2 \\ 3 & 4 \end{bmatrix}^{-1} = \dfrac{1}{(1)(4) - (2)(3)} \begin{bmatrix} 4 & -2 \\ -3 & 1 \end{bmatrix} = -\dfrac{1}{2} \begin{bmatrix} 4 & -2 \\ -3 & 1 \end{bmatrix}$

$\phantom{\textbf{1.} } = \begin{bmatrix} -2 & 1 \\ \frac{3}{2} & -\frac{1}{2} \end{bmatrix}$

2. $\begin{bmatrix} 1 & -1 \\ 2 & -2 \end{bmatrix}$ has determinant $ad - bc = (1)(-2) - (-1)(2) = 0$ and so is singular.

The formula for the inverse of a 2×2 matrix can be obtained using the technique of row reduction. (See the Communication and Reasoning Exercises at the end of the section.)

As we have mentioned earlier, not every square matrix has an inverse, as we see in the next example.

EXAMPLE 3 Singular 3 × 3 Matrix

Find the inverse of the matrix $S = \begin{bmatrix} 1 & 1 & 2 \\ -2 & 0 & 4 \\ 3 & 1 & -2 \end{bmatrix}$, if it exists.

Solution We proceed as before.

$$
\begin{matrix} S & & I \end{matrix}
$$

$$
\begin{bmatrix} 1 & 1 & 2 & | & 1 & 0 & 0 \\ -2 & 0 & 4 & | & 0 & 1 & 0 \\ 3 & 1 & -2 & | & 0 & 0 & 1 \end{bmatrix} \begin{matrix} \\ R_2 + 2R_1 \\ R_3 - 3R_1 \end{matrix} \rightarrow \begin{bmatrix} 1 & 1 & 2 & | & 1 & 0 & 0 \\ 0 & 2 & 8 & | & 2 & 1 & 0 \\ 0 & -2 & -8 & | & -3 & 0 & 1 \end{bmatrix} \begin{matrix} 2R_1 - R_2 \\ \\ R_3 + R_2 \end{matrix}
$$

$$
\rightarrow \begin{bmatrix} 2 & 0 & -4 & | & 0 & -1 & 0 \\ 0 & 2 & 8 & | & 2 & 1 & 0 \\ 0 & 0 & 0 & | & -1 & 1 & 1 \end{bmatrix}
$$

We stopped here, even though the reduction is incomplete, because there is *no hope* of getting the identity on the left-hand side. Completing the row reduction will not change the three zeros in the bottom row. So what is wrong? Nothing. As in Example 1, we have here a singular matrix. Any square matrix that, after row reduction, winds up with a row of zeros is singular. (See Exercise 77.)

➡ **Before we go on...** In practice, deciding whether a given matrix is invertible or singular is easy: Simply try to find its inverse. If the process works, then the matrix is invertible, and we get its inverse. If the process fails, then the matrix is singular. If you try to invert a singular matrix using a spreadsheet, calculator, or computer program, you should get an error. Sometimes, instead of an error, you will get a spurious answer due to round-off errors in the device. ∎

Using the Inverse to Solve a System of *n* Linear Equations in *n* Unknowns

Having used systems of equations and row reduction to find matrix inverses, we will now use matrix inverses to solve systems of equations. Recall that, at the end of the previous section, we saw that a system of linear equations could be written in the form

$$AX = B,$$

where A is the coefficient matrix, X is the column matrix of unknowns, and B is the column matrix of right-hand sides. Now suppose that there are as many unknowns as equations, so that A is a square matrix, and suppose that A is invertible. The object is to solve for the matrix X of unknowns, so we multiply both sides of the equation by the inverse A^{-1} of A, getting

$$A^{-1}AX = A^{-1}B.$$

Notice that we put A^{-1} on the left on both sides of the equation. Order matters when multiplying matrices, so we have to be careful to do the same thing to both sides of the equation. But now $A^{-1}A = I$, so we can rewrite the last equation as

$$IX = A^{-1}B.$$

Also, $IX = X$ (I being the identity matrix), so we really have

$$X = A^{-1}B,$$

and we have solved for X!

Moreover, we have shown that, if A is invertible and $AX = B$, then the only *possible* solution is $X = A^{-1}B$. We should check that $A^{-1}B$ is actually a solution by substituting back into the original equation.

$$AX = A(A^{-1}B) = (AA^{-1})B = IB = B$$

Thus, $X = A^{-1}B$ is a solution and is the only solution. Therefore, if A is invertible, $AX = B$ has exactly one solution.

On the other hand, if $AX = B$ has no solutions or has infinitely many solutions, we can conclude that A is not invertible (why?). To summarize:

Solving the Matrix Equation $AX = B$

If A is an invertible matrix, then the matrix equation $AX = B$ has the unique solution

$$X = A^{-1}B.$$

Quick Example

The system of linear equations

$$2x \qquad + z = 9$$
$$2x + y - z = 6$$
$$3x + y - z = 9$$

can be written as $AX = B$, where

$$A = \begin{bmatrix} 2 & 0 & 1 \\ 2 & 1 & -1 \\ 3 & 1 & -1 \end{bmatrix}, X = \begin{bmatrix} x \\ y \\ z \end{bmatrix} \quad \text{and} \quad B = \begin{bmatrix} 9 \\ 6 \\ 9 \end{bmatrix}.$$

The matrix A is invertible with inverse

$$A^{-1} = \begin{bmatrix} 0 & -1 & 1 \\ 1 & 5 & -4 \\ 1 & 2 & -2 \end{bmatrix}. \qquad \text{You should check this.}$$

Thus,

$$X = A^{-1}B = \begin{bmatrix} 0 & -1 & 1 \\ 1 & 5 & -4 \\ 1 & 2 & -2 \end{bmatrix}\begin{bmatrix} 9 \\ 6 \\ 9 \end{bmatrix} = \begin{bmatrix} 3 \\ 3 \\ 3 \end{bmatrix}$$

so that $(x, y, z) = (3, 3, 3)$ is the (unique) solution to the system.

using Technology

Here is an outline on the use of technology to do the calculations in Example 4 (see the Technology Guides at the end of the chapter for additional details on using a TI-83/84 Plus or a spreadsheet):

TI-83/84 Plus
Enter the four matrices `[A]`, `[B]`, `[C]`, `[D]` using `MATRX`; EDIT
Home Screen: `[A]`$^{-1}$`*[B]`, `[A]`$^{-1}$`*[C]`, `[A]`$^{-1}$`*[D]`
[More details on page 305.]

Spreadsheet
Enter the matrices A and B in convenient blocks of cells (e.g., A1–C3, E1–E3).
Highlight a 3×1 block for the answer.
Type `=MMULT(MINVERSE(A1:C3), E1:E3)`
Press Control+Shift+Enter.
[More details on page 309.]

Website
www.WanerMath.com
   Student Website
      → On Line Utilities
      → Matrix Algebra Tool
Enter `A^-1*B`, `A^-1*C`, and `A^-1*D` to compute these products after entering the matrices A, B, C, and D as shown earlier.

EXAMPLE 4 Solving Systems of Equations Using an Inverse

Solve the following three systems of equations.

a. $2x \qquad + z = 1$
$2x + y - z = 1$
$3x + y - z = 1$

b. $2x \qquad + z = 0$
$2x + y - z = 1$
$3x + y - z = 2$

c. $2x \qquad + z = 0$
$2x + y - z = 0$
$3x + y - z = 0$

Solution We *could* go ahead and row-reduce all three augmented matrices as we did in Chapter 3, but this would require a lot of work. Notice that the coefficients are the same in all three systems. In other words, we can write the three systems in matrix form as

a. $AX = B$ **b.** $AX = C$ **c.** $AX = D$

where the matrix A is the same in all three cases:

$$A = \begin{bmatrix} 2 & 0 & 1 \\ 2 & 1 & -1 \\ 3 & 1 & -1 \end{bmatrix}.$$

Now the solutions to these systems are

a. $X = A^{-1}B$ **b.** $X = A^{-1}C$ **c.** $X = A^{-1}D$

so the main work is the calculation of the single matrix A^{-1}, which we have already noted (Quick Example above) is

$$A^{-1} = \begin{bmatrix} 0 & -1 & 1 \\ 1 & 5 & -4 \\ 1 & 2 & -2 \end{bmatrix}.$$

Thus, the three solutions are:

a. $X = A^{-1}B = \begin{bmatrix} 0 & -1 & 1 \\ 1 & 5 & -4 \\ 1 & 2 & -2 \end{bmatrix} \begin{bmatrix} 1 \\ 1 \\ 1 \end{bmatrix} = \begin{bmatrix} 0 \\ 2 \\ 1 \end{bmatrix}$

b. $X = A^{-1}C = \begin{bmatrix} 0 & -1 & 1 \\ 1 & 5 & -4 \\ 1 & 2 & -2 \end{bmatrix} \begin{bmatrix} 0 \\ 1 \\ 2 \end{bmatrix} = \begin{bmatrix} 1 \\ -3 \\ -2 \end{bmatrix}$

c. $X = A^{-1}D = \begin{bmatrix} 0 & -1 & 1 \\ 1 & 5 & -4 \\ 1 & 2 & -2 \end{bmatrix} \begin{bmatrix} 0 \\ 0 \\ 0 \end{bmatrix} = \begin{bmatrix} 0 \\ 0 \\ 0 \end{bmatrix}$

➡ **Before we go on...** We have been speaking of *the* inverse of a matrix A. Is there only one? It is not hard to prove that a matrix A cannot have more than one inverse: If B and C were both inverses of A, then

$B = BI$ 　　　　Property of the identity
$\quad = B(AC)$ 　　Because C is an inverse of A
$\quad = (BA)C$ 　　Associative law
$\quad = IC$ 　　　Because B is an inverse of A
$\quad = C.$ 　　　Property of the identity

In other words, if B and C were both inverses of A, then B and C would have to be equal. ∎

FAQs

Which Method to Use in Solving a System

Q: *Now we have two methods to solve a system of linear equations $AX = B$: (1) Compute $X = A^{-1}B$, or (2) row-reduce the augmented matrix. Which is the better method?*

A: Each method has its advantages and disadvantages. Method (1), as we have seen, is very efficient when you must solve several systems of equations with the same coefficients, but it works only when the coefficient matrix is *square* (meaning that you have the same number of equations as unknowns) *and invertible* (meaning that there is a unique solution). The row-reduction method will work for all systems. Moreover, for all but the smallest systems, the most efficient way to find A^{-1} is to use row reduction. Thus, in practice, the two methods are essentially the same when both apply.

4.3 EXERCISES

▼ more advanced   ◆ challenging
Ⓣ indicates exercises that should be solved using technology

In Exercises 1–6, determine whether or not the given pairs of matrices are inverse pairs. HINT [See Quick Examples page 257.]

1. $A = \begin{bmatrix} 0 & 1 \\ 1 & 0 \end{bmatrix}$, $B = \begin{bmatrix} 0 & 1 \\ 1 & 0 \end{bmatrix}$

2. $A = \begin{bmatrix} 2 & 0 \\ 0 & 3 \end{bmatrix}$, $B = \begin{bmatrix} \frac{1}{2} & 0 \\ 0 & \frac{1}{2} \end{bmatrix}$

3. $A = \begin{bmatrix} 2 & 1 & 1 \\ 0 & 1 & 1 \\ 0 & 0 & 1 \end{bmatrix}$, $B = \begin{bmatrix} \frac{1}{2} & -\frac{1}{2} & 0 \\ 0 & 1 & -1 \\ 0 & 0 & 1 \end{bmatrix}$

4. $A = \begin{bmatrix} 1 & 1 & 1 \\ 0 & 1 & 1 \\ 0 & 0 & 1 \end{bmatrix}$, $B = \begin{bmatrix} 1 & -1 & 0 \\ 0 & 1 & -1 \\ 0 & 0 & 1 \end{bmatrix}$

5. $A = \begin{bmatrix} a & 0 & 0 \\ 0 & b & 0 \\ 0 & 0 & 0 \end{bmatrix}$, $B = \begin{bmatrix} a^{-1} & 0 & 0 \\ 0 & b^{-1} & 0 \\ 0 & 0 & 0 \end{bmatrix}$ $(a, b \neq 0)$

6. $A = \begin{bmatrix} a & 0 & 0 \\ 0 & b & 0 \\ 0 & 0 & c \end{bmatrix}$, $B = \begin{bmatrix} a^{-1} & 0 & 0 \\ 0 & b^{-1} & 0 \\ 0 & 0 & c^{-1} \end{bmatrix}$ $(a, b, c \neq 0)$

In Exercises 7–26, use row reduction to find the inverses of the given matrices if they exist, and check your answers by multiplication. HINT [See Example 2.]

7. $\begin{bmatrix} 1 & 1 \\ 2 & 1 \end{bmatrix}$ **8.** $\begin{bmatrix} 0 & 1 \\ 1 & 1 \end{bmatrix}$ **9.** $\begin{bmatrix} 0 & 1 \\ 1 & 0 \end{bmatrix}$ **10.** $\begin{bmatrix} 4 & 0 \\ 0 & 2 \end{bmatrix}$

11. $\begin{bmatrix} 2 & 1 \\ 1 & 1 \end{bmatrix}$ **12.** $\begin{bmatrix} 3 & 0 \\ 0 & \frac{1}{2} \end{bmatrix}$ **13.** $\begin{bmatrix} 2 & 1 \\ 4 & 2 \end{bmatrix}$ **14.** $\begin{bmatrix} 1 & 1 \\ 6 & 6 \end{bmatrix}$

15. $\begin{bmatrix} 1 & 1 & 1 \\ 0 & 1 & 1 \\ 0 & 0 & 1 \end{bmatrix}$ **16.** $\begin{bmatrix} 1 & 2 & 3 \\ 0 & 1 & 2 \\ 0 & 0 & 1 \end{bmatrix}$ **17.** $\begin{bmatrix} 1 & 1 & 1 \\ 1 & 0 & 2 \\ 1 & -1 & 1 \end{bmatrix}$

18. $\begin{bmatrix} 1 & 2 & 3 \\ 0 & 2 & 3 \\ 1 & 0 & 1 \end{bmatrix}$ **19.** $\begin{bmatrix} 1 & 1 & 1 \\ 1 & -1 & 0 \\ 1 & 2 & 3 \end{bmatrix}$ **20.** $\begin{bmatrix} 1 & -1 & 3 \\ 0 & 1 & 3 \\ 1 & 1 & 1 \end{bmatrix}$

21. $\begin{bmatrix} 1 & 1 & 1 \\ 1 & 0 & 1 \\ 1 & -1 & 1 \end{bmatrix}$ **22.** $\begin{bmatrix} 1 & 1 & 1 \\ 0 & 1 & 1 \\ 1 & 0 & 0 \end{bmatrix}$

23. $\begin{bmatrix} 1 & 0 & 1 & 0 \\ -1 & 1 & 0 & 1 \\ -1 & 0 & 0 & 1 \\ 0 & -1 & 0 & 1 \end{bmatrix}$ **24.** $\begin{bmatrix} 0 & 1 & 1 & 0 \\ -1 & 1 & 1 & 1 \\ -1 & 1 & 0 & 1 \\ 0 & -1 & 0 & 1 \end{bmatrix}$

25. $\begin{bmatrix} 1 & 2 & 3 & 4 \\ 0 & 1 & 2 & 3 \\ 0 & 0 & 1 & 2 \\ 0 & 0 & 0 & 1 \end{bmatrix}$ **26.** $\begin{bmatrix} 0 & 0 & 0 & 1 \\ 0 & 0 & 1 & 0 \\ 0 & 1 & 0 & 0 \\ 1 & 0 & 0 & 0 \end{bmatrix}$

In Exercises 27–34, compute the determinant of the given matrix. If the determinant is nonzero, use the formula for inverting a 2×2 matrix to calculate the inverse of the given matrix. HINT [See Quick Examples page 260.]

27. $\begin{bmatrix} 1 & 1 \\ 1 & -1 \end{bmatrix}$ **28.** $\begin{bmatrix} 4 & 1 \\ 0 & 2 \end{bmatrix}$ **29.** $\begin{bmatrix} 1 & 2 \\ 3 & 4 \end{bmatrix}$

30. $\begin{bmatrix} 1 & 0 \\ 0 & 1 \end{bmatrix}$ **31.** $\begin{bmatrix} \frac{1}{6} & -\frac{1}{6} \\ 0 & \frac{1}{6} \end{bmatrix}$ **32.** $\begin{bmatrix} 2 & 1 \\ 4 & 2 \end{bmatrix}$

33. $\begin{bmatrix} 1 & 0 \\ \frac{3}{4} & 0 \end{bmatrix}$ **34.** $\begin{bmatrix} 1 & 1 \\ 1 & 1 \end{bmatrix}$

T *In Exercises 35–42, use technology to find the inverse of the given matrix (when it exists). Round all entries in your answer to two decimal places. [Caution: Because of rounding errors, technology sometimes produces an "inverse" of a singular matrix. These often can be recognized by their huge entries.]*

35. $\begin{bmatrix} 1.1 & 1.2 \\ 1.3 & -1 \end{bmatrix}$

36. $\begin{bmatrix} 0.1 & -3.2 \\ 0.1 & -1.5 \end{bmatrix}$

37. $\begin{bmatrix} 3.56 & 1.23 \\ -1.01 & 0 \end{bmatrix}$

38. $\begin{bmatrix} 9.09 & -5.01 \\ 1.01 & 2.20 \end{bmatrix}$

39. $\begin{bmatrix} 1.1 & 3.1 & 2.4 \\ 1.7 & 2.4 & 2.3 \\ 0.6 & -0.7 & -0.1 \end{bmatrix}$

40. $\begin{bmatrix} 2.1 & 2.4 & 3.5 \\ 6.1 & -0.1 & 2.3 \\ -0.3 & -1.2 & 0.1 \end{bmatrix}$

41. $\begin{bmatrix} 0.01 & 0.32 & 0 & 0.04 \\ -0.01 & 0 & 0 & 0.34 \\ 0 & 0.32 & -0.23 & 0.23 \\ 0 & 0.41 & 0 & 0.01 \end{bmatrix}$

42. $\begin{bmatrix} 0.01 & 0.32 & 0 & 0.04 \\ -0.01 & 0 & 0 & 0.34 \\ 0 & 0.32 & -0.23 & 0.23 \\ 0.01 & 0.96 & -0.23 & 0.65 \end{bmatrix}$

In Exercises 43–48, use matrix inversion to solve the given systems of linear equations. (You previously solved similar systems using row reduction in Chapter 3.)
HINT [See Quick Example page 261.]

43. $x + y = 4$
   $x - y = 1$

44. $2x + y = 2$
   $2x - 3y = 2$

45. $\dfrac{x}{3} + \dfrac{y}{2} = 0$
   $\dfrac{x}{2} + y = -1$

46. $\dfrac{2x}{3} - \dfrac{y}{2} = \dfrac{1}{6}$
   $\dfrac{x}{2} - \dfrac{y}{2} = -1$

47. $-x + 2y - z = 0$
   $-x - y + 2z = 0$
   $2x \quad - z = 6$

48. $x + 2y \quad = 4$
   $y - z = 0$
   $x + 3y - 2z = 5$

In Exercises 49 and 50, use matrix inversion to solve each collection of systems of linear equations. HINT [See Example 4.]

49. **a.** $-x - 4y + 2z = 4$
   $x + 2y - z = 3$
   $x + y - z = 8$

   b. $-x - 4y + 2z = 0$
   $x + 2y - z = 3$
   $x + y - z = 2$

   c. $-x - 4y + 2z = 0$
   $x + 2y - z = 0$
   $x + y - z = 0$

50. **a.** $-x - 4y + 2z = 8$
   $x \quad - z = 3$
   $x + y - z = 8$

   b. $-x - 4y + 2z = 8$
   $x \quad - z = 3$
   $x + y - z = 2$

   c. $-x - 4y + 2z = 0$
   $x \quad - z = 0$
   $x + y - z = 0$

APPLICATIONS

Some of the following exercises are similar or identical to exercises and examples in Chapter 3. Use matrix inverses to find the solutions. We suggest you invert some of the matrices by hand, and others using technology.

51. **Nutrition** One serving of Campbell Soup Company's Campbell's® Pork & Beans contains 5 grams of protein and 21 grams of carbohydrates.[16] A typical slice of "lite" rye bread contains 4 grams of protein and 12 grams of carbohydrates.

   a. I am planning a meal of "beans-on-toast" and I want it to supply 20 grams of protein and 80 grams of carbohydrates. How should I prepare my meal?

   b. If I require A grams of protein and B grams of carbohydrates, give a formula that tells me how many slices of bread and how many servings of Pork & Beans to use.

52. **Nutrition** According to the nutritional information on a package of General Mills' Honey Nut Cheerios® brand cereal, each 1-ounce serving of Cheerios contains 3 grams protein and 24 grams carbohydrates.[17] Each half-cup serving of enriched skim milk contains 4 grams protein and 6 grams carbohydrates.

   a. I am planning a meal of cereal and milk and I want it to supply 26 grams of protein and 78 grams of carbohydrates. How should I prepare my meal?

   b. If I require A grams of protein and B grams of carbohydrates, give a formula that tells me how many servings of milk and Cheerios to use.

53. **Resource Allocation** You manage an ice cream factory that makes three flavors: Creamy Vanilla, Continental Mocha, and Succulent Strawberry. Into each batch of Creamy Vanilla go two eggs, one cup of milk, and two cups of cream. Into each batch of Continental Mocha go one egg, one cup of milk, and two cups of cream. Into each batch of Succulent Strawberry go one egg, two cups of milk, and one cup of cream. Your stocks of eggs, milk, and cream vary from day to day. How many batches of each flavor should you make in order to use up all of your ingredients if you have the following amounts in stock?

   a. 350 eggs, 350 cups of milk, and 400 cups of cream

   b. 400 eggs, 500 cups of milk, and 400 cups of cream

   c. A eggs, B cups of milk, and C cups of cream

54. **Resource Allocation** The *Arctic Juice Company* makes three juice blends: PineOrange, using 2 quarts of pineapple juice and 2 quarts of orange juice per gallon; PineKiwi, using 3 quarts of pineapple juice and 1 quart of kiwi juice per gallon; and OrangeKiwi, using 3 quarts of orange juice and 1 quart of kiwi juice per gallon. The amount of each kind of juice the company has on hand varies from day to day. How many gallons of each blend can it make on a day with the following stocks?

---

[16]According to the label information on a 16-oz. can.

[17]Actually, it is 23 grams carbohydrates. We made it 24 grams to simplify the calculation.

a. 800 quarts of pineapple juice, 650 quarts of orange juice, 350 quarts of kiwi juice.

b. 650 quarts of pineapple juice, 800 quarts of orange juice, 350 quarts of kiwi juice.

c. A quarts of pineapple juice, B quarts of orange juice, C quarts of kiwi juice.

Investing: Inverse Mutual Funds *Inverse mutual funds, sometimes referred to as "bear market" or "short" funds, are designed to deliver the opposite of the performance of the index or category they track, and so can be used by traders to bet against the stock market. Exercises 55–56 are based on the following table, which shows the performance of three such funds as of August 12, 2011.*[18]

	Year-to-Date Loss
SHPIX (Short Smallcap Profund)	6%
RYURX (Rydex Inverse S&P 500)	5%
RYIHX (Rydex Inverse High Yield)	7%

55. You invested a total of $9,000 in the three funds at the beginning of 2011, including an equal amount in RYURX and RYIHX. Your year-to-date loss from the first two funds amounted to $400. How much did you invest in each of the three funds?

56. You invested a total of $6,000 in the three funds at the beginning of 2011, including an equal amount in SHPIX and RYURX. Your total year-to-date loss amounted to $360. How much did you invest in each of the three funds?

Investing: Lesser-Known Stocks *Exercises 57–58 are based on the following information about the stocks of* KT Corporation, International Flavors & Fragrances, *and* Quality Systems.[19]

	Price	**Dividend Yield**
KT (KT Corporation)	$16	7%
IFF (International Flavors & Fragrances)	56	2
QSII (Quality Systems)	80	2

57. ▼ You invested a total of $8,400 in shares of the three stocks at the given prices and expected to earn $248 in annual dividends. If you purchased a total of 200 shares, how many shares of each stock did you purchase?

58. ▼ You invested a total of $11,200 in shares of the three stocks at the given prices and expected to earn $304 in annual dividends. If you purchased a total of 250 shares, how many shares of each stock did you purchase?

[18]Based on prices at the close of the stock market on August 12, 2011. YTD losses rounded to the nearest percentage point. Source: www. fidelity.com.

[19]Yields rounded to the nearest percentage point and stock prices at the close of the stock market on August 12, 2011 rounded to the nearest $1. Source: www.google.com/finance.

59. 🔢 ▼ *Population Movement* In 2009, the population of the U.S., broken down by regions, was 54.6 million in the Northeast, 66.0 million in the Midwest, 111.8 million in the South, and 70.6 million in the West. The table below shows the population movement during the period 2008–2009. (Thus, 99.23% of the population in the Northeast stayed there, while 0.16% of the population in the Northeast moved to the Midwest, and so on.)[20]

	To	**Northeast**	**Midwest**	**South**	**West**
From	**Northest**	0.9923	0.0016	0.0042	0.0019
	Midwest	0.0018	0.9896	0.0047	0.0039
	South	0.0056	0.0059	0.9827	0.0058
	West	0.0024	0.0033	0.0044	0.9899

Set up the 2009 population figures as a row vector. Use matrix inversion and multiplication to estimate the population in each region in 2008. (Round all answers to the nearest 0.1 million.)

60. ▼ 🔢 *Population Movement* Assume that the percentages given in the preceding exercise also describe the population movements from 2007 to 2008. Use two matrix multiplications to estimate from the data in the preceding exercise the population in each region in 2007.

61. ◆ 🔢 *Rotations* If a point (x, y) in the plane is rotated counterclockwise about the origin through an angle of 45°, its new coordinates (x', y') are given by

$$\begin{bmatrix} x' \\ y' \end{bmatrix} = R \begin{bmatrix} x \\ y \end{bmatrix}$$

where R is the 2×2 matrix $\begin{bmatrix} a & -a \\ a & a \end{bmatrix}$ and $a = \sqrt{1/2} \approx 0.7071$.

a. If the point $(2, 3)$ is rotated counterclockwise through an angle of 45°, what are its (approximate) new coordinates?

b. Multiplication by what matrix would result in a counterclockwise rotation of 90°? 135°? (Express the matrices in terms of R.) HINT [Think of a rotation through 90° as two successive rotations through 45°.]

c. Multiplication by what matrix would result in a *clockwise* rotation of 45°?

62. ◆ 🔢 *Rotations* If a point (x, y) in the plane is rotated counterclockwise about the origin through an angle of 60°, its new coordinates are given by

$$\begin{bmatrix} x' \\ y' \end{bmatrix} = S \begin{bmatrix} x \\ y \end{bmatrix}$$

where S is the 2×2 matrix $\begin{bmatrix} a & -b \\ b & a \end{bmatrix}$ and $a = 1/2$ and $b = \sqrt{3/4} \approx 0.8660$.

[20]Note that this exercise ignores migration into or out of the country. Source: U.S. Census Bureau, Current Population Survey, 2009 Annual Social and Economic Supplement.

a. If the point (2, 3) is rotated counterclockwise through an angle of 60°, what are its (approximate) new coordinates?

b. Referring to Exercise 61, multiplication by what matrix would result in a counterclockwise rotation of 105°? (Express the matrices in terms of S and the matrix R from Exercise 61.) HINT [Think of a rotation through 105° as a rotation through 60° followed by one through 45°.]

c. Multiplication by what matrix would result in a *clockwise* rotation of 60°?

☐ *Encryption Matrices are commonly used to encrypt data. Here is a simple form such an encryption can take. First, we represent each letter in the alphabet by a number, so let us take <space> = 0, A = 1, B = 2, and so on. Thus, for example, "ABORT MISSION" becomes*

[1   2   15   18   20   0   13   9   19   19   9   15   14]

To encrypt this coded phrase, we use an invertible matrix of any size with integer entries. For instance, let us take A to be the 2 × 2 matrix $\begin{bmatrix} 1 & 2 \\ 3 & 4 \end{bmatrix}$. We can first arrange the coded sequence of numbers in the form of a matrix with two rows (using zero in the last place if we have an odd number of characters) and then multiply on the left by A.

$$Encrypted\ Matrix = \begin{bmatrix} 1 & 2 \\ 3 & 4 \end{bmatrix}\begin{bmatrix} 1 & 15 & 20 & 13 & 19 & 9 & 14 \\ 2 & 18 & 0 & 9 & 19 & 15 & 0 \end{bmatrix}$$

$$= \begin{bmatrix} 5 & 51 & 20 & 31 & 57 & 39 & 14 \\ 11 & 117 & 60 & 75 & 133 & 87 & 42 \end{bmatrix},$$

which we can also write as

[5   11   51   117   20   60   31   75   57   133   39   87   14   42].

To decipher the encoded message, multiply the encrypted matrix by A^{-1}. Exercises 63–66 use the above matrix A for encoding and decoding.

63. ▼ Use the matrix A to encode the phrase "GO TO PLAN B".

64. ▼ Use the matrix A to encode the phrase "ABANDON SHIP".

65. ▼ Decode the following message, which was encrypted using the matrix A.

[33 69 54 126 11 27 20 60 29 59 65 149 41 87]

66. ▼ Decode the following message, which was encrypted using the matrix A.

[59   141   43   101   7   21   29   59   65   149   41   87]

COMMUNICATION AND REASONING EXERCISES

67. Multiple Choice: If A and B are square matrices with $AB = I$ and $BA = I$, then

(A) B is the inverse of A.

(B) A and B must be equal.

(C) A and B must both be singular.

(D) At least one of A and B is singular.

68. Multiple Choice: If A is a square matrix with $A^3 = I$, then

(A) A must be the identity matrix.

(B) A is invertible.

(C) A is singular.

(D) A is both invertible and singular.

69. What can you say about the inverse of a 2 × 2 matrix of the form $\begin{bmatrix} a & b \\ a & b \end{bmatrix}$?

70. If you think of numbers as 1 × 1 matrices, which numbers are invertible 1 × 1 matrices?

71. ▼ Use matrix multiplication to check that the inverse of a general 2 × 2 matrix is given by

$$\begin{bmatrix} a & b \\ c & d \end{bmatrix}^{-1} = \frac{1}{ad - bc}\begin{bmatrix} d & -b \\ -c & a \end{bmatrix} \text{ (provided } ad - bc \neq 0).$$

72. ◆ Derive the formula in Exercise 71 using row reduction. (Assume that $ad - bc \neq 0$.)

73. ▼ A **diagonal** matrix D has the following form.

$$D = \begin{bmatrix} d_1 & 0 & 0 & \cdots & 0 \\ 0 & d_2 & 0 & \cdots & 0 \\ 0 & 0 & d_3 & \cdots & 0 \\ \vdots & \vdots & \vdots & \ddots & \vdots \\ 0 & 0 & 0 & \cdots & d_n \end{bmatrix}$$

When is D singular? Why?

74. ▼ If a square matrix A row-reduces to the identity matrix, must it be invertible? If so, say why, and if not, give an example of such a (singular) matrix.

75. ▼ If A and B are invertible, check that $B^{-1}A^{-1}$ is the inverse of AB.

76. ▼ Solve the matrix equation $A(B + CX) = D$ for X. (You may assume that A and C are invertible square matrices.)

77. ◆ In Example 3 we said that, if a square matrix A row-reduces to a matrix with a row of zeros, then it is singular. Why?

78. ◆ Your friend has two square matrices A and B, neither of them the zero matrix, with the property that AB is the zero matrix. You immediately tell him that neither A nor B can possibly be invertible. How can you be so sure?

Game Theory

It frequently happens that you are faced with making a decision or choosing a best strategy from several possible choices. For instance, you might need to decide whether to invest in stocks or bonds, whether to cut prices of the product you sell, or what offensive play to use in a football game. In these examples, the result depends on something you cannot control. In the first case, your success depends on the future behavior of the economy. In the second case, it depends in part on whether your competitors also cut prices, and in the third case, it depends on the defensive strategy chosen by the opposing team.

We can model situations like these using **game theory**. We represent the various options and payoffs in a matrix and can then calculate the best single strategy or combination of strategies using matrix algebra and other techniques.

Game theory is very new compared with most of the mathematics you learn. It was invented in the 1920s by the noted mathematicians Emile Borel (1871–1956) and John von Neumann (1903–1957). Game theory's connection with linear programming was discovered even more recently, in 1947, by von Neumann, and further advances were made by the mathematician John Nash[*] (1928–), for which he received the 1994 Nobel Prize for Economics.

* Nash's turbulent life is the subject of the biography *A Beautiful Mind* by Sylvia Nasar (Simon & Schuster, 1998). The 2001 Academy Award-winning movie of the same title is a somewhat fictionalized account.

The Payoff Matrix and Expected Payoff

We have probably all played the simple game "Rock, Paper, Scissors" at some time in our lives. It goes as follows: There are two players—let us call them A and B—and at each turn, both players produce, by a gesture of the hand, either paper, a pair of scissors, or a rock. Rock beats scissors (since a rock can crush scissors), but is beaten by paper (since a rock can be covered by paper), while scissors beat paper (since scissors can cut paper). The round is a draw if both A and B show the same item. We could turn this into a betting game if, at each turn, we require the loser to pay the winner 1¢. For instance, if A shows a rock and B shows paper, then A pays B 1¢.

Rock, Paper, Scissors is an example of a **two-person zero-sum game**. It is called a zero-sum game because each player's loss is equal to the other player's gain.[†] We can represent this game by a matrix, called the **payoff matrix**.

† An example of a *nonzero-sum game* would be one in which the government taxed the earnings of the winner. In that case the winner's gain would be less than the loser's loss.

$$
\begin{array}{c}
 \\
\mathbf{A} \begin{array}{c} r \\ p \\ s \end{array}
\end{array}
\begin{array}{c}
\mathbf{B} \\
\begin{array}{ccc} r & p & s \end{array} \\
\left[\begin{array}{ccc} 0 & -1 & 1 \\ 1 & 0 & -1 \\ -1 & 1 & 0 \end{array} \right]
\end{array}
\quad \text{or just} \quad
P = \left[\begin{array}{ccc} 0 & -1 & 1 \\ 1 & 0 & -1 \\ -1 & 1 & 0 \end{array} \right]
$$

if we choose to omit the labels. In the payoff matrix, Player A's options, or **moves**, are listed on the left, while Player B's options are listed on top. We think of A as playing the rows and B as playing the columns. Positive numbers indicate a win for the row player, while negative numbers indicate a loss for the row player. Thus, for example, the p, s entry represents the outcome if A plays p (paper) and B plays s (scissors). In this event, B wins, and the −1 entry there indicates that A loses 1¢. (If that entry were −2 instead, it would have meant that A loses 2¢.)

Two-Person Zero-Sum Game

A **two-person zero-sum game** is one in which one player's loss equals the other's gain. We assume that the outcome is determined by each player's choice from among a fixed, finite set of moves. If Player A has m moves to choose from and Player B has n, we can represent the game using the **payoff matrix**, the $m \times n$ matrix showing the result of each possible pair of choices of moves.

In each round of the game, the way a player chooses a move is called a **strategy**. A player using a **pure strategy** makes the same move each round of the game. For example, if a player in the above game chooses to play scissors at each turn, then that player is using the pure strategy s. A player using a **mixed strategy** chooses each move a certain percentage of the time in a random fashion; for instance, Player A might choose to play p 50% of the time, and each of s and r 25% of the time.

Our ultimate goal is to be able to determine which strategy is best for each player to use. To do that, we need to know how to evaluate strategies. The fundamental calculation we need is that of the **expected payoff** resulting from a pair of strategies. Let's look at a simple example.

EXAMPLE 1 Expected Payoff

Consider the following game:

$$
\begin{array}{cc}
 & \mathbf{B} \\
 & \begin{array}{cc} a & b \end{array} \\
\mathbf{A}\ \begin{array}{c} p \\ q \end{array} & \begin{bmatrix} 3 & -1 \\ -2 & 3 \end{bmatrix}.
\end{array}
$$

Player A decides to pick moves at random, choosing to play p 75% of the time and q 25% of the time. Player B also picks moves at random, choosing a 20% of the time and b 80% of the time. On average, how much does A expect to win or lose?

Solution Suppose they play the game 100 times. Each time they play there are four possible outcomes:

Case 1: A plays p, B plays a.
Because A plays p only 75% of the time and B plays a only 20% of the time, we expect this case to occur $0.75 \times 0.20 = 0.15$, or 15% of the time, or 15 times out of 100. Each time this happens, A gains 3 points, so we get a contribution of $15 \times 3 = 45$ points to A's total winnings.

Case 2: A plays p, B plays b.
Because A plays p only 75% of the time and B plays b only 80% of the time, we expect this case to occur $0.75 \times 0.80 = 0.60$, or 60 times out of 100. Each time this happens, A loses 1 point, so we get a contribution of $60 \times -1 = -60$ to A's total winnings.

Case 3: A plays q, B plays a.
This case occurs $0.25 \times 0.20 = 0.05$, or 5 out of 100 times, with a loss of 2 points to A each time, giving a contribution of $5 \times -2 = -10$ to A's total winnings.

Case 4: A plays q, B plays b.
This case occurs $0.25 \times 0.80 = 0.20$, or 20 out of 100 times, with a gain of 3 points to A each time, giving a contribution of $20 \times 3 = 60$ to A's total winnings.

Summing to get A's total winnings and then dividing by the number of times the game is played gives the average value of

$$(45 - 60 - 10 + 60)/100 = 0.35$$

so that A can expect to win an average of 0.35 points per play of the game. We call 0.35 the **expected payoff** of the game resulting from these particular strategies for A and B.

This calculation was somewhat tedious and it would only get worse if A and B had many moves to choose from. There is a far more convenient way of doing exactly the same calculation, using matrix multiplication: We start by representing the player's strategies as matrices. For reasons to become clear in a moment, we record A's strategy as a row matrix:

$$R = [0.75 \quad 0.25].$$

▦▦ **using** Technology

The use of technology becomes indispensable when we need to do several calculations or when the matrices involved are big. See the technology note accompanying Example 3 in Section 4.2 on page 246 for instructions on multiplying matrices using a TI-83/84 Plus, a spreadsheet, and the Matrix Algebra Tool at the Website.

We record B's strategy as a column matrix:

$$C = \begin{bmatrix} 0.20 \\ 0.80 \end{bmatrix}.$$

(We will sometimes write column vectors using transpose notation, writing, for example, $[0.20 \quad 0.80]^T$ for the column above, to save space.) Now: *The expected payoff is the matrix product RPC, where P is the payoff matrix!*

$$\text{Expected payoff} = RPC = [0.75 \quad 0.25] \begin{bmatrix} 3 & -1 \\ -2 & 3 \end{bmatrix} \begin{bmatrix} 0.20 \\ 0.80 \end{bmatrix}$$

$$= [1.75 \quad 0] \begin{bmatrix} 0.20 \\ 0.80 \end{bmatrix} = [0.35].$$

Why does this work? Write out the arithmetic involved in the matrix product RPC to see what we calculated:

$$[0.75 \times 3 + 0.25 \times (-2)] \times 0.20 + [0.75 \times (-1) + 0.25 \times 3] \times 0.80$$
$$= 0.75 \times 3 \times 0.20 + 0.25 \times (-2) \times 0.20 + 0.75 \times (-1) \times 0.80 + 0.25 \times 3 \times 0.80$$
$$= \quad \text{Case 1} \quad + \quad \text{Case 3} \quad + \quad \text{Case 2} \quad + \quad \text{Case 4.}$$

So, the matrix product does all at once the various cases we considered above.

To summarize what we just saw:

The Expected Payoff resulting from Mixed Strategies R and C

The **expected payoff of a game resulting from given mixed strategies** is the average payoff that occurs if the game is played a large number of times with the row and column players using the given strategies.

To compute the expected payoff resulting from mixed strategies R and C:

1. Write the row player's mixed strategy as a row matrix R.

2. Write the column player's mixed strategy as a column matrix C.

3. Calculate the product RPC, where P is the payoff matrix. This product is a 1×1 matrix whose entry is the expected payoff e.

Quick Example

Consider "Rock, Paper, Scissors."

$$
\mathbf{A} \begin{array}{c} r \\ p \\ s \end{array}
\overset{\displaystyle \mathbf{B}}{\overset{\begin{array}{ccc} r & p & s \end{array}}{\begin{bmatrix} 0 & -1 & 1 \\ 1 & 0 & -1 \\ -1 & 1 & 0 \end{bmatrix}}}
$$

Suppose that the row player plays *rock* half the time and each of the other two strategies a quarter of the time, and the column player always plays *paper*. We write

$$
R = \begin{bmatrix} \dfrac{1}{2} & \dfrac{1}{4} & \dfrac{1}{4} \end{bmatrix}, \quad C = \begin{bmatrix} 0 \\ 1 \\ 0 \end{bmatrix}.
$$

So,

$$
e = RPC = \begin{bmatrix} \dfrac{1}{2} & \dfrac{1}{4} & \dfrac{1}{4} \end{bmatrix} \begin{bmatrix} 0 & -1 & 1 \\ 1 & 0 & -1 \\ -1 & 1 & 0 \end{bmatrix} \begin{bmatrix} 0 \\ 1 \\ 0 \end{bmatrix}
$$

$$
= \begin{bmatrix} \dfrac{1}{2} & \dfrac{1}{4} & \dfrac{1}{4} \end{bmatrix} \begin{bmatrix} -1 \\ 0 \\ 1 \end{bmatrix} = -\dfrac{1}{4}.
$$

Thus, player A can expect to lose an average of once every four plays.

Solving a Game

Now that we know how to evaluate particular strategies, we want to find the *best* strategy. The next example takes us another step toward that goal.

EXAMPLE 2 Television Ratings Wars

Commercial TV station RTV and cultural station CTV are competing for viewers in the Tuesday prime-time 9–10 PM time slot. RTV is trying to decide whether to show a sitcom, a docudrama, a reality show, or a movie, while CTV is thinking about either a nature documentary, a symphony concert, a ballet, or an opera. A television rating company estimates the payoffs for the various alternatives as follows. (Each point indicates a shift of 1,000 viewers from one channel to the other; thus, for instance, -2 indicates a shift of 2,000 viewers from RTV to CTV.)

		CTV			
		Nature Doc.	Symphony	Ballet	Opera
RTV	Sitcom	2	1	−2	2
	Docudrama	−1	1	−1	2
	Reality Show	−2	0	0	1
	Movie	3	1	−1	1

a. If RTV notices that CTV is showing nature documentaries half the time and symphonies the other half, what would RTV's best strategy be, and how many viewers would it gain if it followed this strategy?

b. If, on the other hand, CTV notices that RTV is showing docudramas half the time and reality shows the other half, what would CTV's best strategy be, and how many viewers would it gain or lose if it followed this strategy?

Solution

a. We are given the matrix of the game, P, in the table above, and we are given CTV's strategy $C = [0.50 \ 0.50 \ 0 \ 0]^T$. We are not given RTV's strategy R. To say that RTV is looking for its best strategy is to say that it wants the resulting expected payoff $e = RPC$ to be as high as possible. So, we take $R = [x \ y \ z \ t]$ and look for values for x, y, z, and t that make RPC as high as possible. First, we calculate e in terms of these unknowns:

$$e = RPC = [x \quad y \quad z \quad t] \begin{bmatrix} 2 & 1 & -2 & 2 \\ -1 & 1 & -1 & 2 \\ -2 & 0 & 0 & 1 \\ 3 & 1 & -1 & 1 \end{bmatrix} \begin{bmatrix} 0.50 \\ 0.50 \\ 0 \\ 0 \end{bmatrix}$$

$$= [x \quad y \quad z \quad t] \begin{bmatrix} 1.5 \\ 0 \\ -1 \\ 2 \end{bmatrix} = 1.5x - z + 2t.$$

Now, the unknowns x, y, z, and t must be nonnegative and add up to 1 (why?). Because t has the largest coefficient, 2, we'll get the best result by making it as large as possible, namely, $t = 1$, leaving $x = y = z = 0$. Thus, RTV's best strategy is $R = [0 \ 0 \ 0 \ 1]$. In other words, RTV should use the pure strategy of showing a movie every Tuesday evening. If it does so, the expected payoff will be

$$e = 1.5(0) - 0 + 2(1) = 2$$

so RTV can expect to gain 2,000 viewers.

b. Here, we are given $R = [0 \ 0.50 \ 0.50 \ 0]$ and are not given CTV's strategy C, so this time we take $C = [x \ y \ z \ t]^T$ and calculate the resulting expected payoff e:

$$e = RPC = [0 \quad 0.50 \quad 0.50 \quad 0] \begin{bmatrix} 2 & 1 & -2 & 2 \\ -1 & 1 & -1 & 2 \\ -2 & 0 & 0 & 1 \\ 3 & 1 & -1 & 1 \end{bmatrix} \begin{bmatrix} x \\ y \\ z \\ t \end{bmatrix}$$

$$= [-1.5 \quad 0.5 \quad -0.5 \quad 1.5] \begin{bmatrix} x \\ y \\ z \\ t \end{bmatrix} = -1.5x + 0.5y - 0.5z + 1.5t.$$

Now, CTV wants e to be as *low* as possible (why?). Because x has the largest negative coefficient, CTV would like it to be as large as possible: $x = 1$, so the rest of the unknowns must be zero. Thus, CTV's best strategy is $C = [1 \ 0 \ 0 \ 0]^T$; that is, show a nature documentary every night. If it does so, the expected payoff will be

$$e = -1.5(1) + 0.5(0) - 0.5(0) + 1.5(0) = -1.5.$$

So CTV can expect to gain 1,500 viewers.

This example illustrates the fact that, no matter what mixed strategy one player selects, the other player can choose an appropriate *pure* counterstrategy in order to maximize its gain. How does this affect what decisions you should make as one of the players? If you were on the board of directors of RTV, you might reason as follows: Since for every mixed strategy you try, CTV can find a best counterstrategy (as in part (b)), it is in your company's best interest to select a mixed strategy that *minimizes* the effect of CTV's best counterstrategy. This is called the **minimax criterion**.

Minimax Criterion

A player using the **minimax criterion** chooses a strategy that, among all possible strategies, minimizes the effect of the other player's best counterstrategy. That is, an optimal (best) strategy according to the minimax criterion is one that minimizes the maximum damage the opponent can cause.

This criterion assumes that your opponent is determined to win. More precisely, it assumes the following.

Fundamental Principle of Game Theory

Each player tries to use its best possible strategy, and assumes that the other player is doing the same.

This principle is not always followed by every player. For example, one of the players may be nature and may choose its move at random, with no particular purpose in mind. In such a case, criteria other than the minimax criterion may be more appropriate. For example, there is the "maximax" criterion, which maximizes the maximum possible payoff (also known as the "reckless" strategy), or the criterion that seeks to minimize "regret" (the difference between the payoff you get and the payoff you *would have gotten* if you had known beforehand what was going to happen).[*] But, we shall assume here the fundamental principle and try to find optimal strategies under the minimax criterion.

* See *Location in Space: Theoretical Perspectives in Economic Geography,* 3rd Edition, by Peter Dicken and Peter E. Lloyd, HarperCollins Publishers, 1990, p. 276.

Finding the optimal strategy is called **solving the game**. In general, solving a game can be done using linear programming, as we shall see in the next chapter. However, we can solve 2×2 games "by hand," as we shall see in the next example. First, we notice that some large games can be reduced to smaller games.

Consider the game in the preceding example, which had the following matrix:

$$P = \begin{bmatrix} 2 & 1 & -2 & 2 \\ -1 & 1 & -1 & 2 \\ -2 & 0 & 0 & 1 \\ 3 & 1 & -1 & 1 \end{bmatrix}.$$

Compare the second and third columns through the eyes of the column player, CTV. Every payoff in the third column is as good as or better, from CTV's point of view, than the corresponding entry in the second column. Thus, no matter what RTV does, CTV will do better showing a ballet (third column) than a symphony (second column). We say that the third column **dominates** the second column. As far as CTV is concerned, we might as well forget about symphonies entirely, so we remove the second column. Similarly, the third column dominates the fourth, so we can remove the fourth column, too. This gives us a smaller game to work with:

$$P = \begin{bmatrix} 2 & -2 \\ -1 & -1 \\ -2 & 0 \\ 3 & -1 \end{bmatrix}.$$

Now compare the first and last rows. Every payoff in the last row is larger than the corresponding payoff in the first row, so the last row is always better to RTV. Again, we say that the last row *dominates* the first row, and we can discard the first row. Similarly, the last row dominates the second row, so we discard the second row as well. This reduces us to the following game:

$$P = \begin{bmatrix} -2 & 0 \\ 3 & -1 \end{bmatrix}.$$

In this matrix, neither row dominates the other and neither column dominates the other. So, this is as far as we can go with this line of argument. We call this **reduction by dominance**.

Reduction by Dominance

One *row* **dominates** another if every entry in the former is greater than or equal to the corresponding entry in the latter. Put another way, one row dominates another if it is always at least as good for the row player.

One *column* **dominates** another if every entry in the former is less than or equal to the corresponding entry in the latter. Put another way, one column dominates another if it is always at least as good for the column player.

Procedure for Reducing by Dominance:
1. Check whether there is any row in the (remaining) matrix that is dominated by another row. Remove all dominated rows.

2. Check whether there is any column in the (remaining) matrix that is dominated by another column. Remove all dominated columns.

3. Repeat steps 1 and 2 until there are no dominated rows or columns.

Let us now go back to the "television ratings wars" example and see how we can solve a game using the minimax criterion once we are down to a 2×2 payoff matrix.

EXAMPLE 3 Solving a 2 × 2 Game

Continuing the preceding example:

a. Find the optimal strategy for RTV.

b. Find the optimal strategy for CTV.

c. Find the expected payoff of the game if RTV and CTV use their optimal strategies.

Solution As in the text, we begin by reducing the game by dominance, which brings us down to the following 2×2 game:

		CTV Nature Doc.	**CTV** Ballet
RTV	**Reality Show**	-2	0
	Movie	3	-1

a. Now let's find RTV's optimal strategy. Because we don't yet know what it is, we write down a general strategy:

$$R = [x \quad y].$$

Because $x + y = 1$, we can replace y by $1 - x$:

$$R = [x \quad 1 - x].$$

We know that CTV's best counterstrategy to R will be a pure strategy (see the discussion after Example 2), so let's compute the expected payoff that results from each of CTV's possible pure strategies:

$$e = [x \quad 1-x] \begin{bmatrix} -2 & 0 \\ 3 & -1 \end{bmatrix} \begin{bmatrix} 1 \\ 0 \end{bmatrix}$$

$$= (-2)x + 3(1 - x) = -5x + 3$$

$$f = [x \quad 1-x] \begin{bmatrix} -2 & 0 \\ 3 & -1 \end{bmatrix} \begin{bmatrix} 0 \\ 1 \end{bmatrix}$$

$$= 0x - (1 - x) = x - 1.$$

Figure 1

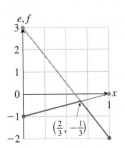

Figure 2

Because both e and f depend on x, we can graph them as in Figure 1.

If, for instance, RTV happened to choose $x = 0.5$, then the expected payoffs resulting from CTV's two pure strategies are $e = -5(1/2) + 3 = 1/2$ and $f = 1/2 - 1 = -1/2$. The worst outcome for RTV is the lower of the two, f, and this will be true wherever the graph of f is below the graph of e. On the other hand, if RTV chose $x = 1$, the graph of e would be lower and the worst possible expected value would be $e = -5(1) + 3 = -2$. Since RTV can choose x to be any value between 0 and 1, the worst possible outcomes are those shown by the colored portion of the graph in Figure 2.

Because RTV is trying to make the worst possible outcome as large as possible (that is, to minimize damages), it is seeking the point on the colored portion of the graph that is highest. This is the intersection point of the two lines. To calculate its coordinates, it's easiest to equate the two functions of x:

$$-5x + 3 = x - 1,$$

$$-6x = -4,$$

or $$x = \frac{2}{3}.$$

The e (or f) coordinate is then obtained by substituting $x = 2/3$ into the expression for e (or f), giving:

$$e = -5 \left(\frac{2}{3} \right) + 3$$

$$= -\frac{1}{3}.$$

We conclude that RTV's best strategy is to take $x = 2/3$, giving an expected value of $-1/3$. In other words, RTV's optimal mixed strategy is:

$$R = \begin{bmatrix} \dfrac{2}{3} & \dfrac{1}{3} \end{bmatrix}.$$

Going back to the original game, RTV should show reality shows 2/3 of the time and movies 1/3 of the time. It should not bother showing any sitcoms or docudramas. It expects to lose, on average, 333 viewers to CTV, but all of its other options are worse.

b. To find CTV's optimal strategy, we must reverse roles and start by writing its unknown strategy as follows:

$$C = \begin{bmatrix} x \\ 1 - x \end{bmatrix}.$$

We calculate the expected payoffs for the two pure row strategies:

$$e = \begin{bmatrix} 1 & 0 \end{bmatrix} \begin{bmatrix} -2 & 0 \\ 3 & -1 \end{bmatrix} \begin{bmatrix} x \\ 1 - x \end{bmatrix}$$

$$= -2x$$

and

$$f = \begin{bmatrix} 0 & 1 \end{bmatrix} \begin{bmatrix} -2 & 0 \\ 3 & -1 \end{bmatrix} \begin{bmatrix} x \\ 1 - x \end{bmatrix}$$

$$= 3x - (1 - x)$$

$$= 4x - 1.$$

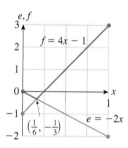

As with the row player, we know that the column player's best strategy will correspond to the intersection of the graphs of e and f (Figure 3). (Why is the upper edge colored, rather than the lower edge?) The graphs intersect when

$$-2x = 4x - 1$$

or

$$x = \frac{1}{6}.$$

The corresponding value of e (or f) is

$$e = -2\left(\frac{1}{6}\right) = -\frac{1}{3}.$$

Thus, CTV's optimal mixed strategy is $\begin{bmatrix} \frac{1}{6} & \frac{5}{6} \end{bmatrix}^T$ and the expected payoff is $-1/3$. So, CTV should show nature documentaries 1/6 of the time and ballets 5/6 of the time. It should not bother to show symphonies or operas. It expects to gain, on average, 333 viewers from RTV.

c. We can now calculate the expected payoff as usual, using the optimal strategies we found in parts (a) and (b).

$$e = RPC$$

$$= \begin{bmatrix} \dfrac{2}{3} & \dfrac{1}{3} \end{bmatrix} \begin{bmatrix} -2 & 0 \\ 3 & -1 \end{bmatrix} \begin{bmatrix} \dfrac{1}{6} \\ \dfrac{5}{6} \end{bmatrix}$$

$$= -\frac{1}{3}$$

Figure 3

➡ **Before we go on...** In Example 3, it is no accident that the expected payoff resulting from the optimal strategies equals the expected payoff we found in (a) and (b). If we call the expected payoff resulting from the optimal strategies the **expected value of the game**, the row player's optimal strategy guarantees an expected payoff no smaller than the expected value, while the column player's optimal strategy guarantees an expected payoff no larger. Together they force the average payoff to be the expected value of the game. ■

Expected Value of a Game

The **expected value of a game** is its expected payoff that results when the row and column players use their optimal (minimax) strategies. By using its optimal strategy, the row player guarantees an expected payoff no lower than the expected value of the game, no matter what the column player does. Similarly, by using its optimal strategy, the column player guarantees an expected payoff no higher than the expected value of the game, no matter what the row player does.

Q: *What about games that don't reduce to 2 × 2 matrices? Are these solved in a similar way?*

A: The method illustrated in the previous example cannot easily be generalized to solve bigger games (i.e., games that cannot be reduced to 2 × 2 matrices); solving even a 2 × 3 game using this approach would require us to consider graphs in three dimensions. To be able to solve games of arbitrary size, we need to wait until the next chapter (Section 5.5), where we describe a method for solving a game, using the simplex method, that works for all payoff matrices.

Strictly Determined Games

Although we haven't yet discussed how to solve general $m \times n$ games, there are certain kinds of games that can be solved quite simply regardless of size, as illustrated by the following example.

EXAMPLE 4 **Strictly Determined Game**

Solve the following game:

$$
\mathbf{A} \begin{array}{c} \\ s \\ t \\ u \end{array} \begin{array}{c} \mathbf{B} \\ \begin{array}{ccc} p & q & r \end{array} \\ \left[\begin{array}{ccc} -4 & -3 & 3 \\ 2 & -1 & -2 \\ 1 & 0 & 2 \end{array} \right] \end{array} .
$$

Solution If we look carefully at this matrix, we see that no row dominates another and no column dominates another, so we can't reduce it. Nor do we know how to solve a 3 × 3 game, so it looks as if we're stuck. However, there is a way to understand this particular game. With the minimax criterion in mind, let's begin by considering the worst possible outcomes for the row player for each possible move. We do this by circling the smallest payoff in each row, the **row minima**:

$$
\mathbf{A}\ \begin{array}{c} \\ s \\ t \\ u \end{array}
\begin{array}{ccc}
p & q & r \\
\end{array}
$$

So, for example, if A plays move *s*, the worst possible outcome is to lose 4. Player A takes the least risk by using move *u*, which has the largest row minimum.

We do the same thing for the column player, remembering that smaller payoffs are better for B and larger payoffs worse. We draw a box around the largest payoff in each column, the **column maxima**:

Player B takes the least risk by using move *q*, which has the smallest column maximum.

Now put the circles and boxes together:

Notice that the *uq* entry is both circled and boxed: It is both a row minimum and a column maximum. We call such an entry a **saddle point.**

Now we claim that the optimal strategy for A is to always play *u* while the optimal strategy for B is to always play *q*. By playing *u*, A guarantees that the payoff will be 0 or higher, no matter what B does, so the expected value of the game has to be *at least* 0. On the other hand, by playing *q*, B guarantees that the payoff will be 0 or less, so the expected value of the game has to be *no more than* 0. Combining these facts, we conclude that the expected value of the game must be exactly 0, and A and B have no strategies that could do any better for them than the pure strategies *u* and *q*.

➡ **Before we go on...** You should consider what happens in an example like the television rating wars game of Example 3. In that game, the largest row minimum is −1 while the smallest column maximum is 0; there is no saddle point. The row player can force a payoff of at least −1 by playing a pure strategy (always showing movies, for example), but can do better, forcing an expected payoff of −1/3, by playing a mixed strategy as we saw in Example 3. Similarly, the column player can force the payoff to be 0 or less with a pure strategy, but can do better, forcing an expected payoff of −1/3, with a mixed strategy. Only when there is a saddle point will pure strategies be optimal. ■

Strictly Determined Game

A **saddle point** is a payoff v that is simultaneously a row minimum and a column maximum (both boxed and circled in our approach). If a game has a saddle point, the corresponding row and column strategies are the optimal ones, the expected value of the game is the payoff v, and we say that the game is **strictly determined**.

 using Technology

Website

www.WanerMath.com
To play a strictly determined game against your computer, and also to automatically reduce by dominance and solve arbitrary games up to 5×5, follow

Student Website

→ On Line Utilities

→ Game Theory Tool

FAQs

Solving a Game

Q: *We've seen several ways of trying to solve a game. What should I do and in what order?*

A: Here are the steps you should take when trying to solve a game:

1. Reduce by dominance. This should always be your first step.
2. If you were able to reduce to a 1×1 game, you're done. The optimal strategies are the corresponding pure strategies, as they dominate all the others.
3. Look for a saddle point in the reduced game. If it has one, the game is strictly determined, and the corresponding pure strategies are optimal.
4. If your reduced game is 2×2 and has no saddle point, use the method of Example 3 to find the optimal mixed strategies.
5. If your reduced game is larger than 2×2 and has no saddle point, you have to use linear programming to solve it, but that will have to wait until the following chapter.

4.4   EXERCISES

▼ more advanced   ◆ challenging
T indicates exercises that should be solved using technology

In Exercises 1–4, calculate the expected payoff of the game with payoff matrix

$$P = \begin{bmatrix} 2 & 0 & -1 & 2 \\ -1 & 0 & 0 & -2 \\ -2 & 0 & 0 & 1 \\ 3 & 1 & -1 & 1 \end{bmatrix}$$

using the mixed strategies supplied. HINT [See Example 1.]

1. $R = \begin{bmatrix} 0 & 1 & 0 & 0 \end{bmatrix}, C = \begin{bmatrix} 1 & 0 & 0 & 0 \end{bmatrix}^T$
2. $R = \begin{bmatrix} 0 & 0 & 0 & 1 \end{bmatrix}, C = \begin{bmatrix} 0 & 1 & 0 & 0 \end{bmatrix}^T$
3. $R = \begin{bmatrix} 0.5 & 0.5 & 0 & 0 \end{bmatrix}, C = \begin{bmatrix} 0 & 0 & 0.5 & 0.5 \end{bmatrix}^T$
4. $R = \begin{bmatrix} 0 & 0.5 & 0 & 0.5 \end{bmatrix}, C = \begin{bmatrix} 0.5 & 0.5 & 0 & 0 \end{bmatrix}^T$

In Exercises 5–8, either a mixed column or row strategy is given. In each case, use

$$P = \begin{bmatrix} 0 & -1 & 5 \\ 2 & -2 & 4 \\ 0 & 3 & 0 \\ 1 & 0 & -5 \end{bmatrix}$$

and find the optimal pure strategy (or strategies) the other player should use. Express the answer as a row or column matrix. Also determine the resulting expected payoff. HINT [See Example 2.]

5. $C = \begin{bmatrix} 0.25 & 0.75 & 0 \end{bmatrix}^T$

6. $C = \begin{bmatrix} \frac{1}{3} & \frac{1}{3} & \frac{1}{3} \end{bmatrix}^T$

7. $R = \begin{bmatrix} \frac{1}{2} & 0 & \frac{1}{4} & \frac{1}{4} \end{bmatrix}$

8. $R = \begin{bmatrix} 0.8 & 0.2 & 0 & 0 \end{bmatrix}$

Reduce the payoff matrices in Exercises 9–14 by dominance.

9.
$$\begin{array}{c} \\ a \\ b \end{array} \begin{array}{ccc} p & q & r \\ \begin{bmatrix} 1 & 1 & 10 \\ 2 & 3 & -4 \end{bmatrix} \end{array}$$

10.
$$\begin{array}{c} \\ a \\ b \end{array} \begin{array}{ccc} p & q & r \\ \begin{bmatrix} 2 & 0 & 10 \\ 15 & -4 & -5 \end{bmatrix} \end{array}$$

11.
$$\begin{array}{c} \\ 1 \\ 2 \\ 3 \end{array} \begin{array}{ccc} a & b & c \\ \begin{bmatrix} 2 & -4 & -9 \\ -1 & -2 & -3 \\ 5 & 0 & -1 \end{bmatrix} \end{array}$$

12.
$$\begin{array}{c} \\ 1 \\ 2 \\ 3 \end{array} \begin{array}{ccc} a & b & c \\ \begin{bmatrix} 0 & -1 & -5 \\ -3 & -10 & 10 \\ 2 & 3 & -4 \end{bmatrix} \end{array}$$

13.

$$\begin{array}{c} \\ p \\ q \\ r \\ s \end{array} \begin{array}{ccc} a & b & c \\ \begin{bmatrix} 1 & -1 & -5 \\ 4 & 0 & 2 \\ 3 & -3 & 10 \\ 3 & -5 & -4 \end{bmatrix} \end{array}$$

14.

$$\begin{array}{c} \\ p \\ q \\ r \\ s \end{array} \begin{array}{ccc} a & b & c \\ \begin{bmatrix} 2 & -4 & 9 \\ 1 & 1 & 0 \\ -1 & -2 & -3 \\ 1 & 1 & -1 \end{bmatrix} \end{array}$$

In Exercises 15–20, decide whether the game is strictly determined. If it is, give the players' optimal pure strategies and the value of the game. HINT [See Example 4.]

15.

$$\begin{array}{c} \\ a \\ b \end{array} \begin{array}{cc} p & q \\ \begin{bmatrix} 1 & 1 \\ 2 & -4 \end{bmatrix} \end{array}$$

16.

$$\begin{array}{c} \\ a \\ b \end{array} \begin{array}{cc} p & q \\ \begin{bmatrix} -1 & 2 \\ 10 & -1 \end{bmatrix} \end{array}$$

17.

$$\begin{array}{c} \\ a \\ b \end{array} \begin{array}{ccc} p & q & r \\ \begin{bmatrix} 2 & 0 & -2 \\ -1 & 3 & 0 \end{bmatrix} \end{array}$$

18.

$$\begin{array}{c} \\ a \\ b \end{array} \begin{array}{ccc} p & q & r \\ \begin{bmatrix} -2 & 1 & -3 \\ -2 & 3 & -2 \end{bmatrix} \end{array}$$

19.

$$\begin{array}{c} \\ P \\ Q \\ R \\ S \end{array} \begin{array}{ccc} a & b & c \\ \begin{bmatrix} 1 & -1 & -5 \\ 4 & -4 & 2 \\ 3 & -3 & -10 \\ 5 & -5 & -4 \end{bmatrix} \end{array}$$

20.

$$\begin{array}{c} \\ P \\ Q \\ R \\ S \end{array} \begin{array}{ccc} a & b & c \\ \begin{bmatrix} -2 & -4 & 9 \\ 1 & 1 & 0 \\ -1 & -2 & -3 \\ 1 & 1 & -1 \end{bmatrix} \end{array}$$

In Exercises 21–24, find: **(a)** *the optimal mixed row strategy;* **(b)** *the optimal mixed column strategy, and* **(c)** *the expected value of the game in the event that each player uses his or her optimal mixed strategy.* HINT [See Example 3.]

21. $P = \begin{bmatrix} -1 & 2 \\ 0 & -1 \end{bmatrix}$

22. $P = \begin{bmatrix} -1 & 0 \\ 1 & -1 \end{bmatrix}$

23. $P = \begin{bmatrix} -1 & -2 \\ -2 & 1 \end{bmatrix}$

24. $P = \begin{bmatrix} -2 & -1 \\ -1 & -3 \end{bmatrix}$

APPLICATIONS

Set up the payoff matrix in each of Exercises 25–32.

25. Games to Pass the Time You and your friend have come up with the following simple game to pass the time: at each round, you simultaneously call "heads" or "tails." If you have both called the same thing, your friend wins 1 point; if your calls differ, you win 1 point.

26. Games to Pass the Time Bored with the game in Exercise 25, you decide to use the following variation instead: If you both call "heads" your friend wins 2 points; if you both call "tails" your friend wins 1 point; if your calls differ, then you win 2 points if you called "heads," and 1 point if you called "tails."

27. War Games You are deciding whether to invade France, Sweden, or Norway, and your opponent is simultaneously deciding which of these three countries to defend. If you invade a country that your opponent is defending, you will be defeated (payoff: -1), but if you invade a country your opponent is not defending, you will be successful (payoff: $+1$).

28. War Games You must decide whether to attack your opponent by sea or air, and your opponent must simultaneously decide whether to mount an all-out air defense, an all-out coastal defense (against an attack from the sea), or a combined air and coastal defense. If there is no defense for your mode of attack, you win 100 points. If your attack is met by a shared air and coastal defense, you win 50 points. If your attack is met by an all-out defense, you lose 200 points.

29. ▼**Marketing** Your fast-food outlet, *Burger Queen*, has obtained a license to open branches in three closely situated South African cities: Brakpan, Nigel, and Springs. Your market surveys show that Brakpan and Nigel each provide a potential market of 2,000 burgers a day, while Springs provides a potential market of 1,000 burgers per day. Your company can finance an outlet in only one of those cities. Your main competitor, Burger Princess, has also obtained licenses for these cities, and is similarly planning to open only one outlet. If you both happen to locate at the same city, you will share the total business from all three cities equally, but if you locate in different cities, you will each get all the business in the cities in which you have located, plus half the business in the third city. The payoff is the number of burgers you will sell per day minus the number of burgers your competitor will sell per day.

30. ▼**Marketing** Repeat Exercise 29, given that the potential sales markets in the three cities are: Brakpan, 2,500 per day; Nigel, 1,500 per day; Springs, 1,200 per day.

31. ▼**Betting** When you bet on a racehorse with odds of *m–n*, you stand to win *m* dollars for every bet of *n* dollars if your horse wins; for instance, if the horse you bet is running at 5–2 and wins, you will win $5 for every $2 you bet. (Thus a $2 bet will return $7.) Here are some actual odds from a 1992 race at Belmont Park, NY.[21] The favorite at 5–2 was Pleasant Tap. The second choice was Thunder Rumble at 7–2, while the third choice was Strike the Gold at 4–1. Assume you are making a $10 bet on one of these horses. The payoffs are your winnings. (If your horse does not win, you lose your entire bet. Of course, it is possible for none of your horses to win.)

32. ▼**Betting** Referring to Exercise 31, suppose that just before the race there has been frantic betting on Thunder Rumble with the result that the odds have dropped to 2–5. The odds on the other two horses remain unchanged.

33. Retail Discount Wars Just one week after your *Abercrom B* men's fashion outlet has opened at a new location opposite *Burger Prince* in the Mall, your rival, *Abercrom A*, opens up

---

[21]Source: *New York Times*, September 18, 1992, p. B14.

directly across from you. You have been informed that Abercrom A is about to launch either a 30% off everything sale or a 50% off everything sale. You, on the other hand, have decided to either *increase* prices (to make your store seem more exclusive) or do absolutely nothing. You construct the following payoff matrix, where the payoffs represent the number of customers your outlet can expect to gain from Abercrom A:

Abercrom A

$$\text{Abercrom B} \quad \begin{matrix} \text{Do Nothing} \\ \text{Increase Prices} \end{matrix} \begin{bmatrix} -60 & -40 \\ 30 & -50 \end{bmatrix}.$$

There is a 20% chance that Abercrom A will opt for the "30% off" sale and an 80% chance that they will opt for the "50% Off" sale. Your sense from upper management at Abercrom B is that there is a 50% chance you will be given the go-ahead to raise prices. What is the expected resulting effect on your customer base?

34. *More Retail Discount Wars* Your *Abercrom B* men's fashion outlet has a 30% chance of launching an expensive new line of used auto-mechanic dungarees (complete with grease stains) and a 70% chance of staying instead with its traditional torn military-style dungarees. Your rival across from you in the mall, *Abercrom A*, appears to be deciding between a line of torn gym shirts and a more daring line of "empty shirts" (that is, empty shirt boxes). Your corporate spies reveal that there is a 20% chance that Abercrom A will opt for the empty shirt option. The following payoff matrix gives the number of customers your outlet can expect to gain from Abercrom A in each situation:

Abercrom A

$$\text{Abercrom B} \quad \begin{matrix} \text{Mechanics} \\ \text{Military} \end{matrix} \begin{bmatrix} 10 & -40 \\ -30 & 50 \end{bmatrix}.$$

What is the expected resulting effect on your customer base?

35. *Factory Location*[22] A manufacturer of electrical machinery is located in a cramped, though low-rent, factory close to the center of a large city. The firm needs to expand, and it could do so in one of three ways: (1) Remain where it is and install new equipment, (2) move to a suburban site in the same city, or (3) relocate in a different part of the country where labor is cheaper. Its decision will be influenced by the fact that one of the following will happen: (I) The government may introduce a program of equipment grants, (II) a new suburban highway may be built, or (III) the government may institute a policy of financial help to companies who move into regions of high unemployment. The value to the company of each combination is given in the following payoff matrix.

Government's Options

Manufacturer's Options		I	II	III
	1	200	150	140
	2	130	220	130
	3	110	110	220

If the manufacturer judges that there is a 20% probability that the government will go with option I, a 50% probability that they will go with option II, and a 30% probability that they will go with option III, what is the manufacturer's best option?

36. *Crop Choice*[23] A farmer has a choice of growing wheat, barley, or rice. Her success will depend on the weather, which could be dry, average, or wet. Her payoff matrix is as follows.

Weather

Crop Choices		Dry	Average	Wet
	Wheat	20	20	10
	Barley	10	15	20
	Rice	10	20	20

If the probability that the weather will be dry is 10%, the probability that it will be average is 60%, and the probability that it will be wet is 30%, what is the farmer's best choice of crop?

37. *Study Techniques* Your mathematics test is tomorrow and will cover the following topics: game theory, linear programming, and matrix algebra. You have decided to do an "all-nighter" and must determine how to allocate your eight hours of study time among the three topics. If you were to spend the entire eight hours on any one of these topics (thus using a pure strategy), you feel confident that you would earn a 90% score on that portion of the test but would not do so well on the other topics. You have come up with the following table, where the entries are your expected scores. (The fact that linear programming and matrix algebra are used in game theory is reflected in these numbers.)

Test

Your Strategies	Game Theory	Linear Programming	Matrix Algebra
Game Theory	90	70	70
Linear Programming	40	90	40
Matrix Algebra	60	40	90

You have been told that the test will be weighted as follows: game theory: 25%; linear programming: 50%; matrix algebra: 25%.

---

[22]Adapted from an example in *Location in Space: Theoretical Perspectives in Economic Geography* by P. Dicken and P.E. Lloyd (Harper & Row, 1990).

[23]*Ibid.*

a. If you spend 25% of the night on game theory, 50% on linear programming, and 25% on matrix algebra, what score do you expect to get on the test?

b. Is it possible to improve on this by altering your study schedule? If so, what is the highest score you can expect on the test?

c. If your study schedule is according to part (a) and your teacher decides to forget her promises about how the test will be weighted and instead base it all on a single topic, which topic would be worst for you, and what score could you expect on the test?

38. *Study Techniques* Your friend Joe has been spending all of his time on fraternity activities and thus knows absolutely nothing about any of the three topics on tomorrow's math test. (See Exercise 37.) Because you are recognized as an expert on the use of game theory to solve study problems, he has turned to you for advice as to how to spend his "all-nighter." As the following table shows, his situation is not so rosy. (Since he knows no linear programming or matrix algebra, the table shows, for instance, that studying game theory all night will not be much use in preparing him for this topic.)

Test

Joe's Strategies	Game Theory	Linear Programming	Matrix Algebra
Game Theory	30	0	20
Linear Programming	0	70	0
Matrix Algebra	0	0	70

Assuming that the test will be weighted as described in Exercise 37, what are the answers to parts (a), (b), and (c) as they apply to Joe?

39. ▼*Staff Cutbacks* Frank Tempest manages a large snowplow service in Manhattan, Kansas, and is alarmed by the recent weather trends; there have been no significant snowfalls in recent years. He is therefore contemplating laying off some of his workers, but is unsure about whether to lay off 5, 10, or 15 of his 50 workers. Being very methodical, he estimates his annual net profits based on four possible annual snowfall figures: 0 inches, 20 inches, 40 inches, and 60 inches. (He takes into account the fact that, if he is running a small operation in the face of a large annual snowfall, he will lose business to his competitors because he will be unable to discount on volume.)

	0 Inches	20 Inches	40 Inches	60 Inches
5 Laid Off	−$500,000	−$200,000	$10,000	$200,000
10 Laid Off	−$200,000	$0	$0	$0
15 Laid Off	−$100,000	$10,000	−$200,000	−$300,000

a. During the past 10 years, the region has had 0 inches twice, 20 inches twice, 40 inches three times, and 60 inches three times. Based on this information, how

many workers should Tempest lay off, and how much would it cost him?

b. There is a 50% chance that Tempest will lay off 5 workers and a 50% chance that he will lay off 15 workers. What is the worst thing Nature can do to him in terms of snowfall? How much would it cost him?

c. The Gods of Chaos (who control the weather) know that Tempest is planning to use the strategy in part (a), and are determined to hurt Tempest as much as possible. Tempest, being somewhat paranoid, suspects it too. What should he do?

40. ▼*Textbook Writing* You are writing a college-level textbook on finite mathematics and are trying to come up with the best combination of word problems. Over the years, you have accumulated a collection of amusing problems, serious applications, long complicated problems, and "generic" problems.[24] Before your book is published, it must be scrutinized by several reviewers, who, it seems, are never satisfied with the mix you use. You estimate that there are three kinds of reviewers: the "no-nonsense" types, who prefer applications and generic problems; the "dead serious" types, who feel that a college-level text should be contain little or no humor and lots of long complicated problems; and the "laid-back" types, who believe that learning best takes place in a light-hearted atmosphere bordering on anarchy. You have drawn up the following chart, where the payoffs represent the reactions of reviewers on a scale of −10 (ballistic) to +10 (ecstatic):

Reviewers

		No-Nonsense	Dead Serious	Laid-Back
	Amusing	−5	−10	10
You	**Serious**	5	3	0
	Long	−5	5	3
	Generic	5	3	−10

a. Your first draft of the book contained no generic problems, and equal numbers of the other categories. If half the reviewers of your book were "dead serious" and the rest were equally divided between the "no-nonsense" and "laid-back" types, what score would you expect?

b. In your second draft of the book, you tried to balance the content by including some generic problems and eliminating several amusing ones, and wound up with a mix of which one eighth were amusing, one quarter were serious, three eighths were long, and a quarter were generic. What kind of reviewer would be *least* impressed by this mix?

c. What kind of reviewer would be *most* impressed by the mix in your second draft?

---

[24]Of the following type: "A certain company has three processing plants: A, B, and C, each of which uses three processes: P_1, P_2, and P_3. Process P_1 uses 100 units of chemical C_1, 50 units of C_2, ... " and so on.

41. Price Wars *Computer Electronics, Inc.* (CE) and the *Gigantic Computer Store* (GCS) are planning to discount the price they charge for the HAL Laptop Computer, of which they are the only distributors. Because Computer Electronics provides a free warranty service, they can generally afford to charge more. A market survey provides the following data on the gains to CE's market share that will result from different pricing decisions:

GCS

		$900	$1,000	$1,200
	$1,000	15%	60%	80%
CE	$1,200	15%	60%	60%
	$1,300	10%	20%	40%

a. Use reduction by dominance to determine how much each company should charge. What is the effect on CE's market share?

b. CE is aware that GCS is planning to use reduction by dominance to determine its pricing policy, and wants its market share to be as large as possible. What effect, if any, would the information about GCS have on CE's best strategy?

42. More Price Wars (Refer to Exercise 41.) A new market survey results in the following revised data:

GCS

		$900	$1,000	$1,200
	$1,000	20%	60%	60%
CE	$1,200	15%	60%	60%
	$1,300	10%	20%	40%

a. Use reduction by dominance to determine how much each company should charge. What is the effect on CE's market share?

b. In general, why do price wars tend to force prices down?

43. Wrestling Tournaments City Community College (CCC) plans to host Midtown Military Academy (MMA) for a wrestling tournament. Each school has three wrestlers in the 190 lb. weight class: CCC has Pablo, Sal, and Edison, while MMA has Carlos, Marcus, and Noto. Pablo can beat Carlos and Marcus, Marcus can beat Edison and Sal, Noto can beat Edison, while the other combinations will result in an even match. Set up a payoff matrix, and use reduction by dominance to decide which wrestler each team should choose as their champion. Does one school have an advantage over the other?

44. Wrestling Tournaments (Refer to Exercise 43.) One day before the wrestling tournament discussed in Exercise 43, Pablo sustains a hamstring injury and is replaced by Hans, who (unfortunately for CCC) can be beaten by both Carlos and Marcus. Set up the payoff matrix, and use reduction by dominance to decide which wrestler each team should

choose as their champion. Does one school have an advantage over the other?

45. The Battle of Rabaul-Lae[25] In the Second World War, during the struggle for New Guinea, intelligence reports revealed that the Japanese were planning to move a troop and supply convoy from the port of Rabaul at the Eastern tip of New Britain to Lae, which lies just west of New Britain on New Guinea. It could either travel via a northern route, which was plagued by poor visibility, or by a southern route, where the visibility was clear. General Kenney, who was the commander of the Allied Air Forces in the area, had the choice of concentrating reconnaissance aircraft on one route or the other and bombing the Japanese convoy once it was sighted. Kenney's staff drafted the following outcomes for his choices, where the payoffs are estimated days of bombing time:

		Japanese Commander's Strategies	
		Northern Route	Southern Route
Kenney's	Northern Route	2	2
Strategies	Southern Route	1	3

What would you have recommended to General Kenney? What would you have recommended to the Japanese Commander?[26] How much bombing time results if these recommendations are followed?

46. The Battle of Rabaul-Lae Referring to Exercise 45, suppose that General Kenney had a third alternative: splitting his reconnaissance aircraft between the two routes, which would result in the following estimates:

		Japanese Commander's Strategies	
		Northern Route	Southern Route
Kenney's	Northern Route	2	2
Strategies	Split Reconnaissance	1.5	2.5
	Southern Route	1	3

What would you have recommended to General Kenney? What would you have recommended to the Japanese Commander? How much bombing time results if these recommendations are followed?

---

[25]As discussed in *Games and Decisions* by R. D. Luce and H. Raiffa Section 11.3 (New York: Wiley, 1957). This is based on an article in the *Journal of the Operations Research Society of America* 2 (1954) 365–385.

[26]The correct answers to these two questions correspond to the actual decisions both commanders made.

47. ▼ *The Prisoner's Dilemma* Slim Lefty and Joe Rap have been arrested for grand theft auto, having been caught red-handed driving away in a stolen 2012 Porsche. Although the police have more than enough evidence to convict them both, they feel that a confession would simplify the work of the prosecution. They decide to interrogate the prisoners separately. Slim and Joe are both told of the following plea-bargaining arrangement: If both confess, they will each receive a 2-year sentence; if neither confesses, they will both receive 5-year sentences, and if only one confesses (and thus squeals on the other), he will receive a suspended sentence, while the other will receive a 10-year sentence. What should Slim do?

48. ▼ *More Prisoners' Dilemmas* Jane Good and Prudence Brown have been arrested for robbery, but the police lack sufficient evidence for a conviction, and so decide to interrogate them separately in the hope of extracting a confession. Both Jane and Prudence are told the following: If they both confess, they will each receive a 5-year sentence; if neither confesses, they will be released; if one confesses, she will receive a suspended sentence, while the other will receive a 10-year sentence. What should Jane do?

49. ▼ *Campaign Strategies*[27] Florida and Ohio are "swing states" that have a large bounty of electoral votes and are therefore highly valued by presidential campaign strategists. Suppose it is now the weekend before Election Day 2012, and each candidate (Romney and Obama) can visit only one more state. Further, to win the election, Romney needs to win both of these states. Currently Romney has a 40% chance of winning Ohio and a 60% chance of winning Florida. Therefore, he has a $0.40 \times 0.60 = 0.24$, or 24% chance of winning the election. Assume that each candidate can increase his probability of winning a state by 10% if he, and not his opponent, visits that state. If both candidates visit the same state, there is no effect.

    a. Set up a payoff matrix with Romney as the row player and Obama as the column player, where the payoff for a specific set of circumstances is the probability (expressed as a percentage) that Romney will win both states.

    b. Where should each candidate visit under the circumstances?

50. ▼ *Campaign Strategies* Repeat Exercise 49, this time assuming that Romney has an 80% chance of winning Ohio and a 90% chance of winning Florida.

51. *Advertising* The *Softex Shampoo Company* is considering how to split its advertising budget between ads on two radio stations: WISH and WASH. Its main competitor, Splish Shampoo, Inc. has found out about this and is considering countering Softex's ads with its own, on the same radio stations. (Proposed jingle: *Softex, Shmoftex; Splash with Splish*) Softex has calculated that, were it to devote its entire advertising budget to ads on WISH, it would increase revenues in the coming month by $100,000 in the event that Splish was running all its ads on the less popular WASH, but would lose $20,000 in revenues if Splish ran its ads on WISH. If, on the other hand, it devoted its entire budget to WASH ads, it would neither increase nor decrease revenues in the event that Splish was running all its ads on the more popular WISH, and would in fact lose $20,000 in revenues if Splish ran its ads on WASH. What should Softex do, and what effect will this have on revenues?

52. *Labor Negotiations* The management team of the *Abstract Concrete Company* is negotiating a 3-year contract with the labor unions at one of its plants and is trying to decide on its offer for a salary increase. If it offers a 5% increase and the unions accept the offer, Abstract Concrete will gain $20 million in projected profits in the coming year, but if labor rejects the offer, the management team predicts that it will be forced to increase the offer to the union demand of 15%, thus halving the projected profits. If Abstract Concrete offers a 15% increase, the company will earn $10 million in profits over the coming year if the unions accept. If the unions reject, they will probably go out on strike (because management has set 15% as its upper limit) and management has decided that it can then in fact gain $12 million in profits by selling out the defunct plant in retaliation. What intermediate percentage should the company offer, and what profit should it project?

COMMUNICATION AND REASONING EXERCISES

53. Why is a saddle point called a "saddle point"?

54. Can the payoff in a saddle point ever be larger than all other payoffs in a game? Explain.

55. ◆One day, while browsing through an old *Statistical Abstract of the United States,* you came across the following data, which show the number of females employed (in thousands) in various categories according to their educational attainment.[28]

	Managerial/ Professional	Technical/Sales/ Administrative	Service	Precision Production	Operators/ Fabricators
Less Than 4 Years High School	260	1,080	2,020	260	1,400
4 Years of High School Only	2,430	9,510	3,600	570	2,130
1 to 3 Years of College	2,690	5,080	1,080	160	350
At Least 4 Years of College	7,210	2,760	380	70	110

Because you had been studying game theory that day, the first thing you did was to search for a saddle point. Having

---

[27]Based on *Game Theory for Swingers: What states should the candidates visit before Election Day?* by Jordan Ellenberg. Source: www.slate.com.

[28]Source: *Statistical Abstract of the United States 1991* (111th Ed.) U.S. Department of Commerce, Economics and Statistics Administration, and Bureau of the Census.

found one, you conclude that, as a female, your best strategy in the job market is to forget about a college career. Find the flaw in this reasoning.

56. ◆Exercises 37 and 38 seem to suggest that studying a single topic prior to an exam is better than studying all the topics in that exam. Comment on this discrepancy between the game theory result and common sense.

57. ◆Explain what is wrong with a decision to play the mixed strategy [0.5 0.5] by alternating the two strategies: Play the first strategy on the odd-numbered moves and the second strategy on the even-numbered moves. Illustrate your argument by devising a game in which your best strategy is [0.5 0.5].

58. ◆Describe a situation in which a both a mixed strategy and a pure strategy are equally effective.

4.5 Input-Output Models

In this section we look at an application of matrix algebra developed by Wassily Leontief (1906–1999) in the middle of the twentieth century. In 1973, he won the Nobel Prize in Economics for this work. The application involves analyzing national and regional economies by looking at how various parts of the economy interrelate. We'll work out some of the details by looking at a simple scenario.

First, we can think of the economy of a country or a region as being composed of various **sectors**, or groups of one or more industries. Typical sectors are the manufacturing sector, the utilities sector, and the agricultural sector. To introduce the basic concepts, we shall consider two specific sectors: the coal-mining sector (Sector 1) and the electric utilities sector (Sector 2). Both produce a commodity: The coal-mining sector produces coal, and the electric utilities sector produces electricity. We measure these products by their dollar value. By **one unit** of a product, we mean $1 worth of that product.

Here is the scenario.

1. To produce one unit ($1 worth) of coal, assume that the coal-mining sector uses 50¢ worth of coal (to power mining machinery, say) and 10¢ worth of electricity.

2. To produce one unit ($1 worth) of electricity, assume that the electric utilities sector uses 25¢ worth of coal and 25¢ worth of electricity.

These are *internal* usage figures. In addition to this, assume that there is an *external* demand (from the rest of the economy) of 7,000 units ($7,000 worth) of coal and 14,000 units ($14,000 worth) of electricity over a specific time period (one year, say). Our basic question is: How much should each of the two sectors supply in order to meet both internal and external demand?

The key to answering this question is to set up equations of the form:

Total supply = Total demand.

The unknowns, the values we are seeking, are

x_1 = the total supply (in units) from Sector 1 (coal) and
x_2 = the total supply (in units) from Sector 2 (electricity).

Our equations then take the following form:

Total supply from Sector 1 = Total demand for Sector 1 products

$$x_1 = 0.50x_1 \quad + \quad 0.25x_2 \quad + \quad 7,000$$

↑   ↑   ↑

Coal required by Sector 1   Coal required by Sector 2   External demand for coal

Total supply from Sector 2 = Total demand for Sector 2 products

$$x_2 = 0.10x_1 \qquad + \qquad 0.25x_2 \qquad + \qquad 14{,}000.$$

$$\uparrow \qquad\qquad\qquad \uparrow \qquad\qquad\qquad \uparrow$$

Electricity required by Sector 1   Electricity required by Sector 2   External demand for electricity

This is a system of two linear equations in two unknowns:

$$x_1 = 0.50x_1 + 0.25x_2 + 7{,}000$$
$$x_2 = 0.10x_1 + 0.25x_2 + 14{,}000.$$

We can rewrite this system of equations in matrix form as follows:

$$\underbrace{\begin{bmatrix} x_1 \\ x_2 \end{bmatrix}}_{\text{Production}} = \underbrace{\begin{bmatrix} 0.50 & 0.25 \\ 0.10 & 0.25 \end{bmatrix} \begin{bmatrix} x_1 \\ x_2 \end{bmatrix}}_{\text{Internal demand}} + \underbrace{\begin{bmatrix} 7{,}000 \\ 14{,}000 \end{bmatrix}}_{\text{External demand}}.$$

In symbols,

$$X = AX + D.$$

Here,

$$X = \begin{bmatrix} x_1 \\ x_2 \end{bmatrix}$$

is called the **production vector**. Its entries are the amounts produced by the two sectors. The matrix

$$D = \begin{bmatrix} 7{,}000 \\ 14{,}000 \end{bmatrix}$$

is called the **external demand** vector, and

$$A = \begin{bmatrix} 0.50 & 0.25 \\ 0.10 & 0.25 \end{bmatrix} \qquad \text{Organization: } \begin{bmatrix} 1 \to 1 & 1 \to 2 \\ 2 \to 1 & 2 \to 2 \end{bmatrix}$$

is called the **technology matrix**. The entries of the technology matrix have the following meanings:

a_{11} = units of Sector 1 needed to produce one unit of Sector 1
a_{12} = units of Sector 1 needed to produce one unit of Sector 2
a_{21} = units of Sector 2 needed to produce one unit of Sector 1
a_{22} = units of Sector 2 needed to produce one unit of Sector 2.

Now that we have the matrix equation

$$X = AX + D$$

we can solve it as follows. First, subtract AX from both sides:

$$X - AX = D.$$

Because $X = IX$, where I is the 2×2 identity matrix, we can rewrite this as

$$IX - AX = D.$$

Now factor out X:

$$(I - A)X = D.$$

If we multiply both sides by the inverse of $(I - A)$, we get the solution

$$X = (I - A)^{-1}D.$$

Input-Output Model

In an input-output model, an economy (or part of one) is divided into n **sectors**. We then record the $n \times n$ **technology matrix** A, whose ijth entry is the number of units from Sector i used in producing one unit from Sector j (in symbols, "$i \to j$"). To meet an **external demand** of D, the economy must produce X, where X is the **production vector**. These are related by the equations

$$X = AX + D$$

or

$$X = (I - A)^{-1}D. \qquad \text{Provided } (I - A) \text{ is invertible}$$

Quick Example

In the previous scenario, $A = \begin{bmatrix} 0.50 & 0.25 \\ 0.10 & 0.25 \end{bmatrix}$, $X = \begin{bmatrix} x_1 \\ x_2 \end{bmatrix}$, and $D = \begin{bmatrix} 7{,}000 \\ 14{,}000 \end{bmatrix}$.

The solution is

$$X = (I - A)^{-1}D$$

$$\begin{bmatrix} x_1 \\ x_2 \end{bmatrix} = \left(\begin{bmatrix} 1 & 0 \\ 0 & 1 \end{bmatrix} - \begin{bmatrix} 0.50 & 0.25 \\ 0.10 & 0.25 \end{bmatrix} \right)^{-1} \begin{bmatrix} 7{,}000 \\ 14{,}000 \end{bmatrix} \qquad \text{Calculate } I - A.$$

$$= \begin{bmatrix} 0.50 & -0.25 \\ -0.10 & 0.75 \end{bmatrix}^{-1} \begin{bmatrix} 7{,}000 \\ 14{,}000 \end{bmatrix} \qquad \text{Calculate } (I - A)^{-1}.$$

$$= \begin{bmatrix} \frac{15}{7} & \frac{5}{7} \\ \frac{2}{7} & \frac{10}{7} \end{bmatrix} \begin{bmatrix} 7{,}000 \\ 14{,}000 \end{bmatrix}$$

$$= \begin{bmatrix} 25{,}000 \\ 22{,}000 \end{bmatrix}.$$

In other words, to meet the demand, the economy must produce $25,000 worth of coal and $22,000 worth of electricity.

The next example uses actual data from the U.S. economy (we have rounded the figures to make the computations less complicated). It is rare to find input-output data already packaged for you as a technology matrix. Instead, the data commonly found in statistical sources come in the form of "input-output tables," from which we will have to construct the technology matrix.

EXAMPLE 1   Petroleum and Natural Gas

Consider two sectors of the U.S. economy: crude petroleum and natural gas (*crude*) and petroleum refining and related industries (*refining*). According to government figures,[29] in 1998 the crude sector used $27,000 million worth of its own products and $750 million worth of the products of the refining sector to produce $87,000 million worth of goods (crude oil and natural gas). The refining sector in the same

---

[29]The data have been rounded to two significant digits. Source: *Survey of Current Business*, December, 2001, U.S. Department of Commerce. The *Survey of Current Business* and the input-output tables themselves are available at the Web site of the Department of Commerce's Bureau of Economic Analysis (www.bea.gov).

year used $59,000 million worth of the products of the crude sector and $15,000 million worth of its own products to produce $140,000 million worth of goods (refined oil and the like). What was the technology matrix for these two sectors? What was left over from each of these sectors for use by other parts of the economy or for export?

Solution First, for convenience, we record the given data in the form of a table, called the **input-output table**. (All figures are in millions of dollars.)

	To	**Crude**	**Refining**
From	**Crude**	27,000	59,000
	Refining	750	15,000
	Total Output	87,000	140,000

The entries in the top portion are arranged in the same way as those of the technology matrix: The ijth entry represents the number of units of Sector i that went to Sector j. Thus, for instance, the 59,000 million entry in the 1, 2 position represents the number of units of Sector 1, crude, that were used by Sector 2, refining. ("From the side, to the top.")

We now construct the technology matrix. The technology matrix has entries a_{ij} = units of Sector i used to produce *one* unit of Sector j. Thus,

a_{11} = units of crude to produce one unit of crude. We are told that 27,000 million units of crude were used to produce 87,000 million units of crude. Thus, to produce *one* unit of crude, $27,000/87,000 \approx 0.31$ units of crude were used, and so $a_{11} \approx 0.31$. (We have rounded this value to two significant digits; further digits are not reliable due to rounding of the original data.)

a_{12} = units of crude to produce one unit of refined:
$a_{12} = 59,000/140,000 \approx 0.42$

a_{21} = units of refined to produce one unit of crude:
$a_{21} = 750/87,000 \approx 0.0086$

a_{22} = units of refined to produce one unit of refined:
$a_{22} = 15,000/140,000 \approx 0.11.$

This gives the technology matrix

$$A = \begin{bmatrix} 0.31 & 0.42 \\ 0.0086 & 0.11 \end{bmatrix}. \quad \text{Technology matrix}$$

In short *we obtained the technology matrix from the input-output table by dividing the Sector 1 column by the Sector 1 total, and the Sector 2 column by the Sector 2 total.*

Now we also know the total output from each sector, so *we have already been given the production vector:*

$$X = \begin{bmatrix} 87,000 \\ 140,000 \end{bmatrix}. \quad \text{Production vector}$$

What we are asked for is the external demand vector D, the amount available for the outside economy. To find D, we use the equation

$$X = AX + D, \quad \text{Relationship of } X, A, \text{ and } D$$

where, this time, we are given A and X, and must solve for D. Solving for D gives

$$D = X - AX$$

$$= \begin{bmatrix} 87,000 \\ 140,000 \end{bmatrix} - \begin{bmatrix} 0.31 & 0.42 \\ 0.0086 & 0.11 \end{bmatrix} \begin{bmatrix} 87,000 \\ 140,000 \end{bmatrix}$$

✱ Why?

$$\approx \begin{bmatrix} 87,000 \\ 140,000 \end{bmatrix} - \begin{bmatrix} 86,000 \\ 16,000 \end{bmatrix} = \begin{bmatrix} 1,000 \\ 124,000 \end{bmatrix}.$$ We rounded to 2 digits.**✱**

The first number, $1,000 million, is the amount produced by the crude sector that is available to be used by other parts of the economy or to be exported. (In fact, because something has to happen to all that crude petroleum and natural gas, this is the amount actually used or exported, where use can include stockpiling.) The second number, $124,000 million, represents the amount produced by the refining sector that is available to be used by other parts of the economy or to be exported.

Note that we could have calculated D more simply from the input-output table. The internal use of units from the crude sector was the sum of the outputs from that sector:

$$27,000 + 59,000 = 86,000.$$

using Technology
See the Technology Guides at the end of the chapter to see how to compute the technology matrix and the external demand vector in Example 1 using a TI-83/84 Plus or a spreadsheet.

Because 87,000 units were actually produced by the sector, that left a surplus of $87,000 - 86,000 = 1,000$ units for export. We could compute the surplus from the refining sector similarly. (The two calculations actually come out slightly different, because we rounded the intermediate results.) The calculation in Example 2 below cannot be done as trivially, however.

Input-Output Table

National economic data are often given in the form of an **input-output table**. The ijth entry in the top portion of the table is the number of units that go from Sector i to Sector j. The "Total outputs" are the total numbers of units produced by each sector. We obtain the technology matrix from the input-output table by dividing the Sector 1 column by the Sector 1 total, the Sector 2 column by the Sector 2 total, and so on.

Quick Example

Input-Output Table:

	To	**Skateboards**	**Wood**
From	**Skateboards**	20,000[†]	0
	Wood	100,000	500,000
	Total Output	200,000	5,000,000

† The production of skateboards required skateboards due to the fact that skateboard workers tend to commute to work on (what else?) skateboards!

Technology Matrix:

$$A = \begin{bmatrix} \frac{20,000}{200,000} & \frac{0}{5,000,000} \\ \frac{100,000}{200,000} & \frac{500,000}{5,000,000} \end{bmatrix} = \begin{bmatrix} 0.1 & 0 \\ 0.5 & 0.1 \end{bmatrix}.$$

EXAMPLE 2 Rising Demand

Suppose that external demand for refined petroleum rises to $200,000 million, but the demand for crude remains $1,000 million (as in Example 1). How do the production levels of the two sectors considered in Example 1 have to change?

Solution We are being told that now

$$D = \begin{bmatrix} 1,000 \\ 200,000 \end{bmatrix}$$

and we are asked to find X. Remember that we can calculate X from the formula

$$X = (I - A)^{-1}D.$$

Now

$$I - A = \begin{bmatrix} 1 & 0 \\ 0 & 1 \end{bmatrix} - \begin{bmatrix} 0.31 & 0.42 \\ 0.0086 & 0.11 \end{bmatrix} = \begin{bmatrix} 0.69 & -0.42 \\ -0.0086 & 0.89 \end{bmatrix}.$$

* Because A is accurate to two digits, we should use more than two significant digits in intermediate calculations so as not to lose additional accuracy. We must, of course, round the final answer to two digits.

We take the inverse using our favorite technique and find that, to four significant digits,*

$$(I - A)^{-1} \approx \begin{bmatrix} 1.458 & 0.6880 \\ 0.01409 & 1.130 \end{bmatrix}.$$

Now we can compute X:

$$X = (I - A)^{-1}D = \begin{bmatrix} 1.458 & 0.6880 \\ 0.01409 & 1.130 \end{bmatrix}\begin{bmatrix} 1,000 \\ 200,000 \end{bmatrix} \approx \begin{bmatrix} 140,000 \\ 230,000 \end{bmatrix}.$$

(As in Example 1, we have rounded all the entries in the answer to two significant digits.) Comparing this vector to the production vector used in Example 1, we see that production in the crude sector has to increase from $87,000 million to $140,000 million, while production in the refining sector has to increase from $140,000 million to $230,000 million.

Note Using the matrix $(I - A)^{-1}$, we have a slightly different way of solving Example 2. We are asking for the effect on production of a *change* in the final demand of 0 for crude and $200,000 - 124,000 = \$76,000$ million for refined products. If we multiply $(I - A)^{-1}$ by the matrix representing this *change,* we obtain

$$\begin{bmatrix} 1.458 & 0.6880 \\ 0.01409 & 1.130 \end{bmatrix}\begin{bmatrix} 0 \\ 76,000 \end{bmatrix} \approx \begin{bmatrix} 53,000 \\ 90,000 \end{bmatrix}.$$

$(I - A)^{-1} \times$ Change in Demand $=$ Change in Production

We see the changes required in production: an increase of $53,000 million in the crude sector and an increase of $90,000 million in the refining sector.

Notice that the increase in external demand for the products of the refining sector requires the crude sector to increase production as well, even though there is no increase in the *external* demand for its products. The reason is that, in order to increase production, the refining sector needs to use more crude oil, so that the *internal* demand for crude oil goes up. The inverse matrix $(I - A)^{-1}$ takes these **indirect effects** into account in a nice way.

By replacing the $76,000 by $1 in the computation we just did, we see that a $1 increase in external demand for refined products will require an increase in production of $0.6880 in the crude sector, as well as an increase in production of $1.130 in the refining sector. This is how we interpret the entries in $(I - A)^{-1}$, and this is why it is useful to look at this matrix inverse rather than just solve $(I - A)X = D$ for X using, say, Gauss-Jordan reduction. Looking at $(I - A)^{-1}$, we can also find the effects of an increase of $1 in external demand for crude: an increase in production of $1.458 in the crude sector and an increase of $0.01409 in the refining sector.

Here are some questions to think about: Why are the diagonal entries of $(I - A)^{-1}$ (slightly) larger than 1? Why is the entry in the lower left so small compared to the others? ∎

Interpreting $(I - A)^{-1}$: Indirect Effects

If A is the technology matrix, then the ijth entry of $(I - A)^{-1}$ is the change in the number of units Sector i must produce in order to meet a one-unit increase in external demand for Sector j products. To meet a rising external demand, the necessary change in production for each sector is given by

$$\text{Change in production} = (I - A)^{-1}D^{+},$$

where D^{+} is the change in external demand.

Quick Example

Take Sector 1 to be skateboards, and Sector 2 to be wood, and assume that

$$(I - A)^{-1} = \begin{bmatrix} 1.1 & 0 \\ 0.6 & 1.1 \end{bmatrix}.$$

Then

$a_{11} = 1.1 =$ number of additional units of skateboards that must be produced to meet a one-unit increase in the demand for skateboards (Why is this number larger than 1?)

$a_{12} = 0 =$ number of additional units of skateboards that must be produced to meet a one-unit increase in the demand for wood (Why is this number 0?)

$a_{21} = 0.6 =$ number of additional units of wood that must be produced to meet a one-unit increase in the demand for skateboards

$a_{22} = 1.1 =$ number of additional units of wood that must be produced to meet a one-unit increase in the demand for wood.

To meet an increase in external demand of 100 skateboards and 400 units of wood, the necessary change in production is

$$(I - A)^{-1}D^{+} = \begin{bmatrix} 1.1 & 0 \\ 0.6 & 1.1 \end{bmatrix}\begin{bmatrix} 100 \\ 400 \end{bmatrix} = \begin{bmatrix} 110 \\ 500 \end{bmatrix}$$

so 110 additional skateboards and 500 additional units of wood will need to be produced.

In the preceding examples, we used only two sectors of the economy. The data used in Examples 1 and 2 were taken from an input-output table published by the U.S. Department of Commerce, in which the whole U.S. economy was broken down into 85 sectors. This in turn was a simplified version of a model in which the economy was broken into about 500 sectors. Obviously, computers are required to make a realistic input-output analysis possible. Many governments collect and publish input-output data as part of their national planning. The United Nations collects these data and publishes collections of national statistics. The United Nations also has a useful set of links to government statistics at the following URL:

www.un.org/Depts/unsd/sd_natstat.htm

EXAMPLE 3 Kenya Economy

Consider four sectors of the economy of Kenya[30]: (1) the traditional economy, (2) agriculture, (3) manufacture of metal products and machinery, and (4) wholesale and retail trade. The input-output table for these four sectors for 1976 looks like this (all numbers are thousands of K£):

	To	1	2	3	4
From	1	8,600	0	0	0
	2	0	20,000	24	0
	3	1,500	530	15,000	660
	4	810	8,500	5,800	2,900
Total Output		87,000	530,000	110,000	180,000

using Technology

Technology can be used to do the computations in Example 3. Here is an outline for part (a) (see the Technology Guides at the end of the chapter for additional details on using a TI-83/84 Plus or a spreadsheet):

TI-83/84 Plus
Enter the matrices *A* and *D* using MATRX ; EDIT.
(For *A* type the entries as quotients: Column entry/ Column total.) Home Screen: `(identity(4)-[A])`$^{-1}$`[D]`
[More details on page 306.]

Spreadsheet
Obtain the technology matrix as in Example 1.
Insert the 4×4 identity matrix and then use MINVERSE and MMULT to compute $(I - A)^{-1}D$.
[More details on page 310.]

 Website
www.WanerMath.com
   Student Website
      → On Line Utilities
      → Matrix Algebra Tool

Enter the matrices *A* and *D*. (For *A* type the entries as quotients: Column entry/Column total.)
Type `(I-A)^(-1)*D` in the formula box and press "Compute".

Suppose that external demand for agriculture increased by K£50,000,000 and that external demand for metal products and machinery increased by K£10,000,000. How would production in these four sectors have to change to meet this rising demand?

Solution To find the change in production necessary to meet the rising demand, we need to use the formula

$$\text{Change in production} = (I - A)^{-1}D^+,$$

where *A* is the technology matrix and D^+ is the change in demand:

$$D^+ = \begin{bmatrix} 0 \\ 50,000 \\ 10,000 \\ 0 \end{bmatrix}.$$

With entries shown rounded to two significant digits, the matrix *A* is

$$A = \begin{bmatrix} 0.099 & 0 & 0 & 0 \\ 0 & 0.038 & 0.00022 & 0 \\ 0.017 & 0.001 & 0.14 & 0.0037 \\ 0.0093 & 0.016 & 0.053 & 0.016 \end{bmatrix}.$$

Entries shown are rounded to two significant digits.

---

[30]Figures are rounded. Source: *Input-Output Tables for Kenya 1976,* Central Bureau of Statistics of the Ministry of Economic Planning and Community Affairs, Kenya.

The next calculation is best done using technology:

$$\text{Change in production} = (I - A)^{-1}D^{+} = \begin{bmatrix} 0 \\ 52{,}000 \\ 12{,}000 \\ 1{,}500 \end{bmatrix}.$$
Entries shown are rounded to two significant digits.

Looking at this result, we see that the changes in external demand will leave the traditional economy unaffected, production in agriculture will rise by K£52 million, production in the manufacture of metal products and machinery will rise by K£12 million, and activity in wholesale and retail trade will rise by K£1.5 million.

➡ **Before we go on...** Can you see why the traditional economy was unaffected in Example 3? Although it takes inputs from other parts of the economy, it is not itself an input to any other part. In other words, there is no intermediate demand for the products of the traditional economy coming from any other part of the economy, and so an increase in production in any other sector of the economy will require no increase from the traditional economy. On the other hand, the wholesale and retail trade sector does provide input to the agriculture and manufacturing sectors, so increases in those sectors do require an increase in the trade sector.

One more point: If you calculate $(I - A)^{-1}$ you will notice how small the off-diagonal entries are. This says that increases in each sector have relatively small effects on the other sectors. We say that these sectors are **loosely coupled**. Regional economies, where many products are destined to be shipped out to the rest of the country, tend to show this phenomenon even more strongly. Notice in Example 2 that those two sectors are **strongly coupled**, because a rise in demand for refined products requires a comparable rise in the production of crude. ■

4.5 EXERCISES

▼ more advanced ◆ challenging
T indicates exercises that should be solved using technology

1. Let A be the technology matrix $A = \begin{bmatrix} 0.2 & 0.05 \\ 0.8 & 0.01 \end{bmatrix}$, where Sector 1 is paper and Sector 2 is wood. Fill in the missing quantities.

a. ___ units of wood are needed to produce one unit of paper.

b. ___ units of paper are used in the production of one unit of paper.

c. The production of each unit of wood requires the use of ___ units of paper.

2. Let A be the technology matrix $A = \begin{bmatrix} 0.01 & 0.001 \\ 0.2 & 0.004 \end{bmatrix}$, where Sector 1 is computer chips and Sector 2 is silicon. Fill in the missing quantities.

a. ___ units of silicon are required in the production of one unit of silicon.

b. ___ units of computer chips are used in the production of one unit of silicon.

c. The production of each unit of computer chips requires the use of ___ units of silicon.

3. Each unit of television news requires 0.2 units of television news and 0.5 units of radio news. Each unit of radio news requires 0.1 units of television news and no radio news. With Sector 1 as television news and Sector 2 as radio news, set up the technology matrix A.

4. Production of one unit of cologne requires no cologne and 0.5 units of perfume. Into one unit of perfume go 0.1 units of cologne and 0.3 units of perfume. With Sector 1 as cologne and Sector 2 as perfume, set up the technology matrix A.

In each of Exercises 5–12, you are given a technology matrix A and an external demand vector D. Find the corresponding production vector X. HINT [See Quick Example page 286.]

5. $A = \begin{bmatrix} 0.5 & 0.4 \\ 0 & 0.5 \end{bmatrix}$, $D = \begin{bmatrix} 10{,}000 \\ 20{,}000 \end{bmatrix}$

6. $A = \begin{bmatrix} 0.5 & 0.4 \\ 0 & 0.5 \end{bmatrix}$, $D = \begin{bmatrix} 20{,}000 \\ 10{,}000 \end{bmatrix}$

7. $A = \begin{bmatrix} 0.1 & 0.4 \\ 0.2 & 0.5 \end{bmatrix}$, $D = \begin{bmatrix} 25{,}000 \\ 15{,}000 \end{bmatrix}$

8. $A = \begin{bmatrix} 0.1 & 0.2 \\ 0.4 & 0.5 \end{bmatrix}$, $D = \begin{bmatrix} 24{,}000 \\ 14{,}000 \end{bmatrix}$

9. $A = \begin{bmatrix} 0.5 & 0.1 & 0 \\ 0 & 0.5 & 0.1 \\ 0 & 0 & 0.5 \end{bmatrix}, D = \begin{bmatrix} 1,000 \\ 1,000 \\ 2,000 \end{bmatrix}$

10. $A = \begin{bmatrix} 0.5 & 0.1 & 0 \\ 0 & 0.5 & 0.1 \\ 0 & 0 & 0.5 \end{bmatrix}, D = \begin{bmatrix} 3,000 \\ 3,800 \\ 2,000 \end{bmatrix}$

11. $A = \begin{bmatrix} 0.2 & 0.2 & 0 \\ 0.2 & 0.4 & 0.2 \\ 0 & 0.2 & 0.2 \end{bmatrix}, D = \begin{bmatrix} 16,000 \\ 8,000 \\ 8,000 \end{bmatrix}$

12. $A = \begin{bmatrix} 0.2 & 0.2 & 0.2 \\ 0.2 & 0.4 & 0.2 \\ 0.2 & 0.2 & 0.2 \end{bmatrix}, D = \begin{bmatrix} 7,000 \\ 14,000 \\ 7,000 \end{bmatrix}$

13. Given $A = \begin{bmatrix} 0.1 & 0.4 \\ 0.2 & 0.5 \end{bmatrix}$, find the changes in production required to meet an increase in demand of 50 units of Sector 1 products and 30 units of Sector 2 products.

14. Given $A = \begin{bmatrix} 0.5 & 0.4 \\ 0 & 0.5 \end{bmatrix}$, find the changes in production required to meet an increase in demand of 20 units of Sector 1 products and 10 units of Sector 2 products.

15. Let $(I - A)^{-1} = \begin{bmatrix} 1.5 & 0.1 & 0 \\ 0.2 & 1.2 & 0.1 \\ 0.1 & 0.7 & 1.6 \end{bmatrix}$ and assume that the external demand for the products in Sector 1 increases by 1 unit. By how many units should each sector increase production? What do the columns of the matrix $(I - A)^{-1}$ tell you? HINT [See Quick Example on page 290.]

16. Let $(I - A)^{-1} = \begin{bmatrix} 1.5 & 0.1 & 0 \\ 0.1 & 1.1 & 0.1 \\ 0 & 0 & 1.3 \end{bmatrix}$, and assume that the external demand for the products in each of the sectors increases by 1 unit. By how many units should each sector increase production? HINT [See Quick Example on page 290.]

In Exercises 17 and 18, obtain the technology matrix from the given input-output table. HINT [See Example 1.]

17.

To	A	B	C
From A	1,000	2,000	3,000
B	0	4,000	0
C	0	1,000	3,000
Total Output	5,000	5,000	6,000

18.

To	A	B	C
From A	0	100	300
B	500	400	300
C	0	0	600
Total Output	1,000	2,000	3,000

APPLICATIONS

19. **Campus Food** The two campus cafeterias, the Main Dining Room and Bits & Bytes, typically use each other's food in doing business on campus. One weekend, the input-output table was as follows.[31]

	To	Main DR	Bits & Bytes
From	**Main DR**	$10,000	$20,000
	Bits & Bytes	5,000	0
	Total Output	50,000	40,000

Given that the demand for food on campus last weekend was $45,000 from the Main Dining Room and $30,000 from Bits & Bytes, how much did the two cafeterias have to produce to meet the demand last weekend? HINT [See Example 1.]

20. **Plagiarism** Two student groups at Enormous State University, the Choral Society and the Football Club, maintain files of term papers that they write and offer to students for research purposes. Some of these papers they use themselves in generating more papers. In order to avoid suspicion of plagiarism by faculty members (who seem to have astute memories), each paper is given to students or used by the clubs only once (no copies are kept). The number of papers that were used in the production of new papers last year is shown in the following input-output table:

	To	Choral Soc.	Football Club
From	**Choral Soc.**	20	10
	Football Club	10	30
	Total Output	100	200

Given that 270 Choral Society papers and 810 Football Club papers will be used by students outside of these two clubs next year, how many new papers do the two clubs need to write?

21. **T** **Communication Equipment** Two sectors of the U.S. economy are (1) audio, video, and communication equipment and (2) electronic components and accessories. In 1998, the input-output table involving these two sectors was as follows (all figures are in millions of dollars):[32]

	To	Equipment	Components
From	**Equipment**	6,000	500
	Components	24,000	30,000
	Total Output	90,000	140,000

Determine the production levels necessary in these two sectors to meet an external demand for $80,000 million of communication equipment and $90,000 million of electronic components. Round answers to two significant digits.

---

[31]For some reason, the Main Dining Room consumes a lot of its own food!

[32]The data have been rounded. Source: *Survey of Current Business,* December, 2001, U.S. Department of Commerce.

22. ▣ *Wood and Paper* Two sectors of the U.S. economy are (1) lumber and wood products and (2) paper and allied products. In 1998 the input-output table involving these two sectors was as follows (all figures are in millions of dollars).[33]

	To	**Wood**	**Paper**
From	**Wood**	36,000	7,000
	Paper	100	17,000
	Total Output	120,000	120,000

If external demand for lumber and wood products rises by $10,000 million and external demand for paper and allied products rises by $20,000 million, what increase in output of these two sectors is necessary? Round answers to two significant digits.

23. *Australia Economy* Two sectors of the Australian economy are (1) textiles and (2) clothing and footwear. The 1977 input-output table[34] involving these two sectors results in the following value for $(I - A)^{-1}$:

$$(I - A)^{-1} = \begin{bmatrix} 1.228 & 0.182 \\ 0.006 & 1.1676 \end{bmatrix}.$$

Complete the following sentences.

a. ____ additional dollars worth of clothing and footwear must be produced to meet a $1 increase in the demand for textiles.

b. 0.182 additional dollars worth of ____ must be produced to meet a one-dollar increase in the demand for ____.

24. *Australia Economy* Two sectors of the Australian economy are (1) community services and (2) recreation services. The 1978–79 input-output table[35] involving these two sectors results in the following value for $(I - A)^{-1}$:

$$(I - A)^{-1} = \begin{bmatrix} 1.0066 & 0.00576 \\ 0.00496 & 1.04206 \end{bmatrix}.$$

Complete the following sentences.

a. 0.00496 additional dollars worth of ____ must be produced to meet a $1 increase in the demand for ____.

b. ____ additional dollars worth of community services must be produced to meet a one-dollar increase in the demand for community services.

▣ *Exercises 25–28 require the use of technology.*

25. ▣ *United States Input-Output Table* Four sectors of the U.S. economy are (1) livestock and livestock products,

(2) other agricultural products, (3) forestry and fishery products, and (4) agricultural, forestry, and fishery services. In 1977 the input-output table involving these four sectors was as follows (all figures are in millions of dollars):[36]

	To	**1**	**2**	**3**	**4**
From	**1**	11,937	9	109	855
	2	26,649	4,285	0	4,744
	3	0	0	439	61
	4	5,423	10,952	3,002	216
Total Output		97,795	120,594	14,642	47,473

Determine how these four sectors would react to an increase in demand for livestock (Sector 1) of $1,000 million, how they would react to an increase in demand for other agricultural products (Sector 2) of $1,000 million, and so on.

26. ▣ *United States Input-Output Table* Four sectors of the U.S. economy are (1) motor vehicles, (2) truck and bus bodies, trailers, and motor vehicle parts, (3) aircraft and parts, and (4) other transportation equipment. In 1998 the input-output table involving these four sectors was (all figures in millions of dollars):[37]

	To	**1**	**2**	**3**	**4**
From	**1**	75	1,092	0	1,207
	2	64,858	13,081	7	1,070
	3	0	0	21,782	0
	4	0	0	0	1,375
Total Output		230,676	135,108	129,376	44,133

Determine how these four sectors would react to an increase in demand for motor vehicles (Sector 1) of $1,000 million, how they would react to an increase in demand for truck and bus bodies (Sector 2) of $1,000 million, and so on.

27. ▽ *Australia Input-Output Table* Four sectors of the Australian economy are (1) agriculture, (2) forestry, fishing, and hunting, (3) meat and milk products, and (4) other food products. In 1978–79 the input-output table involving these four sectors was as follows (all figures are in millions of Australian dollars).[38]

---

[33] The data have been rounded. Source: *Survey of Current Business,* December, 2001, U.S. Department of Commerce.

[34] Source: *Australian National Accounts and Input-Output Tables 1978–1979,* Australian Bureau of Statistics.

[35] *Ibid.*

[36] Source: *Survey of Current Business,* December 2001, U.S. Department of Commerce.

[37] *Ibid.*

[38] Source: *Australian National Accounts and Input-Output Tables 1978–1979,* Australian Bureau of Statistics.

	To	1	2	3	4
From	1	678.4	3.7	3,341.5	1,023.5
	2	15.5	6.9	17.1	124.5
	3	47.3	4.3	893.1	145.8
	4	312.5	22.1	83.2	693.5
Total Output		9,401.3	685.8	6,997.3	4,818.3

a. How much additional production by the meat and milk sector is necessary to accommodate a $100 increase in the demand for agriculture?

b. Which sector requires the most of its own product in order to meet a $1 increase in external demand for that product?

28. ▼ *Australia Input-Output Table* Four sectors of the Australian economy are (1) petroleum and coal products, (2) nonmetallic mineral products, (3) basic metals and products, and (4) fabricated metal products. In 1978–79 the input-output table involving these four sectors was as follows (all figures are in millions of Australian dollars).[39]

	To	1	2	3	4
From	1	174.1	30.5	120.3	14.2
	2	0	190.1	55.8	12.6
	3	2.1	40.2	1,418.7	1,242.0
	4	0.1	7.3	40.4	326.0
Total Output		3,278.0	2,188.8	6,541.7	4,065.8

---

[39]Source: *Australian National Accounts and Input-Output Tables 1978–1979*, Australian Bureau of Statistics.

a. How much additional production by the petroleum and coal products sector is necessary to accommodate a $1,000 increase in the demand for fabricated metal products?

b. Which sector requires the most of the product of some other sector in order to meet a $1 increase in external demand for that product?

COMMUNICATION AND REASONING EXERCISES

29. What would it mean if the technology matrix A were the zero matrix?

30. Can an external demand be met by an economy whose technology matrix A is the identity matrix? Explain.

31. ▼ What would it mean if the total output figure for a particular sector of an input-output table were equal to the sum of the figures in the row for that sector?

32. ▼ What would it mean if the total output figure for a particular sector of an input-output table were less than the sum of the figures in the row for that sector?

33. ▼ What does it mean if an entry in the matrix $(I - A)^{-1}$ is zero?

34. ▼ Why do we expect the diagonal entries in the matrix $(I - A)^{-1}$ to be slightly larger than 1?

35. ▼ Why do we expect the off-diagonal entries of $(I - A)^{-1}$ to be less than 1?

36. ▼ Why do we expect all the entries of $(I - A)^{-1}$ to be nonnegative?

KEY CONCEPTS

 Website www.WanerMath.com
Go to the Website at www.WanerMath
.com to find a comprehensive and
interactive Web-based summary
of Chapter 4.

4.1 Matrix Addition and Scalar Multiplication

$m \times n$ matrix, dimensions, entries
p. 232
Referring to the entries of a matrix
p. 232
Matrix equality p. 233
Row, column, and square matrices
p. 234
Addition and subtraction of matrices
p. 234
Scalar multiplication p. 236
Properties of matrix addition and scalar
multiplication p. 237
The transpose of a matrix p. 238
Properties of transposition p. 238

4.2 Matrix Multiplication

Multiplying a row by a column
p. 242
Linear equation as a matrix
equation p. 244

The product of two matrices: general
case p. 244
Identity matrix p. 248
Properties of matrix addition and
multiplication p. 249
Properties of transposition and
multiplication p. 250
A system of linear equations can be
written as a single matrix equation
p. 250

4.3 Matrix Inversion

The inverse of a matrix, singular matrix
p. 256
Procedure for finding the inverse of a
matrix p. 256
Formula for the inverse of a 2×2
matrix; determinant of a 2×2
matrix p. 257
Using an inverse matrix to solve a
system of equations p. 261

4.4 Game Theory

Two-person zero-sum game, payoff
matrix p. 268
A strategy specifies how a player
chooses a move p. 268
The expected payoff of a game for given
mixed strategies R and C p. 269

An optimal strategy, according to the
minimax criterion, is one that minimizes the maximum damage your
opponent can cause you. p. 272
The Fundamental Principle of Game
Theory p. 272
Procedure for reducing by dominance
p. 273
Procedure for solving a 2×2 game
p. 273
The expected value of a game is its
expected payoff when the players use
their optimal strategies p. 276
A strictly determined game is one with
a saddle point p. 278
Steps to follow in solving a game
p. 278

4.5 Input-Output Models

An input-output model divides an
economy into sectors. The technology matrix records the interactions of
these sectors and allows us to relate
external demand to the production
vector. p. 286
Procedure for finding a technology
matrix from an input-output table
p. 288
The entries of $(I - A)^{-1}$ p. 290

REVIEW EXERCISES

For Exercises 1–10, let

$$A = \begin{bmatrix} 1 & 2 & 3 \\ 4 & 5 & 6 \end{bmatrix}, B = \begin{bmatrix} 1 & -1 \\ 0 & 1 \end{bmatrix},$$

$$C = \begin{bmatrix} -1 & 0 \\ 1 & 1 \\ 0 & 1 \end{bmatrix}, \text{ and } D = \begin{bmatrix} -3 & -2 & -1 \\ 1 & 2 & 3 \end{bmatrix}.$$

*Determine whether each expression is defined, and if it is,
evaluate it.*

1. $A + B$
2. $A - D$
3. $2A^T + C$
4. AB
5. $A^T B$
6. A^2
7. B^2
8. B^3
9. $AC + B$
10. $CD + B$

*In Exercises 11–16, find the inverse of the given matrix or
determine that the matrix is singular.*

11. $\begin{bmatrix} 1 & -1 \\ 0 & 1 \end{bmatrix}$

12. $\begin{bmatrix} 1 & 2 \\ 0 & 0 \end{bmatrix}$

13. $\begin{bmatrix} 1 & 2 & 3 \\ 0 & 4 & 1 \\ 0 & 0 & 1 \end{bmatrix}$

14. $\begin{bmatrix} 1 & 2 & 3 & 4 \\ 1 & 3 & 4 & 2 \\ 0 & 1 & 2 & 3 \\ 0 & 0 & 1 & 2 \end{bmatrix}$

15. $\begin{bmatrix} 1 & 2 & 3 & 4 \\ 2 & 3 & 3 & 3 \\ 0 & 1 & 2 & 3 \\ 0 & 0 & 1 & 2 \end{bmatrix}$

16. $\begin{bmatrix} 0 & 1 & 0 & 0 \\ 1 & 0 & 0 & 0 \\ 0 & 0 & 0 & 1 \\ 0 & 0 & 1 & 0 \end{bmatrix}$

*In Exercises 17–20, write the given system of linear equations as
a matrix equation, and solve by inverting the coefficient matrix.*

17. $x + 2y = 0$
    $3x + 4y = 2$

18. $x + y + z = 3$
    $y + 2z = 4$
    $y - z = 1$

19. $\begin{aligned} x + y + z &= 2 \\ x + 2y + z &= 3 \\ x + y + 2z &= 1 \end{aligned}$ 20. $\begin{aligned} x + y \quad\;\; &= 0 \\ y + z \quad\;\; &= 1 \\ z + w &= 0 \\ x \qquad\;\; - w &= 3 \end{aligned}$

In each of Exercises 21–24, solve the game with the given payoff matrix and give the expected value of the game.

21. $P = \begin{bmatrix} 2 & 1 & 3 & 2 \\ -1 & 0 & -2 & 1 \\ 2 & 0 & 1 & 3 \end{bmatrix}$ 22. $P = \begin{bmatrix} 3 & -3 & -2 \\ -1 & 3 & 0 \\ 2 & 2 & 1 \end{bmatrix}$

23. $P = \begin{bmatrix} -1 & -3 & -2 \\ -1 & 3 & 0 \\ 3 & 3 & -1 \end{bmatrix}$ 24. $P = \begin{bmatrix} 1 & 4 & 3 & 3 \\ 0 & -1 & 2 & 3 \\ 2 & 0 & -1 & 2 \end{bmatrix}$

In each of Exercises 25–28, find the production vector X corresponding to the given technology matrix A and external demand vector D.

25. $A = \begin{bmatrix} 0.3 & 0.1 \\ 0 & 0.3 \end{bmatrix}, D = \begin{bmatrix} 700 \\ 490 \end{bmatrix}$

26. $A = \begin{bmatrix} 0.7 & 0.1 \\ 0.1 & 0.7 \end{bmatrix}, D = \begin{bmatrix} 1{,}000 \\ 2{,}000 \end{bmatrix}$

27. $A = \begin{bmatrix} 0.2 & 0.2 & 0.2 \\ 0 & 0.2 & 0.2 \\ 0 & 0 & 0.2 \end{bmatrix}, D = \begin{bmatrix} 32{,}000 \\ 16{,}000 \\ 8{,}000 \end{bmatrix}$

28. $A = \begin{bmatrix} 0.5 & 0.1 & 0 \\ 0.1 & 0.5 & 0.1 \\ 0 & 0.1 & 0.5 \end{bmatrix}, D = \begin{bmatrix} 23{,}000 \\ 46{,}000 \\ 23{,}000 \end{bmatrix}$

APPLICATIONS: OHaganBooks.com

It is now July 1 and online sales of romance, science fiction, and horror novels at OHaganBooks.com were disappointingly slow over the past month. Exercises 29–34 are based on the following tables:

Inventory of books in stock on June 1 at the OHaganBooks.com warehouses in Texas and Nevada:

Books in Stock (June 1)

	Romance	Sci Fi	Horror
Texas	2,500	4,000	3,000
Nevada	1,500	3,000	1,000

Online sales during June:

June Sales

	Romance	Sci Fi	Horror
Texas	300	500	100
Nevada	100	600	200

New books purchased each month:

Monthly Purchases

	Romance	Sci Fi	Horror
Texas	400	400	300
Nevada	200	400	300

July Sales (Projected)

	Romance	Sci Fi	Horror
Texas	280	550	100
Nevada	50	500	120

29. *Inventory* Use matrix algebra to compute the inventory at each warehouse at the end of June.

30. *Inventory* Use matrix algebra to compute the change in inventory at each warehouse during June.

31. *Inventory* Assuming that sales continue at the level projected for July for the next few months, write down a matrix equation showing the inventory N at each warehouse x months after July 1. How many months from now will OHaganBooks.com run out of Sci Fi novels at the Nevada warehouse?

32. *Inventory* Assuming that sales continue at the level projected for July for the next few months, write down a matrix equation showing the change in inventory N at each warehouse x months after July 1. How many months from now will OHaganBooks.com have 1,000 more horror novels in stock in Texas than currently?

33. *Revenue* It is now the end of July and OHaganBooks.com's e-commerce manager bursts into the CEO's office. "I thought you might want to know, John, that our sales figures are exactly what I projected a month ago. Is that good market analysis or what?" OHaganBooks.com has charged an average of $5 for romance novels, $6 for science fiction novels, and $5.50 for horror novels. Use the projected July sales figures from above and matrix arithmetic to compute the total revenue OHaganBooks.com earned at each warehouse in July.

34. *Cost* OHaganBooks.com pays an average of $2 for romance novels, $3.50 for science fiction novels, and $1.50 for horror novels. Use this information together with the monthly purchasing information to compute the monthly purchasing cost.

Acting on a "tip" from Marjory Duffin, John O'Hagan decided that his company should invest a significant sum in shares of Duffin House Publishers (DHP) and Duffin Subprime Ventures (DSV). Exercises 35–38 are based on the following table, which shows what information John was able to piece together later, after some of the records had been deleted by an angry student intern.

Date	Number of Shares: DHP	Price per Share: DHP	Number of Shares: DSV	Price per Share: DSV
July 1	?	$20	?	$10
August 1	?	$10	?	$20
September 1	?	$5	?	$40
Total	5,000		7,000	

35. *Investments* Over the three months shown, the company invested a total of $50,000 in DHP stock, and, on August 15, was paid dividends of 10¢ per share held on that date, for a total of $300. Use matrix inversion to determine how many shares of DHP OHaganBooks.com purchased on each of the three dates shown.

36. *Investments* Over the three months shown, the company invested a total of $150,000 in DSV stock, and, on July 15, was paid dividends of 20¢ per share held on that date, for a total of $600. Use matrix inversion to determine how many shares of DSV OHaganBooks.com purchased on each of the three dates shown.

37. *Investments* (Refer to Exercise 35.) On October 1, the shares of DHP purchased on July 1 were sold at $3 per share. The remaining shares were sold one month later at $1 per share. Use matrix algebra to determine the total loss (taking into account the dividends paid on August 15) incurred as a result of the Duffin stock debacle.

38. *Investments* (Refer to Exercise 36.) On September 15, DSV announced a two-for-one stock split, so that each share originally purchased was converted into two shares. On October 1, the company paid an additional special dividend of 10¢ per share. On October 15, OHaganBooks.com sold 3,000 shares at $20 per share. One week later the subprime market crashed, Duffin Subprime Ventures declared bankruptcy (after awarding its fund manager a $10 million bonus), and DSV stock became worthless. Use matrix algebra to determine the total loss (taking into account the dividends paid on July 15) incurred as a result of the Duffin stock debacle.

OHaganBooks.com has two main competitors: JungleBooks.com and FarmerBooks.com, and no other competitors of any significance on the horizon. Exercises 39–42 are based on the following table, which shows the movement of customers during July.[40] (Thus, for instance, the first row tells us that 80% of OHaganBooks.com's customers remained loyal, 10% of them went to JungleBooks.com, and the remaining 10% went to FarmerBooks.com.)

	To OHagan	To Jungle	To Farmer
From OHagan	0.8	0.1	0.1
From Jungle	0.4	0.6	0
From Farmer	0.2	0	0.8

At the beginning of July, OHaganBooks.com had an estimated 2,000 customers, while its two competitors had 4,000 each.

39. *Competition* Set up the July 1 customer numbers in a row matrix, and use matrix arithmetic to estimate the number of customers each company has at the end of July.

40. *Competition* Assuming the July trends continue in August, predict the number of customers each company will have at the end of August.

---

41. *Competition* Assuming the July trends continue in August, why is it not possible for a customer of FarmerBooks.com on July 1 to have ended up as a JungleBooks.com customer two months later without having ever been an OHaganBooks.com customer?

42. *Competition* Name one or more important factors that the model we have used does not take into account.

Publisher Marjory Duffin reveals that JungleBooks may be launching a promotional scheme in which it will offer either two books for the price of one, or three books for the price of two (Marjory can't quite seem to remember which, and is not certain whether they will go with the scheme at all). John O'Hagan's marketing advisers Flood and O'Lara seem to have different ideas as to how to respond. Flood suggests that the company counter by offering three books for the price of one, while O'Lara suggests that it offer instead a free copy of the Finite Mathematics Student Solutions Manual *with every purchase. After a careful analysis, O'Hagan comes up with the following payoff matrix, where the payoffs represent the number of customers, in thousands, he expects to gain from JungleBooks.*

		JungleBooks		
		No Promo	2 for Price of 1	3 for Price of 2
O'Hagan	**No Promo**	0	−60	−40
	3 for Price of 1	30	20	10
	Finite Math	20	0	15

Use the above information in Exercises 43–48.

43. *Competition* After a very expensive dinner at an exclusive restaurant, Marjory suddenly "remembers" that the JungleBooks CEO mentioned to her (at a less expensive restaurant) that there is only a 20% chance JungleBooks will launch a "2 for the price of 1" promotion, and a 40% chance that it will launch a "3 for the price of 2" promotion. What should OHaganBooks.com do in view of this information, and what will the expected effect be on its customer base?

44. *Competition* JungleBooks CEO François Dubois has been told by someone with personal ties to OHaganBooks.com staff that OHaganBooks is in fact 80% certain to opt for the "3 for the price of 1" option and will certainly go with one of the two possible promos. What should JungleBooks.com do in view of this information, and what will the expected effect be on its customer base?

45. *Corporate Spies* One of John O'Hagan's trusted marketing advisers has, without knowing it, accidentally sent him a copy of the following e-mail:

> To: René, JungleBooks Marketing Department
>
> From: O'Lara
>
> Hey René somehow the CEO here says he has learned that there is a 20% chance that you will opt for the "2 for the price of 1" promotion, and a 40% chance that you will opt for the "3 for the price of 2" promotion. Thought you might want to know. So when do I get my "commission"? —Jim

---

[40]By a "customer" of one of the three e-commerce sites, we mean someone who purchases more at that site than at either of the two competitors.

What will each company do in view of this new information, and what will the expected effect be on its customer base?

46. **More Corporate Spies** The next day, everything changes: OHaganBooks.com's mole at JungleBooks, Davíde DuPont, is found unconscious in the coffee room at JungleBooks.com headquarters, clutching in his hand the following correspondence he had apparently received moments earlier:

To: Davíde
From: John O'Hagan
Subject: Re: Urgent Information
Davíde: This information is much appreciated and definitely changes my plans—J

>
>To: John O
>From: Davíde
>Subject: Urgent Information
>Thought you might want to know that JungleBooks
>thinks you are 80% likely to opt for 3 for 1 and 20%
>likely to opt for Finite Math.
>—D

What will each company do in view of this information, and what will the expected effect be on its customer base?

47. **Things Unravel** John O'Hagan is about to go with the option chosen in Exercise 45 when he hears word about an exposé in the *Publisher Enquirer* on corporate spying in the two companies. Each company now knows that no information about the other's intentions can be trusted. Now what should OHaganBooks.com do, and how many customers should it expect to gain or lose?

48. **Competition** It is now apparent as a result of the *Publisher Enquirer* exposé that, not only can each company make no assumptions about the strategies the other might be using, but the payoff matrix they have been using is wrong: A crack investigative reporter at the *Enquirer* publishes the following revised matrix:

$$P = \begin{bmatrix} 0 & -60 & -40 \\ 30 & 20 & 10 \\ 20 & 0 & 20 \end{bmatrix}.$$

Now what should JungleBooks.com do, and how many customers should it expect to gain or lose?

Some of the books sold by OHaganBooks.com are printed at Bruno Mills, Inc., a combined paper mill and printing company. Exercises 49–52 are based on the following typical monthly input-output table for Bruno Mills' paper and book printing sectors.

		To	**Paper**	**Books**
From	**Paper**		$20,000	$50,000
	Books		2,000	5,000
Total Output			200,000	100,000

49. **Production** Find the technology matrix for Bruno Mills' paper and book printing sectors.

50. **Production** Compute $(I - A)^{-1}$. What is the significance of the $(1, 2)$-entry?

51. **Production** Approximately $1,700 worth of the books sold each month by OHaganBooks.com are printed at Bruno Mills, Inc., and OHaganBooks.com uses approximately $170 worth of Bruno Mills' paper products each month. What is the total value of paper and books that must be produced by Bruno Mills, Inc. in order to meet demand from OHaganBooks.com?

52. **Production** Currently, Bruno Mills, Inc. has a monthly capacity of $500,000 of paper products and $200,000 of books. What level of external demand would cause Bruno to meet the capacity for both products?

Case Study | **Projecting Market Share**

You are the sales director at *Selular*, a cellphone provider, and things are not looking good for your company: The recently launched *iClone* competitor is beginning to chip away at Selular's market share. Particularly disturbing are rumors of fierce brand loyalty by iClone customers, with several bloggers suggesting that iClone retains close to 100% of their customers. Worse, you will shortly be presenting a sales report to the board of directors, and the CEO has "suggested" that your report include 2-, 5-, and 10-year projections of Selular's market share given the recent impact on the market by iClone, and also a "worst-case" scenario projecting what would happen if iClone customers are so loyal that none of them ever switch services.

The sales department has conducted two market surveys, taken one quarter apart, of the major cellphone providers, which are *iClone, Selular, AB&C*, and some smaller companies lumped together as "Other," and has given you the data shown in Figure 4, which shows the percentages of subscribers who switched from one service to another during the quarter.*

∗ If you go on to study probability theory in Chapter 7, you will see how this scenario can be interpreted as a Markov system, and you will revisit the analysis below in that context.

The percentages in the figure and market shares below reflect actual data for several cellphone services in the United States during a single quarter of 2003. (See the exercises for Section 7.7.)

Figure 4

For example, by the end of the quarter 0.5% of iClone's customers had switched to Selular, 0.5% to AB&C, and 0.9% to Other. The current market shares are as follows: iClone: 29.7%, Selular: 19.3%, AB&C: 18.1%, Other: 32.9%.

"This is simple," you tell yourself. "Since I know the current market shares and percentage movements over one quarter, I can easily calculate the market shares next quarter (assuming the percentages that switch services remain the same), then repeat the calculation for the following quarter, and so on, until I get the long-term prediction I am seeking." So you begin your calculations by computing the market shares next quarter. First you note that, since a total of $0.5 + 0.5 + 0.9 = 1.9\%$ of iClone users switched to other brands, the rest, 98.1%, stayed with iClone. Similarly, 97.2% of Selular users, 97.3% of AB&C, and 98.1% of Other stayed with their respective brands. Then you compute:

iClone share after one quarter

$= 98.1\%$ of iClone $+1.0\%$ of Selular $+1.0\%$ of AB&C $+ 0.8\%$ of Other

$= (0.981)(0.297) + (0.010)(0.193) + (0.010)(0.181) + (0.008)(0.329)$

$= 0.297729$, or 29.7729%.

Similarly,

Selular share:

$= (0.005)(0.297) + (0.972)(0.193) + (0.006)(0.181) + (0.006)(0.329)$

$= 0.192141$

AB&C share:

$= (0.005)(0.297) + (0.006)(0.193) + (0.973)(0.181) + (0.005)(0.329)$

$= 0.180401$

Other share:

$= (0.009)(0.297) + (0.012)(0.193) + (0.011)(0.181) + (0.981)(0.329)$

$= 0.329729$.

So, you project the market shares after one quarter to be: iClone: 29.7729%, Selular: 19.2141%, AB&C: 18.0401%, Other: 32.9729%. You now begin to realize that repeating this kind of calculation for the large number of quarters required for long-term projections will be tedious. You call in your student intern (who happens to be a mathematics major) to see if she can help. After taking one look at the calculations, she makes the observation that all you have really done is compute the product of two matrices:

$$[0.297729 \quad 0.192141 \quad 0.180401 \quad 0.329729]$$

$$= [0.297 \quad 0.193 \quad 0.181 \quad 0.329] \begin{bmatrix} .981 & .005 & .005 & .009 \\ .010 & .972 & .006 & .012 \\ .010 & .006 & .973 & .011 \\ .008 & .006 & .005 & .981 \end{bmatrix}.$$

Market shares after one quarter = Market shares at start of quarter $\times A$

The 4×4 matrix A is organized as follows:

		To			
		iClone	Selular	AB&C	Other
	iClone	.981	.005	.005	.009
From	Selular	.010	.972	.006	.012
	AB&C	.010	.006	.973	.011
	Other	.008	.006	.005	.981

Since the market shares one quarter later can be obtained from the shares at the start of the quarter, you realize that you can now obtain the shares *two* quarters later by multiplying the result by A—and at this point you start using technology (such as the Matrix Algebra Tool at www.WanerMath.com) to continue the calculation:

Market shares after two quarters = Market shares after one quarter $\times A$

$$= [0.297729 \quad 0.192141 \quad 0.180401 \quad 0.329729] \begin{bmatrix} .981 & .005 & .005 & .009 \\ .010 & .972 & .006 & .012 \\ .010 & .006 & .973 & .011 \\ .008 & .006 & .005 & .981 \end{bmatrix}$$

$$\approx [0.298435 \quad 0.191310 \quad 0.179820 \quad 0.330434].$$

Although the use of matrices has simplified your work, continually multiplying the result by A over and over again to get the market shares for successive months is still tedious. Would it not be possible to get, say, the market share after 10 years (40 quarters) with a single calculation? To explore this, you decide to use symbols for the various market shares:

$m_0 =$ Starting market shares $= [0.297 \quad 0.193 \quad 0.181 \quad 0.329]$

$m_1 =$ Market shares after 1 quarter
    $= [0.297729 \quad 0.192141 \quad 0.180401 \quad 0.329729]$

$m_2 =$ Market shares after 2 quarters

$\ldots$

$m_n =$ Market share after n quarters.

You then rewrite the relationships above as

$m_1 = m_0 A$ Shares after one quarter = Shares at start of quarter $\times A$

$m_2 = m_1 A$ Shares after two quarters = Shares after one quarter $\times A$

On an impulse, you substitute the first equation in the second:

$$m_2 = m_1 A = (m_0 A)A = m_0 A^2.$$

Continuing,

$$m_3 = m_2 A = (m_0 A^2)A = m_0 A^3$$

$$\cdots$$

$$m_n = m_0 A^n,$$

which is exactly the formula you need! You can now obtain the 2-, 5-, and 10-year projections each in a single step (with the aid of technology):

2-year projection: $m_8 = m_0 A^8$

$$= [0.297 \quad 0.193 \quad 0.181 \quad 0.329] \begin{bmatrix} .981 & .005 & .005 & .009 \\ .010 & .972 & .006 & .012 \\ .010 & .006 & .973 & .011 \\ .008 & .006 & .005 & .981 \end{bmatrix}^8$$

$$\approx [0.302237 \quad 0.186875 \quad 0.176691 \quad 0.334198]$$

5-year projection: $m_{20} = m_0 A^{20} \approx [0.307992 \quad 0.180290 \quad 0.171938 \quad 0.33978]$

10-year projection: $m_{40} = m_0 A^{40} \approx [0.313857 \quad 0.173809 \quad 0.167074 \quad 0.34526].$

In particular, Selular's market shares are projected to decline slightly: 2-year projection: 18.7%, 5-year projection: 18.0%, 10-year projection: 17.4%.

You now move on to the "worst-case" scenario, which you represent by assuming 100% loyalty by iClone users with the remaining percentages staying the same (Figure 5).

Figure 5

The matrix A corresponding to this diagram is $\begin{bmatrix} 1 & 0 & 0 & 0 \\ .010 & .972 & .006 & .012 \\ .010 & .006 & .973 & .011 \\ .008 & .006 & .005 & .981 \end{bmatrix}$, and you find:

2-year projection: $m_8 = m_0 A^8 \approx [0.346335 \quad 0.175352 \quad 0.165200 \quad 0.313113]$

5-year projection: $m_{20} = m_0 A^{20} \approx [0.413747 \quad 0.152940 \quad 0.144776 \quad 0.288536]$

10-year projection: $m_{40} = m_0 A^{40} \approx [0.510719 \quad 0.123553 \quad 0.117449 \quad 0.248279].$

Thus, in the worst-case scenario, Selular's market shares are projected to decline more rapidly: 2-year projection: 17.5%, 5-year projection: 15.3%, 10-year projection: 12.4%.

EXERCISES

1. Project Selular's market share 20 and 30 years from now based on the original data shown in Figure 4. (Round all figures to the nearest 0.1%.)

2. Using the original data, what can you say about each company's share in 60 and 80 years (assuming current trends continue)? (Round all figures to the nearest 0.1%.)

3. Obtain a sequence of projections several hundreds of years into the future using the scenarios in both Figure 4 and Figure 5. What do you notice?

4. Compute a sequence of larger and larger powers of the matrix A for both scenarios with all figures rounded to four decimal places. What do you notice?

5. Suppose the trends noted in the market survey were in place for several quarters *before* the current quarter. Using the scenario in Figure 4, determine what the companies' market shares were one quarter before the present and one year before the present (to the nearest 0.1%). Do the same for the scenario in Figure 5.

6. If A is the matrix from the scenario in Figure 4, compute A^{-1}. In light of the preceding exercise, what do the entries in A^{-1} mean?

TI-83/84 Plus   Technology Guide

Section 4.1

Example 2 (page 235)   The A-Plus auto parts store chain has two outlets, one in Vancouver and one in Quebec. Among other things, it sells wiper blades, windshield cleaning fluid, and floor mats. The monthly sales of these items at the two stores for two months are given in the following tables:

January Sales

	Vancouver	Quebec
Wiper Blades	20	15
Cleaning Fluid (bottles)	10	12
Floor Mats	8	4

February Sales

	Vancouver	Quebec
Wiper Blades	23	12
Cleaning Fluid (bottles)	8	12
Floor Mats	4	5

Use matrix arithmetic to calculate the change in sales of each product in each store from January to February.

Solution with Technology

On the TI-83/84 Plus, matrices are referred to as [A], [B], and so on through [J]. To enter a matrix, press MATRX to bring up the matrix menu, select EDIT, select a matrix, and press ENTER. Then enter the dimensions of the matrix followed by its entries. When you want to use a matrix, press MATRX, select the matrix and press ENTER.

On the TI-83/84 Plus, adding matrices is similar to adding numbers. The sum of the matrices [A] and [B] is [A]+[B]; their difference, of course, is [A]-[B]. As in the text, for this example,

1. Create two matrices, [J] and [F].
2. Compute their difference, [F]-[J] using [F]-[J] → [D].

Note that we have stored the difference in the matrix [D] in case we need it for later use.

Section 4.2

Example 3(a) (page 245)   Calculate

$$\begin{bmatrix} 2 & 0 & -1 & 3 \\ 1 & -1 & 2 & -2 \end{bmatrix} \begin{bmatrix} 1 & 1 & -8 \\ 1 & 0 & 0 \\ 0 & 5 & 2 \\ -2 & 8 & -1 \end{bmatrix}.$$

Solution with Technology

On the TI-83/84 Plus, the format for multiplying matrices is the same as for multiplying numbers: [A][B] or [A]*[B] will give the product. We enter the matrices and then multiply them. (Note that, while editing, you can see only three columns of [A] at a time.)

Note that if you try to multiply two matrices whose product is not defined, you will get the error "DIM MISMATCH" (dimension mismatch).

Example 6 (page 248)—Identity Matrix   On the TI-83/84 Plus, the function `identity(n)` (in the [MATRX] MATH menu) returns the $n \times n$ identity matrix.

Section 4.3

Example 2(b) (page 259)

Find the inverse of

$$Q = \begin{bmatrix} 1 & 0 & 1 \\ 2 & -2 & -1 \\ 3 & 0 & 0 \end{bmatrix}.$$

Solution with Technology

On a TI-83/84 Plus, you can invert the square matrix [A] by entering [A] [X^{-1}] [ENTER].

(Note that you can use the right and left arrow keys to scroll the answer, which cannot be shown on the screen all at once.) You could also use the calculator to help you go through the row reduction, as described in Chapter 2.

Example 4 (page 262)

Solve the following three systems of equations.

a. $2x \qquad + z = 1$
$2x + y - z = 1$
$3x + y - z = 1$

b. $2x \qquad + z = 0$
$2x + y - z = 1$
$3x + y - z = 2$

c. $2x \qquad + z = 0$
$2x + y - z = 0$
$3x + y - z = 0$

Solution with Technology

1. Enter the four matrices A, B, C, and D:

2. Compute the solutions $A^{-1}B$, $A^{-1}C$, and $A^{-1}D$:

Section 4.5

Example 1 (page 286)   Recall that the input-output table in Example 1 looks like this:

	To	Crude	Refining
From	**Crude**	27,000	59,000
	Refining	750	15,000
	Total Output	87,000	140,000

What was the technology matrix for these two sectors? What was left over from each of these sectors for use by other parts of the economy or for export?

Solution with Technology

There are several ways to use these data to create the technology matrix in your TI-83/84 Plus. For small matrices like this, the most straightforward is to use the matrix editor, where you can give each entry as the appropriate quotient:

and so on. Once we have the technology matrix [A] and the production vector [B] (remember that we can't use [X] as a matrix name), we can calculate the external demand vector:

Of course, when interpreting these numbers, we must remember to round to two significant digits, because our original data were accurate to only that many digits.

Here is an alternative way to calculate the technology matrix that may be better for examples with more sectors.

1. Begin by entering the columns of the input-output table as lists in the list editor (STAT EDIT) (see below left).

2. We now want to divide each column by the total output of its sector and assemble the results into a matrix. We can do this using the List ▶ matr function (under the MATRX MATH menu) shown on the right above.

Example 3 (page 291)   Consider four sectors of the economy of Kenya[41]: (1) the traditional economy, (2) agriculture, (3) manufacture of metal products and machinery, and (4) wholesale and retail trade. The input-output table for these four sectors for 1976 looks like this (all numbers are thousands of K£):

	To	1	2	3	4
From	1	8,600	0	0	0
	2	0	20,000	24	0
	3	1,500	530	15,000	660
	4	810	8,500	5,800	2,900
Total Output		87,000	530,000	110,000	180,000

Suppose that external demand for agriculture increased by K£50,000,000 and that external demand for metal products and machinery increased by K£10,000,000. How would production in these four sectors have to change to meet this rising demand?

Solution with Technology

1. Enter the technology matrices A as [A] and D^+ as [D] using one of the techniques above:

2. You can then compute the change in production with the formula: (identity(4)-[A])$^{-1}$ [D].

---

[41]Figures are rounded. Source: *Input-Output Tables for Kenya 1976*, Central Bureau of Statistics of the Ministry of Economic Planning and Community Affairs, Kenya.

SPREADSHEET Technology Guide

Section 4.1

Example 2 (page 235)   The A-Plus auto parts store chain has two outlets, one in Vancouver and one in Quebec. Among other things, it sells wiper blades, windshield cleaning fluid, and floor mats. The monthly sales of these items at the two stores for two months are given in the following tables:

January Sales

	Vancouver	Quebec
Wiper Blades	20	15
Cleaning Fluid (bottles)	10	12
Floor Mats	8	4

February Sales

	Vancouver	Quebec
Wiper Blades	23	12
Cleaning Fluid (bottles)	8	12
Floor Mats	4	5

Use matrix arithmetic to calculate the change in sales of each product in each store from January to February.

Solution with Technology

To enter a matrix in a spreadsheet, we put its entries in any convenient block of cells. For example, the matrix A in the first Quick Example of this section might look like this:

	A	B	C
1	2	0	1
2	33	-22	0

Spreadsheets refer to such blocks of data as **arrays**, which it can handle in much the same way as it handles single cells of data. For instance, when typing a formula, just as clicking on a cell creates a reference to that cell, selecting a whole array of cells will create a reference to that array. An array is referred to using an **array range** consisting of the top-left and bottom-right cell coordinates, separated by a colon. For example, the array range A1:C2 refers to the 2×3 matrix above, with top-left corner A1 and bottom-right corner C2.

1. To add or subtract two matrices in a spreadsheet, first input their entries in two separate arrays in the spreadsheet (we've also added labels as in the previous tables, which you might do if you wanted to save the spreadsheet for later use):

	A	B	C
1	January Sales		
2		Vancouver	Quebec
3	wiper blades	20	15
4	cleaning fluid (bottles)	10	12
5	floor mats	8	4
6			
7	February Sales		
8		Vancouver	Quebec
9	wiper blades	23	12
10	cleaning fluid (bottles)	8	12
11	floor mats	4	5

2. Select (highlight) a block of the same size (3×2 in this case) where you would like the answer, $F - J$, to appear, enter the formula =B9:C11-B3:C5, and then type Control+Shift+Enter. The easiest way to do this is as follows:

- Highlight cells B15:C17.   Where you want the answer to appear
- Type "=".
- Highlight the matrix F.   Cells B9 through C11
- Type "-".
- Highlight the matrix J.   Cells B3 through C5
- Press Control+Shift+Enter.   Not just Enter

	A	B	C
1	January Sales		
2		Vancouver	Quebec
3	wiper blades	20	15
4	cleaning fluid (bottles)	10	12
5	floor mats	8	4
6			
7	February Sales		
8		Vancouver	Quebec
9	wiper blades	23	12
10	cleaning fluid (bottles)	8	12
11	floor mats	4	5
12			
13	Change in Sales		
14		Vancouver	Quebec
15	wiper blades	=B9:C11-B3:C5	
16	cleaning fluid (bottles)		
17	floor mats		

Typing Control+Shift+Enter (instead of Enter) tells the spreadsheet that your formula is an *array formula,* one that returns a matrix rather than a single number.[42] Once entered, the formula bar will show the formula you entered enclosed in "curly braces," indicating that it is an array formula. Note that you must use Control+Shift+Enter to delete any array you create: Select the block you wish to delete and press Delete followed by Control+Shift+Enter.

Section 4.2

Example 3(a) (page 245) Calculate the product

$$\begin{bmatrix} 2 & 0 & -1 & 3 \\ 1 & -1 & 2 & -2 \end{bmatrix} \begin{bmatrix} 1 & 1 & -8 \\ 1 & 0 & 0 \\ 0 & 5 & 2 \\ -2 & 8 & -1 \end{bmatrix}.$$

Solution with Technology

In a spreadsheet, the function we use for matrix multiplication is MMULT. (Ordinary multiplication, *, will *not* work.)

1. Enter the two matrices as shown in the spreadsheet and highlight a block where you want the answer to appear. (Note that it should have the correct dimensions for the product: 2 × 3.)

2. Enter the formula =MMULT(A1:D2,F1:H4) (using the mouse to avoid typing the array ranges if you like) and press Control+Shift+Enter. The product will appear in the region you highlighted. If you try to multiply two matrices whose product is not defined, you will get the error "#VALUE!".

Example 6—Identity Matrix (page 248) There is no spreadsheet function that returns an identity matrix. If you need a small identity matrix, it's simplest to just

enter the 1s and 0s by hand. If you need a large identity matrix, here is one way to get it quickly.

1. Say we want a 4 × 4 identity matrix in the cells B1:E4. Enter the following formula in cell B1:

```
=IF(ROW(B1)-ROW($B$1)
=COLUMN(B1)-COLUMN($B$1),1,0)
```

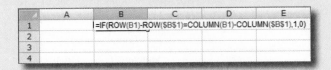

2. Press Enter, then copy cell B1 to cells B1:E4. The formula will return 1s along the diagonal of the matrix and 0s elsewhere, giving you the identity matrix. Why does this formula work?

Section 4.3

Example 2(b) (page 259) Find the inverse of

$$Q = \begin{bmatrix} 1 & 0 & 1 \\ 2 & -2 & -1 \\ 3 & 0 & 0 \end{bmatrix}.$$

Solution with Technology

In a spreadsheet, the function MINVERSE computes the inverse of a matrix.

1. Enter Q somewhere convenient, for example, in cells A1:C3.

2. Choose the block where you would like the inverse to appear, highlight the whole block.

3. Enter the formula =MINVERSE(A1:C3) and press Control+Shift+Enter.

[42]Note that on a Mac, Command-Enter has the same effect as Control+Shift+Enter.

The inverse will appear in the region you highlighted. (To convert the answer to fractions, format the cells as fractions.)

If a matrix is singular, a spreadsheet will register an error by showing #NUM! in each cell.

	A	B	C	D	E	F	G
1	1	0	1		0	0	0.3333333
2	2	-2	-1		-0.5	-0.5	0.5
3	3	0	0		1	0	-0.3333333

Although the spreadsheet appears to invert the matrix in one step, it is going through the procedure in the text or some variation of it to find the inverse. Of course, you could also use the spreadsheet to help you go through the row reduction, just as in Chapter 3.

Example 4 (page 262) Solve the following three systems of equations.

a.
$$2x \quad\quad + z = 1$$
$$2x + y - z = 1$$
$$3x + y - z = 1$$

b.
$$2x \quad\quad + z = 0$$
$$2x + y - z = 1$$
$$3x + y - z = 2$$

c.
$$2x \quad\quad + z = 0$$
$$2x + y - z = 0$$
$$3x + y - z = 0$$

Solution with Technology

Spreadsheets instantly update calculated results every time the contents of a cell are changed. We can take advantage of this to solve the three systems of equations given above using the same worksheet as follows.

1. Enter the matrices A and B from the matrix equation $AX = B$.

2. Select a 3×1 block of cells for the matrix X.

3. The Excel formula we can use to calculate X is:

`=MMULT(MINVERSE(A1:C3),E1:E3)` $A^{-1}B$

	A	B	C	D	E
1	2	0	1		1
2	2	1	-1		1
3	3	1	-1		1
4		A			B
5					
6	=MMULT(MINVERSE(A1:C3),E1:E3)				
7					
8					
9	$A^{-1}B$				

(As usual, use the mouse to select the ranges for A and B while typing the formula, and don't forget to press Control+Shift+Enter.) Having obtained the solution to

part (a), you can now simply modify the entries in Column E to see the solutions for parts (b) and (c).

Note Your spreadsheet for part (a) may look like this:

	A	B	C	D	E
1	2	0	1		1
2	2	1	-1		1
3	3	1	-1		1
4		A			B
5					
6	1.11022E-16				
7	2				
8	1				
9	$A^{-1}B$				

What is that strange number doing in cell A6? "E-16" represents "$\times 10^{-16}$", so the entry is really

$$1.11022 \times 10^{-16} = 0.000\,000\,000\,000\,000\,111022 \approx 0.$$

Mathematically, it is supposed to be *exactly* zero (see the solution to part (a) in the text) but Excel made a small error in computing the inverse of A, resulting in this spurious value. Note, however, that it is accurate (agrees with zero) to 15 decimal places! In practice, when we see numbers arise in matrix calculations that are far smaller than all the other entries, we can usually assume they are supposed to be zero. ∎

Section 4.5

Example 1 (page 286) Recall that the input-output table in Example 1 looks like this:

	To	Crude	Refining
From **Crude**		27,000	59,000
Refining		750	15,000
Total Output		87,000	140,000

What was the technology matrix for these two sectors? What was left over from each of these sectors for use by other parts of the economy or for export?

Solution with Technology

1. Enter the input-output table in a spreadsheet:

	A	B	C	D
1			To	
2			Crude	Refining
3	From	Crude	27000	59000
4		Refining	750	15000
5		Total Output	87000	140000

2. To obtain the technology matrix, we divide each column by the total output of its sector:

	A	B	C	D
1			To	
2			Crude	Refining
3	From	Crude	27000	59000
4		Refining	750	15000
5		Total Output	87000	140000
6				
7			=C3/C$5	
8				

	A	B	C	D
1			To	
2			Crude	Refining
3	From	Crude	27000	59000
4		Refining	750	15000
5		Total Output	87000	140000
6				
7			0.3103448	0.4214286
8			0.0086207	0.1071429

The formula =C3/C$5 is copied into the shaded 2×2 block shown above. (The $ sign in front of the 5 forces the program to always divide by the total in Row 5 even when the formula is copied from Row 7 to Row 8.) The result is the technology matrix shown in the bottom screenshot above.

3. Using the techniques discussed in the second section, we can now compute $D = X - AX$ to find the demand vector.

Example 3 (page 291) Consider four sectors of the economy of Kenya[43]: (1) the traditional economy, (2) agriculture, (3) manufacture of metal products and machinery, and (4) wholesale and retail trade. The input-output table for these four sectors for 1976 looks like this (all numbers are thousands of K£):

	To	1	2	3	4
From	1	8,600	0	0	0
	2	0	20,000	24	0
	3	1,500	530	15,000	660
	4	810	8,500	5,800	2,900
Total Output		87,000	530,000	110,000	180,000

[43]Figures are rounded. Source: *Input-Output Tables for Kenya 1976*, Central Bureau of Statistics of the Ministry of Economic Planning and Community Affairs, Kenya.

Suppose that external demand for agriculture increased by K£50,000,000 and that external demand for metal products and machinery increased by K£10,000,000. How would production in these four sectors have to change to meet this rising demand?

Solution with Technology

1. Enter the input-output table in the spreadsheet.

2. Compute the technology matrix by dividing each column by the column total.

3. Insert the identity matrix I in preparation for the next step.

	A	B	C	D	E	F	G	H	I
1	8600	0	0	0					
2	0	20000	24	0					
3	1500	530	15000	660					
4	810	8500	5800	2900					
5	87000	530000	110000	180000	Totals				
6									
7		Technology Matrix					Identity Matrix		
8	=A1/A$5						1	0	0	0
9							0	1	0	0
10							0	0	1	0
11							0	0	0	1

4. To see how each sector reacts to rising external demand, you must calculate the inverse matrix $(I - A)^{-1}$, as shown below. (Remember to use Control+Shift+Enter each time.)

	A	B	C	D	E	F	G	H	I
1	8600	0	0	0					
2	0	20000	24	0					
3	1500	530	15000	660					
4	810	8500	5800	2900					
5	87000	530000	110000	180000	Totals				
6									
7		Technology Matrix					Identity Matrix		
8	0.0988506	0	0	0			1	0	0	0
9	0	0.0377358	0.0002182	0			0	1	0	0
10	0.0172414	0.001	0.1363636	0.0036667			0	0	1	0
11	0.0093103	0.0160377	0.0527273	0.0161111			0	0	0	1
12									
13		(I−A)					(I - A)⁻¹		
14	=F8:I11-A8:D11						=MINVERSE(A14:D17)		
15									
16									
17									

5. To compute $(I - A)^{-1}D^{+}$, enter D^{+} as a column and use the MMULT operation. (See Example 3 in Section 4.2.)

	A	B	C	D	E	F	G	H	I
13		(I - A)					(I - A)⁻¹		
14	0.9011494	0	0	0		1.1096939	0	0	0
15	0	0.9622642	-0.0002182	0		5.034E-06	1.039216	0.0002626	9.786E-07
16	-0.0172414	-0.001	0.8636364	-0.0036667		0.0222032	0.0012755	1.1581586	0.0043161
17	-0.0093103	-0.0160377	-0.0527273	0.9838889		0.0116908	0.0170079	0.0620708	1.0166062
18									
19		D		(I - A)⁻¹D					
20		0		0					
21		50000		51963.425					
22		10000		11645.361					
23		0		1471.105					

Note Here is one of the beauties of spreadsheet programs: Once you are done with the calculation, you can use the spreadsheet as a template for any 4×4 input-output table by just changing the entries of the input-output matrix and/or D^{+}. The rest of the computation will then be done automatically as the spreadsheet is updated. In other words, you can use it to do your homework! ■

5

Linear Programming

 Website

www.WanerMath.com

At the Website you will find:

- Section-by-section tutorials, including game tutorials with randomized quizzes

- A detailed chapter summary

- A true/false quiz

- Additional review exercises

- A linear programming grapher

- A pivot and Gauss-Jordan tool

- A simplex method tool

Case Study The Diet Problem

The Galaxy Nutrition health-food mega-store chain provides free online nutritional advice and support to its customers. As Web site technical consultant, you are planning to construct an interactive Web page to assist customers prepare a diet tailored to their nutritional and budgetary requirements. Ideally, the customer would select foods to consider and specify nutritional and/or budgetary constraints, and the tool should return the optimal diet meeting those requirements. You would also like the Web page to allow the customer to decide whether, for instance, to find the cheapest possible diet meeting the requirements, the diet with the lowest number of calories, or the diet with the least total carbohydrates. **How do you go about constructing such a Web page?**

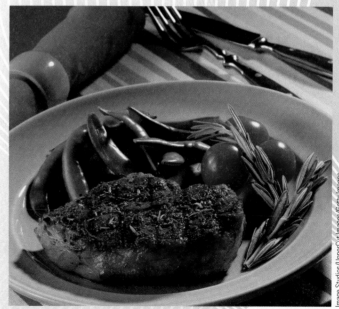

Image Studios/UpperCut Images/Getty Images

Introduction

In this chapter we begin to look at one of the most important types of problems for business and the sciences: finding the largest or smallest possible value of some quantity (such as profit or cost) under certain constraints (such as limited resources). We call such problems **optimization** problems because we are trying to find the best, or optimum, value. The optimization problems we look at in this chapter involve linear functions only and are known as **linear programming** (LP) problems. One of the main purposes of calculus, which you may study later, is to solve nonlinear optimization problems.

Linear programming problems involving only two unknowns can usually be solved by a graphical method that we discuss in Sections 5.1 and 5.2. When there are three or more unknowns, we must use an algebraic method, as we had to do for systems of linear equations. The method we use is called the **simplex method**. Invented in 1947 by George B. Dantzig* (1914–2005), the simplex method is still the most commonly used technique to solve LP problems in real applications, from finance to the computation of trajectories for guided missiles.

The simplex method can be used for hand calculations when the numbers are fairly small and the unknowns are few. Practical problems often involve large numbers and many unknowns, however. Problems such as routing telephone calls or airplane flights, or allocating resources in a manufacturing process can involve tens of thousands of unknowns. Solving such problems by hand is obviously impractical, and so computers are regularly used. Although computer programs most often use the simplex method, mathematicians are always seeking faster methods. The first radically different method of solving LP problems was the **ellipsoid algorithm** published in 1979 by the Soviet mathematician Leonid G. Khachiyan[2] (1952–2005). In 1984, Narendra Karmarkar (1957–), a researcher at Bell Labs, created a more efficient method now known as **Karmarkar's algorithm**. Although these methods (and others since developed) can be shown to be faster than the simplex method in the worst cases, it seems to be true that the simplex method is still the fastest in the applications that arise in practice.

Calculators and spreadsheets are very useful aids in the simplex method. In practice, software packages do most of the work, so you can think of what we teach you here as a peek inside a "black box." What the software cannot do for you is convert a real situation into a mathematical problem, so the most important lessons to get out of this chapter are (1) how to recognize and set up a linear programming problem, and (2) how to interpret the results.

* Dantzig is the real-life source of the story of the student who, walking in late to a math class, copies down two problems on the board, thinking they're homework. After much hard work he hands in the solutions, only to discover that he's just solved two famous unsolved problems. This actually happened to Dantzig in graduate school in 1939.[1]

5.1 Graphing Linear Inequalities

By the end of the next section, we will be solving linear programming (LP) problems with two unknowns. We use inequalities to describe the constraints in a problem, such as limitations on resources. Recall the basic notation for inequalities.

---

[1] Sources: D. J. Albers, and C. Reid, "An Interview of George B. Dantzig: The Father of Linear Programming," *College Math. Journal*, v. 17 (1986), pp. 293–314. Quoted and discussed in the context of the urban legends it inspired at www.snopes.com/college/homework/unsolvable.asp.

[2] Dantzig and Khachiyan died approximately two weeks apart in 2005. The *New York Times* ran their obituaries together on May 23, 2005.

Non-Strict Inequalities

$a \le b$ means that a **is less than or equal to** b.

$a \ge b$ means that a **is greater than or equal to** b.

Quick Examples

$3 \le 99, -2 \le -2, 0 \le 3$

$3 \ge 3, 1.78 \ge 1.76, \dfrac{1}{3} \ge \dfrac{1}{4}$

There are also the inequalities $<$ and $>$, called **strict** inequalities because they do not permit equality. We do not use them in this chapter.

Following are some of the basic rules for manipulating inequalities. Although we illustrate all of them with the inequality $\le$, they apply equally well to inequalities with $\ge$ and to the strict inequalities $<$ and $>$.

Rules for Manipulating Inequalities

Quick Examples

1. The same quantity can be added to or subtracted from both sides of an inequality:
   If $x \le y$, then $x + a \le y + a$ for any real number a.

   $x \le y$ implies $x - 4 \le y - 4$

2. Both sides of an inequality can be multiplied or divided by a positive constant:

   If $x \le y$ and a is positive, then $ax \le ay$.

   $x \le y$ implies $3x \le 3y$

3. Both sides of an inequality can be multiplied or divided by a negative constant if the inequality is *reversed*:

   If $x \le y$ and a is negative, then $ax \ge ay$.

   $x \le y$ implies $-3x \ge -3y$

4. The left and right sides of an inequality can be switched if the inequality is *reversed*:

   If $x \le y$, then $y \ge x$; if $y \ge x$, then $x \le y$.

   $3x \ge 5y$ implies $5y \le 3x$

Here are the particular kinds of inequalities in which we're interested:

Linear Inequalities and Solving Inequalities

An **inequality in the unknown** x is the statement that one expression involving x is less than or equal to (or greater than or equal to) another. Similarly, we can have an **inequality in x and y**, which involves expressions that contain x and y; an **inequality in x, y, and z**; and so on. A **linear inequality** in one or more unknowns is an inequality of the form

$$ax \le b \;(\text{or } ax \ge b), \quad a \text{ and } b \text{ real constants}$$
$$ax + by \le c \;(\text{or } ax + by \ge c), \quad a, b, \text{ and } c \text{ real constants}$$
$$ax + by + cz \le d, \quad a, b, c, \text{ and } d \text{ real constants}$$
$$ax + by + cz + dw \le e, \quad a, b, c, d, \text{ and } e \text{ real constants}$$

and so on.

A **solution** of an inequality in the unknown x is a value for x that makes the inequality true. For example, $2x + 8 \geq 89$ has a solution $x = 50$ because $2(50) + 8 \geq 89$. Of course, it has many other solutions as well. Similarly, a solution of an inequality in x and y is a pair of values (x, y) making the inequality true. For example, $(5, 1)$ is a solution of $3x - 2y \geq 8$ because $3(5) - 2(1) \geq 8$. To **solve** an inequality is to find the set of *all* solutions.

Solving Linear Inequalities in Two Variables

Figure 1

Our first goal is to solve linear inequalities in two variables—that is, inequalities of the form $ax + by \leq c$. As an example, let's solve

$$2x + 3y \leq 6.$$

We already know how to solve the *equation* $2x + 3y = 6$. As we saw in Chapter 1, the solution of this equation may be pictured as the set of all points (x, y) on the straight-line graph of the equation. This straight line has x-intercept 3 (obtained by putting $y = 0$ in the equation) and y-intercept 2 (obtained by putting $x = 0$ in the equation) and is shown in Figure 1.

Notice that, if (x, y) is any point on the line, then x and y not only satisfy the *equation* $2x + 3y = 6$, but they also satisfy the *inequality* $2x + 3y \leq 6$, because being equal to 6 qualifies as being less than or equal to 6.

Figure 2

Q: *Do the points on the line give all possible solutions to the inequality?*

A: No. For example, try the origin, $(0, 0)$. Because $2(0) + 3(0) = 0 \leq 6$, the point $(0, 0)$ is a solution that does not lie on the line. In fact, here is a possibly surprising fact: The solution to any linear inequality in two unknowns is represented by an entire **half plane**: the set of all points on one side of the line (including the line itself). Thus, because $(0, 0)$ is a solution of $2x + 3y \leq 6$ and is not on the line, every point on the same side of the line as $(0, 0)$ is a solution as well (the colored region below the line in Figure 2 shows which half plane constitutes the solution set).

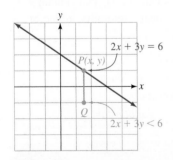

Figure 3

To see why the solution set of $2x + 3y \leq 6$ is the entire half plane shown in Figure 2, start with any point P on the line $2x + 3y = 6$. We already know that P is a solution of $2x + 3y \leq 6$. If we choose any point Q directly below P, the x-coordinate of Q will be the same as that of P, and the y-coordinate will be smaller. So the value of $2x + 3y$ at Q will be smaller than the value at P, which is 6. Thus, $2x + 3y < 6$ at Q, and so Q is another solution of the inequality. (See Figure 3.) In other words, *every point beneath the line is a solution of* $2x + 3y \leq 6$.

On the other hand, any point above the line is directly above a point on the line, and so $2x + 3y > 6$ for such a point. Thus, *no point above the line is a solution of* $2x + 3y \leq 6$.

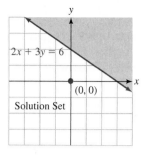

$2x + 3y = 6$

$(0, 0)$

Solution Set

Figure 4

The same kind of argument can be used to show that the solution set of every inequality of the form $ax + by \leq c$ or $ax + by \geq c$ consists of the half plane above or below the line $ax + by = c$. The "test-point" procedure we describe below gives us an easy method for deciding whether the solution set includes the region above or below the corresponding line.

Now we are going to do something that will appear backward at first (but makes it simpler to sketch sets of solutions of *systems* of linear inequalities). For our standard drawing of the region of solutions of $2x + 3y \leq 6$, we are going to *shade only the part that we do not want and leave the solution region blank*. Think of covering over or "blocking out" the unwanted points, leaving those that we do want in full view (but remember that the points on the boundary line are also points that we want). The result is Figure 4. The reason we do this should become clear in Example 2.

Sketching the Region Represented by a Linear Inequality in Two Variables

1. Sketch the straight line obtained by replacing the given inequality with an equality.

2. Choose a test point not on the line; $(0, 0)$ is a good choice if the line does not pass through the origin.

3. If the test point satisfies the inequality, then the set of solutions is the entire region on the same side of the line as the test point. Otherwise, it is the region on the other side of the line. In either case, shade (block out) the side that does *not* contain the solutions, leaving the solution set unshaded.

Quick Example

Here are the three steps used to graph the inequality $x + 2y \geq 5$:

1. Sketch the line $x + 2y = 5$.

2. Test the point $(0, 0)$ $0 + 2(0) \not\geq 5$. Inequality is not satisfied.

3. Because the inequality is not satisfied, shade the region containing the test point.

EXAMPLE 1 Graphing Single Inequalities

Sketch the regions determined by each of the following inequalities:

a. $3x - 2y \leq 6$ **b.** $6x \leq 12 + 4y$ **c.** $x \leq -1$ **d.** $y \geq 0$ **e.** $x \geq 3y$

using Technology

Technology can be used to graph inequalities. Here is an outline (see the Technology Guides at the end of the chapter for additional details on using a TI-83/84 Plus or a spreadsheet):

TI-83/84 Plus

Solve the inequality for *y* and enter the resulting function of *x*; for example,

`Y₁=-(2/3)*X+2.`

Position the cursor on the icon to the left of `Y₁` and press `ENTER` until you see the kind of shading desired (above or below the line). [More details on page 391.]

Spreadsheet

Solve the inequality for *y* and create a scattergraph using two points on the line. Then use the drawing palette to create a polygon to provide the shading.
[More details on page 393.]

Website
www.WanerMath.com
→ On Line Utilities
→ Linear Programming Grapher

Type "graph" and enter one or more inequalities (each one on a new line) as shown:

Adjust the graph window settings, and press "Graph".

Solution

a. The boundary line $3x - 2y = 6$ has x-intercept 2 and y-intercept -3 (Figure 5). We use $(0, 0)$ as a test point (because it is not on the line). Because $3(0) - 2(0) \leq 6$, the inequality is satisfied by the test point $(0, 0)$, and so it lies inside the solution set. The solution set is shown in Figure 5.

b. The given inequality, $6x \leq 12 + 4y$, can be rewritten in the form $ax + by \leq c$ by subtracting $4y$ from both sides:

$$6x - 4y \leq 12.$$

Dividing both sides by 2 gives the inequality $3x - 2y \leq 6$, which we considered in part (a). Now, *applying the rules for manipulating inequalities does not affect the set of solutions.* Thus, the inequality $6x \leq 12 + 4y$ has the same set of solutions as $3x - 2y \leq 6$. (See Figure 5.)

Figure 5

Figure 6

c. The region $x \leq -1$ has as boundary the vertical line $x = -1$. The test point $(0, 0)$ is not in the solution set, as shown in Figure 6.

d. The region $y \geq 0$ has as boundary the horizontal line $y = 0$ (that is, the x-axis). We cannot use $(0, 0)$ for the test point because it lies on the boundary line. Instead, we choose a convenient point not on the line $y = 0$—say, $(0, 1)$. Because $1 \geq 0$, this point is in the solution set, giving us the region shown in Figure 7.

e. The line $x \geq 3y$ has as boundary the line $x = 3y$ or, solving for y,

$$y = \frac{1}{3}x.$$

This line passes through the origin with slope $1/3$, so again we cannot choose the origin as a test point. Instead, we choose $(0, 1)$. Substituting these coordinates in $x \geq 3y$ gives $0 \geq 3(1)$, which is false, so $(0, 1)$ is not in the solution set, as shown in Figure 8.

Figure 7

Figure 8

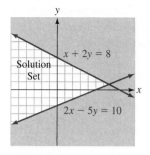

Figure 9

* Although these graphs are quite easy to do by hand, the more lines we have to graph the more difficult it becomes to get everything in the right place, and this is where graphing technology can become important. This is especially true when, for instance, three or more lines intersect in points that are very close together and hard to distinguish in hand-drawn graphs.

EXAMPLE 2 Graphing Simultaneous Inequalities

Sketch the region of points that satisfy both inequalities:

$$2x - 5y \leq 10$$
$$x + 2y \leq 8.$$

Solution Each inequality has a solution set that is a half plane. If a point is to satisfy *both* inequalities, it must lie in both sets of solutions. Put another way, if we cover the points that are not solutions to $2x - 5y \leq 10$ and then also cover the points that are not solutions to $x + 2y \leq 8$, the points that remain uncovered must be the points we want, those that are solutions to both inequalities. The result is shown in Figure 9, where the unshaded region is the set of solutions.*

As a check, we can look at points in various regions in Figure 9. For example, our graph shows that $(0, 0)$ should satisfy both inequalities, and it does:

$$2(0) - 5(0) = 0 \leq 10 \quad ✔$$
$$0 + 2(0) = 0 \leq 8. \quad ✔$$

On the other hand, $(0, 5)$ should fail to satisfy one of the inequalities:

$$2(0) - 5(5) = -25 \leq 10 \quad ✔$$
$$0 + 2(5) = 10 > 8 \quad ✗$$

One more: $(5, -1)$ should fail one of the inequalities:

$$2(5) - 5(-1) = 15 > 10 \quad ✗$$
$$5 + 2(-1) = 3 \leq 8. \quad ✔$$

EXAMPLE 3 Corner Points

Sketch the region of solutions of the following system of inequalities and list the coordinates of all the corner points.

$$3x - 2y \leq 6$$
$$x + y \geq -5$$
$$y \leq 4$$

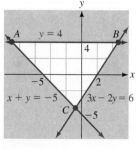

Figure 10

Solution Shading the regions that we do not want leaves us with the triangle shown in Figure 10. We label the corner points A, B, and C as shown.

Each of these corner points lies at the intersection of two of the bounding lines. So, to find the coordinates of each corner point, we need to solve the system of equations given by the two lines. To do this systematically, we make the following table:

Point	Lines through Point	Coordinates
A	$y = 4$ $x + y = -5$	$(-9, 4)$
B	$y = 4$ $3x - 2y = 6$	$\left(\dfrac{14}{3}, 4\right)$
C	$x + y = -5$ $3x - 2y = 6$	$\left(-\dfrac{4}{5}, -\dfrac{21}{5}\right)$

✱ Technology Note Using the trace feature makes it easy to locate corner points graphically. Remember to zoom in for additional accuracy when appropriate. Of course, you can also use technology to help solve the systems of equations, as we discussed in Chapter 3.

Here, we have solved each system of equations in the middle column to get the point on the right, using the techniques of Chapter 2. You should do this for practice.*

As a partial check that we have drawn the correct region, let us choose any point in its interior—say, (0, 0). We can easily check that (0, 0) satisfies all three given inequalities. It follows that all of the points in the triangular region containing (0, 0) are also solutions.

Take another look at the regions of solutions in Examples 2 and 3 (Figure 11).

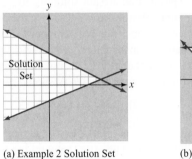

(a) Example 2 Solution Set   (b) Example 3 Solution Set

Figure 11

Notice that the solution set in Figure 11(a) extends infinitely far to the left, whereas the one in Figure 11(b) is completely enclosed by a boundary. Sets that are completely enclosed are called **bounded**, and sets that extend infinitely in one or more directions are **unbounded**. For example, all the solution sets in Example 1 are unbounded.

EXAMPLE 4 Resource Allocation

Socaccio Pistachio Inc. makes two types of pistachio nuts: Dazzling Red and Organic. Pistachio nuts require food color and salt, and the following table shows the amount of food color and salt required for a 1-kilogram batch of pistachios, as well as the total amount of these ingredients available each day.

	Dazzling Red	*Organic*	*Total Available*
Food Color (g)	2	1	20
Salt (g)	10	20	220

Use a graph to show the possible numbers of batches of each type of pistachio Socaccio can produce each day. This region (the solution set of a system of inequalities) is called the **feasible region**.

Solution As we did in Chapter 3, we start by identifying the unknowns: Let x be the number of batches of Dazzling Red manufactured per day and let y be the number of batches of Organic manufactured each day.

Now, because of our experience with systems of linear equations, we are tempted to say: For food color $2x + y = 20$ and for salt, $10x + 20y = 220$. However, no one is saying that Socaccio has to use all available ingredients; the company might choose to use fewer than the total available amounts if this proves more profitable. Thus, $2x + y$ can be anything *up to a total of* 20. In other words,

$$2x + y \leq 20.$$

Similarly,

$$10x + 20y \leq 220.$$

Figure 12

There are two more restrictions not explicitly mentioned: Neither x nor y can be negative. (The company cannot produce a negative number of batches of nuts.) Therefore, we have the additional restrictions

$$x \geq 0 \quad y \geq 0.$$

These two inequalities tell us that the feasible region (solution set) is restricted to the first quadrant, because in the other quadrants, either x or y or both x and y are negative. So instead of shading out all other quadrants, we can simply restrict our drawing to the first quadrant.

The (bounded) feasible region shown in Figure 12 is a graphical representation of the limitations the company faces.

➡ **Before we go on...** Every point in the feasible region in Example 4 represents a value for x and a value for y that do not violate any of the company's restrictions. For example, the point $(5, 6)$ lies well inside the region, so the company can produce five batches of Dazzling Red nuts and six batches of Organic without exceeding the limitations on ingredients [that is, $2(5) + 6 = 16 \leq 20$ and $10(5) + 20(6) = 170 \leq 220$]. The corner points A, B, C, and D are significant if the company wishes to realize the greatest profit, as we will see in Section 5.2. We can find the corners as in the following table:

Point	Lines through Point	Coordinates
A		$(0, 0)$
B		$(10, 0)$
C		$(0, 11)$
D	$2x + y = 20$ $10x + 20y = 220$	$(6, 8)$

(We have not listed the lines through the first three corners because their coordinates can be read easily from the graph.) Points on the line segment DB represent use of all the food color (because the segment lies on the line $2x + y = 20$), and points on the line segment CD represent use of all the salt (because the segment lies on the line $10x + 20y = 220$). Note that the point D is the only solution that uses all of both ingredients. ∎

FAQs

Recognizing Whether to Use a Linear Inequality or a Linear Equation

Q : *How do I know whether to model a situation by a linear inequality like $3x + 2y \leq 10$ or by a linear equation like $3x + 2y = 10$?*

A : Here are some key phrases to look for: *at most, up to, no more than, at least, or more, exactly.* Suppose, for instance, that nuts cost 3¢, bolts cost 2¢, x is the number of nuts you can buy, and y is the number of bolts you can buy.

- If you have *up to* 10¢ to spend, then $3x + 2y \leq 10$.
- If you must spend *exactly* 10¢, then $3x + 2y = 10$.
- If you plan to spend *at least* 10¢, then $3x + 2y \geq 10$.

The use of inequalities to model a situation is often more realistic than the use of equations; for instance, one cannot always expect to exactly fill all orders, spend the exact amount of one's budget, or keep a plant operating at exactly 100% capacity.

5.1 EXERCISES

▼ more advanced   ◆ challenging

▼ indicates exercises that should be solved using technology

In Exercises 1–26, sketch the region that corresponds to the given inequalities, say whether the region is bounded or unbounded, and find the coordinates of all corner points (if any). HINT [See Example 1.]

1. $2x + y \leq 10$

2. $4x - y \leq 12$

3. $-x - 2y \leq 8$

4. $-x + 2y \geq 4$

5. $3x + 2y \geq 5$

6. $2x - 3y \leq 7$

7. $x \leq 3y$

8. $y \geq 3x$

9. $\dfrac{3x}{4} - \dfrac{y}{4} \leq 1$

10. $\dfrac{x}{3} + \dfrac{2y}{3} \geq 2$

11. $x \geq -5$

12. $y \leq -4$

13. $4x - \ y \leq 8$

$\quad x + 2y \leq 2$

HINT [See Examples 2 and 3.]

14. $2x + \ y \leq 4$

$\quad x - 2y \geq 2$

HINT [See Examples 2 and 3.]

15. $3x + 2y \geq 6$

$\quad 3x - 2y \leq 6$

$\quad x \qquad \geq 0$

16. $3x + 2y \leq 6$

$\quad 3x - 2y \geq 6$

$\quad -y \geq 2$

17. $x + y \geq 5$

$\quad x \qquad \leq 10$

$\quad \qquad y \leq 8$

$\quad x \geq 0, y \geq 0$

18. $2x + 4y \geq 12$

$\quad x \qquad \leq 5$

$\quad \qquad y \leq 3$

$\quad x \geq 0, y \geq 0$

19. $20x + 10y \leq 100$

$\quad 10x + 20y \leq 100$

$\quad 10x + 10y \leq 60$

$\quad x \geq 0, y \geq 0$

20. $30x + 20y \leq 600$

$\quad 10x + 40y \leq 400$

$\quad 20x + 30y \leq 450$

$\quad x \geq 0, y \geq 0$

21. $20x + 10y \geq 100$

$\quad 10x + 20y \geq 100$

$\quad 10x + 10y \geq 80$

$\quad x \geq 0, y \geq 0$

22. $30x + 20y \geq 600$

$\quad 10x + 40y \geq 400$

$\quad 20x + 30y \geq 600$

$\quad x \geq 0, y \geq 0$

23. $-3x + 2y \leq 5$

$\quad 3x - 2y \leq 6$

$\quad x \qquad \leq 2y$

$\quad x \geq 0, y \geq 0$

24. $-3x + 2y \leq 5$

$\quad 3x - 2y \geq 6$

$\quad \qquad y \leq x/2$

$\quad x \geq 0, y \geq 0$

25. $2x - \ y \geq 0$

$\quad x - \ 3y \leq 0$

$\quad x \geq 0, y \geq 0$

26. $-x + \ y \geq 0$

$\quad 4x - 3y \geq 0$

$\quad x \geq 0, y \geq 0$

▼ *In Exercises 27–32, we suggest you use technology. Graph the regions corresponding to the inequalities, and find the coordinates of all corner points (if any) to two decimal places.*

27. $2.1x - 4.3y \geq 9.7$

28. $-4.3x + 4.6y \geq 7.1$

29. $-0.2x + 0.7y \geq 3.3$

$\quad 1.1x + 3.4y \geq 0$

30. $0.2x + 0.3y \geq 7.2$

$\quad 2.5x - 6.7y \leq 0$

31. $4.1x - 4.3y \leq 4.4$

$\quad 7.5x - 4.4y \leq 5.7$

$\quad 4.3x + 8.5y \leq 10$

32. $2.3x - 2.4y \leq 2.5$

$\quad 4.0x - 5.1y \leq 4.4$

$\quad 6.1x + 6.7y \leq 9.6$

APPLICATIONS

33. *Resource Allocation* You manage an ice cream factory that makes two flavors: Creamy Vanilla and Continental Mocha. Into each quart of Creamy Vanilla go 2 eggs and 3 cups of cream. Into each quart of Continental Mocha go 1 egg and 3 cups of cream. You have in stock 500 eggs and 900 cups of cream. Draw the feasible region showing the number of quarts of vanilla and number of quarts of mocha that can be produced. Find the corner points of the region. HINT [See Example 4.]

34. *Resource Allocation* Podunk Institute of Technology's Math Department offers two courses: Finite Math and Applied Calculus. Each section of Finite Math has 60 students, and each section of Applied Calculus has 50. The department is allowed to offer a total of up to 110 sections. Furthermore, no more than 6,000 students want to take a math course. (No student will take more than one math course.) Draw the feasible region that shows the number of sections of each class that can be offered. Find the corner points of the region. HINT [See Example 4.]

35. *Nutrition* Ruff Inc. makes dog food out of chicken and grain. Chicken has 10 grams of protein and 5 grams of fat per ounce, and grain has 2 grams of protein and 2 grams of fat per ounce. A bag of dog food must contain at least 200 grams of protein and at least 150 grams of fat. Draw the feasible region that shows the number of ounces of chicken and number of ounces of grain Ruff can mix into each bag of dog food. Find the corner points of the region.

36. *Purchasing* Enormous State University's Business School is buying computers. The school has two models to choose from: the Pomegranate and the iZac. Each Pomegranate comes with 400 GB of memory and 80 TB of disk space, and each iZac has 300 GB of memory and 100 TB of disk space. For reasons related to its accreditation, the school would like to be able to say that it has a total of at least 48,000 GB of memory and at least 12,800 TB of disk space. Draw the feasible region that shows the number of each kind of computer it can buy. Find the corner points of the region.

37. *Nutrition* **Gerber Products'** Gerber Mixed Cereal for Baby contains, in each serving, 60 calories and 11 grams of carbohydrates. Gerber Mango Tropical Fruit Dessert contains, in each serving, 80 calories and 21 grams of carbohydrates.[3] You want to provide your child with at least 140 calories and at least 32 grams of carbohydrates. Draw the feasible region that shows the number of servings of cereal and number of servings of dessert that you can give your child. Find the corner points of the region.

38. *Nutrition* **Gerber Products'** Gerber Mixed Cereal for Baby contains, in each serving, 60 calories, 11 grams of carbohydrates, and no vitamin C. Gerber Apple Banana Juice contains, in each serving, 60 calories, 15 grams of carbohydrates, and 120 percent of the U.S. Recommended Daily Allowance (RDA) of Vitamin C for infants.[4] You want to provide your child with at least 120 calories, at least 26 grams of carbohydrates, and at least 50 percent of the U.S. RDA of vitamin C for infants. Draw the feasible region that shows the number of servings of cereal and number of servings of juice that you can give your child. Find the corner points of the region.

39. *Municipal Bond Funds* The **Pimco** New York Municipal Bond Fund (PNF) and the **Fidelity** Spartan Mass Fund (FDMMX) are tax-exempt municipal bond funds. In 2003, the Pimco fund yielded 6% while the Fidelity fund yielded 5%.[5] You would like to invest a total of up to $80,000 and earn at least $4,200 in interest in the coming year (based on the given yields). Draw the feasible region that shows how much money you can invest in each fund. Find the corner points of the region.

40. *Municipal Bond Funds* In 2003, the **Fidelity** Spartan Mass Fund (FDMMX) yielded 5%, and the Fidelity Spartan Florida Fund (FFLIX) yielded 7%.[6] You would like to invest a total of up to $60,000 and earn at least $3,500 in interest. Draw the feasible region that shows how much money you can invest in each fund (based on the given yields). Find the corner points of the region.

41. ▼ *Investments: Financial Stocks* (Compare Exercise 37 in Section 3.1.) In August 2011, **Bank of Hawaii** (BOH) stock cost $45 per share and yielded 4% per year in dividends, while **JPMorgan Chase** (JPM) stock cost $40 per share and yielded 2.5% per year in dividends.[7] You have up to $25,000 to invest in these stocks and would like to earn at least $760 in dividends over the course of a year. (Assume the dividend to be unchanged for the year.) Draw the feasible region that shows how many shares in each company you can buy. Find the corner points of the region. (Round each coordinate to the nearest whole number.)

42. ▼ *Investments: Utility Stocks* (Compare Exercise 38 in Section 3.1.) In April 2011, **Consolidated Edison** (ED) stock cost $50 per share and yielded 5% per year in dividends, while **National Grid** (NGG) stock cost $50 per share and yielded 6% per year in dividends.[8] You have up to $45,000 to invest in these stocks and would like to earn at least $2,400 in dividends over the course of a year. (Assume the dividend to be unchanged for the year.) Draw the feasible region that shows how many shares in each company you can buy. Find the corner points of the region. (Round each coordinate to the nearest whole number.)

43. ▼ *Advertising* You are the marketing director for a company that manufactures bodybuilding supplements and you are planning to run ads in *Sports Illustrated* and *GQ Magazine*. Based on readership data, you estimate that each one-page ad in *Sports Illustrated* will be read by 650,000 people in your target group, while each one-page ad in *GQ* will be read by 150,000.[9] You would like your ads to be read by at least three million people in the target group and, to ensure the broadest possible audience, you would like to place at least three full-page ads in each magazine. Draw the feasible region that shows how many pages you can purchase in each magazine. Find the corner points of the region. (Round each coordinate to the nearest whole number.)

44. ▼ *Advertising* You are the marketing director for a company that manufactures bodybuilding supplements and you are planning to run ads in *Sports Illustrated* and *Muscle and Fitness*. Based on readership data, you estimate that each one-page ad in *Sports Illustrated* will be read by 650,000 people in your target group, while each one-page ad in *Muscle and Fitness* will be read by 250,000 people in your target group.[10] You would like your ads to be read by at least four million people in the target group and, to ensure the broadest possible audience, you would like to place at least three full-page ads in each magazine during the year. Draw the feasible region showing how many pages you can purchase in each magazine. Find the corner points of the region. (Round each coordinate to the nearest whole number.)

COMMUNICATION AND REASONING EXERCISES

45. Find a system of inequalities whose solution set is unbounded.

46. Find a system of inequalities whose solution set is empty.

47. How would you use linear inequalities to describe the triangle with corner points $(0, 0)$, $(2, 0)$, and $(0, 1)$?

---

[3]Source: Nutrition information supplied with the products.

[4]*Ibid.*

[5]Yields are rounded. Sources: www.pimcofunds.com, www.fidelity.com

[6]Yields are rounded. Source: www.fidelity.com

[7]Stock prices and yields are approximate. Source: http://finance.google.com

[8]*Ibid.*

[9]The readership data for *Sports Illustrated* is based, in part, on the results of a readership survey taken in March 2000. The readership data for *GQ* is fictitious. Source: Mediamark Research Inc./*New York Times*, May 29, 2000, p. C1.

[10]The readership data for both magazines are based on the results of a readership survey taken in March 2000. Source: Mediamark Research Inc./*New York Times*, May 29, 2000, p. C1.

48. Explain the advantage of shading the region of points that do not satisfy the given inequalities. Illustrate with an example.

49. Describe at least one drawback to the method of finding the corner points of a feasible region by drawing its graph, when the feasible region arises from real-life constraints.

50. Draw several bounded regions described by linear inequalities. For each region you draw, find the point that gives the greatest possible value of $x + y$. What do you notice?

In Exercises 51–54, you are mixing x grams of ingredient A and y grams of ingredient B. Choose the equation or inequality that models the given requirement.

51. There should be at least 3 more grams of ingredient A than ingredient B.

(A) $3x - y \leq 0$ (B) $x - 3y \geq 0$
(C) $x - y \geq 3$ (D) $3x - y \geq 0$

52. The mixture should contain at least 25% of ingredient A by weight.

(A) $4x - y \leq 0$ (B) $x - 4y \geq 0$
(C) $x - y \geq 4$ (D) $3x - y \geq 0$

53. ▼ There should be at least 3 parts (by weight) of ingredient A to 2 parts of ingredient B.

(A) $3x - 2y \geq 0$ (B) $2x - 3y \geq 0$
(C) $3x + 2y \geq 0$ (D) $2x + 3y \geq 0$

54. ▼ There should be no more of ingredient A (by weight) than ingredient B.

(A) $x - y = 0$ (B) $x - y \leq 0$
(C) $x - y \geq 0$ (D) $x + y \geq y$

55. ▼ You are setting up a system of inequalities in the unknowns x and y. The inequalities represent constraints faced by Fly-by-Night Airlines, where x represents the number of first-class tickets it should issue for a specific flight and y represents the number of business-class tickets it should issue for that flight. You find that the feasible region is empty. How do you interpret this?

56. ▼ In the situation described in the preceding exercise, is it possible instead for the feasible region to be unbounded? Explain your answer.

57. ▼ Create an interesting scenario that leads to the following system of inequalities:

$$20x + 40y \leq 1{,}000$$
$$30x + 20y \leq 1{,}200$$
$$x \geq 0, y \geq 0.$$

58. ▼ Create an interesting scenario that leads to the following system of inequalities:

$$20x + 40y \geq 1{,}000$$
$$30x + 20y \geq 1{,}200$$
$$x \geq 0, y \geq 0.$$

5.2 Solving Linear Programming Problems Graphically

As we saw in Example 4 in Section 5.1, in some scenarios the possibilities are restricted by a system of linear inequalities. In that example, it would be natural to ask which of the various possibilities gives the company the largest profit. This is a kind of problem known as a *linear programming problem* (commonly referred to as an LP problem).

Linear Programming (LP) Problems

A **linear programming problem** in two unknowns x and y is one in which we are to find the maximum or minimum value of a linear expression

$$ax + by$$

called the **objective function**, subject to a number of linear **constraints** of the form

$$cx + dy \leq e \quad \text{or} \quad cx + dy \geq e.$$

The largest or smallest value of the objective function is called the **optimal value**, and a pair of values of x and y that gives the optimal value constitutes an **optimal solution**.

Maximize $p = x + y$ Objective function
subject to $x + 2y \le 12$
              $2x + y \le 12$ Constraints
              $x \ge 0, y \ge 0.$

See Example 1 for a method of solving this LP problem (that is, finding an optimal solution and value).

The set of points (x, y) satisfying all the constraints is the **feasible region** for the problem. Our methods of solving LP problems rely on the following facts:

Fundamental Theorem of Linear Programming

- If an LP problem has optimal solutions, then at least one of these solutions occurs at a corner point of the feasible region.
- Linear programming problems with bounded, nonempty feasible regions always have optimal solutions.

Let's see how we can use this to solve an LP problem, and then we'll discuss why it's true.

EXAMPLE 1 Solving an LP Problem

Maximize $p = x + y$
subject to $x + 2y \le 12$
             $2x + y \le 12$
             $x \ge 0, y \ge 0.$

Solution We begin by drawing the feasible region for the problem. We do this using the techniques of Section 5.1, and we get Figure 13.

Each **feasible point** (point in the feasible region) gives an x and a y satisfying the constraints. The question now is, which of these points gives the largest value of the objective function $p = x + y$? The Fundamental Theorem of Linear Programming tells us that the largest value must occur at one (or more) of the corners of the feasible region. In the following table, we list the coordinates of each corner point and we compute the value of the objective function at each corner.

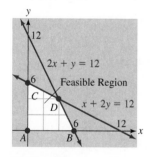

Figure 13

Corner Point	Lines through Point	Coordinates	$p = x + y$
A		$(0, 0)$	0
B		$(6, 0)$	6
C		$(0, 6)$	6
D	$x + 2y = 12$ $2x + y = 12$	$(4, 4)$	8

Now we simply pick the one that gives the largest value for p, which is D. Therefore, the optimal value of p is 8, and an optimal solution is $(4, 4)$.

Figure 14

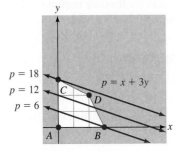

Figure 15

Now we owe you an explanation of why one of the corner points should be an optimal solution. The question is, which point in the feasible region gives the largest possible value of $p = x + y$?

Consider first an easier question: Which points result in a *particular value* of p? For example, which points result in $p = 2$? These would be the points on the line $x + y = 2$, which is the line labeled $p = 2$ in Figure 14.

Now suppose we want to know which points make $p = 4$: These would be the points on the line $x + y = 4$, which is the line labeled $p = 4$ in Figure 14. Notice that this line is parallel to but higher than the line $p = 2$. (If p represented profit in an application, we would call these **isoprofit lines**, or **constant-profit lines**.) Imagine moving this line up or down in the picture. As we move the line down, we see smaller values of p, and as we move it up, we see larger values. Several more of these lines are drawn in Figure 14. Look, in particular, at the line labeled $p = 10$. This line does not meet the feasible region, meaning that no feasible point makes p as large as 10. Starting with the line $p = 2$, as we move the line up, increasing p, there will be a last line that meets the feasible region. In the figure it is clear that this is the line $p = 8$, and this meets the feasible region in only one point, which is the corner point D. Therefore, D gives the greatest value of p of all feasible points.

If we had been asked to maximize some other objective function, such as $p = x + 3y$, then the optimal solution might be different. Figure 15 shows some of the isoprofit lines for this objective function. This time, the last point that is hit as p increases is C, not D. This tells us that the optimal solution is $(0, 6)$, giving the optimal value $p = 18$.

This discussion should convince you that the optimal value in an LP problem will always occur at one of the corner points. By the way, it is possible for the optimal value to occur at *two* corner points and at all points along an edge connecting them. (Do you see why?) We will see this in Example 3(b).

Here is a summary of the method we have just been using.

Graphical Method for Solving Linear Programming Problems in Two Unknowns (Bounded Feasible Regions)

1. Graph the feasible region and check that it is bounded.

2. Compute the coordinates of the corner points.

3. Substitute the coordinates of the corner points into the objective function to see which gives the maximum (or minimum) value of the objective function.

4. Any such corner point is an optimal solution.

Note If the feasible region is unbounded, this method will work only if there are optimal solutions; otherwise, it will not work. We will show you a method for deciding this on page 328. ∎

APPLICATIONS

EXAMPLE 2 Resource Allocation

Acme Baby Foods mixes two strengths of apple juice. One quart of Beginner's juice is made from 30 fluid ounces of water and 2 fluid ounces of apple juice concentrate. One quart of Advanced juice is made from 20 fluid ounces of water and 12 fluid ounces of concentrate. Every day Acme has available 30,000 fluid ounces of water and 3,600 fluid ounces of concentrate. Acme makes a profit of 20¢ on each quart of Beginner's juice and 30¢ on each quart of Advanced juice. How many quarts of each should Acme make each day to get the largest profit? How would this change if Acme made a profit of 40¢ on Beginner's juice and 20¢ on Advanced juice?

Solution Looking at the question that we are asked, we see that our unknown quantities are

$$x = \text{number of quarts of Beginner's juice made each day}$$
$$y = \text{number of quarts of Advanced juice made each day.}$$

(In this context, x and y are often called the **decision variables**, because we must decide what their values should be in order to get the largest profit.) We can write down the data given in the form of a table (the numbers in the first two columns are amounts per quart of juice):

	Beginner's, x	Advanced, y	Available
Water (ounces)	30	20	30,000
Concentrate (ounces)	2	12	3,600
Profit (¢)	20	30	

Because nothing in the problem says that Acme must use up all the water or concentrate, just that it can use no more than what is available, the first two rows of the table give us two inequalities:

$$30x + 20y \leq 30,000$$
$$2x + 12y \leq 3,600.$$

Dividing the first inequality by 10 and the second by 2 gives

$$3x + 2y \leq 3,000$$
$$x + 6y \leq 1,800.$$

We also have that $x \geq 0$ and $y \geq 0$ because Acme can't make a negative amount of juice. To finish setting up the problem, we are asked to maximize the profit, which is

$$p = 20x + 30y. \qquad \text{Expressed in ¢}$$

This gives us our LP problem:

Maximize $p = 20x + 30y$
subject to $3x + 2y \leq 3,000$
$\qquad\qquad x + 6y \leq 1,800$
$\qquad\qquad x \geq 0, y \geq 0.$

The (bounded) feasible region is shown in Figure 16.

The corners and the values of the objective function are listed in the following table:

Figure 16

Point	Lines through Point	Coordinates	p = 20x + 30y
A		(0, 0)	0
B		(1,000, 0)	20,000
C		(0, 300)	9,000
D	$3x + 2y = 3,000$ $x + 6y = 1,800$	(900, 150)	22,500

We are seeking to maximize the objective function p, so we look for corner points that give the maximum value for p. Because the maximum occurs at the point D, we conclude that the (only) optimal solution occurs at D. Thus, the company should make 900 quarts of Beginner's juice and 150 quarts of Advanced juice, for a largest possible profit of 22,500¢, or $225.

If, instead, the company made a profit of 40¢ on each quart of Beginner's juice and 20¢ on each quart of Advanced juice, then we would have $p = 40x + 20y$. This gives the following table:

Point	Lines through Point	Coordinates	$p = 40x + 20y$
A		$(0, 0)$	0
B		$(1,000, 0)$	40,000
C		$(0, 300)$	6,000
D	$3x + 2y = 3,000$ $x + 6y = 1,800$	$(900, 150)$	39,000

We can see that, in this case, Acme should make 1,000 quarts of Beginner's juice and no Advanced juice, for a largest possible profit of 40,000¢, or $400.

⇒ **Before we go on...** Notice that, in the first version of the problem in Example 2, the company used all the water and juice concentrate:

Water: $30(900) + 20(150) = 30,000$

Concentrate: $2(900) + 12(150) = 3,600.$

In the second version, it used all the water but not all the concentrate:

Water: $30(100) + 20(0) = 30,000$

Concentrate: $2(100) + 12(0) = 200 < 3,600.$ ∎

EXAMPLE 3 Investments

The Solid Trust Savings & Loan Company has set aside $25 million for loans to home buyers. Its policy is to allocate at least $10 million annually for luxury condominiums. A government housing development grant it receives requires, however, that at least one third of its total loans be allocated to low-income housing.

a. Solid Trust's return on condominiums is 12% and its return on low-income housing is 10%. How much should the company allocate for each type of housing to maximize its total return?

b. Redo part (a), assuming that the return is 12% on both condominiums and low-income housing.

Solution

a. We first identify the unknowns: Let x be the annual amount (in millions of dollars) allocated to luxury condominiums and let y be the annual amount allocated to low-income housing.

We now look at the constraints. The first constraint is mentioned in the first sentence: The total the company can invest is $25 million. Thus,

$x + y \leq 25.$

(The company is not required to invest all of the $25 million; rather, it can invest *up to* $25 million.) Next, the company has allocated at least $10 million to condos. Rephrasing this in terms of the unknowns, we get

The amount allocated to condos is at least $10 million.

The phrase "is at least" means $\geq$. Thus, we obtain a second constraint:

$$x \geq 10.$$

The third constraint is that at least one third of the total financing must be for low-income housing. Rephrasing this, we say:

The amount allocated to low-income housing is at least one third of the total.

Because the total investment will be $x + y$, we get

$$y \geq \frac{1}{3}(x + y).$$

We put this in the standard form of a linear inequality as follows:

$$3y \geq x + y \qquad \text{Multiply both sides by 3.}$$
$$-x + 2y \geq 0. \qquad \text{Subtract } x + y \text{ from both sides.}$$

There are no further constraints.

Now, what about the return on these investments? According to the data, the annual return is given by

$$p = 0.12x + 0.10y.$$

We want to make this quantity p as large as possible. In other words, we want to

$$
\begin{aligned}
\text{Maximize} \quad & p = 0.12x + 0.10y \\
\text{subject to} \quad & x + y \leq 25 \\
& x \geq 10 \\
& -x + 2y \geq 0 \\
& x \geq 0, y \geq 0.
\end{aligned}
$$

(Do you see why the inequalities $x \geq 0$ and $y \geq 0$ are slipped in here?) The feasible region is shown in Figure 17.

We now make a table that gives the return on investment at each corner point:

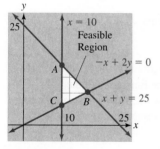

Figure 17

Point	Lines through Point	Coordinates	$p = 0.12x + 0.10y$
A	$x = 10$ $x + y = 25$	$(10, 15)$	2.7
B	$x + y = 25$ $-x + 2y = 0$	$(50/3, 25/3)$	2.833
C	$x = 10$ $-x + 2y = 0$	$(10, 5)$	1.7

From the table, we see that the values of x and y that maximize the return are $x = 50/3$ and $y = 25/3$, which give a total return of $2.833 million. In other words, the most profitable course of action is to invest $16.667 million in loans for condominiums and $8.333 million in loans for low-income housing, giving a maximum annual return of $2.833 million.

b. The LP problem is the same as for part (a) except for the objective function:

Maximize $p = 0.12x + 0.12y$
subject to
$$x + y \leq 25$$
$$x \geq 10$$
$$-x + 2y \geq 0$$
$$x \geq 0, y \geq 0.$$

Here are the values of p at the three corners:

Point	Coordinates	$p = 0.12x + 0.12y$
A	$(10, 15)$	3
B	$(50/3, 25/3)$	3
C	$(10, 5)$	1.8

Looking at the table, we see that a curious thing has happened: We get the same maximum annual return at both A and B. Thus, we could choose either option to maximize the annual return. In fact, any point along the line segment AB will yield an annual return of \$3 million. For example, the point $(12, 13)$ lies on the line segment AB and also yields an annual revenue of \$3 million. This happens because the "isoreturn" lines are parallel to that edge.

➡ **Before we go on...** What breakdowns of investments would lead to the *lowest* return for parts (a) and (b)? ∎

The preceding examples all had bounded feasible regions. If the feasible region is unbounded, then, *provided there are optimal solutions,* the fundamental theorem of linear programming guarantees that the above method will work. The following procedure determines whether or not optimal solutions exist and finds them when they do.

Solving Linear Programming Problems in Two Unknowns (Unbounded Feasible Regions)

If the feasible region of an LP problem is unbounded, proceed as follows:

1. Draw a rectangle large enough so that all the corner points are inside the rectangle (and not on its boundary):

Corner points: A, B, C Corner points inside the rectangle

2. Shade the outside of the rectangle so as to define a new bounded feasible region, and locate the new corner points:

New corner points: D, E, and F

3. Obtain the optimal solutions using this bounded feasible region.
4. If any optimal solutions occur at one of the original corner points (A, B, and C in the figure), then the LP problem has that corner point as an optimal solution. Otherwise, the LP problem has no optimal solutions. When the latter occurs, we say that the **objective function is unbounded**, because it can assume arbitrarily large (positive or negative) values.

In the next two examples, we work with unbounded feasible regions.

EXAMPLE 4 Cost

You are the manager of a small store that specializes in hats, sunglasses, and other accessories. You are considering a sales promotion of a new line of hats and sunglasses. You will offer the sunglasses only to those who purchase two or more hats, so you will sell at least twice as many hats as pairs of sunglasses. Moreover, your supplier tells you that, due to seasonal demand, your order of sunglasses cannot exceed 100 pairs. To ensure that the sale items fill out the large display you have set aside, you estimate that you should order at least 210 items in all.

a. Assume that you will lose $3 on every hat and $2 on every pair of sunglasses sold. Given the constraints above, how many hats and pairs of sunglasses should you order to lose the least amount of money in the sales promotion?

b. Suppose instead that you lose $1 on every hat sold but make a profit of $5 on every pair of sunglasses sold. How many hats and pairs of sunglasses should you order to make the largest profit in the sales promotion?

c. Now suppose that you make a profit of $1 on every hat sold but lose $5 on every pair of sunglasses sold. How many hats and pairs of sunglasses should you order to make the largest profit in the sales promotion?

Solution

a. The unknowns are:

x = number of hats you order
y = number of pairs of sunglasses you order.

The objective is to minimize the total loss:

$$c = 3x + 2y.$$

Now for the constraints. The requirement that you will sell at least twice as many hats as sunglasses can be rephrased as:

The number of hats is at least twice the number of pairs of sunglasses,

or

$$x \geq 2y$$

which, in standard form, is

$$x - 2y \geq 0.$$

Next, your order of sunglasses cannot exceed 100 pairs, so

$$y \leq 100.$$

Finally, you would like to sell at least 210 items in all, giving

$$x + y \geq 210.$$

Thus, the LP problem is the following:

$$\begin{aligned}
\text{Minimize} \quad & c = 3x + 2y \\
\text{subject to} \quad & x - 2y \geq 0 \\
& y \leq 100 \\
& x + \ y \geq 210 \\
& x \geq 0, y \geq 0.
\end{aligned}$$

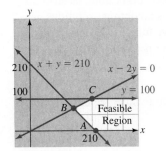

Figure 18

The feasible region is shown in Figure 18. This region is unbounded, so there is no guarantee that there are any optimal solutions. Following the procedure described above, we enclose the corner points in a rectangle as shown in Figure 19. (There are many infinitely many possible rectangles we could have used. We chose one that gives convenient coordinates for the new corners.)

We now list all the corners of this bounded region along with the corresponding values of the objective function c:

Figure 19

Point	Lines through Point	Coordinates	$c = 3x + 2y$ ($)
A		$(210, 0)$	630
B	$x + \ y = 210$ $x - 2y = 0$	$(140, 70)$	560
C	$x - 2y = 0$ $y = 100$	$(200, 100)$	800
D		$(300, 100)$	1,100
E		$(300, 0)$	900

The corner point that gives the minimum value of the objective function c is B. Because B is one of the corner points of the original feasible region, we conclude that our linear programming problem has an optimal solution at B. Thus, the combination that gives the smallest loss is 140 hats and 70 pairs of sunglasses.

b. The LP problem is the following:

$$\text{Maximize} \quad p = -x + 5y$$
$$\text{subject to} \quad x - 2y \geq 0$$
$$y \leq 100$$
$$x + y \geq 210$$
$$x \geq 0, y \geq 0.$$

Because most of the work is already done for us in part (a), all we need to do is change the objective function in the table that lists the corner points:

Point	Lines through Point	Coordinates	$p = -x + 5y$ ($)
A		(210, 0)	−210
B	$x + y = 210$ $x - 2y = 0$	(140, 70)	210
C	$x - 2y = 0$ $y = 100$	(200, 100)	300
D		(300, 100)	200
E		(300, 0)	−300

The corner point that gives the maximum value of the objective function p is C. Because C is one of the corner points of the original feasible region, we conclude that our LP problem has an optimal solution at C. Thus, the combination that gives the largest profit ($300) is 200 hats and 100 pairs of sunglasses.

c. The objective function is now $p = x - 5y$, which is the negative of the objective function used in part (b). Thus, the table of values of p is the same as in part (b), except that it has opposite signs in the p column. This time we find that the maximum value of p occurs at E. However, E is not a corner point of the original feasible region, so the LP problem has no optimal solution. Referring to Figure 18, we can make the objective p as large as we like by choosing a point far to the right in the unbounded feasible region. Thus, the objective function is unbounded; that is, it is possible to make an arbitrarily large profit.

EXAMPLE 5 Resource Allocation

You are composing a very avant-garde ballade for violins and bassoons. In your ballade, each violinist plays a total of two notes and each bassoonist only one note. To make your ballade long enough, you decide that it should contain at least 200 instrumental notes. Furthermore, after playing the requisite two notes, each violinist will sing one soprano note, while each bassoonist will sing three soprano notes.* To make the ballade sufficiently interesting, you have decided on a minimum of 300 soprano notes. To give your composition a sense of balance, you wish to have no more than three times as many bassoonists as violinists. Violinists charge $200 per performance and bassoonists $400 per performance. How many of each should your ballade call for in order to minimize personnel costs?

* Whether or not these musicians are capable of singing decent soprano notes will be left to chance. You reason that a few bad notes will add character to the ballade.

Solution First, the unknowns are x = number of violinists and y = number of bassoonists. The constraint on the number of instrumental notes implies that

$$2x + y \geq 200$$

because the total number is to be *at least* 200. Similarly, the constraint on the number of soprano notes is

$$x + 3y \geq 300.$$

The next one is a little tricky. As usual, we reword it in terms of the quantities x and y.

The number of bassoonists should be no more than three times the number of violinists.

Thus, $y \leq 3x$

or $3x - y \geq 0.$

Finally, the total cost per performance will be

$$c = 200x + 400y.$$

We wish to minimize total cost. So, our linear programming problem is as follows:

Minimize $c = 200x + 400y$
subject to $2x + \;\; y \geq 200$
$x + 3y \geq 300$
$3x - \;\; y \geq 0$
$x \geq 0, y \geq 0.$

Figure 20

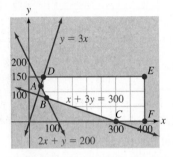

Figure 21

We get the feasible region shown in Figure 20.* The feasible region is unbounded, and so we add a convenient rectangle as before (Figure 21).

* In Figure 20 you can see how graphing technology would help in determining the corner points: Unless you are very confident in the accuracy of your sketch, how do you know that the line $y = 3x$ falls to the left of the point B? If it were to fall to the right, then B would not be a corner point and the solution would be different. You could (and should) check that B satisfies the inequality $3x - y \geq 0$, so that the line falls to the left of B as shown. However, if you use a graphing calculator or computer, you can be fairly confident of the picture produced without doing further calculations.

Point	Lines through Point	Coordinates	$c = 200x + 400y$
A	$2x + y = 200$ $3x - y = 0$	$(40, 120)$	$56{,}000$
B	$2x + \;\; y = 200$ $x + 3y = 300$	$(60, 80)$	$44{,}000$
C		$(300, 0)$	$60{,}000$
D	$3x - y = 0$ $y = 150$	$(50, 150)$	$70{,}000$
E		$(400, 150)$	$140{,}000$
F		$(400, 0)$	$80{,}000$

From the table we see that the minimum cost occurs at B, a corner point of the original feasible region. The linear programming problem thus has an optimal solution, and the minimum cost is $\$44{,}000$ per performance, employing 60 violinists and 80 bassoonists. (Quite a wasteful ballade, one might say.)

using Technology

Website
www.WanerMath.com
For an online utility that does everything (solves linear programming problems with two unknowns and even draws the feasible region), go to the Website and follow

→ On Line Utilities
→ Linear Programming Grapher.

FAQs

Recognizing a Linear Programming Problem, Setting Up Inequalities, and Dealing with Unbounded Regions

Q: *How do I recognize when an application leads to an LP problem as opposed to a system of linear equations?*

A: Here are some cues that suggest an LP problem:

- Key phrases suggesting inequalities rather than equalities, like *at most, up to, no more than, at least*, and *or more*.
- A quantity that is being maximized or minimized (this will be the objective). Key phrases are *maximum, minimum, most, least, largest, greatest, smallest, as large as possible*, and *as small as possible*.

Q: *How do I deal with tricky phrases like "there should be no more than twice as many nuts as bolts" or "at least 50% of the total should be bolts"?*

A: The easiest way to deal with phrases like this is to use the technique we discussed in Chapter 3: reword the phrases using "the number of . . . ", as in

The number of nuts (x) is no more than twice the number of bolts (y) $x \leq 2y$
The number of bolts is at least 50% of the total $y \geq 0.50(x + y)$

Q: *Do I always have to add a rectangle to deal with unbounded regions?*

A: Under some circumstances, you can tell right away whether optimal solutions exist, even when the feasible region is unbounded.

Note that the following apply only when we have the constraints $x \geq 0$ and $y \geq 0$.

1. If you are minimizing $c = ax + by$ with a and b nonnegative, then optimal solutions always exist. (Examples 4(a) and 5 are of this type.)
2. If you are maximizing $p = ax + by$ with a and b nonnegative (and not both zero), then there is no optimal solution unless the feasible region is bounded.

Do you see why statements (1) and (2) are true?

5.2   EXERCISES

▼ more advanced   ◆ challenging
T indicates exercises that should be solved using technology

In Exercises 1–20, solve the LP problems. If no optimal solution exists, indicate whether the feasible region is empty or the objective function is unbounded. HINT [See Example 1.]

1. Maximize $p = x + y$
subject to $x + 2y \leq 9$
$2x + y \leq 9$
$x \geq 0, y \geq 0.$

2. Maximize $p = x + 2y$
subject to $x + 3y \leq 24$
$2x + y \leq 18$
$x \geq 0, y \geq 0.$

3. Minimize $c = x + y$
subject to $x + 2y \geq 6$
$2x + y \geq 6$
$x \geq 0, y \geq 0.$

4. Minimize $c = x + 2y$
subject to $x + 3y \geq 30$
$2x + y \geq 30$
$x \geq 0, y \geq 0.$

5. Maximize $p = 3x + y$
subject to $3x - 7y \leq 0$
$7x - 3y \geq 0$
$x + y \leq 10$
$x \geq 0, y \geq 0.$

6. Maximize $p = x - 2y$
subject to $x + 2y \leq 8$
$x - 6y \leq 0$
$3x - 2y \geq 0$
$x \geq 0, y \geq 0.$

7. Maximize $p = 3x + 2y$

subject to $0.2x + 0.1y \leq 1$

$0.15x + 0.3y \leq 1.5$

$10x + 10y \leq 60$

$x \geq 0, y \geq 0.$

8. Maximize $p = x + 2y$

subject to $30x + 20y \leq 600$

$0.1x + 0.4y \leq 4$

$0.2x + 0.3y \leq 4.5$

$x \geq 0, y \geq 0.$

9. Minimize $c = 0.2x + 0.3y$

subject to $0.2x + 0.1y \geq 1$

$0.15x + 0.3y \geq 1.5$

$10x + 10y \geq 80$

$x \geq 0, y \geq 0.$

10. Minimize $c = 0.4x + 0.1y$

subject to $30x + 20y \geq 600$

$0.1x + 0.4y \geq 4$

$0.2x + 0.3y \geq 4.5$

$x \geq 0, y \geq 0.$

11. Maximize and minimize $p = x + 2y$

subject to $x + y \geq 2$

$x + y \leq 10$

$x - y \leq 2$

$x - y \geq -2.$

12. Maximize and minimize $p = 2x - y$

subject to $x + y \geq 2$

$x - y \leq 2$

$x - y \geq -2$

$x \leq 10, y \leq 10.$

13. Maximize $p = 2x + 3y$

subject to $0.1x + 0.2y \geq 1$

$2x + y \geq 10$

$x \geq 0, y \geq 0.$

14. Maximize $p = 3x + 2y$

subject to $0.1x + 0.1y \geq 0.2$

$y \leq 10$

$x \geq 0, y \geq 0.$

15. Minimize $c = 2x + 4y$

subject to $0.1x + 0.1y \geq 1$

$x + 2y \geq 14$

$x \geq 0, y \geq 0.$

16. Maximize $p = 2x + 3y$

subject to $-x + y \geq 10$

$x + 2y \leq 12$

$x \geq 0, y \geq 0.$

17. Minimize $c = 3x - 3y$

subject to $\dfrac{x}{4} \leq y$

$y \leq \dfrac{2x}{3}$

$x + y \geq 5$

$x + 2y \leq 10$

$x \geq 0, y \geq 0.$

18. Minimize $c = -x + 2y$

subject to $y \leq \dfrac{2x}{3}$

$x \leq 3y$

$y \geq 4$

$x \geq 6$

$x + y \leq 16.$

19. Maximize $p = x + y$

subject to $x + 2y \geq 10$

$2x + 2y \leq 10$

$2x + y \geq 10$

$x \geq 0, y \geq 0.$

20. Minimize $c = 3x + y$

subject to $10x + 20y \geq 100$

$0.3x + 0.1y \geq 1$

$x \geq 0, y \geq 0.$

APPLICATIONS

21. *Resource Allocation* You manage an ice cream factory that makes two flavors: Creamy Vanilla and Continental Mocha. Into each quart of Creamy Vanilla go 2 eggs and 3 cups of cream. Into each quart of Continental Mocha go 1 egg and 3 cups of cream. You have in stock 500 eggs and 900 cups of cream. You make a profit of $3 on each quart of Creamy Vanilla and $2 on each quart of Continental Mocha. How many quarts of each flavor should you make in order to earn the largest profit? HINT [See Example 2.]

22. *Resource Allocation* Podunk Institute of Technology's Math Department offers two courses: Finite Math and Applied Calculus. Each section of Finite Math has 60 students, and each section of Applied Calculus has 50. The department is allowed to offer a total of up to 110 sections. Furthermore, no more than 6,000 students want to take a math course (no student will take more than one math course). Suppose the university makes a profit of $100,000 on each section of Finite Math and $50,000 on each section of Applied Calculus (the profit is the difference between what the students are charged and what the professors are paid). How many sections of each course should the department offer to make the largest profit? HINT [See Example 2.]

23. Nutrition *Ruff, Inc.* makes dog food out of chicken and grain. Chicken has 10 grams of protein and 5 grams of fat per ounce, and grain has 2 grams of protein and 2 grams of fat per ounce. A bag of dog food must contain at least 200 grams of protein and at least 150 grams of fat. If chicken costs 10¢ per ounce and grain costs 1¢ per ounce, how many ounces of each should Ruff use in each bag of dog food in order to minimize cost? HINT [See Example 4.]

24. Purchasing Enormous State University's Business School is buying computers. The school has two models from which to choose, the Pomegranate and the iZac. Each Pomegranate comes with 400 GB of memory and 80 TB of disk space; each iZac has 300 GB of memory and 100 TB of disk space. For reasons related to its accreditation, the school would like to be able to say that it has a total of at least 48,000 GB of memory and at least 12,800 TB of disk space. If the Pomegranate and the iZac cost $2,000 each, how many of each should the school buy to keep the cost as low as possible? HINT [See Example 4.]

25. Nutrition Gerber Products' Gerber Mixed Cereal for Baby contains, in each serving, 60 calories and 11 grams of carbohydrates. Gerber Mango Tropical Fruit Dessert contains, in each serving, 80 calories and 21 grams of carbohydrates.[11] If the cereal costs 30¢ per serving and the dessert costs 50¢ per serving, and you want to provide your child with at least 140 calories and at least 32 grams of carbohydrates, how can you do so at the least cost? (Fractions of servings are permitted.)

26. Nutrition Gerber Products' Gerber Mixed Cereal for Baby contains, in each serving, 60 calories, 10 grams of carbohydrates, and no Vitamin C. Gerber Apple Banana Juice contains, in each serving, 60 calories, 15 grams of carbohydrates, and 120% of the U.S. Recommended Daily Allowance (RDA) of Vitamin C for infants.[12] The cereal costs 10¢ per serving and the juice costs 30¢ per serving. If you want to provide your child with at least 120 calories, at least 25 grams of carbohydrates, and at least 60% of the U.S. RDA of Vitamin C for infants, how can you do so at the least cost? (Fractions of servings are permitted.)

27. Energy Efficiency You are thinking of making your home more energy efficient by replacing some of the light bulbs with compact fluorescent bulbs, and insulating part or all of your exterior walls. Each compact fluorescent light bulb costs $4 and saves you an average of $2 per year in energy costs, and each square foot of wall insulation costs $1 and saves you an average of $0.20 per year in energy costs.[13] Your home has 60 light fittings and 1,100 sq. ft. of uninsulated exterior wall.

You can spend no more than $1,200 and would like to save as much per year in energy costs as possible. How many compact fluorescent light bulbs and how many square feet of insulation should you purchase? How much will you save in energy costs per year?

28. Energy Efficiency (Compare with the preceding exercise.) You are thinking of making your mansion more energy efficient by replacing some of the light bulbs with compact fluorescent bulbs, and insulating part or all of your exterior walls. Each compact fluorescent light bulb costs $4 and saves you an average of $2 per year in energy costs, and each square foot of wall insulation costs $1 and saves you an average of $0.20 per year in energy costs.[14] Your mansion has 200 light fittings and 3,000 sq. ft. of uninsulated exterior wall. To impress your friends, you would like to spend as much as possible, but save no more than $800 per year in energy costs (you are proud of your large utility bills). How many compact fluorescent light bulbs and how many square feet of insulation should you purchase? How much will you save in energy costs per year?

Bodybuilding Supplements *Exercises 29 and 30 are based on the following data on three bodybuilding supplements. (Figures shown correspond to a single serving.)*[15]

	Creatine (g)	Carbohydrates (g)	Taurine (g)	Alpha Lipoic Acid (mg)	Cost ($)
Cell-Tech® (MuscleTech)	10	75	2	200	2.20
RiboForce HP® (EAS)	5	15	1	0	1.60
Creatine Transport® (Kaizen)	5	35	1	100	0.60

29. You are thinking of combining Cell-Tech and RiboForce HP to obtain a 10-day supply that provides at least 80 grams of creatine and at least 10 grams of taurine, but no more than 750 grams of carbohydrates and no more than 1,000 milligrams of alpha lipoic acid. How many servings of each supplement should you combine to meet your specifications at the least cost?

30. You are thinking of combining Cell-Tech and Creatine Transport to obtain a 10-day supply that provides at least 80 grams of creatine and at least 10 grams of taurine, but no more than 600 grams of carbohydrates and no more than 2,000 milligrams of alpha lipoic acid. How many servings of each supplement should you combine to meet your specifications at the least cost?

31. Resource Allocation Your salami manufacturing plant can order up to 1,000 pounds of pork and 2,400 pounds of beef per day for use in manufacturing its two specialties: "Count Dracula Salami" and "Frankenstein Sausage." Production of the Count Dracula variety requires 1 pound of pork and

---

[11]Source: Nutrition information supplied with the products.

[12]*Ibid.*

[13]Source: American Council for an Energy-Efficient Economy/*New York Times*, December 1, 2003, p. C6.

[14]*Ibid.*

[15]Source: Nutritional information supplied by the manufacturers (www.netrition.com). Cost per serving is approximate and varies.

3 pounds of beef for each salami, while the Frankenstein variety requires 2 pounds of pork and 2 pounds of beef for every sausage. In view of your heavy investment in advertising Count Dracula Salami, you have decided that at least one-third of the total production should be Count Dracula. On the other hand, due to the health-conscious consumer climate, your Frankenstein Sausage (sold as having less beef) is earning your company a profit of $3 per sausage, while sales of the Count Dracula variety are down and it is earning your company only $1 per salami. Given these restrictions, how many of each kind of sausage should you produce to maximize profits, and what is the maximum possible profit? HINT [See Example 3.]

32. **Project Design** The *Megabuck Hospital Corp.* is to build a state-subsidized nursing home catering to homeless patients as well as high-income patients. State regulations require that every subsidized nursing home must house a minimum of 1,000 homeless patients and no more than 750 high-income patients in order to qualify for state subsidies. The overall capacity of the hospital is to be 2,100 patients. The board of directors, under pressure from a neighborhood group, insists that the number of homeless patients should not exceed twice the number of high-income patients. Due to the state subsidy, the hospital will make an average profit of $10,000 per month for every homeless patient it houses, whereas the profit per high-income patient is estimated at $8,000 per month. How many of each type of patient should it house in order to maximize profit? HINT [See Example 3.]

33. **Television Advertising** Each Monday evening in August 2011, each episode of *WWE Raw* was typically watched by 1.8 million viewers, while each episode of *Family Guy* was typically watched by 1.5 million viewers.[16] Your marketing services firm has been hired to promote *Bald No More's* hair replacement process by buying at least 30 commercial spots during episodes of *WWE Raw* and *Family Guy*. You have been quoted a price of $3,000 per spot for *WWE Raw* and $1,000 per spot for *Family Guy*. Bald No More's advertising budget for TV commercials is $120,000, and, because of the company president's fondness for wrestling, it would like no more than 50% of the total number of spots to appear on *Family Guy*. How many spots should you purchase on each show to maximize exposure? HINT [Calculate exposure as Number of ads × Number of viewers.]

34. **Television Advertising** Each Friday evening in August 2011, each episode of *Family Guy* was typically watched by 1.3 million viewers, while each episode of *American Dad* was typically watched by 0.9 million viewers.[17] Your marketing services firm has been hired to promote *Gauss Jordan* Sneakers by buying at least 30 commercial spots during episodes of *Family Guy* and *American Dad*. You have been quoted a price of $2,000 per spot for *Family Guy* and $3,000 per spot for *American Dad*. Gauss Jordan Inc.'s advertising budget for TV commercials is $70,000, and it would like at

least 75% of the total number of spots to appear on *Family Guy*. How many spots should you purchase on each show to maximize exposure? HINT [Calculate exposure as Number of ads × Number of viewers.]

Investing Exercises 35 and 36 are based on the following data on four stocks.[18]

	Price	Dividend Yield	52-Week Price Change ($)
FDX (FedEx)	$90	1%	−1.9
WU (Western Union)	20	2%	0.61
DO (Diamond Offshore Drilling)	70	0%	5.5
WERN (Werner Enterprises)	25	1%	3.6

35. ▼ You are planning to invest up to $10,000 in FDX and WU shares. You want your investment to yield at least $120 in dividends, and, for tax reasons, you want to minimize the 52-week gain (or maximize the loss) in the total value of the shares. How many shares of each company should you purchase? (Fractions of shares permitted.)

36. ▼ You are planning to invest up to $43,000 in DO and WERN shares. For tax reasons, you want your investment to yield no more than $10 in dividends. You want to maximize the 52-week gain in the total value of the shares. How many shares of each company should you purchase? (Fractions of shares permitted.)

37. ▼ **Investments: Financial Stocks** (Compare Exercise 41 in Section 5.1.) In August 2011, **Bank of Hawaii** (BOH) stock cost $45 per share, yielded 4% per year in dividends, and had a risk index of 3.0 per share, while **JPMorgan Chase** (JPM) stock cost $40 per share, yielded 2.5% per year in dividends, and had a risk index of 2.0 per share.[19] You have up to $25,000 to invest in these stocks, and would like to earn at least $760 in dividends over the course of a year. (Assume the dividend to be unchanged for the year.) How many shares (to the nearest tenth of a unit) of each stock should you purchase to meet your requirements and minimize the total risk index for your portfolio? What is the minimum total risk index?

38. ▼ **Investments: Utlity Stocks** (Compare Exercise 42 in Section 5.1.) In April 2011, **Consolidated Edison** (ED) stock cost $50 per share, yielded 5% per year in dividends, and had a risk index of 2.0, while **National Grid** (NGG) stock cost $50 per share, yielded 6% per year in dividends, and had a risk index of 3.0.[20] You have up to $45,000 to invest in

---

[16]Ratings are for August 29, 2011. Source: Nielsen Media Research/www.tvbythenumbers.com

[17]*Ibid.*

[18]Approximate 150-day average price as of August 31, 2011. 52-week price changes are approximate. Source: http://finance.google.com

[19]Stock prices and yields are approximate, and risk indices are fictitious. Source: http://finance.google.com

[20]*Ibid.*

these stocks, and would like to earn at least $2,400 in dividends over the course of a year. (Assume the dividend to be unchanged for the year.) How many shares of each stock should you purchase to meet your requirements and minimize the total risk index for your portfolio? What is the minimum total risk index?

39. ▼ *Planning* My friends: I, the mighty Brutus, have decided to prepare for retirement by instructing young warriors in the arts of battle and diplomacy. For each hour spent in battle instruction, I have decided to charge 50 ducats. For each hour in diplomacy instruction I shall charge 40 ducats. Due to my advancing years, I can spend no more than 50 hours per week instructing the youths, although the great Jove knows that they are sorely in need of instruction! Due to my fondness for physical pursuits, I have decided to spend no more than one third of the total time in diplomatic instruction. However, the present border crisis with the Gauls is a sore indication of our poor abilities as diplomats. As a result, I have decided to spend at least 10 hours per week instructing in diplomacy. Finally, to complicate things further, there is the matter of Scarlet Brew: I have estimated that each hour of battle instruction will require 10 gallons of Scarlet Brew to quench my students' thirst, and that each hour of diplomacy instruction, being less physically demanding, requires half that amount. Because my harvest of red berries has far exceeded my expectations, I estimate that I'll have to use at least 400 gallons per week in order to avoid storing the fine brew at great expense. Given all these restrictions, how many hours per week should I spend in each type of instruction to maximize my income?

40. ▼ *Planning* Repeat the preceding exercise with the following changes: I would like to spend no more than half the total time in diplomatic instruction, and I must use at least 600 gallons of Scarlet Brew.

41. ▼ *Resource Allocation* One day, Gillian the magician summoned the wisest of her women. "Devoted followers," she began, "I have a quandary: As you well know, I possess great expertise in sleep spells and shock spells, but unfortunately, these are proving to be a drain on my aural energy resources; each sleep spell costs me 500 pico-shirleys of aural energy, while each shock spell requires 750 pico-shirleys. Clearly, I would like to hold my overall expenditure of aural energy to a minimum, and still meet my commitments in protecting the Sisterhood from the ever-present threat of trolls. Specifically, I have estimated that each sleep spell keeps us safe for an average of two minutes, while every shock spell protects us for about three minutes. We certainly require enough protection to last 24 hours of each day, and possibly more, just to be safe. At the same time, I have noticed that each of my sleep spells can immobilize three trolls at once, while one of my typical shock spells (having a narrower range) can immobilize only two trolls at once. We are faced, my sisters, with an onslaught of 1,200 trolls per day! Finally, as you are no doubt aware, the bylaws dictate that for a Magician of the Order to remain in good standing, the number of shock spells must be between one quarter and one third the number of shock and sleep spells combined. What do I do, oh Wise Ones?"

42. ▼ *Risk Management* The Grand Vizier of the Kingdom of Um is being blackmailed by numerous individuals and is having a very difficult time keeping his blackmailers from going public. He has been keeping them at bay with two kinds of payoff: gold bars from the Royal Treasury and political favors. Through bitter experience, he has learned that each payoff in gold gives him peace for an average of about 1 month, while each political favor seems to earn him about a month and a half of reprieve. To maintain his flawless reputation in the Court, he feels he cannot afford any revelations about his tainted past to come to light within the next year. Thus it is imperative that his blackmailers be kept at bay for 12 months. Furthermore, he would like to keep the number of gold payoffs at no more than one quarter of the combined number of payoffs because the outward flow of gold bars might arouse suspicion on the part of the Royal Treasurer. The Grand Vizier feels that he can do no more than seven political favors per year without arousing undue suspicion in the Court. The gold payoffs tend to deplete his travel budget. (The treasury has been subsidizing his numerous trips to the Himalayas.) He estimates that each gold bar removed from the treasury will cost him four trips. On the other hand, because the administering of political favors tends to cost him valuable travel time, he suspects that each political favor will cost him about two trips. Now, he would obviously like to keep his blackmailers silenced and lose as few trips as possible. What is he to do? How many trips will he lose in the next year?

43. ◆ *Management*[21] You are the service manager for a supplier of closed-circuit television systems. Your company can provide up to 160 hours per week of technical service for your customers, although the demand for technical service far exceeds this amount. As a result, you have been asked to develop a model to allocate service technicians' time between new customers (those still covered by service contracts) and old customers (whose service contracts have expired). To ensure that new customers are satisfied with your company's service, the sales department has instituted a policy that at least 100 hours per week be allocated to servicing new customers. At the same time, your superiors have informed you that the company expects your department to generate at least $1,200 per week in revenues. Technical service time for new customers generates an average of $10 per hour (because much of the service is still under warranty) and for old customers generates $30 per hour. How many hours per week should you allocate to each type of customer to generate the most revenue?

---

[21]Loosely based on a similiar problem in *An Introduction to Management Science* (6th Ed.) by D. R. Anderson, D. J. Sweeney, and T. A. Williams (West, 1991).

44. ◆ *Scheduling*[22] The *Scottsville Textile Mill* produces several different fabrics on eight dobby looms which operate 24 hours per day and are scheduled for 30 days in the coming month. The Scottsville Textile Mill will produce only Fabric 1 and Fabric 2 during the coming month. Each dobby loom can turn out 4.63 yards of either fabric per hour. Assume that there is a monthly demand of 16,000 yards of Fabric 1 and 12,000 yards of Fabric 2. Profits are calculated as 33¢ per yard for each fabric produced on the dobby looms.

a. Will it be possible to satisfy total demand?

b. In the event that total demand is not satisfied, the Scottsville Textile Mill will need to purchase the fabrics from another mill to make up the shortfall. Its profits on resold fabrics ordered from another mill amount to 20¢ per yard for Fabric 1 and 16¢ per yard for Fabric 2. How many yards of each fabric should it produce to maximize profits?

COMMUNICATION AND REASONING EXERCISES

45. If a linear programming problem has a bounded, nonempty feasible region, then optimal solutions

(A) must exist   **(B)** may or may not exist

(C) cannot exist

46. If a linear programming problem has an unbounded, nonempty feasible region, then optimal solutions

(A) must exist   **(B)** may or may not exist

(C) cannot exist

47. What can you say if the optimal value occurs at two adjacent corner points?

48. Describe at least one drawback to using the graphical method to solve a linear programming problem arising from a real-life situation.

49. Create a linear programming problem in two variables that has no optimal solution.

---

[22]Adapted from *The Calhoun Textile Mill Case* by J. D. Camm, P. M. Dearing, and S. K. Tadisina as presented for case study in *An Introduction to Management Science* (6th Ed.) by D. R. Anderson, D. J. Sweeney, and T. A. Williams (West, 1991). Our exercise uses a subset of the data given in the cited study.

50. Create a linear programming problem in two variables that has more than one optimal solution.

51. Create an interesting scenario leading to the following linear programming problem:

Maximize $p = 10x + 10y$
subject to $20x + 40y \le 1{,}000$
$30x + 20y \le 1{,}200$
$x \ge 0, y \ge 0.$

52. Create an interesting scenario leading to the following linear programming problem:

Minimize $c = 10x + 10y$
subject to $20x + 40y \ge 1{,}000$
$30x + 20y \ge 1{,}200$
$x \ge 0, y \ge 0.$

53. ▼ Use an example to show why there may be no optimal solution to a linear programming problem if the feasible region is unbounded.

54. ▼ Use an example to illustrate why, in the event that an optimal solution does occur despite an unbounded feasible region, that solution corresponds to a corner point of the feasible region.

55. ▼ You are setting up an LP problem for Fly-by-Night Airlines with the unknowns x and y, where x represents the number of first-class tickets it should issue for a specific flight and y represents the number of business-class tickets it should issue for that flight, and the problem is to maximize profit. You find that there are two different corner points that maximize the profit. How do you interpret this?

56. ▼ In the situation described in the preceding exercise, you find that there are no optimal solutions. How do you interpret this?

57. ◆ Consider the following example of a *nonlinear* programming problem: Maximize $p = xy$ subject to $x \ge 0, y \ge 0,$ $x + y \le 2$. Show that p is zero on every corner point, but is greater than zero at many non-corner points.

58. ◆ Solve the nonlinear programming problem in Exercise 57.

5.3 The Simplex Method: Solving Standard Maximization Problems

The method discussed in Section 5.2 works quite well for LP problems in two unknowns, but what about three or more unknowns? Because we need an axis for each unknown, we would need to draw graphs in three dimensions (where we have x-, y-, and z-coordinates) to deal with problems in three unknowns, and we would have to draw in hyperspace to answer questions involving four or more unknowns. Given the state of technology as this book is being written, we can't easily do this. So we need another method for solving LP problems that will work for any number of unknowns. One such method, called the **simplex method**, has been the method of choice since it was invented by George Dantzig in 1947. (See the Introduction to this chapter for more about Dantzig.) To illustrate it best, we first use it to solve only so-called standard maximization problems.

General Linear Programming Problem

A **linear programming problem in n unknowns** $x_1, x_2, \ldots, x_n$ is one in which we are to find the maximum or minimum value of a linear **objective function**

$$a_1 x_1 + a_2 x_2 + \cdots + a_n x_n,$$

where $a_1, a_2, \ldots, a_n$ are numbers, subject to a number of linear **constraints** of the form

$$b_1 x_1 + b_2 x_2 + \cdots + b_n x_n \leq c \quad \text{or} \quad b_1 x_1 + b_2 x_2 + \cdots + b_n x_n \geq c,$$

where $b_1, b_2, \ldots, b_n, c$ are numbers.

Standard Maximization Problem

A **standard maximization problem** is an LP problem in which we are required to *maximize* (not minimize) an objective function of the form

$$p = a_1 x_1 + a_2 x_2 + \cdots + a_n x_n$$

subject to the constraints

$$x_1 \geq 0, x_2 \geq 0, \ldots, x_n \geq 0$$

and further constraints of the form

$$b_1 x_1 + b_2 x_2 + \cdots + b_n x_n \leq c$$

with c *nonnegative*. It is important that the inequality here be $\leq$, *not* $=$ or $\geq$.

Note As in the chapter on linear equations, we will almost always use $x, y, z, \ldots$ for the unknowns. Subscripted variables $x_1, x_2, \ldots$ are very useful names when you start running out of letters of the alphabet, but we should not find ourselves in that predicament. ■

Quick Examples

1. Maximize $p = 2x - 3y + 3z$
   subject to $2x \qquad + z \leq 7$
   $-x + 3y - 6z \leq 6$
   $x \geq 0, y \geq 0, z \geq 0.$

   This is a standard maximization problem.

2. Maximize $p = 2x_1 + x_2 - x_3 + x_4$
   subject to $x_1 - 2x_2 \qquad + x_4 \leq 0$
   $3x_1 \qquad\qquad \leq 1$
   $\qquad x_2 + x_3 \qquad \leq 2$
   $x_1 \geq 0, x_2 \geq 0, x_3 \geq 0, x_4 \geq 0.$

   This is a standard maximization problem.

3. Maximize $p = 2x - 3y + 3z$
subject to $2x \quad\quad + z \geq 7$
$-x + 3y - 6z \leq 6$ This is *not* a standard maximization problem.
$x \geq 0, y \geq 0, z \geq 0.$

The inequality $2x + z \geq 7$ cannot be written in the required form. If we reverse the inequality by multiplying both sides by -1, we get $-2x - z \leq -7$, but a negative value on the right side is not allowed.

The idea behind the simplex method is this: In any linear programming problem, there is a feasible region. If there are only two unknowns, we can draw the region; if there are three unknowns, it is a solid region in space; and if there are four or more unknowns, it is an abstract higher-dimensional region. But it is a faceted region with corners (think of a diamond), and it is at one of these corners that we will find the optimal solution. Geometrically, what the simplex method does is to start at the corner where all the unknowns are 0 (possible because we are talking of standard maximization problems) and then walk around the region, from corner to adjacent corner, always increasing the value of the objective function, until the best corner is found. In practice, we will visit only a small number of the corners before finding the right one. Algebraically, as we are about to see, this walking around is accomplished by matrix manipulations of the same sort as those used in the chapter on systems of linear equations.

We describe the method while working through an example.

EXAMPLE 1 **Meet the Simplex Method**

Maximize $p = 3x + 2y + z$
subject to $2x + 2y + z \leq 10$
$x + 2y + 3z \leq 15$
$x \geq 0, \ y \geq 0, \ z \geq 0.$

Solution

Step 1 *Convert to a system of linear equations.* The inequalities $2x + 2y + z \leq 10$ and $x + 2y + 3z \leq 15$ are less convenient than equations. Look at the first inequality. It says that the left-hand side, $2x + 2y + z$, must have some positive number (or zero) *added to it* if it is to equal 10. Because we don't yet know what x, y, and z are, we are not yet sure what number to add to the left-hand side. So we invent a new unknown, $s \geq 0$, called a **slack variable**, to "take up the slack," so that

$$2x + 2y + z + s = 10.$$

Turning to the next inequality, $x + 2y + 3z \leq 15$, we now add a slack variable to its left-hand side, to get it up to the value of the right-hand side. We might have to add a different number than we did the last time, so we use a new slack variable, $t \geq 0$, and obtain

$$x + 2y + 3z + t = 15.$$ Use a different slack variable for each constraint.

Now we write the system of equations we have (including the one that defines the objective function) in standard form.

$$
\begin{aligned}
2x + 2y + \;z + s \qquad\qquad &= 10 \\
x + 2y + 3z \quad\; + t \quad\; &= 15 \\
-3x - 2y - \;z \qquad\quad + p &= 0
\end{aligned}
$$

Note three things: First, all the variables are neatly aligned in columns, as they were in Chapter 3. Second, in rewriting the objective function $p = 3x + 2y + z$, we have left the coefficient of p as $+1$ and brought the other variables over to the same side of the equation as p. This will be our standard procedure from now on. *Don't* write $3x + 2y + z - p = 0$ (even though it means the same thing) because the negative coefficients will be important in later steps. Third, the above system of equations has fewer equations than unknowns, and hence cannot have a unique solution.

Step 2 *Set up the initial tableau.* We represent our system of equations by the following table (which is simply the augmented matrix in disguise), called **the initial tableau**:

	x	y	z	s	t	p	
	2	2	1	1	0	0	10
	1	2	3	0	1	0	15
	−3	−2	−1	0	0	1	0

The labels along the top keep track of which columns belong to which variables.

Now notice a peculiar thing. If we rewrite the matrix using the variables s, t, and p first, we get the matrix

$$
\begin{array}{cccccc}
s & t & p & x & y & z \\
\left[\begin{array}{cccccc}
1 & 0 & 0 & 2 & 2 & 1 \\
0 & 1 & 0 & 1 & 2 & 3 \\
0 & 0 & 1 & -3 & -2 & -1
\end{array}\right.
& & & & &
\begin{array}{c}
10 \\ 15 \\ 0
\end{array}
\end{array}
\Big],
$$

Matrix with s, t, and p columns first

which is already in reduced form. We can therefore read off the general solution (see Section 3.2) to our system of equations as

$$
\begin{aligned}
s &= 10 - 2x - 2y - z \\
t &= 15 - \;x - 2y - 3z \\
p &= 0 + \;3x + 2y + z \\
&x, y, z \text{ arbitrary.}
\end{aligned}
$$

Thus, we get a whole family of solutions, one for each choice of x, y, and z. One possible choice is to set x, y, and z all equal to 0. This gives the particular solution

$$s = 10, t = 15, p = 0, x = 0, y = 0, z = 0. \qquad \text{Set } x = y = z = 0 \text{ above.}$$

This solution is called the **basic solution** associated with the tableau. The variables s and t are called the **active** variables, and x, y, and z are the **inactive** variables. (Other terms used are **basic** and **nonbasic** variables.)

We can obtain the basic solution directly from the tableau as follows.

- The active variables correspond to the cleared columns (columns with only one nonzero entry).

- The values of the active variables are calculated as shown below.
- All other variables are inactive, and set equal to zero.

	Inactive $x = 0$	Inactive $y = 0$	Inactive $z = 0$	Active $s = \frac{10}{1}$	Active $t = \frac{15}{1}$	Active $p = \frac{0}{1}$	
	x	y	z	s	t	p	
	2	2	1	1	0	0	**10**
	1	2	3	0	1	0	**15**
	−3	−2	−1	0	0	1	**0**

As an additional aid to recognizing which variables are active and which are inactive, we label each row with the name of the corresponding active variable. Thus, the complete initial tableau looks like this.

	x	y	z	s	t	p	
s	2	2	1	1	0	0	10
t	1	2	3	0	1	0	15
p	−3	−2	−1	0	0	1	0

This basic solution represents our starting position $x = y = z = 0$ in the feasible region in xyz space.

We now need to move to another corner point. To do so, we choose a pivot* in one of the first three columns of the tableau and clear its column. Then we will get a different basic solution, which corresponds to another corner point. Thus, in order to move from corner point to corner point, all we have to do is choose suitable pivots and clear columns in the usual manner.

The next two steps give the procedure for choosing the pivot.

Step 3 *Select the pivot column* (the column that contains the pivot we are seeking).

Selecting the Pivot Column

Choose the negative number with the largest magnitude on the left-hand side of the bottom row (that is, don't consider the last number in the bottom row). Its column is the pivot column. (If there are two or more candidates, choose any one.) If all the numbers on the left-hand side of the bottom row are zero or positive, then we are done, and the basic solution is the optimal solution.

Simple enough. The most negative number in the bottom row is −3, so we choose the x column as the pivot column:

	x	y	z	s	t	p	
s	**2**	2	1	1	0	0	10
t	**1**	2	3	0	1	0	15
p	**−3**	−2	−1	0	0	1	0

↑
Pivot column

* Also see Section 3.2 for a discussion of pivots and pivoting.

Q: *Why choose the pivot column this way?*

A: The variable labeling the pivot column is going to be increased from 0 to something positive. In the equation $p = 3x + 2y + z$, the fastest way to increase p is to increase x because p would increase by 3 units for every 1-unit increase in x.

(If we chose to increase y, then p would increase by only 2 units for every 1-unit increase in y, and if we increased z instead, p would grow even more slowly.) In short, choosing the pivot column this way makes it likely that we'll increase p as much as possible.

Step 4 *Select the pivot in the pivot column.*

Selecting the Pivot

1. The pivot must always be a positive number. (This rules out zeros and negative numbers, such as the -3 in the bottom row.)

2. For each positive entry b in the pivot column, compute the ratio a/b, where a is the number in the rightmost column in that row. We call this a **test ratio**.

3. Of these ratios, choose the smallest one. (If there are two or more candidates, choose any one.) The corresponding number b is the pivot.

In our example, the test ratio in the first row is $10/2 = 5$, and the test ratio in the second row is $15/1 = 15$. Here, 5 is the smallest, so the 2 in the upper left is our pivot.

	x	y	z	s	t	p		Test Ratios
s	$\boxed{2}$	2	1	1	0	0	10	$10/2 = 5$
t	1	2	3	0	1	0	15	$15/1 = 15$
p	-3	-2	-1	0	0	1	0	

Q: *Why select the pivot this way?*

A: The rule given above guarantees that, after pivoting, all variables will be nonnegative in the basic solution. In other words, it guarantees that we will remain in the feasible region. We will explain further after finishing this example.

Step 5 *Use the pivot to clear the column in the normal manner and then relabel the pivot row with the label from the pivot column.* It is important to follow the exact prescription described in Section 3.2 for formulating the row operations:

$$a R_c \pm b R_p.$$

↑   ↑

Row to change   Pivot row

a and b both positive

All entries in the last column should remain nonnegative after pivoting. Furthermore, because the x column (and no longer the s column) will be cleared, x will become an active variable. In other words, the s on the left of the pivot will be replaced by x. We call s the **departing**, or **exiting variable** and x the **entering variable** for this step.

Entering variable
↓

Departing variable →		x	y	z	s	t	p		
	s	$\boxed{2}$	2	1	1	0	0	10	
	t	1	2	3	0	1	0	15	$2R_2 - R_1$
	p	-3	-2	-1	0	0	1	0	$2R_3 + 3R_1$

This gives

	x	y	z	s	t	p	
x	2	2	1	1	0	0	10
t	0	2	5	−1	2	0	20
p	0	2	1	3	0	2	30

This is the second tableau.

Step 6 *Go to Step 3.* But wait! According to Step 3, we are finished because there are no negative numbers in the bottom row. Thus, we can read off the answer. Remember, though, that the solution for x, the first active variable, is not just $x = 10$, but is $x = 10/2 = 5$ because the pivot has not been reduced to a 1. Similarly, $t = 20/2 = 10$ and $p = 30/2 = 15$. All the other variables are zero because they are inactive. Thus, the solution is as follows: p has a maximum value of 15, and this occurs when $x = 5$, $y = 0$, and $z = 0$. (The slack variables then have the values $s = 0$ and $t = 10$.)

Q: *Why can we stop when there are no negative numbers in the bottom row? Why does this tableau give an optimal solution?*

A: The bottom row corresponds to the equation $2y + z + 3s + 2p = 30$, or

$$p = 15 - y - \frac{1}{2}z - \frac{3}{2}s.$$

Think of this as part of the general solution to our original system of equations, with y, z, and s as the parameters. Because these variables must be nonnegative, *the largest possible value of p in any feasible solution of the system comes when all three of the parameters are 0.* Thus, the current basic solution must be an optimal solution.*

✱ Calculators or spreadsheets could obviously be a big help in the calculations here, just as in Chapter 3. We'll say more about that after the next couple of examples.

We owe some further explanation for Step 4 of the simplex method. After Step 3, we knew that x would be the entering variable, and we needed to choose the departing variable. In the next basic solution, x was to have some positive value and we wanted this value to be as large as possible (to make p as large as possible) without making any other variables negative. Look again at the equations written in Step 2:

$$s = 10 - 2x - 2y - z$$
$$t = 15 - x - 2y - 3z.$$

We needed to make either s or t into an inactive variable and hence zero. Also, y and z were to remain inactive. If we had made s inactive, then we would have had $0 = 10 - 2x$, so $x = 10/2 = 5$. This would have made $t = 15 - 5 = 10$, which would be fine. On the other hand, if we had made t inactive, then we would have had $0 = 15 - x$, so $x = 15$, and this would have made $s = 10 - 2 \cdot 15 = -20$, which would *not* be fine, because slack variables must be nonnegative. In other words, we had a choice of making $x = 10/2 = 5$ or $x = 15/1 = 15$, but making x larger than 5 would have made another variable negative. We were thus compelled to choose the smaller ratio, 5, and make s the departing variable. Of course, we do not have to think it through this way every time. We just use the rule stated in Step 4. (For a graphical explanation, see Example 3.)

EXAMPLE 2 Simplex Method

Find the maximum value of $p = 12x + 15y + 5z$, subject to the constraints:

$$2x + 2y + z \le 8$$
$$x + 4y - 3z \le 12$$
$$x \ge 0, \ y \ge 0, \ z \ge 0.$$

Solution Following Step 1, we introduce slack variables and rewrite the constraints and objective function in standard form:

$$2x + 2y + z + s = 8$$
$$x + 4y - 3z + t = 12$$
$$-12x - 15y - 5z + p = 0.$$

We now follow with Step 2, setting up the initial tableau:

	x	y	z	s	t	p	
s	2	2	1	1	0	0	8
t	1	4	-3	0	1	0	12
p	-12	-15	-5	0	0	1	0

For Step 3, we select the column over the negative number with the largest magnitude in the bottom row, which is the y column. For Step 4, finding the pivot, we see that the test ratios are 8/2 and 12/4, the smallest being $12/4 = 3$. So we select the pivot in the t row and clear its column:

	x	y	z	s	t	p		
s	2	2	1	1	0	0	8	$2R_1 - R_2$
t	1	④	-3	0	1	0	12	
p	-12	-15	-5	0	0	1	0	$4R_3 + 15R_2$

The departing variable is t and the entering variable is y. This gives the second tableau.

	x	y	z	s	t	p	
s	3	0	5	2	-1	0	4
y	1	4	-3	0	1	0	12
p	-33	0	-65	0	15	4	180

We now go back to Step 3. Because we still have negative numbers in the bottom row, we choose the one with the largest magnitude (which is –65), and thus our pivot column is the z column. Because negative numbers can't be pivots, the only possible choice for the pivot is the 5. (We need not compute the test ratios because there would only be one from which to choose.) We now clear this column, remembering to take care of the departing and entering variables.

	x	y	z	s	t	p		
s	3	0	⑤	2	-1	0	4	
y	1	4	-3	0	1	0	12	$5R_2 + 3R_1$
p	-33	0	-65	0	15	4	180	$R_3 + 13R_1$

This gives

	x	y	z	s	t	p	
z	3	0	5	2	−1	0	4
y	14	20	0	6	2	0	72
p	6	0	0	26	2	4	232

Notice how the value of p keeps climbing: It started at 0 in the first tableau, went up to $180/4 = 45$ in the second, and is currently at $232/4 = 58$. Because there are no more negative numbers in the bottom row, we are done and can write down the solution: p has a maximum value of $232/4 = 58$, and this occurs when

$$x = 0$$

$$y = \frac{72}{20} = \frac{18}{5} \quad \text{and}$$

$$z = \frac{4}{5}.$$

The slack variables are both zero.

As a partial check on our answer, we can substitute these values into the objective function and the constraints:

$$58 = 12(0) + 15(18/5) + 5(4/5) \qquad ✔$$

$$2(0) + 2(18/5) + (4/5) = 8 \le 8 \qquad ✔$$

$$0 + 4(18/5) - 3(4/5) = 12 \le 12. \qquad ✔$$

We say that this is only a partial check, because it shows only that our solution is feasible and that we have correctly calculated p. It does not show that we have the optimal solution. This check will *usually* catch any arithmetic mistakes we make, but it is not foolproof.

APPLICATIONS

In the next example (further exploits of Acme Baby Foods—compare Example 2 in Section 2) we show how the simplex method relates to the graphical method.

EXAMPLE 3   Resource Allocation

Acme Baby Foods makes two puddings, vanilla and chocolate. Each serving of vanilla pudding requires 2 teaspoons of sugar and 25 fluid ounces of water, and each serving of chocolate pudding requires 3 teaspoons of sugar and 15 fluid ounces of water. Acme has available each day 3,600 teaspoons of sugar and 22,500 fluid ounces of water. Acme makes no more than 600 servings of vanilla pudding because that is all that it can sell each day. If Acme makes a profit of 10¢ on each serving of vanilla pudding and 7¢ on each serving of chocolate, how many servings of each should it make to maximize its profit?

Solution   We first identify the unknowns. Let

     $x = $ the number of servings of vanilla pudding

     $y = $ the number of servings of chocolate pudding.

The objective function is the profit $p = 10x + 7y$, which we need to maximize. For the constraints, we start with the fact that Acme will make no more than 600 servings of vanilla: $x \leq 600$. We can put the remaining data in a table as follows:

	Vanilla	*Chocolate*	*Total Available*
Sugar (teaspoons)	2	3	3,600
Water (ounces)	25	15	22,500

Because Acme can use no more sugar and water than is available, we get the two constraints:

$$2x + 3y \leq 3,600$$
$$25x + 15y \leq 22,500. \qquad \text{Note that all the terms are divisible by 5.}$$

Thus our linear programming problem is this:

Maximize $p = 10x + 7y$
subject to $x \leq 600$
$2x + 3y \leq 3,600$
$5x + 3y \leq 4,500 \qquad \text{We divided } 25x + 15y \leq 22,500 \text{ by 5.}$
$x \geq 0, \ y \geq 0.$

Next, we introduce the slack variables and set up the initial tableau.

$$x \qquad + s \qquad\qquad\qquad = 600$$
$$2x + 3y \qquad + t \qquad\qquad = 3,600$$
$$5x + 3y \qquad\qquad + u \qquad = 4,500$$
$$-10x - 7y \qquad\qquad\qquad + p = 0$$

Note that we have had to introduce a third slack variable, u. There need to be as many slack variables as there are constraints (other than those of the $x \geq 0$ variety).

Q: What do the slack variables say about Acme puddings?

A: The first slack variable, s, represents the number you must add to the number of servings of vanilla pudding actually made to obtain the maximum of 600 servings. The second slack variable, t, represents the amount of sugar that is left over once the puddings are made, and u represents the amount of water left over.

We now use the simplex method to solve the problem:

	x	y	s	t	u	p		
s	$\boxed{1}$	0	1	0	0	0	600	
t	2	3	0	1	0	0	3,600	$R_2 - 2R_1$
u	5	3	0	0	1	0	4,500	$R_3 - 5R_1$
p	-10	-7	0	0	0	1	0	$R_4 + 10R_1$

	x	y	s	t	u	p		
x	1	0	1	0	0	0	600	
t	0	3	-2	1	0	0	2,400	$R_2 - R_3$
u	0	$\boxed{3}$	-5	0	1	0	1,500	
p	0	-7	10	0	0	1	6,000	$3R_4 + 7R_3$

using Technology

See the Technology Guides at the end of the chapter for a discussion of using a TI-83/84 Plus to help with the simplex method in Example 3. Or, go to the Website at www.WanerMath.com and follow the path

→ On Line Utilities

→ Pivot and Gauss-Jordan Tool

to find a utility that allows you to avoid doing the calculations in each pivot step: Just highlight the entry you wish to use as a pivot, and press "Pivot on Selection."

	x	y	s	t	u	p		
x	1	0	1	0	0	0	600	$3R_1 - R_2$
t	0	0	3	1	-1	0	900	
y	0	3	-5	0	1	0	1,500	$3R_3 + 5R_2$
p	0	0	-5	0	7	3	28,500	$3R_4 + 5R_2$

	x	y	s	t	u	p	
x	3	0	0	-1	1	0	900
s	0	0	3	1	-1	0	900
y	0	9	0	5	-2	0	9,000
p	0	0	0	5	16	9	90,000

Thus, the solution is as follows: The maximum value of p is $90,000/9 = 10,000¢ = \$100$, which occurs when $x = 900/3 = 300$, and $y = 9,000/9 = 1,000$. (The slack variables are $s = 900/3 = 300$ and $t = u = 0$.)

Figure 22

➡ **Before we go on...** Because the problem in Example 3 had only two variables, we could have solved it graphically. It is interesting to think about the relationship between the two methods. Figure 22 shows the feasible region. Each tableau in the simplex method corresponds to a corner of the feasible region, given by the corresponding basic solution. In this example, the sequence of basic solutions is

$$(x, y) = (0, 0), (600, 0), (600, 500), (300, 1,000).$$

This is the sequence of corners shown in Figure 23. In general, we can think of the simplex method as walking from corner to corner of the feasible region, until it locates the optimal solution. In problems with many variables and many constraints, the simplex method usually visits only a small fraction of the total number of corners.

We can also explain again, in a different way, the reason we use the test ratios when choosing the pivot. For example, when choosing the first pivot we had to choose among the test ratios 600, 1,800, and 900 (look at the first tableau). In Figure 22, you can see that those are the three x-intercepts of the lines that bound the feasible region. If we had chosen 1,800 or 900, we would have jumped along the x-axis to a point outside of the feasible region, which we do not want to do. In general, the test ratios measure the distance from the current corner to the constraint lines, and we must choose the smallest such distance to avoid crossing any of them into the unfeasible region.

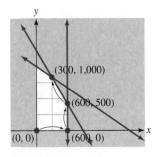

Figure 23

It is also interesting in an application like this to think about the values of the slack variables. We said above that s is the difference between the maximum 600 servings of vanilla that might be made and the number that is actually made. In the optimal solution, $s = 300$, which says that 300 fewer servings of vanilla were made than the maximum possible. Similarly, t was the amount of sugar left over. In the optimal solution, $t = 0$, which tells us that all of the available sugar is used. Finally, $u = 0$, so all of the available water is used as well. ∎

using Technology

Website
www.WanerMath.com
On the
→ On Line Utilities
page you will find utilities that automate the simplex method to varying
extents:

• Pivot and Gauss-Jordan Tool
(Pivots and does row operations)
• Simplex Method Tool (Solves
entire LP problems; shows all
tableaux)

Summary: The Simplex Method for Standard Maximization Problems

To solve a standard maximization problem using the simplex method, we take the following steps:

1. Convert to a system of equations by introducing **slack variables** to turn the constraints into equations and by rewriting the objective function in standard form.

2. Write down the initial **tableau**.

3. Select the pivot column: Choose the negative number with the largest magnitude in the left-hand side of the bottom row. Its column is the pivot column. (If there are two or more candidates, choose any one.) If all the numbers in the left-hand side of the bottom row are zero or positive, then we are finished, and the basic solution maximizes the objective function. (See below for the basic solution.)

4. Select the pivot in the pivot column: The pivot must always be a positive number. For each positive entry b in the pivot column, compute the ratio a/b, where a is the number in the last column in that row. Of these **test ratios**, choose the smallest one. (If there are two or more candidates, choose any one.) The corresponding number b is the pivot.

5. Use the pivot to clear the column in the normal manner (taking care to follow the exact prescription for formulating the row operations described in Chapter 3) and then relabel the pivot row with the label from the pivot column. The variable originally labeling the pivot row is the **departing**, or **exiting**, **variable**, and the variable labeling the column is the **entering variable**.

6. Go to Step 3.

To get the **basic solution** corresponding to any tableau in the simplex method, set to zero all variables that do not appear as row labels. The value of a variable that does appear as a row label (an **active variable**) is the number in the rightmost column in that row divided by the number in that row in the column labeled by the same variable.

FAQs

Troubleshooting the Simplex Method

Q: *What if there is no candidate for the pivot in the pivot column? For example, what do we do with a tableau like the following?*

	x	y	z	s	t	p	
z	0	0	5	2	0	0	4
y	−8	20	0	6	5	0	72
p	−20	0	0	26	15	4	232

A: Here, the pivot column is the *x* column, but there is no suitable entry for a pivot (because zeros and negative numbers can't be pivots). This happens when the feasible region is unbounded and there is also no optimal solution. In other words, *p* can be made as large as we like without violating the constraints.

Q: *What should we do if there is a negative number in the rightmost column?*

A: A negative number will not appear above the bottom row in the rightmost column if we follow the procedure correctly. (The bottom right entry is allowed to be negative if the objective takes on negative values as in a negative profit, or loss.) Following are the most likely errors leading to this situation:

- The pivot was chosen incorrectly. (Don't forget to choose the *smallest* test ratio.) When this mistake is made, one or more of the variables will be negative in the corresponding basic solution.
- The row operation instruction was written backward or performed backward (for example, instead of $R_2 - R_1$, it was $R_1 - R_2$). This mistake can be corrected by multiplying the row by -1.
- An arithmetic error occurred. (We all make those annoying errors from time to time.)

Q: *What about zeros in the rightmost column?*

A: Zeros are permissible in the rightmost column. For example, the constraint $x - y \leq 0$ will lead to a zero in the rightmost column.[*]

Q: *What happens if we choose a pivot column other than the one with the most negative number in the bottom row?*

A: There is no harm in doing this as long as we choose the pivot in that column using the smallest test ratio. All it might do is slow the whole calculation by adding extra steps.

✱ When there are zeros in the rightmost column there is a potential problem of *cycling*, where a sequence of pivots brings you back to a tableau you already considered, with no change in the objective function. You can usually break out of a cycle by choosing a different pivot. This problem should not arise in the exercises.

One last suggestion: If it is possible to do a simplification step (dividing a row by a positive number) *at any stage*, we should do so. As we saw in Chapter 3, this can help prevent the numbers from getting out of hand.

5.3 EXERCISES

▼ more advanced　　◆ challenging
[T] indicates exercises that should be solved using technology

1. Maximize $p = 2x + y$
subject to $x + 2y \leq 6$
$-x + y \leq 4$
$x + y \leq 4$
$x \geq 0, y \geq 0.$

HINT [See Examples 1 and 2.]

2. Maximize $p = x$
subject to $x - y \leq 4$
$-x + 3y \leq 4$
$x \geq 0, y \geq 0.$

HINT [See Examples 1 and 2.]

3. Maximize $p = x - y$
subject to $5x - 5y \leq 20$
$2x - 10y \leq 40$
$x \geq 0, y \geq 0.$

4. Maximize $p = 2x + 3y$
subject to $3x + 8y \leq 24$
$6x + 4y \leq 30$
$x \geq 0, y \geq 0.$

5. Maximize $p = 5x - 4y + 3z$
subject to $5x + 5z \leq 100$
$5y - 5z \leq 50$
$5x - 5y \leq 50$
$x \geq 0, y \geq 0, z \geq 0.$

6. Maximize $p = 6x + y + 3z$
subject to $3x + y \quad\quad \le 15$
$2x + 2y + 2z \le 20$
$x \ge 0, y \ge 0, z \ge 0.$

7. Maximize $p = 7x + 5y + 6z$
subject to $x + y - z \le 3$
$x + 2y + z \le 8$
$x + y \quad\quad \le 5$
$x \ge 0, y \ge 0, z \ge 0.$

8. Maximize $p = 3x + 4y + 2z$
subject to $3x + y + z \le 5$
$x + 2y + z \le 5$
$x + y + z \le 4$
$x \ge 0, y \ge 0, z \ge 0.$

9. Maximize $z = 3x_1 + 7x_2 + 8x_3$
subject to $5x_1 - x_2 + x_3 \le 1{,}500$
$2x_1 + 2x_2 + x_3 \le 2{,}500$
$4x_1 + 2x_2 + x_3 \le 2{,}000$
$x_1 \ge 0, x_2 \ge 0, x_3 \ge 0.$

10. Maximize $z = 3x_1 + 4x_2 + 6x_3$
subject to $5x_1 - x_2 + x_3 \le 1{,}500$
$2x_1 + 2x_2 + x_3 \le 2{,}500$
$4x_1 + 2x_2 + x_3 \le 2{,}000$
$x_1 \ge 0, x_2 \ge 0, x_3 \ge 0.$

11. Maximize $p = x + y + z + w$
subject to $x + y + z \le 3$
$y + z + w \le 4$
$x + z + w \le 5$
$x + y + w \le 6$
$x \ge 0, y \ge 0, z \ge 0, w \ge 0.$

12. Maximize $p = x - y + z + w$
subject to $x + y + z \le 3$
$y + z + w \le 3$
$x + z + w \le 4$
$x + y + w \le 4$
$x \ge 0, y \ge 0, z \ge 0, w \ge 0.$

13. ▼ Maximize $p = x + y + z + w + v$
subject to $x + y \le 1$
$y + z \le 2$
$z + w \le 3$
$w + v \le 4$
$x \ge 0, y \ge 0, z \ge 0, w \ge 0, v \ge 0.$

14. ▼ Maximize $p = x + 2y + z + 2w + v$
subject to $x + y \le 1$
$y + z \le 2$
$z + w \le 3$
$w + v \le 4$
$x \ge 0, y \ge 0, z \ge 0, w \ge 0, v \ge 0.$

🔲 *In Exercises 15–20 we suggest the use of technology. Round all answers to two decimal places.*

15. Maximize $p = 2.5x + 4.2y + 2z$
subject to $0.1x + y - 2.2z \le 4.5$
$2.1x + y + z \le 8$
$x + 2.2y \quad\quad \le 5$
$x \ge 0, y \ge 0, z \ge 0.$

16. Maximize $p = 2.1x + 4.1y + 2z$
subject to $3.1x + 1.2y + z \le 5.5$
$x + 2.3y + z \le 5.5$
$2.1x + y + 2.3z \le 5.2$
$x \ge 0, y \ge 0, z \ge 0.$

17. Maximize $p = x + 2y + 3z + w$
subject to $x + 2y + 3z \quad\quad \le 3$
$y + z + 2.2w \le 4$
$x + z + 2.2w \le 5$
$x + y + 2.2w \le 6$
$x \ge 0, y \ge 0, z \ge 0, w \ge 0.$

18. Maximize $p = 1.1x - 2.1y + z + w$
subject to $x + 1.3y + z \quad\quad \le 3$
$1.3y + z + w \le 3$
$x + z + w \le 4.1$
$x + 1.3y + w \le 4.1$
$x \ge 0, y \ge 0, z \ge 0, w \ge 0.$

19. Maximize $p = x - y + z - w + v$
subject to $x + y \le 1.1$
$y + z \le 2.2$
$z + w \le 3.3$
$w + v \le 4.4$
$x \ge 0, y \ge 0, z \ge 0, w \ge 0, v \ge 0.$

20. Maximize $p = x - 2y + z - 2w + v$
subject to $x + y \le 1.1$
$y + z \le 2.2$
$z + w \le 3.3$
$w + v \le 4.4$
$x \ge 0, y \ge 0, z \ge 0, w \ge 0, v \ge 0.$

APPLICATIONS

21. *Purchasing* You are in charge of purchases at the student-run used-book supply program at your college, and you must decide how many introductory calculus, history, and marketing texts should be purchased from students for resale. Due to budget limitations, you cannot purchase more than 650 of these textbooks each semester. There are also shelf-space limitations: Calculus texts occupy 2 units of shelf space each, history books 1 unit each, and marketing texts 3 units each, and you can spare at most 1,000 units of shelf space for the texts. If the used-book program makes a profit of $10 on each calculus text, $4 on each history text, and $8 on each marketing text, how many of each type of text should you purchase to maximize profit? What is the maximum profit the program can make in a semester? **HINT** [See Example 3.]

22. **Sales** The Marketing Club at your college has decided to raise funds by selling three types of T-shirts: one with a single-color "ordinary" design, one with a two-color "fancy" design, and one with a three-color "very fancy" design. The club feels that it can sell up to 300 T-shirts. "Ordinary" T-shirts will cost the club $6 each, "fancy" T-shirts $8 each, and "very fancy" T-shirts $10 each, and the club has a total purchasing budget of $3,000. It will sell "ordinary" T-shirts at a profit of $4 each, "fancy" T-shirts at a profit of $5 each, and "very fancy" T-shirts at a profit of $4 each. How many of each kind of T-shirt should the club order to maximize profit? What is the maximum profit the club can make? **HINT** [See Example 3.]

23. **Resource Allocation** *Arctic Juice Company* makes three juice blends: PineOrange, using 2 portions of pineapple juice and 2 portions of orange juice per gallon; PineKiwi, using 3 portions of pineapple juice and 1 portion of kiwi juice per gallon; and OrangeKiwi, using 3 portions of orange juice and 1 portion of kiwi juice per gallon. Each day the company has 800 portions of pineapple juice, 650 portions of orange juice, and 350 portions of kiwi juice available. Its profit on PineOrange is $1 per gallon, its profit on PineKiwi is $2 per gallon, and its profit on OrangeKiwi is $1 per gallon. How many gallons of each blend should it make each day to maximize profit? What is the largest possible profit the company can make?

24. **Purchasing** *Trans Global Tractor Trailers* has decided to spend up to $1,500,000 on a fleet of new trucks, and it is considering three models: the Gigahaul, which has a capacity of 6,000 cubic feet and is priced at $60,000; the Megahaul, with a capacity of 5,000 cubic feet, priced at $50,000; and the Picohaul, with a capacity of 2,000 cubic feet, priced at $40,000. The anticipated annual revenues are $500,000 for each new truck purchased (regardless of size). Trans Global would like a total capacity of up to 130,000 cubic feet, and feels that it cannot provide drivers and maintenance for more than 30 trucks. How many of each should it purchase to maximize annual revenue? What is the largest possible revenue it can make?

25. **Resource Allocation** The Enormous State University History Department offers three courses, Ancient, Medieval, and Modern History, and the department chairperson is trying to decide how many sections of each to offer this semester. They may offer up to 45 sections total, up to 5,000 students would like to take a course, and there are 60 professors to teach them (no student will take more than one history course, and no professor will teach more than one section). Sections of Ancient History have 100 students each, sections of Medieval History have 50 students each, and sections of Modern History have 200 students each. Modern History sections are taught by a team of two professors, while Ancient and Medieval History need only one professor per section. Ancient History nets the university $10,000 per section, Medieval nets $20,000, and Modern History nets $30,000 per section. How many sections of each course should the department offer in order to generate the largest profit? What is the largest profit possible? Will there be any unused time slots, any students who did not get into classes, or any professors without anything to teach?

26. **Resource Allocation** You manage an ice cream factory that makes three flavors: Creamy Vanilla, Continental Mocha, and Succulent Strawberry. Into each batch of Creamy Vanilla go 2 eggs, 1 cup of milk, and 2 cups of cream. Into each batch of Continental Mocha go 1 egg, 1 cup of milk, and 2 cups of cream. Into each batch of Succulent Strawberry go 1 egg, 2 cups of milk, and 2 cups of cream. You have in stock 200 eggs, 120 cups of milk, and 200 cups of cream. You make a profit of $3 on each batch of Creamy Vanilla, $2 on each batch of Continental Mocha, and $4 on each batch of Succulent Strawberry.

   a. How many batches of each flavor should you make to maximize your profit?

   b. In your answer to part (a), have you used all the ingredients?

   c. Due to the poor strawberry harvest this year, you cannot make more than 10 batches of Succulent Strawberry. Does this affect your maximum profit?

27. **Agriculture** Your small farm encompasses 100 acres, and you are planning to grow tomatoes, lettuce, and carrots in the coming planting season. Fertilizer costs per acre are: $5 for tomatoes, $4 for lettuce, and $2 for carrots. Based on past experience, you estimate that each acre of tomatoes will require an average of 4 hours of labor per week, while tending to lettuce and carrots will each require an average of 2 hours per week. You estimate a profit of $2,000 for each acre of tomatoes, $1,500 for each acre of lettuce, and $500 for each acre of carrots. You can afford to spend no more than $400 on fertilizer, and your farm laborers can supply up to 500 hours per week. How many acres of each crop should you plant to maximize total profits? In this event, will you be using all 100 acres of your farm?

28. **Agriculture** Your farm encompasses 500 acres, and you are planning to grow soybeans, corn, and wheat in the coming planting season. Fertilizer costs per acre are: $5 for soybeans, $2 for corn, and $1 for wheat. You estimate that each acre of soybeans will require an average of 5 hours of labor per week, while tending to corn and wheat will each require an average of 2 hours per week. Based on past yields and current market prices, you estimate a profit of $3,000 for each acre of soybeans, $2,000 for each acre of corn, and $1,000 for each acre of wheat. You can afford to spend no more than $3,000 on fertilizer, and your farm laborers can supply 3,000 hours per week. How many acres of each crop should you plant to maximize total profits? In this event, will you be using all the available labor?

29. **Resource Allocation** (Compare Exercise 36 in Chapter 3 Review) The Enormous State University Choral Society is planning its annual Song Festival, when it will serve three kinds of delicacies: granola treats, nutty granola treats, and nuttiest granola treats. The following table shows some of the ingredients required (in ounces) for a single serving of each delicacy, as well as the total amount of each ingredient available.

	Granola	Nutty Granola	Nuttiest Granola	Total Available
Toasted Oats	1	1	5	1,500
Almonds	4	8	8	10,000
Raisins	2	4	8	4,000

The society makes a profit of $6 on each serving of granola, $8 on each serving of nutty granola, and $3 on each serving of nuttiest granola. Assuming that the Choral Society can sell all that it makes, how many servings of each will maximize profits? How much of each ingredient will be left over?

30. *Resource Allocation* Repeat the preceding exercise, but this time assume that the Choral Society makes a $3 profit on each of its delicacies.

31. *Recycling* Safety-Kleen operates the world's largest oil re-refinery at Elgin, Illinois. You have been hired by the company to determine how to allocate its intake of up to 50 million gallons of used oil to its three refinery processes: A, B, and C. You are told that electricity costs for process A amount to $150,000 per million gallons treated, while for processes B and C, the costs are, respectively, $100,000 and $50,000 per million gallons treated. Process A can recover 60 percent of the used oil, process B can recover 55 percent, and process C can recover only 50 percent. Assuming a revenue of $4 million per million gallons of recovered oil and an annual electrical budget of $3 million, how much used oil would you allocate to each process in order to maximize total revenues?[23]

32. *Recycling* Repeat the preceding exercise, but this time assume that process C can handle only up to 20 million gallons per year.

Creatine Supplements *Exercises 33 and 34 are based on the following data on four popular bodybuilding supplements. (Figures shown correspond to a single serving.)*[24]

	Creatine (g)	Carbohydrates (g)	Taurine (g)	Alpha Lipoic Acid (mg)
Cell-Tech® (MuscleTech)	10	75	2	200
RiboForce HP® (EAS)	5	15	1	0
Creatine Transport® (Kaizen)	5	35	1	100
Pre-Load Creatine® (Optimum)	6	35	1	25

33. You are thinking of combining the first three supplements in the previous table to obtain a 10-day supply that gives you the maximum possible amount of creatine, but no more than 1,000 milligrams of alpha lipoic acid and 225 grams of carbohydrates. How many servings of each supplement should you combine to meet your specifications, and how much creatine will you get?

34. Repeat Exercise 33, but use the last three supplements in the table instead.

Investing *Exercises 35 and 36 are based on the following data on three stocks.*[25]

	Price	Dividend Yield	52-Week Price Change ($)
FDX (FedEx)	$90	1%	−2
WU (Western Union)	$20	2%	1
DO (Diamond Offshore Drilling)	$70	0%	6

35. ▼ You are planning to invest up to $10,000 in FDX, WU, and DO shares. You desire to maximize the 52-week gain but, for tax reasons, want to earn no more than $200 in dividends. Your broker suggests that because DO stock pays no dividends, you should invest only in DO. Is she right?

36. ▼ Repeat Exercise 35 under the assumption that the 52-week change in DO stock is $3, but its price is unchanged.

37. 🔲 ▼ ***Loan Planning***[26] Enormous State University's employee credit union has $5 million available for loans in the coming year. As VP in charge of finances, you must decide how much capital to allocate to each of four different kinds of loans, as shown in the following table.

Type of Loan	*Annual Rate of Return*
Automobile	8%
Furniture	10%
Signature	12%
Other secured	10%

State laws and credit union policies impose the following restrictions:

- Signature loans may not exceed 10 percent of the total investment of funds.

---

[23]These figures are realistic: Safety-Kleen's actual 1993 capacity was 50 million gallons, its recycled oil sold for approximately $4 per gallon, its recycling process could recover approximately 55 percent of the used oil, and its electrical bill was $3 million. Source: Oil Recycler Greases Rusty City's Economy, *Chicago Tribune*, May 30, 1993, Section 7, p.1.

[24]Source: Nutritional information supplied by the manufacturers (www.netrition.com).

[25]Approximate 150-day average price as of August 31, 2011. 52-week price changes are approximate. Source: http://finance.google.com

[26]Adapted from an exercise in *An Introduction to Management Science* (6th. ed.) by D. R. Anderson, D. J. Sweeney, and T. A. Williams (West, 1991).

- Furniture loans plus other secured loans may not exceed automobile loans.
- Other secured loans may not exceed 200 percent of automobile loans.

How much should you allocate to each type of loan to maximize the annual return?

38. ▯ ▼ *Investments* You have $100,000 that you are considering investing in three dividend-yielding bank stocks: **Banco Santander Brasil**, **Bank of Hawaii**, and **Banco Santander Chile**. You have the following data:[27]

Stock	Yield
BSBR (Banco Santander Brasil)	7%
BOH (Bank of Hawaii)	5%
SAN (Banco Santander Chile)	4%

Your broker has made the following suggestions:

- At least 50 percent of your total investment should be in SAN.
- No more than 10 percent of your total investment should be in BSBR.

How much should you invest in each stock to maximize your anticipated dividends while following your broker's advice?

39. ▼ *Portfolio Management* If x dollars are invested in a company that controls, say, 30 percent of the market with five brand names, then $0.30x$ is a measure of market exposure and $5x$ is a measure of brand-name exposure. Now suppose you are a broker at a large securities firm, and one of your clients would like to invest up to $100,000 in recording industry stocks. You decide to recommend a combination of stocks in four of the world's largest recording companies: **Warner Music**, **Universal Music**, **Sony**, and **EMI**. (See the table.)[28]

	Warner Music	Universal Music	Sony	EMI
Market share	12%	20%	20%	15%
Number of labels (brands)	8	20	10	15

You would like your client's brand-name exposure to be as large as possible but his total market exposure to be $15,000 or less. (This would reflect an average of 15 percent.) Furthermore, you would like at least 20 percent of the investment to be in **Universal** because you feel that its control of the DGG and Phillips labels is advantageous for its classical music operations. How much should you advise your client to invest in each company?

40. ▼ *Portfolio Management* Referring to Exercise 39, suppose instead that you wanted your client to maximize his total market exposure but limit his brand-name exposure to 1.5 million or less (representing an average of 15 labels or fewer per company), and still invest at least 20 percent of the total in **Universal**. How much should you advise your client to invest in each company?

41. ▯ ▼ *Transportation Scheduling* (This exercise is almost identical to Exercise 26 in Section 3.3 but is more realistic; one cannot always expect to fill all orders exactly and keep all plants operating at 100 percent capacity.) The *Tubular Ride Boogie Board Company* has manufacturing plants in Tucson, Arizona, and Toronto, Ontario. You have been given the job of coordinating distribution of the latest model, the Gladiator, to their outlets in Honolulu and Venice Beach. The Tucson plant, when operating at full capacity, can manufacture 620 Gladiator boards per week, while the Toronto plant, beset by labor disputes, can produce only 410 boards per week. The outlet in Honolulu orders 500 Gladiator boards per week, while Venice Beach orders 530 boards per week. Transportation costs are as follows: Tucson to Honolulu: $10 per board; Tucson to Venice Beach: $5 per board; Toronto to Honolulu: $20 per board; Toronto to Venice Beach: $10 per board. Your manager has informed you that the company's total transportation budget is $6,550. You realize that it may not be possible to fill all the orders, but you would like the total number of boogie boards shipped to be as large as possible. Given this, how many Gladiator boards should you order shipped from each manufacturing plant to each distribution outlet?

42. ▯ ▼ *Transportation Scheduling* Repeat the preceding exercise, but use a transportation budget of $5,050.

43. ▯ ▼ *Transportation Scheduling* Your publishing company is about to start a promotional blitz for its new book, *Advanced Quantum Mechanics for the Liberal Arts*. You have 20 salespeople stationed in Chicago and 10 in Denver. You would like to fly at most 10 into Los Angeles and at most 15 into New York. A round-trip plane flight from Chicago to LA costs $195;[29] from Chicago to New York costs $182; from Denver to LA costs $395; and from Denver to New York costs $166. You want to spend at most $4,520 on plane flights. How many salespeople should you fly from each of Chicago and Denver to each of LA and New York to have the most salespeople on the road?

44. ▯ ▼ *Transportation Scheduling* Repeat the preceding exercise, but this time, spend at most $5,770.

COMMUNICATION AND REASONING EXERCISES

45. Can the following linear programming problem be stated as a standard maximization problem? If so, do it; if not, explain why.

$$\text{Maximize} \quad p = 3x - 2y$$
$$\text{subject to} \quad x - y + z \geq 0$$
$$x - y - z \leq 6$$
$$x \geq 0, y \geq 0, z \geq 0.$$

---

[27]Yields are as of September 2011. Source: www.google.com/finance

[28]The number of labels includes only major labels. Market shares are approximate and represent the period 2000–2002. Sources: various, including www.emigroup.com, http://finance.vivendi.com/discover/financial, and http://business2.com, March 2002.

[29]Prices from Travelocity, at www.travelocity.com, for the week of June 3, 2002, as of May 5, 2002.

46. Can the following linear programming problem be stated as a standard maximization problem? If so, do it; if not, explain why.

Maximize $p = -3x - 2y$

subject to $x - y + z \geq 0$

$x - y - z \geq -6$

$x \geq 0, y \geq 0, z \geq 0.$

47. Why is the simplex method useful? (After all, we do have the graphical method for solving LP problems.)

48. Are there any types of linear programming problems that cannot be solved with the methods of this section but that can be solved using the methods of the preceding section? Explain.

49. ▼ Your friend Janet is going around telling everyone that if there are only two constraints in a linear programming problem, then, in any optimal basic solution, at most two unknowns (other than the objective) will be nonzero. Is she correct? Explain.

50. ▼ Your other friend Jason is going around telling everyone that if there is only one constraint in a standard linear programming problem, then you will have to pivot at most once to obtain an optimal solution. Is he correct? Explain.

51. ▼ What is a "basic solution"? How might one find a basic solution of a given system of linear equations?

52. ▼ In a typical simplex method tableau, there are more unknowns than equations, and we know from the chapter on systems of linear equations that this typically implies the existence of infinitely many solutions. How are the following types of solutions interpreted in the simplex method?

a. Solutions in which all the variables are positive.

b. Solutions in which some variables are negative.

c. Solutions in which the inactive variables are zero.

53. ◆ Can the value of the objective function decrease in passing from one tableau to the next? Explain.

54. ◆ Can the value of the objective function remain unchanged in passing from one tableau to the next? Explain.

5.4 The Simplex Method: Solving General Linear Programming Problems

As we saw in Section 5.2, not all LP problems are standard maximization problems. We might have constraints like $2x + 3y \geq 4$ or perhaps $2x + 3y = 4$. Or, we might have to minimize, rather than maximize, the objective function. General problems like this are almost as easy to deal with as the standard kind: There is a modification of the simplex method that works very nicely. The best way to illustrate it is by means of examples. First, we discuss nonstandard maximization problems.

Nonstandard Maximization Problems

EXAMPLE 1 Maximizing with Mixed Constraints

Maximize $p = 4x + 12y + 6z$

subject to $x + y + z \leq 100$

$4x + 10y + 7z \leq 480$

$x + y + z \geq 60$

$x \geq 0, y \geq 0, z \geq 0.$

Solution We begin by turning the first two inequalities into equations as usual because they have the standard form. We get

$x + y + z + s = 100$

$4x + 10y + 7z + t = 480.$

We are tempted to use a slack variable for the third inequality, $x + y + z \geq 60$, but *adding* something positive to the left-hand side will not make it equal to the right: It will get even bigger. To make it equal to 60, we must *subtract* some nonnegative number. We will call this number u (because we have already used s and t) and refer to u as a **surplus variable** rather than a slack variable. Thus, we write

$$x + y + z - u = 60.$$

Continuing with the setup, we have

$$
\begin{aligned}
x + y + z + s &= 100 \\
4x + 10y + 7z + t &= 480 \\
x + y + z - u &= 60 \\
-4x - 12y - 6z + p &= 0.
\end{aligned}
$$

This leads to the initial tableau:

	x	y	z	s	t	u	p	
s	1	1	1	1	0	0	0	100
t	4	10	7	0	1	0	0	480
*u	1	1	1	0	0	-1	0	60
p	-4	-12	-6	0	0	0	1	0

We put a star next to the third row because the basic solution corresponding to this tableau is

$$x = y = z = 0, \ s = 100, \ t = 480, \ u = 60/(-1) = -60.$$

Several things are wrong here. First, the values $x = y = z = 0$ do not satisfy the third inequality $x + y + z \geq 60$. Thus, this basic solution is *not feasible*. Second—and this is really the same problem—the surplus variable u is negative, whereas we said that it should be nonnegative. The star next to the row labeled u alerts us to the fact that the present basic solution is not feasible and that the problem is located in the starred row, where the active variable u is negative.

Whenever an active variable is negative, we star the corresponding row.

In setting up the initial tableau, we star those rows coming from $\geq$ inequalities.

The simplex method as described in the preceding section assumed that we began in the feasible region, but now we do not. Our first task is to get ourselves into the feasible region. In practice, we can think of this as getting rid of the stars on the rows. Once we get into the feasible region, we go back to the method of the preceding section.

There are several ways to get into the feasible region. The method we have chosen is one of the simplest to state and carry out. (We will see why this method works at the end of the example.)

The Simplex Method for General Linear Programming Problems

Star all rows that give a negative value for the associated active variable (except for the objective variable, which is allowed to be negative). If there are starred rows, you will need to begin with Phase I.

Phase I: Getting into the Feasible Region (Getting Rid of the Stars)
In the first starred row, find the largest positive number. Use test ratios as in Section 5.3 to find the pivot in that column (exclude the bottom row), and then pivot on that entry. (If the lowest ratio occurs both in a starred row and an unstarred row, pivot in a starred row rather than the unstarred one.) Check to

see which rows should now be starred. Repeat until no starred rows remain, and then go on to Phase II.

Phase II: Use the Simplex Method for Standard Maximization Problems

If there are any negative entries on the left side of the bottom row after Phase I, use the method described in the preceding section.

Because there is a starred row, we need to use Phase I. The largest positive number in the starred row is 1, which occurs three times. Arbitrarily select the first, which is in the first column. In that column, the smallest test ratio happens to be given by the 1 in the u row, so this is our first pivot.

Pivot column
↓

	x	y	z	s	t	u	p		
s	1	1	1	1	0	0	0	100	$R_1 - R_3$
t	4	10	7	0	1	0	0	480	$R_2 - 4R_3$
*u	[1]	1	1	0	0	−1	0	60	
p	−4	−12	−6	0	0	0	1	0	$R_4 + 4R_3$

This gives

	x	y	z	s	t	u	p	
s	0	0	0	1	0	1	0	40
t	0	6	3	0	1	4	0	240
x	1	1	1	0	0	−1	0	60
p	0	−8	−2	0	0	−4	1	240

Notice that we removed the star from row 3. To see why, look at the basic solution given by this tableau:

$$x = 60, y = 0, z = 0, s = 40, t = 240, u = 0.$$

None of the variables is negative anymore, so there are no rows to star. The basic solution is therefore feasible—it satisfies all the constraints.

Now that there are no more stars, we have completed Phase I, so we proceed to Phase II, which is just the method of the preceding section.

	x	y	z	s	t	u	p		
s	0	0	0	1	0	1	0	40	
t	0	[6]	3	0	1	4	0	240	
x	1	1	1	0	0	−1	0	60	$6R_3 - R_2$
p	0	−8	−2	0	0	−4	1	240	$3R_4 + 4R_2$

	x	y	z	s	t	u	p	
s	0	0	0	1	0	1	0	40
y	0	6	3	0	1	4	0	240
x	6	0	3	0	−1	−10	0	120
p	0	0	6	0	4	4	3	1,680

And we are finished. Thus the solution is

$$p = 1{,}680/3 = 560, x = 120/6 = 20, y = 240/6 = 40, z = 0.$$

The slack and surplus variables are

$$s = 40, t = 0, u = 0.$$

⇒ **Before we go on...** We owe you an explanation of why this method works. When we perform a pivot in Phase I, one of two things will happen. As in Example 1, we may pivot in a starred row. In that case, the negative active variable in that row will become inactive (hence zero) and some other variable will be made active with a positive value because we are pivoting on a positive entry. Thus, at least one star will be eliminated. (We will not introduce any new stars because pivoting on the entry with the smallest test ratio will keep all nonnegative variables nonnegative.)

The second possibility is that we may pivot on some row other than a starred row. Choosing the pivot via test ratios again guarantees that no new starred rows are created. A little bit of algebra shows that the value of the negative variable in the first starred row must increase toward zero. (Choosing the *largest* positive entry in the starred row will make it a little more likely that we will increase the value of that variable as much as possible; the rationale for choosing the largest entry is the same as that for choosing the most negative entry in the bottom row during Phase II.) Repeating this procedure as necessary, the value of the variable must eventually become zero or positive, assuming that there are feasible solutions to begin with.

So, one way or the other, we can eventually get rid of all of the stars. ∎

Here is an example that begins with two starred rows.

EXAMPLE 2 **More Mixed Constraints**

Maximize $p = 2x + y$
subject to $x + y \geq 35$
$x + 2y \leq 60$
$2x + y \geq 60$
$x \leq 25$
$x \geq 0, y \geq 0.$

Solution We introduce slack and surplus variables, and write down the initial tableau:

$$
\begin{aligned}
x + y - s &= 35 \\
x + 2y + t &= 60 \\
2x + y - u &= 60 \\
x + v &= 25 \\
-2x - y + p &= 0.
\end{aligned}
$$

	x	y	s	t	u	v	p	
*s	1	1	−1	0	0	0	0	35
t	1	2	0	1	0	0	0	60
*u	2	1	0	0	−1	0	0	60
v	1	0	0	0	0	1	0	25
p	−2	−1	0	0	0	0	1	0

We locate the largest positive entry in the first starred row (row 1). There are two to choose from (both 1s); let's choose the one in the x column. The entry with the smallest test ratio in that column is the 1 in the v row, so that is the entry we use as the pivot:

Pivot column
↓

	x	y	s	t	u	v	p		
*s	1	1	−1	0	0	0	0	35	$R_1 - R_4$
t	1	2	0	1	0	0	0	60	$R_2 - R_4$
*u	2	1	0	0	−1	0	0	60	$R_3 - 2R_4$
v	☐1	0	0	0	0	1	0	25	
p	−2	−1	0	0	0	0	1	0	$R_5 + 2R_4$

	x	y	s	t	u	v	p	
*s	0	1	−1	0	0	−1	0	10
t	0	2	0	1	0	−1	0	35
*u	0	1	0	0	−1	−2	0	10
x	1	0	0	0	0	1	0	25
p	0	−1	0	0	0	2	1	50

Notice that both stars are still there because the basic solutions for s and u remain negative (but less so). The only positive entry in the first starred row is the 1 in the y column, and that entry also has the smallest test ratio in its column. (Actually, it is tied with the 1 in the u column, so we could choose either one.)

	x	y	s	t	u	v	p		
*s	0	☐1	−1	0	0	−1	0	10	
t	0	2	0	1	0	−1	0	35	$R_2 - 2R_1$
*u	0	1	0	0	−1	−2	0	10	$R_3 - R_1$
x	1	0	0	0	0	1	0	25	
p	0	−1	0	0	0	2	1	50	$R_5 + R_1$

	x	y	s	t	u	v	p	
y	0	1	−1	0	0	−1	0	10
t	0	0	2	1	0	1	0	15
u	0	0	1	0	−1	−1	0	0
x	1	0	0	0	0	1	0	25
p	0	0	−1	0	0	1	1	60

The basic solution is $x = 25$, $y = 10$, $s = 0$, $t = 15$, $u = 0/(-1) = 0$, and $v = 0$. Because there are no negative variables left (even u has become 0), we are in the feasible region, so we can go on to Phase II, shown next. (Filling in the instructions for the row operations is an exercise.)

	x	y	s	t	u	v	p	
y	0	1	−1	0	0	−1	0	10
t	0	0	2	1	0	1	0	15
u	0	0	$\boxed{1}$	0	−1	−1	0	0
x	1	0	0	0	0	1	0	25
p	0	0	−1	0	0	1	1	60

	x	y	s	t	u	v	p	
y	0	1	0	0	−1	−2	0	10
t	0	0	0	1	$\boxed{2}$	3	0	15
s	0	0	1	0	−1	−1	0	0
x	1	0	0	0	0	1	0	25
p	0	0	0	0	−1	0	1	60

	x	y	s	t	u	v	p	
y	0	2	0	1	0	−1	0	35
u	0	0	0	1	2	3	0	15
s	0	0	2	1	0	1	0	15
x	1	0	0	0	0	1	0	25
p	0	0	0	1	0	3	2	135

The optimal solution is

$$x = 25, y = 35/2 = 17.5, p = 135/2 = 67.5 \quad (s = 7.5, t = 0, u = 7.5).$$

➡ **Before we go on...** Because Example 2 had only two unknowns, we can picture the sequence of basic solutions on the graph of the feasible region. This is shown in Figure 24.

You can see that there was no way to jump from (0, 0) in the initial tableau directly into the feasible region because the first jump must be along an axis. (Why?) Also notice that the third jump did not move at all. To which step of the simplex method does this correspond? ∎

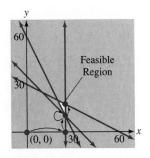

Figure 24

Minimization Problems

Now that we know how to deal with nonstandard constraints, we consider **minimization** problems, problems in which we have to minimize, rather than maximize, the objective function. The idea is to *convert a minimization problem into a maximization problem*, which we can then solve as usual.

Suppose, for instance, we want to minimize $c = 10x - 30y$ subject to some constraints. The technique is as follows: Define a new variable p by taking p to be the negative of c, so that $p = -c$. Then, the larger we make p, the smaller c becomes. For example, if we can make p increase from −10 to −5, then c will decrease from 10 to 5. So, if we are looking for the smallest value of c, we might as well look for the largest value of p instead. More concisely,

Minimizing c is the same as maximizing p $= -c$.

Now because $c = 10x - 30y$, we have $p = -10x + 30y$, and the requirement that we "minimize $c = 10x - 30y$" is now replaced by "maximize $p = -10x + 30y$."

Minimization Problems

We convert a minimization problem into a maximization problem by taking the negative of the objective function. All the constraints remain unchanged.

Quick Example

Minimization Problem	$\rightarrow$	**Maximization Problem**
Minimize $c = 10x - 30y$		Maximize $p = -10x + 30y$
subject to $2x + y \le 160$		subject to $2x + y \le 160$
$x + 3y \ge 120$		$x + 3y \ge 120$
$x \ge 0, y \ge 0.$		$x \ge 0, y \ge 0.$

EXAMPLE 3 Purchasing

You are in charge of ordering furniture for your company's new headquarters. You need to buy at least 200 tables, 500 chairs, and 300 computer desks. Wall-to-Wall Furniture (WWF) is offering a package of 20 tables, 25 chairs, and 18 computer desks for $2,000, whereas rival Acme Furniture (AF) is offering a package of 10 tables, 50 chairs, and 24 computer desks for $3,000. How many packages should you order from each company to minimize your total cost?

Solution The unknowns here are

x = number of packages ordered from WWF
y = number of packages ordered from AF.

We can put the information about the various kinds of furniture in a table:

	WWF	*AF*	*Needed*
Tables	20	10	200
Chairs	25	50	500
Computer Desks	18	24	300
Cost ($)	2,000	3,000	

From this table we get the following LP problem:

Minimize $c = 2{,}000x + 3{,}000y$
subject to $20x + 10y \ge 200$
$25x + 50y \ge 500$
$18x + 24y \ge 300$
$x \ge 0, y \ge 0.$

Before we start solving this problem, notice that all the inequalities may be simplified. The first is divisible by 10, the second by 25, and the third by 6. (However, this affects the meaning of the surplus variables; see *Before we go on* below.) Dividing gives the following simpler problem:

Minimize $c = 2{,}000x + 3{,}000y$
subject to $2x + y \ge 20$
$x + 2y \ge 20$
$3x + 4y \ge 50$
$x \ge 0, y \ge 0.$

Following the discussion that preceded this example, we convert to a maximization problem:

$$\begin{array}{ll}
\text{Maximize} & p = -2{,}000x - 3{,}000y \\
\text{subject to} & 2x + y \geq 20 \\
& x + 2y \geq 20 \\
& 3x + 4y \geq 50 \\
& x \geq 0, y \geq 0.
\end{array}$$

We introduce surplus variables.

$$\begin{array}{rcrcrcrcl}
2x & + & y & - s & & & & = & 20 \\
x & + & 2y & & - t & & & = & 20 \\
3x & + & 4y & & & - u & & = & 50 \\
2{,}000x & + & 3{,}000y & & & & + p & = & 0.
\end{array}$$

The initial tableau is then

	x	y	s	t	u	p	
*s	2	1	−1	0	0	0	20
*t	1	2	0	−1	0	0	20
*u	3	4	0	0	−1	0	50
p	2,000	3,000	0	0	0	1	0

The largest entry in the first starred row is the 2 in the upper left, which happens to give the smallest test ratio in its column.

	x	y	s	t	u	p		
*s	[2]	1	−1	0	0	0	20	
*t	1	2	0	−1	0	0	20	$2R_2 - R_1$
*u	3	4	0	0	−1	0	50	$2R_3 - 3R_1$
p	2,000	3,000	0	0	0	1	0	$R_4 - 1{,}000R_1$

	x	y	s	t	u	p		
x	2	1	−1	0	0	0	20	$3R_1 - R_2$
*t	0	[3]	1	−2	0	0	20	
*u	0	5	3	0	−2	0	40	$3R_3 - 5R_2$
p	0	2,000	1,000	0	0	1	−20,000	$3R_4 - 2{,}000R_2$

	x	y	s	t	u	p		
x	6	0	−4	2	0	0	40	$5R_1 - R_3$
y	0	3	1	−2	0	0	20	$5R_2 + R_3$
*u	0	0	4	[10]	−6	0	20	
p	0	0	1,000	4,000	0	3	−100,000	$R_4 - 400R_3$

	x	y	s	t	u	p		
x	30	0	−24	0	6	0	180	$R_1/6$
y	0	15	9	0	−6	0	120	$R_2/3$
t	0	0	4	10	−6	0	20	$R_3/2$
p	0	0	−600	0	2,400	3	−108,000	$R_4/3$

This completes Phase I. We are not yet at the optimal solution, so after performing the simplifications indicated we proceed with Phase II.

	x	y	s	t	u	p		
x	5	0	−4	0	1	0	30	$R_1 + 2R_3$
y	0	5	3	0	−2	0	40	$2R_2 − 3R_3$
t	0	0	$\boxed{2}$	5	−3	0	10	
p	0	0	−200	0	800	1	−36,000	$R_4 + 100R_3$

	x	y	s	t	u	p	
x	5	0	0	10	−5	0	50
y	0	10	0	−15	5	0	50
s	0	0	2	5	−3	0	10
p	0	0	0	500	500	1	−35,000

The optimal solution is

$x = 50/5 = 10$, $y = 50/10 = 5$, $p = −35,000$, so $c = 35,000$
($s = 5$, $t = 0$, $u = 0$).

You should buy 10 packages from Wall-to-Wall Furniture and 5 from Acme Furniture, for a minimum cost of $35,000.

➡ **Before we go on...** The surplus variables in the preceding example represent pieces of furniture over and above the minimum requirements. The order you place will give you 50 extra tables ($s = 5$, but s was introduced after we divided the first inequality by 10, so the actual surplus is $10 \times 5 = 50$), the correct number of chairs ($t = 0$), and the correct number of computer desks ($u = 0$). ■

The preceding LP problem is an example of a **standard minimization problem**—in a sense the opposite of a standard maximization problem: We are *minimizing* an objective function, where all the constraints have the form $Ax + By + Cz + \cdots \geq N$. We will discuss standard minimization problems more fully in Section 5.5, as well as another method of solving them.

FAQs

When to Switch to Phase II, Equality Constraints, and Troubleshooting

Q: *How do I know when to switch to Phase II?*

A: After each step, check the basic solution for starred rows. You are not ready to proceed with Phase II until all the stars are gone.

Q: *How do I deal with an equality constraint, such as $2x + 7y − z = 90$?*

A: Although we haven't given examples of equality constraints, they can be treated by the following trick: Replace an equality by two inequalities. For example, replace the equality $2x + 7y − z = 90$ by the two inequalities $2x + 7y − z \leq 90$ and $2x + 7y − z \geq 90$. A little thought will convince you that these two inequalities amount to the same thing as the original equality!

> **Q**: *What happens if it is impossible to choose a pivot using the instructions in Phase I?*
>
> **A**: In that case, the LP problem has no solution. In fact, the feasible region is empty. If it is impossible to choose a pivot in Phase II, then the feasible region is unbounded and there is no optimal solution.

5.4   EXERCISES

▼ more advanced   ◆ challenging
T indicates exercises that should be solved using technology

1. Maximize $p = x + y$
  subject to $x + 2y \geq 6$
            $-x + y \leq 4$
            $2x + y \leq 8$
            $x \geq 0, y \geq 0$. HINT [See Examples 1 and 2.]

2. Maximize $p = 3x + 2y$
  subject to $x + 3y \geq 6$
            $-x + y \leq 4$
            $2x + y \leq 8$
            $x \geq 0, y \geq 0$. HINT [See Examples 1 and 2.]

3. Maximize $p = 12x + 10y$
  subject to $x + y \leq 25$
            $x \geq 10$
            $-x + 2y \geq 0$
            $x \geq 0, y \geq 0$.

4. Maximize $p = x + 2y$
  subject to $x + y \leq 25$
            $y \geq 10$
            $2x - y \geq 0$
            $x \geq 0, y \geq 0$.

5. Maximize $p = 2x + 5y + 3z$
  subject to $x + y + z \leq 150$
         $x + y + z \geq 100$
         $x \geq 0, y \geq 0, z \geq 0$.

6. Maximize $p = 3x + 2y + 2z$
  subject to $x + y + 2z \leq 38$
            $2x + y + z \geq 24$
            $x \geq 0, y \geq 0, z \geq 0$.

7. Maximize $p = 10x + 20y + 15z$
  subject to $x + 2y + z \leq 40$
            $2y - z \geq 10$
            $2x - y + z \geq 20$
            $x \geq 0, y \geq 0, z \geq 0$.

8. Maximize $p = 10x + 10y + 15z$
  subject to $x - y + z \leq 12$
            $2x - 2y + z \geq 15$
            $-y + z \geq 3$
            $x \geq 0, y \geq 0, z \geq 0$.

9. Maximize $p = x + y + 3z + w$
  subject to $x + y + z + w \leq 40$
          $2x + y - z - w \geq 10$
          $x + y + z + w \geq 10$
          $x \geq 0, y \geq 0, z \geq 0, w \geq 0$.

10. Maximize $p = x + y + 4z + 2w$
  subject to $x + y + z + w \leq 50$
          $2x + y - z - w \geq 10$
          $x + y + z + w \geq 20$
          $x \geq 0, y \geq 0, z \geq 0, w \geq 0$.

11. Minimize $c = 6x + 6y$
  subject to $x + 2y \geq 20$
          $2x + y \geq 20$
          $x \geq 0, y \geq 0$. HINT [See Example 3.]

12. Minimize $c = 3x + 2y$
  subject to $x + 2y \geq 20$
          $2x + y \geq 10$
          $x \geq 0, y \geq 0$. HINT [See Example 3.]

13. Minimize $c = 2x + y + 3z$
  subject to $x + y + z \geq 100$
          $2x + y \geq 50$
          $y + z \geq 50$
          $x \geq 0, y \geq 0, z \geq 0$.

14. Minimize $c = 2x + 2y + 3z$
  subject to $x + z \geq 100$
          $2x + y \geq 50$
          $y + z \geq 50$
          $x \geq 0, y \geq 0, z \geq 0$.

15. Minimize $c = 50x + 50y + 11z$
subject to
$$2x \quad + z \geq 3$$
$$2x + y - z \geq 2$$
$$3x + y - z \leq 3$$
$$x \geq 0, y \geq 0, z \geq 0.$$

16. Minimize $c = 50x + 11y + 50z$
subject to
$$3x \quad + z \geq 8$$
$$3x + y - z \geq 6$$
$$4x + y - z \leq 8$$
$$x \geq 0, y \geq 0, z \geq 0.$$

17. Minimize $c = x + y + z + w$
subject to
$$5x - y \quad + w \geq 1,000$$
$$z + w \leq 2,000$$
$$x + y \quad \leq 500$$
$$x \geq 0, y \geq 0, z \geq 0, w \geq 0.$$

18. Minimize $c = 5x + y + z + w$
subject to
$$5x - y \quad + w \geq 1,000$$
$$z + w \leq 2,000$$
$$x + y \quad \leq 500$$
$$x \geq 0, y \geq 0, z \geq 0, w \geq 0.$$

T *In Exercises 19–24, we suggest the use of technology. Round all answers to two decimal places.*

19. Maximize $p = 2x + 3y + 1.1z + 4w$
subject to
$$1.2x + y + z + \quad w \leq 40.5$$
$$2.2x + y - z - \quad w \geq 10$$
$$1.2x + y + z + 1.2w \geq 10.5$$
$$x \geq 0, y \geq 0, z \geq 0, w \geq 0.$$

20. Maximize $p = 2.2x + 2y + 1.1z + 2w$
subject to
$$x + 1.5y + 1.5z + \quad w \leq 50.5$$
$$2x + 1.5y - \quad z - \quad w \geq 10$$
$$x + 1.5y + \quad z + 1.5w \geq 21$$
$$x \geq 0, y \geq 0, z \geq 0, w \geq 0.$$

21. Minimize $c = 2.2x + y + 3.3z$
subject to
$$x + 1.5y + 1.2z \geq 100$$
$$2x + 1.5y \quad \geq 50$$
$$1.5y + 1.1z \geq 50$$
$$x \geq 0, y \geq 0, z \geq 0.$$

22. Minimize $c = 50.3x + 10.5y + 50.3z$
subject to
$$3.1x \quad + 1.1z \geq 28$$
$$3.1x + y - 1.1z \geq 23$$
$$4.2x + y - 1.1z \geq 28$$
$$x \geq 0, y \geq 0, z \geq 0.$$

23. Minimize $c = 1.1x + y + 1.5z - w$
subject to
$$5.12x - y \quad + w \leq 1,000$$
$$z + w \geq 2,000$$
$$1.22x + y \quad \leq 500$$
$$x \geq 0, y \geq 0, z \geq 0, w \geq 0.$$

24. Minimize $c = 5.45x + y + 1.5z + w$
subject to
$$5.12x - y \quad + w \geq 1,000$$
$$z + w \geq 2,000$$
$$1.12x + y \quad \leq 500$$
$$x \geq 0, y \geq 0, z \geq 0, w \geq 0.$$

APPLICATIONS

25. *Agriculture* (Compare Exercise 27 in Section 5.3.) Your small farm encompasses 100 acres, and you are planning to grow tomatoes, lettuce, and carrots in the coming planting season. Fertilizer costs per acre are: $5 for tomatoes, $4 for lettuce, and $2 for carrots. Based on past experience, you estimate that each acre of tomatoes will require an average of 4 hours of labor per week, while tending to lettuce and carrots will each require an average of 2 hours per week. You estimate a profit of $2,000 for each acre of tomatoes, $1,500 for each acre of lettuce, and $500 for each acre of carrots. You would like to spend at least $400 on fertilizer (your niece owns the company that manufactures it) and your farm laborers can supply up to 500 hours per week. How many acres of each crop should you plant to maximize total profits? In this event, will you be using all 100 acres of your farm? HINT [See Example 3.]

26. *Agriculture* (Compare Exercise 28 in Section 5.3.) Your farm encompasses 900 acres, and you are planning to grow soybeans, corn, and wheat in the coming planting season. Fertilizer costs per acre are: $5 for soybeans, $2 for corn, and $1 for wheat. You estimate that each acre of soybeans will require an average of 5 hours of labor per week, while tending to corn and wheat will each require an average of 2 hours per week. Based on past yields and current market prices, you estimate a profit of $3,000 for each acre of soybeans, $2,000 for each acre of corn, and $1,000 for each acre of wheat. You can afford to spend no more than $3,000 on fertilizer, but your labor union contract stipulates at least 2,000 hours per week of labor. How many acres of each crop should you plant to maximize total profits? In this event, will you be using more than 2,000 hours of labor? HINT [See Example 3.]

27. *Politics* The political pollster Canter is preparing for a national election. It would like to poll at least 1,500 Democrats and 1,500 Republicans. Each mailing to the East Coast gets responses from 100 Democrats and 50 Republicans. Each mailing to the Midwest gets responses from 100 Democrats and 100 Republicans. And each mailing to the West Coast gets responses from 50 Democrats and 100 Republicans. Mailings to the East Coast cost $40 each to produce and mail, mailings to the Midwest cost $60 each, and mailings to the West Coast cost $50 each. How many mailings should Canter send to each area of the country to get the responses it needs at the least possible cost? What will it cost?

28. *Purchasing* Bingo's *Copy Center* needs to buy white paper and yellow paper. Bingo's can buy from three suppliers. Harvard Paper sells a package of 20 reams of white and 10 reams of yellow for $60, Yale Paper sells a package of

10 reams of white and 10 reams of yellow for $40, and Dartmouth Paper sells a package of 10 reams of white and 20 reams of yellow for $50. If Bingo's needs 350 reams of white and 400 reams of yellow, how many packages should it buy from each supplier to minimize the cost? What is the least possible cost?

29. *Resource Allocation Succulent Citrus* produces orange juice and orange concentrate. This year the company anticipates a demand of at least 10,000 quarts of orange juice and 1,000 quarts of orange concentrate. Each quart of orange juice requires 10 oranges, and each quart of concentrate requires 50 oranges. The company also anticipates using at least 200,000 oranges for these products. Each quart of orange juice costs the company 50¢ to produce, and each quart of concentrate costs $2.00 to produce. How many quarts of each product should Succulent Citrus produce to meet the demand and minimize total costs?

30. *Resource Allocation Fancy Pineapple* produces pineapple juice and canned pineapple rings. This year the company anticipates a demand of at least 10,000 pints of pineapple juice and 1,000 cans of pineapple rings. Each pint of pineapple juice requires 2 pineapples, and each can of pineapple rings requires 1 pineapple. The company anticipates using at least 20,000 pineapples for these products. Each pint of pineapple juice costs the company 20¢ to produce, and each can of pineapple rings costs 50¢ to produce. How many pints of pineapple juice and cans of pineapple rings should Fancy Pineapple produce to meet the demand and minimize total costs?

31. *Latin Music Sales (Digital)* You are about to go live with a Latin music download service called *iYayay* that will compete head-to-head with **Apple's** *iTunes*® (good luck!). You will be selling digital albums of regional (Mexican/Tejano) music for $5 each, pop/rock albums for $4 each, and tropical (salsa/merengue/cumbia/bachata) at $6 per album. Your servers can handle up to 40,000 downloaded albums per day, and you anticipate that, based on national sales,[30] revenues from regional music will be at least fives times those from tropical music. You also anticipate that that you will sell at least 10,000 pop/rock albums per day due to the very attractive $4 price. Based on these assumptions, how many of each type of album should you sell for a maximum daily revenue, and what will your daily revenue be?

32. *Latin Music Sales (Digital)* It seems that your biggest rival, Lupita Pelogrande, has learned about your music store and has decided to launch *iRico*, a competitor Latin Music download service that will also offer regional (Mexican/Tejano) music albums for $5 each and pop/rock albums for $4 each. However, instead of tropical music, *iRico* will offer reggaeton albums at only $3 per album. Lupita's servers are more robust than yours, and can handle up to 60,000 downloaded albums per day. She anticipates that revenues from

regional music can total to up to double those from reggaeton, and that *iRico* can sell at least 50,000 albums per day, not even counting reggaeton. Based on these assumptions, how many of each type of album should *iRico* sell for a maximum daily revenue, and what will the daily revenue be?

33. 🔲 *Nutrition* **Gerber Products'** Gerber Mixed Cereal for Baby contains, in each serving, 60 calories and no Vitamin C. Gerber Mango Tropical Fruit Dessert contains, in each serving, 80 calories and 45% of the U.S. Recommended Daily Allowance (RDA) of Vitamin C for infants. Gerber Apple Banana Juice contains, in each serving, 60 calories and 120% of the RDA of Vitamin C for infants.[31] The cereal costs 10¢/serving, the dessert costs 53¢/serving, and the juice costs 27¢/serving. If you want to provide your child with at least 120 calories and at least 120% of the RDA of Vitamin C, how can you do so at the least cost?

34. 🔲 *Nutrition* **Gerber Products'** Gerber Mixed Cereal for Baby contains, in each serving, 60 calories, no Vitamin C, and 11 grams of carbohydrates. Gerber Mango Tropical Fruit Dessert contains, in each serving, 80 calories, 45% of the RDA of Vitamin C for infants, and 21 grams of carbohydrates. Gerber Apple Banana Juice contains, in each serving, 60 calories, 120% of the RDA of Vitamin C for infants, and 15 grams of carbohydrates.[32] Assume that the cereal costs 11¢/serving, the dessert costs 50¢/serving, and the juice costs 30¢/serving. If you want to provide your child with at least 180 calories, at least 120% of the RDA of Vitamin C, and at least 37 grams of carbohydrates, how can you do so at the least cost?

35. 🔲 *Purchasing Cheapskate Electronics Store* needs to update its inventory of stereos, TVs, and DVD players. There are three suppliers it can buy from: Nadir offers a bundle consisting of 5 stereos, 10 TVs, and 15 DVD players for $3,000. Blunt offers a bundle consisting of 10 stereos, 10 TVs, and 10 DVD players for $4,000. Sonny offers a bundle consisting of 15 stereos, 10 TVs, and 10 DVD players for $5,000. Cheapskate Electronics needs at least 150 stereos, 200 TVs, and 150 DVD players. How can it update its inventory at the least possible cost? What is the least possible cost?

36. 🔲 *Purchasing Federal Rent-a-Car* is putting together a new fleet. It is considering package offers from three car manufacturers. Fred Motors is offering 5 small cars, 5 medium cars, and 10 large cars for $500,000. Admiral Motors is offering 5 small, 10 medium, and 5 large cars for $400,000. Chrysalis is offering 10 small, 5 medium, and 5 large cars for $300,000. Federal would like to buy at least 550 small cars, at least 500 medium cars, and at least 550 large cars. How many packages should it buy from each car maker to keep the total cost as small as possible? What will be the total cost?

---

[30]In 2010, total U.S. revenues from regional music were about five times those from tropical music. Source: Recording Industry Association of America http://riaa.org

[31]Source: Nutrition information supplied with the products.
[32]*Ibid.*

T *Bodybuilding Supplements* *Exercises 37 and 38 are based on the following data on four bodybuilding supplements. (Figures shown correspond to a single serving.)*[33]

	Creatine (g)	Carbohydrates (g)	Taurine (g)	Alpha Lipoic Acid (mg)	Cost ($)
Cell-Tech® (MuscleTech)	10	75	2	200	2.20
RiboForce HP® (EAS)	5	15	1	0	1.60
Creatine Transport® (Kaizen)	5	35	1	100	0.60
Pre-Load Creatine® (Optimum)	6	35	1	25	0.50

37. (Compare Exercise 29 in Section 5.2.) You are thinking of combining Cell-Tech, RiboForce HP, and Creatine Transport to obtain a 10-day supply that provides at least 80 grams of creatine and at least 10 grams of taurine, but no more than 750 grams of carbohydrates and 1,000 milligrams of alpha lipoic acid. How many servings of each supplement should you combine to meet your specifications for the least cost?

38. (Compare Exercise 30 in Section 5.2.) You are thinking of combining RiboForce HP, Creatine Transport, and Pre-Load Creatine to obtain a 10-day supply that provides at least 80 grams of creatine and at least 10 grams of taurine, but no more than 600 grams of carbohydrates and 2,000 milligrams of alpha lipoic acid. How many servings of each supplement should you combine to meet your specifications for the least cost?

39. ▼ *Subsidies* The Miami Beach City Council has offered to subsidize hotel development in Miami Beach, and it is hoping for at least two hotels with a total capacity of at least 1,400. Suppose that you are a developer interested in taking advantage of this offer by building a small group of hotels in Miami Beach. You are thinking of three prototypes: a convention-style hotel with 500 rooms costing $100 million, a vacation-style hotel with 200 rooms costing $20 million, and a small motel with 50 rooms costing $4 million. The City Council will approve your plans, provided you build at least one convention-style hotel and no more than two small motels.

   a. How many of each type of hotel should you build to satisfy the city council's wishes and stipulations while minimizing your total cost?

   b. Now assume that the city council will give developers 20 percent of the cost of building new hotels in Miami Beach, up to $50 million.[34] Will the city's $50 million subsidy be sufficient to cover 20 percent of your total costs?

40. ▼ *Subsidies* Refer back to the preceding exercise. You are about to begin the financial arrangements for your new hotels when the city council informs you that it has changed its mind and now requires at least two vacation-style hotels and no more than four small motels.

   a. How many of each type of hotel should you build to satisfy the city council's wishes and stipulations while minimizing your total costs?

   b. Will the city's $50 million subsidy limit still be sufficient to cover 20 percent of your total costs?

41. ▼ *Transportation Scheduling* We return to your exploits coordinating distribution for the Tubular Ride Boogie Board Company.[35] You will recall that the company has manufacturing plants in Tucson, Arizona, and Toronto, Ontario, and you have been given the job of coordinating distribution of their latest model, the Gladiator, to their outlets in Honolulu and Venice Beach. The Tucson plant can manufacture up to 620 boards per week, while the Toronto plant, beset by labor disputes, can produce no more than 410 Gladiator boards per week. The outlet in Honolulu orders 500 Gladiator boards per week, while Venice Beach orders 530 boards per week. Transportation costs are as follows: Tucson to Honolulu: $10/board; Tucson to Venice Beach: $5/board; Toronto to Honolulu: $20/board; Toronto to Venice Beach: $10/board. Your manager has said that you are to be sure to fill all orders and ship the boogie boards at a minimum total transportation cost. How will you do it?

42. ▼ *Transportation Scheduling* In the situation described in the preceding exercise, you have just been notified that workers at the Toronto boogie board plant have gone on strike, resulting in a total work stoppage. You are to come up with a revised delivery schedule by tomorrow with the understanding that the Tucson plant can push production to a maximum of 1,000 boards per week. What should you do?

43. ▼ *Finance* Senator Porkbarrel habitually overdraws his three bank accounts, at the *Congressional Integrity Bank, Citizens' Trust,* and *Checks R Us*. There are no penalties because the overdrafts are subsidized by the taxpayer. The Senate Ethics Committee tends to let slide irregular banking activities as long as they are not flagrant. At the moment (due to Congress's preoccupation with a Supreme Court nominee), a total overdraft of up to $10,000 will be overlooked. Porkbarrel's conscience makes him hesitate to overdraw accounts at banks whose names include expressions like "integrity" and "citizens' trust." The effect is that his overdrafts at the first two banks combined amount to no more than one quarter of the total. On the other hand, the financial officers at Integrity Bank, aware that Senator Porkbarrel is a member of the Senate Banking Committee, "suggest" that he overdraw at least $2,500 from their bank. Find the amount he should overdraw from each bank in order to avoid investigation by the Ethics Committee and overdraw his account at Integrity by as much as his sense of guilt will allow.

---

[33]Source: Nutritional information supplied by the manufacturers (www.netrition.com). Cost per serving is approximate.

[34]The Miami Beach City Council made such an offer in 1993. (*Chicago Tribune*, June 20, 1993, Section 7, p. 8).

[35]See Exercise 26 in Section 3.3 and also Exercise 41 in Section 5.3. This time, we will use the simplex method to solve the version of this problem we first considered in the chapter on systems of equations.

44. ▼ *Scheduling* Because Joe Slim's brother was recently elected to the State Senate, Joe's financial advisement concern, *Inside Information Inc.,* has been doing a booming trade, even though the financial counseling he offers is quite worthless. (None of his seasoned clients pays the slightest attention to his advice.) Slim charges different hourly rates to different categories of individuals: $5,000/hour for private citizens, $50,000/hour for corporate executives, and $10,000/hour for presidents of universities. Due to his taste for leisure, he feels that he can spend no more than 40 hours/week in consultation. On the other hand, Slim feels that it would be best for his intellect were he to devote at least 10 hours of consultation each week to university presidents. However, Slim always feels somewhat uncomfortable dealing with academics, so he would prefer to spend no more than half his consultation time with university presidents. Furthermore, he likes to think of himself as representing the interests of the common citizen, so he wishes to offer at least 2 more hours of his time each week to private citizens than to corporate executives and university presidents combined. Given all these restrictions, how many hours each week should he spend with each type of client in order to maximize his income?

45. ▼ *Transportation Scheduling* Your publishing company is about to start a promotional blitz for its new book, *Advanced Quantum Mechanics for the Liberal Arts*. You have 20 salespeople stationed in Chicago and 10 in Denver. You would like to fly at least 10 into Los Angeles and at least 15 into New York. A round-trip plane flight from Chicago to LA costs $200; from Chicago to NY costs $125; from Denver to LA costs $225; and from Denver to NY costs $280.[36] How many salespeople should you fly from each of Chicago and Denver to each of LA and NY to spend the least amount on plane flights?

46. ▼ *Transportation Scheduling* Repeat Exercise 45, but now suppose that you would like at least 15 salespeople in Los Angeles.

47. ⊤ ▼ *Hospital Staffing* As the staff director of a new hospital, you are planning to hire cardiologists, rehabilitation specialists, and infectious disease specialists. According to recent data, each cardiology case averages $12,000 in revenue, each physical rehabilitation case $19,000, and each infectious disease case, $14,000.[37] You judge that each specialist you employ will expand the hospital caseload by about 10 patients per week. You already have 3 cardiologists on staff, and the hospital is equipped to admit up to 200 patients per week. Based on past experience, each cardiologist and rehabilitation specialist brings in one government research grant per year, while each infectious disease specialist brings in three. Your board of directors would like to see

a total of at least 30 grants per year and would like your weekly revenue to be as large as possible. How many of each kind of specialist should you hire?

48. ⊤ ▼ *Hospital Staffing* Referring to Exercise 47, you completely misjudged the number of patients each type of specialist would bring to the hospital per week. It turned out that each cardiologist brought in 120 new patients per *year,* each rehabilitation specialist brought in 90 per year, and each infectious disease specialist brought in 70 per year.[38] It also turned out that your hospital could deal with no more than 1,960 new patients per year. Repeat the preceding exercise in light of this corrected data.

COMMUNICATION AND REASONING EXERCISES

49. Explain the need for Phase I in a nonstandard LP problem.

50. Explain the need for Phase II in a nonstandard LP problem.

51. Explain briefly why we would need to use Phase I in solving a linear programming problem with the constraint $x + 2y - z \geq 3$.

52. Which rows do we star, and why?

53. Consider the following linear programming problem:

Maximize $p = x + y$
subject to $x - 2y \geq 0$
              $2x + y \leq 10$
              $x \geq 0, y \geq 0.$

This problem

(A) must be solved using the techniques of Section 5.4.
(B) must be solved using the techniques of Section 5.3.
(C) can be solved using the techniques of either section.

54. Consider the following linear programming problem:

Maximize $p = x + y$
subject to $x - 2y \geq 1$
              $2x + y \leq 10$
              $x \geq 0, y \geq 0.$

This problem

(A) must be solved using the techniques of Section 5.4.
(B) must be solved using the techniques of Section 5.3.
(C) can be solved using the techniques of either section.

55. ▼ Find a linear programming problem in three variables that requires one pivot in Phase I.

56. ▼ Find a linear programming problem in three variables that requires two pivots in Phase I.

57. ▼ Find a linear programming problem in two or three variables with no optimal solution, and show what happens when you try to solve it using the simplex method.

58. ▼ Find a linear programming problem in two or three variables with more than one optimal solution, and investigate which solution is found by the simplex method.

---

[36]Approximate prices advertised on various Web sites in September 2011.

[37]These (rounded) figures are based on an Illinois survey of 1.3 million hospital admissions (*Chicago Tribune,* March 29, 1993, Section 4, p. 1). Source: Lutheran General Health System, Argus Associates, Inc.

[38]These (rounded) figures were obtained from the survey referenced in the preceding exercise by dividing the average hospital revenue per physician by the revenue per case.

| 5.5 | # The Simplex Method and Duality |

We mentioned **standard minimization problems** in the last section. These problems have the following form.

Standard Minimization Problem

A **standard minimization problem** is an LP problem in which we are required to *minimize* (not maximize) a linear objective function

$$c = as + bt + cu + \cdots$$

of the variables $s, t, u, \ldots$ (in this section, we will always use the letters $s, t, u, \ldots$ for the unknowns in a standard minimization problem) subject to the constraints

$$s \geq 0, t \geq 0, u \geq 0, \ldots$$

and further constraints of the form

$$As + Bt + Cu + \cdots \geq N$$

where $A, B, C, \ldots$ and N are numbers with N nonnegative.

A **standard linear programming problem** is an LP problem that is either a standard maximization problem or a standard minimization problem. An LP problem satisfies the **nonnegative objective condition** if all the coefficients in the objective function are nonnegative.

Quick Examples

Standard Minimization and Maximization Problems

1. Minimize $c = 2s + 3t + 3u$
   subject to $2s \quad\;\; + u \geq 10$ This is a standard minimization problem
   $\qquad\qquad s + 3t - 6u \geq 5$ satisfying the nonnegative objective
   $\qquad\qquad s \geq 0, t \geq 0, u \geq 0.$ condition.

2. Maximize $p = 2x + 3y + 3z$
   subject to $2x \quad\;\; + z \leq 7$ This is a standard maximization problem
   $\qquad\qquad x + 3y - 6z \leq 6$ satisfying the nonnegative objective
   $\qquad\qquad x \geq 0, y \geq 0, z \geq 0.$ condition.

3. Minimize $c = 2s - 3t + 3u$
   subject to $2s \quad\;\; + u \geq 10$ This is a standard minimization problem
   $\qquad\qquad s + 3t - 6u \geq 5$ that does *not* satisfy the nonnegative
   $\qquad\qquad s \geq 0, t \geq 0, u \geq 0.$ objective condition.

We saw a way of solving minimization problems in Section 5.4, but a mathematically elegant relationship between maximization and minimization problems gives us another way of solving minimization problems that satisfy the nonnegative objective condition. This relationship is called **duality**.

To describe duality, we must first represent an LP problem by a matrix. This matrix is *not* the first tableau but something simpler: Pretend you forgot all about slack

* Forgetting these things is exactly what happens to many students under test conditions!

† Although duality does not require the problems to be standard, it does require them to be written in so-called *standard form*: In the case of a maximization problem all constraints need to be (re)written using $\leq$, while for a minimization problem all constraints need to be (re)written using $\geq$. It is least confusing to stick with standard problems, which is what we will do in this section.

variables and also forgot to change the signs of the objective function.* As an example, consider the following two standard† problems:

Problem 1

$$\text{Maximize} \quad p = 20x + 20y + 50z$$
$$\text{subject to} \quad 2x + y + 3z \leq 2{,}000$$
$$x + 2y + 4z \leq 3{,}000$$
$$x \geq 0, y \geq 0, z \geq 0.$$

We represent this problem by the matrix

$$\begin{bmatrix} 2 & 1 & 3 & 2{,}000 \\ 1 & 2 & 4 & 3{,}000 \\ 20 & 20 & 50 & 0 \end{bmatrix} \quad \begin{matrix} \text{Constraint 1} \\ \text{Constraint 2} \\ \text{Objective} \end{matrix}$$

Notice that the coefficients of the objective function go in the bottom row, and we place a zero in the bottom right corner.

Problem 2 (from Example 3 in Section 5.4)

$$\text{Minimize} \quad c = 2{,}000s + 3{,}000t$$
$$\text{subject to} \quad 2s + t \geq 20$$
$$s + 2t \geq 20$$
$$3s + 4t \geq 50$$
$$s \geq 0, t \geq 0.$$

Problem 2 is represented by

$$\begin{bmatrix} 2 & 1 & 20 \\ 1 & 2 & 20 \\ 3 & 4 & 50 \\ 2{,}000 & 3{,}000 & 0 \end{bmatrix} \quad \begin{matrix} \text{Constraint 1} \\ \text{Constraint 2} \\ \text{Constraint 3} \\ \text{Objective} \end{matrix}$$

These two problems are related: The matrix for Problem 1 is the transpose of the matrix for Problem 2. (Recall that the transpose of a matrix is obtained by writing its rows as columns; see Section 4.1.) When we have a pair of LP problems related in this way, we say that the two are *dual* LP problems.

Dual Linear Programming Problems

Two LP problems, one a maximization and one a minimization problem, are **dual** if the matrix that represents one is the transpose of the matrix that represents the other.

Finding the Dual of a Given Problem

Given an LP problem, we find its dual as follows:

1. Represent the problem as a matrix (see above).

2. Take the transpose of the matrix.

3. Write down the dual, which is the LP problem corresponding to the new matrix. If the original problem was a maximization problem, its dual will be a minimization problem, and vice versa.

The original problem is called the **primal problem**, and its dual is referred to as the **dual problem**.

> **Quick Example**
>
> Primal problem
> Minimize $c = s + 2t$
> subject to $5s + 2t \geq 60$
> $3s + 4t \geq 80$
> $s + t \geq 20$
> $s \geq 0, t \geq 0.$
>
> $\xrightarrow{1}$ $\begin{bmatrix} 5 & 2 & 60 \\ 3 & 4 & 80 \\ 1 & 1 & 20 \\ 1 & 2 & 0 \end{bmatrix}$
>
> $\xrightarrow{2}$ $\begin{bmatrix} 5 & 3 & 1 & 1 \\ 2 & 4 & 1 & 2 \\ 60 & 80 & 20 & 0 \end{bmatrix}$ $\xrightarrow{3}$
>
> Dual problem
> Maximize $p = 60x + 80y + 20z$
> subject to $5x + 3y + z \leq 1$
> $2x + 4y + z \leq 2$
> $x \geq 0, y \geq 0, z \geq 0.$

The following theorem justifies what we have been doing, and says that solving the dual problem of an LP problem is equivalent to solving the original problem.

Fundamental Theorem of Duality

a. If an LP problem has an optimal solution, then so does its dual. Moreover, the primal problem and the dual problem have the same optimal value for their objective functions.

b. Contained in the final tableau of the simplex method applied to an LP problem is the solution to its dual problem: It is given by the bottom entries in the columns associated with the slack variables, divided by the entry under the objective variable.

✱ The proof of the theorem is beyond the scope of this book but can be found in a textbook devoted to linear programming, like *Linear Programming* by Vašek Chvátal (San Francisco: W. H. Freeman and Co., 1983), which has a particularly well-motivated discussion.

The theorem✱ gives us an alternative way of solving minimization problems that satisfy the nonnegative objective condition. Let's illustrate by solving Problem 2 above.

EXAMPLE 1   Solving by Duality

Minimize $c = 2{,}000s + 3{,}000t$
subject to $2s + t \geq 20$
$s + 2t \geq 20$
$3s + 4t \geq 50$
$s \geq 0, t \geq 0.$

Solution

Step 1 *Find the dual problem.* Write the primal problem in matrix form and take the transpose:

$$\begin{bmatrix} 2 & 1 & 20 \\ 1 & 2 & 20 \\ 3 & 4 & 50 \\ 2{,}000 & 3{,}000 & 0 \end{bmatrix} \rightarrow \begin{bmatrix} 2 & 1 & 3 & 2{,}000 \\ 1 & 2 & 4 & 3{,}000 \\ 20 & 20 & 50 & 0 \end{bmatrix}.$$

The dual problem is:

Maximize $p = 20x + 20y + 50z$
subject to $2x + y + 3z \leq 2{,}000$
$x + 2y + 4z \leq 3{,}000$
$x \geq 0, y \geq 0, z \geq 0.$

Step 2 *Use the simplex method to solve the dual problem.* Because we have a standard maximization problem, we do not have to worry about Phase I but go straight to Phase II.

	x	y	z	s	t	p	
s	2	1	$\boxed{3}$	1	0	0	2,000
t	1	2	4	0	1	0	3,000
p	−20	−20	−50	0	0	1	0

	x	y	z	s	t	p	
z	2	1	3	1	0	0	2,000
t	−5	$\boxed{2}$	0	−4	3	0	1,000
p	40	−10	0	50	0	3	100,000

	x	y	z	s	t	p	
z	9	0	6	6	−3	0	3,000
y	−5	2	0	−4	3	0	1,000
p	15	0	0	30	15	3	105,000

Note that the maximum value of the objective function is $p = 105,000/3 = 35,000$. By the theorem, this is also the optimal value of c in the primal problem!

Step 3 *Read off the solution to the primal problem by dividing the bottom entries in the columns associated with the slack variables by the entry in the p column.* Here is the final tableau again with the entries in question highlighted.

	x	y	z	s	t	p	
z	9	0	6	6	−3	0	3,000
y	−5	2	0	−4	3	0	1,000
p	15	0	0	**30**	**15**	**3**	**105,000**

The solution to the primal problem is

$$s = 30/3 = 10, t = 15/3 = 5, c = 105,000/3 = 35,000.$$

(Compare this with the method we used to solve Example 3 in the preceding section. Which method seems more efficient?)

➡ **Before we go on...**   Can you now see the reason for using the variable names $s, t, u, \ldots$ in standard minimization problems? ■

Q: *Is the theorem also useful for solving problems that do not satisfy the nonnegative objective condition?*

A: Consider a standard minimization problem that does not satisfy the nonnegative objective condition, such as

Minimize $c = 2s - t$
subject to $2s + 3t \geq 2$
             $s + 2t \geq 2$
             $s \geq 0, t \geq 0.$

Its dual would be

$$\begin{aligned} \text{Maximize} \quad & p = 2x + 2y \\ \text{subject to} \quad & 2x + \ y \le 2 \\ & 3x + 2y \le -1 \\ & x \ge 0, y \ge 0. \end{aligned}$$

This is not a standard maximization problem because the right-hand side of the second constraint is negative. In general, if a problem does not satisfy the nonnegative objective condition, its dual is not standard. Therefore, to solve the dual by the simplex method will require using Phase I as well as Phase II, and we may as well just solve the primal problem that way to begin with. Thus, duality helps us solve problems only when the primal problem satisfies the nonnegative objective condition.

In many economic applications, the solution to the dual problem also gives us useful information about the primal problem, as we will see in the following example.

EXAMPLE 2 Shadow Costs

You are trying to decide how many vitamin pills to take. SuperV brand vitamin pills each contain 2 milligrams of vitamin X, 1 milligram of vitamin Y, and 1 milligram of vitamin Z. Topper brand vitamin pills each contain 1 milligram of vitamin X, 1 milligram of vitamin Y, and 2 milligrams of vitamin Z. You want to take enough pills daily to get at least 12 milligrams of vitamin X, 10 milligrams of vitamin Y, and 12 milligrams of vitamin Z. However, SuperV pills cost 4¢ each and Toppers cost 3¢ each, and you would like to minimize the total cost of your daily dosage. How many of each brand of pill should you take? How would changing your daily vitamin requirements affect your minimum cost?

Solution This is a straightforward minimization problem. The unknowns are

$$\begin{aligned} s &= \text{number of SuperV brand pills} \\ t &= \text{number of Topper brand pills.} \end{aligned}$$

The linear programming problem is

$$\begin{aligned} \text{Minimize} \quad & c = 4s + 3t \\ \text{subject to} \quad & 2s + \ t \ge 12 \\ & s + \ t \ge 10 \\ & s + 2t \ge 12 \\ & s \ge 0, t \ge 0. \end{aligned}$$

We solve this problem by using the simplex method on its dual, which is

$$\begin{aligned} \text{Maximize} \quad & p = 12x + 10y + 12z \\ \text{subject to} \quad & 2x + y + \ z \le 4 \\ & x + y + 2z \le 3 \\ & x \ge 0, y \ge 0, z \ge 0. \end{aligned}$$

After pivoting three times, we arrive at the final tableau:

	x	y	z	s	t	p	
x	6	0	−6	6	−6	0	6
y	0	1	3	−1	2	0	2
p	0	0	6	2	8	1	32

Therefore, the answer to the original problem is that you should take two SuperV vitamin pills and eight Toppers at a cost of 32¢ per day.

Now, the key to answering the last question, which asks you to determine how changing your daily vitamin requirements would affect your minimum cost, is to look at the solution to the dual problem. From the tableau we see that $x = 1$, $y = 2$, and $z = 0$. To see what x, y, and z might tell us about the original problem, let's look at their units. In the inequality $2x + y + z \leq 4$, the coefficient 2 of x has units "mg of vitamin X/SuperV pill," and the 4 on the right-hand side has units "¢/SuperV pill." For $2x$ to have the same units as the 4 on the right-hand side, x must have units "¢/mg of vitamin X." Similarly, y must have units "¢/mg of vitamin Y" and z must have units "¢/mg of vitamin Z." One can show (although we will not do it here) that x gives the amount that would be added to the minimum cost for each increase* of 1 milligram of vitamin X in our daily requirement. For example, if we were to increase our requirement from 12 milligrams to 14 milligrams, an increase of 2 milligrams, the minimum cost would change by $2x = 2$¢, from 32¢ to 34¢. (Try it; you'll end up taking four SuperV pills and six Toppers.) Similarly, each increase of 1 milligram of vitamin Y in the requirements would increase the cost by $y = 2$¢. These costs are called the **marginal costs** or the **shadow costs** of the vitamins.

What about $z = 0$? The shadow cost of vitamin Z is 0¢/mg, meaning that you can increase your requirement of vitamin Z without changing your cost. In fact, the solution $s = 2$ and $t = 8$ provides you with 18 milligrams of vitamin Z, so you can increase the required amount of vitamin Z up to 18 milligrams without changing the solution at all.

We can also interpret the shadow costs as the effective cost to you of each milligram of each vitamin in the optimal solution. You are paying 1¢/milligram of vitamin X, 2¢/milligram of vitamin Y, and getting the vitamin Z for free. This gives a total cost of $1 \times 12 + 2 \times 10 + 0 \times 12 = 32$¢, as we know. Again, if you change your requirements slightly, these are the amounts you will pay per milligram of each vitamin.

* To be scrupulously correct, this works only for relatively small changes in the requirements, not necessarily for very large ones.

Game Theory

We return to a topic we discussed in Section 4.4: solving two-person zero-sum games. In that section, we described how to solve games that could be reduced to 2×2 games or smaller. It turns out that we can solve larger games using linear programming and duality. We summarize the procedure, work through an example, and then discuss why it works.

Solving a Matrix Game

Step 1 Reduce the payoff matrix by dominance.

Step 2 Add a fixed number k to each of the entries so that they all become nonnegative and no column is all zero.

Step 3 Write 1s to the right of and below the matrix, and then write down the associated standard maximization problem. Solve this primal problem using the simplex method.

Step 4 Find the optimal strategies and the expected value as follows:

Column Strategy

1. Express the solution to the primal problem as a column vector.
2. Normalize by dividing each entry of the solution vector by p (which is also the sum of all the entries).
3. Insert zeros in positions corresponding to the columns deleted during reduction.

Row Strategy

1. Express the solution to the dual problem as a row vector.
2. Normalize by dividing each entry by p, which will once again be the sum of all the entries.
3. Insert zeros in positions corresponding to the rows deleted during reduction.

Value of the Game

$$e = \frac{1}{p} - k$$

EXAMPLE 3 Restaurant Inspector

You manage two restaurants, Tender Steaks Inn (TSI) and Break for a Steak (BFS). Even though you run the establishments impeccably, the Department of Health has been sending inspectors to your restaurants on a daily basis and fining you for minor infractions. You've found that you can head off a fine if you're present, but you can cover only one restaurant at a time. The Department of Health, on the other hand, has two inspectors, who sometimes visit the same restaurant and sometimes split up, one to each restaurant. The average fines you have been getting are shown in the following matrix.

		Health Inspectors		
		Both at BFS	*Both at TSI*	*One at Each*
You go to	**TSI**	$8,000	0	$2,000
	BFS	0	$10,000	$4,000

How should you choose which restaurant to visit to minimize your expected fine?

Solution This matrix is not quite the payoff matrix because fines, being penalties, should be negative payoffs. Thus, the payoff matrix is the following:

$$P = \begin{bmatrix} -8,000 & 0 & -2,000 \\ 0 & -10,000 & -4,000 \end{bmatrix}.$$

We follow the steps above to solve the game using the simplex method.

Step 1 There are no dominated rows or columns, so this game does not reduce.

Step 2 We add $k = 10,000$ to each entry so that none are negative, getting the following new matrix (with no zero column):

$$\begin{bmatrix} 2,000 & 10,000 & 8,000 \\ 10,000 & 0 & 6,000 \end{bmatrix}.$$

Step 3 We write 1s to the right and below this matrix:

$$\begin{bmatrix} 2{,}000 & 10{,}000 & 8{,}000 & 1 \\ 10{,}000 & 0 & 6{,}000 & 1 \\ 1 & 1 & 1 & 0 \end{bmatrix}.$$

The corresponding standard maximization problem is the following:

$$\begin{aligned}
\text{Maximize} \quad & p = x + y + z \\
\text{subject to} \quad & 2{,}000x + 10{,}000y + 8{,}000z \le 1 \\
& 10{,}000x \quad\quad\quad\; + 6{,}000z \le 1 \\
& x \ge 0, \, y \ge 0, \, z \ge 0.
\end{aligned}$$

Step 4 We use the simplex method to solve this problem. After pivoting twice, we arrive at the final tableau:

	x	y	z	s	t	p	
y	0	50,000	34,000	5	−1	0	4
x	10,000	0	6,000	0	1	0	1
p	0	0	14,000	5	4	50,000	9

Column Strategy The solution to the primal problem is

$$\begin{bmatrix} x \\ y \\ z \end{bmatrix} = \begin{bmatrix} \frac{1}{10{,}000} \\ \frac{4}{50{,}000} \\ 0 \end{bmatrix}.$$

We divide each entry by $p = 9/50{,}000$, which is also the sum of the entries. This gives the optimal column strategy:

$$C = \begin{bmatrix} \frac{5}{9} \\ \frac{4}{9} \\ 0 \end{bmatrix}.$$

Thus, the inspectors' optimal strategy is to stick together, visiting BFS with probability $5/9$ and TSI with probability $4/9$.

Row Strategy The solution to the dual problem is

$$[s \quad t] = \begin{bmatrix} \dfrac{5}{50{,}000} & \dfrac{4}{50{,}000} \end{bmatrix}.$$

Once again, we divide by $p = 9/50{,}000$ to find the optimal row strategy:

$$R = \begin{bmatrix} \dfrac{5}{9} & \dfrac{4}{9} \end{bmatrix}.$$

Thus, you should visit TSI with probability $5/9$ and BFS with probability $4/9$.

Value of the Game Your expected average fine is

$$e = \frac{1}{p} - k = \frac{50{,}000}{9} - 10{,}000 = -\frac{40{,}000}{9} \approx -\$4{,}444.$$

➡ **Before we go on...** We owe you an explanation of why the procedure we used in Example 3 works. The main point is to understand how we turn a game into a linear programming problem. It's not hard to see that adding a fixed number k to all the payoffs will change only the payoff, increasing it by k, and not change the optimal strategies. So let's pick up Example 3 from the point where we were considering the following game:

$$P = \begin{bmatrix} 2{,}000 & 10{,}000 & 8{,}000 \\ 10{,}000 & 0 & 6{,}000 \end{bmatrix}.$$

We are looking for the optimal strategies R and C for the row and column players, respectively; if e is the value of the game, we will have $e = RPC$. Let's concentrate first on the column player's strategy $C = [u \ \ v \ \ w]^T$, where u, v, and w are the unknowns we want to find. Because e is the value of the game, if the column player uses the optimal strategy C and the row player uses any old strategy S, the expected value with these strategies has to be e or better for the column player, so $SPC \leq e$. Let's write that out for two particular choices of S. First, consider $S = [1 \ \ 0]$:

$$[1 \ \ 0] \begin{bmatrix} 2{,}000 & 10{,}000 & 8{,}000 \\ 10{,}000 & 0 & 6{,}000 \end{bmatrix} \begin{bmatrix} u \\ v \\ w \end{bmatrix} \leq e.$$

Multiplied out, this gives

$$2{,}000u + 10{,}000v + 8{,}000w \leq e.$$

Next, do the same thing for $S = [0 \ \ 1]$:

$$[0 \ \ 1] \begin{bmatrix} 2{,}000 & 10{,}000 & 8{,}000 \\ 10{,}000 & 0 & 6{,}000 \end{bmatrix} \begin{bmatrix} u \\ v \\ w \end{bmatrix} \leq e$$

$$10{,}000u + 6{,}000w \leq e.$$

It turns out that if these two inequalities are true, then $SPC \leq e$ for any S at all, which is what the column player wants. These are starting to look like constraints in a linear programming problem, but the e appearing on the right is in the way. We get around this by dividing by e, which we know to be positive because all of the payoffs are nonnegative and no column is all zero (so the column player can't force the value of the game to be 0; here is where we need these assumptions). We get the following inequalities:

$$2{,}000 \left(\frac{u}{e}\right) + 10{,}000 \left(\frac{v}{e}\right) + 8{,}000 \left(\frac{w}{e}\right) \leq 1$$

$$10{,}000 \left(\frac{u}{e}\right) + 6{,}000 \left(\frac{w}{e}\right) \leq 1.$$

Now we're getting somewhere. To make these look even more like linear constraints, we replace our unknowns u, v, and w with new unknowns, $x = u/e$, $y = v/e$, and $z = w/e$. Our inequalities then become.

$$2{,}000x + 10{,}000y + 8{,}000z \leq 1$$

$$10{,}000x + 6{,}000z \leq 1.$$

What about an objective function? From the point of view of the column player, the objective is to find a strategy that will minimize the expected value e. In order to write e in terms of our new variables x, y, and z, we use the fact that our original variables, being the entries in the column strategy, have to add up to 1: $u + v + w = 1$. Dividing by e gives

$$\frac{u}{e} + \frac{v}{e} + \frac{w}{e} = \frac{1}{e}$$

or

$$x + y + z = \frac{1}{e}.$$

Now we notice that, if we *maximize* $p = x + y + z = 1/e$, it will have the effect of minimizing e, which is what we want. So, we get the following linear programming problem:

$$
\begin{aligned}
\text{Maximize} \quad & p = x + y + z \\
\text{subject to} \quad & 2{,}000x + 10{,}000y + 8{,}000z \le 1 \\
& 10{,}000x \qquad\qquad + 6{,}000z \le 1 \\
& x \ge 0,\ y \ge 0,\ z \ge 0.
\end{aligned}
$$

Why can we say that x, y, and z should all be nonnegative? Because the unknowns u, v, w, and e must all be nonnegative.

So now, if we solve this linear programming problem to find x, y, z, and p, we can find the column player's optimal strategy by computing $u = xe = x/p$, $v = y/p$, and $w = z/p$. Moreover, the value of the game is $e = 1/p$. (If we added k to all the payoffs, we should now adjust by subtracting k again to find the correct value of the game.)

Turning now to the row player's strategy, if we repeat the above type of argument from the row player's viewpoint, we'll end up with the following linear programming problem to solve:

$$
\begin{aligned}
\text{Minimize} \quad & c = s + t \\
\text{subject to} \quad & 2{,}000s + 10{,}000t \ge 1 \\
& 10{,}000s \qquad\qquad \ge 1 \\
& 8{,}000s + \ \ 6{,}000t \ge 1 \\
& s \ge 0,\ t \ge 0.
\end{aligned}
$$

This is, of course, the dual to the problem we solved to find the column player's strategy, so we know that we can read its solution off of the same final tableau. The optimal value of c will be the same as the value of p, so $c = 1/e$ also. The entries in the optimal row strategy will be s/c and t/c. ∎

FAQs

When to Use Duality

Q: *Given a minimization problem, when should I use duality, and when should I use the two-phase method in Section 5.4?*

A: If the original problem satisfies the nonnegative objective condition (none of the coefficients in the objective function are negative), then you can use duality to convert the problem to a standard maximization one, which can be solved with the one-phase method. If the original problem does not satisfy the nonnegative objective condition, then dualizing results in a nonstandard LP problem, so dualizing may not be worthwhile.

Q: *When is it absolutely necessary to use duality?*

A: Never. Duality gives us an efficient but not necessary alternative for solving standard minimization problems.

5.5   EXERCISES

In Exercises 1–8, write down (without solving) the dual LP problem. HINT *[See the Quick Example on page 371.]*

1. Maximize $p = 2x + y$
   subject to $x + 2y \le 6$
          $-x + y \le 2$
          $x \ge 0, y \ge 0.$

2. Maximize $p = x + 5y$
   subject to $x + y \le 6$
          $-x + 3y \le 4$
          $x \ge 0, y \ge 0.$

3. Minimize $c = 2s + t + 3u$
   subject to $s + t + u \ge 100$
          $2s + t \quad \ge 50$
          $s \ge 0, t \ge 0, u \ge 0.$

4. Minimize $c = 2s + 2t + 3u$
   subject to $s \quad + u \ge 100$
          $2s + t \quad \ge 50$
          $s \ge 0, t \ge 0, u \ge 0.$

5. Maximize $p = x + y + z + w$
   subject to $x + y + z \quad \le 3$
          $y + z + w \le 4$
          $x + z + w \le 5$
          $x + y + w \le 6$
          $x \ge 0, y \ge 0, z \ge 0, w \ge 0.$

6. Maximize $p = x + y + z + w$
   subject to $x + y + z \quad \le 3$
          $y + z + w \le 3$
          $x + z + w \le 4$
          $x + y + w \le 4$
          $x \ge 0, y \ge 0, z \ge 0, w \ge 0.$

7. Minimize $c = s + 3t + u$
   subject to $5s - t \quad + v \ge 1{,}000$
          $u - v \ge 2{,}000$
          $s + t \quad \ge 500$
          $s \ge 0, t \ge 0, u \ge 0, v \ge 0.$

8. Minimize $c = 5s + 2u + v$
   subject to $s - t \quad + 2v \ge 2{,}000$
          $u + v \ge 3{,}000$
          $s + t \quad \ge 500$
          $s \ge 0, t \ge 0, u \ge 0, v \ge 0.$

In Exercises 9–22, solve the standard minimization problems using duality. (You may already have seen some of them in earlier sections, but now you will be solving them using a different method.) HINT *[See Example 1.]*

9. Minimize $c = s + t$
   subject to $s + 2t \ge 6$
          $2s + t \ge 6$
          $s \ge 0, t \ge 0.$

10. Minimize $c = s + 2t$
   subject to $s + 3t \ge 30$
          $2s + t \ge 30$
          $s \ge 0, t \ge 0.$

11. Minimize $c = 6s + 6t$
   subject to $s + 2t \ge 20$
          $2s + t \ge 20$
          $s \ge 0, t \ge 0.$

12. Minimize $c = 3s + 2t$
   subject to $s + 2t \ge 20$
          $2s + t \ge 10$
          $s \ge 0, t \ge 0.$

13. Minimize $c = 0.2s + 0.3t$
   subject to $2s + t \ge 10$
          $s + 2t \ge 10$
          $s + t \ge 8$
          $s \ge 0, t \ge 0.$

14. Minimize $c = 0.4s + 0.1t$
   subject to $3s + 2t \ge 60$
          $s + 2t \ge 40$
          $2s + 3t \ge 45$
          $s \ge 0, t \ge 0.$

15. Minimize $c = 2s + t$
   subject to $3s + t \ge 30$
          $s + t \ge 20$
          $s + 3t \ge 30$
          $s \ge 0, t \ge 0.$

16. Minimize $c = s + 2t$
   subject to $4s + t \ge 100$
          $2s + t \ge 80$
          $s + 3t \ge 150$
          $s \ge 0, t \ge 0.$

17. Minimize $c = s + 2t + 3u$
   subject to $3s + 2t + u \ge 60$
          $2s + t + 3u \ge 60$
          $s \ge 0, t \ge 0, u \ge 0.$

18. Minimize $c = s + t + 2u$
   subject to $s + 2t + 2u \geq 60$
                  $2s + t + 3u \geq 60$
                  $s \geq 0, t \geq 0, u \geq 0.$

19. Minimize $c = 2s + t + 3u$
   subject to $s + t + u \geq 100$
                  $2s + t \quad \geq 50$
                  $t + u \geq 50$
                  $s \geq 0, t \geq 0, u \geq 0.$

20. Minimize $c = 2s + 2t + 3u$
   subject to $s \quad + u \geq 100$
                  $2s + t \quad \geq 50$
                  $t + u \geq 50$
                  $s \geq 0, t \geq 0, u \geq 0.$

21. Minimize $c = s + t + u$
   subject to $3s + 2t + u \geq 60$
                  $2s + t + 3u \geq 60$
                  $s + 3t + 2u \geq 60$
                  $s \geq 0, t \geq 0, u \geq 0.$

22. Minimize $c = s + t + 2u$
   subject to $s + 2t + 2u \geq 60$
                  $2s + t + 3u \geq 60$
                  $s + 3t + 6u \geq 60$
                  $s \geq 0, t \geq 0, u \geq 0.$

In Exercises 23–28, solve the games with the given payoff matrices. HINT [See Example 3.]

23. $P = \begin{bmatrix} -1 & 1 & 2 \\ 2 & -1 & -2 \end{bmatrix}$ **24.** $P = \begin{bmatrix} 1 & -1 & 2 \\ 1 & 2 & 0 \end{bmatrix}$

25. $P = \begin{bmatrix} -1 & 1 & 2 \\ 2 & -1 & -2 \\ 1 & 2 & 0 \end{bmatrix}$ **26.** $P = \begin{bmatrix} 1 & -1 & 2 \\ 1 & 2 & 0 \\ 0 & 1 & 1 \end{bmatrix}$

27. ⊡ $P = \begin{bmatrix} -1 & 1 & 2 & -1 \\ 2 & -1 & -2 & -3 \\ 1 & 2 & 0 & 1 \\ 0 & 2 & 3 & 3 \end{bmatrix}$

28. ⊡ $P = \begin{bmatrix} 1 & -1 & 2 & 0 \\ 1 & 2 & 0 & 1 \\ 0 & 1 & 1 & 0 \\ 2 & 0 & -2 & 2 \end{bmatrix}$

APPLICATIONS

Exercises 29–38 are similar to ones in preceding exercise sets. Use duality to answer them.

29. *Nutrition* Meow makes cat food out of fish and cornmeal. Fish has 8 grams of protein and 4 grams of fat per ounce, and cornmeal has 4 grams of protein and 8 grams of fat. A jumbo can of cat food must contain at least 48 grams of

protein and 48 grams of fat. If fish and cornmeal both cost 5¢/ounce, how many ounces of each should Meow use in each can of cat food to minimize costs? What are the shadow costs of protein and of fat? HINT [See Example 2.]

30. *Nutrition* Oz makes lion food out of giraffe and gazelle meat. Giraffe meat has 18 grams of protein and 36 grams of fat per pound, while gazelle meat has 36 grams of protein and 18 grams of fat per pound. A batch of lion food must contain at least 36,000 grams of protein and 54,000 grams of fat. Giraffe meat costs $2/pound and gazelle meat costs $4/pound. How many pounds of each should go into each batch of lion food in order to minimize costs? What are the shadow costs of protein and fat? HINT [See Example 2.]

31. *Nutrition* Ruff makes dog food out of chicken and grain. Chicken has 10 grams of protein and 5 grams of fat/ounce, and grain has 2 grams of protein and 2 grams of fat/ounce. A bag of dog food must contain at least 200 grams of protein and at least 150 grams of fat. If chicken costs 10¢/ounce and grain costs 1¢/ounce, how many ounces of each should Ruff use in each bag of dog food in order to minimize cost? What are the shadow costs of protein and fat?

32. *Purchasing* The Enormous State University's Business School is buying computers. The school has two models to choose from, the Pomegranate and the iZac. Each Pomegranate comes with 400 GB of memory and 80 TB of disk space, while each iZac has 300 GB of memory and 100 TB of disk space. For reasons related to its accreditation, the school would like to be able to say that it has a total of at least 48,000 GB of memory and at least 12,800 TB of disk space. If both the Pomegranate and the iZac cost $2,000 each, how many of each should the school buy to keep the cost as low as possible? What are the shadow costs of memory and disk space?

33. *Nutrition* Each serving of Gerber Mixed Cereal for Baby contains 60 calories and no vitamin C. Each serving of Gerber Mango Tropical Fruit Dessert contains 80 calories and 45 percent of the U.S. Recommended Daily Allowance (RDA) of vitamin C for infants. Each serving of Gerber Apple Banana Juice contains 60 calories and 120 percent of the U.S. RDA of vitamin C for infants.[39] The cereal costs 10¢/serving, the dessert costs 53¢/serving, and the juice costs 27¢/serving. If you want to provide your child with at least 120 calories and at least 120 percent of the U.S. RDA of vitamin C, how can you do so at the least cost? What are your shadow costs for calories and vitamin C?

34. *Nutrition* Each serving of Gerber Mixed Cereal for Baby contains 60 calories, no vitamin C, and 11 grams of carbohydrates. Each serving of Gerber Mango Tropical Fruit Dessert contains 80 calories, 45 percent of the U.S. Recommended Daily Allowance (RDA) of vitamin C for infants, and 21 grams of carbohydrates. Each serving of Gerber Apple Banana Juice contains 60 calories, 120 percent of the U.S. RDA of vitamin C for infants, and 15 grams of carbohydrates.[40]

---

[39]Source: Nutrition information supplied with the products.
[40]*Ibid.*

Assume that the cereal costs 11¢/serving, the dessert costs 50¢/serving, and the juice costs 30¢/serving. If you want to provide your child with at least 180 calories, at least 120 percent of the U.S. RDA of vitamin C, and at least 37 grams of carbohydrates, how can you do so at the least cost? What are your shadow costs for calories, vitamin C, and carbohydrates?

35. *Politics* The political pollster Canter is preparing for a national election. It would like to poll at least 1,500 Democrats and 1,500 Republicans. Each mailing to the East Coast gets responses from 100 Democrats and 50 Republicans. Each mailing to the Midwest gets responses from 100 Democrats and 100 Republicans. And each mailing to the West Coast gets responses from 50 Democrats and 100 Republicans. Mailings to the East Coast cost $40 each to produce and mail, mailings to the Midwest cost $60 each, and mailings to the West Coast cost $50 each. How many mailings should Canter send to each area of the country to get the responses it needs at the least possible cost? What will it cost? What are the shadow costs of a Democratic response and a Republican response?

36. *Purchasing* *Bingo's Copy Center* needs to buy white paper and yellow paper. Bingo's can buy from three suppliers. Harvard Paper sells a package of 20 reams of white and 10 reams of yellow for $60; Yale Paper sells a package of 10 reams of white and 10 reams of yellow for $40, and Dartmouth Paper sells a package of 10 reams of white and 20 reams of yellow for $50. If Bingo's needs 350 reams of white and 400 reams of yellow, how many packages should it buy from each supplier so as to minimize the cost? What is the lowest possible cost? What are the shadow costs of white paper and yellow paper?

37. ▼ *Resource Allocation* One day Gillian the Magician summoned the wisest of her women. "Devoted followers," she began, "I have a quandary: As you well know, I possess great expertise in sleep spells and shock spells, but unfortunately, these are proving to be a drain on my aural energy resources; each sleep spell costs me 500 pico-shirleys of aural energy, while each shock spell requires 750 pico-shirleys. Clearly, I would like to hold my overall expenditure of aural energy to a minimum, and still meet my commitments in protecting the Sisterhood from the ever-present threat of trolls. Specifically, I have estimated that each sleep spell keeps us safe for an average of 2 minutes, while every shock spell protects us for about 3 minutes. We certainly require enough protection to last 24 hours of each day, and possibly more, just to be safe. At the same time, I have noticed that each of my sleep spells can immobilize 3 trolls at once, while one of my typical shock spells (having a narrower range) can immobilize only 2 trolls at once. We are faced, my sisters, with an onslaught of 1,200 trolls per day! Finally, as you are no doubt aware, the bylaws dictate that for a Magician of the Order to remain in good standing, the number of shock spells must be between one quarter and one third the number of shock and sleep spells combined. What do I do, oh Wise Ones?"

38. ▼ *Risk Management* The Grand Vizier of the Kingdom of Um is being blackmailed by numerous individuals and is having a very difficult time keeping his blackmailers from going public. He has been keeping them at bay with two kinds of payoff: gold bars from the Royal Treasury and political favors. Through bitter experience, he has learned that each payoff in gold gives him peace for an average of about one month, and each political favor seems to earn him about a month and a half of reprieve. To maintain his flawless reputation in the court, he feels he cannot afford any revelations about his tainted past to come to light within the next year. Thus, it is imperative that his blackmailers be kept at bay for 12 months. Furthermore, he would like to keep the number of gold payoffs at no more than one quarter of the combined number of payoffs because the outward flow of gold bars might arouse suspicion on the part of the Royal Treasurer. The gold payoffs tend to deplete the Grand Vizier's travel budget. (The treasury has been subsidizing his numerous trips to the Himalayas.) He estimates that each gold bar removed from the treasury will cost him four trips. On the other hand, because the administering of political favors tends to cost him valuable travel time, he suspects that each political favor will cost him about two trips. Now, he would obviously like to keep his blackmailers silenced and lose as few trips as possible. What is he to do? How many trips will he lose in the next year?

39. ▼ *Game Theory—Politics* Incumbent Tax N. Spend and challenger Trick L. Down are running for county executive, and polls show them to be in a dead heat. The election hinges on three cities: Littleville, Metropolis, and Urbantown. The candidates have decided to spend the last weeks before the election campaigning in those three cities; each day each candidate will decide in which city to spend the day. Pollsters have determined the following payoff matrix, where the payoff represents the number of votes gained or lost for each one-day campaign trip.

T. N. Spend

		Littleville	Metropolis	Urbantown
	Littleville	−200	−300	300
T. L. Down	**Metropolis**	−500	500	−100
	Urbantown	−500	0	0

What percentage of time should each candidate spend in each city in order to maximize votes gained? If both candidates use their optimal strategies, what is the expected vote?

40. ▼ *Game Theory—Marketing* Your company's new portable phone/music player/PDA/bottle washer, the RunMan, will compete against the established market leader, the iNod, in a saturated market. (Thus, for each device you sell, one fewer iNod is sold.) You are planning to launch the RunMan with a traveling road show, concentrating on two cities,

New York and Boston. The makers of the iNod will do the same to try to maintain their sales. If, on a given day, you both go to New York, you will lose 1,000 units in sales to the iNod. If you both go to Boston, you will lose 750 units in sales. On the other hand, if you go to New York and your competitor to Boston, you will gain 1,500 units in sales from them. If you go to Boston and they to New York, you will gain 500 units in sales. What percentage of time should you spend in New York and what percentage in Boston, and how do you expect your sales to be affected?

41. ▼ *Game Theory—Morra Games* A three-finger *Morra game* is a game in which two players simultaneously show one, two, or three fingers at each round. The outcome depends on a predetermined set of rules. Here is an interesting example: If the numbers of fingers shown by A and B differ by 1, then A loses one point. If they differ by more than 1, the round is a draw. If they show the same number of fingers, A wins an amount equal to the sum of the fingers shown. Determine the optimal strategy for each player and the expected value of the game.

42. ◼ ▼ *Game Theory—Morra Games* Referring to the preceding exercise, consider the following rules for a three-finger Morra game: If the sum of the fingers shown is odd, then A wins an amount equal to that sum. If the sum is even, B wins the sum. Determine the optimal strategy for each player and the expected value of the game. HINT [Use technology to do the pivoting in the associated linear programming problem.]

43. ◼ ◆ *Game Theory—Military Strategy* Colonel Blotto is a well-known game in military strategy.[41] Here is a version of this game: Colonel Blotto has four regiments under his command, while his opponent, Captain Kije, has three. The armies are to try to occupy two locations, and each commander must decide how many regiments to send to each location. The army that sends more regiments to a location captures that location as well as the other army's regiments. If both armies send the same number of regiments to a location, then there is a draw. The payoffs are one point for each

location captured and one point for each regiment captured. Find the optimum strategy for each commander and also the value of the game.

44. ◼ ◆ *Game Theory—Military Strategy* Referring to the preceding exercise, consider the version of Colonel Blotto with the same payoffs given there except that Captain Kije earns two points for each location captured, while Colonel Blotto continues to earn only one point. Find the optimum strategy for each commander and also the value of the game. Round all figures to two decimal places.

COMMUNICATION AND REASONING EXERCISES

45. Give one possible advantage of using duality to solve a standard minimization problem.

46. To ensure that the dual of a minimization problem will result in a standard maximization problem,

   (A) the primal problem should satisfy the nonnegative objective condition.

   (B) the primal problem should be a standard minimization problem.

   (C) the primal problem should not satisfy the nonnegative objective condition.

47. Give an example of a standard minimization problem whose dual is *not* a standard maximization problem. How would you go about solving your problem?

48. Give an example of a nonstandard minimization problem whose dual is a standard maximization problem.

49. ▼ Given a minimization problem, when would you solve it by applying the simplex method to its dual, and when would you apply the simplex method to the minimization problem itself?

50. ▼ Create an interesting application that leads to a standard maximization problem. Solve it using the simplex method and note the solution to its dual problem. What does the solution to the dual tell you about your application?

---

[41]See Samuel Karlin, *Mathematical Methods and Theory in Games, Programming and Economics* (Addison-Wesley, 1959).

CHAPTER 5 REVIEW

KEY CONCEPTS

 Website www.WanerMath.com
Go to the Website at www.WanerMath
.com to find a comprehensive and
interactive Web-based summary
of Chapter 5.

5.1 Graphing Linear Inequalities

Inequalities, strict and nonstrict *p. 313*
Linear inequalities *p. 313*
Solution of an inequality *p. 313*
Sketching the region represented by a
linear inequality in two variables
p. 315
Bounded and unbounded regions *p. 318*
Feasible region *p. 318*

5.2 Solving Linear Programming Problems Graphically

Linear programming (LP) problem in
two unknowns; objective function;
constraints; optimal value; optimal
solution *p. 322*
Feasible region *p. 323*
Fundamental Theorem of Linear
Programming *p. 323*

Graphical method for solving an
LP problem *p. 324*
Decision variables *p. 325*
Procedure for solving an LP problem
with an unbounded feasible
region *p. 328*

5.3 The Simplex Method: Solving Standard Maximization Problems

General linear programming problem in
n unknowns *p. 339*
Standard maximization problem
p. 339
Slack variable *p. 340*
Tableau *p. 341*
Active (or basic) variables; inactive
(or nonbasic) variables; basic
solution *p. 341*
Rules for selecting the pivot
column *p. 342*
Rules for selecting the pivot; test
ratios *p. 343*
Departing or exiting variable, entering
variable *p. 343*

5.4 The Simplex Method: Solving General Linear Programming Problems

Surplus variable *p. 356*
Phase I and Phase II for solving
general LP problems *p. 356*
Using the simplex method to solve
a minimization problem *p. 361*

5.5 The Simplex Method and Duality

Standard minimization problem
p. 369
Standard LP problem *p. 369*
Nonnegative objective condition
p. 369
Dual LP problems; primal problem;
dual problem *p. 370*
Fundamental Theorem of Duality
p. 371
Shadow costs *p. 374*
Game theory: The LP problem
associated with a two-person
zero-sum game *p. 374*

REVIEW EXERCISES

In each of Exercises 1–4, sketch the region corresponding to the given inequalities, say whether it is bounded, and give the coordinates of all corner points.

1. $2x - 3y \le 12$

2. $x \le 2y$

3. $x + 2y \le 20$
$3x + 2y \le 30$
$x \ge 0, y \ge 0$

4. $3x + 2y \ge 6$
$2x - 3y \le 6$
$3x - 2y \ge 0$
$x \ge 0, y \ge 0$

In each of Exercises 5–8, solve the given linear programming problem graphically.

5. Maximize $p = 2x + y$
subject to $3x + y \le 30$
$x + y \le 12$
$x + 3y \le 30$
$x \ge 0, y \ge 0.$

6. Maximize $p = 2x + 3y$
subject to $x + y \ge 10$
$2x + y \ge 12$
$x + y \le 20$
$x \ge 0, y \ge 0.$

7. Minimize $c = 2x + y$
subject to $3x + y \ge 30$
$x + 2y \ge 20$
$2x - y \ge 0$
$x \ge 0, y \ge 0.$

8. Minimize $c = 3x + y$
subject to $3x + 2y \ge 6$
$2x - 3y \le 0$
$3x - 2y \ge 0$
$x \ge 0, y \ge 0.$

In each of Exercises 9–18, solve the given linear programming problem using the simplex method. If no optimal solution exists, indicate whether the feasible region is empty or the objective function is unbounded.

9. Maximize $p = x + y + 2z$
subject to $x + 2y + 2z \le 60$
$2x + y + 3z \le 60$
$x \ge 0, y \ge 0, z \ge 0.$

10. Maximize $p = x + y + 2z$
subject to $x + 2y + 2z \le 60$
$2x + y + 3z \le 60$
$x + 3y + 6z \le 60$
$x \ge 0, y \ge 0, z \ge 0.$

11. Maximize $p = x + y + 3z$
subject to $x + y + z \ge 100$
$y + z \le 80$
$x \quad\quad + z \le 80$
$x \ge 0, y \ge 0, z \ge 0.$

12. Maximize $p = 2x + y$
subject to $x + 2y \ge 12$
$2x + y \le 12$
$x + y \le 5$
$x \ge 0, y \ge 0.$

13. Minimize $c = x + 2y + 3z$
subject to $3x + 2y + z \geq 60$
$2x + y + 3z \geq 60$
$x \geq 0, y \geq 0, z \geq 0.$

14. Minimize $c = 5x + 4y + 3z$
subject to $x + y + 4z \geq 30$
$2x + y + 3z \geq 60$
$x \geq 0, y \geq 0, z \geq 0.$

15. ▌ Minimize $c = x - 2y + 4z$
subject to $3x + 2y - z \geq 10$
$2x + y + 3z \geq 20$
$x + 3y - 2z \geq 30$
$x \geq 0, y \geq 0, z \geq 0.$

16. ▌ Minimize $c = x + y - z$
subject to $3x + 2y + z \geq 60$
$2x + y + 3z \geq 60$
$x + 3y + 2z \geq 60$
$x \geq 0, y \geq 0, z \geq 0.$

17. Minimize $c = x + y + z + w$
subject to $x + y \qquad \geq 30$
$x \quad + z \qquad \geq 20$
$x + y \quad - w \leq 10$
$y + z - w \leq 10$
$x \geq 0, y \geq 0, z \geq 0, w \geq 0.$

18. Minimize $c = 4x + y + z + w$
subject to $x + y \qquad \geq 30$
$y - z \qquad \leq 20$
$z - w \leq 10$
$x \geq 0, y \geq 0, z \geq 0, w \geq 0.$

In each of Exercises 19–22, solve the given linear programming problem using duality.

19. Minimize $c = 2x + y$
subject to $3x + 2y \geq 60$
$2x + y \geq 60$
$x + 3y \geq 60$
$x \geq 0, y \geq 0.$

20. Minimize $c = 2x + y + 2z$
subject to $3x + 2y + z \geq 100$
$2x + y + 3z \geq 200$
$x \geq 0, y \geq 0, z \geq 0.$

21. Minimize $c = 2x + y$
subject to $3x + 2y \geq 10$
$2x - y \leq 30$
$x + 3y \geq 60$
$x \geq 0, y \geq 0.$

22. Minimize $c = 2x + y + 2z$
subject to $3x - 2y + z \geq 100$
$2x + y - 3z \leq 200$
$x \geq 0, y \geq 0, z \geq 0.$

In each of Exercises 23–26, solve the game with the given payoff matrix.

23. $P = \begin{bmatrix} -1 & 2 & -1 \\ 1 & -2 & 1 \\ 3 & -1 & 0 \end{bmatrix}$ **24.** $P = \begin{bmatrix} -3 & 0 & 1 \\ -4 & 0 & 0 \\ 0 & -1 & -2 \end{bmatrix}$

25. $P = \begin{bmatrix} -3 & -2 & 3 \\ 1 & 0 & 0 \\ -2 & 2 & 1 \end{bmatrix}$ **26.** $P = \begin{bmatrix} -4 & -2 & -3 \\ 1 & -3 & -2 \\ -3 & 1 & -4 \end{bmatrix}$

Exercises 27–30 are adapted from the Actuarial Exam on Operations Research.

27. You are given the following linear programming problem:

Minimize $c = x + 2y$
subject to $-2x + y \geq 1$
$x - 2y \geq 1$
$x \geq 0, y \geq 0.$

Which of the following is true?

(A) The problem has no feasible solutions.
(B) The objective function is unbounded.
(C) The problem has optimal solutions.

28. Repeat the preceding exercise with the following linear programming problem:

Maximize $p = x + y$
subject to $-2x + y \leq 1$
$x - 2y \leq 2$
$x \geq 0, y \geq 0.$

29. Determine the optimal value of the objective function. You are given the following linear programming problem.

Maximize $Z = x_1 + 4x_2 + 2x_3 - 10$
subject to $4x_1 + x_2 + x_3 \leq 45$
$-x_1 + x_2 + 2x_3 \leq 0$
$x_1, x_2, x_3 \geq 0.$

30. Determine the optimal value of the objective function. You are given the following linear programming problem.

Minimize $Z = x_1 + 4x_2 + 2x_3 + x_4 + 40$
subject to $4x_1 + x_2 + x_3 \leq 45$
$-x_1 + 2x_2 + x_4 \geq 40$
$x_1, x_2, x_3 \geq 0.$

APPLICATIONS: OHaganBooks.com

In Exercises 31–34, you are the buyer for OHaganBooks.com and are considering increasing stocks of romance and horror novels at the new OHaganBooks.com warehouse in Texas. You have offers from several publishers: Duffin House, Higgins Press, McPhearson Imprints, and O'Conell Books. Duffin offers a package of 5 horror novels and 5 romance novels for $50, Higgins offers a package of 5 horror and 10 romance novels for $80, McPhearson offers a package of 10 horror novels and 5 romance novels for $80, and

O'Conell offers a package of 10 horror novels and 10 romance novels for $90.

31. How many packages should you purchase from Duffin House and Higgins Press to obtain at least 4,000 horror novels and 6,000 romance novels at minimum cost? What is the minimum cost?

32. How many packages should you purchase from McPhearson Imprints and O'Conell Books to obtain at least 5,000 horror novels and 4,000 romance novels at minimum cost? What is the minimum cost?

33. Refer to the scenario in Exercise 31. As it turns out, John O'Hagan promised Marjory Duffin that OHaganBooks.com would buy at least 20 percent more packages from Duffin as from Higgins, but you still want to obtain at least 4,000 horror novels and 6,000 romance novels at minimum cost.

   a. *Without solving the problem,* say which of the following statements are possible:

     (A) The cost will stay the same.
     (B) The cost will increase.
     (C) The cost will decrease.
     (D) It will be impossible to meet all the conditions.
     (E) The cost will become unbounded.

   b. If you wish to meet all the requirements at minimum cost, how many packages should you purchase from each publisher? What is the minimum cost?

34. Refer to Exercise 32. You are about to place the order meeting the requirements of Exercise 32 when you are told that you can order no more than a total of 500 packages, and that at least half of the packages should be from McPhearson. Explain why this is impossible by referring to the feasible region for Exercise 32.

35. *Investments* Marjory Duffin's portfolio manager has suggested two high-yielding stocks: European Emerald Emporium (EEE) and Royal Ruby Retailers (RRR).[42] EEE shares cost $50, yield 4.5% in dividends, and have a risk index of 2.0 per share. RRR shares cost $55, yield 5% in dividends, and have a risk index of 3.0 per share. Marjory has up to $12,100 to invest and would like to earn at least $550 in dividends. How many shares of each stock should she purchase to meet her requirements and minimize the total risk index for her portfolio? What is the minimum total risk index?

36. *Investments* Marjory Duffin's other portfolio manager has suggested another two high-yielding stocks: Countrynarrow Mortgages (CNM) and Scotland Subprime (SS).[43] CNM shares cost $40, yield 5.5% in dividends, and have a risk index of 1.0 per share. SS shares cost $25, yield 7.5% in

dividends, and have a risk index of 1.5 per share. Marjory can invest up to $30,000 in these stocks and would like to earn at least $1,650 in dividends. How many shares of each stock should she purchase in order to meet her requirements and minimize the total risk index for her portfolio?

37. *Resource Allocation* Billy-Sean O'Hagan has joined the Physics Society at Suburban State University, and the group is planning to raise money to support the dying space program by making and selling umbrellas. The society intends to make three models: the Sprinkle, the Storm, and the Hurricane. The amounts of cloth, metal, and wood used in making each model are given in this table:

	Sprinkle	Storm	Hurricane	Total Available
Cloth (sq. yd)	1	2	2	600
Metal (lbs)	2	1	3	600
Wood (lbs)	1	3	6	600
Profit ($)	1	1	2	

The table also shows the amounts of each material available in a given day and the profits to be made from each model. How many of each model should the society make in order to maximize its profit?

38. *Profit* Duffin House, which is now the largest publisher of books sold at the OHaganBooks.com site, prints three kinds of books: paperback, quality paperback, and hardcover. The amounts of paper, ink, and time on the presses required for each kind of book are given in this table:

	Paperback	Quality Paperback	Hardcover	Total Available
Paper (pounds)	3	2	1	6,000
Ink (gallons)	2	1	3	6,000
Time (minutes)	10	10	10	22,000
Profit ($)	1	2	3	

The table also lists the total amounts of paper, ink, and time available in a given day and the profits made on each kind of book. How many of each kind of book should Duffin print to maximize profit?

39. *Purchases* You are just about to place book orders from Duffin and Higgins (see Exercise 31) when everything changes: Duffin House informs you that, due to a global romance crisis, its packages now each will contain 5 horror novels but only 2 romance novels and still cost $50 per package. Packages from Higgins will now contain 10 of each type of novel, but now cost $150 per package. Ewing Books enters the fray and offers its own package of 5 horror and 5 romance novels for $100. The sales manager now tells you that at least 50% of the packages must come from Higgins Press

---

[42]RRR and EEE happen to be, respectively, the ticker symbols of RSC Holdings (an equipment rental provider) and Evergreen Energy Inc. (a environmentally friendly energy technology company) and thus have nothing to do with rubies and emeralds.

[43]CNM is actually the ticker symbol of Carnegie Wave, whereas SS is not the ticker symbol of any U.S.-based company we are aware of.

and, as before, you want to obtain at least 4,000 horror novels and 6,000 romance novels at minimum cost. Taking all of this into account, how many packages should you purchase from each publisher? What is the minimum cost?

40. *Purchases* You are about to place book orders from McPhearson and O'Conell (see Exercise 32) when you get an e-mail from McPhearson Imprints saying that, sorry, but they have stopped publishing romance novels due to the global romance crisis and can now offer only packages of 10 horror novels for $50. O'Conell is still offering packages of 10 horror novels and 10 romance novels for $90, and now the United States Treasury, in an attempt to bolster the floundering romance industry, is offering its own package of 20 romance novels for $120. Furthermore, Congress, in approving this measure, has passed legislation dictating that at least two thirds of the packages in every order must come from the U.S. Treasury. As before, you wish to obtain at least 5,000 horror novels and 4,000 romance novels at minimum cost. Taking all of this into account, how many packages should you purchase from each supplier? What is the minimum cost?

41. *Degree Requirements* During his lunch break, John O'Hagan decides to devote some time to assisting his son Billy-Sean, who continues to have a terrible time planning his college course schedule. The latest Bulletin of Suburban State University claims to have added new flexibility to its course requirements, but it remains as complicated as ever. It reads as follows:

> *All candidates for the degree of Bachelor of Arts at SSU must take at least 120 credits from the Sciences, Fine Arts, Liberal Arts, and Mathematics combined, including at least as many Science credits as Fine Arts credits, and at most twice as many Mathematics credits as Science credits, but with Liberal Arts credits exceeding Mathematics credits by no more than one third of the number of Fine Arts credits.*

Science and fine arts credits cost $300 each, and liberal arts and mathematics credits cost $200 each. John would like to have Billy-Sean meet all the requirements at a minimum total cost.

a. Set up (without solving) the associated linear programming problem.
b. ⊤ Use technology to determine how many of each type of credit Billy-Sean should take. What will the total cost be?

42. *Degree Requirements* No sooner had the "new and flexible" course requirement been released than the English Department again pressured the University Senate to include their vaunted "Verbal Expression" component in place of the fine arts requirement in all programs (including the sciences):

> *All candidates for the degree of Bachelor of Science at SSU must take at least 120 credits from the Liberal Arts, Sciences, Verbal Expression, and Mathematics, including at most as many Science credits as Liberal Arts credits, and at least twice as many Verbal Expression credits as Science credits and Liberal Arts*

credits combined, with Liberal Arts credits exceeding Mathematics credits by at least a quarter of the number of Verbal Expression credits.

Science credits cost $300 each, while each credit in the remaining subjects now costs $400. John would like to have Billy-Sean meet all the requirements at a minimum total cost.

a. Set up (without solving) the associated linear programming problem.
b. ⊤ Use technology to determine how many of each type of credit Billy-Sean should take. What will the total cost be?

43. *Shipping* On the same day that the sales department at Duffin House received an order for 600 packages from the OHaganBooks.com Texas headquarters, it received an additional order for 200 packages from FantasyBooks.com, based in California. Duffin House has warehouses in New York and Illinois. The New York warehouse has 600 packages in stock, but the Illinois warehouse is closing down and has only 300 packages in stock. Shipping costs per package of books are as follows: New York to Texas: $20; New York to California: $50; Illinois to Texas: $30; Illinois to California: $40. What is the lowest total shipping cost for which Duffin House can fill the orders? How many packages should be sent from each warehouse to each online bookstore at a minimum shipping cost?

44. *Transportation Scheduling* Duffin House is about to start a promotional blitz for its new book, *Advanced String Theory for the Liberal Arts*. The company has 25 salespeople stationed in Austin and 10 in San Diego, and would like to fly at least 15 to sales fairs in each of Houston and Cleveland. A round-trip plane flight from Austin to Houston costs $200; from Austin to Cleveland costs $150; from San Diego to Houston costs $400; and from San Diego to Cleveland costs $200. How many salespeople should the company fly from each of Austin and San Diego to each of Houston and Cleveland for the lowest total cost in air fare?

45. *Marketing* Marjory Duffin, head of Duffin House, reveals to John O'Hagan that FantasyBooks.com is considering several promotional schemes: It may offer two books for the price of one, three books for the price of two, or possibly a free copy of *Brain Surgery for Klutzes* with each order. OHaganBooks.com's marketing advisers Floody and O'Lara seem to have different ideas as to how to respond. Floody suggests offering *three* books for the price of one, while O'Lara suggests instead offering a free copy of the *Finite Mathematics Student Solutions Manual* with every purchase. After a careful analysis, O'Hagan comes up with the following payoff matrix, where the payoffs represent the number of customers, in thousands, O'Hagan expects to gain from FantasyBooks.com.

	FantasyBooks.com			
	No Promo	2 for Price of 1	3 for Price of 2	Brain Surgery
OHaganBooks.com No Promo	0	−60	−40	10
3 for Price of 1	30	20	10	15
Finite Math	20	0	15	10

Find the optimal strategies for both companies and the expected shift in customers.

46. *Study Techniques* Billy-Sean's friend Pat from college has been spending all of his time in fraternity activities, and thus knows absolutely nothing about any of the three topics on tomorrow's math test. He has turned to Billy-Sean for advice as to how to spend his "all-nighter." The table below shows the scores Pat could expect to earn if the entire test were to be in a specific subject. (Because he knows no linear programming or matrix algebra, the table shows, for instance, that studying game theory all night will not be much use in preparing him for this topic.)

	Test		
Pat's Strategies ↓	**Game Theory**	**Linear Programming**	**Matrix Algebra**
Study Game Theory	30	0	20
Study Linear Programming	0	70	0
Study Matrix Algebra	0	0	70

What percentage of the night should Pat spend on each topic, assuming the principles of game theory, and what score can he expect to get?

Case Study   The Diet Problem

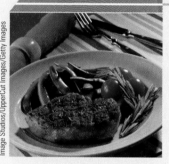

The Galaxy Nutrition health-food mega-store chain provides free online nutritional advice and support to its customers. As Web site technical consultant, you are planning to construct an interactive Web page to assist customers in preparing a diet tailored to their nutritional and budgetary requirements. Ideally, the customer would select foods to consider and specify nutritional and/or budgetary constraints, and the tool should return the optimal diet meeting those requirements. You would also like the Web page to allow the customer to decide whether, for instance, to find the cheapest possible diet meeting the requirements, the diet with the lowest number of calories, or the diet with the least total carbohydrates.

After doing a little research, you notice that the kind of problem you are trying is solve is quite well known and referred to as the *diet problem*, and that solving the diet problem is a famous example of linear programming. Indeed, there are already some online pages that solve versions of the problem that minimize total cost, so you have adequate information to assist you as you plan the page.*

✳ See, for instance, the Diet Problem Demo at the NEOS Wiki: www.neos-guide.org/NEOS/index.php/Diet_Problem_Demo

You decide to start on a relatively small scale, starting with a program that uses a list of 10 foods, and minimizes either total caloric intake or total cost and satisfies a small list of requirements. Following is a small part of a table of nutritional information from the demo at the NEOS Wiki (all the values shown are for a single serving) as well as approximate minimum daily requirements:

	Price per Serving	*Calories*	*Total Fat g*	*Carbs g*	*Dietary Fiber g*	*Protein g*	*Vit C IU*
Tofu	$0.31	88.2	5.5	2.2	1.4	9.4	0.1
Roast Chicken	$0.84	277.4	10.8	0	0	42.2	0
Spaghetti w/Sauce	$0.78	358.2	12.3	58.3	11.6	8.2	27.9
Tomato	$0.27	25.8	0.4	5.7	1.4	1.0	23.5
Oranges	$0.15	61.6	0.2	15.4	3.1	1.2	69.7
Wheat Bread	$0.05	65.0	1.0	12.4	1.3	2.2	0
Cheddar Cheese	$0.25	112.7	9.3	0.4	0	7.0	0
Oatmeal	$0.82	145.1	2.3	25.3	4.0	6.1	0
Peanut Butter	$0.07	188.5	16.0	6.9	2.1	7.7	0
White Tuna in Water	$0.69	115.6	2.1	0	0	22.7	0
Minimum Requirements		2,200	20	80	25	60	90

Source: www.neos-guide.org/NEOS/index.php/Diet_Problem_Demo

Now you get to work. As always, you start by identifying the unknowns. Since the output of the Web page will consist of a recommended diet, the unknowns should logically be the number of servings of each item of food selected by the user. In your first trial run, you decide to include all the 10 food items listed, so you take

$x_1 =$ Number of servings of tofu

$x_2 =$ Number of servings of roast chicken

$\vdots$

$x_{10} =$ Number of servings of white tuna in water.

You now set up a linear programming problem for two sample scenarios:

Scenario 1 (Minimum Cost): Satisfy all minimum nutritional requirements at a minimum cost. Here the linear programming problem is:

Minimize

$$c = 0.31x_1 + 0.84x_2 + 0.78x_3 + 0.27x_4 + 0.15x_5 + 0.05x_6 + 0.25x_7$$
$$+ 0.82x_8 + 0.07x_9 + 0.69x_{10}$$

subject to

$$88.2x_1 + 277.4x_2 + 358.2x_3 + 25.8x_4 + 61.6x_5 + 65x_6 + 112.7x_7$$
$$+ 145.1x_8 + 188.5x_9 + 115.6x_{10} \geq 2{,}200$$

$$5.5x_1 + 10.8x_2 + 12.3x_3 + 0.4x_4 + 0.2x_5 + 1x_6 + 9.3x_7 + 2.3x_8$$
$$+ 16x_9 + 2.1x_{10} \geq 20$$

$$2.2x_1 + 58.3x_3 + 5.7x_4 + 15.4x_5 + 12.4x_6 + 0.4x_7 + 25.3x_8 + 6.9x_9 \geq 80$$

$$1.4x_1 + 11.6x_3 + 1.4x_4 + 3.1x_5 + 1.3x_6 + 4x_8 + 2.1x_9 \geq 25$$

$$9.4x_1 + 42.2x_2 + 8.2x_3 + 1x_4 + 1.2x_5 + 2.2x_6 + 7x_7 + 6.1x_8 + 7.7x_9$$
$$+ 22.7x_{10} \geq 60$$

$$0.1x_1 + 27.9x_3 + 23.5x_4 + 69.7x_5 \geq 90.$$

This is clearly the kind of linear programming problem no one in their right mind would like to do by hand (solving it requires 16 tableaus!) so you decide to use the online simplex method tool at the Website (www.WanerMath.com → Student Web Site → On Line Utilities → Simplex Method Tool).

Here is a picture of the input, entered almost exactly as written above (you need to enter each constraint on a new line, and "Minimize c = 0.31x1 + ⋯ Subject to" must be typed on a single line):

```
                Type your linear programming problem below. (Press "Example" to see how to set it up.)
Minimize   c =
0.31x1+0.84x2+0.78x3+0.27x4+0.15x5+0.05x6+0.25x7+0.82x8+0.07x9+0.69x10 Subject to
88.2x1+277.4x2+358.2x3+25.8x4+61.6x5+65x6+112.7x7+145.1x8+188.5x9+115.6x10 >= 2200
5.5x1+10.8x2+12.3x3+0.4x4+0.2x5+1x6+9.3x7+2.3x8+16x9+2.1x10 >= 20
2.2x1+58.3x3+5.7x4+15.4x5+12.4x6+0.4x7+25.3x8+6.9x9 >= 80
1.4x1+11.6x3+1.4x4+3.1x5+1.3x6+4x8+2.1x9 >= 25
9.4x1+42.2x2+8.2x3+1x4+1.2x5+2.2x6+7x7+6.1x8+7.7x9+22.7x10 >= 60
0.1x1+0x2+27.9x3+23.5x4+69.7x5 >= 90
```

Clicking "Solve" results in the following solution:

$$c = 0.981126;\ x_1 = 0,\ x_2 = 0,\ x_3 = 0,\ x_4 = 0,\ x_5 = 1.29125,\ x_6 = 0,\ x_7 = 0,$$
$$x_8 = 0,\ x_9 = 11.2491,\ x_{10} = 0.$$

This means that you can satisfy all the daily requirements for less than \$1 on a diet of 1.3 servings of orange juice and 11.2 servings of peanut butter! Although you enjoy peanut butter, 11.2 servings seems a little over the top, so you modify the LP problem by adding a new constraint (which also suggests to you that some kind of flexibility needs to be built into the site to allow users to set limits on the number of servings of any one item):

$$x_9 \le 3.$$

This new constraint results in the following solution:

$$c = 1.59981;\; x_1 = 0,\, x_2 = 0,\, x_3 = 0,\, x_4 = 0,\, x_5 = 1.29125,\, x_6 = 23.9224,$$
$$x_7 = 0,\, x_8 = 0,\, x_9 = 3,\, x_{10} = 0.$$

Because wheat bread is cheap and, in large enough quantities, supplies ample protein, the program has now substituted 23.9 servings of wheat bread for the missing peanut butter for a total cost of \$1.60.

Unfettered, you now add

$$x_6 \le 4$$

and obtain the following spaghetti, bread, and peanut butter diet for \$3.40 per day:

$$c = 3.40305;\; x_1 = 0,\, x_2 = 0,\, x_3 = 3.83724,\, x_4 = 0,\, x_5 = 0,\, x_6 = 4,\, x_7 = 0,$$
$$x_8 = 0,\, x_9 = 3,\, x_{10} = 0.$$

Scenario 2 (Minimum Calories): Minimize total calories and satisfy all minimum nutritional requirements (except for caloric intake).

Here, the linear programming problem is

Minimize
$$c = 88.2x_1 + 277.4x_2 + 358.2x_3 + 25.8x_4 + 61.6x_5 + 65x_6 + 112.7x_7$$
$$+ 145.1x_8 + 188.5x_9 + 115.6x_{10}$$

subject to
$$5.5x_1 + 10.8x_2 + 12.3x_3 + 0.4x_4 + 0.2x_5 + 1x_6 + 9.3x_7 + 2.3x_8 + 16x_9$$
$$+ 2.1x_{10} \ge 20$$
$$2.2x_1 + 58.3x_3 + 5.7x_4 + 15.4x_5 + 12.4x_6 + 0.4x_7 + 25.3x_8 + 6.9x_9 \ge 80$$
$$1.4x_1 + 11.6x_3 + 1.4x_4 + 3.1x_5 + 1.3x_6 + 4x_8 + 2.1x_9 \ge 25$$
$$9.4x_1 + 42.2x_2 + 8.2x_3 + 1x_4 + 1.2x_5 + 2.2x_6 + 7x_7 + 6.1x_8 + 7.7x_9$$
$$+ 22.7x_{10} \ge 60$$
$$0.1x_1 + 27.9x_3 + 23.5x_4 + 69.7x_5 \ge 90.$$

You obtain the following 716-calorie tofu, tomato, and tuna diet:

$$x_1 = 2.07232,\, x_2 = 0,\, x_3 = 0,\, x_4 = 15.7848,\, x_5 = 0,\, x_6 = 0,\, x_7 = 0,\, x_8 = 0,$$
$$x_9 = 0,\, x_{10} = 1.08966.$$

As 16 servings of tomatoes seems a little over the top, you add the new constraint $x_4 \le 3$ and obtain a 783-calorie tofu, tomato, orange, and tuna diet:

$$x_1 = 2.81682,\, x_2 = 0,\, x_3 = 0,\, x_4 = 3,\, x_5 = 5.43756,\, x_6 = 0,\, x_7 = 0,\, x_8 = 0,$$
$$x_9 = 0,\, x_{10} = 1.05713.$$

What the trial runs have shown you is that your Web site will need to allow the user to set reasonable upper bounds for the number of servings of each kind of food considered. You now get to work writing the algorithm, which appears here:

www.WanerMath.com → Student Web Site → On Line Utilities → Diet Problem Solver

EXERCISES

1. Briefly explain why roast chicken, which supplies protein more cheaply than either tofu or tuna, does not appear in the optimal solution in either scenario.

2. Consider the optimal solution obtained in Scenario 1 when peanut butter and bread were restricted. Experiment on the Simplex Method Tool by increasing the protein requirement 10 grams at a time until chicken appears in the optimal diet. At what level of protein does the addition of chicken first become necessary?

3. What constraints would you add for a person who wants to eat at most two servings of chicken a day and is allergic to tomatoes and peanut butter? What is the resulting diet for Scenario 2?

4. What is the linear programming problem for someone who wants as much protein as possible at a cost of no more than $6 per day with no more than 50 g of carbohydrates per day assuming they want to satisfy the minimum requirements for all the remaining nutrients? What is the resulting diet?

5. Is it possible to obtain a diet with no bread or peanut butter in Scenario 1 costing less than $4 per day?

TI-83/84 Plus **Technology Guide**

Section 5.1

Some calculators, including the TI-83/84 Plus, will shade one side of a graph, but you need to tell the calculator which side to shade. For instance, to obtain the solution set of $2x + 3y \leq 6$ shown in Figure 4:

1. Solve the corresponding equation $2x + 3y = 6$ for y and use the input shown below:

2. The icon to the left of "Y_1" tells the calculator to shade above the line. You can cycle through the various shading options by positioning the cursor to the left of Y_1 and pressing ENTER until you see the one you want. Here's what the graph will look like:

Section 5.3

Example 3 (page 346) The Acme Baby Foods example in the text leads to the following linear programming problem:

$$\begin{aligned}
\text{Maximize} \quad & p = 10x + 7y \\
\text{subject to} \quad & x \leq 600 \\
& 2x + 3y \leq 3,600 \\
& 5x + 3y \leq 4,500 \\
& x \geq 0, \ y \geq 0.
\end{aligned}$$

Solve it using technology.

Solution with Technology

When we introduce slack variables, we get the following system of equations:

$$\begin{aligned}
x \quad\quad + s \quad\quad\quad\quad &= 600 \\
2x + 3y \quad + t \quad\quad\quad &= 3,600 \\
5x + 3y \quad\quad\quad + u \quad &= 4,500 \\
-10x - 7y \quad\quad\quad\quad + p &= 0.
\end{aligned}$$

We use the PIVOT program for the TI-83/84 Plus to help with the simplex method. This program is available at the Website by following

Everything for Finite Math → Math Tools for Chapter 5.

Because the calculator handles decimals as easily as integers, there is no need to avoid them, except perhaps to save limited screen space. If we don't need to avoid decimals, we can use the traditional Gauss-Jordan method (see the discussion at the end of Section 3.2): After selecting your pivot, and prior to clearing the pivot column, *divide the pivot row by the value of the pivot, thereby turning the pivot into a 1.*

The main drawback to using the TI-83/84 Plus is that we can't label the rows and columns. We can mentally label them as we go, but we can do without labels entirely if we wish. We begin by entering the initial tableau as the matrix [A]. (Another drawback to using the TI-83/84 Plus is that it can't show the whole tableau at once. Here and below we show tableaux across several screens. Use the TI-83/84 Plus's arrow keys to scroll a matrix left and right so you can see all of it.)

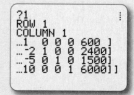

The following is the sequence of tableaux we get while using the simplex method with the help of the PIVOT program.

TECHNOLOGY GUIDE

After determining that the next pivot is in the third row and second column, we divide the third row by the pivot, 3, and then pivot:

```
?2                    :
DIVIDE ROW 3
BY 3
[[1  0   1        ...
 [0  3  -2        ...
 [0  1  -1.66666...
 [0 -7  10        ...
```

```
?2                    :
DIVIDE ROW 3
BY 3
...       0 0    ...
          1 0
...667 0 .3333333...
...       0 0    ...
```

```
?2                    :
DIVIDE ROW 3
BY 3
...       0 600 ]
          0 2400]
...333333 0 500 ]
...       1 6000]]
```

```
?1                    :
ROW 3
COLUMN 2
[[1  0   1        ...
 [0  0   3        ...
 [0  1  -1.666666...
 [0  0  -1.666666...
```

```
?1                    :
ROW 3
COLUMN 2
...       0 0    ...
          1 -1
...667 0 .3333333...
...667 0 2.333333...
```

```
?1                    :
ROW 3
COLUMN 2
...       0 600 ]
          0 900 ]
...333333 0 500 ]
...333333 1 9500]]
```

The next pivot is the 3 in the second row, third column. We divide its row by 3 and pivot:

```
?2                    :
DIVIDE ROW 2
BY 3
[[1  0   1        ...
 [0  0   1        ...
 [0  1  -1.666666...
 [0  0  -1.666666...
```

```
?2                    :
DIVIDE ROW 2
BY 3
...       0        ...
          .33333333...
...6667 0          ...
...6667 0          ...
```

```
?2                    :
DIVIDE ROW 2
BY 3
...       0
...33 -.333333333...
...       .3333333333...
...       2.333333333...
```

```
?2                    :
DIVIDE ROW 2
BY 3
...       0 600 ]
...333333 0 300 ]
...33333  0 500 ]
...33333  1 9500]]
```

```
?1                    :
ROW 2
COLUMN 3
[[1  0  0  -.33333...
 [0  0  1  .333333...
 [0  1  0  .555555...
 [0  0  0  .555555...
```

```
?1                    :
ROW 2
COLUMN 3
...3333 .33333333...
...333  -.3333333...
...556  -.7777777...
...556  1.7777777...
```

```
?1                    :
ROW 2
COLUMN 3
...3333   0 300  ]
...33333  0 300  ]
...22222  0 1000 ]
...7778   1 10000]]
```

There are no negative numbers in the bottom row, so we're finished. How do we read off the optimal solutions if we don't have labels, though? Look at the columns containing one 1 and three 0s. They are the x column, the y column, the s column, and the p column. Think of the 1 that appears in each of these columns as a pivot whose column has been cleared. If we had labels, the row containing a pivot would have the same label as the column containing that pivot. We can now read off the solution as follows:

x column: The pivot is in the first row, so row 1 would have been labeled with x. We look at the rightmost column to read off the value $x = 300$.

y column: The pivot is in row 3, so we look at the rightmost column to read off the value $y = 1,000$.

s column: The pivot is in row 2, so we look at the rightmost column to read off the value $s = 300$.

p column: The pivot is in row 3, so we look at the rightmost column to read off the value $p = 10,000$.

Thus, the maximum value of p is $10,000¢ = \$100$, which occurs when $x = 300$ and $y = 1,000$. The values of the slack variables are $s = 300$ and $t = u = 0$. (Look at the t and u columns to see that they must be inactive.)

SPREADSHEET   Technology Guide

Section 5.1

Excel is not a particularly good tool for graphing linear inequalities because it cannot easily shade one side of a line. One solution available in Excel, for instance, is to use the "error bar" feature to indicate which side of the line *should* be shaded. For example, here is how we might graph the inequality $2x + 3y \leq 6$.

1. Create a scatter graph using two points to construct a line segment (as in Chapter 1). (Notice that we had to solve the equation $2x + 3y = 6$ for y.)

2. Double-click on the line segment, and use the "X-Error Bars" feature to obtain a diagram similar to the one on the left below, where the error bars indicate the direction of shading.

Alternatively, you can use the Drawing Palette to create a polygon with a semi-transparent fill, as shown above.

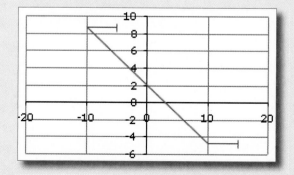

6

Sets and Counting

Website

www.WanerMath.com

At the Website you will find:

- Section-by-section tutorials, including game tutorials with randomized quizzes

- A detailed chapter summary

- A true/false quiz

- A utility to compute factorials, permutations, and combinations

- Additional review exercises

Case Study Designing a Puzzle

As Product Design Manager for Cerebral Toys, Inc., you are constantly on the lookout for ideas for intellectually stimulating yet inexpensive toys. Your design team recently came up with an idea for a puzzle consisting of a number of plastic cubes. Each cube will have two faces colored red, two white, and two blue, and there will be exactly two cubes with each possible configuration of colors. The goal of the puzzle is to seek out the matching pairs, thereby enhancing a child's geometric intuition and three-dimensional manipulation skills. **If the kit is to include every possible configuration of colors, how many cubes will the kit contain?**

Image Source/Getty Images

Introduction

The theory of sets is the foundation for most of mathematics. It also has direct applications—for example, in searching computer databases. We will use set theory extensively in the chapter on probability, and thus much of this chapter revolves around the idea of a **set of outcomes** of a procedure such as rolling a pair of dice or choosing names from a database. Also important in probability is the theory of **counting** the number of elements in a set, which is called **combinatorics**.

Counting elements is not a trivial proposition; for example, the betting game Lotto (used in many state lotteries) has you pick six numbers from some range—say, 1–55. If your six numbers match the six numbers chosen in the "official drawing," you win the top prize. How many Lotto tickets would you need to buy to guarantee that you will win? That is, how many Lotto tickets are possible? By the end of this chapter, we will be able to answer these questions.

6.1   Sets and Set Operations

In this section we introduce some of the basic ideas of set theory. Some of the examples and applications we see here are derived from the theory of probability and will recur throughout the rest of this chapter and the next.

Sets

Sets and Elements

A **set** is a collection of items, referred to as the **elements** of the set.

Visualizing a Set

Set

Elements of the Set

We usually use a capital letter to name a set and braces to enclose the elements of a set.

$x \in A$ means that x **is an element of** the set A. If x is not an element of A, we write $x \notin A$.

$B = A$ means that A and B have the same elements. The order in which the elements are listed does not matter.

$B \subseteq A$ means that B is a **subset** of A; every element of B is also an element of A.

$B \subset A$ means that B is a **proper subset** of A: $B \subseteq A$, but $B \neq A$.

Quick Examples

$W = \{\text{Amazon, eBay, Apple}\}$
$N = \{1, 2, 3, \ldots\}$

Amazon $\in W$ (W as above)
Microsoft $\notin W$ $2 \in N$

$\{5, -9, 1, 3\} = \{-9, 1, 3, 5\}$
$\{1, 2, 3, 4\} \neq \{1, 2, 3, 6\}$

$\{\text{eBay, Apple}\} \subseteq W$
$\{1, 2, 3, 4\} \subseteq \{1, 2, 3, 4\}$

$\{\text{eBay, Apple}\} \subset W$
$\{1, 2, 3\} \subset \{1, 2, 3, 4\}$
$\{1, 2, 3\} \subset N$ (N as above)

Ø is the **empty set**, the set containing no elements. It is a subset of every set.

$\emptyset \subseteq W$
$\emptyset \subset W$

A **finite** set has finitely many elements. An **infinite** set does not have finitely many elements.

$W = \{\text{Amazon, eBay, Apple}\}$ is a finite set.
$N = \{1, 2, 3, \ldots\}$ is an infinite set.

One type of set we'll use often is the **set of outcomes** of some activity or experiment. For example, if we toss a coin and observe which side faces up, there are two possible outcomes, heads (H) and tails (T). The set of outcomes of tossing a coin once can be written

$$S = \{\text{H, T}\}.$$

As another example, suppose we roll a die that has faces numbered 1 through 6, as usual, and observe which number faces up. The set of outcomes *could* be represented as

$$S = \left\{ \boxdot, \boxdot, \boxdot, \boxdot, \boxdot, \boxdot \right\}.$$

However, we can much more easily write

$$S = \{1, 2, 3, 4, 5, 6\}.$$

EXAMPLE 1 Two Dice: Distinguishable vs. Indistinguishable

a. Suppose we have two dice that we can distinguish in some way—say, one is green and one is red. If we roll both dice, what is the set of outcomes?

b. Describe the set of outcomes if the dice are indistinguishable.

Solution

a. A systematic way of laying out the set of outcomes for a distinguishable pair of dice is shown in Figure 1.

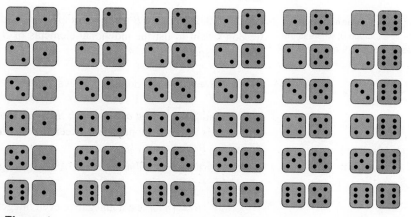

Figure 1

In the first row all the green dice show a 1, in the second row a 2, in the third row a 3, and so on. Similarly, in the first column all the red dice show a 1, in the second column a 2, and so on. The diagonal pairs (top left to bottom right) show all the "doubles." Using the picture as a guide, we can write the set of 36 outcomes as follows.

$$S = \begin{cases} (1, 1), \ (1, 2), \ (1, 3), \ (1, 4), \ (1, 5), \ (1, 6), \\ (2, 1), \ (2, 2), \ (2, 3), \ (2, 4), \ (2, 5), \ (2, 6), \\ (3, 1), \ (3, 2), \ (3, 3), \ (3, 4), \ (3, 5), \ (3, 6), \\ (4, 1), \ (4, 2), \ (4, 3), \ (4, 4), \ (4, 5), \ (4, 6), \\ (5, 1), \ (5, 2), \ (5, 3), \ (5, 4), \ (5, 5), \ (5, 6), \\ (6, 1), \ (6, 2), \ (6, 3), \ (6, 4), \ (6, 5), \ (6, 6) \end{cases} \qquad \text{Distinguishable dice}$$

Notice that S is also the set of outcomes if we roll a single die twice, if we take the first number in each pair to be the outcome of the first roll and the second number the outcome of the second roll.

b. If the dice are truly indistinguishable, we will have no way of knowing which die is which once they are rolled. Think of placing two identical dice in a closed box and then shaking the box. When we look inside afterward, there is no way to tell which die is which. (If we make a small marking on one of the dice or somehow keep track of it as it bounces around, we are *distinguishing* the dice.) We regard two dice as **indistinguishable** if we make no attempt to distinguish them. Thus, for example, the two different outcomes $(1, 3)$ and $(3, 1)$ from part (a) would represent the same outcome in part (b) (one die shows a 3 and the other a 1). Because the set of outcomes should contain each outcome only once, we can remove $(3, 1)$. Following this approach gives the following smaller set of outcomes:

$$S = \begin{cases} (1, 1), \ (1, 2), \ (1, 3), \ (1, 4), \ (1, 5), \ (1, 6), \\ (2, 2), \ (2, 3), \ (2, 4), \ (2, 5), \ (2, 6), \\ (3, 3), \ (3, 4), \ (3, 5), \ (3, 6), \\ (4, 4), \ (4, 5), \ (4, 6), \\ (5, 5), \ (5, 6), \\ (6, 6) \end{cases}. \qquad \text{Indistinguishable dice}$$

EXAMPLE 2   Set-Builder Notation

Let $B = \{0, 2, 4, 6, 8\}$. B is the set of all nonnegative✱ even integers less than 10. If we don't want to list the individual elements of B, we can instead use "set-builder notation," and write

$$B = \{n \mid n \text{ is a nonnegative even integer less than } 10\}.$$

This is read "*B is the set of all n such that n is a nonnegative even integer less than 10*." Here is the correspondence between the words and the symbols:

B is the set of all n such that n is a nonnegative even integer less than 10

$$B = \{n \mid n \text{ is a nonnegative even integer less than } 10\}.$$

Figure 2

Venn Diagrams

We can visualize sets and relations between sets using **Venn diagrams**. In a Venn diagram, we represent a set as a region, often a disk (Figure 2).

The elements of A are the points inside the region. The following Venn diagrams illustrate the relations we've discussed so far.

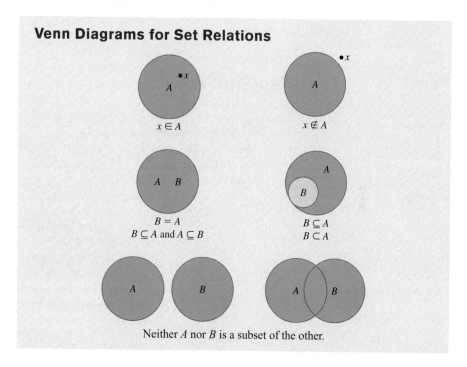

Venn Diagrams for Set Relations

$x \in A$

$x \notin A$

$B = A$
$B \subseteq A$ and $A \subseteq B$

$B \subseteq A$
$B \subset A$

Neither A nor B is a subset of the other.

Note Although the diagram for $B \subseteq A$ suggests a proper subset, it is customary to use the same diagram for both subsets and proper subsets. ■

EXAMPLE 3 **Customer Interests**

NobelBooks.com (a fierce competitor of OHaganBooks.com) maintains a database of customers and the types of books they have purchased. In the company's database is the set of customers

$$S = \{\text{Einstein, Bohr, Millikan, Heisenberg, Schrödinger, Dirac}\}.$$

A search of the database for customers who have purchased cookbooks yields the subset

$$A = \{\text{Einstein, Bohr, Heisenberg, Dirac}\}.$$

Another search, this time for customers who have purchased mysteries, yields the subset

$$B = \{\text{Bohr, Heisenberg, Schrödinger}\}.$$

NobelBooks.com wants to promote a new combination mystery/cookbook, and wants to target two subsets of customers: those who have purchased either cookbooks or mysteries (or both) and, for additional promotions, those who have purchased both cookbooks and mysteries. Name the customers in each of these subsets.

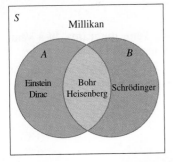

Figure 3

Solution We can picture the database and the two subsets using the Venn diagram in Figure 3.

The set of customers who have purchased either cookbooks or mysteries (or both) consists of the customers who are in *A* or *B* or both: Einstein, Bohr, Heisenberg, Schrödinger, and Dirac. The set of customers who have purchased both cookbooks and mysteries consists of the customers in the overlap of *A* and *B*, Bohr and Heisenberg.

Set Operations

Set Operations

$A \cup B$ is the **union** of *A* and *B*, the set of all elements that are either in *A* or in *B* (or in both).

$$A \cup B = \{x \,|\, x \in A \text{ or } x \in B\}$$

$A \cap B$ is the **intersection** of *A* and *B*, the set of all elements that are common to *A* and *B*.

$$A \cap B = \{x \,|\, x \in A \text{ and } x \in B\}$$

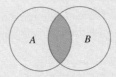

Logical Equivalents
Union: For an element to be in $A \cup B$, it must be in *A* **or** in *B*.
Intersection: For an element to be in $A \cap B$, it must be in *A* **and** in *B*.

Quick Examples

If $A = \{a, b, c, d\}$ and $B = \{c, d, e, f\}$, then

$$A \cup B = \{a, b, c, d, e, f\}$$
$$A \cap B = \{c, d\}.$$

Note Mathematicians always use "or" in its *inclusive* sense: one thing or another or both. ■

There is one other operation we use, called the **complement** of a set *A*, which, roughly speaking, is the set of things *not* in *A*.

Q : *Why only "roughly"? Why not just form the set of things not in A?*

A : This would amount to assuming that there is a set of *all things*. (It would be the complement of the empty set.) Although tempting, talking about entities such as the "set of all things" leads to paradoxes.* Instead, we first need to fix a set *S* of *all objects under consideration,* or the *universe of discourse,* which we generally call the **universal set** for the discussion. For example, when we search the Web, we take *S* to be the set of all Web pages. When talking about integers, we take *S* to be the set of all integers. In other words, our choice of universal set depends on the context. The complement of a set $A \subseteq S$ is then the set of *things in S* that are not in *A*.

* The most famous such paradox is called "Russell's Paradox," after the mathematical logician (and philosopher and pacifist) Bertrand Russell. It goes like this: If there were a set of all things, then there would also be a (smaller) set of all sets. Call it *S*. Now, because *S* is the *set of all* sets, it must contain itself as a member. In other words, $S \in S$. Let *P* be the subset of *S* consisting of all sets that are *not* members of themselves. Now we pose the following question: Is *P* a member of itself? If it is, then, because it is the set of all sets that are *not* members of themselves, it is not a member of itself. On the other hand, if it is *not* a member of itself, then it qualifies as an element of *P*. In other words, it *is* a member of itself! Because neither can be true, something is wrong. What is wrong is the assumption that there is such a thing as the set of all sets or the set of all things.

Complement

If *S* is the universal set and $A \subseteq S$, then A' is the **complement** of *A* (in *S*), the set of all elements of *S* not in *A*.

$$A' = \{x \in S \mid x \notin A\} = \text{Green Region Below}$$

Logical Equivalent

For an element to be in A', it must be in *S* but **not** in *A*.

Quick Example

If $S = \{a, b, c, d, e, f, g\}$ and $A = \{a, b, c, d\}$, then

$$A' = \{e, f, g\}.$$

In the following example we use set operations to describe the sets we found in Example 3, as well as some others.

Joe Hawkins Photography/Alamy

EXAMPLE 4 **Customer Interests**

NobelBooks.com maintains a database of customers and the types of books they have purchased. In the company's database is the set of customers

$$S = \{\text{Einstein, Bohr, Millikan, Heisenberg, Schrödinger, Dirac}\}.$$

A search of the database for customers who have purchased cookbooks yields the subset

$$A = \{\text{Einstein, Bohr, Heisenberg, Dirac}\}.$$

Another search, this time for customers who have purchased mysteries, yields the subset

$$B = \{\text{Bohr, Heisenberg, Schrödinger}\}.$$

Figure 4

Figure 5

A third search, for customers who had registered with the site but not used their first-time customer discount, yields the subset

$$C = \{\text{Millikan}\}.$$

Use set operations to describe the following subsets:

a. The subset of customers who have purchased either cookbooks or mysteries

b. The subset of customers who have purchased both cookbooks and mysteries

c. The subset of customers who have not purchased cookbooks

d. The subset of customers who have purchased cookbooks but have not used their first-time customer discount

Solution   Figure 4 shows two alternative Venn diagram representations of the database. Although the second version shows C overlapping A and B, the placement of the names inside shows that there are no customers in those overlaps.

a. The subset of customers who have bought either cookbooks *or* mysteries is

$$A \cup B = \{\text{Einstein, Bohr, Heisenberg, Schrödinger, Dirac}\}.$$

b. The subset of customers who have bought both cookbooks *and* mysteries is

$$A \cap B = \{\text{Bohr, Heisenberg}\}.$$

c. The subset of customers who have *not* bought cookbooks is

$$A' = \{\text{Millikan, Schrödinger}\}.$$

Note that, for the universal set, we are using the set S of all customers in the database.

d. The subset of customers who have bought cookbooks but have not used their first-time purchase discount is the empty set

$$A \cap C = \varnothing.$$

When the intersection of two sets is empty, we say that the two sets are **disjoint**. In a Venn diagram, disjoint sets are drawn as regions that don't overlap, as in Figure 5.*

✳ People new to set theory sometimes find it strange to consider the empty set a valid set. Here is one of the times where it is very useful to do so. If we did not, we would have to say that $A \cap C$ was defined only when A and C had something in common. Having to deal with the fact that this set operation was not always defined would quickly get tiresome.

➡ **Before we go on...** Computer databases and the Web can be searched using so-called "Boolean searches." These are search requests using "and," "or," and "not." Using "and" gives the intersection of separate searches, using "or" gives the union, and using "not" gives the complement. In the next section we'll see how Web search engines allow such searches. ∎

Cartesian Product

There is one more set operation we need to discuss.

Cartesian Product

The **Cartesian product** of two sets, A and B, is the set of all ordered pairs (a, b) with $a \in A$ and $b \in B$.

$$A \times B = \{(a, b) \mid a \in A \text{ and } b \in B\}$$

In words, $A \times B$ is the set of all ordered pairs whose first component is in A and whose second component is in B.

1. If $A = \{a, b\}$ and $B = \{1, 2, 3\}$, then

$$A \times B = \{(a, 1), (a, 2), (a, 3), (b, 1), (b, 2), (b, 3)\}.$$

Visualizing A $\times$ B

2. If $S = \{H, T\}$, then

$$S \times S = \{(H, H), (H, T), (T, H), (T, T)\}.$$

In other words, if S is the set of outcomes of tossing a coin once, then $S \times S$ is the set of outcomes of tossing a coin twice.

3. If $S = \{1, 2, 3, 4, 5, 6\}$, then

$$S \times S = \left\{ \begin{array}{llllll} (1, 1), & (1, 2), & (1, 3), & (1, 4), & (1, 5), & (1, 6), \\ (2, 1), & (2, 2), & (2, 3), & (2, 4), & (2, 5), & (2, 6), \\ (3, 1), & (3, 2), & (3, 3), & (3, 4), & (3, 5), & (3, 6), \\ (4, 1), & (4, 2), & (4, 3), & (4, 4), & (4, 5), & (4, 6), \\ (5, 1), & (5, 2), & (5, 3), & (5, 4), & (5, 5), & (5, 6), \\ (6, 1), & (6, 2), & (6, 3), & (6, 4), & (6, 5), & (6, 6) \end{array} \right\}.$$

In other words, if S is the set of outcomes of rolling a die once, then $S \times S$ is the set of outcomes of rolling a die twice (or rolling two distinguishable dice).

4. If $A = \{\text{red, yellow}\}$ and $B = \{\text{Mustang, Firebird}\}$, then

$A \times B = \{(\text{red, Mustang}), (\text{red, Firebird}), (\text{yellow, Mustang}), (\text{yellow, Firebird})\}$ which we might also write as

$A \times B = \{\text{red Mustang, red Firebird, yellow Mustang, yellow Firebird}\}$.

EXAMPLE 5 Representing Cartesian Products

The manager of an automobile dealership has collected data on the number of pre-owned Acura, Infiniti, Lexus, and Mercedes cars the dealership has from the 2009, 2010, and 2011 model years. In entering this information on a spreadsheet, the manager would like to have each spreadsheet cell represent a particular year and make. Describe this set of cells.

Solution Because each cell represents a year and a make, we can think of the cell as a pair (year, make), as in (2009, Acura). Thus, the set of cells can be thought of as a Cartesian product:

$$Y = \{2009, 2010, 2011\} \qquad \text{Year of car}$$

$$M = \{\text{Acura, Infiniti, Lexus, Mercedes}\} \qquad \text{Make of car}$$

$$Y \times M = \left\{ \begin{array}{llll} (2009, \text{Acura}) & (2009, \text{Infiniti}) & (2009, \text{Lexus}) & (2009, \text{Mercedes}) \\ (2010, \text{Acura}) & (2010, \text{Infiniti}) & (2010, \text{Lexus}) & (2010, \text{Mercedes}) \\ (2011, \text{Acura}) & (2011, \text{Infiniti}) & (2011, \text{Lexus}) & (2011, \text{Mercedes}) \end{array} \right\}. \qquad \text{Cells}$$

Thus, the manager might arrange the spreadsheet as follows:

	A	B	C	D	E
1		**Acura**	**Infiniti**	**Lexus**	**Mercedes**
2	**2009**	(2009 Acura)	(2009 Infiniti)	(2009 Lexus)	(2009 Mercedes)
3	**2010**	(2010 Acura)	(2010 Infiniti)	(2010 Lexus)	(2010 Mercedes)
4	**2011**	(2011 Acura)	(2011 Infiniti)	(2011 Lexus)	(2011 Mercedes)

The highlighting shows the 12 cells to be filled in, representing the numbers of cars of each year and make. For example, in cell B2 should go the number of 2009 Acuras the dealership has.

➡ **Before we go on...** The arrangement in the spreadsheet in Example 5 is consistent with the matrix notation in Chapter 2. We could also have used the elements of Y as column labels along the top and the elements of M as row labels down the side. Along those lines, we can also visualize the Cartesian product $Y \times M$ as a set of points in the xy-plane ("Cartesian plane") as shown in Figure 6.

Figure 6

6.1 EXERCISES

▼ more advanced   ◆ challenging
[T] indicates exercises that should be solved using technology

List the elements in each of the sets in Exercises 1–16.

1. The set F consisting of the four seasons

2. The set A consisting of the authors of this book

3. The set I of all positive integers no greater than 6

4. The set N of all negative integers greater than -3

5. $A = \{n \mid n$ is a positive integer and $0 \le n \le 3\}$
   HINT [See Example 2.]

6. $A = \{n \mid n$ is a positive integer and $0 < n < 8\}$
   HINT [See Example 2.]

7. $B = \{n \mid n$ is an even positive integer and $0 \le n \le 8\}$

8. $B = \{n \mid n$ is an odd positive integer and $0 \le n \le 8\}$

9. The set of all outcomes of tossing a pair of **(a)** distinguishable coins **(b)** indistinguishable coins HINT [See Example 1.]

10. The set of outcomes of tossing three **(a)** distinguishable coins **(b)** indistinguishable coins HINT [See Example 1.]

11. The set of all outcomes of rolling two distinguishable dice such that the numbers add to 6

12. The set of all outcomes of rolling two distinguishable dice such that the numbers add to 8

13. The set of all outcomes of rolling two indistinguishable dice such that the numbers add to 6

14. The set of all outcomes of rolling two indistinguishable dice such that the numbers add to 8

15. The set of all outcomes of rolling two distinguishable dice such that the numbers add to 13

16. The set of all outcomes of rolling two distinguishable dice such that the numbers add to 1

In each of Exercises 17–20, draw a Venn diagram that illustrates the relationships among the given sets. HINT [See Example 3.]

17. $S = \{$eBay, Google™, Amazon, OHaganBooks, Hotmail$\}$, $A = \{$Amazon, OHaganBooks$\}$, $B = \{$eBay, Amazon$\}$, $C = \{$Amazon, Hotmail$\}$

18. $S = \{$Apple, Dell, Gateway, Pomegranate, Compaq$\}$, $A = \{$Gateway, Pomegranate, Compaq$\}$, $B = \{$Dell, Gateway, Pomegranate, Compaq$\}$, $C = \{$Apple, Dell, Compaq$\}$

19. $S = \{$eBay, Google™, Amazon, OHaganBooks, Hotmail$\}$, $A = \{$Amazon, Hotmail$\}$, $B = \{$eBay, Google™, Amazon, Hotmail$\}$, $C = \{$Amazon, Hotmail$\}$

20. $S = \{$Apple, Dell, Gateway, Pomegranate, Compaq$\}$, $A = \{$Apple, Dell, Pomegranate, Compaq$\}$, $B = \{$Pomegranate$\}$, $C = \{$Pomegranate$\}$

Let $A = \{$June, Janet, Jill, Justin, Jeffrey, Jello$\}$, $B = \{$Janet, Jello, Justin$\}$, and $C = \{$Sally, Solly, Molly, Jolly, Jello$\}$. Find each set in Exercises 21–34. HINT [See Quick Examples on page 400.]

21. $A \cup B$

22. $A \cup C$

23. $A \cup \emptyset$

24. $B \cup \emptyset$

25. $A \cup (B \cup C)$

26. $(A \cup B) \cup C$

27. $C \cap B$

28. $C \cap A$

29. $A \cap \emptyset$

30. $\emptyset \cap B$

31. $(A \cap B) \cap C$

32. $A \cap (B \cap C)$

33. $(A \cap B) \cup C$

34. $A \cup (B \cap C)$

In Exercises 35–42, $A = \{$small, medium, large$\}$, $B = \{$blue, green$\}$, and $C = \{$triangle, square$\}$. HINT [See Quick Examples on page 403.]

35. List the elements of $A \times C$.

36. List the elements of $B \times C$.

37. List the elements of $A \times B$.

38. The elements of $A \times B \times C$ are the ordered triples (a, b, c) with $a \in A, b \in B$, and $c \in C$. List all the elements of $A \times B \times C$.

39. Represent $B \times C$ as cells in a spreadsheet. HINT [See Example 5.]

40. Represent $A \times C$ as cells in a spreadsheet. HINT [See Example 5.]

41. Represent $A \times B$ as cells in a spreadsheet.

42. Represent $A \times A$ as cells in a spreadsheet.

Let $A = \{$H, T$\}$ be the set of outcomes when a coin is tossed, and let $B = \{1, 2, 3, 4, 5, 6\}$ be the set of outcomes when a die is rolled. Write each set in Exercises 43–46 in terms of A and/or B and list its elements.

43. The set of outcomes when a die is rolled and then a coin tossed

44. The set of outcomes when a coin is tossed twice

45. The set of outcomes when a coin is tossed three times

46. The set of outcomes when a coin is tossed twice and then a die is rolled

Let S be the set of outcomes when two distinguishable dice are rolled, let E be the subset of outcomes in which at least one die shows an even number, and let F be the subset of outcomes in which at least one die shows an odd number. List the elements in each subset given in Exercises 47–52.

47. E'

48. F'

49. $(E \cup F)$

50. $(E \cap F)'$

51. $E' \cup F'$

52. $E' \cap F'$

Use Venn diagrams to illustrate the following identities for subsets A, B, and C of S.

53. ▼ $(A \cup B)' = A' \cap B'$ DeMorgan's law

54. ▼ $(A \cap B)' = A' \cup B'$ DeMorgan's law

55. ▼ $(A \cap B) \cap C = A \cap (B \cap C)$ Associative law

56. ▼ $(A \cup B) \cup C = A \cup (B \cup C)$ Associative law

57. ▼ $A \cup (B \cap C) = (A \cup B) \cap (A \cup C)$ Distributive law

58. ▼ $A \cap (B \cup C) = (A \cap B) \cup (A \cap C)$ Distributive law

59. ▼ $S' = \emptyset$ **60.** ▼ $\emptyset' = S$

APPLICATIONS

Databases *A freelance computer consultant keeps a database of her clients, which contains the names*

$S = \{$Acme, Brothers, Crafts, Dion, Effigy, Floyd, Global, Hilbert$\}$.

The following clients owe her money:

$A = \{$Acme, Crafts, Effigy, Global$\}$.

The following clients have done at least $10,000 worth of business with her:

$B = \{$Acme, Brothers, Crafts, Dion$\}$.

The following clients have employed her in the last year:

$C = \{$Acme, Crafts, Dion, Effigy, Global, Hilbert$\}$.

In Exercises 61–68, a subset of clients is described that the consultant could find using her database. Write each subset in terms of A, B, and C and list the clients in that subset.
HINT [See Example 4.]

61. The clients who owe her money and have done at least $10,000 worth of business with her

62. The clients who owe her money or have done at least $10,000 worth of business with her

63. The clients who have done at least $10,000 worth of business with her or have employed her in the last year

64. The clients who have done at least $10,000 worth of business with her and have employed her in the last year

65. The clients who do not owe her money and have employed her in the last year

66. The clients who do not owe her money or have employed her in the last year

67. ▼ The clients who owe her money, have not done at least $10,000 worth of business with her, and have not employed her in the last year

68. ▼ The clients who either do not owe her money, have done at least $10,000 worth of business with her, or have employed her in the last year

69. ▣ ***Boat Sales*** You are given data on revenues from sales of sail boats, motor boats, and yachts for each of the years 2003 through 2006. How would you represent these data in a spreadsheet? The cells in your spreadsheet represent elements of which set?

70. ▣ ***Health-Care Spending*** Spending in most categories of health care in the United States increased dramatically in the last 30 years of the 1900s.[1] You are given data showing total spending on prescription drugs, nursing homes, hospital care, and professional services for each of the last three decades of the 1900s. How would you represent these data in a spreadsheet? The cells in your spreadsheet represent elements of which set?

COMMUNICATION AND REASONING EXERCISES

71. You sell iPads® and jPads. Let I be the set of all iPads you sold last year, and let J be the set of all jPads you sold last year. What set represents the collection of all iPads and jPads you sold combined?

72. You sell two models of music players: the *yoVaina Grandote* and the *yoVaina Minúsculito,* and each comes in three colors: Infraroja, Ultravioleta, and Radiografía. Let M be the set of models and let C be the set of colors. What set represents the different choices a customer can make?

73. You are searching online for techno music that is neither European nor Dutch. In set notation, which set of music files are you searching for?

   (A) Techno $\cap$ (European $\cap$ Dutch$)'$
   (B) Techno $\cap$ (European $\cup$ Dutch$)'$
   (C) Techno $\cup$ (European $\cap$ Dutch$)'$
   (D) Techno $\cup$ (European $\cup$ Dutch$)'$

74. You would like to see either a World War II movie, or one that that is based on a comic book character but does not feature aliens. Which set of movies are you interested in seeing?

   (A) WWII $\cap$ (Comix $\cap$ Aliens$')$
   (B) WWII $\cap$ (Comix $\cup$ Aliens$')$
   (C) WWII $\cup$ (Comix $\cap$ Aliens$')$
   (D) WWII $\cup$ (Comix $\cup$ Aliens$')$

75. ▼ Explain, illustrating by means of an example, why $(A \cap B) \cup C \neq A \cap (B \cup C)$.

76. ▼ Explain, making reference to operations on sets, why the statement "He plays soccer or rugby and cricket" is ambiguous.

77. ▼ Explain the meaning of a universal set, and give two different universal sets that could be used in a discussion about sets of positive integers.

78. ▼ Is the set of outcomes when two indistinguishable dice are rolled (Example 1) a Cartesian product of two sets? If so, which two sets; if not, why not?

79. ▼ Design a database scenario that leads to the following statement: To keep the factory operating at maximum capacity, the plant manager should select the suppliers in $A \cap (B \cup C')$.

80. ▼ Design a database scenario that leads to the following statement: To keep her customers happy, the bookstore owner should stock periodicals in $A \cup (B \cap C')$.

---

[1]Source: Department of Health and Human Services/*New York Times*, January 8, 2002, p. A14.

81. ▼ Rewrite in set notation: She prefers movies that are not violent, are shorter than two hours, and have neither a tragic ending nor an unexpected ending.

82. ▼ Rewrite in set notation: He will cater for any event as long as there are no more than 1,000 people, it lasts for at least three hours, and it is within a 50-mile radius of Toronto.

83. ▼ When this book was being written, the copy editor wanted to delete the comma in the following sentence (see Exercise 74): "You would like to see either a World War II movie, or one that that is based on a comic book character but does not feature aliens." Explain why this would have resulted in an ambiguity.

84. ▼ When an older version of this book was being written, the copy editor wanted to delete the comma in the following sentence: "You would like to see a World War II movie, based on a comic book character but not featuring aliens." Explain why removing the comma would have had no effect on the meaning of the sentence.

6.2   Cardinality

In this section, we begin to look at a deceptively simple idea: the size of a set, which we call its **cardinality**.

Cardinality

If A is a finite set, then its **cardinality** is

$$n(A) = \text{number of elements in } A.$$

Visualizing Cardinality

$n(A) = 6$

Quick Examples

1. Let $S = \{a, b, c\}$. Then $n(S) = 3$.

2. Let S be the set of outcomes when two distinguishable dice are rolled. Then $n(S) = 36$ (see Example 1 in Section 6.1).

3. $n(\varnothing) = 0$ because the empty set has no elements.

Counting the elements in a small, simple set is straightforward. To count the elements in a large, complicated set, we try to describe the set as built of simpler sets using the set operations. We then need to know how to calculate the number of elements in, for example, a union, based on the number of elements in the simpler sets whose union we are taking.

The Cardinality of a Union

How can we calculate $n(A \cup B)$ if we know $n(A)$ and $n(B)$? Our first guess might be that $n(A \cup B)$ is $n(A) + n(B)$. But consider a simple example. Let

$$A = \{a, b, c\}$$

and

$$B = \{b, c, d\}.$$

Then $A \cup B = \{a, b, c, d\}$ so $n(A \cup B) = 4$, but $n(A) + n(B) = 3 + 3 = 6$. The calculation $n(A) + n(B)$ gives the wrong answer because the elements b and c are counted twice, once for being in A and again for being in B. To correct for this overcounting, we need to subtract the number of elements that get counted twice, which is the number of elements that A and B have in common, or $n(A \cap B) = 2$ in this case. So, we get the right number for $n(A \cup B)$ from the following calculation:

$$n(A) + n(B) - n(A \cap B) = 3 + 3 - 2 = 4.$$

This argument leads to the following general formula.

Cardinality of a Union

If A and B are finite sets, then

$$n(A \cup B) = n(A) + n(B) - n(A \cap B).$$

In particular, if A and B are disjoint (meaning that $A \cap B = \emptyset$), then

$$n(A \cup B) = n(A) + n(B).$$

(When A and B are disjoint we say that $A \cup B$ is a **disjoint union**.)

Visualizing Cardinality of a Union

Disjoint Sets

$n(A \cup B) = n(A) + n(B)$
$\qquad\quad = \ 3 \ + \ 1$

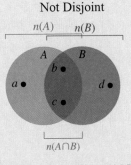

Not Disjoint

$n(A \cup B) = n(A) + n(B) - n(A \cap B)$
$\qquad\quad = \ 3 \ + \ 3 \ - \ 2$

Quick Examples

1. If $A = \{a, b, c, d\}$ and $B = \{b, c, d, e, f\}$, then

$$n(A \cup B) = n(A) + n(B) - n(A \cap B) = 4 + 5 - 3 = 6.$$

In fact, $A \cup B = \{a, b, c, d, e, f\}$.

2. If $A = \{a, b, c\}$ and $B = \{d, e, f\}$, then $A \cap B = \emptyset$, so

$$n(A \cup B) = n(A) + n(B) = 3 + 3 = 6.$$

EXAMPLE 1 Web Searches

In October 2011, a search on Bing™ for "Lt. William Burrows" yielded 29 Web sites containing that phrase, and a search for "Romulan probe" yielded 17 sites. A search for sites containing both phrases yielded 4 Web sites. How many Web sites contained either "Lt. William Burrows," "Romulan probe," or both?

Solution Let A be the set of sites containing "Lt. William Burrows" and let B be the set of sites containing "Romulan probe." We are told that

$$n(A) = 29$$

$$n(B) = 17$$

$$n(A \cap B) = 4. \quad \text{"Lt. William Burrows" AND "Romulan probe"}$$

The formula for the cardinality of the union tells us that

$$n(A \cup B) = n(A) + n(B) - n(A \cap B) = 29 + 17 - 4 = 42.$$

So, 42 sites in the Bing database contained one or both of the phrases "Lt. William Burrows" or "Romulan probe."

➡ **Before we go on...** Each search engine has a different way of specifying a search for a union or an intersection. At Bing or Google™, you can use "OR" for the union and "AND" for the intersection.

Although the formula $n(A \cup B) = n(A) + n(B) - n(A \cap B)$ always holds mathematically, you may sometimes find that, in an actual search, the numbers don't add up. Google, for example, appears not to adhere strictly to the search rule you enter, but instead presents results that it thinks you want.* ∎

✱ For example, in October 2011, a search on Google gave the following results:
"Romulan probe": 471 results
"Abraham Lincoln is born on Earth": 8 results
"Romulan probe" OR "Abraham Lincoln is born on Earth": 1,600 results!

Q: Is there a similar formula for $n(A \cap B)$?

A: The formula for the cardinality of a union can also be thought of as a formula for the cardinality of an intersection. We can solve for $n(A \cap B)$ to get

$$n(A \cap B) = n(A) + n(B) - n(A \cup B).$$

In fact, we can think of this formula as an equation relating four quantities. If we know any three of them, we can use the equation to find the fourth. (See Example 2 on next page).

Q: Is there a similar formula for $n(A')$?

A: We can get a formula for the cardinality of a complement as follows: If S is our universal set and $A \subseteq S$, then S is the disjoint union of A and its complement. That is,

$$S = A \cup A' \quad \text{and} \quad A \cap A' = \emptyset.$$

Applying the cardinality formula for a disjoint union, we get

$$n(S) = n(A) + n(A').$$

We can then solve for $n(A')$ or for $n(A)$ to get the formulas shown below:

Cardinality of a Complement

If S is a finite universal set and A is a subset of S, then

$$n(A') = n(S) - n(A)$$

and

$$n(A) = n(S) - n(A').$$

Visualizing Cardinality of a Complement

$$n(A') = n(S) - n(A)$$
$$= 6 \ - \ 4$$

Quick Example

If $S = \{a, b, c, d, e, f\}$ and $A = \{a, b, c, d\}$, then

$$n(A') = n(S) - n(A) = 6 - 4 = 2.$$

In fact, $A' = \{e, f\}$.

EXAMPLE 2 **Cookbooks**

In November 2011, a search at Amazon.com found 132,000 books on cooking.[2] Of these, 20,000 were on regional cooking, 5,000 were on vegetarian cooking, and 24,000 were on either regional or vegetarian cooking (or both). How many of these books were not on both regional and vegetarian cooking?

Solution Let S be the set of all 132,000 books on cooking, let A be the set of books on regional cooking, and let B be the set of books on vegetarian cooking. We wish to find the size of the complement of the set of books on both regional and vegetarian cooking—that is, $n((A \cap B)')$. Using the formula for the cardinality of a complement, we have

$$n((A \cap B)') = n(S) - n(A \cap B) = 132,000 - n(A \cap B).$$

To find $n(A \cap B)$, we use the formula for the cardinality of a union:

$$n(A \cup B) = n(A) + n(B) - n(A \cap B).$$

Substituting the values we were given, we find

$$24,000 = 20,000 + 5,000 - n(A \cap B),$$

which we can solve to get

$$n(A \cap B) = 1,000.$$

Therefore,

$$n((A \cap B)') = 132,000 - n(A \cap B) = 132,000 - 1,000 = 131,000.$$

So, 131,000 of the books on cooking were not on both regional and vegetarian cooking.

---

[2]Precisely, it found that many books under the subject "Cooking, Food & Wine." Regional cooking falls under "Regional & International." Figures are rounded to the nearest 1,000.

EXAMPLE 3 iPods, iPhones, and iPads

The following table shows sales, in millions of units, of iPods®, iPhones®, and iPads® in the last three quarters of 2011.[3]

	iPods (*A*)	iPhones (*B*)	iPads (*C*)	Total
2011 Q2 (*U*)	9.0	18.7	4.7	32.4
2011 Q3 (*V*)	7.5	20.3	9.3	37.1
2011 Q4 (*W*)	6.6	17.1	11.1	34.8
Total	23.1	56.1	25.1	104.3

Let *S* be the set of all these iPods, iPhones, and iPads, and label the sets representing the sales in each row and column as shown (so that, for example, *A* is the set of all iPods sold during the three quarters). Describe the following sets and compute their cardinality:

a. U' **b.** $A \cap U'$ **c.** $(A \cap U)'$ **d.** $C \cup U$

Solution Because all the figures are stated in millions of units, we'll give our calculations and results in millions of units as well.

a. U' is the set of all items not sold in the second quarter of 2011. To compute its cardinality, we could add the totals for all the other quarters listed in the rightmost column:

$$n(U') = n(V) + n(W) = 37.1 + 34.8 = 71.9 \text{ million items.}$$

Alternatively, we can use the formula for the cardinality of a complement (referring again to the totals in the table):

$$n(U') = n(S) - n(U) = 104.3 - 32.4 = 71.9 \text{ million items.}$$

b. $A \cap U'$ is the intersection of the set of all iPods and the set of all items not sold in 2011 Q2. In other words, it is the set of all iPods not sold in the second quarter of 2011. Here is the table with the corresponding sets *A* and U' shaded ($A \cap U'$ is the overlap):

	iPods (*A*)	iPhones (*B*)	iPads (*C*)	Total
2011 Q2 (*U*)	9.0	18.7	4.7	32.4
2011 Q3 (*V*)	7.5	20.3	9.3	37.1
2011 Q4 (*W*)	6.6	17.1	11.1	34.8
Total	23.1	56.1	25.1	104.3

From the table:

$$n(A \cap U') = 7.5 + 6.6 = 14.1 \text{ million items.}$$

---

[3]Figures are rounded to one decimal place. Source: Apple quarterly press releases (www.investor.apple.com).

c. $A \cap U$ is the set of all iPods sold in 2011 Q2, and so $(A \cap U)'$ is the set of all items remaining if we exclude iPods sold in 2011 Q2:

	iPods (*A*)	iPhones (*B*)	iPads (*C*)	Total
2011 Q2 (*U*)	9.0	18.7	4.7	32.4
2011 Q3 (*V*)	7.5	20.3	9.3	37.1
2011 Q4 (*W*)	6.6	17.1	11.1	34.8
Total	23.1	56.1	25.1	104.3

From the formula for the cardinality of a complement:

$$n((A \cap U)') = n(S) - n(A \cap U)$$
$$= 104.3 - 9.0 = 95.3 \text{ million items.}$$

d. $C \cup U$ is the set of items that were either iPads or sold in 2011 Q2:

	iPods (*A*)	iPhones (*B*)	iPads (*C*)	Total
2011 Q2 (*U*)	9.0	18.7	4.7	32.4
2011 Q3 (*V*)	7.5	20.3	9.3	37.1
2011 Q4 (*W*)	6.6	17.1	11.1	34.8
Total	23.1	56.1	25.1	104.3

To compute it, we can use the formula for the cardinality of a union:

$$n(C \cup U) = n(C) + n(U) - n(C \cap U)$$
$$= 25.1 + 32.4 - 4.7 = 52.8 \text{ million items.}$$

To determine the cardinality of a union of three or more sets, like $n(A \cup B \cup C)$, we can think of $A \cup B \cup C$ as a union of two sets, $(A \cup B)$ and C, and then analyze each piece using the techniques we already have. Alternatively, there are formulas for the cardinalities of unions of any number of sets, but these formulas get more and more complicated as the number of sets grows. In many applications, like the following example, we can use Venn diagrams instead.

EXAMPLE 4 Reading Lists

A survey of 300 college students found that 100 had read *War and Peace,* 120 had read *Crime and Punishment,* and 100 had read *The Brothers Karamazov.* It also found that 40 had read only *War and Peace,* 70 had read *War and Peace* but not *The Brothers Karamazov,* and 80 had read *The Brothers Karamazov* but not *Crime and Punishment.* Only 10 had read all three novels. How many had read none of these three novels?

Solution There are four sets mentioned in the problem: the universe S consisting of the 300 students surveyed, the set W of students who had read *War and Peace,* the set C of students who had read *Crime and Punishment,* and the set K of students who had read *The Brothers Karamazov.* Figure 7 shows a Venn diagram representing these sets.

We have put labels in the various regions of the diagram to represent the number of students in each region. For example, x represents the number of students in

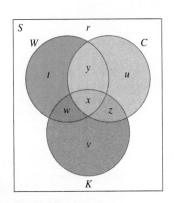

Figure 7

$W \cap C \cap K$, which is the number of students who have read all three novels. We are told that this number is 10, so

$$x = 10.$$

(You should draw the diagram for yourself and fill in the numbers as we go along.) We are also told that 40 students had read only *War and Peace,* so

$$t = 40.$$

We are given none of the remaining regions directly. However, because 70 had read *War and Peace* but not *The Brothers Karamazov,* we see that t and y must add up to 70. Because we already know that $t = 40$, it follows that $y = 30$. Further, because a total of 100 students had read *War and Peace,* we have

$$x + y + t + w = 100.$$

Substituting the known values of x, y, and t gives

$$10 + 30 + 40 + w = 100$$

so $w = 20$. Because 80 students had read *The Brothers Karamazov* but not *Crime and Punishment,* we see that $v + w = 80$, so $v = 60$ (because we know $w = 20$). We can now calculate z using the fact that a total of 100 students had read *The Brothers Karamazov:*

$$60 + 20 + 10 + z = 100$$

giving $z = 10$. Similarly, we can now get u using the fact that 120 students had read *Crime and Punishment:*

$$10 + 30 + 10 + u = 120,$$

giving $u = 70$. Of the 300 students surveyed, we've now found $x + y + z + w + t + u + v = 240$. This leaves

$$r = 60$$

who had read none of the three novels.

The Cardinality of a Cartesian Product

We've covered all the operations except Cartesian product. To find a formula for $n(A \times B)$, consider the following simple example:

$$A = \{H, T\}$$
$$B = \{1, 2, 3, 4, 5, 6\}$$

so that

$$A \times B = \{H1, H2, H3, H4, H5, H6, T1, T2, T3, T4, T5, T6\}.$$

As we saw in Example 5 in Section 6.1, the elements of $A \times B$ can be arranged in a table or spreadsheet with $n(A) = 2$ rows and $n(B) = 6$ elements in each row.

	A	B	C	D	E	F	G
1		1	2	3	4	5	6
2	**H**	H1	H2	H3	H4	H5	H6
3	**T**	T1	T2	T3	T4	T5	T6

In a region with 2 rows and 6 columns, there are $2 \times 6 = 12$ cells. So,

$$n(A \times B) = n(A)n(B)$$

in this case. There is nothing particularly special about this example, however, and that formula holds true in general.

Cardinality of a Cartesian Product

If A and B are finite sets, then

$$n(A \times B) = n(A)n(B).$$

Quick Example

If $A = \{a, b, c\}$ and $B = \{x, y, z, w\}$, then

$$n(A \times B) = n(A)n(B) = 3 \times 4 = 12.$$

EXAMPLE 5 Coin Tosses

a. If we toss a coin twice and observe the sequence of heads and tails, how many possible outcomes are there?

b. If we toss a coin three times, how many possible outcomes are there?

c. If we toss a coin ten times, how many possible outcomes are there?

Solution

a. Let $A = \{H, T\}$ be the set of possible outcomes when a coin is tossed once. The set of outcomes when a coin is tossed twice is $A \times A$, which has

$$n(A \times A) = n(A)n(A) = 2 \times 2 = 4$$

possible outcomes.

b. When a coin is tossed three times, we can think of the set of outcomes as the product of the set of outcomes for the first two tosses, which is $A \times A$, and the set of outcomes for the third toss, which is just A. The set of outcomes for the three tosses is then $(A \times A) \times A$, which we usually write as $A \times A \times A$ or A^3. The number of outcomes is

$$n((A \times A) \times A) = n(A \times A)n(A) = (2 \times 2) \times 2 = 8.$$

c. Considering the result of part (b), we can easily see that the set of outcomes here is $A^{10} = A \times A \times \cdots \times A$ (10 copies of A), or the set of ordered sequences of ten Hs and Ts. It's also easy to see that

$$n(A^{10}) = [n(A)]^{10} = 2^{10} = 1,024.$$

➡ **Before we go on...** We can start to see the power of these formulas for cardinality. In Example 5, we were able to calculate that there are 1,024 possible outcomes when we toss a coin 10 times without writing out all 1,024 possibilities and counting them. ∎

6.2 EXERCISES

▼ more advanced   ◆ challenging

 indicates exercises that should be solved using technology

Let A = {Dirk, Johan, Frans, Sarie}, *B* = {Frans, Sarie, Tina, Klaas, Henrika}, *C* = {Hans, Frans}. *Find the numbers indicated in Exercises 1–6.* HINT [See Quick Examples on page 408.]

1. $n(A) + n(B)$ **2.** $n(A) + n(C)$ **3.** $n(A \cup B)$

4. $n(A \cup C)$ **5.** $n(A \cup (B \cap C))$ **6.** $n(A \cap (B \cup C))$

7. Verify that $n(A \cup B) = n(A) + n(B) - n(A \cap B)$ with *A* and *B* as above.

8. Verify that $n(A \cup C) = n(A) + n(C) - n(A \cap C)$ with *A* and *C* as above.

Let A = {H, T}, *B* = {1, 2, 3, 4, 5, 6}, *and C* = {red, green, blue}. *Find the numbers indicated in Exercises 9–14.* HINT [See Example 5.]

9. $n(A \times A)$ **10.** $n(B \times B)$ **11.** $n(B \times C)$

12. $n(A \times C)$ **13.** $n(A \times B \times B)$ **14.** $n(A \times B \times C)$

15. If $n(A) = 43$, $n(B) = 20$, and $n(A \cap B) = 3$, find $n(A \cup B)$.

16. If $n(A) = 60$, $n(B) = 20$, and $n(A \cap B) = 1$, find $n(A \cap B)$.

17. If $n(A \cup B) = 100$ and $n(A) = n(B) = 60$, find $n(A \cap B)$.

18. If $n(A) = 100$, $n(A \cup B) = 150$, and $n(A \cap B) = 40$, find $n(B)$.

Let S = {Barnsley, Manchester United, Southend, Sheffield United, Liverpool, Maroka Swallows, Witbank Aces, Royal Tigers, Dundee United, Lyon} *be a universal set, A* = {Southend, Liverpool, Maroka Swallows, Royal Tigers}, *and B* = {Barnsley, Manchester United, Southend}. *Find the numbers indicated in Exercises 19–24.* HINT [See Quick Example on page 410.]

19. $n(A')$ **20.** $n(B')$ **21.** $n((A \cap B)')$

22. $n((A \cup B)')$ **23.** $n(A' \cap B')$ **24.** $n(A' \cup B')$

25. With *S*, *A*, and *B* as above, verify that $n((A \cap B)') = n(A') + n(B') - n((A \cup B)')$.

26. With *S*, *A*, and *B* as above, verify that $n(A' \cap B') + n(A \cup B) = n(S)$.

In Exercises 27–30, use the given information to complete the solution of each partially solved Venn diagram. HINT [See Example 4.]

27.

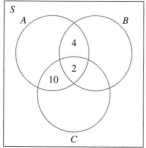

$n(A) = 20$, $n(B) = 20$,
$n(C) = 28$, $n(B \cap C) = 8$,
$n(S) = 50$

28.

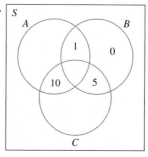

$n(A) = 16$, $n(B) = 11$, $n(C) = 30$, $n(S) = 40$

29. ▼

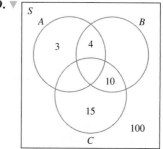

$n(A) = 10$, $n(B) = 19$, $n(S) = 140$

30. ▼

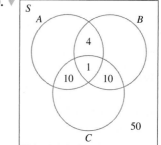

$n(A \cup B) = 30$, $n(B \cup C) = 30$, $n(A \cup C) = 35$

APPLICATIONS

31. *Web Searches* In November 2011, a search using the Web search engine Bing™ for "asteroid" yielded 25.0 million Web sites containing that word. A search for "comet" yielded 93.5 million sites. A search for sites containing both words yielded 3.1 million sites.[4] How many Web sites contained either "asteroid" or "comet" or both? HINT [See Example 1.]

---

[4]Rounded to the nearest 0.1 million.

32. Web Searches In November 2011, a search using the Web search engine Bing™ for "tea party" yielded 58.0 million Web sites containing that phrase. A search for "coffee party" yielded 0.6 million sites. A search for sites containing both phrases yielded 0.1 million sites.[5] How many Web sites contained either "tea party" or "coffee party" or both? HINT [See Example 1.]

33. Amusement On a particularly boring transatlantic flight, one of the authors amused himself by counting the heads of the people in the seats in front of him. He noticed that all 37 of them either had black hair or had a whole row to themselves (or both). Of this total, 33 had black hair and 6 were fortunate enough to have a whole row of seats to themselves. How many of the black-haired people had whole rows to themselves?

34. Restaurant Menus Your favorite restaurant offers a total of 14 desserts, of which 8 have ice cream as a main ingredient and 9 have fruit as a main ingredient. Assuming that all of them have either ice cream or fruit or both as a main ingredient, how many have both?

Publishing Exercises 35–40 are based on the following table, which shows the results of a survey of authors by a fictitious publishing company.

	New Authors	Established Authors	Total
Successful	5	25	30
Unsuccessful	15	55	70
Total	20	80	100

Consider the following subsets of the set S of all authors represented in the table: C, the set of successful authors; U, the set of unsuccessful authors; N, the set of new authors; and E, the set of established authors. HINT [See Example 3.]

35. Describe the sets $C \cap N$ and $C \cup N$ in words. Use the table to compute $n(C)$, $n(N)$, $n(C \cap N)$, and $n(C \cup N)$. Verify that $n(C \cup N) = n(C) + n(N) - n(C \cap N)$.

36. Describe the sets $N \cap U$ and $N \cup U$ in words. Use the table to compute $n(N)$, $n(U)$, $n(N \cap U)$, and $n(N \cup U)$. Verify that $n(N \cup U) = n(N) + n(U) - n(N \cap U)$.

37. Describe the set $C \cap N'$ in words, and find the number of elements it contains.

38. Describe the set $U \cup E'$ in words, and find the number of elements it contains.

39. ▼ What percentage of established authors are successful? What percentage of successful authors are established?

40. ▼ What percentage of new authors are unsuccessful? What percentage of unsuccessful authors are new?

Home Sales Exercises 41–46 are based on the following table, which shows the number of sales of existing homes, in millions, in the different regions of the United States during 2009–2011.[6] Take S to be the set of all home sales represented in the table and label the sets representing the home sales in each row and column as shown (so that, for example, N is the set of all sales of existing homes in the Northeast during 2009–2011)

	Northeast (N)	Midwest (M)	South (T)	West (W)	Total
2009 (A)	0.9	1.2	1.9	1.2	5.2
2010 (B)	0.8	1.1	1.9	1.2	5.0
2011 (C)	0.8	1.1	1.9	1.1	4.9
Total	2.5	3.4	5.7	3.5	15.1

In each exercise, use symbols to describe the given set, and compute its cardinality.

41. The set of sales of existing homes in the Midwest in 2011

42. The set of sales of existing homes either in the West or in 2009

43. The set of sales of existing homes in 2010 excluding sales in the South

44. The set of sales of existing homes in the Northeast after 2009

45. ▼ The set of sales of existing homes in 2010 in the West and Midwest

46. ▼ The set of sales of existing homes in the South and West in years other than 2009

Stock Prices Exercises 47–52 are based on the following table, which shows the performance of a selection of 100 fictitious stocks after one year. (Take S to be the set of all stocks represented in the table.)

	Companies			
	Pharmaceutical (P)	Electronic (E)	Internet (I)	Total
Increased (V)	10	5	15	30
Unchanged[7] (N)	30	0	10	40
Decreased (D)	10	5	15	30
Total	50	10	40	100

47. Use symbols to describe the set of non-Internet stocks that increased. How many elements are in this set?

---

[5]Rounded to the nearest 0.1 million.

[6]Figures are rounded (2011 figure is an estimate based on sales through September). Source: Realtor.org (www.realtor.org).

[7]If a stock stayed within 20% of its original value, it is classified as "unchanged."

48. Use symbols to describe the set of Internet stocks that did not increase. How many elements are in this set?

49. Compute $n(P' \cup N)$. What does this number represent?

50. Compute $n(P \cup N')$. What does this number represent?

51. Calculate $\dfrac{n(V \cap I)}{n(I)}$. What does the answer represent?

52. Calculate $\dfrac{n(D \cap I)}{n(D)}$. What does the answer represent?

53. ▼ *Medicine* In a study of Tibetan children,[8] a total of 1,556 children were examined. Of these, 1,024 had rickets. Of the 243 urban children in the study, 93 had rickets.

    a. How many children living in nonurban areas had rickets?

    b. How many children living in nonurban areas did not have rickets?

54. ▼ *Medicine* In a study of Tibetan children,[9] a total of 1,556 children were examined. Of these, 615 had caries (cavities). Of the 1,313 children living in nonurban areas, 504 had caries.

    a. How many children living in urban areas had caries?

    b. How many children living in urban areas did not have caries?

55. *Entertainment* According to a survey of 100 people regarding their movie attendance in the last year, 40 had seen a science fiction movie, 55 had seen an adventure movie, and 35 had seen a horror movie. Moreover, 25 had seen a science fiction movie and an adventure movie, 5 had seen an adventure movie and a horror movie, and 15 had seen a science fiction movie and a horror movie. Only 5 people had seen a movie from all three categories.

    a. Use the given information to set up a Venn diagram and solve it. HINT [See Example 4.]

    b. Complete the following sentence: The survey suggests that __ % of science fiction movie fans are also horror movie fans.

56. *Athletics* Of the 4,700 students at Medium Suburban College (MSC), 50 play collegiate soccer, 60 play collegiate lacrosse, and 96 play collegiate football. Only 4 students play both collegiate soccer and lacrosse, 6 play collegiate

soccer and football, and 16 play collegiate lacrosse and football. No students play all three sports.

    a. Use the given information to set up a Venn diagram and solve it. HINT [See Example 4.]

    b. Complete the following sentence: __ % of the college soccer players also play one of the other two sports at the collegiate level.

57. *Entertainment* In a survey of 100 Enormous State University students, 21 enjoyed classical music, 22 enjoyed rock music, and 27 enjoyed house music. Five of the students enjoyed both classical and rock. How many of those that enjoyed rock did not enjoy classical music?

58. *Entertainment* Refer back to the preceding exercise. You are also told that 5 students enjoyed all three kinds of music while 53 enjoyed music in none of these categories. How many students enjoyed both classical and rock but disliked house music?

COMMUNICATION AND REASONING EXERCISES

59. If A and B are finite sets with $A \subset B$, how are $n(A)$ and $n(B)$ related?

60. If A and B are subsets of the finite set S with $A \subset B$, how are $n(A')$ and $n(B')$ related?

61. Why is the Cartesian product referred to as a "product"? HINT [Think about cardinality.]

62. Refer back to your answer to Exercise 61. What set operation could you use to represent the *sum* of two disjoint sets A and B? Why?

63. Formulate an interesting application whose answer is $n(A \cap B) = 20$.

64. Formulate an interesting application whose answer is $n(A \times B) = 120$.

65. ▼ When is $n(A \cup B) \neq n(A) + n(B)$?

66. ▼ When is $n(A \times B) = n(A)$?

67. ▼ When is $n(A \cup B) = n(A)$?

68. ▼ When is $n(A \cap B) = n(A)$?

69. ◆ Use a Venn diagram or some other method to obtain a formula for $n(A \cup B \cup C)$ in terms of $n(A)$, $n(B)$, $n(C)$, $n(A \cap B)$, $n(A \cap C)$, $n(B \cap C)$, and $n(A \cap B \cap C)$.

70. ◆ Suppose that A and B are sets with $A \subset B$ and $n(A)$ at least 2. Arrange the following numbers from smallest to largest (if two numbers are equal, say so): $n(A)$, $n(A \times B)$, $n(A \cap B)$, $n(A \cup B)$, $n(B \times A)$, $n(B)$, $n(B \times B)$.

---

[8]Source: N. S. Harris et al., Nutritional and Health Status of Tibetan Children Living at High Altitudes, *New England Journal of Medicine*, 344(5), February 1, 2001, pp. 341–347.

[9]*Ibid.*

6.3 Decision Algorithms: The Addition and Multiplication Principles

Let's start with a really simple example. You walk into an ice cream parlor and find that you can choose between ice cream, of which there are 15 flavors, and frozen yogurt, of which there are 5 flavors. How many different selections can you make? Clearly, you have $15 + 5 = 20$ different desserts from which to choose. Mathematically, this is an example of the formula for the cardinality of a disjoint union: If we let A be the set of ice creams you can choose from, and B the set of frozen yogurts, then $A \cap B = \emptyset$ and we want $n(A \cup B)$. But the formula for the cardinality of a disjoint union is $n(A \cup B) = n(A) + n(B)$, which gives $15 + 5 = 20$ in this case.

This example illustrates a very useful general principle.

Addition Principle

When choosing among r disjoint alternatives, suppose that

alternative 1 has n_1 possible outcomes,

alternative 2 has n_2 possible outcomes,

...

alternative r has n_r possible outcomes,

with no two of these outcomes the same. Then there are a total of $n_1 + n_2 + \cdots + n_r$ possible outcomes.

Quick Example

At a restaurant you can choose among 8 chicken dishes, 10 beef dishes, 4 seafood dishes, and 12 vegetarian dishes. This gives a total of $8 + 10 + 4 + 12 = 34$ different dishes to choose from.

Here is another simple example. In that ice cream parlor, not only can you choose from 15 flavors of ice cream, but you can also choose from 3 different sizes of cone. How many different ice cream cones can you select from? This time, we want to choose both a flavor and a size, or, in other words, a pair (flavor, size). Therefore, if we let A again be the set of ice cream flavors and now let C be the set of cone sizes, the pair we want to choose is an element of $A \times C$, the Cartesian product. To find the number of choices we have, we use the formula for the cardinality of a Cartesian product: $n(A \times C) = n(A)n(C)$. In this case, we get $15 \times 3 = 45$ different ice cream cones we can select.

This example illustrates another general principle.

Multiplication Principle

When making a sequence of choices with r steps, suppose that

step 1 has n_1 possible outcomes

step 2 has n_2 possible outcomes

...

step r has n_r possible outcomes

✱ See Example 3 for a case in which different sequences of choices can lead to the same outcome, with the result that the multiplication principle does not apply.

and that each sequence of choices results in a distinct outcome.✱ Then there are a total of $n_1 \times n_2 \times \cdots \times n_r$ possible outcomes.

Quick Example

At a restaurant you can choose among 5 appetizers, 34 main dishes, and 10 desserts. This gives a total of $5 \times 34 \times 10 = 1{,}700$ different meals (each including one appetizer, one main dish, and one dessert) from which you can choose.

Things get more interesting when we have to use the addition and multiplication principles in tandem.

EXAMPLE 1 Desserts

You walk into an ice cream parlor and find that you can choose between ice cream, of which there are 15 flavors, and frozen yogurt, of which there are 5 flavors. In addition, you can choose among 3 different sizes of cones for your ice cream or 2 different sizes of cups for your yogurt. How many different desserts can you choose from?

Solution It helps to think about a definite procedure for deciding which dessert you will choose. Here is one we can use:

Alternative 1: An ice cream cone
    Step 1 Choose a flavor.
    Step 2 Choose a size.

Alternative 2: A cup of frozen yogurt
    Step 1 Choose a flavor.
    Step 2 Choose a size.

That is, we can choose between alternative 1 and alternative 2. If we choose alternative 1, we have a sequence of two choices to make: flavor and size. The same is true of alternative 2. We shall call a procedure in which we make a sequence of decisions a **decision algorithm**.✱ Once we have a decision algorithm, we can use the addition and multiplication principles to count the number of possible outcomes.

✱ An algorithm is a procedure with definite rules for what to do at every step.

Alternative 1: An ice cream cone
    Step 1 Choose a flavor: 15 choices.
    Step 2 Choose a size: 3 choices.
    There are $15 \times 3 = 45$ possible choices in alternative 1.   Multiplication Principle

Alternative 2: A cup of frozen yogurt
    Step 1 Choose a flavor: 5 choices.
    Step 2 Choose a size: 2 choices.
    There are $5 \times 2 = 10$ possible choices in alternative 2.   Multiplication Principle

So, there are $45 + 10 = 55$ possible choices of desserts.   Addition Principle

➡ **Before we go on...** Decision algorithms can be illustrated by **decision trees**. To simplify the picture, suppose we had fewer choices in Example 1—say, only two choices of ice cream flavor: vanilla and chocolate, and two choices of yogurt flavor: banana and raspberry. This gives us a total of $2 \times 3 + 2 \times 2 = 10$ possible desserts.

We can illustrate the decisions we need to make when choosing what to buy in the diagram in Figure 8, called a decision tree.

Figure 8

We do not use decision trees much in this chapter because, while they provide a good way of thinking about decision algorithms, they're not really practical for counting large sets. Similar diagrams will be very useful, however, in the chapter on probability. ■

To count the number of possible gadgets, pretend you are *designing* a gadget, and list the decisions to be made at each stage.

Decision Algorithm

A **decision algorithm** is a procedure in which we make a sequence of decisions. We can use decision algorithms to determine the number of possible items by pretending we are *designing* such an item (for example, an ice-cream cone) and listing the decisions or choices we should make at each stage of the process.

Quick Example

An iPod is available in two sizes. The larger size comes in two colors and the smaller size (the Mini) comes in four colors. A decision algorithm for "designing" an iPod is:

Alternative 1: Select Large:
   Step 1 Choose a color: Two choices.
   (So, there are two choices for alternative 1.)

Alternative 2: Select a Mini:
   Step 1 Choose a color: Four choices.
   (So, there are four choices for alternative 2.)

Thus, there are $2 + 4 = 6$ possible choices of iPods.

> **Caution**
> For a decision algorithm to give the correct number of possible items, there must be a one-to-one correspondence between sequences of choices and resulting items. So, it is necessary that each sequence of choices results in a distinct item. In other words, *changing one or more choices must result in a different item.* (See Example 3.)

EXAMPLE 2 **Exams**

An exam is broken into two parts, Part A and Part B, both of which you are required to do. In Part A you can choose between answering 10 true-false questions or answering 4 multiple-choice questions, each of which has 5 answers to choose from. In Part B you can choose between answering 8 true-false questions and answering 5 multiple-choice questions, each of which has 4 answers to choose from. How many different collections of answers are possible?

Solution While deciding what answers to write down, we use the following decision algorithm:

Step 1 Do Part A.

Alternative 1: Answer the 10 true-false questions.

> **Steps 1–10** Choose true or false for each question: 2 choices each.
> There are $2 \times 2 \times \cdots \times 2 = 2^{10} = 1{,}024$ choices in alternative 1.

Alternative 2: Answer the 4 multiple-choice questions.

> **Steps 1–4** Choose one answer for each question: 5 choices each.
> There are $5 \times 5 \times 5 \times 5 = 5^4 = 625$ choices in alternative 2.

$1{,}024 + 625 = 1{,}649$ choices in step 1

Step 2 Do Part B.

Alternative 1: Answer the 8 true-false questions: 2 choices each.

> $2^8 = 256$ choices in alternative 1

Alternative 2: Answer the 5 multiple-choice questions, 4 choices each.

> $4^5 = 1{,}024$ choices in alternative 2

$256 + 1{,}024 = 1{,}280$ choices in step 2

There are $1{,}649 \times 1{,}280 = 2{,}110{,}720$ different collections of answers possible.

The next example illustrates the need to select your decision algorithm with care.

EXAMPLE 3 **Scrabble®**

You are playing Scrabble and have the following letters to work with: k, e, r, e. Because you are losing the game, you would like to use all your letters to make a single word, but you can't think of any four-letter words using all these letters. In desperation, you decide to list *all* the four-letter sequences possible to see if there are any valid words among them. How large is your list?

Solution It may first occur to you to try the following decision algorithm.

Step 1 Select the first letter: 4 choices.
Step 2 Select the second letter: 3 choices.

Step 3 Select the third letter: 2 choices.
Step 4 Select the last letter: 1 choice.

This gives $4 \times 3 \times 2 \times 1 = 24$ choices. However, something is wrong with the algorithm.

Q: *What is wrong with this decision algorithm?*

A: We didn't take into account the fact that there are two "e"s;* different decisions in Steps 1–4 can produce the same sequence. Suppose, for example, that we selected the first "e" in Step 1, the second "e" in Step 2, and then the "k" and the "r." This would produce the sequence "eekr." If we selected the *second* "e" in Step 1, the *first* "e" in Step 2, and then the "k" and "r," we would obtain the *same* sequence: "eekr." In other words, the decision algorithm produces two copies of the sequence "eekr" in the associated decision tree. (In fact, it produces two copies of each possible sequence of the letters.) In short, different sequences of choices produce the same result, violating the requirement in the note of caution that precedes Example 2:

For a decision algorithm to be valid, each sequence of choices must produce a different result.

* Consider the following extreme case: If all four letters were "e", then there would be only a single sequence: "eeee" and not the 24 predicted by the decision algorithm.

Because our original algorithm is not valid, we need a new one. Here is a strategy that works nicely for this example. Imagine, as before, that we are going to construct a sequence of four letters. This time we are going to imagine that we have a sequence of four empty slots: ☐☐☐☐, and instead of selecting letters to fill the slots from left to right, we are going to select *slots* in which to place each of the letters. Remember that we have to use these letters: k, e, r, e. We proceed as follows, leaving the "e"s until last.

Step 1 Select an empty slot for the k: 4 choices. (e.g., ☐☐⟦k⟧☐)
Step 2 Select an empty slot for the r: 3 choices. (e.g., ⟦r⟧☐⟦k⟧☐)
Step 3 Place the "e"s in the remaining two slots: 1 choice!

Thus the multiplication principle yields $4 \times 3 \times 1 = 12$ choices.

➡ **Before we go on...** You should try constructing a decision tree for Example 3, and you will see that each sequence of four letters is produced exactly once when we use the correct (second) decision algorithm. ■

FAQs

Creating and Testing a Decision Algorithm

Q: *How do I set up a decision algorithm to count how many items there are in a given scenario?*

A: Pretend that you are *designing* such an item (for example, pretend that you are designing an ice-cream cone) and come up with a step-by-step procedure for doing so, listing the decisions you should make at each stage.

Q: *Once I have my decision algorithm, how do I check if it is valid?*

A: Ask yourself the following question: "Is it possible to get the same item (the exact same ice-cream cone, say) by making different decisions when applying the algorithm?" If the answer is "yes," then your decision algorithm is invalid. Otherwise, it is valid.

6.3 EXERCISES

▼ more advanced   ◆ challenging

Ⓣ indicates exercises that should be solved using technology

1. An experiment requires a choice among 3 initial setups. The first setup can result in 2 possible outcomes, the second in 3 possible outcomes, and the third in 5 possible outcomes. What is the total number of outcomes possible? HINT [See Quick Example on page 418.]

2. A surgical procedure requires choosing among 4 alternative methodologies. The first can result in 4 possible outcomes, the second in 3 possible outcomes, and the remaining methodologies can each result in 2 possible outcomes. What is the total number of outcomes possible? HINT [See Quick Example on page 418.]

3. An experiment requires a sequence of 3 steps. The first step can result in 2 possible outcomes, the second in 3 possible outcomes, and the third in 5 possible outcomes. What is the total number of outcomes possible? HINT [See Quick Example on page 419.]

4. A surgical procedure requires 4 steps. The first can result in 4 possible outcomes, the second in 3 possible outcomes, and the remaining 2 can each result in 2 possible outcomes. What is the total number of outcomes possible? HINT [See Quick Example on page 419.]

For the decision algorithms in Exercises 5–12, find how many outcomes are possible. HINT [See Example 1.]

5. Alternative 1:   Alternative 2:
      Step 1: 1 outcome   Step 1: 2 outcomes
      Step 2: 2 outcomes   Step 2: 2 outcomes
                                  Step 3: 1 outcome

6. Alternative 1:   Alternative 2:
      Step 1: 1 outcome   Step 1: 2 outcomes
      Step 2: 2 outcomes   Step 2: 2 outcomes
      Step 3: 2 outcomes

7. Step 1:   Step 2:
      Alternative 1: 1 outcome   Alternative 1: 2 outcomes
      Alternative 2: 2 outcomes   Alternative 2: 2 outcomes
                                  Alternative 3: 1 outcome

8. Step 1:   Step 2:
      Alternative 1: 1 outcome   Alternative 1: 2 outcomes
      Alternative 2: 2 outcomes   Alternative 2: 2 outcomes
      Alternative 3: 2 outcomes

9. Alternative 1:   Alternative 2: 5 outcomes
      Step 1:
        Alternative 1: 3 outcomes
        Alternative 2: 1 outcome
      Step 2: 2 outcomes

10. Alternative 1: 2 outcomes   Alternative 2:
                                         Step 1:
                                           Alternative 1: 4 outcomes
                                           Alternative 2: 1 outcome
                                           Step 2: 2 outcomes

11. Step 1:   Step 2: 5 outcomes
       Alternative 1:
         Step 1: 3 outcomes
         Step 2: 1 outcome
       Alternative 2: 2 outcomes

12. Step 1: 2 outcomes   Step 2:
                                         Alternative 1:
                                           Step 1: 4 outcomes
                                           Step 2: 1 outcome
                                           Alternative 2: 2 outcomes

13. How many different four-letter sequences can be formed from the letters a, a, a, b? HINT [See Example 3.]

14. How many different five-letter sequences can be formed from the letters a, a, a, b, c? HINT [See Example 3.]

APPLICATIONS

15. *Ice Cream* When **Baskin-Robbins** was founded in 1945, it made 31 different flavors of ice cream.[10] If you had a choice of having your ice cream in a cone, a cup, or a sundae, how many different desserts could you have?

16. *Ice Cream* At the beginning of 2002, **Baskin-Robbins** claimed to have "nearly 1,000 different ice cream flavors."[11] Assuming that you could choose from 1,000 different flavors, that you could have your ice cream in a cone, a cup, or a sundae, and that you could choose from a dozen different toppings, how many different desserts could you have?

17. *Binary Codes* A binary digit, or "bit," is either 0 or 1. A nybble is a four-bit sequence. How many different nybbles are possible?

18. *Ternary Codes* A ternary digit is either 0, 1, or 2. How many sequences of six ternary digits are possible?

19. *Ternary Codes* A ternary digit is either 0, 1, or 2. How many sequences of six ternary digits containing a single 1 and a single 2 are possible?

20. *Binary Codes* A binary digit, or "bit," is either 0 or 1. A nybble is a four-bit sequence. How many different nybbles containing a single 1 are possible?

21. *Reward* While selecting candy for students in his class, Professor Murphy must choose between gummy candy and licorice nibs. Gummy candy packets come in three sizes, while packets of licorice nibs come in two. If he chooses gummy candy, he must select gummy bears, gummy worms, or gummy dinos. If he chooses licorice nibs, he must choose between red and black. How many choices does he have? HINT [See Example 2.]

---

[10] Source: Company Web site (www.baskinrobbins.com).
[11] *Ibid.*

22. *Productivity* Professor Oger must choose between an extra writing assignment and an extra reading assignment for the upcoming spring break. For the writing assignment, there are two essay topics to choose from and three different mandatory lengths (30 pages, 35 pages, or 40 pages). The reading topic would consist of one scholarly biography combined with one volume of essays. There are five biographies and two volumes of essays to choose from. How many choices does she have? HINT [See Example 2.]

23. *CD Discs* CD discs at your local computer store are available in two types (CD-R and CD-RW), packaged singly, in spindles of 50, or in spindles of 100. When purchasing singly, you can choose from five colors; when purchasing in spindles of 50 or 100 you have two choices, silver or an assortment of colors. If you are purchasing CD discs, how many possibilities do you have to choose from?

24. *Radar Detectors* Radar detectors are either powered by their own battery or plug into the cigarette lighter socket. All radar detectors come in two models: no-frills and fancy. In addition, detectors powered by their own batteries detect either radar or laser, or both, whereas the plug-in types come in models that detect either radar or laser, but not both. How many different radar detectors can you buy?

25. *Multiple-Choice Tests* Professor Easy's final examination has 10 true-false questions followed by 2 multiple-choice questions. In each of the multiple-choice questions, you must select the correct answer from a list of five. How many answer sheets are possible?

26. *Multiple-choice Tests* Professor Tough's final examination has 20 true-false questions followed by 3 multiple-choice questions. In each of the multiple-choice questions, you must select the correct answer from a list of six. How many answer sheets are possible?

27. *Tests* A test requires that you answer either Part A or Part B. Part A consists of eight true-false questions, and Part B consists of five multiple-choice questions with one correct answer out of five. How many different completed answer sheets are possible?

28. *Tests* A test requires that you answer first Part A and then either Part B or Part C. Part A consists of four true-false questions, Part B consists of four multiple-choice questions with one correct answer out of five, and Part C consists of three questions with one correct answer out of six. How many different completed answer sheets are possible?

29. *Stock Portfolios* Your broker has suggested that you diversify your investments by splitting your portfolio among mutual funds, municipal bond funds, stocks, and precious metals. She suggests four good mutual funds, three municipal bond funds, eight stocks, and three precious metals (gold, silver, and platinum).

   a. Assuming your portfolio is to contain one of each type of investment, how many different portfolios are possible?

   b. Assuming your portfolio is to contain three mutual funds, two municipal bond funds, one stock, and two precious metals, how many different portfolios are possible?

30. *Menus* The local diner offers a meal combination consisting of an appetizer, a soup, a main course, and a dessert. There are five appetizers, two soups, four main courses, and five desserts. Your diet restricts you to choosing between a dessert and an appetizer. (You cannot have both.) Given this restriction, how many three-course meals are possible?

31. *Computer Codes* A computer "byte" consists of eight "bits," each bit being either a 0 or a 1. If characters are represented using a code that uses a byte for each character, how many different characters can be represented?

32. *Computer Codes* Some written languages, like Chinese and Japanese, use tens of thousands of different characters. If a language uses roughly 50,000 characters, a computer code for this language would have to use how many bytes per character? (See Exercise 31.)

33. *Symmetries of a Five-Pointed Star* A five-pointed star will appear unchanged if it is rotated through any one of the angles 0°, 72°, 144°, 216°, or 288°. It will also appear unchanged if it is flipped about the axis shown in the figure. A *symmetry* of the five-pointed star consists of either a rotation, or a rotation followed by a flip. How many different symmetries are there altogether?

34. *Symmetries of a Six-Pointed Star* A six-pointed star will appear unchanged if it is rotated through any one of the angles 0°, 60°, 120°, 180°, 240°, or 300°. It will also appear unchanged if it is flipped about the axis shown in the figure. A *symmetry* of the six-pointed star consists of either a rotation, or a rotation followed by a flip. How many different symmetries are there altogether?

35. *Variables in BASIC*[12] A variable name in the programming language BASIC can be either a letter or a letter followed by a decimal digit—that is, one of the numbers 0, 1, . . . , 9. How many different variables are possible?

36. *Employee IDs* A company assigns to each of its employees an ID code that consists of one, two, or three letters followed by a digit from 0 through 9. How many employee codes does the company have available?

37. *Tournaments* How many ways are there of filling in the blanks for the following (fictitious) soccer tournament?

North Carolina

Central Connecticut

Virginia

Syracuse

38. *Tournaments* How many ways are there of filling in the blanks for a (fictitious) soccer tournament involving the four teams San Diego State, De Paul, Colgate, and Hofstra?

San Diego State

De Paul

Colgate

39. ▼ *Telephone Numbers* A telephone number consists of a sequence of seven digits not starting with 0 or 1.

a. How many telephone numbers are possible?
b. How many of them begin with either 463, 460, or 400?
c. How many telephone numbers are possible if no two adjacent digits are the same? (For example, 235-9350 is permitted, but not 223-6789.)

40. ▼ *Social Security Numbers* A Social Security Number is a sequence of nine digits.

a. How many Social Security Numbers are possible?
b. How many of them begin with either 023 or 003?
c. How many Social Security Numbers are possible if no two adjacent digits are the same? (For example, 235-93-2345 is permitted, but not 126-67-8189.)

41. ▼ *DNA Chains* DNA (deoxyribonucleic acid) is the basic building block of reproduction in living things. A DNA chain is a sequence of chemicals called *bases*. There are four possible bases: thymine (T), cytosine (C), adenine (A), and guanine (G).

a. How many three-element DNA chains are possible?
b. How many *n*-element DNA chains are possible?

c. A human DNA chain has 2.1×10^{10} elements. How many human DNA chains are possible?

42. ▼ *Credit Card Numbers*[13] Each customer of Mobil Credit Corporation is given a 9-digit number for computer identification purposes.

a. If each digit can be any number from 0 to 9, are there enough different account numbers for 10 million credit-card holders?
b. Would there be if the digits were only 0 or 1?

43. ▼ *HTML* Colors in HTML (the language in which many Web pages are written) can be represented by 6-digit hexadecimal codes: sequences of six integers ranging from 0 to 15 (represented as 0, . . . , 9, A, B, . . . , F).

a. How many different colors can be represented?
b. Some monitors can only display colors encoded with pairs of repeating digits (such as 44DD88). How many colors can these monitors display?
c. Grayscale shades are represented by sequences *xyxyxy* consisting of a repeated pair of digits. How many grayscale shades are possible?
d. The pure colors are pure red: *xy*0000; pure green: 00*xy*00; and pure blue: 0000*xy*. (*xy* = *FF* gives the brightest pure color, while *xy* = 00 gives the darkest: black.) How many pure colors are possible?

44. ▼ *Telephone Numbers* In the past, a local telephone number in the United States consisted of a sequence of two letters followed by five digits. Three letters were associated with each number from 2 to 9 (just as in the standard telephone layout shown in the figure) so that each telephone number corresponded to a sequence of seven digits. How many different sequences of seven digits were possible?

45. ▼ *Romeo and Juliet* Here is a list of the main characters in Shakespeare's *Romeo and Juliet*. The first 7 characters are male and the last 4 are female.

Escalus, *prince of Verona*
Paris, *kinsman to the prince*
Romeo, *of Montague Household*
Mercutio, *friend of Romeo*
Benvolio, *friend of Romeo*

---

[12]From *Applied Combinatorics* by F. S. Roberts (Prentice-Hall, New Jersey, 1984).

[13]Taken from a exercise in *Applied Combinatorics* by F. S. Roberts (Prentice-Hall, New Jersey, 1984).

Tybalt, *nephew to Lady Capulet*
Friar Lawrence, *a Franciscan*
Lady Montague, *of Montague Household*
Lady Capulet, *of Capulet Household*
Juliet, *of Capulet Household*
Juliet's Nurse

A total of 10 male and 8 female actors are available to play these roles. How many possible casts are there? (All roles are to be played by actors of the same gender as the character.)

46. ▼ *Swan Lake* The Enormous State University's Accounting Society has decided to produce a version of the ballet *Swan Lake,* in which all the female roles (including all of the swans) will be danced by men, and vice versa. Here are the main characters:

Prince Siegfried
Prince Siegfried's Mother
Princess Odette, *the White Swan*
The Evil Duke Rotbart
Odile, *the Black Swan*
Cygnet #1, *young swan*
Cygnet #2, *young swan*
Cygnet #3, *young swan*

The ESU Accounting Society has on hand a total of 4 female dancers and 12 male dancers who are to be considered for the main roles. How many possible casts are there?

47. ▼ *License Plates* Many U.S. license plates display a sequence of three letters followed by three digits.

   a. How many such license plates are possible?
   b. In order to avoid confusion of letters with digits, some states do not issue standard plates with the last letter an I, O, or Q. How many license plates are still possible?
   c. Assuming that the letter combinations VET, MDZ, and DPZ are reserved for disabled veterans, medical practitioners, and disabled persons, respectively, how many license plates are possible, also taking the restriction in part (b) into account?

48. ▼ *License Plates*[14] License plates in Montana have a sequence consisting of: (1) a digit from 1 to 9, (2) a letter, (3) a dot, (4) a letter, and (5) a four-digit number.

   a. How many different license plates are possible?
   b. How many different license plates are available for citizens if numbers that end with 0 are reserved for official state vehicles?

49. ▼ *Mazes*

   a. How many four-letter sequences are possible that contain only the letters R and D, with D occurring only once?
   b. Use part (a) to calculate the number of possible routes from Start to Finish in the maze shown in the figure, where each move is either to the right or down.

   c. Comment on what would happen if we also allowed left and up moves.

50. ▼ *Mazes*

   a. How many six-letter sequences are possible that contain only the letters R and D, with D occurring only once?
   b. Use part (a) to calculate the number of possible routes from Start to Finish in the maze shown in the figure, where each move is either to the right or down.

   c. Comment on what would happen if we also allowed left and up moves.

51. ▼ *Car Engines*[15] In a six-cylinder V6 engine, the even-numbered cylinders are on the left and the odd-numbered cylinders are on the right. A good firing order is a sequence of the numbers 1 through 6 in which right and left sides alternate.

   a. How many possible good firing sequences are there?
   b. How many good firing sequences are there that start with a cylinder on the left?

52. ▼ *Car Engines* Repeat the preceding exercise for an eight-cylinder V8 engine.

53. ▼ *Minimalist Art* You are exhibiting your collection of minimalist paintings. Art critics have raved about your paintings, each of which consists of 10 vertical colored lines set against a white background. You have used the following rule to produce your paintings: Every second line, starting with the first, is to be either blue or gray, while the remaining five lines are to be either all light blue, all red, or all purple. Your collection is complete: Every possible combination that satisfies the rules occurs. How many paintings are you exhibiting?

54. ▼ *Combination Locks* Dripping wet after your shower, you have clean forgotten the combination of your lock. It is one

---

[14]Source: The License Plates of the World Web site (http://servo.oit.gatech.edu/~mk5/).

[15]Adapted from an exercise in *Basic Techniques of Combinatorial Theory* by D. I. A. Cohen (New York: John Wiley, 1978).

of those "standard" combination locks, which uses a three-number combination with each number in the range 0 through 39. All you remember is that the second number is either 27 or 37, while the third number ends in a 5. In desperation, you decide to go through all possible combinations using the information you remember. Assuming that it takes about 10 seconds to try each combination, what is the longest possible time you may have to stand dripping in front of your locker?

55. ▼ *Product Design* Your company has patented an electronic digital padlock that a user can program with his or her own four-digit code. (Each digit can be 0 through 9.) The padlock is designed to open if either the correct code is keyed in or—and this is helpful for forgetful people—if exactly one of the digits is incorrect.

   a. How many incorrect codes will open a programmed padlock?
   b. How many codes will open a programmed padlock?

56. ▼ *Product Design* Your company has patented an electronic digital padlock that has a telephone-style keypad. Each digit from 2 through 9 corresponds to three letters of the alphabet (see the figure for Exercise 44). How many different four-letter sequences correspond to a single four-digit sequence using digits in the range 2 through 9?

57. ▼ *Calendars* The World Almanac[16] features a "perpetual calendar," a collection of 14 possible calendars. Why does this suffice to be sure there is a calendar for every conceivable year?

58. ▼ *Calendars* How many possible calendars are there that have February 12 falling on a Sunday, Monday, or Tuesday?

59. ▼ *Programming in BASIC* (Some programming knowledge assumed for this exercise.) How many iterations will be carried out in the following routine?

```
For i = 1 to 10
    For j = 2 to 20
        For k = 1 to 10
            Print i, j, k
        Next k
    Next j
Next i
```

60. ▼ *Programming in JAVASCRIPT* (Some programming knowledge assumed for this exercise.) How many iterations will be carried out in the following routine?

```
for (i = 1; i <= 2; i++) {
    for (j = 1; j <= 2; j++) {
        for (k = 1; k <= 2; k++)
            sum += i+j+k;
    }
}
```

61. ◆ *Building Blocks* Use a decision algorithm to show that a rectangular solid with dimensions $m \times n \times r$ can be constructed with $m \cdot n \cdot r$ cubical $1 \times 1 \times 1$ blocks. (See the figure.)

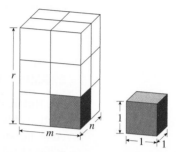

Rectangular Solid Made Up of $1 \times 1 \times 1$ Cubes

62. ◆ *Matrices* (Some knowledge of matrices is assumed for this exercise.) Use a decision algorithm to show that an $m \times n$ matrix must have $m \cdot n$ entries.

63. ◆ *Morse Code* In Morse Code, each letter of the alphabet is encoded by a different sequence of dots and dashes. Different letters may have sequences of different lengths. How long should the longest sequence be in order to allow for every possible letter of the alphabet?

64. ◆ *Numbers* How many odd numbers between 10 and 99 have distinct digits?

COMMUNICATION AND REASONING EXERCISES

65. Complete the following sentences: The multiplication principle is based on the cardinality of the _____ of two sets.

66. Complete the following sentences: The addition principle is based on the cardinality of the _____ of two disjoint sets.

67. You are packing for a short trip and want to take 2 of the 10 shirts you have hanging in your closet. Critique the following decision algorithm and calculation of how many different ways you can choose two shirts to pack: Step 1, choose one shirt, 10 choices. Step 2, choose another shirt, 9 choices. Hence there are 90 possible choices of two shirts.

68. You are designing an advertising logo that consists of a tower of five squares. Three are yellow, one is blue, and one is green. Critique the following decision algorithm and calculation of the number of different five-square sequences: Step 1: Choose the first square, 5 choices. Step 2: Choose the second square, 4 choices. Step 3: Choose the third square: 3 choices. Step 4: Choose the fourth square, 2 choices. Step 5: Choose the last square: 1 choice. Hence there are 120 possible five-square sequences.

69. ▼ Construct a decision algorithm that gives the correct number of five-square sequences in Exercise 68.

70. ▼ Find an interesting application that requires a decision algorithm with two steps in which each step has two alternatives.

[16]Source: *The World Almanac and Book of Facts* 1992 (New York: Pharos Books, 1992).

6.4 Permutations and Combinations

Certain classes of counting problems come up frequently, and it is useful to develop formulas to deal with them.

EXAMPLE 1 Casting

Ms. Birkitt, the English teacher at Brakpan Girls High School, wanted to stage a production of R. B. Sheridan's play, *The School for Scandal*. The casting was going well until she was left with five unfilled characters and five seniors who were yet to be assigned roles. The characters were Lady Sneerwell, Lady Teazle, Mrs. Candour, Maria, and Snake; while the unassigned seniors were April, May, June, Julia, and Augusta. How many possible assignments are there?

Solution To decide on a specific assignment, we use the following algorithm:

Step 1 Choose a senior to play Lady Sneerwell: 5 choices.

Step 2 Choose one of the remaining seniors to play Lady Teazle: 4 choices.

Step 3 Choose one of the now remaining seniors to play Mrs. Candour: 3 choices.

Step 4 Choose one of the now remaining seniors to play Maria: 2 choices.

Step 5 Choose the remaining senior to play Snake: 1 choice.

Thus, there are $5 \times 4 \times 3 \times 2 \times 1 = 120$ possible assignments of seniors to roles.

What the situation in Example 1 has in common with many others is that we start with a set—here the set of seniors—and we want to know how many ways we can put the elements of that set in order in a list. In this example, an ordered list of the five seniors, for instance

1. May

2. Augusta

3. June

4. Julia

5. April

corresponds to a particular casting:

Cast

Lady Sneerwell	May
Lady Teazle	Augusta
Mrs. Candour	June
Maria	Julia
Snake	April

We call an ordered list of items a **permutation** of those items.

If we have *n* items, how many permutations of those items are possible? We can use a decision algorithm similar to the one we used in the preceding example to select a permutation.

Step 1 Select the first item: n choices.
Step 2 Select the second item: $n - 1$ choices.
Step 3 Select the third item: $n - 2$ choices.
...
Step $n - 1$ Select the next-to-last item: 2 choices.
Step n Select the last item: 1 choice.
Thus, there are $n \times (n - 1) \times (n - 2) \times \cdots \times 2 \times 1$ possible permutations. We call this number **n factorial**, which we write as $n!$.

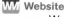 **using** Technology

Technology can be used to compute factorials. For instance, to compute 5!:

TI-83/84 Plus
Home screen: 5 !
(To obtain the ! symbol, press
MATH , choose PRB, and
select 4 : !.)

Spreadsheet
Use the formula
=FACT(5)

Website
www.WanerMath.com
On the Main Page enter 5! and
press "Calculate".

Permutations

A **permutation of n items** is an ordered list of those items. The number of possible permutations of n items is given by **n factorial**, which is

$$n! = n \times (n - 1) \times (n - 2) \times \cdots \times 2 \times 1$$

for n a positive integer, and

$$0! = 1.$$

Visualizing Permutations
Permutations of three colors in a flag:

$3! = 3 \times 2 \times 1 = 6$ Possible Flags

Quick Examples

1. The number of permutations of five items is
   $5! = 5 \times 4 \times 3 \times 2 \times 1 = 120.$

2. The number of ways four CDs can be played in sequence is
   $4! = 4 \times 3 \times 2 \times 1 = 24.$

3. The number of ways three cars can be matched with three drivers is $3! = 6.$

Sometimes, instead of constructing an ordered list of *all* the items of a set, we might want to construct a list of only *some* of the items, as in the next example.

EXAMPLE 2 Corporations[17]

At the end of 2008, the 10 largest companies (by market capitalization) listed on the New York Stock Exchange were, in alphabetical order, AT&T Inc., Berkshire Hathaway Inc., Chevron Corporation, China Mobile Ltd. (ADR), Exxon Mobil Corporation, Johnson & Johnson, PetroChina Company Limited (ADR), Royal Dutch Shell plc (ADR), The Procter & Gamble Company, and Wal-Mart Stores, Inc. You would like to apply to six of these

[17]Source: New York Stock Exchange Web site (www.nyse.com).

Scott Barrow, Inc./SuperStock

companies for a job and you would like to list them in order of job preference. How many such ordered lists are possible?

Solution We want to count ordered lists, but we can't use the permutation formula because we don't want all 10 companies in the list, just 6 of them. So we fall back to a decision algorithm.

Step 1 Choose the first company: 10 choices.

Step 2 Choose the second company: 9 choices.

Step 3 Choose the third one: 8 choices;

Step 4 Choose the fourth one: 7 choices.

Step 5 Choose the fifth one: 6 choices.

Step 6 Choose the sixth one: 5 choices.

Thus, there are $10 \times 9 \times 8 \times 7 \times 6 \times 5 = 151,200$ possible lists of 6. We call this number the **number of permutations of 6 items chosen from 10**, or the **number of permutations of 10 items taken 6 at a time**.

➡ **Before we go on...** We wrote the answer as the product $10 \times 9 \times 8 \times 7 \times 6 \times 5$. But it is useful to notice that we can write this number in a more compact way:

$$10 \times 9 \times 8 \times 7 \times 6 \times 5 = \frac{10 \times 9 \times 8 \times 7 \times 6 \times 5 \times 4 \times 3 \times 2 \times 1}{4 \times 3 \times 2 \times 1}$$

$$= \frac{10!}{4!} = \frac{10!}{(10-6)!} \qquad ■$$

So, we can generalize our definition of permutation to allow for the case in which we use only some of the items, not all. Check that, if $r = n$ below, this is the same definition we gave above.

Permutations of *n* items taken *r* at a time

A **permutation of *n* items taken *r* at a time** is an ordered list of *r* items chosen from a set of *n* items. The number of permutations of *n* items taken *r* at a time is given by

$$P(n, r) = n \times (n - 1) \times (n - 2) \times \cdots \times (n - r + 1)$$

(there are *r* terms multiplied together). We can also write

$$P(n, r) = \frac{n!}{(n - r)!}.$$

Quick Example

The number of permutations of six items taken two at a time is

$$P(6, 2) = 6 \times 5 = 30$$

which we could also calculate as

$$P(6, 2) = \frac{6!}{(6 - 2)!} = \frac{6!}{4!} = \frac{720}{24} = 30.$$

What if we don't care about the order of the items we're choosing? Consider the following example:

EXAMPLE 3 Corporations

Suppose we simply wanted to pick two of the 10 companies listed in Example 2 to apply to, without regard to order. How many possible choices do we have? What if we wanted to choose six to apply to, without regard to order?

Solution Our first guess might be $P(10, 2) = 10 \times 9 = 90$. However, that is the number of *ordered lists* of two companies. We said that we don't care which is first and which second. For example, we consider the list

1. AT&T   **2.** Johnson & Johnson

to be the same as

1. Johnson & Johnson   **2.** AT&T.

Because every set of two companies occurs twice in the 90 lists, once in one order and again in the reverse order, we would count every set of two twice. Thus, there are $90/2 = 45$ possible choices of two companies.

Now, if we wish to pick six companies, again we might start with $P(10, 6) = 151{,}200$. But now, every set of six companies appears as many times as there are different orders in which they could be listed. Six things can be listed in $6! = 720$ different orders, so the number of ways of choosing six companies is $151{,}200/720 = 210$.

In Example 3 we were concerned with counting not the number of ordered lists, but the number of *unordered sets* of companies. For ordered lists we used the word *permutation*; for unordered sets we use the word **combination**.

Permutations and Combinations

A **permutation** of n items taken r at a time is an *ordered list* of r items chosen from n. A **combination** of n items taken r at a time is an *unordered set* of r items chosen from n.

Visualizing

Permutation   Combination

Note Because lists are usually understood to be ordered, when we refer to a list of items, we will always mean an *ordered* list. Similarly, because sets are understood to be unordered, when we refer to a set of items we will always mean an *unordered* set. In short:

Lists are ordered. Sets are unordered. ∎

> **Quick Example**
>
> There are six permutations of the three letters a, b, c taken two at a time:
>
> **1.** a, b;   **2.** b, a;   **3.** a, c;   **4.** c, a;   **5.** b, c;   **6.** c, b.
>
> There are six lists containing two of the letters a, b, c.
>
> There are three combinations of the three letters a, b, c taken two at a time:
>
> **1.** {a, b};   **2.** {a, c};   **3.** {b, c}.
>
> There are three sets containing two of the letters a, b, c.

How do we count the number of possible combinations of n items taken r at a time? We generalize the calculation done in Example 3. The number of permutations is $P(n, r)$, but each set of r items occurs $r!$ times because this is the number of ways in which those r items can be ordered. So, the number of combinations is $P(n, r)/r!$.

> ## Combinations of n items taken r at a time
>
> The number of **combinations of n items taken r at a time** is given by
>
> $$C(n, r) = \frac{P(n, r)}{r!} = \frac{n \times (n - 1) \times (n - 2) \times \cdots \times (n - r + 1)}{r!}.$$
>
> We can also write
>
> $$C(n, r) = \frac{n!}{r!(n - r)!}.$$
>
> **Quick Examples**
>
> **1.** The number of combinations of six items taken two at a time is
>
> $$C(6, 2) = \frac{6 \times 5}{2 \times 1} = 15,$$
>
> which we can also calculate as
>
> $$C(6, 2) = \frac{6!}{2!(6 - 2)!} = \frac{6!}{2!4!} = \frac{720}{2 \times 24} = 15.$$
>
> **2.** The number of sets of four marbles chosen from six is
>
> $$C(6, 4) = \frac{6 \times 5 \times 4 \times 3}{4 \times 3 \times 2 \times 1} = 15.$$

Note There are other common notations for $C(n, r)$. Calculators often have $_nC_r$. In mathematics we often write $\binom{n}{r}$ which is also known as a **binomial coefficient**. Because $C(n, r)$ is the number of ways of choosing a set of r items from n, it is often read "n choose r." ∎

EXAMPLE 4   Calculating Combinations

Calculate   **a.** $C(11, 3)$ **b.** $C(11, 8)$

Solution The easiest way to calculate $C(n, r)$ by hand is to use the first formula above:

$$C(n, r) = \frac{P(n, r)}{r!}$$
$$= \frac{n \times (n - 1) \times (n - 2) \times \cdots \times (n - r + 1)}{r \times (r - 1) \times (r - 2) \times \cdots \times 1}.$$

Both the numerator and the denominator have r factors, so we can begin with n/r and then continue multiplying by decreasing numbers on the top and the bottom until we hit 1 in the denominator. When calculating, it helps to cancel common factors from the numerator and denominator before doing the multiplication in either one.

a. $C(11, 3) = \dfrac{11 \times 10 \times 9}{3 \times 2 \times 1} = \dfrac{11 \times \overset{5}{\cancel{10}} \times \overset{3}{\cancel{9}}}{\cancel{3} \times \cancel{2} \times 1} = 165$

b. $C(11, 8) = \dfrac{11 \times 10 \times 9 \times 8 \times 7 \times 6 \times 5 \times 4}{8 \times 7 \times 6 \times 5 \times 4 \times 3 \times 2 \times 1}$

$$= \dfrac{11 \times \overset{5}{\cancel{10}} \times \overset{3}{\cancel{9}}}{\cancel{3} \times \cancel{2} \times 1} = 165$$

 using Technology

Technology can be used to compute combinations. For instance, to compute $C(11, 8)$:

TI-83/84 Plus
Home screen: `11 nCr 8`
(To obtain the `nCr` symbol, press MATH, choose PRB, and select `3:nCr`.)

Spreadsheet
Use the formula
`=COMBIN(11,8)`

Website
www.WanerMath.com
On the Main Page enter
`comb(11,8)`
and press "Calculate".

➡ **Before we go on...** It is no coincidence that the answers for parts (a) and (b) of Example 4 are the same. Consider what each represents. $C(11, 3)$ is the number of ways of choosing 3 items from 11—for example, electing 3 trustees from a slate of 11. Electing those 3 is the same as choosing the 8 who *do not* get elected. Thus, there are exactly as many ways to choose 3 items from 11 as there are ways to choose 8 items from 11. So, $C(11, 3) = C(11, 8)$. In general,

$$C(n, r) = C(n, n - r).$$

We can also see this equality by using the formula

$$C(n, r) = \frac{n!}{r!(n - r)!}.$$

If we substitute $n - r$ for r, we get exactly the same formula.
   Use the equality $C(n, r) = C(n, n - r)$ to make your calculations easier. Choose the one with the smaller denominator to begin with. ∎

EXAMPLE 5   Calculating Combinations

Calculate   **a.** $C(11, 11)$ **b.** $C(11, 0)$.

Solution

a. $C(11, 11) = \dfrac{11 \times 10 \times 9 \times 8 \times 7 \times 6 \times 5 \times 4 \times 3 \times 2 \times 1}{11 \times 10 \times 9 \times 8 \times 7 \times 6 \times 5 \times 4 \times 3 \times 2 \times 1} = 1$

b. What do we do with that 0? What does it mean to multiply 0 numbers together? We know from above that $C(11, 0) = C(11, 11)$, so we must have $C(11, 0) = 1$. How does this fit with the formulas? Go back to the calculation of $C(11, 11)$:

$$1 = C(11, 11) = \frac{11!}{11!(11 - 11)!} = \frac{11!}{11!0!}.$$

This equality is true only if we agree that $0! = 1$, which we do. Then

$$C(11, 0) = \frac{11!}{0!11!} = 1.$$

➡ **Before we go on...** There is nothing special about 11 in the calculation in Example 5. In general,

$$C(n, n) = C(n, 0) = 1.$$

After all, there is only one way to choose n items out of n: Choose them all. Similarly, there is only one way to choose 0 items out of n: Choose none of them. ■

Now for a few more complicated examples that illustrate the applications of the counting techniques we've discussed.

EXAMPLE 6 **Lotto**

In the betting game Lotto, used in many state lotteries, you choose six different numbers in the range 1–55 (the upper number varies). The order in which you choose them is irrelevant. If your six numbers match the six numbers chosen in the "official drawing," you win the top prize. If Lotto tickets cost $1 for two sets of numbers and you decide to buy tickets that cover every possible combination, thereby guaranteeing that you will win the top prize, how much money will you have to spend?

Solution We first need to know how many sets of numbers are possible. Because order does not matter, we are asking for the number of combinations of 55 numbers taken 6 at a time. This is

$$C(55, 6) = \frac{55 \times 54 \times 53 \times 52 \times 51 \times 50}{6 \times 5 \times 4 \times 3 \times 2 \times 1} = 28{,}989{,}675.$$

Because $1 buys you two of these, you need to spend $28{,}989{,}675/2 = \$14{,}494{,}838$ (rounding up to the nearest dollar) to be assured of a win!

➡ **Before we go on...** The calculation in Example 6 shows that you should not bother buying all these tickets if the winning prize is less than about $14.5 million. Even if the prize is higher, you need to account for the fact that many people will play and the prize may end up split among several winners, not to mention the impracticality of filling out millions of betting slips. ■

EXAMPLE 7 **Marbles**

A bag contains three red marbles, three blue ones, three green ones, and two yellow ones (all distinguishable from one another).

a. How many sets of four marbles are possible?

b. How many sets of four are there such that each one is a different color?

c. How many sets of four are there in which at least two are red?

d. How many sets of four are there in which none are red, but at least one is green?

Solution

a. We simply need to find the number of ways of choosing 4 marbles out of 11, which is

$$C(11, 4) = 330 \text{ possible sets of 4 marbles}$$

b. We use a decision algorithm for choosing such a set of marbles.

Step 1 Choose one red one from the three red ones: $C(3, 1) = 3$ choices.
Step 2 Choose one blue one from the three blue ones: $C(3, 1) = 3$ choices.
Step 3 Choose one green one from the three green ones: $C(3, 1) = 3$ choices.
Step 4 Choose one yellow one from the two yellow ones: $C(2, 1) = 2$ choices.

This gives a total of $3 \times 3 \times 3 \times 2 = 54$ possible sets.

c. We need another decision algorithm. To say that at least two must be red means that either two are red or three are red (with a total of three red ones). In other words, we have two *alternatives*.

Alternative 1: Exactly two red marbles
Step 1 Choose two red ones: $C(3, 2) = 3$ choices.
Step 2 Choose two nonred ones. There are eight of these, so we get $C(8, 2) = 28$ possible choices.

Thus, the total number of choices for this alternative is $3 \times 28 = 84$.

Alternative 2: Exactly three red marbles.
Step 1 Choose the three red ones: $C(3, 3) = 1$ choice.
Step 2 Choose one nonred one: $C(8, 1) = 8$ choices.

Thus, the total number of choices for this alternative is $1 \times 8 = 8$.

By the addition principle, we get a total of $84 + 8 = 92$ sets.

d. The phrase "at least one green" tells us that we again have some alternatives.

Alternative 1: One green marble
Step 1 Choose one green marble from the three: $C(3, 1) = 3$ choices.
Step 2 Choose three nongreen, nonred marbles: $C(5, 3) = 10$ choices.

Thus, the total number of choices for alternative 1 is $3 \times 10 = 30$.

Alternative 2: Two green marbles
Step 1 Choose two green marbles from the three: $C(3, 2) = 3$ choices.
Step 2 Choose two nongreen, nonred marbles: $C(5, 2) = 10$ choices.

Thus, the total number of choices for alternative 2 is $3 \times 10 = 30$.

Alternative 3: Three green marbles
Step 1 Choose three green marbles from the three: $C(3, 3) = 1$ choice.
Step 2 Choose one nongreen, nonred marble: $C(5, 1) = 5$ choices.

Thus, the total number of choices for alternative 3 is $1 \times 5 = 5$.

The addition principle now tells us that the number of sets of four marbles with none red, but at least one green, is $30 + 30 + 5 = 65$.

➡ **Before we go on...** Here is an easier way to answer part (d) of Example 7. First, the total number of sets having *no* red marbles is $C(8, 4) = 70$. Next, of those, the number containing no green marbles is $C(5, 4) = 5$. This leaves $70 - 5 = 65$ sets that contain no red marbles but have at least one green marble. (We have really used here the formula for the cardinality of the complement of a set.) ∎

The last example concerns poker hands. For those unfamiliar with playing cards, here is a short description. A standard deck consists of 52 playing cards. Each card is in one of 13 denominations: ace, 2, 3, 4, 5, 6, 7, 8, 9, 10, jack (J), queen (Q), and king (K), and in one of four suits: hearts (♥), diamonds (♦), clubs (♣), and spades (♠). Thus, for instance, the jack of spades, J♠, refers to the denomination of jack in the suit of spades. The entire deck of cards is thus

A♥	2♥	3♥	4♥	5♥	6♥	7♥	8♥	9♥	10♥	J♥	Q♥	K♥
A♦	2♦	3♦	4♦	5♦	6♦	7♦	8♦	9♦	10♦	J♦	Q♦	K♦
A♣	2♣	3♣	4♣	5♣	6♣	7♣	8♣	9♣	10♣	J♣	Q♣	K♣
A♠	2♠	3♠	4♠	5♠	6♠	7♠	8♠	9♠	10♠	J♠	Q♠	K♠

EXAMPLE 8 Poker Hands

In the card game poker, a hand consists of a set of 5 cards from a standard deck of 52. A **full house** is a hand consisting of three cards of one denomination ("three of a kind"—e.g., three 10s) and two of another ("two of a kind"—e.g., two queens). Here is an example of a full house: 10♣, 10♦, 10♠, Q♥, Q♣.

a. How many different poker hands are there?

b. How many different full houses are there that contain three 10s and two queens?

c. How many different full houses are there altogether?

Solution

a. Because the order of the cards doesn't matter, we simply need to know the number of ways of choosing a set of 5 cards out of 52, which is

$$C(52, 5) = 2,598,960 \text{ hands.}$$

b. Here is a decision algorithm for choosing a full house with three 10s and two queens.

Step 1 Choose three 10s. Because there are four 10s to choose from, we have $C(4, 3) = 4$ choices.

Step 2 Choose two queens: $C(4, 2) = 6$ choices.

Thus, there are $4 \times 6 = 24$ possible full houses with three 10s and two queens.

c. Here is a decision algorithm for choosing a full house.

Step 1 Choose a denomination for the three of a kind; 13 choices.

Step 2 Choose three cards of that denomination. Because there are four cards of each denomination (one for each suit), we get $C(4, 3) = 4$ choices.

Step 3 Choose a different denomination for the two of a kind. There are only 12 denominations left, so we have 12 choices.

Step 4 Choose two of that denomination: $C(4, 2) = 6$ choices.

Thus, by the multiplication principle, there are a total of $13 \times 4 \times 12 \times 6 = 3,744$ possible full houses.

FAQs

Recognizing When to Use Permutations or Combinations

Q: *How can I tell whether a given application calls for permutations or combinations?*

A: Decide whether the application calls for ordered lists (as in situations where order is implied) or for unordered sets (as in situations where order is not relevant). Ordered lists are permutations, whereas unordered sets are combinations.

6.4 EXERCISES

▼ more advanced   ◆ challenging
T indicates exercises that should be solved using technology

Evaluate each number in Exercises 1–16. HINT [See Quick Examples on pp. 430 and 432.]

1. 6!

2. 7!

3. 8!/6!

4. 10!/8!

5. $P(6, 4)$

6. $P(8, 3)$

7. $P(6, 4)/4!$

8. $P(8, 3)/3!$

9. $C(3, 2)$

10. $C(4, 3)$

11. $C(10, 8)$

12. $C(11, 9)$

13. $C(20, 1)$

14. $C(30, 1)$

15. $C(100, 98)$

16. $C(100, 97)$

17. How many ordered lists are there of four items chosen from six?

18. How many ordered sequences are possible that contain three objects chosen from seven?

19. How many unordered sets are possible that contain three objects chosen from seven?

20. How many unordered sets are there of four items chosen from six?

21. How many five-letter sequences are possible that use the letters b, o, g, e, y once each?

22. How many six-letter sequences are possible that use the letters q, u, a, k, e, s once each?

23. How many three-letter sequences are possible that use the letters q, u, a, k, e, s at most once each?

24. How many three-letter sequences are possible that use the letters b, o, g, e, y at most once each?

25. How many three-letter (unordered) sets are possible that use the letters q, u, a, k, e, s at most once each?

26. How many three-letter (unordered) sets are possible that use the letters b, o, g, e, y at most once each?

27. ▼ How many six-letter sequences are possible that use the letters a, u, a, a, u, k? HINT [Use the decision algorithm discussed in Example 3 of Section 6.3.]

28. ▼ How many six-letter sequences are possible that use the letters f, f, a, a, f, f? HINT [See the hint for the preceding exercise.]

Marbles For Exercises 29–42, a bag contains 3 red marbles, 2 green ones, 1 lavender one, 2 yellows, and 2 orange marbles. HINT [See Example 7.]

29. How many possible sets of four marbles are there?

30. How many possible sets of three marbles are there?

31. How many sets of four marbles include all the red ones?

32. How many sets of three marbles include all the yellow ones?

33. How many sets of four marbles include none of the red ones?

34. How many sets of three marbles include none of the yellow ones?

35. How many sets of four marbles include one of each color other than lavender?

36. How many sets of five marbles include one of each color?

37. How many sets of five marbles include at least two red ones?

38. How many sets of five marbles include at least one yellow one?

39. How many sets of five marbles include at most one of the yellow ones?

40. How many sets of five marbles include at most one of the red ones?

41. ▼ How many sets of five marbles include either the lavender one or exactly one yellow one but not both colors?

42. ▼ How many sets of five marbles include at least one yellow one but no green ones?

Dice If a die is rolled 30 times, there are 6^{30} different sequences possible. Exercises 43–46 ask how many of these sequences satisfy certain conditions. HINT [Use the decision algorithm discussed in Example 3 of Section 6.3.]

43. ▼ What fraction of these sequences have exactly five 1s?

44. ▼ What fraction of these sequences have exactly five ones and five 2s?

45. ▼ What fraction of these sequences have exactly 15 even numbers?

46. ▼ What fraction of these sequences have exactly 10 numbers less than or equal to 2?

In Exercises 47–52, calculate how many different sequences can be formed that use the letters of each given word. [Decide where, for example, all the s's will go, rather than what will go in each position. Leave your answer as a product of terms of the form $C(n, r)$.]

47. ▼ mississippi

48. ▼ mesopotamia

49. ▼ megalomania

50. ▼ schizophrenia

51. ▼ casablanca

52. ▼ desmorelda

APPLICATIONS

53. *Itineraries* Your international diplomacy trip requires stops in Thailand, Singapore, Hong Kong, and Bali. How many possible itineraries are there? HINT [See Examples 1 and 2.]

54. *Itineraries* Refer back to the preceding exercise. How many possible itineraries are there in which the last stop is Thailand?

Poker Hands *A poker hand consists of 5 cards from a standard deck of 52. (See the chart preceding Example 8.) In Exercises 55–60, find the number of different poker hands of the specified type.* HINT [See Example 8.]

55. Two pairs (two of one denomination, two of another denomination, and one of a third)

56. Three of a kind (three of one denomination, one of another denomination, and one of a third)

57. Two of a kind (two of one denomination and three of different denominations)

58. Four of a kind (all four of one denomination and one of another)

59. ▼ Straight (five cards of consecutive denominations: A, 2, 3, 4, 5 up through 10, J, Q, K, A, not all of the same suit) (Note that the ace counts either as a 1 or as the denomination above king.)

60. ▼ Flush (five cards all of the same suit, but not consecutive denominations)

Dogs of the Dow *The "Dogs of the Dow" refer to the stocks listed on the Dow with the highest dividend yield. Exercises 61 and 62 are based on the following table, which shows the top 10 stocks of the "Dogs of the Dow" list in November 2011:*[18]

Symbol	Company	Price	Yield
T	AT&T	29.46	5.84%
VZ	Verizon	37.52	5.20%
MRK	Merck	34.47	4.41%
PFE	Pfizer	20.08	3.98%
JNJ	Johnson & Johnson	64.86	3.52%
INTC	Intel	24.75	3.39%
KFT	Kraft	35.48	3.27%
DD	DuPont	49.81	3.29%
CVX	Chevron	108.86	2.87%
MCD	McDonald's	94.60	2.58%

61. You decide to make a small portfolio consisting of a collection of 5 of the top 10 Dogs of the Dow.

   a. How many portfolios are possible?

   b. How many of these portfolios contain VZ and KFT but neither JNJ nor DD?

   c. How many of these portfolios contain at least four stocks with yields above 3.5%?

62. You decide to make a small portfolio consisting of a collection of 6 of the top 10 Dogs of the Dow.

   a. How many portfolios are possible?

   b. How many of these portfolios contain MRK but not PFE?

   c. How many of these portfolios contain at most one stock priced above $60?

Day Trading *Day traders typically buy and sell stocks (or other investment instruments) during the trading day and sell all investments by the end of the day. Exercises 63 and 64 are based on the following table, which shows the closing prices on November 20, 2011, of 12 stocks selected by your broker, Prudence Swift, as well as the change that day.*

Tech Stocks	Close	Change
AAPL (Apple)	$385.22	−10.06
MSFT (Microsoft)	$26.28	0.08
GOOG (Google)	$595.08	−5.87
INTC (Intel)	$24.06	0.22
SNE (Sony Corp.)	$17.11	−0.09
NOK (Nokia)	$6.45	0.07
Non-Tech Stocks		
F (Ford Motor Co.)	$10.99	−0.05
LCC (US Airways)	$4.86	−0.20
ED (Con Ed)	$58.88	0.66
HD (Home Depot)	$37.20	0.04
MO (Altria Group)	$27.63	0.46
ANF (Abercrombie & Fitch)	$55.46	−0.82

63. On the morning of November 20, 2011, Swift advised you to purchase a collection of three tech stocks and two non-tech stocks, all chosen at random from those listed in the table. You were to sell all the stocks at the end of the trading day.

   a. How many possible collections are possible?

   b. You tend to have bad luck with stocks—they usually start going down the moment you buy them. How many of the collections in part (a) consist entirely of stocks that declined in value by the end of the day?

   c. Using the answers to parts (a) and (b), what would you say your chances were of choosing a collection consisting entirely of stocks that declined in value by the end of the day?

64. On the morning of November 20, 2011, Swift advised your friend to purchase a collection of three stocks chosen at random from those listed in the table. Your friend was to sell all the stocks at the end of the trading day.

   a. How many possible collections are possible?

   b. How many of the collections in part (a) included exactly two tech stocks that increased in value by the end of the day?

---

[18]Source: www.dogsofthedow.com.

c. Using the answers to parts (a) and (b), what would you say the chances were that your friend chose a collection that included exactly two tech stocks that increased in value by the end of the day?

Movies Exercises 65 and 66 are based on the following list of top DVD rentals (based on revenue) for the weekend ending November 6, 2011:[19]

Name	*Rank*
Captain America: The First Avenger	1
Bad Teacher	2
Fast Five	3
Cars 2	4
Trespass	5
Bridesmaids	6
Zookeeper	7
Transformers: Dark of the Moon	8
Scream	9
Thor	10

65. ▼ Rather than study for math, you and your buddies decide to get together for a marathon movie-watching, popcorn-guzzling event on Saturday night. You decide to watch four movies selected at random from the above list.

a. How many sets of four movies are possible?
b. Your best friends, the Lara twins, refuse to see *Bridesmaids* on the grounds that it is "for girlie men" and also insist that at least one of *Captain America* or *Thor* be among the movies selected. How many of the possible groups of four will satisfy the twins?
c. Comparing the answers in parts (a) and (b), would you say the Lara twins are more likely than not to be satisfied with your random selection?

66. ▼ Rather than study for astrophysics, you and your friends decide to get together for a marathon movie-watching, gummy-bear-munching event on Saturday night. You decide to watch three movies selected at random from the above list.

a. How many sets of three movies are possible?
b. Your best friends, the Pelogrande twins, refuse to see either *Cars 2* or *Zookeeper* on the grounds that they are "for idiots" and also insist that no more than one of *Bad Teacher* and *Fast Five* should be among the movies selected. How many of the possible groups of three will satisfy the twins?
c. Comparing the answers in parts (a) and (b), would you say the Pelogrande twins are more likely than not to be satisfied with your random selection?

[19]Source: Home Media Magazine (www.imdb.com/Charts/videolast).

67. ▼ *Traveling Salesperson* Suppose you are a salesperson who must visit the following 23 cities: Dallas, Tampa, Orlando, Fairbanks, Seattle, Detroit, Chicago, Houston, Arlington, Grand Rapids, Urbana, San Diego, Aspen, Little Rock, Tuscaloosa, Honolulu, New York, Ithaca, Charlottesville, Lynchville, Raleigh, Anchorage, and Los Angeles. Leave all your answers in factorial form.

a. How many possible itineraries are there that visit each city exactly once?
b. Repeat part (a) in the event that the first five stops have already been determined.
c. Repeat part (a) in the event that your itinerary must include the sequence Anchorage, Fairbanks, Seattle, Chicago, and Detroit, in that order.

68. ▼ *Traveling Salesperson* Refer back to the preceding exercise (and leave all your answers in factorial form).

a. How many possible itineraries are there that start and end at Detroit, and visit every other city exactly once?
b. How many possible itineraries are there that start and end at Detroit, and visit Chicago twice and every other city once?
c. Repeat part (a) in the event that your itinerary must include the sequence Anchorage, Fairbanks, Seattle, Chicago, and New York, in that order.

69. ▼ *(From the GMAT)* Ben and Ann are among seven contestants from which four semifinalists are to be selected. Of the different possible selections, how many contain neither Ben nor Ann?

(A) 5   **(B)** 6   **(C)** 7   **(D)** 14   **(E)** 21

70. ▼ *(Based on a Question from the GMAT)* Ben and Ann are among seven contestants from which four semifinalists are to be selected. Of the different possible selections, how many contain Ben but not Ann?

(A) 5   **(B)** 8   **(C)** 9   **(D)** 10   **(E)** 20

71. ◆ *(From the GMAT exam)* If 10 persons meet at a reunion and each person shakes hands exactly once with each of the others, what is the total number of handshakes?

(A) $10 \cdot 9 \cdot 8 \cdot 7 \cdot 6 \cdot 5 \cdot 4 \cdot 3 \cdot 2 \cdot 1$ **(B)** $10 \cdot 10$
(C) $10 \cdot 9$ **(D)** 45   **(E)** 36

72. ◆ *(Based on a question from the GMAT exam)* If 12 businesspeople have a meeting and each pair exchanges business cards, how many business cards, total, get exchanged?

(A) $12 \cdot 11 \cdot 10 \cdot 9 \cdot 8 \cdot 7 \cdot 6 \cdot 5 \cdot 4 \cdot 3 \cdot 2 \cdot 1$ **(B)** $12 \cdot 12$
(C) $12 \cdot 11$ **(D)** 66   **(E)** 72

73. ◆ *Product Design* The Honest Lock Company plans to introduce what it refers to as the "true combination lock." The lock will open if the correct set of three numbers from 0 through 39 is entered in any order.

a. How many different combinations of three different numbers are possible?
b. If it is allowed that a number appear twice (but not three times), how many more possibilities are created?

c. If it is allowed that any or all of the numbers may be the same, what is the total number of combinations that will open the lock?

74. ◆ *Product Design* Repeat Exercise 73 for a lock based on selecting from the numbers 0 through 19.

75. ◆ *Theory of Linear Programming* (Some familiarity with linear programming is assumed for this exercise.) Suppose you have a linear programming problem with two unknowns and 20 constraints. You decide that graphing the feasible region would take a lot of work, but then you recall that corner points are obtained by solving a system of two equations in two unknowns obtained from two of the constraints. Thus, you decide that it might pay instead to locate all the possible corner points by solving all possible combinations of two equations and then checking whether each solution is a feasible point.

a. How many systems of two equations in two unknowns will you be required to solve?

b. Generalize this to n constraints.

76. ◆ *More Theory of Linear Programming* (Some familiarity with linear programming is assumed for this exercise.) Before the advent of the simplex method for solving linear programming problems, the following method was used: Suppose you have a linear programming problem with three unknowns and 20 constraints. You locate corner points as follows: Selecting three of the constraints, you turn them into equations (by replacing the inequalities with equalities), solve the resulting system of three equations in three unknowns, and then check to see whether the solution is feasible.

a. How many systems of three equations in three unknowns will you be required to solve?

b. Generalize this to n constraints.

COMMUNICATION AND REASONING EXERCISES

77. If you were hard pressed to study for an exam on counting and had only enough time to study one topic, would you choose the formula for the number of permutations or the multiplication principle? Give reasons for your choice.

78. The formula for $C(n, r)$ is written as a ratio of two whole numbers. Can $C(n, r)$ ever be a fraction and not a whole number? Explain (without actually discussing the formula itself).

79. Which of the following represent permutations?

(A) An arrangement of books on a shelf
(B) A group of 10 people in a bus
(C) A committee of 5 senators chosen from 100
(D) A presidential cabinet of 5 portfolios chosen from 20

80. Which of the following represent combinations?

(A) A portfolio of five stocks chosen from the S&P Top Ten
(B) A group of 5 tenors for a choir chosen from 12 singers
(C) A new company CEO and a new CFO chosen from five
(D) The *New York Times* Top Ten Bestseller list

81. When you click on "Get Driving Directions" on Mapquest .com do you get a permutation or a combination of driving instructions? Explain, and give a simple example to illustrate why the answer is important.

82. If you want to know how many possible lists, arranged in alphabetical order, there are of five students selected from your class, you would use the formula for permutations, right? (Explain your answer.)

83. You are tutoring your friend for a test on sets and counting and she asks the question: "How do I know what formula to use for a given problem?" What is a good way to respond?

84. Complete the following. If a counting procedure has five alternatives, each of which has four steps of two choices each, then there are ____ outcomes. On the other hand, if there are five steps, each of which has four alternatives of two choices each, then there are ____ outcomes.

85. ▼ A textbook has the following exercise. "Three students from a class of 50 are selected to take part in a play. How many casts are possible?" Comment on this exercise.

86. ▼ Explain why the coefficient of $a^2 b^4$ in $(a + b)^6$ is $C(6, 2)$ (this is a consequence of the **binomial theorem**). HINT [In the product $(a + b)(a + b) \cdots (a + b)$ (six times), in how many different ways can you pick two a's and four b's to multiply together?]

CHAPTER 6 REVIEW

KEY CONCEPTS

 Website www.WanerMath.com

Go to the Website at www.WanerMath .com to find a comprehensive and interactive Web-based summary of Chapter 6, along with section-by-section tutorials.

6.1 Sets and Set Operations

Sets, elements, subsets, proper subsets, empty set, finite and infinite sets *pp. 396 & 397*

Visualizing sets and relations between sets using Venn diagrams *p. 399*

Union:
$A \cup B = \{x \mid x \in A \text{ or } x \in B\}$ *p. 400*

Intersection: $A \cap B =$ $\{x \mid x \in A \text{ and } x \in B\}$ *p. 400*

Universal sets, complements *p. 401*

Disjoint sets: $A \cap B = \emptyset$ *p. 402*

Cartesian product: $A \times B =$ $\{(a, b) \mid a \in A \text{ and } b \in B\}$ *p. 402*

6.2 Cardinality

Cardinality: $n(A) =$ number of elements in A. *p. 407*

If A and B are finite sets, then $n(A \cup B) =$ $n(A) + n(B) - n(A \cap B)$. *p. 408*

If A and B are disjoint finite sets, then $n(A \cup B) = n(A) + n(B)$. In this case, we say that $A \cup B$ is a **disjoint union**. *p. 408*

If S is a finite universal set and A is a subset of S, then $n(A') = n(S) - n(A)$ and $n(A) = n(S) - n(A')$. *p. 409*

If A and B are finite sets, then $n(A \times B) = n(A)n(B)$. *p. 414*

6.3 Decision Algorithms: The Addition and Multiplication Principles

Addition principle *p. 418*

Multiplication principle *p. 418*

Decision algorithm: a procedure for making a sequence of decisions to choose an element of a set *p. 420*

6.4 Permutations and Combinations

n factorial:
$n! = n \times (n - 1) \times (n - 2) \times \cdots \times 2 \times 1$ *p. 429*

Permutation of n items taken r at a time:
$$P(n, r) = \frac{n!}{(n - r)!} \quad \textit{p. 430}$$

Combination of n items taken r at a time:
$$C(n, r) = P(n, r)/r! = \frac{n!}{r!(n - r)!}$$
p. 432

Using the equality
$C(n, r) = C(n, n - r)$ to simplify calculations of combinations *p. 433*

REVIEW EXERCISES

In each of Exercises 1–5, list the elements of the given set.

1. The set N of all negative integers greater than or equal to -3

2. The set of all outcomes of tossing a coin five times

3. The set of all outcomes of tossing two distinguishable dice such that the numbers are different

4. The sets $(A \cap B) \cup C$ and $A \cap (B \cup C)$, where $A = \{1, 2, 3, 4, 5\}$, $B = \{3, 4, 5\}$, and $C = \{1, 2, 5, 6, 7\}$

5. The sets $A \cup B'$ and $A \times B'$, where $A = \{a, b\}$, $B = \{b, c\}$, and $S = \{a, b, c, d\}$

In each of Exercises 6–10, write the indicated set in terms of the given sets.

6. S: the set of all customers; A: the set of all customers who owe money; B: the set of all customers who owe at least $1,000. The set of all customers who owe money but owe less than $1,000

7. A: the set of outcomes when a day in August is selected; B: the set of outcomes when a time of day is selected. The set of outcomes when a day in August and a time of that day are selected

8. S: the set of outcomes when two dice are rolled; E: those outcomes in which at most one die shows an even number, F: those outcomes in which the sum of the numbers is 7. The set of outcomes in which both dice show an even number or sum to seven

9. S: the set of all integers; P: the set of all positive integers; E: the set of all even integers; Q: the set of all integers that are perfect squares ($Q = \{0, 1, 4, 9, 16, 25, \ldots\}$). The set of all integers that are not positive odd perfect squares

10. S: the set of all integers; N: the set of all negative integers; E: the set of all even integers; T: the set of all integers that are multiples of 3 ($T = \{0, 3, -3, 6, -6, 9, -9, \ldots\}$). The set of all even integers that are neither negative nor multiples of three

In each of Exercises 11–14, give a formula for the cardinality rule or rules needed to answer the question, and then give the solution.

11. You have read 150 of the 400 novels in your home, but your sister Roslyn has read 200, of which only 50 are novels you have read as well. How many have neither of you read?

12. There are 32 students in categories A and B combined; 24 are in A and 24 are in B. How many are in both A and B?

13. You roll two dice, one red and one green. Losing combinations are doubles (both dice show the same number) and outcomes in which the green die shows an odd number and the red die shows an even number. The other combinations are winning ones. How many winning combinations are there?

14. The *Apple iMac* used to come in three models, each with five colors to choose from. How many combinations were possible?

Recall that a poker hand consists of 5 cards from a standard deck of 52. In each of Exercises 15–18, find the number of different poker hands of the specified type. Leave your answer in terms of combinations.

15. Two of a kind with no aces

16. A full house with either two kings and three queens or two queens and three kings

17. Straight Flush (five cards of the same suit with consecutive denominations: A, 2, 3, 4, 5 up through 10, J, Q, K, A)

18. Three of a kind with no aces

In each of Exercises 19–24, consider a bag containing four red marbles, two green ones, one transparent one, three yellow ones, and two orange ones.

19. How many possible sets of five marbles are there in which all of them are red or green?

20. How many possible sets of five marbles are there in which none of them are red or green?

21. How many sets of five marbles include all the red ones?

22. How many sets of five marbles do not include all the red ones?

23. How many sets of five marbles include at least two yellow ones?

24. How many sets of five marbles include at most one of the red ones but no yellow ones?

APPLICATIONS: OHaganBooks.com

Inventories OHaganBooks.com currently operates three warehouses: one in Washington, one in California, and the new one in Texas. Exercises 25–30 are based on the following table, which shows the book inventories at each warehouse:

	Sci Fi	Horror	Romance	Other	Total
Washington	10,000	12,000	12,000	30,000	64,000
California	8,000	12,000	6,000	16,000	42,000
Texas	15,000	15,000	20,000	44,000	94,000
Total	33,000	39,000	38,000	90,000	200,000

Take the first letter of each category to represent the corresponding set of books; for instance, S is the set of sci fi books in stock, W is the set of books in the Washington warehouse, and so on. In each exercise describe the given set in words and compute its cardinality.

25. $S \cup T$

26. $H \cap C$

27. $C \cup S'$

28. $(R \cap T) \cup H$

29. $R \cap (T \cup H)$

30. $(S \cap W) \cup (H \cap C')$

Customers OHaganBooks.com has two main competitors: JungleBooks.com and FarmerBooks.com. At the beginning of

August, OHaganBooks.com had 3,500 customers. Of these, a total of 2,000 customers were shared with JungleBooks.com and 1,500 with FarmerBooks.com. Furthermore, 1,000 customers were shared with both. JungleBooks.com has a total of 3,600 customers, FarmerBooks.com has 3,400, and they share 1,100 customers between them. Use these data for Exercises 31–36.

31. How many of all these customers are exclusive OHaganBooks.com customers?

32. How many customers of the other two companies are not customers of OHaganBooks.com?

33. Which of the three companies has the largest number of exclusive customers?

34. Which of the three companies has the smallest number of exclusive customers?

35. OHaganBooks.com is interested in merging with one of its two competitors. Which merger would give it the largest combined customer base, and how large would that be?

36. Referring to the preceding exercise, which merger would give OHaganBooks.com the largest *exclusive* customer base, and how large would that be?

Online IDs As the customer base at OHaganBooks.com grows, software manager Ruth Nabarro is thinking of introducing identity codes for all the online customers. Help her with the questions in Exercises 37–40.

37. If she uses 3-letter codes, how many different customers can be identified?

38. If she uses codes with three different letters, how many different customers can be identified?

39. It appears that Nabarro has finally settled on codes consisting of two letters followed by two digits. For technical reasons, the letters must be different and the first digit cannot be a zero. How many different customers can be identified?

40. O'Hagan sends Nabarro the following memo:

```
To: Ruth Nabarro, Software Manager
From: John O'Hagan, CEO
Subject: Customer Identity Codes

I have read your proposal for the cus-
tomer ID codes. However, due to our
ambitious expansion plans, I would
like our system software to allow for
at least 500,000 customers. Please
adjust your proposal accordingly.
```

Nabarro is determined to have a sequence of letters followed by some digits, and, for reasons too complicated to explain, there cannot be more than two letters, the letters must be different, the digits must all be different, and the first digit cannot be a zero. What is the form of the shortest code she can use to satisfy the CEO, and how many different customers can be identified?

Degree Requirements *After an exhausting day at the office, John O'Hagan returns home and finds himself having to assist his son Billy-Sean, who continues to have a terrible time planning his first-year college course schedule. The latest Bulletin of Suburban State University reads as follows:*

> *All candidates for the degree of Bachelor of Arts at SSU must take, in their first year, at least 10 courses in the Sciences, Fine Arts, Liberal Arts, and Mathematics combined, of which at least 2 must be in each of the Sciences and Fine Arts, and exactly 3 must be in each of the Liberal Arts and Mathematics.*

Help him with the answers to Exercises 41–43.

41. If the Bulletin lists exactly five first-year-level science courses and six first-year-level courses in each of the other categories, how many course combinations are possible that meet the minimum requirements?

42. Reading through the course descriptions in the bulletin a second time, John O'Hagan notices that Calculus I (listed as one of the mathematics courses) is a required course for many of the other courses, and so decides that it would be best if Billy-Sean included Calculus I. Further, two of the Fine Arts courses cannot both be taken in the first year. How many course combinations are possible that meet the minimum requirements and include Calculus I?

43. To complicate things further, in addition to the requirement in Exercise 42, Physics II has Physics I as a prerequisite (both are listed as first-year science courses, but it is not necessary to take both). How many course combinations are possible that include Calculus I and meet the minimum requirements?

Case Study   Designing a Puzzle

As Product Design Manager for Cerebral Toys Inc., you are constantly on the lookout for ideas for intellectually stimulating yet inexpensive toys. You recently received the following memo from Felix Frost, the developmental psychologist on your design team.

> To: Felicia
> From: Felix
> Subject: Crazy Cubes
>
> We've hit on an excellent idea for a new educational puzzle (which we are calling "Crazy Cubes" until Marketing comes up with a better name). Basically, Crazy Cubes will consist of a set of plastic cubes. Two faces of each cube will be colored red, two will be colored blue, and two white, and there will be exactly two cubes with each possible configuration of colors. The goal of the puzzle is to seek out the matching pairs, thereby enhancing a child's geometric intuition and three-dimensional manipulation skills. The kit will include every possible configuration of colors. We are, however, a little stumped on the following question: How many cubes will the kit contain? In other words, how many possible ways can one color the faces of a cube so that two faces are red, two are blue, and two are white?

Looking at the problem, you reason that the following three-step decision algorithm ought to suffice:

Step 1 Choose a pair of faces to color red; $C(6, 2) = 15$ choices.

Step 2 Choose a pair of faces to color blue; $C(4, 2) = 6$ choices.

Step 3 Choose a pair of faces to color white; $C(2, 2) = 1$ choice.

This algorithm appears to give a total of $15 \times 6 \times 1 = 90$ possible cubes. However, before sending your reply to Felix, you realize that something is wrong, because there are different choices that result in the same cube. To describe some of these choices, imagine a cube oriented so that four of its faces are facing the four compass directions (Figure 9). Consider choice 1, with the top and bottom faces blue, north and south faces white, and east and west faces red; and choice 2, with the top and bottom

Figure 9

Figure 10

Figure 11

Figure 12

faces blue, north and south faces red, and east and west faces white. These cubes are actually the same, as you see by rotating the second cube 90 degrees (Figure 10).

You therefore decide that you need a more sophisticated decision algorithm. Here is one that works.

Alternative 1: Faces with the same color opposite each other. Place one of the blue faces down. Then the top face is also blue. The cube must look like the one drawn in Figure 10. Thus there is only one choice here.

Alternative 2: Red faces opposite each other and the other colors on adjacent pairs of faces. Again there is only one choice, as you can see by putting the red faces on the top and bottom and then rotating.

Alternative 3: White faces opposite each other and the other colors on adjacent pairs of faces; one possibility.

Alternative 4: Blue faces opposite each other and the other colors on adjacent pairs of faces; one possibility.

Alternative 5: Faces with the same color adjacent to each other. Look at the cube so that the edge common to the two red faces is facing you and horizontal (Figure 11). Then the faces on the left and right must be of different colors because they are opposite each other. Assume that the face on the right is white. (If it's blue, then rotate the die with the red edge still facing you to move it there, as in Figure 12.) This leaves two choices for the other white face, on the upper or the lower of the two back faces. This alternative gives two choices.

It follows that there are $1 + 1 + 1 + 1 + 2 = 6$ choices. Because the Crazy Cubes kit will feature two of each cube, the kit will require 12 different cubes.*

EXERCISES

In all of the following exercises, there are three colors to choose from: red, white, and blue.

1. In order to enlarge the kit, Felix suggests including two each of two-colored cubes (using two of the colors red, white, and blue) with three faces one color and three another. How many additional cubes will be required?

2. If Felix now suggests adding two each of cubes with two faces one color, one face another color, and three faces the third color, how many additional cubes will be required?

3. Felix changes his mind and suggests the kit use tetrahedral blocks with two colors instead (see the figure). How many of these would be required?

4. Once Felix finds the answer to the preceding exercise, he decides to go back to the cube idea, but this time insists that all possible combinations of up to three colors should be included. (For instance, some cubes will be all one color, others will be two colors.) How many cubes should the kit contain?

* There is a beautiful way of calculating this and similar numbers, called Pólya enumeration, but it requires a discussion of topics well outside the scope of this book. Take this as a hint that counting techniques can use some of the most sophisticated mathematics.

A tetrahedron

7

Probability

Website

www.WanerMath.com

At the Website you will find:

- Section-by-section tutorials, including game tutorials with randomized quizzes

- A detailed chapter summary

- A true/false quiz

- A Markov system simulation and matrix algebra tool

- Additional review exercises

Case Study The Monty Hall Problem

On the game show *Let's Make a Deal*, you are shown three doors, A, B, and C, and behind one of them is the Big Prize. After you select one of them—say, door A—to make things more interesting the host (Monty Hall) opens one of the other doors—say, door B—revealing that the Big Prize is not there. He then offers you the opportunity to change your selection to the remaining door, door C. Should you switch or stick with your original guess? **Does it make any difference?**

Everett Collection

Introduction

What is the probability of winning the lottery twice? What are the chances that a college athlete whose drug test is positive for steroid use is actually using steroids? You are playing poker and have been dealt two jacks. What is the likelihood that one of the next three cards you are dealt will also be a jack? These are all questions about probability.

Understanding probability is important in many fields, ranging from risk management in business through hypothesis testing in psychology to quantum mechanics in physics. Historically, the theory of probability arose in the sixteenth and seventeenth centuries from attempts by mathematicians such as Gerolamo Cardano, Pierre de Fermat, Blaise Pascal, and Christiaan Huygens to understand games of chance. Andrey Nikolaevich Kolmogorov set forth the foundations of modern probability theory in his 1933 book *Foundations of the Theory of Probability.*

The goal of this chapter is to familiarize you with the basic concepts of modern probability theory and to give you a working knowledge that you can apply in a variety of situations. In the first two sections, the emphasis is on translating real-life situations into the language of sample spaces, events, and probability. Once we have mastered the language of probability, we spend the rest of the chapter studying some of its theory and applications. The last section gives an interesting application of both probability and matrix arithmetic.

7.1 Sample Spaces and Events

Sample Spaces

At the beginning of a football game, to ensure fairness, the referee tosses a coin to decide who will get the ball first. When the ref tosses the coin and observes which side faces up, there are two possible results: heads (H) and tails (T). These are the *only* possible results, ignoring the (remote) possibility that the coin lands on its edge. The act of tossing the coin is an example of an **experiment**. The two possible results, H and T, are possible **outcomes** of the experiment, and the set $S = \{H, T\}$ of all possible outcomes is the **sample space** for the experiment.

Experiments, Outcomes, and Sample Spaces

An **experiment** is an occurrence with a result, or **outcome**, that is uncertain before the experiment takes place. The set of all possible outcomes is called the **sample space** for the experiment.

Quick Examples

1. *Experiment:* Flip a coin and observe the side facing up.
   Outcomes: H, T
   Sample Space: $S = \{H, T\}$

2. *Experiment:* Select a student in your class.
   Outcomes: The students in your class
   Sample Space: The set of students in your class

3. *Experiment:* Select a student in your class and observe the color of his or her hair.
Outcomes: red, black, brown, blond, green, . . .
Sample Space: {red, black, brown, blond, green, . . .}

4. *Experiment:* Cast a die and observe the number facing up.
Outcomes: 1, 2, 3, 4, 5, 6
Sample Space: $S = \{1, 2, 3, 4, 5, 6\}$

5. *Experiment:* Cast two distinguishable dice (see Example 1(a) of Section 6.1) and observe the numbers facing up.
Outcomes: (1, 1), (1, 2), . . . , (6, 6)   (36 outcomes)

$$Sample\ Space:\ S = \begin{Bmatrix} (1,1), & (1,2), & (1,3), & (1,4), & (1,5), & (1,6), \\ (2,1), & (2,2), & (2,3), & (2,4), & (2,5), & (2,6), \\ (3,1), & (3,2), & (3,3), & (3,4), & (3,5), & (3,6), \\ (4,1), & (4,2), & (4,3), & (4,4), & (4,5), & (4,6), \\ (5,1), & (5,2), & (5,3), & (5,4), & (5,5), & (5,6), \\ (6,1), & (6,2), & (6,3), & (6,4), & (6,5), & (6,6) \end{Bmatrix}$$

$n(S) =$ the number of outcomes in $S = 36$

6. *Experiment:* Cast two indistinguishable dice (see Example 1(b) of Section 6.1) and observe the numbers facing up.
Outcomes: (1, 1), (1, 2), . . . , (6, 6)   (21 outcomes)

$$Sample\ Space:\ S = \begin{Bmatrix} (1,1), & (1,2), & (1,3), & (1,4), & (1,5), & (1,6), \\ & (2,2), & (2,3), & (2,4), & (2,5), & (2,6), \\ & & (3,3), & (3,4), & (3,5), & (3,6), \\ & & & (4,4), & (4,5), & (4,6), \\ & & & & (5,5), & (5,6), \\ & & & & & (6,6) \end{Bmatrix}$$

$n(S) = 21$

7. *Experiment:* Cast two dice and observe the *sum* of the numbers facing up.
Outcomes: 2, 3, 4, 5, 6, 7, 8, 9, 10, 11, 12
Sample Space: $S = \{2, 3, 4, 5, 6, 7, 8, 9, 10, 11, 12\}$

8. *Experiment:* Choose 2 cars (without regard to order) at random from a fleet of 10.
Outcomes: Collections of 2 cars chosen from 10
Sample Space: The set of all collections of 2 cars chosen from 10

$n(S) = C(10, 2) = 45$

The following example introduces a sample space that we'll use in several other examples.

EXAMPLE 1 **School and Work**

In a survey conducted by the Bureau of Labor Statistics,[1] the high school graduating class of 2010 was divided into those who went on to college and those who did not. Those who went on to college were further divided into those who went to 2-year colleges and those who went to 4-year colleges. All graduates were also asked whether they were working or not. Find the sample space for the experiment "Select a member of the high school graduating class of 2010 and classify his or her subsequent school and work activity."

Solution The tree in Figure 1 shows the various possibilities.

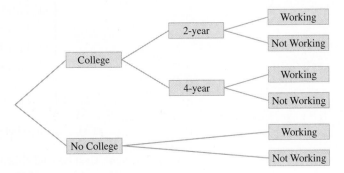

Figure 1

The sample space is

$$S = \{\text{2-year college \& working, 2-year college \& not working,} \\ \text{4-year college \& working, 4-year college \& not working,} \\ \text{no college \& working, no college \& not working}\}.$$

Events

In Example 1, suppose we are interested in the event that a 2010 high school graduate was working. In mathematical language, we are interested in the *subset* of the sample space consisting of all outcomes in which the graduate was working.

Events

Given a sample space S, an **event** E is a subset of S. The outcomes in E are called the **favorable** outcomes. We say that E **occurs** in a particular experiment if the outcome of that experiment is one of the elements of E—that is, if the outcome of the experiment is favorable.

---

[1]"College Enrollment and Work Activity of High School Graduates," U.S. Bureau of Labor Statistics, www.bls.gov/news.release/hsgec.htm.

Visualizing an Event

In the following figure, the favorable outcomes (events in E) are shown in green.

Sample Space S

Quick Examples

1. *Experiment:* Roll a die and observe the number facing up.

   $S = \{1, 2, 3, 4, 5, 6\}$

   Event: E: The number observed is odd.

   $E = \{1, 3, 5\}$

2. *Experiment:* Roll two distinguishable dice and observe the numbers facing up.

   $S = \{(1, 1), (1, 2), \ldots, (6, 6)\}$

   Event: F: The dice show the same number.

   $F = \{(1, 1), (2, 2), (3, 3), (4, 4), (5, 5), (6, 6)\}$

3. *Experiment:* Roll two distinguishable dice and observe the numbers facing up.

   $S = \{(1, 1), (1, 2), \ldots, (6, 6)\}$

   Event: G: The sum of the numbers is 1.

   $G = \emptyset$ There are no favorable outcomes.

4. *Experiment:* Select a city beginning with "J."
   Event: E: The city is Johannesburg.

   $E = \{\text{Johannesburg}\}$ An event can consist of a single outcome.

5. *Experiment:* Roll a die and observe the number facing up.
   Event: E: The number observed is either even or odd.

   $E = S = \{1, 2, 3, 4, 5, 6\}$ An event can consist of all possible outcomes.

6. *Experiment:* Select a student in your class.
   Event: E: The student has red hair.

   $E = \{\text{red-haired students in your class}\}$

7. *Experiment:* Draw a hand of 2 cards from a deck of 52.
   Event: H: Both cards are diamonds.

   H is the set of all hands of 2 cards chosen from 52 such that both cards are diamonds.

Here are some more examples of events.

EXAMPLE 2 Dice

We roll a red die and a green die and observe the numbers facing up. Describe the following events as subsets of the sample space.

a. E: The sum of the numbers showing is 6.

b. F: The sum of the numbers showing is 2.

Solution Here (again) is the sample space for the experiment of throwing two dice.

$$S = \begin{cases} (1,1), & (1,2), & (1,3), & (1,4), & (1,5), & (1,6), \\ (2,1), & (2,2), & (2,3), & (2,4), & (2,5), & (2,6), \\ (3,1), & (3,2), & (3,3), & (3,4), & (3,5), & (3,6), \\ (4,1), & (4,2), & (4,3), & (4,4), & (4,5), & (4,6), \\ (5,1), & (5,2), & (5,3), & (5,4), & (5,5), & (5,6), \\ (6,1), & (6,2), & (6,3), & (6,4), & (6,5), & (6,6) \end{cases}$$

a. In mathematical language, E is the subset of S that consists of all those outcomes in which the sum of the numbers showing is 6. Here is the sample space once again, with the outcomes in question shown in color:

$$S = \begin{cases} (1,1), & (1,2), & (1,3), & (1,4), & (1,5), & (1,6), \\ (2,1), & (2,2), & (2,3), & (2,4), & (2,5), & (2,6), \\ (3,1), & (3,2), & (3,3), & (3,4), & (3,5), & (3,6), \\ (4,1), & (4,2), & (4,3), & (4,4), & (4,5), & (4,6), \\ (5,1), & (5,2), & (5,3), & (5,4), & (5,5), & (5,6), \\ (6,1), & (6,2), & (6,3), & (6,4), & (6,5), & (6,6) \end{cases}$$

Thus, $E = \{(1,5), (2,4), (3,3), (4,2), (5,1)\}$.

b. The only outcome in which the numbers showing add to 2 is $(1, 1)$. Thus,

$$F = \{(1, 1)\}.$$

EXAMPLE 3 School and Work

Let S be the sample space of Example 1. List the elements in the following events:

a. The event E that a 2010 high school graduate was working.

b. The event F that a 2010 high school graduate was not going to a 2-year college.

Solution

a. We had this sample space:

$$S = \{\text{2-year college \& working, two-year college \& not working,}$$
$$\text{4-year college \& working, four-year college \& not working,}$$
$$\text{no college \& working, no college \& not working}\}.$$

We are asked for the event that a graduate was working. Whenever we encounter a phrase involving "the event that . . . ," we mentally translate this into mathematical language by changing the wording.

Replace the phrase "the event that . . ." by the phrase "the subset of the sample space consisting of all outcomes in which . . . ."

Thus we are interested in the subset of the sample space consisting of all outcomes in which the graduate was working. This gives

$E = \{$2-year college & working, 4-year college & working, no college & working$\}$.

The outcomes in E are illustrated by the shaded cells in Figure 2.

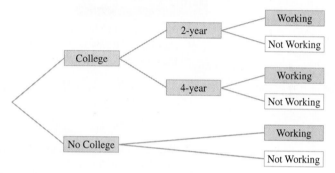

Figure 2

b. We are looking for the event that a graduate was not going to a 2-year college; that is, the subset of the sample space consisting of all outcomes in which the graduate was not going to a 2-year college. Thus,

$F = \{$4-year college & working, 4-year college & not working, no college & working, no college & not working$\}$.

The outcomes in F are illustrated by the shaded cells in Figure 3.

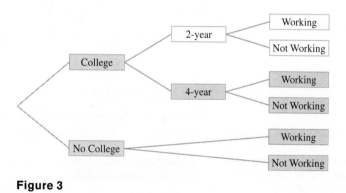

Figure 3

Complement, Union, and Intersection of Events

Events may often be described in terms of other events, using set operations such as complement, union, and intersection.

Complement of an Event

The **complement** of an event E is the set of outcomes not in E. Thus, the complement of E represents the event that E *does not occur*.

Visualizing the Complement

Sample Space S

Quick Examples

1. You take four shots at the goal during a soccer game and record the number of times you score. Describe the event that you score at least twice, and also its complement.

   $S = \{0, 1, 2, 3, 4\}$ Set of outcomes

   $E = \{2, 3, 4\}$ Event that you score at least twice

   $E' = \{0, 1\}$ Event that you do not score at least twice

2. You roll a red die and a green die and observe the two numbers facing up. Describe the event that the sum of the numbers is not 6.

   $S = \{(1, 1), (1, 2), \ldots, (6, 6)\}$

   $F = \{(1, 5), (2, 4), (3, 3), (4, 2), (5, 1)\}$ Sum of numbers is 6.

   $$F' = \begin{cases} (1,1), & (1,2), & (1,3), & (1,4), & & & (1,6), \\ (2,1), & (2,2), & (2,3), & & (2,5), & (2,6), \\ (3,1), & (3,2), & & (3,4), & (3,5), & (3,6), \\ (4,1), & & (4,3), & (4,4), & (4,5), & (4,6), \\ & (5,2), & (5,3), & (5,4), & (5,5), & (5,6), \\ (6,1), & (6,2), & (6,3), & (6,4), & (6,5), & (6,6) \end{cases}$$

   Sum of numbers is not 6.

Union of Events

The **union** of the events E and F is the set of all outcomes in E or F (or both). Thus, $E \cup F$ represents the event that E occurs *or* F occurs (or both).[*]

* As in the preceding chapter, when we use the word *or*, we agree to mean one or the other *or both*. This is called the **inclusive or** and mathematicians have agreed to take this as the meaning of *or* to avoid confusion.

Quick Example

Roll a die.

   E: The outcome is a 5; $E = \{5\}$.

   F: The outcome is an even number; $F = \{2, 4, 6\}$.

   $E \cup F$: The outcome is either a 5 *or* an even number;
   $E \cup F = \{2, 4, 5, 6\}$.

Intersection of Events

The **intersection** of the events E and F is the set of all outcomes common to E and F. Thus, $E \cap F$ represents the event that both E *and* F occur.

Quick Example

Roll two dice; one red and one green.

E: The red die is 2.

F: The green die is odd.

$E \cap F$: The red die is 2 and the green die is odd;
$E \cap F = \{(2, 1), (2, 3), (2, 5)\}$.

EXAMPLE 4 **Weather**

Let R be the event that it will rain tomorrow, let P be the event that it will be pleasant, let C be the event that it will be cold, and let H be the event that it will be hot.

a. Express in words: $R \cap P'$, $R \cup (P \cap C)$.

b. Express in symbols: Tomorrow will be either a pleasant day or a cold and rainy day; it will not, however, be hot.

Solution The key here is to remember that intersection corresponds to *and* and union to *or*.

a. $R \cap P'$ is the event that it will rain *and* it will not be pleasant.
$R \cup (P \cap C)$ is the event that either it will rain, or it will be pleasant and cold.

b. If we rephrase the given statement using *and* and *or* we get "Tomorrow will be either a pleasant day or a cold and rainy day, and it will not be hot."

$$[P \cup (C \cap R)] \cap H' \qquad \text{Pleasant, or cold and rainy, and not hot.}$$

The nuances of the English language play an important role in this formulation. For instance, the effect of the pause (comma) after "rainy day" suggests placing the preceding clause $P \cup (C \cap R)$ in parentheses. In addition, the phrase "cold and rainy" suggests that C and R should be grouped together in their own parentheses.

EXAMPLE 5 **iPods, iPhones, and iPads**

(Compare Example 3 in Section 6.2.) The following table shows sales, in millions of units, of iPods®, iPhones®, and iPads® in the last three quarters of 2011.[2]

	iPods (A)	iPhones (B)	iPads (C)	**Total**
2011 Q2 (U)	9.0	18.7	4.7	32.4
2011 Q3 (V)	7.5	20.3	9.3	37.1
2011 Q4 (W)	6.6	17.1	11.1	34.8
Total	23.1	56.1	25.1	104.3

---

[2]Figures are rounded to one decimal place. Source: Apple quarterly press releases (www.investor.apple.com).

Consider the experiment in which a device is selected at random from those represented in the table. Let A be the event that it was an iPod, let C be the event that it was an iPad, and let U be the event that it was sold in the second quarter of 2011. Describe the following events and compute their cardinality:

a. U' **b.** $A \cap U'$ **c.** $C \cup U$

Solution Before we answer the questions, note that S is the set of all items represented in the table, so S has a total of 104.3 million outcomes.

a. U' is the event that the item was not sold in the second quarter of 2011. Its cardinality is

$$n(U') = n(S) - n(U) = 104.3 - 32.4 = 71.9 \text{ million items.}$$

b. $A \cap U'$ is the event that it was an iPod not sold in the second quarter of 2011.

	iPods (A)	iPhones (B)	iPads (C)	Total
2011 Q2 (U)	9.0	18.7	4.7	32.4
2011 Q3 (V)	7.5	20.3	9.3	37.1
2011 Q4 (W)	6.6	17.1	11.1	34.8
Total	23.1	56.1	25.1	104.3

Referring to the table, we find

$$n(A \cap U') = 7.5 + 6.6 = 14.1 \text{ million items.}$$

c. $C \cup U$ is the event that either it was an iPad or it was sold in the second quarter of 2011:

	iPods (A)	iPhones (B)	iPads (C)	Total
2011 Q2 (U)	9.0	18.7	4.7	32.4
2011 Q3 (V)	7.5	20.3	9.3	37.1
2011 Q4 (W)	6.6	17.1	11.1	34.8
Total	23.1	56.1	25.1	104.3

To compute its cardinality, we can use the formula for the cardinality of a union:

$$n(C \cup U) = n(C) + n(U) - n(C \cap U)$$
$$= 25.1 + 32.4 - 4.7 = 52.8 \text{ million items.}$$

The case where $E \cap F$ is empty is interesting, and we give it a name.

Mutually Exclusive Events

If E and F are events, then E and F are said to be **disjoint** or **mutually exclusive** if $E \cap F$ is empty. (Hence, they have no outcomes in common.)

Visualizing Mutually Exclusive Events

Sample Space S

Interpretation
It is impossible for mutually exclusive events to occur simultaneously.

Quick Examples

In each of the following examples, E and F are mutually exclusive events.

1. Roll a die and observe the number facing up. E: The outcome is even; F: The outcome is odd.

$$E = \{2, 4, 6\}, F = \{1, 3, 5\}$$

2. Toss a coin three times and record the sequence of heads and tails. E: All three tosses land the same way up, F: One toss shows heads and the other two show tails.

$$E = \{HHH, TTT\}, F = \{HTT, THT, TTH\}$$

3. Observe tomorrow's weather. E: It is raining; F: There is not a cloud in the sky.

FAQs

Specifying the Sample Space

Q : *How do I determine the sample space in a given application?*

A : Strictly speaking, an experiment should include a description of what kinds of objects are in the sample space, as in:

Cast a die and observe the number facing up.
Sample space: the possible numbers facing up, {1, 2, 3, 4, 5, 6}.

Choose a person at random and record her Social Security number and whether she is blonde.
Sample space: pairs (9-digit number, Y/N).

However, in many of the scenarios discussed in this chapter and the next, an experiment is specified more vaguely, as in "Select a student in your class." In cases like this, the nature of the sample space should be determined from the context. For example, if the discussion is about grade-point averages and gender, the sample space can be taken to consist of pairs (grade-point average, M/F).

7.1 EXERCISES

▼ more advanced   ◆ challenging
T indicates exercises that should be solved using technology

In Exercises 1–18, describe the sample space S of the experiment and list the elements of the given event. (Assume that the coins are distinguishable and that what is observed are the faces or numbers that face up.) HINT [See Examples 1–3.]

1. Two coins are tossed; the result is at most one tail.

2. Two coins are tossed; the result is one or more heads.

3. Three coins are tossed; the result is at most one head.

4. Three coins are tossed; the result is more tails than heads.

5. Two distinguishable dice are rolled; the numbers add to 5.

6. Two distinguishable dice are rolled; the numbers add to 9.

7. Two indistinguishable dice are rolled; the numbers add to 4.

8. Two indistinguishable dice are rolled; one of the numbers is even and the other is odd.

9. Two indistinguishable dice are rolled; both numbers are prime.[3]

10. Two indistinguishable dice are rolled; neither number is prime.

11. A letter is chosen at random from those in the word *Mozart*; the letter is a vowel.

12. A letter is chosen at random from those in the word *Mozart*; the letter is neither *a* nor *m*.

13. A sequence of two different letters is randomly chosen from those of the word *sore*; the first letter is a vowel.

14. A sequence of two different letters is randomly chosen from those of the word *hear*; the second letter is not a vowel.

15. A sequence of two different digits is randomly chosen from the digits 0–4; the first digit is larger than the second.

16. A sequence of two different digits is randomly chosen from the digits 0–4; the first digit is twice the second.

17. You are considering purchasing either a domestic car, an imported car, a van, an antique car, or an antique truck; you do not buy a car.

18. You are deciding whether to enroll for Psychology 1, Psychology 2, Economics 1, General Economics, or Math for Poets; you decide to avoid economics.

19. A packet of gummy candy contains four strawberry gums, four lime gums, two black currant gums, and two orange gums. April May sticks her hand in and selects four at random. Complete the following sentences:

  a. The sample space is the set of . . . .

  b. April is particularly fond of combinations of two strawberry and two black currant gums. The event that April will get the combination she desires is the set of . . . .

20. A bag contains three red marbles, two blue ones, and four yellow ones, and Alexandra Great pulls out three of them at random. Complete the following sentences:

  a. The sample space is the set of . . . .

  b. The event that Alexandra gets one of each color is the set of . . . .

21. ▼ President Barack H. Obama's cabinet consisted of the Secretaries of Agriculture, Commerce, Defense, Education, Energy, Health and Human Services, Homeland Security, Housing and Urban Development, Interior, Labor, State, Transportation, Treasury, Veterans Affairs, and the Attorney General.[4] Assuming that President Obama had 20 candidates, including Hillary Clinton, to fill these posts (and wished to

assign no one to more than one post), complete the following sentences:

  a. The sample space is the set of . . . .

  b. The event that Hillary Clinton is the Secretary of State is the set of . . . .

22. ▼ A poker hand consists of a set of 5 cards chosen from a standard deck of 52 playing cards. You are dealt a poker hand. Complete the following sentences:

  a. The sample space is the set of . . . .

  b. The event "a full house" is the set of . . . . (Recall that a full house is three cards of one denomination and two of another.)

Suppose two dice (one red, one green) are rolled. Consider the following events. A: the red die shows 1; B: the numbers add to 4; C: at least one of the numbers is 1; and D: the numbers do not add to 11. In Exercises 23–30, express the given event in symbols and say how many elements it contains. HINT [See Example 5.]

23. The red die shows 1 and the numbers add to 4.

24. The red die shows 1 but the numbers do not add to 11.

25. The numbers do not add to 4.

26. The numbers add to 11.

27. The numbers do not add to 4, but they do add to 11.

28. Either the numbers add to 11 or the red die shows a 1.

29. At least one of the numbers is 1 or the numbers add to 4.

30. Either the numbers add to 4, or they add to 11, or at least one of them is 1.

Let W be the event that you will use the book's Website tonight, let I be the event that your math grade will improve, and let E be the event that you will use the Website every night. In Exercises 31–38, express the given event in symbols.

31. You will use the Website tonight and your math grade will improve.

32. You will use the Website tonight or your math grade will not improve.

33. Either you will use the Website every night, or your math grade will not improve.

34. Your math grade will not improve even though you use the Website every night.

35. ▼ Either your math grade will improve, or you will use the Website tonight but not every night.

36. ▼ You will use the Website either tonight or every night, and your grade will improve.

37. ▼ (Compare Exercise 35.) Either your math grade will improve or you will use the Website tonight, but you will not use it every night.

38. ▼ (Compare Exercise 36.) Either you will use the Website tonight, or you will use it every night and your grade will improve.

---

[3]A positive integer is **prime** if it is neither 1 nor a product of smaller integers.

[4]Source: The White House Web site (www.whitehouse.gov).

In Exercises 39–42, Pablo randomly picks three marbles from a bag of eight marbles (four red ones, two green ones, and two yellow ones).

39. How many outcomes are there in the sample space? How many outcomes in the event that none of the marbles he picks are red?

40. How many outcomes are there in the sample space? How many outcomes in the event that all of the marbles he picks are red?

41. ▼ How many outcomes are there in the event that Pablo picks one marble of each color?

42. ▼ How many outcomes are there in the event that the marbles Pablo picks are not all the same color?

APPLICATIONS

Housing Prices Exercises 43–48 are based on the map below, which shows the percentage change in housing prices from June 2010 to June 2011 in each of nine regions (U.S. Census divisions).[5]

43. You are choosing a region of the country to move to. Describe the event *E* that the region you choose saw a decrease in housing prices of 7% or more.

44. You are choosing a region of the country to move to. Describe the event *E* that the region you choose saw a decrease in housing prices of less than 3%.

45. You are choosing a region of the country to move to. Let *E* be the event that the region you choose saw a decrease in housing prices of 7% or more, and let *F* be the event that the region you choose is on the east coast. Describe the events $E \cup F$ and $E \cap F$ both in words and by listing the outcomes of each.

46. You are choosing a region of the country to move to. Let *E* be the event that the region you choose saw a decrease in housing prices of less than 3%, and let *F* be the event that the region you choose is not on the east coast. Describe the events $E \cup F$ and $E \cap F$ both in words and by listing the outcomes of each.

47. ▼ You are choosing a region of the country to move to. Which of the following pairs of events are mutually exclusive?

a. *E*: You choose a region from among the two with the highest percentage decrease in housing prices.
F: You choose a region that is not on the east or west coast.

b. *E*: You choose a region from among the two with the highest percentage decrease in housing prices.
F: You choose a region that is on the east coast.

48. ▼ You are choosing a region of the country to move to. Which of the following pairs of events are mutually exclusive?

a. *E*: You choose a region from among the three with the least decline in housing prices.
F: You choose a region from among the central divisions.

b. *E*: You choose a region from among the three with the least decline in housing prices.
F: You choose a region on the east or west coast.

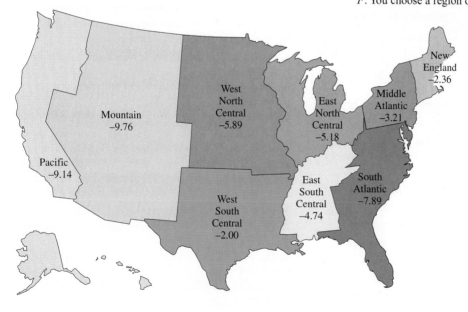

Publishing Exercises 49–56 are based on the accompanying table, which shows the results of a survey of authors by a (fictitious) publishing company. HINT [See Example 5.]

	New Authors	Established Authors	Total
Successful	5	25	30
Unsuccessful	15	55	70
Total	20	80	100

[5]Source: Office of Federal Housing Enterprise Oversight (www.ofheo.gov).

Consider the following events: *S: an author is successful; U: an author is unsuccessful; N: an author is new;* and *E: an author is established.*

49. Describe the events $S \cap N$ and $S \cup N$ in words. Use the table to compute $n(S \cap N)$ and $n(S \cup N)$.

50. Describe the events $N \cap U$ and $N \cup U$ in words. Use the table to compute $n(N \cap U)$ and $n(N \cup U)$.

51. Which of the following pairs of events are mutually exclusive: *N* and *E; N* and *S; S* and *E?*

52. Which of the following pairs of events are mutually exclusive: *U* and *E; U* and *S; S* and *N?*

53. Describe the event $S \cap N'$ in words and find the number of elements it contains.

54. Describe the event $U \cup E'$ in words and find the number of elements it contains.

55. ▼ What percentage of established authors are successful? What percentage of successful authors are established?

56. ▼ What percentage of new authors are unsuccessful? What percentage of unsuccessful authors are new?

Stock Prices *Exercises 57–64 are based on the following table, which shows the performance of a selection of 100 stocks after one year. (Take S to be the set of all stocks represented in the table.)*

	Companies			
	Pharmaceutical *P*	Electronic *E*	Internet *I*	Total
Increased *V*	10	5	15	30
Unchanged[6] *N*	30	0	10	40
Decreased *D*	10	5	15	30
Total	50	10	40	100

57. Use symbols to describe the event that a stock's value increased but it was not an Internet stock. How many elements are in this event?

58. Use symbols to describe the event that an Internet stock did not increase. How many elements are in this event?

59. Compute $n(P' \cup N)$. What does this number represent?

60. Compute $n(P \cup N')$. What does this number represent?

61. Find all pairs of mutually exclusive events among the events *P, E, I, V, N,* and *D.*

62. Find all pairs of events that are not mutually exclusive among the events *P, E, I, V, N,* and *D.*

63. ▼ Calculate $\dfrac{n(V \cap I)}{n(I)}$. What does the answer represent?

64. ▼ Calculate $\dfrac{n(D \cap I)}{n(D)}$. What does the answer represent?

---

[6]If a stock stayed within 20% of its original value, it is classified as "unchanged."

Animal Psychology *Exercises 65–70 concern the following chart, which shows the way in which a dog moves its facial muscles when torn between the drives of fight and flight.[7] The "fight" drive increases from left to right; the "flight" drive increases from top to bottom. (Notice that an increase in the "fight" drive causes its upper lip to lift, while an increase in the "flight" drive draws its ears downward.)*

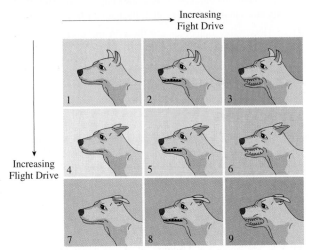

65. ▼ Let *E* be the event that the dog's flight drive is the strongest, let *F* be the event that the dog's flight drive is weakest, let *G* be the event that the dog's fight drive is the strongest, and let *H* be the event that the dog's fight drive is weakest. Describe the following events in terms of *E, F, G,* and *H* using the symbols $\cap$, $\cup$, and ′.

    a. The dog's flight drive is not strongest and its fight drive is weakest.

    b. The dog's flight drive is strongest or its fight drive is weakest.

    c. Neither the dog's flight drive nor its fight drive is strongest.

66. ▼ Let *E* be the event that the dog's flight drive is the strongest, let *F* be the event that the dog's flight drive is weakest, let *G* be the event that the dog's fight drive is the strongest, and let *H* be the event that the dog's fight drive is weakest. Describe the following events in terms of *E, F, G,* and *H* using the symbols $\cap$, $\cup$, and ′.

    a. The dog's flight drive is weakest and its fight drive is not weakest.

    b. The dog's flight drive is not strongest or its fight drive is weakest.

    c. Either the dog's flight drive or its fight drive fails to be strongest.

67. ▼ Describe the following events explicitly (as subsets of the sample space):

    a. The dog's fight and flight drives are both strongest.

    b. The dog's fight drive is strongest, but its flight drive is neither weakest nor strongest.

---

[7]Source: *On Aggression* by Konrad Lorenz (Fakenham, Norfolk: University Paperback Edition, Cox & Wyman Limited, 1967).

68. ▼ Describe the following events explicitly (as subsets of the sample space):

a. Neither the dog's fight drive nor its flight drive is strongest.

b. The dog's fight drive is weakest, but its flight drive is neither weakest nor strongest.

69. ▼ Describe the following events in words:

a. $\{1, 4, 7\}$
b. $\{1, 9\}$
c. $\{3, 6, 7, 8, 9\}$

70. ▼ Describe the following events in words:

a. $\{7, 8, 9\}$
b. $\{3, 7\}$
c. $\{1, 2, 3, 4, 7\}$

Exercises 71–74 use counting arguments from the preceding chapter.

71. ▼ *Gummy Bears* A bag contains six gummy bears. Noel picks four at random. How many possible outcomes are there? If one of the gummy bears is raspberry, how many of these outcomes include the raspberry gummy bear?

72. ▼ *Chocolates* My couch potato friend enjoys sitting in front of the TV and grabbing handfuls of 5 chocolates at random from his snack jar. Unbeknownst to him, I have replaced one of the 20 chocolates in his jar with a cashew. (He hates cashews with a passion.) How many possible outcomes are there the first time he grabs 5 chocolates? How many of these include the cashew?

73. ▼ *Horse Races* The seven contenders in the fifth horse race at Aqueduct on February 18, 2002, were: Pipe Bomb, Expect a Ship, All That Magic, Electoral College, Celera, Cliff Glider, and Inca Halo.[8] You are interested in the first three places (winner, second place, and third place) for the race.

a. Find the cardinality $n(S)$ of the sample space S of all possible finishes of the race. (A finish for the race consists of a first, second, and third place winner.)

b. Let E be the event that Electoral College is in second or third place, and let F be the event that Celera is the winner. Express the event $E \cap F$ in words, and find its cardinality.

74. ▼ *Intramurals* The following five teams will be participating in Urban University's hockey intramural tournament: the Independent Wildcats, the Phi Chi Bulldogs, the Gate Crashers, the Slide Rule Nerds, and the City Slickers. Prizes will be awarded for the winner and runner-up.

a. Find the cardinality $n(S)$ of the sample space S of all possible outcomes of the tournament. (An outcome of the tournament consists of a winner and a runner-up.)

b. Let E be the event that the City Slickers are runners-up, and let F be the event that the Independent Wildcats are neither the winners nor runners-up. Express the event $E \cup F$ in words, and find its cardinality.

COMMUNICATION AND REASONING EXERCISES

75. Complete the following sentence. An event is a ____.

76. Complete the following sentence. Two events E and F are mutually exclusive if their intersection is _____.

77. If E and F are events, then $(E \cap F)'$ is the event that ____.

78. If E and F are events, then $(E' \cap F')$ is the event that ____.

79. Let E be the event that you meet a tall dark stranger. Which of the following could reasonably represent the experiment and sample space in question?

(A) You go on vacation and lie in the sun; S is the set of cloudy days.

(B) You go on vacation and spend an evening at the local dance club; S is the set of people you meet.

(C) You go on vacation and spend an evening at the local dance club; S is the set of people you do not meet.

80. Let E be the event that you buy a Porsche. Which of the following could reasonably represent the experiment and sample space in question?

(A) You go to an auto dealership and select a Mustang; S is the set of colors available.

(B) You go to an auto dealership and select a red car; S is the set of cars you decide not to buy.

(C) You go to an auto dealership and select a red car; S is the set of car models available.

81. ▼ True or false? Every set S is the sample space for some experiment. Explain.

82. ▼ True or false? Every sample space S is a finite set. Explain.

83. ▼ Describe an experiment in which a die is cast and the set of outcomes is $\{0, 1\}$.

84. ▼ Describe an experiment in which two coins are flipped and the set of outcomes is $\{0, 1, 2\}$.

85. ▼ Two distinguishable dice are rolled. Could there be two mutually exclusive events that both contain outcomes in which the numbers facing up add to 7?

86. ▼ Describe an experiment in which two dice are rolled and describe two mutually exclusive events that both contain outcomes in which both dice show a 1.

---

[8]Source: *Newsday*, Feb. 18, 2002, p. A36.

7.2 Relative Frequency

Suppose you have a coin that you think is not fair and you would like to determine the likelihood that heads will come up when it is tossed. You could estimate this likelihood by tossing the coin a large number of times and counting the number of times heads comes up. Suppose, for instance, that in 100 tosses of the coin, heads comes up 58 times. The fraction of times that heads comes up, $58/100 = .58$, is the **relative frequency**, or **estimated probability** of heads coming up when the coin is tossed. In other words, saying that the relative frequency of heads coming up is .58 is the same as saying that heads came up 58% of the time in your series of experiments.

Now let's think about this example in terms of sample spaces and events. First of all, there is an experiment that has been repeated $N = 100$ times: Toss the coin and observe the side facing up. The sample space for this experiment is $S = \{H, T\}$. Also, there is an event E in which we are interested: the event that heads comes up, which is $E = \{H\}$. The number of times E has occurred, or the **frequency** of E, is $fr(E) = 58$. The relative frequency of the event E is then

$$P(E) = \frac{fr(E)}{N} \qquad \frac{\text{Frequency of event } E}{\text{Number of repetitions } N}$$
$$= \frac{58}{100} = .58.$$

Notes

1. The relative frequency gives us an *estimate* of the likelihood that heads will come up when that particular coin is tossed. This is why statisticians often use the alternative term *estimated probability* to describe it.

2. The larger the number of times the experiment is performed, the more accurate an estimate we expect this estimated probability to be. ∎

Relative Frequency

When an experiment is performed a number of times, the **relative frequency** or **estimated probability** of an event E is the fraction of times that the event E occurs. If the experiment is performed N times and the event E occurs $fr(E)$ times, then the relative frequency is given by

$$P(E) = \frac{fr(E)}{N}. \qquad \text{Fraction of times } E \text{ occurs}$$

The number $fr(E)$ is called the **frequency** of E. N, the number of times that the experiment is performed, is called the number of **trials** or the **sample size**. If E consists of a single outcome s, then we refer to $P(E)$ as the relative frequency or estimated probability of the outcome s, and we write $P(s)$.

Visualizing Relative Frequency

$$P(E) = \frac{fr(E)}{N} = \frac{4}{10} = .4$$

The collection of the estimated probabilities of *all* the outcomes is the **relative frequency distribution** or **estimated probability distribution**.

> ### Quick Examples
>
> 1. **Experiment:** Roll a pair of dice and add the numbers that face up.
>
>   **Event:** E: The sum is 5.
>
>   If the experiment is repeated 100 times and E occurs on 10 of the rolls, then the relative frequency of E is
>
> $$P(E) = \frac{fr(E)}{N} = \frac{10}{100} = .10.$$
>
> 2. If 10 rolls of a single die resulted in the outcomes 2, 1, 4, 4, 5, 6, 1, 2, 2, 1, then the associated relative frequency distribution is shown in the following table:
>
> | Outcome | 1 | 2 | 3 | 4 | 5 | 6 |
> |---|---|---|---|---|---|---|
> | Rel. Frequency | .3 | .3 | 0 | .2 | .1 | .1 |
>
> 3. **Experiment:** Note the cloud conditions on a particular day in April.
>
>   If the experiment is repeated a number of times, and it is clear 20% of those times, partly cloudy 30% of those times, and overcast the rest of those times, then the relative frequency distribution is:
>
> | Outcome | Clear | Partly Cloudy | Overcast |
> |---|---|---|---|
> | Rel. Frequency | .20 | .30 | .50 |

EXAMPLE 1 Sales of Hybrid Vehicles

* The official plural form of Prius according to Toyota.

In a survey of 250 hybrid vehicles sold in the United States, 125 were Toyota Prii,* 30 were Honda Civics, 20 were Toyota Camrys, 15 were Ford Escapes, and the rest were other makes.[9] What is the relative frequency that a hybrid vehicle sold in the United States is not a Toyota Camry?

Solution The experiment consists of choosing a hybrid vehicle sold in the United States and determining its make. The sample space suggested by the information given is

$$S = \{\text{Toyota Prius, Honda Civic, Toyota Camry, Ford Escape, Other}\}$$

and we are interested in the event

$$E = \{\text{Toyota Prius, Honda Civic, Ford Escape, Other}\}.$$

The sample size is $N = 250$, of which 20 were Toyota Camrys. Thus, the frequency of E is $fr(E) = 250 - 20 = 230$ and the relative frequency of E is

$$P(E) = \frac{fr(E)}{N} = \frac{230}{250} = .92.$$

---

[9] The proportions are based on approximate actual cumulative sales through October 2011 (www.wikipedia.com).

➡ **Before we go on...** In Example 1, you might ask how accurate the estimate of .92 is or how well it reflects *all* of the hybrid vehicles sold in the United States absent any information about national sales figures. The field of statistics provides the tools needed to say to what extent this estimated probability can be trusted. ∎

EXAMPLE 2 Auctions on eBay

The following chart shows the results of a survey of the bid prices for 50 paintings on eBay with the highest number of bids.[10]

Bid Price	$0–$9.99	$10–$49.99	$50–$99.99	≥ $100
Frequency	6	23	15	6

Consider the experiment in which a painting is chosen and the bid price is observed.

a. Find the relative frequency distribution.

b. Find the relative frequency that a painting in the survey had a bid price of less than $50.

Solution

a. The following table shows the relative frequency of each outcome, which we find by dividing each frequency by the sum $N = 50$:

Bid Price	$0–$9.99	$10–$49.99	$50–$99.99	≥ $100
Rel. Frequency	$\dfrac{6}{50} = .12$	$\dfrac{23}{50} = .46$	$\dfrac{15}{50} = .30$	$\dfrac{6}{50} = .12$

b. Method 1: Computing Directly

$E = \{\$0–\$9.99, \$10–\$49.99\}$

Thus,

$$P(E) = \frac{fr(E)}{N} = \frac{6 + 23}{50} = \frac{29}{50} = .58.$$

Method 2: Using the Relative Frequency Distribution

Notice that we can obtain the same answer from the distribution in part (a) by simply adding the relative frequencies of the outcomes in E:

$$P(E) = .12 + .46 = .58.$$

---

[10]In the category "Art—Direct from Artist" on November 14, 2011 (www.eBay.com).

Q : *Why did we get the same result in part (b) of Example 2 by simply adding the relative frequencies of the outcomes in E?*

A : The reason can be seen by doing the calculation in the first method a slightly different way:

$$P(E) = \frac{fr(E)}{N} = \frac{6+23}{50}$$

$$= \frac{6}{50} + \frac{23}{50}. \qquad \text{Sum of rel. frequencies of the individual outcomes}$$

This property of relative frequency distributions is discussed below.

Following are some important properties of estimated probability that we can observe in Example 2.

Some Properties of Relative Frequency Distributions

Let $S = \{s_1, s_2, \ldots, s_n\}$ be a sample space and let $P(s_i)$ be the relative frequency of the event $\{s_i\}$. Then

1. $0 \le P(s_i) \le 1$
2. $P(s_1) + P(s_2) + \cdots + P(s_n) = 1$
3. If $E = \{e_1, e_2, \ldots, e_r\}$, then $P(E) = P(e_1) + P(e_2) + \cdots + P(e_r)$.

In words:

1. The relative frequency of each outcome is a number between 0 and 1 (inclusive).
2. The relative frequencies of all the outcomes add up to 1.
3. The relative frequency of an event E is the sum of the relative frequencies of the individual outcomes in E.

Relative Frequency and Increasing Sample Size

 using Technology

See the Technology Guides at the end of the chapter to see how to use a TI-83/84 Plus or a spreadsheet to simulate experiments.

A "fair" coin is one that is as likely to come up heads as it is to come up tails. In other words, we expect heads to come up 50% of the time if we toss such a coin many times. Put more precisely, we expect the relative frequency to approach .5 as the number of trials gets larger. Figure 4 shows how the relative frequency behaved for one sequence of coin tosses. For each N we have plotted what fraction of times the coin came up heads in the first N tosses.

Figure 4

Notice that the relative frequency graph meanders as N increases, sometimes getting closer to .5, and sometimes drifting away again. However, the graph tends to meander within smaller and smaller distances of .5 as N increases.*

In general, this is how relative frequency seems to behave; as N gets large, the relative frequency appears to approach some fixed value. Some refer to this value as the "actual" probability, whereas others point out that there are difficulties with this this notion. For instance, how can we actually determine this limit to any accuracy by experiment? How exactly is the experiment conducted? Technical and philosophical issues aside, the relative frequencies do approach a fixed value and, in the next section, we will talk about how we use probability models to predict this limiting value.

* This can be made more precise by the concept of "limit" used in calculus.

7.2   EXERCISES

▼ more advanced   ◆ challenging
🆃 indicates exercises that should be solved using technology

In Exercises 1–6, calculate the relative frequency $P(E)$ using the given information.

1. $N = 100$, $fr(E) = 40$ 2. $N = 500$, $fr(E) = 300$

3. Eight hundred adults are polled and 640 of them support universal health-care coverage. E is the event that an adult supports universal health coverage. HINT [See Example 1.]

4. Eight Hundred adults are polled and 640 of them support universal health-care coverage. E is the event that an adult does not support universal health coverage. HINT [See Example 1.]

5. A die is rolled 60 times with the following result: 1, 2, and 3 each come up 8 times, and 4, 5, and 6 each come up 12 times. E is the event that the number that comes up is at most 4.

6. A die is rolled 90 times with the following result: 1 and 2 never come up, 3 and 4 each come up 30 times, and 5 and 6 each come up 15 times. E is the event that the number that comes up is at least 4.

Exercises 7–12 are based on the following table, which shows the frequency of outcomes when two distinguishable coins were tossed 4,000 times and the uppermost faces were observed. HINT [See Example 2.]

Outcome	HH	HT	TH	TT
Frequency	1,100	950	1,200	750

7. Determine the relative frequency distribution.

8. What is the relative frequency that heads comes up at least once?

9. What is the relative frequency that the second coin lands with heads up?

10. What is the relative frequency that the first coin lands with heads up?

11. Would you judge the second coin to be fair? Give a reason for your answer.

12. Would you judge the first coin to be fair? Give a reason for your answer.

In Exercises 13–18, say whether the given distribution can be a relative frequency distribution. If your answer is no, indicate why not. HINT [See the properties of relative frequency distributions on page 463.]

13.

Outcome	1	2	3	5
Rel. Frequency	.4	.6	0	0

14.

Outcome	A	B	C	D
Rel. Frequency	.2	.1	.2	.1

15.

Outcome	HH	HT	TH	TT
Rel. Frequency	.5	.4	.5	−.4

16.

Outcome	2	4	6	8
Rel. Frequency	25	25	25	25

17.

Outcome	−3	−2	−1	0
Rel. Frequency	.2	.3	.2	.3

18.

Outcome	HH	HT	TH	TT
Rel. Frequency	0	0	0	1

In Exercises 19 and 20, complete the given relative frequency distribution and compute the stated relative frequencies. HINT [See the properties of relative frequency distributions on page 463.]

19.

Outcome	1	2	3	4	5
Rel. Frequency	.2	.3	.1	.1	

   a. $P(\{1, 3, 5\})$ b. $P(E')$ where $E = \{1, 2, 3\}$

20.

Outcome	1	2	3	4	5
Rel. Frequency	.4		.3	.1	.1

   a. $P(\{2, 3, 4\})$ b. $P(E')$ where $E = \{3, 4\}$

Ⅰ *Exercises 21–24 require the use of a calculator or computer with a random number generator.*

21. Simulate 100 tosses of a fair coin, and compute the estimated probability that heads comes up.

22. Simulate 100 throws of a fair die, and calculate the estimated probability that the result is a 6.

23. Simulate 50 tosses of two coins, and compute the estimated probability that the outcome is one head and one tail (in any order).

24. Simulate 100 throws of two fair dice, and calculate the estimated probability that the result is a double 6.

APPLICATIONS

25. *Latin Music Sales* In a survey of 500 Latin music downloads, 250 were regional (Mexican/Tejano), 165 were pop-rock, 55 were tropical (salsa/merengue/cumbia/bachata), and 30 were urban (reggaeton).[11] Calculate the following relative frequencies:

   a. That a music download was regional
   b. That a music download was either tropical or urban
   c. That a music download was not urban HINT [See Example 1.]

26. *Latin Music Sales* In a survey of 400 Latin music downloads, 200 were regional (Mexican/Tejano), 130 were pop-rock, 45 were tropical (salsa/merengue/cumbia/bachata), and 25 were urban (reggaeton).[12] Calculate the following relative frequencies:

   a. That a music download was pop/rock
   b. That a music download was neither tropical nor regional.
   c. That a music download was not regional HINT [See Example 1.]

27. *Subprime Mortgages during the 2000–2008 Housing Bubble* The following chart shows the results of a survey of the status of subprime home mortgages in Texas in November 2008:[13]

Mortgage Status	Current	Past Due	In Foreclosure	Repossessed
Frequency	134	52	9	5

(The four categories are mutually exclusive; for instance, "Past Due" refers to a mortgage whose payment status is past due but is not in foreclosure, and "In Foreclosure" refers to a mortgage that is in the process of being fore-closed but not yet repossessed.)

   a. Find the relative frequency distribution for the experiment of randomly selecting a subprime mortgage in Texas and determining its status.

   b. What is the relative frequency that a randomly selected subprime mortgage in Texas was not current? HINT [See Example 2.]

28. *Subprime Mortgages during the 2000–2008 Housing Bubble* The following chart shows the results of a survey of the status of subprime home mortgages in Florida in November 2008:[14]

Mortgage Status	Current	Past Due	In Foreclosure	Repossessed
Frequency	110	65	60	15

(The four categories are mutually exclusive; for instance, "Past Due" refers to a mortgage whose payment status is past due but is not in foreclosure, and "In Foreclosure" refers to a mortgage that is in the process of being fore-closed but not yet repossessed.)

   a. Find the relative frequency distribution for the experiment of randomly selecting a subprime mortgage in Florida and determining its status.

   b. What is the relative frequency that a randomly selected subprime mortgage in Florida was neither in foreclosure nor repossessed? HINT [See Example 2.]

29. *Population Age in Mexico* The following table shows the results of a survey of randomly selected residents of Mexico:[15]

Age	0–14	15–29	30–64	>64
Percentage	30	27	37	6

   a. Find the associated relative frequency distribution. HINT [See Quick Example 3, page 461.]

   b. Find the relative frequency that a resident of Mexico is *not* from 15 to 64 years old.

30. *Population Age in the United States* The following table shows the results of a survey of randomly selected U.S. residents:[16]

Age	0–14	15–29	30–64	>64
Percentage	20	21	46	13

   a. Find the associated relative frequency distribution. HINT [See Quick Example 3, page 461.]

   b. Find the relative frequency that a resident of the United States is 30 years old or older.

[11] Based on revenues in 2010. Source: The Recording Industry Association of America (www.riaa.com).

[12] Based on revenues in 2009. Source: The Recording Industry Association of America (www.riaa.com).

[13] Based on actual data in 2008. Source: Federal Reserve Bank of New York (www.newyorkfed.org/regional/subprime.html).

[14] *Ibid.*

[15] Based on population distribution in 2010. Source: Instituto Nacional de Estadística y Geografía (www.inegi.org.mx).

[16] *Ibid.* (The data for the U.S. was also provided by the Instituto Nacional de Estadística y Geografía.)

31. *Motor Vehicle Safety* The following table shows crashworthiness ratings for 10 small SUVs.[17] (3 = Good, 2 = Acceptable, 1 = Marginal, 0 = Poor)

Frontal Crash Test Rating	3	2	1	0
Frequency	1	4	4	1

a. Find the relative frequency distribution for the experiment of choosing a small SUV at random and determining its frontal crash rating.

b. What is the relative frequency that a randomly selected small SUV will have a crash test rating of "Acceptable" or better?

32. *Motor Vehicle Safety* The following table shows crashworthiness ratings for 16 small cars.[18] (3 = Good, 2 = Acceptable, 1 = Marginal, 0 = Poor)

Frontal Crash Test Rating	3	2	1	0
Frequency	1	11	2	2

a. Find the relative frequency distribution for the experiment of choosing a small car at random and determining its frontal crash rating.

b. What is the relative frequency that a randomly selected small car will have a crash test rating of "Marginal" or worse?

33. *Internet Connections* The following pie chart shows the relative frequency distribution resulting from a survey of 2,000 U.S. households with Internet connections back in 2003.[19]

Determine the **frequency distribution**; that is, the total number of households with each type of Internet connection in the survey.

34. *Internet Connections* The following pie chart shows the relative frequency distribution resulting from a survey of 3,000 U.S. rural households with Internet connections back in 2003.[20]

Determine the **frequency distribution**; that is, the total number of households with each type of Internet connection in the survey.

35. ▼ *Stock Market Gyrations* The following chart shows the day-by-day change in the Dow Jones Industrial Average during 20 successive business days in October 2008 during the 2008 financial crisis:[21]

Use the chart to construct the relative frequency distribution using the following three outcomes. Surge: The Dow was up by more than 300 points; Plunge: The Dow was down by more than 300 points; Steady: The Dow changed by 300 points or less.

36. ▼ *Stock Market Gyrations* Repeat Exercise 35 using the following chart for November–December 2008:[22]

---

[17] Ratings by the Insurance Institute for Highway Safety. Sources: Oak Ridge National Laboratory: "An Analysis of the Impact of Sport Utility Vehicles in the United States" Stacy C. Davis, Lorena F. Truett (August 2000) Insurance Institute for Highway Safety (www-cta.ornl.gov/Publications/Final SUV report.pdf).

[18] Ratings by the Insurance Institute for Highway Safety. Sources: Oak Ridge National Laboratory: "An Analysis of the Impact of Sport Utility Vehicles in the United States" Stacy C. Davis, Lorena F. Truett (August 2000) Insurance Institute for Highway Safety (www-cta.ornl.gov/Publications/Final SUV report.pdf www.highwaysafety.org/vehicle_ratings/).

[19] Based on a 2003 survey. Source: "A Nation Online: Entering the Broadband Age," U.S. Department of Commerce, September 2004 (www.ntia.doc.gov/reports/anol/index.html).

[20] *Ibid.*

[21] Source: http://finance.google.com.

[22] *Ibid.*

Publishing Exercises 37–46 are based on the following table, which shows the results of a survey of 100 authors by a (fictitious) publishing company.

	New Authors	**Established Authors**	**Total**
Successful	5	25	30
Unsuccessful	15	55	70
Total	20	80	100

Compute the relative frequencies of the given events if an author as specified is chosen at random.

37. ▼ An author is established and successful.

38. ▼ An author is unsuccessful and new.

39. ▼ An author is a new author.

40. ▼ An author is successful.

41. ▼ An author is unsuccessful.

42. ▼ An author is established.

43. ▼ A successful author is established.

44. ▼ An unsuccessful author is established.

45. ▼ An established author is successful.

46. ▼ A new author is unsuccessful.

47. ▼ *Public Health* A random sampling of chicken in supermarkets revealed that approximately 80% was contaminated with the organism *Campylobacter*.[23] Of the contaminated chicken, 20% had the strain resistant to antibiotics. Construct a relative frequency distribution showing the following outcomes when chicken is purchased at a supermarket: *U:* the chicken is not infected with *Campylobacter*; *C:* the chicken is infected with nonresistant *Campylobacter*; *R:* the chicken is infected with resistant *Campylobacter*.

48. ▼ *Public Health* A random sampling of turkey in supermarkets found 58% to be contaminated with *Campylobacter*, and 84% of those to be resistant to antibiotics.[24] Construct a relative frequency distribution showing the following outcomes when turkey is purchased at a supermarket: *U:* the turkey is not infected with *Campylobacter*; *C:* the turkey is infected with nonresistant *Campylobacter*; and *R:* the turkey is infected with resistant *Campylobacter*.

49. ▼ *Organic Produce* A 2001 Agriculture Department study of more than 94,000 samples from more than 20 crops showed that 73% of conventionally grown foods had residues from at least one pesticide. Moreover, conventionally grown foods were six times as likely to contain multiple pesticides as organic foods. Of the organic foods tested, 23% had pesticide residues, which includes 10% with multiple pesticide residues.[25] Compute two estimated probability distributions: one for conventional produce and one for organic produce, showing the relative frequencies that a randomly selected product has no pesticide residues, has residues from a single pesticide, and has residues from multiple pesticides.

50. ▼ *Organic Produce* Repeat Exercise 49 using the following information for produce from California: 31% of conventional food and 6.5% of organic food had residues from at least one pesticide. Assume that, as in Exercise 49, conventionally grown foods were six times as likely to contain multiple pesticides as organic foods. Also assume that 3% of the organic food has residues from multiple pesticides.

51. ▼ *Steroids Testing* A pharmaceutical company is running trials on a new test for anabolic steroids. The company uses the test on 400 athletes known to be using steroids and 200 athletes known not to be using steroids. Of those using steroids, the new test is positive for 390 and negative for 10. Of those not using steroids, the test is positive for 10 and negative for 190. What is the relative frequency of a **false negative** result (the probability that an athlete using steroids will test negative)? What is the relative frequency of a **false positive** result (the probability that an athlete not using steroids will test positive)?

52. ▼ *Lie Detectors* A manufacturer of lie detectors is testing its newest design. It asks 300 subjects to lie deliberately and another 500 to tell the truth. Of those who lied, the lie detector caught 200. Of those who told the truth, the lie detector accused 200 of lying. What is the relative frequency of the machine wrongly letting a liar go, and what is the probability that it will falsely accuse someone who is telling the truth?

53. 🖳 ◆ *Public Health* Refer back to Exercise 47. Simulate the experiment of selecting chicken at a supermarket and determining the following outcomes: *U:* The chicken is not infected with *campylobacter; C:* The chicken is infected with nonresistant *campylobacter; R:* The chicken is infected with resistant *campylobacter.* HINT [Generate integers in the range 1–100. The outcome is determined by the range. For instance if the number is in the range 1–20, regard the outcome as *U*, etc.]

54. 🖳 ◆ *Public Health* Repeat the preceding exercise, but use turkeys and the data given in Exercise 48.

---

[23]*Campylobacter* is one of the leading causes of food poisoning in humans. Thoroughly cooking the meat kills the bacteria. Source: *New York Times*, October 20, 1997, p. A1. Publication of this article first brought *Campylobacter* to the attention of a wide audience.
[24]*Ibid.*

---

[25]The 10% figure is an estimate. Source: *New York Times*, May 8, 2002, p. A29.

COMMUNICATION AND REASONING EXERCISES

55. Complete the following. The relative frequency of an event E is defined to be _____.

56. If two people each flip a coin 100 times and compute the relative frequency that heads comes up, they will both obtain the same result, right?

57. How many different answers are possible if you flip a coin 100 times and compute the relative frequency that heads comes up? What are the possible answers?

58. Interpret the popularity rating of the student council president as a relative frequency by specifying an appropriate experiment and also what is observed.

59. ▼ Ruth tells you that when you roll a pair of fair dice, the probability of obtaining a pair of matching numbers is 1/6. To test this claim, you roll a pair of fair dice 20 times, and never once get a pair of matching numbers. This proves that either Ruth is wrong or the dice are not fair, right?

60. ▼ Juan tells you that when you roll a pair of fair dice, the probability that the numbers add up to 7 is 1/6. To test this claim, you roll a pair of fair dice 24 times, and the numbers add up to 7 exactly four times. This proves that Juan is right, right?

61. ▼ How would you measure the relative frequency that the weather service accurately predicts the next day's high temperature?

62. ▼ Suppose that you toss a coin 100 times and get 70 heads. If you continue tossing the coin, the estimated probability of heads overall should approach 50% if the coin is fair. Will you have to get more tails than heads in subsequent tosses to "correct" for the 70 heads you got in the first 100 tosses?

7.3   **Probability and Probability Models**

It is understandable if you are a little uncomfortable with using relative frequency as the estimated probability because it does not always agree with what you intuitively feel to be true. For instance, if you toss a fair coin (one as likely to come up heads as tails) 100 times and heads happen to come up 62 times, the experiment seems to suggest that the probability of heads is .62, even though you *know* that the "actual" probability is .50 (because the coin is fair).

Q: *So what do we mean by "actual" probability?*

A: There are various philosophical views as to exactly what we should mean by "actual" probability. For example, (finite) *frequentists* say that there is no such thing as "actual probability"—all we should really talk about is what we can actually measure, the relative frequency. *Propensitists* say that the actual probability *p* of an event is a (often physical) property of the event that makes its relative frequency tend to *p* in the long run; that is, *p* will be the limiting value of the relative frequency as the number of trials in a repeated experiment gets larger and larger. (See Figure 4 in the preceding section.) *Bayesians*, on the other hand, argue that the actual probability of an event is the degree to which we *expect* it to occur, given our knowledge about the nature of the experiment. These and other viewpoints have been debated in considerable depth in the literature.✶

✶ The interested reader should consult references in the philosophy of probability. For an online summary, see, for example, the Stanford Encyclopedia of Philosophy (http://plato.stanford.edu/contents.html).

Mathematicians tend to avoid the whole debate, and talk instead about *abstract* probability, or **probability distributions**, based purely on the properties of relative frequency listed in Section 7.2. Specific probability distributions can then be used as *models* in real-life situations, such as flipping a coin or tossing a die, to predict (or model) relative frequency.

Probability Distribution; Probability

(Compare with the properties of relative frequency distributions in Section 7.2.) A (finite) **probability distribution** is an assignment of a number $P(s_i)$, the **probability of s_i**, to each outcome of a finite sample space $S = \{s_1, s_2, \ldots, s_n\}$. The probabilities must satisfy

1. $0 \leq P(s_i) \leq 1$

and

2. $P(s_1) + P(s_2) + \cdots + P(s_n) = 1$.

We find the **probability of an event E**, written $P(E)$, by adding up the probabilities of the outcomes in E.

If $P(E) = 0$, we call E an **impossible event**. The empty event $\emptyset$ is always impossible, since *something* must happen.

Quick Examples

1. All the examples of estimated probability distributions in Section 7.2 are examples of probability distributions. (See page 463.)

2. Let us take $S = \{H, T\}$ and make the assignments $P(H) = .5$, $P(T) = .5$. Because these numbers are between 0 and 1 and add to 1, they specify a probability distribution.

3. In Quick Example 2, we can instead make the assignments $P(H) = .2$, $P(T) = .8$. Because these numbers are between 0 and 1 and add to 1, they, too, specify a probability distribution.

4. With $S = \{H, T\}$ again, we could also take $P(H) = 1$, $P(T) = 0$, so that $\{T\}$ is an impossible event.

5. The following table gives a probability distribution for the sample space $S = \{1, 2, 3, 4, 5, 6\}$.

Outcome	1	2	3	4	5	6
Probability	.3	.3	0	.1	.2	.1

It follows that

$$P(\{1, 6\}) = .3 + .1 = .4$$
$$P(\{2, 3\}) = .3 + 0 = .3$$
$$P(3) = 0. \qquad \text{\{3\} is an impossible event.}$$

✻ Just how large is a "large number of times"? That depends on the nature of the experiment. For example, if you toss a fair coin 100 times, then the relative frequency of heads will be between .45 and .55 about 73% of the time. If an outcome is extremely unlikely (such as winning the lotto), you might need to repeat the experiment billions or trillions of times before the relative frequency approaches any specific number.

The above Quick Examples included models for the experiments of flipping fair and unfair coins. In general:

Probability Models

A **probability model** for a particular experiment is a probability distribution that predicts the relative frequency of each outcome if the experiment is performed a large number of times (see Figure 4 at the end of the preceding section).✻ Just as we think of relative frequency as *estimated probability*, we can think of modeled probability as *theoretical probability*.

Quick Examples

1. **Fair Coin Model:** (See Quick Example 2 on the previous page.) Flip a fair coin and observe the side that faces up. Because we expect that heads is as likely to come up as tails, we model this experiment with the probability distribution specified by $S = \{H, T\}$, $P(H) = .5$, $P(T) = .5$. Figure 4 on p. 463 suggests that the relative frequency of heads approaches .5 as the number of coin tosses gets large, so the fair coin model predicts the relative frequency for a large number of coin tosses quite well.

2. **Unfair Coin Model:** (See Quick Example 3 on the previous page.) Take $S = \{H, T\}$ and $P(H) = .2$, $P(T) = .8$. We can think of this distribution as a model for the experiment of flipping an unfair coin that is four times as likely to land with tails uppermost than heads.

3. **Fair Die Model:** Roll a fair die and observe the uppermost number. Because we expect to roll each specific number one sixth of the time, we model the experiment with the probability distribution specified by $S = \{1, 2, 3, 4, 5, 6\}$, $P(1) = 1/6$, $P(2) = 1/6, \ldots, P(6) = 1/6$. This model predicts, for example, that the relative frequency of throwing a 5 approaches $1/6$ as the number of times you roll the die gets large.

4. Roll a pair of fair dice (recall that there are a total of 36 outcomes if the dice are distinguishable). Then an appropriate model of the experiment has

$$
S = \begin{cases}
(1, 1), \ (1, 2), \ (1, 3), \ (1, 4), \ (1, 5), \ (1, 6), \\
(2, 1), \ (2, 2), \ (2, 3), \ (2, 4), \ (2, 5), \ (2, 6), \\
(3, 1), \ (3, 2), \ (3, 3), \ (3, 4), \ (3, 5), \ (3, 6), \\
(4, 1), \ (4, 2), \ (4, 3), \ (4, 4), \ (4, 5), \ (4, 6), \\
(5, 1), \ (5, 2), \ (5, 3), \ (5, 4), \ (5, 5), \ (5, 6), \\
(6, 1), \ (6, 2), \ (6, 3), \ (6, 4), \ (6, 5), \ (6, 6)
\end{cases}
$$

with each outcome being assigned a probability of $1/36$.

5. In the experiment in Quick Example 4, take E to be the event that the sum of the numbers that face up is 5, so

$$E = \{(1, 4), (2, 3), (3, 2), (4, 1)\}.$$

By the properties of probability distributions,

$$P(E) = \frac{1}{36} + \frac{1}{36} + \frac{1}{36} + \frac{1}{36} = \frac{4}{36} = \frac{1}{9}.$$

Notice that, in all of the Quick Examples above except for the unfair coin, all the outcomes are equally likely, and each outcome s has a probability of

$$P(s) = \frac{1}{\text{Total number of outcomes}} = \frac{1}{n(S)}.$$

More generally, in the last Quick Example we saw that adding the probabilities of the individual outcomes in an event E amounted to computing the ratio (Number of favorable outcomes)/(Total number of outcomes):

$$P(E) = \frac{\text{Number of favorable outcomes}}{\text{Total number of outcomes}} = \frac{n(E)}{n(S)}.$$

Probability Model for Equally Likely Outcomes

In an experiment in which all outcomes are equally likely, we model the experiment by taking the probability of an event E to be

$$P(E) = \frac{\text{Number of favorable outcomes}}{\text{Total number of outcomes}} = \frac{n(E)}{n(S)}.$$

Visualizing Probability for Equally Likely Outcomes

Sample Space S

$$P(E) = \frac{n(E)}{n(S)} = \frac{6}{10} = .6$$

Note

Remember that this formula will work *only* when the outcomes are equally likely. If, for example, a die is *weighted*, then the outcomes may not be equally likely, and the formula above will not give an appropriate probability model.

Quick Examples

1. Toss a fair coin three times, so $S = \{$HHH, HHT, HTH, HTT, THH, THT, TTH, TTT$\}$. The probability that we throw exactly two heads is

   $$P(E) = \frac{n(E)}{n(S)} = \frac{3}{8}.$$ There are eight equally likely outcomes and $E = \{$HHT, HTH, THH$\}$.

2. Roll a pair of fair dice. The probability that we roll a double (both dice show the same number) is

   $$P(E) = \frac{n(E)}{n(S)} = \frac{6}{36} = \frac{1}{6}.$$ $E = \{(1, 1), (2, 2), (3, 3), (4, 4), (5, 5), (6, 6)\}$

3. Randomly choose a person from a class of 40, in which 6 have red hair. If E is the event that a randomly selected person in the class has red hair, then

   $$P(E) = \frac{n(E)}{n(S)} = \frac{6}{40} = .15.$$

EXAMPLE 1 Sales of Hybrid Vehicles

(Compare Example 1 in Section 7.2.) A total of 1.9 million hybrid vehicles had been sold in the United States through October of 2011. Of these, 955,000 were Toyota Prii, 205,000 were Honda Civics, 170,000 were Toyota Camrys, 105,000 were Ford Escapes, and the rest were other makes.[26]

a. What is the probability that a randomly selected hybrid vehicle sold in the United States was either a Toyota Prius or a Honda Civic?

b. What is the probability that a randomly selected hybrid vehicle sold in the United States was not a Toyota Camry?

---

[26]Source for sales data: www.wikipedia.com.

Solution

a. The experiment suggested by the question consists of randomly choosing a hybrid vehicle sold in the United States and determining its make. We are interested in the event E that the hybrid vehicle was either a Toyota Prius or a Honda Civic. So,

$$S = \text{the set of hybrid vehicles sold; } n(S) = 1{,}900{,}000$$

$$E = \text{the set of Toyota Prii and Honda Civics sold;}$$
$$n(E) = 955{,}000 + 205{,}000 = 1{,}160{,}000.$$

Are the outcomes equally likely in this experiment? Yes, because we are as likely to choose one vehicle as another. Thus,

$$P(E) = \frac{n(E)}{n(S)} = \frac{1{,}160{,}000}{1{,}900{,}000} \approx .61.$$

b. Let the event F consist of those hybrid vehicles sold that were not Toyota Camrys.

$$n(F) = 1{,}900{,}000 - 170{,}000 = 1{,}730{,}000$$

Hence,

$$P(F) = \frac{n(F)}{n(S)} = \frac{1{,}730{,}000}{1{,}900{,}000} \approx .91.$$

Q: *In Example 1 of Section 7.2 we had a similar example about hybrid vehicles, but we called the probabilities calculated there relative frequencies. Here they are probabilities. What is the difference?*

A: In Example 1 of Section 7.2, the data were based on the results of a survey, or sample, of only 250 hybrid vehicles (out of a total of about 1.9 million sold in the United States), and were therefore incomplete. (A statistician would say that we were given *sample data*.) It follows that any inference we draw from the 250 surveyed, such as the probability that a hybrid vehicle sold in the United States is not a Toyota Camry, is uncertain, and this is the cue that tells us that we are working with relative frequency, or estimated probability. Think of the survey as an experiment (choosing a hybrid vehicle) repeated 250 times—exactly the setting for estimated probability.

In Example 1 above, on the other hand, the data do not describe how *some* hybrid vehicle sales are broken down into the categories described, but they describe how *all 1.9 million* hybrid vehicle sales in the United States are broken down. (The statistician would say that we were given *population data* in this case, because the data describe the entire "population" of hybrid vehicles sold in the United States.)

EXAMPLE 2 Indistinguishable Dice

We recall from Section 7.1 that the sample space when we roll a pair of indistinguishable dice is

$$S = \left\{ \begin{array}{l} (1,1),\ (1,2),\ (1,3),\ (1,4),\ (1,5),\ (1,6), \\ \quad (2,2),\ (2,3),\ (2,4),\ (2,5),\ (2,6), \\ \qquad\quad (3,3),\ (3,4),\ (3,5),\ (3,6), \\ \qquad\qquad\quad (4,4),\ (4,5),\ (4,6), \\ \qquad\qquad\qquad\quad (5,5),\ (5,6), \\ \qquad\qquad\qquad\qquad\quad (6,6) \end{array} \right\}.$$

Construct a probability model for this experiment.

Solution Because there are 21 outcomes, it is tempting to say that the probability of each outcome should be taken to be 1/21. However, the outcomes are not all equally likely. For instance, the outcome (2, 3) is twice as likely as (2, 2), because (2, 3) can occur in two ways (it corresponds to the event {(2, 3), (3, 2)} for distinguishable dice). For purposes of calculating probability, it is easiest to use calculations for distinguishable dice.* Here are some examples.

✱ Note that any pair of real dice can be distinguished in principle because they possess slight differences, although we may regard them as indistinguishable by not attempting to distinguish them. Thus, the probabilities of events must be the same as for the corresponding events for distinguishable dice.

Outcome (indistinguishable dice)	(1, 1)	(1, 2)	(2, 2)	(1, 3)	(2, 3)	(3, 3)
Corresponding Event (distinguishable dice)	{(1, 1)}	{(1, 2), (2, 1)}	{(2, 2)}	{(1, 3), (3, 1)}	{(2, 3), (3, 2)}	{(3, 3)}
Probability	$\dfrac{1}{36}$	$\dfrac{2}{36} = \dfrac{1}{18}$	$\dfrac{1}{36}$	$\dfrac{2}{36} = \dfrac{1}{18}$	$\dfrac{2}{36} = \dfrac{1}{18}$	$\dfrac{1}{36}$

If we continue this process for all 21 outcomes, we will find that they add to 1. Figure 5 illustrates the complete probability distribution:

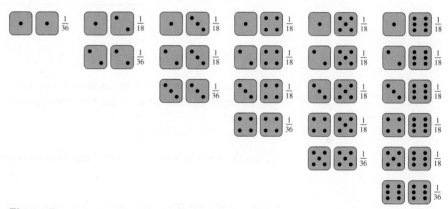

Figure 5

EXAMPLE 3 Weighted Dice

In order to impress your friends with your die-rolling skills, you have surreptitiously weighted your die in such a way that 6 is three times as likely to come up as any one of the other numbers. (All the other outcomes are equally likely.) Obtain a probability distribution for a roll of the die and use it to calculate the probability of an even number coming up.

Solution Let us label our unknowns (there appear to be two of them):

x = probability of rolling a 6

y = probability of rolling any one of the other numbers

We are first told that "6 is three times as likely to come up as any one of the other numbers." If we rephrase this in terms of our unknown probabilities we get, "the probability of rolling a 6 is three times the probability of rolling any one of the other numbers." In symbols,

$x = 3y.$

We must also use a piece of information not given to us, but one we know must be true: The sum of the probabilities of all the outcomes is 1:

$$x + y + y + y + y + y = 1$$

or

$$x + 5y = 1.$$

We now have two linear equations in two unknowns, and we solve for x and y. Substituting the first equation ($x = 3y$) in the second ($x + 5y = 1$) gives

$$8y = 1$$

or

$$y = \frac{1}{8}.$$

To get x, we substitute the value of y back into either equation and find

$$x = \frac{3}{8}.$$

Thus, the probability model we seek is the one shown in the following table.

Outcome	1	2	3	4	5	6
Probability	$\frac{1}{8}$	$\frac{1}{8}$	$\frac{1}{8}$	$\frac{1}{8}$	$\frac{1}{8}$	$\frac{3}{8}$

We can use the distribution to calculate the probability of an even number coming up by adding the probabilities of the favorable outcomes.

$$P(\{2,\ 4,\ 6\}) = \frac{1}{8} + \frac{1}{8} + \frac{3}{8} = \frac{5}{8}.$$

Thus there is a $5/8 = .625$ chance that an even number will come up.

➡ **Before we go on...** We should check that the probability distribution in Example 3 satisfies the requirements: 6 is indeed three times as likely to come up as any other number. Also, the probabilities we calculated do add up to 1:

$$\frac{1}{8} + \frac{1}{8} + \frac{1}{8} + \frac{1}{8} + \frac{1}{8} + \frac{3}{8} = 1. \ ■$$

Probability of Unions, Intersections, and Complements

So far, all we know about computing the probability of an event E is that $P(E)$ is the sum of the probabilities of the individual outcomes in E. Suppose, though, that we do not know the probabilities of the individual outcomes in E but we do know that $E = A \cup B$, where we happen to know $P(A)$ and $P(B)$. How do we compute the probability of $A \cup B$? We might be tempted to say that $P(A \cup B)$ is $P(A) + P(B)$, but let us look at an example using the probability distribution in Quick Example 5 at the beginning of this section:

Outcome	1	2	3	4	5	6
Probability	.3	.3	0	.1	.2	.1

For A let us take the event $\{2, 4, 5\}$, and for B let us take $\{2, 4, 6\}$. $A \cup B$ is then the event $\{2, 4, 5, 6\}$. We know that we can find the probabilities $P(A)$, $P(B)$, and $P(A \cup B)$ by adding the probabilities of all the outcomes in these events, so

$$P(A) = P(\{2, 4, 5\}) = .3 + .1 + .2 = .6$$
$$P(B) = P(\{2, 4, 6\}) = .3 + .1 + .1 = .5, \text{ and}$$
$$P(A \cup B) = P(\{2, 4, 5, 6\}) = .3 + .1 + .2 + .1 = .7.$$

Our first guess was wrong: $P(A \cup B) \neq P(A) + P(B)$. Notice, however, that the outcomes in $A \cap B$ are counted twice in computing $P(A) + P(B)$, but only once in computing $P(A \cup B)$:

$$P(A) + P(B) = P(\{2, 4, 5\}) + P(\{2, 4, 6\}) \qquad A \cap B = \{2, 4\}$$
$$= (.3 + .1 + .2) + (.3 + .1 + .1) \qquad P(A \cap B) \text{ counted twice}$$
$$= 1.1$$

whereas

$$P(A \cup B) = P(\{2, 4, 5, 6\}) = .3 + .1 + .2 + .1 \qquad P(A \cap B) \text{ counted once}$$
$$= .7.$$

Thus, if we take $P(A) + P(B)$ and then subtract the surplus $P(A \cap B)$, we get $P(A \cup B)$. In symbols,

$$P(A \cup B) = P(A) + P(B) - P(A \cap B)$$
$$.7 = .6 + .5 - .4$$

(see Figure 6). We call this formula the **addition principle**. One more thing: Notice that our original guess $P(A \cup B) = P(A) + P(B)$ would have worked if we had chosen A and B with no outcomes in common; that is, if $A \cap B = \emptyset$. When $A \cap B = \emptyset$, recall that we say that A and B are mutually exclusive.

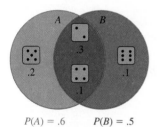

$P(A) = .6$ $P(B) = .5$
$P(A \cap B) = .4$
$P(A \cup B) = .6 + .5 - .4$

Figure 6

Addition Principle

If A and B are any two events, then

$$P(A \cup B) = P(A) + P(B) - P(A \cap B).$$

Visualizing the Addition Principle
In the figure, the area of the union is obtained by adding the areas of A and B and then subtracting the overlap (because it is counted twice when we add the areas).

$P(A \cup B) = P(A) + P(B) - P(A \cap B)$

Addition Principle for Mutually Exclusive Events

If $A \cap B = \emptyset$, we say that A and B are **mutually exclusive**, and we have

$$P(A \cup B) = P(A) + P(B). \qquad \text{Because } P(A \cap B) = 0$$

Visualizing the Addition Principle for Mutually Exclusive Events

If A and B do not overlap, then the area of the union is obtained by adding the areas of A and B.

$$P(A \cup B) = P(A) + P(B)$$

This holds true also for more than two events: If $A_1, A_2, \ldots, A_n$ are mutually exclusive events (that is, the intersection of every pair of them is empty), then

$$P(A_1 \cup A_2 \cup \cdots \cup A_n) = P(A_1) + P(A_2) + \cdots + P(A_n).$$

Addition principle for many mutually exclusive events

Quick Examples

1. There is a 10% chance of rain (R) tomorrow, a 20% chance of high winds (W), and a 5% chance of both. The probability of either rain or high winds (or both) is

$$\begin{aligned} P(R \cup W) &= P(R) + P(W) - P(R \cap W) \\ &= .10 + .20 - .05 = .25. \end{aligned}$$

2. The probability that you will be in Cairo at 6:00 am tomorrow (C) is .3, while the probability that you will be in Alexandria at 6:00 am tomorrow (A) is .2. Thus, the probability that you will be either in Cairo or Alexandria at 6:00 am tomorrow is

$$\begin{aligned} P(C \cup A) &= P(C) + P(A) \qquad \text{A and C are mutually exclusive.} \\ &= .3 + .2 = .5. \end{aligned}$$

3. When a pair of fair dice is rolled, the probability of the numbers that face up adding to 7 is 6/36, the probability of their adding to 8 is 5/36, and the probability of their adding to 9 is 4/36. Thus, the probability of the numbers adding to 7, 8, or 9 is

$$\begin{aligned} P(\{7\} \cup \{8\} \cup \{9\}) &= P(7) + P(8) + P(9) \qquad \text{The events are mutually exclusive.*} \\ &= \frac{6}{36} + \frac{5}{36} + \frac{4}{36} = \frac{15}{36} = \frac{5}{12}. \end{aligned}$$

* The sum of the numbers that face up cannot equal two different numbers at the same time.

You can use the formula
$P(A \cup B) = P(A) + P(B) - P(A \cap B)$
to calculate any of the four quantities in the formula if you know the other three.

EXAMPLE 4 School and Work

A survey[27] conducted by the Bureau of Labor Statistics found that 68% of the high school graduating class of 2010 went on to college the following year, while 42% of the class was working. Furthermore, 92% were either in college or working, or both.

a. What percentage went on to college and work at the same time?

b. What percentage went on to college but not work?

Solution We can think of the experiment of choosing a member of the high school graduating class of 2010 at random. The sample space is the set of all these graduates.

a. We are given information about two events:

A: A graduate went on to college; $P(A) = .68$.

B: A graduate went on to work; $P(B) = .42$.

We are also told that $P(A \cup B) = .92$. We are asked for the probability that a graduate went on to both college and work, $P(A \cap B)$. To find $P(A \cap B)$, we take advantage of the fact that the formula

$$P(A \cup B) = P(A) + P(B) - P(A \cap B)$$

can be used to calculate any one of the four quantities that appear in it as long as we know the other three. Substituting the quantities we know, we get

$$.92 = .68 + .42 - P(A \cap B)$$

so

$$P(A \cap B) = .68 + .42 - .92 = .18.$$

Thus, 18% of the graduates went on to college and work at the same time.

b. We are asked for the probability of a new event:

C: A graduate went on to college but not work.

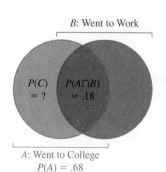

B: Went to Work

$P(C)$ $= ?$ $P(A \cap B)$ $= .18$

A: Went to College
$P(A) = .68$

Figure 7

C is the part of A outside of $A \cap B$, so $C \cup (A \cap B) = A$, and C and $A \cap B$ are mutually exclusive. (See Figure 7.)

Thus, applying the addition principle, we have

$$P(C) + P(A \cap B) = P(A).$$

From part (a), we know that $P(A \cap B) = .18$, so

$$P(C) + .18 = .68$$

giving

$$P(C) = .50.$$

In other words, 50% of the graduates went on to college but not work.

We can use the addition principle to deduce other useful properties of probability distributions.

[27]Source: "College Enrollment and Work Activity of High School Graduates," U.S. Bureau of Labor Statistics (www.bls.gov/news.release/hsgec.htm).

More Principles of Probability Distributions

The following rules hold for any sample space S and any event A:

$$P(S) = 1 \qquad \text{The probability of } \textit{something} \text{ happening is 1.}$$

$$P(\emptyset) = 0 \qquad \text{The probability of } \textit{nothing} \text{ happening is 0.}$$

$$P(A') = 1 - P(A). \qquad \text{The probability of } A \textit{ not} \text{ happening is 1 minus the probability of } A.$$

Note

We can also write the third equation as

$$P(A) = 1 - P(A')$$

or

$$P(A) + P(A') = 1. \qquad \blacksquare$$

Visualizing the Rule for Complements

Think of A' as the portion of S outside of A. Adding the two areas gives the area of all of S, equal to 1.

Sample Space S

$P(A) + P(A') = 1$

Quick Examples

1. There is a 10% chance of rain (R) tomorrow. Therefore, the probability that it will *not* rain is

$$P(R') = 1 - P(R) = 1 - .10 = .90.$$

2. The probability that Eric Ewing will score at least two goals is .6. Therefore, the probability that he will score at most one goal is

$$1 - .6 = .4.$$

Q: *Can you persuade me that all of these principles are true?*

A: Let us take them one at a time.

We know that $S = \{s_1, s_2, \ldots, s_n\}$ is the set of all outcomes, and so

$$
\begin{aligned}
P(S) &= P(\{s_1, s_2, \ldots, s_n\}) && \text{We add the probabilities of the outcomes} \\
&= P(s_1) + P(s_2) + \cdots + P(s_n) && \text{to obtain the probability of an event.} \\
&= 1. && \text{By the definition of a probability distribution}
\end{aligned}
$$

Now, note that $S \cap \emptyset = \emptyset$, so that S and $\emptyset$ are mutually exclusive. Applying the addition principle gives

$$P(S) = P(S \cup \emptyset) = P(S) + P(\emptyset).$$

Subtracting $P(S)$ from both sides gives $0 = P(\emptyset)$.

If A is any event in S, then we can write

$$S = A \cup A'$$

where A and A' are mutually exclusive. (Why?) Thus, by the addition principle,

$$P(S) = P(A) + P(A').$$

Because $P(S) = 1$, we get

$$1 = P(A) + P(A')$$

or $$P(A') = 1 - P(A).$$

EXAMPLE 5 Subprime Mortgages during the Housing Bubble

A home loan is either current, 30–59 days past due, 60–89 days past due, 90 or more days past due, in foreclosure, or repossessed by the lender. In November 2008, the probability that a randomly selected subprime home mortgage in California was not current was .51. The probability that a mortgage was not current, but neither in foreclosure nor repossessed, was .28.[28] Calculate the probabilities of the following events.

a. A California home mortgage was current.

b. A California home mortgage was in foreclosure or repossessed.

Solution

a. Let us write C for the event that a randomly selected subprime home mortgage in California was current. The event that the home mortgage was *not* current is its complement C', and we are given that $P(C') = .51$. We have

$$P(C) + P(C') = 1$$
$$P(C) + .51 = 1,$$
so $$P(C) = 1 - .51 = .49.$$

b. Take

F: A mortgage was in foreclosure or repossessed.

N: A mortgage was neither current, in foreclosure, nor repossessed.

We are given $P(N) = .28$. Further, the events F and N are mutually exclusive with union C', the set of all non-current mortgages. Hence,

$$P(C') = P(F) + P(N)$$
$$.51 = P(F) + .28$$

giving

$$P(F) = .51 - .28 = .23.$$

Thus, there was a 23% chance that a subprime home mortgage was either in foreclosure or repossessed.

---

[28]Source: Federal Reserve Bank of New York (www.newyorkfed.org/regional/subprime.html).

EXAMPLE 6 iPods, iPhones, and iPads

The following table shows sales, in millions of units, of iPods®, iPhones®, and iPads® in the last three quarters of 2011.[29]

	iPods (A)	iPhones (B)	iPads (C)	Total
2011 Q2 (U)	9.0	18.7	4.7	32.4
2011 Q3 (V)	7.5	20.3	9.3	37.1
2011 Q4 (W)	6.6	17.1	11.1	34.8
Total	23.1	56.1	25.1	104.3

If one of the items sold is selected at random, find the probabilities of the following events:

a. It is an iPod.

b. It was sold in the third quarter of 2011.

c. It is an iPod sold in the third quarter of 2011.

d. It either is an iPod or was sold in the third quarter of 2011.

e. It is not an iPod.

Solution Before we answer the questions, note that S is the set of all items represented in the table, so S has a total of 104.3 million outcomes.

a. Because an item is being selected at random, all the outcomes are equally likely. If A is the event that the selected item is an iPod, then

$$P(A) = \frac{n(A)}{n(S)} = \frac{23.1}{104.3} \approx .221.$$

The event A is represented by the pink shaded region in the table:

	iPods (A)	iPhones (B)	iPads (C)	Total
2011 Q2 (U)	9.0	18.7	4.7	32.4
2011 Q3 (V)	7.5	20.3	9.3	37.1
2011 Q4 (W)	6.6	17.1	11.1	34.8
Total	23.1	56.1	25.1	104.3

b. If V is the event that the selected item was sold in the third quarter of 2011, then

$$P(V) = \frac{n(V)}{n(S)} = \frac{37.1}{104.3} \approx .356.$$

---

[29] Figures are rounded to one decimal place. Source: Apple quarterly press releases (www.investor.apple.com).

In the table, V is represented as shown:

	iPods (A)	iPhones (B)	iPads (C)	Total
2011 Q2 (U)	9.0	18.7	4.7	32.4
2011 Q3 (V)	7.5	20.3	9.3	37.1
2011 Q4 (W)	6.6	17.1	11.1	34.8
Total	23.1	56.1	25.1	104.3

c. The event that the selected item is an iPod sold in the third quarter of 2011 is the event $A \cap V$.

$$P(A \cap V) = \frac{n(A \cap V)}{n(S)} = \frac{7.5}{104.3} \approx .072$$

In the table, $A \cap V$ is represented by the overlap of the regions representing A and V:

	iPods (A)	iPhones (B)	iPads (C)	Total
2011 Q2 (U)	9.0	18.7	4.7	32.4
2011 Q3 (V)	7.5	20.3	9.3	37.1
2011 Q4 (W)	6.6	17.1	11.1	34.8
Total	23.1	56.1	25.1	104.3

d. The event that the selected item either is an iPod or was sold in the third quarter of 2011 is the event $A \cup V$, and is represented by the pink shaded area in the table:

	iPods (A)	iPhones (B)	iPads (C)	Total
2011 Q2 (U)	9.0	18.7	4.7	32.4
2011 Q3 (V)	7.5	20.3	9.3	37.1
2011 Q4 (W)	6.6	17.1	11.1	34.8
Total	23.1	56.1	25.1	104.3

We can compute its probability in two ways:

1. Directly from the table:

$$P(A \cup V) = \frac{n(A \cup V)}{n(S)} = \frac{23.1 + 37.1 - 7.5}{104.3} \approx .505$$

2. Using the addition principle:

$$P(A \cup V) = P(A) + P(V) - P(A \cap V)$$
$$\approx .221 + .356 - .072 = .505$$

e. The event that the selected item is not an iPod is the event A'. Its probability may be computed using the formula for the probability of the complement:

$$P(A') = 1 - P(A) \approx 1 - .221 = .779.$$

Distinguishing Probability from Relative Frequency

Q : *Relative frequency and modeled probability using equally likely outcomes have essentially the same formula: (Number of favorable outcomes)/(Total number of outcomes). How do I know whether a given probability is one or the other?*

A : Ask yourself this: Has the probability been arrived at experimentally, by performing a number of trials and counting the number of times the event occurred? If so, the probability is estimated; that is, relative frequency. If, on the other hand, the probability was computed by analyzing the experiment under consideration rather than by performing actual trials of the experiment, it is a probability model.

Q : *Out of every 100 homes, 22 have broadband Internet service. Thus, the probability that a house has broadband service is .22. Is this probability estimated (relative frequency) or theoretical (a probability model)?*

A : That depends on how the ratio 22 out of 100 was arrived at. If it is based on a poll of *all* homes, then the probability is theoretical. If it is based on a survey of only a *sample* of homes, it is estimated (see the Q/A following Example 1).

7.3   EXERCISES

▼ more advanced   ◆ challenging
T indicates exercises that should be solved using technology

1. Complete the following probability distribution table and then calculate the stated probabilities. HINT [See Quick Example 5, page 469.]

Outcome	a	b	c	d	e
Probability	.1	.05	.6	.05	

  a. $P(\{a, c, e\})$
  b. $P(E \cup F)$, where $E = \{a, c, e\}$ and $F = \{b, c, e\}$
  c. $P(E')$, where E is as in part (b)
  d. $P(E \cap F)$, where E and F are as in part (b)

2. Repeat the preceding exercise using the following table. HINT [See Quick Example 5, page 469.]

Outcome	a	b	c	d	e
Probability	.1		.65	.1	.05

In Exercises 3–8, calculate the (modeled) probability $P(E)$ using the given information, assuming that all outcomes are equally likely. HINT [See Quick Examples on page 471.]

  3. $n(S) = 20$, $n(E) = 5$ **4.** $n(S) = 8$, $n(E) = 4$
  5. $n(S) = 10$, $n(E) = 10$ **6.** $n(S) = 10$, $n(E) = 0$
  7. $S = \{a, b, c, d\}$, $E = \{a, b, d\}$
  8. $S = \{1, 3, 5, 7, 9\}$, $E = \{3, 7\}$

In Exercises 9–18, an experiment is given together with an event. Find the (modeled) probability of each event, assuming that the coins and dice are distinguishable and fair, and that what is observed are the faces or numbers uppermost. (Compare with Exercises 1–10 in Section 7.1.)

  9. Two coins are tossed; the result is at most one tail.

  10. Two coins are tossed; the result is one or more heads.

  11. Three coins are tossed; the result is at most one head.

  12. Three coins are tossed; the result is more tails than heads.

  13. Two dice are rolled; the numbers add to 5.

  14. Two dice are rolled; the numbers add to 9.

  15. Two dice are rolled; the numbers add to 1.

  16. Two dice are rolled; one of the numbers is even, the other is odd.

  17. Two dice are rolled; both numbers are prime.[30]

  18. Two dice are rolled; neither number is prime.

  19. If two indistinguishable dice are rolled, what is the probability of the event $\{(4, 4), (2, 3)\}$? What is the corresponding event for a pair of distinguishable dice? HINT [See Example 2.]

  20. If two indistinguishable dice are rolled, what is the probability of the event $\{(5, 5), (2, 5), (3, 5)\}$? What is the corresponding event for a pair of distinguishable dice? HINT [See Example 2.]

---

[30]A positive integer is prime if it is neither 1 nor a product of smaller integers.

21. A die is weighted in such a way that each of 2, 4, and 6 is twice as likely to come up as each of 1, 3, and 5. Find the probability distribution. What is the probability of rolling less than 4? HINT [See Example 3.]

22. Another die is weighted in such a way that each of 1 and 2 is three times as likely to come up as each of the other numbers. Find the probability distribution. What is the probability of rolling an even number?

23. A tetrahedral die has four faces, numbered 1–4. If the die is weighted in such a way that each number is twice as likely to land facing down as the next number (1 twice as likely as 2, 2 twice as likely as 3, and 3 twice as likely as 4), what is the probability distribution for the face landing down?

24. A dodecahedral die has 12 faces, numbered 1–12. If the die is weighted in such a way that 2 is twice as likely to land facing up as 1, 3 is three times as likely to land facing up as 1, and so on, what is the probability distribution for the face landing up?

In Exercises 25–40, use the given information to find the indicated probability. HINT [See Quick Examples, page 476.]

25. $P(A) = .1$, $P(B) = .6$, $P(A \cap B) = .05$. Find $P(A \cup B)$.

26. $P(A) = .3$, $P(B) = .4$, $P(A \cap B) = .02$. Find $P(A \cup B)$.

27. $A \cap B = \emptyset$, $P(A) = .3$, $P(A \cup B) = .4$. Find $P(B)$.

28. $A \cap B = \emptyset$, $P(B) = .8$, $P(A \cup B) = .8$. Find $P(A)$.

29. $A \cap B = \emptyset$, $P(A) = .3$, $P(B) = .4$. Find $P(A \cup B)$.

30. $A \cap B = \emptyset$, $P(A) = .2$, $P(B) = .3$. Find $P(A \cup B)$.

31. $P(A \cup B) = .9$, $P(B) = .6$, $P(A \cap B) = .1$. Find $P(A)$.

32. $P(A \cup B) = 1.0$, $P(A) = .6$, $P(A \cap B) = .1$. Find $P(B)$.

33. $P(A) = .75$. Find $P(A')$.

34. $P(A) = .22$. Find $P(A')$.

35. A, B, and C are mutually exclusive. $P(A) = .3$, $P(B) = .4$, $P(C) = .3$. Find $P(A \cup B \cup C)$.

36. A, B, and C are mutually exclusive. $P(A) = .2$, $P(B) = .6$, $P(C) = .1$. Find $P(A \cup B \cup C)$.

37. A and B are mutually exclusive. $P(A) = .3$, $P(B) = .4$. Find $P((A \cup B)')$.

38. A and B are mutually exclusive. $P(A) = .4$, $P(B) = .4$. Find $P((A \cup B)')$.

39. $A \cup B = S$ and $A \cap B = \emptyset$. Find $P(A) + P(B)$.

40. $P(A \cup B) = .3$ and $P(A \cap B) = .1$. Find $P(A) + P(B)$.

In Exercises 41–46, determine whether the information shown is consistent with a probability distribution. If not, say why.

41. $P(A) = .2$; $P(B) = .1$; $P(A \cup B) = .4$

42. $P(A) = .2$; $P(B) = .4$; $P(A \cup B) = .2$

43. $P(A) = .2$; $P(B) = .4$; $P(A \cap B) = .2$

44. $P(A) = .2$; $P(B) = .4$; $P(A \cap B) = .3$

45. $P(A) = 0.1$; $P(B) = 0$; $P(A \cup B) = 0$

46. $P(A) = .1$; $P(B) = 0$; $P(A \cap B) = 0$

APPLICATIONS

47. *Subprime Mortgages during the 2000–2008 Housing Bubble* (Compare Exercise 27 in Section 7.2.) The following chart shows the (approximate) total number of subprime home mortgages in Texas in November 2008, broken down into four categories:[31]

Mortgage Status	Current	Past Due	In Foreclosure	Repossessed	Total
Number	136,330	53,310	8,750	5,090	203,480

(The four categories are mutually exclusive; for instance, "Past Due" refers to a mortgage whose payment status is past due but is not in foreclosure, and "In Foreclosure" refers to a mortgage that is in the process of being foreclosed but not yet repossessed.)

a. Find the probability that a randomly selected subprime mortgage in Texas during November 2008 was neither in foreclosure nor repossessed. HINT [See Example 1.]

b. What is the probability that a randomly selected subprime mortgage in Texas during November 2008 was not current?

48. *Subprime Mortgages during the 2000–2008 Housing Bubble* (Compare Exercise 28 in Section 7.2.) The following chart shows the (approximate) total number of subprime home mortgages in Florida in November 2008, broken down into four categories:[32]

Mortgage Status	Current	Past Due	In Foreclosure	Repossessed	Total
Number	130,400	73,260	72,380	17,000	293,040

(The four categories are mutually exclusive; for instance, "Past Due" refers to a mortgage whose payment status is past due but is not in foreclosure, and "In Foreclosure" refers to a mortgage that is in the process of being foreclosed but not yet repossessed.)

a. Find the probability that a randomly selected subprime mortgage in Florida during November 2008 was either in foreclosure or repossessed. HINT [See Example 1.]

b. What is the probability that a randomly selected subprime mortgage in Florida during November 2008 was not repossessed?

49. *Ethnic Diversity* The following pie chart shows the ethnic makeup of California schools in the 2006–2007 academic year.[33]

---

[31]Data are rounded to the nearest 10 units. Source: Federal Reserve Bank of New York (www.newyorkfed.org/regional/subprime.html).

[32]*Ibid.*

[33]Source: CBEDS data collection, Educational Demographics, October 2006 (www.cde.ca.gov/resrc/factbook/).

Write down the probability distribution showing the probability that a randomly selected California student in 2006–2007 belonged to one of the ethnic groups named. What is the probability that a student is neither white nor Asian?

50. ***Ethnic Diversity*** (Compare Exercise 49.) The following pie chart shows the ethnic makeup of California schools in the 1981–1982 academic year.[34]

Write down the probability distribution showing the probability that a randomly selected California student in 1981–1982 belonged to one of the ethnic groups named. What is the probability that a student is neither Hispanic, Latino, nor African American?

51. ▼ ***Internet Investments in the 1990s*** The following excerpt is from an article in *The New York Times* in July 1999.[35]

> While statistics are not available for Web entrepreneurs who fail, the venture capitalists that finance such Internet start-up companies have a rule of thumb. For every 10 ventures that receive financing—and there are plenty who do not—2 will be stock market successes, which means spectacular profits for early investors; 3 will be sold to other concerns, which translates into more modest profits; and the rest will fail.

   a. What is a sample space for the scenario?
   b. Write down the associated probability distribution.
   c. What is the probability that a start-up venture that receives financing will realize profits for early investors?

52. ▼ ***Internet Investments in the 1990s*** The following excerpt is from an article in *The New York Times* in July 1999.[36]

---

[34]Source: CBEDS data collection, Educational Demographics, October 2006 (www.cde.ca.gov/resrc/factbook/).

[35]Article: "Not All Hit It Rich in the Internet Gold Rush," *New York Times*, July 20, 1999, p. A1.

[36]Article: Ibid. Source for data: Comm-Scan/*New York Times*, July 20, 1999, p. A1.

> Right now, the market for Web stocks is sizzling. Of the 126 initial public offerings of Internet stocks priced this year, 73 are trading above the price they closed on their first day of trading. . . . Still, 53 of the offerings have failed to live up to their fabulous first-day billings, and 17 [of these] are below the initial offering price.

Assume that, on the first day of trading, all stocks closed higher than their initial offering price.

   a. What is a sample space for the scenario?
   b. Write down the associated probability distribution. (Round your answers to two decimal places.)
   c. What is the probability that an Internet stock purchased during the period reported ended either below its initial offering price or above the price it closed on its first day of trading? HINT [See Example 3.]

53. ▼ ***Market Share: Light Vehicles*** In 2003, 25% of all light vehicles sold (SUVs, pickups, passenger cars, and minivans) in the United States were SUVs and 15% were pickups. Moreover, a randomly chosen vehicle sold that year was five times as likely to be a passenger car as a minivan.[37] Find the associated probability distribution.

54. ▼ ***Market Share: Light Vehicles*** In 2000, 15% of all light vehicles (SUVs, pickups, passenger cars, and minivans) sold in the United States were pickups and 55% were passenger cars. Moreover, a randomly chosen vehicle sold that year was twice as likely to be an SUV as a minivan.[38] Find the associated probability distribution.

Gambling *In Exercises 55–62 are detailed some of the nefarious dicing practices of the Win Some/Lose Some Casino. In each case, find the probabilities of all the possible outcomes and also the probability that an odd number or an odd sum faces up.* HINT [See Example 3.]

55. Some of the dice are specially designed so that 1 and 6 never come up, and all the other outcomes are equally likely.

56. Other dice are specially designed so that 1 comes up half the time, 6 never comes up, and all the other outcomes are equally likely.

57. Some of the dice are cleverly weighted so that each of 2, 3, 4, and 5 is twice as likely to come up as 1 is, and 1 and 6 are equally likely.

58. Other dice are weighted so that each of 2, 3, 4, and 5 is half as likely to come up as 1 is, and 1 and 6 are equally likely.

59. ▼ Some pairs of dice are magnetized so that each pair of mismatching numbers is twice as likely to come up as each pair of matching numbers.

---

[37]Source: Environmental Protection Agency/*New York Times*, June 28, 2003.

[38]*Ibid.*

60. ▼ Other pairs of dice are so strongly magnetized that mismatching numbers never come up.

61. ▼ Some dice are constructed in such a way that deuce (2) is five times as likely to come up as 4 and three times as likely to come up as each of 1, 3, 5, and 6.

62. ▼ Other dice are constructed in such a way that deuce is six times as likely to come up as 4 and four times as likely to come up as each of 1, 3, 5, and 6.

63. *Astrology* The astrology software package, Turbo Kismet,[39] works by first generating random number sequences and then interpreting them numerologically. When I ran it yesterday, it informed me that there was a 1/3 probability that I would meet a tall dark stranger this month, a 2/3 probability that I would travel this month, and a 1/6 probability that I would meet a tall dark stranger and also travel this month. What is the probability that I will either meet a tall dark stranger or that I will travel this month? HINT [See Quick Example 1, page 476 and Example 4.]

64. *Astrology* Another astrology software package, Java Kismet, is designed to help day traders choose stocks based on the position of the planets and constellations. When I ran it yesterday, it informed me that there was a .5 probability that Amazon.com will go up this afternoon, a .2 probability that Yahoo.com will go up this afternoon, and a .2 chance that both will go up this afternoon. What is the probability that either Amazon.com or Yahoo.com will go up this afternoon? HINT [See Quick Example 1 on page 476 and Example 4.]

65. *Polls* According to a *New York Times*/CBS poll released in March 2005, 61% of those polled ranked jobs or health care as the top domestic priority.[40] What is the probability that a randomly selected person polled did not rank either as the top domestic priority? HINT [See Example 5.]

66. *Polls* According to *The New York Times*/CBS poll of March 2005 referred to in Exercise 65, 72% of those polled ranked neither Iraq nor North Korea as the top foreign policy issue.[41] What is the probability that a randomly selected person polled ranked either Iraq or North Korea as the top foreign policy issue? HINT [See Example 5.]

67. *Hybrid Auto Sales* In 2010, the probability that a randomly chosen hybrid vehicle sold in the United States was manufactured by Toyota was .70, while the probability that it was manufactured by Honda was .05.[42] What is the probability that a randomly chosen hybrid vehicle was manufactured by neither company?

68. *Hybrid Auto Sales* In 2010, the probability that a randomly chosen hybrid vehicle sold in the United States was manufactured by Ford was .12, while the probability that it was manufactured by Nissan was .02.[43] What is the probability that a randomly chosen hybrid vehicle was manufactured by neither company?

Student Admissions Exercises 69–84 are based on the following table, which shows the profile, by the math section of the SAT Reasoning Test, of admitted students at UCLA for the Fall 2011 semester.[44]

SAT Reasoning Test—Math Section

	700–800	600–699	500–599	400–499	200–399	Total
Admitted	6,611	3,981	1,388	385	8	12,373
Not admitted	6,622	13,876	9,890	4,974	1,363	36,725
Total applicants	13,233	17,857	11,278	5,359	1,371	49,098

Determine the probabilities of the following events. (Round your answers to the nearest .01.) HINT [Example 6.]

69. An applicant was admitted.

70. An applicant had a Math SAT below 400.

71. An applicant had a Math SAT below 400 and was admitted.

72. An applicant had a Math SAT of 700 or above and was admitted.

73. An applicant was not admitted.

74. An applicant did not have a Math SAT below 400.

75. An applicant had a Math SAT in the range 500–599 or was admitted.

76. An applicant had a Math SAT of 700 or above or was admitted.

77. An applicant neither was admitted nor had a Math SAT in the range 500–599.

78. An applicant neither had a Math SAT of 700 or above nor was admitted.

79. ▼ An applicant who had a Math SAT below 400 was admitted.

80. ▼ An applicant who had a Math SAT of 700 or above was admitted.

81. ▼ An admitted student had a Math SAT of 700 or above.

82. ▼ An admitted student had a Math SAT below 400.

83. ▼ A rejected applicant had a Math SAT below 600.

84. ▼ A rejected applicant had a Math SAT of at least 600.

---

[39]The name and concept were borrowed from a hilarious (as yet unpublished) novel by the science-fiction writer William Orr, who also happens to be a faculty member at Hofstra University.

[40]Source: *New York Times*, March 3, 2005, p. A20.

[41]*Ibid.*

[42]Source for sales data: www.wikipedia.com.

[43]Source for sales data: www.wikipedia.com.

[44]Source: University of California (www.admissions.ucla.edu/Prospect/Adm_fr/Frosh_Prof11.htm).

85. ▼ *Social Security* According to *The New York Times*/CBS poll of March 2005 referred to in Exercise 65, 79% agreed that it should be the government's responsibility to provide a decent standard of living for the elderly, and 43% agreed that it would be a good idea to invest part of their Social Security taxes on their own. What is the smallest percentage of people who could have agreed with both statements? What is the largest percentage of people who could have agreed with both statements?

86. ▼ *Social Security* According to *The New York Times*/CBS poll of March 2005 referred to in Exercise 65, 49% agreed that Social Security taxes should be raised if necessary to keep the system afloat, and 43% agreed that it would be a good idea to invest part of their Social Security taxes on their own. What is the largest percentage of people who could have agreed with at least one of these statements? What is the smallest percentage of people who could have agreed with at least one of these statements?

87. ▼ *Greek Life* The ΤΦΦ Sorority has a tough pledging program—it requires its pledges to master the Greek alphabet forward, backward, and "sideways." During the last pledge period, two-thirds of the pledges failed to learn it backward and three quarters of them failed to learn it sideways; 5 of the 12 pledges failed to master it either backward or sideways. Because admission into the sisterhood requires both backward and sideways mastery, what fraction of the pledges were disqualified on this basis?

88. ▼ *Swords and Sorcery* Lance the Wizard has been informed that tomorrow there will be a 50% chance of encountering the evil Myrmidons and a 20% chance of meeting up with the dreadful Balrog. Moreover, Hugo the Elf has predicted that there is a 10% chance of encountering both tomorrow. What is the probability that Lance will be lucky tomorrow and encounter neither the Myrmidons nor the Balrog?

89. ▼ *Public Health* A study shows that 80% of the population has been vaccinated against the Venusian flu, but 2% of the vaccinated population gets the flu anyway. If 10% of the total population gets this flu, what percent of the population either gets the vaccine or gets the disease?

90. ▼ *Public Health* A study shows that 75% of the population has been vaccinated against the Martian ague, but 4% of this group gets this disease anyway. If 10% of the total population gets this disease, what is the probability that a randomly selected person has been neither vaccinated nor has contracted Martian ague?

COMMUNICATION AND REASONING EXERCISES

91. Design an experiment based on rolling a fair die for which there are exactly three outcomes with the same probabilities.

92. Design an experiment based on rolling a fair die for which there are at least three outcomes with different probabilities.

93. ▼ Tony has had a "losing streak" at the casino—the chances of winning the game he is playing are 40%, but he has lost five times in a row. Tony argues that, because he should have won two times, the game must obviously be "rigged." Comment on his reasoning.

94. ▼ Maria is on a winning streak at the casino. She has already won four times in a row and concludes that her chances of winning a fifth time are good. Comment on her reasoning.

95. Complete the following sentence. The probability of the union of two events is the sum of the probabilities of the two events if _____.

96. A friend of yours asserted at lunch today that, according to the weather forecast for tomorrow, there is a 52% chance of rain and a 60% chance of snow. "But that's impossible!" you blurted out, "the percentages add up to more than 100%." Explain why you were wrong.

97. ▼ A certain experiment is performed a large number of times, and the event E has relative frequency equal to zero. This means that it should have modeled probability zero, right? HINT [See the definition of a probability model on page 469.]

98. ▼ (Refer to the preceding exercise.) How can the modeled probability of winning the lotto be nonzero if you have never won it, despite playing 600 times? HINT [See the definition of a probability model on page 469.]

99. ▼ Explain how the addition principle for mutually exclusive events follows from the general addition principle.

100. ▼ Explain how the property $P(A') = 1 - P(A)$ follows directly from the properties of a probability distribution.

101. ◆ It is said that lightning never strikes twice in the same spot. Assuming this to be the case, what should be the modeled probability that lightning will strike a given spot during a thunderstorm? Explain. HINT [See the definition of a probability model on page 469.]

102. ◆ A certain event has modeled probability equal to zero. This means it will never occur, right? HINT [See the definition of a probability model on page 469.]

103. ◆ Find a formula for the probability of the union of three (not necessarily mutually exclusive) events A, B, and C.

104. ◆ Four events A, B, C, and D have the following property: If any two events have an outcome in common, that outcome is common to all four events. Find a formula for the probability of their union.

7.4 Probability and Counting Techniques

We saw in the preceding section that, when all outcomes in a sample space are equally likely, we can use the following formula to model the probability of each event:

Modeling Probability: Equally Likely Outcomes

In an experiment in which all outcomes are equally likely, the probability of an event E is given by

$$P(E) = \frac{\text{Number of favorable outcomes}}{\text{Total number of outcomes}} = \frac{n(E)}{n(S)}.$$

This formula is simple, but calculating $n(E)$ and $n(S)$ may not be. In this section, we look at some examples in which we need to use the counting techniques discussed in Chapter 6.

EXAMPLE 1 **Marbles**

A bag contains four red marbles and two green ones. Upon seeing the bag, Suzan (who has compulsive marble-grabbing tendencies) sticks her hand in and grabs three at random. Find the probability that she will get both green marbles.

S is the set of all outcomes that can occur, and has nothing to do with having green marbles.

Solution According to the formula, we need to know these numbers:

• The number of elements in the sample space S.

• The number of elements in the event E.

First of all, what is the sample space? The sample space is the set of all possible outcomes, and each outcome consists of a set of three marbles (in Suzan's hand). So, the set of outcomes is the set of all sets of three marbles chosen from a total of six marbles (four red and two green). Thus,

$$n(S) = C(6, 3) = 20.$$

Now what about E? This is the event that Suzan gets both green marbles. We must *rephrase this as a subset of S* in order to deal with it: "E is the collection of sets of three marbles such that one is red and two are green." Thus, $n(E)$ is the *number* of such sets, which we determine using a decision algorithm.

Step 1 Choose a red marble: $C(4, 1) = 4$ possible outcomes.

Step 2 Choose the two green marbles: $C(2, 2) = 1$ possible outcome.

We get $n(E) = 4 \times 1 = 4$. Now,

$$P(E) = \frac{n(E)}{n(S)} = \frac{4}{20} = \frac{1}{5}.$$

Thus, there is a one in five chance of Suzan's getting both the green marbles.

EXAMPLE 2 Investment Lottery

After a down day on the stock market, you decide to ignore your broker's cautious advice and purchase three stocks at random from the six most active stocks listed on the New York Stock Exchange at the end of the day's trading.[45]

Company	Symbol	Price	Change
Bank of America	BAC	$5.80	−$1.00
PowerShares QQQ	QQQ	$55.83	−$1.34
Och-Ziff Capital Mgmt	OZM	$7.98	−$0.43
UBS AG Common Stock	UBS	$11.21	−$0.30
iShares Silver Trust	SLV	$30.64	−$2.18
Direxion Small Cap Bull	TNA	$42.80	−$1.92

Find the probabilities of the following events:

a. You purchase BAC and QQQ.

b. At most two of the stocks you purchase declined in value by more than $1.

Solution First, the sample space is the set of all collections of 3 stocks chosen from the 6. Thus,

$$n(S) = C(6, 3) = 20.$$

a. The event E of interest is the event that you purchase BAC and QQQ. Thus, E is the set of all groups of 3 stocks that include BAC and QQQ. Because there is only one more stock left to choose,

$$n(E) = C(4, 1) = 4.$$

We now have

$$P(E) = \frac{n(E)}{n(S)} = \frac{4}{20} = \frac{1}{5} = .2.$$

b. Let F be the event that at most two of the stocks you purchase declined in value by more than $1. Thus, F is the set of all groups of three stocks of which at most two declined in value by more than $1. To calculate $n(F)$, we use the following decision algorithm.

   Alternative 1: None of the stocks declined in value by more than $1.
      Step 1 Choose three stocks that did not decline in value by more than $1:
         $C(3, 3) = 1$ possibility.

   Alternative 2: One of the stocks declined in value by more than $1.
      Step 1 Choose one stock that declined in value by more than $1: $C(3, 1) = 3$ possibilities.
      Step 2 Choose two stocks that did not decline in value by more than $1:
         $C(3, 2) = 3$ possibilities.
      This gives $3 \times 3 = 9$ possibilities for this alternative.

   Alternative 3: Two of the stocks declined in value by more than $1.
      Step 1 Choose two stocks that declined in value by more than $1:
         $C(3, 2) = 3$ possibilities.
      Step 2 Choose one stock that did not decline in value by more than $1:
         $C(3, 1) = 3$ possibilities.
      This gives $3 \times 3 = 9$ possibilities for this alternative.

---

[45]Most active stocks on November 17, 2011. Source: Yahoo! Finance (http://finance.yahoo.com).

So, we have a total of $1 + 9 + 9 = 19$ possible outcomes. Thus,

$$n(F) = 19$$

and

$$P(F) = \frac{n(F)}{n(S)} = \frac{19}{20} = .95.$$

➡ **Before we go on...** When counting the number of outcomes in an event, the calculation is sometimes easier if we look at the *complement* of that event. In the case of part (b) of Example 2, the complement of the event F is

> F': At least three of the stocks you purchase declined in value by more than $1.

Because there are only three stocks in your portfolio, this is the same as the event that all three you purchase declined in value by more than $1. The decision algorithm for $n(F')$ is far simpler:

> **Step 1** Choose three stocks that declined in value by more than $1: $C(3, 3) = 1$ possibility.

So, $n(F') = 1$, giving

$$n(F) = n(S) - n(F') = 20 - 1 = 19$$

as we calculated above. ∎

At most two of the stocks declined in value by more than $1.

Complementary Events

At least three of the stocks declined in value by more than $1.

EXAMPLE 3 **Poker Hands**

You are dealt 5 cards from a well-shuffled standard deck of 52. Find the probability that you have a full house. (Recall that a full house consists of 3 cards of one denomination and 2 of another.)

Solution The sample space S is the set of all possible 5-card hands dealt from a deck of 52. Thus,

$$n(S) = C(52, 5) = 2,598,960.$$

If the deck is thoroughly shuffled, then each of these 5-card hands is equally likely. Now consider the event E, the set of all possible 5-card hands that constitute a full house. To calculate $n(E)$, we use a decision algorithm, which we show in the following compact form.

$$n(E) = C(13, 1) \times C(4, 3) \times C(12, 1) \times C(4, 2) = 3,744$$

Thus,

$$P(E) = \frac{n(E)}{n(S)} = \frac{3,744}{2,598,960} \approx .00144.$$

In other words, there is an approximately 0.144% chance that you will be dealt a full house.

EXAMPLE 4 **More Poker Hands**

You are playing poker, and you have been dealt the following hand:

$$J\spadesuit, J\diamondsuit, J\heartsuit, 2\clubsuit, 10\spadesuit.$$

You decide to exchange the last two cards. The exchange works as follows: The two cards are discarded (not replaced in the deck), and you are dealt two new cards.

a. Find the probability that you end up with a full house.

b. Find the probability that you end up with four jacks.

c. What is the probability that you end up with either a full house or four jacks?

Solution

a. In order to get a full house, you must be dealt two of a kind. The sample space S is the set of all pairs of cards selected from what remains of the original deck of 52. You were dealt 5 cards originally, so there are $52 - 5 = 47$ cards left in the deck. Thus, $n(S) = C(47, 2) = 1{,}081$. The event E is the set of all pairs of cards that constitute two of a kind. Note that you cannot get two jacks because only one is left in the deck. Also, only three 2s and three 10s are left in the deck. We have

Thus,

$$P(E) = \frac{n(E)}{n(S)} = \frac{66}{1{,}081} \approx .0611.$$

b. We have the same sample space as in part (a). Let F be the set of all pairs of cards that include the missing jack of clubs. So,

1. Choose the jack of clubs.

2. Choose 1 card from the remaining 46.

$$n(F) = C(1, 1) \times C(46, 1) = 46.$$

Thus,

$$P(F) = \frac{n(F)}{n(S)} = \frac{46}{1{,}081} \approx .0426.$$

c. We are asked to calculate the probability of the event $E \cup F$. From the addition principle, we have

$$P(E \cup F) = P(E) + P(F) - P(E \cap F).$$

Because $E \cap F$ means "E and F," $E \cap F$ is the event that the pair of cards you are dealt are two of a kind and include the jack of clubs. But this is impossible because only one jack is left. Thus $E \cap F = \emptyset$, and so $P(E \cap F) = 0$. This gives us

$$P(E \cup F) = P(E) + P(F) \approx .0611 + .0426 = .1037.$$

In other words, there is slightly better than a one in ten chance that you will wind up with either a full house or four of a kind, given the original hand.

➡ **Before we go on...** A more accurate answer to part (c) of Example 4 is $(66 + 46)/1{,}081 \approx .1036$; we lost some accuracy in rounding the answers to parts (a) and (b). ∎

EXAMPLE 5 Committees

The University Senate bylaws at Hofstra University state the following:[46]

> The Student Affairs Committee shall consist of one elected faculty senator, one faculty senator-at-large, one elected student senator, five student senators-at-large (including one from the graduate school), two delegates from the Student Government Association, the President of the Student Government Association or his/her designate, and the President of the Graduate Student Organization. It shall be chaired by the elected student senator on the Committee and it shall be advised by the Dean of Students or his/her designate.

You are an undergraduate student and, even though you are not an elected student senator, you would very much like to serve on the Student Affairs Committee. The senators-at-large as well as the Student Government delegates are chosen by means of a random drawing from a list of candidates. There are already 13 undergraduate candidates for the position of senator-at-large, and 6 candidates for Student Government delegates, and you have been offered a position on the Student Government Association by the President (who happens to be a good friend of yours), should you wish to join it. (This would make you ineligible for a senator-at-large position.) What should you do?

Solution You have two options. Option 1 is to include your name on the list of candidates for the senator-at-large position. Option 2 is to join the Student Government Association (SGA) and add your name to its list of candidates. Let us look at the two options separately.

Option 1: Add your name to the senator-at-large list.
This will result in a list of 14 undergraduates for 4 undergraduate positions. The sample space is the set of all possible outcomes of the random drawing. Each outcome consists of a set of 4 lucky students chosen from 14. Thus,

$$n(S) = C(14, 4) = 1{,}001.$$

We are interested in the probability that you are among the chosen four. Thus, E is the set of sets of four that include you.

1. Choose yourself.

2. Choose 3 from the remaining 13.

$$n(E) = C(1, 1) \times C(13, 3) = 286.$$

---

[46]As of 2011. Source: Hofstra University Senate Bylaws.

So,

$$P(E) = \frac{n(E)}{n(S)} = \frac{286}{1,001} = \frac{2}{7} \approx .2857.$$

Option 2: Join the SGA and add your name to its list.
This results in a list of seven candidates from which two are selected. For this case, the sample space consists of all sets of two chosen from seven, so

$$n(S) = C(7, 2) = 21$$

and

1. Choose yourself.

2. Choose one from the remaining six.

$$n(E) = C(1, 1) \times C(6, 1) = 6.$$

Thus,

$$P(E) = \frac{n(E)}{n(S)} = \frac{6}{21} = \frac{2}{7} \approx .2857.$$

In other words, the probability of being selected is exactly the same for Option 1 as it is for Option 2! Thus, you can choose either option, and you will have slightly less than a 29% chance of being selected.

7.4   EXERCISES

▼ more advanced   ◆ challenging
🔳 indicates exercises that should be solved using technology

Recall from Example 1 that whenever Suzan sees a bag of marbles, she grabs a handful at random. In Exercises 1–10, she has seen a bag containing four red marbles, three green ones, two white ones, and one purple one. She grabs five of them. Find the probabilities of the following events, expressing each as a fraction in lowest terms. HINT [See Example 1.]

1. She has all the red ones.

2. She has none of the red ones.

3. She has at least one white one.

4. She has at least one green one.

5. She has two red ones and one of each of the other colors.

6. She has two green ones and one of each of the other colors.

7. She has at most one green one.

8. She has no more than one white one.

9. She does not have all the red ones.

10. She does not have all the green ones.

Dogs of the Dow *The phrase "Dogs of the Dow" refers to the stocks listed on the Dow with the highest dividend yield.*

Exercises 11–16 are based on the following table, which shows the top ten stocks of the "Dogs of the Dow" list in November 2011:[47] HINT [See Example 2.]

Symbol	Company	Price	Yield
T	AT&T	29.46	5.84%
VZ	Verizon	37.52	5.20%
MRK	Merck	34.47	4.41%
PFE	Pfizer	20.08	3.98%
JNJ	Johnson & Johnson	64.86	3.52%
INTC	Intel	24.75	3.39%
KFT	Kraft	35.48	3.27%
DD	DuPont	49.81	3.29%
CVX	Chevron	108.86	2.87%
MCD	McDonald's	94.60	2.58%

---

[47]Source: www.dogsofthedow.com.

11. If you selected two of these stocks at random, what is the probability that both the stocks in your selection had yields of 4% or more?

12. If you selected three of these stocks at random, what is the probability that all three of the stocks in your selection had yields of 4% or more?

13. If you selected four of these stocks at random, what is the probability that your selection included the company with the highest yield and excluded the company with the lowest yield?

14. If you selected four of these stocks at random, what is the probability that your selection included T and VZ but excluded PFE and DD?

15. ▼ If your portfolio included 100 shares of PFE and you then purchased 100 shares each of any two companies on the list at random, find the probability that you ended up with a total of 200 shares of PFE.

16. ▼ If your portfolio included 100 shares of PFE and you then purchased 100 shares each of any three companies on the list at random, find the probability that you ended up with a total of 200 shares of PFE.

17. *Tests* A test has three parts. Part A consists of eight true-false questions, Part B consists of five multiple choice questions with five choices each, and Part C requires you to match five questions with five different answers one-to-one. Assuming that you make random guesses in filling out your answer sheet, what is the probability that you will earn 100% on the test? (Leave your answer as a formula.)

18. *Tests* A test has three parts. Part A consists of four true-false questions, Part B consists of four multiple choice questions with five choices each, and Part C requires you to match six questions with six different answers one-to-one. Assuming that you make random choices in filling out your answer sheet, what is the probability that you will earn 100% on the test? (Leave your answer as a formula.)

Poker In Exercises 19–24, you are asked to calculate the probability of being dealt various poker hands. (Recall that a poker player is dealt 5 cards at random from a standard deck of 52.) Express each of your answers as a decimal rounded to four decimal places, unless otherwise stated. HINT [See Example 3.]

19. **Two of a kind:** Two cards with the same denomination and three cards with other denominations (different from each other and that of the pair). Example: K♣, K♥, 2♠, 4♦, J♠

20. **Three of a kind:** Three cards with the same denomination and two cards with other denominations (different from each other and that of the three). Example: Q♣, Q♥, Q♠, 4♦, J♠

21. **Two pairs:** Two cards with one denomination, two with another, and one with a third. Example: 3♣, 3♥, Q♠, Q♥, 10♠

22. **Straight Flush:** Five cards of the same suit with consecutive denominations but not a royal flush (a royal flush consists of the 10, J, Q, K, and A of one suit). Round the answer to one significant digit. Examples: A♣, 2♣, 3♣, 4♣, 5♣, or

9♦, 10♦, J♦, Q♦, K♦, or A♥, 2♥, 3♥, 4♥, 5♥, but *not* 10♦, J♦, Q♦, K♦, A♦

23. **Flush:** Five cards of the same suit, but not a straight flush or royal flush. Example: A♣, 5♣, 7♣, 8♣, K♣

24. **Straight:** Five cards with consecutive denominations, but not all of the same suit. Examples: 9♦, 10♦, J♣, Q♥, K♦, and 10♥, J♦, Q♦, K♦, A♦.

25. ***The Monkey at the Typewriter*** Suppose that a monkey is seated at a computer keyboard and randomly strikes the 26 letter keys and the space bar. Find the probability that its first 39 characters (including spaces) will be "to be or not to be that is the question". (Leave your answer as a formula.)

26. ***The Cat on the Piano*** A standard piano keyboard has 88 different keys. Find the probability that a cat, jumping on 4 keys in sequence and at random (possibly with repetition), will strike the first four notes of Beethoven's Fifth Symphony. (Leave your answer as a formula.)

27. **(Based on a question from the GMAT)** Tyler and Gebriella are among seven contestants from which four semifinalists are to be selected at random. Find the probability that neither Tyler nor Gebriella is selected.

28. **(Based on a question from the GMAT)** Tyler and Gebriella are among seven contestants from which four semifinalists are to be selected at random. Find the probability that Tyler but not Gebriella is selected.

29. ▼ *Lotteries* The Sorry State Lottery requires you to select five different numbers from 0 through 49. (Order is not important.) You are a Big Winner if the five numbers you select agree with those in the drawing, and you are a Small-Fry Winner if four of your five numbers agree with those in the drawing. What is the probability of being a Big Winner? What is the probability of being a Small-Fry Winner? What is the probability that you are either a Big Winner or a Small-Fry winner?

30. ▼ *Lotto* The Sad State Lottery requires you to select a sequence of three different numbers from 0 through 49. (Order is important.) You are a Winner if your sequence agrees with that in the drawing, and you are a Booby Prize Winner if your selection of numbers is correct, but in the wrong order. What is the probability of being a Winner? What is the probability of being a Booby Prize Winner? What is the probability that you are either a Winner or a Booby Prize Winner?

31. ▼ *Transfers* Your company is considering offering 400 employees the opportunity to transfer to its new headquarters in Ottawa and, as personnel manager, you decide that it would be fairest if the transfer offers are decided by means of a lottery. Assuming that your company currently employs 100 managers, 100 factory workers, and 500 miscellaneous staff, find the following probabilities, leaving the answers as formulas:

   a. All the managers will be offered the opportunity.

   b. You will be offered the opportunity.

32. ▼ *Transfers* (Refer back to the preceding exercise.) After thinking about your proposed method of selecting employees for the opportunity to move to Ottawa, you decide it might be a better idea to select 50 managers, 50 factory workers, and 300 miscellaneous staff, all chosen at random. Find the probability that you will be offered the opportunity. (Leave your answer as a formula.)

33. ▼ *Lotteries* In a New York State daily lottery game, a sequence of three digits (not necessarily different) in the range 0–9 are selected at random. Find the probability that all three are different.

34. ▼ *Lotteries* Refer back to the preceding exercise. Find the probability that two of the three digits are the same.

35. ▼ *Sports* The following table shows the results of the Big Eight Conference for the 1988 college football season.[48]

Team	Won	Lost
Nebraska (NU)	7	0
Oklahoma (OU)	6	1
Oklahoma State (OSU)	5	2
Colorado (CU)	4	3
Iowa State (ISU)	3	4
Missouri (MU)	2	5
Kansas (KU)	1	6
Kansas State (KSU)	0	7

This is referred to as a "perfect progression." Assuming that the "Won" score for each team is chosen at random in the range 0–7, find the probability that the results form a perfect progression.[49] (Leave your answer as a formula.)

36. ▼ *Sports* Refer back to Exercise 35. Find the probability of a perfect progression with Nebraska scoring seven wins and zero losses. (Leave your answer as a formula.)

37. ▼ *Graph Searching* A graph consists of a collection of **nodes** (the dots in the figure) connected by **edges** (line segments from one node to another). A **move on a graph** is a move from one node to another along a single edge. Find the probability of going from Start to Finish in a sequence of two random moves in the graph shown. (All directions are equally likely.)

38. ▼ *Graph Searching* Refer back to Exercise 37. Find the probability of going from Start to one of the Finish nodes in a sequence of two random moves in the following figure. (All directions are equally likely.)

39. ▼ *Tournaments* What is the probability that North Carolina will beat Central Connecticut but lose to Virginia in the following (fictitious) soccer tournament? (Assume that all outcomes are equally likely.)

40. ▼ *Tournaments* In a (fictitious) soccer tournament involving the four teams San Diego State, De Paul, Colgate, and Hofstra, find the probability that Hofstra will play Colgate in the finals and win. (Assume that all outcomes are equally likely and that the teams not listed in the first round slots are placed at random.)

41. ◆ *Product Design* Your company has patented an electronic digital padlock that a user can program with his or her own four-digit code. (Each digit can be 0 through 9, and repetitions are allowed.) The padlock is designed to open either if the correct code is keyed in or—and this is helpful for forgetful people—if exactly one of the digits is incorrect. What is the probability that a randomly chosen sequence of four digits will open a programmed padlock?

---

[48]Source: On the probability of a perfect progression, *The American Statistician*, August 1991, vol. 45, no. 3, p. 214.

[49]Even if all the teams are equally likely to win each game, the chances of a perfect progression actually coming up are a little more difficult to estimate, because the number of wins by one team impacts directly on the number of wins by the others. For instance, it is impossible for all eight teams to show a score of seven wins and zero losses at the end of the season—someone must lose! It is, however, not too hard to come up with a counting argument to estimate the total number of win-loss scores actually possible.

42. ◆ *Product Design* Assume that you already know the first digit of the combination for the lock described in Exercise 41. Find the probability that a random guess of the remaining three digits will open the lock. HINT [See Example 5.]

43. ◆ *Committees* An investigatory committee in the Kingdom of Utopia consists of a chief investigator (a Royal Party member), an assistant investigator (a Birthday Party member), two at-large investigators (either party), and five ordinary members (either party). Royal Party member Larry Sifford is hoping to avoid serving on the committee, unless he is the Chief Investigator and Otis Taylor, a Birthday Party member, is the Assistant Investigator. The committee is to be selected at random from a pool of 12 candidates (including Larry Sifford and Otis Taylor), half of whom are Royal Party and half of whom are Birthday Party.

a. How many different committees are possible? HINT [See Example 5.]

b. How many committees are possible in which Larry's hopes are fulfilled? (This includes the possibility that he's not on the committee at all.)

c. What is the probability that he'll be happy with a randomly selected committee?

44. ◆ *Committees* A committee is to consist of a chair, three hagglers, and four do-nothings. The committee is formed by choosing randomly from a pool of 10 people and assigning them to the various "jobs."

a. How many different committees are possible? HINT [See Example 5.]

b. Norman is eager to be the chair of the committee. What is the probability that he will get his wish?

c. Norman's girlfriend Norma is less ambitious and would be happy to hold any position on the committee provided Norman is also selected as a committee member. What is the probability that she will get her wish and serve on the committee?

d. Norma does not get along with Oona (who is also in the pool of prospective members) and would be most unhappy if Oona were to chair the committee. Find the probability that all her wishes will be fulfilled: She and Norman are on the committee and it is not chaired by Oona.

COMMUNICATION AND REASONING EXERCISES

45. What is wrong with the following argument? A bag contains two blue marbles and two red ones; two are drawn at random. Because there are four possibilities—(red, red), (blue, blue), (red, blue) and (blue, red)—the probability that both are red is 1/4.

46. What is wrong with the following argument? When we roll two indistinguishable dice, the number of possible outcomes (unordered groups of two not necessarily distinct numbers) is 21 and the number of outcomes in which both numbers are the same is 6. Hence, the probability of throwing a double is 6/21 = 2/7.

47. ▼ Suzan grabs two marbles out of a bag of five red marbles and four green ones. She could do so in two ways: She could take them out one at a time, so that there is a first and a second marble, or she could grab two at once so that there is no order. Does the method she uses to grab the marbles affect the probability that she gets two red marbles?

48. ▼ If Suzan grabs two marbles, one at a time, out of a bag of five red marbles and four green ones, find an event with a probability that depends on the order in which the two marbles are drawn.

49. Create an interesting application whose solution requires finding a probability using combinations.

50. Create an interesting application whose solution requires finding a probability using permutations.

7.5 Conditional Probability and Independence

Cyber Video Games, Inc., ran a television ad in advance of the release of its latest game, "Ultimate Hockey." As Cyber Video's director of marketing, you would like to assess the ad's effectiveness, so you ask your market research team to survey video game players. The results of its survey of 2,000 video game players are summarized in the following table:

	Saw Ad	Did Not See Ad	Total
Purchased Game	100	200	300
Did Not Purchase Game	200	1,500	1,700
Total	300	1,700	2,000

The market research team concludes in its report that the ad is highly persuasive, and recommends using the company that produced the ad for future projects.

But wait, how could the ad possibly have been persuasive? Only 100 people who saw the ad purchased the game, while 200 people purchased the game without seeing the ad at all! At first glance, it looks as though potential customers are being *put off* by the ad. But let us analyze the figures a little more carefully.

First, let us restrict attention to those players who saw the ad (first column of data: "Saw Ad") and compute the estimated probability that a player *who saw the ad* purchased Ultimate Hockey.

	Saw Ad
Purchased Game	100
Did Not Purchase Game	200
Total	300

To compute this probability, we calculate

Probability that someone who saw the ad purchased the game

$$= \frac{\text{Number of people who saw the ad and bought the game}}{\text{Total number of people who saw the ad}} = \frac{100}{300} \approx .33.$$

In other words, 33% of game players who saw the ad went ahead and purchased the game. Let us compare this with the corresponding probability for those players who did *not* see the ad (second column of data "Did Not See Ad"):

	Did Not See Ad
Purchased Game	200
Did Not Purchase Game	1,500
Total	1,700

Probability that someone who did not see the ad purchased the game

$$= \frac{\text{Number of people who did not see the ad and bought the game}}{\text{Total number of people who did not see the ad}} = \frac{200}{1,700} \approx .12.$$

In other words, only 12% of game players who did not see the ad purchased the game, whereas 33% of those who *did* see the ad purchased the game. Thus, it appears that the ad *was* highly persuasive.

Here's some terminology. In this example there were two related events of importance:

A: A video game player purchased Ultimate Hockey.

B: A video game player saw the ad.

The first probability we computed was the estimated probability that a video game player purchased Ultimate Hockey *given that* he or she saw the ad. We call the latter probability the (estimated) **probability of *A*, given *B***, and we write it as $P(A \mid B)$. We call $P(A \mid B)$ a **conditional probability**—it is the probability of *A* under the condition that B occurred. Put another way, it is the probability of A occurring if the sample space is reduced to just those outcomes in B.

$$P(\text{Purchased game } given \text{ } that \text{ saw the ad}) = P(A \mid B) \approx .33$$

The second probability we computed was the estimated probability that a video game player purchased Ultimate Hockey *given that* he or she did not see the ad, or the **probability of A, given B'**.

$$P(\text{Purchased game } given \text{ } that \text{ did not see the ad}) = P(A \mid B') \approx .12$$

Calculating Conditional Probabilities

How do we calculate conditional probabilities? In the example above we used the ratio

$$P(A \mid B) = \frac{\text{Number of people who saw the ad and bought the game}}{\text{Total number of people who saw the ad}}.$$

The numerator is the frequency of $A \cap B$, and the denominator is the frequency of B:

$$P(A \mid B) = \frac{fr(A \cap B)}{fr(B)}.$$

Now, we can write this formula in another way:

$$P(A \mid B) = \frac{fr(A \cap B)}{fr(B)} = \frac{fr(A \cap B)/N}{fr(B)/N} = \frac{P(A \cap B)}{P(B)}.$$

We therefore have the following definition, which applies to general probability distributions.

Conditional Probability

If A and B are events with $P(B) \neq 0$, then the probability of A given B is

$$P(A \mid B) = \frac{P(A \cap B)}{P(B)}.$$

Visualizing Conditional Probability

In the figure, $P(A \mid B)$ is represented by the fraction of B that is covered by A.

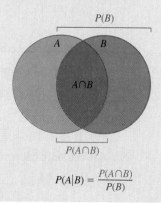

$$P(A|B) = \frac{P(A \cap B)}{P(B)}$$

Quick Examples

1. If there is a 50% chance of rain (R) and a 10% chance of both rain and lightning (L), then the probability of lightning, given that it rains, is

$$P(L \mid R) = \frac{P(L \cap R)}{P(R)} = \frac{.10}{.50} = .20.$$

Here are two more ways to express the result:

- If it rains, the probability of lightning is .20.
- Assuming that it rains, there is a 20% chance of lightning.

2. Referring to the Cyber Video data at the beginning of this section, the probability that a video game player did not purchase the game (A'), given that she did not see the ad (B'), is

$$P(A' \mid B') = \frac{P(A' \cap B')}{P(B')} = \frac{1{,}500/2{,}000}{1{,}700/2{,}000} = \frac{15}{17} \approx .88.$$

Q: *Returning to the video game sales survey, how do we compute the* ordinary probability *of A, not "given" anything?*

A: We look at the event A that a randomly chosen game player purchased Ultimate Hockey *regardless of whether or not he or she saw the ad*. In the "Purchased Game" row we see that a total of 300 people purchased the game out of a total of 2,000 surveyed. Thus, the (estimated) probability of A is

$$P(A) = \frac{fr(A)}{N} = \frac{300}{2{,}000} = .15.$$

We sometimes refer to $P(A)$ as the **unconditional** probability of A to distinguish it from conditional probabilities like $P(A|B)$ and $P(A|B')$.

Now, let's see some more examples involving conditional probabilities.

EXAMPLE 1   Dice

If you roll a fair die twice and observe the numbers that face up, find the probability that the sum of the numbers is 8, given that the first number is 3.

Solution We begin by recalling that the sample space when we roll a fair die twice is the set $S = \{(1, 1), (1, 2), \ldots, (6, 6)\}$ containing the 36 different equally likely outcomes.

The two events under consideration are

     A: The sum of the numbers is 8.

     B: The first number is 3.

We also need

     $A \cap B$: The sum of the numbers is 8 and the first number is 3.

But this can only happen in one way: $A \cap B = \{(3, 5)\}$. From the formula, then,

$$P(A \mid B) = \frac{P(A \cap B)}{P(B)} = \frac{1/36}{6/36} = \frac{1}{6}.$$

➡ **Before we go on...** There is another way to think about Example 1. When we say that the first number is 3, we are restricting the sample space to the six outcomes $(3, 1), (3, 2), \ldots, (3, 6)$, all still equally likely. Of these six, only one has a sum of 8, so the probability of the sum being 8, given that the first number is 3, is $1/6$. ■

Notes

1. Remember that, in the expression $P(A \mid B)$, A is the event whose probability you want, given that you know the event B has occurred.
2. From the formula, notice that $P(A \mid B)$ is not defined if $P(B) = 0$. Could $P(A \mid B)$ make any sense if the event B were impossible? ■

EXAMPLE 2 School and Work

A survey[50] of the high school graduating class of 2010, conducted by the Bureau of Labor Statistics, found that, if a graduate went on to college, there was a 40% chance that he or she would work at the same time. On the other hand, there was a 68% chance that a randomly selected graduate would go on to college. What is the probability that a graduate went to college and work at the same time?

Solution To understand what the question asks and what information is given, it is helpful to rephrase everything using the standard wording "*the probability that ___*" and "*the probability that ___ given that ___.*" Now we have, "The probability that a graduate worked, given that the graduate went on to college, equals .40. (See Figure 8.) The probability that a graduate went on to college is .68." The events in question are as follows:

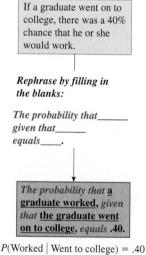

If a graduate went on to college, there was a 40% chance that he or she would work.

Rephrase by filling in the blanks:

The probability that_____ given that_____ equals____.

*The probability that **a graduate worked**, given that **the graduate went on to college**, equals .40.*

$P(\text{Worked} \mid \text{Went to college}) = .40$

Figure 8

    W: A high school graduate went on to work.

    C: A high school graduate went on to college.

From our rephrasing of the question we can write:

$$P(W \mid C) = .40. \qquad P(C) = .68. \qquad \text{Find } P(W \cap C).$$

The definition

$$P(W \mid C) = \frac{P(W \cap C)}{P(C)}$$

can be used to find $P(W \cap C)$:

$$P(W \cap C) = P(W \mid C)P(C)$$
$$= (.40)(.68) \approx .27.$$

Thus there is a 27% chance that a member of the high school graduating class of 2010 went on to college and work at the same time.

The Multiplication Principle and Trees

In Example 2, we saw that the formula

$$P(A \mid B) = \frac{P(A \cap B)}{P(B)}$$

---

[50]Source: "College Enrollment and Work Activity of High School Graduates," U.S. Bureau of Labor Statistics (www.bls.gov/news.release/hsgec.htm).

can be used to calculate $P(A \cap B)$ if we rewrite the formula in the following form, known as the **multiplication principle for conditional probability**:

Multiplication Principle for Conditional Probability

If A and B are events, then

$$P(A \cap B) = P(A \mid B)P(B).$$

Quick Example

If there is a 50% chance of rain (R) and a 20% chance of a lightning (L) if it rains, then the probability of both rain and lightning is

$$P(R \cap L) = P(L \mid R)P(R) = (.20)(.50) = .10.$$

The multiplication principle is often used in conjunction with **tree diagrams**. Let's return to Cyber Video Games, Inc., and its television ad campaign. Its marketing survey was concerned with the following events:

A: A video game player purchased Ultimate Hockey.

B: A video game player saw the ad.

We can illustrate the various possibilities by means of the two-stage "tree" shown in Figure 9.

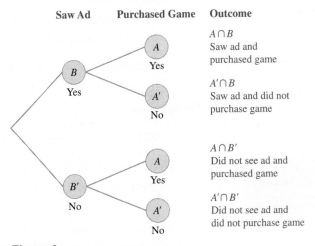

Figure 9

Consider the outcome $A \cap B$. To get there from the starting position on the left, we must first travel up to the B node. (In other words, B must occur.) Then we must travel up the branch from the B node to the A node. We are now going to associate a probability with each branch of the tree: the probability of traveling along that branch *given that we have gotten to its beginning node.* For instance, the probability of traveling up the branch from the starting position to the B node is $P(B) = 300/2{,}000 = .15$ (see the data in the survey). The probability of going up the branch from the B node to the A node is the probability that A occurs, given that B has occurred. In other words, it is the *conditional* probability $P(A \mid B) \approx .33$.

(We calculated this probability at the beginning of the section.) The probability of the outcome $A \cap B$ can then be computed using the multiplication principle:

$$P(A \cap B) = P(B)P(A \mid B) \approx (.15)(.33) \approx .05.$$

In other words, *to obtain the probability of the outcome $A \cap B$, we multiply the probabilities on the branches leading to that outcome* (Figure 10).

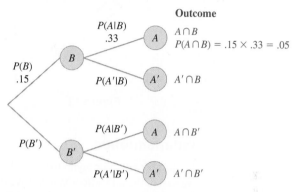

Figure 10

The same argument holds for the remaining three outcomes, and we can use the table given at the beginning of this section to calculate all the conditional probabilities shown in Figure 11.

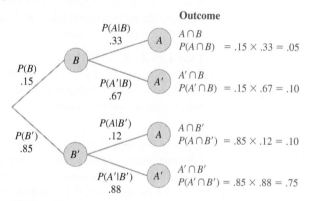

Figure 11

Note The sum of the probabilities on the branches leaving any node is always 1 (why?). This observation often speeds things up because after we have labeled one branch (or, all but one, if a node has more than two branches leaving it), we can easily label the remaining one. ■

EXAMPLE 3 Unfair Coins

An experiment consists of tossing two coins. The first coin is fair, while the second coin is twice as likely to land with heads facing up as it is with tails facing up. Draw a tree diagram to illustrate all the possible outcomes, and use the multiplication principle to compute the probabilities of all the outcomes.

Solution A quick calculation shows that the probability distribution for the second coin is $P(\text{H}) = 2/3$ and $P(\text{T}) = 1/3$. (How did we get that?) Figure 12 shows the tree diagram and the calculations of the probabilities of the outcomes.

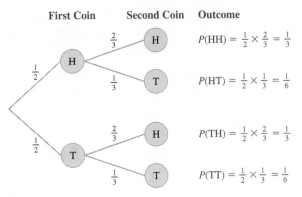

Figure 12

Independence

Let us go back once again to Cyber Video Games, Inc., and its ad campaign. How did we assess the ad's effectiveness? We considered the following events.

> A: A video game player purchased Ultimate Hockey.
>
> B: A video game player saw the ad.

We used the survey data to calculate $P(A)$, the probability that a video game player purchased Ultimate Hockey, and $P(A \mid B)$, the probability that a video game player *who saw the ad* purchased Ultimate Hockey. When these probabilities are compared, one of three things can happen.

Case 1 $P(A \mid B) > P(A)$
This is what the survey data actually showed: A video game player was more likely to purchase Ultimate Hockey if he or she saw the ad. This indicates that the ad is effective; seeing the ad had a positive effect on a player's decision to purchase the game.

Case 2 $P(A \mid B) < P(A)$
If this had happened, then a video game player would have been *less* likely to purchase Ultimate Hockey if he or she saw the ad. This would have indicated that the ad had "backfired"; it had, for some reason, put potential customers off. In this case, just as in the first case, the event B would have had an effect—a negative one—on the event A.

Case 3 $P(A \mid B) = P(A)$
In this case seeing the ad would have had absolutely no effect on a potential customer's buying Ultimate Hockey. Put another way, the probability of A occurring *does not depend* on whether B occurred or not. We say in a case like this that the events A and B are **independent**.

    In general, we say that two events A and B are independent if $P(A \mid B) = P(A)$. When this happens, we have

$$P(A) = P(A \mid B) = \frac{P(A \cap B)}{P(B)}$$

so

$$P(A \cap B) = P(A)P(B).$$

✳ We shall only discuss the independence of two events in cases where their probabilities are both nonzero.

Conversely, if $P(A \cap B) = P(A)P(B)$, then, assuming $P(B) \neq 0,$✳ $P(A) = P(A \cap B)/P(B) = P(A \mid B)$. Thus, saying that $P(A) = P(A \mid B)$ is the same as saying that $P(A \cap B) = P(A)P(B)$. Also, we can switch A and B in this last formula and conclude that saying that $P(A \cap B) = P(A)P(B)$ is the same as saying that $P(B \mid A) = P(B)$.

Independent Events

The events A and B are **independent** if

$$P(A \cap B) = P(A)P(B).$$

Equivalent formulas (assuming neither A nor B is impossible) are

$$P(A \mid B) = P(A)$$

and $$P(B \mid A) = P(B).$$

If two events A and B are not independent, then they are **dependent**.

The property $P(A \cap B) = P(A)P(B)$ can be extended to three or more independent events. If, for example, A, B, and C are three mutually independent events (that is, each one of them is independent of each of the other two and of their intersection), then, among other things,

$$P(A \cap B \cap C) = P(A)P(B)P(C).$$

Quick Examples

To test for independence, calculate the three quantities $P(A)$, $P(B)$, and $P(A \cap B)$ separately, and then see if $P(A \cap B) = P(A) \cdot P(B)$.

1. If A and B are independent, and if A has a probability of .2 and B has a probability of .3, then $A \cap B$ has a probability of $(.2)(.3) = .06$.

2. Let us assume that the phase of the moon has no effect on whether or not my newspaper is delivered. The probability of a full moon (M) on a randomly selected day is about .034, and the probability that my newspaper will be delivered (D) on the random day is .20. Therefore, the probability that it is a full moon and my paper is delivered is

$$P(M \cap D) = P(M)P(D) = (.034)(.20) = .0068.$$

Testing for Independence

To check whether two events A and B are independent, we compute $P(A)$, $P(B)$, and $P(A \cap B)$. If $P(A \cap B) = P(A)P(B)$, the events are independent; otherwise, they are dependent. Sometimes it is obvious that two events, by their nature, are independent, so a test is not necessary. For example, the event that a die you roll comes up 1 is clearly independent of whether or not a coin you toss comes up heads.

Quick Examples

1. Roll two distinguishable dice (one red, one green) and observe the numbers that face up.

A: The red die is even; $P(A) = \dfrac{18}{36} = \dfrac{1}{2}$.

B: The dice have the same parity*; $P(B) = \dfrac{18}{36} = \dfrac{1}{2}$.

$A \cap B$: Both dice are even; $P(A \cap B) = \dfrac{9}{36} = \dfrac{1}{4}$.

$P(A \cap B) = P(A)P(B)$, and so A and B are independent.

* Two numbers have the **same parity** if both are even or both are odd. Otherwise, they have **opposite parity**.

2. Roll two distinguishable dice and observe the numbers that face up.

A: The sum of the numbers is 6; $P(A) = \dfrac{5}{36}$.

B: Both numbers are odd; $P(B) = \dfrac{9}{36} = \dfrac{1}{4}$.

$A \cap B$: The sum is 6, and both are odd; $P(A \cap B) = \dfrac{3}{36} = \dfrac{1}{12}$.

$P(A \cap B) \neq P(A)P(B)$, and so A and B are dependent.

EXAMPLE 4 Weather Prediction

According to the weather service, there is a 50% chance of rain in New York and a 30% chance of rain in Honolulu. Assuming that New York's weather is independent of Honolulu's, find the probability that it will rain in at least one of these cities.

Solution We take A to be the event that it will rain in New York and B to be the event that it will rain in Honolulu. We are asked to find the probability of $A \cup B$, the event that it will rain in at least one of the two cities. We use the addition principle:

$$P(A \cup B) = P(A) + P(B) - P(A \cap B).$$

We know that $P(A) = .5$ and $P(B) = .3$. But what about $P(A \cap B)$? Because the events A and B are independent, we can compute

$$P(A \cap B) = P(A)P(B)$$
$$= (.5)(.3) = .15.$$

Thus,

$$P(A \cup B) = P(A) + P(B) - P(A \cap B)$$
$$= .5 + .3 - .15$$
$$= .65.$$

So, there is a 65% chance that it will rain either in New York or in Honolulu (or in both).

EXAMPLE 5 Roulette

You are playing roulette and have decided to leave all 10 of your $1 chips on black for five consecutive rounds, hoping for a sequence of five blacks which, according to the rules, will leave you with $320. There is a 50% chance of black coming up on each spin, ignoring the complicating factor of zero or double zero. What is the probability that you will be successful?

Solution Because the roulette wheel has no memory, each spin is independent of the others. Thus, if A_1 is the event that black comes up the first time, A_2 the event that it comes up the second time, and so on, then

$$P(A_1 \cap A_2 \cap A_3 \cap A_4 \cap A_5) = P(A_1)P(A_2)P(A_3)P(A_4)P(A_5) = \left(\frac{1}{2}\right)^5 = \frac{1}{32}.$$

The next example is a version of a well known "brain teaser" that forces one to think carefully about conditional probability.

EXAMPLE 6 Legal Argument

A man was arrested for attempting to smuggle a bomb on board an airplane. During the subsequent trial, his lawyer claimed that, by means of a simple argument, she would prove beyond a shadow of a doubt that her client was not only innocent of any crime, but was in fact contributing to the safety of the other passengers on the flight. This was her eloquent argument: "Your Honor, first of all, my client had absolutely no intention of setting off the bomb. As the record clearly shows, the detonator was unarmed when he was apprehended. In addition—and your Honor is certainly aware of this—there is a small but definite possibility that there will be a bomb on any given flight. On the other hand, the chances of there being *two* bombs on a flight are so remote as to be negligible. There is in fact no record of this having *ever* occurred. Thus, because my client had already brought one bomb on board (with no intention of setting it off) and because we have seen that the chances of there being a second bomb on board were vanishingly remote, it follows that the flight was far safer as a result of his action! I rest my case." This argument was so elegant in its simplicity that the judge acquitted the defendant. Where is the flaw in the argument? (Think about this for a while before reading the solution.)

Solution The lawyer has cleverly confused the phrases "two bombs on board" and "a second bomb on board." To pinpoint the flaw, let us take B to be the event that there is one bomb on board a given flight, and let A be the event that there are two independent bombs on board. Let us assume for argument's sake that $P(B) = 1/1,000,000 = .000\,001$. Then the probability of the event A is

$$(.000\,001)(.000\,001) = .000\,000\,000\,001.$$

This *is* vanishingly small, as the lawyer contended. It was at this point that the lawyer used a clever maneuver: She assumed in concluding her argument that the probability of having two bombs on board was the same as the probability of having a *second* bomb on board. But to say that there is a *second* bomb on board is to imply that there already is one bomb on board. This is therefore a *conditional* event: the event that there are two bombs on board, *given that there is already one bomb on board.* Thus, the probability that there is a second bomb on board is the probability that there are two bombs on board, given that there is already one bomb on board, which is

$$P(A \mid B) = \frac{P(A \cap B)}{P(B)} = \frac{.000\,000\,000\,001}{.000\,001} = .000\,001.$$

In other words, it is the same as the probability of there being a single bomb on board to begin with! Thus the man's carrying the bomb onto the plane did not improve the flight's safety at all.[*]

[*] If we want to be picky, there was a *slight* decrease in the probability of a second bomb because there was one less seat for a potential second bomb bearer to occupy. In terms of our analysis, this is saying that the event of one passenger with a bomb and the event of a second passenger with a bomb are not completely independent.

Probability of what given what?

Q : *How do I tell if a statement in an application is talking about conditional proba-bility or unconditional probability? And if it is talking about conditional probabil-ity, how do I determine what to use as A and B in P(A|B)?*

A : Look carefully at the wording of the statement. If there is some kind of qualifica-tion or restriction to a smaller set than the entire sample space, then it is probably talking about conditional probability, as in the following examples:

60% of veterans vote Republican while 40% of the entire voting population vote Republican.
Here the sample space can be taken to be the entire voting population.
Reworded (see Example 2): *The probability of voting Republican (R) is 60% given that the person is a veteran (V); P(R|V) = .60, whereas the probability of voting Republican is .40: P(R) = .40.*

The likelihood of being injured if in an accident is 80% for a driver not wear-ing a seatbelt but it is 50% for all drivers.
Here, the sample space can be taken to be the set of drivers involved in an accident—these are the only drivers discussed.
Reworded: *The probability of a driver being injured (I) is .80 given that the driver is not wearing a seatbelt (B); P(I|B) = .80 whereas, for all drivers, the probability of being injured is .50: P(I) = .50.*

7.5   EXERCISES

▼ more advanced   ◆ challenging
T indicates exercises that should be solved using technology

In Exercises 1–10, compute the indicated quantity.

1. $P(B) = .5$, $P(A \cap B) = .2$. Find $P(A \mid B)$.

2. $P(B) = .6$, $P(A \cap B) = .3$. Find $P(A \mid B)$.

3. $P(A \mid B) = .2$, $P(B) = .4$. Find $P(A \cap B)$.

4. $P(A \mid B) = .1$, $P(B) = .5$. Find $P(A \cap B)$.

5. $P(A \mid B) = .4$, $P(A \cap B) = .3$. Find $P(B)$.

6. $P(A \mid B) = .4$, $P(A \cap B) = .1$. Find $P(B)$.

7. $P(A) = .5$, $P(B) = .4$. A and B are independent. Find $P(A \cap B)$.

8. $P(A) = .2$, $P(B) = .2$. A and B are independent. Find $P(A \cap B)$.

9. $P(A) = .5$, $P(B) = .4$. A and B are independent. Find $P(A \mid B)$.

10. $P(A) = .3$, $P(B) = .6$. A and B are independent. Find $P(B \mid A)$.

In Exercises 11–14, supply the missing quantities.

11.

Outcome

C $P(A \cap C) = \underline{\quad}$

A

D $P(A \cap D) = \underline{\quad}$

C $\underline{\quad} = \underline{\quad}$

B

D $\underline{\quad} = \underline{\quad}$

12.

Outcome

C $P(A \cap C) = \underline{\quad}$

A

D $\underline{\quad} = \underline{\quad}$

C $P(B \cap C) = \underline{\quad}$

B

D $\underline{\quad} = \underline{\quad}$

13.

14.

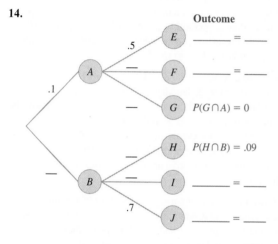

In Exercises 15–20, find the conditional probabilities of the indicated events when two fair dice (one red and one green) are rolled. HINT [See Example 1.]

15. The sum is 5, given that the green one is not a 1.

16. The sum is 6, given that the green one is either 4 or 3.

17. The red one is 5, given that the sum is 6.

18. The red one is 4, given that the green one is 4.

19. The sum is 5, given that the dice have opposite parity.

20. The sum is 6, given that the dice have opposite parity.

Exercises 21–26 require the use of counting techniques from the last chapter. A bag contains three red marbles, two green ones, one fluorescent pink one, two yellow ones, and two orange ones. Suzan grabs four at random. Find the probabilities of the indicated events.

21. She gets all the red ones, given that she gets the fluorescent pink one.

22. She gets all the red ones, given that she does not get the fluorescent pink one.

23. She gets none of the red ones, given that she gets the fluorescent pink one.

24. She gets one of each color other than fluorescent pink, given that she gets the fluorescent pink one.

25. She gets one of each color other than fluorescent pink, given that she gets at least one red one.

26. She gets at least two red ones, given that she gets at least one green one.

In Exercises 27–30, say whether the given pairs of events are independent, mutually exclusive, or neither.

27. *A*: Your new skateboard design is a success.

　　B: Your new skateboard design is a failure.

28. *A*: Your new skateboard design is a success.

　　B: There is life in the Andromeda galaxy.

29. *A*: Your new skateboard design is a success.

　　B: Your competitor's new skateboard design is a failure.

30. *A*: Your first coin flip results in heads.

　　B: Your second coin flip results in heads.

In Exercises 31–36, two dice (one red and one green) are rolled, and the numbers that face up are observed. Test the given pairs of events for independence. HINT [See Quick Example on Testing for Independence, page 503.]

31. *A*: The red die is 1, 2, or 3; *B*: The green die is even.

32. *A*: The red die is 1; *B*: The sum is even.

33. *A*: Exactly one die is 1; *B*: The sum is even.

34. *A*: Neither die is 1 or 6; *B*: The sum is even.

35. *A*: Neither die is 1; *B*: Exactly one die is 2.

36. *A*: Both dice are 1; *B*: Neither die is 2.

37. If a coin is tossed 11 times, find the probability of the sequence H, T, T, H, H, H, T, H, H, T, T. HINT [See Example 5.]

38. If a die is rolled four times, find the probability of the sequence 4, 3, 2, 1. HINT [See Example 5.]

In Exercises 39–44, fill in the blanks using the named events. HINT [See Example 2 and also the FAQ on page 506.]

39. 10% of all Anchovians detest anchovies (*D*), whereas 30% of all married Anchovians (*M*) detest them. $P(\_\_\_) = \_\_\_$; $P(\_\_\_ | \_\_\_) = \_\_\_$

40. 95% of all music composers can read music (*M*), whereas 99% of all classical music composers (*C*) can read music. $P(\_\_\_) = \_\_\_$; $P(\_\_\_ | \_\_\_) = \_\_\_$

41. 30% of all lawyers who lost clients (*L*) were antitrust lawyers (*A*), whereas 10% of all antitrust lawyers lost clients. $P(\_\_\_ | \_\_\_) = \_\_\_$; $P(\_\_\_ | \_\_\_) = \_\_\_$

42. 2% of all items bought on my auction site (*B*) were works of art (*A*), whereas only 1% of all works of art on the site were bought. $P(\_\_\_ | \_\_\_) = \_\_\_$; $P(\_\_\_ | \_\_\_) = \_\_\_$

43. 55% of those who go out in the midday sun (M) are Englishmen (E) whereas only 5% of those who do not go out in the midday sun are Englishmen. $P(\_\_\mid\_\_) = \_\_$; $P(\_\_\mid\_\_) = \_\_$

44. 80% of those who have a Mac now (M) will purchase a Mac next time (X) whereas 20% of those who do not have a Mac now will purchase a Mac next time. $P(\_\_\mid\_\_) = \_\_$; $P(\_\_\mid\_\_) = \_\_$

APPLICATIONS

45. *Personal Bankruptcy* In 2004, the probability that a person in the United States would declare personal bankruptcy was .006. The probability that a person in the United States would declare personal bankruptcy and had recently experienced a "big three" event (loss of job, medical problem, or divorce or separation) was .005.[51] What was the probability that a person had recently experienced one of the "big three" events, given that she had declared personal bankruptcy? (Round your answer to one decimal place.)

46. *Personal Bankruptcy* In 2004, the probability that a person in the United States would declare personal bankruptcy was .006. The probability that a person in the United States would declare personal bankruptcy and had recently overspent credit cards was .0004.[52] What was the probability that a person had recently overspent credit cards given that he had declared personal bankruptcy?

47. *Existing Home Sales* During the year ending February 28, 2011, there were approximately 4.9 million sales of existing homes in the United States, of which 1.2 million were sold in the West. In February 2011 there were a total of 293,000 existing homes sold in the United States, of which 71,000 were sold in the West.[53]

a. Find the probability that a home sale in the year ending February 28, 2011, took place in the West, given that the home was sold in February 2011.

b. Find the probability that a home sale in the year ending February 28, 2011, took place in February 2011, given that it took place in the West.

48. *Existing Home Sales* Refer to the data given in the preceding exercise.

a. Find the probability that a home sale in the year ending February 28, 2011, took place outside the West, given that the home was sold in February 2011.

b. Find the probability that a home sale in the year ending February 28, 2011, took place in February 2011, given that it took place outside the West.

49. *Social Security* According to a *New York Times*/CBS poll released in March 2005, 79% agreed that it should be the government's responsibility to provide a decent standard of living for the elderly, and 43% agreed that it would be a good idea to invest part of their Social Security taxes on their own.[54] If agreement with one of these propositions is independent of agreement with the other, what is the probability that a person agreed with both propositions? (Round your answer to two decimal places.) HINT [See Quick Examples on Independence on page 503.]

50. *Social Security* According to *The New York Times*/CBS poll of March 2005 referred to in Exercise 43, 49% agreed that Social Security taxes should be raised if necessary to keep the system afloat, and 43% agreed that it would be a good idea to invest part of their Social Security taxes on their own.[55] If agreement with one of these propositions is independent of agreement with the other, what is the probability that a person agreed with both propositions? (Round your answer to two decimal places.) HINT [See Quick Examples on Independence on page 503.]

51. *Marketing* A market survey shows that 40% of the population used Brand X laundry detergent last year, 5% of the population gave up doing its laundry last year, and 4% of the population used Brand X and then gave up doing laundry last year. Are the events of using Brand X and giving up doing laundry independent? Is a user of Brand X detergent more or less likely to give up doing laundry than a randomly chosen person?

52. *Marketing* A market survey shows that 60% of the population used Brand Z computers last year, 5% of the population quit their jobs last year, and 3% of the population used Brand Z computers and then quit their jobs. Are the events of using Brand Z computers and quitting your job independent? Is a user of Brand Z computers more or less likely to quit a job than a randomly chosen person?

53. *Road Safety* In 1999, the probability that a randomly selected vehicle would be involved in a deadly tire-related accident was approximately 3×10^{-6}, whereas the probability that a tire-related accident would prove deadly was .02.[56] What was the probability that a vehicle would be involved in a tire-related accident?

54. *Road Safety* In 1998, the probability that a randomly selected vehicle would be involved in a deadly tire-related accident was approximately 2.8×10^{-6}, while the probability that a tire-related accident would prove deadly

---

[51] Probabilities are approximate. Source: *New York Times*, March 13, 2005, p, WK3.

[52] Ibid. The .0004 figure is an estimate by the authors.

[53] Source: National Association of Realtors (www.realtor.org).

[54] Source: *New York Times*, March 3, 2005, p. A20.

[55] *Ibid.*

[56] The original data reported three tire-related deaths per million vehicles. Source: *New York Times* analysis of National Traffic Safety Administration crash data/Polk Company vehicle registration data/ *New York Times*, Nov. 22, 2000, p. C5.

was .016.[57] What was the probability that a vehicle would be involved in a tire-related accident?

Publishing Exercises 55–62 are based on the following table, which shows the results of a survey of 100 authors by a publishing company.

	New Authors	Established Authors	Total
Successful	5	25	30
Unsuccessful	15	55	70
Total	20	80	100

Compute the following conditional probabilities:

55. An author is established, given that she is successful.

56. An author is successful, given that he is established.

57. An author is unsuccessful, given that he is a new author.

58. An author is a new author, given that she is unsuccessful.

59. An author is unsuccessful, given that she is established.

60. An author is established, given that he is unsuccessful.

61. An unsuccessful author is established.

62. An established author is successful.

In Exercises 63–68, draw an appropriate tree diagram and use the multiplication principle to calculate the probabilities of all the outcomes. HINT [See Example 3.]

63. *Sales* Each day, there is a 40% chance that you will sell an automobile. You know that 30% of all the automobiles you sell are two-door models, and the rest are four-door models.

64. *Product Reliability* You purchase Brand X memory chips one quarter of the time and Brand Y memory chips the rest of the time. Brand X memory chips have a 1% failure rate, while Brand Y memory chips have a 3% failure rate.

65. *Car Rentals* Your auto rental company rents out 30 small cars, 24 luxury sedans, and 46 slightly damaged "budget" vehicles. The small cars break down 14% of the time, the luxury sedans break down 8% of the time, and the "budget" cars break down 40% of the time.

66. *Travel* It appears that there is only a one in five chance that you will be able to take your spring vacation to the Greek Islands. If you are lucky enough to go, you will visit either Corfu (20% chance) or Rhodes. On Rhodes, there is a 20% chance of meeting a tall dark stranger, while on Corfu, there is no such chance.

67. *Weather Prediction* There is a 50% chance of rain today and a 50% chance of rain tomorrow. Assuming that the event that it rains today is independent of the event that it rains tomorrow, draw a tree diagram showing the probabilities of all outcomes. What is the probability that there will be no rain today or tomorrow?

68. *Weather Prediction* There is a 20% chance of snow today and a 20% chance of snow tomorrow. Assuming that the event that it snows today is independent of the event that it snows tomorrow, draw a tree diagram showing the probabilities of all outcomes. What is the probability that it will snow by the end of tomorrow?

Education and Employment Exercises 69–78 are based on the following table, which shows U.S. employment figures for August 2011, broken down by educational attainment.[58] All numbers are in millions, and represent civilians aged 25 years and over. Those classed as "not in labor force" were not employed nor actively seeking employment. Round all answers to two decimal places.

	Employed	Unemployed	Not in Labor Force	Total
Less Than High School Diploma	9.9	1.6	17.7	29.2
High School Diploma Only	34.1	3.5	24.4	62.0
Some College or Associate's Degree	34.4	3.0	15.6	53.0
Bachelor's Degree or Higher	46.4	2.0	12.2	60.6
Total	124.8	10.1	69.9	204.8

69. Find the probability that a person was employed, given that the person had a bachelor's degree or higher.

70. Find the probability that a person was employed, given that the person had attained less than a high school diploma.

71. Find the probability that a person had a bachelor's degree or higher, given that the person was employed.

72. Find the probability that a person had attained less than a high school diploma, given that the person was employed.

73. ▼ Find the probability that a person who had not completed a bachelor's degree or higher was not in the labor force.

74. ▼ Find the probability that a person who had completed at least a high school diploma was not in the labor force.

75. ▼ Find the probability that a person who had completed a bachelor's degree or higher and was in the labor force was employed.

---

[57] The original data reported 2.8 tire-related deaths per million vehicles. Source: *Ibid.*

[58] Source: Bureau of Labor Statistics (www.bls.gov).

76. ▼ Find the probability that a person who had completed less than a high school diploma and was in the labor force was employed.

77. ▼ Your friend claims that an unemployed person is more likely to have a high school diploma only than an employed person. Respond to this claim by citing actual probabilities.

78. ▼ Your friend claims that a person not in the labor force is more likely to have less than a high school diploma than an employed person. Respond to this claim by citing actual probabilities.

79. ▼ *Airbag Safety* According to a study conducted by the Harvard School of Public Health, a child seated in the front seat who was wearing a seatbelt was 31% more likely to be killed in an accident if the car had an air bag that deployed than if it did not.[59] Let the sample space S be the set of all accidents involving a child seated in the front seat wearing a seatbelt. Let K be the event that the child was killed and let D be the event that the airbag deployed. Fill in the missing terms and quantities: $P(\_\_ \mid \_\_) = \_\_ \times P(\_\_ \mid \_\_)$.
HINT [When we say "A is 31% more likely than B" we mean that the probability of A is 1.31 times the probability of B.]

80. ▼ *Airbag Safety* According to the study cited in Exercise 73, a child seated in the front seat not wearing a seatbelt was 84% more likely to be killed in an accident if the car had an air bag that deployed than if it did not.[60] Let the sample space S be the set of all accidents involving a child seated in the front seat not wearing a seatbelt. Fill in the missing terms and quantities: $P(\_\_ \mid \_\_) = \_\_ \times P(\_\_ \mid \_\_)$.
HINT [When we say "A is 84% more likely than B" we mean that the probability of A is 1.84 times the probability of B.]

81. ▼ *Productivity* A company wishes to enhance productivity by running a one-week training course for its employees. Let T be the event that an employee participated in the course, and let I be the event that an employee's productivity improved the week after the course was run.

  a. Assuming that the course has a positive effect on productivity, how are $P(I \mid T)$ and $P(I)$ related?
  b. If T and I are independent, what can one conclude about the training course?

82. ▼ *Productivity* Consider the events T and I in the preceding exercise.

  a. Assuming that everyone who improved took the course but that not everyone took the course, how are $P(T \mid I)$ and $P(T)$ related?
  b. If half the employees who improved took the course and half the employees took the course, are T and I independent?

83. ▼ *Internet Use in 2000* The following pie chart shows the percentage of the population that used the Internet in 2000, broken down further by family income, and based on a survey taken in August 2000.[61]

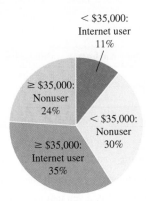

  a. Determine the probability that a randomly chosen person was an Internet user, given that his or her family income was at least $35,000.

  b. Based on the data, was a person more likely to be an Internet user if his or her family income was less than $35,000 or $35,000 or more? (Support your answer by citing the relevant conditional probabilities.)

84. ▼ *Internet Use in 2001* Repeat Exercise 83 using the following pie chart, which shows the results of a similar survey taken in September 2001.[62]

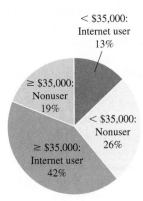

---

[59] The study was conducted by Dr. Segul-Gomez at the Harvard School of Public Health. Source: *New York Times*, December 1, 2000, p. F1.
[60] *Ibid.*

[61] Source: *Falling Through the Net: Toward Digital Inclusion, A Report on Americans' Access to Technology Tools*, U.S. Department of Commerce, October, 2000. Available at www.ntia.doc.gov/ntiahome/fttn00/contents00.html.

[62] Source: *A Nation Online: How Americans Are Expanding Their Use of the Internet*, U.S. Department of Commerce, February, 2002. Available at www.ntia.doc.gov/ntiahome/dn/index.html.

Auto Theft *Exercises 85–90 are based on the following table, which shows the probability that an owner of the given model would report his or her vehicle stolen in a one-year period.*[63]

Brand	Jeep Wrangler	Suzuki Sidekick (two-door)	Toyota Land Cruiser	Geo Tracker (two-door)	Acura Integra (two-door)
Probability	.0170	.0154	.0143	.0142	.0123
Brand	Mitsubishi Montero	Acura Integra (four-door)	BMW 3-series (two-door)	Lexus GS300	Honda Accord (two-door)
Probability	.0108	.0103	.0077	.0074	.0070

In an experiment in which a vehicle is selected, consider the following events:

   R: The vehicle was reported stolen.
   J: The vehicle was a Jeep Wrangler.
   A2: The vehicle was an Acura Integra (two-door).
   A4: The vehicle was an Acura Integra (four-door).
   A: The vehicle was an Acura Integra (either two-door or four-door).

85. ▼ Fill in the blanks: $P(\_\_\_ \mid \_\_\_) = .0170$.

86. ▼ Fill in the blanks: $P(\_\_\_ \mid A4) = \_\_\_$.

87. ▼ Which of the following is true?

   (A) There is a 1.43% chance that a vehicle reported stolen was a Toyota Land Cruiser.
   (B) Of all the vehicles reported stolen, 1.43% of them were Toyota Land Cruisers.
   (C) Given that a vehicle was reported stolen, there is a .0143 probability that it was a Toyota Land Cruiser.
   (D) Given that a vehicle was a Toyota Land Cruiser, there was a 1.43% chance that it was reported stolen.

88. ▼ Which of the following is true?

   (A) $P(R \mid A) = .0123 + .0103 = .0226$
   (B) $P(R' \mid A2) = 1 - .0123 = .9877$
   (C) $P(A2 \mid A) = .0123/(.0123 + .0103) \approx .544$
   (D) $P(R \mid A2') = 1 - .0123 = .9877$

89. ▼ It is now January, and I own a BMW 3-series and a Lexus GS300. Because I house my vehicles in different places, the event that one of my vehicles gets stolen does not depend on the event that the other gets stolen. Compute each probability to six decimal places.

   a. Both my vehicles will get stolen this year.
   b. At least one of my vehicles will get stolen this year.

90. ▼ It is now December, and I own a Mitsubishi Montero and a Jeep Wrangler. Because I house my vehicles in different places, the event that one of my vehicles gets stolen does not depend on the event that the other gets stolen. I have just returned from a one-year trip to the Swiss Alps.

   a. What is the probability that my Montero, but not my Wrangler, has been stolen?

   b. Which is more likely: the event that my Montero was stolen or the event that *only* my Montero was stolen?

91. ▼ *Drug Tests* If 90% of the athletes who test positive for steroids in fact use them, and 10% of all athletes use steroids and test positive, what percentage of athletes test positive?

92. ▼ *Fitness Tests* If 80% of candidates for the soccer team pass the fitness test, and only 20% of all athletes are soccer team candidates who pass the test, what percentage of the athletes are candidates for the soccer team?

93. ▼ *Food Safety* According to a University of Maryland study of 200 samples of ground meats,[64] the probability that a sample was contaminated by *salmonella* was .20. The probability that a *salmonella*-contaminated sample was contaminated by a strain resistant to at least three antibiotics was .53. What was the probability that a ground meat sample was contaminated by a strain of *salmonella* resistant to at least three antibiotics?

94. ▼ *Food Safety* According to the study mentioned in Exercise 87,[65] the probability that a ground meat sample was contaminated by *salmonella* was .20. The probability that a *salmonella*-contaminated sample was contaminated by a strain resistant to at least one antibiotic was .84. What was the probability that a ground meat sample was contaminated by a strain of *salmonella* resistant to at least one antibiotic?

95. ◆ *Food Safety* According to a University of Maryland study of 200 samples of ground meats,[66] the probability that one of the samples was contaminated by *salmonella* was .20. The probability that a *salmonella*-contaminated sample was contaminated by a strain resistant to at least one antibiotic was .84, and the probability that a *salmonella*-contaminated sample was contaminated by a strain resistant to at least three antibiotics was .53. Find the probability that a ground meat sample that was contaminated by an antibiotic-resistant strain was contaminated by a strain resistant to at least three antibiotics.

96. ◆ *Food Safety* According to a University of Maryland study of 200 samples of ground meats,[67] the probability that

---

[63] Data are for insured vehicles, for 1995 to 1997 models except Wrangler, which is for 1997 models only. Source: Highway Loss Data Institute/*New York Times,* March 28, 1999, p. WK3.

[64] As cited in the *New York Times*, October 16, 2001, p. A12.
[65] *Ibid.*
[66] *Ibid.*
[67] *Ibid.*

a ground meat sample was contaminated by a strain of *salmonella* resistant to at least three antibiotics was .11. The probability that someone infected with any strain of *salmonella* will become seriously ill is .10. What is the probability that someone eating a randomly chosen ground meat sample will not become seriously ill with a strain of *salmonella* resistant to at least three antibiotics?

COMMUNICATION AND REASONING EXERCISES

97. Name three events, each independent of the others, when a fair coin is tossed four times.

98. Name three pairs of independent events when a pair of distinguishable and fair dice is rolled and the numbers that face up are observed.

99. You wish to ascertain the probability of an event E, but you happen to know that the event F has occurred. Is the probability you are seeking $P(E)$ or $P(E|F)$? Give the reason for your answer.

100. Your television advertising campaign seems to have been very persuasive: 10,000 people who saw the ad purchased your product, while only 2,000 people purchased the product without seeing the ad. Explain how additional data could show that your ad campaign was, in fact, unpersuasive.

101. You are having trouble persuading your friend Iliana that conditional probability is different from unconditional probability. She just said: "Look here, Saul, the probability of throwing a double-six is 1/36, and that's that! That probability is not affected by anything, including the 'given' that the sum is larger than 7." How do you persuade her otherwise?

102. Your other friend Giuseppe is spreading rumors that the conditional probability $P(E|F)$ is always bigger than $P(E)$. Is he right? (If he is, explain why; if not, give an example to prove him wrong.)

103. ▼ If $A \subseteq B$ and $P(B) \neq 0$, why is $P(A\,|\,B) = \dfrac{P(A)}{P(B)}$?

104. ▼ If $B \subseteq A$ and $P(B) \neq 0$, why is $P(A\,|\,B) = 1$?

105. ▼ Your best friend thinks that it is impossible for two mutually exclusive events with nonzero probabilities to be independent. Establish whether or not he is correct.

106. ▼ Another of your friends thinks that two mutually exclusive events with nonzero probabilities can never be dependent. Establish whether or not she is correct.

107. ◆ Show that if A and B are independent, then so are A' and B' (assuming none of these events has zero probability). HINT [$A' \cap B'$ is the complement of $A \cup B$.]

108. ◆ Show that if A and B are independent, then so are A and B' (assuming none of these events has zero probability). HINT [$P(B'\,|\,A) + P(B\,|\,A) = 1$.]

7.6 Bayes' Theorem and Applications

Should schools test their athletes for drug use? A problem with drug testing is that there are always false positive results, so one can never be certain that an athlete who tests positive is in fact using drugs. Here is a typical scenario.

EXAMPLE 1 Steroids Testing

Gamma Chemicals advertises its anabolic steroid detection test as being 95% effective at detecting steroid use, meaning that it will show a positive result on 95% of all anabolic steroid users. It also states that its test has a false positive rate of 6%. This means that the probability of a nonuser testing positive is .06. Estimating that about 10% of its athletes are using anabolic steroids, Enormous State University (ESU) begins testing its football players. The quarterback, Hugo V. Huge, tests positive and is promptly dropped from the team. Hugo claims that he is not using anabolic steroids. How confident can we be that he is not telling the truth?

Solution There are two events of interest here: the event T that a person tests positive, and the event A that the person tested uses anabolic steroids. Here are the probabilities we are given:

$$P(T\,|\,A) = .95$$
$$P(T\,|\,A') = .06$$
$$P(A) = .10$$

We are asked to find $P(A \mid T)$, the probability that someone who tests positive is using anabolic steroids. We can use a tree diagram to calculate $P(A \mid T)$. The trick to setting up the tree diagram is to use as the first branching the events with *unconditional* probabilities we know. Because the only unconditional probability we are given is $P(A)$, we use A and A' as our first branching (Figure 13).

Figure 13

For the second branching, we use the outcomes of the drug test: positive (T) or negative (T'). The probabilities on these branches are conditional probabilities because they depend on whether or not an athlete uses steroids. (See Figure 14.) (We fill in the probabilities that are not supplied by remembering that the sum of the probabilities on the branches leaving any node must be 1.)

Figure 14

We can now calculate the probability we are asked to find:

$$P(A \mid T) = \frac{P(A \cap T)}{P(T)} = \frac{P(\text{Uses anabolic steroids and tests positive})}{P(\text{Tests positive})}$$

$$= \frac{P(\text{Using } A \text{ and } T \text{ branches})}{\text{Sum of } P(\text{Using branches ending in } T)}.$$

From the tree diagram, we see that $P(A \cap T) = .095$. To calculate $P(T)$, the probability of testing positive, notice that there are two outcomes on the tree diagram that reflect a positive test result. The probabilities of these events are .095 and .054. Because these two events are mutually exclusive (an athlete either uses steroids or does not, but not both), the probability of a test being positive (ignoring whether or not steroids are used) is the sum of these probabilities, .149. Thus,

$$P(A \mid T) = \frac{.095}{.095 + .054} = \frac{.095}{.149} \approx .64.$$

Thus there is a 64% chance that a randomly selected athlete who tests positive, like Hugo, is using steroids. In other words, we can be 64% confident that Hugo is lying.

➡ **Before we go on...** Note that the correct answer in Example 1 is 64%, *not* the 94% we might suspect from the test's false positive rating. In fact, we can't answer the question asked without knowing the percentage of athletes who actually use steroids. For instance, if *no* athletes at all use steroids, then Hugo must be telling the truth, and so the test result has no significance whatsoever. On the other hand, if *all* athletes use steroids, then Hugo is definitely lying, regardless of the outcome of the test.

✳ *Drug Testing in the Workplace,*
ACLU Briefing Paper, 1996.

False positive rates are determined by testing a large number of samples known not to contain drugs and computing estimated probabilities. False negative rates are computed similarly by testing samples known to contain drugs. However, the accuracy of the tests depends also on the skill of those administering them. False positives were a significant problem when drug testing started to become common, with estimates of false positive rates for common immunoassay tests ranging from 10% to 30% on the high end,✳ but the accuracy has improved since then. Because of the possibility of false positive results, positive immunoassay tests need to be confirmed by the more expensive and much more reliable gas chromatograph/mass spectrometry (GC/MS) test. See also the National Collegiate Athletic Association's (NCAA) Drug-Testing Program Handbook, available at www.ncaa.org. (The section on Institutional Drug Testing addresses the problem of false positives.) ■

Bayes' Theorem

The calculation we used to answer the question in Example 1 can be recast as a formula known as **Bayes' theorem**. Figure 15 shows a general form of the tree we used in Example 1.

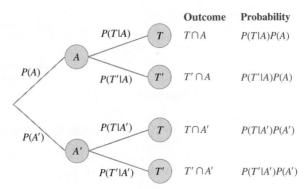

Figure 15

We first calculated

$$P(A \mid T) = \frac{P(A \cap T)}{P(T)}$$

as follows. We first calculated the numerator $P(A \cap T)$ using the multiplication principle:

$$P(A \cap T) = P(T \mid A)P(A).$$

We then calculated the denominator $P(T)$ by using the addition principle for mutually exclusive events together with the multiplication principle:

$$P(T) = P(A \cap T) + P(A' \cap T)$$
$$= P(T \mid A)P(A) + P(T \mid A')P(A').$$

Substituting gives

$$P(A \mid T) = \frac{P(T \mid A)P(A)}{P(T \mid A)P(A) + P(T \mid A')P(A')}.$$

This is the short form of Bayes' theorem.

Bayes' Theorem (Short Form)

If A and T are events, then

Bayes' Formula

$$P(A \mid T) = \frac{P(T \mid A)P(A)}{P(T \mid A)P(A) + P(T \mid A')P(A')}.$$

Using a Tree

$$P(A \mid T) = \frac{P(\text{Using } A \text{ and } T \text{ branches})}{\text{Sum of } P(\text{Using branches ending in } T)}$$

Quick Example

Let us calculate the probability that an athlete from Example 1 who tests positive is actually using steroids if only 5% of ESU athletes are using steroids. Thus,

$$P(T \mid A) = .95$$
$$P(T \mid A') = .06$$
$$P(A) = .05$$
$$P(A') = .95$$

and so

$$P(A \mid T) = \frac{P(T \mid A)P(A)}{P(T \mid A)P(A) + P(T \mid A')P(A')}$$
$$= \frac{(.95)(.05)}{(.95)(.05) + (.06)(.95)} \approx .45.$$

In other words, it is actually more likely that such an athlete does *not* use steroids than he does.[*]

✳ Without knowing the results of the test, we would have said that there was a probability of $P(A) = 0.05$ that the athlete is using steroids. The positive test result raises the probability to $P(A \mid T) = 0.45$, but the test gives too many false positives for us to be any more than 45% certain that the athlete is actually using steroids.

Remembering the Formula

Although the formula looks complicated at first sight, it is not hard to remember if you notice the pattern. Or, you could re-derive it yourself by thinking of the tree diagram.

The next example illustrates that we can use either a tree diagram or the Bayes' theorem formula.

EXAMPLE 2 Lie Detectors

† The reason for this is that many people show physical signs of distress when asked accusatory questions. Many people are nervous around police officers even if they have done nothing wrong.

The Sherlock Lie Detector Company manufactures the latest in lie detectors, and the Count-Your-Pennies (CYP) store chain is eager to use them to screen its employees for theft. Sherlock's advertising claims that the test misses a lie only once in every 100 instances. On the other hand, an analysis by a consumer group reveals 20% of people who are telling the truth fail the test anyway.[†] The local police department estimates that 1 out of every 200 employees has engaged in theft. When the CYP store first screened its employees, the test indicated Mrs. Prudence V. Good was lying when she claimed that she had never stolen from CYP. What is the probability that she was lying and had in fact stolen from the store?

Solution We are asked for the probability that Mrs. Good was lying, and in the preceding sentence we are told that the lie detector test showed her to be lying. So, we are looking for a conditional probability: the probability that she is lying, given that the lie detector test is positive. Now we can start to give names to the events:

> L: A subject is lying.
>
> T: The test is positive (indicated that the subject was lying).

We are looking for $P(L \mid T)$. We know that 1 out of every 200 employees engages in theft; let us assume that no employee admits to theft while taking a lie detector test, so the probability $P(L)$ that a test subject is lying is $1/200$. We also know the false negative and false positive rates $P(T' \mid L)$ and $P(T \mid L')$.

Using a Tree Diagram

Figure 16 shows the tree diagram.

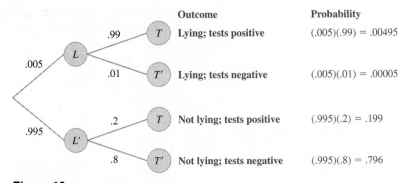

		Outcome	Probability
.99	T	Lying; tests positive	$(.005)(.99) = .00495$
.01	T'	Lying; tests negative	$(.005)(.01) = .00005$
.2	T	Not lying; tests positive	$(.995)(.2) = .199$
.8	T'	Not lying; tests negative	$(.995)(.8) = .796$

Figure 16

We see that

$$P(L \mid T) = \frac{P(\text{Using } L \text{ and } T \text{ branches})}{\text{Sum of } P(\text{Using branches ending in } T)}$$

$$= \frac{.00495}{.00495 + .199} \approx .024.$$

This means that there was only a 2.4% chance that poor Mrs. Good was lying and had stolen from the store!

Using Bayes' Theorem

We have

$$P(L) = .005$$
$$P(T' \mid L) = .01, \text{ from which we obtain}$$
$$P(T \mid L) = .99$$
$$P(T \mid L') = .2$$

and so

$$P(L \mid T) = \frac{P(T \mid L)P(L)}{P(T \mid L)P(L) + P(T \mid L')P(L')} = \frac{(.99)(.005)}{(.99)(.005) + (.2)(.995)} \approx .024.$$

A and A′ form a partition of S.

Figure 17

A_1, A_2, and A_3 form a partition of S.

Figure 18

Expanded Form of Bayes' Theorem

We have seen the "short form" of Bayes' theorem. What is the "long form?" To motivate an expanded form of Bayes' theorem, look again at the formula we've been using:

$$P(A \mid T) = \frac{P(T \mid A)P(A)}{P(T \mid A)P(A) + P(T \mid A')P(A')}.$$

The events A and A' form a **partition** of the sample space S; that is, their union is the whole of S and their intersection is empty (Figure 17).

The expanded form of Bayes' theorem applies to a partition of S into three or more events, as shown in Figure 18.

By saying that the events A_1, A_2, and A_3 form a partition of S, we mean that their union is the whole of S and the intersection of any two of them is empty, as in the figure. When we have a partition into three events as shown, the formula gives us $P(A_1 \mid T)$ in terms of $P(T \mid A_1)$, $P(T \mid A_2)$, $P(T \mid A_3)$, $P(A_1)$, $P(A_2)$, and $P(A_3)$.

Bayes' Theorem (Expanded Form)

If the events A_1, A_2, and A_3 form a partition of the sample space S, then

$$P(A_1 \mid T) = \frac{P(T \mid A_1)P(A_1)}{P(T \mid A_1)P(A_1) + P(T \mid A_2)P(A_2) + P(T \mid A_3)P(A_3)}$$

As for why this is true, and what happens when we have a partition into *four or more* events, we will wait for the exercises. In practice, as was the case with a partition into two events, we can often compute $P(A_1 \mid T)$ by constructing a tree diagram.

EXAMPLE 3 School and Work

A survey[68] conducted by the Bureau of Labor Statistics found that approximately 27% of the high school graduating class of 2010 went on to a 2-year college, 41% went on to a 4-year college, and the remaining 32% did not go on to college. Of those who went on to a 2-year college, 52% worked at the same time, 32% of those going on to a 4-year college worked, and 78% of those who did not go on to college worked. What percentage of those working had not gone on to college?

Solution We can interpret these percentages as probabilities if we consider the experiment of choosing a member of the high school graduating class of 2010 at random. The events we are interested in are these:

R_1: A graduate went on to a 2-year college

R_2: A graduate went on to a 4-year college

R_3: A graduate did not go to college

A: A graduate went on to work.

---

[68] Source: "College Enrollment and Work Activity of High School Graduates," U.S. Bureau of Labor Statistics (www.bls.gov/news.release/hsgec.htm).

The three events R_1, R_2, and R_3 partition the sample space of all graduates into three events. We are given the following probabilities:

$$P(R_1) = .27 \qquad P(R_2) = .41 \qquad P(R_3) = .32$$
$$P(A \mid R_1) = .52 \quad P(A \mid R_2) = .32 \quad P(A \mid R_3) = .78.$$

We are asked to find the probability that a graduate who went on to work did not go to college, so we are looking for $P(R_3 \mid A)$. Bayes' formula for these events is

$$P(R_3 \mid A) = \frac{P(A \mid R_3)P(R_3)}{P(A \mid R_1)P(R_1) + P(A \mid R_2)P(R_2) + P(A \mid R_3)P(R_3)}$$

$$= \frac{(.78)(.32)}{(.52)(.27) + (.32)(.41) + (.78)(.32)} \approx .48.$$

Thus we conclude that 48% of all those working had not gone on to college.

➡ **Before we go on...** We could also solve Example 3 using a tree diagram. As before, the first branching corresponds to the events with unconditional probabilities that we know: R_1, R_2, and R_3. You should complete the tree and check that you obtain the same result as above. ∎

7.6 EXERCISES

▼ more advanced   ◆ challenging

🖥 indicates exercises that should be solved using technology

In Exercises 1–8, use Bayes' theorem or a tree diagram to calculate the indicated probability. Round all answers to four decimal places. HINT [See Quick Example on page 515 and Example 3.]

1. $P(A \mid B) = .8$, $P(B) = .2$, $P(A \mid B') = .3$. Find $P(B \mid A)$.

2. $P(A \mid B) = .6$, $P(B) = .3$, $P(A \mid B') = .5$. Find $P(B \mid A)$.

3. $P(X \mid Y) = .8$, $P(Y') = .3$, $P(X \mid Y') = .5$. Find $P(Y \mid X)$.

4. $P(X \mid Y) = .6$, $P(Y') = .4$, $P(X \mid Y') = .3$. Find $P(Y \mid X)$.

5. Y_1, Y_2, Y_3 form a partition of S. $P(X \mid Y_1) = .4$, $P(X \mid Y_2) = .5$, $P(X \mid Y_3) = .6$, $P(Y_1) = .8$, $P(Y_2) = .1$. Find $P(Y_1 \mid X)$.

6. Y_1, Y_2, Y_3 form a partition of S. $P(X \mid Y_1) = .2$, $P(X \mid Y_2) = .3$, $P(X \mid Y_3) = .6$, $P(Y_1) = .3$, $P(Y_2) = .4$. Find $P(Y_1 \mid X)$.

7. Y_1, Y_2, Y_3 form a partition of S. $P(X \mid Y_1) = .4$, $P(X \mid Y_2) = .5$, $P(X \mid Y_3) = .6$, $P(Y_1) = .8$, $P(Y_2) = .1$. Find $P(Y_2 \mid X)$.

8. Y_1, Y_2, Y_3 form a partition of S. $P(X \mid Y_1) = .2$, $P(X \mid Y_2) = .3$, $P(X \mid Y_3) = .6$, $P(Y_1) = .3$, $P(Y_2) = .4$. Find $P(Y_2 \mid X)$.

APPLICATIONS

9. *Music Downloading* According to a study on the effect of music downloading on spending on music, 11% of all Internet users had decreased their spending on music.[69] We estimate that 40% of all music fans used the Internet at the time of the study.[70] If 20% of non–Internet users had decreased their spending on music, what percentage of those who had decreased their spending on music were Internet users? HINT [See Examples 1 and 2.]

10. *Music Downloading* According to the study cited in the preceding exercise, 36% of experienced file-sharers with broadband access had decreased their spending on music. Let us estimate that 3% of all music fans were experienced file-sharers with broadband access at the time of the study.[71] If 20% of the other music fans had decreased their spending on music, what percentage of those who had decreased their spending on music were experienced file-sharers with broadband access? HINT [See Examples 1 and 2.]

[69] Regardless of whether they used the Internet to download music. Source: *New York Times*, May 6, 2002, p. C6.

[70] According to the U.S. Department of Commerce, 51% of all U.S. households had computers in 2001.

[71] Around 15% of all online households had broadband access in 2001 according to a *New York Times* article (Dec. 24, 2001, p. C1).

11. **Weather** It snows in Greenland an average of once every 25 days, and when it does, glaciers have a 20% chance of growing. When it does not snow in Greenland, glaciers have only a 4% chance of growing. What is the probability that it is snowing in Greenland when glaciers are growing?

12. **Weather** It rains in Spain an average of once every 10 days, and when it does, hurricanes have a 2% chance of happening in Hartford. When it does not rain in Spain, hurricanes have a 1% chance of happening in Hartford. What is the probability that it rains in Spain when hurricanes happen in Hartford?

13. **University Admissions** In Fall 2011, 34% of applicants with a Math SAT of 700 or more were admitted by the University of California, Los Angeles (UCLA), while 10% with a Math SAT of less than 700 were admitted. Further, 63% of all applicants had a Math SAT score of 700 or more.[72] What percentage of admitted applicants had an SAT of 700 or more? (Round your answer to the nearest percentage point.)

14. **University Admissions** In Fall 2011, 44% of rejected applicants to UCLA had a Math SAT of less than 700, while 15% of accepted applicants to UCLA had a Math SAT of 700. Further, 75% of all applicants were rejected.[73] What percentage of applicants with a Math SAT of less than 700 were rejected? (Round your answer to the nearest percentage point.)

15. **Side-Impact Hazard** In 2004, 45.4% of all light vehicles were cars, and the rest were pickups or SUVs. The probability that a severe side-impact crash would prove deadly to a driver depended on the type of vehicle he or she was driving at the time, as shown in the table:[74]

Car	1.0
Light Truck or SUV	.3

What is the probability that the victim of a deadly side-impact accident was driving a car?

16. **Side-Impact Hazard** In 2004, 27.3% of all light vehicles were light trucks, and the rest were cars or SUVs. The probability that a severe side-impact crash would prove deadly to a driver depended on the type of vehicle he or she was driving at the time, as shown in the table:[75]

Light Truck	.2
Car or SUV	.7

What is the probability that the victim of a deadly side-impact accident was driving a car or SUV?

17. **Athletic Fitness Tests** Any athlete who fails the Enormous State University's women's soccer fitness test is automatically dropped from the team. Last year, Mona Header failed the test, but claimed that this was due to the early hour. (The fitness test is traditionally given at 5 am on a Sunday morning.) In fact, a study by the ESU Physical Education Department suggested that 50% of athletes fit enough to play on the team would fail the soccer test, although no unfit athlete could possibly pass the test. It also estimated that 45% of the athletes who take the test are fit enough to play soccer. Assuming these estimates are correct, what is the probability that Mona was justifiably dropped?

18. **Academic Testing** Professor Frank Nabarro insists that all senior physics majors take his notorious physics aptitude test. The test is so tough that anyone *not* going on to a career in physics has no hope of passing, whereas 60% of the seniors who do go on to a career in physics still fail the test. Further, 75% of all senior physics majors in fact go on to a career in physics. Assuming that you fail the test, what is the probability that you will not go on to a career in physics?

19. **Side-Impact Hazard** (Compare Exercise 15.) In 2004, 27.3% of all light vehicles were light trucks, 27.3% were SUVs, and 45.4% were cars. The probability that a severe side-impact crash would prove deadly to a driver depended on the type of vehicle he or she was driving at the time, as shown in the table:[76]

Light Truck	.210
SUV	.371
Car	1.000

What is the probability that the victim of a deadly side-impact accident was driving an SUV? HINT [See Example 3.]

20. **Side-Impact Hazard** In 1986, 23.9% of all light vehicles were pickups, 5.0% were SUVs, and 71.1% were cars. Refer to Exercise 19 for the probabilities that a severe side-impact crash would prove deadly. What is the probability that the victim of a deadly side-impact accident was driving a car? HINT [See Example 3.]

21. **University Admissions** In fall 2008, UCLA admitted 22% of its California resident applicants, 28% of its applicants from other U.S. states, and 22% of its international student applicants. Of all its applicants, 84% were California residents, 10% were from other U.S. states, and 6% were international students.[77] What percentage of all admitted students were California residents? (Round your answer to the nearest 1%.)

22. **University Admissions** In fall 2002, UCLA admitted 26% of its California resident applicants, 18% of its applicants from other U.S. states, and 13% of its international student applicants. Of all its applicants, 86% were California residents,

---

[72] Percentages are rounded. Source: University of California (www.admissions.ucla.edu/Prospect/Adm_fr/Frosh_Prof11.htm).

[73] *Ibid.*

[74] A "serious" side-impact accident is defined as one in which the driver of a car would be killed. Source: National Highway Traffic Safety Administration/*New York Times*, May 30, 2004, p. BU 9.

[75] *Ibid.*

[76] A "serious" side-impact accident is defined as one in which the driver of a car would be killed. Source: National Highway Traffic Safety Administration/*New York Times*, May 30, 2004, p. BU 9.

[77] Source: University of California (www.admissions.ucla.edu/Prospect/Adm_fr/Frosh_Prof08.htm).

11% were from other U.S. states, and 3% were international students.[78] What percentage of all admitted students were California residents? (Round your answer to the nearest 1%.)

23. *Internet Use (Historical)* In 2000, 86% of all Caucasians in the United States, 77% of all African-Americans, 77% of all Hispanics, and 85% of residents not classified into one of these groups used the Internet for email.[79] At that time, the U.S. population was 69% Caucasian, 12% African-American, and 13% Hispanic. What percentage of U.S. residents who used the Internet for email were Hispanic?

24. *Internet Use (Historical)* In 2000, 59% of all Caucasians in the United States, 57% of all African-Americans, 58% of all Hispanics, and 54% of residents not classified into one of these groups used the Internet to search for information.[80] At that time, the U.S. population was 69% Caucasian, 12% African-American, and 13% Hispanic. What percentage of U.S. residents who used the Internet for information search were African-American?

25. ▼ *Market Surveys* A *New York Times* survey of homeowners in the 1990s showed that 86% of those with swimming pools were married couples, and the other 14% were single.[81] It also showed that 15% of all homeowners had pools.

   a. Assuming that 90% of all homeowners without pools are married couples, what percentage of homes owned by married couples have pools?

   b. Would it have been more profitable for pool manufacturers to go after single homeowners or married homeowners? Explain.

26. ▼ *Crime and Preschool.* A *New York Times* survey[82] of needy and disabled youths showed that 51% of those who had no preschool education were arrested or charged with a crime by the time they were 19, whereas only 31% who had preschool education wound up in this category. The survey did not specify what percentage of the youths in the survey had preschool education, so let us take a guess at that and estimate that 20% of them had attended preschool.

   a. What percentage of the youths arrested or charged with a crime had no preschool education?

   b. What would this figure be if 80% of the youths had attended preschool? Would youths who had preschool education be more likely to be arrested or charged with a crime than those who did not? Support your answer by quoting probabilities.

27. ▼ *Grade Complaints* Two of the mathematics professors at Enormous State are Professor A (known for easy grading) and Professor F (known for tough grading). Last semester, roughly three quarters of Professor F's class consisted of former students of Professor A; these students apparently felt encouraged by their (utterly undeserved) high grades. (Professor F's own former students had fled in droves to Professor A's class to try to shore up their grade-point averages.) At the end of the semester, as might have been predicted, all of Professor A's former students wound up with a C– or lower. The rest of the students in the class—former students of Professor F who had decided to "stick it out"—fared better, and two-thirds of them earned higher than a C–. After discovering what had befallen them, all the students who earned C– or lower got together and decided to send a delegation to the Department Chair to complain that their grade-point averages had been ruined by this callous and heartless beast! The contingent was to consist of 10 representatives selected at random from among them. How many of the 10 would you estimate to have been former students of Professor A?

28. ▼ *Weather Prediction* A local TV station employs Desmorelda, "Mistress of the Zodiac," as its weather forecaster. Now, when it rains, Sagittarius is in the shadow of Jupiter one-third of the time, and it rains on 4 out of every 50 days. Sagittarius falls in Jupiter's shadow on only 1 in every 5 rainless days. The powers that be at the station notice a disturbing pattern to Desmorelda's weather predictions. It seems that she always predicts that it will rain when Sagittarius is in the shadow of Jupiter. What percentage of the time is she correct? Should they replace her?

29. ▼ *Employment in the 1980s* In a 1987 survey of married couples with earnings, 95% of all husbands were employed. Of all employed husbands, 71% of their wives were also employed.[83] Noting that either the husband or wife in a couple with earnings had to be employed, find the probability that the husband of an employed woman was also employed.

30. ▼ *Employment in the 1980s* Repeat the preceding exercise in the event that 50% of all husbands were employed.

31. ▼ *Juvenile Delinquency* According to a study at the Oregon Social Learning Center, boys who had been arrested by age 14 were 17.9 times more likely to become chronic offenders than those who had not.[84] Use these data to estimate the percentage of chronic offenders who had been arrested by age 14 in a city where 0.1% of all boys have been arrested by age 14. HINT [Use Bayes' formula rather than a tree.]

---

[78] Source: UCLA Web site, May 2002 (www.admissions.ucla.edu/Prospect/Adm_fr/Frosh_Prof.htm).

[79] Source: NTIA and ESA, U.S. Department of Commerce, using August 2000 U.S. Bureau of The Census Current Population Survey Supplement.

[80] *Ibid.*

[81] Source: "All about Swimming Pools," *New York Times*, September 13, 1992.

[82] Source: "Governors Develop Plan to Help Preschool Children," *New York Times*, August 2, 1992.

[83] Source: *Statistical Abstract of the United States*, 111th Ed., 1991, U.S. Dept. of Commerce/U.S. Bureau of Labor Statistics. Figures rounded to the nearest 1%.

[84] Based on a study, by Marion S. Forgatch, of 319 boys from high-crime neighborhoods in Eugene, Oregon. Source: W. Wayt Gibbs, "Seeking the Criminal Element," *Scientific American*, March 1995, pp. 101–107.

32. ▼ Crime According to the same study at the Oregon Social Learning Center, chronic offenders were 14.3 times more likely to commit violent offenses than people who were not chronic offenders.[85] In a neighborhood where 2 in every 1,000 residents is a chronic offender, estimate the probability that a violent offender is also a chronic offender. HINT [Use Bayes' formula rather than a tree.]

33. ▼ Benefits of Exercise According to a study in *The New England Journal of Medicine*,[86] 202 of a sample of 5,990 middle-aged men had developed diabetes. It also found that men who were very active (burning about 3,500 calories daily) were half as likely to develop diabetes compared with men who were sedentary. Assume that one-third of all middle-aged men are very active, and the rest are classified as sedentary. What is the probability that a middle-aged man with diabetes is very active?

34. ▼ Benefits of Exercise Repeat Exercise 33 assuming that only 1 in 10 middle-aged men is very active.

35. ◆ Air Bag Safety According to a study conducted by the Harvard School of Public Health, a child seated in the front seat who was wearing a seatbelt was 31% more likely to be killed in an accident if the car had an air bag that deployed than if it did not.[87] Air bags deployed in 25% of all accidents. For a child seated in the front seat wearing a seatbelt, what is the probability that the air bag deployed in an accident in which the child was killed? (Round your answer to two decimal places.) HINT [When we say "A is 31% more likely than B" we mean that the probability of A is 1.31 times the probability of B.]

36. ◆ Air Bag Safety According to the study cited in Exercise 35, a child seated in the front seat who was not wearing a seatbelt was 84% more likely to be killed in an accident if the car had an air bag that deployed than if it did not.[88] Air bags deployed in 25% of all accidents. For a child seated in the front seat not wearing a seatbelt, what is the probability that the air bag deployed in an accident in which the child was killed? (Round your answer to two decimal places.) HINT [When we say "A is 84% more likely than B" we mean that the probability of A is 1.84 times the probability of B.]

---

[85]*Ibid.*
[86]As cited in an article in *New York Times* on July 18, 1991.
[87]The study was conducted by Dr. Segul-Gomez at the Harvard School of Public Health. Source: *New York Times*, December 1, 2000, p. F1.
[88]*Ibid.*

COMMUNICATION AND REASONING EXERCISES

37. Your friend claims that the probability of *A* given *B* is the same as the probability of *B* given *A*. How would you convince him that he is wrong?

38. Complete the following sentence. To use Bayes' formula to compute $P(E \mid F)$, you need to be given _____.

39. ▼ Give an example in which a steroids test gives a false positive only 1% of the time, and yet if an athlete tests positive, the chance that he or she has used steroids is under 10%.

40. ▼ Give an example in which a steroids test gives a false positive 30% of the time, and yet if an athlete tests positive, the chance that he or she has used steroids is over 90%.

41. ▼ Use a tree to derive the expanded form of Bayes' theorem for a partition of the sample space *S* into three events R_1, R_2, and R_3.

42. ▼ Write down an expanded form of Bayes' theorem that applies to a partition of the sample space *S* into four events R_1, R_2, R_3, and R_4.

43. ◆ Politics The following letter appeared in *The New York Times*.[89]

> To the Editor:
>
> It stretches credulity when William Safire contends (column, Jan. 11) that 90 percent of those who agreed with his Jan. 8 column, in which he called the First Lady, Hillary Rodham Clinton, "a congenital liar," were men and 90 percent of those who disagreed were women.
>
> Assuming these percentages hold for Democrats as well as Republicans, only 10 percent of Democratic men disagreed with him. Is Mr. Safire suggesting that 90 percent of Democratic men supported him? How naive does he take his readers to be?
>
> A. D.
> New York, Jan. 12, 1996

Comment on the letter writer's reasoning.

44. ◆ Politics Refer back to the preceding exercise. If the letter writer's conclusion was correct, what percentage of all Democrats would have agreed with Safire's column?

---

[89]The original letter appeared in *New York Times*, January 16, 1996, p. A16. The authors have edited the first phrase of the second paragraph slightly for clarity; the original sentence read: "Assuming the response was equally divided between Democrats and Republicans, . . . "

7.7 Markov Systems

Many real-life situations can be modeled by processes that pass from state to state with given probabilities. A simple example of such a **Markov system** is the fluctuation of a gambler's fortune as he or she continues to bet. Other examples come from the study of trends in the commercial world and the study of neural networks and artificial intelligence. The mathematics of Markov systems is an interesting combination of probability and matrix arithmetic.

Here is a basic example we shall use many times: A market analyst for Gamble Detergents is interested in whether consumers prefer powdered laundry detergents or liquid detergents. Two market surveys taken one year apart revealed that 20% of powdered detergent users had switched to liquid one year later, while the rest were still using powder. Only 10% of liquid detergent users had switched to powder one year later, with the rest still using liquid.

We analyze this example as follows: Every year a consumer may be in one of two possible **states**: He may be a powdered detergent user or a liquid detergent user. Let us number these states: A consumer is in state 1 if he uses powdered detergent and in state 2 if he uses liquid. There is a basic **time step** of one year. If a consumer happens to be in state 1 during a given year, then there is a probability of 20% = .2 (the chance that a randomly chosen powder user will switch to liquid) that he will be in state 2 the next year. We write

$$p_{12} = .2$$

to indicate that the probability of going *from* state 1 *to* state 2 in one time step is .2. The other 80% of the powder users are using powder the next year. We write

$$p_{11} = .8$$

to indicate that the probability of *staying* in state 1 from one year to the next is .8.[*]
What if a consumer is in state 2? Then the probability of going to state 1 is given as 10% = .1, so the probability of remaining in state 2 is .9. Thus,

$$p_{21} = .1$$

* Notice that these are actually *conditional* probabilities. For instance, p_{12} is the probability that the system (the consumer in this case) will go into state 2, *given that the system* (the consumer) *is in state 1.*

and

$$p_{22} = .9.$$

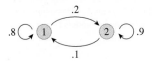

Figure 19

We can picture this system as in Figure 19, which shows the **state transition diagram** for this example. The numbers p_{ij}, which appear as labels on the arrows, are the **transition probabilities**.

† Named after the Russian mathematician A.A. Markov (1856–1922), who first studied these "nondeterministic" processes.

Markov System, States, and Transition Probabilities

A **Markov system**[†] (or **Markov process** or **Markov chain**) is a system that can be in one of several specified **states**. There is specified a certain **time step**, and at each step the system will randomly change states or remain where it is. The probability of going from state i to state j is a fixed number p_{ij}, called the **transition probability**.

Quick Example

The Markov system depicted in Figure 19 has two states: state 1 and state 2. The transition probabilities are as follows:

$$p_{11} = \text{Probability of going from state 1 to state 1} = .8$$
$$p_{12} = \text{Probability of going from state 1 to state 2} = .2$$
$$p_{21} = \text{Probability of going from state 2 to state 1} = .1$$
$$p_{22} = \text{Probability of going from state 2 to state 2} = .9.$$

Notice that, because the system must go somewhere at each time step, the transition probabilities originating at a particular state always add up to 1. For example, in the transition diagram above, when we add the probabilities originating at state 1, we get $.8 + .2 = 1$.

The transition probabilities may be conveniently arranged in a matrix.

Transition Matrix

The **transition matrix** associated with a given Markov system is the matrix P whose ijth entry is the transition probability p_{ij}, the transition probability of going *from* state i *to* state j. In other words, the entry in position ij is the *label on the arrow going from state i to state j* in a state transition diagram.

Thus, the transition matrix for a system with two states would be set up as follows:

$$\text{From:} \begin{array}{c} \\ 1 \\ 2 \end{array} \overset{\displaystyle \text{To:}}{\overset{\displaystyle \begin{array}{cc} 1 & 2 \end{array}}{\begin{bmatrix} p_{11} & p_{12} \\ p_{21} & p_{22} \end{bmatrix}}} \quad \begin{array}{l} \text{Arrows Originating in State 1} \\ \text{Arrows Originating in State 2} \end{array}$$

Quick Example

In the system pictured in Figure 19, the transition matrix is

$$P = \begin{bmatrix} .8 & .2 \\ .1 & .9 \end{bmatrix}.$$

Note Notice that because the sum of the transition probabilities that originate at any state is 1, *the sum of the entries in any row of a transition matrix is 1.* ∎

Now, let's start doing some calculations.

EXAMPLE 1 Laundry Detergent Switching

Consider the Markov system found by Gamble Detergents at the beginning of this section. Suppose that 70% of consumers are now using powdered detergent, while the other 30% are using liquid.

a. What will be the distribution one year from now? (That is, what percentage will be using powdered and what percentage liquid detergent?)

b. Assuming that the probabilities remain the same, what will be the distribution two years from now? Three years from now?

Solution

a. First, let us think of the statement that 70% of consumers are using powdered detergent as telling us a probability: The probability that a randomly chosen consumer uses powdered detergent is .7. Similarly, the probability that a randomly chosen consumer uses liquid detergent is .3. We want to find the corresponding probabilities one year from now. To do this, consider the tree diagram in Figure 20.

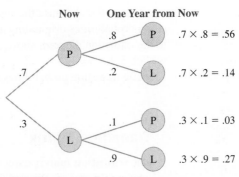

Figure 20

The first branching shows the probabilities now, while the second branching shows the (conditional) transition probabilities. So, if we want to know the probability that a consumer is using powdered detergent one year from now, it will be

Probability of using powder after one year $= .7 \times .8 + .3 \times .1 = .59$.

On the other hand, we have:

Probability of using liquid after one year $= .7 \times .2 + .3 \times .9 = .41$.

Now, here's the crucial point: *These are exactly the same calculations as in the matrix product*

$$[.7 \quad .3] \begin{bmatrix} .8 & .2 \\ .1 & .9 \end{bmatrix} = [.59 \quad .41].$$

$\qquad\quad\uparrow\qquad\qquad\uparrow\qquad\qquad\uparrow$

Initial distribution   Transition matrix   Distribution after 1 step

Thus, to get the distribution of detergent users after one year, all we have to do is multiply the **initial distribution vector** [.7 .3] by the transition matrix P. The result is [.59 .41], the **distribution vector after one step**.

b. Now what about the distribution after *two* years? If we assume that the same fraction of consumers switch or stay put in the second year as in the first, we can simply repeat the calculation we did above, using the new distribution vector:

$$[.59 \quad .41] \begin{bmatrix} .8 & .2 \\ .1 & .9 \end{bmatrix} = [.513 \quad .487].$$

$\quad\uparrow\qquad\qquad\qquad\uparrow\qquad\qquad\uparrow$

Distribution after 1 step   Transition matrix   Distribution after 2 steps

Thus, after two years we can expect 51.3% of consumers to be using powdered detergent and 48.7% to be using liquid detergent. Similarly, after three years we have

$$[.513 \quad .487] \begin{bmatrix} .8 & .2 \\ .1 & .9 \end{bmatrix} = [.4591 \quad .5409].$$

So, after three years, 45.91% of consumers will be using powdered detergent and 54.09% will be using liquid. Slowly but surely, liquid detergent seems to be winning.

➡ **Before we go on...** Note that the sum of the entries is 1 in each of the distribution vectors in Example 1. In fact, these vectors are giving the probability distributions for each year of finding a randomly chosen consumer using either powdered or liquid detergent. A vector having nonnegative entries adding up to 1 is called a **probability vector**. ∎

 using Technology

Technology can be used to compute the distribution vectors in Example 1:

TI-83/84 Plus
Define [A] as the initial distribution and [B] as the transition matrix. Then compute [A]*[B] for the distribution after 1 step. Ans*[B] gives the distribution after successive steps. [More details on page 542.]

Spreadsheet
Use the MMULT command to multiply the associated matrices. [More details on page 544.]

Website
www.WanerMath.com
Student Home
→ On Line Utilities
→ Matrix Algebra Tool
You can enter the transition matrix P and the initial distribution vector v in the input area, and compute the various distribution vectors using the following formulas:

v*P   1 step
v*P^2   2 steps
v*P^3   3 steps.

Distribution Vector after m Steps

A **distribution vector** is a probability vector giving the probability distribution for finding a Markov system in its various possible states. If v is a distribution vector, then the distribution vector one step later will be vP. The distribution m steps later will be

Distribution after m steps $= v \cdot P \cdot P \cdot \ldots \cdot P$ (m times) $= vP^m$.

Quick Example

If $P = \begin{bmatrix} 0 & 1 \\ .5 & .5 \end{bmatrix}$ and $v = [.2 \quad .8]$, then we can calculate the following distribution vectors:

$$vP = [.2 \quad .8] \begin{bmatrix} 0 & 1 \\ .5 & .5 \end{bmatrix} = [.4 \quad .6] \qquad \text{Distribution after one step}$$

$$vP^2 = (vP)P = [.4 \quad .6] \begin{bmatrix} 0 & 1 \\ .5 & .5 \end{bmatrix} = [.3 \quad .7] \qquad \text{Distribution after two steps}$$

$$vP^3 = (vP^2)P = [.3 \quad .7] \begin{bmatrix} 0 & 1 \\ .5 & .5 \end{bmatrix} = [.35 \quad .65]. \qquad \text{Distribution after three steps}$$

What about the matrix P^m that appears above? Multiplying a distribution vector v times P^m gives us the distribution m steps later, so we can think of P^m as the m-step transition matrix. More explicitly, consider the following example.

EXAMPLE 2 Powers of the Transition Matrix

Continuing the example of detergent switching, suppose that a consumer is now using powdered detergent. What are the probabilities that the consumer will be using powdered or liquid detergent two years from now? What if the consumer is now using liquid detergent?

Solution To record the fact that we know that the consumer is using powdered detergent, we can take as our initial distribution vector $v = [1 \quad 0]$. To find the distribution two years from now, we compute vP^2. To make a point, we do the calculation slightly differently:

$$vP^2 = [1 \quad 0] \begin{bmatrix} .8 & .2 \\ .1 & .9 \end{bmatrix} \begin{bmatrix} .8 & .2 \\ .1 & .9 \end{bmatrix}$$

$$= [1 \quad 0] \begin{bmatrix} .66 & .34 \\ .17 & .83 \end{bmatrix}$$

$$= [.66 \quad .34].$$

So, the probability that our consumer is using powdered detergent two years from now is .66, while the probability of using liquid detergent is .34. The point to notice is that these are the entries in the first row of P^2. Similarly, if we consider a consumer now using liquid detergent, we should take the initial distribution vector to be $v = [0 \quad 1]$ and compute

$$vP^2 = [0 \quad 1] \begin{bmatrix} .66 & .34 \\ .17 & .83 \end{bmatrix} = [.17 \quad .83].$$

Thus, the bottom row gives the probabilities that a consumer, now using liquid detergent, will be using either powdered or liquid detergent two years from now.

In other words, the ijth entry of P^2 gives the probability that a consumer, starting in state i, will be in state j after two time steps.

What is true in Example 2 for two time steps is true for any number of time steps:

Powers of the Transition Matrix

P^m $(m = 1, 2, 3, \ldots)$ is the *m*-step transition matrix. The ijth entry in P^m is the probability of a transition from state i to state j in m steps.

Quick Example

If $P = \begin{bmatrix} 0 & 1 \\ .5 & .5 \end{bmatrix}$ then

$$P^2 = P \cdot P = \begin{bmatrix} .5 & .5 \\ .25 & .75 \end{bmatrix} \qquad \text{2-step transition matrix}$$

$$P^3 = P \cdot P^2 = \begin{bmatrix} .25 & .75 \\ .375 & .625 \end{bmatrix}. \qquad \text{3-step transition matrix}$$

The probability of going from state 1 to state 2 in two steps = $(1, 2)$-entry of $P^2 = .5$.

The probability of going from state 1 to state 2 in three steps = $(1, 2)$-entry of $P^3 = .75$.

What happens if we follow our laundry detergent–using consumers for many years?

EXAMPLE 3 Long-Term Behavior

Suppose that 70% of consumers are now using powdered detergent while the other 30% are using liquid. Assuming that the transition matrix remains valid the whole time, what will be the distribution 1, 2, 3, . . . , and 50 years later?

Solution Of course, to do this many matrix multiplications, we're best off using technology. We already did the first three calculations in an earlier example.

Distribution after 1 year: $[.7 \quad .3] \begin{bmatrix} .8 & .2 \\ .1 & .9 \end{bmatrix} = [.59 \quad .41].$

Distribution after 2 years: $[.59 \quad .41] \begin{bmatrix} .8 & .2 \\ .1 & .9 \end{bmatrix} = [.513 \quad .487].$

Distribution after 3 years: $[.513 \quad .487] \begin{bmatrix} .8 & .2 \\ .1 & .9 \end{bmatrix} = [.4591 \quad .5409].$

. . .

Distribution after 48 years: $[.33333335 \quad .66666665].$

Distribution after 49 years: $[.33333334 \quad .66666666].$

Distribution after 50 years: $[.33333334 \quad .66666666].$

Thus, the distribution after 50 years is approximately $[.33333334 \quad .66666666].$

Something interesting seems to be happening in Example 3. The distribution seems to be getting closer and closer to

$$[.333333\ldots \quad .666666\ldots] = \begin{bmatrix} \dfrac{1}{3} & \dfrac{2}{3} \end{bmatrix}.$$

Let's call this distribution vector v_∞. Notice two things about v_∞:

- v_∞ is a probability vector.
- If we calculate $v_\infty P$, we find

$$v_\infty P = \begin{bmatrix} \dfrac{1}{3} & \dfrac{2}{3} \end{bmatrix}\begin{bmatrix} .8 & .2 \\ .1 & .9 \end{bmatrix} = \begin{bmatrix} \dfrac{1}{3} & \dfrac{2}{3} \end{bmatrix} = v_\infty.$$

In other words,

$$v_\infty P = v_\infty.$$

We call a probability vector v with the property that $vP = v$ a **steady-state (probability) vector**.

Q: *Where does the name steady-state vector come from?*

A: If $vP = v$, then v is a distribution that will not change from time step to time step. In the example above, because [1/3 2/3] is a steady-state vector, if 1/3 of consumers use powdered detergent and 2/3 use liquid detergent one year, then the proportions will be the same the next year. Individual consumers may still switch from year to year, but as many will switch from powder to liquid as switch from liquid to powder, so the number using each will remain constant.

But how do we find a steady-state vector?

EXAMPLE 4 Calculating the Steady-State Vector

Calculate the steady-state probability vector for the transition matrix in the preceding examples:

$$P = \begin{bmatrix} .8 & .2 \\ .1 & .9 \end{bmatrix}.$$

Solution We are asked to find

$$v_\infty = [x \quad y].$$

This vector must satisfy the equation

$$v_\infty P = v_\infty$$

or

$$[x \quad y]\begin{bmatrix} .8 & .2 \\ .1 & .9 \end{bmatrix} = [x \quad y].$$

Doing the matrix multiplication gives

$$[.8x + .1y \quad .2x + .9y] = [x \quad y].$$

Equating corresponding entries gives

$$.8x + .1y = x$$
$$.2x + .9y = y$$

or

$$-.2x + .1y = 0$$
$$.2x - .1y = 0.$$

 using Technology

Technology can be used to compute the steady-state vector in Example 4.

TI-83/84 Plus
Define `[A]` as the coefficient matrix of the system of equations being solved, and `[B]` as the column matrix of the right-hand sides. Then compute `[A]`$^{-1}$`[B]`
[More details on page 543.]

Spreadsheet
Use the `MMULT` and `MINVERSE` commands to solve the necessary system of equations.
[More details on page 545.]

Website
www.WanerMath.com
Student Home
  → On Line Utilities
  → Pivot and Gauss-Jordan Tool
You can use the Pivot and Gauss-Jordan Tool to solve the system of equations that gives you the steady-state vector.

Now these equations are really the same equation. (Do you see that?) There is one more thing we know, though: Because $[x \quad y]$ is a probability vector, its entries must add up to 1. This gives one more equation:

$$x + y = 1.$$

Taking this equation together with one of the two equations above gives us the following system:

$$x + \quad y = 1$$
$$-.2x + .1y = 0.$$

We now solve this system using any of the techniques we learned for solving systems of linear equations. We find that the solution is $x = 1/3$, and $y = 2/3$, so the steady-state vector is

$$v_\infty = [x \quad y] = \begin{bmatrix} \dfrac{1}{3} & \dfrac{2}{3} \end{bmatrix}$$

as suggested in Example 3.

The method we just used works for any size transition matrix and can be summarized as follows.

Calculating the Steady-State Distribution Vector

To calculate the steady-state probability vector for a Markov system with transition matrix P, we solve the system of equations given by

$$x + y + z + \cdots = 1$$
$$[x \quad y \quad z \ldots]P = [x \quad y \quad z \ldots],$$

where we use as many unknowns as there are states in the Markov system. The steady-state probability vector is then

$$v_\infty = [x \quad y \quad z \ldots].$$

Q: *Is there always a steady-state distribution vector?*

A: Yes, although the explanation why is more involved than we can give here.

Q: *In Example 3, we started with a distribution vector v and found that vP^m got closer and closer to v_∞ as m got larger. Does that always happen?*

A: It does if the Markov system is **regular**, as we define below, but may not for other kinds of systems. Again, we shall not prove this fact here.

Regular Markov Systems

A **regular** Markov system is one for which some power of its transition matrix P has no zero entries. If a Markov system is regular, then

1. It has a unique steady-state probability vector v_∞, and
2. If v is any probability vector whatsoever, then vP^m approaches v_∞ as m gets large. We say that the **long-term behavior** of the system is to have distribution (close to) v_∞.

Interpreting the Steady-State Vector

In a regular Markov system, the entries in the steady-state probability vector give the long-term probabilities that the system will be in the corresponding states, or the fractions of time one can expect to find the Markov system in the corresponding states.

Quick Examples

1. The system with transition matrix $P = \begin{bmatrix} .8 & .2 \\ .1 & .9 \end{bmatrix}$ is regular because $P(= P^1)$ has no zero entries.

2. The system with transition matrix $P = \begin{bmatrix} 0 & 1 \\ .5 & .5 \end{bmatrix}$ is regular because

   $P^2 = \begin{bmatrix} .5 & .5 \\ .25 & .75 \end{bmatrix}$ has no zero entries.

3. The system with transition matrix $P = \begin{bmatrix} 0 & 1 \\ 1 & 0 \end{bmatrix}$ is *not* regular:

   $P^2 = \begin{bmatrix} 1 & 0 \\ 0 & 1 \end{bmatrix}$ and $P^3 = P$ again, so the powers of P alternate between these two matrices. Thus, every power of P has zero entries. Although this system has a steady-state vector, namely $[.5\ .5]$, if we take $v = [1\ 0]$, then $vP = [0\ 1]$ and $vP^2 = v$, so the distribution vectors vP^m just alternate between these two vectors, not approaching v_∞.

We finish with one more example.

EXAMPLE 5 Gambler's Ruin

A timid gambler, armed with her annual bonus of $20, decides to play roulette using the following scheme. At each spin of the wheel, she places $10 on red. If red comes up, she wins an additional $10; if black comes up, she loses her $10. For the sake of simplicity, assume that she has a probability of $1/2$ of winning. (In the real game, the probability is slightly lower—a fact that many gamblers forget.) She keeps playing until she has either gotten up to $30 or lost it all. In either case, she then packs up and leaves. Model this situation as a Markov system and find the associated transition matrix. What can we say about the long-term behavior of this system?

Solution We must first decide on the states of the system. A good choice is the gambler's financial state, the amount of money she has at any stage of the game. According to her rules, she can be broke, have $10, $20, or $30. Thus, there are four states: $1 = \$0, 2 = \$10, 3 = \$20$, and $4 = \$30$. Because she bets $10 each time, she moves down $10 if she loses (with probability $1/2$) and up $10 if she wins (with probability also $1/2$), until she reaches one of the extremes. The transition diagram is shown in Figure 21.

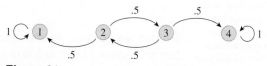

Figure 21

* These states are like "Roach Motels" ("Roaches check in, but they don't check out")!

Note that once the system enters state 1 or state 4, it does not leave; with probability 1, it stays in the same state.* We call such states **absorbing states**. We can now write down the transition matrix:

$$P = \begin{bmatrix} 1 & 0 & 0 & 0 \\ .5 & 0 & .5 & 0 \\ 0 & .5 & 0 & .5 \\ 0 & 0 & 0 & 1 \end{bmatrix}.$$

(Notice all the 0 entries, corresponding to possible transitions that we did not draw in the transition diagram because they have 0 probability of occurring. We usually leave out such arrows.) Is this system regular? Take a look at P^2:

$$P^2 = \begin{bmatrix} 1 & 0 & 0 & 0 \\ .5 & .25 & 0 & .25 \\ .25 & 0 & .25 & .5 \\ 0 & 0 & 0 & 1 \end{bmatrix}.$$

Notice that the first and last rows haven't changed. After two steps, there is still no chance of leaving states 1 or 4. In fact, no matter how many powers we take, no matter how many steps we look at, there will still be no way to leave either of those states, and the first and last rows will still have plenty of zeros. This system is not regular.

Nonetheless, we can try to find a steady-state probability vector. If we do this (and you should set up the system of linear equations and solve it), we find that there are infinitely many steady-state probability vectors, namely all vectors of the form $[x \ 0 \ 0 \ 1 - x]$ for $0 \le x \le 1$. (You can check directly that these are all steady-state vectors.) As with a regular system, if we start with any distribution, the system will tend toward one of these steady-state vectors. In other words, eventually the gambler will either lose all her money or leave the table with $30.

But which outcome is more likely, and with what probability? One way to approach this question is to try computing the distribution after many steps. The distribution that represents the gambler starting with $20 is $v = [0 \ 0 \ 1 \ 0]$. Using technology, it's easy to compute vP^n for some large values of n:

$$vP^{10} \approx [.333008 \ \ 0 \ \ .000976 \ \ .666016]$$
$$vP^{50} \approx [.333333 \ \ 0 \ \ 0 \ \ .666667].$$

So, it looks like the probability that she will leave the table with $30 is approximately $2/3$, while the probability that she loses it all is $1/3$.

What if she started with only $10? Then our initial distribution would be $v = [0 \ 1 \ 0 \ 0]$ and

$$vP^{10} \approx [.666016 \ \ .000976 \ \ 0 \ \ .333008]$$
$$vP^{50} \approx [.666667 \ \ 0 \ \ 0 \ \ .333333].$$

So, this time, the probability of her losing everything is about $2/3$ while the probability of her leaving with $30 is $1/3$. There is a way of calculating these probabilities exactly using matrix arithmetic; however, it would take us too far afield to describe it here.

Website
www.WanerMath.com
Follow the path
Chapter 7
→ On Line Utilities
→ Markov Simulation
where you can enter the transition matrix and watch a visual simulation showing the system hopping from state to state. Run the simulation a number of times to get an experimental estimate of the time to absorption. (Take the average time to absorption over many runs.) Also, try varying the transition probabilities to study the effect on the time to absorption.

➡ **Before we go on...** Another interesting question is, how long will it take the gambler in Example 5 to get to $30 or lose it all? This is called the *time to absorption* and can be calculated using matrix arithmetic. ∎

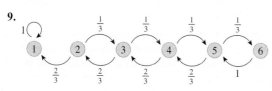

7.7 EXERCISES

▼ more advanced   ◆ challenging
⊤ indicates exercises that should be solved using technology

In Exercises 1–10, write down the transition matrix associated with each state transition diagram.

1.

2.

3.

4.

5.

6.

7.

8.

9.

10.

In each of Exercises 11–24, you are given a transition matrix P and initial distribution vector v. Find

(a) *the two-step transition matrix and*
(b) *the distribution vectors after one, two, and three steps.*
  HINT [See Quick Examples on pages 525 and 526.]

11. $P = \begin{bmatrix} .5 & .5 \\ 0 & 1 \end{bmatrix}, v = [1 \quad 0]$

12. $P = \begin{bmatrix} 1 & 0 \\ .5 & .5 \end{bmatrix}, v = [0 \quad 1]$

13. $P = \begin{bmatrix} .2 & .8 \\ .4 & .6 \end{bmatrix}, v = [.5 \quad .5]$

14. $P = \begin{bmatrix} 1/3 & 2/3 \\ 1/2 & 1/2 \end{bmatrix}, v = [1/4 \quad 3/4]$

15. $P = \begin{bmatrix} 1/2 & 1/2 \\ 1 & 0 \end{bmatrix}, v = [2/3 \quad 1/3]$

16. $P = \begin{bmatrix} 0 & 1 \\ 1/4 & 3/4 \end{bmatrix}, v = [1/5 \quad 4/5]$

17. $P = \begin{bmatrix} 3/4 & 1/4 \\ 3/4 & 1/4 \end{bmatrix}, v = [1/2 \quad 1/2]$

18. $P = \begin{bmatrix} 2/3 & 1/3 \\ 2/3 & 1/3 \end{bmatrix}, v = [1/7 \quad 6/7]$

19. $P = \begin{bmatrix} .5 & .5 & 0 \\ 0 & 1 & 0 \\ 0 & .5 & .5 \end{bmatrix}, v = [1 \quad 0 \quad 0]$

20. $P = \begin{bmatrix} .5 & 0 & .5 \\ 1 & 0 & 0 \\ 0 & .5 & .5 \end{bmatrix}, v = [0 \quad 1 \quad 0]$

21. $P = \begin{bmatrix} 0 & 1 & 0 \\ 1/3 & 1/3 & 1/3 \\ 1 & 0 & 0 \end{bmatrix}, v = [1/2 \quad 0 \quad 1/2]$

22. $P = \begin{bmatrix} 1/2 & 1/2 & 0 \\ 1/2 & 1/2 & 0 \\ 1/2 & 0 & 1/2 \end{bmatrix}, v = [0 \quad 0 \quad 1]$

23. $P = \begin{bmatrix} .1 & .9 & 0 \\ 0 & 1 & 0 \\ 0 & .2 & .8 \end{bmatrix}, v = [.5 \quad 0 \quad .5]$

24. $P = \begin{bmatrix} .1 & .1 & .8 \\ .5 & 0 & .5 \\ .5 & 0 & .5 \end{bmatrix}, v = [0 \quad 1 \quad 0]$

In each of Exercises 25–36, you are given a transition matrix P. Find the steady-state distribution vector. HINT [See Example 4.]

25. $P = \begin{bmatrix} 1/2 & 1/2 \\ 1 & 0 \end{bmatrix}$ **26.** $P = \begin{bmatrix} 0 & 1 \\ 1/4 & 3/4 \end{bmatrix}$

27. $P = \begin{bmatrix} 1/3 & 2/3 \\ 1/2 & 1/2 \end{bmatrix}$ **28.** $P = \begin{bmatrix} .2 & .8 \\ .4 & .6 \end{bmatrix}$

29. $P = \begin{bmatrix} .1 & .9 \\ .6 & .4 \end{bmatrix}$ **30.** $P = \begin{bmatrix} .2 & .8 \\ .7 & .3 \end{bmatrix}$

31. $P = \begin{bmatrix} .5 & 0 & .5 \\ 1 & 0 & 0 \\ 0 & .5 & .5 \end{bmatrix}$ **32.** $P = \begin{bmatrix} 0 & .5 & .5 \\ .5 & .5 & 0 \\ 1 & 0 & 0 \end{bmatrix}$

33. $P = \begin{bmatrix} 0 & 1 & 0 \\ 1/3 & 1/3 & 1/3 \\ 1 & 0 & 0 \end{bmatrix}$ **34.** $P = \begin{bmatrix} 1/2 & 1/2 & 0 \\ 1/2 & 1/2 & 0 \\ 1/2 & 0 & 1/2 \end{bmatrix}$

35. $P = \begin{bmatrix} .1 & .9 & 0 \\ 0 & 1 & 0 \\ 0 & .2 & .8 \end{bmatrix}$ **36.** $P = \begin{bmatrix} .1 & .1 & .8 \\ .5 & 0 & .5 \\ .5 & 0 & .5 \end{bmatrix}$

APPLICATIONS

37. *Marketing* A market survey shows that half the owners of Sorey State Boogie Boards became disenchanted with the product and switched to C&T Super Professional Boards the next surf season, while the other half remained loyal to Sorey State. On the other hand, three quarters of the C&T Boogie Board users remained loyal to C&T, while the rest switched to Sorey State. Set these data up as a Markov transition matrix, and calculate the probability that a Sorey State Board user will be using the same brand two seasons later. HINT [See Example 1.]

38. *Major Switching* At Suburban Community College, 10% of all business majors switched to another major the next semester, while the remaining 90% continued as business majors. Of all non–business majors, 20% switched to a business major the following semester, while the rest did not. Set up these data as a Markov transition matrix, and calculate the probability that a business major will no longer be a business major in two semesters' time. HINT [See Example 1.]

39. *Pest Control* In an experiment to test the effectiveness of the latest roach trap, the "Roach Resort," 50 roaches were placed in the vicinity of the trap and left there for an hour. At the end of the hour, it was observed that 30 of them had "checked in," while the rest were still scurrying around. (Remember that "once a roach checks in, it never checks out.")

   a. Set up the transition matrix P for the system with decimal entries, and calculate P^2 and P^3.

   b. If a roach begins outside the "Resort," what is the probability of it "checking in" by the end of 1 hour? 2 hours? 3 hours?

   c. What do you expect to be the long-term impact on the number of roaches? HINT [See Example 5.]

40. *Employment* You have worked for the Department of Administrative Affairs (DAA) for 27 years, and you still have little or no idea exactly what your job entails. To make your life a little more interesting, you have decided on the following course of action. Every Friday afternoon, you will use your desktop computer to generate a random digit from 0 to 9 (inclusive). If the digit is a zero, you will immediately quit your job, never to return. Otherwise, you will return to work the following Monday.

   a. Use the states (1) employed by the DAA and (2) not employed by the DAA to set up a transition probability matrix P with decimal entries, and calculate P^2 and P^3.

   b. What is the probability that you will still be employed by the DAA after each of the next three weeks?

   c. What are your long-term prospects for employment at the DAA? HINT [See Example 5.]

41. *Risk Analysis* An auto insurance company classifies each motorist as "high risk" if the motorist has had at least one moving violation during the past calendar year and "low risk" if the motorist has had no violations during the past calendar year. According to the company's data, a high-risk motorist has a 50% chance of remaining in the high-risk category the next year and a 50% chance of moving to the low-risk category. A low-risk motorist has a 10% chance of moving to the high-risk category the next year and a 90% chance of remaining in the low-risk category. In the long term, what percentage of motorists fall in each category?

42. *Debt Analysis* A credit card company classifies its cardholders as falling into one of two credit ratings: "good" and "poor." Based on its rating criteria, the company finds that a cardholder with a good credit rating has an 80% chance of remaining in that category the following year and a 20% chance of dropping into the poor category. A cardholder with a poor credit rating has a 40% chance of moving into the good rating the following year and a 60% chance of remaining in the poor category. In the long term, what percentage of cardholders fall in each category?

43. *Textbook Adoptions* College instructors who adopt this book are (we hope!) twice as likely to continue to use the book the following semester as they are to drop it, whereas nonusers are nine times as likely to remain nonusers the following year as they are to adopt this book.

   a. Determine the probability that a nonuser will be a user in two years.

   b. In the long term, what proportion of college instructors will be users of this book?

44. *Confidence Level* Tommy the Dunker's performance on the basketball court is influenced by his state of mind: If he scores, he is twice as likely to score on the next shot as he is to miss, whereas if he misses a shot, he is three times as likely to miss the next shot as he is to score.

   a. If Tommy has missed a shot, what is the probability that he will score two shots later?

   b. In the long term, what percentage of shots are successful?

45. *Debt Analysis* As the manager of a large retailing outlet, you have classified all credit customers as falling into one of the following categories: Paid Up, Outstanding 0–90 Days, Bad

Debts. Based on an audit of your company's records, you have come up with the following table, which gives the probabilities that a single credit customer will move from one category to the next in the period of 1 month.

	To		
	Paid Up	**0–90 Days**	**Bad Debts**
From **Paid Up**	.5	.5	0
0–90 Days	.5	.3	.2
Bad Debts	0	.5	.5

How do you expect the company's credit customers to be distributed in the long term?

46. Debt Analysis Repeat the preceding exercise using the following table:

	To		
	Paid Up	**0–90 Days**	**Bad Debts**
From **Paid Up**	.8	.2	0
0–90 Days	.5	.3	.2
Bad Debts	0	.5	.5

47. ▼ Income Brackets The following diagram shows the movement of U.S. households among three income groups—affluent, middle class, and poor—over the 11-year period 1980–1991.[90]

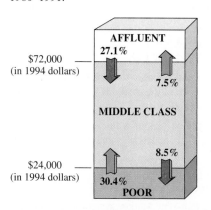

a. Use the transitions shown in the diagram to construct a transition matrix (assuming zero probabilities for the transitions between affluent and poor).

b. Assuming that the trend shown was to continue, what percent of households classified as affluent in 1980 were predicted to become poor in 2002? (Give your answer to the nearest 0.1%.)

c. ▣ According to the model, what percentage of all U.S. households will be in each income bracket in the long term? (Give your answer to the nearest 0.1%.)

48. ▼ Income Brackets The following diagram shows the movement of U.S. households among three income groups—affluent, middle class, and poor—over the 12-year period 1967–1979.[91]

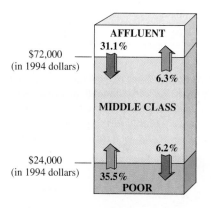

a. Use the transitions shown in the diagram to construct a transition matrix (assuming zero probabilities for the transitions between affluent and poor).

b. Assuming that the trend shown had continued, what percent of households classified as affluent in 1967 would have been poor in 1991? (Give your answer to the nearest 0.1%.)

c. ▣ According to the model, what percentage of all U.S. households will be in each income bracket in the long term? (Give your answer to the nearest 0.1%.)

49. ▣ ▼ Income Distribution A University of Michigan study shows the following one-generation transition probabilities among four major income groups.[92]

Father's Income	Eldest Son's Income			
	Bottom 10%	**10–50%**	**50–90%**	**Top 10%**
Bottom 10%	.30	.52	.17	.01
10–50%	.10	.48	.38	.04
50–90%	.04	.38	.48	.10
Top 10%	.01	.17	.52	.30

In the long term, what percentage of male earners would you expect to find in each category? Why are the long-range figures not necessarily 10% in the lowest 10% income bracket, 40% in the 10–50% range, 40% in the 50–90% range, and 10% in the top 10% range? (Use technology to compute an approximation of the steady-state transition matrix.)

---

[90] The figures were based on household after-tax income. The study was conducted by G. J. Duncan of Northwestern University and T. Smeeding of Syracuse University and based on annual surveys of the personal finances of 5,000 households since the late 1960s. (The surveys were conducted by the University of Michigan.) Source: *New York Times*, June 4, 1995, p. E4.

[91] *Ibid.*

[92] Source: Gary Solon, University of Michigan/*New York Times*, May 18, 1992, p. D5. We have adjusted some of the figures so that the probabilities add to 1; they did not do so in the original table due to rounding.

50. ▢ ▼ *Income Distribution* Repeat Exercise 49, using the following data:

Father's Income	Son's income			
	Bottom 10%	10–50%	50–90%	Top 10%
Bottom 10%	.50	.32	.17	.01
10–50%	.10	.48	.38	.04
50–90%	.04	.38	.48	.10
Top 10%	.01	.17	.32	.50

Market Share: Cell Phones Three of the largest cellular phone companies in 2004 were **Verizon**, **Cingular**, *and* **AT&T Wireless**. *Exercises 51 and 52 are based on the following figure, which shows percentages of subscribers who switched from one company to another during the third quarter of 2003:*[93]

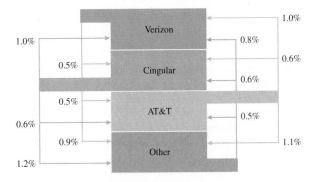

51. a. ▢ ▼ Use the diagram to set up an associated transition matrix.
 b. At the end of the third quarter of 2003, the market shares were: **Verizon**: 29.7%, **Cingular**: 19.3%, **AT&T**: 18.1%, and Other: 32.9%. Use your Markov system to estimate the percentage shares at the *beginning* of the third quarter of 2003.
 c. Using the information from part (b), estimate the market shares at the end of 2005. Which company is predicted to gain the most in market share?

52. a. ▢ ▼ Use the diagram to set up an associated transition matrix.
 b. At the end of the third quarter of 2003, the market shares were: **Verizon**: 29.7%, **Cingular**: 19.3%, **AT&T**: 18.1%, Other: 32.9%. Use your Markov system to estimate the percentage shares one year earlier.
 c. Using the information from part (b), estimate the market shares at the end of 2010. Which company is predicted to lose the most in market share?

---

[93] Published market shares and "churn rate" (percentage drops for each company) were used to estimate the individual transition percentages. "Other" consists of Sprint, Nextel, and T Mobile. No other cellular companies are included in this analysis. Source: The Yankee Group/ *New York Times*, January 21, 2004, p. C1.

53. ▼ *Dissipation* Consider the following five-state model of one-dimensional dissipation without drift:

Find the steady-state distribution vector.

54. ▼ *Dissipation with Drift* Consider the following five-state model of one-dimensional dissipation with drift:

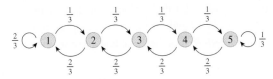

Find the steady-state distribution vector.

COMMUNICATION AND REASONING EXERCISES

55. Describe an interesting situation that can be modeled by the transition matrix
$$P = \begin{bmatrix} .2 & .8 & 0 \\ 0 & 1 & 0 \\ .4 & .6 & 0 \end{bmatrix}.$$

56. Describe an interesting situation that can be modeled by the transition matrix
$$P = \begin{bmatrix} .8 & .1 & .1 \\ 1 & 0 & 0 \\ .3 & .3 & .4 \end{bmatrix}.$$

57. ▼ Describe some drawbacks to using Markov processes to model the behavior of the stock market with states (1) bull market (2) bear market.

58. ▼ Can the repeated toss of a fair coin be modeled by a Markov process? If so, describe a model; if not, explain the reason.

59. ▼ Explain: If Q is a matrix whose rows are steady-state distribution vectors for P, then $QP = Q$.

60. ▼ Construct a four-state Markov system so that both [.5 .5 0 0] and [0 0 .5 .5] are steady-state vectors. HINT [Try one in which no arrows link the first two states to the last two.]

61. ▼ Refer to the following state transition diagram and explain in words (without doing any calculation) why the steady-state vector has a zero in position 1.

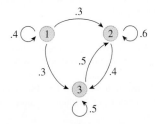

62. ▼ Without doing any calculation, find the steady-state distribution of the following system and explain the reasoning behind your claim.

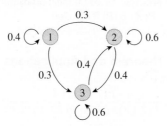

63. ◆ Construct a regular state transition diagram that possesses the steady-state vector [.3 .3 .4].

64. ◆ Construct a regular state transition diagram possessing a steady-state vector [.6 .3 0 .1].

65. ◆ Show that if a Markov system has two distinct steady-state distributions v and w, then $\dfrac{v + w}{2}$ is another steady-state distribution.

66. ◆ If higher and higher powers of P approach a fixed matrix Q, explain why the rows of Q must be steady-state distributions vectors.

CHAPTER 7 REVIEW

KEY CONCEPTS

Website www.WanerMath.com

Go to the Website at www.WanerMath.com to find a comprehensive and interactive Web-based summary of Chapter 7.

7.1 Sample Spaces and Events

Experiment, outcome, sample space *p. 446*

Event *p. 448*

The complement of an event *p. 452*

Unions of events *p. 452*

Intersections of events *p. 453*

Mutually exclusive events *p. 454*

7.2 Relative Frequency

Relative frequency or estimated probability *p. 460*

Relative frequency distribution *p. 460*

Properties of relative frequency distribution *p. 463*

7.3 Probability and Probability Models

Probability distribution, probability: $0 \le P(s_i) \le 1$ and $P(s_1) + \cdots + P(s_n) = 1$ *p. 469*

If $P(E) = 0$, we call E an impossible event *p. 469*

Probability models *p. 469*

Probability models for equally likely outcomes: $P(E) = n(E)/n(S)$ *p. 471*

Addition principle: $P(A \cup B) = P(A) + P(B) - P(A \cap B)$ *p. 475*

If A and B are mutually exclusive, then $P(A \cup B) = P(A) + P(B)$ *p. 476*

If S is the sample space, then $P(S) = 1$, $P(\emptyset) = 0$, and $P(A') = 1 - P(A)$ *p. 478*

7.4 Probability and Counting Techniques

Use counting techniques from Chapter 6 to calculate probability *p. 487*

7.5 Conditional Probability and Independence

Conditional probability: $P(A \mid B) = P(A \cap B)/P(B)$ *p. 497*

Multiplication principle for conditional probability: $P(A \cap B) = P(A \mid B)P(B)$ *p. 500*

Independent events: $P(A \cap B) = P(A)P(B)$ *p. 503*

7.6 Bayes' Theorem and Applications

Bayes' theorem (short form):

$$P(A \mid T) = \frac{P(T \mid A)P(A)}{P(T \mid A)P(A) + P(T \mid A')P(A')} \quad p.\ 515$$

Bayes' theorem (partition of sample space into three events):

$$P(A_1 \mid T) = \frac{P(T \mid A_1)P(A_1)}{P(T \mid A_1)P(A_1) + P(T \mid A_2)P(A_2) + P(T \mid A_3)P(A_3)}$$

p. 517

7.7 Markov Systems

Markov system, Markov process, states, transition probabilities *p. 522*

Transition matrix associated with a given Markov system *p. 523*

A vector having non-negative entries adding up to 1 is called a probability vector *p. 524*

A distribution vector is a probability vector giving the probability distribution for finding a Markov system in its various possible states *p. 524*

If v is a distribution vector, then the distribution vector one step later will be vP. The distribution after m steps will be vP^m *p. 524*

P^m is the m-step transition matrix. The ijth entry in P^m is the probability of a transition from state i to state j in m steps *p. 526*

A steady-state (probability) vector is a probability vector v such that $vP = v$ *p. 527*

Calculation of the steady-state distribution vector *p. 528*

A regular Markov system, long-term behavior of a regular Markov system *p. 528*

An absorbing state is one for which the probability of staying in the state is 1 (and the probability of leaving it for any other state is 0) *p. 530*

REVIEW EXERCISES

In each of Exercises 1–6, say how many elements are in the sample space S, list the elements of the given event E, and compute the probability of E.

1. Three coins are tossed; the result is one or more tails.

2. Four coins are tossed; the result is fewer heads then tails.

3. Two distinguishable dice are rolled; the numbers facing up add to 7.

4. Three distinguishable dice are rolled; the number facing up add to 5.

5. A die is weighted so that each of 2, 3, 4, and 5 is half as likely to come up as either 1 or 6; however, 2 comes up.

6. Two indistinguishable dice are rolled; the numbers facing up add to 7.

In each of Exercises 7–10, calculate the relative frequency P(E).

7. Two coins are tossed 50 times, and two heads come up 12 times. *E* is the event that at least one tail comes up.

8. Ten stocks are selected at random from a portfolio. Seven of them have increased in value since their purchase, and the rest have decreased. Eight of them are Internet stocks and two of those have decreased in value. E is the event that a stock has either increased in value or is an Internet stock.

9. You have read 150 of the 400 novels in your home, but your sister Roslyn has read 200, of which only 50 are novels you have read as well. E is the event that a novel has been read by neither you nor your sister.

10. You roll two dice 10 times. Both dice show the same number 3 times, and on 2 rolls, exactly one number is odd. E is the event that the sum of the numbers is even.

In each of Exercises 11–14, calculate the probability $P(E)$.

11. There are 32 students in categories A and B combined. Some are in both, 24 are in A, and 24 are in B. E is the event that a randomly selected student (among the 32) is in both categories.

12. You roll two dice, one red and one green. Losing combinations are doubles (both dice showing the same number) and outcomes in which the green die shows an odd number and the red die shows an even number. The other combinations are winning ones. E is the event that you roll a winning combination.

13. The *jPlay* portable music/photo/video player and bottle opener comes in three models: A, B, and C, each with five colors to choose from, and there are equal numbers of each combination. E is the event that a randomly selected *jPlay* is either orange (one of the available colors), a Model A, or both.

14. The Heavy Weather Service predicts that for tomorrow there is a 50% chance of tornadoes, a 20% chance of a monsoon, and a 10% chance of both. What is the probability that we will be lucky tomorrow and encounter neither tornadoes nor a monsoon?

A bag contains four red marbles, two green ones, one transparent one, three yellow ones, and two orange ones. You select five at random. In each of Exercises 15–20, compute the probability of the given event.

15. You have selected all the red ones.

16. You have selected all the green ones.

17. All are different colors.

18. At least one is not red.

19. At least two are yellow.

20. None are yellow and at most one is red.

In each of Exercises 21–26, find the probability of being dealt the given type of 5-card hand from a standard deck of 52 cards. (None of these is a recognized poker hand.) Express your answer in terms of combinations.

21. **Kings and Queens:** Each of the five cards is either a king or a queen.

22. **Five Pictures:** Each card is a picture card (J, Q, K).

23. **Fives and Queens:** Three fives, the queen of spades, and one other queen.

24. **Prime Full House:** A full house (three cards of one denomination, two of another) with the face value of each card a prime number (Ace $= 1$, J $= 11$, Q $= 12$, K $= 13$).

25. **Full House of Commons:** A full house (three cards of one denomination, two of another) with no royal cards (that is, no J, Q, K, or Ace).

26. **Black Two Pair:** Five black cards (spades or clubs), two with one denomination, two with another, and one with a third.

Two dice, one green and one yellow, are rolled. In each of Exercises 27–32, find the conditional probability, and also say whether the indicated pair of events is independent.

27. The sum is 5, given that the green one is not 1 and the yellow one is 1.

28. The sum is 6, given that the green one is either 1 or 3 and the yellow one is 1.

29. The yellow one is 4, given that the green one is 4.

30. The yellow one is 5, given that the sum is 6.

31. The dice have the same parity, given that both of them are odd.

32. The sum is 7, given that the dice do not have the same parity.

A poll shows that half the consumers who use Brand A switched to Brand B the following year, while the other half stayed with Brand A. Three quarters of the Brand B users stayed with Brand B the following year, while the rest switched to Brand A. Use this information to answer Exercises 33–36.

33. Give the associated Markov transition matrix, with state 1 representing using Brand A and state 2 representing using Brand B.

34. Compute the associated two- and three-step transition matrices. What is the probability that a Brand A user will be using Brand B three years later?

35. If two thirds of consumers are presently using Brand A and one third are using Brand B, how are these consumers distributed in three years' time?

36. In the long term, what fraction of the time will a user spend using each of the two brands?

APPLICATIONS: OHaganBooks.com

OHaganBooks.com currently operates three warehouses: one in Washington, one in California, and the new one in Texas. Book inventories are shown in the following table.

	Sci Fi	Horror	Romance	Other	Total
Washington	10,000	12,000	12,000	30,000	64,000
California	8,000	12,000	6,000	16,000	42,000
Texas	15,000	15,000	20,000	44,000	94,000
Total	33,000	39,000	38,000	90,000	200,000

A book is selected at random. In each of Exercises 37–42, compute the probability of the given event.

37. That it is either a sci-fi book or stored in Texas (or both)

38. That it is a sci-fi book stored in Texas

39. That it is a sci-fi book, given that it is stored in Texas

40. That it was stored in Texas, given that it was a sci-fi book

41. That it was stored in Texas, given that it was not a sci-fi book

42. That it was not stored in Texas, given that it was a sci-fi book

In order to gauge the effectiveness of the OHaganBooks.com site, you recently commissioned a survey of online shoppers. According to the results, 2% of online shoppers visited OHaganBooks.com during a one-week period, while 5% of them visited at least one of OHaganBooks.com's two main competitors: JungleBooks.com and FarmerBooks.com. Use this information to answer Exercises 43–50.

43. What percentage of online shoppers never visited OHaganBooks.com?

44. What percentage of shoppers never visited either of OHaganBooks.com's main competitors?

45. Assuming that visiting OHaganBooks.com was independent of visiting a competitor, what percentage of online shoppers visited either OHaganBooks.com or a competitor?

46. Assuming that visiting OHaganBooks.com was independent of visiting a competitor, what percentage of online shoppers visited OHaganBooks.com but not a competitor?

47. Under the assumption of Exercise 45, what is the probability that an online shopper will visit none of the three sites during a week?

48. If no one who visited OHaganBooks.com ever visited any of the competitors, what is the probability that an online shopper will visit none of the three sites during a week?

49. Actually, the assumption in Exercise 45 is not what was found by the survey, because an online shopper visiting a competitor was in fact more likely to visit OHaganBooks.com than a randomly selected online shopper. Let H be the event that an online shopper visits OHaganBooks.com, and let C be the event that he visits a competitor. Which is greater: $P(H \cap C)$ or $P(H)P(C)$? Why?

50. What the survey found is that 25% of online shoppers who visited a competitor also visited OHaganBooks.com. Given this information, what percentage of online shoppers visited OHaganBooks.com and neither of its competitors?

51. *Sales* According to statistics gathered by OHaganBooks.com, 2% of online shoppers visited the OHaganBooks.com Web site during the course of a week, and 8% of those purchased books from the company. Further, 0.5% of online shoppers who did not visit the OHaganBooks.com Web site during the course of a week nonetheless purchased books from the company (through mail-order catalogs and other

sites like LemmaZorn.com). What is the probability that an online shopper who purchased books from OHaganBooks .com during a given week visited the site?

52. *Sales* Repeat Exercise 51 in the event that 1% of online shoppers visited OHaganBooks.com during the week.

53. *University Admissions* In the year Billy-Sean O'Hagan applied to Suburban State U, 56% of in-state applicants were admitted, while only 15% of out-of-state applicants were admitted. Further, 72% of all applicants were in-state. What percentage of admitted applicants were in-state? (Round your answer to the nearest percentage point.)

54. *University Admissions* Billy-Sean O'Hagan had also applied to Gigantic State U, at which time 75% of all applicants were from the United States and 22% of those applicants were admitted. Also, 14% of the applicants from foreign countries were admitted. What percentage of admitted applicants were from the United States? (Round your answer to the nearest percentage point.)

As mentioned earlier, OHaganBooks.com has two main competitors, JungleBooks.com and FarmerBooks.com, and no other competitors of any significance. The following table shows the movement of customers during July.[94] (Thus, for instance, the first row tells us that 80% of OHaganBooks.com's customers remained loyal, 10% of them went to JungleBooks.com and the remaining 10% to FarmerBooks.com.)

		To		
		OHaganBooks	**JungleBooks**	**FarmerBooks**
From	**OHaganBooks**	80%	10%	10%
	JungleBooks	40%	60%	0%
	FarmerBooks	20%	0%	80%

At the beginning of July, OHaganBooks.com had an estimated market share of one fifth of all customers, while its two competitors had two fifths each. Use this information to answer Exercises 55–58.

55. Estimate the market shares each company had at the end of July.

56. Assuming the July trends continue in August, predict the market shares of each company at the end of August.

57. Name one or more important factors that the Markov model does not take into account.

58. Assuming the July trend were to continue indefinitely, predict the market share enjoyed by each of the three e-commerce sites.

---

[94] By a "customer" of one of the three e-commerce sites, we mean someone who purchases more at that site than at any of the two competitors' sites.

The Monty Hall Problem

Here is a famous "paradox" that even mathematicians find counterintuitive. On the game show *Let's Make a Deal*, you are shown three doors, A, B, and C, and behind one of them is the Big Prize. After you select one of them—say, door A—to make things more interesting the host (Monty Hall), who knows what is behind each door, opens one of the other doors—say, door B—to reveal that the Big Prize is not there. He then offers you the opportunity to change your selection to the remaining door, door C. Should you switch or stick with your original guess? Does it make any difference?

Most people would say that the Big Prize is equally likely to be behind door A or door C, so there is no reason to switch.* In fact, this is wrong: The prize is more likely to be behind door C! There are several ways of seeing why this is so. Here is how you might work it out using Bayes' theorem.

* This problem caused quite a stir in late 1991 when this problem was discussed in Marilyn vos Savant's column in *Parade* magazine. Vos Savant gave the answer that you should switch. She received about 10,000 letters in response, most of them disagreeing with her, including several from mathematicians.

Let A be the event that the Big Prize is behind door A, B the event that it is behind door B, and C the event that it is behind door C. Let F be the event that Monty has opened door B and revealed that the prize is not there. You wish to find $P(C \mid F)$ using Bayes' theorem. To use that formula you need to find $P(F \mid A)$ and $P(A)$ and similarly for B and C. Now, $P(A) = P(B) = P(C) = 1/3$ because at the outset, the prize is equally likely to be behind any of the doors. $P(F \mid A)$ is the probability that Monty will open door B if the prize is actually behind door A, and this is $1/2$ because we assume that he will choose either B or C randomly in this case. On the other hand, $P(F \mid B) = 0$, because he will never open the door that hides the prize. Also, $P(F \mid C) = 1$ because if the prize is behind door C, he must open door B to keep from revealing that the prize is behind door C. Therefore,

$$P(C \mid F) = \frac{P(F \mid C)P(C)}{P(F \mid A)P(A) + P(F \mid B)P(B) + P(F \mid C)P(C)}$$

$$= \frac{1 \cdot \frac{1}{3}}{\frac{1}{2} \cdot \frac{1}{3} + 0 \cdot \frac{1}{3} + 1 \cdot \frac{1}{3}} = \frac{2}{3}.$$

You conclude from this that you *should* switch to door C because it is more likely than door A to be hiding the Prize.

Here is a more elementary way you might work it out. Consider the tree diagram of possibilities shown in Figure 22. The top two branches of the tree give the cases in which the prize is behind door A, and there is a total probability of $1/3$ for that case. The remaining two branches with nonzero probabilities give the cases in which the prize is behind the door that you did not choose, and there is a total probability of $2/3$ for that case. Again, you conclude that you should switch your choice of doors because the one you did not choose is twice as likely as door A to be hiding the Big Prize.

Prize Behind   Monty Opens

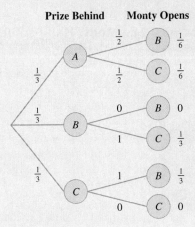

Figure 22

EXERCISES

1. The answer you came up with, to switch to the other door, depends on the strategy Monty Hall uses in picking the door to open. Suppose that he actually picks one of doors B and C at random, so that there is a chance that he will reveal the Big Prize. If he opens door B and it happens that the Prize is not there, should you switch or not?

2. What if you know that Monty's strategy is always to open door B if possible (i.e., it does not hide the Big Prize) after you choose A?

   a. If he opens door B, should you switch?
   b. If he opens door C, should you switch?

3. Repeat the analysis of the original game, but suppose that the game uses four doors instead of three (and still only one prize).

4. Repeat the analysis of the original game, but suppose that the game uses 1,000 doors instead of 3 (and still only one prize).

TI-83/84 Plus Technology Guide

Section 7.2

The TI-83/84 Plus has a random number generator that we can use to simulate experiments. For the following example, recall that a fair coin has probability 1/2 of coming up heads and 1/2 of coming up tails.

Example Use a simulated experiment to check the following.

a. The estimated probability of heads coming up in a toss of a fair coin approaches 1/2 as the number of trials gets large.

b. The estimated probability of heads coming up in two consecutive tosses of a fair coin approaches 1/4 as the number of trials gets large.[95]

Solution with Technology

a. Let us use 1 to represent heads and 0 to represent tails. We need to generate a list of **random binary digits** (0 or 1). One way to do this—and a method that works for most forms of technology—is to generate a random number between 0 and 1 and then round it to the nearest whole number, which will be either 0 or 1.

We generate random numbers on the TI-83/84 Plus using the "rand" function. To round the number X to the nearest whole number on the TI-83/84 Plus, follow MATH →NUM, select "round," and enter round(X,0). This instruction rounds X to zero decimal places—that is, to the nearest whole number. Since we wish to round a random number we need to enter

round(rand,0)   To obtain rand,
                 follow MATH →PRB.

The result will be either 0 or 1. Each time you press ENTER you will now get another 0 or 1. The TI-83/84 Plus can also generate a random integer directly (without the need for rounding) through the instruction

randInt(0,1)   To obtain randInt,
                follow MATH →PRB.

In general, the command randInt(m, n) generates a random integer in the range [m, n]. The following sequence of 100 random binary digits was produced using technology.[96]

0	1	0	0	1	1	0	1	0	0
0	1	0	0	0	0	0	0	1	0
1	1	0	0	0	1	0	0	1	1
1	1	1	0	1	0	0	0	1	0
1	1	1	1	1	1	1	0	0	1
1	0	1	1	1	0	0	1	1	0
0	1	0	1	1	1	0	1	1	1
1	0	0	0	0	0	0	1	1	1
1	1	1	1	0	0	1	1	1	0
1	1	1	0	1	1	0	1	0	0

If we use only the first row of data (corresponding to the first ten tosses), we find

$$P(\text{H}) = \frac{fr(1)}{N} = \frac{4}{10} = .4.$$

Using the first two rows ($N = 20$) gives

$$P(\text{H}) = \frac{fr(1)}{N} = \frac{6}{20} = .3.$$

Using all ten rows ($N = 100$) gives

$$P(\text{H}) = \frac{fr(1)}{N} = \frac{54}{100} = .54.$$

This is somewhat closer to the theoretical probability of 1/2 and supports our intuitive notion that the larger the number of trials, the more closely the estimated probability should approximate the theoretical value.[97]

b. We need to generate pairs of random binary digits and then check whether they are both 1s. Although the TI-83/84 Plus will generate a pair of random digits if you enter round(rand(2),0), it would be a lot more convenient if the calculator could tell you right away whether both digits are 1s (corresponding to two consecutive heads in a coin toss). Here is a simple way of accomplishing this. Notice that if we *add* the two random binary digits, we obtain either 0, 1, or 2, telling us the number of heads that result from the two consecutive throws. Therefore, all we need to do is add the pairs of random digits and then count the number of times 2 comes up. A formula we can use is

randInt(0,1)+randInt(0,1)

---

[95] Since the set of outcomes of a pair of coin tosses is {HH, HT, TH, TT}, we expect HH to come up once in every four trials, on average.

[96] The instruction randInt(0,1,100)→L₁ will generate a list of 100 random 0s and 1s and store it in L₁, where it can be summed with Sum(L₁) (under 2ND LIST →MATH).

[97] Do not expect this to happen every time. Compare, for example, $P(\text{H})$ for the first five rows and for all ten rows.

What would be even *more* convenient is if the result of the calculation would be either 0 or 1, with 1 signifying success (two consecutive heads) and 0 signifying failure. Then, we could simply add up all the results to obtain the number of times two heads occurred. To do this, we first divide the result of the previous calculation above by 2 (obtaining 0, .5, or 1, where now 1 signifies success) and then round *down* to an integer using a function called "int":

```
int(0.5*(randInt(0,1)+randInt(0,1)))
```

Following is the result of 100 such pairs of coin tosses, with 1 signifying success (two heads) and 0 signifying failure (all other outcomes). The last column records the number of successes in each row and the total number at the end.

1	1	0	0	0	0	0	0	0	0	2
0	1	0	0	0	0	0	1	0	1	3
0	1	0	0	1	1	0	0	0	1	4
0	0	0	0	0	0	0	0	1	0	1
0	1	0	0	1	0	0	1	0	0	3
1	0	1	0	0	0	0	0	0	0	2
0	0	0	0	0	0	0	0	0	1	1
0	1	1	1	1	0	0	0	0	1	5
1	1	0	1	0	0	1	1	0	0	5
0	0	0	0	0	0	0	0	1	0	1
										27

Now, as in part (a), we can compute estimated probabilities, with D standing for the outcome "two heads":

First 10 trials: $P(D) = \dfrac{fr(1)}{N} = \dfrac{2}{10} = .2$

First 20 trials: $P(D) = \dfrac{fr(1)}{N} = \dfrac{5}{20} = .25$

First 50 trials: $P(D) = \dfrac{fr(1)}{N} = \dfrac{13}{50} = .26$

100 trials: $P(D) = \dfrac{fr(1)}{N} = \dfrac{27}{100} = .27.$

Q: *What is happening with the data? The probabilities seem to be getting* less *accurate as N increases!*

A: Quite by chance, exactly 5 of the first 20 trials resulted in success, which matches the theoretical probability. Figure 23 shows an Excel plot of estimated probability versus N (for N a multiple of 10). Notice that, as N increases, the graph seems to meander within smaller distances of .25.

Figure 23

Q: *The previous techniques work fine for simulating coin tosses. What about rolls of a fair die, where we want outcomes between 1 and 6?*

A: We can simulate a roll of a die by generating a random integer in the range 1 through 6. The following formula accomplishes this:

$$1 + \text{int}(5.99999*\text{rand}).$$

(We used 5.99999 instead of 6 to avoid the outcome 7.)

Section **7.7**

Example 1 (page 523)   Consider the Markov system found by Gamble Detergents at the beginning of this section. Suppose that 70% of consumers are now using powdered detergent while the other 30% are using liquid. What will be the distribution one year from now? Two years from now? Three years from now?

Solution with Technology

In Chapter 4 we saw how to set up and multiply matrices. For this example, we can use the matrix editor to define [A] as the initial distribution and [B] as the transition matrix (remember that the only names we can use are [A] through [J]).

Entering [A] (obtained by pressing MATRX 1 ENTER) will show you the initial distribution. To obtain the distribution after 1 step, press X MATRX 2 ENTER, which has the effect of multiplying the previous answer by the transition matrix [B]. Now, just press ENTER repeatedly to continue multiplying by the transition matrix and obtain the distribution after any number of steps. The screenshot shows the initial distribution [A] and the distributions after 1, 2, and 3 steps.

```
[A]
          [[.7 .3]]
Ans*[B]
          [[.59 .41]]
        [[.513 .487]]
      [[.4591 .5409]]
```

Example 4 (page 527)   Calculate the steady-state probability vector for the transition matrix in the preceding examples.

Solution with Technology

Finding the steady-state probability vector comes down to solving a system of equations. As discussed in Chapters 3 and 4, there are several ways to use a calculator to help. The most straightforward is to use matrix inversion to solve the matrix form of the system. In this case, as in the text, the system of equations we need to solve is

$$x + y = 1$$
$$-.2x + .1y = 0.$$

We write this as the matrix equation $AX = B$ with

$$A = \begin{bmatrix} 1 & 1 \\ -.2 & .1 \end{bmatrix} \qquad B = \begin{bmatrix} 1 \\ 0 \end{bmatrix}.$$

To find $X = A^{-1}B$ using the TI-83/84 Plus, we first use the matrix editor to enter these matrices as [A] and [B], then compute [A]$^{-1}$[B] on the home screen.

```
[A]⁻¹[B]
   [[.3333333333]
    [.6666666667]]
```

To convert the entries to fractions, we can follow this by the command.

▶ Frac   [MATH] [ENTER] [ENTER]

```
[A]⁻¹[B]
   [[.3333333333]
    [.6666666667]]
Ans▶Frac
          [[1/3]
           [2/3]]
```

SPREADSHEET   **Technology Guide**

Section 7.2

Spreadsheets have random number generators that we can use to simulate experiments. For the following example, recall that a fair coin has probability 1/2 of coming up heads and 1/2 of coming up tails.

Example   Use a simulated experiment to check the following.

a. The estimated probability of heads coming up in a toss of a fair coin approaches 1/2 as the number of trials gets large.

b. The estimated probability of heads coming up in two consecutive tosses of a fair coin approaches 1/4 as the number of trials gets large.[98]

Solution with Technology

a. Let us use 1 to represent heads and 0 to represent tails. We need to generate a list of **random binary digits** (0 or 1). One way to do this—and a method that works for most forms of technology—is to generate a random number between 0 and 1 and then round it to the nearest whole number, which will be either 0 or 1.

In a spreadsheet, the formula RAND() gives a random number between 0 and 1.[99] The function ROUND(X,0) rounds X to zero decimal places—that is, to the nearest integer. Therefore, to obtain a random binary digit in any cell, just enter the following formula:

```
=ROUND(RAND(),0)
```

---

[98] Because the set of outcomes of a pair of coin tosses is {HH, HT, TH, TT}, we expect HH to come up once in every four trials, on average.

[99] The parentheses after RAND are necessary even though the function takes no arguments.

Spreadsheets can also generate a random integer directly (without the need for rounding) through the formula

```
=RANDBETWEEN(0,1)
```

To obtain a whole array of random numbers, just drag this formula into the cells you wish to use.

b. We need to generate pairs of random binary digits and then check whether they are both 1s. It would be convenient if the spreadsheet could tell you right away whether both digits are 1s (corresponding to two consecutive heads in a coin toss). Here is a simple way of accomplishing this. Notice that if we *add* two random binary digits, we obtain either 0, 1, or 2, telling us the number of heads that result from the two consecutive throws. Therefore, all we need to do is add pairs of random digits and then count the number of times 2 comes up. Formulas we can use are

```
=RANDBETWEEN(0,1)+RANDBETWEEN(0,1)
```

What would be even *more* convenient is if the result of the calculation would be either 0 or 1, with 1 signifying success (two consecutive heads) and 0 signifying failure. Then, we could simply add up all the results to obtain the number of times two heads occurred. To do this, we first divide the result of the calculation above by 2 (obtaining 0, .5, or 1, where now 1 signifies success) and then round *down* to an integer using a function called "int":

```
=INT(0.5*(RANDBETWEEN(0,1)+
RANDBETWEEN(0,1)))
```

Following is the result of 100 such pairs of coin tosses, with 1 signifying success (two heads) and 0 signifying failure (all other outcomes). The last column records the number of successes in each row and the total number at the end.

1	1	0	0	0	0	0	0	0	0	2
0	1	0	0	0	0	0	1	0	1	3
0	1	0	0	1	1	0	0	0	1	4
0	0	0	0	0	0	0	0	1	0	1
0	1	0	0	1	0	0	1	0	0	3
1	0	1	0	0	0	0	0	0	0	2
0	0	0	0	0	0	0	0	0	1	1
0	1	1	1	1	0	0	0	0	1	5
1	1	0	1	0	0	1	1	0	0	5
0	0	0	0	0	0	0	0	1	0	1
										27

Now, as in part (a), we can compute estimated probabilities, with D standing for the outcome "two heads":

First 10 trials: $P(D) = \dfrac{fr(1)}{N} = \dfrac{2}{10} = .2$

First 20 trials: $P(D) = \dfrac{fr(1)}{N} = \dfrac{5}{20} = .25$

First 50 trials: $P(D) = \dfrac{fr(1)}{N} = \dfrac{13}{50} = .26$

100 trials: $P(D) = \dfrac{fr(1)}{N} = \dfrac{27}{100} = .27.$

Q: *What is happening with the data? The probabilities seem to be getting less accurate as N increases!*

A: Quite by chance, exactly 5 of the first 20 trials resulted in success, which matches the theoretical probability. Figure 24 shows an Excel plot of estimated probability versus N (for N a multiple of 10). Notice that, as N increases, the graph seems to meander within smaller distances of .25.

Figure 24

Q: *The previous techniques work fine for simulating coin tosses. What about rolls of a fair die, where we want outcomes between 1 and 6?*

A: We can simulate a roll of a die by generating a random integer in the range 1 through 6. The following formula accomplishes this:

```
=1 + INT(5.99999*RAND())
```

(We used 5.99999 instead of 6 to avoid the outcome 7.)

Section 7.7

Example 1 (page 523)   Consider the Markov system found by Gamble Detergents at the beginning of this section. Suppose that 70% of consumers are now using powdered detergent while the other 30% are using liquid. What will be the distribution one year from now? Two years from now? Three years from now?

Solution with Technology

In your spreadsheet, enter the initial distribution vector in cells A1 and B1 and the transition matrix to the right of that, as shown.

	A	B	C	D	E
1	0.7	0.3		0.8	0.2
2				0.1	0.9

To calculate the distribution after one step, use the array formula

$$\texttt{=MMULT(A1:B1,\$D\$1:\$E\$2)}$$

The absolute cell references (dollar signs) ensure that the formula always refers to the same transition matrix, even if we copy it into other cells. To use the array formula, select cells A2 and B2, where the distribution vector will go, enter this formula, and then press Control+Shift+Enter.[100]

	A	B	C	D	E
1	0.7	0.3		0.8	0.2
2	=MMULT(A1:B1,$D$1:$E$2)			0.1	0.9

The result is the following, with the distribution after one step highlighted.

	A	B	C	D	E
1	0.7	0.3		0.8	0.2
2	0.59	0.41		0.1	0.9

To calculate the distribution after two steps, select cells A2 and B2 and drag the fill handle down to copy the formula to cells A3 and B3. Note that the formula now takes the vector in A2:B2 and multiplies it by the transition matrix to get the vector in A3:B3. To calculate several more steps, drag down as far as desired.

	A	B	C	D	E
1	0.7	0.3		0.8	0.2
2	0.59	0.41		0.1	0.9
3					
4					

	A	B	C	D	E
1	0.7	0.3		0.8	0.2
2	0.59	0.41		0.1	0.9
3	0.513	0.487			
4	0.4591	0.5409			

Example 4 (page 527) Calculate the steady-state probability vector for the transition matrix in the preceding examples.

Solution with Technology

Finding the steady-state probability vector comes down to solving a system of equations. As discussed in Chapters 3 and 4, there are several ways to use Excel to help. The most straightforward is to use matrix inversion to solve the matrix form of the system. In this case, as in the text, the system of equations we need to solve is

$$x + \quad y = 1$$
$$-.2x + .1y = 0.$$

We write this as the matrix equation $AX = B$ with

$$A = \begin{bmatrix} 1 & 1 \\ -.2 & .1 \end{bmatrix} \qquad B = \begin{bmatrix} 1 \\ 0 \end{bmatrix}.$$

We enter A in cells A1:B2, B in cells D1:D2, and the formula for $X = A^{-1}B$ in a convenient location, say B4:B5.

	A	B	C	D
1	1	1		1
2	-0.2	0.1		0
3				
4		=MMULT(MINVERSE(A1:B2),D1:D2)		
5				

When we press Control+Shift+Enter we see the result:

	A	B	C	D
1	1	1		1
2	-0.2	0.1		0
3				
4		0.3333333		
5		0.6666667		

If we want to see the answer in fraction rather than decimal form, we format the cells as fractions.

	A	B	C	D
1	1	1		1
2	-0.2	0.1		0
3				
4		1/3		
5		2/3		

---

[100] On a Macintosh, you can also use Command+Enter.

8

Random Variables and Statistics

 Website

www.WanerMath.com

At the Website you will find:

- Section-by-section tutorials, including game tutorials with randomized quizzes

- A detailed chapter summary

- A true/false quiz

- Additional review exercises

- Histogram, Bernoulli trials, and normal distribution utilities

- The following optional extra sections:

    Sampling Distributions and the Central Limit Theorem

    Confidence Intervals

    Calculus and Statistics

Case Study Spotting Tax Fraud with Benford's Law

You are a tax fraud specialist working for the Internal Revenue Service (IRS), and you have just been handed a portion of the tax return from Colossal Conglomerate. The IRS suspects that the portion you were handed may be fraudulent and would like your opinion. **Is there any mathematical test, you wonder, that can point to a suspicious tax return based on nothing more than the numbers entered?**

age fotostock/SuperStock

547

Introduction

Statistics is the branch of mathematics concerned with organizing, analyzing, and interpreting numerical data. For example, given the current annual incomes of 1,000 lawyers selected at random, you might wish to answer some questions: If I become a lawyer, what income am I likely to earn? Do lawyers' salaries vary widely? How widely?

To answer questions like these, it helps to begin by organizing the data in the form of tables or graphs. This is the topic of the first section of the chapter. The second section describes an important class of examples that are applicable to a wide range of situations, from tossing a coin to product testing.

Once the data are organized, the next step is to apply mathematical tools for analyzing the data and answering questions like those posed above. Numbers such as the **mean** and the **standard deviation** can be computed to reveal interesting facts about the data. These numbers can then be used to make predictions about future events.

The chapter ends with a section on one of the most important distributions in statistics, the **normal distribution**. This distribution describes many sets of data and also plays an important role in the underlying mathematical theory.

8.1   Random Variables and Distributions

Random Variables

In many experiments we can assign numerical values to the outcomes. For instance, if we roll a die, each outcome has a value from 1 through 6. If you select a lawyer and ascertain his or her annual income, the outcome is again a number. We call a rule that assigns a number to each outcome of an experiment a **random variable**.

> ✳ In the language of functions (Chapter 1), a random variable is a *real-valued function* whose domain is the sample space.

> ### Random Variable
>
> A **random variable** X is a rule that assigns a number, or **value**, to each outcome in the sample space of an experiment.✳
>
> **Visualizing a Random Variable**
>
>

> **Quick Examples**
>
> **1.** Roll a die; $X =$ the number facing up.
> **2.** Select a mutual fund; $X =$ the number of companies in the fund portfolio.
> **3.** Select a computer; $X =$ the number of gigabytes of memory it has.
> **4.** Survey a group of 20 college students; $X =$ the mean SAT.

Discrete and Continuous Random Variables

A **discrete** random variable can take on only specific, isolated numerical values, like the outcome of a roll of a die, or the number of dollars in a randomly chosen bank account. A **continuous** random variable, on the other hand, can take on any values within a continuum or an interval, like the temperature in Central Park, or the height of an athlete in centimeters. Discrete random variables that can take on only finitely many values (like the outcome of a roll of a die) are called **finite** random variables.

Random Variable	Values	Type
1. Select a mutual fund; $X =$ the number of companies in the fund portfolio.	$\{1, 2, 3, \ldots\}$	Discrete Infinite
2. Take five shots at the goal during a soccer match; $X =$ the number of times you score.	$\{0, 1, 2, 3, 4, 5\}$	Finite
3. Measure the length of an object; $X =$ its length in centimeters.	Any positive real number	Continuous
4. Roll a die until you get a 6; $X =$ the number of times you roll the die.	$\{1, 2, \ldots\}$	Discrete Infinite
5. Bet a whole number of dollars in a race where the betting limit is \$100; $X =$ the amount you bet.	$\{0, 1, \ldots, 100\}$	Finite
6. Bet a whole number of dollars in a race where there is no betting limit; $X =$ the amount you bet.	$\{0, 1, \ldots, 100, 101, \ldots\}$	Discrete Infinite

Notes

1. In Chapter 7, the only sample spaces we considered in detail were finite sample spaces. However, in general, sample spaces can be infinite, as in many of the experiments mentioned above.

2. There are some "borderline" situations. For instance, if X is the salary of a factory worker, then X is, strictly speaking, discrete. However, the values of X are so numerous and close together that in some applications it makes sense to model X as a continuous random variable. ∎

For the moment, we shall consider only finite random variables.

EXAMPLE 1 Finite Random Variable

Let X be the number of heads that come up when a coin is tossed three times. List the value of X for each possible outcome. What are the possible values of X?

Solution First, we describe X as a random variable.

X is the rule that assigns to each outcome the number of heads that come up.

2 Heads ($X = 2$)

We take as the outcomes of this experiment all possible sequences of three heads and tails. Then, for instance, if the outcome is HTH, the value of X is 2. An easy way to list the values of X for all the outcomes is by means of a table.

Outcome	HHH	HHT	HTH	HTT	THH	THT	TTH	TTT
Value of X	3	2	2	1	2	1	1	0

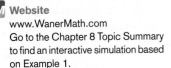

Website
www.WanerMath.com
Go to the Chapter 8 Topic Summary to find an interactive simulation based on Example 1.

From the table, we also see that the possible values of X are 0, 1, 2, and 3.

➡ **Before we go on...** Remember that X is just a rule we decide on. In Example 1, we could have taken X to be a different rule, such as the number of tails or perhaps the number of heads minus the number of tails. These different rules are examples of different random variables associated with the same experiment. ■

EXAMPLE 2 Stock Prices

You have purchased $10,000 worth of stock in a biotech company whose newest arthritis drug is awaiting approval by the Food and Drug Administration (FDA). If the drug is approved this month, the value of the stock will double by the end of the month. If the drug is rejected this month, the stock's value will decline by 80%. If no decision is reached this month, its value will decline by 10%. Let X be the value of your investment at the end of this month. List the value of X for each possible outcome.

Solution There are three possible outcomes: the drug is approved this month, it is rejected this month, and no decision is reached. Once again, we express the random variable as a rule.

The random variable X is the rule that assigns to each outcome the value of your investment at the end of this month.

We can now tabulate the values of X as follows:

Outcome	Approved This Month	Rejected This Month	No Decision
Value of X	$20,000	$2,000	$9,000

Probability Distribution of a Finite Random Variable

Given a random variable X, it is natural to look at certain *events*—for instance, the event that $X = 2$. By this, we mean the event consisting of all outcomes that have an assigned X-value of 2. Looking once again at the chart in Example 1, with X being the number of heads that face up when a coin is tossed three times, we find the following events:

The event that $X = 0$ is {TTT}.
The event that $X = 1$ is {HTT, THT, TTH}.
The event that $X = 2$ is {HHT, HTH, THH}.
The event that $X = 3$ is {HHH}.
The event that $X = 4$ is Ø.   There are no outcomes with four heads.

Each of these events has a certain probability. For instance, the probability of the event that $X = 2$ is 3/8 because the event in question consists of three of the eight possible (equally likely) outcomes. We shall abbreviate this by writing

$$P(X = 2) = \frac{3}{8}.$$ The probability that $X = 2$ is 3/8.

Similarly,

$$P(X = 4) = 0.$$ The probability that $X = 4$ is 0.

When X is a finite random variable, the collection of the probabilities of X equaling each of its possible values is called the **probability distribution** of X. Because the probabilities in a probability distribution can be estimated or theoretical, we shall discuss both *estimated probability distributions* (or *relative frequency distributions*) and *theoretical (modeled) probability distributions* of random variables. (See the next two examples.)

Probability Distribution of a Finite Random Variable

If X is a finite random variable, with values $n_1, n_2, \ldots$ then its **probability distribution** lists the probabilities that $X = n_1$, $X = n_2$, ... The sum of these probabilities is always 1.

Visualizing the Probability Distribution of a Random Variable

If each outcome in S is equally likely, we get the probability distribution shown for the random variable X.

S

| •0 | •0 | •5 |
| •2 | | •−1 |

Probability Distribution of X

x	-1	0	2	5
$P(X = x)$	$\frac{1}{5} = .2$	$\frac{2}{5} = .4$	$\frac{1}{5} = .2$	$\frac{1}{5} = .2$

Here $P(X = x)$ means "the probability that the random variable X has the specific value x."

Quick Example

Roll a fair die; $X =$ the number facing up. Then, the probability that any specific value of X occurs is $\frac{1}{6}$. So, the probability distribution of X is the following (notice that the probabilities add up to 1):

x	1	2	3	4	5	6
$P(X = x)$	$\frac{1}{6}$	$\frac{1}{6}$	$\frac{1}{6}$	$\frac{1}{6}$	$\frac{1}{6}$	$\frac{1}{6}$

Using this probability distribution, we can calculate the probabilities of certain events; for instance:

$$P(X < 3) = \frac{1}{3}$$ The event that $X < 3$ is the event $\{1, 2\}$.

$$P(1 < X < 5) = \frac{1}{2}$$ The event that $1 < X < 5$ is the event $\{2, 3, 4\}$.

Note The distinction between X (uppercase) and x (lowercase) in the tables above is important; X stands for the random variable in question, whereas x stands for a specific *value* of X (so that x is always a number). Thus, if, say $x = 2$, then $P(X = x)$ means $P(X = 2)$, the probability that X is 2. Similarly, if Y is a random variable, then $P(Y = y)$ is the probability that Y has the specific value y. ■

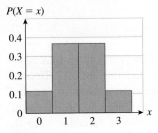

Figure 1

EXAMPLE 3 **Probability Distribution**

Let X be the number of heads that face up in three tosses of a coin. Give the probability distribution of X. What is the probability of throwing at least two heads?

Solution X is the random variable of Example 1, so its values are 0, 1, 2, and 3. The probability distribution of X is given in the following table:

x	0	1	2	3
$P(X = x)$	$\dfrac{1}{8}$	$\dfrac{3}{8}$	$\dfrac{3}{8}$	$\dfrac{1}{8}$

Notice that the probabilities add to 1, as we might expect. From the distribution, the probability of throwing at least two heads is

$$P(X \geq 2) = P(\{2, 3\}) = \frac{3}{8} + \frac{1}{8} = \frac{1}{2}.$$

We can use a bar graph to visualize a probability distribution. Figure 1 shows the bar graph for the probability distribution we obtained. Such a graph is sometimes called a **histogram**.

➡ **Before we go on...** The probabilities in the table in Example 3 are *modeled* probabilities. To obtain a similar table of relative frequencies, we would have to repeatedly toss a coin three times and calculate the fraction of times we got 0, 1, 2, and 3 heads. ∎

Note The table of probabilities in Example 3 looks like the probability distribution associated with an experiment, as we studied in Section 7.3. In fact, the probability distribution of a random variable is not really new. Consider the following experiment: toss three coins and count the number of heads. The associated probability distribution (as per Section 7.3) would be this:

Outcome	0	1	2	3
Probability	$\dfrac{1}{8}$	$\dfrac{3}{8}$	$\dfrac{3}{8}$	$\dfrac{1}{8}$

The difference is that in this chapter we are thinking of 0, 1, 2, and 3 not as the outcomes of the experiment, but as values of the random variable X. ∎

EXAMPLE 4 **Relative Frequency Distribution**

The following table shows the (fictitious) income brackets of a sample of 1,000 lawyers in their first year out of law school.

Income Bracket	\$20,000–\$29,999	\$30,000–\$39,999	\$40,000–\$49,999	\$50,000–\$59,999	\$60,000–\$69,999	\$70,000–\$79,999	\$80,000–\$89,999
Number	20	80	230	400	170	70	30

Think of the experiment of choosing a first-year lawyer at random (all being equally likely) and assign to each lawyer the number X that is the midpoint of his or her income bracket. Find the relative frequency distribution of X.

Solution Statisticians refer to the income brackets as **measurement classes**. Because the first measurement class contains incomes that are at least \$20,000, but less

∗ One might argue that the midpoint should be $(20,000 + 29,999)/2 = 24,999.50$, but we round this to 25,000. So, technically we are using "rounded" midpoints of the measurement classes.

 using Technology

Technology can be used to automate the calculations in Example 4. Here is an outline.

TI-83/84 Plus

STAT EDIT values of x in L_1 and frequencies in L_2.
Home screen: $L_2/\text{sum}(L_2) \rightarrow L_3$
[More details on page 615.]

Spreadsheet
Headings x, Fr, and $P(X = x)$ in A1–C1
x-values and frequencies in Columns A2–B8
$=B2/\text{SUM}(B:B)$ in C2
Copy down column C.
[More details on page 616.]

 Website
www.WanerMath.com
Student Home
  → On Line Utilities
  → Histogram Utility

Enter the x-values and frequencies as shown:

```
25000, 20
35000, 80
45000, 230
55000, 400
65000, 170
75000, 70
85000, 30
```

Make sure "Show probability distribution" is checked, and press "Results". The relative frequency distribution will appear at the bottom of the page.

than \$30,000, its midpoint is \$25,000.∗ Similarly the second measurement class has midpoint \$35,000, and so on. We can rewrite the table with the midpoints, as follows:

x	25,000	35,000	45,000	55,000	65,000	75,000	85,000
Frequency	20	80	230	400	170	70	30

We have used the term *frequency* rather than *number*, although it means the same thing. This table is called a **frequency table**. It is *almost* the relative frequency distribution for X, except that we must replace frequencies by relative frequencies. (We did this in calculating relative frequencies in the preceding chapter.) We start with the lowest measurement class. Because 20 of the 1,000 lawyers fall in this group, we have

$$P(X = 25,000) = \frac{20}{1,000} = .02.$$

We can calculate the remaining relative frequencies similarly to obtain the following distribution:

x	25,000	35,000	45,000	55,000	65,000	75,000	85,000
$P(X = x)$	.02	.08	.23	.40	.17	.07	.03

Note again the distinction between X and x: X stands for the random variable in question, whereas x stands for a specific value (25,000, 35,000, . . . , or 85,000) of X.

EXAMPLE 5 Probability Distribution: Greenhouse Gases

The following table shows per capita emissions of greenhouse gases for the 30 countries with the highest per capita carbon dioxide emissions. (Emissions are rounded to the nearest 5 metric tons.)[1]

Country	Per Capita Emissions (metric tons)	Country	Per Capita Emissions (metric tons)
Qatar	70	Estonia	15
Kuwait	40	Faroe Islands	15
United Arab Emirates	40	Saudi Arabia	15
Luxembourg	25	Kazakhstan	15
Trinidad and Tobago	25	Gibraltar	15
Brunei	25	Finland	15
Bahrain	25	Oman	15
Netherlands Antilles	20	Singapore	10
Aruba	20	Palau	10
United States	20	Montserrat	10
Canada	20	Czech Republic	10
Norway	20	Equatorial Guinea	10
Australia	15	New Caledonia	10
Falkland Islands	15	Israel	10
Nauru	15	Russia	10

[1]Figures are based on 2004 data. Source: United Nations Millennium Development Goals Indicators (http://mdgs.un.org/unsd/mdg/Data.aspx).

Consider the experiment in which a country is selected at random from this list, and let X be the per capita carbon dioxide emissions for that country. Find the probability distribution of X and graph it with a histogram. Use the probability distribution to compute $P(X \geq 20)$ (the probability that X is 20 or more) and interpret the result.

Solution The values of X are the possible emissions figures, which we can take to be $0, 5, 10, 15, \ldots, 70$. In the table below, we first compute the frequency of each value of X by counting the number of countries that produce that per capita level of greenhouse gases. For instance, there are seven countries that have $X = 15$. Then, we divide each frequency by the sample size $N = 30$ to obtain the probabilities.*

* Even though we are using the term "frequency," we are really calculating *modeled* probability based on the assumption of equally likely outcomes. In this context, the frequencies are the number of favorable outcomes for each value of X. (See the Q&A discussion at the end of Section 7.3.)

x	0	5	10	15	20	25	30	35	40	45	50	55	60	65	70
Frequency	0	0	8	10	5	4	0	0	2	0	0	0	0	0	1
$P(X = x)$	0	0	$\frac{8}{30}$	$\frac{10}{30}$	$\frac{5}{30}$	$\frac{4}{30}$	0	0	$\frac{2}{30}$	0	0	0	0	0	$\frac{1}{30}$

Figure 2 shows the resulting histogram.

Finally, we compute $P(X \geq 20)$, the probability of the event that X has a value of 20 or more, which is the sum of the probabilities $P(X = 20)$, $P(X = 25)$, and so on. From the table, we obtain

$$P(X \geq 20) = \frac{5}{30} + \frac{4}{30} + \frac{2}{30} + \frac{1}{30} = \frac{12}{30} = .4.$$

Thus, there is a 40% chance that a country randomly selected from the given list produces 20 or more metric tons per capita of carbon dioxide.

$P(X = x)$

Per Capita Emissions

Figure 2

FAQs

Recognizing What to Use as a Random Variable and Deciding on Its Values

Q : *In an application, how, exactly, do I decide what to use as a random variable X?*

A : Be as systematic as possible: First, decide what the experiment is and what its sample space is. Then, based on what is asked for in the application, complete the following sentence: "*X* assigns ___ to each outcome." For instance, "*X* assigns the number of flavors to each packet of gummy bears selected," or "*X* assigns the average faculty salary to each college selected."

Q : *Once I have decided what X should be, how do I decide what values to assign it?*

A : Ask yourself: What are the conceivable values I could get for *X*? Then choose a collection of values that includes all of these. For instance, if *X* is the number of heads obtained when a coin is tossed five times, then the possible values of *X* are 0, 1, 2, 3, 4, and 5. If *X* is the average faculty salary in dollars, rounded to the nearest $5,000, then possible values of *X* could be 20,000, 25,000, 30,000, and so on, up to the highest salary in your data.

8.1   EXERCISES

▼ more advanced   ◆ challenging
T indicates exercises that should be solved using technology

In Exercises 1–10, classify each random variable X as finite, discrete infinite, or continuous, and indicate the values that X can take. HINT [See Quick Examples on page 549.]

1. Roll two dice; $X =$ the sum of the numbers facing up.

2. Open a 500-page book on a random page; $X =$ the page number.

3. Select a stock at random; $X =$ your profit, to the nearest dollar, if you purchase one share and sell it one year later.

4. Select an electric utility company at random; $X =$ the exact amount of electricity, in gigawatt hours, it supplies in a year.

5. Look at the second hand of your watch; X is the time it reads in seconds.

6. Watch a soccer game; $X =$ the total number of goals scored.

7. Watch a soccer game; $X =$ the total number of goals scored, up to a maximum of 10.

8. Your class is given a mathematics exam worth 100 points; X is the average score, rounded to the nearest whole number.

9. According to quantum mechanics, the energy of an electron in a hydrogen atom can assume only the values $k/1$, $k/4$, $k/9$, $k/16$, … for a certain constant value k. $X =$ the energy of an electron in a hydrogen atom.

10. According to classical mechanics, the energy of an electron in a hydrogen atom can assume any positive value. $X =$ the energy of an electron in a hydrogen atom.

*In Exercises 11–18, **(a)** say what an appropriate sample space is; **(b)** complete the following sentence: "X is the rule that assigns to each … "; **(c)** list the values of X for all the outcomes.* HINT [See Example 1.]

11. X is the number of tails that come up when a coin is tossed twice.

12. X is the largest number of consecutive times heads comes up in a row when a coin is tossed three times.

13. X is the sum of the numbers that face up when two dice are rolled.

14. X is the value of the larger number when two dice are rolled.

15. X is the number of red marbles that Tonya has in her hand after she selects four marbles from a bag containing four red marbles and two green ones and then notes how many there are of each color.

16. X is the number of green marbles that Stej has in his hand after he selects four marbles from a bag containing three red marbles and two green ones and then notes how many there are of each color.

17. The mathematics final exam scores for the students in your study group are 89%, 85%, 95%, 63%, 92%, and 80%.

18. The capacities of the hard drives of your dormitory suite mates' computers are 1,000 GB, 1,500 GB, 2,000 GB, 2,500 GB, 3,000 GB, and 3,500 GB.

19. The random variable X has this probability distribution table:

x	2	4	6	8	10
$P(X = x)$	.1	.2	–	–	.1

  a. Assuming $P(X = 8) = P(X = 6)$, find each of the missing values. HINT [See Quick Example on page 551.]

  b. Calculate $P(X \geq 6)$ and $P(2 < X < 8)$.

20. The random variable X has the probability distribution table shown below:

x	-2	-1	0	1	2
$P(X = x)$	–	–	.4	.1	.1

  a. Calculate $P(X \geq 0)$ and $P(X < 0)$. HINT [See Quick Example on page 551.]

  b. Assuming $P(X = -2) = P(X = -1)$, find each of the missing values.

In Exercises 21–28, give the probability distribution for the indicated random variable and draw the corresponding histogram, and calculate the indicated probability. HINT [See Example 3.]

21. A fair die is rolled, and X is the number facing up. Calculate $P(X < 5)$.

22. A fair die is rolled, and X is the square of the number facing up. Calculate $P(X > 9)$.

23. Three fair coins are tossed, and X is the square of the number of heads showing. Calculate $P(1 \leq X \leq 9)$.

24. Three fair coins are tossed, and X is the number of heads minus the number of tails. Calculate $P(-3 \leq X \leq -1)$.

25. A red die and a green die are rolled, and X is the sum of the numbers facing up. Calculate $P(X \neq 7)$.

26. A red die and a green die are rolled, and
$$X = \begin{cases} 0 & \text{if the numbers are the same} \\ 1 & \text{if the numbers are different} \end{cases}$$
Calculate $P(X > 1)$.

27. ▼ A red die and a green die are rolled, and X is the larger of the two numbers facing up. Calculate $P(X \leq 3)$.

28. ▼ A red die and a green die are rolled, and X is the smaller of the two numbers facing up. Calculate $P(X \geq 4)$.

APPLICATIONS

29. *2010 Income Distribution up to $100,000* The following table shows the distribution of household incomes in 2010 for a sample of 1,000 households in the U.S. with incomes up to $100,000.[2]

Income Bracket ($)	0–19,999	20,000–39,999	40,000–59,000	60,000–79,999	80,000–99,999
Households	240	290	180	170	120

a. Let X be the (rounded) midpoint of a bracket in which a household falls. Find the relative frequency distribution of X and graph its histogram. HINT [See Example 4.]

b. Shade the area of your histogram corresponding to the probability that a randomly selected U.S. household in the sample has a value of X above 50,000. What is this probability?

30. *2003 Income Distribution up to $100,000* Repeat Exercise 29, using the following data from a sample of 1,000 households in the U.S. in 2003.[3]

Income Bracket ($)	0–19,999	20,000–39,999	40,000–59,000	60,000–79,999	80,000–99,999
Households	270	280	200	150	100

31. *Population Age in Mexico* The following chart shows the ages of 250 randomly selected residents of Mexico:[4]

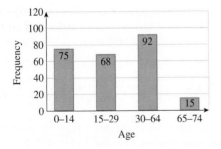

What is the associated random variable? Represent the data as a relative frequency distribution using the (rounded) midpoints of the given measurement classes. HINT [See Example 4.]

32. *Population Age in the U.S.* Repeat the preceding exercise, using the following chart, which shows the ages of 250 randomly selected residents of the U.S.:[5]

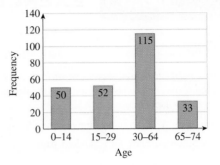

33. *Sport Utility Vehicles—Tow Ratings* The following table shows tow ratings (in pounds) for some popular sports utility vehicles in 2000:[6]

Mercedes Grand Marquis V8	2,000
Jeep Wrangler I6	2,000
Ford Explorer V6	3,000
Dodge Dakota V6	4,000
Mitsubishi Montero V6	5,000
Ford Explorer V8	6,000
Dodge Durango V8	6,000
Dodge Ram 1500 V8	8,000
Ford Expedition V8	8,000
Hummer 2-door Hardtop	8,000

Let X be the tow rating of a randomly chosen popular SUV from the list above.

a. What are the values of X?

b. Compute the frequency and probability distributions of X. HINT [See Example 5.]

c. What is the probability that an SUV (from the list above) is rated to tow no more than 5,000 pounds?

34. *Housing Prices Going into the Real Estate Bubble* The following table shows the average percentage increase in the price of a house from 1980 to 2001 in nine regions of the United States.[7]

---

[2]Based on actual income distribution in 2010. Source: U.S. Census Bureau, Current Population Survey, 2010 American Community Survey (www.census.gov).

[3]Based on actual income distribution in 2003 (not adjusted for inflation). Source: U.S. Census Bureau, Current Population Survey, 2004 Annual Social and Economic Supplement (www.census.gov).

[4]Based on population distribution in 2010. Source: Instituto Nacional de Estadística y Geografía (www.inegi.org.mx).

[5]*Ibid.* (The data for the U.S. was also provided by the Instituto Nacional de Estadística y Geografía.)

[6]Tow ratings are for 2000 models and vary considerably within each model. Figures cited are rounded. For more detailed information, consult www.rvsafety.com/towrate2k.htm.

[7]Percentages are rounded to the nearest 25%. Source: Third Quarter 2001 House Price Index, released November 30, 2001 by the Office of Federal Housing Enterprise Oversight; available online at www.ofheo.gov/ house/3q01hpi.pdf.

New England	300
Pacific	225
Middle Atlantic	225
South Atlantic	150
Mountain	150
West North Central	125
West South Central	75
East North Central	150
East South Central	125

Let X be the percentage increase in the price of a house in a randomly selected region.

a. What are the values of X?

b. Compute the frequency and probability distribution of X. HINT [See Example 5.]

c. What is the probability that, in a randomly selected region, the percentage increase in the cost of a house exceeded 200%?

35. Stock Market Gyrations The following chart shows the day-by-day change, rounded to the nearest 100 points, in the Dow Jones Industrial Average during 20 successive business days around the start of the financial crisis in October 2008:[8]

Change in DJIA

October 2　　　　　　　　　　　　October 30

Let X be the (rounded) change in the Dow on a randomly selected day.

a. What are the values of X?

b. Compute the frequency and probability distribution of X. HINT [See Example 5.]

c. What is the probability that, on a randomly selected day, the Dow decreased by more than 250 points?

36. Stock Market Gyrations Repeat Exercise 35 using the following chart for November–December 2008:[9]

Change in DJIA

November 4　　　　　　　　　　　　December 2

37. Grade-Point Averages The grade-point averages of the students in your mathematics class are

3.2, 3.5, 4.0, 2.9, 2.0, 3.3, 3.5, 2.9, 2.5, 2.0,
2.1, 3.2, 3.6, 2.8, 2.5, 1.9, 2.0, 2.2, 3.9, 4.0

Use these raw data to construct a frequency table with the following measurement classes: 1.1–2.0, 2.1–3.0, 3.1–4.0, and find the probability distribution using the (rounded) midpoint values as the values of X. HINT [See Example 5.]

38. Test Scores Your scores for the 20 surprise math quizzes last semester were (out of 10)

4.5, 9.5, 10.0, 3.5, 8.0, 9.5,　7.5, 6.5, 7.0, 8.0,
8.0, 8.5,　7.5, 7.0, 8.0, 9.0, 10.0, 8.5, 7.5, 8.0.

Use these raw data to construct a frequency table with the following brackets: 2.1–4.0, 4.1–6.0, 6.1–8.0, 8.1–10.0, and find the probability distribution using the (rounded) midpoint values as the values of X. HINT [See Example 5.]

39. ▼ Car Purchases To persuade his parents to contribute to his new car fund, Carmine has spent the last week surveying the ages of 2,000 cars on campus. His findings are reflected in the following frequency table:

Age of Car (years)	0	1	2	3	4	5	6	7	8	9	10
Number of Cars	140	350	450	650	200	120	50	10	5	15	10

Carmine's jalopy is 6 years old. He would like to make the following claim to his parents: "x percent of students have cars newer than mine." Use a relative frequency distribution to find x.

[8]Source: http://finance.google.com.

[9]Ibid.

40. ▼ *Car Purchases* Carmine's parents, not convinced of his need for a new car, produced the following statistics showing the ages of cars owned by students on the Dean's List:

Age of Car (years)	0	1	2	3	4	5	6	7	8	9	10
Number of Cars	0	2	5	5	10	10	15	20	20	20	40

They then claimed that if he kept his 6-year-old car for another year, his chances of getting on the Dean's List would be increased by x percent. Use a relative frequency distribution to find x.

Highway Safety Exercises 41–50 are based on the following table, which shows crashworthiness ratings for several categories of motor vehicles.[10] In all of these exercises, take X as the crash-test rating of a small car, Y as the crash-test rating for a small SUV, and so on, as shown in the table.

	Number Tested	Overall Frontal Crash Test Rating			
		3 (Good)	2 (Acceptable)	1 (Marginal)	0 (Poor)
Small Cars X	16	1	11	2	2
Small SUVs Y	10	1	4	4	1
Medium SUVs Z	15	3	5	3	4
Passenger Vans U	13	3	0	3	7
Midsize Cars V	15	3	5	0	7
Large Cars W	19	9	5	3	2

41. Compute the relative frequency distribution for X.

42. Compute the relative frequency distribution for Y.

43. Compute $P(X \geq 2)$ and interpret the result.

44. Compute $P(Y \leq 1)$ and interpret the result.

45. Compare $P(Y \geq 2)$ and $P(Z \geq 2)$. What does the result suggest about SUVs?

46. Compare $P(V \geq 2)$ and $P(Z \geq 2)$. What does the result suggest?

47. ▼ Which of the six categories shown has the *lowest* probability of a Good rating?

48. ▼ Which of the six categories shown has the *highest* probability of a Poor rating?

49. ▼ You choose, at random, a small car and a small SUV. What is the probability that both will be rated at least 2?

[10]Ratings are by the Insurance Institute for Highway Safety. Sources: Oak Ridge National Laboratory: "An Analysis of the Impact of Sport Utility Vehicles in the United States," Stacy C. Davis, Lorena F. Truett (August 2000)/Insurance Institute for Highway Safety (www-cta.ornl.gov/Publications/Final SUV report.pdf, www.highwaysafety.org/vehicle_ratings).

50. ▼ You choose, at random, a small car and a midsize car. What is the probability that both will be rated at most 1?

Exercises 51 and 52 assume familiarity with counting arguments and probability (Section 7.4).

51. ▼ *Camping* Kent's Tents has four red tents and three green tents in stock. Karin selects four of them at random. Let X be the number of red tents she selects. Give the probability distribution and find $P(X \geq 2)$.

52. ▼ *Camping* Kent's Tents has five green knapsacks and four yellow ones in stock. Curt selects four of them at random. Let X be the number of green knapsacks he selects. Give the probability distribution and find $P(X \leq 2)$.

53. ◆ *Testing Your Calculator* Use your calculator or computer to generate a sequence of 100 random digits in the range 0–9, and test the random number generator for uniformness by drawing the distribution histogram.

54. ◆ *Testing Your Dice* Repeat Exercise 53, but this time, use a die to generate a sequence of 50 random numbers in the range 1–6.

COMMUNICATION AND REASONING EXERCISES

55. Are all infinite random variables necessarily continuous? Explain.

56. Are all continuous random variables necessarily infinite? Explain.

57. If you are unable to compute the (theoretical) probability distribution for a random variable X, how can you estimate the distribution?

58. What do you expect to happen to the probabilities in a probability distribution as you make the measurement classes smaller?

59. ▼ Give an example of a real-life situation that can be modeled by a random variable with a probability distribution whose histogram is highest on the left.

60. ▼ Give an example of a real-life situation that can be modeled by a random variable with a probability distribution whose histogram is highest on the right.

61. ▼ How wide should the bars in a histogram be so that the area of each bar equals the probability of the corresponding range of values of X?

62. ▼ How wide should the bars in a histogram be so that the probability $P(a \leq X \leq b)$ equals the area of the corresponding portion of the histogram?

63. ▼ Give at least one scenario in which you might prefer to model the number of pages in a randomly selected book using a continuous random variable rather than a discrete random variable.

64. ▼ Give at least one scenario in which you might prefer to model a temperature using a discrete random variable rather than a continuous random variable.

8.2 Bernoulli Trials and Binomial Random Variables

Your electronic production plant produces video game joysticks. Unfortunately, quality control at the plant leaves much to be desired, and 10% of the joysticks the plant produces are defective. A large corporation has expressed interest in adopting your product for its new game console, and today an inspection team will be visiting to test video game joysticks as they come off the assembly line. If the team tests five joysticks, what is the probability that none will be defective? What is the probability that more than one will be defective?

In this scenario we are interested in the following, which is an example of a particular type of finite random variable called a **binomial random variable**: Think of the experiment as a sequence of five "trials" (in each trial the inspection team chooses one joystick at random and tests it) each with two possible outcomes: "success" (a defective joystick) and "failure" (a non-defective one).[*] If we now take X to be the number of successes (defective joysticks) the inspection team finds, we can recast the questions above as follows: Find $P(X = 0)$ and $P(X > 1)$.

[*] These are customary names for the two possible outcomes, and often do not indicate actual success or failure at anything. "Success" is the label we give the outcome of interest—in this case, finding a defective joystick.

[†] Jakob Bernoulli (1654–1705) was one of the pioneers of probability theory.

Bernoulli Trial

A **Bernoulli**[†] **trial** is an experiment that has two possible outcomes, called **success** and **failure**. If the probability of success is p, then the probability of failure is $q = 1 - p$.

Visualizing a Bernoulli Trial

Tossing a coin three times is an example of a **sequence of independent Bernoulli trials**: a sequence of Bernoulli trials in which the outcomes in any one trial are independent (in the sense of the preceding chapter) of those in any other trial, and in which the probability of success is the same for all the trials.

Quick Examples

1. Roll a die, and take success to be the event that you roll a 6. Then $p = 1/6$ and $q = 5/6$. Rolling the die 10 times is then an example of a sequence of 10 independent Bernoulli trials.

2. Provide a property with flood insurance for 20 years, and take success to be the event that the property is flooded during a particular year. Observing whether or not the property is flooded each year for 20 years is then an example of 20 independent Bernoulli trials (assuming that the occurrence of flooding one year is independent of whether there was flooding in earlier years).

✱ Choosing a "loser" (a fund that will depreciate next year) slightly depletes the pool of "losers" and hence slightly decreases the probability of choosing another one. However, the fact that the pool of funds is very large means that this decrease is extremely small. Hence, p is very nearly constant.

3. You know that 60% of all bond funds will depreciate in value next year. Take success to be the event that a randomly chosen fund depreciates next year. Then $p = .6$ and $q = .4$. Choosing five funds at random for your portfolio from a very large number of possible funds is, approximately,✱ an example of five independent Bernolli trials.

4. Suppose that E is an event in an experiment with sample space S. Then we can think of the experiment as a Bernoulli trial with two outcomes; success if E occurs, and failure if E' occurs. The probability of success is then

$$p = P(E)$$ Success is the occurrence of E.

and the probability of failure is

$$q = P(E') = 1 - P(E) = 1 - p.$$ Failure is the occurrence of E'.

Repeating the experiment 30 times, say, is then an example of 30 independent Bernoulli trials.

Note Quick Example 4 above tells us that Bernoulli trials are not very special kinds of experiments; in fact, we are performing a Bernoulli trial every time we repeat *any* experiment and observe whether a specific event E occurs. Thinking of an experiment in this way amounts, mathematically, to thinking of $\{E, E'\}$ as our sample space (E = success, E' = failure). ■

Binomial Random Variable

A **binomial random variable** is one that counts the number of successes in a sequence of independent Bernoulli trials, where the number of trials is fixed.

Visualizing a Binomial Random Variable

Quick Examples

1. Roll a die 10 times; X is the number of times you roll a 6.

2. Provide a property with flood insurance for 20 years; X is the number of years, during the 20-year period, during which the property is flooded (assuming that the occurrence of flooding one year is independent of whether there was flooding in earlier years).

3. You know that 60% of all bond funds will depreciate in value next year, and you randomly select four from a very large number of possible choices; X is the number of bond funds you hold that will depreciate next year. (X is approximately binomial; see the margin note on p. 560.)

EXAMPLE 1 **Probability Distribution of a Binomial Random Variable**

Suppose that we have a possibly unfair coin with the probability of heads p and the probability of tails $q = 1 - p$.

a. Let X be the number of heads you get in a sequence of five tosses. Find $P(X = 2)$.

b. Let X be the number of heads you get in a sequence of n tosses. Find $P(X = x)$.

Solution

a. We are looking for the probability of getting exactly two heads in a sequence of five tosses. Let's start with a simpler question: What is the probability that we will get the sequence HHTTT?

> The probability that the first toss will come up heads is p.
>
> The probability that the second toss will come up heads is also p.
>
> The probability that the third toss will come up tails is q.
>
> The probability that the fourth toss will come up tails is q.
>
> The probability that the fifth toss will come up tails is q.

The probability that the first toss will be heads *and* the second will be heads *and* the third will be tails *and* the fourth will be tails *and* the fifth will be tails equals the probability of the *intersection* of these five events. Because these are independent events, the probability of the intersection is the product of the probabilities, which is

$$p \times p \times q \times q \times q = p^2 q^3.$$

Now HHTTT is only one of several outcomes with two heads and three tails. Two others are HTHTT and TTTHH. How many such outcomes are there altogether? This is the number of "words" with two H's and three T's, and we know from Chapter 6 that the answer is $C(5, 2) = 10$.

Each of the 10 outcomes with two H's and three T's has the same probability: $p^2 q^3$. (Why?) Thus, the probability of getting one of these 10 outcomes is the probability of the union of all these (mutually exclusive) events, and we saw in the preceding chapter that this is just the sum of the probabilities. In other words, the probability we are after is

$$P(X = 2) = p^2 q^3 + p^2 q^3 + \cdots + p^2 q^3 \qquad \text{\small $C(5, 2)$ times}$$
$$= C(5, 2) p^2 q^3.$$

The structure of this formula is as follows:

Number of heads Number of tails

$$P(X = 2) = C(5, 2)\, p^2 q^3$$

Number of tosses | | Probability of tails
Number of heads Probability of heads

b. What we did using the numbers 5 and 2 in part (a) works as well in general. For the general case, with n tosses and x heads, replace 5 with n and replace 2 with x to get:

$$P(X = x) = C(n, x)\, p^x q^{n-x}.$$

(Note that the coefficient of q is the number of tails, which is $n - x$.)

The calculation in Example 1 applies to any binomial random variable, so we can say the following:

Probability Distribution of Binomial Random Variables

If X is the number of successes in a sequence of n independent Bernoulli trials, then

$$P(X = x) = C(n, x)\, p^x q^{n-x},$$

where

$n =$ number of trials
$p =$ probability of success
$q =$ probability of failure $= 1 - p$.

Quick Example

If you roll a fair die five times, the probability of throwing exactly two 6s is

$$P(X = 2) = C(5, 2) \left(\frac{1}{6}\right)^2 \left(\frac{5}{6}\right)^3 = 10 \times \frac{1}{36} \times \frac{125}{216} \approx .1608.$$

Here, we used $n = 5$ and $p = 1/6$, the probability of rolling a 6 on one roll of the die.

EXAMPLE 2 Aging

By 2030, the probability that a randomly chosen resident in the United States will be 65 years old or older is projected to be .2.[11]

a. What is the probability that, in a randomly selected sample of six U.S. residents, exactly four of them will be 65 or older?

b. If X is the number of people aged 65 or older in a sample of six, construct the probability distribution of X and plot its histogram.

---

[11]Source: U.S. Census Bureau, Decennial Census, Population Estimates and Projections (www.agingstats .gov/agingstatsdotnet/Main_Site/Data/2008_Documents/Population.aspx).

c. Compute $P(X \leq 2)$.

d. Compute $P(X \geq 2)$.

Solution

a. The experiment is a sequence of Bernoulli trials; in each trial we select a person and ascertain his or her age. If we take "success" to mean selection of a person aged 65 or older, then the probability distribution is

$$P(X = x) = C(n, x)p^x q^{n-x}$$

where n = number of trials = 6
p = probability of success = .2
q = probability of failure = .8

So,

$$P(X = 4) = C(6, 4)(.2)^4(.8)^2$$
$$= 15 \times .0016 \times .64 = .01536$$

b. We have already computed $P(X = 4)$. Here are all the calculations:

$$P(X = 0) = C(6, 0)(.2)^0(.8)^6$$
$$= 1 \times 1 \times .262144 = .262144$$

$$P(X = 1) = C(6, 1)(.2)^1(.8)^5$$
$$= 6 \times .2 \times .32768 = .393216$$

$$P(X = 2) = C(6, 2)(.2)^2(.8)^4$$
$$= 15 \times .04 \times .4096 = .24576$$

$$P(X = 3) = C(6, 3)(.2)^3(.8)^3$$
$$= 20 \times .008 \times .512 = .08192$$

$$P(X = 4) = C(6, 4)(.2)^4(.8)^2$$
$$= 15 \times .0016 \times .64 = .01536$$

$$P(X = 5) = C(6, 5)(.2)^5(.8)^1$$
$$= 6 \times .00032 \times .8 = .001536$$

$$P(X = 6) = C(6, 6)(.2)^6(.8)^0$$
$$= 1 \times .000064 \times 1 = .000064.$$

The probability distribution is therefore as follows:

$P(X = x)$

Figure 3

x	0	1	2	3	4	5	6
$P(X = x)$	.262144	.393216	.24576	.08192	.01536	.001536	.000064

Figure 3 shows its histogram.

c. $P(X \leq 2)$—the probability that the number of people selected who are at least 65 years old is either 0, 1, or 2—is the probability of the union of these events and is thus the sum of the three probabilities:

$$P(X \leq 2) = P(X = 0) + P(X = 1) + P(X = 2)$$
$$= .262144 + .393216 + .24576$$
$$= .90112.$$

 using Technology

Technology can be used to replicate the histogram in Example 2.

TI-83/84 Plus

Y= screen: Y_1=6 nCr
X*0.2^X*0.8^(6-X)

2ND TBLSET Set Indpt to Ask.

2ND TABLE Enter x-values

0, 1, . . . , 6.

[More details on page 613.]

Spreadsheet
Headings x and $P(X = x)$ in A1, B1
x-values 0, 1, . . . , 6 in A2–A8
=BINOMDIST(A2,6,0,.2,0) in B2
Copy down to B6.
[More details on page 616.]

 Website
www.WanerMath.com
  Student Home
    → On Line Utilities
    → Binomial Distribution Utility
Enter $n = 6$ and $p = .2$ and press "Generate Distribution."

d. To compute $P(X \geq 2)$, we *could* compute the sum

$$P(X \geq 2) = P(X = 2) + P(X = 3) + P(X = 4) + P(X = 5) + P(X = 6)$$

but it is far easier to compute the probability of the complement of the event:

$$P(X < 2) = P(X = 0) + P(X = 1)$$
$$= .262144 + .393216 = .65536$$

and then subtract the answer from 1:

$$P(X \geq 2) = 1 - P(X < 2)$$
$$= 1 - .65536 = .34464.$$

FAQs

Terminology and Recognizing when to Use the Binomial Distribution

Q: *What is the difference between Bernoulli trials and a binomial random variable?*

A: A Bernoulli trial is a type of experiment, whereas a binomial random variable is the resulting kind of random variable. More precisely, if your experiment consists of performing a sequence of n Bernoulli trials (think of throwing a dart n times at random points on a dartboard hoping to hit the bull's eye), then the random variable X that counts the number of successes (the number of times you actually hit the bull's eye) is a binomial random variable.

Q: *How do I recognize when a situation gives a binomial random variable?*

A: Make sure that the experiment consists of a sequence of independent Bernoulli trials; that is, a sequence of a fixed number of trials of an experiment that has two outcomes, where the outcome of each trial does not depend on the outcomes in previous trials, and where the probability of success is the same for all the trials. For instance, repeatedly throwing a dart at a dartboard hoping to hit the bull's eye does not constitute a sequence of Bernoulli trials if you adjust your aim each time depending on the outcome of your previous attempt. This dart-throwing experiment can be modeled by a sequence of Bernoulli trials if you make no adjustments after each attempt and your aim does not improve (or deteriorate) with time.

8.2   EXERCISES

▼ more advanced   ◆ challenging
Ⓣ indicates exercises that should be solved using technology

In Exercises 1–10, you are performing 5 independent Bernoulli trials with $p = .1$ and $q = .9$. Calculate the probability of each of the stated outcomes. Check your answer using technology.
HINT [See Quick Example on page 562.]

1. Two successes
2. Three successes
3. No successes
4. No failures
5. All successes
6. All failures
7. At most two successes
8. At least four successes
9. At least three successes
10. At most three successes

In Exercises 11–18, X is a binomial variable with $n = 6$ and $p = .4$. Compute the given probabilities. Check your answer using technology. HINT [See Example 2.]

11. $P(X = 3)$
12. $P(X = 4)$
13. $P(X \leq 2)$
14. $P(X \leq 1)$
15. $P(X \geq 5)$
16. $P(X \geq 4)$
17. $P(1 \leq X \leq 3)$
18. $P(3 \leq X \leq 5)$

In Exercises 19 and 20, graph the histogram of the given binomial distribution. Check your answer using technology.

19. $n = 5$, $p = \dfrac{1}{4}$, $q = \dfrac{3}{4}$
20. $n = 5$, $p = \dfrac{1}{3}$, $q = \dfrac{2}{3}$

In Exercises 21 and 22, graph the histogram of the given binomial distribution and compute the given quantity, indicating the corresponding region on the graph.

21. $n = 4, p = \dfrac{1}{3}, q = \dfrac{2}{3}; P(X \le 2)$

22. $n = 4, p = \dfrac{1}{4}, q = \dfrac{3}{4}; P(X \le 1)$

APPLICATIONS

23. *Internet Addiction* The probability that a randomly chosen person in the Netherlands connects to the Internet immediately upon waking is approximately .25.[12] What is the probability that, in a randomly selected sample of five people, two connect to the Internet immediately upon waking? HINT [See Example 2.]

24. *Alien Retirement* The probability that a randomly chosen citizen-entity of Cygnus is of pension age[13] is approximately .8. What is the probability that, in a randomly selected sample of four citizen-entities, all of them are of pension age? HINT [See Example 2.]

25. *1990s Internet Stock Boom* According to a July 1999 article in *The New York Times*,[14] venture capitalists had this "rule of thumb": The probability that an Internet start-up company will be a "stock market success" resulting in "spectacular profits for early investors" is .2. If you were a venture capitalist who invested in 10 Internet start-up companies, what was the probability that at least 1 of them would be a stock market success? (Round your answer to four decimal places.)

26. *1990s Internet Stock Boom* According to the article cited in Exercise 25, 13.5% of Internet stocks that entered the market in 1999 ended up trading below their initial offering prices. If you were an investor who purchased five Internet stocks at their initial offering prices, what was the probability that at least four of them would end up trading at or above their initial offering price? (Round your answer to four decimal places.)

27. *Job Training (from the GRE Exam in Economics)* In a large on-the-job training program, half of the participants are female and half are male. In a random sample of three participants, what is the probability that an investigator will draw at least one male?

28. *Job Training (based on a question from the GRE Exam in Economics)* In a large on-the-job training program, half of the participants are female and half are male. In a random sample of five participants, what is the probability that an investigator will draw at least two males?

29. *Manufacturing* Your manufacturing plant produces air bags, and it is known that 10% of them are defective. Five air bags are tested.

  a. Find the probability that three of them are defective.
  b. Find the probability that at least two of them are defective.

30. *Manufacturing* Compute the probability distribution of the binomial variable described in the preceding exercise, and use it to compute the probability that if five air bags are tested, at least one will be defective and at least one will not.

31. *Teenage Pastimes* According to a study,[15] the probability that a randomly selected teenager watched a rented video at least once during a week was .71. What is the probability that at least 8 teenagers in a group of 10 watched a rented movie at least once last week?

32. *Other Teenage Pastimes* According to the study cited in the preceding exercise, the probability that a randomly selected teenager studied at least once during a week was only .52. What is the probability that less than half of the students in your study group of 10 have studied in the last week?

33. *Subprime Mortgages during the Housing Bubble* In November 2008 the probability that a randomly selected subprime home mortgage in Florida was in foreclosure was .24.[16] Choose 10 subprime home mortgages at random.

  a. What is the probability that exactly 5 of them were in foreclosure?
  b. ▢ Use technology to generate the probability distribution for the associated binomial random variable.
  c. Fill in the blank: If 10 subprime home mortgages were chosen at random, the number of them most likely to have been in foreclosure was _____.

34. *Subprime Mortgages during the Housing Bubble* In November 2008 the probability that a randomly selected subprime home mortgage in Texas was current in its payments was .67.[17] Choose 10 subprime home mortgages at random.

  a. What is the probability that exactly 4 of them were current?
  b. ▢ Use technology to generate the probability distribution for the associated binomial random variable.
  c. Fill in the blank: If 10 subprime home mortgages were chosen at random, the number of them most likely to have been current was _____.

35. ▼ *Triple Redundancy* In order to ensure reliable performance of vital computer systems, aerospace engineers sometimes employ the technique of "triple redundancy," in which three identical computers are installed in a space vehicle. If one of the three computers gives results different

[12]Source: *Webwereld* November 17, 2008 (http://webwereld.nl/article/view/id/53599).

[13]The retirement age in Cygnus is 12,000 bootlags, which is equivalent to approximately 20 minutes Earth time.

[14]"Not All Hit It Rich in the Internet Gold Rush," *New York Times*, July 20, 1999, p. A1.

[15]Sources: Rand Youth Poll/Teen-Age Research Unlimited/*New York Times*, March 14, 1998, p. D1.

[16]Source: Federal Reserve Bank of New York (www.newyorkfed.org/regional/subprime.html).

[17]*Ibid.*

from the other two, it is assumed to be malfunctioning and it is ignored. This technique will work as long as no more than one computer malfunctions. Assuming that an onboard computer is 99% reliable (that is, the probability of its failing is .01), what is the probability that at least two of the three computers will malfunction?

36. ▼ *IQ Scores* Mensa is a club for people who have high IQ scores. To qualify, your IQ must be at least 132, putting you in the top 2% of the general population. If a group of 10 people are chosen at random, what is the probability that at least 2 of them qualify for Mensa?

37. ▮T▮ ▼ *Standardized Tests* Assume that on a standardized test of 100 questions, a person has a probability of 80% of answering any particular question correctly. Find the probability of answering between 75 and 85 questions, inclusive, correctly. (Assume independence, and round your answer to 4 decimal places.)

38. ▮T▮ ▼ *Standardized Tests* Assume that on a standardized test of 100 questions, a person has a probability of 80% of answering any particular question correctly. Find the probability of answering at least 90 questions correctly. (Assume independence, and round your answer to 4 decimal places.)

39. ▮T▮ ▼ *Product Testing* It is known that 43% of all the ZeroFat hamburger patties produced by your factory actually contain more than 10 grams of fat. Compute the probability distribution for $n = 50$ Bernoulli trials.

  a. What is the most likely value for the number of burgers in a sample of 50 that contain more than 10 grams of fat?

  b. Complete the following sentence: There is an approximately 71% chance that a batch of 50 ZeroFat patties contains _____ or more patties with more than 10 grams of fat.

  c. Compare the graphs of the distributions for $n = 50$ trials and $n = 20$ trials. What do you notice?

40. ▮T▮ ▼ *Product Testing* It is known that 65% of all the ZeroCal hamburger patties produced by your factory actually contain more than 1,000 calories. Compute the probability distribution for $n = 50$ Bernoulli trials.

  a. What is the most likely value for the number of burgers in a sample of 50 that contain more than 1,000 calories?

  b. Complete the following sentence: There is an approximately 73% chance that a batch of 50 ZeroCal patties contains _____ or more patties with more than 1,000 calories.

  c. Compare the graphs of the distributions for $n = 50$ trials and $n = 20$ trials. What do you notice?

41. ▮T▮ ▼ *Quality Control* A manufacturer of light bulbs chooses bulbs at random from its assembly line for testing. If the probability of a bulb's being bad is .01, how many bulbs does the manufacturer need to test before the probability of finding at least one bad one rises to more than .5? (You may have to use trial and error to solve this.)

42. ▮T▮ ▼ *Quality Control* A manufacturer of light bulbs chooses bulbs at random from its assembly line for testing. If the probability of a bulb's being bad is .01, how many bulbs does the manufacturer need to test before the probability of finding at least two bad ones rises to more than .5? (You may have to use trial and error to solve this.)

43. ▼ *Highway Safety* According to a study,[18] a male driver in the United States will average 562 accidents per 100 million miles. Regard an n-mile trip as a sequence of n Bernoulli trials with "success" corresponding to having an accident during a particular mile. What is the probability that a male driver will have an accident in a 1-mile trip?

44. ▼ *Highway Safety*: According to the study cited in the preceding exercise, a female driver in the United States will average 611 accidents per 100 million miles. Regard an n-mile trip as a sequence of n Bernoulli trials with "success" corresponding to having an accident during a particular mile. What is the probability that a female driver will have an accident in a 1-mile trip?

45. ◆ *Mad Cow Disease* In March 2004, the U.S. Department of Agriculture announced plans to test approximately 243,000 slaughtered cows per year for mad cow disease (bovine spongiform encephalopathy).[19] When announcing the plan, the Agriculture Department stated that "by the laws of probability, that many tests should detect mad cow disease even if it is present in only 5 cows out of the 45 million in the nation."[20] Test the Department's claim by computing the probability that, if only 5 out of 45 million cows had mad cow disease, at least 1 cow would test positive in a year (assuming the testing was done randomly).

46. ◆ *Mad Cow Disease* According to the article cited in Exercise 45, only 223,000 of the cows being tested for bovine spongiform encephalopathy were to be "downer cows"; cows unable to walk to their slaughter. Assuming that just one downer cow in 500,000 is infected on average, use a binomial distribution to find the probability that 2 or more cows would test positive in a year. Your associate claims that "by the laws of probability, that many tests should detect at least 2 cases of mad cow disease even if it is present in only 2 cows out of a million downers." Comment on that claim.

COMMUNICATION AND REASONING EXERCISES

47. A soccer player is more likely to score on his second shot if he was successful on his first. Can we model a succession of shots a player takes as a sequence of Bernoulli trials? Explain.

---

[18]Data are based on a report by National Highway Traffic Safety Administration released in January, 1996. Source for data: U.S. Department of Transportation/*New York Times*, April 9, 1999, p. F1.

[19]Source: *New York Times*, March 17, 2004, p. A19.

[20]As stated in the *New York Times* article.

48. A soccer player takes repeated shots on goal. What assumption must we make if we want to model a succession of shots by a player as a sequence of Bernoulli trials?

49. Your friend just told you that "misfortunes always occur in threes." If life is just a sequence of Bernoulli trials, is this possible? Explain.

50. Suppose an experiment consists of repeatedly (every week) checking whether your graphing calculator battery has died. Is this a sequence of Bernoulli trials? Explain.

51. In an experiment with sample space S, a certain event E has a probability p of occurring. What has this scenario to do with Bernoulli trials?

52. An experiment consists of removing a gummy bear from a bag originally containing 10, and then eating it. Regard eating a lime-flavored bear as success. Repeating the experiment five times is a sequence of Bernoulli trials, right?

53. ▼ Why is the following not a binomial random variable? Select, without replacement, five marbles from a bag containing six red marbles and two blue ones, and let X be the number of red marbles you have selected.

54. ▼ By contrast with Exercise 53, why can the following be modeled by a binomial random variable? Select, without replacement, 5 electronic components from a batch of 10,000 in which 1,000 are defective, and let X be the number of defective components you select.

8.3 Measures of Central Tendency

Mean, Median, and Mode of a Set of Data

One day you decide to measure the popularity rating of your statistics instructor, Mr. Pelogrande. Ideally, you should poll all of Mr. Pelogrande's students, which is what statisticians would refer to as the **population**. However, it would be difficult to poll all the members of the population in question (Mr. Pelogrande teaches more than 400 students). Instead, you decide to survey 10 of his students, chosen at random, and ask them to rate Mr. Pelogrande on a scale of 0–100. The survey results in the following set of data:

$$60, 50, 55, 0, 100, 90, 40, 20, 40, 70.$$

Such a collection of data is called a **sample**, because the 10 people polled represent only a (small) sample of Mr. Pelogrande's students. We should think of the individual scores $60, 50, 55, \ldots$ as values of a random variable: Choose one of Mr. Pelogrande's students at random and let X be the rating the student gives to Mr. Pelogrande.

How do we distill a single measurement, or **statistic**, from this sample that would describe Mr. Pelogrande's popularity? Perhaps the most commonly used statistic is the **average**, or **mean**, which is computed by adding the scores and dividing the sum by the number of scores in the sample:

$$\text{Sample Mean} = \frac{60 + 50 + 55 + 0 + 100 + 90 + 40 + 20 + 40 + 70}{10}$$

$$= \frac{525}{10} = 52.5.$$

We might then conclude, based on the sample, that Mr. Pelogrande's average popularity rating is about 52.5. The usual notation for the sample mean is $\bar{x}$, and the formula we use to compute it is

$$\bar{x} = \frac{x_1 + x_2 + \cdots + x_n}{n},$$

where $x_1, x_2, \ldots, x_n$ are the values of X in the sample.

A convenient way of writing the sum that appears in the numerator is to use **summation** or **sigma notation**. We write the sum $x_1 + x_2 + \cdots + x_n$ as

$$\sum_{i=1}^{n} x_i.$$

$\sum_{i=1}^{n}$ by itself stands for "the sum, from $i = 1$ to n."

$\sum_{i=1}^{n} x_i$ stands for "the sum of the x_i, from $i = 1$ to n."

We think of i as taking on the values $1, 2, \ldots, n$ in turn, making x_i equal $x_1, x_2, \ldots, x_n$ in turn, and we then add up these values.

Sample and Mean

A **sample** is a sequence of values (or scores) of a random variable X. (The process of collecting such a sequence is sometimes called **sampling** X.) The **sample mean** is the average of the values, or **scores**, in the sample. To compute the sample mean, we use the following formula:

$$\bar{x} = \frac{x_1 + x_2 + \cdots + x_n}{n} = \frac{\sum_{i=1}^{n} x_i}{n}$$

or simply

$$\bar{x} = \frac{\sum_i x_i}{n}. \qquad \sum_i \text{ stands for "sum over all } i\text{."}*$$

* In Section 1.4 we simply wrote $\sum x$ for the sum of all the x_i, but here we will use the subscripts to make it easier to interpret formulas in this and the next section.

† When we talk about *populations*, the understanding is that the underlying experiment consists of selecting a member of a given population and ascertaining the value of X.

Here, n is the **sample size** (number of scores), and $x_1, x_2, \ldots, x_n$ are the individual values.

If the sample $x_1, x_2, \ldots, x_n$ consists of all the values of X from the entire population† (for instance, the ratings given Mr. Pelogrande by *all* of his students), we refer to the mean as the **population mean**, and write it as μ (Greek "mu") instead of $\bar{x}$.

Visualizing the Mean

$$\bar{x} = \frac{8 + 5 + 2}{3} = 5$$

Quick Examples

1. The mean of the sample 1, 2, 3, 4, 5 is $\bar{x} = 3$.

2. The mean of the sample -1, 0, 2 is $\bar{x} = \dfrac{-1 + 0 + 2}{3} = \dfrac{1}{3}$.

3. The mean of the population -3, -3, 0, 0, 1 is

$$\mu = \frac{-3 - 3 + 0 + 0 + 1}{5} = -1.$$

Note: Sample Mean versus Population Mean
Determining a population mean can be difficult or even impossible. For instance, computing the mean household income for the United States would entail recording the income of every single household in the United States. Instead of attempting to do this, we usually use sample means instead. The larger the sample used, the more accurately we expect the sample mean to approximate the population mean. Estimating how accurately a sample mean based on a given sample size approximates the population mean is possible, but we will not go into that in this book. ∎

The mean $\bar{x}$ is an attempt to describe where the "center" of the sample is. It is therefore called a **measure of central tendency**. There are two other common measures of central tendency: the "middle score," or **median**, and the "most frequent score," or **mode**. These are defined as follows.

Median and Mode

The **sample median** m is the middle score (in the case of an odd-size sample), or average of the two middle scores (in the case of an even-size sample) when the scores in a sample are arranged in ascending order.

A **sample mode** is a score that appears most often in the collection. (There may be more than one mode in a sample.)

Visualizing the Median and Mode

Median = Middle Score = 4

Mode = Most Frequent Score = 2

As before, we refer to the **population median** and **population mode** if the sample consists of the data from the entire population.

Quick Examples

1. The sample median of 2, –3, –1, 4, 2 is found by first arranging the scores in ascending order: –3, –1, 2, 2, 4 and then selecting the middle (third) score: $m = 2$. The sample mode is also 2 because this is the score that appears most often.
2. The sample 2, 5, 6, –1, 0, 6 has median $m = (2 + 5)/2 = 3.5$ and mode 6.

The mean tends to give more weight to scores that are further away from the center than does the median. For example, if you take the largest score in a collection of more than two numbers and make it larger, the mean will increase but the median will remain the same. For this reason the median is often preferred for collections that contain a wide range of scores. The mode can sometimes lie far from the center and is thus used less often as an indication of where the "center" of a sample lies.

EXAMPLE 1 **Teenage Spending in the 1990s**

A 10-year survey of spending patterns of U.S. teenagers in the 1990s yielded the following figures (in billions of dollars spent in a year):[21] 90, 90, 85, 80, 80, 80, 80, 85, 90, 100. Compute and interpret the mean, median, and mode, and illustrate the data on a graph.

Solution The *mean* is given by

$$\bar{x} = \frac{\sum_i x_i}{n}$$

$$= \frac{90 + 90 + 85 + 80 + 80 + 80 + 80 + 85 + 90 + 100}{10} = \frac{860}{10} = 86.$$

Thus, spending by teenagers averaged $86 billion per year.

For the *median*, we arrange the sample data in ascending order:

80, 80, 80, 80, 85, 85, 90, 90, 90, 100.

We then take the average of the two middle scores:

$$m = \frac{85 + 85}{2} = 85.$$

This means that in half the years in question, teenagers spent $85 billion or less, and in half they spent $85 billion or more.

For the *mode* we choose the score (or scores) that occurs most frequently: $80 billion. Thus, teenagers spent $80 billion per year more often than any other amount.

The frequency histogram in Figure 4 illustrates these three measures.

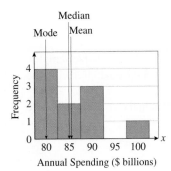

Mode | Median | Mean

Annual Spending ($ billions)

Figure 4

➡ **Before we go on...** There is a nice geometric interpretation of the difference between the median and mode: The median line shown in Figure 4 divides the total area of the histogram into two equal pieces, whereas the mean line passes through its "center of gravity"; if you placed the histogram on a knife-edge along the mean line, it would balance. ∎

Expected Value of a Finite Random Variable

Now, instead of looking at a sample of values of a given random variable, let us look at the probability distribution of the random variable itself and see if we can predict the sample mean without actually taking a sample. This prediction is what we call the *expected value* of the random variable.

EXAMPLE 2 **Expected Value of a Random Variable**

Suppose you roll a fair die a large number of times. What do you expect to be the average of the numbers that face up?

Solution Suppose we take a sample of *n* rolls of the die (where *n* is large). Because the probability of rolling a 1 is 1/6, we would expect that we would roll a 1 one sixth

---

[21]Spending figures are rounded, and cover the years 1988 through 1997. Source: Rand Youth Poll/ Teen-Age Research Unlimited/*New York Times*, March 14, 1998, p. D1.

of the time, or $n/6$ times. Similarly, each other number should also appear $n/6$ times. The frequency table should then look like this:

x	1	2	3	4	5	6
Number of Times x Is Rolled (frequency)	$\dfrac{n}{6}$	$\dfrac{n}{6}$	$\dfrac{n}{6}$	$\dfrac{n}{6}$	$\dfrac{n}{6}$	$\dfrac{n}{6}$

Note that we would not really expect the scores to be evenly distributed in practice, although for very large values of n we would expect the frequencies to vary only by a small percentage. To calculate the sample mean, we would add up all the scores and divide by the sample size. Now, the table tells us that there are $n/6$ ones, $n/6$ twos, $n/6$ threes, and so on, up to $n/6$ sixes. Adding these all up gives

$$\sum_i x_i = \frac{n}{6} \cdot 1 + \frac{n}{6} \cdot 2 + \frac{n}{6} \cdot 3 + \frac{n}{6} \cdot 4 + \frac{n}{6} \cdot 5 + \frac{n}{6} \cdot 6.$$

(Notice that we can obtain this number by multiplying the frequencies by the values of X and then adding.) Thus, the mean is

$$\bar{x} = \frac{\sum_i x_i}{n}$$

$$= \frac{\frac{n}{6} \cdot 1 + \frac{n}{6} \cdot 2 + \frac{n}{6} \cdot 3 + \frac{n}{6} \cdot 4 + \frac{n}{6} \cdot 5 + \frac{n}{6} \cdot 6}{n}$$

$$= \frac{1}{6} \cdot 1 + \frac{1}{6} \cdot 2 + \frac{1}{6} \cdot 3 + \frac{1}{6} \cdot 4 + \frac{1}{6} \cdot 5 + \frac{1}{6} \cdot 6 \qquad \text{Divide top and bottom by } n.$$

$$= 3.5.$$

This is the average value we expect to get after a large number of rolls or, in short, the **expected value** of a roll of the die. More precisely, we say that this is the expected value of the random variable X whose value is the number we get by rolling a die. Notice that n, the number of rolls, does not appear in the expected value. In fact, we could redo the calculation more simply by dividing the frequencies in the table by n *before* adding. Doing this replaces the frequencies with the *probabilities*, $1/6$. That is, it *replaces the frequency distribution with the probability distribution.*

x	1	2	3	4	5	6
$P(X = x)$	$\dfrac{1}{6}$	$\dfrac{1}{6}$	$\dfrac{1}{6}$	$\dfrac{1}{6}$	$\dfrac{1}{6}$	$\dfrac{1}{6}$

The expected value of X is then the sum of the products $x \cdot P(X = x)$. This is how we shall compute it from now on.

Expected Value of a Finite Random Variable

If X is a finite random variable that takes on the values $x_1, x_2, \ldots, x_n$, then the **expected value** of X, written $E(X)$ or μ, is

$$\mu = E(X) = x_1 \cdot P(X = x_1) + x_2 \cdot P(X = x_2) + \cdots + x_n \cdot P(X = x_n)$$

$$= \sum_i x_i \cdot P(X = x_i).$$

To obtain the expected value, multiply the values of X by their probabilities, and then add the results.

In Words

To compute the expected value from the probability distribution of X, we multiply the values of X by their probabilities and add up the results.

Interpretation

We interpret the expected value of X as a *prediction* of the mean of a large random sample of measurements of X; in other words, it is what we "expect" the mean of a large number of scores to be. (The larger the sample, the more accurate this prediction will tend to be.)

Quick Example

If X has the distribution shown,

x	-1	0	4	5
$P(X = x)$	.3	.5	.1	.1

then $\mu = E(X) = -1(.3) + 0(.5) + 4(.1) + 5(.1) = -.3 + 0 + .4 + .5$
$= .6$.

EXAMPLE 3 **Sports Injuries**

According to historical data, the number of injuries that a member of the Enormous State University women's soccer team will sustain during a typical season is given by the following probability distribution table:

Injuries	0	1	2	3	4	5	6
Probability	.20	.20	.22	.20	.15	.01	.02

If X denotes the number of injuries sustained by a player during one season, compute $E(X)$ and interpret the result.

using Technology

Technology can be used to compute the expected values in Example 3.

TI-83/84 Plus

STAT EDIT values of X in L_1 and probabilities in L_2.
Home screen: sum(L_1*L_2)
[More details on page 614.]

Spreadsheet

Headings x and $P(X = x)$ in A1, B1.
x-values and probabilities in A2–B8.
=A2*B2 in C2, copied down to B6.
=SUM(C2:C8) in C9.
[More details on page 616.]

Solution We can compute the expected value using the following tabular approach: Take the probability distribution table, add another row in which we compute the product $xP(X = x)$, and then add these products together.

x	0	1	2	3	4	5	6	
$P(X = x)$	.20	.20	.22	.20	.15	.01	.02	**Total:**
$xP(X = x)$	0	.20	.44	.60	.60	.05	.12	2.01

The total of the entries in the bottom row is the expected value. Thus,

$$E(X) = 2.01.$$

We interpret the result as follows: If many soccer players are observed for a season, we predict that the average number of injuries each will sustain is about two.

Website
www.WanerMath.com
  Student Home
    → On Line Utilities
    → Histogram Utility
Enter the *x*-values and frequencies as shown:

```
0, .2
1, .2
2, .22
3, .2
4, .15
5, .01
6, .02
```

Make sure "Show expected value and standard deviation" is checked, and press "Results." The results will appear at the bottom of the page.

EXAMPLE 4 **Roulette**

A roulette wheel (of the kind used in the United States) has the numbers 1 through 36, 0 and 00. A bet on a single number pays 35 to 1. This means that if you place a $1 bet on a single number and win (your number comes up), you get your $1 back plus $35 (that is, you gain $35). If your number does not come up, you lose the $1 you bet. What is the expected gain from a $1 bet on a single number?

Solution The probability of winning is 1/38, so the probability of losing is 37/38. Let X be the gain from a $1 bet. X has two possible values: $X = -1$ if you lose and $X = 35$ if you win. $P(X = -1) = 37/38$ and $P(X = 35) = 1/38$. This probability distribution and the calculation of the expected value are given in the following table:

x	-1	35	
$P(X = x)$	$\frac{37}{38}$	$\frac{1}{38}$	**Total:**
$xP(X = x)$	$-\frac{37}{38}$	$\frac{35}{38}$	$-\frac{2}{38}$

So, we expect to average a small loss of $2/38 \approx \$0.0526$ on each spin of the wheel.

➡ **Before we go on...** Of course, you cannot actually lose the expected $0.0526 on one spin of the roulette wheel in Example 4. However, if you play many times, this is what you expect your *average* loss per bet to be. For example, if you played 100 times, you could expect to lose about $100 \times 0.0526 = \$5.26$. ∎

A betting game in which the expected value is zero is called a **fair game**. For example, if you and I flip a coin, and I give you $1 each time it comes up heads but you give me $1 each time it comes up tails, then the game is fair. Over the long run, we expect to come out even. On the other hand, a game like roulette, in which the expected value is not zero, is **biased**. Most casino games are slightly biased in favor of the house.* Thus, most gamblers will lose only a small amount and many gamblers will actually win something (and return to play some more). However, when the earnings are averaged over the huge numbers of people playing, the house is guaranteed to come out ahead. This is how casinos make (lots of) money.

* Only rarely are games not biased in favor of the house. However, blackjack played without continuous shuffle machines can be beaten by card counting.

Expected Value of a Binomial Random Variable

Suppose you guess all the answers to the questions on a multiple-choice test. What score can you expect to get? This scenario is an example of a sequence of Bernoulli trials (see the preceding section), and the number of correct guesses is therefore a binomial random variable whose expected value we wish to know. There is a simple formula for the expected value of a binomial random variable.

> ### Expected Value of Binomial Random Variable
>
> If X is the binomial random variable associated with n independent Bernoulli trials, each with probability p of success, then the expected value of X is
>
> $$\mu = E(X) = np.$$

Quick Examples

1. If X is the number of successes in 20 Bernoulli trials with $p = .7$, then the expected number of successes is $\mu = E(X) = (20)(.7) = 14$.

2. If an event F in some experiment has $P(F) = .25$, the experiment is repeated 100 times, and X is the number of times F occurs, then $E(X) = (100)(.25) = 25$ is the number of times we expect F to occur.

Where does this formula come from? We *could* use the formula for expected value and compute the sum

$$E(X) = 0C(n, 0)p^0 q^n + 1C(n, 1)p^1 q^{n-1} + 2C(n, 2)p^2 q^{n-2} + \cdots + nC(n, n)p^n q^0$$

directly (using the binomial theorem), but this is one of the many places in mathematics where a less direct approach is much easier. X is the number of successes in a sequence of n Bernoulli trials, each with probability p of success. Thus, p is the fraction of time we expect a success, so out of n trials we expect np successes. Because X counts successes, we expect the value of X to be np. (With a little more effort, this can be made into a formal proof that the sum above equals np.)

EXAMPLE 5 Guessing on an Exam

An exam has 50 multiple-choice questions, each having four choices. If a student randomly guesses on each question, how many correct answers can he or she expect to get?

Solution Each guess is a Bernoulli trial with probability of success 1 in 4, so $p = .25$. Thus, for a sequence of $n = 50$ trials,

$$\mu = E(X) = np = (50)(.25) = 12.5.$$

Thus, the student can expect to get about 12.5 correct answers.

Q : *Wait a minute. How can a student get a fraction of a correct answer?*

A : Remember that the expected value is the average number of correct answers a student will get if he or she guesses on a large number of such tests. Or, we can say that if many students use this strategy of guessing, they will average about 12.5 correct answers each.

Estimating the Expected Value from a Sample

It is not always possible to know the probability distribution of a random variable. For instance, if we take X to be the income of a randomly selected lawyer, we could not be expected to know the probability distribution of X. However, we can still obtain a good *estimate* of the expected value of X (the average income of all lawyers) by using the relative frequency distribution based on a large random sample.

EXAMPLE 6 Estimating an Expected Value

The following table shows the (fictitious) incomes of a random sample of 1,000 lawyers in the United States in their first year out of law school.

Income Bracket	$20,000–$29,999	$30,000–$39,999	$40,000–$49,999	$50,000–$59,999	$60,000–$69,999	$70,000–$79,999	$80,000–$89,999
Number	20	80	230	400	170	70	30

Estimate the average of the incomes of all lawyers in their first year out of law school.

Solution We first interpret the question in terms of a random variable. Let X be the income of a lawyer selected at random from among all currently practicing first-year lawyers in the United States. We are given a sample of 1,000 values of X, and we are asked to find the expected value of X. First, we use the midpoints of the income brackets to set up a relative frequency distribution for X:

x	25,000	35,000	45,000	55,000	65,000	75,000	85,000
$P(X = x)$	.02	.08	.23	.40	.17	.07	.03

Our estimate for $E(X)$ is then

$$E(X) = \sum_i x_i \cdot P(X = x_i)$$

$$= (25,000)(.02) + (35,000)(.08) + (45,000)(.23) + (55,000)(.40)$$
$$+ (65,000)(.17) + (75,000)(.07) + (85,000)(.03) = \$54,500.$$

Thus, $E(X)$ is approximately $54,500. That is, the average income of all currently practicing first-year lawyers in the United States is approximately $54,500.

FAQ

Recognizing when to Compute the Mean and when to Compute the Expected Value

Q: *When am I supposed to compute the mean (add the values of X and divide by n) and when am I supposed to use the expected value formula?*

A: The formula for the mean (adding and dividing by the number of observations) is used to compute the mean of a sequence of random scores, or sampled values of X. If, on the other hand, you are given the probability distribution for X (even if it is only an estimated probability distribution), then you need to use the expected value formula.

▼ more advanced   ◆ challenging
T indicates exercises that should be solved using technology

Compute the mean, median, and mode of the data samples in Exercises 1–8. HINT *[See Quick Examples on pages 568 and 569.]*

1. −1, 5, 5, 7, 14

2. 2, 6, 6, 7, −1

3. 2, 5, 6, 7, −1, −1

4. 3, 1, 6, −3, 0, 5

5. $\frac{1}{2}, \frac{3}{2}, -4, \frac{5}{4}$

6. $-\frac{3}{2}, \frac{3}{8}, -1, \frac{5}{2}$

7. 2.5, −5.4, 4.1, −0.1, −0.1

8. 4.2, −3.2, 0, 1.7, 0

9. ▼ Give a sample of six scores with mean 1 and with median ≠ mean. (Arrange the scores in ascending order.)

10. ▼ Give a sample of five scores with mean 100 and median 1. (Arrange the scores in ascending order.)

In Exercises 11–16, calculate the expected value of X for the given probability distribution. HINT *[See Quick Example on page 572.]*

11.

x	0	1	2	3
$P(X = x)$	.5	.2	.2	.1

12.

x	1	2	3	4
$P(X = x)$	.1	.2	.5	.2

13.

x	10	20	30	40
$P(X = x)$	$\frac{15}{50}$	$\frac{20}{50}$	$\frac{10}{50}$	$\frac{5}{50}$

14.

x	2	4	6	8
$P(X = x)$	$\frac{1}{20}$	$\frac{15}{20}$	$\frac{2}{20}$	$\frac{2}{20}$

15.

x	−5	−1	0	2	5	10
$P(X = x)$	.2	.3	.2	.1	.2	0

16.

x	−20	−10	0	10	20	30
$P(X = x)$	.2	.4	.2	.1	0	.1

In Exercises 17–28, calculate the expected value of the given random variable X. [Exercises 23, 24, 27, and 28 assume familiarity with counting arguments and probability (Section 7.4).] HINT *[See Quick Example page 572.]*

17. *X* is the number that faces up when a fair die is rolled.

18. *X* is a number selected at random from the set {1, 2, 3, 4}.

19. *X* is the number of tails that come up when a coin is tossed twice.

20. *X* is the number of tails that come up when a coin is tossed three times.

21. ▼ *X* is the higher number when two dice are rolled.

22. ▼ *X* is the lower number when two dice are rolled.

23. ▼ *X* is the number of red marbles that Suzan has in her hand after she selects four marbles from a bag containing four red marbles and two green ones.

24. ▼ *X* is the number of green marbles that Suzan has in her hand after she selects four marbles from a bag containing three red marbles and two green ones.

25. ▼ Twenty darts are thrown at a dartboard. The probability of hitting a bull's-eye is .1. Let *X* be the number of bull's-eyes hit.

26. ▼ Thirty darts are thrown at a dartboard. The probability of hitting a bull's-eye is $\frac{1}{5}$. Let *X* be the number of bull's-eyes hit.

27. **T** ▼ Select 5 cards without replacement from a standard deck of 52, and let *X* be the number of queens you draw.

28. **T** ▼ Select 5 cards without replacement from a standard deck of 52, and let *X* be the number of red cards you draw.

APPLICATIONS

29. *Stock Market Gyrations* Following is a sample of the day-by-day change, rounded to the nearest 100 points, in the Dow Jones Industrial Average during 10 successive business days around the start of the financial crisis in October 2008:[22]

−400, −500, −200, −700, −100, 900, −100, −700, 400, −100

Compute the mean and median of the given sample. Fill in the blank: There were as many days with a change in the Dow above _____ points as there were with changes below that. HINT *[See Quick Examples on pages 568 and 569.]*

30. *Stock Market Gyrations* Following is a sample of the day-by-day change, rounded to the nearest 100 points, in the Dow Jones Industrial Average during 10 successive business days around the start of the financial crisis in October 2008:[23]

−100, 400, −200, −500, 200, −300, −200, 900, −100, 200

Compute the mean and median of the given sample. Fill in the blank: There were as many days with a change in the Dow above _____ points as there were with changes below that. HINT *[See Quick Examples on pages 568 and 569.]*

31. *Gold* The following figures show the price of gold per ounce, in dollars, for the 10-business-day period Nov. 17–Nov. 30, 2011:[24]

1,756, 1,730, 1,704, 1,698, 1,686, 1,699, 1,676, 1,714, 1,717, 1,704

Find the sample mean, median, and mode(s). What do your answers tell you about the price of gold?

---

[22]Source: http://finance.google.com.

[23]*Ibid.*

[24]Prices rounded to the nearest $1. Source: www.kitco.com/gold .londonfix.html.

32. Silver The following figures show the price of silver per ounce, in dollars, for the 10-business-day period Nov. 17–Nov. 30, 2011:[25]

$$33, 33, 31, 32, 32, 32, 31, 32, 32, 32$$

Find the sample mean, median, and mode(s). What do your answers tell you about the price of silver?

33. Supermarkets A survey of 52 U.S. supermarkets yielded the following relative frequency table, where X is the number of checkout lanes at a randomly chosen supermarket.[26]

x	1	2	3	4	5	6	7	8	9	10
$P(X = x)$	.01	.04	.04	.08	.10	.15	.25	.20	.08	.05

a. Compute $\mu = E(X)$ and interpret the result.
HINT [See Example 3.]

b. Which is larger, $P(X < \mu)$ or $P(X > \mu)$? Interpret the result.

34. Video Arcades Your company, *Sonic Video, Inc.*, has conducted research that shows the following probability distribution, where X is the number of video arcades in a randomly chosen city with more than 500,000 inhabitants.

x	0	1	2	3	4	5	6	7	8	9
$P(X = x)$	.07	.09	.35	.25	.15	.03	.02	.02	.01	.01

a. Compute $\mu = E(X)$ and interpret the result.
HINT [See Example 3.]

b. Which is larger, $P(X < \mu)$ or $P(X > \mu)$? Interpret the result.

35. School Enrollment The following table shows the approximate numbers of school goers in the United States (residents who attended some educational institution) in 1998, broken down by age group.[27]

Age	3–6.9	7–12.9	13–16.9	17–22.9	23–26.9	27–42.9
Population (millions)	12	24	15	14	2	5

Use the rounded midpoints of the given measurement classes to compute the probability distribution of the age X of a school goer. (Round probabilities to 2 decimal places.) Hence compute the expected value of X. What information does the expected value give about residents enrolled in schools?

36. School Enrollment Repeat Exercise 35, using the following data from 1980.[28]

Age	3–6.9	7–12.9	13–16.9	17–22.9	23–26.9	27–42.9
Population (millions)	8	20	11	13	1	3

37. Population Age in Mexico The following chart shows the ages of 250 randomly selected residents of Mexico:[29]

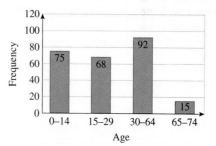

Use the relative frequency distribution based on the (rounded) midpoints of the given measurement classes to obtain an estimate of the average age of a resident in Mexico. (Round the answer to 1 decimal place). HINT [See Example 6.]

38. Population Age in the U.S. Repeat the preceding exercise, using the following chart, which shows the ages of 250 randomly selected residents of the U.S.:[30]

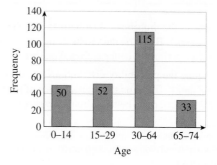

[25] Prices rounded to the nearest $1. Source: www.kitco.com/gold .londonfix.html.

[26] Sources: J.T. McClave, P.G. Benson, T. Sincich, *Statistics for Business and Economics*, 7th Ed. (Prentice Hall, 1998), p. 177; W. Chow *et al.* "A model for predicting a supermarket's annual sales per square foot," Graduate School of Management, Rutgers University.

[27] Data are approximate. Source: Statistical Abstract of the United States: 2000.

[28] *Ibid.*

[29] Based on population distribution in 2010. Source: Instituto Nacional de Estadística y Geografía (www.inegi.org.mx).

[30] *Ibid.*

39. *2010 Income Distribution up to $100,000* The following table shows the distribution of household incomes in 2010 for a sample of 1,000 households in the U.S. with incomes up to $100,000.[31]

Income Bracket ($)	0–19,999	20,000–39,999	40,000–59,000	60,000–79,999	80,000–99,999
Households	240	290	180	170	120

Use this information to estimate, to the nearest $1,000, the average household income for such households. HINT [See Example 6.]

40. *2003 Income Distribution up to $100,000* Repeat Exercise 39, using the following data from a sample of 1,000 households in the U.S. in 2003.[32]

Income Bracket ($)	0–19,999	20,000–39,999	40,000–59,000	60,000–79,999	80,000–99,999
Households	270	280	200	150	100

Highway Safety Exercises 41–44 are based on the following table, which shows crashworthiness ratings for several categories of motor vehicles.[33] In all of these exercises, take X as the crash-test rating of a small car, Y as the crash-test rating for a small SUV, and so on as shown in the table.

		Overall Frontal Crash-Test Rating			
	Number Tested	3 (Good)	2 (Acceptable)	1 (Marginal)	0 (Poor)
Small Cars X	16	1	11	2	2
Small SUVs Y	10	1	4	4	1
Medium SUVs Z	15	3	5	3	4
Passenger Vans U	13	3	0	3	7
Midsize Cars V	15	3	5	0	7
Large Cars W	19	9	5	3	2

41. ▼ Compute the probability distributions and expected values of X and Y. Based on the results, which of the two types of vehicles performed better in frontal crashes?

42. ▼ Compute the probability distributions and expected values of Z and V. Based on the results, which of the two types of vehicles performed better in frontal crashes?

43. ▼ Based on expected values, which of the following categories performed best in crash tests: small cars, midsize cars, or large cars?

44. ▼ Based on expected values, which of the following categories performed best in crash tests: small SUVs, medium SUVs, or passenger vans?

45. ▼ ***Roulette*** A roulette wheel has the numbers 1 through 36, 0, and 00. Half of the numbers from 1 through 36 are red, and a bet on red pays even money (that is, if you win, you will get back your $1 plus another $1). How much do you expect to win with a $1 bet on red? HINT [See Example 4.]

46. ▼ ***Roulette*** A roulette wheel has the numbers 1 through 36, 0, and 00. A bet on two numbers pays 17 to 1 (that is, if one of the two numbers you bet comes up, you get back your $1 plus another $17). How much do you expect to win with a $1 bet on two numbers? HINT [See Example 4.]

47. *Teenage Pastimes* According to a study,[34] the probability that a randomly selected teenager shopped at a mall at least once during a week was .63. How many teenagers in a randomly selected group of 40 would you expect to shop at a mall during the next week? HINT [See Example 5.]

48. *Other Teenage Pastimes* According to the study referred to in the preceding exercise, the probability that a randomly selected teenager played a computer game at least once during a week was .48. How many teenagers in a randomly selected group of 30 would you expect to play a computer game during the next 7 days? HINT [See Example 5.]

49. ▼ ***Manufacturing*** Your manufacturing plant produces air bags, and it is known that 10% of them are defective. A random collection of 20 air bags is tested.

  a. How many of them would you expect to be defective?
  b. In how large a sample would you expect to find 12 defective airbags?

50. ▼ ***Spiders*** Your pet tarantula, Spider, has a .12 probability of biting an acquaintance who comes into contact with him. Next week, you will be entertaining 20 friends (all of whom will come into contact with Spider).

  a. How many guests should you expect Spider to bite?
  b. At your last party, Spider bit 6 of your guests. Assuming that Spider bit the expected number of guests, how many guests did you have?

Exercises 51 and 52 assume familiarity with counting arguments and probability (Section 7.4).

51. ▼ ***Camping*** Kent's Tents has four red tents and three green tents in stock. Karin selects four of them at random. Let X be the number of red tents she selects. Give the probability distribution of X and find the expected number of red tents selected.

52. ▼ ***Camping*** Kent's Tents has five green knapsacks and four yellow ones in stock. Curt selects four of them at random.

---

[31]Based on actual income distribution in 2010. Source: U.S. Census Bureau, Current Population Survey, 2010 American Community Survey (www.census.gov).

[32]Based on actual income distribution in 2003 (not adjusted for inflation). Source: U.S. Census Bureau, Current Population Survey, 2004 Annual Social and Economic Supplement (www.census.gov).

[33]Ratings are by the Insurance Institute for Highway Safety. Sources: Oak Ridge National Laboratory: "An Analysis of the Impact of Sport Utility Vehicles in the United States," Stacy C. Davis, Lorena F. Truett, August 2000, Insurance Institute for Highway Safety (www-cta.ornl.gov/Publications/Final SUV report.pdf, www.highwaysafety.org/vehicle_ratings).

[34]Source: Rand Youth Poll/Teen-Age Research Unlimited/*New York Times*, March 14, 1998, p. D1.

Let X be the number of green knapsacks he selects. Give the probability distribution of X, and find the expected number of green knapsacks selected.

53. ⬛ ▼ *Stock Portfolios* You are required to choose between two stock portfolios, *FastForward Funds* and *SolidState Securities*. Stock analysts have constructed the following probability distributions for next year's rate of return for the two funds.

FastForward Funds

Rate of Return	−.4	−.3	−.2	−.1	0	.1	.2	.3	.4
Probability	.015	.025	.043	.132	.289	.323	.111	.043	.019

SolidState Securities

Rate of Return	−.4	−.3	−.2	−.1	0	.1	.2	.3	.4
Probability	.012	.023	.050	.131	.207	.330	.188	.043	.016

Which of the two funds gives the higher expected rate of return?

54. ⬛ ▼ *Risk Management* Before making your final decision whether to invest in *FastForward Funds* or *SolidState Securities* (see Exercise 53), you consult your colleague in the risk management department of your company. She informs you that, in the event of a stock market crash, the following probability distributions for next year's rate of return would apply:

FastForward Funds

Rate of Return	−.8	−.7	−.6	−.5	−.4	−.2	−.1	0	.1
Probability	.028	.033	.043	.233	.176	.230	.111	.044	.102

SolidState Securities

Rate of Return	−.8	−.7	−.6	−.5	−.4	−.2	−.1	0	.1
Probability	.033	.036	.038	.167	.176	.230	.211	.074	.035

Which of the two funds offers the lowest risk in case of a market crash?

55. ◆ *Insurance Schemes* The *Acme Insurance Company* is launching a drive to generate greater profits, and it decides to insure racetrack drivers against wrecking their cars. The company's research shows that, on average, a racetrack driver races 4 times a year and has a 1 in 10 chance of wrecking a vehicle, worth an average of $100,000, in every race. The annual premium is $5,000, and Acme automatically drops any driver who is involved in an accident (after paying for a new car), but does not refund the premium. How much profit (or loss) can the company expect to earn from a typical driver in a year? HINT [Use a tree diagram to compute the probabilities of the various outcomes.]

56. ◆ *Insurance* The *Blue Sky Flight Insurance Company* insures passengers against air disasters, charging a prospective passenger $20 for coverage on a single plane ride. In the event of a fatal air disaster, it pays out $100,000 to the named beneficiary. In the event of a nonfatal disaster, it pays out an average of $25,000 for hospital expenses. Given that the probability of a plane's crashing on a single trip is .00000087,[35]

and that a passenger involved in a plane crash has a .9 chance of being killed, determine the profit (or loss) per passenger that the insurance company expects to make on each trip. HINT [Use a tree to compute the probabilities of the various outcomes.]

COMMUNICATION AND REASONING EXERCISES

57. In a certain set of scores, there are as many values above the mean as below it. It follows that

(A) The median and mean are equal.
(B) The mean and mode are equal.
(C) The mode and median are equal.
(D) The mean, mode, and median are all equal.

58. In a certain set of scores, the median occurs more often than any other score. It follows that

(A) The median and mean are equal.
(B) The mean and mode are equal.
(C) The mode and median are equal.
(D) The mean, mode, and median are all equal.

59. Your friend Charlesworth claims that the median of a collection of data is always close to the mean. Is he correct? If so, say why; if not, give an example to prove him wrong.

60. Your other friend Imogen asserts that Charlesworth is wrong and that it is the mode and the median that are always close to each other. Is she correct? If so, say why; if not, give an example to prove her wrong.

61. Must the expected number of times you hit a bull's-eye after 50 attempts always be a whole number? Explain.

62. Your statistics instructor tells you that the expected score of the upcoming midterm test is 75%. That means that 75% is the most likely score to occur, right?

63. ▼ Your grade in a recent midterm was 80%, but the class average was 83%. Most people in the class scored better than you, right?

64. ▼ Your grade in a recent midterm was 80%, but the class median was 100%. Your score was lower than the average score, right?

65. ▼ Slim tells you that the population mean is just the mean of a suitably large sample. Is he correct? Explain.

66. ▼ Explain how you can use a sample to estimate an expected value.

67. ▼ Following is an excerpt from a full-page ad by MoveOn.org in *The New York Times* criticizing President G.W. Bush:[36]

On Tax Cuts:

George Bush: ". . . Americans will keep, this year, an average of almost $1,000 more of their own money."

The Truth: Nearly half of all taxpayers get less than $100. And 31% of all taxpayers get nothing at all.

The statements referred to as "The Truth" contradict the statement attributed to President Bush, right? Explain.

---

[35] This was the probability of a passenger plane crashing per departure in 1990. (Source: National Transportation Safety Board)

[36] Source: Full-page ad in the *New York Times*, September 17, 2003, p. A25.

68. ▼ Following is an excerpt from a five-page ad by WeissneggerForGov.org in *The Martian Enquirer* criticizing Supreme Martian Administrator, Gov. Red Davis:

On Worker Accommodation:

Gov. Red Davis: "The median size of Government worker habitats in Valles Marineris is at least 400 square feet."

Weissnegger: "The average size of a Government worker habitat in Valles Marineris is a mere 150 square feet."

The statements attributed to Weissnegger do not contradict the statement attributed to Gov. Davis, right? Explain.

69. ▼ Sonia has just told you that the expected household income in the United States is the same as the population mean of all U.S. household incomes. Clarify her statement by describing an experiment and an associated random variable X so that the expected household income is the expected value of X.

70. ▼ If X is a random variable, what is the difference between a sample mean of measurements of X and the expected value of X? Illustrate by means of an example.

8.4 Measures of Dispersion

Variance and Standard Deviation of a Set of Scores

Your grade on a recent midterm was 68%; the class average was 72%. How do you stand in comparison with the rest of the class? If the grades were widely scattered, then your grade may be close to the mean and a fair number of people may have done a lot worse than you (Figure 5a). If, on the other hand, almost all the grades were within a few points of the average, then your grade may not be much higher than the lowest grade in the class (Figure 5b).

This scenario suggests that it would be useful to have a way of measuring not only the central tendency of a set of scores (mean, median, or mode) but also the amount of "scatter" or "dispersion" of the data.

If the scores in our set are $x_1, x_2, \ldots, x_n$ and their mean is $\bar{x}$ (or μ in the case of a population mean), we are really interested in the distribution of the differences $x_i - \bar{x}$. We could compute the *average* of these differences, but this average will always be 0. (Why?) It is really the *sizes* of these differences that interest us, so we might try computing the average of the absolute values of the differences. This idea is reasonable, but it leads to technical difficulties that are avoided by a slightly different approach: The statistic we use is based on the average of the *squares* of the differences, as explained in the following definitions.

$P(X = x)$

Figure 5(a)

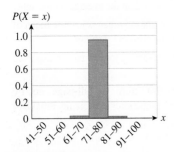

$P(X = x)$

Figure 5(b)

Population Variance and Standard Deviation

If the values $x_1, x_2, \ldots, x_n$ are all the measurements of X in the entire population, then the **population variance** is given by

$$\sigma^2 = \frac{(x_1 - \mu)^2 + (x_2 - \mu)^2 + \cdots + (x_n - \mu)^2}{n} = \frac{\sum_{i=1}^{n}(x_i - \mu)^2}{n}.$$

(Remember that μ is the symbol we use for the *population* mean.) The **population standard deviation** is the square root of the population variance:

$$\sigma = \sqrt{\sigma^2}.$$

Sample Variance and Standard Deviation

The **sample variance** of a sample $x_1, x_2, \ldots, x_n$ of n values of X is given by

$$s^2 = \frac{(x_1 - \bar{x})^2 + (x_2 - \bar{x})^2 + \cdots + (x_n - \bar{x})^2}{n - 1} = \frac{\sum_{i=1}^{n} (x_i - \bar{x})^2}{n - 1}.$$

The **sample standard deviation** is the square root of the sample variance:

$$s = \sqrt{s^2}.$$

Visualizing Small and Large Variance

Small Variance

Large Variance

Quick Examples

1. The sample variance of the scores 1, 2, 3, 4, 5 is the sum of the squares of the differences between the scores and the mean $\bar{x} = 3$, divided by $n - 1 = 4$:

$$s^2 = \frac{(1 - 3)^2 + (2 - 3)^2 + (3 - 3)^2 + (4 - 3)^2 + (5 - 3)^2}{4}$$

$$= \frac{10}{4} = 2.5$$

so

$$s = \sqrt{2.5} \approx 1.58.$$

2. The population variance of the scores 1, 2, 3, 4, 5 is the sum of the squares of the differences between the scores and the mean $\mu = 3$, divided by $n = 5$:

$$\sigma^2 = \frac{(1 - 3)^2 + (2 - 3)^2 + (3 - 3)^2 + (4 - 3)^2 + (5 - 3)^2}{5} = \frac{10}{5} = 2$$

so

$$\sigma = \sqrt{2} \approx 1.41.$$

using Technology

Technology can be used to compute means and standard deviations as follows:

TI-83/84 Plus
[STAT] EDIT Enter the values $x_1, x_2, \ldots, x_n$ in L_1
[STAT] CALC 1-Var Stats
[ENTER]
s will appear as "Sx" and σ as "σx".

Spreadsheet
Enter the values $x_1, x_2, \ldots, x_n$ in column A
=AVERAGE(A:A) computes the mean.
=STDEV(A:A) computes s.
=STDEVP(A:A) computes σ.

Q: *The population variance is the average of the squares of the differences between the values and the mean. But why do we divide by $n - 1$ instead of n when calculating the sample variance?*

A: In real-life applications, we would like the variance we calculate from a sample to approximate the variance of the whole population. In statistical terms, we would like the expected value of the sample variance s^2 to be the same as the population variance σ^2. The sample variance s^2 as we have defined it is the "unbiased estimator" of the population variance σ^2 that accomplishes this task; if, instead, we divided by n in the formula for s^2, we would, on average, tend to underestimate the population variance. (See the online text on Sampling Distributions at the Website for further discussion of unbiased estimators.) Note that as the sample size gets larger and larger, the discrepancy between the formulas for s^2 and σ^2 becomes negligible; dividing by n gives almost the same answer as dividing by $n - 1$. It is traditional, nonetheless, to use the sample variance in preference to the population variance when working with samples, and we do that here. In practice we should not try to draw conclusions about the entire population from samples so small that the difference between the two formulas matters. As one book puts it, "If the difference between n and $n - 1$ ever matters to you, then you are probably up to no good anyway—e.g., trying to substantiate a questionable hypothesis with marginal data."[*]

[*] W. H. Press, S. A. Teukolsky, E. T. Vetterling, and B. P. Flannery, *Numerical Recipes: The Art of Scientific Computing*, Cambridge University Press, 2007.

Here's a simple example of calculating standard deviation.

EXAMPLE 1   Income

Following is a sample of the incomes (in thousands of dollars) of eight U.S. residents selected at random:[37]

$$50, 40, 60, 20, 90, 10, 30, 20.$$

Compute the sample mean and standard deviation, rounded to one decimal place. What percentage of the scores fall within one standard deviation of the mean? What percentage fall within two standard deviations of the mean?

Solution The sample mean is

$$\bar{x} = \frac{\sum_i x_i}{n} = \frac{50 + 40 + 60 + 20 + 90 + 10 + 30 + 20}{8} = \frac{320}{8} = 40.$$

The sample variance is

$$s^2 = \frac{\sum_i (x_i - \bar{x})^2}{n - 1}$$

$$= \frac{1}{7}[(50 - 40)^2 + (40 - 40)^2 + (60 - 40)^2 + (20 - 40)^2$$

$$+ (90 - 40)^2 + (10 - 40)^2 + (30 - 40)^2 + (20 - 40)^2]$$

$$= \frac{1}{7}(100 + 0 + 400 + 400 + 2{,}500 + 900 + 100 + 400)$$

$$= \frac{4{,}800}{7}.$$

Thus, the sample standard deviation is

$$s = \sqrt{\frac{4{,}800}{7}} \approx 26.2. \qquad \text{Rounded to one decimal place}$$

To ask which scores fall "within one standard deviation of the mean" is to ask which scores fall in the interval $[\bar{x} - s, \bar{x} + s]$, or about $[40 - 26.2, 40 + 26.2] = [13.8, 66.2]$. Six out of the eight scores fall in this interval, so the percentage of scores that fall within one standard deviation of the mean is $6/8 = .75$, or 75%.

For two standard deviations, the interval in question is $[\bar{x} - 2s, \bar{x} + 2s] \approx [40 - 52.4, 40 + 52.4] = [-12.4, 92.4]$, which includes all of the scores. In other words, 100% of the scores fall within two standard deviations of the mean.

---

[37] The sample is roughly statistically representative of the actual income distribution in the U.S. in 2010 for incomes up to $100,000. (See Exercise 35.) Source for income distribution: U.S. Census Bureau (www.census.gov).

Q: *In Example 1, 75% of the scores fell within one standard deviation of the mean and all of them fell within two standard deviations of the mean. Is this typical?*

A: Actually, the percentage of scores within a number of standard deviations of the mean depends a great deal on the way the scores are distributed. There are two useful methods for *estimating* the percentage of scores that fall within any number of standard deviations of the mean. The first method applies to any set of data and is due to P.L. Chebyshev (1821–1894), while the second applies to "nice" sets of data and is based on the "normal distribution," which we shall discuss in Section 5.

Chebyshev's Rule

For any set of data, the following statements are true:

At least $3/4$ of the scores fall within two standard deviations of the mean (within the interval $[\bar{x} - 2s, \bar{x} + 2s]$ for samples or $[\mu - 2\sigma, \mu + 2\sigma]$ for populations).

At least $8/9$ of the scores fall within three standard deviations of the mean (within the interval $[\bar{x} - 3s, \bar{x} + 3s]$ for samples or $[\mu - 3\sigma, \mu + 3\sigma]$ for populations).

At least $15/16$ of the scores fall within four standard deviations of the mean (within the interval $[\bar{x} - 4s, \bar{x} + 4s]$ for samples or $[\mu - 4\sigma, \mu + 4\sigma]$ for populations).

. . .

At least $1 - 1/k^2$ of the scores fall within k standard deviations of the mean (within the interval $[\bar{x} - ks, \bar{x} + ks]$ for samples or $[\mu - k\sigma, \mu + k\sigma]$ for populations).

Visualizing Chebyshev's Rule

* Unlike Chebyshev's rule, which is a precise theorem, the empirical rule is a "rule of thumb" that is intentionally vague about what exactly is meant by a "bell shaped distribution" and "approximately such-and-such %." (As a result, the rule is often stated differently in different textbooks.) We will see in Section 8.5 that if the distribution is a *normal* one, the empirical rule translates to a precise statement.

Empirical Rule*

For a set of data whose frequency distribution is bell shaped and symmetric (see Figure 6), the following is true:

Bell Shaped Symmetric Distribution
Figure 6(a)

Not Symmetric
Figure 6(b)

Not Bell-Shaped
Figure 6(c)

Approximately 68% of the scores fall within one standard deviation of the mean (within the interval $[\bar{x} - s, \bar{x} + s]$ for samples or $[\mu - \sigma, \mu + \sigma]$ for populations).

Approximately 95% of the scores fall within two standard deviations of the mean (within the interval $[\bar{x} - 2s, \bar{x} + 2s]$ for samples or $[\mu - 2\sigma, \mu + 2\sigma]$ for populations).

Approximately 99.7% of the scores fall within three standard deviations of the mean (within the interval $[\bar{x} - 3s, \bar{x} + 3s]$ for samples or $[\mu - 3\sigma, \mu + 3\sigma]$ for populations).

Visualizing the Empirical Rule

Quick Examples

1. If the mean of a sample is 20 with standard deviation $s = 2$, then at least 15/16, or 93.75% of the scores lie within four standard deviations of the mean—that is, in the interval [12, 28].

2. If the mean of a sample with a bell shaped symmetric distribution is 20 with standard deviation $s = 2$, then approximately 95% of the scores lie in the interval [16, 24].

The empirical rule could not be applied in Example 1. The distribution there is not symmetric (sketch it to see for yourself) and the fact that there were only 8 scores limits the accuracy further. The empirical rule is, however, accurate in distributions that are bell shaped and symmetric, even if not perfectly so. Chebyshev's rule, on the other hand, is always valid (and applies in Example 1 in particular) but tends to be "overcautious" and in practice underestimates how much of a distribution lies in a given interval.

EXAMPLE 2 Automobile Life

The average life span of a Batmobile is 9 years, with a standard deviation of 2 years. My own Batmobile lasted less than 3 years before being condemned to the bat-junkyard.

a. Without any further knowledge about the distribution of Batmobile life spans, what can one say about the percentage of Batmobiles that last less than 3 years?

b. Refine the answer in part (a), assuming that the distribution of Batmobile life spans is bell shaped and symmetric.

Figure 7

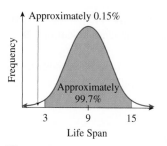

Figure 8

Solution

a. If we are given no further information about the distribution of Batmobile life spans, we need to use Chebyshev's rule. Because the life span of my Batmobile was more than 6 years (or three standard deviations) shorter than the mean, it lies outside the range $[\mu - 3\sigma, \mu + 3\sigma] = [3, 15]$. Because *at least* 8/9 of the life spans of all Batmobiles lie in this range, *at most* 1/9, or 11%, of the life spans lie outside this range (see Figure 7). Some of these, like the life span of my own Batmobile, are less than 3 years, while the rest are more than $\mu + 3\sigma = 15$ years.

b. Because we know more about the distribution now than we did in part (a), we can use the empirical rule and obtain sharper results. The empirical rule predicts that approximately 99.7% of the life spans of Batmobiles lie in the range $[\mu - 3\sigma, \mu + 3\sigma] = [3, 15]$. Thus, approximately $1 - 99.7\% = 0.3\%$ of them lie outside that range. Because the distribution is symmetric, however, more can be said: half of that 0.3%, or 0.15% of Batmobiles will last longer than 15 years, while the other 0.15% are, like my own ill-fated Batmobile, doomed to a life span of less than 3 years (see Figure 8).

Variance and Standard Deviation of a Finite Random Variable

Recall that the expected value of a random variable X is a prediction of the average of a large sample of values of X. Can we similarly predict the variance of a large sample? Suppose we have a sample $x_1, x_2, \ldots, x_n$. If n is large, the sample and population variances are essentially the same, so we concentrate on the population variance, which is the average of the numbers $(x_i - \bar{x})^2$. This average can be predicted using $E([X - \mu]^2)$ the expected value of $(X - \mu)^2$. In general, we make the following definition.

Variance and Standard Deviation of a Finite Random Variable

If X is a finite random variable taking on values $x_1, x_2, \ldots, x_n$, then the **variance** of X is

$$\sigma^2 = E([X - \mu]^2)$$
$$= (x_1 - \mu)^2 P(X = x_1) + (x_2 - \mu)^2 P(X = x_2) + \cdots + (x_n - \mu)^2 P(X = x_n)$$
$$= \sum_i (x_i - \mu)^2 P(X = x_i).$$

The **standard deviation** of X is then the square root of the variance:

$$\sigma = \sqrt{\sigma^2}.$$

To compute the variance from the probability distribution of X, first compute the expected value μ and then compute the expected value of $(X - \mu)^2$.

Quick Example

The following distribution has expected value $\mu = E(X) = 2$:

x	-1	2	3	10
$P(X = x)$	.3	.5	.1	.1

The variance of X is

$$\sigma^2 = (x_1 - \mu)^2 P(X = x_1) + (x_2 - \mu)^2 P(X = x_2) + \cdots + (x_n - \mu)^2 P(X = x_n)$$
$$= (-1 - 2)^2(.3) + (2 - 2)^2(.5) + (3 - 2)^2(.1) + (10 - 2)^2(.1) = 9.2.$$

The standard deviation of X is

$$\sigma = \sqrt{9.2} \approx 3.03.$$

Note We can interpret the variance of X as the number we expect to get for the variance of a large sample of values of X, and similarly for the standard deviation. ∎

We can calculate the variance and standard deviation of a random variable using a tabular approach just as when we calculated the expected value in Example 3 in the preceding section.

using Technology

Technology can be used to automate the calculations of Example 3.

TI-83/84 Plus

STAT EDIT values of x in L_1, probabilities in L_2.
Home screen: sum($L_1 * L_2$) → M
Then sum((L_1-M)^2*L_2)
[More details on page 614.]

Spreadsheet
x-values in A2–A7, probabilities in B2–B7
=A2*B2 in C2; copy down to C7.
=SUM(C2:C7) in C8
=(A2-$C$8)^2*B2 in D2; copy down to D7.
=SUM(D2:D7) in D8
[More details on page 617.]

WW Website
www.WanerMath.com
Student Home
→ On Line Utilities
→ Histogram Utility
Enter the x-values and probabilities as shown:

```
10, .2
20, .2
30, .3
40, .1
50, .1
60, .1
```

Make sure "Show expected value and standard deviation" is checked, and press "Results".

EXAMPLE 3 **Variance of a Random Variable**

Compute the variance and standard deviation for the following probability distribution.

x	10	20	30	40	50	60
$P(X = x)$	.2	.2	.3	.1	.1	.1

Solution We first compute the expected value, μ, in the usual way:

x	10	20	30	40	50	60	
$P(X = x)$	.2	.2	.3	.1	.1	.1	
$xP(X = x)$	2	4	9	4	5	6	$\mu = 30$

Next, we add an extra three rows:

- a row for the differences $(x - \mu)$, which we get by subtracting μ from the values of X
- a row for the squares $(x - \mu)^2$, which we obtain by squaring the values immediately above
- a row for the products $(x - \mu)^2 P(X = x)$, which we obtain by multiplying the values in the second and the fifth rows.

x	10	20	30	40	50	60	
$P(X = x)$	.2	.2	.3	.1	.1	.1	
$xP(X = x)$	2	4	9	4	5	6	$\mu = 30$
$x - \mu$	−20	−10	0	10	20	30	
$(x - \mu)^2$	400	100	0	100	400	900	
$(x - \mu)^2 P(X = x)$	80	20	0	10	40	90	$\sigma^2 = 240$

The sum of the values in the last row is the variance. The standard deviation is then the square root of the variance:

$$\sigma = \sqrt{240} \approx 15.49.$$

Note Chebyshev's rule and the empirical rule apply to random variables just as they apply to samples and populations, as we illustrate in the following example. ∎

EXAMPLE 4 Internet Commerce

Your newly launched company, CyberPromo, Inc., sells computer games on the Internet.

a. Statistical research indicates that the lifespan of an Internet marketing company such as yours is symmetrically distributed with an expected value of 30 months and standard deviation of 4 months. Complete the following sentence:

There is (at least/at most/approximately)_____ a _____ percent chance that CyberPromo will still be around for more than 3 years.

b. How would the answer to part (a) be affected if the distribution of lifespans was not known to be symmetric?

Solution

a. Do we use Chebyshev's rule or the empirical rule? Because the empirical rule requires that the distribution be both symmetric and bell shaped—not just symmetric—we cannot conclude that it applies here, so we are forced to use Chebyshev's rule instead.

Let X be the lifespan of an Internet commerce site. The expected value of X is 30 months, and the hoped-for lifespan of CyberPromo, Inc., is 36 months, which is 6 months, or $6/4 = 1.5$ standard deviations, above the mean. Chebyshev's rule tells us that X is within $k = 1.5$ standard deviations of the mean at least $1 - 1/k^2$ of the time; that is,

$$P(24 \leq X \leq 36) \geq 1 - \frac{1}{k^2} = 1 - \frac{1}{1.5^2} \approx .56.$$

In other words, at least 56% of all Internet marketing companies have life spans in the range of 24 to 36 months. Thus, *at most* 44 % have life spans outside this range. Because the distribution is symmetric, at most 22% have life spans longer than 36 months. Thus we can complete the sentence as follows:

There is at most a 22 percent chance that CyberPromo will still be around for more than 3 years.

b. If the given distribution was not known to be symmetric, how would this affect the answer? We saw above that regardless of whether the distribution is symmetric or not, at most 44% have lifespans outside the range 24 to 36 months. Because the distribution is not symmetric, we cannot conclude that at most half of the 44% have lifespans longer than 36 months, and all we can say is that *no more than 44% can possibly have life spans longer than 36 years.* In other words:

There is at most a 44 percent chance that CyberPromo will still be around for more than 3 years.

Variance and Standard Deviation of a Binomial Random Variable

We saw that there is an easy formula for the expected value of a binomial random variable: $\mu = np$, where n is the number of trials and p is the probability of success. Similarly, there is a simple formula for the variance and standard deviation.

Variance and Standard Deviation of a Binomial Random Variable

If X is a binomial random variable associated with n independent Bernoulli trials, each with probability p of success, then the variance and standard deviation of X are given by

$$\sigma^2 = npq \quad \text{and} \quad \sigma = \sqrt{npq}$$

where $q = 1 - p$ is the probability of failure.

Quick Example

If X is the number of successes in 20 Bernoulli trials with $p = .7$, then the standard deviation is $\sigma = \sqrt{npq} = \sqrt{(20)(.7)(.3)} \approx 2.05$.

For values of p near $1/2$ and large values of n, a binomial distribution is bell shaped and (nearly) symmetric, hence the empirical rule applies. One rule of thumb is that we can use the empirical rule when both $np \geq 10$ and $nq \geq 10$.[*]

✻ Remember that the empirical rule only gives an *estimate* of probabilities. In Section 8.5 we give a more accurate approximation that takes into account the fact that the binomial distribution is not continuous.

EXAMPLE 5 Internet Commerce

You have calculated that there is a 40% chance that a hit on your Web page results in a fee paid to your company CyberPromo, Inc. Your Web page receives 25 hits per day. Let X be the number of hits that result in payment of the fee ("successful hits").

a. What are the expected value and standard deviation of X?

b. Complete the following: On approximately 95 out of 100 days, I will get between ____ and ____ successful hits.

Solution

a. The random variable X is binomial with $n = 25$ and $p = .4$. To compute μ and σ, we use the formulas

$$\mu = np = (25)(.4) = 10 \text{ successful hits}$$

$$\sigma = \sqrt{npq} = \sqrt{(25)(.4)(.6)} \approx 2.45 \text{ hits.}$$

b. Because $np = 10 \geq 10$ and $nq = (25)(.6) = 15 \geq 10$, we can use the empirical rule, which tells us that there is an approximately 95% probability that the number of successful hits is within two standard deviations of the mean—that is, in the interval

$$[\mu - 2\sigma, \mu + 2\sigma] = [10 - 2(2.45), 10 + 2(2.45)] = [5.1, 14.9].$$

Thus, on approximately 95 out of 100 days, I will get between <u>5.1</u> and <u>14.9</u> successful hits.

FAQ

Recognizing when to Use the Empirical Rule or Chebyshev's Rule

Q : *How do I decide whether to use Chebyshev's rule or the empirical rule?*

A : Check to see whether the probability distribution you are considering is both symmetric and bell shaped. If so, you can use the empirical rule. If not, then you must use Chebyshev's rule. Thus, for instance, if the distribution is symmetric but not known to be bell shaped, you must use Chebyshev's rule.

8.4 EXERCISES

▼ more advanced   ◆ challenging

Ⓣ indicates exercises that should be solved using technology

Compute the (sample) variance and standard deviation of the data samples given in Exercises 1–8. (You calculated the means in the last exercise set. Round all answers to two decimal places.) HINT [See Quick Examples on page 581.]

1. $-1, 5, 5, 7, 14$

2. $2, 6, 6, 7, -1$

3. $2, 5, 6, 7, -1, -1$

4. $3, 1, 6, -3, 0, 5$

5. $\dfrac{1}{2}, \dfrac{3}{2}, -4, \dfrac{5}{4}$

6. $-\dfrac{3}{2}, \dfrac{3}{8}, -1, \dfrac{5}{2}$

7. $2.5, -5.4, 4.1, -0.1, -0.1$

8. $4.2, -3.2, 0, 1.7, 0$

In Exercises 9–14, calculate the standard deviation of X for each probability distribution. (You calculated the expected values in the last exercise set. Round all answers to two decimal places.) HINT [See Quick Example on page 585.]

9.

x	0	1	2	3
$P(X = x)$	.5	.2	.2	.1

10.

x	1	2	3	4
$P(X = x)$	.1	.2	.5	.2

11.

x	10	20	30	40
$P(X = x)$	$\dfrac{3}{10}$	$\dfrac{2}{5}$	$\dfrac{1}{5}$	$\dfrac{1}{10}$

12.

x	2	4	6	8
$P(X = x)$	$\dfrac{1}{20}$	$\dfrac{15}{20}$	$\dfrac{2}{20}$	$\dfrac{2}{20}$

13.

x	-5	-1	0	2	5	10
$P(X = x)$	.2	.3	.2	.1	.2	0

14.

x	-20	-10	0	10	20	30
$P(X = x)$	.2	.4	.2	.1	0	.1

In Exercises 15–24, calculate the expected value, the variance, and the standard deviation of the given random variable X. (You calculated the expected values in the last exercise set. Round all answers to two decimal places.)

15. X is the number that faces up when a fair die is rolled.

16. X is the number selected at random from the set $\{1, 2, 3, 4\}$.

17. X is the number of tails that come up when a coin is tossed twice.

18. X is the number of tails that come up when a coin is tossed three times.

19. ▼ X is the higher number when two dice are rolled.

20. ▼ X is the lower number when two dice are rolled.

21. ▼ X is the number of red marbles that Suzan has in her hand after she selects four marbles from a bag containing four red marbles and two green ones.

22. ▼ X is the number of green marbles that Suzan has in her hand after she selects four marbles from a bag containing three red marbles and two green ones.

23. ▼ Twenty darts are thrown at a dartboard. The probability of hitting a bull's-eye is .1. Let X be the number of bull's-eyes hit.

24. ▼ Thirty darts are thrown at a dartboard. The probability of hitting a bull's-eye is $\frac{1}{5}$. Let X be the number of bull's-eyes hit.

APPLICATIONS

25. *Popularity Ratings* In your bid to be elected class representative, you have your election committee survey five randomly chosen students in your class and ask them to rank you on a scale of 0–10. Your rankings are 3, 2, 0, 9, 1.

a. Find the sample mean and standard deviation. (Round your answers to two decimal places.) HINT [See Example 1 and Quick Examples on page 581.]

b. Assuming the sample mean and standard deviation are indicative of the class as a whole, in what range does the empirical rule predict that approximately 68% of the class will rank you? What other assumptions must we make to use the rule?

26. *Popularity Ratings* Your candidacy for elected class representative is being opposed by Slick Sally. Your election committee has surveyed six of the students in your class and had them rank Sally on a scale of 0–10. The rankings were 2, 8, 7, 10, 5, 8.

a. Find the sample mean and standard deviation. (Round your answers to two decimal places.) HINT [See Example 1 and Quick Examples on page 581.]

b. Assuming the sample mean and standard deviation are indicative of the class as a whole, in what range does the empirical rule predict that approximately 95% of the class will rank Sally? What other assumptions must we make to use the rule?

27. *Unemployment* Following is a sample of unemployment rates (in percentage points) in the United States sampled from the period 1990–2004:[38]

4.2, 4.7, 5.4, 5.8, 4.9.

a. Compute the mean and standard deviation of the given sample. (Round your answers to one decimal place.)

---

[38] Sources for data: Bureau of Labor Statistics (BLS) (www.bls.gov).

b. Assuming the distribution of unemployment rates in the population is symmetric and bell shaped, 95% of the time, the unemployment rate is between ____ and ____ percent.

28. Unemployment Following is a sample of unemployment rates among Hispanics (in percentage points) in the US sampled from the period 1990–2004:[39]

7.7, 7.5, 9.3, 6.9, 8.6

a. Compute the mean and standard deviation of the given sample. (Round your answers to one decimal place.)

b. Assuming the distribution of unemployment rates in the population of interest is symmetric and bell shaped, 68% of the time, the unemployment rate is between ____ and ____ percent.

29. Stock Market Gyrations Following is a sample of the day-by-day change, rounded to the nearest 100 points, in the Dow Jones Industrial Average during 10 successive business days around the start of the financial crisis in October 2008:[40]

−400, −500, −200, −700, −100, 900, −100, −700, 400, −100

a. Compute the mean and standard deviation of the given sample. (Round your answers to the nearest whole number.)

b. Assuming the distribution of day-by-day changes of the Dow during financial crises is symmetric and bell shaped, then the Dow falls by more than ____ points 16% of the time. What is the percentage of times in the sample that the Dow actually fell by more than that amount? HINT [See Example 2(b).]

30. Stock Market Gyrations Following is a sample of the day-by-day change, rounded to the nearest 100 points, in the Dow Jones Industrial Average during 10 successive business days around the start of the financial crisis in October 2008:[41]

−100, 400, −200, −500, 200, −300, −200, 900, −100, 200.

a. Compute the mean and standard deviation of the given sample. (Round your answers to the nearest whole number.)

b. Assuming the distribution of day-by-day changes of the Dow during financial crises is symmetric and bell shaped, then the Dow rises by more than ____ points 2.5% of the time. What is the percentage of times in the sample that the Dow actually rose by more than that amount? HINT [See Example 2(b).]

31. ▣ Sport Utility Vehicles Following are highway driving gas mileages of a selection of medium-sized sport utility vehicles (SUVs):[42]

17, 18, 17, 18, 21, 16, 21, 18, 16, 14, 15, 22, 17, 19, 17, 18.

a. Find the sample standard deviation (rounded to two decimal places).

b. In what gas mileage range does Chebyshev's inequality predict that at least 8/9 (approximately 89%) of the selection will fall?

c. What is the actual percentage of SUV models of the sample that fall in the range predicted in part (b)? Which gives the more accurate prediction of this percentage: Chebyshev's rule or the empirical rule?

32. ▣ Sport Utility Vehicles Following are the city driving gas mileages of a selection of sport utility vehicles (SUVs):[43]

14, 15, 14, 15, 13, 16, 12, 14, 19, 18, 16, 16, 12, 15, 15, 13.

a. Find the sample standard deviation (rounded to two decimal places).

b. In what gas mileage range does Chebyshev's inequality predict that at least 75% of the selection will fall?

c. What is the actual percentage of SUV models of the sample that fall in the range predicted in part (b)? Which gives the more accurate prediction of this percentage: Chebyshev's rule or the empirical rule?

33. Shopping Malls A survey of all the shopping malls in your region yields the following probability distribution, where X is the number of movie theater screens in a selected mall:

Number of Movie Screens	0	1	2	3	4
Probability	.4	.1	.2	.2	.1

Compute the expected value μ and the standard deviation σ of X. (Round answers to two decimal places.) What percentage of malls have a number of movie theater screens within two standard deviations of μ?

34. Pastimes A survey of all the students in your school yields the following probability distribution, where X is the number of movies that a selected student has seen in the past week:

Number of Movies	0	1	2	3	4
Probability	.5	.1	.2	.1	.1

Compute the expected value μ and the standard deviation σ of X. (Round answers to two decimal places.) For what percentage of students is X within two standard deviations of μ?

35. ▣ 2010 Income Distribution up to $100,000 The following table shows the distribution of household incomes in 2010 for a sample of 1,000 households in the U.S. with incomes up to $100,000.[44]

[39] Sources for data: Bureau of Labor Statistics (BLS) (www.bls.gov).

[40] Source: http://finance.google.com.

[41] Ibid.

[42] Figures are the low-end of ranges for 1999 models tested. Source: Oak Ridge National Laboratory: "An Analysis of the Impact of Sport Utility Vehicles in the United States" Stacy C. Davis, Lorena F. Truett (August 2000)/Insurance Institute for Highway Safety (http://cta.ornl.gov/cta/Publications/pdf/ORNL_TM_2000_147.pdf).

[43] Ibid.

[44] Based on actual income distribution in 2010. Source: U.S. Census Bureau, Current Population Survey, 2010 American Community Survey (www.census.gov).

Income ($ Thousands)	10	30	50	70	90
Households	240	290	180	170	120

Compute the expected value μ and the standard deviation σ of the associated random variable X. If we define a "lower income" family as one whose income is more than one standard deviation below the mean, and a "higher income" family as one whose income is at least one standard deviation above the mean, what is the income gap between higher- and lower-income families in the U.S.? (Round your answers to the nearest $1,000.)

36. ▣ *2003 Income Distribution up to $100,000* Repeat Exercise 35, using the following data from a sample of 1,000 households in the U.S. in 2003.[45]

Income ($ thousands)	10	30	50	70	90
Households	270	280	200	150	100

37. *Hispanic Employment: Male* The following table shows the approximate number of males of Hispanic origin employed in the United States in 2005, broken down by age group.[46]

Age	15–24.9	25–54.9	55–64.9
Employment (thousands)	16,000	13,000	1,600

a. Use the rounded midpoints of the given measurement classes to compute the expected value and the standard deviation of the age X of a male Hispanic worker in the United States. (Round all probabilities and intermediate calculations to two decimal places.)

b. In what age interval does the empirical rule predict that 68% of all male Hispanic workers will fall? (Round answers to the nearest year.)

38. *Hispanic Employment: Female* Repeat Exercise 37, using the corresponding data for females of Hispanic origin.[47]

Age	15–24.9	25–54.9	55–64.9
Employment (thousands)	1,200	5,000	600

39. *Commerce* You have been told that the average life span of an Internet-based company is 2 years, with a standard deviation of 0.15 years. Further, the associated distribution is highly skewed (not symmetric). Your Internet company is now 2.6 years old. What percentage of all Internet-based companies have enjoyed a life span at least as long as yours? Your answer should contain one of the following phrases: *At least; At most; Approximately*. HINT [See Example 2.]

40. *Commerce* You have been told that the average life span of a car-compounding service is 3 years, with a standard deviation of 0.2 years. Further, the associated distribution is symmetric but not bell shaped. Your car-compounding service is exactly 2.6 years old. What fraction of car-compounding services last at most as long as yours? Your answer should contain one of the following phrases: *At least; At most; Approximately*. HINT [See Example 2.]

41. *Batmobiles* The average life span of a Batmobile is 9 years, with a standard deviation of 2 years.[48] Further, the probability distribution of the life spans of Batmobiles is symmetric, but not known to be bell shaped.

Because my old Batmobile has been sold as bat-scrap, I have decided to purchase a new one. According to the above information, there is

(A) at least   **(B)** at most   **(C)** approximately

a _____ percent chance that my new Batmobile will last 13 years or more.

42. *Spiderman Coupés* The average life span of a Spiderman Coupé is 8 years, with a standard deviation of 2 years. Further, the probability distribution of the life spans of Spiderman Coupés is not known to be bell shaped or symmetric. I have just purchased a brand-new Spiderman Coupé. According to the above information, there is

(A) at least   **(B)** at most   **(C)** approximately

a _____ percent chance that my new Spiderman Coupé will last for less than 4 years.

43. *Teenage Pastimes* According to a study,[49] the probability that a randomly selected teenager shopped at a mall at least once during a week was .63. Let X be the number of students in a randomly selected group of 40 that will shop at a mall during the next week.

[45] Based on actual income distribution in 2003 (not adjusted for inflation). Source: U.S. Census Bureau, Current Population Survey, 2004 Annual Social and Economic Supplement (www.census.gov).

[46] Figures are rounded. Bounds for the age groups for the first and third categories were adjusted for computational convenience. Source: Bureau of Labor Statistics (ftp://ftp.bls.gov/pub/suppl/empsit.cpseed15.txt).

[47] Ibid.

[48] See Example 2.

[49] Source: Rand Youth Poll/Teen-Age Research Unlimited/*New York Times*, March 14, 1998, p. D1.

a. Compute the expected value and standard deviation of X. (Round answers to two decimal places.) HINT [See Example 5.]

b. Fill in the missing quantity: There is an approximately 2.5% chance that ___ or more teenagers in the group will shop at a mall during the next week.

44. **Other Teenage Pastimes** According to the study referred to in the preceding exercise, the probability that a randomly selected teenager played a computer game at least once during a week was .48. Let X be the number of teenagers in a randomly selected group of 30 who will play a computer game during the next 7 days.

a. Compute the expected value and standard deviation of X. (Round answers to two decimal places.) HINT [See Example 5.]

b. Fill in the missing quantity: There is an approximately 16% chance that ___ or more teenagers in the group will play a computer game during the next 7 days.

45. ▼ **Teenage Marketing** In 2000, 22% of all teenagers in the United States had checking accounts.[50] Your bank, *TeenChex Inc.*, is interested in targeting teenagers who do not already have a checking account.

a. If TeenChex selects a random sample of 1,000 teenagers, what number of teenagers *without* checking accounts can it expect to find? What is the standard deviation of this number? (Round the standard deviation to one decimal place.)

b. Fill in the missing quantities: There is an approximately 95% chance that between ___ and ___ teenagers in the sample will not have checking accounts. (Round answers to the nearest whole number.)

46. ▼ **Teenage Marketing** In 2000, 18% of all teenagers in the United States owned stocks or bonds.[51] Your brokerage company, *TeenStox Inc.*, is interested in targeting teenagers who do not already own stocks or bonds.

a. If TeenStox selects a random sample of 2,000 teenagers, what number of teenagers who *do not* own stocks or bonds can it expect to find? What is the standard deviation of this number? (Round the standard deviation to one decimal place.)

b. Fill in the missing quantities: There is an approximately 99.7% chance that between ___ and ___ teenagers in the sample will not own stocks or bonds. (Round answers to the nearest whole number.)

47. ⏸ ▼ **Supermarkets** A survey of supermarkets in the United States yielded the following relative frequency table, where X is the number of checkout lanes at a randomly chosen supermarket:[52]

x	1	2	3	4	5	6	7	8	9	10
$P(X = x)$	.01	.04	.04	.08	.10	.15	.25	.20	.08	.05

a. Compute the mean, variance, and standard deviation (accurate to one decimal place).

b. As financial planning manager at *Express Lane Mart*, you wish to install a number of checkout lanes that is in the range of at least 75% of all supermarkets. What is this range according to Chebyshev's inequality? What is the *least* number of checkout lanes you should install so as to fall within this range?

48. ⏸ ▼ **Video Arcades** Your company, *Sonic Video, Inc.,* has conducted research that shows the following probability distribution, where X is the number of video arcades in a randomly chosen city with more than 500,000 inhabitants:

x	0	1	2	3	4	5	6	7	8	9
$P(X = x)$	.07	.09	.35	.25	.15	.03	.02	.02	.01	.01

a. Compute the mean, variance, and standard deviation (accurate to one decimal place).

b. As CEO of Sonic Video, you wish to install a chain of video arcades in Sleepy City, U.S.A. The city council regulations require that the number of arcades be within the range shared by at least 75% of all cities. What is this range? What is the *largest* number of video arcades you should install so as to comply with this regulation?

Distribution of Wealth *If we model after-tax household income by a normal distribution, then the figures of a 1995 study imply the information in the following table, which should be used for Exercises 49–60.*[53] *Assume that the distribution of incomes in each country is bell shaped and symmetric.*

Country	United States	Canada	Switzerland	Germany	Sweden
Mean Household Income	$38,000	$35,000	$39,000	$34,000	$32,000
Standard Deviation	$21,000	$17,000	$16,000	$14,000	$11,000

---

[50] Source: Teen-Age Research Unlimited, January 25, 2001 (www.teenresearch.com).

[51] *Ibid.*

[52] Source: J.T. McClave, P.G. Benson, T. Sincich, *Statistics for Business and Economics*, 7th Ed. (Prentice Hall, 1998) p. 177, W. Chow *et al.* "A model for predicting a supermarket's annual sales per square foot," Graduate School of Management, Rutgers University.

[53] The data are rounded to the nearest $1,000 and based on a report published by the Luxembourg Income Study. The report shows after-tax income, including government benefits (such as food stamps) of households with children. Our figures were obtained from the published data by assuming a normal distribution of incomes. All data were based on constant 1991 U.S. dollars and converted foreign currencies (adjusted for differences in buying power). Source: Luxembourg Income Study/*New York Times*, August 14, 1995, p. A9.

49. If we define a "poor" household as one whose after-tax income is at least 1.3 standard deviations below the mean, what is the household income of a poor family in the United States?

50. If we define a "poor" household as one whose after-tax income is at least 1.3 standard deviations below the mean, what is the household income of a poor family in Switzerland?

51. If we define a "rich" household as one whose after-tax income is at least 1.3 standard deviations above the mean, what is the household income of a rich family in the United States?

52. If we define a "rich" household as one whose after-tax income is at least 1.3 standard deviations above the mean, what is the household income of a rich family in Sweden?

53. ▼ Refer to Exercise 49. Which of the five countries listed has the poorest households (i.e., the lowest cutoff for considering a household poor)?

54. ▼ Refer to Exercise 52. Which of the five countries listed has the wealthiest households (i.e., the highest cutoff for considering a household rich)?

55. ▼ Which of the five countries listed has the largest gap between rich and poor?

56. ▼ Which of the five countries listed has the smallest gap between rich and poor?

57. What percentage of U.S. families earned an after-tax income of $17,000 or less?

58. What percentage of U.S. families earned an after-tax income of $80,000 or more?

59. What was the after-tax income range of approximately 99.7% of all Germans?

60. What was the after-tax income range of approximately 99.7% of all Swedes?

▯ *Aging* Exercises 61–68 are based on the following list, which shows the percentage of aging population (residents of age 65 and older) in each of the 50 states in 1990, 2000, and 2010:[54]

1990

4, 9, 10, 10, 10, 10, 10, 11, 11, 11, 11, 11, 11, 11, 11, 11, 12, 12, 12, 12, 12, 12, 13, 13, 13, 13, 13, 13, 13, 13, 13, 13, 13, 13, 13, 13, 14, 14, 14, 14, 14, 14, 14, 15, 15, 15, 15, 15, 15, 18

2000

6, 9, 10, 10, 10, 11, 11, 11, 11, 11, 11, 11, 12, 12, 12, 12, 12, 12, 12, 12, 12, 12, 12, 13, 13, 13, 13, 13, 13, 13, 13, 13, 13, 13, 13, 14, 14, 14, 14, 14, 14, 15, 15, 15, 15, 16, 18

2010

8, 9, 10, 11, 11, 11, 12, 12, 12, 12, 12, 12, 12, 13, 13, 13, 13, 13, 13, 13, 13, 13, 14, 14, 14, 14, 14, 14, 14, 14, 14, 14, 14, 14, 14, 14, 14, 14, 15, 15, 15, 15, 15, 16, 16, 17

61. ▯ Compute the population mean and standard deviation for the 2000 and 2010 data.

62. ▯ Compute the population mean and standard deviation for the 1990 and 2000 data.

63. The answer to Exercise 61 suggests that the 2010 population was:

   (A) older on average and more diverse with respect to age
   (B) older on average and less diverse with respect to age
   (C) younger on average and more diverse with respect to age
   (D) younger on average and less diverse with respect to age than the 2000 population.

64. The answer to Exercise 62 suggests that the 1990 population was:

   (A) older on average and more diverse with respect to age
   (B) older on average and less diverse with respect to age
   (C) younger on average and more diverse with respect to age
   (D) younger on average and less diverse with respect to age than the 2000 population.

65. ▯ Compare the actual percentage of states whose aging population in 2010 was within one standard deviation of the mean to the percentage predicted by the empirical rule. Comment on your answer.

66. ▯ Compare the actual percentage of states whose aging population in 1990 was within one standard deviation of the mean to the percentage predicted by the empirical rule. Comment on your answer.

67. ▯ What was the actual percentage of states whose aging population in 2010 was within two standard deviations of the mean? Does Chebyshev's rule apply to the data? Explain.

68. ▯ What was the actual percentage of states whose aging population in 2000 was within two standard deviations of the mean? Does Chebyshev's rule apply to the data? Explain.

Electric Grid Stress In early 2000, a Federal Energy Regulatory Commission order (FERC Order 888, first issued in 1996 and advocated by various energy companies, including **Enron**) went into effect, mandating that owners of power transmission lines make them available on the open market. The subsequent levels of stress on the electric grid are believed by many to have led to the Northeast blackout of August 14, 2003. Exercises 69–72 deal with the stress on the national electric grid before and after Order 888 went into effect.

69. ▼ The following chart shows the approximate standard deviation of the power grid frequency, in 1/1,000 cycles per second, taken over 6-month periods. (0.9 is the average standard deviation.)[55]

---

[54] Percentages are rounded and listed in ascending order. Source: U.S. Census Bureau, Census 2000 Summary File 1 (www.census.gov/prod/2001pubs/c2kbr01-10.pdf), Age and Sex Composition: 2010 (www.census.gov/prod/cen2010/briefs/c2010br-03.pdf).

[55] Source Robert Blohm, energy consultant and adviser to the North American Electric Reliability Council/*New York Times*, August 20, 2003, p. A16.

Which of the following statements are true? (More than one may be true.)

(A) The power grid frequency was at or below the mean until late 1999.

(B) The power grid frequency was more stable in mid-1999 than in 1995.

(C) The power grid frequency was more stable in mid-2002 than in mid-1999.

(D) The greatest fluctuations in the power grid frequency occurred in 2000–2001.

(E) The power grid frequency was more stable around January 1995 than around January 1999.

70. ▼ The following chart shows the approximate monthly means of the power grid frequency, in 1/1,000 cycles per second. 0.0 represents the desired frequency of exactly 60 cycles per second.[56]

Which of the following statements are true? (More than one may be true.)

(A) Both the mean and the standard deviation show an upward trend from 2000 on.

(B) The mean, but not the standard deviation, shows an upward trend from 2000 on.

(C) The demand for electric power peaked in the second half of 2001.

(D) The standard deviation was larger in the second half of 2002 than in the second half of 1999.

(E) The mean of the monthly means in 2000 was lower than that for 2002, but the standard deviation of the monthly means was higher.

71. ▼ The following chart shows the approximate monthly means of the power grid frequency, in 1/1,000 cycles per second. 0.0 represents the desired frequency of exactly 60 cycles per second. (Note that this is the same data as in Exercise 70 but over a different period of time.)[57]

---

[56] Source Robert Blohm, energy consultant and adviser to the North American Electric Reliability Council/*New York Times*, August 20, 2003, p. A16.

[57] Source: Eric J. Lerner, *What's wrong with the electric grid? The Industrial Physicist,* Oct./Nov. 2003, American Institute of Physics (www.aip.org/tip/INPHFA/vol-9/iss-5/p8.pdf).

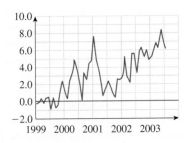

Which of the following statements are true? (More than one may be true.)

(A) Both the mean and the standard deviation show an upward trend from 2002 on.

(B) The mean, but not the standard deviation, shows an upward trend from 2002 on.

(C) The standard deviation, but not the mean, shows an upward trend from 2002 on.

(D) The standard deviation was greater in 2003 than in 2001.

(E) The mean of the monthly means in 2002 was higher than that for 2000, but the standard deviation of the monthly means was lower.

72. ▼ The following chart shows the number of transmission loading relief procedures (procedures undertaken to relieve excessive transmission loads by shifting power to other lines) per month.[58]

Which of the following statements are true? (More than one may be true.)

(A) Both the annual mean and the standard deviation show a significant upward trend from 2000 on.

(B) The annual mean, but not the standard deviation, shows a significant upward trend from 2000 on.

(C) The annual standard deviation, but not the mean, shows a significant upward trend from 2000 on.

(D) The standard deviation in the second half of 2000 is significantly greater than that in the first half.

(E) The standard deviation in 2000 is significantly greater than that in 2001.

COMMUNICATION AND REASONING EXERCISES

73. Which is greater for a given set of data: the sample standard deviation or the population standard deviation? Explain.

---

[58] *Ibid.*

74. Suppose you take larger and larger samples of a given population. Would you expect the sample and population standard deviations to get closer or further apart? Explain.

75. In one Finite Math class, the average grade was 75 and the standard deviation of the grades was 5. In another Finite Math class, the average grade was 65 and the standard deviation of the grades was 20. What conclusions can you draw about the distributions of the grades in each class?

76. You are a manager in a precision manufacturing firm and you must evaluate the performance of two employees. You do so by examining the quality of the parts they produce. One particular item should be 50.0 ± 0.3 mm long to be usable. The first employee produces parts that are an average of 50.1 mm long with a standard deviation of 0.15 mm.

The second employee produces parts that are an average of 50.0 mm long with a standard deviation of 0.4 mm. Which employee do you rate higher? Why? (Assume that the empirical rule applies.)

77. ▼ If a finite random variable has an expected value of 10 and a standard deviation of 0, what must its probability distribution be?

78. ▼ If the values of X in a population consist of an equal number of 1s and −1s, what is its standard deviation?

79. ◆ Find an algebraic formula for the population standard deviation of a sample $\{x, y\}$ of two scores $(x \leq y)$.

80. ◆ Find an algebraic formula for the sample standard deviation of a sample $\{x, y\}$ of two scores $(x \leq y)$.

8.5 Normal Distributions

Continuous Random Variables

Figure 9 shows the probability distributions for the number of successes in sequences of 10 and 15 independent Bernoulli trials, each with probability of success $p = .5$.

Figure 9(a)   **Figure 9(b)**

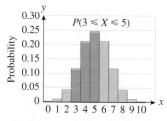

Figure 10

Because each column is 1 unit wide, its area is numerically equal to its height. Thus, the area of each rectangle can be interpreted as a probability. For example, in Figure 9(a) the area of the rectangle over $X = 3$ represents $P(X = 3)$. If we want to find $P(3 \leq X \leq 5)$, we can add up the areas of the three rectangles over 3, 4, and 5, shown shaded in Figure 10. Notice that if we add up the areas of *all* the rectangles in Figure 9(a), the total is 1 because $P(0 \leq X \leq 10) = 1$. We can summarize these observations.

Properties of the Probability Distribution Histogram

In a probability distribution histogram where each column is 1 unit wide:

- The total area enclosed by the histogram is 1 square unit.
- $P(a \leq X \leq b)$ is the area enclosed by the rectangles lying between and including $X = a$ and $X = b$.

This discussion is motivation for considering another kind of random variable, one whose probability distribution is specified not by a bar graph, as above, but by the graph of a function.

Continuous Random Variable; Probability Density Function

A **continuous random variable** X may take on any real value whatsoever. The probabilities $P(a \leq X \leq b)$ are defined by means of a **probability density function**, a function whose graph lies above the x-axis with the total area between the graph and the x-axis being 1. The probability $P(a \leq X \leq b)$ is defined to be the area enclosed by the curve, the x-axis, and the lines $x = a$ and $x = b$ (see Figure 11).

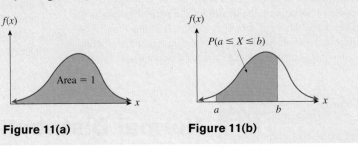

Figure 11(a)   **Figure 11(b)**

Notes

1. In Chapter 7, we defined probability distributions only for *finite* sample spaces. Because continuous random variables have infinite sample spaces, we need the definition above to give meaning to $P(a \leq X \leq b)$ if X is a continuous random variable.

2. If $a = b$, then $P(X = a) = P(a \leq X \leq a)$ is the area under the curve between the lines $x = a$ and $x = a$—no area at all! Thus, when X is a continuous random variable, $P(X = a) = 0$ for every value of a.

3. Whether we take the region in Figure 11(b) to include the boundary or not does not affect the area. The probability $P(a < X < b)$ is defined as the area strictly between the vertical lines $x = a$ and $x = b$, but is, of course, the same as $P(a \leq X \leq b)$, because the boundary contributes nothing to the area. When we are calculating probabilities associated with a continuous random variable,

$$P(a \leq X \leq b) = P(a < X \leq b) = P(a \leq X < b) = P(a < X < b). \quad \blacksquare$$

Normal Density Functions

Among all the possible probability density functions, there is an important class of functions called **normal density functions**, or **normal distributions**. The graph of a normal density function is bell shaped and symmetric, as the following figure shows. The formula for a normal density function is rather complicated looking:

$$f(x) = \frac{1}{\sigma \sqrt{2\pi}} e^{-\frac{(x-\mu)^2}{2\sigma^2}}.$$

The quantity μ is called the **mean** and can be any real number. The quantity σ is called the **standard deviation** and can be any positive real number. The number $e = 2.7182\ldots$ is a useful constant that shows up many places in mathematics, much as the constant π does. Finally, the constant $1/(\sigma \sqrt{2\pi})$ that appears in front is there to make the total area come out to be 1. We rarely use the actual formula in computations; instead, we use tables or technology.

Normal Density Function; Normal Distribution

A **normal density function**, or **normal distribution**, is a function of the form

$$f(x) = \frac{1}{\sigma\sqrt{2\pi}} e^{-\frac{(x-\mu)^2}{2\sigma^2}},$$

where μ is the mean and σ is the standard deviation. Its graph is bell shaped and symmetric, and has the following form:

The "inflection points" are the points where the curve changes from bending in one direction to bending in another.*

* Pretend you were driving along the curve in a car. Then the points of inflection are the points where you would change the direction in which you are steering (from left to right or right to left).

Figure 12 shows the graphs of several normal density functions. The third of these has mean 0 and standard deviation 1, and is called the **standard normal distribution**. We use Z rather than X to refer to the standard normal variable.

 using Technology

The graphs in Figure 12 can be drawn on a TI-83/84 Plus or the Website grapher.

TI-83/84 Plus
Figure 12(a):
Y_1=normalpdf(x,2,1)
Figure 12(b):
Y_1=normalpdf(x,0,2)
Figure 12(c):
Y_1=normalpdf(x)

 Website
www.WanerMath.com
   Student Home
      → On Line Utilities
         → Function Evaluator and
            Grapher
Figure 12(a):
normalpdf(x,2,1)
Figure 12(b):
normalpdf(x,0,2)
Figure 12(c):
normalpdf(x)

Figure 12(a)

Figure 12(b)

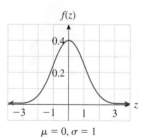

Standard Normal Distribution

Figure 12(c)

Calculating Probabilities for the Standard Normal Distribution

The standard normal distribution has $\mu = 0$ and $\sigma = 1$. The corresponding variable is called the **standard normal variable**, which we always denote by Z. Recall that to calculate the probability $P(a \le Z \le b)$, we need to find the area under the distribution curve between the vertical lines $z = a$ and $z = b$. We can use the table in the Appendix to look up these areas, or we can use technology. Here is an example.

EXAMPLE 1 Standard Normal Distribution

Let Z be the standard normal variable. Calculate the following probabilities:

a. $P(0 \le Z \le 2.4)$ **b.** $P(0 \le Z \le 2.43)$
c. $P(-1.37 \le Z \le 2.43)$ **d.** $P(1.37 \le Z \le 2.43)$

Solution

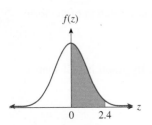

$f(z)$

0   2.4

Figure 13

a. We are asking for the shaded area under the standard normal curve shown in Figure 13. We can find this area, correct to four decimal places, by looking at the table in the Appendix, which lists the area under the standard normal curve from $Z = 0$ to $Z = b$ for any value of b between 0 and 3.09. To use the table, write 2.4 as 2.40, and read the entry in the row labeled 2.4 and the column labeled 0.00 $(2.4 + 0.00 = 2.40)$. Here is the relevant portion of the table:

	Z	**0.00**	**0.01**	**0.02**	**0.03**
	2.3	.4893	.4896	.4898	.4901
→	**2.4**	.4918	.4920	.4922	.4925
	2.5	.4938	.4940	.4941	.4943

Thus, $P(0 \leq Z \leq 2.40) = .4918$.

b. The area we require can be read from the same portion of the table shown above. Write 2.43 as $2.4 + 0.03$, and read the entry in the row labeled 2.4 and the column labeled 0.03:

	Z	**0.00**	**0.01**	**0.02**	**0.03**
	2.3	.4893	.4896	.4898	.4901
→	**2.4**	.4918	.4920	.4922	.4925
	2.5	.4938	.4940	.4941	.4943

Thus, $P(0 \leq Z \leq 2.43) = .4925$.

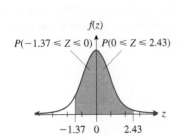

$f(z)$

$P(-1.37 \leqslant Z \leqslant 0)$ $P(0 \leqslant Z \leqslant 2.43)$

−1.37 0   2.43

Figure 14

c. Here we cannot use the table directly because the range $-1.37 \leq Z \leq 2.43$ does not start at 0. But we can break the area up into two smaller areas that start or end at 0:

$$P(-1.37 \leq Z \leq 2.43) = P(-1.37 \leq Z \leq 0) + P(0 \leq Z \leq 2.43).$$

In terms of the graph, we are splitting the desired area into two smaller areas (Figure 14).

We already calculated the area of the right-hand piece in part (b):

$$P(0 \leq Z \leq 2.43) = .4925.$$

For the left-hand piece, the symmetry of the normal curve tells us that

$$P(-1.37 \leq Z \leq 0) = P(0 \leq Z \leq 1.37).$$

This we can find on the table. Look at the row labeled 1.3 and the column labeled .07, and read

$$P(-1.37 \leq Z \leq 0) = P(0 \leq Z \leq 1.37) = .4147.$$

Thus,

$$P(-1.37 \leq Z \leq 2.43) = P(-1.37 \leq Z \leq 0) + P(0 \leq Z \leq 2.43)$$
$$= .4147 + .4925$$
$$= .9072.$$

using Technology

Technology can be used to calculate the probabilities in Example 1. For instance, the calculation for part (c) is as follows:

TI-83/84 Plus
Home   Screen: normal-
cdf(−1.37, 2.43)
(normalcdf is in 2ND VARS.)
[More details on page 614.]

Spreadsheet
=NORMSDIST(2.43)
−NORMSDIST(−1.37)
[More details on page 617.]

d. The range $1.37 \leq Z \leq 2.43$ does not contain 0, so we cannot use the technique of part (c). Instead, the corresponding area can be computed as the *difference* of two areas:

$$P(1.37 \leq Z \leq 2.43) = P(0 \leq Z \leq 2.43) - P(0 \leq Z \leq 1.37)$$
$$= .4925 - .4147$$
$$= .0778.$$

Calculating Probabilities for Any Normal Distribution

Although we have tables to compute the area under the *standard* normal curve, there are no readily available tables for nonstandard distributions. For example, if $\mu = 2$ and $\sigma = 3$, then how would we calculate $P(0.5 \leq X \leq 3.2)$? The following conversion formula provides a method for doing so:

Standardizing a Normal Distribution

If X has a normal distribution with mean μ and standard deviation σ, and if Z is the standard normal variable, then

$$P(a \leq X \leq b) = P\left(\frac{a - \mu}{\sigma} \leq Z \leq \frac{b - \mu}{\sigma}\right).$$

Quick Example

If $\mu = 2$ and $\sigma = 3$, then

$$P(0.5 \leq X \leq 3.2) = P\left(\frac{0.5 - 2}{3} \leq Z \leq \frac{3.2 - 2}{3}\right)$$
$$= P(-0.5 \leq Z \leq 0.4) = .1915 + .1554 = .3469.$$

To completely justify the above formula requires more mathematics than we shall discuss here. However, here is the main idea: If X is normal with mean μ and standard deviation σ, then $X - \mu$ is normal with mean 0 and standard deviation still σ, while $(X - \mu)/\sigma$ is normal with mean 0 and standard deviation 1. In other words, $(X - \mu)/\sigma = Z$. Therefore,

$$P(a \leq X \leq b) = P\left(\frac{a - \mu}{\sigma} \leq \frac{X - \mu}{\sigma} \leq \frac{b - \mu}{\sigma}\right) = P\left(\frac{a - \mu}{\sigma} \leq Z \leq \frac{b - \mu}{\sigma}\right).$$

EXAMPLE 2 Quality Control

Pressure gauges manufactured by Precision Corp. must be checked for accuracy before being placed on the market. To test a pressure gauge, a worker uses it to measure the pressure of a sample of compressed air known to be at a pressure of exactly 50 pounds per square inch. If the gauge reading is off by more than 1% (0.5 pounds), it is rejected. Assuming that the reading of a pressure gauge under these circumstances is a normal random variable with mean 50 and standard deviation 0.4, find the percentage of gauges rejected.

using Technology

Technology can be used to calculate the probability $P(49.5 \leq X \leq 50.5)$ in Example 2:

TI-83/84 Plus
Home Screen:
`normalcdf(49.5,50.5,50,0.4)`
(`normalcdf` is in [2ND] [VARS].)
[More details on page 615.]

Spreadsheet
`=NORMDIST(50.5,50,0.4,1)`
`-NORMDIST(49.5,50,0.4,1)`
[More details on page 618.]

Website
www.WanerMath.com
    Student Home
        → On Line Utilities
        → Normal Distribution
           Utility
Set up as shown and press "Calculate Probability".

Solution If X is the reading of the gauge, then X has a normal distribution with $\mu = 50$ and $\sigma = 0.4$. We are asking for $P(X < 49.5 \text{ or } X > 50.5) = 1 - P(49.5 \leq X \leq 50.5)$. We calculate

$$P(49.5 \leq X \leq 50.5) = P\left(\frac{49.5 - 50}{0.4} \leq Z \leq \frac{50.5 - 50}{0.4}\right) \quad \text{Standardize}$$
$$= P(-1.25 \leq Z \leq 1.25)$$
$$= 2 \cdot P(0 \leq Z \leq 1.25)$$
$$= 2(.3944) = .7888.$$

So, $P(X < 49.5 \text{ or } X > 50.5) = 1 - P(49.5 \leq X \leq 50.5)$
$$= 1 - .7888 = .2112.$$

In other words, about 21% of the gauges will be rejected.

In many applications, we need to know the probability that a value of a normal random variable will lie within one standard deviation of the mean, or within two standard deviations, or within some number of standard deviations. To compute these probabilities, we first notice that, if X has a normal distribution with mean μ and standard deviation σ, then

$$P(\mu - k\sigma \leq X \leq \mu + k\sigma) = P(-k \leq Z \leq k)$$

by the standardizing formula. We can compute these probabilities for various values of k using the table in the Appendix, and we obtain the following results.

Probability of a Normal Distribution Being within k Standard Deviations of Its Mean

$P(\mu - \sigma \leq X \leq \mu + \sigma) =$
$P(-1 \leq Z \leq 1) = .6826$

$P(\mu - 2\sigma \leq X \leq \mu + 2\sigma) =$
$P(-2 \leq Z \leq 2) = .9544$

$P(\mu - 3\sigma \leq X \leq \mu + 3\sigma) =$
$P(-3 \leq Z \leq 3) = .9974$

Now you can see where the empirical rule in Section 8.4 comes from! Notice also that the probabilities above are a good deal larger than the lower bounds given by Chebyshev's rule. Chebyshev's rule must work for distributions that are skew or any shape whatsoever.

EXAMPLE 3 Loans

The values of mortgage loans made by a certain bank one year were normally distributed with a mean of \$120,000 and a standard deviation of \$40,000.

a. What is the probability that a randomly selected mortgage loan was in the range of \$40,000–\$200,000?

b. You would like to state in your annual report that 50% of all mortgage loans were in a certain range with the mean in the center. What is that range?

Solution

a. We are asking for the probability that a loan was within two standard deviations ($80,000) of the mean. By the calculation done previously, this probability is .9544.

b. We look for the k such that

$$P(120{,}000 - k \cdot 40{,}000 \le X \le 120{,}000 + k \cdot 40{,}000) = .5.$$

Because

$$P(120{,}000 - k \cdot 40{,}000 \le X \le 120{,}000 + k \cdot 40{,}000) = P(-k \le Z \le k)$$

we look in the Appendix to see for which k we have

$$P(0 \le Z \le k) = .25$$

so that $P(-k \le Z \le k) = .5$. That is, we look *inside* the table to see where 0.25 is, and find the corresponding k. We find

$$P(0 \le Z \le 0.67) = .2486$$
and $$P(0 \le Z \le 0.68) = .2517.$$

Therefore, the k we want is about halfway between 0.67 and 0.68, call it 0.675. This tells us that 50% of all mortgage loans were in the range

$$120{,}000 - 0.675 \cdot 40{,}000 = \$93{,}000$$
to $$120{,}000 + 0.675 \cdot 40{,}000 = \$147{,}000.$$

Normal Approximation to a Binomial Distribution

You might have noticed that the histograms of some of the binomial distributions we have drawn (for example, those in Figure 9) have a very rough bell shape. In fact, in many cases it is possible to draw a normal curve that closely approximates a given binomial distribution.

Normal Approximation to a Binomial Distribution

If X is the number of successes in a sequence of n independent Bernoulli trials, with probability p of success in each trial, and if the range of values of X within three standard deviations of the mean lies entirely within the range 0 to n (the possible values of X), then

$$P(a \le X \le b) \approx P(a - 0.5 \le Y \le b + 0.5)$$

where Y has a normal distribution with the same mean and standard deviation as X; that is, $\mu = np$ and $\sigma = \sqrt{npq}$, where $q = 1 - p$.

Notes

1. The condition that $0 \le \mu - 3\sigma < \mu + 3\sigma \le n$ is satisfied if n is sufficiently large and p is not too close to 0 or 1; it ensures that most of the normal curve lies in the range 0 to n.

2. In the formula $P(a \le X \le b) \approx P(a - 0.5 \le Y \le b + 0.5)$, we assume that a and b are integers. The use of $a - 0.5$ and $b + 0.5$ is called the **continuity correction**. To see that it is necessary, think about what would happen if you wanted to approximate, say, $P(X = 2) = P(2 \le X \le 2)$. Should the answer be 0? ∎

Figures 15 and 16 show two binomial distributions with their normal approximations superimposed, and illustrate how closely the normal approximation fits the binomial distribution.

Figure 15

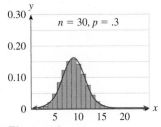

Figure 16

EXAMPLE 4 Coin Tosses

a. If you flip a fair coin 100 times, what is the probability of getting more than 55 heads or fewer than 45 heads?

b. What number of heads (out of 100) would make you suspect that the coin is not fair?

Solution

a. We are asking for

$$P(X < 45 \text{ or } X > 55) = 1 - P(45 \le X \le 55).$$

We *could* compute this by calculating

$$1 - [C(100, 45)(.5)^{45}(.5)^{55} + C(100, 46)(.5)^{46}(.5)^{54} + \cdots + C(100, 55)(.5)^{55}(.5)^{45}]$$

but we can much more easily *approximate* it by looking at a normal distribution with mean $\mu = 50$ and standard deviation $\sigma = \sqrt{(100)(.5)(.5)} = 5$. (Notice that three standard deviations above and below the mean is the range 35 to 65, which is well within the range of possible values for X, which is 0 to 100, so the approximation should be a good one.) Let Y have this normal distribution. Then

$$P(45 \le X \le 55) \approx P(44.5 \le Y \le 55.5)$$
$$= P(-1.1 \le Z \le 1.1)$$
$$= .7286.$$

Therefore,

$$P(X < 45 \text{ or } X > 55) \approx 1 - .7286 = .2714.$$

b. This is a deep question that touches on the concept of **statistical significance**: What evidence is strong enough to overturn a reasonable assumption (the assumption that the coin is fair)? Statisticians have developed sophisticated ways of answering this question, but we can look at one simple test now. Suppose we tossed a coin 100 times and got 66 heads. If the coin were fair, then $P(X > 65) \approx P(Y > 65.5) = P(Z > 3.1) \approx .001$. This is small enough to raise a reasonable doubt that the coin is fair. However, we should not be too surprised if we threw 56 heads because we can calculate $P(X > 55) \approx .1357$, which is not such a small probability. As we said, the actual tests of statistical significance are more sophisticated than this, but we shall not go into them.

FAQ

When to Subtract from .5 and when Not to

Q: *When computing probabilities like, say* $P(Z \leq 1.2)$, $P(Z \geq 1.2)$, *or* $P(1.2 \leq Z \leq 2.1)$ *using a table, just looking up the given values (1.2, 2.1, or whatever) is not enough. Sometimes you have to subtract from .5, sometimes not. Is there a simple rule telling me what to do when?*

A: The simplest—and also most instructive—way of knowing what to do is to draw a picture of the standard normal curve, and shade in the area you are looking for. Drawing pictures also helps you come up with the following mechanical rules:

1. To compute $P(a \leq Z \leq b)$, look up the areas corresponding to $|a|$ and $|b|$ in the table. If a and b have opposite signs, add these areas. Otherwise, subtract the smaller area from the larger.

2. To compute $P(Z \leq a)$, look up the area corresponding to $|a|$. If a is positive, add .5. Otherwise, subtract from .5.

3. To compute $P(Z \geq a)$, look up the area corresponding to $|a|$. If a is positive, subtract from .5. Otherwise, add .5.

8.5 EXERCISES

▼ more advanced   ◆ challenging
T indicates exercises that should be solved using technology

Note: Answers for Section 8.5 were computed using the 4-digit table in the Appendix, and may differ slightly from the more accurate answers generated using technology.

In Exercises 1–8, Z is the standard normal distribution. Find the indicated probabilities. HINT [See Example 1.]

1. $P(0 \leq Z \leq 0.5)$ **2.** $P(0 \leq Z \leq 1.5)$

3. $P(-0.71 \leq Z \leq 0.71)$ **4.** $P(-1.71 \leq Z \leq 1.71)$

5. $P(-0.71 \leq Z \leq 1.34)$ **6.** $P(-1.71 \leq Z \leq 0.23)$

7. $P(0.5 \leq Z \leq 1.5)$ **8.** $P(0.71 \leq Z \leq 1.82)$

In Exercises 9–14, X has a normal distribution with the given mean and standard deviation. Find the indicated probabilities. HINT [See Quick Example on page 599.]

9. $\mu = 50$, $\sigma = 10$, find $P(35 \leq X \leq 65)$

10. $\mu = 40$, $\sigma = 20$, find $P(35 \leq X \leq 45)$

11. $\mu = 50$, $\sigma = 10$, find $P(30 \leq X \leq 62)$

12. $\mu = 40$, $\sigma = 20$, find $P(30 \leq X \leq 53)$

13. $\mu = 100$, $\sigma = 15$, find $P(110 \leq X \leq 130)$

14. $\mu = 100$, $\sigma = 15$, find $P(70 \leq X \leq 80)$

15. ▼ Find the probability that a normal variable takes on values within 0.5 standard deviations of its mean.

16. ▼ Find the probability that a normal variable takes on values within 1.5 standard deviations of its mean.

17. ▼ Find the probability that a normal variable takes on values more than $\frac{2}{3}$ standard deviations away from its mean.

18. ▼ Find the probability that a normal variable takes on values more than $\frac{5}{3}$ standard deviations away from its mean.

19. ▼ Suppose X is a normal random variable with mean $\mu = 100$ and standard deviation $\sigma = 10$. Find b such that $P(100 \leq X \leq b) = .3$. HINT [See Example 3.]

20. ▼ Suppose X is a normal random variable with mean $\mu = 10$ and standard deviation $\sigma = 5$. Find b such that $P(10 \leq X \leq b) = .4$. HINT [See Example 3.]

21. ▼ Suppose X is a normal random variable with mean $\mu = 100$ and standard deviation $\sigma = 10$. Find a such that $P(X \geq a) = .04$.

22. ▼ Suppose X is a normal random variable with mean $\mu = 10$ and standard deviation $\sigma = 5$. Find a such that $P(X \geq a) = .03$.

23. If you roll a die 100 times, what is the approximate probability that you will roll between 10 and 15 ones, inclusive? (Round your answer to two decimal places.) HINT [See Example 4.]

24. If you roll a die 100 times, what is the approximate probability that you will roll between 15 and 20 ones, inclusive? (Round your answer to two decimal places.) HINT [See Example 4.]

25. If you roll a die 200 times, what is the approximate probability that you will roll fewer than 25 ones, inclusive? (Round your answer to two decimal places.)

26. If you roll a die 200 times, what is the approximate probability that you will roll more than 40 ones? (Round your answer to two decimal places.)

APPLICATIONS

27. *SAT Scores* SAT test scores are normally distributed with a mean of 500 and a standard deviation of 100. Find the probability that a randomly chosen test-taker will score between 450 and 550. HINT [See Example 3.]

28. *SAT Scores* SAT test scores are normally distributed with a mean of 500 and a standard deviation of 100. Find the probability that a randomly chosen test-taker will score 650 or higher. HINT [See Example 3.]

29. *LSAT Scores* LSAT test scores are normally distributed with a mean of 151 and a standard deviation of 7. Find the probability that a randomly chosen test-taker will score between 137 and 158.

30. *LSAT Scores* LSAT test scores are normally distributed with a mean of 151 and a standard deviation of 7. Find the probability that a randomly chosen test-taker will score 144 or lower.

31. *IQ Scores* IQ scores (as measured by the Stanford-Binet intelligence test) are normally distributed with a mean of 100 and a standard deviation of 16. What percentage of the population has an IQ score between 110 and 140? (Round your answer to the nearest percentage point.)

32. *IQ Scores* Refer to Exercise 31. What percentage of the population has an IQ score between 80 and 90? (Round your answer to the nearest percentage point.)

33. *IQ Scores* Refer to Exercise 31. Find the approximate number of people in the United States (assuming a total population of 313,000,000) with an IQ of 120 or higher.

34. *IQ Scores* Refer to Exercise 31. Find the approximate number of people in the United States (assuming a total population of 313,000,000) with an IQ of 140 or higher.

35. *SAT Scores* SAT test scores are normally distributed with a mean of 500 and a standard deviation of 100. What score would place you in the top 5% of test-takers? HINT [See Example 3.]

36. *LSAT Scores* LSAT test scores are normally distributed with a mean of 151 and a standard deviation of 7. What score would place you in the top 2% of test-takers? HINT [See Example 3.]

37. *Baseball* The mean batting average in major league baseball is about 0.250. Supposing that batting averages are normally distributed, that the standard deviation in the averages is 0.03, and that there are 250 batters, what is the expected number of batters with an average of at least 0.400?

38. *Baseball* The mean batting average in major league baseball is about 0.250. Supposing that batting averages are normally distributed, that the standard deviation in the averages is 0.05, and that there are 250 batters, what is the expected number of batters with an average of at least 0.400?[59]

39. *Marketing* Your pickle company rates its pickles on a scale of spiciness from 1 to 10. Market research shows that customer preferences for spiciness are normally distributed, with a mean of 7.5 and a standard deviation of 1. Assuming that you sell 100,000 jars of pickles, how many jars with a spiciness of 9 or above do you expect to sell?

40. *Marketing* Your hot sauce company rates its sauce on a scale of spiciness of 1 to 20. Market research shows that customer preferences for spiciness are normally distributed, with a mean of 12 and a standard deviation of 2.5. Assuming that you sell 300,000 bottles of sauce, how many bottles with a spiciness below 9 do you expect to sell?

Distribution of Income If we model after-tax household income with a normal distribution, then the figures of a 1995 study imply the information in the following table, which should be used for Exercises 41–46.[60] Assume that the distribution of incomes in each country was normal, and round all percentages to the nearest whole number.

Country	United States	Canada	Switzerland	Germany	Sweden
Mean Household Income	$38,000	$35,000	$39,000	$34,000	$32,000
Standard Deviation	$21,000	$17,000	$16,000	$14,000	$11,000

---

[59] The last time that a batter ended the year with an average above 0.400 was in 1941. The batter was Ted Williams of the Boston Red Sox, and his average was 0.406. Over the years, as pitching and batting have improved, the standard deviation in batting averages has declined from around 0.05 when professional baseball began to around 0.03 by the end of the twentieth century. For a very interesting discussion of statistics in baseball and in evolution, see Stephen Jay Gould, *Full House: The Spread of Excellence from Plato to Darwin*, Random House, 1997.

[60] The data are rounded to the nearest $1,000 and are based on a report published by the Luxembourg Income Study. The report shows after-tax income, including government benefits (such as food stamps) of households with children. Our figures were obtained from the published data by assuming a normal distribution of incomes. All data were based on constant 1991 U.S. dollars and converted foreign currencies (adjusted for differences in buying power). Source: Luxembourg Income Study/ *New York Times*, August 14, 1995, p. A9.

41. What percentage of U.S. households had an income of $50,000 or more?

42. What percentage of German households had an income of $50,000 or more?

43. What percentage of Swiss households were either very wealthy (income at least $100,000) or very poor (income at most $12,000)?

44. What percentage of Swedish households were either very wealthy (income at least $100,000) or very poor (income at most $12,000)?

45. Which country had a higher proportion of very poor families (income $12,000 or less): the United States or Canada?

46. Which country had a higher proportion of very poor families (income $12,000 or less): Canada or Switzerland?

47. ▼ *Comparing IQ Tests* IQ scores as measured by both the Stanford-Binet intelligence test and the Wechsler intelligence test have a mean of 100. The standard deviation for the Stanford-Binet test is 16, while that for the Wechsler test is 15. For which test do a smaller percentage of test-takers score less than 80? Why?

48. ▼ *Comparing IQ Tests* Referring to Exercise 47, for which test do a larger percentage of test-takers score more than 120?

49. ▼ *Product Repairs* The new copier your business bought lists a mean time between failures of 6 months, with a standard deviation of 1 month. One month after a repair, it breaks down again. Is this surprising? (Assume that the times between failures are normally distributed.)

50. ▼ *Product Repairs* The new computer your business bought lists a mean time between failures of 1 year, with a standard deviation of 2 months. Ten months after a repair, it breaks down again. Is this surprising? (Assume that the times between failures are normally distributed.)

Software Testing Exercises 51–56 are based on the following information, gathered from student testing of a statistical software package called MODSTAT.[61] Students were asked to complete certain tasks using the software, without any instructions. The results were as follows. (Assume that the time for each task is normally distributed.)

Task	Mean Time (minutes)	Standard Deviation
Task 1: Descriptive Analysis of Data	11.4	5.0
Task 2: Standardizing Scores	11.9	9.0
Task 3: Poisson Probability Table	7.3	3.9
Task 4: Areas under Normal Curve	9.1	5.5

51. Find the probability that a student will take at least 10 minutes to complete Task 1.

52. Find the probability that a student will take at least 10 minutes to complete Task 3.

53. ▼ Assuming that the time it takes a student to complete each task is independent of the others, find the probability that a student will take at least 10 minutes to complete each of Tasks 1 and 2.

54. ▼ Assuming that the time it takes a student to complete each task is independent of the others, find the probability that a student will take at least 10 minutes to complete each of Tasks 3 and 4.

55. ◆ It can be shown that if X and Y are independent normal random variables with means μ_X and μ_Y, and standard deviations σ_X and σ_Y respectively, then their sum $X + Y$ is also normally distributed and has mean $\mu = \mu_X + \mu_Y$ and standard deviation $\sigma = \sqrt{\sigma_X^2 + \sigma_Y^2}$. Assuming that the time it takes a student to complete each task is independent of the others, find the probability that a student will take at least 20 minutes to complete both Tasks 1 and 2.

56. ◆ Referring to Exercise 55, compute the probability that a student will take at least 20 minutes to complete both Tasks 3 and 4.

57. *Internet Access* In 2010, 71% of all households in the United States had Internet access.[62] Find the probability that, in a small town with 1,200 households, at least 840 had Internet access in 2010. HINT [See Example 4.]

58. *Television Ratings* Based on data from the **Nielsen Company**, there is a 1.8% chance that any television that is turned on during the time of the evening newscasts will be tuned to **ABC**'s evening news show.[63] Your company wishes to advertise on a local station carrying ABC that serves a community with 5,000 households that regularly tune in during this time slot. Find the approximate probability that at least 100 households will be tuned in to the show. HINT [See Example 4.]

59. *Aviation* The probability of a plane crashing on a single trip in 2010 was .00000276.[64] Find the approximate probability that in 10,000,000 flights, there will be fewer than 35 crashes.

60. *Aviation* The probability of a plane crashing on a single trip in 1990 was .00000087. Find the approximate probability that in 100,000,000 flights, there will be more than 110 crashes.

---

[61] Data are rounded to one decimal place. Source: *Student Evaluations of MODSTAT,* by Joseph M. Nowakowski, Muskingum College, New Concord, OH, 1997.

[62] Source: *Digital Nation: Expanding Internet Usage,* National Telecommunications and Information Administration, February 2011 (www.ntia.doc.gov/data).

[63] As of November 2011. Source: The Nielsen Company via the TVbytheNumbers Web site (http://tvbythenumbers.zap2it.com/category/ratings/evening-news).

[64] Figures are for scheduled commercial flights. Source for this exercise and the following three: National Transportation Safety Board (www.ntsb.gov).

61. ▼ *Insurance* Your company issues flight insurance. You charge $3 and, in the event of a plane crash, you will pay out $1 million to the victim or his or her family. In 2010, the probability of a plane crashing on a single trip was .00000276. If 10 people per flight buy insurance from you, what was your approximate probability of losing money over the course of 10 million flights in 2010? HINT [First determine how many crashes there must be for you to lose money.]

62. ▼ *Insurance* Refer back to the preceding exercise. What is your approximate probability of losing money over the course of 100 million flights?

63. ◆ *Polls* In a certain political poll, each person polled has a 90% probability of telling his or her real preference. Suppose that 55% of the population really prefer candidate Goode, and 45% prefer candidate Slick. First find the probability that a person polled will say that he or she prefers Goode. Then find the approximate probability that, if 1,000 people are polled, more than 52% will say they prefer Goode.

64. ◆ *Polls* In a certain political poll, each person polled has a 90% probability of telling his or her real preference. Suppose that 1,000 people are polled and 51% say that they prefer candidate Goode, while 49% say that they prefer candidate Slick. Find the approximate probability that Goode could do at least this well if, in fact, only 49% prefer Goode.

65. ◆ *IQ Scores* Mensa is a club for people with high IQs. To qualify, you must be in the top 2% of the population. One way of qualifying is by having an IQ of at least 148, as measured by the Cattell intelligence test. Assuming that scores on this test are normally distributed with a mean of 100, what is the standard deviation? HINT [Use the table in the Appendix "backward."]

66. ◆ *SAT Scores* Another way to qualify for Mensa (see the previous exercise) is to score at least 1,250 on the SAT [combined Critical Reading (Verbal, before March 2005) and Math

scores], which puts you in the top 2%. Assuming that SAT scores are normally distributed with a mean of 1,000, what is the standard deviation? (See the hint for the previous exercise.)

COMMUNICATION AND REASONING EXERCISES

67. Under what assumptions are the estimates in the empirical rule exact?

68. If X is a continuous random variable, what values can the quantity $P(X = a)$ have?

69. Which is larger for a continuous random variable, $P(X \leq a)$ or $P(X < a)$?

70. Which of the following is greater: $P(X \leq b)$ or $P(a \leq X \leq b)$?

71. ▼ A uniform continuous distribution is one with a probability density curve that is a horizontal line. If X takes on values between the numbers a and b with a uniform distribution, find the height of its probability density curve.

72. ▼ Which would you expect to have the greater variance: the standard normal distribution or the uniform distribution taking values between -1 and 1? Explain.

73. ◆ Which would you expect to have a density curve that is higher at the mean: the standard normal distribution, or a normal distribution with standard deviation 0.5? Explain.

74. ◆ Suppose students must perform two tasks: Task 1 and Task 2. Which of the following would you expect to have a smaller standard deviation?

(A) The time it takes a student to perform both tasks if the time it takes to complete Task 2 is independent of the time it takes to complete Task 1.

(B) The time it takes a student to perform both tasks if students will perform similarly in both tasks.

Explain.

KEY CONCEPTS

 Website www.WanerMath.com

Go to the Website at www.WanerMath.com to find a comprehensive and interactive Web-based summary of Chapter 8.

8.1 Random Variables and Distributions

Random variable; discrete vs continuous random variable *pp. 548–549*

Probability distribution of a finite random variable *p. 551*

Using measurement classes *p. 552*

8.2 Bernoulli Trials and Binomial Random Variables

Bernoulli trial; binomial random variable *pp. 559, 560*

Probability distribution of binomial random variable:

$P(X = x) = C(n, x)p^x q^{n-x}$
p. 562

8.3 Measures of Central Tendency

Sample, sample mean; population, population mean *p. 568*

Sample median, sample mode *p. 569*

Expected value of a random variable:

$\mu = E(X) = \sum_i x_i \cdot P(X = x_i)$
p. 571

Expected value of a binomial random variable: $\mu = E(X) = np$ *p. 573*

8.4 Measures of Dispersion

Population variance:

$$\sigma^2 = \frac{\sum_{i=1}^{n}(x_i - \mu)^2}{n}$$

Population standard deviation:

$\sigma = \sqrt{\sigma^2}$ *p. 580*

Sample variance:

$$s^2 = \frac{\sum_{i=1}^{n}(x_i - \bar{x})^2}{n - 1}$$

Sample standard deviation:

$s = \sqrt{s^2}$ *p. 581*

Chebyshev's rule *p. 583*

Empirical rule *p. 583*

Variance of a random variable:

$\sigma^2 = \sum_i (x_i - \mu)^2 P(X = x_i)$ *p. 585*

Standard deviation of X: $\sigma = \sqrt{\sigma^2}$ *p. 585*

Variance and standard deviation of a binomial random variable:

$\sigma^2 = npq, \sigma = \sqrt{npq}$ *p. 588*

8.5 Normal Distributions

Probability density function *p. 596*

Normal density function; normal distribution; standard normal distribution *p. 597*

Calculating probabilities based on the standard normal distribution *p. 597*

Standardizing a normal distribution *p. 599*

Calculating probabilities based on non-standard normal distributions *p. 599*

Normal approximation to a binomial distribution *p. 601*

REVIEW EXERCISES

In Exercises 1–6, find the probability distribution for the given random variable and draw a histogram.

1. A couple has two children; $X = $ the number of boys. (Assume an equal likelihood of a child being a boy or a girl.)

2. A couple has three children; $X = $ the number of girls. (Assume an equal likelihood of a child being a boy or a girl.)

3. A four-sided die (with sides numbered 1 through 4) is rolled twice in succession; $X = $ the sum of the two numbers.

4. 48.2% of *Xbox* players are in their teens, 38.6% are in their twenties, 11.6% are in their thirties, and the rest are in their forties; $X = $ age of an *Xbox* player. (Use the midpoints of the measurement classes.)

5. From a bin that contains 20 defective joysticks and 30 good ones, 3 are chosen at random; $X = $ the number of defective joysticks chosen. (Round all probabilities to four decimal places.)

6. Two dice are weighted so that each number 2, 3, 4, and 5 is half as likely to face up as each 1 and 6; $X = $ the number of 1s that face up when both are thrown.

7. Use any method to calculate the sample mean, median, and standard deviation of the following sample of scores: $-1, 2, 0, 3, 6$.

8. Use any method to calculate the sample mean, median, and standard deviation of the following sample of scores: 4, 4, 5, 6, 6.

9. Give an example of a sample of four scores with mean 1 and median 0. (Arrange them in ascending order.)

10. Give an example of a sample of six scores with sample standard deviation 0 and mean 2.

11. Give an example of a population of six scores with mean 0 and population standard deviation 1.

12. Give an example of a sample of five scores with mean 0 and sample standard deviation 1.

A die is constructed in such a way that rolling a 6 is twice as likely as rolling each other number. That die is rolled four times. Let X be the number of times a 6 is rolled. Evaluate the probabilities in Exercises 13–20.

13. $P(X = 1)$

14. $P(X = 3)$

15. The probability that 6 comes up at most twice

16. The probability that 6 comes up at most once

17. The probability that X is more than 3

18. The probability that X is at least 2

19. $P(1 \le X \le 3)$

20. $P(X \le 3)$

21. A couple has three children; $X = $ the number of girls. (Assume an equal likelihood of a child being a boy or a girl.) Find the expected value and standard deviation of X, and complete the following sentence with the smallest possible whole number: All values of X lie within ___ standard deviations of the expected value.

22. A couple has four children; $X =$ the number of boys. (Assume only a 25% chance of a child being a boy.) Find the expected value and standard deviation of X, and complete the following sentence with the smallest possible whole number: All values of X lie within ___ standard deviations of the expected value.

23. A random variable X has the following frequency distribution.

x	-3	-2	-1	0	1	2	3
$fr(X = x)$	1	2	3	4	3	2	1

Find the probability distribution, expected value, and standard deviation of X, and complete the following sentence: 87.5% (or 14/16) of the time, X is within ___ (round to one decimal place) standard deviations of the expected value.

24. A random variable X has the following frequency distribution.

x	-4	-2	0	2	4	6
$fr(X = x)$	3	3	4	5	3	2

Find the probability distribution, expected value, and standard deviation of X, and complete the following sentence: ___ percent of the values of X lie within one standard deviation of the expected value.

25. A random variable X has expected value $\mu = 100$ and standard deviation $\sigma = 16$. Use Chebyshev's rule to find an interval in which X is guaranteed to lie with a probability of at least 90%.

26. A random variable X has a symmetric distribution and an expected value $\mu = 200$ and standard deviation $\sigma = 5$. Use Chebyshev's rule to find a value that X is guaranteed to exceed with a probability of at most 10%.

27. A random variable X has a bell shaped, symmetric distribution, with expected value $\mu = 200$ and standard deviation $\sigma = 20$. The empirical rule tells us that X has a value greater than ___ approximately 0.15% of the time.

28. A random variable X has a bell shaped, symmetric distribution, with expected value $\mu = 100$ and standard deviation $\sigma = 30$. Use the empirical rule to give an interval in which X lies approximately 95% of the time.

In Exercises 29–34 the mean and standard deviation of a normal variable X are given. Find the indicated probability.

29. X is the standard normal variable Z; $P(0 \le X \le 1.5)$.

30. X is the standard normal variable Z; $P(X \le -1.5)$.

31. X is the standard normal variable Z; $P(|X| \ge 2.1)$.

32. $\mu = 100, \sigma = 16; P(80 \le X \le 120)$

33. $\mu = 0, \sigma = 2; P(X \le -1)$

34. $\mu = -1, \sigma = 0.5; P(X \ge 1)$

APPLICATIONS: OHaganBooks.com

Marketing As a promotional gimmick, OHaganBooks.com has been selling copies of the Encyclopædia Galactica at an extremely low price that is changed each week at random in a nationally televised drawing. Exercises 35–40 are based on the following table, which summarizes the anticipated sales.

Price	$5.50	$10	$12	$15
Frequency (weeks)	1	2	3	4
Weekly Sales	6,200	3,500	3,000	1,000

35. What is the expected value of the price of *Encyclopædia Galactica*?

36. What are the expected weekly sales of *Encyclopædia Galactica*?

37. What is the expected weekly revenue from sales of *Encyclopædia Galactica*? (Revenue = Price per copy sold × Number of copies sold.)

38. OHaganBooks.com originally paid Duffin House $20 per copy for the *Encyclopædia Galactica*. What is the expected weekly loss from sales of the encyclopædia? (Loss = Loss per copy sold × Number of copies sold.)

39. True or false? If X and Y are two random variables, then $E(XY) = E(X)E(Y)$ (the expected value of the product of two random variables is the product of the expected values). Support your claim by referring to the answers of Exercises 35, 36, and 37.

40. True or false? If X and Y are two random variables, then $E(X/Y) = E(X)/E(Y)$ (the expected value of the ratio of two random variables is the ratio of the expected values). Support your claim by referring to the answers of Exercises 36 and 38.

41. *Online Sales* The following table shows the number of online orders at OHaganBooks.com per million residents in 100 U.S. cities during one month:

Orders (per million residents)	1–2.9	3–4.9	5–6.9	7–8.9	9–10.9
Number of Cities	25	35	15	15	10

a. Let X be the number of orders per million residents in a randomly chosen U.S. city (use rounded midpoints of the given measurement classes). Construct the probability distribution for X and hence compute the expected value μ of X and standard deviation σ. (Round answers to four decimal places.)

b. What range of orders per million residents does the empirical rule predict from approximately 68% of all cities? Would you judge that the empirical rule applies? Why?

c. The actual percentage of cities from which you obtain between 3 and 8 orders per million residents is (choose the correct answer that gives the most specific information):
(A) Between 50% and 65%　(B) At least 65%
(C) At least 50%　(D) 57.5%

42. _Pollen_ Marjory Duffin is planning a joint sales meeting with OHaganBooks.com in Atlanta at the end of March, but is extremely allergic to pollen, so she went online to find pollen counts for the period. The following table shows the results of her search:

Pollen Count	0–1.9	2–3.9	4–5.9	6–7.9	8–9.9	10–11.9
Number of Days	3	5	7	2	1	2

a. Let X be the pollen count on a given day (use rounded midpoints of the given measurement classes). Construct the probability distribution for X and hence compute the expected value μ of X and standard deviation σ. (Round answers to four decimal places.)

b. What range of pollen counts does the empirical rule predict on approximately 95% of the days? Would you judge that the empirical rule applies? Why?

c. The actual percentage of days on which the pollen count is between 2 and 7 is (choose the correct answer that gives the most specific information):

(A) Between 50% and 60%   **(B)** At least 60%
(C) At most 70%   **(D)** Between 60% and 70%

**Mac vs. Windows** On average, 5% of all hits by Mac OS users and 10% of all hits by Windows users result in orders for books at OHaganBooks.com. Due to online promotional efforts, the site traffic is approximately 10 hits per hour by Mac OS users, and 20 hits per hour by Windows users. Compute the probabilities in Exercises 43–48. (Round all answers to three decimal places.)

43. What is the probability that exactly three Windows users will order books in the next hour?

44. What is the probability that at most three Windows users will order books in the next hour?

45. What is the probability that exactly one Mac OS user and three Windows users will order books in the next hour?

46. What assumption must you make to justify your calculation in Exercise 45?

47. How many orders for books can OHaganBooks.com expect in the next hour from Mac OS users?

48. How many orders for books can OHaganBooks.com expect in the next hour from Windows users?

**Online Cosmetics** OHaganBooks.com has launched a subsidiary, GnuYou.com, which sells beauty products online. Most products sold by GnuYou.com are skin creams and hair products. Exercises 49–52 are based on the following table, which shows monthly revenues earned through sales of these products. (Assume a normal distribution. Round all answers to three decimal places.)

Product	Skin Creams	Hair Products
Mean Monthly Revenue	$38,000	$34,000
Standard Deviation	$21,000	$14,000

49. What is the probability that GnuYou.com will sell _at least_ $50,000 worth of skin cream next month?

50. What is the probability that GnuYou.com will sell _at most_ $50,000 worth of hair products next month?

51. What is the probability that GnuYou.com will sell less than $12,000 of skin creams next month?

52. What is the probability that GnuYou.com will sell less than $12,000 of hair products next month?

53. _Intelligence_ Billy-Sean O'Hagan, now a senior at Suburban State University, has done exceptionally well and has just joined Mensa, a club for people with high IQs. Within Mensa is a group called the Three Sigma Club because their IQ scores are at least 3 standard deviations higher than the U.S. mean. Assuming a U.S. population of 313,000,000, how many people in the United States are qualified for the Three Sigma Club? (Round your answer to the nearest 1,000 people.)

54. _Intelligence_ To join Mensa (not necessarily the Three Sigma Club), one needs an IQ of at least 132, corresponding to the top 2% of the population. Assuming that scores on this test are normally distributed with a mean of 100, what is the standard deviation? (Round your answer to the nearest whole number.)

55. _Intelligence_ Based on the information given in Exercises 53 and 54, what score must Billy-Sean have to get into the Three Sigma Club? (Assume that IQ scores are normally distributed with a mean of 100, and use the rounded standard deviation.)

56. _Intelligence_ Mensa allows the results of various standardized tests to be used to gain membership. Suppose that there was such a test with a mean of 500 on which one needed to score at least 600 to be in the top 2% of the population, hence eligible to join Mensa. What would Billy-Sean need to score on this test to get into the Three Sigma Club?

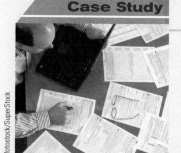

Case Study

Spotting Tax Fraud with Benford's Law[65]

You are a tax fraud specialist working for the Internal Revenue Service (IRS), and you have just been handed a portion of the tax return from Colossal Conglomerate. The IRS suspects that the portion you were handed may be fraudulent, and would like your opinion. Is there any mathematical test, you wonder, that can point to a suspicious tax return based on nothing more than the numbers entered?

[65] The discussion is based on the article "Following Benford's Law, or Looking Out for No. 1" by Malcolm W. Browne, _New York Times_, August 4, 1998, p. F4. The use of Benford's Law in detecting tax evasion is discussed in a Ph.D. dissertation by Dr. Mark J. Nigrini (Southern Methodist University, Dallas).

You decide, on an impulse, to make a list of the first digits of all the numbers entered in the portion of the Colossal Conglomerate tax return (there are 625 of them). You reason that, if the tax return is an honest one, the first digits of the numbers should be uniformly distributed. More precisely, if the experiment consists of selecting a number at random from the tax return, and the random variable X is defined to be the first digit of the selected number, then X should have the following probability distribution:

x	1	2	3	4	5	6	7	8	9
$P(X = x)$	$\frac{1}{9}$	$\frac{1}{9}$	$\frac{1}{9}$	$\frac{1}{9}$	$\frac{1}{9}$	$\frac{1}{9}$	$\frac{1}{9}$	$\frac{1}{9}$	$\frac{1}{9}$

You then do a quick calculation based on this probability distribution and find an expected value of $E(X) = 5$. Next, you turn to the Colossal Conglomerate tax return data and calculate the relative frequency (estimated probability) of the actual numbers in the tax return. You find the following results.

Colossal Conglomerate Return

y	1	2	3	4	5	6	7	8	9
$P(Y = y)$	.29	.1	.04	.15	.31	.08	.01	.01	.01

It certainly does look suspicious! For one thing, the digits 1 and 5 seem to occur a lot more often than any of the other digits, and roughly three times what you predicted. Moreover, when you compute the expected value, you obtain $E(Y) = 3.48$, considerably lower than the value of 5 you predicted. Gotcha! you exclaim.

You are about to file a report recommending a detailed audit of Colossal Conglomerate when you recall an article you once read about first digits in lists of numbers. The article dealt with a remarkable discovery in 1938 by Dr. Frank Benford, a physicist at General Electric. What Dr. Benford noticed was that the pages of logarithm tables that listed numbers starting with the digits 1 and 2 tended to be more soiled and dog-eared than the pages that listed numbers starting with higher digits— say, 8. For some reason, numbers that start with low digits seemed more prevalent than numbers that start with high digits. He subsequently analyzed more than 20,000 sets of numbers, such as tables of baseball statistics, listings of widths of rivers, half-lives of radioactive elements, street addresses, and numbers in magazine articles. The result was always the same: Inexplicably, numbers that start with low digits tended to appear more frequently than those that start with high ones, with numbers beginning with the digit 1 most prevalent of all.[66] Moreover, the expected value of the first digit was not the expected 5, but 3.44.

Because the first digits in Colossal Conglomerate's return have an expected value of 3.48, very close to Benford's value, it might appear that your suspicion was groundless after all. (Back to the drawing board . . .)

Out of curiosity, you decide to investigate Benford's discovery more carefully. What you find is that Benford did more than simply observe a strange phenomenon in lists of numbers. He went further and derived the following formula for the probability distribution of first digits in lists of numbers:

$$P(X = x) = \log(1 + 1/x) \qquad (x = 1, 2, \ldots, 9).$$

---

[66] This does not apply to all lists of numbers. For instance, a list of randomly chosen numbers between 100 and 999 will have first digits uniformly distributed between 1 and 9.

Benford
Colossal Conglomerate

Figure 17

You compute these probabilities, and find the following distribution (the probabilities are all rounded, and thus do not add to exactly 1).

x	1	2	3	4	5	6	7	8	9
$P(X = x)$	.30	.18	.12	.10	.08	.07	.06	.05	.05

You then enter these data along with the Colossal Conglomerate tax return data in your spreadsheet program and obtain the graph shown in Figure 17.

The graph shows something awfully suspicious happening with the digit 5. The percentage of numbers in the Colossal Conglomerate return that begin with 5 far exceeds Benford's prediction that approximately 8% of all numbers should begin with 5.

Now it seems fairly clear that you are justified in recommending Colossal Conglomerate for an audit, after all.

Q: *Because no given set of data can reasonably be expected to satisfy Benford's law exactly, how can I be certain that the Colossal Conglomerate data is not simply due to chance?*

A: You can never be 100% certain. It is certainly conceivable that the tax figures just happen to result in the "abnormal" distribution in the Colossal Conglomerate tax return. However—and this is the subject of "inferential statistics"—there is a method for deciding whether you can be, say "95% certain" that the anomaly reflected in the data is not due to chance. To check, you must first compute a statistic that determines how far a given set of data deviates from satisfying a theoretical prediction (Benford's law, in this case). This statistic is called a **sum-of-squares error** and is given by the following formula (reminiscent of the variance):

$$\text{SSE} = n \left[\frac{[P(y_1) - P(x_1)]^2}{P(x_1)} + \frac{[P(y_2) - P(x_2)]^2}{P(x_2)} + \cdots + \frac{[P(y_9) - P(x_9)]^2}{P(x_9)} \right].$$

Here, n is the sample size: 625 in the case of Colossal Conglomerate. The quantities $P(x_i)$ are the theoretically predicted probabilities according to Benford's Law, and the $P(y_i)$ are the probabilities in the Colossal Conglomerate return. Notice that if the Colossal Conglomerate return probabilities had exactly matched the theoretically predicted probabilities, then SSE would have been zero. Notice also the effect of multiplying by the sample size n: The larger the sample, the more likely that the discrepancy between the $P(x_i)$ and the $P(y_i)$ is not due to chance. Substituting the numbers gives

$$\text{SSE} \approx 625 \left[\frac{[.29 - .30]^2}{.30} + \frac{[.1 - .18]^2}{.18} + \cdots + \frac{[.01 - .05]^2}{.05} \right]$$
$$\approx 552.[67]$$

Q: *The value of SSE does seem quite large. But how can I use this figure in my report? I would like to say something impressive, such as "Based on the portion of the Colossal Conglomerate tax return analyzed, one can be 95% certain that the figures are anomalous."*

A: The error SSE is used by statisticians to answer exactly such a question. What they would do is compare this figure to the largest SSE we would have expected to get

---

[67] If you use more accurate values for the probabilities in Benford's distribution, the value is approximately 560.

by chance in 95 out of 100 selections of data that *do* satisfy Benford's law. This "biggest error" is computed using a "chi-squared" distribution and can be found in Excel by entering

```
=CHIINV(0.05,8)
```

Here, the 0.05 is $1 - 0.95$, encoding the "95% certainty," and the 8 is called the "number of degrees of freedom" = number of outcomes (9) minus 1.

You now find, using Excel, that the chi-squared figure is 15.5, meaning that the largest SSE that you could have expected purely by chance is 15.5. Because Colossal Conglomerate's error is much larger at 552, you can now justifiably say in your report that there is a 95% certainty that the figures are anomalous.[68]

EXERCISES

Which of the following lists of data would you expect to follow Benford's law? If the answer is "no," give a reason.

1. Distances between cities in France, measured in kilometers
2. Distances between cities in France, measured in miles
3. The grades (0–100) in your math instructor's grade book
4. The Dow Jones averages for the past 100 years
5. Verbal SAT scores of college-bound high school seniors
6. Life spans of companies

⊤ *Use technology to determine whether the given distribution of first digits fails, with 95% certainty, to follow Benford's law.*

7. Good Neighbor Inc.'s tax return ($n = 1,000$)

y	1	2	3	4	5	6	7	8	9
$P(Y = y)$	.31	.16	.13	.11	.07	.07	.05	.06	.04

8. Honest Growth Funds Stockholder Report ($n = 400$)

y	1	2	3	4	5	6	7	8	9
$P(Y = y)$	.28	.16	.1	.11	.07	.09	.05	.07	.07

[68] What this actually means is that, if you were to do a similar analysis on a large number of tax returns, and you designated as "not conforming to Benford's law" all of those whose value of SSE was larger than 15.5, you would be justified in 95% of the cases.

TI-83/84 Plus **Technology Guide**

Section 8.1

Example 3 (page 552) Let X be the number of heads that face up in three tosses of a coin. We obtained the following probability distribution of X in the text:

x	0	1	2	3
$P(X = x)$	$\frac{1}{8}$	$\frac{3}{8}$	$\frac{3}{8}$	$\frac{1}{8}$

Use technology to obtain the corresponding histogram.

Solution with Technology

1. In the TI-83/84 Plus, you can enter a list of probabilities as follows: press $\boxed{\text{STAT}}$, choose EDIT, and then press $\boxed{\text{ENTER}}$. Clear columns L_1 and L_2 if they are not already cleared. (Select the heading of a column and press $\boxed{\text{CLEAR}}$ $\boxed{\text{ENTER}}$ to clear it.) Enter the values of X in the column under L_1 (pressing $\boxed{\text{ENTER}}$ after each entry) and enter the frequencies in the column under L_2.

2. To graph the data as in Figure 1, first set the $\boxed{\text{WINDOW}}$ to $0 \leq X \leq 4$, $0 \leq Y \leq 0.5$, and Xscl = 1 (the width of the bars). Then turn STAT PLOT on ([2nd] $\boxed{\text{Y=}}$), and configure it by selecting the histogram icon, setting Xlist = L_1 and Freq = L_2. Then hit $\boxed{\text{GRAPH}}$.

Example 4 (page 552) We obtained the following frequency table in the text:

x	25,000	35,000	45,000	55,000	65,000	75,000	85,000
Frequency	20	80	230	400	170	70	30

Find the probability distribution of X.

Solution with Technology

We need to divide each frequency by the sum. Although the computations in this example (dividing the seven frequencies by 1,000) are simple to do by hand, they could become tedious in general, so technology is helpful.

1. On the TI-83/84 Plus, press $\boxed{\text{STAT}}$, select EDIT, enter the values of X in the L_1 list, and enter the frequencies in the L_2 list as in Example 3 (below left).

2. Then, on the home screen, enter

$L_2/1,000 \rightarrow L_3$ L_2 is $\boxed{\text{2nd}}$ $\boxed{2}$, L_3 is $\boxed{\text{2nd}}$ $\boxed{3}$.

or, better yet,

$L_2/\text{sum}(L_2) \rightarrow L_3$ Sum is found in $\boxed{\text{2nd}}$ $\boxed{\text{STAT}}$, under MATH.

3. After pressing $\boxed{\text{ENTER}}$ you can now go back to the $\boxed{\text{STAT}}$ EDIT screen, and you will find the probabilities displayed in L_3 as shown above on the right.

Section 8.2

Example 2(b) (page 562) By 2030, the probability that a randomly chosen resident in the United States will be 65 years old or older is projected to be .2. If X is the number of people aged 65 or older in a sample of 6, construct the probability distribution of X.

Solution with Technology

In the "Y=" screen, you can enter the binomial distribution formula

$$Y_1 = 6 \text{ nCr } X*0.2\char`^X*0.8\char`^(6-X)$$

directly (to get nCr, press $\boxed{\text{MATH}}$ and select PRB), and hit $\boxed{\text{TABLE}}$. You can then replicate the table in the text by choosing $X = 0, 1, \ldots, 6$ (use the TBLSET screen to set "Indpnt" to "Ask" if you have not already done so).

The TI-83/84 Plus also has a built-in binomial distribution function that you can use in place of the explicit formula:

Y_1 = binompdf(6, 0.2, X)   Press [2nd] [VARS] [0].

The TI-83/84 Plus function binompcf (directly following binompdf) gives the value of the *cumulative* distribution function, $P(0 \leq X \leq x)$.

    To graph the resulting probability distribution on your calculator, follow the instructions for graphing a histogram in Section 8.1.

Section 8.3

Example 3 (page 572) According to historical data, the number of injuries that a member of the Enormous State University women's soccer team will sustain during a typical season is given by the following probability distribution table:

Injuries	0	1	2	3	4	5	6
Probability	.20	.20	.22	.20	.15	.01	.02

If X denotes the number of injuries sustained by a player during one season, compute $E(X)$.

Solution with Technology

To obtain the expected value of a probability distribution on the TI-83/84 Plus, press [STAT], select EDIT, and then press [ENTER], and enter the values of X in the L_1 list and the probabilities in the column in the L_2 list. Then, on the home screen, you can obtain the expected value as

sum ($L_1 * L_2$) L_1 is [2nd] [1] L_2 is [2nd] [2]
             Sum is found in [2nd] [STAT], under MATH

Section 8.4

Example 3 (page 586) Compute the variance and standard deviation for the following probability distribution.

x	10	20	30	40	50	60
$P(X = x)$	.2	.2	.3	.1	.1	.1

Solution with Technology

1. As in Example 3 in the preceding section, begin by entering the probability distribution of X into columns L_1 and L_2 in the LIST screen (press [STAT] and select EDIT). (See below left.)

2. Then, on the home screen, enter

    sum($L_1 * L_2$)→M   Stores the value of μ as M
                          Sum is found in [2nd] [STAT], under MATH.

3. To obtain the variance, enter the following.

    sum((L_1-M)^2*L_2)   Computation of
                              $\sum (x - \mu)^2 P(X = x)$

Section 8.5

Example 1(b), (c) (page 598) Let Z be the standard normal variable. Calculate the following probabilities.

b. $P(0 \leq Z \leq 2.43)$

c. $P(-1.37 \leq Z \leq 2.43)$

Solution with Technology

On the TI-83/84 Plus, press [2nd] [VARS] to obtain the selection of distribution functions. The first function, normalpdf, gives the values of the normal density function (whose graph is the normal curve). The second, normalcdf, gives $P(a \leq Z \leq b)$. For example, to compute $P(0 \leq Z \leq 2.43)$, enter

    normalcdf(0, 2.43)

To compute $P(-1.37 \leq Z \leq 2.43)$, enter

```
normalcdf(-1.37, 2.43)
```

```
normalcdf(0,2.43
)
        .4924505885
normalcdf(-1.37,
2.43)
        .9071070809
■
```

Example 2 (page 599) Pressure gauges manufactured by Precision Corp. must be checked for accuracy before being placed on the market. To test a pressure gauge, a worker uses it to measure the pressure of a sample of compressed air known to be at a pressure of exactly 50 pounds per square inch. If the gauge reading is off by more than 1% (0.5 pounds), it is rejected. Assuming that the reading of a pressure gauge under these circumstances is a normal random variable with mean 50 and standard deviation 0.4, find the percentage of gauges rejected.

Solution with Technology

As seen in the text, we need to compute $1 - P(49.5 \leq X \leq 50.5)$ with $\mu = 50$ and $\sigma = 0.4$. On the TI-83/84 Plus, the built-in `normalcdf` function permits us to compute $P(a \leq X \leq b)$ for nonstandard normal distributions as well. The format is

$$\texttt{normalcdf(a, b, } \mu \texttt{, } \sigma \texttt{)} \quad P(a \leq X \leq b)$$

For example, we can compute $P(49.5 \leq X \leq 50.5)$ by entering

```
normalcdf(49.5, 50.5, 50, 0.4)
```

Then subtract it from 1 to obtain the answer:

```
normalcdf(49.5,5
0.5,50,.4)
        .7887003221
1-Ans
        .2112996779
■
```

SPREADSHEET Technology Guide

Section 8.1

Example 3 (page 552) Let X be the number of heads that face up in three tosses of a coin. We obtained the following probability distribution of X in the text:

x	0	1	2	3
$P(X = x)$	$\frac{1}{8}$	$\frac{3}{8}$	$\frac{3}{8}$	$\frac{1}{8}$

Use technology to obtain the corresponding histogram.

Solution with Technology

1. In your spreadsheet, enter the values of X in one column and the probabilities in another.

	A	B
1	x	P(X=x)
2	0	0.125
3	1	0.375
4	2	0.375
5	3	0.125

2. Next, select *only* the column of probabilities (B2–B5) and then choose Insert → Column Chart. The procedure for doing this depends heavily on the spreadsheet and platform you are using.

TECHNOLOGY GUIDE

Example 4 (page 552)   We obtained the following frequency table in the text:

x	25,000	35,000	45,000	55,000	65,000	75,000	85,000
Frequency	20	80	230	400	170	70	30

Find the probability distribution of X.

Solution with Technology

We need to divide each frequency by the sum. Although the computations in this example (dividing the seven frequencies by 1,000) are simple to do by hand, they could become tedious in general, so technology is helpful. Spreadsheets manipulate lists with ease. Set up your spreadsheet as shown.

	A	B	C
1	x	Fr	P(X=x)
2	25000	20	=B2/SUM(B:B)
3	35000	80	
4	45000	230	
5	55000	400	
6	65000	170	
7	75000	70	
8	85000	30	

↓

	A	B	C
1	x	Fr	P(X=x)
2	25000	20	0.02
3	35000	80	0.08
4	45000	230	0.23
5	55000	400	0.4
6	65000	170	0.17
7	75000	70	0.07
8	85000	30	0.03

The formula `SUM(B:B)` gives the sum of all the numerical entries in Column B. You can now change the frequencies to see the effect on the probabilities. You can also add new values and frequencies to the list if you copy the formula in column C further down the column.

Section 8.2

Example 2(b) (page 562)   By 2030, the probability that a randomly chosen resident in the United States will be 65 years old or older is projected to be .2. If X is the number of people aged 65 or older in a sample of 6, construct the probability distribution of X.

Solution with Technology

You can generate the binomial distribution as follows in your spreadsheet:

	A	B
1	x	P(X=x)
2	0	=BINOMDIST(A2,6,0.2,0)
3	1	
4	2	
5	3	
6	4	
7	5	
8	6	

↓

	A	B
1	x	P(X=x)
2	0	0.262144
3	1	0.393216
4	2	0.24576
5	3	0.08192
6	4	0.01536
7	5	0.001536
8	6	6.4E-05

The values of X are shown in column A, and the probabilities are computed in column B. The arguments of the `BINOMDIST` function are as follows:

$$\text{BINOMDIST}(x, n, p, \text{Cumulative } (0 = \text{no}, 1 = \text{yes})).$$

Setting the last argument to 0 (as shown) gives $P(X = x)$. Setting it to 1 gives $P(X \le x)$.

To graph the resulting probability distribution using your spreadsheet, insert a bar chart as in Section 8.1.

Section 8.3

Example 3 (page 572)   According to historical data, the number of injuries that a member of the Enormous State University women's soccer team will sustain during a typical season is given by the following probability distribution table:

Injuries	0	1	2	3	4	5	6
Probability	.20	.20	.22	.20	.15	.01	.02

If X denotes the number of injuries sustained by a player during one season, compute $E(X)$.

Solution with Technology

As the method we used suggests, the calculation of the expected value from the probability distribution is particularly easy to do using a spreadsheet program such as Excel.

The following worksheet shows one way to do it. (The first two columns contain the probability distribution of X; the quantities $xP(X=x)$ are summed in cell C9.)

	A	B	C
1	x	P(X=x)	x*P(X=x)
2	0	0.2	=A2*B2
3	1	0.2	
4	2	0.22	
5	3	0.2	
6	4	0.15	
7	5	0.01	
8	6	0.02	
9			=SUM(C2:C8)

↓

	A	B	C
1	x	P(X=x)	x*P(X=x)
2	0	0.2	0
3	1	0.2	0.2
4	2	0.22	0.44
5	3	0.2	0.6
6	4	0.15	0.6
7	5	0.01	0.05
8	6	0.02	0.12
9			2.01

An alternative is to use the SUMPRODUCT function: Once we enter the first two columns above, the formula

=SUMPRODUCT(A2:A8,B2:B8)

computes the sum of the products of corresponding entries in the columns, giving us the expected value.

Section 8.4

Example 3 (page 586) Compute the variance and standard deviation for the following probability distribution.

x	10	20	30	40	50	60
$P(X=x)$	.2	.2	.3	.1	.1	.1

Solution with Technology

As in Example 3 in the preceding section, begin by entering the probability distribution into columns A and B, and then proceed as shown:

The variance then appears in cell D8:

	A	B	C	D
1	x	P(X=x)	x*P(X=x)	(x-Mu)^2 * P(X=x)
2	10	0.2	2	80
3	20	0.2	4	20
4	30	0.3	9	0
5	40	0.1	4	10
6	50	0.1	5	40
7	60	0.1	6	90
8			30	240
9			Expected Value	Variance

Section 8.5

Example 1(b), (c) (page 598) Let Z be the standard normal variable. Calculate the following probabilities.
b. $P(0 \le Z \le 2.43)$
c. $P(-1.37 \le Z \le 2.43)$

Solution with Technology

In spreadsheets, the function NORMSDIST (Normal Standard Distribution) gives the area shown on the left in Figure 18. (Tables such as the one in the Appendix give the area shown on the right.)

Figure 18

To compute a general area, $P(a \le Z \le b)$ in your spreadsheet, subtract the cumulative area to a from that to b:

=NORMSDIST(b)-NORMSDIST(a) $P(a \le Z \le b)$

In particular, to compute $P(0 \le Z \le 2.43)$, use

=NORMSDIST(2.43)-NORMSDIST(0)

and to compute $P(-1.37 \le Z \le 2.43)$, use

=NORMSDIST(2.43)-NORMSDIST(-1.37)

TECHNOLOGY GUIDE

Example 2 (page 599)   Pressure gauges manufactured by Precision Corp. must be checked for accuracy before being placed on the market. To test a pressure gauge, a worker uses it to measure the pressure of a sample of compressed air known to be at a pressure of exactly 50 pounds per square inch. If the gauge reading is off by more than 1% (0.5 pounds), it is rejected. Assuming that the reading of a pressure gauge under these circumstances is a normal random variable with mean 50 and standard deviation 0.4, find the percentage of gauges rejected.

Solution with Technology

In spreadsheets, we use the function NORMDIST instead of NORMSDIST. Its format is similar to NORMSDIST, but includes extra arguments as shown.

$$=\text{NORMDIST}(a,\ \mu,\ \sigma,\ 1)   P(X \le a)$$

(The last argument, set to 1, tells the spreadsheet that we want the cumulative distribution.) To compute $P(a \le X \le b)$ we enter the following in any vacant cell:

$$=\text{NORMDIST}(b,\ \mu,\ \sigma,\ 1)$$
$$-\text{NORMDIST}(a,\ \mu,\ \sigma,\ 1)   P(a \le X \le b)$$

For example, we can compute $P(49.5 \le X \le 50.5)$ by entering

$$=\text{NORMDIST}(50.5,50,0.4,1)$$
$$-\text{NORMDIST}(49.5,50,0.4,1)$$

We then subtract it from 1 to obtain the answer:

	A	B	C	D
1	=NORMDIST(50.5,50,0.4,1)-NORMDIST(49.5,50,0.4,1)			
2	=1-A1			

↓

	A
1	0.78870045
2	0.21129955

Appendix A   Logic

Introduction

Logic is the underpinning of all reasoned argument. The ancient Greeks recognized its role in mathematics and philosophy, and studied it extensively. Aristotle, in his *Organon*, wrote the first systematic treatise on logic. His work had a heavy influence on philosophy, science and religion through the Middle Ages.

But Aristotle's logic was expressed in ordinary language, so was subject to the ambiguities of ordinary language. Philosophers came to want to express logic more formally and symbolically, more like the way that mathematics is written (Leibniz, in the 17th century, was probably the first to envision and call for such a formalism). It was with the publication in 1847 of G. Boole's *The Mathematical Analysis of Logic* and A. DeMorgan's *Formal Logic* that **symbolic logic** came into being, and logic became recognized as part of mathematics. Since Boole and DeMorgan, logic and mathematics have been inextricably intertwined. Logic is part of mathematics, but at the same time it is the language of mathematics.

The study of symbolic logic is usually broken into several parts. The first and most fundamental is the **propositional logic**. Built on top of this is the **predicate logic**, which is the language of mathematics. In this appendix we give an introduction to propositional logic.

A.1   Statements and Logical Operators

Propositional logic is the study of *propositions*. A **statement**, or **proposition**, is any declarative sentence which is either true (T) or false (F). We refer to T or F as the **truth value** of the statement.

EXAMPLE 1   Statements

a. "$2 + 2 = 4$" is a statement because it can be either true or false.[1] Because it happens to be a true statement, its truth value is T.

b. "$1 = 0$" is also a statement, but its truth value is F.

c. "It will rain tomorrow" is a statement. To determine its truth value, we shall have to wait for tomorrow.

d. "Solve the following equation for x" is not a statement, because it cannot be assigned any truth value whatsoever. It is an imperative, or command, rather than a declarative sentence.

e. "The number 5" is not a statement, because it is not even a complete sentence.

For a much more extensive interactive treatment of logic, including discussion of proofs, rules of inference, and an introduction to the predicate calculus, go online and follow:

Online Text

→ On Line Topics in Finite Mathematics

→ Introduction to Logic

---

[1]Is "$2 + 2 = 4$" a sentence? Read it aloud: "Two plus two equals four," is a perfectly respectable English sentence.

f. "This statement is false" gets us into a bind: If it were true, then, because it is declaring itself to be false, it must be false. On the other hand, if it were false, then its declaring itself false is a lie, so it is true! In other words, if it is true, then it is false, and if it is false, then it is true, and we go around in circles. We get out of this bind by saying that because the sentence cannot be either true or false, we refuse to call it a statement. An equivalent pseudo-statement is: "I am lying," so this sentence is known as **the liar's paradox**.

Note Sentences that refer to themselves, or *self-referential sentences*, as illustrated in Example 1(f), are not permitted to be statements. This eliminates the liar's paradox and several similar problems. ∎

We shall use letters like p, q, r, and so on to stand for statements. Thus, for example, we might decide that p should stand for the statement "the moon is round." We write

p: "the moon is round" p is the statement that the moon is round

to express this.

We can form new statements from old ones in several different ways. For example, starting with p: "I am an Anchovian," we can form the **negation** of p: "It is not the case that I am an Anchovian" or simply "I am not an Anchovian."

Negation of a Statement

If p is a statement, then its **negation** is the statement "not p" and is denoted by $\sim p$. We mean by this that, if p is true, then $\sim p$ is false, and vice versa.

Quick Examples

1. If p: "$2 + 2 = 4$," then $\sim p$: "It is not the case that $2 + 2 = 4$," or, more simply, $\sim p$: "$2 + 2 \neq 4$."
2. If q: "$1 = 0$," then $\sim q$: "$1 \neq 0$."
3. If r: "Diamonds are a pearl's best friend," then $\sim r$: "Diamonds are not a pearl's best friend."
4. If s: "All politicians are crooks," then $\sim s$: "Not all politicians are crooks."
5. **Double Negation:** If p is any statement, then the negation of $\sim p$ is $\sim(\sim p)$: "not (not p)," or, in other words, p. Thus $\sim(\sim p)$ has the same meaning as p.

Notes

1. Notice in Quick Example 1 above that $\sim p$ is false, because p is true. However, in Quick Example 2, $\sim q$ is true, because q is false. A statement of the form $\sim q$ can very well be true; it is a common mistake to think it must be false.
2. Saying that not all politicians are crooks is not the same as saying that no politicians are crooks, but is the same as saying that some (meaning one or more) politicians are not crooks.
3. The symbol $\sim$ is our first example of a **logical operator**.
4. When we say in Quick Example 5 above that $\sim(\sim p)$ has the same meaning as p, we mean that they are *logically equivalent*—a notion we will make precise below. ∎

Here is another way we can form a new statement from old ones. Starting with p: "I am wise," and q: "I am strong," we can form the statement "I am wise and I am strong." We denote this new statement by $p \wedge q$, read "p and q." In order for $p \wedge q$ to be true, *both p and q* must be true. Thus, for example, if I am wise but not strong, then $p \wedge q$ is false. The symbol $\wedge$ is another logical operator. The statement $p \wedge q$ is called the **conjunction** of p and q.

Conjunction

The **conjunction** of p and q is the statement $p \wedge q$, which we read "p and q." It can also be said in a number of different ways, such as "p even though q." The statement $p \wedge q$ is true when both p and q are true and false otherwise.

Quick Examples

1. If p: "This galaxy will ultimately disappear into a black hole" and q: "$2 + 2 = 4$," then $p \wedge q$ is the statement "Not only will this galaxy ultimately disappear into a black hole, but $2 + 2 = 4$!"

2. If p: "$2 + 2 = 4$" and q: "$1 = 0$," then $p \wedge q$: "$2 + 2 = 4$ and $1 = 0$." Its truth value is F because q is F.

3. With p and q as in Quick Example 1, the statement $p \wedge (\sim q)$ says: "This galaxy will ultimately disappear into a black hole and $2 + 2 \neq 4$," or, more colorfully, as "Contrary to your hopes, this galaxy is doomed to disappear into a black hole; moreover, two plus two is decidedly *not* equal to four!"

Notes

1. We sometimes use the word "but" as an emphatic form of "and." For instance, if p: "It is hot," and q: "It is not humid," then we can read $p \wedge q$ as "It is hot but not humid." There are always many ways of saying essentially the same thing in a natural language; one of the purposes of symbolic logic is to strip away the verbiage and record the underlying logical structure of a statement.

2. A **compound statement** is a statement formed from simpler statements via the use of logical operators. Examples are $\sim p$, $(\sim p) \wedge (q \wedge r)$ and $p \wedge (\sim p)$. A statement that cannot be expressed as a compound statement is called an **atomic statement**.[2] For example, "I am clever" is an atomic statement. In a compound statement such as $(\sim p) \wedge (q \wedge r)$, we refer to p, q, and r as the **variables** of the statement. Thus, for example, $\sim p$ is a compound statement in the single variable p. ∎

Before discussing other logical operators, we pause for a moment to talk about **truth tables**, which give a convenient way to analyze compound statements.

Truth Table

The **truth table** for a compound statement shows, for each combination of possible truth values of its variables, the corresponding truth value of the statement.

---

[2]"Atomic" comes from the Greek for "not divisible." Atoms were originally thought to be the indivisible components of matter, but the march of science proved that wrong. The name stuck, though.

Quick Examples

1. The truth table for negation, that is, for $\sim p$, is:

p	$\sim p$
T	F
F	T

Each row shows a possible truth value for p and the corresponding value of $\sim p$.

2. The truth table for conjunction, that is, for $p \wedge q$, is:

p	q	$p \wedge q$
T	T	T
T	F	F
F	T	F
F	F	F

Each row shows a possible combination of truth values of p and q and the corresponding value of $p \wedge q$.

EXAMPLE 2 **Construction of Truth Tables**

Construct truth tables for the following compound statements.

a. $\sim(p \wedge q)$ **b.** $(\sim p) \wedge q$

Solution

a. Whenever we encounter a complex statement, we work from the inside out, just as we might do if we had to evaluate an algebraic expression like $-(a + b)$. Thus, we start with the p and q columns, then construct the $p \wedge q$ column, and finally, the $\sim(p \wedge q)$ column.

p	q	$p \wedge q$	$\sim(p \wedge q)$
T	T	T	F
T	F	F	T
F	T	F	T
F	F	F	T

Notice how we get the $\sim(p \wedge q)$ column from the $p \wedge q$ column: we reverse all the truth values.

b. Because there are two variables, p and q, we again start with the p and q columns. We then evaluate $\sim p$, and finally take the conjunction of the result with q.

p	q	$\sim p$	$(\sim p) \wedge q$
T	T	F	F
T	F	F	F
F	T	T	T
F	F	T	F

Because we are "and-ing" $\sim p$ with q, we look at the values in the $\sim p$ and q columns and combine these according to the instructions for "and." Thus, for example, in the first row we have $F \wedge T = F$ and in the third row we have $T \wedge T = T$.

Here is a third logical operator. Starting with p: "You are over 18" and q: "You are accompanied by an adult," we can form the statement "You are over 18 or are accompanied by an adult," which we write symbolically as $p \vee q$, read "p or q." Now in English the word "or" has several possible meanings, so we have to agree on which one we want here. Mathematicians have settled on the **inclusive or:** $p \vee q$ means p is true or q is true *or both are true*.[3] With p and q as above, $p \vee q$ stands for "You are over 18 or are accompanied by an adult, or both." We shall sometimes include the phrase "or both" for emphasis, but even if we leave it off we still interpret "or" as inclusive.

Disjunction

The **disjunction** of p and q is the statement $p \vee q$, which we read "p or q." Its truth value is defined by the following truth table.

p	q	$p \vee q$
T	T	T
T	F	T
F	T	T
F	F	F

This is the **inclusive** or, so $p \vee q$ is true when p is true or q is true *or both* are true.

Quick Examples

1. Let p: "The butler did it" and let q: "The cook did it." Then $p \vee q$: "Either the butler or the cook did it."

2. Let p: "The butler did it," and let q: "The cook did it," and let r: "The lawyer did it." Then $(p \vee q) \wedge (\sim r)$: "Either the butler or the cook did it, but not the lawyer."

Note The only way for $p \vee q$ to be false is for *both* p and q to be false. For this reason, we can say that $p \vee q$ also means "p and q are not both false." ∎

To introduce our next logical operator, we ask you to consider the following statement: "If you earn an A in logic, then I'll buy you a new car." It seems to be made up out of two simpler statements,

p: "You earn an A in logic," and
q: "I will buy you a new car."

---

[3]There is also the **exclusive or:** "p or q but not both." This can be expressed as $(p \vee q) \wedge \sim(p \wedge q)$. Do you see why?

The original statement says: *if p is true, then q is true*, or, more simply, **if** *p*, **then** *q*. We can also phrase this as *p* **implies** *q*, and we write the statement symbolically as $p \rightarrow q$.

Now let us suppose for the sake of argument that the original statement: "If you earn an A in logic, then I'll buy you a new car," is true. This does *not* mean that you *will* earn an A in logic. All it says is that *if* you do so, then I will buy you that car. Thinking of this as a promise, the only way that it can be broken is if you *do* earn an A and I do *not* buy you a new car. With this in mind, we define the logical statement $p \rightarrow q$ as follows.

Conditional

The **conditional** $p \rightarrow q$, which we read "if *p*, then *q*" or "*p* implies *q*," is defined by the following truth table:

p	q	$p \rightarrow q$
T	T	T
T	F	F
F	T	T
F	F	T

The arrow "$\rightarrow$" is the **conditional** operator, and in $p \rightarrow q$ the statement *p* is called the **antecedent,** or **hypothesis,** and *q* is called the **consequent,** or **conclusion.** A statement of the form $p \rightarrow q$ is also called an **implication.**

Quick Examples

1. "If $1 + 1 = 2$ then the sun rises in the east" has the form $p \rightarrow q$ where *p*: "$1 + 1 = 2$" is true and *q*: "the sun rises in the east." is also true. Therefore the statement is true.

2. "If the moon is made of green cheese, then I am Arnold Schwartzenegger" has the form $p \rightarrow q$ where *p* is false. From the truth table, we see that $p \rightarrow q$ is therefore true, regardless of whether or not I am Arnold Schwartzenegger.

3. "If $1 + 1 = 2$ then $0 = 1$" has the form $p \rightarrow q$ where this time *p* is true but *q* is false. Therefore, by the truth table, the given statement is false.

Notes

1. The only way that $p \rightarrow q$ can be false is if *p* is true and *q* is false—this is the case of the "broken promise" in the car example above.

2. If you look at the last two rows of the truth table, you see that we say that "$p \rightarrow q$" is true when *p* is false, *no matter what the truth value of q.* Think again about the promise—if you don't get that A, then whether or not I buy you a new car, I have not broken my promise. It may seem strange at first to say that F $\rightarrow$ T is T and F $\rightarrow$ F is also T, but, as they did in choosing to say that "or" is always inclusive, mathematicians agreed that the truth table above gives the most useful definition of the conditional. ■

It is usually misleading to think of "if *p* then *q*" as meaning that *p causes q.* For instance, tropical weather conditions cause hurricanes, but one cannot claim that if there are tropical weather conditions, then there are (always) hurricanes. Here is a list of some English phrases that *do* have the same meaning as $p \rightarrow q$.

Some Phrasings of the Conditional

We interpret each of the following as equivalent to the conditional $p \to q$.

If p then q.	p implies q.
q follows from p.	Not p unless q.
q if p.	p only if q.
Whenever p, q.	q whenever p.
p is sufficient for q.	q is necessary for p.
p is a sufficient condition for q.	q is a necessary condition for p.

Quick Example

"If it's Tuesday, this must be Belgium" can be rephrased in several ways as follows:

"Its being Tuesday implies that this is Belgium."
"This is Belgium if it's Tuesday."
"It's Tuesday only if this is Belgium."
"It can't be Tuesday unless this is Belgium."
"Its being Tuesday is sufficient for this to be Belgium."
"That this is Belgium is a necessary condition for its being Tuesday."

Notice the difference between "if" and "only if." We say that "p only if q" means $p \to q$ because, assuming that $p \to q$ is true, p can be true only if q is also. In other words, the only line of the truth table that has $p \to q$ true and p true also has q true. The phrasing "p is a sufficient condition for q" says that it suffices to know that p is true to be able to conclude that q is true. For example, it is sufficient that you get an A in logic for me to buy you a new car. Other things might induce me to buy you the car, but an A in logic would suffice. The phrasing "q is necessary for p" says that for p to be true, q must be true (just as we said for "p only if q").

Q : *Does the commutative law hold for the conditional? In other words, is $p \to q$ the same as $q \to p$?*

A : No, as we can see in the following truth table:

p	q	$p \to q$	$q \to p$
T	T	T	T
T	F	F	T
F	T	T	F
F	F	T	T

not the same

Converse and Contrapositive

The statement $q \to p$ is called the **converse** of the statement $p \to q$. A conditional and its converse are *not* the same.

The statement $\sim q \to \sim p$ is the **contrapositive** of the statement $p \to q$. A conditional and its contrapositive are logically equivalent in the sense we define below: they have the same truth value for all possible values of p and q.

EXAMPLE 3 **Converse and Contrapositive**

Give the converse and contrapositive of the statement "If you earn an A in logic, then I'll buy you a new car."

Solution This statement has the form $p \to q$ where p: "you earn an A" and q: "I'll buy you a new car." The converse is $q \to p$. In words, this is "If I buy you a new car then you earned an A in logic."

The contrapositive is $(\sim q) \to (\sim p)$. In words, this is "If I don't buy you a new car, then you didn't earn an A in logic."

Assuming that the original statement is true, notice that the converse is not necessarily true. There is nothing in the original promise that prevents me from buying you a new car if you do not earn the A. On the other hand, the contrapositive is true. If I don't buy you a new car, it must be that you didn't earn an A; otherwise I would be breaking my promise.

It sometimes happens that we do want both a conditional and its converse to be true. The conjunction of a conditional and its converse is called a **biconditional**.

Biconditional

The **biconditional**, written $p \leftrightarrow q$, is defined to be the statement $(p \to q) \wedge (q \to p)$. Its truth table is the following:

p	q	$p \leftrightarrow q$
T	T	T
T	F	F
F	T	F
F	F	T

Phrasings of the Biconditional

We interpret each of the following as equivalent to $p \leftrightarrow q$.

p if and only if q.
p is necessary and sufficient for q.
p is equivalent to q.

Quick Example

"I teach math if and only if I am paid a large sum of money" can be rephrased in several ways as follows:

"I am paid a large sum of money if and only if I teach math."
"My teaching math is necessary and sufficient for me to be paid a large sum of money."
"For me to teach math, it is necessary and sufficient that I be paid a large sum of money."

A.2 Logical Equivalence

We mentioned above that we say that two statements are **logically equivalent** if for all possible truth values of the variables involved the two statements always have the same truth values. If s and t are equivalent, we write $s \equiv t$. This is *not* another logical statement. It is simply the claim that the two statements s and t are logically equivalent. Here are some examples.

EXAMPLE 4 Logical Equivalence

Use truth tables to show the following:

a. $p \equiv \sim(\sim p)$. This is called **double negation**.

b. $\sim(p \wedge q) \equiv (\sim p) \vee (\sim q)$. This is one of **DeMorgan's Laws**.

Solution

a. To demonstrate the logical equivalence of these two statements, we construct a truth table with columns for both p and $\sim(\sim p)$.

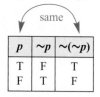

same

p	$\sim p$	$\sim(\sim p)$
T	F	T
F	T	F

Because the p and $\sim(\sim p)$ columns contain the same truth values in all rows, the two statements are logically equivalent.

b. We construct a truth table showing both $\sim(p \wedge q)$ and $(\sim p) \vee (\sim q)$.

same

p	q	$p \wedge q$	$\sim(p \wedge q)$	$\sim p$	$\sim q$	$(\sim p) \vee (\sim q)$
T	T	T	F	F	F	F
T	F	F	T	F	T	T
F	T	F	T	T	F	T
F	F	F	T	T	T	T

Because the $\sim(p \wedge q)$ column and $(\sim p) \vee (\sim q)$ column agree, the two statements are equivalent.

➡ **Before we go on...** The statement $\sim(p \wedge q)$ can be read as "It is not the case that both p and q are true" or "p and q are not both true." We have just shown that this is equivalent to "Either p is false or q is false." ∎

Here are the two equivalences known as DeMorgan's Laws.

DeMorgan's Laws

If p and q are statements, then
$$\sim(p \wedge q) \equiv (\sim p) \vee (\sim q)$$
$$\sim(p \vee q) \equiv (\sim p) \wedge (\sim q)$$

> **Quick Example**
>
> Let p: "the President is a Democrat," and q: "the President is a Republican." Then the following two statements say the same thing:
>
> $\sim(p \wedge q)$: "the President is not both a Democrat and a Republican."
>
> $(\sim p) \vee (\sim q)$: "either the President is not a Democrat, or he is not a Republican (or he is neither)."

Here is a list of some important logical equivalences, some of which we have already encountered. All of them can be verified using truth tables as in Example 4. (The verifications of some of these are in the exercise set.)

Important Logical Equivalences

$\sim(\sim p) \equiv p$	the Double Negative Law
$p \wedge q \equiv q \wedge p$	the Commutative Law for Conjunction
$p \vee q \equiv q \vee p$	the Commutative Law for Disjunction
$(p \wedge q) \wedge r \equiv p \wedge (q \wedge r)$	the Associative Law for Conjunction
$(p \vee q) \vee r \equiv p \vee (q \vee r)$	the Associative Law for Disjunction
$\sim(p \vee q) \equiv (\sim p) \wedge (\sim q)$	DeMorgan's Laws
$\sim(p \wedge q) \equiv (\sim p) \vee (\sim q)$	
$p \wedge (q \vee r) \equiv (p \wedge q) \vee (p \wedge r)$	the Distributive Laws
$p \vee (q \wedge r) \equiv (p \vee q) \wedge (p \vee r)$	
$p \wedge p \equiv p$	Absorption Laws
$p \vee p \equiv p$	
$p \rightarrow q \equiv (\sim q) \rightarrow (\sim p)$	Contrapositive Law

Note that these logical equivalences apply to *any* statement. The ps, qs, and rs can stand for atomic statements or compound statements, as we see in the next example.

EXAMPLE 5 Applying Logical Equivalences

a. Apply DeMorgan's law (once) to the statement $\sim([p \wedge (\sim q)] \wedge r)$.

b. Apply the distributive law to the statement $(\sim p) \wedge [q \vee (\sim r)]$.

c. Consider: "You will get an A if either you are clever and the sun shines, or you are clever and it rains." Rephrase the condition more simply using the distributive law.

Solution

a. We can analyze the given statement from the outside in. It is first of all a negation, but further, it is the negation $\sim(A \wedge B)$, where A is the compound statement $[p \wedge (\sim q)]$ and B is r:

$$\sim(\quad \overset{A}{} \quad \wedge \quad B)$$
$$\sim(\ \overbrace{[p \wedge (\sim q)]} \wedge \quad r)$$

Now one of DeMorgan's laws is

$$\sim(A \wedge B) \equiv (\sim A) \vee (\sim B)$$

Applying this equivalence gives

$$\sim([p \wedge (\sim q)] \wedge r) \equiv (\sim[p \wedge (\sim q)]) \vee (\sim r)$$

b. The given statement has the form $A \wedge [B \vee C]$, where $A = (\sim p)$, $B = q$, and $C = (\sim r)$. So, we apply the distributive law $A \wedge [B \vee C], \equiv [A \wedge B] \vee [A \wedge C]$:

$$(\sim p) \wedge [q \vee (\sim r)] \equiv [(\sim p) \wedge q] \vee [(\sim p) \wedge (\sim r)]$$

(We need not stop here: The second expression on the right is just begging for an application of DeMorgan's law...)

c. The condition is "either you are clever and the sun shines, or you are clever and it rains." Let's analyze this symbolically: Let p: "You are clever," q: "The sun shines," and r: "It rains." The condition is then $(p \wedge q) \vee (p \wedge r)$. We can "factor out" the p using one of the distributive laws in reverse, getting

$$(p \wedge q) \vee (p \wedge r) \equiv p \wedge (q \vee r)$$

We are taking advantage of the fact that the logical equivalences we listed can be read from right to left as well as from left to right. Putting $p \wedge (q \vee r)$ back into English, we can rephrase the sentence as "You will get an A if you are clever and either the sun shines or it rains."

➧ **Before we go on...** In part (a) of Example 5 we could, if we wanted, apply DeMorgan's law again, this time to the statement $\sim[p \wedge (\sim q)]$ that is part of the answer. Doing so gives

$$\sim[p \wedge (\sim q)] \equiv (\sim p) \vee \sim(\sim q) \equiv (\sim p) \vee q$$

Notice that we've also used the double negative law. Therefore, the original expression can be simplified as follows:

$$\sim([p \wedge (\sim q)] \wedge r) \equiv (\sim[p \wedge (\sim q)]) \vee (\sim r) \equiv ((\sim p) \vee q) \vee (\sim r)$$

which we can write as

$$(\sim p) \vee q \vee (\sim r)$$

because the associative law tells us that it does not matter which two expressions we "or" first. ∎

A.3 Tautologies, Contradictions, and Arguments

Tautologies and Contradictions

A compound statement is a **tautology** if its truth value is always T, regardless of the truth values of its variables. It is a **contradiction** if its truth value is always F, regardless of the truth values of its variables.

Quick Examples

1. $p \vee (\sim p)$ has truth table

p	$\sim p$	$p \vee (\sim p)$
T	F	T
F	T	T

— all T's

and is therefore a tautology.

2. $p \wedge (\sim p)$ has truth table

p	$\sim p$	$p \wedge (\sim p)$
T	F	F
F	T	F

and is therefore a contradiction.

When a statement is a tautology, we also say that the statement is **tautological**. In common usage this sometimes means simply that the statement is self-evident. In logic it means something stronger: that the statement is always true, under all circumstances. In contrast, a contradiction, or **contradictory** statement, is *never* true, under any circumstances.

Some of the most important tautologies are the **tautological implications**, tautologies that have the form of implications. We look at two of them: Direct Reasoning, and Indirect Reasoning:

Modus Ponens or Direct Reasoning

The following tautology is called *modus ponens* or **direct reasoning:**

$$[(p \rightarrow q) \wedge p] \rightarrow q$$

In Words
If an implication and its antecedent (p) are both true, then so is its consequent (q).

Quick Example

If my loving math implies that I will pass this course, and if I do love math, then I will pass this course.

Note You can check that the statement $[(p \rightarrow q) \wedge p] \rightarrow q$ is a tautology by drawing its truth table. ∎

Tautological implications are useful mainly because they allow us to check the validity of **arguments**.

Argument

An **argument** is a list of statements called **premises** followed by a statement called the **conclusion**. If the premises are $P_1, P_2, \ldots, P_n$ and the conclusion is C, then we say that the argument is **valid** if the statement $(P_1 \wedge P_2 \wedge \ldots \wedge P_n) \to C$ is a tautology. In other words, an argument is valid if the truth of all its premises logically implies the truth of its conclusion.

Quick Examples

1. The following is a valid argument:

$$p \to q$$
$$\underline{p}$$
$$\therefore \quad q$$

(This is the traditional way of writing an argument: We list the premises above a line and then put the conclusion below; the symbol "$\therefore$" stands for the word "therefore.") This argument is valid because the statement $[(p \to q) \wedge p] \to q$ is a tautology, namely *modus ponens*.

2. The following is an invalid argument:

$$p \to q$$
$$\underline{q}$$
$$\therefore \quad p$$

The argument is invalid because the statement $[(p \to q) \wedge q] \to p$ is not a tautology. In fact, if p is F and q is T, then the whole statement is F.

The argument in Quick Example 2 above is known as the *fallacy of affirming the consequent*. It is a common invalid argument and not always obviously flawed at first sight, so is often exploited by advertisers. For example, consider the following claim: All Olympic athletes drink Boors, so you should too. The suggestion is that, if you drink Boors, you will be an Olympic athlete:

If you are an Olympic Athlete you drink Boors.	Premise (Let's pretend this is True)
You drink Boors.	Premise (True)
$\therefore$ You are an Olympic Athlete.	Conclusion (May be false!)

This is an error that Boors hopes you will make!

There is, however, a correct argument in which we *deny* the consequent:

Modus Tollens or Indirect Reasoning

The following tautology is called *modus tollens* or **indirect reasoning**:

$$[(p \to q) \wedge (\sim q)] \to (\sim p)$$

In Words

If an implication is true but its consequent (q) is false, then its antecedent (p) is false.

In Argument Form

$$p \to q$$
$$\sim q$$
$$\therefore \quad \sim p$$

Quick Example

If my loving math implies that I will pass this course, and if I do not pass the course, then it must be the case that I do not love math.
In argument form:

> If I love math, then I will pass this course.
>
> I will not pass the course.
>
> Therefore, I do not love math.

Note This argument is not as direct as *modus ponens;* it contains a little twist: "If I loved math I would pass this course. However, I will not pass this course. Therefore, it must be that I don't love math (else I *would* pass this course)." Hence the name "indirect reasoning."

Note that, again, there is a similar, but fallacious argument to avoid, for instance: "If I were an Olympic athlete then I would drink Boors ($p \to q$). However, I am not an Olympic athlete ($\sim p$). Therefore, I won't drink Boors. ($\sim q$)." This is a mistake Boors certainly hopes you do *not* make! ∎

There are other interesting tautologies that we can use to justify arguments. We mention one more and refer the interested reader to the website for more examples and further study.

For an extensive list of tautologies go online and follow:

Chapter L Logic

→ List of Tautologies and
  Tautological Implications

Disjunctive Syllogism or "One or the Other"

The following tautologies are both known as the **disjunctive syllogism** or **one-or-the-other:**

$$[(p \vee q) \wedge (\sim p)] \to q \qquad [(p \vee q) \wedge (\sim q)] \to p$$

In Words
If one or the other of two statements is true, but one is known to be false, then the other must be true.

In Argument Form

$$p \vee q \qquad\qquad p \vee q$$
$$\sim p \qquad\qquad\quad \sim q$$
$$\therefore \quad q \qquad\qquad \therefore \quad p$$

Quick Example

The butler or the cook did it. The butler didn't do it. Therefore, the cook did it.
In argument form:

> The butler or the cook did it.
>
> The butler did not do it.
>
> Therefore, the cook did it.

A   EXERCISES

Which of Exercises 1–10 are statements? Comment on the truth values of all the statements you encounter. If a sentence fails to be a statement, explain why. HINT [See Example 1.]

1. All swans are white.   **2.** The fat cat sat on the mat.

3. Look in thy glass and tell whose face thou viewest.[4]

4. My glass shall not persuade me I am old.[5]

5. There is no largest number.

6. 1,000,000,000 is the largest number.

7. Intelligent life abounds in the universe.

8. There may or may not be a largest number.

9. This is exercise number 9.   **10.** This sentence no verb.[6]

Let p: "Our mayor is trustworthy," q: "Our mayor is a good speller," and r = "Our mayor is a patriot." Express each of the statements in Exercises 11–16 in logical form: HINT [See Quick Examples on pages A2, A3, A5.]

11. Although our mayor is not trustworthy, he is a good speller.

12. Either our mayor is trustworthy, or he is a good speller.

13. Our mayor is a trustworthy patriot who spells well.

14. While our mayor is both trustworthy and patriotic, he is not a good speller.

15. It may or may not be the case that our mayor is trustworthy.

16. Our mayor is either not trustworthy or not a patriot, yet he is an excellent speller.

Let p: "Willis is a good teacher," q: "Carla is a good teacher," r: "Willis' students hate math," s: "Carla's students hate math." Express the statements in Exercises 17–24 in words.

17. $p \wedge (\sim r)$ **18.** $(\sim p) \wedge (\sim q)$

19. $q \vee (\sim q)$ **20.** $((\sim p) \wedge (\sim s)) \vee q$

21. $r \wedge (\sim r)$ **22.** $(\sim s) \vee (\sim r)$

23. $\sim(q \vee s)$ **24.** $\sim(p \wedge r)$

Assume that it is true that "Polly sings well," it is false that "Quentin writes well," and it is true that "Rita is good at math." Determine the truth of each of the statements in Exercises 25–32.

25. Polly sings well and Quentin writes well.

26. Polly sings well or Quentin writes well.

27. Polly sings poorly and Quentin writes well.

28. Polly sings poorly or Quentin writes poorly.

29. Either Polly sings well and Quentin writes poorly, or Rita is good at math.

30. Either Polly sings well and Quentin writes poorly, or Rita is not good at math.

31. Either Polly sings well or Quentin writes well, or Rita is good at math.

32. Either Polly sings well and Quentin writes well, or Rita is bad at math.

Find the truth value of each of the statements in Exercises 33–48. HINT [See Quick Examples on page A6.]

33. "If 1 = 1, then 2 = 2."   **34.** "If 1 = 1, then 2 = 3."

35. "If 1 ≠ 0, then 2 ≠ 2."   **36.** "If 1 = 0, then 1 = 1."

37. "A sufficient condition for 1 to equal 2 is 1 = 3."

38. "1 = 1 is a sufficient condition for 1 to equal 0."

39. "1 = 0 is a necessary condition for 1 to equal 1."

40. "1 = 1 is a necessary condition for 1 to equal 2."

41. "If I pay homage to the great Den, then the sun will rise in the east."

42. "If I fail to pay homage to the great Den, then the sun will still rise in the east."

43. "In order for the sun to rise in the east, it is necessary that it sets in the west."

44. "In order for the sun to rise in the east, it is sufficient that it sets in the west."

45. "The sun rises in the west only if it sets in the west."

46. "The sun rises in the east only if it sets in the east."

47. "In order for the sun to rise in the east, it is necessary and sufficient that it sets in the west."

48. "In order for the sun to rise in the west, it is necessary and sufficient that it sets in the east."

Construct the truth tables for the statements in Exercises 49–62. HINT [See Example 2.]

49. $p \wedge (\sim q)$ **50.** $p \vee (\sim q)$

51. $\sim(\sim p) \vee p$ **52.** $p \wedge (\sim p)$

53. $(\sim p) \wedge (\sim q)$ **54.** $(\sim p) \vee (\sim q)$

55. $(p \wedge q) \wedge r$ **56.** $p \wedge (q \wedge r)$

57. $p \wedge (q \vee r)$ **58.** $(p \wedge q) \vee (p \wedge r)$

59. $p \rightarrow (q \vee p)$ **60.** $(p \vee q) \rightarrow \sim p$

61. $p \leftrightarrow (p \vee q)$ **62.** $(p \wedge q) \leftrightarrow \sim p$

Use truth tables to verify the logical equivalences given in Exercises 63–72.

63. $p \wedge p \equiv p$ **64.** $p \vee p \equiv p$

65. $p \vee q \equiv q \vee p$ **66.** $p \wedge q \equiv q \wedge p$
(Commutative law for disjunction)   (Commutative law for conjunction)

---

[4] William Shakespeare Sonnet 3.

[5] *Ibid.*, Sonnet 22.

[6] From *Metamagical Themas: Questing for the Essence of Mind and Pattern* by Douglas R. Hofstadter (Bantam Books, New York 1986).

67. $\sim(p \vee q) \equiv (\sim p) \wedge (\sim q)$

68. $\sim(p \wedge (\sim q)) \equiv (\sim p) \vee q$

69. $(p \wedge q) \wedge r \equiv p \wedge (q \wedge r)$
(Associative law for conjunction)

70. $(p \vee q) \vee r \equiv p \vee (q \vee r)$
(Associative law for disjunction)

71. $p \rightarrow q \equiv (\sim q) \rightarrow (\sim p)$ **72.** $\sim(p \rightarrow q) \equiv p \wedge (\sim q)$

In Exercises 73–78, use truth tables to check whether the given statement is a tautology, a contradiction, or neither. HINT [See Quick Examples on page A11.]

73. $p \wedge (\sim p)$

74. $p \wedge p$

75. $p \wedge \sim(p \vee q)$

76. $p \vee \sim(p \vee q)$

77. $p \vee \sim(p \wedge q)$

78. $q \vee \sim(p \wedge (\sim p))$

Apply the stated logical equivalence to the given statement in Exercises 79–84. HINT [See Example 5a, b.]

79. $p \vee (\sim p)$; the commutative law

80. $p \wedge (\sim q)$; the commutative law

81. $\sim(p \wedge (\sim q))$; DeMorgan's law

82. $\sim(q \vee (\sim q))$; DeMorgan's law

83. $p \vee ((\sim p) \wedge q)$; the distributive law

84. $(\sim q) \wedge ((\sim p) \vee q)$; the distributive law

In Exercises 85–88, use the given logical equivalence to rewrite the given sentence. HINT [See Example 5c.]

85. It is not true that both I am Julius Caesar and you are a fool. DeMorgan's law.

86. It is not true that either I am Julius Caesar or you are a fool. DeMorgan's law.

87. Either it is raining and I have forgotten my umbrella, or it is raining and I have forgotten my hat. The distributive law.

88. I forgot my hat or my umbrella, and I forgot my hat or my glasses. The distributive law.

Give the contrapositive and converse of each of the statements in Exercises 89 and 90, phrasing your answers in words.

89. "If I think, then I am."

90. "If these birds are of a feather, then they flock together."

Exercises 91 and 92 are multiple choice. Indicate which statement is equivalent to the given statement, and say why that statement is equivalent to the given one.

91. "In order for you to worship Den, it is necessary for you to sacrifice beasts of burden."
  (A) "If you are not sacrificing beasts of burden, then you are not worshiping Den."
  (B) "If you are sacrificing beasts of burden, then you are worshiping Den."
  (C) "If you are not worshiping Den, then you are not sacrificing beasts of burden."

92. "In order to read the Tarot, it is necessary for you to consult the Oracle."
  (A) "In order to consult the Oracle, it is necessary to read the Tarot."
  (B) "In order not to consult the Oracle, it is necessary not to read the Tarot."
  (C) "In order not to read the Tarot, it is necessary not to read the Oracle."

In Exercises 93–102, write the given argument in symbolic form (use the underlined letters to represent the statements containing them), then decide whether it is valid or not, If it is valid, name the validating tautology. HINT [See Quick Examples on pages A12, A13, A14.]

93. If I am <u>h</u>ungry I am also <u>t</u>hirsty. I am hungry. Therefore, I am thirsty.

94. If I am not <u>h</u>ungry, then I certainly am not <u>t</u>hirsty either. I am not thirsty, and so I cannot be hungry.

95. For me to bring my <u>u</u>mbrella, it's sufficient that it <u>r</u>ain. It is not raining. Therefore, I will not bring my umbrella.

96. For me to bring my <u>u</u>mbrella, it's necessary that it <u>r</u>ain. But it is not raining. Therefore, I will not bring my umbrella.

97. For me to pass <u>m</u>ath, it is sufficient that I have a <u>g</u>ood teacher. I will not pass math. Therefore, I have a bad teacher.

98. For me to pass <u>m</u>ath, it is necessary that I have a <u>g</u>ood teacher. I will pass math. Therefore, I have a good teacher.

99. I will either pass <u>m</u>ath or I have a <u>b</u>ad teacher. I have a good teacher. Therefore, I will pass math.

100. Either <u>r</u>oses are not red or <u>v</u>iolets are not blue. But roses are red. Therefore, violets are not blue.

101. I am either <u>s</u>mart or <u>a</u>thletic, and I am athletic. So I must not be smart.

102. The president is either <u>w</u>ise or <u>s</u>trong. She is strong. Therefore, she is not wise.

In Exercises 103–108, use the stated tautology to complete the argument.

103. If John is a swan, it is necessary that he is green. John is indeed a swan. Therefore, ____. (*Modus ponens.*)

104. If Jill had been born in Texas, then she would be able to ride horses. But Jill cannot ride horses. Therefore, ___. (*Modus tollens.*)

105. If John is a swan, it is necessary that he is green. But John is not green. Therefore, ____. (*Modus tollens.*)

106. If Jill had been born in Texas, then she would be able to ride horses. Jill was born in Texas. Therefore, ___ (*Modus ponens.*)

107. Peter is either a scholar or a gentleman. He is not, however, a scholar. Therefore, ___. (*Disjunctive syllogism.*)

108. Pam is either a plumber or an electrician. She is not, however, an electrician. Therefore, ___ (*Disjunctive syllogism.*)

COMMUNICATION AND REASONING EXERCISES

109. If two statements are logically equivalent, what can be said about their truth tables?

110. If a proposition is neither a tautology nor a contradiction, what can be said about its truth table?

111. If A and B are two compound statements such that $A \vee B$ is a contradiction, what can you say about A and B?

112. If A and B are two compound statements such that $A \wedge B$ is a tautology, what can you say about A and B?

113. Give an example of an instance where $p \rightarrow q$ means that q causes p.

114. Complete the following. If $p \rightarrow q$, then its converse, ___ , is the statement that ___ and (is/is not) logically equivalent to $p \rightarrow q$.

115. Give an instance of a biconditional $p \leftrightarrow q$ where neither one of p or q causes the other.

Area Under a Normal Curve

$P(0 \le Z \le b)$

The table below gives the probabilities $P(0 \le Z \le b)$ where Z is a standard normal variable. For example, to find $P(0 \le Z \le 2.43)$, write 2.43 as $2.4 + 0.03$, and read the entry in the row labeled 2.4 and the column labeled 0.03. From the portion of the table shown at left, you will see that $P(0 \le Z \le 2.43) = .4925$.

Z	0.00	0.01	0.02	0.03
2.3	.4893	.4896	.4898	.4901
2.4	.4918	.4920	.4922	.4925
2.5	.4938	.4940	.4941	.4943

Z	0.00	0.01	0.02	0.03	0.04	0.05	0.06	0.07	0.08	0.09
0.0	.0000	.0040	.0080	.0120	.0160	.0199	.0239	.0279	.0319	.0359
0.1	.0398	.0438	.0478	.0517	.0557	.0596	.0636	.0675	.0714	.0753
0.2	.0793	.0832	.0871	.0910	.0948	.0987	.1026	.1064	.1103	.1141
0.3	.1179	.1217	.1255	.1293	.1331	.1368	.1406	.1443	.1480	.1517
0.4	.1554	.1591	.1628	.1664	.1700	.1736	.1772	.1808	.1844	.1879
0.5	.1915	.1950	.1985	.2019	.2054	.2088	.2123	.2157	.2190	.2224
0.6	.2257	.2291	.2324	.2357	.2389	.2422	.2454	.2486	.2517	.2549
0.7	.2580	.2611	.2642	.2673	.2704	.2734	.2764	.2794	.2823	.2852
0.8	.2881	.2910	.2939	.2967	.2995	.3023	.3051	.3078	.3106	.3133
0.9	.3159	.3186	.3212	.3238	.3264	.3289	.3315	.3340	.3365	.3389
1.0	.3413	.3438	.3461	.3485	.3508	.3531	.3554	.3577	.3599	.3621
1.1	.3643	.3665	.3686	.3708	.3729	.3749	.3770	.3790	.3810	.3830
1.2	.3849	.3869	.3888	.3907	.3925	.3944	.3962	.3980	.3997	.4015
1.3	.4032	.4049	.4066	.4082	.4099	.4115	.4131	.4147	.4162	.4177
1.4	.4192	.4207	.4222	.4236	.4251	.4265	.4279	.4292	.4306	.4319
1.5	.4332	.4345	.4357	.4370	.4382	.4394	.4406	.4418	.4429	.4441
1.6	.4452	.4463	.4474	.4484	.4495	.4505	.4515	.4525	.4535	.4545
1.7	.4554	.4564	.4573	.4582	.4591	.4599	.4608	.4616	.4625	.4633
1.8	.4641	.4649	.4656	.4664	.4671	.4678	.4686	.4693	.4699	.4706
1.9	.4713	.4719	.4726	.4732	.4738	.4744	.4750	.4756	.4761	.4767
2.0	.4772	.4778	.4783	.4788	.4793	.4798	.4803	.4808	.4812	.4817
2.1	.4821	.4826	.4830	.4834	.4838	.4842	.4846	.4850	.4854	.4857
2.2	.4861	.4864	.4868	.4871	.4875	.4878	.4881	.4884	.4887	.4890
2.3	.4893	.4896	.4898	.4901	.4904	.4906	.4909	.4911	.4913	.4916
2.4	.4918	.4920	.4922	.4925	.4927	.4929	.4931	.4932	.4934	.4936
2.5	.4938	.4940	.4941	.4943	.4945	.4946	.4948	.4949	.4951	.4952
2.6	.4953	.4955	.4956	.4957	.4959	.4960	.4961	.4962	.4963	.4964
2.7	.4965	.4966	.4967	.4968	.4969	.4970	.4971	.4972	.4973	.4974
2.8	.4974	.4975	.4976	.4977	.4977	.4978	.4979	.4979	.4980	.4981
2.9	.4981	.4982	.4982	.4983	.4984	.4984	.4985	.4985	.4986	.4986
3.0	.4987	.4987	.4987	.4988	.4988	.4989	.4989	.4989	.4990	.4990

Answers to Selected Exercises

Chapter 0

Section 0.1

1. -48 **3.** $2/3$ **5.** -1 **7.** 9 **9.** 1 **11.** 33 **13.** 14
15. $5/18$ **17.** 13.31 **19.** 6 **21.** $43/16$ **23.** 0
25. `3*(2-5)` **27.** `3/(2-5)` **29.** `(3-1)/(8+6)`
31. `3-(4+7)/8` **33.** `2/(3+x)-x*y^2`
35. `3.1x^3-4x^(-2)-60/(x^2-1)`
37. `(2/3)/5` **39.** `3^(4-5)*6`
41. `3*(1+4/100)^(-3)` **43.** `3^(2*x-1)+4^x-1`
45. `2^(2x^2-x+1)` **47.** `4*e^(-2*x)/`
`(2-3e^(-2*x))` or `4(*e^(-2*x))/`
`(2-3e^(-2*x))` **49.** `3(1-(-1/2)^2)^2+1`

Section 0.2

1. 27 **3.** -36 **5.** $4/9$ **7.** $-1/8$ **9.** 16 **11.** 2
13. 32 **15.** 2 **17.** x^5 **19.** $-\dfrac{y}{x}$ **21.** $\dfrac{1}{x}$ **23.** $x^3 y$
25. $\dfrac{z^4}{y^3}$ **27.** $\dfrac{x^6}{y^6}$ **29.** $\dfrac{x^4 y^6}{z^4}$ **31.** $\dfrac{3}{x^4}$ **33.** $\dfrac{3}{4x^{2/3}}$
35. $1 - 0.3x^2 - \dfrac{6}{5x}$ **37.** 2 **39.** $1/2$ **41.** $4/3$
43. $2/5$ **45.** 7 **47.** 5 **49.** -2.668 **51.** $3/2$ **53.** 2
55. 2 **57.** ab **59.** $x + 9$ **61.** $x\sqrt[3]{a^3 + b^3}$ **63.** $\dfrac{2y}{\sqrt{x}}$
65. $3^{1/2}$ **67.** $x^{3/2}$ **69.** $(xy^2)^{1/3}$ **71.** $x^{3/2}$
73. $\dfrac{3}{5}x^{-2}$ **75.** $\dfrac{3}{2}x^{-1.2} - \dfrac{1}{3}x^{-2.1}$
77. $\dfrac{2}{3}x - \dfrac{1}{2}x^{0.1} + \dfrac{4}{3}x^{-1.1}$
79. $\dfrac{3}{4}x^{1/2} - \dfrac{5}{3}x^{-1/2} + \dfrac{4}{3}x^{-3/2}$ **81.** $\dfrac{3}{4}x^{2/5} - \dfrac{7}{2}x^{-3/2}$
83. $(x^2 + 1)^{-3} - \dfrac{3}{4}(x^2 + 1)^{-1/3}$ **85.** $\sqrt[3]{2^2}$ **87.** $\sqrt[3]{x^4}$
89. $\sqrt[5]{\sqrt{x}\sqrt[3]{y}}$ **91.** $-\dfrac{3}{2\sqrt[4]{x}}$ **93.** $\dfrac{0.2}{\sqrt[3]{x^2}} + \dfrac{3\sqrt{x}}{7}$
95. $\dfrac{3}{4\sqrt{(1-x)^5}}$ **97.** 64 **99.** $\sqrt{3}$ **101.** $1/x$
103. xy **105.** $\left(\dfrac{y}{x}\right)^{1/3}$ **107.** ± 4 **109.** $\pm 2/3$
111. $-1, -1/3$ **113.** -2 **115.** 16 **117.** ± 1
119. $33/8$

Section 0.3

1. $4x^2 + 6x$ **3.** $2xy - y^2$ **5.** $x^2 - 2x - 3$
7. $2y^2 + 13y + 15$ **9.** $4x^2 - 12x + 9$

11. $x^2 + 2 + 1/x^2$ **13.** $4x^2 - 9$ **15.** $y^2 - 1/y^2$
17. $2x^3 + 6x^2 + 2x - 4$
19. $x^4 - 4x^3 + 6x^2 - 4x + 1$
21. $y^5 + 4y^4 + 4y^3 - y$
23. $(x + 1)(2x + 5)$
25. $(x^2 + 1)^5(x + 3)^3(x^2 + x + 4)$
27. $-x^3(x^3 + 1)\sqrt{x + 1}$ **29.** $(x + 2)\sqrt{(x + 1)^3}$
31. a. $x(2 + 3x)$ **b.** $x = 0, -2/3$ **33. a.** $2x^2(3x - 1)$
b. $x = 0, 1/3$ **35. a.** $(x - 1)(x - 7)$ **b.** $x = 1, 7$
37. a. $(x - 3)(x + 4)$ **b.** $x = 3, -4$
39. a. $(2x + 1)(x - 2)$ **b.** $x = -1/2, 2$
41. a. $(2x + 3)(3x + 2)$ **b.** $x = -3/2, -2/3$
43. a. $(3x - 2)(4x + 3)$ **b.** $x = 2/3, -3/4$
45. a. $(x + 2y)^2$ **b.** $x = -2y$
47. a. $(x^2 - 1)(x^2 - 4)$ **b.** $x = \pm 1, \pm 2$

Section 0.4

1. $\dfrac{2x^2 - 7x - 4}{x^2 - 1}$ **3.** $\dfrac{3x^2 - 2x + 5}{x^2 - 1}$ **5.** $\dfrac{x^2 - x + 1}{x + 1}$
7. $\dfrac{x^2 - 1}{x}$ **9.** $\dfrac{2x - 3}{x^2 y}$ **11.** $\dfrac{(x + 1)^2}{(x + 2)^4}$ **13.** $\dfrac{-1}{\sqrt{(x^2 + 1)^3}}$
15. $\dfrac{-(2x + y)}{x^2(x + y)^2}$

Section 0.5

1. -1 **3.** 5 **5.** $13/4$ **7.** $43/7$ **9.** -1
11. $(c - b)/a$ **13.** $x = -4, 1/2$ **15.** No solutions
17. $\pm\sqrt{\dfrac{5}{2}}$ **19.** -1 **21.** $-1, 3$ **23.** $\dfrac{1 \pm \sqrt{5}}{2}$ **25.** 1
27. $\pm 1, \pm 3$ **29.** $\pm\sqrt{\dfrac{-1 \pm \sqrt{5}}{2}}$ **31.** $-1, -2, -3$
33. -3 **35.** 1 **37.** -2 **39.** $1, \pm\sqrt{5}$ **41.** $\pm 1, \pm\dfrac{1}{\sqrt{2}}$
43. $-2, -1, 2, 3$

Section 0.6

1. $0, 3$ **3.** $\pm\sqrt{2}$ **5.** $-1, -5/2$ **7.** -3 **9.** $0, -1, 1$
11. $x = -1$ ($x = -2$ is not a solution.)
13. $-2, -3/2, -1$ **15.** -1 **17.** $\pm\sqrt[4]{2}$ **19.** ± 1
21. ± 3 **23.** $2/3$ **25.** $-4, -1/4$

Section 0.7

1. $P(0, 2)$, $Q(4, -2)$, $R(-2, 3)$, $S(-3.5, -1.5)$,
$T(-2.5, 0)$, $U(2, 2.5)$

3.

5.

7.

9.

11.

13. $\sqrt{2}$

15. $\sqrt{a^2 + b^2}$

17. 1/2

19. Circle with center (0, 0) and radius 3

23.

$1/x^2$

25. a. (I) **b.** (IV) **c.** (V) **d.** (VI) **e.** (III) **f.** (II)

27. $0.1*x^2-4*x+5$

x	0	1	2	3
$f(x)$	5	1.1	−2.6	−6.1
x	4	5	6	7
$f(x)$	−9.4	−12.5	−15.4	−18.1
x	8	9	10	
$f(x)$	−20.6	−22.9	−25	

29. $(x^2-1)/(x^2+1)$

x	0.5	1.5	2.5	3.5
$h(x)$	−0.6000	0.3846	0.7241	0.8491
x	4.5	5.5	6.5	7.5
$h(x)$	0.9059	0.9360	0.9538	0.9651
x	8.5	9.5	10.5	
$h(x)$	0.9727	0.9781	0.9820	

31. a. −1 **b.** 2 **c.** 2   **33. a.** 1 **b.** 0 **c.** 1

$x*(x<0)+2*(x>=0)$

$(x^2)*(x<=0)+(1/x)*$
$(0<x)$

35. a. 0 **b.** 2 **c.** 3 **d.** 3

$x*(x<=0)+(x+1)*$
$(0<x)*(x<=2)+x*$
$(2<x)$

37. a. $h(2x+h)$ **b.** $2x+h$ **39. a.** $-h(2x+h)$
b. $-(2x+h)$ **41. a.** $s(1) = 3.8$. In 2006, Pemex sold
3.8 billion metric tons of petrochemicals domestically
(i.e., in Mexico). $s(4) = 4.0$. In 2009, Pemex sold

Chapter 1

Section 1.1

1. a. 2 **b.** 0.5 **3. a.** −1.5 **b.** 8 **c.** −8 **5. a.** 20 **b.** 30
c. 30 **d.** 20 **e.** 0 **7. a.** −1 **b.** 1.25 **c.** 0 **d.** 1 **e.** 1
9. a. Yes; $f(4) = 63/16$ **b.** Not defined **c.** Not defined
11. a. Not defined **b.** Not defined **c.** Yes, $f(-10) = 0$
13. a. −7 **b.** −3 **c.** 1 **d.** $4y - 3$ **e.** $4(a + b) - 3$
15. a. 3 **b.** 6 **c.** 2 **d.** 6 **e.** $a^2 + 2a + 3$
f. $(x + h)^2 + 2(x + h) + 3$ **17. a.** 2 **b.** 0 **c.** 65/4
d. $x^2 + 1/x$ **e.** $(s + h)^2 + 1/(s + h)$
f. $(s + h)^2 + 1/(s + h) - (s^2 + 1/s)$

19.

$-(x^3)$

21.

x^4

4.0 billion metric tons of petrochemicals domestically. $s(5) = 4.1$. In 2010, Pemex sold 4.1 billion metric tons of petrochemicals domestically. **b.** [0, 5] **c.** Graph:

$s(1.5) \approx 3.9$. Pemex sold about 3.9 billion metric tons of petrochemicals domestically in the year ending June 30, 2007. **43.** $f(4) \approx 1{,}600$, $f(5) \approx 1{,}700$, $f(7.5) \approx 800$. There were 1.6 million housing starts in 2004, 1.7 million housing starts in 2005, and 800,000 housing starts in the year beginning July 2007. **45.** $f(8) - f(0)$. The change in the number of housing starts from 2000 to 2008 was larger in magnitude than the change from 2000 to 2005. **47. a.** $P(0) \approx -100$; $P(4) \approx -400$; $P(1.5) \approx 400$. Continental Airlines lost about \$100 million in 2005, lost about \$400 million in 2009, and made a profit of about \$400 million in the year starting July 1, 2006. **b.** 0; Continental's net income was increasing most rapidly in 2005. **c.** 2.5; Continental's net income was decreasing most rapidly midway through 2007. **49. a.** [0, 10]. $t \geq 0$ is not an appropriate domain because it would predict U.S. trade with China into the indefinite future with no basis. **b.** \$280 billion; U.S. trade with China in 2004 was valued at approximately \$280 billion. **51. a.** `100*(1-12200/t^4.48)` **b.** Graph:

c. Table:

t	9	10	11	12	13	14
$p(t)$	35.2	59.6	73.6	82.2	87.5	91.1
t	15	16	17	18	19	20
$p(t)$	93.4	95.1	96.3	97.1	97.7	98.2

d. 82.2% **e.** 14 months
53. a. $v(10) \approx 58$, $v(16) = 200$, $v(28) = 3{,}800$. Processor speeds were about 58 MHz in 1990, 200 MHz in 1996, and 3,800 MHz in 2008.
b. `(8*(1.22)^x)*(x<16)+(400*x-6200)*` `(x>=16)*(x<25)+3800*(x>=25)`

c. Graph:

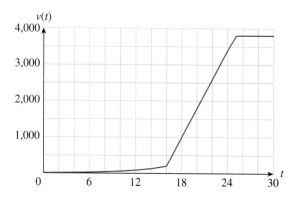

Table:

t	0	2	4	6	8	10
$v(t)$	8.0	12	18	26	39	58
t	12	14	16	18	20	22
$v(t)$	87	130	200	1,000	1,800	2,600
t	24	26	28	30		
$v(t)$	3,400	3,800	3,800	3,800		

d. 2003
55. a.

$$T(x) =$$

$$\begin{cases} 0.10x & \text{if } 0 < x \leq 8{,}375 \\ 837.50 + 0.15(x - 8{,}375) & \text{if } 8{,}375 < x \leq 34{,}000 \\ 4{,}663.25 + 0.25(x - 34{,}000) & \text{if } 34{,}000 < x \leq 82{,}400 \\ 16{,}763.25 + 0.28(x - 82{,}400) & \text{if } 82{,}400 < x \leq 171{,}850 \\ 41{,}809.25 + 0.33(x - 171{,}850) & \text{if } 171{,}850 < x \leq 373{,}650 \\ 108{,}403.25 + 0.35(x - 373{,}650) & \text{if } 373{,}650 < x \end{cases}$$

b. \$5,163.25 **57.** t; m **59.** $y(x) = 4x^2 - 2$ (or $f(x) = 4x^2 - 2$) **61.** False. A graph usually gives infinitely many values of the function while a numerical table will give only a finite number of values.
63. False. In a numerically specified function, only certain values of the function are specified so we cannot know its value on every real number in [0, 10], whereas an algebraically specified function would give values for every real number in [0, 10]. **65.** False: Functions with infinitely many points in their domain (such as $f(x) = x^2$) cannot be specified numerically. **67.** As the text reminds us: to evaluate f of a quantity (such as $x + h$) replace x everywhere by the *whole quantity* $x + h$, getting $f(x + h) = (x + h)^2 - 1$.
69. They are different portions of the graph of the associated equation $y = f(x)$. **71.** The graph of g is the same as the graph of f, but shifted 5 units to the right.

Section 1.2

1. a. $s(x) = x^2 + x$ **b.** Domain: All real numbers **c.** 6
3. a. $p(x) = (x - 1)\sqrt{x + 10}$ **b.** Domain: $[-10, 0)$
c. -14 **5. a.** $q(x) = \frac{\sqrt{10 - x}}{x - 1}$
b. Domain: $0 \leq x \leq 10; x \neq 1$
c. Undefined **7. a.** $m(x) = 5(x^2 + 1)$ **b.** Domain: All
real numbers **c.** 10 **9.** $N(t) = 200 + 10t$
(N = number of music files, t = time in days)
11. $A(x) = x^2/2$ **13.** $C(x) = 12x$

15. $h(n) = \begin{cases} 4 & \text{if } 1 \leq n \leq 5 \\ 0 & \text{if } n > 5 \end{cases}$

17. $C(x) = 1{,}500x + 1{,}200$ per day **a.** $5{,}700$
b. $1{,}500$ **c.** $1{,}500$ **d.** Variable cost = $1{,}500x$; Fixed
cost = $1{,}200$; Marginal cost = $1{,}500$ per piano
e. Graph:

19. a.
$C(x) = 0.4x + 70$, $R(x) = 0.5x$, $P(x) = 0.1x - 70$
b. $P(500) = -20$; a loss of $20 **c.** 700 copies
21. $R(x) = 100x$, $P(x) = -2{,}000 + 90x - 0.2x^2$; at
least 24 jerseys. **23.** $P(x) = -1.7 - 0.02x + 0.0001x^2$;
approximately 264 thousand square feet
25. $P(x) = 100x - 5{,}132$, with domain $[0, 405]$.
For profit, $x \geq 52$ **27.** 5,000 units
29. $FC/(SP - VC)$ **31.** $P(x) = 579.7x - 20{,}000$,
with domain $x \geq 0$; $x = 34.50$ g per day for breakeven
33. a. Graph:

b. Ridership drops by about 3,070 rides per day.
35. a. Graph:

b. 210 million units **c.** 233 million units
d. $R(p) = 0.0009p^3 - 0.63p^2 + 245p$ million dollars/
year; $13 billion/year **37.** $240 per skateboard.
39. a. $110 per phone. **b.** Shortage of 25 million phones

41. a. $3.50 per ride.
Graph:

b. A surplus of around 9,170 rides. **43. a.** $12,000
b. $N(q) = 2{,}000 + 100q^2 - 500q$; This is the cost of
removing q pounds of PCPs per day after the subsidy is
taken into account. **c.** $N(20) = 32{,}000$; The net cost
of removing 20 pounds of PCPs per day is $32,000.
45. a. (B) b. $36.8 billion **47. a. (C) b.** $20.80 per
shirt if the team buys 70 shirts
Graph:

49. a. Graph:

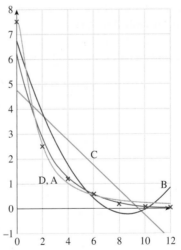

(A), (D) **b.** Model (A); Approximately $0.0021
51. A linear model (A) is the best choice; a plot of the
given points gives a straight line. **53.** Model (D) is
the best choice; the exponential models predict either
perpetually increasing or perpetually decreasing sales,
and Model (C) would give a concave-up parabola.
55. $A(t) = 5{,}000(1 + 0.003/12)^{12t}$; $5,106 **57.** 2024
59. 31.0 grams, 9.25 grams, 2.76 grams **61.** 20,000
years **63. a.** 1,000 years: 65%, 2,000 years: 42%,
3,000 years: 27% **b.** 1,600 years **65.** 30
67. Curve fitting. The model is based on fitting a
curve to a given set of observed data.

69. The cost of downloading a movie was $4 in January and is decreasing by 20¢ per month.   **71.** Variable; marginal.   **73.** Yes, as long as the supply is going up at a faster rate, as illustrated by the following graph:

75. Extrapolate both models and choose the one that gives the most reasonable predictions.
77. They are ≥ 0.   **79.** Books per person

Section 1.3

1. 11; $m = 3$ **3.** -4; $m = -1$ **5.** 7; $m = 3/2$
7. $f(x) = -x/2 - 2$ **9.** $f(0) = -5$, $f(x) = -x - 5$
11. f is linear: $f(x) = 4x + 6$ **13.** g is linear:
$g(x) = 2x - 1$ **15.** $-3/2$ **17.** $1/6$ **19.** Undefined
21. 0   **23.** $-4/3$

25.

27.

29.

31.

33.

35.

37.

39. 2   **41.** 2   **43.** -2 **45.** Undefined   **47.** 1.5
49. -0.09 **51.** $1/2$ **53.** $(d - b)/(c - a)$
55. Undefined   **57.** $-b/a$ **59. a.** 1 **b.** 1/2 **c.** 0
d. 3 **e.** $-1/3$ **f.** -1 **g.** Undefined **h.** $-1/4$ **i.** -2

61. $y = 3x$ **63.** $y = \dfrac{1}{4}x - 1$

65. $y = 10x - 203.5$ **67.** $y = -5x + 6$
69. $y = -3x + 2.25$ **71.** $y = -x + 12$

73. $y = 2x + 4$ **75.** $y = \dfrac{q}{p}x$ **77.** $y = q$

79. Fixed cost $= \$8,000$, marginal cost $= \$25$ per bicycle   **81.** $C = 188x + 20$; $188 per iPhone; $7,540
83. $q = -40p + 2,000$ **85. a.** $q = -2p + 273$;
123 million phones **b.** $1; 2 million
87. a. $q = -4,500p + 41,500$ **b.** Rides/day per $1 increase in the fare; ridership decreases by 4,500 rides per day for every $1 increase in the fare.
c. 14,500 rides/day   **89. a.** $y = 40t + 290$ million pounds of pasta **b.** 890 million pounds
91. a. $N = 5t - 20$ **b.** Billions of dollars per year; Amazon's net income grew at a rate of $5 billion per year. **c.** $20 billion   **93. a.** 2.5 ft/sec **b.** 20 feet along the track **c.** after 6 seconds   **95. a.** 130 miles per hour **b.** $s = 130t - 1,300$ **97. a.** $L = 55n + 475$
b. Pages per edition; *Applied Calculus* is growing at a rate of 55 pages per edition. **c.** 19th edition
99. $F = 1.8C + 32$; 86°F; 72°F; 14°F; 7°F
101. a. $A = 2.4C - 730$ **b.** $100 million lower than the actual $450 million net income American earned in 2007 **c.** Millions of dollars of American's net income per million dollars of Continental's net income; American earned an additional net income of $2.40 per $1 additional net income earned by Continental.
103. $I(N) = 0.05N + 50,000$; $N = \$1,000,000$; marginal income is $m = 5$¢ per dollar of net profit
105. Increasing at 400 MHz per year
107. a. $y = 31.1t + 78$ **b.** $y = 90t - 1,100$

c. $y = \begin{cases} 31.1t + 78 & \text{if } 0 \leq t < 20 \\ 90t - 1,100 & \text{if } 20 \leq t \leq 40 \end{cases}$ or

$y = \begin{cases} 31.1t + 78 & \text{if } 0 \leq t \leq 20 \\ 90t - 1,100 & \text{if } 20 < t \leq 40 \end{cases}$

d. $1,960,000, considerably lower than the actual shown on the graph. The actual cost is not linear in the range 1990–2010.

109. $N = \begin{cases} 0.22t + 3 & \text{if } 0 \leq t \leq 5 \\ -0.15t + 4.85 & \text{if } 5 < t \leq 9 \end{cases}$

3.8 million jobs

111. Compute the corresponding successive changes Δx in x and Δy in y, and compute the ratios $\Delta y/\Delta x$. If the answer is always the same number, then the values in the table come from a linear function.

113. $f(x) = -\dfrac{a}{b}x + \dfrac{c}{b}$. If $b = 0$, then $\dfrac{a}{b}$ is undefined, and y cannot be specified as a function of x. (The graph of the resulting equation would be a vertical line.)
115. slope, 3.   **117.** If m is positive, then y will increase as x increases; if m is negative, then y will decrease as x increases; if m is zero, then y will not change as x changes.   **119.** The slope increases, because an increase in the y-coordinate of the second point increases Δy while leaving Δx fixed.
121. Bootlags per zonar; bootlags   **123.** It must increase by 10 units each day, including the third.
125. (B)   **127.** It is linear with slope $m + n$.
129. Answers may vary. For example, $f(x) = x^{1/3}$, $g(x) = x^{2/3}$ **131.** Increasing the number of items from the break-even number results in a profit: Because the slope of the revenue graph is larger than the slope of the cost graph, it is higher than the cost graph to the right of the point of intersection, and hence corresponds to a profit.

Section 1.4

1. 6   **3.** 86   **5. a.** 0.5 (better fit) **b.** 0.75
7. a. 27.42 **b.** 27.16 (better fit)
9. $y = 1.5x - 0.6667$
Graph:

11. $y = 0.7x + 0.85$
Graph:

13. a. $r = 0.9959$ (best, not perfect) **b.** $r = 0.9538$
c. $r = 0.3273$ (worst)
15.

x	y	xy	x^2
2	0	0	4
6	70	420	36
10	900	9,000	100
18	970	9,420	140

$y = 112.5x - 351.7$; 998.3 million

17. $y = 3.4t + 5$; $25.4 billion   **19.** $y = 0.135x + 0.15$; 6.9 million jobs   **21. a.** $I = 44S - 220$ **b.** Amazon.com earned $44 million in net income per billion dollars in net sales. **c.** $28 billion
d. Graph:

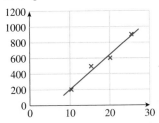

The graph shows a close fit, so the linear model seems reasonable.   **23. a.** $L = 52.70n + 486.30$
Graph:

b. *Applied Calculus* is growing at a rate of 52.7 pages per edition.   **25. a.** $y = 1.62x - 23.87$.
Graph:

b. Each acre of cultivated land produces about 1.62 tons of soybeans.
27. a. $y = -11.85x + 797.71$; $r \approx -0.414$
b. Continental's net income is not correlated to the price of oil. **c.** The points are nowhere near the regression line, confirming the conclusion in (b).
Graph:

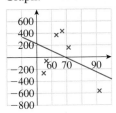

29. a. Regression line: $y = 0.582x + 35.4$ Graph:

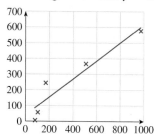

b. There are about 582 additional doctorates in engineering per additional 1,000 doctorates in the natural sciences. **c.** $r \approx 0.949$; a strong correlation. **d.** No, the data points suggest a concave down curve rather than a straight line. **31. a.** $y = 44.0t - 67.8$; $r \approx 0.912$ Graph:

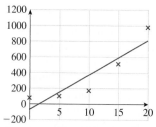

b. The number of natural science doctorates has been increasing at a rate of about 44 per year. **c.** Faster and faster rate; the slopes of successive pairs of points increase as we go from left to right. **d.** No; If r had been equal to 1, then the points would lie exactly on the regression line, which would indicate that the number of doctorates is growing at a constant rate.
33. a. $p = 0.13t + 0.22$; $r \approx 0.97$
Graph:

b. Yes; the first and last points lie above the regression line, while the central points lie below it, suggesting a curve.
c.

	A	B	C	D
1	t	p (Observed)	p (predicted)	Residual
2	0	0.38	0.22	0.16
3	2	0.4	0.48	-0.08
4	4	0.6	0.74	-0.14
5	6	0.95	1	-0.05
6	8	1.2	1.26	-0.06
7	10	1.6	1.52	0.08
8				

Notice that the residuals are positive at first, then become negative, and then become positive, confirming the impression from the graph.

35. The line that passes through (a, b) and (c, d) gives a sum-of-squares error SSE $= 0$, which is the smallest value possible. **37.** The regression line is the line passing through the given points. **39.** 0 **41.** No. The regression line through $(-1, 1)$, $(0, 0)$, and $(1, 1)$ passes through none of these points. **43.** (Answers may vary.) The data in Exercise 33 give $r \approx 0.97$, yet the plotted points suggest a curve, not a straight line.

Chapter 1 Review

1. a. 1 **b.** -2 **c.** 0 **d.** -1 **3. a.** 1 **b.** 0 **c.** 0 **d.** -1
5.

7.

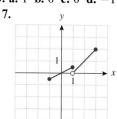

9. Absolute value **11.** Linear **13.** Quadratic
15. $y = -3x + 11$ **17.** $y = 1.25x - 4.25$
19. $y = (1/2)x + 3/2$ **21.** $y = 4x - 12$
23. $y = -x/4 + 1$ **25.** $y = -0.214x + 1.14$, $r \approx -0.33$
27. a. Exponential. Graph:

b. The ratios (rounded to 1 decimal place) are:

$V(1)/V(0)$	$V(2)/V(1)$	$V(3)/V(2)$	$V(4)/V(3)$	$V(5)/V(4)$	$V(6)/V(5)$
3	3.3	3.3	3.2	3.2	3.2

They are close to 3.2. **c.** About 343,700 visits/day
29. a. 2.3; 3.5; 6 **b.** For Web site traffic of up to 50,000 visits per day, the number of crashes is increasing by 0.03 per additional thousand visits.
c. 140,000 **31. a.** (A) **b.** (A) Leveling off (B) Rising (C) Rising; begins to fall after 7 months (D) Rising **33. a.** The number of visits would increase by 30 per day. **b.** No; it would increase at a slower and slower rate and then begin to decrease.
c. Probably not. This model predicts that Web site popularity will start to decrease as advertising increases beyond $8,500 per month, and then drop toward zero. **35. a.** $v = 0.05c + 1,800$
b. 2,150 new visits per day **c.** $14,000 per month
37. $d = 0.95w + 8$; 86 kg **39. a.** Cost:
$C = 5.5x + 500$; Revenue: $R = 9.5x$; Profit
$P = 4x - 500$ **b.** More than 125 albums per week
c. More than 200 albums per week

41. a. $q = -80p + 1,060$ **b.** 100 albums per week
c. $9.50, for a weekly profit of $700
43. a. $q = -74p + 1,015.5$ **b.** 239 albums per week

Chapter 2

Section 2.1

1. $INT = \$120, FV = \$2,120$
3. $INT = \$505, FV = \$20,705$
5. $INT = \$250, FV = \$10,250$ **7.** $PV = \$9,090.91$
9. $PV = \$966.18$ **11.** $PV = \$14,457.83$ **13.** $5,200
15. $787.40 **17.** 5% **19.** About 0.2503%
21. In 2 years **23.** 3.775% **25.** 65% **27.** 10%
29. 86.957% **31.** 48.04% **33.** 58.96% if you had sold
in November 2010 **35.** No. Simple interest increase is
linear. The graph is visibly not linear in that time period.
Further, the slopes of the lines through the successive
pairs of marked points are quite different. **37.** 9.2%
39. 3,260,000 **41.** $P = 500 + 46t$ thousand
($t = $ time in years since 1950)

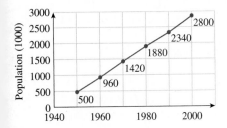

43. Graph (A) is the only possible choice, because the
equation $FV = PV(1 + rt) = PV + PVrt$ gives the
future value as a linear function of time. **45.** Wrong. In
simple interest growth, the change each year is a fixed percentage of the *starting* value, and not the preceding
year's value. (Also see Exercise 46.)
47. Simple interest is always calculated on a constant
amount, PV. If interest is paid into your account, then
the amount on which interest is calculated does not
remain constant.

Section 2.2

1. $13,439.16 **3.** $11,327.08 **5.** $19,154.30
7. $12,709.44 **9.** $613.91 **11.** $810.65
13. $1,227.74 **15.** 5.09% **17.** 10.47% **19.** 10.52%
21. $268.99 **23.** $728.91 **25.** $2,927.15
27. $21,161.79 **29.** $163,414.56
31. $55,526.45 per year **33.** $174,110 **35.** $750.00
37. $27,171.92 **39.** $111,678.96 **41.** $1,039.21

43. The one earning 11.9% compounded monthly
45. Yes. The investment will have grown to about
$394,020 million. **47.** 136 reals **49.** 245 bolivianos
51. 223 bolivars **53.** The Nicaragua investment is
better: It is worth about 1.006 units of currency (in
constant units) per unit invested as opposed to about
1.003 units for Mexico. **55.** 53.81%
57. 65.99% if you had sold in November 2010
59. No. Compound interest increase is exponential,
and exponential curves either increase continually (in
the case of appreciation) or decrease continually (in
the case of depreciation). The graph of the stock price
has both increases and decreases during the given
period, so the curve cannot model compound interest
change. **61.** 31 years; about $26,100 **63.** 2.3 years
65. a. $1,510.31 **b.** $54,701.29 **c.** 23.51%
67. The function $y = P(1 + r/m)^{mx}$ is not a linear
function of x, but an exponential function. Thus, its
graph is not a straight line. **69.** Wrong. Its growth is
exponential and can be modeled by $0.01(1.10)^t$.
71. The graphs are the same because the formulas
give the same function of x; a compound interest
investment behaves as though it was being
compounded once a year at the effective rate.
73. The effective rate exceeds the nominal rate when
the interest is compounded more than once a year
because then interest is being paid on interest accumulated during each year, resulting in a larger effective
rate. Conversely, if the interest is compounded less
often than once a year, the effective rate is less than
the nominal rate. **75.** Compare their future
values in constant dollars. The investment with the
larger future value is the better investment. **77.** The
graphs are approaching a particular curve as m gets
larger, approximately the curve given by the largest
two values of m.

Section 2.3

1. $15,528.23 **3.** $171,793.82 **5.** $23,763.28
7. $147.05 **9.** $491.12 **11.** $105.38 **13.** $90,155.46
15. $69,610.99 **17.** $95,647.68 **19.** $554.60
21. $1,366.41 **23.** $524.14 **25.** $248.85
27. $1,984.65 **29.** $999.61 **31.** $998.47
33. $917.45 **35.** 3.617% **37.** 3.059% **39.** 6.038%
41. You should take the loan from Solid Savings & Loan:
It will have payments of $248.85 per month. The
payments on the other loan would be more than
$300 per month. **43.** $973.54 **45.** $7,451.49

47. Answers using correctly rounded intermediate results:

Year	Interest	Payment on Principal
1	$3,934.98	$1,798.98
2	$3,785.69	$1,948.27
3	$3,623.97	$2,109.99
4	$3,448.84	$2,285.12
5	$3,259.19	$2,474.77
6	$3,053.77	$2,680.19
7	$2,831.32	$2,902.64
8	$2,590.39	$3,143.57
9	$2,329.48	$3,404.48
10	$2,046.91	$3,687.05
11	$1,740.88	$3,993.08
12	$1,409.47	$4,324.49
13	$1,050.54	$4,683.42
14	$661.81	$5,072.15
15	$240.84	$5,491.80

49. 1st 5 years: $402.62/month; last 25 years: $601.73
51. Original monthly payments were $824.79. The new monthly payments will be $613.46. You will save $36,481.77 in interest.   **53.** 10.81%   **55.** 13 years
57. 4.5 years   **59.** 24 years   **61.** He is wrong because his estimate ignores the interest that will be earned by your annuity—both while it is increasing and while it is decreasing. Your payments will be considerably smaller (depending on the interest earned).   **63.** He is not correct. For instance, the payments on a $100,000 10-year mortgage at 12% are $1,434.71, while for a 20-year mortgage at the same rate, they are $1,101.09, which is a lot more than half the 10-year mortgage payment.   **65.** $PV = FV(1 + i)^{-n} =$

$$PMT\frac{(1 + i)^n - 1}{i}(1 + i)^{-n} = PMT\frac{1 - (1 + i)^{-n}}{i}$$

Chapter 2 Review

1. $7,425.00   **3.** $7,604.88   **5.** $6,757.41
7. $4,848.48   **9.** $4,733.80   **11.** $5,331.37
13. $177.58   **15.** $112.54   **17.** $187.57
19. $9,584.17   **21.** 5.346%   **23.** 14.0 years
25. 10.8 years   **27.** 7.0 years   **29.** 168.85%
31. 85.28% if she sold in February 2010.   **33.** No. Simple interest increase is linear. We can compare slopes between successive points to see if the slope remained roughly constant: From December 2002 to August 2004 the slope was $(16.31 - 3.28)/(20/12) = 7.818$ while from August 2004 to March 2005 the slope was $(33.95 - 16.31)/(7/12) = 30.24$. These slopes are quite different.   **35.** 2003

Year	2000	2001	2002	2003	2004
Revenue	$180,000	$216,000	$259,200	$311,040	$373,248

37. At least 52,515 shares   **39.** $3,234.94
41. $231,844   **43.** 7.75%   **45.** $420,275
47. $140,778   **49.** $1,453.06   **51.** $2,239.90 per month
53. $53,055.66   **55.** 5.99%

Chapter 3

Section 3.1

1. $(2, 2)$ **3.** $(3, 1)$ **5.** $(6, 6)$ **7.** $(5/3, -4/3)$
9. $(0, -2)$ **11.** $(x, (1 - 2x)/3)$ or $((1 - 3y)/2, y)$
13. No solution   **15.** $(5, 0)$ **17.** $(0.3, -1.1)$
19. $(116.6, -69.7)$ **21.** $(3.3, 1.8)$ **23.** $(3.4, 1.9)$
25. 200 quarts of vanilla and 100 quarts of mocha
27. 2 servings of Mixed Cereal and 1 serving of Mango Tropical Fruit   **29. a.** 4 servings of beans and 5 slices of bread **b.** No. One of the variables in the solution of the system has a negative value.
31. Mix 12 servings of Designer Whey and 2 servings of Muscle Milk for a cost of $9.20.   **33.** 65 g
35. 20 AAPL, 30 GOOG   **37.** 200 BOH, 400 JPM
39. 242 in favor and 193 against   **41.** 5 soccer games and 7 football games   **43.** 7   **45.** $1.50 each
47. 55 widgets   **49.** Demand: $q = -4p + 47$; supply: $q = 4p - 29$; equilibrium price: $9.50
51. 33 pairs of dirty socks and 11 T-shirts   **53.** $1,200
55. The three lines in a plane must intersect in a single point for there to be a unique solution. This can happen in two ways: (1) The three lines intersect in a single point, or (2) two of the lines are the same, and the third line intersects it in a single point.
57. Yes. Even if two lines have negative slope, they will still intersect if the slopes differ.   **59.** You cannot round both of them up, since there will not be sufficient eggs and cream. Rounding both answers down will ensure that you will not run out of ingredients. It may be possible to round one answer down and the other up, and this should be tried.   **61.** (B)   **63.** (B)
65. Answers will vary.   **67.** It is very likely. Two randomly chosen straight lines are unlikely to be parallel.

Section 3.2

1. $(3, 1)$ **3.** $(6, 6)$ **5.** $\left(\frac{1}{2}(1 - 3y), y\right)$; y arbitrary
7. No solution   **9.** $(1/4, 3/4)$ **11.** No solution
13. $(10/3, 1/3)$ **15.** $(4, 4, 4)$ **17.** $\left(-1, -3, \frac{1}{2}\right)$
19. (z, z, z); z arbitrary   **21.** No solution
23. $(-1, 1, 1)$ **25.** $(1, z - 2, z)$; z arbitrary
27. $(4 + y, y, -1)$; y arbitrary

29. $(4 - y/3 + z/3, y, z)$; y arbitrary, z arbitrary
31. $(-17, 20, -2)$ **33.** $\left(-\frac{3}{2}, 0, 1/2, 0\right)$
35. $(-3z, 1 - 2z, z, 0)$; z arbitrary **37.** $(7/5 - 17z/5 + 8w/5, 1/5 - 6z/5 - 6w/5, z, w)$; z, w arbitrary
39. $(1, 2, 3, 4, 5)$ **41.** $(-2, -2 + z - u, z, u, 0)$;
z, u arbitrary **43.** $(16, 12/7, -162/7, -88/7)$
45. $(-8/15, 7/15, 7/15, 7/15, 7/15)$ **47.** $(1.0, 1.4, 0.2)$
49. $(-5.5, -0.9, -7.4, -6.6)$ **51.** A pivot is an entry in a matrix that is selected to "clear a column"; that is, use the row operations of a certain type to obtain zeros everywhere above and below it. "Pivoting" is the procedure of clearing a column using a designated pivot. **53.** $2R_1 + 5R_4$, or $6R_1 + 15R_4$ (which is less desirable) **55.** It will include a row of zeros.
57. The claim is wrong. If there are more equations than unknowns, there can be a unique solution as well as row(s) of zeros in the reduced matrix, as in Example 6. **59.** Two **61.** The number of pivots must equal the number of variables, since no variable will be used as a parameter. **63.** A simple example is: $x = 1$; $y - z = 1$; $x + y - z = 2$.
65. It has to be the zero solution (each unknown is equal to zero): Putting each unknown equal to zero causes each equation to be satisfied because the right-hand sides are zero. Thus, the zero solution is in fact a solution. Because the solution is unique, this solution is the *only* solution.
67. No: As pointed out in Exercise 65, every homogeneous system has at least one solution (namely, the zero solution), and hence cannot be inconsistent.

Section 3.3

1. 100 batches of vanilla, 50 batches of mocha, and 100 batches of strawberry **3.** 3 sections of Finite Math, 2 sections of Applied Calculus, and 1 section of Computer Methods **5.** $25 million for regional music, $16 million for pop/rock music, and $5 million for tropical music **7.** 4 Airbus A330-300s, 4 Boeing 767-200ERs, and 8 Dreamliners **9.** 22 tons from Cheesy Cream, 56 tons from Super Smooth & Sons, and 22 tons from Bagel's Best Friend **11.** 10 evil sorcerers, 50 trolls, and 500 orcs **13.** $600 to each of the MPBF and the SCN, and $1,200 to the Jets
15. Continental: 120; American: 40; Southwest: 50
17. $5,000 in SHPIX, $2,000 in RYURX, $2,000 in RYIHX **19.** 100 shares of KT, 50 shares of IFF, 50 shares of QSII **21.** Microsoft: 88 million, Time Warner: 79 million, Yahoo: 75 million, Google: 42 million
23. The third equation is $x + y + z + w = 100$.
General Solution: $x = 50.5 - 0.5w$, $y = 33.5 - 0.3w$,

$z = 16 - 0.2w$, w arbitrary. State Farm is most impacted by other companies.
25. a. Brooklyn to Long Island: 500 books; Brooklyn to Manhattan: 500 books; Queens to Long Island: 1,000 books; Queens to Manhattan: 1,000 books.
b. Brooklyn to Long Island: none; Brooklyn to Manhattan: 1,000 books; Queens to Long Island: 1,500 books; Queens to Manhattan: 500 books, giving a total cost of $8,000 **27. a.** The associated system of equations has infinitely many solutions. **b.** No; the associated system of equations still has infinitely many solutions. **c.** Yes; North America to Australia: 440,000, North America to South Africa: 190,000, Europe to Australia: 950,000, Europe to South Africa: 950,000. **29. a.** $x + y = 14,000$; $z + w = 95,000$; $x + z = 63,550$, $y + w = 45,450$. The system does not have a unique solution, indicating that the given data are insufficient to obtain the missing data.
b. $(x, y, z, w) = (5,600, 8,400, 57,950, 37,050)$
31. a. No; The general solution is: Eastward Blvd.: $S + 200$; Northwest La.: $S + 50$; Southwest La.: S, where S is arbitrary. Thus it would suffice to know the traffic along Southwest La. **b.** Yes, as it leads to the solution Eastward Blvd.: 260; Northwest La.: 110; Southwest La.: 60. **c.** 50 vehicles per day
33. a. With $x =$ traffic on middle section of Bree, $y =$ traffic on middle section of Jeppe, $z =$ traffic on middle section of Simmons, $w =$ traffic on middle section of Harrison, the general solution is $x = w - 100$, $y = w$, $z = w$, w arbitrary.
b. No; there are infinitely many possible values for y.
c. 500 cars/minute **d.** 100 cars/minute **e.** No; a large number of cars can circulate around the middle block without affecting the numbers shown. **35. a.** No; the corresponding system of equations is underdetermined. The net flow of traffic along any of the three stretches of Broadway would suffice. **b.** West
37. $10 billion **39.** $x =$ water, $y =$ gray matter, $z =$ tumor **41.** $x =$ water, $y =$ bone, $z =$ tumor, $u =$ air **43.** tumor **45.** 200 Democrats, 20 Republicans, 13 of other parties **47.** Yes; $20m in Company X, $5m in Company Y, $10m in Company Z, and $30m in Company W **49.** It is not realistic to expect to use exactly all of the ingredients. Solutions of the associated system may involve negative numbers or not exist. Only solutions with nonnegative values for all the unknowns correspond to being able to use up all of the ingredients. **51.** Yes; $x = 100$
53. Yes; $0.3x - 0.7y + 0.3z = 0$ is one form of the equation. **55.** No; represented by an inequality rather than an equation. **57.** Answers will vary.

Chapter 3 Review

1. One solution

3. Infinitely many solutions

5. One solution

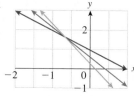

7. $(6/5, 7/5)$ **9.** $(3y/2, y)$; y arbitrary
11. $(-0.7, 1.7)$ **13.** $(-1, -1, -1)$
15. $(z - 2, 4(z - 1), z)$; z arbitrary   **17.** No solution
19. $-40°$ **21.** It is impossible; setting $F = 1.8C$
leads to an inconsistent system of equations.
23. $x + y + z + w = 10$; Linear   **25.** $w = 0$; Linear
27. $-1.3y + z = 0$ or $1.3y - z = 0$; Linear
29. 550 packages from Duffin House, 350 from
Higgins Press   **31.** 1,200 packages from Duffin
House, 200 from Higgins Press   **33.** $40
35. 7 of each   **37.** 5,000 hits per day at
OHaganBooks.com, 1,250 at JungleBooks.com,
3,750 at FarmerBooks.com   **39.** 100 shares of HAL,
20 shares of POM, and 80 shares of WELL
41. Billy-Sean is forced to take exactly the following
combination: Liberal Arts: 52 credits, Sciences:
12 credits, Fine Arts: 12 credits, Mathematics: 48
credits.   **43. a.** $x = 100$, $y = 100 + w$, $z = 300 - w$,
w arbitrary **b.** 100 book orders per day **c.** 300 book
orders per day **d.** $x = 100$, $y = 400$, $z = 0$, $w = 300$
e. 100 book orders per day
45. Yes; New York to OHaganBooks.com: 450 packages, New York to FantasyBooks.com: 50 packages,
Illinois to OHaganBooks.com: 150 packages, Illinois
to FantasyBooks.com: 150 packages

Chapter 4

Section 4.1

1. 1×4; 0   **3.** 4×1; 5/2   **5.** $p \times q$; e_{22} **7.** 2×2; 3
9. $1 \times n$; d_r **11.** $x = 1$, $y = 2$, $z = 3$, $w = 4$

13. $\begin{bmatrix} 0.25 & -2 \\ 1 & 0.5 \\ -2 & 5 \end{bmatrix}$ **15.** $\begin{bmatrix} -0.75 & -1 \\ 0 & -0.5 \\ -1 & 6 \end{bmatrix}$

17. $\begin{bmatrix} -1 & -1 \\ 1 & -1 \\ -1 & 5 \end{bmatrix}$ **19.** $\begin{bmatrix} 0 & 2 & -2 \\ -2 & 0 & 4 \end{bmatrix}$

21. $\begin{bmatrix} 4 & -1 & -1 \\ 5 & 1 & 0 \end{bmatrix}$ **23.** $\begin{bmatrix} -2+x & 0 & 1+w \\ -5+z & 3+r & 2 \end{bmatrix}$

25. $\begin{bmatrix} -1 & -2 & 1 \\ -5 & 5 & -3 \end{bmatrix}$ **27.** $\begin{bmatrix} 9 & 15 \\ 0 & -3 \\ -3 & 3 \end{bmatrix}$

29. $\begin{bmatrix} -8.5 & -22.35 & -24.4 \\ 54.2 & 20 & 42.2 \end{bmatrix}$

31. $\begin{bmatrix} 1.54 & 8.58 \\ 5.94 & 0 \\ 6.16 & 7.26 \end{bmatrix}$ **33.** $\begin{bmatrix} 7.38 & 76.96 \\ 20.33 & 0 \\ 29.12 & 39.92 \end{bmatrix}$

35. $\begin{bmatrix} -19.85 & 115.82 \\ -50.935 & 46 \\ -57.24 & 94.62 \end{bmatrix}$

37. Q1 2010: $[3.3 \quad 21 \quad 8.7]$;   Q1 2011:
$[4.1 \quad 19.4 \quad 16.2]$

39. Sales $= \begin{bmatrix} 700 & 1,300 & 2,000 \\ 400 & 300 & 500 \end{bmatrix}$;

Inventory $-$ Sales $= \begin{bmatrix} 300 & 700 & 3,000 \\ 600 & 4,700 & 1,500 \end{bmatrix}$

41. Profit $=$ Revenue $-$ Cost $= \begin{bmatrix} 8,000 & 7,200 & 8,800 \\ 5,600 & 5,760 & 7,040 \\ 2,800 & 3,500 & 4,000 \end{bmatrix}$

43. 2000 distribution $= A = [53.6 \quad 64.4 \quad 100.2 \quad 63.2]$;
2010 distribution $= B = [55.3 \quad 66.9 \quad 114.6 \quad 71.9]$;
Net change 2000 to 2010 $= D = B - A =$
$[1.7 \quad 2.5 \quad 14.4 \quad 8.7]$; 2020 Distribution $= B + D =$
$[57.0 \quad 69.4 \quad 129.0 \quad 80.6]$
45. Total Foreclosures $=$ Foreclosures in California $+$
Foreclosures in Florida $+$ Foreclosures in Texas $=$
$[55,900 \quad 51,900 \quad 54,100 \quad 56,200 \quad 59,400] +$
$[19,600 \quad 19,200 \quad 23,800 \quad 22,400 \quad 23,600] +$
$[8,800 \quad 9,100 \quad 9,300 \quad 10,600 \quad 10,100] =$
$[84,300 \quad 80,200 \quad 87,200 \quad 89,200 \quad 93,100]$
47. Difference $=$ Foreclosures in California $-$
Foreclosures in Florida $= [55,900 \quad 51,900 \quad 54,100$
$56,200 \quad 59,400] - [19,600 \quad 19,200 \quad 23,800 \quad 22,400$
$23,600] = [36,300 \quad 32,700 \quad 30,300 \quad 33,800 \quad 35,800]$
The difference was greatest in April.

49. a. Use $=$

	Proc	Mem	Tubes
Pom II	2	16	20
Pom Classic	1	4	40

$\begin{bmatrix} 2 & 16 & 20 \\ 1 & 4 & 40 \end{bmatrix}$;

Inventory $= \begin{bmatrix} 500 & 5{,}000 & 10{,}000 \\ 200 & 2{,}000 & 20{,}000 \end{bmatrix}$;

Inventory $- 100 \times$ Use $= \begin{bmatrix} 300 & 3{,}400 & 8{,}000 \\ 100 & 1{,}600 & 16{,}000 \end{bmatrix}$

b. After 4 months

51. a. $A = \begin{bmatrix} 440 & 190 \\ 950 & 950 \\ 1{,}790 & 200 \end{bmatrix}$ $D = \begin{bmatrix} -20 & 40 \\ 50 & 50 \\ 0 & 100 \end{bmatrix}$

2008 Tourism $= A + D = \begin{bmatrix} 420 & 230 \\ 1{,}000 & 1{,}000 \\ 1{,}790 & 300 \end{bmatrix}$

b. $\dfrac{1}{2}(A + B)$; $\begin{bmatrix} 430 & 210 \\ 975 & 975 \\ 1{,}790 & 250 \end{bmatrix}$

53. No; for two matrices to be equal, they must have the same dimension.   **55.** The ijth entry of the sum $A + B$ is obtained by adding the ijth entries of A and B.
57. It would have zeros down the main diagonal:

$A = \begin{bmatrix} 0 & \# & \# & \# & \# \\ \# & 0 & \# & \# & \# \\ \# & \# & 0 & \# & \# \\ \# & \# & \# & 0 & \# \\ \# & \# & \# & \# & 0 \end{bmatrix}$

The symbols # indicate arbitrary numbers.
59. $(A^T)_{ij} = A_{ji}$ **61.** Answers will vary.

a. $\begin{bmatrix} 0 & -4 \\ 4 & 0 \end{bmatrix}$ **b.** $\begin{bmatrix} 0 & -4 & 5 \\ 4 & 0 & 1 \\ -5 & -1 & 0 \end{bmatrix}$

63. The associativity of matrix addition is a consequence of the associativity of addition of numbers, since we add matrices by adding the corresponding entries (which are real numbers).
65. Answers will vary.

Section 4.2

1. [13]   **3.** [5/6]   **5.** $[-2y + z]$ **7.** Undefined
9. $[3 \quad 0 \quad -6 \quad -2]$ **11.** $[-6 \quad 37 \quad 7]$

13. $\begin{bmatrix} -4 & -7 & -1 \\ 9 & 17 & 0 \end{bmatrix}$ **15.** $\begin{bmatrix} 0 & 1 \\ 0 & 0 \end{bmatrix}$ **17.** $\begin{bmatrix} 1 & -1 \\ 1 & -1 \end{bmatrix}$

19. $\begin{bmatrix} 0 & 0 \\ 0 & 0 \end{bmatrix}$ **21.** Undefined **23.** $\begin{bmatrix} 1 & -5 & 3 \\ 0 & 0 & 9 \\ 0 & 4 & 1 \end{bmatrix}$

25. $\begin{bmatrix} 3 \\ -4 \\ 0 \\ 3 \end{bmatrix}$ **27.** $\begin{bmatrix} 0.23 & 5.36 & -21.65 \\ -13.18 & -5.82 & -16.62 \\ -11.21 & -9.9 & 0.99 \\ -2.1 & 2.34 & 2.46 \end{bmatrix}$

29. $A^2 = \begin{bmatrix} 0 & 0 & 1 & 2 \\ 0 & 0 & 0 & 1 \\ 0 & 0 & 0 & 0 \\ 0 & 0 & 0 & 0 \end{bmatrix}$; $A^3 = \begin{bmatrix} 0 & 0 & 0 & 1 \\ 0 & 0 & 0 & 0 \\ 0 & 0 & 0 & 0 \\ 0 & 0 & 0 & 0 \end{bmatrix}$;

$A^4 = \begin{bmatrix} 0 & 0 & 0 & 0 \\ 0 & 0 & 0 & 0 \\ 0 & 0 & 0 & 0 \\ 0 & 0 & 0 & 0 \end{bmatrix}$; $\ldots$; $A^{100} = \begin{bmatrix} 0 & 0 & 0 & 0 \\ 0 & 0 & 0 & 0 \\ 0 & 0 & 0 & 0 \\ 0 & 0 & 0 & 0 \end{bmatrix}$;

31. $\begin{bmatrix} 4 & -1 \\ -1 & -7 \end{bmatrix}$ **33.** $\begin{bmatrix} 4 & -1 \\ -12 & 2 \end{bmatrix}$

35. $\begin{bmatrix} -2 & 1 & -2 \\ 10 & -2 & 2 \\ -10 & 2 & -2 \end{bmatrix}$

37. $\begin{bmatrix} -2 + x - z & 2 - r & -6 + w \\ 10 + 2z & -2 + 2r & 10 \\ -10 - 2z & 2 - 2r & -10 \end{bmatrix}$

39. a.–d. $P^2 = P^4 = P^8 = P^{1{,}000} = \begin{bmatrix} 0.2 & 0.8 \\ 0.2 & 0.8 \end{bmatrix}$

41. a. $P^2 = \begin{bmatrix} 0.01 & 0.99 \\ 0 & 1 \end{bmatrix}$

b. $P^4 = \begin{bmatrix} 0.0001 & 0.9999 \\ 0 & 1 \end{bmatrix}$

c and d. $P^8 \approx P^{1{,}000} \approx \begin{bmatrix} 0 & 1 \\ 0 & 1 \end{bmatrix}$

43. a.–d. $P^2 = P^4 = P^8 = P^{1{,}000} = \begin{bmatrix} 0.3 & 0.3 & 0.4 \\ 0.3 & 0.3 & 0.4 \\ 0.3 & 0.3 & 0.4 \end{bmatrix}$

The rows of P are the same, and the entries in each row add up to 1. If P is any square matrix with identical rows such that the entries in each row add up to 1, then $P \cdot P = P$.
45. $2x - y + 4z = 3$; $-4x + \dfrac{3}{4}y + \dfrac{1}{3}z = -1$; $-3x = 0$
47. $x - y + w = -1$; $x + y + 2z + 4w = 2$

49. $\begin{bmatrix} 1 & -1 \\ 2 & -1 \end{bmatrix} \begin{bmatrix} x \\ y \end{bmatrix} = \begin{bmatrix} 4 \\ 0 \end{bmatrix}$

51. $\begin{bmatrix} 1 & 1 & -1 \\ 2 & 1 & 1 \\ \frac{3}{4} & 0 & \frac{1}{2} \end{bmatrix} \begin{bmatrix} x \\ y \\ z \end{bmatrix} = \begin{bmatrix} 8 \\ 4 \\ 1 \end{bmatrix}$

53. Revenue $=$ Price $\times$ Quantity $=$

$[15 \quad 10 \quad 12] \begin{bmatrix} 50 \\ 40 \\ 30 \end{bmatrix} = [1{,}510]$

55. $32.5 million
57. Revenue $=$ Quantity $\times$ Price $=$

$\begin{bmatrix} 700 & 1{,}300 & 2{,}000 \\ 400 & 300 & 500 \end{bmatrix} \begin{bmatrix} 30 \\ 10 \\ 15 \end{bmatrix} = \begin{bmatrix} 64{,}000 \\ 22{,}500 \end{bmatrix}$

59. $5,100 billion (or $5.1 trillion)
61. $D = N(F - M)$, where N is the income per person, and F and M are, respectively, the female and male populations in 2020; $400 billion
63. [1.2   1.0], which represents the amount, in billions of pounds, by which cheese production in north central states exceeded that in western states.
65. Number of foreclosures filings handled by firm = Percentage handled by firm × Total number = [8,460   8,860   9,140]
67. The number of foreclosures in California and Florida combined in each of the months shown.

69. $[\,1 \quad -1 \quad 1\,] \begin{bmatrix} 54,100 & 56,200 & 59,400 \\ 23,800 & 22,400 & 23,600 \\ 9,300 & 10,600 & 10,100 \end{bmatrix} \begin{bmatrix} 1 \\ 1 \\ 1 \end{bmatrix}$
$= [129,900]$

71. $\begin{bmatrix} 2 & 16 & 20 \\ 1 & 4 & 40 \end{bmatrix} \begin{bmatrix} 100 & 150 \\ 50 & 40 \\ 10 & 15 \end{bmatrix} = \begin{bmatrix} 1,200 & 1,240 \\ 700 & 910 \end{bmatrix}$

73. $AB = \begin{bmatrix} 29.6 \\ 85.5 \\ 97.5 \end{bmatrix}$ $AC = \begin{bmatrix} 22 & 7.6 \\ 47.5 & 38 \\ 89.5 & 8 \end{bmatrix}$

The entries of AB give the number of people from each of the three regions who settle in Australia or South Africa, while the entries in AC break those figures down further into settlers in South Africa and settlers in Australia.   **75.** [54.6   66.0   111.8   70.6]
77. Answers will vary. One example:

$A = [1 \quad 2]$, $B = \begin{bmatrix} 1 & 2 & 3 \\ 4 & 5 & 6 \end{bmatrix}$.

Another example: $A = [1]$, $B = [1 \quad 2]$
79. We finnd that the addition and multiplication of 1×1 matrices is identical to the addition and multiplication of numbers.   **81.** The claim is correct. Every matrix equation represents the equality of two matrices. When two matrices are equal, each of their corresponding entries must be equal. Equating the corresponding entries gives a system of equations.
83. Here is a possible scenario: costs of items A, B, and C in 2013 = [10   20   30], percentage increases in these costs in 2014 = [0.5   0.1   0.20], actual increases in costs = [10 × 0.5   20 × 0.1   30 × 0.20]
85. It produces a matrix whose ij entry is the product of the ij entries of the two matrices.

Section 4.3

1. Yes   **3.** Yes   **5.** No   **7.** $\begin{bmatrix} -1 & 1 \\ 2 & -1 \end{bmatrix}$ **9.** $\begin{bmatrix} 0 & 1 \\ 1 & 0 \end{bmatrix}$

11. $\begin{bmatrix} 1 & -1 \\ -1 & 2 \end{bmatrix}$ **13.** Singular   **15.** $\begin{bmatrix} 1 & -1 & 0 \\ 0 & 1 & -1 \\ 0 & 0 & 1 \end{bmatrix}$

17. $\begin{bmatrix} 1 & -1 & 1 \\ \frac{1}{2} & 0 & -\frac{1}{2} \\ -\frac{1}{2} & 1 & -\frac{1}{2} \end{bmatrix}$

19. $\begin{bmatrix} 1 & \frac{1}{3} & -\frac{1}{3} \\ 1 & -\frac{2}{3} & -\frac{1}{3} \\ -1 & \frac{1}{3} & \frac{2}{3} \end{bmatrix}$

21. Singular   **23.** $\begin{bmatrix} 0 & 1 & -2 & 1 \\ 0 & 1 & -1 & 0 \\ 1 & -1 & 2 & -1 \\ 0 & 1 & -1 & 1 \end{bmatrix}$

25. $\begin{bmatrix} 1 & -2 & 1 & 0 \\ 0 & 1 & -2 & 1 \\ 0 & 0 & 1 & -2 \\ 0 & 0 & 0 & 1 \end{bmatrix}$ **27.** -2; $\begin{bmatrix} \frac{1}{2} & \frac{1}{2} \\ \frac{1}{2} & -\frac{1}{2} \end{bmatrix}$

29. -2; $\begin{bmatrix} -2 & 1 \\ \frac{3}{2} & -\frac{1}{2} \end{bmatrix}$ **31.** $1/36$; $\begin{bmatrix} 6 & 6 \\ 0 & 6 \end{bmatrix}$

33. 0; Singular

35. $\begin{bmatrix} 0.38 & 0.45 \\ 0.49 & -0.41 \end{bmatrix}$ **37.** $\begin{bmatrix} 0.00 & -0.99 \\ 0.81 & 2.87 \end{bmatrix}$

39. Singular

41. $\begin{bmatrix} 91.35 & -8.65 & 0 & -71.30 \\ -0.07 & -0.07 & 0 & 2.49 \\ 2.60 & 2.60 & -4.35 & 1.37 \\ 2.69 & 2.69 & 0 & -2.10 \end{bmatrix}$

43. $(5/2, 3/2)$
45. $(6, -4)$ **47.** $(6, 6, 6)$ **49. a.** $(10, -5, -3)$
b. $(6, 1, 5)$ **c.** $(0, 0, 0)$ **51. a.** $10/3$ servings of beans, and $5/6$ slices of bread

b. $\begin{bmatrix} -1/2 & 1/6 \\ 7/8 & -5/24 \end{bmatrix} \begin{bmatrix} A \\ B \end{bmatrix} = \begin{bmatrix} -A/2 + B/6 \\ 7A/8 - 5B/24 \end{bmatrix}$; that is,

$-A/2 + B/6$ servings of beans and $7A/8 - 5B/24$ slices of bread   **53. a.** 100 batches of vanilla, 50 batches of mocha, 100 batches of strawberry **b.** 100 batches of vanilla, no mocha, 200 batches of strawberry

c. $\begin{bmatrix} 1 & -1/3 & -1/3 \\ -1 & 0 & 1 \\ 0 & 2/3 & -1/3 \end{bmatrix} \begin{bmatrix} A \\ B \\ C \end{bmatrix}$, or

$A - B/3 - C/3$ batches of vanilla, $-A + C$ batches of mocha, and $2B/3 - C/3$ batches of strawberry
55. $5,000 in SHPIX, $2,000 in RYURX, $2,000 in RYIHX   **57.** 100 shares of KT, 50 shares of IFF, 50 shares of QSII   **59.** [54.1   65.7   112.9   70.3]
61. a. $(-0.7071, 3.5355)$ **b.** R^2, R^3 **c.** R^{-1}
63. [37 81 40 80 15 45 40 96 29 59 4 8]
65. CORRECT ANSWER   **67.** (A)   **69.** The inverse does not exist; the matrix is singular. (If two rows of a matrix are the same, then row reducing it will lead to a row of zeros, and so it cannot be reduced to the identity.)

71. Calculation (See the Student Solutions Manual.)
73. When one or more of the d_i are zero. If that is the case, then the matrix $[D \mid I]$ easily reduces to a matrix that has a row of zeros on the left-hand portion, so that D is singular. Conversely, if none of the d_i are zero, then $[D \mid I]$ easily reduces to a matrix of the form $[I \mid E]$, showing that D is invertible.
75. $(AB)(B^{-1}A^{-1}) = A(BB^{-1})A^{-1} = AIA^{-1} = AA^{-1} = I$ **77.** If A has an inverse, then every system of equations $AX = B$ has a unique solution, namely $X = A^{-1}B$. But if A reduces to a matrix with a row of zeros, then such a system has either infinitely many solutions or no solution at all.

Section 4.4

1. -1 **3.** -0.25 **5.** $[0 \quad 0 \quad 1 \quad 0]$; $e = 2.25$
7. $[1 \quad 0 \quad 0]^T$ or $[0 \quad 1 \quad 0]^T$; $e = 1/4$

9.
$$\begin{array}{c} \\ a \\ b \end{array}\begin{array}{cc} p & r \\ \left[\begin{array}{cc} 1 & 10 \\ 2 & -4 \end{array}\right] \end{array}$$
11. $\begin{array}{c} c \\ 3[-1] \end{array}$ **13.** $\begin{array}{c} b \\ q\,[0] \end{array}$

15. Strictly determined. The row player's optimal strategy is a; the column player's optimal strategy is q; Value: 1   **17.** Not strictly determined Circle the row minima and box the row maxima:

$$\begin{array}{c} \\ a \\ b \end{array}\begin{array}{ccc} p & q & r \\ \left[\begin{array}{ccc} 2 & 0 & \boxed{-2} \\ \boxed{-1} & 3 & 0 \end{array}\right] \end{array} \qquad \begin{array}{c} \\ a \\ b \end{array}\begin{array}{ccc} p & q & r \\ \left[\begin{array}{ccc} \boxed{2} & 0 & -2 \\ -1 & \boxed{3} & \boxed{0} \end{array}\right] \end{array}.$$

Since no entry is both circled and boxed, there are no saddle points, and so the game is not strictly determined.

19. Not strictly determined
Circle the row minima and box the row maxima:

$$\begin{array}{c} \\ P \\ Q \\ R \\ S \end{array}\begin{array}{ccc} a & b & c \\ \left[\begin{array}{ccc} 1 & -1 & \boxed{-5} \\ 4 & \boxed{-4} & 2 \\ 3 & -3 & \boxed{-10} \\ 5 & \boxed{-5} & -4 \end{array}\right] \end{array} \qquad \begin{array}{c} \\ P \\ Q \\ R \\ S \end{array}\begin{array}{ccc} a & b & c \\ \left[\begin{array}{ccc} 1 & \boxed{-1} & -5 \\ 4 & -4 & \boxed{2} \\ 3 & -3 & -10 \\ \boxed{5} & -5 & -4 \end{array}\right] \end{array}.$$

Since no entry is both circled and boxed, there are no saddle points, and so the game is not strictly determined.

21. $R = [1/4 \quad 3/4]$, $C = [3/4 \quad 1/4]^T$, $e = -1/4$
23. $R = [3/4 \quad 1/4]$, $C = [3/4 \quad 1/4]^T$, $e = -5/4$
25. Row player: You; Column player: Your friend;

$$\begin{array}{c} \\ H \\ T \end{array}\begin{array}{cc} H & T \\ \left[\begin{array}{cc} -1 & 1 \\ 1 & -1 \end{array}\right] \end{array}$$

27. $F =$ France; $S =$ Sweden; $N =$ Norway

Your Opponent Defends

$$\text{You Invade} \quad \begin{array}{c} F \\ S \\ N \end{array}\begin{array}{ccc} F & S & N \\ \left[\begin{array}{ccc} -1 & 1 & 1 \\ 1 & -1 & 1 \\ 1 & 1 & -1 \end{array}\right] \end{array}$$

29. Row player: You, Column player: Your opponent; $B =$ Brakpan, $N =$ Nigel, $S =$ Springs;

Your Opponent

$$\text{You} \quad \begin{array}{c} B \\ N \\ S \end{array}\begin{array}{ccc} B & N & S \\ \left[\begin{array}{ccc} 0 & 0 & 1{,}000 \\ 0 & 0 & 1{,}000 \\ -1{,}000 & -1{,}000 & 0 \end{array}\right] \end{array}$$

31. P = PleasantTap; T = Thunder Rumble; S = Strike the Gold, N = None;

Winner

$$\text{You Bet} \quad \begin{array}{c} P \\ T \\ S \end{array}\begin{array}{cccc} P & T & S & N \\ \left[\begin{array}{cccc} 25 & -10 & -10 & -10 \\ -10 & 35 & -10 & -10 \\ -10 & -10 & 40 & -10 \end{array}\right] \end{array}$$

33. You can expect to lose 39 customers.
35. Option 2: Move to the suburbs.   **37. a.** About 66%
b. Yes; spend the whole night studying game theory; 75%
c. Game theory; 57.5%   **39. a.** Lay off 10 workers; cost: $40,000   **b.** 60 inches of snow, costing $350,000
c. Lay off 15 workers.   **41. a.** CE should charge $1,000, and GCS should charge $900; 15% gain in market share for CE.   **b.** CE should charge $1,200 (the more CE can charge for the same market, the better!).
43. Pablo vs. Noto; evenly matched   **45.** Both commanders should use the northern route; 2 days.
47. Confess

49. a. $\begin{array}{c} F \\ O \end{array}\begin{array}{cc} F & O \\ \left[\begin{array}{cc} 24 & 21 \\ 25 & 24 \end{array}\right] \end{array}$

b. Both candidates should visit Ohio, leaving Romney with a 24% chance of winning the election.
51. Allocate 1/7 of the budget to WISH and the rest (6/7) to WASH. Softex will lose approximately $2,860.
53. Like a saddle point in a payoff matrix, the center of a saddle is a low point (minimum height) in one direction and a high point (maximum) in a perpendicular direction.   **55.** Although there is a saddle point in the (2, 4) position, you would be wrong to use saddle points (based on the minimax criterion) to reach the conclusion that row strategy 2 is best. One reason is that the entries in the matrix do not represent payoffs, since high numbers of employees in an area do not necessarily represent benefit to the row player. Another reason for this is that there is no opponent deciding what your job will be in such a way as to force you into the least populated job.

57. If you strictly alternate the two strategies, the column player will know which pure strategy you will play on each move and can choose a pure strategy accordingly. For example, consider the game

$$\begin{array}{c} \; a\;\;\; b \\ \begin{array}{c} A \\ B \end{array} \left[\begin{array}{cc} 1 & 0 \\ 0 & 1 \end{array} \right]. \end{array}$$

By the analysis of Example 3 (or the symmetry of the game), the best strategy for the row player is [0.5 0.5] and the best strategy for the column player is $[0.5\ 0.5]^T$. This gives an expected value of 0.5 for the game. However, suppose that the row player alternates A and B strictly and that the column player catches on to this. Then, whenever the row player plays A the column player will play b, and whenever the row player plays B the column player will play a. This gives a payoff of 0 each time, worse for the row player than the expected value of 0.5.

Section 4.5

1. a. 0.8 **b.** 0.2 **c.** 0.05   **3.** $\begin{bmatrix} 0.2 & 0.1 \\ 0.5 & 0 \end{bmatrix}$

5. $[\,52{,}000 \quad 40{,}000\,]^T$ **7.** $[\,50{,}000 \quad 50{,}000\,]^T$

9. $[\,2{,}560 \quad 2{,}800 \quad 4{,}000\,]^T$

11. $[\,27{,}000 \quad 28{,}000 \quad 17{,}000\,]^T$

13. Increase of 100 units in each sector.

15. Increase of $[\,1.5 \quad 0.2 \quad 0.1\,]^T$; the ith column of $(I - A)^{-1}$ gives the change in production necessary to meet an increase in external demand of one unit for the product of Sector i.

17. $A = \begin{bmatrix} 0.2 & 0.4 & 0.5 \\ 0 & 0.8 & 0 \\ 0 & 0.2 & 0.5 \end{bmatrix}$

19. Main DR: $80,000, Bits & Bytes: $38,000

21. Equipment Sector production approximately $86,000 million, Components Sector production approximately $140,000 million   **23. a.** 0.006 **b.** textiles; clothing and footwear

25. Columns of

$$\begin{bmatrix} 1{,}140.99 & 2.05 & 13.17 & 20.87 \\ 332.10 & 1{,}047.34 & 26.05 & 111.18 \\ 0.12 & 0.13 & 1{,}031.19 & 1.35 \\ 93.88 & 95.69 & 215.50 & 1{,}016.15 \end{bmatrix}$$

(in millions of dollars)

27. a. $0.78 **b.** Other food products   **29.** It would mean that all of the sectors require neither their own product nor the product of any other sector.   **31.** It would mean that all of the output of that sector was used internally in the economy; none of the output was available for export and no importing was necessary.

33. If an entry in the matrix $(I - A)^{-1}$ is zero, then an increase in demand for one sector (the column sector) has no effect on the production of another sector (the row sector).   **35.** Usually, to produce one unit of one sector requires less than one unit of input from another. We would expect then that an increase in demand of one unit for one sector would require a smaller increase in production in another sector.

Chapter 4 Review

1. Undefined **3.** $\begin{bmatrix} 1 & 8 \\ 5 & 11 \\ 6 & 13 \end{bmatrix}$ **5.** $\begin{bmatrix} 1 & 3 \\ 2 & 3 \\ 3 & 3 \end{bmatrix}$ **7.** $\begin{bmatrix} 1 & -2 \\ 0 & 1 \end{bmatrix}$

9. $\begin{bmatrix} 2 & 4 \\ 1 & 12 \end{bmatrix}$ **11.** $\begin{bmatrix} 1 & 1 \\ 0 & 1 \end{bmatrix}$ **13.** $\begin{bmatrix} 1 & -1/2 & -5/2 \\ 0 & 1/4 & -1/4 \\ 0 & 0 & 1 \end{bmatrix}$

15. Singular

17. $\begin{bmatrix} 1 & 2 \\ 3 & 4 \end{bmatrix}\begin{bmatrix} x \\ y \end{bmatrix} = \begin{bmatrix} 0 \\ 2 \end{bmatrix}; \begin{bmatrix} x \\ y \end{bmatrix} = \begin{bmatrix} 2 \\ -1 \end{bmatrix}$

19. $\begin{bmatrix} 1 & 1 & 1 \\ 1 & 2 & 1 \\ 1 & 1 & 2 \end{bmatrix}\begin{bmatrix} x \\ y \\ z \end{bmatrix} = \begin{bmatrix} 2 \\ 3 \\ 1 \end{bmatrix}; \begin{bmatrix} x \\ y \\ z \end{bmatrix} = \begin{bmatrix} 2 \\ 1 \\ -1 \end{bmatrix}$

21. $R = [1 \quad 0 \quad 0], C = [0 \quad 1 \quad 0 \quad 0]^T, e = 1$

23. $R = [0 \quad 0.8 \quad 0.2], C = [0.2 \quad 0 \quad 0.8],$ $e = -0.2$

25. $\begin{bmatrix} 1{,}100 \\ 700 \end{bmatrix}$ **27.** $\begin{bmatrix} 48{,}125 \\ 22{,}500 \\ 10{,}000 \end{bmatrix}$

29. Inventory − Sales + Purchases =

$$\begin{bmatrix} 2{,}500 & 4{,}000 & 3{,}000 \\ 1{,}500 & 3{,}000 & 1{,}000 \end{bmatrix} - \begin{bmatrix} 300 & 500 & 100 \\ 100 & 600 & 200 \end{bmatrix} +$$

$$\begin{bmatrix} 400 & 400 & 300 \\ 200 & 400 & 300 \end{bmatrix} = \begin{bmatrix} 2{,}600 & 3{,}900 & 3{,}200 \\ 1{,}600 & 2{,}800 & 1{,}100 \end{bmatrix}$$

31. $N =$

$$\begin{bmatrix} 2{,}600 & 3{,}900 & 3{,}200 \\ 1{,}600 & 2{,}800 & 1{,}100 \end{bmatrix} - x\begin{bmatrix} 280 & 550 & 100 \\ 50 & 500 & 120 \end{bmatrix} +$$

$$x\begin{bmatrix} 400 & 400 & 300 \\ 200 & 400 & 300 \end{bmatrix} = \begin{bmatrix} 2{,}600 & 3{,}900 & 3{,}200 \\ 1{,}600 & 2{,}800 & 1{,}100 \end{bmatrix} +$$

$$x\begin{bmatrix} 120 & -150 & 200 \\ 150 & -100 & 180 \end{bmatrix}; 28 \text{ months from now (July 1)}$$

33. Revenue = Quantity × Price =

$$\begin{bmatrix} 280 & 550 & 100 \\ 50 & 500 & 120 \end{bmatrix}\begin{bmatrix} 5 \\ 6 \\ 5.5 \end{bmatrix} = \begin{bmatrix} 5{,}250 \\ 3{,}910 \end{bmatrix} \begin{array}{l} \text{Texas} \\ \text{Nevada} \end{array}$$

35. July 1: 1,000 shares, August 1: 2,000 shares, September 1: 2,000 shares

37. Loss = Number of shares × (Purchase price − Dividends − Selling price) = [1,000 2,000 2,000]

$$\left(\begin{bmatrix} 20 \\ 10 \\ 5 \end{bmatrix} - \begin{bmatrix} 0.10 \\ 0.10 \\ 0 \end{bmatrix} - \begin{bmatrix} 3 \\ 1 \\ 1 \end{bmatrix}\right) = [42,700]$$

39. $[2,000 \quad 4,000 \quad 4,000]\begin{bmatrix} 0.8 & 0.1 & 0.1 \\ 0.4 & 0.6 & 0 \\ 0.2 & 0 & 0.8 \end{bmatrix} =$

[4,000 2,600 3,400] **41.** The matrix shows that no JungleBooks customers switched directly to FarmerBooks, so the only way to get to FarmerBooks is via OHaganBooks. **43.** Go with the "3 for 1" promotion and gain 20,000 customers from JungleBooks. **45.** JungleBooks will go with "3 for 2" and OHaganBooks will go with Finite Math, resulting in a gain of 15,000 customers to OHaganBooks. **47.** Choose between the "3 for 1" and Finite Math promotions with probabilities 60% and 40%, respectively. You would expect to gain 12,000 customers from JungleBooks (if you played this game many times).

49. $A = \begin{bmatrix} 0.1 & 0.5 \\ 0.01 & 0.05 \end{bmatrix}$

51. $1,190 worth of paper, $1,802 worth of books

Chapter 5

Section 5.1

1.

Unbounded

3.

Unbounded

5.

Unbounded

7.

Unbounded

9.

Unbounded

11.

Unbounded

13.

Unbounded;
corner point: (2, 0)

15.

Unbounded;
corner points:
(2, 0), (0, 3)

17.

Bounded; corner points:
(5, 0), (10, 0), (10, 8),
(0, 8), (0, 5)

19.

Bounded; corner points:
(0, 0), (5, 0), (0, 5),
(2, 4), (4, 2)

21.

Unbounded; corner points:
(0, 10), (10, 0), (2, 6),
(6, 2)

23.

Unbounded;
corner points:(0, 0),
(0, 5/2), (3, 3/2)

25.

Unbounded;
corner point: (0, 0)

27.

29.

Corner point:
$(-7.74, 2.50)$

31.

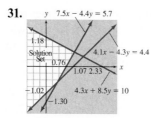

Corner points:
$(0.36, -0.68), (1.12, 0.61)$

33. $x = $ # quarts of Creamy Vanilla,
$y = $ # quarts of Continental Mocha

Corner points: $(0, 0), (250, 0), (0, 300), (200, 100)$

35. $x = $ # ounces of chicken, $y = $ # ounces of grain

Corner points: $(30, 0), (10, 50), (0, 100)$

37. $x = $ # servings of Mixed Cereal for Baby,
$y = $ # servings of Mango Tropical Fruit Dessert

Corner points: $(0, 7/4), (1, 1), (32/11, 0)$

39. $x = $ # dollars in PNF, $y = $ # dollars in FDMMX.

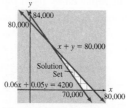

Corner points: $(70,000, 0), (80,000, 0), (20,000, 60,000)$

41. Let $x = $ number of shares of BOH; $y = $ number of shares of JPM.

Corner points: $(200, 400), (556, 0), (422, 0)$

43. $x = $ # full-page ads in Sports Illustrated,
$y = $ # full-page ads in GQ

Corner points: $(3, 7), (4, 3)$ (Rounded)

45. An example is $x \geq 0, y \geq 0, x + y \geq 1$.
47. The given triangle can be described as the solution set of the system $x \geq 0, y \geq 0, x + 2y \leq 2$.
49. Answers may vary. One limitation is that the method is only suitable for situations with two unknown quantities. Accuracy is also limited when graphing. **51. (C)   53. (B)   55.** There are no feasible solutions; that is, it is impossible to satisfy all the constraints. **57.** Answers will vary.

Section 5.2

1. $p = 6, x = 3, y = 3$ **3.** $c = 4, x = 2, y = 2$
5. $p = 24, x = 7, y = 3$ **7.** $p = 16, x = 4, y = 2$
9. $c = 1.8, x = 6, y = 2$ **11.** Max: $p = 16, x = 4$,
$y = 6$. Min: $p = 2, x = 2, y = 0$ **13.** No optimal solution; objective function unbounded **15.** $c = 28$;
$(x, y) = (14, 0)$ and $(6, 4)$ and the line connecting them **17.** $c = 3, x = 3, y = 2$ **19.** No solution; feasible region empty **21.** You should make 200 quarts of vanilla and 100 quarts of mocha. **23.** Ruff, Inc., should use 100 oz of grain and no chicken.
25. Feed your child 1 serving of cereal and 1 serving of dessert. **27.** Purchase 60 compact fluorescent light bulbs and 960 square feet of insulation for a saving of $312 per year in energy costs. **29.** Mix 5 servings of Cell-Tech and 6 servings of RiboForce HP for a cost of $20.60. **31.** Make 200 Dracula Salamis and 400 Frankenstein Sausages, for a profit of $1,400.
33. 30 spots on *WWE Raw* and 30 spots on *Family Guy* **35.** 88.89 shares of FDX and 100 shares of WU

37. 422.2 shares of BOH and no shares of JPM
39. He should instruct in diplomacy for 10 hours per week and in battle for 40 hours per week, giving a weekly profit of 2,400 ducats.   **41.** Gillian could expend a minimum of 360,000 pico-shirleys of energy by using 480 sleep spells and 160 shock spells. (There is actually a whole line of solutions joining the one above with $x = 2,880/7$, $y = 1,440/7$.)   **43.** 100 hours per week for new customers and 60 hours per week for old customers.   **45. (A)   47.** Every point along the line connecting them is also an optimal solution.
49. Answers may vary. Maximize $p = x + y$ subject to $x + y \le 10$; $x + y \ge 11$, $x \ge 0$, $y \ge 0$.
51. Answers may vary.
53. A simple example is the following: Maximize profit $p = 2x + y$ subject to $x \ge 0$, $y \ge 0$. Then p can be made as large as we like by choosing large values of x and/or y. Thus there is no optimal solution to the problem.   **55.** Mathematically, this means that there are infinitely many possible solutions: one for each point along the line joining the two corner points in question. In practice, select those points with integer solutions (since x and y must be whole numbers in this problem) that are in the feasible region and close to this line, and choose the one that gives the largest profit.   **57.** Proof

Section 5.3

1. $p = 8$; $x = 4$, $y = 0$ **3.** $p = 4$; $x = 4$, $y = 0$
5. $p = 80$; $x = 10$, $y = 0$, $z = 10$
7. $p = 53$; $x = 5$, $y = 0$, $z = 3$
9. $z = 14,500$; $x_1 = 0$, $x_2 = 500/3$, $x_3 = 5,000/3$
11. $p = 6$; $x = 2$, $y = 1$, $z = 0$, $w = 3$
13. $p = 7$; $x = 1$, $y = 0$, $z = 2$, $w = 0$, $v = 4$
(or: $x = 1$, $y = 0$, $z = 2$, $w = 1$, $v = 3$.)
15. $p = 21$; $x = 0$, $y = 2.27$, $z = 5.73$
17. $p = 4.52$; $x = 1$, $y = 0$, $z = 0.67$, $w = 1.52$; or: $x = 1.67$, $y = 0.67$, $z = 0$, $w = 1.52$ **19.** $p = 7.7$; $x = 1.1$, $y = 0$, $z = 2.2$, $w = 0$, $v = 4$ **21.** You should purchase 500 calculus texts, no history texts, and no marketing texts. The maximum profit is $5,000 per semester.   **23.** The company can make a maximum profit of $650 by making 100 gallons of PineOrange, 200 gallons of PineKiwi, and 150 gallons of OrangeKiwi.   **25.** The department should offer no Ancient History, 30 sections of Medieval History, and 15 sections of Modern History, for a profit of $1,050,000. There will be 500 students without classes, but all sections and professors are used.   **27.** Plant 80 acres of tomatoes and leave the other 20 acres unplanted. This will give you a profit of $160,000.   **29.** It can make a profit of $10,000 by selling 1,000 servings

of granola, 500 servings of nutty granola, and no nuttiest granola. It is left with 2,000 oz almonds.
31. Allocate 5 million gals to process A and 45 million gals to process C. Another solution: Allocate 10 million gals to process B and 40 million gals to process C.
33. Use 15 servings of RiboForce HP and none of the others for a maximum of 75 g creatine.   **35.** She is right; you should buy 142.9 shares of DO and no others.   **37.** Allocate $2,250,000 to automobile loans, $500,000 to signature loans, and $2,250,000 to any combination of furniture loans and other secured loans.
39. Invest $75,000 in Universal, none in the rest. Another optimal solution is: Invest $18,750 in Universal, and $75,000 in EMI.   **41.** Tucson to Honolulu: 290 boards; Tucson to Venice Beach: 330 boards; Toronto to Honolulu: 0 boards; Toronto to Venice Beach: 200 boards, giving 820 boards shipped.
43. Fly 10 people from Chicago to Los Angeles, 5 people from Chicago to New York, and 10 people from Denver to New York.   **45.** Yes; the given problem can be stated as: Maximize $p = 3x - 2y$ subject to $-x + y - z \le 0$, $x - y - z \le 6$, $x \ge 0$, $y \ge 0$, $z \ge 0$.   **47.** The graphical method applies only to LP problems in two unknowns, whereas the simplex method can be used to solve LP problems with any number of unknowns.   **49.** She is correct. There are only two constraints, so there can be only two active variables, giving two or fewer nonzero values for the unknowns at each stage.   **51.** A basic solution to a system of linear equations is a solution in which all the nonpivotal variables are taken to be zero; that is, all variables whose values are arbitrary are assigned the value zero. To obtain a basic solution for a given system of linear equations, one can row reduce the associated augmented matrix, write down the general solution, and then set all the parameters (variables with "arbitrary" values) equal to zero.   **53.** No. Let us assume for the sake of simplicity that all the pivots are 1s. (They may certainly be changed to 1s without affecting the value of any of the variables.) Because the entry at the bottom of the pivot column is negative, the bottom row gets replaced by itself plus a positive multiple of the pivot row. The value of the objective function (bottom-right entry) is thus replaced by itself plus a positive multiple of the nonnegative rightmost entry of the pivot row. Therefore, it cannot decrease.

Section 5.4

1. $p = 20/3$; $x = 4/3$, $y = 16/3$ **3.** $p = 850/3$; $x = 50/3$, $y = 25/3$ **5.** $p = 750$; $x = 0$, $y = 150$, $z = 0$ **7.** $p = 450$; $x = 10$, $y = 10$, $z = 10$

9. $p = 260/3$; $x = 50/3$, $y = 0$, $z = 70/3$, $w = 0$
11. $c = 80$; $x = 20/3$, $y = 20/3$
13. $c = 100$; $x = 0$, $y = 100$, $z = 0$
15. $c = 111$; $x = 1$, $y = 1$, $z = 1$
17. $c = 200$; $x = 200$, $y = 0$, $z = 0$, $w = 0$
19. $p = 136.75$; $x = 0$, $y = 25.25$, $z = 0$, $w = 15.25$
21. $c = 66.67$; $x = 0$, $y = 66.67$, $z = 0$
23. $c = -250$; $x = 0$, $y = 500$, $z = 500$,
$w = 1,500$ **25.** Plant 100 acres of tomatoes and no other crops. This will give you a profit of $200,000. (You will be using all 100 acres of your farm.)
27. 10 mailings to the East Coast, none to the Midwest, 10 to the West Coast. Cost: $900. Another solution resulting in the same cost is no mailings to the East Coast, 15 to the Midwest, none to the West Coast.   **29.** 10,000 quarts of orange juice and 2,000 quarts of orange concentrate   **31.** Sell 25,000 regional music albums, 10,000 pop/rock music albums, and 5,000 tropical music albums per day for a maximum revenue of $195,000.   **33.** One serving of cereal, one serving of juice, and no dessert!   **35.** 15 bundles from Nadir, 5 from Sonny, and none from Blunt. Cost: $70,000. Another solution resulting in the same cost is 10 bundles from Nadir, none from Sonny, and 10 from Blunt.   **37.** Mix 6 servings of Riboforce HP and 10 servings of Creatine Transport for a cost of $15.60.   **39. a.** Build 1 convention-style hotel, 4 vacation-style hotels, and 2 small motels. The total cost will amount to $188 million.   **b.** Because 20% of this is $37.6 million, you will still be covered by the subsidy.   **41.** Tucson to Honolulu: 500 boards/week; Tucson to Venice Beach: 120 boards/week; Toronto to Honolulu: 0 boards/week; Toronto to Venice Beach: 410 boards/week. Minimum weekly cost is $9,700.
43. $2,500 from Congressional Integrity Bank, $0 from Citizens' Trust, $7,500 from Checks R Us.
45. Fly 5 people from Chicago to LA, 15 from Chicago to New York, 5 from Denver to LA, none from Denver to New York at a total cost of $4,000.
47. Hire no more cardiologists, 12 rehabilitation specialists, and 5 infectious disease specialists.
49. The solution $x = 0$, $y = 0$, . . . , represented by the initial tableau may not be feasible. In Phase I we use pivoting to arrive at a basic solution that is feasible.   **51.** The basic solution corresponding to the initial tableau has all the unknowns equal to zero, and this is not a feasible solution because it does not satisfy the given inequality.   **53. (C)**   **55.** Answers may vary. Examples are Exercises 1 and 2.
57. Answers may vary. A simple example is:
Maximize $p = x + y$ subject to $x + y \leq 10$,
$x + y \geq 20$, $x \geq 0$, $y \geq 0$.

Section 5.5

1. Minimize $c = 6s + 2t$ subject to $s - t \geq 2$,
$2s + t \geq 1$, $s \geq 0$, $t \geq 0$
3. Maximize $p = 100x + 50y$ subject to $x + 2y \leq 2$,
$x + y \leq 1$, $x \leq 3$, $x \geq 0$, $y \geq 0$.   **5.** Minimize
$c = 3s + 4t + 5u + 6v$ subject to $s + u + v \geq 1$,
$s + t + v \geq 1$, $s + t + u \geq 1$, $t + u + v \geq 1$,
$s \geq 0$, $t \geq 0$, $u \geq 0$, $v \geq 0$.   **7.** Maximize
$p = 1,000x + 2,000y + 500z$ subject to $5x + z \leq 1$,
$-x + z \leq 3$, $y \leq 1$, $x - y \leq 0$, $x \geq 0$, $y \geq 0$, $z \geq 0$.
9. $c = 4$; $s = 2$, $t = 2$ **11.** $c = 80$; $s = 20/3$,
$t = 20/3$ **13.** $c = 1.8$; $s = 6$, $t = 2$
15. $c = 25$; $s = 5$, $t = 15$ **17.** $c = 30$; $s = 30$, $t = 0$,
$u = 0$ **19.** $c = 100$; $s = 0$, $t = 100$, $u = 0$
21. $c = 30$; $s = 10$, $t = 10$, $u = 10$
23. $R = [3/5 \quad 2/5]$, $C = [2/5 \quad 3/5 \quad 0]^T$, $e = 1/5$
25. $R = [1/4 \quad 0 \quad 3/4]$, $C = [1/2 \quad 0 \quad 1/2]^T$,
$e = 1/2$ **27.** $R = [0 \quad 3/11 \quad 3/11 \quad 5/11]$,
$C = [8/11 \quad 0 \quad 2/11 \quad 1/11]^T$, $e = 9/11$
29. 4 ounces each of fish and cornmeal, for a total cost of 40¢ per can; 5/12¢ per gram of protein, 5/12¢ per gram of fat.   **31.** 100 oz of grain and no chicken, for a total cost of $1; 1/2¢ per gram of protein, 0¢ per gram of fat.   **33.** One serving of cereal, one serving of juice, and no dessert! for a total cost of 37¢; 1/6¢ per calorie and 17/120¢ per % U.S. RDA of vitamin C.
35. 10 mailings to the East coast, none to the Midwest, 10 to the West Coast. Cost: $900; 20¢ per Democrat and 40¢ per Republican. OR 15 mailings to the Midwest and no mailing to the coasts. Cost: $900; 20¢ per Democrat and 40¢ per Republican.
37. Gillian should use 480 sleep spells and 160 shock spells, costing 360,000 pico-shirleys of energy OR 2,880/7 sleep spells and 1,440/7 shock spells.
39. T. N. Spend should spend about 73% of the days in Littleville, 27% in Metropolis, and skip Urbantown. T. L. Down should spend about 91% of the days in Littleville, 9% in Metropolis, and skip Urbantown. The expected outcome is that T. L. Down will lose about 227 votes per day of campaigning.   **41.** Each player should show one finger with probability 1/2, two fingers with probability 1/3, and three fingers with probability 1/6. The expected outcome is that player A will win 2/3 point per round, on average.   **43.** Write moves as (x, y), where x represents the number of regiments sent to the first location and y represents the number sent to the second location. Colonel Blotto should play $(0, 4)$ with probability 4/9, $(2, 2)$ with probability 1/9, and $(4, 0)$ with probability 4/9. Captain Kije has several optimal strategies, one of which is to play $(0, 3)$ with probability 1/30, $(1, 2)$ with probability 8/15, $(2, 1)$ with probability 16/45,

and (3, 0) with probability 7/90. The expected outcome is that Colonel Blotto will win 14/9 points on average.   **45.** The dual of a standard minimization problem satisfying the nonnegative objective condition is a standard maximization problem, which can be solved using the standard simplex algorithm, thus avoiding the need to do Phase I.   **47.** Answers will vary. An example is: Minimize $c = x - y$ subject to $x - y \geq 100$, $x + y \geq 200$, $x \geq 0$, $y \geq 0$. This problem can be solved using the techniques in Section 5.4.   **49.** If the given problem is a standard minimization problem satisfying the nonnegative objective condition, its dual is a standard maximization problem, and so can be solved using a single-phase simplex method. Otherwise, dualizing may not save any labor, since the dual will not be a standard maximization problem.

Chapter 5 Review

1.

Unbounded

3.

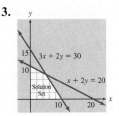

Bounded; corner points: (0, 0), (0, 10), (5, 15/2), (10, 0)

5. $p = 21$; $x = 9$, $y = 3$ **7.** $c = 22$; $x = 8$, $y = 6$
9. $p = 45$; $x = 0$, $y = 15$, $z = 15$
11. $p = 220$; $x = 20$, $y = 20$, $z = 60$
13. $c = 30$; $x = 30$, $y = 0$, $z = 0$
15. No solution; feasible region unbounded
17. $c = 50$; $x = 20$, $y = 10$, $z = 0$, $w = 20$, OR $x = 30$, $y = 0$, $z = 0$, $w = 20$
19. $c = 60$; $x = 24$, $y = 12$ OR $x = 0$, $y = 60$
21. $c = 20$; $x = 0$, $y = 20$
23. $R = [1/2 \quad 1/2 \quad 0]$, $C = [0 \quad 1/3 \quad 2/3]^T$, $e = 0$
25. $R = [1/27 \quad 7/9 \quad 5/27]$,
$C = [8/27 \quad 5/27 \quad 14/27]^T$, $e = 8/27$
27. (A)   **29.** 35   **31.** 400 packages from each for a minimum cost of $52,000   **33. a.** (B), (D) **b.** 450 packages from Duffin House, 375 from Higgins Press for a minimum cost of $52,500   **35.** 220 shares of EEE and 20 shares of RRR. The minimum total risk index is 500.   **37.** 240 Sprinkles, 120 Storms, and no Hurricanes   **39.** Order 600 packages from Higgins and none from the others, for a total cost of $90,000.
41. a. Let $x = $ # science credits, $y = $ # fine arts credits, $z = $ # liberal arts credits, and $w = $ # math credits.

Minimize $C = 300x + 300y + 200z + 200w$ subject to: $x + y + z + w \geq 120$; $x - y \geq 0$; $-2x + w \leq 0$; $-y + 3z - 3w \leq 0$; $x \geq 0$, $y \geq 0$, $z \geq 0$, $w \geq 0$.
b. Billy-Sean should take the following combination: Sciences—24 credits, Fine Arts—no credits, Liberal Arts—48 credits, Mathematics—48 credits, for a total cost of $26,400.   **43.** Smallest cost is $20,000; New York to OHaganBooks.com: 600 packages, New York to FantasyBooks.com: 0 packages, Illinois to OHaganbooks.com: 0 packages, Illinois to FantasyBooks.com: 200 packages.
45. FantasyBooks.com should choose between "2 for 1" and "3 for 2" with probabilities 20% and 80%, respectively. OHaganBooks.com should choose between "3 for 1" and "Finite Math" with probabilities 60% and 40%, respectively. OHaganBooks.com expects to gain 12,000 customers from FantasyBooks.com.

Chapter 6

Section 6.1

1. $F = \{\text{spring, summer, fall, winter}\}$
3. $I = \{1, 2, 3, 4, 5, 6\}$ **5.** $A = \{1, 2, 3\}$
7. $B = \{2, 4, 6, 8\}$ **9. a.** $S = \{(\text{H, H}), (\text{H, T}), (\text{T, H}),$
$(\text{T, T})\}$ **b.** $S = \{(\text{H, H}), (\text{H, T}), (\text{T, T})\}$
11. $S = \{(1, 5), (2, 4), (3, 3), (4, 2), (5, 1)\}$
13. $S = \{(1, 5), (2, 4), (3, 3)\}$ **15.** $S = \emptyset$
17.

19.

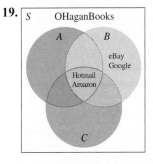

21. A **23.** A **25.** {June, Janet, Jill, Justin, Jeffrey, Jello, Sally, Solly, Molly, Jolly}   **27.** {Jello}   **29.** $\emptyset$
31. {Jello}   **33.** {Janet, Justin, Jello, Sally, Solly,

Molly, Jolly}   **35.** {(small, triangle), (small, square), (medium, triangle), (medium, square), (large, triangle), (large, square)}   **37.** {(small, blue), (small, green), (medium, blue), (medium, green), (large, blue), (large, green)}

39.

	A	B	C
1		Triangle	Square
2	Blue	Blue Triangle	Blue Square
3	Green	Green Triangle	Green Square

41.

	A	B	C
1		Blue	Green
2	Small	Small Blue	Small Green
3	Medium	Medium Blue	Medium Green
4	Large	Large Blue	Large Green

43. $B \times A = \{$1H, 1T, 2H, 2T, 3H, 3T, 4H, 4T, 5H, 5T, 6H, 6T$\}$
45. $A \times A \times A = \{$HHH, HHT, HTH, HTT, THH, THT, TTH, TTT$\}$
47. {(1,1), (1,3), (1,5), (3,1), (3,3), (3,5), (5,1), (5,3), (5,5)}   **49.** $\emptyset$ **51.** {(1,1), (1,3), (1,5), (3,1), (3,3), (3,5), (5,1), (5,3), (5,5), (2,2), (2,4), (2,6), (4,2), (4,4), (4,6), (6,2), (6,4), (6,6)}   **61.** $A \cap B = \{$Acme, Crafts$\}$
63. $B \cup C = \{$Acme, Brothers, Crafts, Dion, Effigy, Global, Hilbert$\}$ **65.** $A' \cap C = \{$Dion, Hilbert$\}$
67. $A \cap B' \cap C' = \emptyset$
69. {2003, 2004, 2005, 2006} $\times$ {Sail Boats, Motor Boats, Yachts}

	A	B	C	D
1		**Sail Boats**	**Motor Boats**	**Yachts**
2	**2003**	(2003 Sail Boats)	(2003 Motor Boats)	(2003 Yachts)
3	**2004**	(2004 Sail Boats)	(2004 Motor Boats)	(2004 Yachts)
4	**2005**	(2005 Sail Boats)	(2005 Motor Boats)	(2005 Yachts)
5	**2006**	(2006 Sail Boats)	(2006 Motor Boats)	(2006 Yachts)

71. $I \cup J$ **73.** (B)   **75.** Answers may vary.
Let $A = \{1\}$, $B = \{2\}$, and $C = \{1, 2\}$.
Then $(A \cap B) \cup C = \{1, 2\}$ but $A \cap (B \cup C) = \{1\}$.
In general, $A \cap (B \cup C)$ must be a subset of A, but $(A \cap B) \cup C$ need not be; also, $(A \cap B) \cup C$ must contain C as a subset, but $A \cap (B \cup C)$ need not.
77. A universal set is a set containing all "things" currently under consideration. When discussing sets of positive integers, the universe might be the set of all positive integers, or the set of all integers (positive, negative, and 0), or any other set containing the set of all positive integers.   **79.** A is the set of suppliers who deliver components on time, B is the set of suppliers

whose components are known to be of high quality, and C is the set of suppliers who do not promptly replace defective components.   **81.** Let $A = \{$movies that are violent$\}$, $B = \{$movies that are shorter than two hours$\}$, $C = \{$movies that have a tragic ending$\}$, and $D = \{$movies that have an unexpected ending$\}$. The given sentence can be rewritten as "She prefers movies in $A' \cap B \cap (C \cup D)'$." It can also be rewritten as "She prefers movies in $A' \cap B \cap C' \cap D'$."
83. Removing the comma would cause the statement to be ambiguous, as it could then correspond to either WWII $\cup$ (Comix $\cap$ Aliens$'$) or to (WWII $\cup$ Comix) $\cap$ Aliens$'$. (See Exercise 76.)

Section 6.2

1. 9   **3.** 7   **5.** 4   **7.** $n(A \cup B) = 7$,
$n(A) + n(B) - n(A \cap B) = 4 + 5 - 2 = 7$
9. 4   **11.** 18   **13.** 72   **15.** 60   **17.** 20   **19.** 6   **21.** 9
23. 4   **25.** $n((A \cap B)') = 9$
$n(A') + n(B') - n((A \cup B)') = 6 + 7 - 4 = 9$

27.

29.

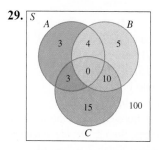

31. 115.4 million   **33.** 2   **35.** $C \cap N$ is the set of authors who are both successful and new. $C \cup N$ is the set of authors who are either successful or new (or both). $n(C) = 30$; $n(N) = 20$; $n(C \cap N) = 5$; $n(C \cup N) = 45$; $45 = 30 + 20 - 5$ **37.** $C \cap N'$ is the set of authors who are successful but not new. $n(C \cap N') = 25$ **39.** 31.25%; 83.33%
41. $M \cap C$; $n(M \cap C) = 1.1$ million
43. $B \cap T'$; $n(B \cap T') = 3.1$ million
45. $B \cap (W \cup M)$; $n(B \cap (W \cup M)) = 2.3$ million
47. $V \cap I'$; $n(V \cap I') = 15$ **49.** 80; The number of stocks that were either not pharmaceutical stocks, or were unchanged in value after a year (or both).

51. $3/8$; the fraction of Internet stocks that increased in value   **53. a.** 931 **b.** 382

55. a.

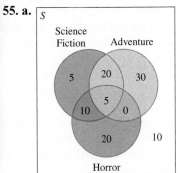

b. 37.5%   **57.** 17   **59.** $n(A) < n(B)$ **61.** The number of elements in the Cartesian product of two finite sets is the product of the number of elements in the two sets.   **65.** When $A \cap B \neq \emptyset$ **67.** When $B \subseteq A$ **69.** $n(A \cup B \cup C) = n(A) + n(B) + n(C) - n(A \cap B) - n(B \cap C) - n(A \cap C) + n(A \cap B \cap C)$

Section 6.3

1. 10   **3.** 30   **5.** 6 outcomes   **7.** 15 outcomes
9. 13 outcomes   **11.** 25 outcomes   **13.** 4   **15.** 93
17. 16   **19.** 30   **21.** 13   **23.** 18   **25.** 25,600
27. 3,381   **29. a.** 288 **b.** 288   **31.** 256   **33.** 10
35. 286   **37.** 4   **39. a.** 8,000,000 **b.** 30,000
c. 4,251,528   **41. a.** $4^3 = 64$ **b.** 4^n **c.** $4^{2.1 \times 10^{10}}$
43. a. $16^6 = 16,777,216$ **b.** $16^3 = 4,096$
c. $16^2 = 256$ **d.** 766
45. $(10 \times 9 \times 8 \times 7 \times 6 \times 5 \times 4) \times (8 \times 7 \times 6 \times 5)$
$= 1,016,064,000$ possible casts   **47. a.** $26^3 \times 10^3 =$
$17,576,000$ **b.** $26^2 \times 23 \times 10^3 = 15,548,000$
c. $15,548,000 - 3 \times 10^3 = 15,545,000$
49. a. 4   **b.** 4   **c.** There would be an infinite
number of routes.   **51. a.** 72   **b.** 36   **53.** 96
55. a. 36 **b.** 37   **57.** Step 1: Choose a day of the week on
which Jan. 1 will fall: 7 choices. Step 2: Decide whether
or not it is a leap year; 2 choices. Total: $7 \times 2 = 14$
possible calendars.   **59.** 1,900   **61.** Step 1: Choose a
position in the left-right direction; m choices. Step 2:
Choose a position in the front-back direction; n choices.
Step 3: Choose a position in the up-down direction; r
choices. Hence, there are $m \cdot n \cdot r$ possible outcomes.
63. 4   **65.** Cartesian product   **67.** The decision algorithm
produces every pair of shirts twice, first in one order and
then in the other.   **69.** Think of placing the five squares
in a row of five empty slots. Step 1: Choose a slot for the
blue square; five choices. Step 2: Choose a slot for the
green square; four choices. Step 3: Choose the remaining three slots for the yellow squares; one choice.
Hence, there are 20 possible five-square sequences.

Section 6.4

1. 720   **3.** 56   **5.** 360   **7.** 15   **9.** 3   **11.** 45   **13.** 20
15. 4,950   **17.** 360   **19.** 35   **21.** 120   **23.** 120
25. 20   **27.** 60   **29.** 210   **31.** 7   **33.** 35   **35.** 24
37. 126   **39.** 196   **41.** 105

43. $\dfrac{C(30, 5) \times 5^{25}}{6^{30}} \approx 0.192$

45. $\dfrac{C(30, 15) \times 3^{15} \times 3^{15}}{6^{30}} \approx 0.144$

47. $C(11, 1)C(10, 4)C(6, 4)C(2, 2)$
49. $C(11, 2)C(9, 1)C(8, 1)C(7, 3)C(4, 1)$
$C(3, 1)C(2, 1)C(1, 1)$
51. $C(10, 2)C(8, 4)C(4, 1)C(3, 1)C(2, 1)C(1, 1)$
53. 24   **55.** $C(13, 2)C(4, 2)C(4, 2) \times 44 = 123,552$
57. $13 \times C(4, 2)C(12, 3) \times 4 \times 4 \times 4 = 1,098,240$
59. 10,200   **61. a.** 252 **b.** 20 **c.** 26   **63. a.** 300 **b.** 3
c. 1 in 100 or .01   **65. a.** 210 **b.** 91 **c.** No   **67. a.** 23!
b. 18! **c.** $19 \times 18!$ **69.** (A)   **71.** (D)   **73. a.** 9,880
b. 1,560 **c.** 11,480
75. a. $C(20, 2) = 190$ **b.** $C(n, 2)$
77. The multiplication principle; it can be used to solve
all problems that use the formulas for permutations.
79. (A), (D)   **81.** A permutation. Changing the order
in a list of driving instructions can result in a different
outcome; for instance, "1. Turn left. 2. Drive one
mile." and "1. Drive one mile. 2. Turn left." will take
you to different locations.   **83.** Urge your friend not to
focus on formulas, but instead learn to formulate decision algorithms and use the principles of counting.
85. It is ambiguous on the following point: Are the
three students to play different characters, or are they to
play a group of three, such as "three guards"? This
should be made clear in the exercise.

Chapter 6 Review

1. $N = \{-3, -2, -1\}$ **3.** $S = \{(1, 2), (1, 3), (1, 4),$
$(1, 5), (1, 6), (2, 1), (2, 3), (2, 4), (2, 5), (2, 6), (3, 1),$
$(3, 2), (3, 4), (3, 5), (3, 6), (4, 1), (4, 2), (4, 3), (4, 5),$
$(4, 6), (5, 1), (5, 2), (5, 3), (5, 4), (5, 6), (6, 1), (6, 2),$
$(6, 3), (6, 4), (6, 5)\}$ **5.** $A \cup B' = \{a, b, d\},$
$A \times B' = \{(a, a), (a, d), (b, a), (b, d)\}$ **7.** $A \times B$
9. $(P \cap E' \cap Q)'$ or $P' \cup E \cup Q'$ **11.** $n(A \cup B) =$
$n(A) + n(B) - n(A \cap B), n(C') = n(S) - n(C); 100$
13. $n(A \times B) = n(A)n(B), n(A \cup B) = n(A) +$
$n(B) - n(A \cap B), n(A') = n(S) - n(A); 21$
15. $C(12, 1)C(4, 2)C(11, 3)C(4, 1)C(4, 1)C(4, 1)$
17. $C(4, 1)C(10, 1)$ **19.** 6   **21.** $C(4, 4)C(8, 1) = 8$
23. $C(3, 2)C(9, 3) + C(3, 3)C(9, 2) = 288$
25. The set of books that are either sci-fi or stored

in Texas (or both); $n(S \cup T) = 112{,}000$ **27.** The set of books that are either stored in California or not sci-fi; $n(C \cup S') = 175{,}000$ **29.** The romance books that are also horror books or stored in Texas; $n(R \cap (T \cup H)) = 20{,}000$ **31.** 1,000
33. FarmerBooks.com; 1,800   **35.** FarmerBooks.com; 5,400   **37.** $26 \times 26 \times 26 = 17{,}576$
39. $26 \times 25 \times 9 \times 10 = 58{,}500$ **41.** 60,000
43. 19,600

Chapter 7

Section 7.1

1. $S = \{HH, HT, TH, TT\}$; $E = \{HH, HT, TH\}$
3. $S = \{HHH, HHT, HTH, HTT, THH, THT, TTH, TTT\}$; $E = \{HTT, THT, TTH, TTT\}$

5. $S = \left\{ \begin{array}{l} (1, 1), (1, 2), (1, 3), (1, 4), (1, 5), (1, 6), \\ (2, 1), (2, 2), (2, 3), (2, 4), (2, 5), (2, 6), \\ (3, 1), (3, 2), (3, 3), (3, 4), (3, 5), (3, 6), \\ (4, 1), (4, 2), (4, 3), (4, 4), (4, 5), (4, 6), \\ (5, 1), (5, 2), (5, 3), (5, 4), (5, 5), (5, 6), \\ (6, 1), (6, 2), (6, 3), (6, 4), (6, 5), (6, 6) \end{array} \right\}$;

$E = \{(1, 4), (2, 3), (3, 2), (4, 1)\}$

7. $S = \left\{ \begin{array}{l} (1, 1), (1, 2), (1, 3), (1, 4), (1, 5), (1, 6), \\ (2, 2), (2, 3), (2, 4), (2, 5), (2, 6), \\ (3, 3), (3, 4), (3, 5), (3, 6), \\ (4, 4), (4, 5), (4, 6), \\ (5, 5), (5, 6), \\ (6, 6) \end{array} \right\}$;

$E = \{(1, 3), (2, 2)\}$
9. S as in Exercise 7; $E = \{(2, 2), (2, 3), (2, 5), (3, 3),$ $(3, 5), (5, 5)\}$ **11.** $S = \{m, o, z, a, r, t\}$: $E = \{o, a\}$
13. $S = \{(s, o), (s, r), (s, e), (o, s), (o, r), (o, e), (r, s),$ $(r, o), (r, e), (e, s), (e, o), (e, r)\}$; $E = \{(o, s), (o, r),$ $(o, e), (e, s), (e, o), (e, r)\}$ **15.** $S = \{01, 02, 03, 04,$ $10, 12, 13, 14, 20, 21, 23, 24, 30, 31, 32, 34, 40, 41,$ $42, 43\}$; $E = \{10, 20, 21, 30, 31, 32, 40, 41, 42, 43\}$
17. $S = \{$domestic car, imported car, van, antique car, antique truck$\}$; $E = \{$van, antique truck$\}$
19. a. All sets of 4 gummy candies chosen from the packet of 12 **b.** All sets of four gummy candies in which two are strawberry and two are black currant
21. a. All lists of 15 people chosen from 20 **b.** All lists of 15 people chosen from 20, in which Hillary Clinton occupies the eleventh position
23. $A \cap B$; $n(A \cap B) = 1$ **25.** B'; $n(B') = 33$
27. $B' \cap D'$; $n(B' \cap D') = 2$
29. $C \cup B$; $n(C \cup B) = 12$
31. $W \cap I$ **33.** $E \cup I'$ **35.** $I \cup (W \cap E')$
37. $(I \cup W) \cap E'$ **39.** 56; 4
41. $C(4, 1)\,C(2, 1)\,C(2, 1) = 16$

43. $E = \{$Pacific, Mountain, South Atlantic$\}$
45. $E \cup F$ is the event that you choose a region that saw a decrease in housing prices of 7% or more or is on the east coast. $E \cup F = \{$Pacific, Mountain, New England, Middle Atlantic, South Atlantic$\}$. $E \cap F$ is the event that you choose a region that saw a decrease in housing prices of 7% or more and is on the east coast. $E \cap F = \{$South Atlantic$\}$.   **47. a.** Not mutually exclusive **b.** Mutually exclusive   **49.** $S \cap N$ is the event that an author is successful and new. $S \cup N$ is the event that an author is either successful or new; $n(S \cap N) = 5$; $n(S \cup N) = 45$
51. N and E **53.** $S \cap N'$ is the event that an author is successful but not a new author. $n(S \cap N') = 25$
55. 31.25%; 83.33%   **57.** $V \cap I'$; $n(V \cap I') = 15$
59. 80; the number of stocks that were either not pharmaceutical stocks, or were unchanged in value after a year (or both)   **61.** P and E, P and I, E and I, N and E, V and N, V and D, N and D **63.** 3/8; the fraction of Internet stocks that increased in value
65. a. $E' \cap H$ **b.** $E \cup H$ **c.** $(E \cup G)' = E' \cap G'$
67. a. $\{9\}$ **b.** $\{6\}$ **69. a.** The dog's fight drive is weakest. **b.** The dog's fight and flight drives are either both strongest or both weakest. **c.** Either the dog's fight drive is strongest, or its flight drive is strongest.   **71.** $C(6, 4) = 15$; $C(1, 1)C(5, 3) = 10$
73. a. $n(S) = P(7, 3) = 210$ **b.** $E \cap F$ is the event that Celera wins and Electoral College is in second or third place. In other words, it is the set of all lists of three horses in which Celera is first and Electoral College is second or third. $n(E \cap F) = 10$ **75.** Subset of the sample space   **77.** E and F do not both occur
79. (B)   **81.** True; consider the following experiment: Select an element of the set S at random.
83. Answers may vary. Cast a die and record the remainder when the number facing up is divided by 2.
85. Yes. For instance, $E = \{(2, 5), (5, 1)\}$ and $F = \{(4, 3)\}$ are two such events.

Section 7.2

1. .4   **3.** .8   **5.** .6
7.

Outcome	HH	HT	TH	TT
Rel. Frequency	.275	.2375	.3	.1875

9. .575   **11.** The second coin *seems* slightly biased in favor of heads, as heads comes up approximately 58% of the time. On the other hand, it is conceivable that the coin is fair and that heads came up 58% of the time purely by chance. Deciding which conclusion is more reasonable requires some knowledge of inferential statistics.   **13.** Yes   **15.** No; relative frequencies cannot be negative.   **17.** Yes   **19.** Missing value: .3 **a.** .6 **b.** .4   **21.** Answers will vary.   **23.** Answers will vary.
25. a. .5 **b.** .17 **c.** .94

27. a.

Mortgage Status	Current	Past Due	In Foreclosure	Repossessed
Rel. Frequency	.67	.26	.045	.025

b. .33
29. a.

Age	0–14	15–29	30–64	>64
Rel. Frequency	.30	.27	.37	.06

b. .36
31. a.

Test Rating	3	2	1	0
Rel. Frequency	.1	.4	.4	.1

b. .5   **33.** Dial-up: 1256, Cable Modem: 412,
DSL: 302, Other: 30
35.

Outcome	Surge	Plunge	Steady
Rel. Frequency	.2	.3	.5

37. .25   **39.** .2   **41.** .7   **43.** 5/6   **45.** 5/16
47.

Outcome	U	C	R
Rel. Frequency	.2	.64	.16

49.

Conventional	No pesticide	Single pesticide	Multiple pesticide
Probability	.27	.13	.60
Organic	No pesticide	Single pesticide	Multiple pesticide
Probability	.77	.13	.10

51. $P(\text{false negative}) = 10/400 = .025$,
$P(\text{false positive}) = 10/200 = .05$ **53.** Answers will
vary.   **55.** The fraction of times E occurs   **57.** 101;
$fr(E)$ can be any number between 0 and 100 inclusive,
so the possible answers are $0/100 = 0$, $1/100 = .01$,
$2/100 = .02, \ldots, 99/100 = .99$, $100/100 = 1$.
59. Wrong. For a pair of fair dice, the probability of a
pair of matching numbers is 1/6, as Ruth says.
However, it is quite possible, although not very likely,
that if you cast a pair of fair dice 20 times, you will
never obtain a matching pair (in fact, there is approximately a 2.6% chance that this will happen). In
general, a nontrivial claim about probability can never
be absolutely validated or refuted experimentally. All
we can say is that the evidence suggests that the dice
are not fair.   **61.** For a (large) number of days, record
the temperature prediction for the next day and then
check the actual high temperature the next day.
Record whether the prediction was accurate (within,
say, 2°F of the actual temperature). The fraction of
times the prediction was accurate is the relative
frequency.

Section 7.3

1. $P(e) = .2$ **a.** .9 **b.** .95 **c.** .1 **d.** .8
3. $P(E) = 1/4$ **5.** $P(E) = 1$ **7.** $P(E) = 3/4$
9. $P(E) = 3/4$ **11.** $P(E) = 1/2$ **13.** $P(E) = 1/9$
15. $P(E) = 0$ **17.** $P(E) = 1/4$
19. 1/12; {(4, 4), (2, 3), (3, 2)}
21.

Outcome	1	2	3	4	5	6
Probability	1/9	2/9	1/9	2/9	1/9	2/9

$P(\{1, 2, 3\}) = 4/9$

23.

Outcome	1	2	3	4
Probability	8/15	4/15	2/15	1/15

25. .65   **27.** .1   **29.** .7   **31.** .4   **33.** .25   **35.** 1.0
37. .3   **39.** 1.0   **41.** No; $P(A \cup B)$ should be $\leq$
$P(A) + P(B)$.   **43.** Yes   **45.** No; $P(A \cup B)$
should be $\geq P(A)$.   **47. a.** .93 **b.** .33
49.

Outcome	Hispanic or Latino	White (not Hispanic)	African American	Asian	Other
Probability	0.48	0.29	0.08	0.08	0.07

$P(\text{Neither White nor Asian}) = .63$
51. a. $S = \{$Stock market success, Sold to other concern, Fail$\}$
b.

Outcome	Stock Market Success	Sold to Other Concern	Fail
Probability	.2	.3	.5

c. .5
53.

Outcome	SUV	Pickup	Passenger Car	Minivan
Probability	.25	.15	.50	.10

55. $P(1) = 0$, $P(6) = 0$; $P(2) = P(3) = P(4) =$
$P(5) = 1/4 = .25$; $P(\text{odd}) = .5$ **57.** $P(1) = P(6) =$
$1/10$; $P(2) = P(3) = P(4) = P(5) = 1/5$, $P(\text{odd}) =$
$1/2$ **59.** $P(1, 1) = P(2, 2) = \ldots = P(6, 6) = 1/66$;
$P(1, 2) = \ldots = P(6, 5) = 1/33$, $P(\text{odd sum}) = 6/11$
61. $P(2) = 15/38$; $P(4) = 3/38$, $P(1) = P(3) =$
$P(5) = P(6) = 5/38$, $P(\text{odd}) = 15/38$ **63.** 5/6
65. .39   **67.** .25   **69.** .25   **71.** .00   **73.** .75   **75.** .45
77. .55   **79.** .01   **81.** .53   **83.** .44   **85.** 22%; 43%
87. All of them   **89.** 88.4%   **91.** Here is one possible
experiment: Roll a die and observe which of the
following outcomes occurs. Outcome A: 1 or 2 facing
up; $P(A) = 1/3$, Outcome B: 3 or 4 facing up;
$P(B) = 1/3$, Outcome C: 5 or 6 facing up;
$P(C) = 1/3$.   **93.** He is wrong. It is possible to have
a run of losses of any length. Tony may have grounds
to *suspect* that the game is rigged, but no proof.
95. They are mutually exclusive.   **97.** Wrong. For
example, the modeled probability of winning a state

lotto is small but nonzero. However, the vast majority of people who play lotto every day of their lives never win no matter how frequently they play, so the relative frequency is zero for these people.   **99.** When $A \cap B = \emptyset$ we have $P(A \cap B) = P(\emptyset) = 0$, so $P(A \cup B) = P(A) + P(B) - P(A \cap B) = P(A) + P(B) - 0 = P(A) + P(B)$.   **101.** Zero. According to the assumption, no matter how many thunderstorms occur, lightning cannot strike a given spot more than once, and so, after n trials the relative frequency will never exceed $1/n$, and so will approach zero as the number of trials gets large. Since the modeled probability models the limit of relative frequencies as the number of trials gets large, it must therefore be zero.   **103.** $P(A \cup B \cup C) = P(A) + P(B) + P(C) - P(A \cap B) - P(A \cap C) - P(B \cap C) + P(A \cap B \cap C)$

Section 7.4

1. $1/42$ **3.** $7/9$ **5.** $1/7$ **7.** $1/2$ **9.** $41/42$ **11.** $1/15$ **13.** $4/15$ **15.** $1/5$ **17.** $1/(2^8 \times 5^5 \times 5!)$ **19.** $.4226$ **21.** $.0475$ **23.** $.0020$ **25.** $1/27^{39}$ **27.** $1/7$ **29.** Probability of being a Big Winner = $1/2,118,760 \approx .000000472$. Probability of being a Small-Fry Winner = $225/2,118,760 \approx .000106194$. Probability of being either a Big Winner or a Small-Fry Winner = $226/2,118,760 \approx .000106666$.   **31. a.** $C(600,300)/C(700,400)$ **b.** $C(699,399)/C(700,400)$ or $400/700$ **33.** $P(10, 3)/10^3 = 18/25 = .72$ **35.** $8!/8^8$ **37.** $1/8$ **39.** $1/8$ **41.** $37/10,000$ **43. a.** $90,720$ **b.** $25,200$ **c.** $25,200/90,720 = 25/90 \approx .28$ **45.** The four outcomes listed are not equally likely; for example, (red, blue) can occur in four ways. The methods of this section yield a probability for (red, blue) of $C(2, 2)/C(4, 2) = 1/6$ **47.** No. If we do not pay attention to order, the probability is $C(5, 2)/C(9, 2) = 10/36 = 5/18$. If we do pay attention to order, the probability is $P(5, 2)/P(9, 2) = 20/72 = 5/18$ again. The difference between permutations and combinations cancels when we compute the probability.   **49.** Answers will vary.

Section 7.5

1. $.4$ **3.** $.08$ **5.** $.75$ **7.** $.2$ **9.** $.5$ **11.**

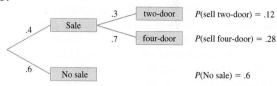

		Outcome
	$.5$ C	$P(A \cap C) = .15$
$.3$ A	$.5$ D	$P(A \cap D) = .15$
$.7$ B	$.2$ C	$P(B \cap C) = .14$
	$.8$ D	$P(B \cap D) = .56$

13.

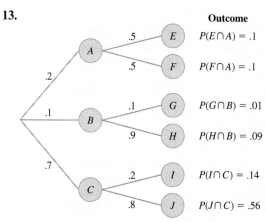

		Outcome
$.2$ A	$.5$ E	$P(E \cap A) = .1$
	$.5$ F	$P(F \cap A) = .1$
$.1$ B	$.1$ G	$P(G \cap B) = .01$
	$.9$ H	$P(H \cap B) = .09$
$.7$ C	$.2$ I	$P(I \cap C) = .14$
	$.8$ J	$P(J \cap C) = .56$

15. $1/10$ **17.** $1/5$ **19.** $2/9$ **21.** $1/84$ **23.** $5/21$ **25.** $24/175$ **27.** Mutually exclusive   **29.** Neither   **31.** $\frac{1}{2} \cdot \frac{1}{2} = \frac{1}{4}$ Independent   **33.** $\frac{5}{18} \cdot \frac{1}{2} \neq \frac{1}{9}$ Dependent   **35.** $\frac{25}{36} \cdot \frac{5}{18} \neq \frac{2}{9}$ Dependent   **37.** $(1/2)^{11} = 1/2,048$ **39.** $P(D) = .10$; $P(D|M) = .30$ **41.** $P(A|L) = .30$; $P(L|A) = .10$ **43.** $P(E|M) = .55$; $P(E|M') = .05$ **45.** $.8$ **47. a.** $.24$ **b.** $.059$ **49.** $.34$ **51.** Not independent; $P(\text{giving up} \mid \text{used Brand X}) = .1$ is larger than $P(\text{giving up}) = .05$.   **53.** $.00015$ **55.** $5/6$ **57.** $3/4$ **59.** $11/16$ **61.** $11/14$

63.

			two-door	$P(\text{sell two-door}) = .12$
	$.4$ Sale	$.3$		
		$.7$	four-door	$P(\text{sell four-door}) = .28$
	$.6$ No sale			$P(\text{No sale}) = .6$

65.

			Breaks down	$P(\text{small and breaks down}) = .042$
$.30$ Small	$.14$			
	$.86$		Does not	$P(\text{small and does not break down}) = .258$
$.24$ Luxury	$.08$		Breaks down	$P(\text{luxury and breaks down}) = .0192$
	$.92$		Does not	$P(\text{luxury and does not break down}) = .2208$
$.46$ Budget	$.4$		Breaks down	$P(\text{budget and breaks down}) = .184$
	$.6$		Does not	$P(\text{budget and does not break down}) = .276$

67.

			Probability
$.5$ Rain today	$.5$	Rain tomorrow	$.25$
	$.5$	No rain tomorrow	$.25$
$.5$ No rain today	$.5$	Rain tomorrow	$.25$
	$.5$	No rain tomorrow	$.25$

69. .77 **71.** .37 **73.** .40 **75.** .96

77. The claim is correct. The probability that an unemployed person has a high school diploma only is .35, while the corresponding figure for an employed person is .27. **79.** $P(K \mid D) = 1.31P(K \mid D')$

81. a. $P(I \mid T) > P(I)$ **b.** It was ineffective.

83. a. .59 **b.** \$35,000 or more: $P(\text{Internet user} \mid < \$35,000) \approx$ .27 $< P(\text{Internet user} \mid \geq \$35,000) \approx$ .59.

85. $P(R \mid J)$ **87.** (D) **89. a.** .000057 **b.** .015043 **91.** 11% **93.** 106 **95.** .631

97. Answers will vary. Here is a simple one: E: the first toss is a head; F: the second toss is a head; G: the third toss is a head. **99.** The probability you seek is $P(E \mid F)$, or should be. If, for example, you were going to place a wager on whether E occurs or not, it is crucial to know that the sample space has been reduced to F (you know that F did occur). If you base your wager on $P(E)$ rather than $P(E \mid F)$ you will misjudge your likelihood of winning.

101. You might explain that the conditional probability of E is not the *a priori* probability of E, but it is the probability of E in a hypothetical world in which the outcomes are restricted to be what is given. In the example she is citing, yes, the probability of throwing a double-six is 1/36, in the absence of any other knowledge. However by the "conditional probability" of throwing a double-six given that the sum is larger than 7, we might mean the probability of a double-six in a situation in which the dice have already been thrown, but all we know is that the sum is greater than 7. Because there are only 15 ways in which that can happen, the conditional probability is 1/15. For a more extreme case, consider the conditional probability of throwing a double-six given that the sum is 12.

103. If $A \subseteq B$ then $A \cap B = A$, so $P(A \cap B) = P(A)$ and $P(A \mid B) = P(A \cap B)/P(B) = P(A)/P(B)$.

105. Your friend is correct. If A and B are mutually exclusive, then $P(A \cap B) = 0$. On the other hand, if A and B are independent, then $P(A \cap B) = P(A)P(B)$. Thus, $P(A)P(B) = 0$. If a product is 0, then one of the factors must be 0, so either $P(A) = 0$ or $P(B) = 0$. Thus, it cannot be true that A and B are mutually exclusive, have nonzero probabilities, and are independent all at the same time.

107. $P(A' \cap B') = 1 - P(A \cup B) =$ $1 - [P(A) + P(B) - P(A \cap B)] =$ $1 - [P(A) + P(B) - P(A)P(B)] =$ $(1 - P(A))(1 - P(B)) = P(A')P(B')$

Section 7.6

1. .4 **3.** .7887 **5.** .7442 **7.** .1163 **9.** 26.8% **11.** .1724 **13.** 85% **15.** .73 **17.** .71 **19.** .165 **21.** 82% **23.** 12% **25. a.** 14.43%; **b.** 19.81% of single homeowners have pools. Thus they should go after the single homeowners. **27.** 9 **29.** .9310

31. 1.76% **33.** .20 **35.** K: child killed; D: Airbag deployed; $P(K \mid D) = 1.31P(K \mid D')$; $P(D \mid K) = 1.31(.25)/[1.31(.25) + .75] = .30$

37. Show him an example like Example 1 of this section, where $P(T \mid A) = .95$ but $P(A \mid T) \approx .64$.

39. Suppose that the steroid test gives 10% false negatives and that only 0.1% of the tested population uses steroids. Then the probability that an athlete uses steroids, given that he or she has tested positive, is

$$\frac{(.9)(.001)}{(.9)(.001) + (.01)(.999)} \approx .083.$$

41. Draw a tree in which the first branching shows which of R_1, R_2, or R_3 occurred, and the second branching shows which of T or T' then occurred. There are three final outcomes in which T occurs: $P(R_1 \cap T) = P(T \mid R_1)P(R_1)$, $P(R_2 \cap T) = P(T \mid R_2)P(R_2)$, and $P(R_3 \cap T) = P(T \mid R_3)P(R_3)$. In only one of these, the first, does R_1 occur. Thus,

$$P(R_1 \mid T) = \frac{P(R_1 \cap T)}{P(T)}$$
$$= \frac{P(T \mid R_1)P(R_1)}{P(T \mid R_1)P(R_1) + P(T \mid R_2)P(R_2) + P(T \mid R_3)P(R_3)}$$

43. The reasoning is flawed. Let A be the event that a Democrat agrees with Safire's column, and let F and M be the events that a Democrat reader is female and male, respectively. Then A. D. makes the following argument:

$P(M \mid A) = 0.9$, $P(F \mid A') = 0.9$. Therefore, $P(A \mid M) = 0.9$.

According to Bayes' theorem, we cannot conclude anything about $P(A \mid M)$ unless we know $P(A)$, the percentage of all Democrats who agreed with Safire's column. This was not given.

Section 7.7

1. $\begin{bmatrix} 1/4 & 3/4 \\ 1/2 & 1/2 \end{bmatrix}$ **3.** $\begin{bmatrix} 0 & 1 \\ 1/6 & 5/6 \end{bmatrix}$

5. $\begin{bmatrix} 0 & .8 & .2 \\ .9 & 0 & .1 \\ 0 & 0 & 1 \end{bmatrix}$ **7.** $\begin{bmatrix} 1 & 0 & 0 \\ 0 & 1 & 0 \\ 0 & 0 & 1 \end{bmatrix}$

9. $\begin{bmatrix} 1 & 0 & 0 & 0 & 0 & 0 \\ 2/3 & 0 & 1/3 & 0 & 0 & 0 \\ 0 & 2/3 & 0 & 1/3 & 0 & 0 \\ 0 & 0 & 2/3 & 0 & 1/3 & 0 \\ 0 & 0 & 0 & 2/3 & 0 & 1/3 \\ 0 & 0 & 0 & 0 & 1 & 0 \end{bmatrix}$

11. a. $\begin{bmatrix} .25 & .75 \\ 0 & 1 \end{bmatrix}$

b. distribution after one step: [.5 .5]; after two steps: [.25 .75]; after three steps: [.125 .875]

13. a. $\begin{bmatrix} .36 & .64 \\ .32 & .68 \end{bmatrix}$ **b.** distribution after one step:
[.3 .7]; after two steps: [.34 .66]; after three steps:
[.332 .668]

15. a. $\begin{bmatrix} 3/4 & 1/4 \\ 1/2 & 1/2 \end{bmatrix}$ **b.** distribution after one step:
[2/3 1/3]; after two steps: [2/3 1/3]; after three
steps: [2/3 1/3]

17. a. $\begin{bmatrix} 3/4 & 1/4 \\ 3/4 & 1/4 \end{bmatrix}$ **b.** distribution after one step:
[3/4 1/4]; after two steps: [3/4 1/4]; after three
steps: [3/4 1/4]

19. a. $\begin{bmatrix} .25 & .75 & 0 \\ 0 & 1 & 0 \\ 0 & .75 & .25 \end{bmatrix}$ **b.** distribution after one step:
[.5 .5 0]; after two steps: [.25 .75 0]; after three
steps: [.125 .875 0]

21. a. $\begin{bmatrix} 1/3 & 1/3 & 1/3 \\ 4/9 & 4/9 & 1/9 \\ 0 & 1 & 0 \end{bmatrix}$ **b.** distribution after one

step: [1/2 1/2 0]; after two steps: [1/6 2/3 1/6];
after three steps: [7/18 7/18 2/9]

23. a. $\begin{bmatrix} .01 & .99 & 0 \\ 0 & 1 & 0 \\ 0 & .36 & .64 \end{bmatrix}$ **b.** distribution after one step:
[.05 .55 .4]; after two steps: [.005 .675 .32]; after
three steps: [.0005 .7435 .256]
25. [2/3 1/3] **27.** [3/7 4/7] **29.** [2/5 3/5]
31. [2/5 1/5 2/5] **33.** [1/3 1/2 1/6]
35. [0 1 0] **37.** 1 = Sorey state, 2 = C&T;

$P = \begin{bmatrix} \frac{1}{2} & \frac{1}{2} \\ \frac{1}{4} & \frac{3}{4} \end{bmatrix}$; 3/8 = .375 **39. a.** 1 =

not checked in; 2 = checked in

$P = \begin{bmatrix} .4 & .6 \\ 0 & 1 \end{bmatrix}$, $P^2 = \begin{bmatrix} .16 & .84 \\ 0 & 1 \end{bmatrix}$,

$P^3 = \begin{bmatrix} .064 & .936 \\ 0 & 1 \end{bmatrix}$ **b.** 1 hour: .6; 2 hours: .84;

3 hours: .936 **c.** Eventually, all the roaches will have
checked in. **41.** 16.67% fall into the high-risk
category and 83.33% into the low-risk category.
43. a. 47/300 ≈ .156667 **b.** 3/13 **45.** 41.67% of the
customers will be in the Paid up category, 41.67% in
the 0–90 days category, and 16.67% in the bad debt
category.

47. a. $P = \begin{bmatrix} .729 & .271 & 0 \\ .075 & .84 & .085 \\ 0 & .304 & .696 \end{bmatrix}$ **b.** 2.3%

c. Affluent: 17.8%; middle class: 64.3%; poor: 18.0%
49. Long-term income distribution (top to bottom):
[8.43%, 41.57%, 41.57%, 8.43%]

51. a. $P = \begin{bmatrix} .981 & .005 & .005 & .009 \\ .01 & .972 & .006 & .012 \\ .01 & .006 & .973 & .011 \\ .008 & .006 & .005 & .981 \end{bmatrix}$

b. Verizon: 29.6%, Cingular: 19.4%, AT&T: 18.2%,
Other: 32.8% **c.** Verizon: 30.3%, Cingular: 18.6%,
AT&T: 17.6%, Other: 33.5%. The biggest gainers
are Verizon and Other, each gaining 0.6%.
53. [1/5 1/5 1/5 1/5 1/5] **55.** Answers
will vary. **57.** There are two assumptions made by
Markov systems that may not be true about the stock
market: the assumption that the transition probabilities
do not change over time, and the assumption that the
transition probability depends only on the current
state. **59.** If q is a row of Q, then by assumption
$qP = q$. Thus, when we multiply the rows of Q by P,
nothing changes, and $QP = Q$. **61.** At each step,
only 0.4 of the population in state 1 remains there,
and nothing enters from any other state. Thus, when
the first entry in the steady-state distribution vector is
multiplied by 0.4 it must remain unchanged. The only
number for which this true is 0.
63. An example is

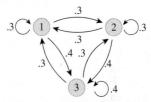

65. If $vP = v$ and $wP = w$, then $\frac{1}{2}(v+w)P =$
$\frac{1}{2}vP + \frac{1}{2}wP = \frac{1}{2}v + \frac{1}{2}w = \frac{1}{2}(v+w)$. Further, if the
entries of v and w add up to 1, then so do the entries
of $(v+w)/2$.

Chapter 7 Review

1. $n(S) = 8$, $E = \{$HHT, HTH, HTT, THH, THT,
TTH, TTT$\}$, $P(E) = 7/8$ **3.** $n(S) = 36$; $E =$
$\{(1, 6), (2, 5), (3, 4), (4, 3), (5, 2), (6, 1)\}$; $P(E) = 1/6$
5. $n(S) = 6$; $E = \{2\}$; $P(E) = 1/8$ **7.** .76 **9.** .25
11. .5 **13.** 7/15 **15.** 8/792 **17.** 48/792
19. 288/792 **21.** $C(8, 5)/C(52, 5)$
23. $C(4, 3)C(1, 1)C(3, 1)/C(52, 5)$
25. $C(9, 1)C(8, 1)C(4, 3)C(4, 2)/C(52, 5)$ **27.** 1/5;
dependent **29.** 1/6; independent **31.** 1; dependent

33. $P = \begin{bmatrix} 1/2 & 1/2 \\ 1/4 & 3/4 \end{bmatrix}$ **35.** Brand A: 65/192 ≈ .339,

Brand B: 127/192 ≈ .661 **37.** 14/25 **39.** 15/94
41. 79/167 **43.** 98% **45.** 6.9% **47.** .931
49. $P(H \cap C)$, since $P(H|C) > P(H)$ gives
$P(H \cap C) > P(H)P(C)$ **51.** .246 **53.** 91%

55. $[.2 \quad .4 \quad .4] \begin{bmatrix} 0.8 & 0.1 & 0.1 \\ 0.4 & 0.6 & 0 \\ 0.2 & 0 & 0.8 \end{bmatrix} = [.4 \quad .26 \quad .34]$,

so 40% for OHaganBooks.com, 26% for
JungleBooks.com, and 34% for FarmerBooks.com
57. Here are three: (1) it is possible for someone to be
a customer at two different enterprises; (2) some customers may stop using all three of the companies; and
(3) new customers can enter the field.

Chapter 8

Section 8.1

1. Finite; $\{2, 3, \ldots, 12\}$ **3.** Discrete infinite;
$\{0, 1, -1, 2, -2, \ldots\}$ (negative profits indicate loss)
5. Continuous; X can assume any value between 0
and 60.   **7.** Finite; $\{0, 1, 2, \ldots, 10\}$ **9.** Discrete
infinite $\{k/1, k/4, k/9, k/16, \ldots\}$
11. a. $S = \{HH, HT, TH, TT\}$
b. X is the rule that assigns to each outcome the number
of tails.
c.

Outcome	HH	HT	TH	TT
Value of X	0	1	1	2

13. a. $S = \{(1, 1), (1, 2), \ldots, (1, 6), (2, 1), (2, 2), \ldots, (6, 6)\}$ **b.** X is the rule that assigns to each outcome the
sum of the two numbers.
c.

Outcome	(1, 1)	(1, 2)	(1, 3)	...	(6, 6)
Value of X	2	3	4	...	12

15. a. $S = \{(4, 0), (3, 1), (2, 2)\}$ (listed in order (red,
green)) **b.** X is the rule that assigns to each outcome the
number of red marbles.
c.

Outcome	(4, 0)	(3, 1)	(2, 2)
Value of X	4	3	2

17. a. $S =$ the set of students in the study group.
b. X is the rule that assigns to each student his or her
final exam score. **c.** The values of X, in the order given,
are 89%, 85%, 95%, 63%, 92%, 80%.
19. a. $P(X = 8) = P(X = 6) = .3$ **b.** .7; .5
21.

x	1	2	3	4	5	6
$P(X = x)$	$\frac{1}{6}$	$\frac{1}{6}$	$\frac{1}{6}$	$\frac{1}{6}$	$\frac{1}{6}$	$\frac{1}{6}$

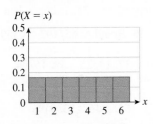

$P(X < 5) = 2/3$

23.

x	0	1	4	9
$P(X = x)$	$\frac{1}{8}$	$\frac{3}{8}$	$\frac{3}{8}$	$\frac{1}{8}$

$P(1 \leq X \leq 9) = 7/8$

25.

x	2	3	4	5	6	7	8	9	10	11	12
$P(X = x)$	$\frac{1}{36}$	$\frac{2}{36}$	$\frac{3}{36}$	$\frac{4}{36}$	$\frac{5}{36}$	$\frac{6}{36}$	$\frac{5}{36}$	$\frac{4}{36}$	$\frac{3}{36}$	$\frac{2}{36}$	$\frac{1}{36}$

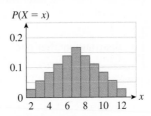

$P(X \neq 7) = 5/6$

27.

x	1	2	3	4	5	6
$P(X = x)$	$\frac{1}{36}$	$\frac{3}{36}$	$\frac{5}{36}$	$\frac{7}{36}$	$\frac{9}{36}$	$\frac{11}{36}$

$P(X \leq 3) = 1/4$

29. a.

x	10,000	30,000	50,000	70,000	90,000
$P(X = x)$	.24	.29	.18	.17	.12

b. .29 Histogram:

31. The random variable is $X =$ age of a resident in Mexico.

x	7	22	47	70
$P(X = x)$	.300	.272	.368	.060

33. a. 2,000, 3,000, 4,000, 5,000, 6,000, 7,000, 8,000 (7,000 is optional)
b.

x	2,000	3,000	4,000	5,000	6,000	7,000	8,000
Freq.	2	1	1	1	2	0	3
$P(X = x)$	.2	.1	.1	.1	.2	0	.3

c. $P(X \leq 5,000) = .5$ **35. a.** $-700, -600, -500,$
$-400, -300, -200, -100, 0, 100, 200, 300, 400, 500,$
$600, 700, 800, 900$ $(-600, 0, 100, 300, 500, 600, 700,$
and 800 are optional.)
b.

x	−700	−600	−500	−400	−300	−200	−100	0
Freq.	2	0	2	1	1	4	4	0
$P(X = x)$	.1	0	.1	.05	.05	.2	.2	0

x	100	200	300	400	500	600	700	800	900
Freq.	0	2	0	2	0	0	0	0	2
$P(X = x)$	0	.1	0	.1	0	0	0	0	.1

c. .3
37.

Class	1.1 − 2.0	2.1 − 3.0	3.1 − 4.0
Freq.	4	7	9

x	1.5	2.5	3.5
$P(X = x)$	.20	.35	.45

39. 95.5%
41.

x	3	2	1	0
$P(X = x)$	.0625	.6875	.125	.125

43. .75 The relative frequency that a randomly selected small car is rated Good or Acceptable is .75.
45. $P(Y \geq 2) = .50$, $P(Z \geq 2) \approx .53$, suggesting that medium SUVs are safer than small SUVs in frontal crashes   **47.** Small cars   **49.** .375
51.

x	1	2	3	4
$P(X = x)$	$\dfrac{4}{35}$	$\dfrac{18}{35}$	$\dfrac{12}{35}$	$\dfrac{1}{35}$

$P(X \geq 2) = 31/35 \approx .886$
53. Answers will vary.   **55.** No; for instance, if X is the number of times you must toss a coin until heads comes up, then X is infinite but not continuous.
57. By measuring the values of X for a large number of outcomes, and then using the estimated probability

(relative frequency)   **59.** Here is an example: Let X be the number of days a diligent student waits before beginning to study for an exam scheduled in 10 days' time.   **61.** The bars should be 1 unit wide, so that their height is numerically equal to their area.   **63.** Answers may vary. If we are interested in exact page counts, then the number of possible values is very large and the values are (relatively speaking) close together, so using a continuous random variable might be advantageous. In general, the finer and more numerous the measurement classes, the more likely it becomes that a continuous random variable could be advantageous.

Section 8.2

1. .0729   **3.** .59049   **5.** .00001   **7.** .99144   **9.** .00856
11. .27648   **13.** .54432   **15.** .04096   **17.** .77414
19. $P(X = x)$

21. $P(X = x)$

$P(X \leq 2) = .8889$
23. .2637   **25.** .8926   **27.** .875   **29. a.** .0081
b. .08146   **31.** .41   **33. a.** .0509   **b.** Probability distribution (entries rounded to four decimal places):

x	0	1	2	3	4
$P(X = x)$	.0643	.2030	.2885	.2429	.1343
5	**6**	**7**	**8**	**9**	**10**
.0509	.0134	.0024	.0003	.0000	.0000

c. 2   **35.** .000298   **37.** .8321   **39. a.** 21 **b.** 20
c. The graph for $n = 50$ trials is more widely distributed than the graph for $n = 20$.   **41.** 69 trials
43. $.562 \times 10^{-5}$ **45.** .0266; because there is only a 2.66% chance of detecting the disease in a given year, the government's claim seems dubious.   **47.** No; in a sequence of Bernoulli trials, the occurrence of one success does not affect the probability of success on the next attempt.   **49.** No; if life is a sequence of Bernoulli trials, then the occurrence of one misfortune ("success") does not affect the probability of a misfortune on the next trial. Hence, misfortunes may very

well not "occur in threes."   **51.** Think of performing the experiment as a Bernoulli trial with "success" being the occurrence of E. Performing the experiment n times independently in succession would then be a sequence of n Bernoulli trials.   **53.** The probability of selecting a red marble changes after each selection, as the number of marbles left in the bag decreases. This violates the requirement that, in a sequence of Bernoulli trials, the probability of "success" does not change.

Section 8.3

1. $\bar{x} = 6$, median $= 5$, mode $= 5$
3. $\bar{x} = 3$, median $= 3.5$, mode $= -1$
5. $\bar{x} = -0.1875$, median $= 0.875$, every value is a mode   **7.** $\bar{x} = 0.2$, median $= -0.1$, mode $= -0.1$
9. Answers may vary. Two examples are: 0, 0, 0, 0, 0, 6 and 0, 0, 0, 1, 2, 3   **11.** 0.9   **13.** 21   **15.** -0.1
17. 3.5   **19.** 1   **21.** 4.472   **23.** 2.667   **25.** 2
27. 0.385   **29.** $\bar{x} = -150$, $m = -150$; -150
31. $\bar{x} = 1{,}708.4$, median $= 1{,}704$; mode $= 1{,}704$;
Over the 10-business-day period sampled, the price of gold averaged \$1,708.4 per ounce. It was above \$1,704 as many times as it was below that price, and stood at \$1,704 per ounce more often than at any other price.
33. a. 6.5; there were, on average, 6.5 checkout lanes in each supermarket that was surveyed.
b. $P(X < \mu) = .42$; $P(X > \mu) = .58$, and is thus larger. Most supermarkets have more than the average number of checkout lanes.
35.

X	5	10	15	20	25	35
P(X)	.17	.33	.21	.19	.03	.07

$E(X) = 14.3$;

the average age of a school goer in 1998 was 14.3.
37. 29.6   **39.** \$43,000
41.

x	3	2	1	0
P(X = x)	.0625	.6875	.125	.125

$E(X) = 1.6875$

y	3	2	1	0
P(Y = y)	.1	.4	.4	.1

$E(Y) = 1.5$;

small cars
43. Large cars   **45.** Expect to lose 5.3¢.   **47.** 25.2 students   **49. a.** Two defective airbags **b.** 120 airbags
51.

x	1	2	3	4
P(X = x)	$\frac{4}{35}$	$\frac{18}{35}$	$\frac{12}{35}$	$\frac{1}{35}$

$E(X) = 16/7 \approx 2.2857$ tents

53. FastForward: 3.97%; SolidState: 5.51%; SolidState gives the higher expected return.   **55.** A loss of \$29,390
57. (A)   **59.** He is wrong; for example, the collection 0, 0, 300 has mean 100 and median 0.   **61.** No. The

expected number of times you will hit the dart-board is the average number of times you will hit the bull's eye per 50 shots; the average of a set of whole numbers need not be a whole number.   **63.** Wrong. It might be the case that only a small fraction of people in the class scored better than you but received exceptionally high scores that raised the class average. Suppose, for instance, that there are 10 people in the class. Four received 100%, you received 80%, and the rest received 70%. Then the class average is 83%, 5 people have lower scores than you, but only 4 have higher scores.   **65.** No; the mean of a very large sample is only an *estimate* of the population mean. The means of larger and larger samples *approach* the population mean as the sample size increases.
67. Wrong. The statement attributed to President Bush asserts that the mean tax refund would be \$1,000, whereas the statements referred to as "The Truth" suggest that the *median* tax refund would be close to \$100 [and that the 31st percentile would be zero].
69. Select a U.S. household at random, and let X be the income of that household. The expected value of X is then the population mean of all U.S. household incomes.

Section 8.4

1. $s^2 = 29$; $s = 5.39$ **3.** $s^2 = 12.4$; $s = 3.52$
5. $s^2 = 6.64$; $s = 2.58$ **7.** $s^2 = 13.01$; $s = 3.61$
9. 1.04   **11.** 9.43   **13.** 3.27   **15.** Expected value $= 3.5$, variance $= 2.918$, standard deviation $= 1.71$
17. Expected value $= 1$, variance $= 0.5$, standard deviation $= 0.71$ **19.** Expected value $= 4.47$, variance $= 1.97$, standard deviation $= 1.40$
21. Expected value $= 2.67$, variance $= 0.36$, standard deviation $= 0.60$ **23.** Expected value $= 2$, variance $= 1.8$, standard deviation $= 1.34$
25. a. $\bar{x} = 3$, $s = 3.54$ **b.** [0, 6.54] We must assume that the population distribution is bell shaped and symmetric.   **27. a.** $\bar{x} = 5.0$, $s = 0.6$ **b.** 3.8, 6.2
29. a. $\bar{x} = -150$, $s \approx 495$ **b.** 645, 20%   **31. a.** 2.18
b. [11.22, 24.28] **c.** 100%; Empirical rule
33. $\mu = 1.5$, $\sigma = 1.43$; 100%   **35.** $\mu = 43$, $\sigma = 27$; \$54,000 **37. a.** $\mu \approx 30.2$ yrs. old, $\sigma = 11.78$ years
b. 18–42   **39.** At most 6.25%   **41.** At most; 12.5%
43. a. $\mu = 25.2$, $\sigma = 3.05$ **b.** 31   **45. a.** $\mu = 780$, $\sigma \approx 13.1$ **b.** 754, 806   **47. a.** $\mu = 6.5$, $\sigma^2 = 4.0$, $\sigma = 2.0$ **b.** [2.5, 10.5]; three checkout lanes
49. \$10,700 or less   **51.** \$65,300 or more   **53.** U.S.
55. U.S.   **57.** 16%   **59.** 0–\$76,000   **61.** 2000 data: $\mu = 12.56\%$, $\sigma \approx 1.8885\%$; 2010 data: $\mu = 13.30\%$, $\sigma \approx 1.6643\%$ **63.** (B)   **65.** 72%;. The empirical rule predicts 68% The associated probability distribution is roughly bell shaped but not symmetric.   **67.** 94%. Chebyshev's rule is valid, since it predicts that *at least* 75% of the scores are in this range.   **69.** (B), (D)
71. (B), (E)   **73.** The sample standard deviation is bigger; the formula for sample standard deviation

involves division by the smaller term $n - 1$ instead of n, which makes the resulting number larger.   **75.** The grades in the first class were clustered fairly close to 75. By Chebyshev's inequality, at least 88% of the class had grades in the range 60–90. On the other hand, the grades in the second class were widely dispersed. The second class had a much wider spread of ability than did the first class.   **77.** The variable must take on only the value 10, with probability 1.   **79.** $(y - x)/2$

Section 8.5

1. .1915   **3.** .5222   **5.** .6710   **7.** .2417   **9.** .8664
11. .8621   **13.** .2286   **15.** .3830   **17.** .5028   **19.** 108.4
21. 117.5   **23.** .35   **25.** .05   **27.** .3830   **29.** .8185
31. 26%   **33.** 33,100,000   **35.** 665   **37.** 0
39. About 6,680   **41.** 28%   **43.** 5%   **45.** The U.S.
47. Wechsler. As this test has a smaller standard deviation, a greater percentage of scores fall within 20 points of the mean.   **49.** This is surprising, because the time between failures was more than five standard deviations away from the mean, which happens with an extremely small probability.   **51.** .6103   **53.** .6103 × .5832 ≈ .3559
55. .6255   **57.** .7881   **59.** .9049   **61.** .2912
63. Probability that a person will say Goode = .54. Probability that Goode polls more than 52% ≈ .8925.
65. 23.4   **67.** When the distribution is normal
69. Neither. They are equal.   **71.** $1/(b - a)$
73. A normal distribution with standard deviation 0.5, because it is narrower near the mean but must enclose the same amount of area as the standard curve, and so it must be higher.

Chapter 8 Review

1.

x	0	1	2
$P(X = x)$	1/4	1/2	1/4

3.

x	2	3	4	5	6	7	8
$P(X = x)$	1/16	2/16	3/16	4/16	3/16	2/16	1/16

5.

x	0	1	2	3
$P(X = x)$	.2071	.4439	.2908	.0582

7. $\bar{x} = 2$, $m = 2$, $s \approx 2.7386$ **9.** Two examples are: 0, 0, 0, 4 and $-1, -1, 1, 5$ **11.** An example is $-1, -1, -1, 1, 1, 1$ **13.** .4165   **15.** .9267   **17.** .0067
19. .7330   **21.** $\mu = 1.5$, $\sigma = 0.8660$; 2
23.

x	-3	-2	-1	0	1	2	3
$P(X = x)$	1/16	2/16	3/16	4/16	3/16	2/16	1/16

$\mu = 0$, $\sigma = 1.5811$; within 1.3 standard deviations of the mean   **25.** [49.4, 150.6]   **27.** 260   **29.** .4332
31. .0358   **33.** .3085   **35.** $12.15   **37.** $27,210
39. False; let X = price and Y = weekly sales. Then weekly Revenue = XY. However, $27,210 \neq 12.15 \times 2,620$. In other words, $E(XY) \neq E(X)E(Y)$.
41. a.

x	2	4	6	8	10
$P(X = x)$	.25	.35	.15	.15	.10

$\mu = 5$, $\sigma = 2.5690$ **b.** Between 2.431 and 7.569 orders per million residents; the empirical rule does not apply because the distribution is not symmetric.
c. (A)   **43.** .190   **45.** .060   **47.** 0.5   **49.** .284
51. .108   **53.** Using normal distribution table: 407,000 people; more accurate answer: 423,000 people
55. 148

Index

Transformations:

The order that will always work when transforming a graph is HSRV. An easy way to remember this order is the following acronym: a **H**uge **S**tation wagon is an **RV**.

Using coordinates to do transformations is very straightforward. It is also very easy to check your work.

Let us do an example together.

Your initial graph is $f(x)=x^2$. Using transformations and the initial graph $f(x)=x^2$, graph $g(x)=-(3x+2)^2-4$.

For the first set of coordinates, pick some ordered pairs. (Remember, you are starting with graph $f(x)$ and transforming this to graph $g(x)$.)

x	$f(x)=x^2$
-2	4
-1	1
0	0
1	1
2	4

Horizontal shift: We will shift the graph 2 units to the left. The horizontal axis is the *x-axis*; so, let us shift the input values by subtracting two from each *x-value*.

x	$(x+2)^2$
-4	4
-3	1
-2	0
-1	1
0	4

Shrinking: We will shrink the graph by dividing each input coordinate by 3. (We know it is the input coordinate for this reason. Notice that the 3 is attached to the input value, *x*.)

x	$(3x+2)^2$
$-\dfrac{4}{3}$	4
-1	1
$-\dfrac{2}{3}$	0
$-\dfrac{1}{3}$	1
0	4

Reflection: We will reflect the graph about the $x-axis$. We will change the sign on each output value.

x	$-(3x+2)^2$
$-\dfrac{4}{3}$	-4
-1	-1
$-\dfrac{2}{3}$	0
$-\dfrac{1}{3}$	-1
0	-4

Vertical shift: Lastly, we will shift the graph 4 units downward. The vertical axis is the *y-axis*; so, let us shift the output values by subtracting four from each *y-value*.

x	$-(3x+2)^2 - 4$
$-\dfrac{4}{3}$	-8
-1	-5
$-\dfrac{2}{3}$	-4
$-\dfrac{1}{3}$	-5
0	-8

The last table of coordinates represents a list of points on your graph, $g(x)$. These are the ordered pairs that are on your final graph:

$$\{(-\tfrac{4}{3},-8),(-1,-5),(-\tfrac{2}{3},-4),(-\tfrac{1}{3},-5),(0,-8)\}\,.$$

Here is another example. Your initial graph is $f(x) = x^2$. Using transformations and the initial graph $f(x) = x^2$, graph $g(x) = 3(-x-2)^2$.

Please note, the horizontal movement will be to the right two units. The graph will be stretched along the *y-axis* by a factor of three. The graph will be reflected about the *y-axis*.
As always, we will perform the transformations in the order of H-S-R-V.
Let us use the same initial set of points as above.

x	$f(x) = x^2$
-2	4
-1	1
0	0
1	1
2	4

Horizontal shift:

x	$f(x) = (x-2)^2$
0	4
1	1
2	0
3	1
4	4

Stretching:

x	$f(x) = 3(x-2)^2$
0	12(3*4=12)
1	3
2	0
3	3
4	12

Reflection:

x	$f(x) = 3(-x-2)^2$
0	12
-1	3
-2	0
-3	3
-4	12

For the graph of $g(x)$, we plot the above ordered pairs:
$\{(-2,12),(-1,3),(-2,0),(-3,3),(-4,12)\}$ to get the graph of a parabola.

Matrices

When we solve a system of linear equations, there are only three possible solutions:

1. Exactly one unique solution (Consistent and Independent)
2. No solution (Inconsistent)
3. Infinitely many solutions (Consistent and Dependent).

Below is one general approach to solving a matrix problem.

1. Work by column. Please remember, each column represents the coefficients of the same variable. This is why we work by column.
2. Get the one in each column first.

3. When getting a zero in a matrix, addition is used. The constant, c, used in the row operation is the same number and opposite sign: $cR_i + R_j \rightarrow R_j$.

4. When getting a one in a matrix, multiplication is used. The constant, c, used in the row operation is the reciprocal number and same sign: $cR_i \rightarrow R_i$.

5. Rows may also be interchanged: $R_i \leftrightarrow R_j$.

Here are a couple of notes before an example.
- Be careful when interchanging rows. Make sure that a column that has already been reduced is not changed.
- Please notice that in steps 3 and 4 above, the row is the same immediately before and after the arrow.
- Think of the arrow as the word 'change'.

Write the augmented matrix of the system below. Solve the system by using Gauss-Jordan elimination.

$$3x + y + 2z = 31$$
$$x + y + 2z = 19$$
$$x + 3y + 2z = 25$$

Call this matrix A.

$$A = \begin{bmatrix} 3 & 1 & 2 & | & 31 \\ 1 & 1 & 2 & | & 19 \\ 1 & 3 & 2 & | & 25 \end{bmatrix}$$

Column 1 represents the coefficients of the x variable.
Column 2 represents the coefficients of the y variable.
Column 3 represents the coefficients of the z variable.

$$\begin{bmatrix} 3 & 1 & 2 & | & 31 \\ 1 & 1 & 2 & | & 19 \\ 1 & 3 & 2 & | & 25 \end{bmatrix} R_1 \leftrightarrow R_2$$

Interchange Row 1 and Row 2.

$$\begin{bmatrix} 1 & 1 & 2 & | & 19 \\ 3 & 1 & 2 & | & 31 \\ 1 & 3 & 2 & | & 25 \end{bmatrix} \begin{matrix} -3R_1 + R_2 \rightarrow R_2 \\ \\ -R_1 + R_3 \rightarrow R_3 \end{matrix}$$

In words, a_{21} and a_{31} both need to be 0. Addition is used, and the constant is the same number AND opposite sign.

$$\begin{bmatrix} 1 & 1 & 2 & | & 19 \\ 0 & -2 & -4 & | & -26 \\ 0 & 2 & 0 & | & 6 \end{bmatrix} -\frac{1}{2} R_2 \rightarrow R_2$$

In words, a_{22} needs to be a 1. Multiplication is used, and the constant is the reciprocal AND same sign.

Remember, column 1 is reduced. Make sure this column does not change throughout the remainder of the matrix solving.

$$\begin{bmatrix} 1 & 1 & 2 & | & 19 \\ 0 & -2 & -4 & | & -26 \\ 0 & 2 & 0 & | & 6 \end{bmatrix} \begin{matrix} -R_2 + R_1 \rightarrow R_1 \\ \\ -2R_2 + R_3 \rightarrow R_3 \end{matrix}$$

In words, a_{12} and a_{32} both need to be 0. Addition is used, and the constant is the same number AND opposite sign.

$$\begin{bmatrix} 1 & 0 & 0 & | & 6 \\ 0 & 1 & 2 & | & 13 \\ 0 & 0 & -4 & | & -20 \end{bmatrix} -\frac{1}{4}R_3 \to R_3$$

In words, a_{33} needs to be a 1. Multiplication is used, and the constant is the reciprocal AND same sign.

Remember, column 2 is now reduced. Make sure column 1 and column 2 do not change throughout the remainder of the matrix solving.

$$\begin{bmatrix} 1 & 0 & 0 & | & 6 \\ 0 & 1 & 2 & | & 13 \\ 0 & 0 & 1 & | & 5 \end{bmatrix} -2R_3 + R_2 \to R_2$$

In words, a_{23} needs to be 0. Addition is used, and the constant is the same number AND opposite sign.

$$\begin{bmatrix} 1 & 0 & 0 & | & 6 \\ 0 & 1 & 0 & | & 3 \\ 0 & 0 & 1 & | & 5 \end{bmatrix}$$

We have reduced our matrix.

A matrix is in reduced form when the following guidelines have been met:

1. If the matrix has a row of zeros, the row of zeros is the last row in the matrix.
2. The first nonzero number in each row is a one.
3. Using step 2 above, look at those values of 1. Make sure that the rest of the elements in the column containing the 1 are 0's.
4. The 1's must be on a principal diagonal: top to bottom, left to right.

Remember, column 1 represents the x variable. Column 2 represents the y variable, and column 3 represents the z variable.

When we read across each row, we have the following:

$$x + 0y + 0z = 6$$
$$0x + y + 0z = 3$$
$$0x + 0y + z = 5$$

or, $x = 6, y = 3, z = 5$. The final answer is given as $(6, 3, 5)$.

MTH 110   Sample Exam 3

Name_____

PID_____

Section_____

Instructions:

You must show your work when directed to do so or credit will not be given. If you use a graph from your calculator, sketch it on your exam paper, along with enough markings on the axes to indicate your viewing rectangle.

This exam consists of problems 1 – 6. Request a new copy of the exam if any of the problems are missing or hard to read.

1.(20 pts) Solve each one of the following systems of linear equations by any method. Show work.

(a)
$$-3x - 9y = -4$$
$$6x + 18y = 8$$

Answer_____

(a)
$$5x + 5y = 0$$
$$x + y = -1$$

Answer_____

2. (10 pts) Consider the matrix $\begin{bmatrix} 1 & 32 & 0 & | & 9 \\ 0 & 0 & 1 & | & 2 \end{bmatrix}$. Answer the following two questions about this matrix.

(a) Is this matrix in reduced form?

(b) Does the system which corresponds to this matrix have solutions?

3.(20 pts) Suppose the supply and demand for a certain type of calculator are given by the following equations (first equation represents the supply, second equation represents the demand):

$p = 45 + 22q$
$p = 135 - 8q$

where p is the price in dollars, and q is the quantity in millions.

    (a) Find the equilibrium price and quantity. Show work.

Answer_____

    (b) Graph the two equations in the same coordinate system and identify the equilibrium point, supply curve and demand curve.

4. (15 pts) Solve the following system using Gauss-Jordan Elimination. Be sure to indicate each one of your steps.

$$4x_1 - 2x_2 - 4x_3 = 4$$
$$x_1 + 2x_2 - 3x_3 = -1$$
$$2x_1 - 6x_2 + 2x_3 = 2$$

Answer_____

5. (15 pts) Graph each one of the following inequalities.

(a) $2y - 10 \geq 0$

(b) $x < -2$

(c) $5x + 2y \leq 10$

6. (20 pts) Find the feasible region (the solution region) and corner points for the following system of linear inequalities. Show work.

$4x + 5y \leq 100$

$3x + 2y \leq 54$

$x \geq 0$

$y \geq 0$

MTH 110   **SAMPLE FINAL EXAM**

Printed Name_____

Signed Name_____

PID_____

Section_____

You will be given 120 minutes to complete this exam. The exam consists of 27 questions on 7 pages. Some formulae are listed on page 8. Request a new copy of the exam if any of the problems are missing or hard to read.

You must show your work when directed to do so or credit will not be given. If you use a graph from your calculator, sketch it on your exam paper, along with enough markings on the axes to indicate your viewing rectangle.

Pg.1	Pg.2	Pg.3	Pg.4	Pg.5	Pg.6	Pg.7	Total /200

Questions 1 – 20 are multiple choice (5 pts each). Circle the correct answer. There is only one correct answer for each problem.

1. What is the domain of $f(x) = \dfrac{2}{\sqrt{x+10}}$?

(A) $x < 10$ (B) $x \geq -10$ (C) $x > -10$ (D) All real numbers

---

2. How many x-intercepts does $g(x) = x^2 + 2x + 10$ have?

(A) One   (B) None   (C) Two

---

3. Which of the following equations represents the line with undefined slope?

(A) $y = 4$ (B) $y = 2x - 5$ (C) $y = x$ (D) $x = -3$ (E) None of these

---

4. Which of the following points represents the vertex of $y = x^2 - 4$?

(A) (0, -4)   (B) (4, 0)   (C) (0, 4)   (D) (-4, 0)   (E) None of these

---

5. Which of the following equations is equivalent to $\ln x = 3$? (Assume that $x > 0$)

(A) $x = 3^e$ (B) $x = e^3$ (C) $x^3 = e$ (D) None of these

---

6. Which of the following is equivalent to $2 \log x - 5 \log y + \log z$? (Assume that $x, y, z > 0$)

(A) $\log(2x - 5y + z)$ (B) $\log(\dfrac{2xz}{5y})$ (C) $\log(\dfrac{x^2 z}{y^5})$ (D) None of these

---

7. What is the monthly payment (to the nearest dollar) on a $20,000 car loan for 5 years at 7% compounded monthly?

(A) $245   (B) $350   (C) $403   (D) $396   (E) None of these

---

2

8. Suppose you invested $1,000 into each of the following accounts: account X which pays 4.5% compounded monthly, and account Y which pays 4.8% compounded annually. Which one of the two accounts will have more money in it at the end of 5 years (no money withdrawn)?

(A) Account X   (B) Account Y

---

9. Consider the system of linear equations: $\begin{array}{l} 2x - 3y = 4 \\ 4x - 6y = 7 \end{array}$. How many solutions does this system have?

(A) Infinitely many   (B) One   (C) Two   (D) None

---

10. Which one of the following matrices is not in reduced form?

(A) $\begin{bmatrix} 1 & 0 & 0 \\ 0 & 1 & 1 \\ 0 & 0 & 1 \end{bmatrix}$ (B) $\begin{bmatrix} 1 & 0 & 7 \\ 0 & 1 & 2 \\ 0 & 0 & 0 \end{bmatrix}$ (C) $\begin{bmatrix} 1 & 4 & 0 \\ 0 & 0 & 1 \end{bmatrix}$ (D) None of these

---

11. A single fair die is rolled once. What is the probability of rolling a 2 or a 6 ?

(A) $\dfrac{1}{3}$ (B) $\dfrac{1}{2}$ (C) $\dfrac{1}{36}$ (D) None of these

---

12. What is the probability that a 5-card hand from a standard 52-card deck will have three diamonds?

(A) 0.0054   (B) 0.017   (C) 0.00011   (D) None of these

---

13. Given that the probability of event E is 0.07, what is the probability of the complement of E?

(A) –0.07   (B) 0.93   (C) –0.93   (D) None of these

---

14. What are the odds in favor of event M if P(M) = 0.3 ?

(A) 3 to 7   (B) 7 to 3   (C) 3 to 10   (D) None of these

---

15. Suppose events F, G, H are independent. Find $P(F \cap G \cap H)$ if $P(F) = 0.5$, $P(G) = 0.4$, and $P(H) = 0.1$.

(A) 0.2   (B) 0.04   (C) 0.02   (D) None of these

---

16. A spinner is numbered from 1 through 8 with each number as likely to occur as any other. Compute the probability that in a single spin the dial will stop at number less than 3 or greater than 6.

(A) 0.5   (B) 0.25   (C) $\dfrac{1}{8}$ (D) None of these

---

17. Consider the sample space S = {X, Y, Z}. Determine if the following probability assignment is acceptable: P(X) = 0.2, P(Y) = 3, P(Z) = 0.8.

(A) Acceptable   (B) Not acceptable

---

18. Find the mean for the data set: 2, 11, 35, 2, 9, 7, 8 .

(A) 8   (B) 10.57   (C) 9.3   (D) None of these

---

19. Find the median for the data set: 2, 8, 2, 5, 11, 8, 13 .

(A) 5   (B) 8   (C) 7   (D) None of these

---

20. Find the mode for the data set: 4, 2, 3, 2, 4, 3, 3, 7, 11, 12, 7 .

(A) 3   (B) 2   (C) 3.5   (D) none of these

---

21. (15 pts) Maximize and minimize $P = 3x_1 + 2x_2$

$$5x_1 + 2x_2 \leq 40$$
Subject to $x_1 + 3x_2 \leq 21$
$$x_1, x_2 \geq 0$$

Show work.

Answer_____

---

22. (15 pts) Solve the following equation: $\log_7 x + \log_7(x-2) = \log_7 24$. Show work.

Answer_____

23. (15 pts) Solve the following system using Gauss – Jordan Elimination. Be sure to indicate each one of your steps.

$$x_1 - 3x_2 - 3x_3 = 13$$
$$x_2 - 4x_3 = 5$$
$$x_1 + x_3 = -4$$

Answer_____

24. (10 pts) A person makes monthly deposits of $500, which earn 5% compounded monthly. At the end of one year, how much interest has been earned? Show work.

Answer_____

25. (15 pts) By testing a large number of individuals, it has been determined that 80% of the population have normal hearts, 15% have some minor heart problems, and 5% have severe heart problems. Ninety – two percent of the persons with normal hearts, 30% of those with minor problems, and 5% of those with severe problems will pass a cardiogram test. What is the probability that a person who passes the cardiogram test has a normal heart? Show work.

Answer_____

26. (15 pts) Find the mean and standard deviation for the following sample data set. Show work.

Interval	Frequency
9.5 – 12.5	3
12.5 – 15.5	2
15.5 – 18.5	7
18.5 – 21.5	4

Mean = _____

Standard deviation = _____

27. (15 pts) Sketch the graph corresponding to each of the following descriptions.

(a) $y = b^{-x}$, $b > 1$

(b) A quadratic function with a < 0 and one x – intercept.

(c) An even – degree polynomial with 3 turning points.

Interesting Formulae:

$$A = P(1 + rt)$$

$$A = P(1 + i)^n$$

$$FV = PMT \frac{(1 + i)^n - 1}{i}$$

$$PV = PMT \frac{1 - (1 + i)^{-n}}{i}$$

$$P_{n,r} = \frac{n!}{(n - r)!}$$

$$C_{n,r} = \frac{n!}{r!(n - r)!}$$

$$P(E) = \frac{n(E)}{n(S)}$$

$$P(E) = \frac{a}{a + b}$$

$$P(A \cup B) = P(A) + P(B) - P(A \cap B)$$

$$P(A \mid B) = \frac{P(A \cap B)}{P(B)}$$

$$P(A \cap B) = P(A)P(B \mid A) = P(B)P(A \mid B)$$

$$P(E') = 1 - P(E)$$

$$\bar{x} = \frac{x_1 + x_2 + \ldots + x_n}{n}$$

$$\bar{x} = \frac{x_1 f_1 + x_2 f_2 + \ldots x_k f_k}{n}$$

$$s^2 = \frac{(x_1 - \bar{x})^2 + (x_2 - \bar{x})^2 + \ldots + (x_n - \bar{x})^2}{n - 1}$$

$$s^2 = \frac{(x_1 - \bar{x})^2 f_1 + (x_2 - \bar{x})^2 f_2 + \ldots + (x_k - \bar{x})^2 f_k}{n - 1}$$

$$s = \sqrt{s^2}$$

Properties of Logarithms

If b is a positive number and $b \neq 1$,

1. $\log_b 1 = 0$
2. $\log_b b = 1$
3. $\log_b b^x = x$
4. $b^{\log_b x} = x$
5. **Product Rule:**
   $\log_b MN = \log_b M + \log_b N$
6. **Quotient Rule:**
   $\log_b \dfrac{M}{N} = \log_b M - \log_b N$
7. **Power Rule:**
   $\log_b M^p = p \log_b M$
8. **One-to-One Property:**
   If $\log_b x = \log_b y$, then $x = y$.

Graphs of $f(x) = e^x$ and $f(x) = \ln x$

$f(x) = e^x$

$f(x) = \ln x$

Natural Logarithm Properties

1. $\ln 1 = 0$
2. $\ln e = 1$
3. $\ln e^x = x$
4. $e^{\ln x} = x$

Theorems

Remainder Theorem:
If $P(x)$ is a polynomial, r is any number, and $P(x)$ is divided by $x - r$, the remainder is $P(r)$.

Factor Theorem:
If $P(x)$ is a polynomial and r is any number, then

If $P(r) = 0$, then $x - r$ is a factor of $P(x)$.

If $x - r$ is a factor of $P(x)$, then $P(r) = 0$.

Binomial Theorem:
If n is any positive integer, then

$$(a + b)^n = a^n + \frac{n!}{1!(n - 1)!}a^{n-1}b$$

$$+ \frac{n!}{2!(n - 2)!}a^{n-2}b^2 + \frac{n!}{3!(n - 3)!}a^{n-3}b^3$$

$$+ \frac{n!}{r!(n - r)!}a^{n-r}b^r + \cdots + b^n$$

Parabolas

A **parabola** is the set of all points in a plane equidistant from a line l (called the **directrix**) and fixed point F (called the **focus**) that is not on line l.

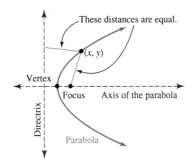

These distances are equal.

(x, y)

Vertex

Focus   Axis of the parabola

Directrix

Parabola

Parabola opening	Vertex at origin	
Right	$y^2 = 4px$	$(p > 0)$
Left	$y^2 = 4px$	$(p < 0)$
Upward	$x^2 = 4py$	$(p > 0)$
Downward	$x^2 = 4py$	$(p < 0)$

- For a parabola that opens right or left with vertex at the origin, the directrix is $x = -p$ and the focus is $(p, 0)$.
- For a parabola that opens upward or downward with vertex at the origin, the directrix is $y = -p$ and the focus is $(0, p)$.

Parabola opening	Vertex at $V(h, k)$	
Right	$(y - k)^2 = 4p(x - h)$	$(p > 0)$
Left	$(y - k)^2 = 4p(x - h)$	$(p < 0)$
Upward	$(x - h)^2 = 4p(y - k)$	$(p > 0)$
Downward	$(x - h)^2 = 4p(y - k)$	$(p < 0)$

- For a parabola that opens right or left with vertex at (h, k), the directrix is $x = -p + h$ and the focus is $(h + p, k)$.
- For a parabola that opens upward or downward with vertex at (h, k), the directrix is $y = -p + k$ and the focus is $(h, k + p)$.

Ellipses

An **ellipse** is the set of all points P in a plane such that the sum of the distances from P to two other fixed points F and F' is a positive constant.

The standard equations of an ellipse with center (h, k) and major axis horizontal is

$$\frac{(x - h)^2}{a^2} + \frac{(y - k)^2}{b^2} = 1,$$

where $a > b > 0$.

$F'(h - c, k)$

$B(h, b + k)$

$F(h + c, k)$

$V'(-a + h, k)$

b a

(h, k)

$V(a + h, k)$

$B'(h, -b + k)$